HALSBURY'S
LAWS OF ENGLAND

ANNUAL ABRIDGMENT
1993

HALSBURY'S
Laws of England

FOURTH EDITION

ANNUAL ABRIDGMENT 1993

BUTTERWORTHS

LONDON 1994

UNITED KINGDOM	Butterworth & Co (Publishers) Ltd Halsbury House, 35 Chancery Lane, **London** WC2A 1EL and 4 Hill Street, **Edinburgh** EH2 3JZ
AUSTRALIA	Butterworths Pty Ltd, **Sydney, Melbourne, Brisbane, Adelaide, Perth, Canberra** and **Hobart**
BELGIUM	Butterworth & Co (Publishers) Ltd, **Brussels**
CANADA	Butterworths Canada Ltd, **Toronto** and **Vancouver**
IRELAND	Butterworth (Ireland) Ltd, **Dublin**
MALAYSIA	Malayan Law Journal Sdn Bhd, **Kuala Lumpur**
NEW ZEALAND	Butterworths of New Zealand Ltd, **Wellington** and **Auckland**
PUERTO RICO	Equity de Puerto Rico Inc, **Hato Rey**
SINGAPORE	Butterworths Asia, **Singapore**
SOUTH AFRICA	Butterworth Publishers (Pty) Ltd, **Durban**
USA	Butterworth Legal Publishers, **Austin**, Texas; **Boston**, Massachusetts; **Clearwater**, Florida (D & S Publishers); **Orford**, New Hampshire (Equity Publishing); **St Paul**, Minnesota; and **Seattle**, Washington

ISBN   0 406 03206 8

Printed in Great Britain by
William Clowes Limited
Beccles and London

PUBLISHERS' NOTE

This is the twentieth *Annual Abridgment* and covers the year 1993. The *Abridgment* constitutes year by year a comprehensive survey of English case law, statute law and subordinate legislation. European Community law and decisions of Commonwealth courts are given attention commensurate with their importance. Further noteworthy items are derived from government papers, reports of committees, legal periodicals and the daily press. The alphabetical arrangement and the comprehensive tables and index make the work an ideal aid to research.

Each *Annual Abridgment* is complete without recourse to any other publication.

When referring to this volume reference should be made to both the year and the relevant paragraph number: eg "1993 Abr para 2039".

This volume covers the law made in 1993 and is compiled from sources available in London on 31 December 1993.

BUTTERWORTH LAW PUBLISHERS LTD

TABLE OF CONTENTS

The text of this *Abridgment* is arranged under the following titles. A list of titles currently used in *Halsbury's Laws* appears on page *13*.

Table of Contents

Table of Contents

ARRANGEMENT OF TITLES
HALSBURY'S LAWS, FOURTH EDITION & REISSUE

The following is the title scheme of *Halsbury's Laws* as it stood in 1993. Where the titles used in the *Annual Abridgment* differ from those in the main work, the new titles appear in brackets.

VOL	TITLE
1(1)	Administrative Law (reissue)
	Admiralty (reissue)
1(2)	Agency (reissue)
	Agriculture (reissue)
2	Allotments and Smallholdings (reissue)
	Animals (reissue)
	Arbitration (reissue)
	Auction (reissue)
	Aviation (reissue)
	Bailment (reissue)
3(1)	Banking (reissue)
	Barristers (reissue)
3(2)	Bankruptcy and Insolvency (reissue)
4(1)	Betting, Gaming and Lotteries (reissue)
	Bills of Exchange and other Negotiable Instruments (reissue)
	Bills of Sale (reissue)
	Boundaries (reissue)
4(2)	British Nationality, Immigration and Race Relations (reissue)
	Building Contracts, Architects, Engineers and Surveyors (reissue)
	Building Societies (reissue)
5(1)	Capital Gains Taxation (reissue)
	Carriers (reissue)
5(2)	Charities (reissue)
	Children and Young Persons (reissue)
6	Choses in Action (reissue)
	Clubs (reissue)
	Commons (reissue)
	Commonwealth and Dependencies (reissue)
7(1), (2)	Companies (reissue)
8	Compulsory Acquisition of Land
	Conflict of Laws
	Constitutional Law

VOL	TITLE
9	Contempt of Court
	Contract
	Copyholds
	Copyright
	Coroners
	Corporations
10	County Courts
	Courts
	Cremation and Burial
11(1),(2)	Criminal Law, Evidence and Procedure (reissue)
	(Criminal Evidence and Procedure / Criminal Law / Sentencing)
	Crown Proceedings and Crown Practice
	(pending the inclusion of this title in Vol 12 (reissue), the revised title Crown Proceedings appears in the Cumulative Supplement)
12	Custom and Usage
	Customs and Excise
	(Customs and Excise / Value Added Tax)
	Damages
	(Damages and Compensation)
	Deeds and other Instruments
13	Discovery, Inspection and Interrogatories
	Distress
	Divorce
14	Easements and Profits à Prendre
	Ecclesiastical Law
15	Education (reissue)
	Elections (reissue)
16(4ed)	Electricity, Atomic Energy and Radioactive Substances
	(Electricity and Atomic Energy)
16	Employment (reissue)
	Equity (reissue)
	Estoppel (reissue)
17	Evidence
	(Evidence [Civil])
	Execution
	Executors and Administrators

Arrangement of Titles

REFERENCES AND ABBREVIATIONS

Abr . . . . Halsbury's Abridgment
AC (preceded by date) . . . . . Law Reports (Appeal Cases)
ACTR . . . . Australian Capital Territory Reports
ADRLJ . . . . Arbitration and Dispute Resolution Law Journal
ALJ . . . . Australian Law Journal
All ER . . . . All England Law Reports
ALJR . . . . Australian Law Journal Reports
ALR . . . . Australian Law Reports
AVMA . . . . AVMA Medical & Legal Journal
BCLC . . . . Butterworth Company Law Cases
BLR . . . . Business Law Review
BMLR . . . . Butterworths Medico-Legal Reports
CCC . . . . Canadian Criminal Cases
Ch (preceded by date) . . . . . Law Reports (Chancery Division)
CJQ . . . . Civil Justice Quarterly
CLJ . . . . Cambridge Law Journal
CLY . . . . Current Law Yearbook
CMLR . . . . Common Market Law Reports
Conv . . . . Conveyancer and Property Lawyer
Cr App Rep . . . . Criminal Appeal Reports
Cr App Rep (S) . . . . Criminal Appeal Reports (Sentencing)
Crim LR . . . . Criminal Law Review
Decisions and Reports . . . . . Decisions and Reports of European Commission on
. . . . Human Rights
DLR . . . . Dominion Law Reports (Canada)
ECR . . . . European Court Reports
EG . . . . Estates Gazette
EGCS . . . . Estates Gazette Case Summaries
EGLR . . . . Estates Gazette Law Reports
EHRR . . . . European Human Rights Reports
EIPR . . . . European Intellectual Property Review
ELJ . . . . Ecclesiastical Law Journal
Fam (preceded by date) . . . . . Law Reports (Family Division)
Fam Law . . . . Family Law (journal)
FCR . . . . Family Court Reporter
FLR . . . . Family Law Reports
FSR . . . . Fleet Street Reports
HC . . . . House of Commons Paper
HLR . . . . Housing Law Reports
ICJ Reports . . . . International Court of Justice Reports
ICLQ . . . . International and Comparative Law Quarterly
ICR . . . . Industrial Cases Reports
ILJ . . . . Industrial Law Journal
Imm AR . . . . Immigration Appeals Reports
IR . . . . Irish Reports
IRLR . . . . Industrial Relations Law Reports
JBL . . . . Journal of Business Law
JIBFL . . . . Journal of International Banking and Financial Law
JP . . . . Justice of the Peace Reports
JP Jo . . . . Justice of the Peace Journal
JPL . . . . Journal of Planning and Environmental Law
JSWFL . . . . Journal of Social Welfare and Family Law
LGR . . . . Local Government Reports
LG Rev . . . . Local Government Review
Lloyd's Rep . . . . Lloyd's Law Reports
LMCLQ . . . . Lloyd's Maritime and Commercial Law Quarterly
LQR . . . . Law Quarterly Review
LS . . . . Legal Studies
LS Gaz . . . . Law Society Gazette

LS Gaz Rep . . . . Law Society Gazette Reports
Med LR . . . . Medical Law Reports
MLJ . . . . Malayan Law Journal
MLR . . . . Modern Law Review
NI . . . . Northern Ireland Law Reports
NLJ . . . . New Law Journal
NLJR . . . . New Law Journal Reports
NTR . . . . Northern Territory Reports
NZLR . . . . New Zealand Law Reports
OJ C . . . . Official Journal of the European Communities—
                                     communications and information series
OJ L . . . . Official Journal of the European Communities—
                                     legislation series
P & CR . . . . Property and Compensation Reports
PIQR . . . . Personal Injuries and Quantum Reports
PLR . . . . (Estates Gazette) Planning Law Reports
QB (preceded by date) . . . . . Law Reports (Queen's Bench Division)
RA . . . . Rating Appeals
RPC . . . . Reports of Patent Etc Cases
RRC . . . . Ryde's Rating Cases
RTR . . . . Road Traffic Reports
RVR . . . . Rating and Valuation Reporter
SA . . . . South African Law Reports
SC . . . . Session Cases
SJ . . . . Solicitors' Journal
SLT . . . . Scots Law Times
STC . . . . Simon's Tax Cases
STI . . . . Simon's Tax Intelligence
TC . . . . Tax Cases
TR . . . . Taxation Reports
VATTR . . . . Value Added Tax Tribunal Reports
WLR . . . . Weekly Law Reports

WORDS AND PHRASES

The following words and phrases have been judicially interpreted and can be found at the relevant paragraph noted below.

TABLE OF STATUTES

TABLE OF STATUTORY INSTRUMENTS

27

TABLE OF CASES

Decisions of the European Court of Human Rights, European Commission of Human Rights, and European Court of Justice are listed numerically after the main table.

A

Decisions of the Decisions of the European Court of Human Rights and European Commission of Human Rights are listed below numerically. These decisions are also included in the preceding alphabetical Table.

COMMAND PAPERS

QUANTUM OF DAMAGES TABLE

Examples of awards of damages in personal injury or fatal accident cases are arranged in the following order. Cases involving more than one injury are classified according to the major injury suffered.

Death
Brain damage and paralysis
Multiple injuries
Psycholgical damage and
  emotional stress

Internal injuries
Burns
Scarring
Head
Neck and shoulder

Back, chest and abdomen
Arm and hand
Leg and foot
Minor injuries

For the purposes of this table the age of the plaintiff is at the date of the accident unless otherwise stated. In fatal accident cases, sex and age are those of the deceased unless otherwise stated.

INJURY	DAMAGES AWARDED	SEX/AGE	CITATION & REVIEW PARA NUMBER
Death	£130,000	Male/—	Sandham v Pettipher (Fam Div), para 922
	£63,000	Male/42	Jones v Liverpool City Council (QBD), para 922
	£45,000	Male/30	Heap v W E Ford & Sons (QBD), para 922
	£15,424	Female/20	Smith v "Marchioness"/ "Bowbelle" (QBD), para 922
	£10,000	Male/14	Devlin v Strathclyde Regional Council (Outer House), para 922
Brain Damage	£916,750	Male/birth	Bould v Wakefield Health Authority (QBD), para 923
	£450,768	Male/44	Potts v Buckley (QBD), para 923
	£344,007	Male/—	(CICB), para 923
	£263,972	Male/19	Boulton v Brammer (QBD), para 923
	£112,628	Female/46	Clark v Austin Rover Group Ltd (QBD), para 923
Brain Damage and Quadriplegia	£612,773	—/birth	Willett v North Bedfordshire Health Authority (QBD), para 923

INJURY	DAMAGES AWARDED	SEX/AGE	CITATION & REVIEW PARA NUMBER
Quadriplegia	£1,270,000	Male/birth	*Pimpalkhare v North West Hertfordshire Health Authority* (QBD), para 924
Paraplegia	£784,197	Male/33	(CICB), para 925
	£750,000	Male/23	*Hall v Witherspoon* (Mold Crown Court), para 925
	£518,625	Male/26	*Brignall v Kelly* (QBD), para 925
	£216,426	Male/59	*Michalski v Martin Stabin Ltd and another* (QBD), para 925
Multiple injuries	£223,674·98	Male/18	*Ward v Holness and Gardner* (QBD), para 926
	£196,457	Male/28	*Cord v Technico Site Services Ltd* (QBD), para 926
	£173,479·11	Male/18	(CICB), para 926
	£86,399	Male/—	(CICB), para 926
	£62,630·04	Male/27	*Cummings v W Lucy & Co* (QBD), para 926
	£50,799·97	Male/61	*Rogers v A & D Walter Ltd* (Portsmouth County Ct), para 926
	£33,750	Female/17	(CICB), para 926
	£32,335	Male/21	*Thorogood v Barron* (Wandsworth County Ct), para 926
	£9,160	Male/32	(CICB), para 926
	£6,648·75	Female/40	*Pitman v Clarke* (CA), para 926
Physical and emotional stress	£31,5000	Females/24, 25 and 28	*P v Keleman* (QBD), para 927
Post-traumatic stress disorder	£271,725	Male/46	*Anderson v Davis* (QBD), para 928
	£147,683·58	Male/39	*Hale v London Underground Limited* (QBD), para 928

INJURY	DAMAGES AWARDED	SEX/AGE	CITATION & REVIEW PARA NUMBER
	£12,500	Female/28	*Barnaby v North Tees Health Authority* (Manchester District Registry), para 928
	£10,000	Male/21	*Fendwick v Chief Constable South Yorkshire Police* (Liverpool County Ct), para 928
	£3,800	Male/37 (at hearing)	(CICB), para 928
Post-traumatic stress disorder and legs	£1,616	Female/27	*Bhudia v Newman* (Willesden County Ct), para 928
Psychological damage	£147,405·12	Male/50	*Page v Smith* (QBD), para 927
	£15,000	Female/18 (at hearing)	(CICB), para 930
	£7,500	Female/10–21	(CICB), para 930
	£2,500	Female/3½	(CICB), para 930
Psychological damage and multiple injuries	£27,500	Male/39	(CICB), para 930
Psychological damage and cheek and neck	£3,500	Female/28	(CICB), para 927
Pain and suffering	£3,000	Female/47	*Patel v Patel* (Brentford County Ct), para 931
Internal injuries	£260,588	Male/40	*Bliman v Appledore Shipbuilders Ltd* (Exeter District Registry), para 932
	£17,778·72	Male/12	*Irwin v The Scout Association* (Watford County Ct), para 932
	£16,816	Female/45	*A v Torbay Health Authority* (settled out of court), para 932
	£16,000	Male/73	*Campbell v Campbell & Isherwood* (Outer House), para 932
	£4,980	Female/44	*Winterbone v West Suffolk Health Authority* (Cambridge County Ct), para 932

INJURY	DAMAGES AWARDED	SEX/AGE	CITATION & REVIEW PARA NUMBER
Burns	£10,286·61	Male/29	*Day v South Wales Upholstery Ltd* (Caerphilly County Ct), para 933
	£6,000	Male/11	*Whorton (A minor) v British Coal Corporation* (Doncaster County Ct), para 933
Scarring	£14,225	Female/23	*Goodall v Hall* (Brentford County Ct), para 934
	£8,000	Male/24	(CICB), para 934
	£8,000	Female/9	*Maloney v Liverpool City Council* (Liverpool County Ct), para 934
	£4,529·38	Female/23	*Greensides v Bath Hair & Beauty Clinic* (Bath County Ct), para 934
Head	£639,386·90	Female/3½	*Feltham v Seaview Services Ltd* (Winchester District Registry), para 935
	£125,000	Male/infant	*Rhodes v Watson* (QBD), para 935
	£57,244	Male/40 (at hearing)	*Williams v Mound-Evans* (QBD), para 935
	£5,000	Male/15	(CICB), para 935
	£250	Female/11	*Caplin v Parkinson* (Birkenhead County Ct), para 935
Hair	£700	Male/40+	*Dickinson v Growth Hair Clinic* (Southport County Ct), para 935
Ear	£1,750	Male/24	*Moffat v Babcock Thorn* (Outer House), para 938
Face	£67,241·47	Male/53	*Woodburn v Liverpool City Council* (QBD), para 936
	£11,250	Male/26	(CICB), para 936

INJURY	DAMAGES AWARDED	SEX/AGE	CITATION & REVIEW PARA NUMBER
Eyes and loss of vision	£22,782	Female/17	(CICB), para 937
Eye	£81,290	Male/34	(CICB), para 937
	£25,076	Female/15	(CICB), para 937
Nose	£5,810	Male/15	(CICB), para 939
Jaw	£1,000	Male/28	(CICB), para 940
Neck	£181,432·13	Female/41	*Jones v Pandis* (Middlesborough County Ct), para 941
	£97,370·20	Male/45	*Loughran v London Buses Ltd* (Clerkenwell County Ct), para 941
	£42,631·99	Male/33	*Willis v Reeby* (Plymouth County Ct), para 941
	£16,017·68	Female/37	*Baker v Keshwala* (Watford County Ct), para 941
	£15,944·48	Female/67	*Holland v Wood* (Torquay County Ct), 93/2021
	£11,718·50	Male/68	*Edwards v GKN Chep Ltd* (Coventry County Ct), para 941
	£10,500	Male/22	*Nelson v Ellis* (Clerkenwell County Ct), para 941
	£8,000	Female/72	*Farmborough v Davies* (Trowbridge County Ct), para 941
	£7,000	Female/53	*Calvert v Greenfield* (Watford County Ct), para 941
	£5,250	Male/18	*Norrington v Struth* (Colchester & Clacton County Ct), para 941
	£4,446·18	Male/42	*Murphy v MRS (Distribution) Ltd* (Outer House), para 941

INJURY	DAMAGES AWARDED	SEX/AGE	CITATION & REVIEW PARA NUMBER
	£4,384·50	Female/21	*Santi v Rothesay* (Barnet County Ct), para 941
	£4,008	Male/25	*Deeley v Western National Ltd* (Aldershot & Farnham County Ct), para 941
	£3,712·23	Male/20	*Callaway v Charles* (Birkenhead County Ct), para 941
	£3,500	Female/38	*Lowe v Kapadia* (Bury County Ct), para 941
	£3,017·32	Male/26	*Brown v Walker* (Birkenhead County Ct), para 941
	£2,807·57	Female/23	*Lyon v Chambers* (Mayor's and City of London County Ct), para 941
	£2,592·64	Female/31	*Rhodes v James* (Birkenhead County Ct), para 941
	£2,044·87	Female/44	*Shipley v Street* (Bristol County Ct), para 941
	£1,750	Male/20 +	*Nakrani v Gajjar* (Reading County Ct), para 941
	£1,750	Male/20 +	*Mandavia v Gajjar* (Reading County Ct), para 941
	£1,750	Male/20 +	*Bajaj v Gajjar* (Reading County Ct), para 941
	£1,560	Male/20 +	*Nakrani v Gajjar* (Reading County Ct), para 941
	£1,558·23	Male/18	*Gregory v Hale (t/a Hale Construction)* (Leeds County Ct), para 941
	£1,500	Female/20 +	*Walsh v Clarke* (Kingston Upon Thames County Ct), para 941

INJURY	DAMAGES AWARDED	SEX/AGE	CITATION & REVIEW PARA NUMBER
	£200	Male/39	*Galtrees v Patten* (Birkenhead County Ct), para 941
Neck and shoulder	£100,000	Male/52	*Huston v Homewood and Mayne Nickless Finances plc* (QBD), para 942
	£5,302	Female/68	*Young v Costello* (Oldham County Ct), para 942
Shoulder	£22,300	Female/37	*Bryg v Fuji Television Network Inc* (Central London County Ct), para 943
	£15,650·18	Male/41	*Creedon v Rainor and Padam (t/a Grange Construction) and Sehmis (t/a Sehmis Builders Merchants)* (Brentford County Ct), para 943
	£4,000	Male/61	(CICB), para 943
	£3,533·69	Male/30	*Berry v Roe* (Bromley County Ct), para 943
Shoulder, arm and thigh	£2,452·54	Male/26	*Foster v Appleton* (Oldham County Ct), para 942
Trunk	£1,850	Male/34	(CICB), para 944
Stomach	£1,250	Male/—	(CICB), para 945
Back	£28,070	Male/44	*Vickers v Chief Constable of West Midlands* (QBD, Birmingham), para 946
	£23,430	Male/48, female/45	*Mochan v Paterson Candy Holst Ltd* (Lincoln County Ct), para 946
	£19,631·25	Male/41	*Maslin v Sankey Jonchu Ltd* (Blackpool County Ct), para 946
	£14,229·30	Male/28	*Hyland v George* (Liverpool County Ct), para 946

INJURY	DAMAGES AWARDED	SEX/AGE	CITATION & REVIEW PARA NUMBER
	£12,000	Female/30	*Bradnock v Liston* (Outer House), para 946
	£9,000	Female/36	*Coonan v Rashid & Rashid* (Brentford County Ct), para 946
	£6,050	Male/25	*Mattinson v Ullah* (Bury County Ct), para 946
	£5,000	Female/42	*Young v Greater Glasgow Health Board* (Outer House), para 946
	£3,300	Male/30	*Jones v Liverpool City Council* (Liverpool County Ct), para 946
	£3,000	Female/57	*Weeks v WJ & SD Williams (t/a Barum Cabs) and Lucas-Farley* (Barnstaple County Ct), para 946
	£2,000	Male/52	*Williams v Parry (t/a Animal Lovers)* (Cardiff County Ct), para 946
	£2,000	Male/—	*Ellaway v Bambergers Transportation Ltd* (QBD), para 946
	£1,200	Male/59	*Hornigold v Taylor (t/a Hesketh Shooting Club)* (Preston County Ct), para 946
	£1,000	Male/—	*Russell v John Williams* (Cardiff County Ct), para 946
Arm	£301,861	Male/34	*Wright v Ramsden* (QBD), para 947
	£5,137	Female/30	*Wickens v Red Shift Theatre Co* (Central London County Ct), para 947
Arm and hands	£189,502	Male/34 (at hearing)	*Cord v Technico* (QBD, Birmingham), para 948

INJURY	DAMAGES AWARDED	SEX/AGE	CITATION & REVIEW PARA NUMBER
Elbows	£104,398·47	Male/39	*Fry v Double A Hydraulics* (QBD, Plymouth), para 949
Elbow	£193,000	Male/38	*Girvan v Inverness Farmers Dairy* (Court of Session), para 950
Elbow, wrist and hand	£5,000	Male/43	*Radford v Giovanni* (Reading County Ct), para 951
Wrist	£26,923·73	Female/27 (at hearing)	*Reynolds v Barratts & Baird* (QBD), para 952
	£6,355	Male/58	*Murphy v West Midlands Regional Heaalth Authority* (QBD, Birmingham), para 952
	£695	Male/33	*Chesham v R K Donnelley Ltd* (Wakefield County Ct), para 952
Hands	£24,750	Male/48 (at hearing)	*Bir v A L Dunn & Co Ltd* (Coventry County Ct), para 954
Hand	£34,000	Male/30	*Gunter v Nicholas & Sons* (CA), para 955
	£33,564·29	Male/32	*Martin v Press Offshore* (Newcastle Upon Tyne County Ct), para 955
	£9,869·31	Male/27	*Albrighton v Townscape Products Ltd* (Mansfield County Ct), para 955
	£2,047·04	Female/34	*Beal v Turner* (Slough County Ct), para 948
Hand and wrist	£3,679	Male/37	(CICB), para 953
	£1,912·50	Male/16	*May v British Railways Board* (Coventry County Ct), para 953
Finger	£10,196·02	Male/38	*Cox v GKN Axles* (Leeds County Ct), para 956

INJURY	DAMAGES AWARDED	SEX/AGE	CITATION & REVIEW PARA NUMBER
	£4,376·26	Male/24	*Scott v Higgins Potato Merchants* (Doncaster County Ct), para 956
	£3,750	Male/36	*Stark v Nairn Floors* (Outer House), para 956
	£1,250	Male/51	*Edge v Stanton plc* (Nottingham County Ct), para 956
	£648·05	Male/45	*Leech v South Yorkshire Transport* (Doncaster County Ct), para 956
Thumb	£47,260·67	Male/50	*Cook v Containerships Ltd* (Middlesborough County Court), para 957
	£5,554·85	Male/50	*Sanderson v Precision Engineering Ltd* (Preston County Ct), para 957
	£1,810	Male/28	*Cook v Ideal Waste Paper Co Ltd* (Slough County Ct), para 957
Hip	£285,546·45	Male/44 (at hearing)	*Houghton v Drayton* (QBD), para 958
Pelvis and leg	£4,800	Male/24	*Friar v Pickup* (Bradford County Ct), para 960
Leg	£258,640·90	Male/44 (at hearing)	*Welch v Albright & Wilson* (QBD), para 961
	£175,644	Male/31	*Frost v Palmer* (CA), para 961
	£21,551	Male/56	(CICB), para 961
	£4,000	Male/24	(CICB), para 959
	£3,500	Male/15	*Richardson v Ravoof* (Birmingham County Ct), para 961
Knee	£152,165	Male/23	*Leadbetter v Blackpool, Wyre and Fylde Health Authority* (QBD), para 962

INJURY	DAMAGES AWARDED	SEX/AGE	CITATION & REVIEW PARA NUMBER
	£91,243·64	Female/26	*Newberry v Warwickshire County Council* (QBD), para 962
	£12,500	Male/18	*Lambert v Walker* (Ipswich County Ct), para 962
	£4,000	Male/9	*Southwell v Calderdate Metropolitan Borough Council* (Halifax County Ct), para 962
Ankle	£100,316·21	Male/38	*Swinburn v London Fire and Civil Defence Authority* (QBD), para 963
	£12,500	Male/49	*Thomson v Hailstone* (Southampton County Ct), para 963
	£9,319·74	Female/26	*Cooper v Salford City Council* (Manchester County Ct), para 963
	£6,500	Female/51	*Dinsdale v Urban Firm Ltd* (Liverpool County Ct), para 963
	£1,858·21	Female/36	*Brelsford v British Railways Board* (Derby County Ct), para 963
Feet	£1,775	Female/55	*Smith v Creedon & Yiasoumi* (Peterborough County Ct), para 960
Foot	£17,500	Female/17	*Redding v Sedgemoor District Council* (Bridgwater County Ct), para 964
	£10,500	Female/23	*Polley v Alasti* (Sunderland County Ct), para 959
	£2,000	Female/37	*Thorpe v Calderdale* (Halifax County Ct), para 964

INJURY	DAMAGES AWARDED	SEX/AGE	CITATION & REVIEW PARA NUMBER
	£1,580·73	Male/16	*Phillips v Southern Vectis plc* (Southampton County Court), para 964
	£1,500	Female/3	*Harcourt v Harper* (Chesterfield County Ct), para 964
Minor injuries	£9,847	Female/28	*McGunnigal v DB Marshall (Newbridge) Ltd* (Outer House), para 965
	£5,821·32	Female/68	*Littlefair v Turner* (Preston County Ct), para 966
Skin	£2,400	—/4½	*MLD v Torbay Health Authority* (settled out of court), para 967

TABLE OF ARTICLES

COMMONWEALTH AND DEPENDENCIES

COMPANIES

CRIMINAL LAW

PRESS, PRINTING AND PUBLISHING

RATING AND THE COUNCIL TAX

REAL PROPERTY

ROAD TRAFFIC

ROYAL FORCES

SALE OF GOODS

SENTENCING

VALUERS AND APPRAISERS

WEIGHTS AND MEASURES

WILLS

HALSBURY'S

Annual Abridgment 1993

ADMINISTRATIVE LAW

Halsbury's Laws of England (4th edn) Vol 1(1) (reissue), paras 1–300

1 Articles

Appeals in Judicial Review Cases, Lee Bridges and Stephen Cragg: 143 NLJ 1745
Collateral Attack—Attacking *Ultra Vires* Action Indirectly in Courts and Tribunals, Carl
Emery: 56 MLR 643
Community Care Assessments—A Practitioner's Guide, Richard Gordon (on the use of judicial
review as a means of challenging assessments): 137 SJ 664
Delays in Judicial Review, Ian Cram: 143 NLJ 1198
Discretion to Prosecute and Judicial Review, Christopher Hilson: [1993] Crim LR 739
Falling at the Last Fence, Richard Gordon and Craig Barlow (on *R v Disciplinary Committee of
the Jockey Club, ex p the Aga Khan* [1993] NLJR 163 (1992 Abr para 27)): 143 NLJ 158
Insuring Against Judicial Review, Richard Gordon and Sam Grodzinski: 144 NLJ 98
Judicial Review and the Detained Patient, Richard Gordon: 137 SJ 43
Judicial Review of Police Cautions, Marcus Tregilgas-Davey: Criminal Lawyer, Issue 39, p 4
Judicial Review of the Pit Closures (on *R v British Coal Corpn and the Secretary of State for Trade,
ex p Vardy* [1993] IRLR 104 (1992 Abr para 17)): (1993) 22 ILJ 211
Judicial Review—Questions of Practice and Costs, Tim Kerr: 137 SJ 302
Public Law "Sins" and Pardons, Alistair Lindsay (on the implications of *R v Home Secretary, ex p
Bentley* (1993) NLJ 1025 (para 30): 143 NLJ 1418
The Black Hole Theory, Richard Gordon and Craig Barlow: 143 NLJ 322
The Jockey Club and Judicial Review, Neil Parpworth (on *R v Disciplinary Committee of the
Jockey Club, ex p the Aga Khan* [1993] NLJR 163 (1992 Abr para 27)): 137 SJ 252
The Lottery of Judicial Review, Maurice Sunkin, Lee Bridges and George Meszaros: Counsel,
July 1993, p 19
The Reform of Judicial Review in Queensland, Timothy Jones: (1993) 12 CJQ 256

2 Administrative powers—modification of legislation—severance of partly invalid legislation—test of substantial severability

See *Comr of Police v Davis*, para 556.

3 Contract entered into by the Crown—Prime Minister's authority—contract for the construction of government building

South Africa
The plaintiff entered into a contract to build a government building which included a private
dwelling enclosing the Prime Minister's office. The contract was concluded by the then Prime
Minister and an issue arose as to whether he had the necessary authority to do so on behalf of the
then government. The plaintiff in an action against the government claimed that the contract
ought to stand and alleged that the Prime Minister had implied authority, that it was common
knowledge that he wielded such power in government and that his decisions were, as a matter
of practice, acted upon by the government. The defendant government, at the close of the
plaintiff's case, applied to be absolved from the case. *Held*, where the purpose of a contract was
to bring about the construction of a government building for use by the government, the
contract would clearly be categorised as one which was entered into in the ordinary or necessary
course of government administration. In following *New South Wales v Bardolph* (1934) 52 CLR

1

455 a contract entered into by the government of a state was enforceable if: (1) the contract was entered into in the ordinary or necessary course of government administration, (2) it was authorised by the responsible Ministers of the State, and (3) the payments which the contractor was seeking to recover from the government were covered by or were referable to a parliamentary grant for the class of service to which the contract related. The failure of the contractor, as plaintiff, to prove requirement (3) ought not to affect the validity of the contract but would be related to the enforcement of the contract rather than to inherent invalidity. The plaintiff had therefore made out a prima facie case that the defendant lawfully incurred the obligation and the Prime Minister had the necessary authority to conclude the contract on behalf of the defendant. Accordingly, the application would be dismissed.

Quintessence Co-Ordinators (Pty) Ltd v Government of the Republic of Transkei (1993) 3 SA 184 (Transkei General Division). (Kindly submitted for publication by IG Farlam, counsel for the plaintiff).

4 Judicial review—British Railways Board—enforcement of statutory duty— private legislation

Scotland

A local council sought an order requiring the defendants to construct barriers at a level crossing, in compliance with their statutory duty under the Highway (Railway Crossings) Act 1839, s 1. At the same time, the defendants were promoting private legislation that would have the effect of closing the crossing and therefore claimed that whilst a draft order was laid before Parliament, the court's function was supervisory and equitable and it therefore had a discretion whether or not to order specific performance of statutory duties. *Held*, the court could not properly refuse the order unless the defendants could establish that they had an exceptional case and cogent reasons for such an order not to be granted. The defendants had to comply with the law as quickly as possible even though there was private legislation which, should it be passed, would render the order invalid. The court would not suspend an order for compliance merely because to do so would cause the defendants to incur costs and inconvenience. Accordingly the order would be granted.

Tayside Regional Council v British Railways Board (1993) Times, 30 December (Outer House).

5 Judicial review—committal—failure to pay community charge

See *R v Alfreton Justices, ex p Gratton*, para 2118.

6 Judicial review—county council's duty to accommodate gypsies—fact-finding exercise

The applicant, a gypsy, purchased land and duly stationed his caravan on the plot. The district council issued enforcement and stop notices on the applicant which he continued to contravene. The applicant sought, by way of judicial review, to challenge the council's attempt to obtain injunctive relief against him. The county council was joined in the application, without previous complaint being made about its performance of its own duties under the Caravan Sites Act 1968, s 6 to supply adequate accommodation for gypsies residing in or resorting to its area. The joinder of the county council led to an investigation of the ethnic origins of the applicant which gave rise to disputed issues of fact. *Held*, judicial review would be inappropriate for the fact-finding exercise involved. A court of first instance or a statutory body with responsibility for investigation would be better equipped to undertake it. Parliament clearly intended that the appropriate remedy for a grievance such as the applicant's was by way of representation to the Secretary of State and intervention by the court would therefore rarely be appropriate. Accordingly, the application would be dismissed.

R v West Sussex County Council, ex p Wenman [1993] LG Rev 201 (Queen's Bench Division: Brooke J).

7 Judicial review—decision of Broadcasting Complaints Commission

See *R v Broadcasting Complaints Commission, ex p Granada Television Ltd*, para 2441.

8 Judicial review—decision of coroner—duty to summon jury

See *R v Merseyside Coroner, ex p Carr*, para 628.

9   Judicial review—decision of coroner—unlawful killing—verdict should be left to jury

A prisoner died in a struggle with prison officers. A fellow prisoner gave evidence that the officers had jumped up and down on the deceased. At the subsequent inquest, the doctor who performed the post-mortem examination stated that it was highly possible that death was caused by acute cardiac failure during the struggle. In summing up, the coroner withdrew the verdict of unlawful killing from the jury on the grounds that no reasonable jury could be satisfied beyond reasonable doubt that the medical cause of death was injury resulting from an unlawful act. The hearing was adjourned whilst judicial review proceedings were brought. *Held*, the coroner erred in considering only the medical cause of death. There was evidence on which a jury could decide that death was caused by cardiac arrest resulting from the deceased's struggle to resist being restrained. There was a risk that the prisoner's evidence was exaggerated, but it was not so inherently unreliable as to justify rejecting it as worthless. Further, although the death was not attributable to the acts of any single officer, the principles of joint enterprise were as applicable in an inquest as they were in a criminal trial. Accordingly, the inquest would be resumed and the verdict of unlawful killing would be left to the jury.

R v Coroner for Inner North London, ex p Diesa Koto (1993) 157 JP 857 (Queen's Bench Division: Lloyd LJ and Blofeld J).

10   Judicial review—decision of Crown Court—appeal against costs—determination of jurisdiction

See *R v Crown Court at Canterbury, ex p Kent County Council*, para 1733.

11   Judicial review—decision of Crown Court—dismissal of appeal—duty to give reasons

See *R v Crown Court at Harrow, ex p Dave*, para 672.

12   Judicial review—decision of Crown Court—limits of judicial review

At the trial of the defendant an order was made that statements taken from the police during an informal resolution of complaints and which were inadmissible at trial under the Police and Criminal Evidence Act 1984, s 104(3) ought to be disclosed to the defence. The prosecution sought judicial review of the decision. *Held*, the Crown Court was in the same position as the High Court and its decisions were not open to challenge in the High Court. However, some of its decisions were subject to the supervisory power of the Divisional Court. That supervisory power was limited to the provisions of the Supreme Court Act 1981, ss 28, 29 and the general power of judicial review under the 1981 Act, s 31, which was subject to those sections. Accordingly, the court did not have jurisdiction to hear the application, and it would be dismissed.

R v Crown Court at Chelmsford, ex p Chief Constable of Essex Police [1994] 1 All ER 325 (Queen's Bench Division: Glidewell LJ and Cresswell J).

13   Judicial review—decision of Crown Prosecution Service—refusal to disclose unused material—susceptibiltiy to judicial review

The applicant had been charged with handling stolen property. The Crown Prosecution Service (CPS) refused to disclose to him prior to committal proceedings certain unused material in his possession. The applicant believed that the material in question would be of use to him in his defence to the charge and sought judicial review of the decision of the CPS, contending that it had failed to comply with the Attorney General's *Guidelines on the Disclosure of Information to the Defence in Cases to be Tried on Indictment* (1981) 74 Cr App Rep 302. *Held*, it would be inappropriate for decisions as to disclosure of unused material to be taken in a lower level of court than the Crown Court because the material in question might be sensitive and, regardless of the attitude adopted on committal, the question as to whether unused material should be disclosed would inevitably have to be determined by a Crown Court judge. A decision by the CPS refusing to disclose unused material upon request prior to committal proceedings was not subject to judicial review. It was for the Crown Court to decide whether the CPS was entitled to withhold unused material. The application would be dismissed.

R v Crown Prosecution Service, ex p Warby (1993) Independent, 16 September (Queen's Bench Division: Watkins LJ and Auld J).

14 Judicial review—decision of district health authority—failure to consult Community Health Council

See *R v North West Thames Regional Health Authority, ex p Daniels*, para 1840.

15 Judicial review—decision of employer as to redundancy—consultation with trade union

An employer proposed to close a number of collieries on the ground that they were no longer economically viable. A union representing miners at the collieries sought judicial review of the employer's decision and obtained an order that the employer could not reach a final decision on the closure until it had followed an agreed procedure for consultation with the union. The employer applied for a declaration that it would not be in breach of the previous order if it implemented the decision to close the collieries, arguing that it had now followed the proper consultation procedure. The union disputed that the appropriate consultation had taken place. *Held*, in the knowledge of the inevitable decline in the market for coal, and of government policy, the employer was entitled to say that at any one of the collieries the requirement for their employees to carry out other work was expected to diminish if not to cease, and thus to treat them as being redundant. It was apparent from the facts that the employer had genuinely consulted the union with a view to seeking agreement on a form of machinery substantially the same as the agreed consultation procedure. The criteria adopted for closing the collieries, that they were operating at a loss and that there was no realistic prospect of them operating at a profit in the foreseeable future, were perfectly reasonable. The earlier order had been based upon the employer's failure to consult and not the irrationality of their criteria. Accordingly, the declaration would be granted.

R v British Coal Corpn, ex p Price (No 3) (1993) Times, 28 May (Queen's Bench Division: Glidewell LJ and Hidden J). For earlier related proceedings, see *R v British Coal Corpn, ex p Vardy* (1992) Times, 30 December (1992 Abr para 17).

16 Judicial review—decision of Football Association—susceptibility to judicial review

The Football Association (the "FA"), as the governing body and rule-making authority of association football in England, sanctioned various leagues including the Football League (the "League") which consisted of four divisions. Football clubs which desired FA recognition and to play in an FA sanctioned league had to be affiliated to the FA or an affiliated association. The League had a contractual arrangement with the FA whereby the League, in accordance with the FA's rules, applied annually for the FA's sanction to run the four divisions comprising the League. The League adopted a regulation requiring any member club to give three seasons' notice to terminate membership, or an indemnity in lieu of notice. The FA subsequently decided to form and run a Premier League consisting of the first division clubs and to amend its regulations so that any League regulation requiring a longer notice period for termination than the FA's was void. The League sought judicial review of the FA's decisions to set up the Premier League and amend its regulations, contending that judicial review was applicable to the FA because it had monopoly control over, and its rules were in effect a legislative code for, the game of association football. *Held*, the FA was not amenable to judicial review because it was a domestic body whose powers and duties existed in private law only. Despite its monopoly and the importance of its decisions to the public, it was not supported by any state body or interest and there was no evidence that in its absence the state would create an equivalent body. It would be inappropriate to apply principles designed to control public abuses of power to such a body. Accordingly, the application would be dismissed.

R v Football Association, ex p Football League; Football Association v Football League [1993] 2 All ER 833 (Queen's Bench Division: Rose J).

17 Judicial review—decision of health authority—conditional offer to disclose patient's medical records

See *R v Mid-Glamorgan Family Health Services Authority, ex p Martin*, para 1770.

18 Judicial review—decision of Home Secretary—refusal to give reasons for decision

See *R v Secretary of State for the Home Department, ex p Doody; R v Secretary of State for the Home Department, ex p Pierson; R v Secretary of State for the Home Department, ex p Smart; R v Secretary of State for the Home Department, ex p Pegg*, para 2084.

19   Judicial review—decision of Investors' Compensation Scheme—right to compensation

See *R v Investors' Compensation Scheme Ltd, ex p Weyell*, para 1268.

20   Judicial review—decision of justices—decision to adjourn hearing

See *R v Kingston upon Thames Justices, ex p Martin*, para 1731.

21   Judicial review—decision of local authority—council's duty to negotiate contractual terms with residential care home owners

See *R v Cleveland County Council, ex p Cleveland Care Homes Association*, para 2399.

22   Judicial review—decision of local authority—duty to provide day care services for children in need—closure of day nursery

See *R v Barnet London Borough Council, ex p B*, para 409.

23   Judicial review—decision of local education authority—exercise of education function—provision of places at single sex school—sex discrimination

See *R v Northamptonshire County Council, ex p K*, para 1084.

24   Judicial review—decision of Lord Chancellor—choice of tender

The applicants submitted a tender for a contract to supply the services of shorthand writers to a court for three years. Although they had provided services to the court for nearly 90 years their application was unsuccessful. The firm applied for judicial review of the Lord Chancellor's decision to award the contract for court reporting services to another firm. *Held*, the procedures adopted by the Lord Chancellor when deciding which tender to adopt were in part at least unfair. The wording of the instructions for tendering issued by the Lord Chancellor, which stated the right to enter into discussions with tenderers to clarify bids, gave rise to a legitimate expectation on the part of the applicants that tenderers would not be able to submit reduced bids. The applicants satisfied all the other criteria but were precluded from submitting a reduced bid. Although the applicants had been treated unfairly it was impossible to provide them with relief by way of judicial review because the decision challenged lacked a sufficient public law element. Accordingly, the application would be dismissed.

R v Lord Chancellor, ex p Hibbit and Saunders (a firm) (1993) Times, 12 March (Queen's Bench Division: Rose LJ and Waller J).

25   Judicial review—decision of Lord Chancellor—legal aid

See *R v Lord Chancellor, ex p the Law Society*, paras 1668, 1669.

26   Judicial review—decision of magistrates—issue of summons—exercise of discretion

See *R v Metropolitan Stipendiary Magistrate, ex p Chaudhry*, para 1739.

27   Judicial review—decision of magistrates—validity of repealed legislation

The Interpretation Act 1978, s 16(1)(c) provides that where an Act repeals an enactment, the repeal does not affect any obligation or liability incurred under that enactment unless the contrary intention appears.

The applicant was charged with contravening the requirements of a noise abatement notice, contrary to the Control of Pollution Act 1974, s 58(4). That provision had been replaced by the Environmental Protection Act 1990, s 162(2), and the notice requiring the applicant to prevent noise escaping from her premises had been served under the 1974 Act, s 58(1) two weeks before the 1990 Act had come into force. The justices ruled that the validity of notices served under the 1974 Act had been preserved by the 1990 Act, and the applicant challenged that ruling and sought a writ of mandamus directing the justices to acquit her on both counts. *Held*, the 1974 Act, s 58(9) specifically preserved the validity of noise abatement notices served under the Noise Abatement Act 1960, but the 1990 Act had not contained a similar provision to preserve the validity of notices served under the 1974 Act, s 58(1), so the notice served upon the applicant had ceased to be valid once the 1990 Act had come into force. The fact that the 1990 Act had not contained a similar provision indicated there had been an intention to abandon the old procedure in favour of the new one which the 1990 Act had introduced, so the Crown could not rely on the provisions of the 1978 Act, s 16 because a "contrary intention" had appeared. The application would be allowed, and a writ would be granted in the terms sought.

R v Folkestone Justices, ex p Kibble [1993] Crim LR 704 (Queen's Bench Division: Watkins LJ and Owen J).

28   Judicial review—decision of Secretary of State—alteration of local authority boundary line

Scotland

The Secretary of State for Scotland decided to make and obtain parliamentary approval for a statutory instrument altering the boundary line between two local authorities. The applicant, one of the authorities which would thereby incur expense of about £300,000, sought judicial review of the decision, contending that the Secretary of State had failed to consider the imminent comprehensive reorganisation of local government. *Held*, the courts could only hold to be ultra vires a statutory instrument which had been laid before Parliament where that instrument was patently defective in that it purported to do what was not authorised by the enabling statute or where the procedure followed in making the instrument departed from the requirements of the enabling statute. The applicant's contention was not a relevant challenge of the Secretary of State's decision and, accordingly, the application would be dismissed.

East Kilbride District Council v Secretary of State for Scotland (1993) Times, 18 August (Outer House).

29   Judicial review—decision of Secretary of State—barring of teacher

See *R v Secretary of State for Education, ex p Standish*, para 1104.

30   Judicial review—decision of Secretary of State—exercise of prerogative of mercy—susceptibility to judicial review

In 1952, the applicant's brother, Derek Bentley, was jointly convicted with Christopher Craig of the murder of a police officer. Although it was Craig who shot the officer, Bentley, aged 19, was convicted as an accomplice because he had shouted, "Let him have it, Chris", before the shot was fired. Bentley was sentenced to death and executed, despite the jury's recommendation for mercy; Craig could not be sentenced to death because he was only 16. The applicant sought judicial review of the Home Secretary's decision not to recommend a posthumous free pardon for her brother. The Home Secretary claimed that the basis upon which he exercised the pardon was a question of policy and not justiciable. However, the applicant contended that the Home Secretary had failed to recognise the wide scope and flexibility of the prerogative of mercy: it could be exercised in differing circumstances and to varying degrees. This failure was an error of law and thus amenable to judicial review. *Held*, a free pardon should only be granted where the technical and moral innocence of the convicted person was established. However, the prerogative's inherent flexibility gave the Home Secretary the option to grant other forms of pardon, for example a conditional pardon, with a lower sentence being substituted. The Home Secretary failed to give sufficient consideration to his power to grant a form of pardon appropriate to the particular case and this failure was reviewable. There were now strong grounds for believing that Bentley should have been reprieved. Although the court did not think it right to make a formal order or declaration, it believed that the grant of a posthumous conditional pardon would be a suitable acknowledgement by the state that a mistake had been made in not granting a reprieve. Accordingly, the Home Secretary would be invited to consider the matter again.

R v Secretary of State for the Home Department, ex p Bentley [1993] 4 All ER 442 (Queen's Bench Division: Watkins and Neill LJJ and Tuckey J).

31   Judicial review—decision of Secretary of State—high security risk prisoner—determination of security category

See *R v Secretary of State for the Home Department, ex p Duggan*, para 2078.

32   Judicial review—decision of Secretary of State—proscription of foreign satellite service

See *R v Secretary of State for the National Heritage, ex p Continental Television BV*, para 1524.

33   Judicial review—decision of spiritual leader—susceptibility to judicial review

The applicants sought judicial review of the decision of an imam to exclude certain persons from the list of those eligible to vote in respect of a mosque's affairs. *Held*, there was no public law element in the imam's function or in the nature of his decision. His power to reach that decision came from an order of the court binding on the parties and based on the private law of contract. His decision was not susceptible to judicial review and, accordingly, the application would be dismissed.

R v Imam of Bury Park Mosque, Luton, ex p Sulaiman Ali (1993) Times, 20 May (Court of Appeal: Balcombe, McCowan and Roch LJJ). Decision of Auld J (1991) Independent, 13 September (1991 Abr para 12) affirmed.

34   Judicial review—decision of Universities Funding Council—reasons for decision—appearance of fairness

The plaintiff college was assessed by the defendant funding council as to the quality of its research. It was assessed at a level lower than that of previous years which had implications for the level of outside funding which the plaintiff would expect to receive. The plaintiff applied for judicial review of the decision on the ground that the defendant failed to give reasons for its decision. *Held*, the defendant's assessment was carried out by a panel of specialists who gave their ratings by secret ballot. There was no general duty to give reasons, as a requirement to do so would place an undue burden on the decision-makers by calling for the articulation of sometimes inexpressible value judgments. Where what was sought to be impugned was no more than an informed decision of academic judgment, fairness alone would not require reasons to be given. Further, the eventual rating was far from being absurd, and therefore it did not call for an explanation. Accordingly, the application would be dismissed.

R v Higher Education Funding Council, ex p Institute of Dental Surgery [1994] 1 All ER 651 (Queen's Bench Division: Mann LJ and Sedley J).

35   Judicial review—decision of university examinations board—conscientious judgment—matters to be taken into account

The applicant took unauthorised material into an examination. At an oral hearing before the Faculty Examinations Disciplinary Committee of his university, at which he was present and represented, he denied referring to the material but was found guilty of attempting to gain an unfair academic advantage rather than the more serious offence of cheating. Evidence, including testimonials and a short report from a psychiatrist, was called. The committee found that there were mitigating circumstances, made no formal recommendations but asked the Examination Board of Examiners of the university to determine the appropriate action or penalty. The board, which did not have before it all the testimonials or the psychiatrist's report, decided that the applicant should be deemed to have failed the examination and not be permitted to resit it. He challenged those decisions. *Held*, the applicant had no right to attend the board meeting and was entirely dependent on what was placed before it. The board did not have before it some important statements in mitigation so that there was a material failure by it to take into account matters which it was obliged to take into account. Given the acceptance of the mitigating evidence and the conclusive finding of a lesser offence than cheating, it was for the decision-making body of the university to decide what was the appropriate penalty or disposal for the applicant. The court would not hold that it could never be, or could not on the limited evidence before the board, have been a rational or proportionate response to fail a student for something less than cheating. Subject to the court's supervisory jurisdiction, the board had to exercise a conscientious judgment on the material before it. Its decisions would be quashed and it would now exercise that judgment having before it all the material which ought to have been before it and also bearing in mind the precise limits and purposes of its function.

R v Manchester Metropolitan University, ex p Nolan (1993) Independent, 15 July (Queen's Bench Division: Mann LJ and Sedley J).

36   Judicial review—decision of waste disposal authority—competitive tendering

See *R v Avon County Council, ex p Terry Adams Ltd*, para 1224.

37   Judicial review—decision to prosecute—abuse of process

See *R v Lincoln Magistrates' Court, ex p Wickes Building Supplies Ltd*, para 2531.

38   Judicial review—decision to prosecute—overseas offender

The applicant, a New Zealand citizen, was wanted for questioning by the police in the United Kingdom. He was arrested in South Africa, sent to the United kingdom, where he was arrested and subsequently committed for trial. He alleged that he had been brought into the country by unlawful means and sought judicial review of the decision to prosecute. It was held that the court had no power to inquire into the circumstances whereby the applicant came into the jurisdiction, and his application was dismissed. On appeal, *held*, Lord Oliver dissenting, it was an abuse of process for a person to be forcibly brought within the jurisdiction in disregard of extradition procedures available for the return of an accused person to the United Kingdom. The High Court in the exercise of its supervisory jurisdiction had the power to inquire into the circumstances by which a person had been brought into the United Kingdom, and if it was satisfied that it was in disregard of extradition procedures, it had the power to stay the prosecution and order the release of the accused. The applicant's appeal would accordingly be allowed.

Bennett v Horseferry Road Magistrates' Court [1993] 3 All ER 138 (House of Lords: Lord Griffiths, Lord Bridge of Harwich, Lord Oliver of Aylmerton, Lord Lowry and Lord Slynn of Hadley). Decision of Queen's Bench Divisional Court [1993] 2 All ER 474 (1992 Abr para 24) reversed.

39   Judicial review—declaration—sole purpose of declaration to support claim for damages

RSC Ord 53, r 1 provides that an application for a declaration may be made by way of an application for judicial review and r 7 provides for an award of damages to be made on an application for judicial review.

A council improperly applied the Housing Act 1985, Pt II, to the applicant's claim for rehousing. Her original claim for judicial review was adjourned and the council then correctly applied Pt III. She sought leave to apply for a declaration that the council's initial approach was improper and for consequential damages. *Held*, this was a private law claim which required the establishment of a public law obligation as a condition precedent. Since the public body made good the default outside the scope of legal proceedings, the applicant's claim for damages had become stranded and could now only be prosecuted within the judicial review procedure if leave was granted to seek the declaration. It would be an abuse of process to bring the claim outside the judicial review procedure and thus, if leave was not granted, any application begun by writ risked being struck out. Although the application for a declaration was an artificial means to enable the claim for ancillary damages to proceed, it was necessary to circumvent procedural rules which might deny an applicant with a viable claim a legal forum. A refusal would be a denial of justice and, accordingly, the application would be allowed.

R v Northavon District Council, ex p Palmer (1993) 25 HLR 674 (Queen's Bench Division: Sedley J).

40   Judicial review—declaration—subsequent variation of declaration

In earlier proceedings, the court had declared that a decision by the Secretary of State and the employer to close 10 coal mines and review the future of 21 others had been unlawful. The applicant sought a variation of that order to prohibit the employer from closing any of the 10 collieries until the modified pit review procedure had been followed, and to notify and consult with certain trades unions if it decided not to implement that procedure. *Held*, the court had already discharged its function, and in those circumstances it had no jurisdiction to grant the relief sought. Even if the court had jurisdiction, it would have been premature to grant relief because the employer had not yet decided whether to close the mines, or even on the form of consultation it would adopt, and any challenge which the applicant wished to make would have to wait until those decisions had been made. Accordingly, the application would be refused.

R v British Coal Corpn, ex p Price (No 2) (1993) Times, 23 February (Queen's Bench Division: Glidewell LJ). For earlier related proceedings, see *R v British Coal Corpn, ex p Vardy* (1992) Times, 30 December (1992 Abr para 17).

41   Judicial review—deportation order—extra-statutory advisory panel—right to legal representation

Scotland

The applicants were subject to proposed deportation orders. The Home Secretary had previously set up an extra-statutory advisory panel to hear representations from persons aggrieved by such decisions and had intimated that each petitioner could make representations to the panel but that he could not be legally represented before it. In judicial review proceedings, the applicants argued that while the panel had no legal personality distinct from the Home Secretary, the Home Secretary would be bound himself to consider representations from legal advisers. *Held*, although the Home Secretary had to exercise a discretionary power with regard to deportation, there was no right to legal representation before the panel. Accordingly, the application would be dismissed.

Abbas v Secretary of State for the Home Department 1993 SLT 502 (Outer House).

42   Judicial review—leave to apply—decision of council—review of market stall rent increase

The plaintiff was a market trader trading at stalls owned by the defendant council. A resolution was passed by the council to change the method of assessment and increase the levels of rent for stalls to be paid by market traders. The plaintiff applied for judicial review of the decision. In seeking to distinguish the case of *R v Barnsley Metropolitan Borough Council, ex p Hook* [1976] 1 WLR 1052, the council asserted that its decision in relation to stall charges was a managerial and commercial one and therefore outside the field of public law. The plaintiff argued that the decision would affect his ability to come to the market and follow his livelihood. *Held*, it was clear that the only way in which the plaintiff would be able to trade was by obtaining and paying for a stall, the council had effectively excluded the plaintiff by putting his rent up to a ridiculously high level and as the underlying relationship was the common law right to trade and to earn a living the case was a public law matter. Accordingly, the council's decision to increase stall charges was susceptible to judicial review.

R v Birmingham City Council, ex p Dredger (1993) Times, 28 January (Queen's Bench Division: Hutchison J).

43   Judicial review—leave to apply—grounds for decision to grant or refuse leave

See *R v Secretary of State for Transport, ex p Richmond London Borough Council*, para 152.

44   Judicial review—letter explaining school's policy—justiciability

The father of the applicant, a pupil at a school in Wales, requested that the majority of the applicant's teaching at the school be in English rather than in Welsh. The headmaster wrote to the father explaining that the school's policy was to teach in the medium of the Welsh language. The father sought judicial review of the alleged decision of the headmaster refusing his request. *Held*, no decision had been made as far as the applicant was concerned. The court had no jurisdiction to consider the application for judicial review which, accordingly, would be dismissed.

R v Gwynedd County Council, ex p W (1993) Times, 25 June (Queen's Bench Division: Watkins LJ and Tucker J).

45   Judicial review—proceedings—costs—legal representative's personal liability for costs

See *R v Horsham District Council, ex p Wenman*, para 2014.

46   Judicial review—Parliamentary Commissioner for Administration—extent of discretionary powers

The Parliamentary Commissioner Act 1967, lays down the procedure for the investigation of complaints of maladministration by members of the public. Section 5(1) states that a complaint must first be made to an MP who then refers it to the Parliamentary Commissioner. Section 5(5) states that subject to certain restrictions the Parliamentary Commissioner acts in accordance with his own discretion in determining whether to initiate or discontinue an investigation. Under s 10 the Parliamentary Commissioner must first send a report of the investigation to the MP and the government department concerned.

The Parliamentary Commissioner carried out an investigation into the mishandling of the applicant's claims for benefit from the Department of Social Security (the "DSS"). The Parliamentary Commissioner had submitted a report to the DSS and to the MP who had referred the case, in which he concluded that the complaint was justified and that an apology and a money payment towards expenses were sufficient compensation. The applicant was not satisfied with the investigation and applied for judicial review of the Parliamentary

Commissioner's refusal to re-open the investigation. *Held,* (1) the fact that the Parliamentary Commissioner was subject to control under the 1967 Act did not displace the supervisory control of the courts. The court was therefore entitled to review the Parliamentary Commissioner's exercise of his discretion. However because of the width of the Parliamentary Commissioner's discretion the court would not readily interfere. (2) With regard to the specific complaints, the Parliamentary Commissioner was permitted to restrict his investigations and it was not essential to investigate all of the complaints. A draft report had been sent to the DSS for comment but it was not also necessary to send it to the complainant. The discretion in s 5(5) did not extend to reopening the investigation without further referring the complaint to an MP, as required under s 5(1).

R v Parliamentary Comr for Administration, ex p Dyer [1994] 1 All ER 375 (Queen's Bench Division: Simon Brown LJ and Buckley J).

47 Judicial review—prerogative power—exercise of prerogative of mercy—susceptibility to judicial review

See *R v Secretary of State for the Home Department, ex p Bentley,* para 30.

48 Judicial review—scope—order of contempt against minister of the Crown

See *M v Home Office,* para 583.

49 Judicial review and statutory appeals—Law Commission consultation paper

The Law Commission has published a consultation paper, *Administrative Law: Judicial Review and Statutory Appeals* (consultation paper No 126), suggesting that some rationalisation of the process of appeals and judicial review should be considered. It queries the composition of the High Court acting in its appellate capacity, and whether all existing appeals and applications could be reduced to two procedures. Consideration is given to differences between the locus standi on appeals and applications for judicial review and to the time limits for initiating the procedures and to extensions of time. It is suggested that some harmonisation might be sought in relation to the provisions for the stay or suspension of orders pending appeals and applications for judicial review. Views are sought on the clarification of the High Court's powers on appeal, the principles which should underlie the right of appeal or the grant of leave to appeal, the continued distinction between cases where there is a right of appeal and those where there is none, and the overlap between appellate and review bodies. Consideration is given to a number of procedural matters, including the originating process, the respondents to proceedings, the clarification of the procedure at appeal hearings, and to the principles governing further appeals.

50 Natural justice—determination of compensation—decision on basis of valuation not relied on by parties—breach of natural justice

A council made a compulsory purchase order in relation to a building and the amount of compensation payable was referred to the Lands Tribunal for determination. At the hearing, the claimants advanced three valuations for the building. The tribunal rejected all of these and adopted a fourth basis of valuation not relied on by the claimants. The council appealed, contending that the tribunal acted in breach of natural justice as the chosen valuation had not been relied on by the claimants and the council had not been given proper opportunity to deal with it. *Held,* although the tribunal, acting as an expert, was entitled to act upon a basis of valuation put forward by neither side at the hearing, it was necessary to ensure that the parties were given proper opportunity to call any evidence with reference to it and to make submissions upon it. The tribunal should have raised the matter at the hearing or called the parties back for further consideration. Accordingly, the appeal would be allowed.

Aquilina and Carberry v London Borough of Havering (1993) 66 P & CR 39 (Court of Appeal: Lloyd and Ralph Gibson LJJ and Sir David Croom-Johnson).

51 Tribunals and inquiries—supervision—friendly societies tribunals

The Tribunals and Inquiries (Friendly Societies) Order 1993, SI 1993/3258 (in force on 1 February 1994), amends the Tribunals and Inquiries Act 1992 to provide for the bringing of tribunals constituted under the Friendly Societies Act 1992, s 59 and adjudicators appointed under s 84 of that Act under the supervision of the Council on Tribunals, and for consultation with the Council before the making of procedural rules or regulations under the Friendly Societies Act 1992, s 60.

ADMIRALTY

Halsbury's Laws of England (4th edn) Vol 1(1) (reissue), paras 301–564

52   Action in rem—arrest of ship—amendment of rules of procedure—effect on issue of warrant for arrest

The owner of cargo on board a motor vessel obtained a warrant for the arrest of the vessel's sister ship. The owners of the vessels successfully applied for the warrant to be set aside on the ground that the cargo owner had failed to make full and frank disclosure of certain material facts in his affidavit, as required by RSC Ord 75, r 5(4). However, the day after the application was heard, counsel for the cargo owner was informed that RSC Ord 75, r 5 had been amended so that the issue of a warrant was no longer a discretionary remedy and the strict obligations regarding disclosure no longer applied. On the basis of that information the cargo owner appealed against the decision to set the warrant aside. *Held*, the cargo owner's affidavit had complied with the requirements of the amended RSC Ord 75 even though he had failed to draw the court's attention to certain material facts, including the fact that proceedings between the parties were pending in another jurisdiction, so there had been no grounds for setting the warrant aside. It was highly regrettable that neither the judge nor the Court of Appeal on the original hearing had been made aware of those changes by either party's legal representatives. Accordingly, the appeal would be allowed.

The Varna [1993] 2 Lloyd's Rep 253 (Court of Appeal: Scott and Rose LJJ). *The Vasso* [1983] 3 All ER 211, DC (1983 Abr para 259) considered.

53   Action in rem—arrest of ship—jurisdiction of court

The defendant owners chartered vessels to the plaintiffs under bareboat charters. The plaintiffs time-chartered the vessels to a firm of freighters, who employed them on a cross-channel ferry service. The defendants subsequently withdrew both vessels on the ground of non-payment of hire. The freighters gave notice terminating the time charters on the ground that the plaintiffs were no longer able to perform their obligations under the time charters. The defendants commenced arbitration proceedings against the plaintiffs, claiming unpaid hire and damages. The plaintiffs served a defence and counterclaim. The defendants entered into fresh bareboat charters with the freighters and the vessels continued to be employed on the ferry service. The plaintiffs issued proceedings in rem against the vessels, having given due warning that they intended to arrest the vessels in order to obtain security for their counterclaim in the arbitration. The vessels were arrested and taken into the custody of the Admiralty Marshal. The defendants issued a motion for a stay of the action in rem under the Arbitration Act 1975, s 1 and for the warrant of arrest to be set aside. The judge, without dealing with the s 1 application, made an interim order that the vessels were to remain under arrest, but could continue to be employed on the ferry service against certain undertakings given by the defendants and the freighters. That order was varied by another judge who ordered that the vessels remain within the jurisdiction of the court pending a full hearing of the defendants' motion. The defendants and the freighters appealed against both the interim order and the variation. *Held*, a vessel could not remain within the custody of the Admiralty Marshal and yet be allowed to trade outside the jurisdiction. The effect of the Civil Jurisdiction and Judgments Act 1982, s 26 was to assimilate in rem proceedings in the Admiralty Court with arbitration claims, so that the discretion to release an arrested vessel was the same in both cases and the court did not have a wider discretion when the claim was subject to an arbitration clause to release the vessel without requiring equivalent security, depending on whether the defendant was likely to be able to meet any arbitration award in the plaintiff's favour. Accordingly, on an application under RSC Ord 75, r 13 for the release of a vessel held as security for a claim in arbitration, the court would only exercise its discretion to release the vessel on the provision of sufficient security to cover the amount of the claim, plus interest and costs, on the basis of the plaintiff's reasonably arguable best case. The fact that there might be no question of the defendant's ability to meet any award that might be made against it or that the defendant might have difficulty in finding sufficient cash in time to put up the security or that the arrest might cause great inconvenience were not good reasons for departing from the usual practice of requiring sufficient security to cover the amount of the claim. The appeal from the variation of the original order would be dismissed, a stay of the action would be granted under s 1 and the two vessels would remain under arrest pending further order.

The Bazias 3, The Bazias 4 [1993] 2 All ER 964 (Court of Appeal: Lloyd, Ralph Gibson and Butler-Sloss LJJ).

54 Jurisdiction—Guernsey

The Admiralty Jurisdiction (Guernsey) Order 1993, SI 1993/2664 (in force on 1 December 1993), extends the provisions of the Supreme Court Act 1981, ss 20–24 to the Bailiwick of Guernsey subject to exceptions, adaptations and modifications set out in the Schedule to the order. The 1966 Order, SI 1966/1186, is revoked.

55 Limitation of liability

See SHIPPING AND NAVIGATION.

56 Practice—harmonisation of practice with Commercial Court practice—interlocutory applications—listing—trials

Clarke J has issued, with the consent of the Lord Chief Justice and with the approval of Saville J as judge in charge of the Commercial Court, the following *Practice Note* ([1993] 2 All ER 671), signed by himself and the Admiralty Registrar.

Preface

1. Practice in the Commercial Court has for some time been governed not only by RSC Ord 72 but also by the *Guide to Commercial Court Practice*, which is at present set out in *The Supreme Court Practice 1993*, Vol 1, paras 72/A1–72/A31.

2. Many of the actions heard in the Admiralty Court raise similar issues to those heard in the Commercial Court. Many of those who regularly practise in the Admiralty Court also practise in the Commercial Court. Since 1987 there has been an Admiralty and Commercial Registry. In these circumstances, it is desirable that there should be as much harmonisation as possible between the practice of the two courts, provided that care is taken to ensure that the two courts remain independent so that each may best serve the interests of those who wish to use it.

3. These aims can best be served by improving the practice of the Admiralty Court in the following areas: the hearing of interlocutory applications by the Admiralty Judge, the listing of actions and the harmonisation of the general practice of the two courts where appropriate.

Interlocutory applications

4. With effect from 8 June 1993 most summonses and other interlocutory applications (including motions) which are to be heard by the Admiralty Judge and which are short enough to be heard on "summons day" will ordinarily be listed for hearing on Fridays. The Admiralty Registrar will continue to hear interlocutory applications as before.

Trials

5.1 With effect from 8 June 1993 trials will thus be heard on Mondays to Thursdays and, save in exceptional circumstances, will not be heard on Fridays.

5.2 Except where the Admiralty Judge otherwise directs, all actions will be heard by the Admiralty Judge. However, the Admiralty and Commercial Registry will maintain a list of all matters to be heard in the Admiralty and Commercial Courts in order to ensure that the judicial resources of both courts are used to best effect. All such listing will be under the direction of the Admiralty and Commercial Court listing officer.

5.3 This will enable the Admiralty Judge to hear actions in the Commercial Court and it will also enable judges of the Commercial Court to hear actions in the Admiralty Court where the facts of the particular case make that course appropriate.

5.4 It is stressed that the purpose of this change is to make both courts operate as efficiently as possible. Care will be taken to ensure that an Admiralty action which involves questions of navigation or other particular matters of an essentially Admiralty nature will be heard by the Admiralty Judge or (where necessary) by a judge nominated by the Admiralty Judge who has experience of such questions or matters.

Practice

6.1 With effect from 8 June 1993 the *Guide to Commercial Court Practice* will govern the practice of the Admiralty Court so far as applications to and hearings before the Admiralty Judge are concerned, save where the provisions of that guide can apply only to commercial actions and save that applications in the Admiralty Court will continue to be heard by the Admiralty Registrar in accordance with the Rules of the Supreme Court.

6.2 Thus the following sections of the *Guide to Commercial Court Practice* will apply to proceedings in the Admiralty Court before the Admiralty Judge:

III	Ex parte applications
IV	Service out of the jurisdiction
V	Mareva and Anton Piller injunctions

VI   Summonses inter partes
VII   Arbitration matters
VIII   Security for costs
IX   Pleadings
X   Amendment of pleadings
XI   Discovery and interrogatories
XII   The summons for directions (except for paras 12.1 and 12.2)
XIII   Preliminary issues
XIV   Exchange of evidence: factual witnesses
XV   Exchange of evidence: expert witnesses
XVI   Documents
XVII   Preparation for long trials (save that the reference in para 17.2 to a single judge shall be a reference to the Admiralty Judge unless he otherwise directs)
XVIII   Pre-trial checklist
XIX   The trial

6.3 The reason that some parts of the *Guide to Commercial Court Practice* have been omitted is that they do not seem to be appropriate to an Admiralty action having regard to the express terms of RSC Ord 75 and to the fact that RSC Ord 72 does not apply to an Admiralty action. However, suggestions from the Admiralty Court Committee (or indeed from any other user of the Admiralty Court) as to how the practice of the court could be improved in this or any other respect would be welcome.

6.4 Admiralty Practice Direction No 4 (see para 4 of *Practice Direction* [1973] 3 All ER 446, [1973] 1 WLR 1146, as amended by *Practice Direction* [1982] 2 All ER 480, [1982] 1 WLR 660), which is at present set out in *The Supreme Court Practice 1993*, Vol 2, para 1326, will cease to have effect.

Conclusion
7 The changes in the practice set out above will come into effect from 8 June 1993, subject to any adjustments which may be necessary as a result of arrangements or orders already made at the date of this Practice Direction.

AGENCY

Halsbury's Laws of England (4th edn) Vol 1(2) (reissue), paras 1–300

57 Articles

Des Res—Oh Yes, Peter Cartwright (on the provisions of the Property Misdescriptions Act 1991): 143 NLJ 859
Legal Protection For Commercial Agents, Robert Bell and Kate O'Toole: 138 SJ 10
Special Agents, Paul Egerton-Vernon (on the differences between agency and distribution agreements within the EC): LS Gaz, 31 March 1993, p 24

58 Agent—self-employed hair stylist—agreement to supply services from taxpayer's premises—supply of services to taxpayer or to customers

See *Customs and Excise Comrs v MacHenrys (Hairdressers) Ltd*, para 2631.

59 Commercial agents—rights and obligations

The Commercial Agents (Council Directive) Regulations 1993, SI 1993/3053 (in force on 1 January 1994) (as amended by SI 1993/3173), implement Council Directive (EC) 86/653 on the co-ordination of the laws of member states relating to self-employed commercial agents. The regulations set out the rights and obligations as between commercial agents and their principals. They also deal with remuneration, the conclusion and termination of the agency contract, the indemnity or compensation payable to an agent on termination of his contract, and the validity of restraint of trade clauses.

60 Duty of care—members' agents and managing agents—Lloyd's of London

See *Arbuthnott v Feltrim; Deeny v Gooda Walker; Henderson v Merrett Syndicates*, para 1552.

61   Estate agent—commission—entitlement—part-exchange transaction

The sale of the defendant's house had been negotiated to a purchaser introduced by the plaintiff estate agents. It had not been an outright cash transaction as the defendant had been paid a sum of money and had received another house in part exchange. The written agency agreement between the plaintiffs and the defendant had stipulated a commission of three per cent on the "purchase price" on the "completion of the sale". The plaintiffs claimed commission on the purchase price and the value of the part-exchanged house. The court held that the agreement was applicable to the transaction but that "purchase price" referred to the cash element alone. On appeal by the plaintiffs, *held*, the court fully accepted that an outright exchange of property without any cash element could not properly be called a sale. The court did however think that a part-exchange transaction could be regarded as a sale given that it was not an uncommon commercial practice. The cash element in these instances need not be large or substantial, as long as it was not nominal. In this case the purchase price had been the aggregate figure of the cash price and the part-exchange value. It would have been artificial to have ignored the value of the house received in part-exchange, especially as it made up almost 50 per cent of the transaction. It had been the defendant's choice to accept the part-exchange and that choice had in no way reduced the work that had been done by the estate agent. Accordingly, the appeal would be allowed.

Connell Estate Agents v Begej [1993] 39 EG 123 (Court of Appeal: Butler-Sloss and Hirst LJJ).

62   Estate agent—commission—entitlement—two agents

The plaintiff firm of estate agents accepted the defendant's instructions to find a purchaser for a property. A number of potential purchasers were introduced by the plaintiffs, including the ultimate purchaser, but at the time no offer nor sale resulted. One month later new planning information was given to the ultimate purchaser by other estate agents who completed the purchase of the property. Both agents claimed commission and the defendant paid the second agents. In proceedings brought by the plaintiffs against the defendant, the court ruled in the plaintiffs' favour. On appeal by the defendant, *held*, it was the plaintiff who generally bore the burden of showing that his introduction had been the effective cause of the purchase. If however he showed that he was the first to introduce the purchaser, and that a purchase followed, and if no other facts were established, then the court in some cases would infer that the plaintiff's introduction was the effective cause of the purchase. The evidential burden in such a case would then pass to the defendant. The first introduction by the plaintiffs had produced no offer from the purchaser whereas the second introduction, which had not depended on the first, had been the cause of the purchase. Accordingly, the appeal would be allowed.

Chasen Ryder & Co v Hedges [1993] 08 EG 119 (Court of Appeal: Sir Donald Nicholls V-C and Staughton LJ).

63   Estate agent—commission—payment out of proceeds of sale—implication of contractual term

The plaintiff estate agents sold a property on behalf of a company which subsequently became insolvent. They brought a claim against a director of the company for the commission on the sale, arguing that it was an implied term of the contract that the commission would be paid out of the proceeds of sale or that the contract created an equitable charge on the proceeds of sale to the extent of the commission. *Held*, there was no law on the question of whether there was normally to be implied into an estate agent's contract with a vendor a term that the agent's fees were recoverable directly from the purchase moneys normally held by the vendor's solicitors. Although in practice the vendor sometimes did discharge the commission out of the purchase moneys, there was no evidence as to how common the practice was. The implication of such a term was not necessary to give the contract business efficacy. If an estate agent wanted such a term to be part of his contract of engagement, express provision had to be made. Accordingly, the plaintiffs' claim would be dismissed.

W A Ellis Services Ltd v Wood [1993] 31 EG 78 (Chancery Division: Antony Watson QC).

64   Ratification—time for ratification—commencement of proceedings without authority—purported ratification—limitation period

A firm of solicitors had issued a writ in 1988 on behalf of the plaintiff; but without his knowledge, in relation to breaches of an agency agreement which took place in 1982 and copyright infringement. The plaintiff purported to ratify the action in 1991 and the question arose as to whether the ratification was valid. It was held on trial of a preliminary issue that the plaintiff had adopted the action, which had been commenced without his authority by the solicitors. The defendants appealed and argued that proceedings issued without authority could not be ratified, if at the time of ratification the causes of action would have been partly statute-barred. *Held*, a writ issued without authority was not a nullity. The plaintiff did not need to make an application to the court to adopt the writ which had been issued in his name. A plaintiff raising a single cause of action, which was begun by solicitors without authority, could adopt the action in spite of the fact that the limitation period on that particular cause of action had expired if the issue of the writ would not have been barred if authorisation had been obtained in advance. However, if a time was fixed for doing an act by statute or by agreement, that time could not be extended by using the doctrine of ratification. In the present case the causes of action were not all statute-barred in 1991. Accordingly, the appeal would be allowed.

Presentaciones Musicales SA v Secunda (1993) Times, 29 November (Court of Appeal: Dillon, Nolan and Roch LJJ).

65 Undisclosed principal—contract of insurance—validity of contract

Hong Kong
Several members of a ship's crew had been killed when their ship was hit by a typhoon. The plaintiffs were administrators of the deceased and had obtained judgment for damages for negligence against the owners of the ship, but the company had been wound up before the damages were paid. The plaintiffs then started proceedings against the defendant insurance company under the Third Parties (Rights Against Insurers) Ordinance, s 2(1), which states that where a company is insured against liability to third parties then, in the event of a winding up any rights to claim in respect of that liability, are transferred to the party to whom the liability was incurred. The defendants claimed that as the company's shipping agents were named as insured, the shipping company was not disclosed as principal and the policy was unlawful contrary to the Life Assurance Act 1774, s 2, which provided that names of the person receiving benefit under any policy on a person's life, or other event or events, should be stated therein. The Hong Kong Court of Appeal upheld the first instance decision that the plaintiffs had no rights under the Ordinance. On appeal, *held*, the contract for insurance was an ordinary commercial contract and the company was therefore entitled to sue as undisclosed principal unless the defendant insurance company had only intended to contract with the shipping agents. There was nothing in the proposal form which expressly or impliedly excluded this. The actual identity of the shipping company was not relevant to the risk and therefore it was not a personal contract of the type which excluded rights of an undisclosed principal. It was accepted that there were some contracts which could not be enforced by an undisclosed principal; there was however, no case in which it had been decided that a contract of insurance was an exception to the rule that an undisclosed principal could sue on a contract made by an agent with actual authority. The words "event or events" in the 1774 Act, s 2 applied to the loss of the ship and not the liability of the company to their employees. Section 2 would be interpreted in accordance with legislative intent and following the case of *Mark Rowlands Ltd v Berni Inns Ltd* [1986] QB 211, CA (1985 Abr para 1434), s 2 would not apply because the Act was not intended to apply to indemnity insurance. Accordingly, the appeal would be allowed.

Siu Yin Kwan v Eastern Insurance Co Ltd [1994] 1 All ER 213 (Privy Council: Lords Templeman, Mustill, Woolf, Lloyd of Berwick, and Sir Thomas Eichelbaum).

AGRICULTURE

Halsbury's Laws of England (4th edn) Vol 1(2) (reissue), paras 301–1133

66 Articles

Arable Farming in the Short-Term, Michael Cardwell: [1993] Conv 138
Milk Quota—A Hybrid Animal, Francis Fitzpatrick: Tax Journal, Issue 207, p 12
Short-Term Farm Agreements, William Barr: 137 SJ 609

67 Agricultural business—grants

The Farm and Conservation Grant (Amendment) Regulations 1993, SI 1993/2900 (in force on 1 December 1993), amend the 1991 Regulations, SI 1991/1630, by changing the closing dates by which, for grant to be payable, expenditure must be incurred in respect of certain items which are eligible for grant in the Isles of Scilly and claims for grant in respect of those items must be received. The regulations also reduce the rates of grant in respect of a number of items, subject to saving provisions.

The Farm and Conservation Grant (Variation) Scheme 1993, SI 1993/2901 (in force on 1 December 1993), further varies the 1989 Regulations, SI 1989/128 and complies with Council Regulation (EC) 2328/91. The variations include changing certain closing dates in relation to applications for grant to be payable and changing provisions for payment of grant in relation to certain expenditure incurred for the purpose of the 1989 Regulations.

68 Agricultural business—grants—claim under "set aside" scheme

A farmer was registered with the Ministry of Agriculture, Fisheries and Food for the "set aside" scheme. An application form was sent to him and was duly completed and returned. He was advised that a claim form would be sent to him and that he would have to return it by 31 August 1992. The appropriate form was not sent to the farmer, however, and he returned two other forms (relating to cereal co-responsibility levy) in the belief that these constituted a valid claim under the "set aside" scheme. The claim under the "set aside" scheme was refused as no claim form had been submitted by the appropriate date. The farmer complained to the Parliamentary Commissioner for Administration about this refusal. Following an investigation, the ministry offered the farmer an ex gratia payment covering the payment under the "set aside" scheme to which he was in principle entitled.

Case C 99/93, Selected Cases 1993, Vol 4, p 8, Parliamentary Commissioner for Administration.

69 Agricultural holding—breach of model clauses—arbitration—staying of action

Under the Agriculture (Maintenance, Repair and Insurance of Fixed Equipment) Regulations 1973, SI 1973/1473, Schedule, para 15, "any claim, question or difference ... between the landlord and the tenant under the foregoing provisions hereof ... shall be determined, in default of agreement, by arbitration" under the Agricultural Holdings Act 1986.

The tenants brought actions for damages and specific performance against the defendant landlords for claimed breaches of repairing obligations imposed by model clauses incorporated into the tenancy under the Agricultural Holdings Act 1986 and the 1973 Regulations, Schedule, para 3. The master stayed both actions pending compulsory arbitration under the 1986 Act pursuant to the 1973 Regulations, Schedule, para 15. Although the 1986 Act, s 84(1) provided that any arbitration was to be determined in accordance with that Act and not the Arbitration Act 1950, the tenants appealed contending that the court retained a discretion to stay proceedings under the 1950 Act, s 4. The court held that it had no discretion to permit the actions to continue and that they had been correctly stayed. On the tenants further appeal, *held*, although the decision of the court would not be questioned on the merits, the stay would be lifted for the purpose only of allowing the tenants to apply for summary judgement in the actions under RSC Ord 14. Accordingly, the appeal would be allowed in part.

Tustian v Johnston [1993] 3 All ER 534n (Court of Appeal: Russell, Evans and Hoffmann LJJ). Decision of Knox J [1993] 2 All ER 673 in part affirmed.

70 Agricultural holding—tenancy—notice to quit

The Agricultural Holdings Act 1986, s 26(3), Sch III, Pt I, Case D provides that if at the date of the giving of a notice to quit, the tenant has failed to comply with a written notice served on him by the landlord requiring him within two months of the service of the notice to pay rent to which the notice related, the tenancy terminates.

A tenant paid a rent cheque into the landlord's account within the two-month notice period but it was dishonoured. On re-presentation, but after the expiry of that period, the cheque was honoured. Three days later, the landlord issued a notice to quit under the 1986 Act, Case D. The tenant sought to challenge the notice by way of arbitration and accordingly sent a letter of appointment to the arbitrator. In his acknowledgement of receipt, the arbitrator informed the parties that their statements of cases should arrive no later than 35 days from the date of appointment. He subsequently wrote to the tenant's solicitors and told them that they were out of time but they disputed that and submitted a statement of case. The judge found that the arbitrator was not appointed until the tenant had been informed of that fact. On the landlord's appeal, *held*, the 35-day time limit under which the parties had to file their statements of cases ran from the time when the arbitrator received his notice of appointment, not when the parties received the arbitrator's acknowledgement of appointment. Further, the landlord's acceptance of the rent, due more than two months earlier, did not constitute a waiver of her entitlement to claim possession by her notice to quit. Accordingly, the appeal would be allowed.

Hannaford v Smallcombe (1993) Times, 30 December (Court of Appeal: Neill, Beldam and Henry LJJ).

71 Agricultural holding—tenancy—rent assessment committees—council tax

See para 1623.

72 Agricultural holding—tenancy—succession to tenancy—calculation of annual income of land

The Agricultural Holdings (Units of Production) Order 1993, SI 1993/2037 (in force on 12 September 1993), supersedes the 1992 Order, SI 1992/1972 and prescribes units of production for the assessment of the productive capacity of agricultural land and sets out the amount which is to be regarded as the net annual income from each such unit for the year 12 September 1993 to 11 September 1994. The units of production are used together with the net annual income of land to determine whether or not the land in question is a commercial unit for the purposes of the succession provisions of the Agricultural Holdings Act 1986.

73 Agricultural marketing—milk and milk products—export sales—commercial risk

A trader successfully tendered for a quantity of salted butter which it undertook to export to the USSR after it had been processed into butteroil. Meanwhile, Soviet authorities had altered quality requirements for imported butteroil. The butter acquired by the trader did not meet the new requirements and could no longer be imported into the USSR. The trader sought the repayment of the tendering security, required under Commission Regulation (EC) 765/86 (which lays down detailed rules for the sale of butter from intervention stock for export to certain destinations), lodged by it on the submission of its tender, on the ground that, for reasons of force majeure it was no longer able to export the butter and, therefore, the security was not forfeit. *Held*, the principle of force majeure was not limited to absolute impossibility. It should be understood in the sense of abnormal and unforeseeable circumstances outside the control of the trader concerned, the consequences of which, in spite of the exercise of all due care, might only be avoided at the cost of excessive sacrifice. Although the alteration of the legislation of a non-member country governing the quality of products imported into that country was a circumstance outside the control of the trader concerned, it constituted a usual commercial risk in commercial transactions with a state-trading country. A prudent trader should take appropriate precautions against such a risk. The circumstances in the instant case did not constitute force majeure within the meaning of Community law and for the purposes of Commission Regulation (EC) 765/86.

Case C-124/92: An Bord Bainne Co-operative Ltd v Intervention Board for Agricultural Produce [1993] 3 CMLR 856 (ECJ: Sixth Chamber).

74 Agricultural marketing—milk and milk products—milk marketing scheme

The Milk Marketing Board Scheme of Reorganisation (Extension of Period for Application) Order 1993, SI 1993/3230 (in force on 31 December 1993), extends the last day on which the Board can apply to the appropriate minister for approval of the reorganisation of arrangements relating to the marketing of milk in England and Wales from 31 December 1993 to 31 March 1994.

75 Agricultural marketing—milk and milk products—milk quota—procedure on application to tribunal

The applicant submitted an application to the Dairy Produce Quota Tribunal for a secondary milk quota, in accordance with the Dairy Produce Regulations 1991, SI 1991/2232. He was dissatisfied with its determination and applied for judicial review to quash the decision on the ground that the tribunal had not given him an explanation of how the decision had been reached. *Held*, in considering an application for a secondary milk quota the tribunal, in accordance with the 1991 Regulations, Sch 9, should have given separate consideration to the production capacity of the farm and the quantity of produce which it might reasonably expect to sell annually. The separation of production capacity from sales potential was important because it allowed an unsuccessful applicant to know why he had failed, and the tribunal's decision could not stand because it had not adopted that procedure. Accordingly, the application would be allowed and the case remitted for rehearing.

R v Dairy Produce Quota Tribunal for England and Wales, ex p P A Cooper & Sons [1993] 19 EG 138 (Queen's Bench Division: Kennedy LJ).

76 Agricultural marketing—milk and milk products—milk quota—terms for transfer

The applicant was a farmer who had bought a milk quota linked to the grant of a grazing licence over farm land. The Milk Marketing Board acting as agent for the Ministry of Agriculture, Fisheries and Food registered the quota in the name of the applicant. She failed to exercise the licence and the ministry wrote to her giving notice of intention to revoke the quota registration. In an application for judicial review of the notice, *held*, as a general rule of law where there was a transfer of part of an agricultural holding, the person to whom the holding had been transferred had to be operating the holding before becoming entitled to the transfer of the dairy quota. Although it was open to the minister to alter the registration, in this case it would have been unfair to deprive the applicant of her quota and oblige her to find a sum to cover the levy for which she had become liable. Accordingly, the application would be allowed.

R v Minister of Agriculture, Fisheries and Food, ex p Cox [1993] 2 CMLR 917 (Queen's Bench Division: Popplewell J).

77 Agriculture Act 1993

The Agriculture Act 1993 makes provision in relation to milk marketing and potato marketing and provides for the payment of grants in connection with the marketing of certain commodities. The Act received the royal assent on 27 July 1993. Certain provisions came into force on that date and on 27 September 1993, except for ss 55, 59, which came into force on 4 August 1993: SI 1993/2038. Sections 1(1)(a), 21 are to come into force on 1 October 1994 or such later date before 1 January 1996 as may be specified. For details of commencement, see the commencement table in the title STATUTES.

Part I (ss 1–24) Milk Marketing
Section 1 provides for the revocation of the Milk Marketing Scheme 1933. Section 2 provides that a milk marketing board may apply to the Minister of Agriculture, Fisheries and Food and the Secretary of State for Wales ("the appropriate authority") for approval of a scheme for the reorganisation of the arrangements relating to its marketing of milk. Section 3 and Sch 1 specify the various matters in respect of which the appropriate authority must be satisfied, and the requirements which the appropriate authority must meet, before an application for approval of a reorganisation scheme can be granted. Section 4 lays down the procedure where the appropriate authority is not satisfied that a scheme is one which ought to be approved, and enables modifications to the scheme to be proposed and accepted. Section 5 enables the appropriate authority to approve a variation of an approved scheme on the application of the milk marketing board before the vesting day under the scheme. Section 6 enables the appropriate authority, on the application of the board to which the reorganisation scheme relates, to withdraw approval for a scheme before the vesting day under that scheme if there has been a material change of circumstances since the scheme's approval, and enables the boards to submit a new scheme for approval within a specified period. Section 7 enables the authority to which an application for approval of a reorganisation scheme under ss 2, 5 or 6 is made to require any person to supply information which the authority considers necessary or desirable for the carrying out of its functions in relation to the application. Section 8 requires the authority granting an application to make public the fact that it has done so.

Section 9 provides for the board to which an approved scheme relates to do whatever is necessary for the carrying out of the scheme in the period up to and including the vesting day under the scheme. Section 10 requires the appropriate authority to satisfy itself in relation to an approved scheme that so much of the scheme as relates to the period prior to the vesting day is carried out. Section 11 gives statutory effect to any transfer under an approved scheme which is a qualifying transfer, and is a transfer which the scheme provides is to have effect under this section. Section 12 and Sch 2 introduce provisions relating to the carrying out of an approved scheme. Section 13 provides that the board administering a milk marketing scheme is not to be dissolved simply by virtue of the revocation of the scheme. Section 14 requires the appropriate authority to make regulations giving effect to so much of the approved scheme as relates to the board in the period after the transfer under s 11. Section 15 sets out the procedure for winding up a milk marketing board in accordance with the Agricultural Marketing Act 1958 where its revocation under s 1(1) has taken place without the statutory transfer of property, rights and liabilities under s 11. Section 16 makes provision in relation to the expiry of the term of office of a member of a milk marketing board or a committee under the marketing scheme administered by the board. Section 17 empowers the appropriate authority to make an order in certain circumstances enabling the board to require eligible producers to make contributions to enable the board to meet any liabilities which cannot be met from existing resources. Section 18 provides that the functions of a milk marketing board are deemed always to have included the function of preparing for the enactment of Pt 1 of the Act. Section 19 precludes acts done in pursuance of Pt I of the Act by a milk marketing board from constituting a breach of any duty to registered producers arising elsewhere. Section 20 provides that the functions of a committee appointed under the Agricultural Marketing Act 1958, s 19, are not to include the consideration of anything done by a milk marketing board by way of preparing for the enactment of Pt I of this Act, or in connection with an application under Pt I for the carrying out of an approved scheme. Section 21 provides that the Agricultural Marketing Act 1958, Pt I, is to cease to have effect in relation to milk once the milk marketing scheme has been revoked under s 1(1) above. Section 22 makes provision for the service of documents under Pt I. Section 23 enables ministers to make any necessary or expedient modifications to any other legislation in consequence of the coming into force of s 1(1) above. Section 24 deals with interpretation.

Part II (ss 25–49) Potato Marketing
Section 25 provides that Pt II will apply if the relevant ministers decide that it is necessary or expedient or in the public interest for the Potato Marketing Scheme to be brought to an end. Section 26 revokes the Potato Marketing Scheme and prescribes the date for such revocation. Section 27 provides for the Potato Marketing Board to apply to the relevant ministers for the approval of a scheme providing for the transfer of its property, rights and liabilities, subject to the approval of a poll of registered producers. Section 28 and Sch 3 specify the various matters and criteria in respect of which the relevant ministers must be satisfied before granting an application for approval of a transfer scheme. Section 29 lays down the procedure where the relevant ministers are not satisfied that the scheme meets the criteria specified by s 28(3), and enables modifications to the scheme to be proposed and accepted. Section 30 enables the relevant ministers to approve the variation of an approved scheme on the application of the Potato Marketing Board before the vesting day under the scheme. Section 31 gives the relevant ministers power to require any person to supply them with information for the purpose of enabling them to carry out their functions in relation to an application under ss 27 or 30 above. Section 32 requires the relevant ministers granting an application under ss 27 or 30 to make public the fact that they have granted the application. Section 33 enables the Potato Marketing Board to do whatever is necessary for the carrying out of an approved scheme up to and including the vesting day under the scheme. Section 34 requires the relevant ministers to satisfy themselves in relation to an approved scheme that any steps that need to be taken to enable the scheme to be carried out are taken before the vesting day under the scheme. Section 35 provides for certain transfers under an approved Scheme to have statutory effect on the vesting day under an approved scheme. Section 36 and Sch 4 introduce provisions in relation to the carrying out of an approved scheme. Section 37 provides that the Potato Marketing Board is not deemed to be dissolved by reason of the revocation of the Potato Marketing Scheme and that so much of the scheme as relates to the winding up of the Board is to continue in force notwithstanding the revocation. Section 38 enables the relevant ministers to make regulations where the property, rights and liabilities of the Board are transferred under an approved scheme. Section 39 sets out the procedure for the winding up of the Board in accordance with the Agricultural Marketing Act 1958, Sch 2, where its revocation by s 26(1) has taken place without the statutory transfer of property, rights and liabilities under s 35.

Section 40 enables the Potato Marketing Board to carry out a poll of registered producers for the purpose of ascertaining the level of support for submitting a transfer scheme to ministers for approval. Section 41 specifies those persons eligible to vote in a poll under s 40. Section 42 provides for the ending of elections to the Potato Marketing Board established under the Potato Marketing Scheme and for the expiry of the term of office of board members. Section 43 precludes acts done in pursuance of Pt II by the Potato Marketing Board or by a member or officer of the Board from constituting a breach of any duty to registered producers arising elsewhere. Section 44 provides that the functions of a committee appointed under the Agricultural Marketing Act 1958, s 19, are not to include the consideration of anything done by the Board in connection with an application under Pt II or the carrying out of an approved scheme. Section 45 prevents a new quota year from being prescribed under the Potato Marketing Scheme after the making of an order under s 25. Section 46 provides for the Agricultural Marketing Act 1958, Pt I, to cease to have effect in relation to potatoes on the day on which s

26(1) comes into force. Section 47 deals with the service of documents under Pt II. Section 48 enables the relevant ministers to make any necessary or expedient modifications to any other legislation in consequence of s 26(1). Section 49 deals with interpretation.

Part III (ss 50–53) Grants for Marketing
Section 50 empowers ministers to make a scheme for the payment of grants for the marketing of agricultural and horticultural produce, the produce of fish farming and other produce specified by order, or anything derived from such produce. Section 51 creates an offence of knowingly or recklessly making a false or misleading statement for the purpose of obtaining a payment under s 50. Section 52 sets time limits for the commencement of prosecutions brought under Pt III. Section 53 deals with finance.

Part IV (54–65) Miscellaneous and Supplementary
Section 54 amends the Agriculture Act 1957, Sch 1, to provide for the termination of the wool guarantee. Section 55 amends the Agriculture Act 1957, Sch 1, to provide for the termination of the potato guarantee as from an appointed date. Section 56 requires the distribution of profits of a milk marketing scheme to be made so as not to discriminate between persons who are registered as producers under the scheme by reference to the identity of the person to whom the milk is sold. Section 57 provides for the British Wool Marketing Board to be treated as a company for the purposes of the Companies Act 1985, s 727. Section 58 requires Ministers to publish annually a report on matters relevant to price support for agricultural produce. Section 59 enables the Joint Consultative Committee under the Potato Marketing Scheme to establish a target area to be planted with potatoes in the following year, provides for the relationship between that area and the setting of the quota area by the Potato Marketing Board and establishes an arbitration procedure in the event of dispute between the two bodies on the size of the areas. Section 60 modifies the Industrial Organisation and Development Act 1947, s 4, to enable levies raised by agricultural development councils established under that Act to be collected by other specified persons. Section 61 makes provision as to offences by bodies corporate. Section 62 contains general provisions as to the making of orders and regulations. Section 63 lays down the parliamentary procedure for extending the Act to Northern Ireland by Order in Council. Section 64 and Sch 5 contain repeals. Section 65 relates to short title, commencement and extent.

78   Agriculture Act 1993—specification of year

The Agriculture Act 1993 (Specification of Year) (Potato Target Area) Order 1993, SI 1993/2039 (in force on 9 August 1993), specifies 1993 as the year for the purposes of the Agriculture Act 1993, s 59(1). The 1993 Act, s 59(1) requires the Joint Consultative Committee constituted under the Potato Marketing Scheme to consider in each year after the year 1993 whether it is desirable to establish a target area, to be used for planting potatoes in the following year.

79   Common agricultural policy—agricultural marketing—wine

The Common Agricultural Policy (Wine) Regulations 1993, SI 1993/517 (in force on 1 April 1993), revoke and re-enact with amendments the provisions of the Common Agricultural Policy (Wine) Regulations 1992, SI 1992/672, as amended. The regulations allow an authorised officer to retain any record, register or document required as evidence in legal proceedings and introduce the defence of due diligence in relation to specified offences. Provision is also made for the enforcement of the relevant Community provisions prohibiting the new planting of vines, on the production level in the United Kingdom exceeding 25,000 hectolitres per wine year. The regulations designate competent authorities and a liaison authority for the purposes of enforcement, define "medium dry" for the purposes of labelling and description and specify conditions for the use of geographical descriptions for the designation of table wine. The regulations also exempt certain products from provisions relating to information required on labels, permit the planting of certain wine varieties for certain purposes and provide for powers of inspection and enforcement. The regulations authorise controls on the movement of wine sector products, relieve authorised officers of personal liability for acts done by them in execution of the regulations, confer on courts powers in relation to the analysis and examination of samples and describe Southern Counties and Northern Counties as the specified regions in the United Kingdom for producing quality wines. The schedules include references to relevant regulations of the European Economic Community which have been adopted since the 1992 Regulations came into force.

The Common Agricultural Policy (Wine) (Amendment) Regulations, SI 1993/3071 (in force on 1 January 1994), amend the 1993 Regulations, SI 1993/517, supra, by implementing the provisions of Commission Regulation (EC) 2238/93, which deals with carriage of wine products and which replaced Commission Regulation (EC) 986/89.

80 Common agricultural policy—organic products—creation of inspection authority

The Organic Products (Amendment) Regulations 1993, SI 1993/405 (in force on 29 March 1993), amend the Organic Products Regulations 1992, SI 1992/2111, by substituting for the reference to a "Specified Community provision" in the 1991 Regulations a reference to a different offence-creating provision.

81 Crop burning—restrictions

The Crop Residues (Burning) Regulations 1993, SI 1993/1366 (in force on 29 June 1993), replace the Crop Residues (Restrictions on Burning) (No 2) Regulations 1991, SI 1991/1590. The regulations prohibit the burning on agricultural land of specified crop residues unless the burning is for a specified purpose. The regulations also impose restrictions and requirements in relation to the burning of linseed residues and other exempted burning. Burning crop residues in contravention of the regulations is an offence punishable on summary conviction by a fine.

82 Feeding stuffs—regulations

The Feeding Stuffs (Amendment) Regulations 1993, SI 1993/1442 (in force in part on 30 June 1993, in part on 1 October 1993 and in part on 31 December 1993), further amend the 1991 Regulations, SI 1991/2840. The main changes include (1) the omission, from the regulation relating to the control of the use of additives in feeding stuffs, of certain provisions relating to the importation into Great Britain of material containing additives; (2) the extension of the provisions relating to the declaration of the ingredients of compound feeding stuffs for animals other than pet animals; (3) the addition of certain substances to the list of substances which may not be contained in material used or sold for use as a compound feeding stuff; and (4) the modification and extension of the provisions which control the use in feeding stuffs and ingredients of undesirable substances.

83 Hill livestock—compensatory allowance

The Hill Livestock (Compensatory Allowances) Regulations 1993, SI 1993/2631 (in force on 15 November 1993), consolidate the 1992 Regulations, SI 1992/269, as amended by SI 1993/70, and implement various Community provisions relating to mountain and hill farming and farming in less-favoured areas, improving the efficiency of agricultural structures, and the administration and enforcement of provisions for payment of compensatory allowances. The main changes include (1) the introduction of new conditions relating to the number of animals in respect of which an allowance may be paid; (2) the requirement that an application for an allowance be made in a specified period; (3) the enlargement of powers of entry and inspection; (4) the prescription of the rate of interest payable on amounts recovered in specified circumstances; (5) the creation of new offences and the prescription of penalties in respect of them; and (6) the specification of time limits for bringing prosecutions and the making of provision for offences committed by corporate bodies.

The Hill Livestock (Compensatory Allowances) (Amendment) (No 2) Regulations 1993, SI 1993/2924 (in force on 21 December 1993), amend SI 1993/2631 supra by changing the rates of compensatory allowance payable for animals kept on severely disadvantaged land to £47·50 per cow, £5·75 per ewe in a specially qualified flock and £3 for other ewes, and on disadvantaged land to £23·75 per cow and £2·44 per ewe. Where both categories of land are occupied the regulations provide for allocating the allowances at the higher and lower rates among cows and ewes maintained on the two categories of land.

84 Home-Grown Cereals Authority—levy scheme

The Home-Grown Cereals Authority (Rate of Levy) Order 1993, SI 1993/1405 (in force on 1 July 1993), specifies, for the purpose of financing the Home-Grown Cereals Authority's non-trading functions for the year beginning 1 July 1993, rates of dealer levy, grower levy and processor levies which appear to ministers to be appropriate to meet the amount apportioned to certain cereals and oilseeds grown in the United Kingdom. The rate of dealer levy in the case of cereals, namely wheat, barley, oats, rye, maize, triticale or any two or more of such cereals grown as one crop, is 37·60 pence per tonne, and the rate of grower levy is 35·25 pence per tonne. The standard rate of processor levy is 7·05 pence per tonne and the reduced rate of processor levy is 1·175 pence per tonne. In the case of oilseeds, namely rapeseed, linseed, soyabean, sunflowerseed or any two or more of such oilseeds grown as one crop, the rate of levy is 58·75 pence per tonne. The levy is imposed in accordance with the provisions of the Home-Grown Cereals Authority Levy Scheme 1987 and the Home-Grown Cereals Authority Oilseeds Levy Scheme 1990.

85 Integrated administration and control system—general

The Integrated Administration and Control System Regulations 1993, SI 1993/1317 (in force on 10 June 1993), implement Council Regulations (EC) 3508/92 (establishing an integrated administration and control system for certain Community aid schemes) and 3887/92 (laying down rules for applying that system). The regulations provide for the calculation of the date from which forage area is available, prescribe the minimum size of an agricultural parcel, authorise the Minister of Agriculture, Fisheries and Food to co-ordinate checks, and confer on authorised persons powers of entry for the purpose of the regulations. Offences and penalties for the obstruction of authorised persons and for failure to comply with requests made by them are created.

86 Livestock—artificial breeding—sheep and goats

The Artificial Breeding of Sheep and Goats Regulations 1993, SI 1993/3248 (in force on 1 January 1994), implement Council Directive (EC) 92/65 regarding the production for intra-Community trade of the semen, ova and embryos of sheep and goats and providing for the approval of semen collection centres and embryo collection teams.

87 Livestock—beef special premium

The Beef Special Premium Regulations 1993, SI 1993/1734 (in force on 1 August 1993), implement the provisions of Council Directive (EC) 805/68 relating to the payment of premia for producers of male bovine animals, and implement other relevant provisions in Commission Regulations (EC) 3886/92 and 3887/92. The regulations (1) specify that the national administrative document, issued by the appropriate minister, must accompany each animal; (2) prohibit the sale of an animal over three months old unless accompanied by such a document; (3) require the surrender of the document to the appropriate minister on the death, loss, theft or export of an animal; (4) provide for the issue of a duplicate or replacement document in certain specified circumstances; (5) confer powers of entry and inspection, and seizure and retention of records, on certain authorised persons and require that they be assisted on reasonable request; (6) specify circumstances in which premium paid to an applicant may be recovered from the appropriate minister and prescribe the rate of interest payable on the amounts recovered; and (7) create offences, prescribe penalties, specify time limits for bringing prosecutions and make provision for dealing with offences committed by corporate bodies.

88 Livestock—bovine embryos

The Bovine Embryo Collection and Transfer Regulations 1993, SI 1993/2921 (in force on 21 December 1993), regulate the collection, storage and use of bovine embryos and implement part of Council Directive (EC) 89/556. The regulations enable the appropriate minister to approve teams for embryo collection and transfer; regulate the collection, processing, storage and transport of embryos; make requirements to use anaesthetics and for record keeping; and provide that breach of the regulations is an offence.

The Bovine Embryo Collection and Transfer (Fees) Regulations 1993, SI 1993/2920 (in force on 21 December 1993), set fees payable for services under the 1993 Regulations supra.

89 Livestock—bovine semen

The Importation of Bovine Semen (Amendment) Regulations 1993, SI 1993/1966 (in force on 25 August 1993), amend the 1984 Regulations, SI 1984/1325, to make provision for the issue of general as well as specific licences for the importation of bovine semen into Great Britain.

90 Meat and Livestock Commission levy scheme—confirmation

The Meat and Livestock Commission Levy (Variation) Scheme (Confirmation) Order 1993, SI 1993/1899 (in force on 22 July 1993), further varies the scheme confirmed by the 1987 Order, SI 1987/1303. The maximum charges payable in respect of general expenses are increased (1) for cattle, from 190p a head to 219p a head; (2) for calves, from 12p a head to 14p a head; (3) for sheep, from 34p a head to 39p a head; (4) for pigs, from 48p a head to 55p a head. The maximum charges payable in respect of species promotion expenses are unchanged except in relation to pigs, where they are increased from 40p to 80p. The rights of slaughterers to recover levy from the sellers of exported livestock and to deduct the expenses in exercising that right from payments to the Meat and Livestock Commission, have been extended to exporters.

91 Plant breeders' rights—fees

The Plant Breeders' Rights (Fees) (Amendment) Regulations 1993, SI 1993/430 (in force on 1 April 1993), amend the Plant Breeders' Rights (Fees) Regulations 1990, SI 1990/618, by prescribing revised fees in respect of matters arising under the Plant Breeders' Rights Regulations 1978, SI 1978/272. Most application, test, grant and renewal fees have been increased. The fee for the purchase of a report from a testing authority in another country has been increased to accord with the international charge of 350 Swiss Francs whilst fees payable in respect of other matters remain unchanged.

92 Plant breeders' rights—reproductive and other plant material

The Plant Breeders' Rights (Amendment) Regulations 1993, SI 1993/2775 (in force on 1 December 1993), further amend the 1978 Regulations, SI 1978/294, by adding sainfoin, birdsfoot trefoil, tomatoes, quince rootstock, herbaceous perennials, trees, shrubs and woody climbers, and miscellaneous ornamentals to the species of plant varieties which may be the subject of plant breeders' rights. It amends the Schedule specifying the reproductive and other material which must be delivered to the Controller of Plant Variety Rights when an application is made for a grant of plant breeders' rights in respect of those species.

93 Plant breeders' rights—reproductive material—infringement

The Plant Varieties and Seeds Act 1964, s 4 provides that: (1) the holder of plant breeders' rights in a plant variety has the exclusive right to sell, or produce for sale, the reproductive material of the plant variety; (2) a sale by the rights-holder does not imply that the seller authorises the buyer to produce the reproductive material of the plant variety for the purpose of selling it; and (3) the sale of reproductive material includes any transactions under which the property in the reproductive material passes from one party to another or is made over from one person to another in pursuance of a contract under which he will use it to grow further reproductive material. Further, s 15 provides that reproductive material includes seeds for sowing.

The plaintiff company had plant breeders' rights for a variety of grass. A subsidiary company sold its surplus seed to a third party on condition that it would not be used for producing seed. Some of this was then sold to the first defendant who subsequently entered into an agreement with the second defendant whereby the latter agreed to produce the seed on his land and deliver it to the first defendant who would use it to grow turf to sell to end-users. The plaintiff sued, claiming that the defendants had infringed its rights under the 1964 Act, s 4. The defendants contended that: (1) the arrangement between them was a tenancy and thus the seeds were grown on the first defendant's land so that no question of a sale arose; (2) the property in the seeds remained with the first defendant at all times, but (3) if not, the contract should be rectified to give effect to that common intention; and (4) the 1964 Act, s 4 should be construed as providing that the rights of the plant breeder were confined to the sale of reproductive material to be used as reproductive material and as implying that the rights-holder authorised a purchaser to make over the reproductive material to a third party to produce further reproductive material. *Held,* the defendants' construction of the Act was incorrect. Further, (1) the defendants' agreement did not create a tenancy; it did not carry the right to exclusive possession since the second defendant retained control over the land. (2) The first defendant did not retain the property in the seeds: this was lost, at the latest, when the seeds were sown and became part of the second defendant's land. There was a making over of the seed, and thus a sale under the 1964 Act, s 4. (3) No error was made in reducing the defendants' agreement into writing, the only mistake was as to the document's legal effect and this was not a ground for rectification. (4) There was an unauthorised sale when the second defendant returned the seed he had grown to the first defendant. Accordingly, an order would be granted restraining the defendants from further infringements of the plaintiff's rights.

Germinal Holdings Ltd v H R Fell & Sons Ltd [1993] FSR 343 (Chancery Division: Judge Paul Baker QC).

94 Plant breeders' rights—schemes

Schemes have been made, and existing schemes replaced or amended, prescribing plant varieties in respect of which plant breeders' rights may be granted. The following table shows the plant variety, the period for which the rights are exercisable and the authority. All the schemes come into force on 1 December 1993.

Plant variety	Period for which rights are exercisable	Authority (SI 1993 No)
trees, shrubs and woody climbers	20–30 years	2776 (revokes SI 1993/1733)
tomatoes	20 years	2777
miscellaneous ornamental plants	20 years	2778
sainfoin and birdsfoot trefoil	25 years	2779
herbaceous perennials	25 years	2880
quince rootstocks	30 years	2881

95 Plant health—general provisions

The Plant Health (Great Britain) Order 1993, SI 1993/1320 (in force on 1 June 1993), revokes and supersedes the 1987 Order, SI 1987/1758, on protective measures against the introduction into member states of the European Community of organisms harmful to plants and plant products and against their spread within the Community. The main provisions under the order include a prohibition on the landing of certain plant pests, the introduction of protected zones of specified plant pests and plant products and the establishment of a register of those involved in activities associated with plants and plant products.

The Plant Health (Great Britain) (Amendment) Order 1993, SI 1993/3213 (in force on 21 January 1994), implements Council Directive (EEC) 93/85 on the control of potato ring rot. It substitutes a new schedule for the 1993 Order, SI 1993/1320, Sch 13, containing more extensive provisions for preventing the spread of potato ring rot following the creation of the single market.

The Plant Passport (Plant Health Fees) (England and Wales) Regulations 1993, SI 1993/1642 (in force 19 July 1993), prescribe fees, charged at an hourly rate, in respect of inspections carried out for the purpose of conferring authority to issue plant passports under the Plant Health (Great Britain) Order 1993 supra.

96 Plant health—import and export services

The Import (Plant Health Fees) (England and Wales) Order 1993, SI 1993/1641 (in force on 19 July 1993), replaces the 1988 Order, SI 1988/1427, as amended. The fees are unchanged.

97 Potatoes—seed potatoes

The Seed Potatoes (Amendment) Regulations 1993, SI 1993/1878 (in force on 20 August 1993), further amend the 1991 Regulations, SI 1991/2206 by modifying the tolerances for tobacco necrosis virus infection and for leafroll, severe mosaic and mosaic infection in crops inspected with a view to classification as certified seed potatoes. The diseases will no longer be separately identified in the tolerances. A drafting error in the 1991 Regulations is corrected.

98 Seeds—beet seeds

The Beet Seeds Regulations 1993, SI 1993/2006 (in force on 1 September 1993), consolidate, with amendments, the provisions of the Beet Seeds Regulations 1985, SI 1985/978 as amended. The regulations, which implement Council Directive (EC) 66/400, continue to restrict the marketing of beet seeds in Great Britain to specified categories meeting prescribed standards, require such seeds to be sold in sealed packages labelled or marked with prescribed particulars and make tampering with labels prescribed by regulations an offence. The regulations also continue to make provision for the taking of samples for the verification of standards and provide that certain particulars stated or implied on a package of seeds are deemed to constitute a statutory warranty by the seller for the protection of the purchaser. The regulations incorporate a provision required under Council Directive (EC) 88/380, relating to the marketing of seed in respect of which no official certificate has been issued.

99 Seeds—cereal seeds

The Cereal Seeds Regulations 1993, SI 1993/2005 (in force on 1 September 1993), consolidate, with amendments, the provisions of the Cereal Seeds Regulations 1985, SI 1985/976 as amended. The regulations, which implement Council Directive (EC) 66/402, continue to restrict the marketing of cereal seeds in Great Britain to specified categories meeting prescribed standards, require such seeds to be sold in sealed packages labelled or marked with prescribed particulars and to make tampering with labels prescribed by regulations an offence. The regulations also continue to make provision for the taking of samples for the verification of standards and provide that certain particulars stated or implied on a package of seeds are deemed to constitute a statutory warranty by the seller for the protection of the purchaser. The regulations incorporate a provision required under Council Directive (EC) 88/380, relating to the marketing of seed in respect of which no official certificate has been issued, and also make provision for the marketing of "naked oat" varieties, as required under Commission Directive) (EC)93/2.

100 Seeds—fees

The Seeds (Fees) (Amendment) Regulations 1993, SI 1993/429 (in force on 1 June 1993), amend the Seeds (Fees) Regulations 1985, SI 1985/981, by prescribing revised fees in respect of matters arising under the Cereal Seeds Regulations 1985, SI 1985/976, the Fodder Plant Seeds Regulations 1985, SI 1985/975, the Oil and Fibre Plant Seeds Regulations 1985, SI 1985/977, the Beet Seeds Regulations 1985, SI 1985/978, the Vegetable Seeds Regulations 1985, SI 1985/979 and the Seeds (Registration, Licensing and Enforcement) Regulations 1985, SI 1985/980. The Seeds (Fees) (Amendment) Regulations 1992, SI 1992/1085 are revoked.

The Seeds (National Lists of Varieties) (Fees) (Amendment) Regulations 1993, SI 1993/416 (in force on 1 April 1993), amend the 1990 Regulations, SI 1990/617. Most application, test, award and renewal fees have been increased, although the test fee for sugar beet and fodder beet varieties has been reduced. The fee for the purchase of a report from a testing authority in another country has been increased to accord with the international charge of 350 Swiss Francs although fees payable in respect of other matters remain unchanged. The Seeds (National Lists of Varieties) (Fees) (Amendment) Regulations 1991, SI 1991/657, reg 2(4) and the Seeds (National Lists of Varieties) (Fees) (Amendment) Regulations 1992, SI 1992/436, are revoked.

101 Seeds—fodder plants

The Fodder Plant Seeds Regulations 1993, SI 1993/2009 (in force on 1 September 1993) consolidate, with amendments, the provisions of the 1985 Regulations, SI 1985/975 as amended. The consolidation incorporates a provision required under Council Directive (EEC) 88/380 relating to the marketing of seed for which an official certificate has not been issued to other member states.

The Fodder Plant Seeds (Amendment) Regulations 1993, SI 1993/2529 (in force on 22 November 1993), amend the 1993 Regulations supra in relation to certain provisions concerning field pea crops.

102 Seeds—oil and fibre plants

The Oil and Fibre Plant Seeds Regulations 1993, SI 1993/2007 (in force on 1 September 1993), consolidate, with amendments, the provisions of the 1985 Regulations, SI 1985/977, as amended. In addition, the consolidation incorporates Council Directive (EC) 88/380 relating to the marketing of seed for which an official certificate has not been issued to other member states. The regulations also implement Council Directive (EC) 69/208 (as amended) on the marketing of oil and fibre plant seed.

103   Seeds—registration, licensing and enforcement

The Seeds (Registration, Licensing and Enforcement) (Amendment) Regulations 1993, SI 1993/2530 (in force on 22 November 1993), further amend the 1985 Regulations, SI 1985/980, by removing the requirement for the result of a test for pea bacterial blight to be noted on the certificate of the result of an official test of seeds.

104   Seeds—vegetable seeds

The Vegetable Seeds Regulations 1993, SI 1993/2008 (in force on 1 September 1993), re-enact, with amendments, the provisions of the Vegetable Seeds Regulations 1985, SI 1985/979 as amended. The regulations, which implement Council Directive (EC) 70/458, continue to restrict the marketing of vegetable seeds in Great Britain to specified categories meeting prescribed standards, require such seeds to be sold in sealed packages labelled or marked with prescribed particulars and make tampering with labels prescribed by regulations an offence. The regulations also continue to make provision for the taking of samples for the verification of standards and provide that certain particulars stated or implied on a package of seeds are deemed to constitute a statutory warranty by the seller for the protection of the purchaser. The regulations incorporate a provision required under Council Directive (EC) 88/380, relating to the marketing to other member states of seed in respect of which no official certificate has been issued.

105   Sheep—annual premium

The Sheep Annual Premium and Suckler Cow Premium Quotas Regulations 1993, SI 1993/1626 (in force on 1 July 1993), make provision for the implementation of Council Regulations (EC) 3013/89 and 805/68 and Commission Regulations 3567/92 and 3886/92 which establish a system of quotas for sheep and suckler cow annual premiums. The main provisions under the regulations include specifying reference years for determining quotas, the laying down of supplementary rules for notifying transfers and leases of quota and specifying a minimum level of suckler cow premium quota that small producers may transfer without a holding or that they may lease to other producers.

The Sheep Annual Premium and Suckler Cow Premium Quotas (Amendment) Regulations 1993, SI 1993/3036 (in force on 7 December 1993), amend the 1993 Regulations supra by making further provision for the implementation of the Community provisions cited above. The main changes include laying down principles to govern allocations of sheep annual premium quota and suckler cow premium quota from the national reserve for 1993 and subsequent years, giving specified persons powers to verify applications for an allocation of quota from a particular national reserve and creating a related offence, listing the categories of persons eligible to be allocated quota and imposing further conditions in relation to such eligibilty, and specifying how much quota is to be allocated to successful applicants and when such allocations are to be effective.

106   Suckler cows—premiums

The Suckler Cow Premium Regulations 1993, SI 1993/1441 (in force on 30 June 1993), provide for the administration and enforcement of provisions relating to the payment of a premium for maintaining suckler cows under part of Council Regulation (EC) 805/68 and other relevant provisions in Commission Regulations (EC) 3886/92 and 3887/92. The regulations specify the period for submission of applications for premium and prohibit the submission of more than one application per year, require applicants to retain specified records and other documents, confer on authorised persons powers of entry and inspection and of seizure and retention of records, specify circumstances in which premium may be recovered by the appropriate minister and prescribe the appropriate rates of interest payable in such circumstances. The regulations create offences, prescribe penalties, specify time limits for bringing prosecutions and make provision for offences committed by corporate bodies.

107   Suckler cows—premiums—quota

See para 105.

108   Wool—guaranteed prices

The British Wool (Guaranteed Prices) (Revocation) Order 1993, SI 1993/1184 (in force on 1 May 1993), revokes SI 1955/487, as amended, which, nevertheless, remains in force in relation to any period before the date of revocation.

ANIMALS

Halsbury's Laws of England (4th edn) Vol 2 (reissue), paras 201–600

109 Articles

Dangerous Dogs and Public Places, Christine Clayson: 157 JP Jo 824
Dangerous Dogs—Time for an Amnesty, Ronald Cottrell: 158 JP Jo 9
Hounded Hunts, Alec Samuels (on banning hunting on council land): LS Gaz, 3 November 1993, p 25
The Dangerous Dogs Act 1991, Gillian B Babington-Browne: 157 JP Jo 531
Unfair Treatment For Dog Owners, Ronald Cotterell: 157 JP Jo 505

110 Abandonment of animals—meaning of abandonment

The Abandonment of Animals Act 1960, s 1 provides that if any person, being the owner or having charge or control of any animal, abandons it without reasonable cause or excuse, whether permanently or not, in circumstances likely to cause the animal any unnecessary suffering, or causes, or procures, or, being the owner, permits it to be so abandoned, he will be guilty of an offence of cruelty.

An information laid against the respondent alleged that he had committed an offence under s 1. The information was dismissed by the magistrates. On appeal, the question arose as to the interpretation of "abandon it, whether permanently or not" within s 1. *Held*, the use by Parliament of the word "abandoned" implied something more than having left or leaving the animal unattended. Emphasis should be on the character of the act of abandonment and what made it an act of abandonment as distinct from leaving unattended. The use of the word "abandoned" implied physical leaving of an unattended animal in circumstances where suffering was likely and where there was sufficient evidence to prove that the defendant had totally disregarded his duty to care for the animal. The appeal in this case would be dismissed.

Hunt v Duckering [1993] Crim LR 678 (Queen's Bench Division: Evans LJ and Morland J).

111 Animal pathogens—import—licence

The Specified Animal Pathogens Order 1993, SI 1993/3250 (in force on 1 January 1993), implements certain provisions of Council Directive (EC) 92/118 relating to pathogens. It removes the requirement for an import licence for animal pathogens imported from another member state but creates a requirement for any person possessing certain animal pathogens, or wishing to introduce them into animals, to do so in accordance with a licence.

112 Bovine animals—identification, marking and breeding of animals—records

The Bovine Animals (Identification, Marking and Breeding Records) (Amendment) Order 1993, SI 1993/503 (in force on 9 March 1993), amends the Bovine Animals (Identification, Marking and Breeding Records) Order 1990, SI 1990/1867, so as to implement parts of Council Directive (EEC) 92/102, on the identification and registration of animals. The order requires records to be kept of the birth or death of each bovine animal and the number of bovine animals kept in the holding and requires that the local Animal Health Office be notified of the name and address of the owner or occupier of a holding on which bovine animals are kept.

113 Diseases of animals—approved disinfectants

The Diseases of Animals (Approved Disinfectants) (Amendment) Order 1993, SI 1993/1194 (in force on 30 April 1993), further amends the 1978 Order, SI 1978/32, by substituting newly approved disinfectants. The regulations revoke SI 1992/238, 2290.

The Diseases of Animals (Approved Disinfectants) (Amendment) (No 2) Order 1993, SI 1993/3086 (in force on 8 December 1993), further amends the 1978 Order supra, by adding specified newly approved disinfectants to the list of approved disinfectants and by deleting from that list other specified disinfectants, which may, however, continue to be used as approved disinfectants until 31 December 1993.

114 Diseases of animals—foot-and-mouth disease

The Foot-and-Mouth Disease (Amendment) (No 2) Order 1993, SI 1993/3119 (in force on 1 January 1994), amends the 1983 Order, SI 1983/1950, by providing for the confinement of animals running on unenclosed land in the event of an outbreak of the disease in that area. It makes consequential amendments to the Swine Vesicular Disease Order 1972, SI 1972/1980 and the African Swine Fever Order 1980, SI 1980/145, and revokes the 1993 Order, SI 1993/1847.

The Foot-and-Mouth Disease (Sera and Glandular Products) (Revocation) Order 1993, SI 1993/1332 (in force on 14 June 1993), revokes the 1939 Order, SR & O 1939/707, so as to remove controls inconsistent with Community legislation concerning labelling of veterinary medicinal products.

115 Diseases of animals—therapeutic substances

The Diseases of Animals (Therapeutic Substances) (Revocation) Order 1993, SI 1993/1331 (in force on 14 June 1993), revokes the 1952 Order, SI 1952/1933, as amended, and amends the Importation of Animal Products and Poultry Products Order 1980, SI 1980/14, and the Channel Tunnel (Amendment of Agriculture, Fisheries and Food Import Legislation) Order 1990, SI 1990/237, so as to remove frontier controls inconsistent with the single market.

116 Dogs—dangerous dogs—detention of dangerous dog by police—failure to tattoo dog

The applicant obtained a certificate of exemption from the Home Office agency which dealt with dangerous dogs, after having neutered and implanted a transponder in his pit bull terrier. The police stopped the applicant for a road traffic offence and, on seeing his dog, charged him with unlawful possession of a dangerous dog which was unmuzzled. The Crown Prosecution Service decided not to prosecute but the police detained the dog because it had not been tattooed. The applicant sought judicial review of the decision to detain on the ground that the certificate of exemption had not been invalidated by the failure to tattoo the dog. *Held*, although it was now a statutory requirement, on the date that the dog was first detained the requirement of tattooing was for administrative reasons only, in order to make it easier for the police to trace a particular dog to its owner. Therefore, as there had been no statutory basis for tattooing at the time of detention, the certificate of exemption was valid and accordingly a declaration would be made to that effect.

R v Metropolitan Police and the Index of Exempted Dogs, ex p Wheeler [1993] Crim LR 942 (Queen's Bench Division: Evans LJ and Morland J).

117 Dogs—dangerous dogs—interpretation of legislation

The Dangerous Dogs Act 1991, s 1 provides that it is an offence for a person to allow any dog "of the type known as the pit bull terrier", of which he is the owner or the person in charge, to be in a public place without being muzzled or kept on a lead.

In two separate cases involving convictions under the Dangerous Dogs Act 1991, s 1, the following questions fell to be determined: (1) the correct interpretation of the word "type" in s 1; and (2) whether a dog's behaviour and dangerous proclivities should be taken into account in determining whether a dog was "of the type known as the pit bull terrier". *Held*, (1) the word "type" should be construed as having a wider meaning than the word "breed". There was no breed standard for pit bull terriers in the United Kingdom but the standard set by the American Dog Breeder's Association (ABDA) could be used by the court as a guide in determining, as a question of fact, the scope of the words "any dog of the type known as the pit bull terrier". However, the court did not have to adhere strictly to the ABDA standard, and, provided that a dog substantially conformed to the ABTA-listed characteristics the court was entitled to find that it was "of the type known as the pit bull terrier" even though it did not meet that standard in every respect. (2) Such evidence was relevant, but not conclusive, to the court's determination and the court ought to have considered it.

R v Crown Court at Knightsbridge, ex p Dunne; Brock v DPP [1993] 4 All ER 491 (Queen's Bench Division: Glidewell LJ and Cresswell J).

118 Dogs—dangerous dogs—public place—car

The defendant was driving a motor car on a public road. He was stopped by the police who found an unmussled pit bull terrier loose in the car. The defendant was convicted of having an unmuzzled pit bull terrier in his possession or custody in a public place contrary to the Dangerous Dogs Act 1991, s 1. The defendant appealed. *Held*, for the purposes of s 1, a dangerous dog in a private car which was on a public highway was in a public place within the meaning of s 10(2) and was therefore required to be muzzled and on a lead as prescribed by s 1(2)(d). The appeal would accordingly be dismissed.

Bates v DPP (1993) 157 JP 1004 (Queen's Bench Division: Rose LJ and Waller J).

119 Dogs—dangerous dogs—public place—garden path

The defendant was convicted of having a dog which was dangerously out of control in a public place and which had caused injury contrary to the Dangerous Dogs Act 1991, s 3(1). The defendant appealed on the question of whether the court was correct in holding that the defendant's garden was a public place for the purposes of the 1991 Act, s 10. *Held*, in considering *R v Llewellyn Edwards* (1978) 67 Cr App R 228, which was concerned with the Public Order Act 1936, a front garden could not be said to be a public place simply on the basis of an implied licence. Therefore, the garden path leading to the appellant's front door was not a public place within the meaning of the 1991 Act, s 10. The terms of the offence were not sufficiently wide to include places to which people were invited in implied or express terms. Accordingly, the appeal would be allowed.

Fellowes v DPP (1993) 157 JP 936 (Queen's Bench Division: Kennedy LJ and Clarke J).

120 Dogs—dangerous dogs—strict liability of owner

The Dangerous Dogs Act 1991, s 3(1) provides that if a dog is dangerously out of control in a public place, the owner or person in charge of the dog for the time being is guilty of an offence, or, if the dog while so out of control injures any person, an aggravated offence.

The defendants had all been convicted of an aggravated offence under the 1991 Act, s 3(1). They appealed on the ground that the offence had been treated as one of strict liability where in fact it ought to have been treated as one in which mens rea was required. *Held*, it had been established that strict liability could apply to a criminal offence where it was created by a statute that was concerned with an issue of social concern such as public safety. This was clearly the case here and, in addition, if Parliament had meant to introduce an element of mens rea, it could have done so as it had in the 1991 Act, s 3(2) and (3). Accordingly, the appeals would be dismissed.

R v Bezzina; R v Codling; R v Elvin (1993) Times, 7 December (Court of Appeal: Kennedy LJ, Waterhouse and Ebsworth JJ). *Gammon (Hong Kong) Ltd v Attorney-General of Hong-Kong* [1984] 2 All ER 503 (1984 Abr para 584) followed.

121 Export of animals—veterinary and zootechnichal checks

The Animals and Animal Products (Import and Export) Regulations 1993, SI 1993/3247 (in force on 1 January 1994), revoke and re-enact with amendments the 1992 Regulations, SI 1992/3295 and revoke the 1993 Regulations, SI 1993/1967. The most important changes include implementing Council Directive (EEC) 92/65, laying down animal health requirements governing trade in and imports of animals, semen, ova and embryos; Council Directive (EEC) 92/118 in relation to intra-Community trade; and Council Directive (EEC) 90/425 in relation to animal pathogens.

122 Import of animals—bees

The Importation of Bees (Amendment) Order 1993, SI 1993/3249 (in force on 1 January 1994) implements Council Directive (EC) 92/65 which deals with animal health requirements relating to the importation and trade in the Community of animals, semen, ova and embryos which are not subject to any other EC animal health requirements. Provision is made for any bee imported from another member state to be accompanied by the correct health certificate. The permitted importation of bees from other member states without a licence is confined to parts of Great Britain which have been designated infected areas under the Bee Disease Control Order 1982, SI 1982/107.

123 Import of animals—post-import controls

The Animals (Post-Import Control) Order 1993, SI 1993/14 (in force on 9 January 1993), establishes controls with regard to cattle from areas not free of warble fly, pigs from areas not free of Aujeszky's disease, and cattle from Canada and specified countries which are the subject of Community decisions. The order empowers an inspector to serve a notice in specified circumstances requiring a person to comply with any duty imposed by this order and is enforceable by the local authority.

124   Import of animals—veterinary and zootechnichal checks
See para 121.

125   Movement of animals—markets
The Welfare of Animals at Markets (Amendment) Order 1993, SI 1993/3085 (in force in part on 1 January 1994, in part on 1 January 1995), amends the 1990 Order, SI 1990/2628, by making further provisions for the protection of lambs and kids at market.

126   Poultry—fees
The Poultry Breeding Flocks, Hatcheries and Processed Animal Protein (Fees) Order 1993, SI 1993/1998 (in force on 30 August 1993), replaces the 1992 Regulations, SI 1992/1490. It prescribes fees to recover the full cost of transactions specified in the order in respect of breeding flocks and hatcheries and for the purpose of authorising laboratories under certain orders relating to poultry and protein processing.

127   Poultry—general
The Poultry Breeding Flocks and Hatcheries Order 1993, SI 1993/1898 (in force on 30 August 1993), replaces the Poultry Breeding Flocks and Hatcheries (Registration and Testing) Order 1989, SI 1989/1963 and revokes SI 1990/347. The order simplifies the requirements for registration and testing for salmonella in breeding flocks and hatcheries; provides for the registration of breeding flocks and hatcheries; and provides for the taking of samples for bacteriological testing for salmonella.

128   Poultry—laying flocks—testing and registration
The Poultry Laying Flocks (Testing and Registration etc) (Revocation) Order 1993, SI 1993/357 (in force on 25 February 1993), revokes the 1989 Order, SI 1989/1964 (as amended), which provided for the testing of samples from, and registration of flocks of, domestic fowls kept for the production of eggs for human consumption.

129   Scientific procedures—establishments—fees
The Animals (Scientific Procedures) Act (Fees) Order 1993, SI 1993/2956 (in force on 1 January 1994), replaces the 1992 Order, SI 1992/3058. The order prescribes the fees payable by the holder of a certificate issued under the Animals (Scientific Procedures) Act 1968, ss 6, 7. The fee for scientific procedure establishments is £120 plus £110 for each personal licence holder whose place of primary availability is that establishment. The fee for a breeding and supplying establishment which is not a scientific procedure establishment is increased to £553.

130   Scientific procedures—protected animals
The Animals (Scientific Procedures) Act (Amendment) Order 1993, SI 1993/2103 (in force on 1 October 1993), extends the scope of the 1986 Act. The Order extends Octopus vulgaris from the time at which it becomes capable of independent feeding to the definition of protected animals. Quail (Coturnix coturnix) is added to the list of animals to be obtained only from designated breeding or supplying establishments.

131   Spring traps
The Spring Traps Approval (Variation) Order 1993, SI 1993/189 (in force on 1 March 1993), adds the Kania Trap 2000 to those already approved in the Spring Traps Approval Order 1975, SI 1975/1647, and specifies the animals for which, and the circumstances in which, it may be used.

132   Veterinary drugs
See MEDICINE, PHARMACY, DRUGS AND MEDICINAL PRODUCTS.

133   Veterinary surgeons—recognition of member states' qualifications
The Veterinary Surgeons Qualifications (EC Recognition) (Amendment) Order 1993, SI 1993/596 (in force on 11 March 1993), amends the Veterinary Surgeons Act 1966 for the

purpose of implementing Council Directive (EC) 89/594 relating to the right of establishment of veterinary surgeons and their freedom to provide veterinary services. Provision is made for the registration of the holder of a European qualification in veterinary surgery granted in a member state which that state treats as equivalent to the recognised European qualification. The holder must produce a certificate to that effect from that member state and the certificate must also state that the holder has been trained in accordance with Council Directive (EC) 78/1027.

134 Veterinary surgeons and veterinary practitioners—registration

The Veterinary Surgeons and Veterinary Practitioners (Registration) (Amendment) Regulations Order in Council 1993, SI 1993/610 (in force on 5 March 1993), approve regulations which further amend the Veterinary Surgeons and Veterinary Practitioners Registration Regulations 1967, SI 1967/395, by increasing the fees payable in respect of the registration and annual retention of names on the Royal College of Veterinary Surgeons by between 2·8 per cent and 4·5 per cent.

ARBITRATION

Halsbury's Laws of England (4th edn) Vol 2 (reissue), paras 601–900

135 Articles

A Real Alternative? ADR Appraised, Elizabeth Jones (on alternative dispute resolution): 137 SJ 378
ADR in Perspective, Michael Upton: 1993 SLT 57
ADR: The Story Since 1979, Alex Bevan: 1993 SLT 80
Alternative Dispute Resolution and Civil Justice: An Unresolved Relationship, Simon Roberts: 56 MLR 452
Alternative Dispute Resolution Processes within the Framework of the World-Wide Access-to-Justice Movement, Mauro Cappelletti: 56 MLR 277
Arbitration Needs Lawyers, Michael Reynolds: 137 SJ 1210
Court Sponsored Mediation: The Case Against Mandatory Participation, Richard Ingleby: 56 MLR 441
Determinations and Experts, Del Williams: Estates Gazette, 21 August 1993, p 75
Forensic Submission as a Bar to Arbitration, Peter Kaye: (1993) 12 CJQ 359
Lawyer Negotiations: Theories and Realities-What We Learn From Mediation, Carrie Menkel-Meadow: 56 MLR 361
Lawyers and Arbitration: The Juridification of Construction Disputes, John Flood and Andrew Caiger: 56 MLR 412
Reaching Agreements, Gillian Howard (on settlements which bypass ACAS): LS Gaz, 25 August 1993, p 26
Stays and Support, Brian Dye (on *Channel Tunnel Group v Balfour Beatty* [1993] 1 All ER 664, HL (1992 Abr para 129)): 137 SJ 433
The Relationship Between Arbitration and the Courts in Scotland and England, Dr Fraser P Davidson: (1993) 12 CJQ 372
The Tribunal and the Truth, Francis Miller: 144 NLJ 50
Tribunals and Informal Justice, Hazel Genn: 56 MLR 393
Undertaking the Undefinable, Francis Miller (on undertakings to pay arbitrator's fees): 143 NLJ 928

136 Arbitration agreement—initial illegality of contract—jurisdiction of arbitrator

It fell to be determined whether, even though a contract was illegal, an arbitration clause contained in it nevertheless conferred jurisdiction on an arbitrator to determine the initial illegality of the contract. *Held*, provided that the arbitration clause itself was not directly impeached, it could survive the invalidity of the contract and thereby confer jurisdiction on the arbitrator to determine the contract's initial validity. The wishes of the parties should be given effect unless there were compelling reasons of principle for that not being possible. The principle of separability applied even where the alleged ground of the invalidity of the contract was its initial illegality.

Harbour Assurance Co (UK) Ltd v Kansa General International Insurance Co Ltd [1993] 3 WLR 42 (Court of Appeal: Ralph Gibson, Leggatt and Hoffmann LJJ). Decision of Steyn J [1992] 1 Lloyd's Rep 81 (1991 Abr para 97) reversed.

137 Arbitration agreement—jurisdiction of arbitrator

See *Bulk Chartering & Consultants Australia Pty Ltd v T & T Metal Pty Ltd,* para 2325.

138 Arbitration agreement—rent review—notice—service out of time

See *Richurst Ltd v Pimenta,* para 1628.

139 Arbitrator—conduct—jurisdiction

The contractor was employed under a contract which provided for payment to be made against interim certificates issued by a supervising officer. The employer retained a right to raise set-offs or defences to the certified sum. When the interim certificate was issued, the employer refused to pay the certified sums to the contractor, and the contractor began court proceedings claiming that he was entitled to payments greater than the certified amount. Following the appointment of an arbitrator, the contractor applied for an interim payment. The employer, while contending that the arbitrator had no jurisdiction to make an award without a full hearing, submitted affidavits in reply. By an interim award, the arbitrator ordered the employer to pay the certified sum to the contractor and decided that the employer's counterclaim would be considered at a full hearing. The employer applied for an order setting aside the interim award and for an order removing the arbitrator for misconduct. *Held,* in exceptional circumstances an arbitrator could make an interim award without a full hearing where an employer raised defences or set-offs to a certified sum in relation to a contract which did not exclude the raising of such defences or set-offs. In other cases there had to be a full hearing. In this case, following these guidelines, the arbitrator had been wrong in law. There had been no finding that the defence and set-off had not been made bona fide or on reasonable grounds, and it would have been impossible for any arbitrator to have reached such a conclusion. The application to set aside the interim award would therefore be allowed, although the application to remove the arbitrator for misconduct would be dismissed.

The Modern Trading Co Ltd v Swale Building and Construction Ltd [1992] ADRLJ 174 (Queen's Bench Division: Waller J).

140 Award—costs—effect of sealed offer

A dispute between shipowners and charterers had been referred to arbitration. The shipowners refused the charterers' sealed offer of settlement of their claim and continued with the arbitration. The arbitration award exceeded the amount of the sealed offer by a small amount. The arbitrators directed that each party pay its own costs but that the shipowners pay the costs of both parties from the date of the sealed offer. The owners contended that they should not be required to pay the charterers' costs because the sealed offer procedure operated according to the same principles which applied when taking account of payments made into court in settlement of litigation. *Held,* Sir Thomas Bingham MR dissenting, an arbitrator was required to act judicially in exercising his discretion as to costs, applying the same principles as applied in the High Court, in particular the principle that costs normally followed the event. A sealed offer made in an arbitration was the arbitral equivalent of a payment into court; accordingly, a respondent was normally entitled to payment of costs from the date of the offer if the claim and interest was less than the offer. The arbitrator was not entitled to take into account whether an award of costs would be made in favour of the claimant as that would require the claimant to assess not only the likelihood of achieving an award on his claim and interest exceeding the offer, but also, if there was a risk of an order that the respondent pay the claimant's costs, the chance of obtaining an award greater than the offer and the respondent's costs. Such a result would hinder settlement and introduce complications inconsistent with the principle that costs should follow the event.

Everglade Maritime Inc v Schiffahrtsgesellschaft Detlef von Appen mbH, The Maria [1993] 3 All ER 748 (Court of Appeal: Sir Thomas Bingham MR, Kennedy and Evans LJJ). Decision of Judge Diamond QC [1992] 3 All ER 851 (1992 Abr para 126) affirmed. Dictum of Donaldson J in *Tramountana Armadora SA v Atlantic Shipping Co SA* [1978] 2 All ER 870 at 877 (1978 Abr para 155) applied. *Gray v Lord Ashburton* [1916–17] All ER Rep 380 distinguished.

141 Award—enforcement of award—foreign award—order for security

The plaintiffs applied for leave to enforce an arbitration award made in Sweden against the defendants. The application was adjourned at first instance pending the outcome of proceedings brought by the defendants in Sweden to set aside the award. On the adjournment the court required the defendants to provide security of US$29·5m, which represented the total value of the award of $9·5m plus interest. The defendants appealed. *Held*, an order for security should not be made automatically. There were two important factors to be taken into account. If the arbitration award was invalid, there should be an adjournment of the application and no order for security. If it was clearly valid, there should be an order for immediate enforcement or substantial security. The court also had to consider the ease or difficulty of enforcement of the award and whether it would be rendered more difficult if enforcement were delayed. In this case, it could not be said that further delay would definitely not prejudice the enforceability of the award in England. The correct course would be to order security in a significant sum, which would provide an incentive for the defendants to proceed with the Swedish proceedings expeditiously and give some protection for the plaintiffs against any deterioration of their prospects of enforcement in England. An order requiring the whole amount of an award including interest for so many years should only have been made as an exceptional measure. The appeal would accordingly be allowed and an order substituted requiring the defendants to provide security in the sum of $5m.

Soleh Boneh International Ltd v Government of the Republic of Uganda [1993] 2 Lloyd's Rep 208 (Court of Appeal: Neill, Staughton and Roch LJJ).

142 Award—enforcement of award—foreign award—parties to Convention

The Arbitration (Foreign Awards) Order 1993, SI 1993/1256 (in force on 3 June 1993), declares Antigua and Barbuda as a party to the New York Convention on the Recognition and Enforcement of Foreign Arbitral Awards. The 1989 Order, SI 1989/1348, is amended by deleting the reference in the Schedule to Antigua and Barbados.

143 Award—remission of award—application out of time

At an arbitration hearing it was held that under a lease of a building the notional lease postulated by the rent review clauses did not itself contain a rent review provision. Three and a quarter years later the plaintiff tenants issued an originating motion seeking an order remitting the award by the arbitrator pursuant to the Arbitration Act 1950, s 22, on the grounds that it contained an error of law, and an order extending time for making such an application. *Held*, the delay in making the applications was excessive and further it would not be possible to set aside the error. It would not be correct to find a way around the limitation on actions imposed by Parliament and as such estoppel per rem judicatam would be applied. The changes made to appealing an arbitrator's award by the Arbitration Act 1979 did not impliedly enlarge the power of the court to remit under the 1950 Act, s 22. Accordingly, the application would be dismissed.

Arnold v National Westminster Bank plc [1993] 01 EG 94 (Chancery Division: Knox J).

144 Reference to arbitration—delay in prosecuting claim—principle against retrospectivity of legislation

The owners of a vessel had brought an arbitration claim which had been struck out on the grounds of inordinate and inexcusable delay under the Arbitration Act 1950, s 13A, which came into force on 1 January 1992. The arbitrator had ruled that s 13A applied retrospectively, and he struck out the claim on the basis of delays which had occured before 1 January 1992, finding that the owners had been guilty of inordinate and inexcusable delay in advancing the arbitration which had created a real risk of an unfair resolution of the dispute, although he had not found the owners guilty of delay after that date. The owners successfully appealed against the decision to strike out their claim, and the charterers' subsequent appeal was dismissed. On further appeal, *held*, the courts were required to approach questions of statutory interpretation with a disposition, and in some cases a very strong disposition, to assume that a statute was not intended to have retrospective effect. However, the basis of the rule was fairness, and how the question of fairness would be answered in respect of a particular statute would depend on the interaction of several factors, capable of varying from case to case. In this case, the words in s 13A were sufficient to demonstrate that the delay encompassed all the delay that had caused the substantial risk of unfairness. The meaning of the section showed that in the interests of reform, Parliament had been willing to tolerate the very qualified kind of hardship implied in giving the legislation a partially retrospective effect. The charterer's appeal would therefore be allowed.

L'Office Cherifien des Phosphates v Yamashita-Shinnihon Steamship Co Ltd [1994] 1 All ER 20 (House of Lords: Lords Templeman, Goff of Chievely, Jauncey of Tullichettle, Browne-Wilkinson and Mustill). Decision of Court of Appeal [1993] 3 All ER 686 reversed.

1950 Act, s 13A inserted by the Courts and Legal Services Act 1990, s 102.

145   Religious court—Beth Din—award of costs—award contrary to established principle

By a written agreement under the Arbitration Acts 1950 and 1979 two parties to an arbitration submitted to the jurisdiction of the Beth Din whereby they agreed that the award of the Beth Din would be final and binding and to pay such costs as the Beth Din ordered. It was an established principle of Jewish law that in a Beth Din arbitration each party ought to bear its own legal costs. The Beth Din found for the plaintiff and ordered that its costs, the arbitrators' fees and expenses, would be divided equally with each side paying a fixed sum. The plaintiff refused to pay and the defendants to the action issued a writ and were given summary judgment under RSC Ord 14. The plaintiff applied for leave to defend contending that the decision on costs was not a judicial exercise of discretion because the arbitrators failed to apply the general rule that costs follow the event and failed to give reasons for departing from that rule. The defendants contended that such matters could not be raised by way of defence because by RSC Ord 73, r 2 the only available challenge was by the procedure under the Arbitration Acts 1950 and 1979. The plaintiff's application was refused and he appealed. *Held*, the Arbitration Act 1979, s 1 laid down that any challenge to an award of costs by arbitrators, on the grounds of misconduct or misapplication of some general principle of Jewish law, had to be brought by way of an application for leave to appeal under the 1979 Act by the procedure in RSC Ord 73. No such application having been made, the arbitrators' award stood as a final, valid and unassailable award, and therefore the plaintiff was precluded from raising those issues by way of defence. Accordingly, the appeal would be dismissed.

Cohen v Baram (1993) Times, 16 December (Court of Appeal: Dillon, Mann and Hirst LJJ).

146   Stay of court proceedings—compulsory submission to arbitration—discretion to stay proceedings

See *Tustian v Johnston*, para 69.

AVIATION

Halsbury's Laws of England (4th edn) Vol 2 (reissue), paras 1001–1800

147   Articles

Aircraft Operating Leases—The Lessee's Perspective: Ian Siddell: (1993) 8 JIBFL 367
The Practice of Aircraft Overbooking, Duncan Nicol and Ronald Herd: [1993] 21 SLT 207

148   Air navigation—flying restrictions—high security prisons

The Air Navigation (Restriction of Flying) (High Security Prisons) (Amendment No 3) Regulations 1993, SI 1993/2123 (in force on 25 August 1993), further amend the 1989 Regulations, SI 1989/2118, by imposing restrictions on helicopters flying in specified airspace around the high security prison at Belmarsh.

149   Air navigation—police air operation licences

The Air Navigation (Fourth Amendment) Order 1993, SI 1993/607 (in force on 1 April 1993), further amends the 1989 Order, SI 1989/2004. Provision is made for flights in the service of the police authority to be conducted under a police air operator's certificate granted to the operator and in accordance with a police operations manual.

150   Air navigation—public transport aircraft

The Air Navigation (General) Regulations 1993, SI 1993/1622 (in force on 19 July 1993), consolidate and amend the 1981 Regulations SI 1981/57. The principal amendments include the bringing of performance group B public transport aircraft within the weight and performance requirements for performance group A aircraft and to exclude helicopters flying under and in accordance with a police air operator's certificate.

The Air Navigation (Third Amendment) Order 1993, SI 1993/231 (in force on 12 March 1993), further amends the 1989 Order, SI 1989/2004. Major changes include the introduction of revised requirements for the marking of nationality and registration marks on aircraft registered in the United Kingdom, a requirement that all public transport aircraft registered in the United Kingdom establish and comply with aerodrome operating minima, and a new requirement that a person holding an air traffic controller's licence must not perform any of the functions specified in respect of a rating included in his licence when suffering from fatigue. Further amendments include a provision that every holder or applicant for an aerodrome licence must submit an aerodrome manual which contains specified information, and a requirement that pilots of aircraft flying for the purposes of public transport undergo tests of proficiency in using instrument approach-to-land systems.

151 Air navigation—route licences

The Air Navigation (Fifth Amendment) Order 1993, SI 1993/2670 (in force on 27 October 1993), amends the 1989 Order, SI 1989/2004, by adding the holder of a route licence granted under the Civil Aviation Act 1982, s 65 to the class of persons against whom unfair, discriminatory or restrictive practices may particularly cause the Secretary of State to exercise his power to revoke a licence.

152 Aircraft noise restrictions—maximum movements of aircraft—judicial review

The Civil Aviation Act 1982, s 78(3)(b) provides that the Secretary of State has power by notice to specify the maximum number of occasions on which aircraft are permitted to take off and land, for the purpose of avoiding aircraft noise.

The existing scheme of restrictions under the 1982 Act, s 78 which restricted night flying by reference to the number of aircraft was due to be replaced with a scheme assigning each aircraft with a quota count according to the amount of noise created. Aircraft movements which exceeded the quota would be prohibited. Under the new scheme it would therefore be possible to fly a smaller number of noisier aircraft or a larger number of quieter aircraft. It was submitted that the new scheme fell outside the wording of s 78. On an application for judicial review of the decision to introduce the new rules, *held*, the argument put forward by the Secretary of State that the scheme implied maximum numbers of aircraft involved an indefinite number of possible combinations of aircraft movements and was therefore impracticable. The concept of a maximum number of movements played no part in the new proposals. However under s 78(3)(b) a maximum number of aircraft had to be the basis of any new scheme and the scheme was not therefore authorised by the section. A number of other arguments were rejected and it was recommended that RSC Ord 53 should be amended so that a judge could refuse leave to apply for judicial review on some grounds whilst granting it on other grounds which had more merit. Accordingly the application would be allowed.

R v Secretary of State for Transport, ex p Richmond upon Thames London Borough Council [1994] 1 All ER 577 (Queen's Bench Division: Laws J).

153 Aircraft noise restrictions—new offences

The Aeroplane Noise (Limitation on Operation of Aeroplanes) Regulations 1993, SI 1993/1409 (in force on 1 July 1993), implement Council Directive (EC) 94/14 on the limitation of the operation of prescribed aircraft. The operation of such aircraft will gradually be phased out between 1 April 1995 and 31 March 2002. The regulations create the offences of operating a relevant aircraft without carrying an appropriate noise certificate, of failing to produce the noise certificate, of failing to comply with a direction not to take off and of obstructing a person acting in the exercise of his powers or the performance of his duties.

154 Airport operations—slots at Community airports—provision for co-ordinators

The Airports Slot Allocation Regulations 1993, SI 1993/1067 (in force on 12 May 1993), implement Council Regulation (EC) 95/93 on common rules for the allocation of slots at Community airports. Provision is made for the publication of any determination that an airport be designated a co-ordinated airport and for the appointment of an approved co-ordinator. Offences are created where a person acts as co-ordinator when not approved as such, where an air carrier fails to give the co-ordinator requested information and where an air carrier exchanges or transfers slots contrary to the requirements of the council regulation.

The Airports Slot Allocation (Amendment) Regulations 1993, SI 1993/3042 (in force on 1 January 1994), amend the 1993 Regulations supra. The definition of the expression "the Council Regulation" is amended so as to take account of the coming into force of Council Decision (EC) 93/453 concerning the amendment of the Agreement between the EEC, the Kingdom of Norway and Kingdom of Sweden on civil aviation.

155   Airports—public airport companies—finance

See para 1692.

156   Airports—removal and disposal of vehicles

The Airports (Designation) (Removal and Disposal of Vehicles) (Amendment) Order 1993, SI 1993/2117 (in force on 1 November 1993), adds Bristol and London Luton airports to the list of airports set out in the 1990 Order, SI 1990/54.

157   Aviation security—air cargo agents

The Aviation Security (Air Cargo Agents) Regulations 1993, SI 1993/1073 (in force on 1 September 1993), enable the Secretary of State to maintain a list of air cargo agents who are approved for purposes related to aviation security. The regulations extend to air cargo agents on the list, the provisions of the Aviation Security Act 1982, Pt II, which apply to persons permitted to have access to a restricted zone of an aerodrome for the activities of a business.

158   Aviation security—extension of provisions to Jersey

The Aviation Security (Jersey) Order 1993, SI 1993/1251 (in force on 12 June 1993), extends to the Bailiwick of Jersey the provisions of the Aviation Security Act 1982. The Aviation and Maritime Security Act 1990, ss 1, 50 are also extended to the Bailiwick of Jersey.

159   Carriage by air—carriers—intra-Community routes—access

The Access for Community Air Carriers to Intra-Community Air Routes (Amendment and Other Provisions) Regulations 1993, SI 1993/3040 (in force on 1 January 1994), further amend the 1992 Regulations, SI 1992/2993, so as to take into account the coming into force of Council Decision (EC) 93/453 concerning the amendment of the Agreement between the EEC, the Kingdom of Norway and Kingdom of Sweden on civil aviation. Further provision has been made to disapply the requirement for a permission under the Air Navigation Order 1989, SI 1989/2004, art 88(1) for Community Air Carriers exercising traffic rights on routes to or from Norway or Sweden in consequence of Council Decision (EC) 93/453.

160   Carriage by air—carriers—intra-Community routes—agreements between carriers—exemption from rules of competition

See para 2730.

161   Carriage by air—dangerous goods

The Air Navigation (Dangerous Goods) (Fourth Amendment) Regulations 1993, SI 1993/179 (in force on 1 January 1993), amend the Air Navigation (Dangerous Goods) Regulations 1985, SI 1985/1939, as amended, by (1) updating the definition of "technical instructions"; (2) requiring a person carrying dangerous goods by air to comply with the Technical Instructions; (3) requiring a shipper of dangerous goods to furnish the operator of the aircraft with specified documents; (4) requiring that an operator must within a reasonable time after being requested to do so by an authorised person produce any documents which relate to dangerous goods; (5) specifying that an authorised person has the power to examine, seize, retain or detain, and dispose of any goods, baggage, package or sample taken from any goods, baggage or package which he has reasonable grounds to suspect may contain dangerous goods.

162   Carriage by air—development of intra-Community markets and direct services—exclusion of territory

See *Government of Gibraltar v EC Council*, para 2739.

163 Carriage by air—loss of goods in transit—carrier's liability—limitation of liability

Carriers lost a consignment of diamonds in transit between Brussels and London. Their liability was limited, under the Warsaw-Hague Convention, art 22(2)(a), to a sum of 250 francs per kilogram of the consignment or a sum not exceeding that declared on consignment by the consignor in a special declaration of interest in delivery at destination. The consignor had made such a special declaration, declaring the value of the diamonds to be £200 which was only a fraction of their actual value which, it claimed, was over £70,000. The consignor sought compensation for the diamonds' actual value. On a preliminary issue, it fell to be determined whether a consignor could recover more than the sum specified in a special declaration if the carrier was proved to have acted intentionally or recklessly. *Held*, a special declaration of the value of cargo under art 22(2)(a) was a limit of liability for the purposes of art 25 (which provided that art 22 did not apply if it was proved that the damage resulted from an act or omission of the carrier, its servants or agents acting within the scope of their employment, done with intent to cause damage or recklessly and with knowledge that damage would probably result) because art 22 was exclusively concerned with the limits of a carrier's absolute liability under arts 17, 18 for death or injury or loss of, or damage to, baggage or cargo occurring during carriage by air. Article 22 restricted the amount that could be recovered but further provided that the carrier and the passenger could agree a higher limit by special contract. Both the limit of 250 francs per kilogram and the alternative special contract limit were "limits of liability" specified in art 22 and, therefore, subject to art 25, under which the carrier was deprived of all limitations on liability conferred by art 22 when the damage was caused by his wilful misconduct, as defined by art 25. Accordingly, if damage to cargo was caused by the carrier's wilful misconduct then, by virtue of art 25, the limit of liability in a special declaration of interest under art 22(2)(a) did not apply.

Antwerp United Diamond BVBA v Air Europe (a firm) [1993] 4 All ER 469 (Queen's Bench Division: Phillips J).

164 Civil Aviation Authority—air carriers—licensing

The Licensing of Air Carriers (Amendment) Regulations 1993, SI 1993/101 (in force on 19 February 1993), amend the 1992 Regulations, SI 1992/2992 by adding a definition for the expression "United Kingdom national".

165 Civil Aviation Authority—air fares—regulations

The Air Fares (Amendment) Regulations 1993, SI 1993/100 (in force on 19 February 1993), amend the 1992 Regulations, SI 1992/2994, by adding a definition for the expression "United Kingdom national".

The Air Fares (Second Amendment) Regulations 1993, SI 1993/3041 (in force on 1 January 1994), further amend the 1992 Regulations, SI 1992/2994. The definition of the expression "the Council Regulations" is amended so as to take account of the coming into force of the Council Decision (EC) 93/453 concerning the amendment of the Agreement between the EC, the Kingdom of Norway and Kingdom of Sweden on civil aviation.

166 Civil Aviation Authority—functions—operator's licence

The Licensing of Air Carriers (Second Amendment and Other Provisions) Regulations 1993, SI 1993/3039 (in force on 1 January 1994), further amend the 1992 Regulations, SI 1992/2992. The definition of the expression "the Council Regulation" has been amended so as to take account of the coming into force of Council Decision(EC) 93/453 concerning the amendment of the Agreement between the EEC, the Kingdom of Norway and the Kingdom of Sweden on civil aviation.

167 Civil Aviation Authority—navigation services—charges

The Civil Aviation (Navigation Services Charges) (Second Amendment) Regulations 1993, SI 1993/499 (in force on 1 April 1993), further amend the 1991 Regulations, SI 1991/470, by changing the charges payable to the Civil Aviation Authority for navigation services provided in connection with the use of specified aerodromes. In respect of the three London Airports, the standard charge for aircraft engaged on international flights is reduced but is unchanged for aircraft engaged on non international flights. The charge payable to the Civil Aviation Authority by the operator of an aircraft which flies within the Shanwick Oceanic Control Area and in respect of which a flight plan is communicated to the appropriate air traffic control unit is reduced. The co-ordinates defining the area of the Northern North Sea, in respect of which flights made by helicopters from any place in the United Kingdom to a vessel or an offshore installation are subject to a charge for the navigation services made available by the Civil Aviation Authority in relation to that flight, are revised.

The Civil Aviation (Navigation Services Charges) (Third Amendment) Regulations 1993, SI 1993/1176 (in force on 1 June 1993), further amend the 1991 Regulations, SI 1991/470. The charge payable to the Civil Aviation Authority by an operator of a helicopter which flies from any place in the United Kingdom to a vessel or an off-shore installation within the area of the Southern North Sea is increased from £46 to £68.

The Civil Aviation (Route Charges for Navigation Services) Regulations 1993, SI 1993/1965 (in force on 1 September 1993), revoke and replace the 1989 Regulations, SI 1989/303. The principal amendments include new unit rates and the introduction of transatlantic charges to take account of the new apportionment of Eurocontrol costs between the member states resulting from the accession of Austria to the Eurocontrol Convention.

The Civil Aviation (Route Charges for Navigation Services) (Amendment) Regulations 1993, SI 1993/2970 (in force 1 January 1994), amend the 1993 Regulations, SI 1993/1965, supra, by introducing new unit rates and transatlantic charges which reflect forecasts of costs and traffic for 1994 and take into account the balance of over and under recoveries of revenue as compared with costs experienced by the countries participating in the Eurocontrol charging system in 1992.

The Civil Aviation (Route Charges for Navigation Services) (Second Amendment) Regulations 1993, SI 1993/3098 (in force on 1 January 1994), revoke and replace the 1993 Regulations, SI 1993/2970. The principal amendments include new unit rates and the introduction of transatlantic charges to take into account the balance of over and under recoveries of revenue as compared with costs experienced by countries participating in the Eurocontrol charging system in 1992. The unit rates in ECUs and the amount of the charges in ECUs for transatlantic flights are calculated by reference to the costs of provision of en route navigation services in the participating countries in the Eurocontrol charges system, the amount of traffic using each country's airspace and the relationship of each country's currency to the ECU over a period agreed by ministers of the participating countries. The Regulations also vary the unit rates for specified countries.

The Civil Aviation (Canadian Navigation Services) (Fourth Amendment) Regulations 1993, SI 1993/2320 (in force on 1 October 1993), further amend the 1986 Regulations, SI 1986/1202, by increasing the charges for certain air navigation services provided by or on behalf of the Government of Canada. The charges must be paid to the Civil Aviation Authority which is required to remit them to the Canadian Government.

The Civil Aviation (Joint Financing) (Fifth Amendment) Regulations 1993, SI 1993/2975 (in force on 1 January 1994), amend the 1988 Regulations, SI 1988/2151 by increasing the charge payable by operators of aircraft to the Civil Aviation Authority (CAA) in respect of crossings between Europe and North America. The charge payable in respect of air navigation services provided by the Government of Denmark is increased from £10· 43 to £11·63 and in relation to Iceland is decreased from £33·22 to £32·23. The CAA must deduct from the charges received a sum of 2 per cent and remit this sum to the Council of International Civil Aviation Organisation in respect of air navigation services provided by it. The charges are required to be remitted to the Governments of Denmark and Iceland subject to the deduction of a fee not exceeding 5 per cent for the CAA's expenses in billing and collection.

168   Rules of the air

The Rules of the Air (Amendment) Regulations 1993, SI 1993/254 (in force on 12 March 1993), amend the 1991 Regulations, SI 1991/2437. The definition of "apron" and "manoeuvring areas" are deleted and the meaning of "simulated instrument flight" in r 7 is clarified so that it is the same as that in r 6.

The Rules of the Air (Second Amendment) Regulations 1993, SI 1993/728 (in force on 1 April 1993), further amend the 1991 Regulations, SI 1991/2437. Provision is made for the exclusion, from a number of specified provisions, of aircraft flying in accordance with a police air operator's certificate. Further, an aircraft flying in accordance with a police air operator's certificate does not need the agreement of the commander of any other aircraft to fly in formation with that aircraft and does not need to maintain its course and speed if it has the right of way.

BANKING

Halsbury's Laws of England (4th edn) Vol 3(1) (reissue), paras 1–350

169 Articles

Banking Contracts—The Influence of Spouses, William Johnston: (1993) 11 JIBFL 523
"Informed Consent" and Acting As Surety: *Barclays Bank plc v O'Brien* – The Implications for Lenders, Linda Clements (see [1992] 4 All ER 983): (1993) 2 JIBFL 68
Policing Banking Transactions, Michael Levi: 141 NLJ 1222
Selling Loan Assets—Some Guidelines and Some Problems, Jeffrey Barratt: (1993) 3 JIBFL 110

170 Banking Act 1987—exempt persons

The Banking Act 1987 (Exempt Persons) Order 1993, SI 1993/953 (in force on 23 April 1993), adds the Council of Europe Resettlement Fund to the list in the Banking Act 1987, Sch 2 of persons exempted from the restrictions on acceptance of deposits.

171 Banking Appeal Tribunal—credit institutions

The Banking Appeal Tribunal (Amendment) Regulations 1993, SI 1993/982 (in force on 30 April 1993), amend the 1987 Regulations, SI 1987/1299. The time limit for lodging an appeal is extended to 10 days from the date on which the bank serves notice. In urgent cases, the chairman can direct that a preliminary hearing should be held less than 21 days after receipt of the notice of appeal. The chairman of the tribunal is also required to take into account, when making directions on discovery of evidence, the need to protect information relating to a person not a party to an appeal which is commercially sensitive or was communicated or obtained in confidence. Procedural effect is given to the extension of rights of appeal under the Banking Act 1987, s 27 by the Banking Co-ordination (Second Council Directive) Regulations 1992, SI 1992/3218.

172 Cheque—forged cheque—liability of bank

A fraudster used a forged cheque, together with a cheque guarantee card, to obtain goods from the plaintiffs. The guarantee card had the same account number as the cheque and bore the name of the account holder. At first instance it was held that the defendant bank were liable to meet the cheque drawn by the fraudster. Following the bank's successful appeal, the plaintiffs appealed. *Held,* Kennedy LJ dissenting, the conditions for use of the card were that (1) no other cheque guaranteed by a card issued by the bank was also used to settle the transaction; (2) the cheque was taken from the bank's cheque book issued in the United Kingdom; (3) the signature on the cheque agreed with the specimen on the card; (4) the signature on the cheque was written in the presence of the seller; (5) the seller recorded the number of the card on the reverse of the cheque. All the conditions had been complied with and the signature on the cheque agreed with the specimen on the card. Provided that the retailer had no reason to believe that the fraudster was not the authorised signatory and the account holder, then the fraudster had ostensible authority to convey the bank's offer on its behalf. If the bank had intended to make it clear to a retailer that some other person had no actual or apparent authority then the statement on the back of the card could have been worded to that effect. The retailer was entitled to rely on that statement, on its true construction, and if he complied with the conditions, then the bank was bound by its undertaking to payees. The appeal would accordingly be allowed.

First Sport Ltd v Barclays Bank plc [1993] 3 All ER 789 (Court of Appeal: Sir Thomas Bingham MR, Kennedy and Evans LJJ).

173 Credit institutions—co-ordination of national laws

The Banking Co-ordination (Second Council Directive) (Amendment) Regulations 1993, SI 1993/3225 (in force on 1 January 1994), amend the 1992 Regulations, SI 1992/3218, so as to give effect to the adaptations made to Council Directive (EC) 89/646 on the co-ordination of laws, regulations and administrative provisions concerning credit institutions in its application to the European Economic Area. Provision is made in relation to Iceland, which is to implement the directive by 1 January 1995. Authorisations granted to credit institutions by the Icelandic authorities are not to have European Economic Area-wide validity before the full application of the directive to Iceland, although Iceland is immediately to recognise authorisations granted to credit institutions by the other contracting parties. The regulations also make provision concerning the treatment of credit institutions within the European Economic Area which are the subsidiaries of undertakings based in third countries which impose restrictions on credit institutions based in the European Economic Area. Following consultation with the Bank of England, the Treasury is empowered to determine that certain credit institutions authorised in a relevant European Free Trade Association state which are not allowed to carry on listed activities in the United Kingdom because they have not yet complied with specified provisions of the 1992 Regulations will not thereafter be allowed to do so. Failure to comply with a determination is an offence.

174 Disclosure of information—specified persons

The Banking Act 1987 (Disclosure of Information) (Specified Persons) (Revocation) Order 1993, SI 1993/836 (in force on 29 March 1993), revokes the 1993 Order, SI 1993/491. The earlier order had added the operator (as defined in the Uncertificated Securities Regulations 1992, SI 1992/225) to the list of persons to whom information, subject to certain restrictions, may be disclosed by the Bank of England in order to allow such persons to discharge certain functions. The list is contained in the Banking Act 1987, s 84(1).

175 Money laundering—prevention

The Money Laundering Regulations 1993, SI 1993/1933 (in force on 1 April 1994), give effect to Council Directive (EEC) 91/308, arts 3, 4, 10 and 11 on the prevention of the use of the financial system for the purposes of money laundering, the remaining provisions of the directive having been implemented by the Criminal Justice Act 1993 (para 93/2242). The regulations provide that where business relationships are formed, or one-off transactions are carried out, in the course of relevant financial business, the persons carrying out that business are required to maintain certain procedures to forestall or prevent money laundering. Such persons are required to train their employees in those procedures and to provide general training in the recognition of, and the law relating to, money laundering. Failure to maintain the procedures and to carry out the training is an offence.

The procedures include the obtaining of evidence of the identity of an applicant for business in certain circumstances, except where prescribed exemptions apply. Payment from a bank or building society account may be acceptable evidence of a person's identity where it is reasonable for the payment to be made by post. Where an applicant for business is, or may be, acting on behalf of another person, reasonable measures must be taken to obtain evidence of the identity of the other person. Records of all identification evidence that has been obtained and of all transactions with applicants for business that have been carried out must be kept for five years. Each relevant financial business must identify a person to whom a report is to be made of any information that gives rise to a knowledge or suspicion that money laundering is taking place, and that person must consider the reports and, if he believes that money laundering may be taking place, he must make a report to the police. Supervisory authorities must also make a report to the police where they obtain information indicative of money laundering, and inspectors and others working with supervisory authorities are required to report any such information to the relevant authority or to the police.

176 Protected deposits—assignment—insolvent bank

The holder of a bank deposit assigned part of that deposit to another. The bank had been served with a winding-up petition. The assignment was made after service of the petition but before winding up, and before the Banking Act 1987 (Means of Deposit) Order 1991, SI 1991/1776, came into force. The assignment was made in order to maximise the levels of compensation from the Deposit Protection Fund set up by the Banking Act 1987 to alleviate hardship when a bank became insolvent. The 1991 Order excluded from the compensation scheme sums to which a person became entitled after presentation of a winding-up petition. An issue arose as to whether assignments made before the 1991 Order came into force had the desired effect. At first instance it was held that the assignee was entitled to compensation from the fund. On appeal by the Fund, held, Simon Brown LJ dissenting, although there were clear differences between legal and equitable assignees, that did not justify a fundamental distinction being drawn so that the fund was liable to one and not to the other. The fund acting as a compensating authority ought to stand in the shoes of the bank and as such there was no reason why it ought to be in any better position regarding the equitable assignees, than it would have been but for the insolvency. Accordingly, the appeal would be dismissed.

Deposit Protection Board v Dalia [1994] 1 All ER 539 (Court of Appeal: Russell and Simon Brown LJJ and Sir Michael Fox). Decision of Sir Donald Nicholls V-C [1992] 3 WLR 945, (1992 Abr para 151) affirmed.

BANKRUPTCY AND INSOLVENCY

Halsbury's Laws of England (4th edn) Vol 3(2) (reissue), paras 1–878

177 Articles

Bankruptcy—Its Associated Crimes, Andrew Campbell: 137 SJ 638
Equitable Accounting Between Co-Owners, Elizabeth Cooke (on *Re Pavlou (a bankrupt)* [1993] 3 All ER 955 (para 178)): [1993] Fam Law 695
Insolvency, David Archer: 137 SJ 149
Liquidation Set-Off: Security over Cash, Alan Berg (on *MS Fashions Ltd v BCCI* (1992) Times, December 24 (1992 Abr para 167): (1993) 2 JIBFL 57
Preserving the Family Home in the Face of Bankruptcy, Lyn Ayrton: [1993] Fam Law 180
Undervalue and Insolvency, Touchstone: 137 SJ 403

178 Bankruptcy—administration of bankrupt's estate—property vesting in trustee—joint tenancy—severance of joint tenancy

The deceased, a former partner in a firm of solicitors, and his wife purchased property as joint tenants in law and in equity. Following allegations of serious defalcations the deceased was subject to inquiries by the Law Society but, before the inquiries were completed, the deceased died and an executor of his estate was appointed. The executor applied to the court for an insolvency administration order and a trustee of the estate was duly appointed. There were substantial claims against the estate both by former clients of the deceased's firm and for tax in respect of partnership income. These claims would have been met if the deceased's share of the jointly owned property devolved as part of his estate. The trustee therefore applied to the court for a declaration under the Insolvency Act 1986, s 283 that his title to the deceased's estate should relate back to the date of death and that that would be sufficient to sever the joint tenancy and thereby create a tenancy in common with the result that the deceased's share in the property would devolve to the estate. The 1986 Act, s 283 provides that a bankrupt's estate comprises all property belonging to him or his personal representative at the commencement of bankruptcy, and that the administration order is to be taken as being made 'on the date of death of the deceased debtor'. *Held,* for the purposes of the definition of the deceased debtor's estate under the 1986 Act, the making of an insolvency administration order was a judicial act, and applying the general rule that such an act was presumed to have been made at the first moment on the day it was done and took precedence over other non-judicial acts on the same day, the order was to be treated as having been made on the date of the debtor's death, since there was no other point of time to which it could relate. Until the act of bankruptcy the deceased was the beneficial owner of all his assets. Upon bankruptcy, however, his title became no longer absolute, but contingent on no order being made. When the administration order was made the whole of his assets vested in his trustee as from the date of bankruptcy. Since the order was to be treated as having been made on the date of death, it was on that date that the whole of the deceased's assets became vested in the trustee. A trust was imposed on the deceased's property for the benefit of the creditors and the joint tenancy was duly severed. Accordingly, the declaration would be granted.

Re Palmer (deceased) (a debtor) [1993] 4 All ER 812 (Chancery Division: Vinelott J).

A married couple were the beneficial joint tenants of the matrimonial home. The husband transferred his interest to the wife, who assumed sole liability for the mortgage and became the registered sole proprietor of the property, and upon the parties' divorce the wife's claim for capital provision in the matrimonial proceedings was dismissed by consent in consideration of the husband having transferred his legal and equitable interest and estate in the matrimonial home to her. A bankruptcy order was subsequently made against the husband, and the trustee in bankruptcy applied to have the transfer order set aside on the ground that the transfer was an undervalue for the purposes of the Insolvency Act 1986, s 339. *Held*, the only consideration granted by the wife for the transfer was her assumption of sole liability for the mortgage. The property had been valued at £140,000 and the mortgage was only £30,000, so the value of her consideration was significantly less than the value of the consideration provided by the husband and, therefore, the transfer had been at an undervalue. Accordingly, the application would be allowed and the transfer set aside.

Re Kumar (a bankrupt), ex p Lewis v Kumar [1993] 2 All ER 700 (Chancery Division: Ferris J).

The respondents, a married couple, bought a house with the assistance of a mortgage. The transfer to them contained an express declaration that they held it as beneficial joint tenants. The husband deserted in 1983, leaving the wife in sole occupation. She paid all the subsequent mortgage payments and spent money on various repairs and improvements. In 1986 she obtained a decree nisi. In 1987 a bankruptcy order was made against the husband and a trustee in bankruptcy was appointed. This severed the joint tenancy, leaving the respondents holding the beneficial interest as tenants in common in equal shares. The trustee in bankruptcy applied for an order for sale and for a declaration of the respondents' equitable interests. He contended that the wife was not entitled to be reimbursed for any expenditure by her before the date of the bankruptcy order because, until then, the respondents were beneficial joint tenants and each owned the entire property. *Held*, with regard to an equitable accounting between the respondents it made no difference whether the respondents held the beneficial interest as joint tenants or tenants in common. On an order for sale, adjustments would be made between the co-owners to reflect any increase in value which was brought about by expenditure by one of them. Accordingly, the wife was entitled to credit for the lesser of one half of her expenditure or of the increase in value so realised. Similarly, she was entitled to credit for one half of the increase in value of the equity of redemption resulting from the capital element of the mortgage payments. However, there should be an inquiry into whether or not any occupation rent payable by the wife should be set off against her mortgage interest payments.

Re Pavlou (a bankrupt) [1993] 1 WLR 1046 (Chancery Division: Millett J).

179 Bankruptcy—administration of bankrupt's estate—property vesting in trustee—statutory assignment—right to appeal against tax assessment

See *Hunt v Customs and Excise Comrs*, para 2594.

180 Bankruptcy—disclaimer of onerous property—interest in leasehold property

An assignment of a lease was granted pursuant to a licence to assign by deed, made between the landlord, the tenant and the assignee. The assignee covenanted with the landlord to pay rent for the residue of the term of the lease and to observe the tenant's covenants. The assignee became bankrupt and his trustee in bankruptcy filed notice of disclaimer of all his interest "in the licence to assign relating to the lease". The disclaimer was held to be of the interest under the licence to assign but not of the interest under the lease. On appeal by the trustee, *held*, in the context of the Insolvency Act 1986, s 315 (which authorised the disclaimer of onerous property) the onerous property was the lease itself under which rent was payable. The trustee could not disclaim the onerous liabilities in relation to the property but retain the property itself. The disclaimer was a disclaimer of all the interest of the bankrupt's estate under the lease and, accordingly, the appeal would be allowed.

MEPC plc v Scottish Amicable Life Assurance Society, Eckley (third party) (1993) Times, 6 April (Court of Appeal: Dillon and Leggatt LJJ).

The Insolvency Act 1986, s 181 provides that where a liquidator has disclaimed property an application may be made by any person who claims an interest in the disclaimed property and that the court may make an order vesting the disclaimed property in a person entitled to it. The 1986 Act, s 182(4) provides that a person claiming under the company as underlessee or mortgagee who declines to accept an order under s 181 is excluded from all interest in the property.

The freehold owners of a property assigned the headlease to a company. Eight-year underleases of two flats at the property were assigned to the applicants who, on the expiry of the terms of those leases, became statutory tenants. A liquidator was subsequently appointed in respect of the company and he served notices of disclaimer on the applicants disclaiming the underleases as onerous property. They had then applied for vesting orders in relation to their respective flats but now sought orders for discontinuance. The freeholders contended that the applicants were only entitled to the same relief which would have been available had they continued with their application but declined to accept the order and thus that, under the 1986 Act, s 182(4), any discontinuance order should be made on terms which excluded the statutory tenants from all interest in the flats. *Held,* the first issue was whether a statutory tenant had locus standi to make an application under the 1986 Act, s 181. "Interest" covered any proprietary or financial interest in the disclaimed property, namely the lease, and also any right which might be adversely affected by the disclaimer, thus including a statutory tenant's personal right to retain possession. Secondly, the 1986 Act, s 182(4) was only applicable to cases where an underlessee or mortgagee declined to accept a vesting order, resulting in their proprietary interest being statutorily extinguished. A statutory tenant was not an underlessee and had no proprietorial right to be extinguished. The 1986 Act, s 182(4) did not deprive the applicants of their status as statutory tenants and, accordingly, irrespective of the outcome of the proceedings, the applicants would not lose their statutory protection.

Re Vedmay Ltd (1993) Times, 21 October (Chancery Division: Mr Gavin Lightman QC).

181 Bankruptcy—distribution of bankrupt's estate—property available for distribution—matrimonial home—order for sale

See *Lloyds Bank plc v Byrne*, para 1442.

182 Bankruptcy—mutual dealings—set-off of liability—assignment of right of action by trustee in bankruptcy

The Insolvency Act 1986, s 323 provides that where there have been mutual dealings between a bankrupt and a creditor before the bankruptcy, an account must be taken of what is due from each party to the other in respect of the mutual dealings and the sums due from one party must be set off against the sums due from the other.

The plaintiff brought consolidated actions against the defendant claiming the defendant was in breach of an agreement to equalise the plaintiff's shareholding in various companies and to give the plaintiff 25 per cent of those companies' profits. The defendant counterclaimed for misrepresentation. The plaintiff became bankrupt and the trustee in bankruptcy assigned to the plaintiff the trustee's claims in the consolidated action. The defendant applied to have the action stayed on the ground that, until an account had been taken under the 1986 Act, s 323, there was nothing to assign. The master and judge allowed the defendant's application. On appeal by the plaintiff, *held,* the purpose of a set-off under s 323 was to ensure that substantial justice was done between the bankrupt and the creditor. Otherwise it would be unjust if the creditor had to discharge his debt to the bankrupt's estate in full while being left with only the right to prove in the bankruptcy. Section 323 therefore applied to all cross-claims in the bankruptcy provided they were mutual and measurable in money terms. Since s 323 did not prohibit a trustee in bankruptcy from assigning to a third party a claim subject to a counterclaim, it was acceptable for him to do so in the present case. In addition, it did not provide that only the trustee in bankruptcy had authority to take the account, which implied that it could be done by whoever was the appropriate authority in the circumstances, including the judge hearing the action between the trustee or his assignee and the creditor. Accordingly, the appeal would be allowed.

Stein v Blake [1993] 4 All ER 225 (Court of Appeal: Balcombe, Staughton and Waite LJJ). *Farley v Housing and Commercial Developments Ltd* [1984] BCLC 442 overruled.

183 Bankruptcy—order—appeal against order—security for costs

On a bankrupt's appeal against a bankruptcy order against him, the petitioning creditor sought security for costs. *Held,* a bankrupt appealing against the order by which he had been rendered bankrupt would be treated in the same way as any other impecunious appellant. An application for security for costs would normally be granted unless the bankrupt could show that such an order would amount to a denial of justice to him because he had an arguable appeal which would be stifled because he could not provide security. It was not sufficient for the bankrupt to show that he did not have the necessary resources if there were evidence before the court that there were sources from which he could obtain the necessary funds or security. The creditor's application would be granted.

Hocking v Walker (1993) Times, 11 August (Court of Appeal: Balcombe, Leggatt and Hoffmann LJJ).

184 Bankruptcy—order—application for annulment—grounds for allowing application

A bank had secured a bankruptcy judgment and a bankruptcy order against a debtor, who applied to have both the order and the judgment set aside. His application to set aside the bankruptcy judgment was unconditionally granted, and the deputy district judge subsequently annulled the bankruptcy order on the ground that it was inherently unjust for a debtor to have an order hanging over him when the judgment had been set aside. The bank appealed, contending the court had lacked the power to set aside the bankruptcy order. *Held*, under the Insolvency Act 1986, s 282(1)(a), the court's power to annul a bankruptcy order was expressly limited. Unless all bankruptcy debts and expenses had been paid since the making of the order, the only grounds for annulling the order were "any grounds existing at the time the order was made". It followed that there had been no scope for the exercise of judicial discretion in annulling the order, and, accordingly, the bank's appeal would be allowed.

Re a debtor (No 68 of 1992) (1993) Times, 12 February (Chancery Division: Harman J).

185 Bankruptcy—petition—expedited petition—outstanding application to set aside statutory demand

By virtue of the Insolvency Act 1986, s 268, for the purposes of s 267(2)(c), a debtor appears to be unable to pay a debt if it is payable immediately and at least three weeks have elapsed since the statutory demand was served.

A statutory demand was served on the debtor by the creditors, the joint liquidators of a company. The debtor applied to set aside the demand. The joint liquidators sought to present a bankruptcy petition which did not refer to the debtor's outstanding application, but stated that there was a serious possibility that the debtor's property and/or its value would be significantly diminished within the three-week period following the date of the service of the demand. The debtor sought to have the petition dismissed. *Held*, by virtue of s 267(2)(d), a creditor's petition might only be presented to the court in respect of a debt which the debtor appeared to be unable to pay or to have no reasonable prospect of paying if there was no outstanding application to set aside a statutory demand. Section 267(2) did not necessarily apply to every case; it was expressly made "subject to" s 270 which entitled a petitioning creditor to present an expedited petition. Where a statutory provision was expressed to be "subject to" another statutory provision, if there was any conflict, the latter, the master provision, prevailed over the former, the subject provision. Since the creditor might require protection against the serious possibility of jeopardy to the debtor's property, during the three-week period referred to in s 268, s 270 relaxed the requirements of s 267(2) by enabling a petition to be presented in respect of a debt demanded before the expiration of that period. A petition was not automatically or necessarily invalidated by a failure to state that no application to set aside the statutory demand was outstanding. If the application to set aside the demand succeeded, the petition would be dismissed but, if it failed, the debtor would still be able to challenge the assertion that there was a serious possibility of jeopardy to his property. If the court was not satisfied on jeopardy, it might dismiss the petition; if it was satisfied, it might, in its discretion, waive any irregularity under the Insolvency Rules 1986, r 7.55 and proceed to make a bankruptcy order. The debtor's application would be dismissed.

A debtor v Focus Insurance Co Ltd (in liquidation) (1993) Times, 12 July (Chancery Division: Mummery J).

186 Bankruptcy—petition—rights of appeal

The applicants had been declared bankrupt, applied for leave to appeal against the judgments upon which their bankruptcy orders were founded. *Held*, the judgment on which a petition of bankruptcy was founded was not sufficiently different to justify a departure from the general principle that a bankrupt could not in his own name appeal from a judgment against him enforceable only against the estate vested in his trustee in bankruptcy. Neither applicant had locus standi to institute an appeal, and the applications for leave to appeal would therefore be refused.

Heath v Tang; Stevens v Peacock [1993] 1 WLR 1421 (Court of Appeal: Sir Thomas Bingham MR, Steyn and Hoffmann LJJ).

187 Bankruptcy—statutory demand—application to set aside

See *Re a debtor (No 960/SD/1992), ex p the debtor v IRC*, para 1454.

188   Bankruptcy—statutory demand—application to set aside—appropriate appeal procedure

The petitioning creditor, a firm of accountants, served a statutory demand for payment of the amount outstanding on invoices for work done in investigating the tax affairs of the debtor and preparing his accounts. The debtor applied to have the statutory demand set aside and the application was dismissed by the court. The debtor then applied under the Insolvency Act 1986, s 375(1), for a review of the application and it came before the same judge accompanied by an affidavit sworn by an accountant from a different firm. The view expressed in that affidavit was that the petitioning creditor's charges were grossly excessive. The court considered that there was no basis for a review of the order as the new evidence should have been available at the earlier hearing and that the proper course open to the debtor was to appeal. The application was refused and on appeal by the debtor, *held*, the court had jurisdiction under the 1986 Act, s 375 to review, rescind or vary an order dismissing an application to set aside a statutory demand. The court could, as a matter of discretion, admit fresh evidence, notwithstanding that the evidence could have been obtained at the time of the original hearing. It was sufficient to show either that there was no debt or that for some other reason the statutory demand ought to have been set aside. The court had either not exercised its discretion or exercised it on the wrong basis. Accordingly, the appeal would be allowed.

Re a debtor (No 32-SD-1991) [1993] 1 WLR 314 (Chancery Division: Millett J).

189   Bankruptcy—statutory demand—application to set aside on a conditional basis

The Insolvency Rules 1986, SI 1986/1925, r 6.5 provides that a court hearing an application to set aside a statutory demand may grant the application if the debt is disputed on grounds which appear to the court to be substantial or the court is satisfied, on other grounds, that the demand ought to be set aside.

A debtor applied to set aside a statutory demand by a bank. The court ordered that on the debtor complying with the statutory demand as to one of the sums claimed in the statutory demand within a specified period then the statutory demand would be set aside on the ground that all the remainder of the claim would be disputed. The debtor appealed. *Held*, the court's order raised difficulties in that the order took no account of the interest claimed and that the scheme of the Insolvency Act 1986 and the 1986 Rules did not contemplate any grey area concerning the extent to which a debt was, or was not, the subject of substantial dispute. It would not be possible for a debtor to be given time to comply with a demand so that if he did, it was set aside, and if he did not, his application to set it aside failed. The 1986 Rules contemplated a definitive rather than a conditional outcome, in that if the application failed under the 1986 Rules, r 6.5(6) the court was positively required to authorise the creditor to present a bankruptcy petition, and as from the date of failure, the time for compliance with the demand began again to run. However, the court had been correct in its conclusion that there was not sufficient substantial ground for dispute of the debt to warrant setting aside the statutory demand. Accordingly, the appeal would be dismissed.

Re a debtor (No 90 of 1992) (1993) Times, 12 July (Chancery Division: Knox J).

190   Bankruptcy—statutory demand—debtor's offer of security—obligation of creditor

The Insolvency Rules 1986, SI 1986/1925, r 6.5 provides that a court hearing an application to set aside a statutory demand may grant the application if the debt is disputed on grounds which appear to the court to be substantial or the court is satisfied, on other grounds, that the demand ought to be set aside.

A statutory demand was served upon a debtor in the sum of almost £900,000. The debtor was unable to pay the debt immediately and he made an offer to the creditor to give security over certain shares which he said were not at present realisable but were worth between £4 million and £18 million. The creditor took the view that it was entitled to immediate payment and did not have to consider that offer. The debtor contended that the creditor was unreasonable in failing to consider his offer, that it was obliged to do so and that, accordingly, the statutory demand ought to be set aside. The debtor's application to set aside was refused. On appeal, *held*, the Insolvency Rules 1986, r 6.5 was concerned with a case in which a statutory demand ought to be set aside because it was defective to the point of being unfair to the debtor, or if it was shown that, in the case of an immediately payable debt, there was evidence that it would in substance be immediately paid. The only inquiries which the court was called upon to make at the statutory demand stage was whether or not it was shown that the debtor was, in the case of the Insolvency Act 1986, s 268(1), "unable to pay a debt" or, under s 268(2), "had no reasonable prospect of being able to pay a debt". The "other grounds" of r 6.5 related only to that question and ancillary matters such as whether the demand was fair. The debtor's offer in the present case did not constitute "other grounds" within the meaning of r 6.5. In addition, in the case of an unsecured debt, the creditor had no security and was not obliged to take the security offered by the debtor however good it might be. Accordingly, the appeal would be dismissed.

Re a debtor (No 415/SD/1993) (1993) Times, 8 December (Chancery Division: Jacob J).

See also *Re a Debtor (No 960/SD/1992), ex p the Debtor v IRC*, para 1454.

191 Bankruptcy—statutory demand—defective demand—application set aside

The debtor owned a commercial property on which he had executed a legal charge in favour of creditors to secure a loan. The debtor defaulted and the creditors sought to enforce the debt by bankruptcy proceedings rather than by enforcing their charge. The debtor contended the creditors were fully secured and therefore not entitled to rely on a statutory demand and applied under the Insolvency Rules 1986, SI 1986/1925, to set aside the statutory demand. At the first hearing of that application the court had before it two surveyors' reports from the creditors' experts. The judge adjourned the case and directed the debtor to file further expert valuation evidence. At the adjourned hearing, the debtor, not having filed any further evidence, wished to adduce oral evidence from his surveyor and to cross-examine the creditor's experts. The court refused the debtor permission and dismissed the application. On appeal by the debtor, *held*, under the 1986 Rules, the court had the power to determine the value of the security following evidence from both parties. In the present case the debtor had not intimated an intention to adduce oral evidence or a wish to cross-examine and had failed to comply with the court's direction to file any further expert evidence. The court had a discretion to dismiss an application on the incomplete evidence before it, without adjourning for full evidence and was still free to go into questions of value on the hearing of the petition. Accordingly, the appeal would be dismissed.

Platts v Western Trust and Savings Ltd [1993] 22 LS Gaz R 38 (Court of Appeal: Nourse and Butler-Sloss LJJ and Sir Christopher Slade).

192 Bankruptcy—statutory demand—statutory demand based on failure to make interim payment—right to present bankruptcy petition

An interim payment order was made against the defendant and, following his failure to pay, the plaintiffs served a statutory demand on him pursuant to the Insolvency Act 1986, s 268(1)(a). They then sought to present to the court a bankruptcy petition. The defendant applied to set aside the statutory demand and for an order that the plaintiffs be prevented from presenting a bankruptcy petition following the expiry of the statutory demand. The defendant contended that as an order for an interim payment was not a final order or judgment it did not constitute a debt on which a statutory demand or a bankruptcy petition could be founded, and as such the failure to make the interim payment would not be an act of bankruptcy under the Bankruptcy Act 1914. *Held*, an order made under RSC Ord 29, r 10 requiring a defendant to make an interim payment created a debt payable for a liquidated sum either immediately or at some certain future time within the meaning of the Insolvency Act 1986, s 267(2)(b). Therefore a creditor, to whom it was immediately payable, would be entitled to serve upon that debtor a statutory demand pursuant to the 1986 Act, s 268(1)(a) and, if unpaid, to present to the court a bankruptcy petition. Accordingly, the application would fail.

Maxwell v Bishopsgate Investment Management Ltd (in liquidation) (1993) Times, 11 February (Chancery Division: Chadwick J). For related proceedings, see *Bishopsgate Investment Management Ltd (in Liquidation) v Maxwell* (1993) Times, 16 February, para 477.

193 Bankruptcy—voluntary arrangement—interim order—effect of order on other legal process—distress

A landlord who was owed rent by a tenant jeweller decided to distrain for arrears and through a bailiff entered the premises and took possession of a quantity of jewellery while an interim order was in force under the Insolvency Act 1986, s 252(2). On the question of whether the distress was lawful, *held*, the landlord was entitled to enter the premises and take the jewellery. Section 252(2)(b), which prevented any other proceedings or other legal process being commenced against a debtor where an interim order was in force, except with the leave of the court, was intended to restrict only those rights which a creditor could enforce by "legal process" against the debtor or his property. It did not prevent a landlord exercising the remedy of distress for arrears of rent when an interim order was in force. Judgment would be given accordingly.

McMullen & Sons Ltd v Cerrone (1993) 66 P & CR 351 (Chancery Division: Roger Kaye QC).

194   Bankruptcy—voluntary arrangement—nominee—order for costs against nominee

A debtor nominated a licensed insolvency practitioner to act in a voluntary arrangement under the Insolvency Act 1986, Pt VIII. The nominee made a report to the court upon the debtor's proposals and acted as chairman of a creditors' meeting held to consider the proposals. The court subsequently found that the report had not been prepared with proper skill and competence and that the nominee's decisions at the meeting were erroneous. On the creditors' application to recover the costs of the court proceedings from the nominee, *held*, the nominee both in making his report and and in acting as chairman of the meeting had a duty to exercise a professional independent judgment. Where he had a duty to the court to report his own opinion of the debtor's proposals, the nominee was not an agent of the debtor. Where a nominee fell significantly below the standards required of a licensed insolvency practitioner, the court could under the 1986 Act, s 262 require him to pay all or part of the costs of legal proceedings arising out of his inadequate discharge of his duties, including his conduct as chairman of the creditors' meeting. Accordingly, the application would be granted.

Re a debtor (No 222 of 1990), ex p Bank of Ireland (No 2) [1993] BCLC 233 (Chancery Division: Harman J). For earlier proceedings see [1992] BCLC 137 (1991 Abr para 140).

195   Bankruptcy—voluntary arrangement—service of notice

The Insolvency Rules 1986, SI 1986/1925, r 12.16 provides that where a meeting of creditors is summoned by notice, the meeting is presumed to have been duly summoned and held, notwithstanding that not all those to whom the notice is to be given have received it.

A debtor sent notice of a creditors' meeting to a corporate creditor, but sent it to an address that was not, at that time, the creditor's head office. The creditor was not therefore aware of the meeting and did not attend. A short time later, the creditor served a statutory demand on the debtor who claimed that the creditor was bound by the voluntary arrangement made at the meeting of which it had had constructive notice and as a result, the statutory demand was invalid. The court at first instance ordered the statutory demand to be set aside. On appeal by the creditor, *held*, the 1986 Rules, r 12.16 presumed that the meeting had been held, not that the creditor had notice of the meeting, when in fact he had not. The creditor would not therefore be bound by any arrangement made at the meeting. A creditor would only have had constructive notice if he could have discovered that the meeting was taking place by making investigations, but had failed to make such investigations, or if he had deliberately or carelessly failed to make enquiries which a prudent person in his position ought to have made and which, if made, would have led him to discovery of the fact. Accordingly, the appeal would be allowed and the statutory demand would be declared valid.

Re a debtor (No 64 of 1992) [1994] 1 WLR 264 (Chancery Division: Mr Colin Rimer).

196   Insolvency—practitioners—regulation

The Insolvency Practitioners (Amendment) Regulations 1993, SI 1993/221 (in force on 1 April 1993), amend the 1990 Regulations, SI 1990/439, in relation to the prescribed requirements regarding security or caution for the proper performance of the functions of an insolvency practitioner and the records in respect of such security or caution to be kept for inspection or submitted to his authorising body by an insolvency practitioner in respect of the estate of each person in relation to whom the practitioner acts. The 1993 Regulations also amend the prescribed educational requirements of insolvency practitioners.

197   Insolvency—proceedings—originating application—definition of pleadings

See *Re Port (A Bankrupt) (No 516 of 1987); Port v Auger*, para 1972.

198   Insolvency—proceedings—writ of fieri facias—defective writ—failure to execute

It has been held that where a sheriff calls at a debtor's home in order to execute a writ of fieri facias, and reports that he is unable to gain access to it, the failure to execute the writ is a failure in the process of execution, and not a formal defect or irregularity in insolvency proceedings. It cannot not therefore be capable of remedy under the Insolvency Rules 1986, SI 1986/1925, r 7.55.

Re a debtor (No 340 of 1992) (1993) Times, 19 July (Chancery Division: Aldous J).

199 Insolvency—rules

The Insolvency (Amendment) Rules 1993, SI 1993/602 (in force on 5 April 1993), amend the 1986 Rules, SI 1986/1925, by replacing the provision setting out the remuneration of shorthand writers appointed in insolvency proceedings with a provision that any question as to their rates of remuneration is to be determined by the court. The 1993 Rules also amend the definition of obligations arising which are not provable as debts in a bankruptcy.

BARRISTERS

Halsbury's Laws of England (4th edn) Vol 3(1) (reissue), paras 351–536

200 Articles

A Very English Form of Corruption (on the judicial appointments system): 143 NLJ 504
Bar None, Dominique Harvie (on discrimination at the Bar): 142 NLJ 892
Boom and Bust, Roger Smith (on the future of the young bar): 143 NLJ 1725
Continuing Professional Development, Richard Southwell: Counsel, July 1993, p 14
Fiddling While the Junior Bar Burns, Steven Woolfe and Paul Whetton (on the effect of standard fees in the magistrates' courts): 143 NLJ 1230
Racism at the Bar, Philip Thomas: 137 SJ 902
Restrictive Practices, Derek Wheatley (on the Bar's professional rules): LS Gaz, 3 November 1993, p 27

201 Professional conduct—duty to court—allegation of bias against judge—application for removal of judge

See *Arab Monetary Fund v Hashim*, para 2045.

202 Professional conduct—negligent, unreasonable or improper conduct of proceedings—wasted costs order—order against counsel

See *Filmlab Systems International Ltd v Pennington*, para 2013 and *Fozal v Gofur*, para 2015.

BETTING, GAMING AND LOTTERIES

Halsbury's Laws of England (4th edn) Vol 4(1) (reissue), paras 1–300

203 Articles

Licensing Jackpot Machines, Susanna FitzGerald: 137 SJ 120
Prize Competitions and Severable Promotions, R Lawson: 157 JP Jo 778

204 Gaming—monetary limits

The Gaming Act (Variation of Monetary Limits) Order 1993, SI 1993/967 (in force on 1 May 1993), increases the maximum permitted aggregate amount of winnings in respect of games of bingo played in one week simultaneously on different club premises to £10,000 and increases the maximum amount by which weekly winnings on any particular bingo club premises may exceed the aggregate amount of the stakes hazarded to £2,500. The 1992 Regulations, 1992/426, and the 1991 Regulations, 1991/870, are revoked.

205 Gaming clubs—charges

The Gaming Clubs (Hours and Charges) (Amendment) Regulations 1993, SI 1993/968 (in force on 1 May 1993), amend the 1984 Regulations, SI 1984/248, by increasing the maximum charges which may be made for admissions to gaming on bingo club premises from £6·20 to £6·40. The 1992 Regulations, SI 1992/431 are revoked.

206   Licensed betting offices—control

The Licensed Betting Offices (Amendment) Regulations 1993, SI 1993/51 (in force on 1 March 1993), amend the 1986 Regulations, SI 1986/103, by providing that a licensed betting office must be closed between 10 pm and midnight on any day between April and August inclusive. Closing hours for the rest of the year remain the same.

207   Lottery—duty

The Lottery Duty Regulations 1993, SI 1993/3212 (in force on 1 February 1994), provide for the registration of promoters, payment and refund of lottery duty including deferred payment, duty on tickets or chances taken abroad and administration and protection of the revenue derived from lottery duty.

208   Lottery—exempt entertainments—variation of monetary limit

The Exempt Entertainments (Variation of Monetary Limit) Order 1993, SI 1993/3222 (in force on 3 May 1994), increases the sum which the promoters of a lottery incidental to an exempt entertainment are permitted to deduct from the proceeds of the entertainment on account of expenses incurred by them in purchasing prizes, from £50 to £250.

209   Lottery—Gaming Board fees

The Lotteries (Gaming Board Fees) Order 1993, SI 1993/3224 (in force on 3 May 1994), increases the fees payable to the Gaming Board under the Lotteries and Amusements Act 1976 for the registration of societies' and local authorities' lottery schemes as well as supplying figures for the new system of fees introduced by the National Lottery etc Act 1993. The 1992 Regulations, SI 1992/94, are revoked.

210   Lottery—promotion of lottery schemes

The Lotteries Regulations 1993, SI 1993/3223 (in force on 3 May1994), replace the 1977 Regulations, SI 1977/256; 1977/238 and relate to lotteries promoted by registered societies or local authorities. Requirements and changes regarding the nature and content of schemes for the promotion of lotteries are set out as are provisions regarding the sale and distribution of tickets or chances and the matters to be specified on such tickets.

211   National Lottery etc Act 1993

The National Lottery etc Act 1993 authorises lotteries to be promoted as part of a National Lottery and makes provision for the running, regulation and distribution of proceeds of the National Lottery. The Act received the royal assent on 21 October 1993 and certain provisions have been brought into force by the National Lottery etc Act 1993 (Commencement No 1 and Transitional Provisions) Order 1993, SI 1993/2632. For details of commencement, see the commencement table in the title STATUTES.

Pt I (ss 1–20) Authorisation and Regulation of the National Lottery
Section 1 defines the National Lottery and sets out conditions for a lottery to form part of the National Lottery. Section 2, Sch 1 make provision for the legality of lotteries forming part of the National Lottery and s 3, Sch 2 make provision for a Director General of the National Lottery. The overriding duties of the Secretary of State and the Director General when exercising functions under Pt I are set out in s 4. Sections 5, 6 make provision for the licensing of a body corporate to run the National Lottery and bodies corporate to promote lotteries. Sections 7–10, Sch 3 contain further provisions relating to licences under ss 5, 6 including the variation and enforcement of conditions in licences and the revocation of licences. The Secretary of State may give directions to the Director General under s 11 and may, under s 12, make regulations as to the promotion of lotteries. Contravention of such regulations is an offence: s 13. The Director General must produce an annual report to the Secretary of State (s 14) and under s 15 the Secretary of State may require the Director General to provide him with information. False representation that a lottery forms part of the National Lottery is an offence: s 16. The Horserace Totalisator Board may hold a licence under s 5 or 6: s 17. Section 18 amends the Betting, Gaming and Lotteries Act 1963 to impose controls on betting on the National

Lottery. The 1993 Act, s 19 prevents certain provisions of the Rehabilitation of Offenders Act 1974 from applying in relation to the grant or revocation by the Director General of a licence. Section 20 deals with the interpretation of Pt I.

Pt II (ss 21–44) Distribution of the Net Proceeds of the National Lottery
Section 21 provides for there to be a National Lottery Distribution Fund. Section 22 provides for the apportionment of money in the fund. Section 23 specifies the bodies who will distribute the apportioned sums from the fund and s 24 provides for payments to be made to the specified bodies from the fund. Section 25 deals with how the money from the fund should be applied by the distributing bodies. The Secretary of State may give directions to distributing bodies and may in certain cases prohibit distribution: ss 26, 27. Sections 28, 29 enable the Secretary of State to amend ss 22, 23. Section 30 provides for the winding up of the fund allocated to projects to mark the year 2000 and the beginning of the third millenium. Payments may be made from the fund in respect of expenses under s 31. Money held in the fund may be invested by the National Debt Commissioners and provision is made as to the preparation of accounts by the commissioners and by the Secretary of State: ss 32, 33. Each distributing body must make an annual report to the Secretary of State and must keep accounts: ss 34, 35. Section 36, Sch 4 amend the National Heritage Act 1980 to increase the number of Trustees of the National Heritage Memorial Fund. The 1993 Act, s 37, Sch 5 provide for there to be a National Lottery Charities Board. The board may make grants for charitable expenditure and must keep accounts: ss 38, 39. Section 40, Sch 6 establishes the Millenium Commission. The commission may make grants to fund projects to mark the year 2000 and the beginning of the third millenium: s 41. The commission must lay an annual report before Parliament and must keep accounts: ss 42, 43. Section 44 deals with the interpretation of Pt II.

Pt III (ss 45–55) Miscellaneous Amendments Relating to Lotteries
Sections 45, 55, deal with interpretation. Section 46 contains importation and exportation restrictions. Section 47 makes provision for the sale of tickets or chances in a private lottery. Sections 48, 49, Schs 7, 8 alter the provisions relating to the registration of societies' lotteries and lottery schemes. Section 50, Sch 9 specify the categories of persons who may manage a society's lottery. Sections 51, 52 make provision as to the frequency of lotteries and in connection with rules for authorised lotteries. Sections 53, 54 create offences and a statutory defence and amend the powers of the Secretary of State to vary monetary limits and to prescribe or vary fees.

Pt IV (ss 56–59) Pool Betting
Section 56 removes the prohibition on the use of premises for the delivery of football pools coupons and stakes. Section 57 reduces the age limit in relation to football pool betting. Sections 58, 59 amend the 1963 Act concerning the roll-over of prize money and pool promoters' dividends.

Pt V (ss 60–66) Supplementary
Sections 60, 61 provide for the making of subordinate legislation and for the giving of directions. Section 62 makes financial provision. Sections 63–66, Sch 10 deal with Northern Ireland, repeals, commencement and short title.

212   Wagering contracts—contracts for differences—interest rate swap transactions

The plaintiffs, as the fixed rate payer, entered into an interest rate swap contract with the defendant local authority, as the floating rate payer. The defendants then, as part of the same transaction and through the same brokers, entered, as the fixed rate payer, into a swap contract with the third party local authority, as the floating rate payer. The defendant and the third party did not have power to enter into the contracts, which were therefore wholly void. The defendant sought restitution in respect of a judgment which held that principal sums paid under ultra vires interest rate swap contracts were recoverable from the recipient. The third party argued that the contract between it and the defendant was a wagering contract and that the Gaming Acts 1845 and 1892 provided them with a defence to the defendant's claim. On the question of whether the contract was a wagering contract, *held*, interest rate swap contracts were contracts which might or might not be wagering transactions depending on the interests of the parties and their purpose in entering into the particular contract. As they provided for the payment of differences, they were capable of being entered into by way of gaming or wagering. Potentially, they had a speculative character deriving from the fact that the obligations of the floating rate payer were to be ascertained by reference to a fluctuating market rate that might be higher or lower than the fixed rate at any given time. However, the mere fact that there was a provision for the payment of differences did not mean that the contract was a wagering contract. This depended on the other features of the transaction. The normal inference in interest rate swap contracts entered into by parties or institutions involved in the capital market and in the making and receiving of loans was that they were commercial or financial transactions to which the law would, in the absence of some other consideration, give full recognition and effect. Only if the purpose of both parties was to wager would the contract be a wagering contract.

Morgan Grenfell and Co Ltd v Welwyn Hatfield District Council, Islington London Borough Council (Third Party) (1993) Times, 1 June (Queen's Bench Division: Hobhouse J). For related proceedings, see *Westdeutsche Landesbank Girozentrale v Islington London Borough Council* (1993) Times, 23 February (para 607).

BRITISH NATIONALITY, IMMIGRATION AND RACE RELATIONS

Halsbury's Laws of England (4th edn) Vol 4(2) (reissue), paras 1–300

213 Articles

Defining Ethnic Origins, Neil Parpworth: 143 NLJ 610

Diminution of Status, Ramnik Shah (on proposals to revise the Immigration Rules): 144 NLJ 62

Goodbye to Appeal Rights, Leon Daniel (on the Asylum and Immigration Appeals Bill): 143 NLJ 280

Here to Stay? Jacqueline Thompson (on immigration investor UK rules): LS Gaz, 17 November 1993, p 23

Immigration and Homeless, Nicholas Dobson: 137 SJ 1436

Immigration Law Threatened by Legal Aid Cuts, Penny Smith: 137 SJ 247

Legal Aid Eligibility Criteria: The Impact for Immigration Law Practitioners and their Clients, Penny Smith: [1993] CJQ 167

One Step Forward and Two Steps Back, Edward Munir (on the Asylum and Immigration Appeals Act 1993): 143 NLJ 1149

Race Relations in Northern Ireland, Ciaran White: 143 NLJ 337

Raising the Barriers, Maria Fernandes (on the rules relating to immigration): 143 NLJ 1576

Transatlantic Staff Transfers, Bernard Andonian (on inter-company transfers and visa procedures): 137 SJ 1238

214 Asylum and Immigration Appeals Act 1993

The Asylum and Immigration Appeals Act 1993 makes provision about persons who claim asylum in the United Kingdom and their dependants, amends the law with respect to certain rights of appeal under the Immigration Act 1971 and extends the provisions of the Immigration (Carriers Liability) Act 1987 to transit passengers. The Act received the royal assent on 1 July 1993 and ss 2, 3, 12–16 and s 1, so far as it relates to those provisions, came into force on that day. The remaining provisions came into force on 26 July 1993: see SI 1993/1655. For details of commencement, see the commencement table in the title STATUTES.

Section 1 provides for the interpretation of the Act and s 2 states that nothing in the immigration rules, made under the Immigration Act 1971, may lay down any practice which would be contrary to the 1951 Geneva Convention relating to the Status of Refugees and the Protocol to the Convention.

Provision is made by s 3 for the fingerprinting of an asylum-seeker and his dependants (with safeguards for dependants under the age of 16) and, if the asylum-seeker fails to comply with a requirement to attend for fingerprinting, for his arrest without warrant and the securing of his fingerprints. Section 4 and Sch 1 ("the housing provisions", as defined by s 5) deal with the allocation of local authority housing to asylum-seekers and their dependants. An authority is not obliged to find accommodation for an asylum-seeker who has available to him accommodation, however temporary, that it is reasonable for him to occupy, but where this is not the case the authority's duty to secure accommodation ceases when the applicant ceases to be an asylum-seeker, following which the homelessness legislation applies to the applicant as if, at the time he ceased to be an asylum-seeker, he were not occupying local authority accommodation and had made an application to the authority for accommodation or assistance in obtaining accommodation: s 4. A person who has made a claim for asylum cannot be removed from, or required to leave, the United Kingdom until he has been notified of the decision on his claim: s 6. The Secretary of State is empowered by s 7 by notice in writing to curtail limited leave to enter or remain in the United Kingdom when an asylum application is refused.

Section 8 provides for appeals to be made to a special adjudicator against a refusal of leave to enter the United Kingdom, against any variation of, or refusal to vary, the leave of a person with limited leave to enter or remain in the United Kingdom, against a deportation order or the refusal to revoke a deportation order, and against directions for removal, in each case on the ground that the person's removal from the United Kingdom would be contrary to the United Kingdom's obligations under the 1951 Geneva Convention. The 1993 Act, Sch 2 makes supplementary provision in respect of appeals under s 8. By virtue of s 9, asylum-seekers have a further right of appeal, with leave, to the Court of Appeal on a point of law arising from a decision of the Immigration Appeal Tribunal on an appeal brought under the Immigration Act 1971, Pt II (ss 15–25); and rules of procedure made under s 22 are to apply to applications to the tribunal for such leave to appeal. Further amendments provide that appeals under Pt II may not be treated as finally determined where any further appeal can be brought by virtue of the 1993 Act, s 9 or, if such an appeal is brought, it is finally determined or withdrawn: s 9. Section 10 amends the 1971 Act, s 13 so as to remove the right of appeal against the refusal of entry clearance, or against the refusal of leave to enter, as a visitor, as a short-term student, as a prospective student, or as a dependant of any of those, unless a current entry clearance is held at the time of refusal and to provide for the independent monitoring of refusals of entry clearance in cases where there is no right of appeal. Further provisions, inserted in ss 13, 14 by the 1993 Act, s 11, remove the right of appeal against refusals of entry clearance or variation of leave to remain where such refusals are mandatory under the immigration rules, disallow an appeal against decisions to refuse entry clearance taken on the grounds that the person, or the person whose dependant he is, does not have the relevant documents required by the immigration rules, fails to satisfy a requirement of those rules as to age, nationality or citizenship, or seeks to enter for a period exceeding that permitted by those rules, and disallow appeal against a refusal to vary leave to enter or remain on any of the above grounds or on the ground that a required fee has not been paid.

Section 12 amends the Immigration (Carriers' Liability) Act 1987, s 1 so as to empower the Secretary of State by order to require transit passengers passing through the United Kingdom, excluding those with right of abode, to hold a visa for that purpose, to specify in that order a description of persons by reference to nationality, citizenship, origin or other connection with any particular country or territory, but not by reference to race, colour or religion, to which the order applies, and to provide for the exemption from the requirements of the order of any specified category of persons.

Section 13 deals with financial provision for the Act, and ss 14–16 with its commencement, extent and short title respectively.

215 British nationality—citizenship—naturalisation—requirements—spouse of British citizen

The British Nationality Act 1981, s 6(2) provides that on an application for naturalisation as a British citizen made by a person of full age and capacity who on the date of the application is married to a British citizen, if the Secretary of State is satisfied that the applicant fulfils the requirements specified for naturalisation as such a citizen, he may, if he thinks fit, grant to him a certificate of naturalisation as such a citizen.

The applicant's husband first came to England in 1979 using a British passport in the name under which the applicant married him. The husband later purported to change his name by deed poll and a passport was issued to him in that name. The applicant, who believed herself married to a British citizen, applied for naturalisation. She was granted a certificate of naturalisation under s 6(2) but, when it transpired that her husband was in fact a citizen of Pakistan, the Home Secretary decided that she was an illegal immigrant. She sought judicial review of that decision. At first instance, it was held that, as the applicant had not been married to a British citizen, despite her belief to the contrary, the grant of the certificate to her was a nullity and her application would be dismissed. On appeal by the applicant, *held*, in the interests of certainty and justice, where a fact leading to naturalisation was subsequently found to be incorrect, this would not nullify the naturalisation. Once a person had been issued with a certificate of naturalisation, it remained valid unless and until the Home Secretary exercised his discretion under the 1981 Act, s 40, whereby he could deprive a person of citizenship if it had been obtained by fraud, false representation or concealment of any material fact. Accordingly the appeal would be allowed.

R v Secretary of State for the Home Department, ex p Ejaz (1993) Times, 7 December (Court of Appeal: Balcombe, Stuart-Smith and Peter Gibson LJJ). Decision of Hutchison J (1993) Times, 23 July reversed.

216 British nationality—Hong Kong citizens—naturalisation or registration

The Hong Kong (British Nationality) (Amendment) Order 1993, SI 1993/1795 (in force on 21 July 1993), amends the 1986 Order, SI 1986/948, by providing that, where any person is registered or naturalised as a British Dependent Territories citizen by virtue, wholly or partly, of his having a connection with Hong Kong, after, or less than three months before, the relevant date (as defined), the Secretary of State must register him as a British National (Overseas) if he applies within three months after the date of his registration or naturalisation as a British Dependent Territories citizen. The 1993 Order also amends the British Nationality Act 1981 by providing that a person who applies for registration or naturalisation as a British Dependent Territories citizen under any provision of the Act by virtue, wholly or partly, of his having a connection with Hong Kong may not be naturalised or registered unless he makes his application on or before 31 March 1996.

217 British nationality—Hong Kong residents—selection scheme

The British Nationality (Hong Kong) (Selection Scheme) (Amendment) Order 1993, SI 1993/1789 (in force on 3 January 1994), amends the Selection Scheme set out in the 1990 Order, SI 1990/2292, by (1) providing for the Governor of Hong Kong to invite a second application for registration as a British citizen in either the sensitive service class or the entrepreneurs class and for him to transfer places between classes if it appears to him that the number of persons to be recommended in any class will fall short of the allocated quota; (2) making new provision for the determination of the quota for each approved occupation and each specified occupational class; (3) removing the special provisions for managers and administrators; (4) making several changes to the number of points allocated in the scheme; (5) making new provision for the determination of the quota for each disciplined service within the disciplined services class; (6) revising the points to be allocated for each year's relevant experience for applicants in the managers and administrators occupational group of the general occupational class; and (7) making amendments with respect to the points to be allocated to accounting associate professionals.

218 Immigration—appeals—procedure

The Immigration Appeals (Procedure) (Amendment) Rules 1993, SI 1993/1662 (in force on 26 July 1993), amend the 1984 Rules, SI 1984/2041, by prescribing the procedure to be followed where application for leave to appeal to the Court of Appeal against the final determination of the Immigration Appeal Tribunal of an appeal against a decision made under the Immigration Act 1971 is made.

219 Immigration—asylum—appeals—procedure

The Asylum Appeals (Procedure) Rules 1993, SI 1993/1661 (in force on 26 July 1993), prescribe the procedure to be followed in respect of asylum appeals under the Asylum and Immigration Appeals Act 1993. The rules deal with (1) the bringing of an appeal to a special adjudicator, prescribing the form to be used for notice of an appeal and the time limits for the determination of an appeal by a special adjudicator; (2) the bringing of appeals, which may only be brought with the leave of the Immigration Appeal Tribunal, from a special adjudicator to the tribunal, prescribing the form to be used on such an application; (3) the making of applications to the tribunal for leave to bring an appeal, which may only be brought on a question of law, from a determination of that tribunal to the Court of Appeal, prescribing the form to be used on such an application; and (4) the procedure to be followed where an appeal is brought under the rules. The Immigration Appeals (Procedure) Rules 1984, SI 1984/2041, are also amended.

220 Immigration—asylum—application lodged in member state—power to return applicant to other member state

The applicant, a Turkish Kurd, flew from Turkey to Paris where he remained in a transit lounge before flying to London. Immigration authorities there refused to consider his claim for political asylum on the ground that, under the unratified Dublin Convention on Asylum and the policy followed by the Secretary of State, the claim had first to be considered by France as the country to which the applicant first went after leaving Turkey. On his application for leave to apply for judicial review of that decision, he claimed that, by virtue of the EC Treaty, art 8a, on the abolition of internal frontiers, there was no power to return him from one member state to another. *Held*, the applicant had only been in transit in France. As he had not been admitted into France so as to be lawfully there, he could not claim the direct application to him of art 8a. The Secretary of State was entitled to follow his existing practice by returning the applicant to France for the determination there of his claim. The application would be dismissed.

  R v Secretary of State for the Home Department, ex p Colak [1993] 3 CMLR 201 (Court of Appeal: Dillon, Stuart-Smith and Evans LJJ).

The applicant left Ethiopia for Sudan and later, using a false passport, travelled to Italy. He then obtained false identity papers before travelling by train through France to the United Kingdom where he sought political asylum. The Secretary of State decided that as the applicant had arrived in the United Kingdom, having come not from the country where he feared persecution but from an intervening third country, his application would not be considered here but he would be returned to that third country as it was one where his application would be appropriately and fairly considered and was not a country which would return him without investigation to the country from which he had originally come. The applicant sought leave to apply for judicial review of the decision on the ground that the EEC Treaty, art 8a which insured the free movement of persons throughout member states of the Community, was inconsistent with the policy adopted by the Secretary of State. *Held*, there was no inconsistency between art 8a and the policy adopted by the Secretary of State in dealing with applications for asylum. Therefore, an applicant who sought asylum in the United Kingdom after travelling from a non-member state where he feared persecution through a member state might properly be returned to the member state for his asylum application to be considered and determined. Accordingly, the application would be dismissed and the applicant would be returned to France.

  R v Secretary of State for the Home Department, ex p Ghebretatios [1993] 3 CMLR 475 (Court of Appeal: Sir Thomas Bingham MR, Steyn and Hoffmann LJJ).

221 Immigration—asylum—"first safe country" policy—reasonableness

The appellant, a member of the government of Sierra Leone, owned property in the United Kingdom and had been educated there. After a coup in Sierra Leone he illegally entered the United Kingdom via Belgium and claimed political asylum. The Secretary of State refused to consider his claim on the ground that he should have sought asylum in Belgium, and he refused to use his discretionary powers to override the "first safe country" policy notwithstanding the appellant's close links with the United Kingdom. On appeal, the appellant contended the decision not to override the "first safe country" policy had been due to his involvement in an allegedly corrupt government in Sierra Leone, and he argued that was an irrelevant factor when considering an application for asylum. He also contended that the Secretary of State's decision departed from a publicly declared policy that applications for asylum made by persons who had links with the United Kingdom would be considered even if the United Kingdom had not been the first safe country which those persons had reached. *Held*, there was no merit to the contention that considering the appellant's involvement in an allegedly corrupt government was irrelevant to the question of whether asylum should be granted, and the Secretary of State's decision had not been rendered irrational by his decision to consider that matter. The statement relating to appellants who had links with the United Kingdom had been intended to assist potential applicants for asylum and the immigration authorities. It was not indicative of government policy, and as such it had not given rise to a legitimate expectation upon which the appellant could rely. Accordingly, the appeal would be dismissed.

  Conteh v Secretary of State for the Home Department [1992] Imm AR 594 (Court of Appeal: Bingham, Butler-Sloss and Farquharson LJJ). *R v Secretary of State for the Home Department, ex p Khan* [1985] 1 All ER 40, CA (1984 Abr para 1296) distinguished.

222 Immigration—asylum—refusal of application—absence of causal link between persecution and decision to seek asylum

The applicant had engaged in political activity in India which had resulted in his being detained without charge on a number of occasions. He sought political asylum in the United Kingdom, but the Secretary of State refused his application on the ground that he had failed to establish a causal link between his detention and his decision to leave India. The applicant sought leave to apply for judicial review on the ground that the law did not require a causal link to be established. He also contended that the Secretary of State had understated the significance of periods of detention without charge, and that the Secretary of State should have given more weight to the fact that politically active persons of the applicant's religion were inevitably subject to persecution in certain Indian states. *Held*, the law did not require a causal link to be established between periods of detention and an applicant's departure from his native country, but the Secretary of State was entitled to take causes and effects, or the absence of them, into account when making his decision. In determining the application the Secretary of State had taken all the relevant factors into account and had given proper weight to questions arising from the applicant's detention without charge and the persecution of politically active persons of the applicant's religion generally. There were no grounds for interfering with the decision, and the application would be refused.

R v Secretary of State for the Home Department, ex p Singh [1992] Imm AR 607 (Queen's Bench Division: Pill J).

223   Immigration—asylum—refusal of application—failure to show exceptional circumstances justifying transfer of refugee status

The appellant was a citizen of Iran who had secured refugee status in France. He was granted leave to enter the United Kingdom as a visitor, and upon arrival in that country he applied for a transfer of his refugee status so that he could remain indefinitely. He based his application on the fact that he had experienced difficulty in assimilating into French society and found his relatives there irksome, but the Secretary of State refused his application on the ground that his case did not disclose any compassionate circumstances which would justify a transfer of his refugee status under the European Agreement on Transfer of Responsibility for Refugees 1980. The adjudicator dismissed his appeal against that decision, and, on his further appeal, *held*, consideration would not normally be given to a request for a transfer of refugee status unless the appellant could show that there were "compassionate circumstances which put the case into an exceptional category", in accordance with the 1980 Agreement. The appellant had failed to show that he came into that category, and the difficulties he had faced in France were not exceptional in comparison to the difficulties faced by refugees generally. There were no grounds for overturning the Secretary of State's decision, and, accordingly, the appeal would be dismissed.

Shramir v Secretary of State for the Home Department [1992] Imm AR 542 (Immigration Appeal Tribunal).

224   Immigration—asylum—refusal of application—subsequent radical changes in applicant's native country

The appellants, husband and wife, were citizens of Uganda. In 1985, they sought political asylum in the United Kingdom after entering the country as visitors the previous year. Their application was refused, and in 1989 the Secretary of State commenced deportation proceedings under the Immigration Act 1971, s 3(5)(a). The adjudication officer upheld the Secretary of State's decision to deport the appellants on the ground that the radical political changes in Uganda between 1985 and 1989 had removed the basis of their original claim. On their further appeal against the decision to deport them, *held*, there was a well-settled policy in immigration law generally that the material date was the date of the decision under appeal. There was no justification for making an exception to that rule in relation to applications for political asylum, or in relation to the review of a claim to be a refugee in the context of a deportation appeal. However, the appeal would fail because there was no evidence that they would have been in danger of persecution if they had returned to Uganda when the decision to deport them had been made. Accordingly, the appeal would be dismissed.

Musisi v Secretary of State for the Home Department [1992] Imm AR 520 (Immigration Appeal Tribunal).

225   Immigration—deportation—appeal—policy

The Immigration Act 1971, Sch 3, para 1(1) provides that where a deportation order is in force against any person, the Secretary of State may give directions for his removal to a country or territory specified in the directions being either (a) a country of which he is a national; or (b) a country or territory to which there is reason to believe that he will be admitted.

The applicant was a British Overseas citizen married to an Indian national living in India with their children. The applicant was admitted to the United Kingdom as a visitor, but she overstayed and the Secretary of State decided to deport her. He proposed removal directions to India, a country which he described as one to which there was reason to believe the applicant would be admitted. The applicant refused to apply for the visa she needed if she was to return to

India, although it was not expected that there would be any difficulty in obtaining the visa. An application by the applicant for leave to seek judicial review of the decision of the Secretary of State was refused at first instance. On a renewed application, the applicant contended that the Secretary of State could not have had reason to believe that the applicant would have been admitted to India, and that para 1(1)(b) had to be read subject to para 1(1)(a). It was also submitted that there had been an established policy under which British Overseas citizens who overstayed were not deported. *Held*, para 1(1)(b) was not to be read subject to para 1(1)(a); the disjunctive "or" between para 1(1)(a) and (b) showed that this was not the case. In addition, to require the applicant to apply for a visa and thus comply with an immigration formality did not stop the Secretary of State from reasonably believing that the applicant would be granted a visa and be admitted to India. In this case, there was no policy or practice from which the applicant could benefit. The judge had also been right in concluding that the conduct of the applicant in declining to apply for a visa did not merit benefiting from the discretionary remedy of judicial review. The application would accordingly be refused.

Patel v Secretary of State for the Home Department [1993] Imm AR 392 (Court of Appeal: Balcombe, Kennedy and Evans LJJ).

226 Immigration—deportation—appeal—related appellants

The appellant and his brother, who were both Pakistani citizens, were convicted of supplying heroin and served with deportation notices. Both appealed to the Immigration Appeal Tribunal. The brother's appeal was allowed because, although it was in the public interest to deport him, the offence of supplying heroin was outweighed by compassionate grounds, namely the fact that his girlfriend was pregnant and unable to accompany him to Pakistan. The tribunal dismissed the appellant's appeal, unaware of the decision reached in his brother's case. On further appeal on the ground that the tribunal had a duty to raise the matter of the outcome of the brother's appeal, *held*, the tribunal was not under a duty to consider the brother's case but was obliged to conform to principles set out in the Statement of Changes in the Immigration Rules (1983) HC 169 and (1990) HC 251. There was no doubt that the brother's case was a material fact which the tribunal would have taken into account had it known about it; otherwise it would not have been exercising its jurisdiction under the rules. Accordingly, the appeal would be allowed and the tribunal's decision would be quashed and remitted to the tribunal for reconsideration in light of the brother's case. This was not an invitation to re-open the whole case but merely to look at the situation as it existed when the decision to deport was made.

R v Immigration Appeal Tribunal, ex p Yasim (1993) Times, 8 December (Queen's Bench Division: Popplewell J).

227 Immigration—deportation—appeal—restricted right of appeal—exemption

The Immigration (Restricted Right of Appeal against Deportation) (Exemption) Order 1993, SI 1993/1656 (in force on 26 July 1993), provides that a person is exempt from the restrictions on the right of appeal against deportation if he would have been last given leave to enter the United Kingdom seven years or more before the date of the decision to make a deportation order against him but for his having obtained a subsequent leave after an absence from the United Kingdom within the period limited for the duration of the earlier leave; and if his limited leave to enter or remain has been curtailed by the Secretary of State under the Asylum and Immigration Appeals Act 1993, s 7(1).

228 Immigration—deportation—application for asylum—removal directions issued—no alternative destination proposed—jurisdiction

The appellant was a Turkish citizen, against whom the Secretary of State had made a deportation order. The appellant then claimed political asylum which was refused. An appeal was lodged after the deportation order had been signed, and when the appeal went before the adjudicator no alternative destination was put forward. The adjudicator considered he was obliged to inquire into the circumstances surrounding the service of the notice of intention to deport the appellant, holding that if the appellant had lodged an appeal against that decision, the Secretary of State would have had no power in law to issue the removal directions. He found however that the notice of intention to deport had been validly served and no appeal had been lodged and that therefore he had no jurisdiction to hear the appeal against removal directions. On appeal to the Immigration Appeal Tribunal, *held*, the adjudicator had misdirected himself in law in seeking to establish the precedent facts in relation to the issue of the notice of intention to deport. There could be no valid appeal before him in relation to removal directions, unless an alternative destination had been put forward by the appellant. The adjudicator had confused his powers in a deportation appeal, where he had jurisdiction to inquire whether the Secretary of State had the power to take the decision he had taken, with his very limited jurisdiction in an appeal against removal directions. In the present case neither the adjudicator nor the tribunal had jurisdiction to entertain the appeal and accordingly the appeal would be dismissed.

Tuglaci v Secretary of State for the Home Department [1993] Imm AR 47 (Immigration Appeal Tribunal).

229 Immigration—deportation—drug trafficking—Community national

The appellant, an Indian and Portuguese national, came to England in 1975. In 1986 he was convicted of conspiracy fraudulently to evade the restriction on importation of a class A drug and his deportation was ordered by the Secretary of State. The appellant's application for judicial review of the decision was dismissed. On appeal, he submitted that he should not be deported as he was an EC national and had no propensity to commit further offences. *Held*, even though the appellant was an EC national, the court had to consider the seriousness of the offence and whether that itself merited deportation. The offence was an affront to the requirements of public policy and disregarded one of the basic tenets in society. The appeal would accordingly be dismissed.

R v Secretary of State for the Home Department, ex p Marchon [1993] 2 CMLR 132 (Court of Appeal: Dillon, Beldam and Roch LJJ).

230 Immigration—deportation—extra-statutory advisory panel—right to legal representation

See *Abbas v Secretary of State for the Home Department*, para 41.

231 Immigration—deportation—recommendation for deportation—deportation following criminal conviction—grant of bail whilst recommendation in force

The defendants had been convicted of handling and attempting to handle stolen cars and were sentenced to two years' imprisonment with recommendations for deportation. They had both served the operative part of their sentences but continued to be detained under the Immigration Act 1971, Sch 3. Both appealed against their conviction and sentence and applied for bail pending their appeal. *Held*, under the Immigration Act 1971, Sch 3, para 2(1), (1A) the courts had the power to release an offender notwithstanding that a recommendation for deportation was in force, at every stage of the process. Any court considering whether to release or grant bail to an offender subject to a recommendation for deportation, ought to consult the Secretary of State to allow him to make representations. In the present case, bail would not be in the public interest as there was a short waiting period before the appeal and the temptation to abscond would be at its highest.

R v Ofori; R v Tackie (1993) Times, 17 November (Court of Appeal: Lord Taylor of Gosforth CJ, Schiemann and Wright JJ).

232 Immigration—deportation—recommendation for deportation—discretion of Secretary of State

The appellant a was a citizen of Jamaica who had received a long custodial sentence for serious criminal offences. Although the issue of deportation had been discussed at the trial the court had not recommended deportation. The Secretary of State however decided to deport the appellant and on appeal against the deportation, *held*, no recommendation, or absence of recommendation, for deportation by a court limited the discretionary powers of the Secretary of State. A decision by a sentencing court to make or not to make a recommendation that a defendant be deported did not mean that the issue of deportation had been conclusively decided. In the present case the decision of the Secretary of State to deport was justified and accordingly the appeal would be dismissed.

Martin v Secretary of State for the Home Department [1993] Imm AR 161 (Immigration Appeal Tribunal).

233 Immigration—deportation—recommendation for deportation— recommendation in relation to refugee

See *R v Villa and Villa*, para 2285.

234 Immigration—deportation—recommendation for deportation—threat to national security

The Secretary of State refused the applicant refugee status and ordered his deportation on the ground that his presence was not conducive to the public good and for reasons of national security. The applicant, who maintained that he was a refugee and entitled to asylum, sought judicial review of this decision. His application for judicial review was dismissed, the judge holding that the Secretary of State, having identified grounds for regarding the applicant as a danger to the security of the country, was required to balance his interests as identified in the Convention and Protocol Relating to the Status of Refugees 1951 (Cmnd 9171) and 1967 (Cmnd 3906). As the Secretary of State had undertaken that task, his decision was not irrational and could not be impugned. On appeal, *held*, the effect of the 1951 Convention, incorporated by the Immigration Rules (HC 251 of 1990) required a balancing exercise to be carried out between the threat to life or freedom contained in the 1951 Convention, art 33(1) and the danger to the security of the country in article 33(2). In this case, a balancing exercise had been carried out, and the Secretary of State's decision could only be interfered with if that decision was irrational or perverse or otherwise unlawful. It was not shown to be any of these things, and the appeal would accordingly be dismissed.

R v Secretary of State for the Home Department, ex p Chahal (1993) Times, 27 October (Court of Appeal: Neill, Staughton and Nolan LJJ). Decision of Potts J [1993] Imm AR 362 affirmed.

235 Immigration—entry—application for entry clearance—application made before payment of statutory fees

A mother who sought entry clearance for her son to join her in the United Kingdom wrote to the entry clearance office asking for the appropriate forms. She completed the forms and apparently sent them to the entry clearance office, but that office had no record of an application being made. By the time the matter was resolved the son had attained the age of 18, and his application was refused because he did not satisfy the rules relating to dependent relatives. He successfully appealed against the decision on the ground that his mother's letter had constituted an application for leave to enter, and as that application had been made while her son was a minor he only had to satisfy the less stringent entry rules relating to children. The entry clearance officer appealed on the ground that the Consular Fees Order 1983, SI 1983/1518, indicated that an application was only regarded as having been made once the statutory fees had been paid. *Held*, if payment of the fee was intended to be a prerequisite of making an application, the 1983 Order should have specifically stated that that was the case. There was no statement to that effect, and the adjudicator had been correct to regard the application as having been made when the letter requesting the appropriate forms was sent. Accordingly, the appeal would be dismissed.

Entry Clearance Officer, Port Louis v Ross [1992] Imm AR 493 (Immigration Appeal Tribunal).

236 Immigration—entry—illegal entry—entry gained by deception—breach of procedure

The applicant was granted entry clearance as a visitor and had intended to spend 15 days in the United Kingdom. To both the entry clearance officer and the immigration officer he stated that he knew no one in the United Kingdom. He was arrested by immigration officers five weeks after his arrival and following his arrest it became clear that he had friends in the United Kingdom. On the basis of that deception the Secretary of State concluded that the applicant was an illegal entrant. While the applicant was being held at the police station, a solicitor, alerted by a friend of the applicant, arrived at the police station to see him. The applicant was not told of the solicitor's arrival. The applicant argued that there had been a lapse of procedure in relation to his interview and that the deception had not been proven to the requisite high standard. *Held*, the Secretary of State had shown to the requisite high standard of proof that there had been material deception and was entitled to conclude the applicant was an illegal entrant. As the alleged conduct of the applicant could have led to a criminal charge, the breach of procedure did not justify the disregarding of the record of interview. Accordingly, the appeal would be dismissed.

R v Secretary of State for the Home Department, ex p Ibrahim [1993] Imm AR 124 (Queen's Bench Division: Macpherson J).

237 Immigration—entry—illegal entry—test of legality of entry

The appellants were involved in the production of forged passports for use by certain persons travelling to the United Kingdom. Those travellers had used the passports to leave other countries but had not relied on them when claiming political asylum on arrival in the United Kingdom. The appellants were convicted of the offence of facilitating the illegal entry of persons into the United Kingdom contrary to the Immigration Act 1971, s 25(1). On appeal against conviction, *held*, s 3 of the Act drew a distinction between arrival and entry. It conferred power to give leave to enter on immigration officers who might examine persons arriving in the United Kingdom. Schedule 2, para 2 provided for a person who had arrived, including transit passengers and those not seeking to enter, to be examined so the immigration officer might determine whether such persons might or might not enter the United Kingdom without leave. A person arriving by air at Heathrow did not enter the United Kingdom when he disembarked nor did he enter when he proceeded towards immigration control, thereby evincing an intention to go through immigration rather than going on to a foreign destination. Merely to disembark without a passport did not mean a person had ipso facto entered illegally. A person only sought to enter when he presented himself to the immigration officer or tried to evade immigration control. If he presented himself to an immigration officer and lied or produced forged documents, he was seeking to enter in breach of immigration laws; if he merely asked for political asylum and did not produce a forged document or otherwise seek to deceive the immigration officer, he was not an illegal entrant. The test of the legality of his entry was whether leave had been lawfully obtained, not whether a valid passport or other relevant document was in his possession. None of the travellers sought to rely on false documents nor did they themselves practise any fraud or deception on the immigration officers or enter clandestinely. There had been no illegal entry for the appellants to facilitate and, accordingly, their appeals would be allowed.

R v Naillie; R v Kanesarajah [1993] 2 All ER 782 (House of Lords: Lords Templeman, Lowry, Browne-Wilkinson, Slynn of Hadley and Woolf). Decision of Court of Appeal [1993] 1 All ER 75 (1992 Abr para 196) affirmed.

238   Immigration—entry—leave to enter—variation of leave

The Immigration (Variation of Leave) (Amendment) Order 1993, SI 1993/1657 (in force on 26 July 1993), further amends the 1976 Order, SI 1976/1572, by excluding from its provisions persons whose leave to enter or remain in the United Kingdom under the Immigration Act 1971 has been curtailed by the Secretary of State under the Asylum and Immigration Appeals Act 1993, s 7(1); and by providing that, where a person's limited leave to enter or remain has been extended under the 1976 Order, the extension is not to have effect beyond the date to which the leave is curtailed.

239   Immigration—entry—leave to enter—variation of leave—medical treatment

The appellant was a citizen of Israel who had been refused a variation of leave to continue medical treatment in the United Kingdom as she had failed to satisfy the Secretary of State that the treatment was for a finite period and that she intended to leave the United Kingdom following its completion. On appeal it was argued that the Secretary of State had incorrectly exercised his discretion. *Held*, before the Secretary of State could exercise his discretion, it was a mandatory requirement that the appellant provide evidence that she would leave the United Kingdom at the end of the treatment. The availability of suitable facilities for the treatment in an applicant's native country was not relevant to an assessment of whether the applicant would leave the United Kingdom in due course, but was a factor to be taken into account in the later exercise of the Secretary of State's discretion. Whilst the Secretary of State was obliged to show that he had reason to believe that an applicant did not intend to leave the United Kingdom at the end of the treatment a failure by an applicant to provide adequate evidence relevant to an application could itself contribute to such a conclusion by the Secretary of State. On the facts the mandatory requirement of proof had not been satisfied and it followed that there was no discretion to be exercised by the Secretary of State. Accordingly, the appeal would be dismissed.

Ganu v Secretary of State for the Home Department [1993] Imm AR 20 (Immigration Appeal Tribunal).

240   Immigration—entry—refusal of leave to enter—appeal—jurisdiction of tribunal

The appellant, a citizen of Ghana, was refused leave to enter the United Kingdom as a visitor. He made an application for political asylum which was also refused, and his appeals against those decisions were dismissed by the adjudicator. His subsequent appeal to the immigration office was made out of time because the immigration office wrongly told him he had 42 days in which to lodge an appeal when the time limit was actually 14 days. The immigration office acknowledged that it had made a mistake and indicated it would be content for the tribunal to assume jurisdiction on the substantive issue. On the question of whether the tribunal could hear the appeal, *held*, the tribunal, being a creature of statute, could not assume a jurisdiction which the statute had not given to it even if the parties to the proceedings had asked it to assume that jurisdiction. There were provisions for agreed determinations in certain circumstances, namely those situations which came within the ambit of the Immigration Appeals (Procedure) Rules 1984, SI 1984/2041, r 37(c), but those provisions did not extend to the issue of jurisdiction. Accordingly, the appeal would be dismissed.

O v Immigration Officer, Heathrow [1992] Imm AR 584 (Immigration Appeal tribunal).

241 Immigration—entry—refusal of leave to enter—judicial review

A citizen of Bangladesh had made a claim for political asylum upon his arrival in the United Kingdom. He was granted temporary admission, but was subsequently refused leave to enter and his asylum application was also refused. The letter refusing asylum was withdrawn while further representations made on his behalf were considered but the refusal was subsequently maintained, although the final letter was sent one month after it had been written. He sought leave to apply for judicial review on the grounds that the Secretary of State had acted too hastily in giving his first refusal, and that had tainted all he had done subsequently. He also contended that (1) the withdrawal of the first refusal of asylum was by implication also a withdrawal of the refusal of leave to enter; and (2) the examination of the applicant had been completed when the final letter of refusal of asylum was written rather than when that letter was sent, and on either basis he had secured six months' leave to enter within the provisions of the Immigration Act 1971, Sch 2, para 6(3). *Held*, the withdrawal of the letter explaining the reasons for the refusal of the application for asylum did not cause the withdrawal of the refusal of leave to enter, and the examination of the applicant had not been completed until the final letter of refusal had been served on him. The Secretary of State had acted fairly and promptly upon the case put to him, but he had been willing to consider further representations and his approach could not be faulted. Accordingly, the application would be dismissed.

Ahmed v Secretary of State for the Home Department [1992] Imm AR 449 (Court of Appeal: Neill, Ralph Gibson and Stocker LJJ).

242 Immigration—entry—refusal of leave of entry—re-application

The applicants sought entry clearance into the United Kingdom, on the basis that their mother was dead and that A, their father, was a British citizen. Their application was refused on the ground that the immigration officer was not satisfied that the applicants were related to A. It was later revealed that the applicants' mother was still alive. DNA tests subsequently showed that the applicants were A's sons. The Home Office, unaware that A had since died, wrote to the applicants stating that arrangements would be made for entry clearance. When A's death became known to the immigration authorities, a formal refusal notice was issued. The applicants unsuccessfully appealed to an adjudicator. Their further appeal to the appeal tribunal was successful, the tribunal holding that the decision under appeal was no longer the initial refusal of entry clearance, but the later refusal notice, and their decision was based on the facts as they had developed since the refusal of entry clearance. An application for judicial review was subsequently granted to quash this decision. The applicants appealed. *Held*, once an application had been decided, both the application and the decision taken upon it were to be regarded as legally incapable of being re-opened. If the decision was adverse to the applicant, the Home Office could review it, and come to a fresh conclusion in the applicant's favour, and the applicant could also appeal any adverse decision to the appellate authorities. However, following an adverse decision, if the applicant wished to gain entry on a revised basis, depending on circumstances occurring after that decision, then a fresh application would have to be made. The appeal would accordingly be dismissed.

R v Immigration Appeal Tribunal, ex p Secretary of State for the Home Department (1993) Times, 15 July (Court of Appeal: Neill, Simon Brown and Waite LJJ). Decision of Popplewell J (1993) Times, 28 January affirmed.

243 Immigration—entry—refusal of leave to enter—return from travel

The applicant was a citizen of India who was given leave to enter the United Kingdom as a visitor for six months. During that period he applied for political asylum and his application was refused. He appealed and accordingly was not required to leave the United Kingdom while the appeal was pending. He decided however to go the United States. When his flight arrived in Ireland it was discovered that he was travelling on a forged passport. He was returned to the

United Kingdom on the first available plane. On arrival in the United Kingdom he was refused leave to enter. He again claimed political asylum and that was refused. In an application challenging the refusals, *held*, the applicant merely had a stay of execution preventing his removal from the United Kingdom while his appeal was pending. The phrasing of the Immigration (Control of Entry through Republic of Ireland) Order 1972, SI 1972/1610, showed that "entered" as used in the Order did not mean "given leave to enter". It was therefore logical to construe the words in the Order "entered that Republic", as including a person who was physically there but was not given leave to land there. On that basis the decision of the immigration officer to refuse the applicant leave to enter the United Kingdom had not been unreasonable and accordingly the appeal would be dismissed.

Singh v Secretary of State for the Home Department [1993] Imm AR 76 (Court of Appeal: Dillon, Russell, Rose LJJ).

244 Immigration—entry—sponsor—dependent relatives—financial dependency

The respondents were British Dependent Territories citizens by virtue of a connection with Hong Kong, who sought entrance clearance to join their sponsor in the United Kingdom as dependent relatives. The applications were refused as the entry clearance officer was unsatisfied the respondents were dependent on the sponsor. Whilst the respondents had a significant amount of capital they argued that there was a constant erosion of capital as it was being drawn for regular medical costs incurred as a result of the disabilities of one of the respondents. An adjudicator reversed the decision of the entry clearance officer on the basis that the rule did not require the exhaustion of capital before a successful application could be made as a dependent relative. On appeal by the entry clearance officer, *held*, emotional dependency was only likely to be of significant weight where there had been fairly close contact between an applicant and the relative; it did not need to be principally a financial dependency. It was not the case that all capital holdings had to be exhausted before an applicant could demonstrate the necessary degree of financial dependency required by the rules. The respondents had failed to show that they were wholly or mainly financially dependent of necessity on the sponsor and accordingly the appeal would be allowed.

Entry Clearance Officer, Hong Kong v Cheng [1993] Imm AR 81 (Immigration Appeal Tribunal).

245 Immigration—legislation—appellate authorities—jurisdiction

The applicant, a Pakistani national who was employed by a German company, entered the United Kingdom on a visitor's permit. He then claimed a right to stay by virtue of the EEC Treaty, art 54(3)(f) in exercise of the company's right of establishment through a branch. He sought a statement that he was lawfully present by virtue of art 54(3)(f) or leave to remain as the representative of an overseas company. The statement was refused but he was granted leave to remain. The applicant and the company appealed to an adjudicator and then to the Immigration Appeal Tribunal against the refusal of the statement, *held*, the appeal procedure through the appellate bodies set up under the Immigration Acts was limited to situations covered by the scheme of those Acts; the applicant's position fell outside that scheme and, accordingly, his appeal did not lie under the statutory appellate procedure. As there was a right to apply to the High Court for judicial review, lack of access to the appellate procedures constituted neither discrimination nor failure to provide adequate protection of Community rights. The appellate tribunals had no jurisdiction to hear the appeal which would be dismissed.

Pasha v Secretary of State for the Home Department [1993] 2 CMLR 350 (Immigration Appeal Tribunal).

246 Immigration—rules

The Immigration Rules, as set out in HC251, have been further amended (see HC725). Provision is now made for the control of persons seeking entry to the United Kingdom through the Channel Tunnel. A passenger in possession of a current entry clearance or named in a current work permit who is refused leave to enter when seeking entry through the tunnel may, on giving notice of appeal, be brought through the tunnel to enable him to pursue his appeal. No application for entry clearance may now be made until the requisite fee has been paid. The "au pair" arrangements now apply to unmarried persons, instead of unmarried girls only, aged 17 to 27. A person who was not given leave to enter the United Kingdom as an "au pair" must be refused an extension if he applies to remain as an "au pair". New provision is made for asylum applications and, until the determination of such an application or any appeal against a refusal of asylum, no action will be taken to require a person's departure from the United Kingdom. A person of any age may qualify for refugee status. Unaccompanied children are entitled to apply for asylum and, in view of their potential vulnerability, particular priority and care is to be given to the handling of their cases. Any application for an extension of stay by a visitor admitted for up to 48 hours for the sole purpose of transit must be refused and a visitor admitted for a stay of six months will not usually be permitted to extend the duration of his visit. Nationals or citizens of Eritrea now require visas for the United Kingdom.

247 Immigration—transit visa

The Immigration (Transit Visa) Order 1993, SI 1993/1678 (in force on 22 July 1993), requires nationals or citizens of specified countries or territories to hold a visa for passing through the United Kingdom to another country or territory unless they have the right of abode in the United Kingdom under the Immigration Act 1971 or are also a national of a member state. An application for a visa must be made to any British High Commission, Embassy or Consulate which accepts such applications.

248 Immigration (Carriers' Liability) Act 1987—Guernsey

The Immigration (Guernsey) Order 1993, SI 1993/1796 (in force on 1 August 1993), consolidates specified Orders and extends to Guernsey, with modifications, the provisions of the Immigration Act 1988.

249 Immigration (Carriers' Liability) Act 1987—Jersey

The Immigration (Jersey) Order 1993, SI 1993/1797 (in force on 1 August 1993), consolidates specified Orders and extends to Jersey, with modifications, the provisions of the Immigration Act 1988.

250 Race relations—discrimination—education—local education authority— exercise of education function

See *R v Bradford Metropolitan Borough Council, ex p Sikander Ali*, para 1085.

251 Race relations—discrimination—employment—comparison of treatment— effect of failure to make comparison

The Race Relations Act 1976, s 1(1)(a) provides that a person discriminates against another on racial grounds if he treats that person less favourably than he treats or would treat other persons.

The applicant was employed as an assistant gaming manager in a casino. He held a Gaming Board green certificate which qualified him to be a supervisor or junior manager and sought to acquire a grey certificate to gain managerial status. He was given the relevant documents, informed that he would have to take an oral examination and warned that, as his spoken English was poor he was unlikely to succeed and should take lessons. He was subsequently dismissed and successfully claimed that he had been unlawfully discriminated against on the grounds of race, contrary to the 1976 Act, s 1(1)(a) because he was not given sufficient opportunity for promotion or training under the 1976 Act, s 4(2)(b), particularly in respect of improving his spoken English. On the employers' appeal, *held*, the industrial tribunal made an error in law by failing to compare the treatment of the applicant and that of a comparator who was not of foreign origin. In the absence of that comparison it could not be inferred that the applicant had received less favourable treatment on racial grounds under the 1976 Act, s 1(1)(a). Accordingly, the appeal would be allowed.

Mecca Leisure Group plc v Chatprachong [1993] ICR 688 (Employment Appeal Tribunal: Wood J presiding). *Webb v Emo Air Cargo (UK) Ltd* [1993] ICR 175, HL (1992 Abr para 2313) applied.

252 Race relations—discrimination—employment—complaint to industrial tribunal—time limit

The Race Relations Act 1976, s 68(1) provides that an industrial tribunal may not consider a complaint unless it is presented to the tribunal before the end of the period of three months beginning when the act complained of was done.

The plaintiff, who had been employed by the defendants for less than two years, was dismissed from her job. Her internal appeal was heard two months later, and a further month later she was informed that the appeal had been unsuccessful. On an originating application to an industrial tribunal, the plaintiff complained that she had been unfairly dismissed, alleging that white employees would not have been dismissed for doing what she was alleged to have done, and that they would not have failed on the internal appeal. The tribunal dismissed her complaint. On appeal, the question arose whether the determination of her appeal was an "act complained of" for the purposes of s 68(1), and therefore whether her complaint had been made within time. *Held*, if, as in this case, there was an allegation of race discrimination in the result of an appeal, that was an act complained of within s 68(1). The appeal would accordingly be allowed.

Adekeye v Post Office [1993] ICR 464 (Employment Appeal Tribunal: May J presiding).

Scotland
The Race Relations Act 1976, s 68(1) provides that complaints of unlawful racial discrimination must be brought within three months from the time that the act complained of was done. Section 68(7)(b) provides that any act extending over a period must be treated as done at the end of that period.

The plaintiff employee alleged that he had been racially abused by his supervisor. The plaintiff met with his employer's management, who agreed to replace the existing supervisor with one who was to receive training in multi-racial management and improving morale and efficiency in the department. Some months later, the plaintiff complained that his employer had failed to implement their commitments. He took voluntary redundancy and brought a complaint of unlawful racial discrimination. An industrial tribunal held that the complaint was out of time, as more than three months had elapsed between the act complained of and the filing of the application to the industrial tribunal. On a fresh application to a different tribunal, it was held that the complaint was not time-barred, because the act of discrimination complained of was continuing. On appeal by the employer, *held*, the plaintiff's complaint related to a continuing act of discrimination rather than to a single act having consequences extending over a period of time. As long as the agreed remedial measures were not actually taken, a situation capable of involving racial discrimination continued. Permitting that situation to continue amounted to a continuing act. The employer's appeal would accordingly be dismissed.

Littlewoods Organisation plc v Traynor [1993] IRLR 154 (Employment Appeal Tribunal: Lord Coulsfield presiding).

253   Race relations—discrimination—employment—engagement in a particular trade

The respondents offered the applicant a position as a sub-postmaster subject to satisfactory references. Following the withdrawal of the offer the applicant made a complaint that he had been unlawfully discriminated against on the ground of his race contrary to the Race Relations Act 1976, s 12. An industrial tribunal dismissed the complaint on the ground that the respondents were not an authority or body that could confer "an authorisation needed for engagement in a particular trade" within the meaning of the 1976 Act, s 12. On appeal, *held*, the granting by the respondents of an appointment to an individual sub-postmaster did not confer an authorisation needed for or facilitating engagement in a particular trade for the purposes of the 1976 Act, s 12. Accordingly, the appeal would be dismissed.

Malik v Post Office Counters Ltd [1993] ICR 93 (Employment Appeal Tribunal: Knox J presiding).

254   Race relations—discrimination—employment—exemplary damages

A local authority appointed the appellant, who was white, to the post of principal housing officer. The appointment was made in the absence of the housing director, who, on his return, refused to confirm the appointment because he felt that the position ought to be awarded to a person of Asian origin who spoke Asian languages. The appellant complained of unlawful racial discrimination contrary to the Race Relations Act 1976, s 1(1)(a) against both the local authority and the housing director personally. An industrial tribunal made an award against the local authority, including an element for injury to feelings, but it did not make an award of exemplary damages nor an award against the director personally. On appeal, *held*, as the housing director had been acting in the course of his employment, any award of damages had to be against the local authority rather than the director personally. Furthermore, exemplary damages could only be awarded in respect of torts which existed prior to 1964, and as the appellant's claim for exemplary damages arose from a statutory tort created by the 1976 Act, that part of the appeal would also fail. However, the tribunal had erroneously estimated the level of injury which the discrimination had caused to the appellant's feelings, and, accordingly, the appeal would be allowed to the extent that damages for injury to feelings would be increased from £500 to £1000.

Deane v Ealing London Borough Council [1993] ICR 329 (Employment Appeal Tribunal: Wood J presiding). *AB v South West Water Services Ltd* [1993] 2 WLR 507, CA (1992 Abr para 879) applied.

255   Race relations—discrimination—employment—jurisdiction of industrial tribunal

The Race Relations Act 1976, s 12 provides that it is unlawful for a body conferring a qualification which was needed for engagement in a profession to discriminate against a person by refusing to grant his application.

The appellant had qualified as a doctor in Pakistan. He entered the United Kingdom and unsuccessfully applied for full registration with the General Medical Council (GMC). He appealed to the GMC's review board in accordance with the Medical Act 1983, s 29, but his appeal failed. He alleged that the GMC's conduct contravened the provisions of the 1976 Act, s 12, and complained of discrimination on the ground of race to an industrial tribunal. The tribunal ruled it had no jurisdiction to hear his complaint, and, on his appeal, *held*, the 1976 Act, s 54 gave a right to complain of discrimination to an industrial tribunal but excluded the right to make a complaint against a decision under the 1976 Act, s 12, in respect of which an appeal or proceedings in the nature of an appeal could be brought. Consequently, the case turned on whether the proceedings before the GMC's review board had been "an appeal or proceedings in the nature of an appeal" within the meaning of the 1976 Act, s 54. The proceedings had been fair and had met with the procedural characteristics identified in *R v Board of the Defence Council, ex p Anderton* [1991] ICR 537, CA, so the provisions of the 1976 Act, s 54 had been complied with and the industrial tribunal had been correct to rule that it had no jurisdiction to hear the complaint. Accordingly, the appeal would be dismissed.

Khan v General Medical Council [1993] ICR 627 (Employment Appeal Tribunal: May J presiding).

256   Race relations—discrimination—employment—justifiable discrimination— condition as to religion

The applicant, a deputy head teacher of Asian origin who was a Roman Catholic but not a communicant, applied for the post of head teacher at her school. The school was run according to the religious tenets of the Anglo-Catholic tradition and pupils were expected to attend mass once a week. A weekly class lesson was set aside to prepare for mass and the head teacher was frequently required to administer communion. The school invited applications from teachers who were "committed communicant Christians" and the applicant was not selected for the post. An industrial tribunal found that the school had discriminated against the applicant within the meaning of the Race Relations Act 1976, s 1(1)(b)(ii). On appeal, the board of governors of the school argued that the school's condition was justifiable irrespective of the colour, race, nationality or ethnic or national origins of the applicant within the meaning of s 1(1)(b)(ii) because of the importance of the church in the life and ethos of the school. *Held*, the correct approach was to ask whether the objective of the governors was a reasonable objective and whether the means used to achieve it were both reasonable in themselves and could also be justified, when balanced on the principle of proportionality between the discriminatory effect upon the applicant's racial group and the reasonable needs of the governors. The governors were entitled to take a decision affecting the way in which their own school was managed in spiritual affairs. Their objective went beyond religious education to encompass religious worship and the ethos of the school. The objective was reasonable and the means used to achieve it were reasonable and justifiable. Accordingly, the appeal would be allowed.

Board of Governors of St Matthias Church of England School v Crizzle [1993] ICR 401 (Employment Appeal Tribunal: Wood J presiding). *Hampson v Department of Education and Science* [1989] ICR 179, CA (1988 Abr para 1976) applied.

257   Race relations—discrimination—employment—meaning of ethnic group

The appellant, a Rastafarian, applied for a job as a government van driver. His application was turned down because he wore his hair long on account of his beliefs, and he refused to have it cut. His claim that he had been discriminated against on racial grounds contrary to the Race Relations Act 1976 was upheld by an industrial tribunal, but the Employment Appeal Tribunal allowed the employer's appeal on the ground that Rastafarians were not a separate ethnic group within the meaning of the 1976 Act. On appeal against that decision, *held*, it was clear that

Rastafarians had a strong cultural tradition and certain identifiable characteristics, but the case turned on whether they had established a separate identity by reference to their ethnic origins. Rastafarians could not be set aside from the rest of the Jamaican or Afro-Caribbean communities in the country because they did not have a long shared history, and consequently they were not a separate group defined by their ethnic origins, as required by the 1976 Act. The decision of the Employment Appeal Tribunal had been correct, and the appeal would be dismissed.

Crown Suppliers (Property Services Agency) Ltd v Dawkins[1993] ICR 517 (Court of Appeal: Neill and Beldam LJJ and Sir John Megaw). Decision of Employment Appeal Tribunal [1991] ICR 583 (1991 Abr para 1982) affirmed.

BUILDING CONTRACTS, ARCHITECTS, ENGINEERS AND SURVEYORS

Halsbury's Laws of England (4th edn) Vol 4(2) (reissue), paras 301–700

258 Articles

Assigning Construction Contracts, Kaz Stepien (on *Linden Gardens Trust Ltd v Lenesta Sludge Disposals Ltd* (1993) Times, 23 July (para 259)): 137 SJ 888

Lenesta Sludge—Rescued from the Black Hole, Lawrance Heller (on *Linden Gardens Trust Ltd v Lenesta Sludge Disposals Ltd* (1993) Times, 23 July (para 259)): Estates Gazette, 28 August 1993, p 108

Listed Buildings—The Continuing Dilemmas of Definition, R Pickard: [1993] Conv 192

Professional Negligence in the Construction Industry, Gillian Birkby: 137 SJ 819

259 Building contract—contractual term—prohibition on assignment— assignment contrary to prohibition—assignee's right of action

In the first case, a lessee of premises entered into a building contract with a building contractor to remove asbestos from the premises. The contract was under the Joint Contracts Tribunal standard form of building contracts cl 17(1) of which prohibits the employer from assigning the contract without the consent of the contractor. The building contractor contracted work to the defendant who failed to remove all the asbestos. The lessee issued a writ against the defendant claiming damages for breach of contract and negligence. The lessee then assigned the lease on the property to a third party and, by a further assignment, his rights of the action as pleaded and rights incidental to the leasehold interest. The contractor did not consent to that assignment. In the second case, a property corporation entered into a building contract, containing an identical clause prohibiting assignment, for the development of a site. It subsequently assigned all its interests in the site to a third party and the full benefit of all its contracts and engagements. The contractor was neither asked for nor gave its consent. Certain breaches of contract took place after the assignment. In both cases, the assignees of the contracts claimed damages against the contractors for breach of contract. *Held*, it was clear that a party to a building contract would have a genuine commercial interest in seeking to ensure that he was in contractual relations only with a person whom he had selected as the other party to the contract. There was no policy reason why a contractual prohibition on assignment of contractual rights should be held contrary to public policy. Clause 17(1) prohibited the assignment by an employer of the benefit of the contract. The purported assignments without the consent of the contractors therefore constituted a breach of that clause. An attempted assignment of contractual rights in breach of a contractual prohibition was ineffective to transfer such contractual rights. Accordingly, the party attempting to assign retained his rights under the contract. He could assert them against the other party in case of a breach of contract by that other party. The claim in the first case would fail. In the second case, where the contract was for a large development of property which would be occupied and, perhaps, purchased by third parties, the corporation was entitled to enforce contractual rights for the benefit of those who suffered from defective performance but who, under the terms of the contract, could not acquire any right to hold the contractor liable for breach.

Linden Gardens Trust Ltd v Lenesta Sludge Disposals Ltd; St Martins Property Corpn Ltd v Robert McAlpine Ltd [1993] 3 All ER 417 (House of Lords: Lords Keith of Kinkel, Bridge of Harwich, Griffiths, Ackner and Browne-Wilkinson). Decision of Court of Appeal (1992) Independent, 6 March (1992 Abr para 214) affirmed.

260 Building contract—liquidated damages—delayed completion—deduction of liquidated damages

The plaintiff builder entered into a contract with the defendant employer for the construction of a number of flats. A date for completion was agreed, as was a rate for liquidated and ascertained damages for non completion. The contract provided that the employer could in writing require the builder to pay damages for the period between the contractual completion date and the date of actual completion. The builder failed to complete the works by the completion date. An interim certificate for the cost of the works was issued and the employer sent a payment of part of the amount due under the certificate together with a note stating that it had deducted the remainder as damages for delayed completion. The builder argued that the deduction was unlawful as the employer had failed to comply with the provisions of the contract. *Held*, the contract created a condition precedent that before any deduction could be made in respect of damages for delayed completion, the employer had to make a requirement of the builder in writing. The note sent with the part payment did not constitute a proper requirement in writing by the employer as such a requirement had to indicate at least the basic details relied on to justify the deduction. Accordingly, the employer's deduction was in breach of contract.

J F Finnegan Ltd v Community Housing Association Ltd (1993) Independent, 11 June (Official Referee's Court: Judge Carr).

261 Building contract—liquidated damages—validity of liquidated damages provision

Hong Kong

A company had sought a ruling, prior to arbitration, on contractual provisions for liquidated damages arising from a delay in completing a highway construction project. The court had held that the company was not liable to pay liquidated damages on the ground that the provisions were penal in effect, but that decision was reversed on appeal. On appeal by the company, *held*, with the possible exception of situations in which one of the parties to the contract was able to dominate the other as to the choice of terms of the contract, the fact that the application of a provision could result in the party recovering a sum larger than his actual loss would not usually result in that provision being regarded as penal. So long as the sum payable in the event of non-compliance with the contract was not extravagant, having regard to the range of losses that could reasonably have been anticipated, it would be a perfectly valid liquidated damages provision. The terms that the parties had agreed should normally be upheld in order to prevent undesirable uncertainty in commercial contract, and there were no grounds for upholding the company's contention that those terms had been penal. Accordingly, the appeal would be dismissed.

Philips Hong Kong Ltd v A-G of Hong Kong (1993) Times, 15 February (Privy Council: Lords Templeman, Goff of Chieveley, Browne-Wilkinson and Woolf and Sir Christopher Slade).

262 Engineer—duty of care—liability for economic loss

Malaysia

The plaintiff employed a firm of consultant engineers, of which the defendant engineer was an employee, to superintend and supervise buildings constructed for the plaintiff. The buildings needed repair which caused the plaintiff to incur substantial loss and he consequently brought an action against the defendant for breach of his duty of care. The defendant claimed that he was not responsible to the plaintiff as he worked under the supervision and instruction of the firm with whom the plaintiff had contracted, and there was therefore no privity of contract between the plaintiff and himself. The plaintiff claimed that although there was no contractual relationship, there was an action in tort, but this was disputed by the defendant who claimed that there could be no action in tort because the only loss suffered was pure economic loss. The defendant applied to the court to have the plaintiff's action against him struck out on the grounds that the plaintiff had no reasonable cause of action against him and that the action was scandalous, frivolous and vexatious and was an abuse of the court. At first instance the action was struck out. On appeal by the plaintiff, *held*, the defendant was not an agent of the firm and therefore, there was no privity of contract between him and the plaintiff. The loss suffered was pure economic loss and there was no action in tort against the defendant as there had been no injury to any person or damage to any property as a result of the defendant's act or misconduct. It was unreasonable to hold an employee of a construction firm liable for negligence where no injury to a person or property of another had resulted. Accordingly, the appeal would be dismissed and the plaintiff's action struck out.

Kerajaan Malaysia lwn Cheah Foong Chiew dan Lain-lain [1993] 2 Malayan LJ 439 (Malaysian High Court).

BUILDING SOCIETIES

Halsbury's Laws of England (4th edn) Vol 4(2) (reissue), paras 701–988

263   Assets and liabilities—aggregation—subsidiaries and associated bodies

The Building Societies (Aggregation) Rules 1993, SI 1993/2833 (in force on 31 December 1993), which revoke the 1990 Rules, SI 1990/2362, provide for the method by which the assets and liabilities of a building society's subsidiaries and other associated bodies are to be aggregated with those of the society for the purposes of the limits under the Building Societies Act 1986, ss 7, 8 and 20.

264   Building Societies Appeal Tribunal

The Building Societies Appeal Tribunal (Amendment) Regulations 1993, SI 1993/983 (in force on 30 April 1993), amend the 1987 Regulations, SI 1987/891. The main changes include provisions that the chairman of the tribunal can direct that a preliminary hearing be held less than 21 days after receipt of the notice of appeal, and that he take into account, when making directions on discovery, the need to protect commercially sensitive or confidential information relating to a person not a party to the appeal. The regulations give procedural effect to the 1992 Regulations, SI 1992/3218, which extended rights of appeal under the Building Societies Act 1986, s 46.

265   Building Societies Commisssion—expenses—general charge

The Building Societies (General Charge and Fees) Regulations 1993, SI 1993/546 (in force on 1 April 1993), replace the 1992 Regulations, SI 1992/497. The regulations provide for the payment of a general charge by authorised building societies towards the expenses of the Building Societies Commission and for fees in respect of particular functions of the commission and of the Central Office of the Registry of Friendly Societies.

266   Investment—power to invest in qualifying bodies—designated bodies

The Building Societies (Designation of Qualifying Bodies) Order 1993, SI 1993/985 (in force on 1 May 1993), adds "funding body" as a further type of designated body under the Building Societies Act 1986, s 18. It is a body corporate which is a subsidiary of a society, formed for the purposes of raising funds, holding assets equivalent to liquid assets held by building societies, entering into hedging contracts and lending money to the society which has invested in the funding body. The Order amends previous orders made under the 1986 Act, s 18 by removing restrictions preventing certain bodies designated by description from lending money and investing in subordinate organisations which lend money. The 1992 Order, SI 1992/650, is amended to remove the restriction that an appropriate holding vehicle must be a wholly-owned subsidiary of the society.

The Building Societies (Designation of Qualifying Bodies) (No 2) Order 1993, SI 1993/989 (in force on 1 May 1993), adds "mortgage indemnity insurance body" as a further type of designated body under the Building Societies Act 1986, s 18. It is a body corporate and the purposes for which it is formed include carrying on mortgage indemnity insurance business.

The Building Societies (Designation of Qualifying Bodies) (No 3) Order 1993, SI 1993/2706 (in force on 1 December 1993), consolidates, with amendments, SI 1990/1434, 1991/357, 1358, 2581, 1992/649, 650, 651, 652. The order designates Girobank plc and various specified types of corporate body for the purposes of the Building Societies Act 1986, s 18, and makes various changes of substance, including the following: (1) designated bodies carrying on specified types of activity may be incorporated in the Isle of Man or the Channel Islands; (2) the threshold up to which a society may invest in a designated body which is carrying on prohibited activities is increased to 5 per cent; (3) the threshold above which a society must be satisfied that 40 per cent of the income of an estate agency body in which the society has invested is derived from estate agency work is increased to 15 per cent; (4) the "group interest provision" has been simplified and is now known as the "qualifying activities condition"; (5) syndicated loans are defined; (6) the types of body corporate which building societies may support only (and are not required to invest in) are specified; the restriction that a society must both invest and support (and may not support only) some of the specified bodies corporate if such bodies have the capacity to have subordinate organisations is removed; and (7) amendments are made to SI 1993/985 and 989.

267 Loans of money—offences in relation to minors

See *Alliance & Leicester Building Society v Leicestershire County Council*, para 1818.

268 Power to hedge—prescribed contracts

The Building Societies (Prescribed Contracts) Order 1993, SI 1993/984 (in force on 1 May 1993), prescribes swap contracts, option contracts, swap option contracts and forward and future contracts in relation to interest rates and currency risks as types of contract which a building society may enter into under the Building Societies Act 1986, s 23 for the purpose of reducing the risk of loss. The power to enter into such contracts is only available to a building society which has adopted the power under s 23. Societies which do not have a qualifying asset holding, commercial assets of at least £100 million, may only enter into certain interest rate swap contracts. The 1988 Order, SI 1988/1153, and the 1991 Order, SI 1991/2582 are revoked, although the validity of prescribed contracts entered into under those orders is preserved.

CAPITAL GAINS TAXATION

Halsbury's Laws of England (4th edn) Vol 5(1) (reissue), paras 1–400

269 Articles

Budgeting for CGT, Gordon Pickering: 138 SJ 48
Capital Gains in Partnerships, Colin Davis: 137 SJ 992
Interaction of Reinvestment Relief with Other Reliefs, Simon McKie: Tax Journal, Issue 237, p 16
More on Capital Gains and Fictions, Sue Porter: Tax Journal, Issue 229, p 13
Multiple Buildings, Sylvia Elwes: Tax Journal, Issue 231, p 13
One Interpretation Leads to Another, Lindsay Pentelow (on options granted over land): Tax Journal, Issue 230, p 14
Retirement Bonus, Angus Gawn and David Small: Tax Journal, Issue 238, p 12
Structuring UK Real Estate for Non-Residents, Jay Sanghrajka and Kaz Stepien: 137 SJ 1137, 1246
The New Share Rollover, Christopher Cox: Tax Journal, Issue 225, p 10, Issue 226, p 16
The Principal Private Residence Exemption from Capital Gains Tax—The Area of Exempt Property, David Wilde: [1993] Conv 435
Trading or Investing? A Fine Line, Brenda Coleman: Tax Journal, Issue 227, p 10
Well What Can They Do Then? Lindsay Pentelow (on reinvestment rollover relief): Tax Journal, Issue 234, p 10
Where Sheps May Safely Graze, David Harris (on the tax treatment of second hand endowment policies): Tax Journal, Issue 239, p 13

270 Disposal of assets—asset held on 6 April 1965—computation of chargeable gains

The taxpayer acquired antiques in 1952 and sold them in 1987. She did not elect for valuation at 6 April 1965 under the Capital Gains Tax Act 1979, Sch 5, para 12, and, therefore, her gain fell to be computed in accordance with the time apportionment basis under Sch 5, para 11. It fell to be determined whether the indexation allowance which, under the Finance Act 1982, s 86(4), was to be set against the unindexed gain so as to give the gain for the purposes of the 1979 Act, was to be applied to the whole of the amount of the gain accruing between the acquisition and disposal of the antiques. *Held*, under s 86(2), the unindexed gain was the actual overall gain made by the taxpayer on the disposal of the asset so that the indexation allowance fell to be set against the unindexed gain before time apportionment under Sch 5, para 11.

Smith (Inspector of Taxes) v Schofield [1993] STC 268 (House of Lords: Lords Templeman, Goff of Chieveley, Jauncey of Tullichettle, Mustill and Woolf). Decision of Court of Appeal [1992] STC 249 reversed.

1979 Act, Sch 5 now Taxation of Chargeable Gains Act 1992, Sch 2. 1982 Act, s 86(4) now 1992 Act, s 53(1).

271 Disposal of assets—capital sum derived from assets—theft of assets—difference between amount of compensation and replacement value

The taxpayer sold a cottage on which a chargeable gain arose. He sought to treat as allowable losses (1) the difference between that gain and the replacement value of the cottage, and (2) the difference between a capital sum received by way of compensation from an insurance company in respect of items of jewellery and antiques stolen from the cottage prior to its sale and the replacement value of the stolen items. *Held*, (1) the supposed loss on the sale of the cottage which the taxpayer sought to offset against the gain was completely impermissible as a loss in accordance with the capital gains tax law. (2) There was no evidence that any of the items purchased to replace those stolen had a market value in excess of the statutory limit under the Capital Gains Tax Act 1979, s 128. The onus was on the taxpayer to put any such evidence before the commissioners. The taxpayer's claims would fail.

Neely v Ward (Inspector of Taxes) (note) [1993] STC 196 (Court of Appeal: Dillon and Rose LJJ and Peter Gibson J). Decision of Sir Donald Nicholls V-C [1991] STC 656n (1991 Abr para 190) affirmed.

1979 Act, s 128 now Taxation of Chargeable Gains Act 1992, s 262.

272 Disposal of assets—insurance company—transfer of long term business

The Inland Revenue has issued a Statement of Practice SP 7/93 explaining its approach to the interpretation of the Taxation of Chargeable Gains Act 1992, s 211, which allows a deferral of a charge to corporation tax on chargeable gains when a life assurance company transfers the whole or part of its long term business to another company. Mixed fund assets are to be treated as being within the scope of the deferral provisions, thereby facilitating any transfer in accordance with a scheme sanctioned by a court under the Insurance Companies Act 1982, s 49. An asset which, in the hands of either the transferor or transferee, is partly referable to taxable life assurance business and partly exempt pension business will not, of itself, be denied the deferral provided by s 139, as applied by s 211. These provisions apply to transfers taking place after 11 June 1993. See further *STI*, 17 June 1993.

273 Disposal of assets—reorganisation of share capital—transfer of shares from parent to subsidiary company

Under the Income and Corporation Taxes Act 1970, s 273, the disposal of an asset by one member of a group of companies to another member of the same group is treated in relation to both companies as taking place for such a consideration as will give rise neither to a chargeable gain nor to an allowable loss for the disposal; the gain or loss only arises when the asset is disposed of outside the group. Under the Capital Gains Tax Act 1979, s 78, the reorganisation of a company's share capital is not to be treated as involving a disposal.

Shares in a company were transferred to the taxpayer company by its parent company in exchange for an issue of shares in the taxpayer company. The transferred shares were subsequently disposed of outside the group by the taxpayer company. The question arose as to the amount of the consideration which the taxpayer company was to be treated as having given for the shares and the amount of capital gain realised by it on the disposal of the shares. A Special Commissioner confirmed the assessment to corporation tax on the taxpayer company. This decision was upheld on appeal, the court holding that in computing the taxpayer company's gain, it was to be treated as having acquired the shares for a consideration equal to the base cost of the shares to the parent company and not their market value at the time of the transaction. The taxpayer company appealed. *Held*, the decision in *Westcott (Inspector of Taxes) v Woolcombers Ltd* [1987] STC 600, CA (1987 Abr para 1288), had been superseded by subsequent legislation. The amount of the consideration that the taxpayer company was to be treated as having given for the acquisition was their market value at the date of their acquisition by it, not by reference to the base cost of the shares to the parent company. The rise in value of the shares was rolled over in the taxpayer company's shares which were still in the group and thus remained unrealised for tax purposes. Accordingly, the appeal would be allowed.

NAP Holdings UK Ltd v Whittles (Inspector of Taxes) [1993] STC 592 (Court of Appeal: Ralph Gibson, Nolan and Hirst LJJ). Decision of Millett J [1992] STC 59 (1991 Abr para 193) reversed.

1970 Act, s 273 now Taxation of Chargeable Gains Act 1992, s 171. 1979 Act, s 78 now 1992 Act, s 127.

274 Exemptions and reliefs—annual exempt amount

The Capital Gains Tax (Annual Exempt Amount) Order 1993, SI 1993/760 (made on 16 March 1993), provides that for the year 1993–94 an individual is exempt from capital gains tax on taxable gains not exceeding £6,000. This applies unless Parliament otherwise determines.

The Capital Gains Tax (Annual Exempt Amount) (No 2) Order 1993, SI 1993/2947 (made on 30 November 1993), provides that for the year 1994–95 an individual is exempt from capital gains tax on taxable gains not exceeding £6,000. This applies unless Parliament otherwise determines.

275 Exemptions and reliefs—disposal of part of business—relief—retirement relief

The taxpayer was a 60-year-old farmer who kept beef cattle and sheep. He sold part of his land including the farmhouse. On the land retained stood a covered cattle yard in which calves were reared. He thereafter reduced his calf-rearing activities, running down his herd in anticipation of planning permission being attained for the cattle yard. A year later, planning permission was granted and the taxpayer sold the yard. He continued farming but on a reduced scale, and later stopped rearing calves. He was assessed for capital gains tax in respect of the sale and was refused retirement relief. On his appeal, the General Commissioners granted him relief. On the Crown's appeal, *held*, the sole issue was whether the disposition by the taxpayer of the cattle yard amounted to a disposal of part of a business for the purposes of the Finance Act 1985, s 69(2)(a). The commissioners had found a fundamental change in the taxpayer's business. However, that change pre-dated the sale of the yard and it was not the sale that caused the taxpayer to change the nature of his business but the prospect of obtaining planning permission. The sale was not a disposal of part of the taxpayer's business of farming within the meaning of s 69. Therefore, retirement relief from capital gains tax was not available to the taxpayer on the sale of a cattle yard for which he had acquired planning permission. Accordingly, the appeal would be allowed.

Pepper (Inspector of Taxes) v Daffurn [1993] STC 466 (Chancery Division: Jonathan Parker J).

Finance Act 1985, s 69 now Taxation of Chargeable Gains Act 1992, s 163.

276 Exemption and reliefs—disposal of private residence—electing principal private residence

The Capital Gains Tax Act 1979, s 101(5) provides that where it is necessary to determine which of two or more residences is an individual's main residence for any period the individual may conclude that question by notice in writing to the inspector given within two years from the beginning of that period.

A year after purchasing a farmhouse the taxpayer purchased another property. Eighteen months later he gave notice to the tax inspector under the Capital Gains Tax Act 1979, s 101(5) that the farmhouse be treated as his principal private residence. A year later he sold the farmhouse which realised a capital gain which was alleged to be subject to capital gains tax. The matter came before the special commissioner who accepted the taxpayer's claim that he was entitled to relief from the tax on the basis that the farm house was to be treated as his principal private residence and that his election took effect for a period of two years prior to the date on which he had given it. On appeal by the Inland Revenue, *held*, where a taxpayer owned more than one house he could, for the purposes of obtaining relief from capital gains tax under the Capital Gains Tax Act 1979, s 101(5), elect which was his principal private residence. That election was to be given to the tax inspector within two years after the beginning of the period of the ownership of the two houses. Accordingly, the appeal would be allowed.

Griffin (Inspector of Taxes) v Craig-Harvey [1994] STC 54 (Chancery Division: Vinelott J).

Capital Gains Tax Act 1979, s 101 now Taxation of Chargeable Gains Act 1992, s 222.

277 Exemptions and reliefs—gilt-edged securities

The Capital Gains Tax (Gilt-edged Securities) Order 1993, SI 1993/950, adds further gilt-edged securities to the list set out in the Taxation of Chargeable Gains Act 1992, Sch 9, Pt II, any gain accruing on the disposal of which is exempt from capital gains tax in accordance with s 115.

278 Exemptions and reliefs—loan—co-guarantors—contributions payable by co-guarantors

The taxpayer company, a member of a group of companies, together with ten other companies in the group, entered into a composite joint and several guarantee with a bank whereby the liabilities of each of the companies in the group to the bank were guaranteed by all the other companies in the group as co-guarantors. Demands in respect of certain debts made by the bank against two of the companies, which were unable to meet the demands, were met by the taxpayer under the guarantee. The taxpayer, which received no contributions from its co-guarantors in respect of the payment, claimed relief under the Capital Gains Tax Act 1979, s 136(4) on the full amount of the payment. A Special Commissioner decided that the taxpayer was entitled to loss relief pursuant to s 136(4), only on one-third of the amount paid by it on the basis that potential contributions from the two other companies in the group which were solvent were "payable" to the taxpayer within the meaning of s 136(4). On appeal by the taxpayer, *held*, there was no compelling reason why the word "payable" in s 136(4) should not bear its ordinary meaning. A sum of money was payable if it ought to be paid forthwith; and it ought to be so paid when all the conditions which entitled the claimant to call for immediate payment had been satisfied. The amount so payable and which could be recovered in the liquidation of an insolvent co-guarantor should be taken into account as a contribution payable by that co-guarantor for the purposes of s 136(4). The possibility of recovery from insolvent co-guarantors should not be disregarded unless it was clear that they were not merely insolvent in the sense that they were unable to pay their debts as they fell due or that the value of their assets was less than the amount of their liabilities but had no assets available to meet the claims of unsecured creditors. The commissioner was not wrong to hold that contributions were payable to the taxpayer by other companies in the group. Accordingly, the appeal would be dismissed.

Leisureking Ltd v Cushing (Inspector of Taxes) [1993] STC 46 (Chancery Division: Chadwick J).

1979 Act, s 136(4) now Taxation of Chargeable Gains Act 1992, s 253(4).

279 Exemptions and reliefs—private residence—residence occupied by dependent relative

The Inland Revenue has published a revised concession D20 concerning the capital gains tax relief for private residences occupied by dependent relatives. Where relief is claimed under the Capital Gains Tax Act 1979, s 105 (repealed with effect for disposals on or after 6 April 1988 and replaced by Taxation of Chargeable Gains Act 1992, s 226) in respect of the disposal by an individual of a dwelling house which has at any time been the sole residence of a dependent relative, payments of council tax by the dependent relative will not be taken into account in calculating the owner's income from the property but any mortgage payments by the dependent relative will be taken into account. See further *STI*, 26 August 1993.

280 Exemptions and reliefs—rollover relief—compulsory acquisition of freehold by tenant

The Inland Revenue has issued a revised Statement of Practice SP 13/93 concerning capital gains tax rollover relief where tenants exercise rights to buy the freehold reversion of a property under the Leasehold Reform Act 1967 or the Leasehold Reform, Housing and Urban Development Act 1993. Subject to the general conditions for relief, where a landlord sells the freehold of his property or grants a new lease to a tenant under those provisions, the Revenue will accept a claim to rollover relief under the Taxation of Chargeable Gains Act 1992, s 247, subject to the general provisions of that section being met. The statement applies to claims made after 29 October 1990, provided that they are within the normal time limits for s 247, and has been issued because the earlier Statement of Practice SP 7/90, which it replaces, did not extend to the 1993 Act. See further *STI*, 23 September 1993.

281 Exemptions and reliefs—rollover relief—replacement of business assets—acquisition of freehold interest without vacant possession

Following its acquisition by another company, the taxpayer company sold its trading premises and moved into the premises of its parent company. Two years later, using gains acquired on the sale of the old premises, the taxpayer acquired the freehold interest in new premises which were subject to a lease and underlease. It was unable to obtain vacant possession but the parent company acquired the underlease some months later and it and the taxpayer thenceforth traded from the new premises. The taxpayer claimed rollover relief on the disposal of the old premises against the cost of the acquisition of the new premises. At first instance, it was held that the new premises had not been "taken into use, and used only, for the purposes of [the taxpayer's] trade" for the purposes of the Capital Gains Tax Act 1979, s 115 under which the claim was made. Section 115, which allowed rollover relief if the consideration obtained for the disposal of old assets was applied by the taxpayer in acquiring other assets, referred to the new assets not an interest in them. Further, only one acquisition was contemplated by that provision. The taxpayer's claim involved two acquisitions, ie its acquisition of the freehold interest and the parent company's acquisition of the underlease. The requirements of s 115 were therefore held not to have been satisfied and, accordingly, the claim would fail. On appeal by the taxpayer, *held*, the court at first instance had been correct in holding that the transactions did not in the face of the plain wording of the 1979 Act, s 115(1) attract the relief. Accordingly, the appeal would be dismissed.

Campbell Connelly & Co Ltd v Barnett (Inspector of Taxes) (1993) Times, 9 December (Court of Appeal: Dillon, Mann and Hirst LJJ). Decision of Knox J [1992] STC 316 (1992 Abr para 245) affirmed.

1979 Act, s 115 now Taxation of Chargeable Gains Act 1992, s 152.

282 Exemptions and reliefs—stock lending

See para 1468.

283 Settled property—creation of overseas trusts—assessment of gain

The Finance Act 1981, s 80 provides that capital gains of non-resident settlements shall be computed as the amount on which the trustees would have been chargeable to capital gains tax if they had been resident or ordinarily resident in the United Kingdom. The Finance Act 1988, Sch 10 provides that, in the case of settled property where the settlor has an interest, where chargeable gains accrue to trustees they shall not be chargeable to tax in respect of those gains which shall instead be treated as having accrued to the settlor.

It has been held that the 1988 Act is intended to prevent a taxpayer from paying a lower rate of tax by settling assets on trustees and deals with the case where trustees are chargeable to tax on realised gains. The amount computed under the 1981 Act, s 80 is to be treated as a chargeable gain accruing to the beneficiaries.

De Rothschild v Lawrenson [1994] STC 8 (Chancery Division: Vinelott J).

Finance Act 1981, s 80 consolidated in the Taxation of Chargeable Gains Act 1992, s 87. Finance Act 1988, Sch 10 repealed by the Taxation of Chargeable Gains Act 1992, s 290(3), Sch 12.

284 Settled property—creation of overseas trusts—identity of settlor

The Finance Act 1965, s 24 provides that dispositions which are varied by a deed of family arrangement not less than two years after a testator's death are to be regarded as being made by the testator.

Under the terms of his will a father, a resident of Jersey, bequeathed one half of his personal estate to his daughter, a United Kingdom resident. By a deed of family arrangement made less than two years after her father's death the daughter settled her share of the estate on Jersey trustees to be held on trusts for herself and her family, and a Special Commissioner assessed her as being liable to the capital gains tax on non-resident settlements but not liable to the capital gains tax on the payments made to her by the trustees. On appeal by the Crown, that assessment was discharged on the ground that on a true construction of the 1965 Act, s 24 the daughter ought to have been regarded as the settlor. On the daughter's appeal, *held*, deeming provisions did not require the abandonment of the rule that in construing a statute the grammatical and ordinary sense of the words used had to be adhered to unless that would lead to an absurdity or inconsistency. The trial judge should have construed the provisions of s 24 literally, and there had been no grounds for his decision to give a limited interpretation to those provisions. Accordingly, the appeal would be allowed.

Marshall (Inspector of Taxes) v Kerr [1993] STC 360 (Court of Appeal: Balcombe and Simon Brown LJJ and Peter Gibson J). Decision of Harman J [1991] STC 686 (1991 Abr para 201) reversed.

1965 Act, s 24 now Taxation of Chargeable Gains Act 1992, s 62.

CARRIERS

Halsbury's Laws of England (4th edn) Vol 5(1) (reissue), paras 401–604

285 Carriage by air
See AVIATION.

286 Carriage by rail
See RAILWAYS, INLAND WATERWAYS AND PIPE-LINES.

287 Carriage by sea
See SHIPPING AND NAVIGATION.

288 Common transport policy
See EUROPEAN COMMUNITIES.

289 International carriage of goods—carriage by road—dangerous goods—fees
The International Carriage of Dangerous Goods by Road (Fees) (Amendment) Regulations 1993, SI 1993/3067 (in force on 2 January 1994), amends the 1988 Regulations, SI 1988/370 (as amended). The amendments reduce the fee payable (1) in respect of certain inspections in relation to an application for an ADR certificate; (2) where a vehicle fails to pass an inspection and arrangements are made for an inspection to be carried out not more than 14 days after the first inspection; (3) for the issue of an ADR certificate which has been lost or destroyed.

290 International carriage of goods—perishable foodstuffs
The International Carriage of Perishable Foodstuffs (Amendment) Regulations 1993, SI 1993/1589 (in force on 18 July 1993), further amend the 1985 Regulations, SI 1985/1071, so as to alter the definition of the Agreement on the International Carriage of Perishable Foodstuffs and on the Special Equipment to be used for such Carriage (ATP) in order to take account of a further amendment to that agreement.

CHARITIES

Halsbury's Laws of England (4th edn) Vol 5(2) (reissue), paras 1–600

291 Articles
Charities Act 1992, William Cohen: Estates Gazette, 20 March 1993, p 103
Charitable Giving, Gordon Pickering (on tax-efficient donations): 137 SJ 1170
Local Authorities and Charities, Francesca Quint: 155 LG Rev 922, 1002
Tax Treatment of Charities, Tim Good: Tax Journal, Issue 231, p 16

292 Accounts—auditors—failure to identify irregularities in accounts
The annual report of the Charity Commissioners 1992 (HC 651), para 95 refers to an instance where an employee of a charity who was involved in fund-raising stole a substantial sum of money from the charity. The irregularities were not identified by the auditors and in a 12-month period it was estimated that some £400,000 had been taken. The report states that, in recognition of this, the auditors had agreed to make a "substantial payment" to the charity.

293 Charitable purpose—efficiency of armed forces—shooting clubs
Reliance has been placed for a number of years on Re Stephens, Giles v Stephens (1892) 8 TLR 792 to establish the charitable status of rifle and pistol clubs. The Charity Commissioners now regard that decision as authority for no more than that the promotion of the teaching of the general public in the use of weapons used by the armed forces is charitable. Even if it were to be

regarded as of wider application, circumstances have so changed since it was delivered that it cannot be relied upon by shooting clubs seeking charitable status by reason of the promotion of the security of the nation and defence of the realm; the modern army does not rely on the expert shooting skills of soldiers in the way in which it did in the late nineteenth century and changes affecting recruitment for the armed forces have rendered anachronistic the view that rifle and pistol clubs fulfil a role as a semi-trained third line of reserve for the armed forces.

Re City of London Rifle and Pistol Club and Burnley Rifle Club, Decisions of the Charity Commissioners, Vol 1, p 4.

294 Charitable purpose—freemen and their widows—extension of class—application to borough as a whole

Two institutions of the borough of Huntingdon were known as the Huntingdon Commons for the benefit of Freemen and Widows of Freemen in the Ancient Borough of Huntingdon, ("the Commons Charity") and the second was called the Lammas Rights in the Ancient Borough of Huntingdon ("the Lammas Charity"). The object of the Commons Charity was described as "provision of income for the freemen and freemen's widows of Huntingdon". In the case of the Lammas Charity the object was described as "general benefits of the freemen and freemen's widows of the former borough of Huntingdon". The class of freemen entitled to benefit had reduced in number whilst the annual benefit to a freeman was more than the Charity Commissioners considered to be consistent with the application of charitable funds. It was suggested that the trustees of both charities apply for a scheme to provide that income only be paid to freemen in need and the surplus applied to help the poor and sick of the borough. In an application issued on behalf of the plaintiffs who were the trustees of both charities, *held*, whilst the original class of freemen had been a suitable class for charitable purposes, the effect of the Municipal Corporations Act 1835, and its statutory successors had been to undermine the social and economic importance of the freemen and there would come a time when the class of freemen would cease to exist altogether. Therefore a scheme should be directed pursuant to the Charities Act 1960, s 13(1)(d) to widen the class to include the inhabitants of the ancient borough as a whole. Accordingly, the application would be allowed.

Peggs v Lamb [1993] 2 WLR 1 (Chancery Division: Morritt J).

295 Charitable trust—variation—pictures given in trust to college as decoration

The Charity Commissioners, in agreeing to a scheme to vary a trust under which pictures had been given to what is now the Royal Holloway and Bedford New College to enable some of them to be sold, noted the concern expressed that their decision might be regarded as a precedent for the sale of items by museums, art galleries and libraries. They stated that any scheme for the sale of items held in trust by a charity would be carefully scrutinised. Further, the pictures in question had been donated to the college for the "decoration" of the college buildings; the commissioners regarded such decoration as a different purpose from the education of the students attending the college and pointed out that works of art, artefacts and books donated to museums, art galleries and libraries were in a different legal position to the pictures in this case.

Re Royal Holloway and Bedford New College, Decisions of the Charity Commissioners, Vol 1, p 21.

296 Charities Act 1993

The Charities Act 1993 consolidates the Charitable Trustees Incorporation Act 1872, the Charities Act 1960 and the Charities Act 1992, Pt I. The Act received the royal assent on 27 May 1993 and comes into force on 1 August 1993. A table showing the destination of enactments consolidated appears opposite.

DESTINATION TABLE

This table shows in column (1) the enactments repealed by the Charities Act 1993, s 98(2), Sch 7 ante, and in column (2) the provisions of that Act corresponding thereto.

In certain cases the enactment in column (1), though having a corresponding provision in column (2) is not, or not wholly, repealed as it is still required, or partly required, for the purposes of other legislation.

A dash adjacent to a repealed or revoked provision indicates that that provision is spent, unnecessary or for some other reason not reproduced.

(1)	(2)	(1)	(2)
Charitable Trustees Incorporation Act 1872 (c 24)	**Charities Act 1993 (c 10)**	**Charities Act 1960 (c 58)**	**Charities Act 1993 (c 10)**
		s 4(2A)	s 3(3)
s 1	s 50	s 4(3)–(7)	s 3(4)–(8)
s 2	s 51	s 4(7A), (7B)	s 3(9), (10)
s 3	s 52	s 4(8)	s 3(11)
s 4	s 53	s 4(8A)	s 3(12)
s 5	s 54	s 4(8B)	s 86(1)
s 6	s 55	s 4(9)	s 3(14)
s 6A	s 56	s 4(10)	Rep 1973 c 16, s 1(4), Sch 2, Pt I
s 7	s 57	s 5	s 4
s 8	s 58	s 6(1)–(5)	s 8(1)–(5)
s 9	Rep 1949 c 47, s 52(10), Sch 11, Pt V	s 6(6)	Rep 1992 c 41, ss 6(4), 78(2), Sch 7
s 10	s 59	s 6(7), (8)	s 8(6), (7)
s 11	Rep 1960 c 46, s 4(2), Schedule	s 6(9)	Rep 1992 c 41, ss 6(6), 78(2), Sch 7
s 12	s 60	s 7(1)–(3)	s 9(1)–(3)
s 12A	s 61	s 7(4)	Rep 1992 c 41, ss 7(3), 78(2), Sch 7
s 13	Rep 1888 c 42, s 13, Schedule	s 7(5), (6)	s 9(4), (5)
s 14	s 62	s 8(1), (2)	Rep 1992 c 41, ss 47, 78(2), Sch 3, para 2(a), Sch 7
s 15	—	s 8(3)–(6)	s 69(1)–(4)
Schedule	Rep 1992 c 41, ss 48, 78(2), Sch 4, para 11	s 8(7)	Rep 1992 c 41, ss 47, 78(2), Sch 3, para 2(e), Sch 7
		s 8(14)	s 86(1)
Imperial War Museum Act 1920 (c 16)	**Charities Act 1993 (c 10)**	s 9	s 84
		s 10(1)–(5)	s 76
s 5	Sch 2, para (u)	s 10(6), (7)	Rep 1972 c 70, s 272(1), Sch 30
		s 11	s 77
National Maritime Museum Act 1934 (c 43)	**Charities Act 1993 (c 10)**	s 12	s 78
		s 13	s 13
s 7	Sch 2, para (v)	s 14(1)	s 14(1)
		s 14(1A)	s 14(2)
Charities Act 1960 (c 58)	**Charities Act 1993 (c 10)**	s 14(2)–(4)	s 14(3)–(5)
		s 14(4A)	s 14(6)
s 1	s 1	s 14(5)	s 14(7)
s 2	Rep 1973 c 16, s 1(1)(a), (4), Sch 2, Pts II, III	s 14(5A), (5B)	s 14(8), (9)
s 3(1)–(7)	s 2	s 14(6), (7)	s 14(10), (11)
s 3(8)	Rep 1973 c 16, s 1(4), Sch 2, Pt III	s 15	s 15
s 4(1), (2)	s 3(1), (2)	s 16(1)	s 21(1)
		s 16(2)	1992 c 41, ss 47, 78(2), Sch 3, para 4(b), Sch 7

(1)	(2)	(1)	(2)
Charities Act 1960 (c 58)	Charities Act 1993 (c 10)	Charities Act 1960 (c 58)	Charities Act 1993 (c 10)
s 16(3), (4)	s 21(2), (3)	s 30BB	s 67
s 16(5)	ss 21(4), 97(3)	s 30C	s 68
s 17(1), (2)	s 22(1), (2)	s 31	Rep 1992 c 41, ss 47, 78(2), Sch 3, para 12, Sch 7
s 17(2A)	s 22(3)		
s 17(3)–(6)	s 22(4)–(7)		
s 18(1)–(6)	s 16(1)–(6)	s 32(1)	s 46(1)
s 18(6A)	s 16(7)	s 32(2), (3)	s 46(2)
s 18(7)–(10)	s 16(8)–(11)	s 33	s 81
s 18(11)	s 16(12), (13)	s 34	s 82
s 18(12), (13)	s 16(14), (15)	s 35(1)–(5)	s 83
s 18(14)	s 86(1)	s 35(6)	—
s 19(1)–(7)	s 17(1)–(7)	s 36	s 93
s 19(8)	s 17(8), (9)	s 37(1)–(5)	s 79(1)–(5)
s 20(1)	s 18(1)	s 37(6)–(9)	s 79(8)–(11)
s 20(1A)	s 18(2)	s 38(1), (2)	Rep 1973 c 16, s 1(4), Sch 2, Pt I
s 20(2)–(7)	s 18(3)–(8)		
s 20(7A), (7B)	s 18(9), (10)	s 39(1)	Rep 1973 c 16, s 1(4), Sch 2, Pt I
s 20(8), (9)	s 18(11), (12)		
s 20(9A)	s 18(13)	s 40(1)–(4)	s 89
s 20(10)	s 18(14)	s 40(5)	Cf Sch 6, paras 1(3), 2, 3(3)
s 20(10A)	s 18(15)		
s 20(11)	Rep 1973 c 16, s 1(4), Sch 2, Pt III	s 40A	s 91
		s 41	s 88
s 20A	s 19	s 42(1), (2)	s 92
s 21	s 20	s 42(3)	Rep 1977 c 38, s 32(4), Sch 5, Pt IV
s 21A	s 35(1)		
s 22(1)–(5)	s 24(1)–(5)	s 43(1)	ss 3(6), (8), 4(2), 19(6), 30(2)
s 22(6)	Rep 1992 c 41, ss 47, 78(2), Sch 3, para 9(a), Sch 7		
		s 43(2A)	s 86(3)
s 22(7)–(9)	s 24(6)–(8)	s 43(3)	s 86(1)
s 22(10)	Rep 1986 c 60, s 212(2), (3), Sch 16, para 1(a), Sch 17, Pt I	s 44	Rep 1992 c 41, s 78(2), Sch 7
		s 45(1)–(5)	s 96(1)–(5)
		s 45(6)	s 3(13)
s 22(11)	s 24(9)	s 46	s 97(1), (2)
s 22(12)	Rep 1973 c 16, s 1(4), Sch 2, Pt III	s 47	Rep 1973 c 36, s 41(1), Sch 6, Pt I
s 22A	s 25	s 49(2)†	s 100(2), (4)
s 23(1)–(4)	s 26(1)–(4)	Sch 1	
s 23(5), (6)	s 26(5)–(7)	para 1(1)–(5)	Sch 1, para 1
s 23A	s 27	para 1(6)	Rep 1973 c 16, s 1(4), Sch 2, Pt I
s 24	s 29		
s 25(1)–(3)	s 30(1)–(3)	para 2(1), (2)	Sch 1, para 2
s 25(4)	s 30(2)	para 2(3)	Rep 1973 c 16, s 1(4), Sch 2, Pt I
s 25(5)	s 30(5)		
s 26	s 31	para 3	Sch 1, para 3
s 26A	s 32	para 4	Sch 1, para 4
s 27	Rep 1992 c 41, ss 37(5), 78(2), Sch 7	Sch 2	
		para (a)	Sch 2, paras (a), (u), (v)
s 28(1)–(8)	s 33	paras (b), (c)	Sch 2, paras (b), (c)
s 28(9)	—	paras (ca)–(cd)	Sch 2, paras (k)–(n)
s 28A	s 34	para (ce)	Sch 2, para (o)
s 29	Rep 1992 c 41, s 78(2), Sch 7	paras (ce)–(ch)	Sch 2, paras (q)–(t)
		para (d)	Sch 2, para (p)
s 30	s 63	paras (da)–(dd)	Rep 1992 c 44, s 11(2), (3), Sch 8, Pt II, para 10(2), Sch 9
s 30A	s 64		
s 30B	s 65		
s 30BA	s 66	para (e)	Sch 2, para (w)

† Not repealed

(1)	(2)
Charities Act 1960 (c 58)	Charities Act 1993 (c 10)

Sch 2	
para (f)	Sch 2, para (x)
para (g)	Sch 2, para (y)
para (h)	Sch 2, para (z)
para (i)	Sch 2, para (za)
para (j)	Rep 1990/1765, art 3
Sch 3	
Sch 4	
Sch 5	Rep 1973 c 16, s 1(4), Sch 2, Pt I
Sch 7	Rep 1973 c 16, s 1(4), Sch 2, Pt I

(1)	(2)
London Government Act 1963 (c 33)	Charities Act 1993 (c 10)

s 4(4)†	s 79(5)
s 81(9)(b)	ss 76(1)–(5), 77, 78
s 81(9)(c)	Sch 3

(1)	(2)
Museum of London Act 1965 (c 17)	Charities Act 1993 (c 10)

s 11	Sch 2, para (z)

(1)	(2)
British Library Act 1972 (c 54)	Charities Act 1993 (c 10)

s 4(2)	Sch 2, para (za)

(1)	(2)
Local Government Act 1972 (c 70)	Charities Act 1993 (c 10)

s 210(9)(a)	s 76(1)
s 210(9)(b)	s 77(1), (4), (5)
s 210(9)(c)	s 78(1)
s 210(9)(d)	—
s 210(9)(e)	s 79(6), (7)
s 210(9)(f)	Sch 3

(1)	(2)
Education Act 1973 (c 16)	Charities Act 1993 (c 10)

s 2(7)★	Sch 4, para 1
Sch 1	
para 1(1)	ss 3(6), (8), 86(1)
para 1(3)	—

(1)	(2)
Endowments and Glebe Measure 1976 (No 4)	Charities Act 1993 (c 10)

s 44	s 96(2)

(1)	(2)
National Heritage Act 1983 (c 47)	Charities Act 1993 (c 10)

Sch 5	
para 4	Sch 2, paras (k)–(n)

(1)	(2)
Companies Consolidation (Consequential Provisions Act 1985 (c 9)	Charities Act 1993 (c 10)

Sch 2★	Cf Sch 8, Pt I, para 1

(1)	(2)
Charities Act 1985 (c 20)	Charities Act 1993 (c 10)

s 1	Cf Sch 8, Pt I, para 2

(1)	(2)
Financial Services Act 1986 (c 60)	Charities Act 1993 (c 10)

Sch 16	
para 1(a)	—
para 1(b)	s 24(9)

(1)	(2)
Education Reform Act 1988 (c 40)	Charities Act 1993 (c 10)

Sch 12, Pt I	
para 9	s 79(9)
para 10	Sch 2, para (d), (w)
Sch 12, Pt III	
para 63	Sch 2, paras (e), (f), (g), (w)
para 64(1), (2)	Sch 2, paras (h), (i)
para 64(3)	Sch 2, para (w)

(1)	(2)
Companies Act 1989 (c 40)	Charities Act 1993 (c 10)

s 111(1)	ss 63(1), 64, 65, 68
s 111(2)	s 97(1)

(1)	(2)
Courts and Legal Services Act 1990 (c 41)	Charities Act 1992 (c 10)

Sch 10, para 14	Sch 1, para 1

(1)	(2)
Further and Higher Education Act 1992 (c 13)	Charities Act 1992 (c 10)

Sch 8	
para 69	Sch 2, paras (j), (w)

★Repealed in part
† Not repealed

(1)	(2)	(1)	(2)
Charities Act 1992 (c 41)	Charities Act 1993 (c 10)	Charities Act 1992 (c 41)	Charities Act 1993 (c 10)
s 1(1)†	s 97(1)	s 25(2)	s 84
s 1(2)	ss 96, 97(1)	s 25(3), (4)	s 47(2), (3)
s 1(3)	s 97(1), (2)	s 26	s 48
s 1(4)†	s 97(3)	s 27	s 49
s 2(1)	—	s 28	s 32
s 2(2), (3)	s 3(1), (2)	s 31	s 23
s 2(4)	s 3(3)	s 32	s 36
s 2(5)	s 3(5)	s 33	s 37
s 2(6)	s 3(9), (10)	s 34	s 38
s 2(7)	ss 3(12), 86(1)	s 35	s 39
s 2(8), (9)	—	s 37(1)–(4)	s 40
s 3	s 5	s 37(5)	—
s 4	s 6	s 38	s 70
s 5	s 7	s 39	s 71
s 6(1)	—	s 40	s 64(2)–(4)
s 6(2)	s 8(3)	s 41	s 66
s 6(3)	s 8(5)	s 42	s 67
s 6(4)	—	s 43	s 74
s 6(5)	s 8(6)	s 44	s 75
s 6(6)	—	s 45(1)–(4)	s 72(1)–(4)
s 7(1)	—	s 45(5)	—
s 7(2)	s 9(1)	s 45(6)–(8)	s 72(5)–(7)
s 7(3)	—	s 46	s 73
s 7(4)	s 9(5)	ss 47, 48	—
s 8(1)	—	s 51(1), (2), (6)	s 85(1), (2)
s 8(2)	s 18(1), (2)	s 51(3)–(5)	s 85(3)–(5)
s 8(3), (4)	s 18(3), (4)	s 52	s 10
s 8(5)	s 18(8)–(10)	s 53	s 12
s 8(6)–(8)	s 18(11)–(13)	s 54(1)	s 11(1), cf Sch 6, para 29(8)
s 8(9)	s 18(14), (15)	s 54(2)	s 11(2)
s 8(10)	—	s 54(3)	s 11(3), cf Sch 6, para 29(8)
s 9	s 19	s 54(4)	s 11(4)
s 10(1)	s 63(2)–(6)	s 55	s 94
s 10(2)	—	s 56(1), (2)	s 87(1), (2)
s 11	s 34	s 56(3)	s 88
s 12(1)	s 80(1), Sch 1, para 3	s 56(4), (5)	s 89(1)–(4), cf Sch 6, para 29(7)
s 12(2)–(6)	s 80(2)–(6)	s 56(6)	ss 87(1), 88, 89
s 13(1)	—	s 57	s 90
s 13(2)–(5)	s 16(4)–(7)	s 75(b)	s 95
s 13(6)	ss 16(5), 86(1)	s 76(1)(a)	s 91(1)
s 14	s 35	s 77★	s 86
s 15(1)	—	s 79(3)†	s 100(2)
s 15(2), (3)	s 14(1), (2)	s 79(4)	s 100(3)
s 15(4), (5)	s 14(5), (6)	s 79(5)	s 100(5)
s 15(6)	s 14(8), (9)	Sch 1	—
s 16	s 25	Sch 2	Sch 5
s 17	s 27	Sch 3	
s 18	s 28	para 1	s 1(2)
s 19	s 41	para 2(a)	—
s 20	s 42	para 2(b), (c)	s 69(1), (2)
s 21(1)–(8)	s 43(1)–(8)	para 2(d)	s 69(4)
s 21(9)	s 43(9), cf Sch 8, Pt I, para 1	para 2(e)	—
s 22	s 44	para 3	s 84
s 23	s 45	para 4(a)	s 21(1)
s 24(1)	s 46(1)	para 4(b)	—
s 24(2)–(7)	s 46(3)–(8)	para 5(a)	s 22(2)
s 25(1)	s 47(1)		

★Repealed in part
† Not repealed

(1)	(2)	(1)	(2)
Charities Act 1992 (c 41)	Charities Act 1993 (c 10)	Museums and Galleries Act 1992 (c 44)	Charities Act 1993 (c 10)
Sch 3		Sch 4	
para 5(b)	s 22(3)	para 3	s 52
para 5(c)	s 22(5), (6)	para 4	s 53
para 6	s 16(1)	para 5	s 54
para 7	s 17(6)	para 6	s 56
para 8	s 20(2), (3)	para 7	s 57
para 9	s 24(8)	para 8	s 58
para 10	s 33(3), (6)	para 9	ss 60, 61
para 11	s 68(1)	para 10	s 62
para 12	—	Sch 6	
para 13	s 46(2)	para 13(2)	—
para 14	s 82(2)	Sch 7	—
para 15	s 91(1)–(5)		
para 16	s 88		
para 17	s 86(3)	Museums and Galleries Act 1992 (c 44)	Charities Act 1993 (c 10)
para 18(a)	s 96(3)		
para 18(b)	ss 96(4), 97(1)		
para 19	s 97(1), (2)		
para 20	Sch 1, para 2	Sch 8, Pt I	
para 21	Sch 1, para 3(4), (6)	para 4	Sch 2, para (p)
para 22	—	Sch 8, Pt II	
Sch 4		para 10(1)	Sch 2, paras (q)–(t)
para 1	s 50	para 10(2)	—
para 2	s 51	Sch 9★	—

*Repealed in part

297   Charities Act 1993—exempt charities

The Exempt Charities Order 1993, SI 1993/2359 (in force on 30 September 1993), exempts Cranfield University from the requirement to be registered with the Charity Commissioners, by declaring the University to be an exempt charity within the meaning of the Charities Act 1993.

298   Fund-raising

In their annual report for 1992 (HC 651), para 97 the Charity Commissioners draw attention to the recruitment of collectors for some charities by unsolicited phone calls, made at random and without checks as to the suitability of the individual concerned. The individuals are supplied with certificates of authority and collection boxes. It seems that some charities take little or no action to pursue the individuals if funds are not forwarded to the charities. The commissioners state that they deprecate this kind of fund-raising and that a number of such cases are under investigation.

299   Land registration—rules

See para 1577.

300   Trustees—sole trustee—local authority

See para 1713.

CHILDREN AND YOUNG PERSONS

Halsbury's Laws of England (4th edn) Vol 5(2) (reissue), paras 601–1392

301   Articles

Adoption, Law and Homosexuality—Can Gay People Adopt a Child?, R Sandland: [1993] 5 JSWFL 321

Adoption Law Reform, Chris Barton: 137 SJ 1198

A Drastic Remedy for a Drastic Situation, Simon Dodgshon (on ex parte residence orders): 157 JP Jo 410

Allocation of Proceedings: Rational or Random Distribution? Glenn Brasse: [1993] Fam Law 178

Applications For Secure Accommodation—A Further Twist in the Labyrinth, Peter Dawson and Robert Stevens: 157 JP Jo 761

Brookside or Stateside: a Residence Battle, Gillian Bishop: 137 SJ 556

Can We Rely on the Children Act? Victor Smith (on the effect of *Nottinghamshire CC v P* [1993] 3 All ER 815 (1992 Abr para 359)): 137 SJ 706

Caring Parents and Absent Parents, Maggie Rae (on the Child Support Act 1991): 143 NLJ 513

Child Abduction—The Hague Convention and Recent Case Law, Christina Sachs: [1993] Fam Law 530, 585

Child Support Act 1991, C E Bazell: 157 JP Jo 101, 117, 131, 151

Child Support Act 1991 Contra-Indications for Ancillary Relief and Contract, Jennifer Bispham and Angeline Greaney: [1993] Fam Law 525

Child Support Act 1991 Net Effect—Dead or Alive? Clifford Bellamy: [1993] Fam Law 633

Child Support Act 1991 Setting Aside Clean Break Consent Orders, Helen Meadows: [1993] Fam Law 635

Children Act 1989, s 34: A Trojan Horse? Glenn Brasse: [1993] Fam Law 55

Children and the Courts, Chris Barton (on the 1992/1993 annual report of the Children Act Advisory Committee): 138 SJ 69

Children's Applications, an Assessment of Understanding in the Light of *Re CT*, David Burrows (see *Re CT (A Minor)* (1993) Independent, 7 May, Times, May 10 (para 420)): [1993] Fam Law 421

Children's Proceedings With a Foreign Element, Michael Nicholls: [1993] Fam Law 685

Complaints About Social and Education Services for Children, Neville Harris: [1993] Fam Law 587

Consent Orders for Periodical Payments, Lesley Vickers: 144 NLJ 55

Contact—Can We Do Better? David McHardy: [1993] Fam Law 528
Contact Implacably Opposed, Robert Stevens: 157 JP Jo 648
Costs Orders Against Legally Aided Persons, District Judge Bullock: [1993] Fam Law 389
Disclosure of Documents in Children Cases, Moira Wright: [1993] Fam Law 348
Failing to Protect Children, Hilaire Barnett: [1993] Fam Law 591
For Better or Worse? Dr Liz Trinder (on the impact of the Children Act 1989 on court processes): [1993] Fam Law 484
Identifying the Issues in Cases Relating to Children, Judith Parker and David Burrows: [1993] Fam Law 637
Injunctive Orders Relating to Children, Judge Nigel Fricker QC: [1993] Fam Law 141, 226
Interviewing Child Witnesses, Brian Ward: 142 NLJ 1547
Involvement of the Punitive Father, Victor Smith: [1993] 157 JP Jo 408
Long-distance Love: Practice Issues in Unmarried Parent Cases, Angela Buckley and Helen Scholar: [1993] Fam Law 81
Maintenance From Abroad, David Hodson and Deborah Wilkin: 137 SJ 1262
Managing Child Maintenance, Prestataire: LS Gaz, 7 April 1993, p 27
On Being a Reasonable Parent, Neil Leighton: [1993] 157 JP Jo 680
Paying Up for Children, Jane Simpson and Louise Spitz (on the Child Support Act 1991): LS Gaz, 24 March 1993, p 2
Payment of Child Support, David Barry: 143 NLJ 1193
Rights of the Child, Dr Dominic McGoldrick (on the UK implementation of the goals agreed by the world summit for children): [1993] Fam Law 536
Say Goodbye to Daddy, P Gallagher (on the Children Act 1989): 137 SJ 906
Section 30—The Acceptable Face of Surrogacy? Eric Blyth (on the Surrogacy Arrangements Act 1985, s 30): [1993] 4 SWFL 248
Spare the Smack? Angela Hodes (on corporal punishment by a child minder): 137 SJ 717
Teething Troubles, Wendy Mantle (on the Child Support Agency): 137 SJ 882
The Child as Client—'Sacking' the Guardian, Philip Bennett and Louise Dunford: [1993] Fam Law 354
The Children Act and the Issue of Delay, Ian Butler et al: [1993] Fam Law 412
The Children Act in Practice—Underlying Themes Revisited, Lorraine M Harding: 157 JP Jo 600, 616
The Dilemma of Parental Choice, Claire Gilham (on withholding medical treatment): 143 NLJ 1219.
The Future of the Civil Court Welfare Service, Jean Graham Hall: 157 JP Jo 613
The Hague Convention on Abduction and Beyond, Alain Cornec (on French practice): [1993] Fam Law 148
The Section 31 Monopoly, Glenn Brasse (on *Nottinghamshire CC v P* [1993] 3 All ER 815 (1992 Abr para 359)): [1993] Fam Law 691
Willing Guardians of Children, Gillian Cockburn and David Hodson (on the testamentary appointment of guardians): 137 SJ 346

302   Adoption—adoption order—contact with natural parent

The mother of a child who had been adopted applied for leave to apply for contact and specific issue orders in respect of the child under the Children Act 1989. No access conditions had been attached pursuant to the Adoption Act 1976, s 12(6) when the adoption order was made. The application stated that the mother wished to have indirect contact. At the hearing of the application, she contended that her application should be considered liberally in the light of research showing that society was moving towards a recognition of the importance of the biological family and that the 1989 Act, by inserting into the 1976 Act machinery for a contact register to which natural parents could apply to be joined on the adoption of their child or at any time thereafter, had recognised the importance of enabling adopted children to re-establish contact with their roots. *Held*, an application by a natural parent for indirect contact with the child after adoption could only be made by way of a condition attached to the adoption order prior to perfection of the order and could not be made afterwards, as such orders were intended to be permanent and final and a fundamental question such as contact, even if confined to indirect contact, ought not to be subsequently reopened unless there was some fundamental change in the circumstances. Notwithstanding any changes in society's understanding of what ought best be done for children whose parenting was through adoption, in the absence of statutory reform, principles determining such applications had to be drawn from current law and practice. There was no evidence of any fundamental change in the circumstances surrounding the case and, accordingly, the application for leave to apply would be dismissed.

Re C (A Minor) (Adopted Child: Contact) [1993] 3 All ER 259 (Family Division: Thorpe J).
Re O (A Minor) (Wardship: Adopted Child) [1978] 2 All ER 27, *Re C (A Minor) (Adoption: Conditions)* [1988] 1 All ER 705, HL (1988 Abr para 1594) applied.

303   Adoption—designation of overseas adoptions—variation

The Adoption (Designation of Overseas Adoptions) (Variation) Order 1993, SI 1993/690 (in force on 5 April 1993), varies the 1973 Order, SI 1973/19, so as to include the People's Republic of China as a designated country so that adoption orders made in any place forming part of the republic are to be recognised in England and Wales.

304   Adoption—freeing order—application—matters to be considered by the court

The Adoption Act 1976, s 6 provides that in reaching any decision relating to the adoption of a child a court or adoption agency must give primary consideration to the need to safeguard and promote the welfare of the child. The 1976 Act, s 18 provides that where, on the application of an adoption agency, the court is satisfied that the child's parents or guardians agree to an adoption order, or that such agreement can be dispensed with under s 16, the court must make an order declaring the child free for adoption.

A local council, which was also an adoption agency within the 1976 Act, made a care order in relation to a child and removed her from her parents after she repeatedly suffered non-accidental injuries. She was placed with foster parents. The council applied for an order freeing the child for adoption. It was common ground that the child would not be returned to her parents and the issue was whether she would be placed with her paternal grandparents or a freeing order made. The judge decided that the child's welfare required that she be placed with her paternal grandparents and made a residence order in their favour. The council appealed, contending that, as an adoption agency, it was subject to the duty to promote the child's welfare under the 1976 Act, s 6 and that reconsideration of that issue by the court constituted a review of the adoption agency's decision. Further, the council contended that the wording of the 1976 Act, s 18 was mandatory and thus where the court had dispensed with the need for parental consent it was required to make a freeing order. *Held*, the fact that an adoption agency had due regard to the 1976 Act, s 6 did not free the court from its duties under that section, nor was the agency's decision binding on the court. The court was required to adopt a two step approach to an application for a freeing order under the 1976 Act, s 18. Only if it considered that a freeing order promoted the child's welfare would it then consider whether parental consent had been given or could be dispensed with. Accordingly, the appeal would be dismissed but the residence order would be varied by adding an order requiring the council to make one of its officers available to assist and advise the paternal grandparents.

Re U (Application to Free for Adoption) [1993] 2 FCR 64 (Court of Appeal: Balcombe, Kennedy and Evans LJJ). *Re D (A Minor) (Adoption: Parental Agreement)* [1990] FCR 615, CA (1991 Abr para 229) applied.

305   Adoption—freeing order—contact order pending adoption

A judge decided that it was in a child's best interests that he be adopted. Dispensing with the agreement of both parents, the judge made an order freeing the child for adoption. Contact between the child and his father was terminated but an order was made for contact for one and a half hours each month with the mother to continue until an adoption order was made. On her appeal against the freeing order, *held*, since the Children Act 1989, a judge could attach a condition of access to a freeing order, thereby both freeing and preserving contact between the child and the natural family pending adoption, because a s 8 application, including a contact application, might be made in any family proceedings which, by virtue of s 8(4)(d), included proceedings under the Adoption Act 1976. The mother, as a former parent (see ss 18(5), 19), retained the right to be heard on contact. Although the contact order could not survive the adoption order, a contact order could now be imposed upon adopters after the making of the adoption order as an alternative to the making of an order with conditions. The mother might still be heard on the question of whether she could have continuing contact after the adoption order was made. When a contact order was made side by side with a freeing order, directions should be given to provide, if possible, for continuity of judicial approach in subsequent hearings to ensure that the judge hearing the adoption application was not faced with an outstanding contact order in favour of a parent who had no right to be heard when the adoption order had the effect of extinguishing the contact order. If a freeing order was made with a s 8 contact order, appropriate directions should be given to ensure that, if possible, the judge who heard the adoption application also heard any contact application affecting the former parent.

Re A (A Minor) (Adoption: Contact Order) [1993] 2 FLR 645 (Court of Appeal: Butler-Sloss, Stuart-Smith and Farquharson LJJ).

306 Adoption—government proposals

The Secretary of State for Health (together with the Welsh Office, the Home Office and the Lord Chancellor's Department) has published a White Paper, *Adoption: The Future* (Cm 2288). It notes the changing background to adoption and puts forward some proposals for changes in the law. These include the possibility of maintaining some contact between an adopted child and his birth family; this would, however, be dependent upon the free consent of the child and his new family. Arrangements will also ensure that adopted children will be made aware of their adoptive status at a suitable age and will be able, if they so desire, to obtain more information about their birth parents provided that the latter agree. Adoption agencies will have a duty to prepare a package of information including health and family history for adopters; the information will be kept in court records and will be available to the adopted child after attaining the age of 18 years. The wishes of the adopted child's parents and guardians as regards religious upbringing will continue to be a matter to which regard will have to be paid so far as is practicable but some status will also be given to the views of the child, so far as these are ascertainable. A broad requirement to have regard to ethnicity or culture will be written into legislation regarding the matching of children and parents; regard will be paid to views on the subject expressed by the birth parents and to the ascertainable wishes of the child. It is also intended to introduce a range of alternatives to adoption. As an alternative to "step-parent" adoption, there would be a "parental responsibility agreement" under which the birth parent and her new spouse would undertake joint parental responsibility, without severing the link between the child and the other birth parent; this would not require a court hearing or an assessment as to suitability, but there would be different consequences under intestacy than under adoption. If adoption is nevertheless preferred, the form of adoption order would not require the birth parent to adopt her own child. Another alternative to adoption would be an inter vivos guardianship order, whereby persons caring for the child would be able to obtain legal recognition for their role without resorting to adoption as such. Any application to dissolve a guardianship order would require prior leave of the court. The paper refers to the 1993 Hague Convention on inter-country adoptions which provides for the mutual recognition of inter-country adoption orders in respect of the parties to the Convention and which ensures that there is no immigration obstacle to such adoptions; the Government intends to ratify the Convention and to adopt the necessary changes in the law. The role of local authorities in inter-country adoptions will be clarified. Efforts have also been made in respect of certain countries where there is no mutual recognition of adoption orders to improve the safeguards against children being released for emigration to the United Kingdom in circumstances which might lead to difficulty or uncertainty about their status and future. Eventually, it will be a criminal offence to bring a child to the United Kingdom for adoption without due authorisation and any person who brings a child to the United Kingdom without entry clearance may become liable for any costs incurred by a local authority in looking after the child. Legislation will be introduced as soon as the legislative programme permits after the 1993–94 parliamentary session.

307 Adoption—parental consent—contact with parents—correct approach

The applicants were the parents of a four-year-old girl. She had been made the subject of a care order and placed with foster parents after a doctor stated that marks appearing on the girl's body indicated sexual abuse, although the parents were given access. The local authority decided that the girl should be rehabilitated with her parents and on that basis the parents withdrew their opposition to the care order. Inquiries were made as to the suitability of the parents and it was decided to abandon plans to rehabilitate the child. The parents applied for residence and/or contact orders whilst the local authority applied for permission to refuse the parents contact with the girl and an order freeing her for adoption. At first instance, the judge determined that there had not been any sexual abuse of the girl but found for the local authority, granting it leave to refuse contact between the girl and her parents and freeing her for adoption. He not only decided that adoption would promote the girl's welfare, but also that the mother was unreasonably withholding her consent. It was acknowledged by all parties that as the parents had never married and the father had no parental responsibility for the girl, his consent was not needed. On appeal by the parents, *held*, the decision regarding adoption was one which the judge was best equipped to make as he had heard and seen the parties and was able to appraise their character and personality, which were a vital basis for any decision. That decision could only be disputed where the judge had erred in law, acted without adequate evidence or made inadequate consideration of the witnesses and their demeanour. The correct approach was for the judge to ask himself whether, in all the circumstances of the case, it was within the band of responses open to the reasonable hypothetical parent to reach the conclusion that, even if the girl were not to live with her natural parents, her welfare could still require that she maintained contact with them. The consent of the parent was not easily overridden but, in this case, the judge had adopted the correct approach and his decision was one which he was entitled to make. Accordingly, the appeal would be dismissed.

Re C (A Minor) (Adoption) (Parental Agreement: Contact) [1993] 2 FLR 260 (Court of Appeal: Balcombe, Steyn and Hoffmann LJJ).

308 Adoption—proceedings—transfer from county court to High Court—foreign children

Senior District Judge Angel, with the approval of the President of the Family Division and the concurrence of the Lord Chancellor, has issued the following *Practice Direction* ([1993] 4 All ER 960).

1. In county court proceedings under the Adoption Act 1976 concerning a child whose place of origin is outside the United Kingdom, the question of the transfer of the case to the High Court might arise.

2. In deciding whether, under the Children (Allocation of Proceedings) Order 1991, SI 1991/1677, such proceedings are appropriate for determination in the High Court, guidance may continue to be derived from *Re N (Minors) (Adoption Proceedings: Venue)* [1987] 1 WLR 829, CA (transfer to be limited to those cases giving rise to issues of complexity, difficulty or gravity).

3. Orders for transfer should not be made of the court's own motion without the parties and the guardian ad litem, if appointed, having the opportunity of making representations on the question of transfer.

4. It will usually be possible for the necessary inquires to be made by letter and for the matter to be determined without a hearing.

5. In the cases where there is an issue as to transfer, a hearing for determination of the issue should be fixed, with notice of the date, time and place given to the parties and the guardian ad litem.

6. It will usually be impracticable to obtain the views of the natural parents or for them to be given notice of any hearing.

309 Adoption—residence requirement

A boy was brought up by his grandparents, who had brought him to the United Kingdom, because his mother was not capable of caring for him and could not be traced. He lived with the grandparents during the week but stayed with his aunt at weekends and holidays. The aunt visited him during the week and made all the decisions as to his upbringing. At the hearing of her application to adopt him, the issue arose as to whether the boy had lived with her for the 13 weeks preceding the making of the order, as required under the Adoption Act 1976, s 13. *Held*, the situation was analogous to one where a child was away at boarding school during the week and so the 1976 Act, s 13 residence requirement was satisfied. Accordingly, the adoption order would be made.

Re KT (A Minor) (Adoption) [1993] Fam Law 567 (Family Division: Ward J).

310 Adoption and contact applications—concurrent applications—confidential information—characteristics of adopters—disclosure to natural parent

A child was placed in care by his mother when he was two months old. He was then made a ward of court and the mother agreed to terminate her access so that the child could be adopted. After the child was placed with prospective adopters the mother changed her mind about adoption and made an application for a contact order. The prospective adopters then made an application to adopt and the two applications were to be heard together. The guardian ad litem felt that information about the health of the adoptive father should be revealed to the natural mother and an order was granted accordingly. The prospective adopters appealed against that order. *Held*, (1) the mother had a right to cross-examine the adopters on the facts available, but she did not have a right to receive the confidential information provided to the judge. In relation to adoption proceedings all the information collected for the case was confidential until it was disclosed. The purpose of the confidentiality was to protect the child. (2) Although it was in the interests of children to be brought up by their natural parents, the presumption in favour of natural parents could be displaced if the parent was not capable of meeting the needs of the child. The assessment of lack of capability was based on the Children Act 1989, s 31. (3) Although the mother had not asked for a residence order, the application for contact was designed to lead to the return of her son and therefore the judge would be bound to consider the prospects of success of a future application for residence. On the facts of the present case if there was any prospect of renewing contact between the mother and the child it would be unlikely that adoption would follow. The question of adoption should therefore not be considered until the issues of contact and future residence had been considered, and the characteristics of the prospective adopters were not relevant to those issues. (4) In relation to the adoption, the matters to be considered included the welfare of the child, in accordance with the Adoption Act 1976, s 6, and whether the parent was unreasonably withholding her agreement under s 16(2)(b) of that Act. A parent had no rights to information about the placement or the adopters but her wishes had to be considered. The views of the adopters on the question of contact were crucial to the reasonableness of the withholding of the agreement. In this case the mother was objecting to the act of adoption itself, and not the particular adopter, therefore information about the disability of the adoptive father would make no difference to her. There should not be unnecessary secrecy, but the provision of information should be balanced against the risk to the child of identification of his placement and destabilisation of his future home. In this case there was a real risk that disclosure would lead to the child being found and the information should not therefore be disclosed. Accordingly, the appeal would be allowed.

Re S (Adoption Application: Disclosure of Information) [1993] 2 FCR 16 (Court of Appeal: Sir Thomas Bingham MR, Butler-Sloss and Hoffmann LJJ).

311 Adoption and contact applications—freeing order—appropriateness of freeing order and interim contact order

A three-year-old girl had been placed with foster parents from the age of three weeks. The local authority applied for a freeing order, claiming that it did not want to subject the foster parents to the stress of making a full adoption application. The girl's natural mother was only prepared to consent to an open adoption whereby she would maintain contact with the child on a regular basis. At first instance, the judge refused the local authority's application but gave leave to the foster parents to commence proceedings for adoption, directing that the girl remain with them in the meantime. He also ordered that the natural parents should have supervised contact with the girl each month. On appeal by the local authority against the judge's orders, *held*, a freeing order was inappropriate in this case, particularly bearing in mind the length of time the girl had lived with her foster parents, the fact that there was no need for confidentiality and that there was no opposition by the natural parents to the child staying with the foster parents. In such circumstances, the court ought to have gone straight to the adoption application. It was wrong to issue an interim contact order before further investigations had been made, preferably with oral evidence. The judge had also been procedurally wrong in not allowing counsel for the local authority to raise arguments as to the unsuitability of an interim contact order being made. Accordingly, the appeal would be dismissed in relation to the freeing order and allowed in relation to the interim contact order.

Re H (A Minor) (Freeing Order) [1993] 2 FLR 325 (Court of Appeal: Ralph Gibson and Butler-Sloss LJJ).

312 Care order—appeal—fresh evidence

Following a history of court actions and domestic violence a supervision order was made in respect of two children and their parents. The local authority appealed against that decision contending the court was wrong in not making a full care order. At the appeal the local authority sought to adduce fresh evidence indicating that subsequent to the order the parents had failed to cooperate and that following another violent incident at the home, the children had been placed with foster parents. The question arose as to how the appellate court was to deal with the fresh evidence that had not been before the court below and for which leave had been given for its production on appeal. *Held*, the appellate court was to consider the original decision in view of the material before the court at that time, ignoring any fresh evidence adduced before the appellate court. If the judge below was plainly wrong or had misdirected himself by including or excluding any matter the appeal would be allowed unless the fresh evidence led to a different conclusion. Where the appellate court was inclined to dismiss the appeal it was necessary to examine the fresh evidence, being mindful of the fact that in this case there were disadvantages in having to decide on affidavit evidence only. In this case it had not been established that the court was wrong on the basis of the original evidence before it, but as the fresh evidence indicated a change in circumstances, the appeal would be allowed.

Croydon London Borough Council v A (No 3) [1992] 2 FLR 350 (Family Division: Hollings J). For earlier related proceedings see [1992] 1 WLR 984 (1992 Abr para 289) and [1992] 3 All ER 788 (1992 Abr para 360).

313 Care order—application for variation of order

In May 1989 the High Court had made an order placing a child in the care of a local authority, and access was terminated. After the Children Act 1989 came into force in October 1991, the child's paternal grandfather made an application for contact under the 1989 Act, s 34, but the local authority contended the application was flawed and applied for it to be dismissed. *Held*, where an order had been made before the 1989 Act had come into force, any application to vary the order had to be made to the High Court, being the court which had made the original order. The application should have been made by way of summons backed by affidavit evidence to the High Court, and the application would be dismissed without prejudice to the applicant making a fresh application in the correct form to the High Court.

Sunderland Borough Council v A [1993] 1 FCR 398 (Family Division: Hollis J).

314 Care order—child in local authority care—authority's breach of obligations

See *Holtom v Barnet London Borough Council*, para 2457.

315 Care order—disclosure of documents—directions

The two children of a family were committed into the care of a local authority and parental access was terminated. The father applied to discharge the care orders and for contact. At the first directions hearing the court fixed a date for the final hearing and directed the local authority to file their written evidence by a certain date. The local authority failed to file their documents. Following a further directions hearing they had still neglected to do so and it was not until the father had applied for a third directions hearing that the local authority filed and served a lengthy statement from a social worker. Leave was also given by the court for the local authority to file outstanding statements. The father appealed on the grounds that the family proceedings court ought not to have extended the time for filing further documents and accordingly, ought not to have looked at the evidence that was filed late. *Held*, it was in the interests of the children that the court ought to have the best up-to-date information available, and therefore it would have been wrong to prevent the local authority from adducing their evidence. Where a party had caused delay by failing to file evidence in accordance with directions the sanction of an order for costs against the defaulting party was available. Accordingly, the appeal would be dismissed.

R v Nottinghamshire County Council [1993] 1 FCR 576 (Family Division: Douglas Brown J).

316 Care order—disclosure of documents—legal professional privilege

A local authority commenced care proceedings under the Children Act 1989, s 31 in respect of two young girls born to the mother by different fathers. At a hearing for directions the court gave leave to the mother and the father of one of the girls to disclose to psychiatrists all the reports and video recordings held by the court on the condition that the reports would then be disclosed to the court and other parties. The mother and father appealed against the condition in respect of certain medical reports on the basis that the documents were covered by legal professional privilege. *Held*, cases involving children were non-adversarial, and it was therefore important that the court reached an informed decision. The 1989 Act established the paramountcy of the child's welfare as the sole and overriding principle in care proceedings. Legal professional privilege would be outweighed by that paramount principle, and therefore in proceedings under the 1989 Act a party would be obliged to disclose all experts' reports. However, communications between lawyer and client would still attract privilege. Accordingly, the appeal would be dismissed.

Oxfordshire County Council v M [1994] 1 FLR 175 (Court of Appeal: Sir Stephen Brown P, Steyn and Kennedy LJJ).

317 Care order—duty of local authority to prepare care plan

It has been held that where a local authority applies for a care order in respect of a child, it must prepare a care plan which accords, as far as is reasonably possible, with the Children Act 1989: Guidance and Regulations (HMSO, 1991) Vol 3, Family Placements, para 2.6.6.

Manchester City Council v F [1993] 1 FCR 1000 (Family Division: Eastham J).

318   Care order—interim order—appeal

An interim care order was made in respect of three children which provided that they were to remain with the father. He appealed, contending that the court should have made an interim residence order in his favour so that he would have parental responsibility. *Held*, the Court of Appeal had repeatedly deprecated the bringing of appeals against interim orders. Legal representatives were obliged to consider the merits and the utility of pursuing an appeal before launching it. They ought to bear in mind the court's power to make orders for costs against those who supported appeals as lacking in merit as the present one, which would have had negligible practical effect on the childrens' lives. Accordingly, the appeal would be dismissed.

Re G (Minors: Costs) [1993] Fam Law 621 (Family Division: Johnson J).

319   Care order—interim order—application for leave to appeal out of time

The mother of children who had been made the subject of an interim care order chose not to appeal against the order at the time it was made because the local authority proposed to allow the children to continue to live with her. The local authority subsequently decided there was a risk that the children would sustain physical injury if they remained with the mother, and they were removed from her care. At that stage, the mother made an application for leave to appeal out of time against the making of the interim care order. *Held*, it should have been clear to the mother and those advising her that a care order would allow the local authority to terminate the arrangement whereby the children lived with the mother if it felt that the arrangement was no longer appropriate in the circumstances. A parent could not wait and see what happened before deciding whether to challenge an interim care order. The mother's application was without merit and, accordingly, it would be dismissed.

Re M (Minors: Interim Order) [1993] 2 FCR 182 (Family Division: Douglas Brown J).

320   Care order—interim order—application for subsequent orders

Two children were the subject of two interim care orders, which together ran for seven weeks and four days from the date on which the first order was made. The substantive hearing for the case was not due to take place until almost two months after the second order expired, and the local authority applied for a third interim care order for four weeks as the first of subsequent orders to run until the substantive hearing. The court refused to make the order on the ground that, by virtue of the Children Act 1989, s 38(4), (5), the maximum period for which interim orders could be made was eight weeks from the making of the first order. On appeal by the local authority, *held*, the effect of the 1989 Act, s 38 was that a first interim care order might last for up to eight weeks while a second and any subsequent orders might last for up to four weeks, or for a period of up to eight weeks from the date of the first order if that was no longer than four weeks. Therefore, the court had had the power to make a further interim care order for four weeks, and there was no limit on the number of such orders which could be made. Accordingly, the appeal would be allowed and an interim care order for four weeks would be made.

Gateshead Metropolitan Borough Council v N [1993] 1 FCR 400 (Family Division: Connell J).

321   Care order—interim order—arrangements to assist children to live abroad—Northern Ireland

A local authority had two children in their temporary care under an interim care order made under the Children Act 1989, s 38. It was decided by the local authority that the children should be allowed to stay with their mother and stepfather in Northern Ireland. The local authority therefore arranged for the children to live in Northern Ireland and applied for the court's consent to the arrangement under the 1989 Act, Sch 2, para 19. It also applied for a full care order to be made which could then be transformed into the Northern Irish equivalent order through application of the Children (Prescribed Orders–Northern Ireland, Guernsey and Isle of Man) Regulations 1991, SI 1991/2032. The judge refused consent and declared that the children were to be made the subject of repeated interim care orders until the Northern Ireland placement was shown to be permanent and satisfactory. On appeal, *held*, the role of the court in determining questions relating to the upbringing of a child was to determine current questions as they arose, and to do so with finality and as much speed as was consistent with justice and the welfare of the child. Once a question had been determined, it was seldom, if ever, right for the court to make continued use of its powers of adjournment under the 1989 Act, s 38. The judge had established that the children were at risk of significant harm and that suitable arrangements had been made for their reception and welfare in Northern Ireland. His duty was therefore to make a care order because the conditions for it had been finally established and only a final care order would bring the 1991 Regulations into effect. Accordingly, the appeal would be allowed.

Cheshire County Council v P [1993] 2 FCR 397 (Court of Appeal: Sir Thomas Bingham MR, Stuart-Smith and Waite LJJ).

322   Care order—interim order—children placed with temporary foster parents

A local authority applied for an interim care order under the Children Act 1989, s 38 in respect of two children whose mother had placed them with temporary foster parents pending the final hearing of applications relating to their residence. The judge refused the application and made a prohibited steps order against the authority to prevent it removing the children from the foster parents. On the authority's appeal, *held*, whilst the judge correctly sought to maintain the status quo pending the hearing, he had made an error of principle and misconstrued the effect of the 1989 Act, s 38. Granting an interim care order would not have given the authority a tactical advantage over the other parties and was in fact the best means of preserving the status quo. It was an impartial step which enabled the court to control any steps taken by an authority exercising reviewable powers and was designed to afford all parties opportunity for frequent review of progress. The interim care order would be granted and the prohibited steps order revoked. Accordingly, the appeal would be allowed.

Re G (Minors) (Interim Care Order) [1993] 2 FCR 557 (Court of Appeal: Sir Thomas Bingham MR, Steyn and Waite LJJ).

323   Care order—interim order—closing submissions—right to be heard

At an interim care hearing there was considerable difference between the mother and local authority on a number of material issues. At the conclusion of the evidence counsel for the mother sought to address the court on both fact and law. The court refused to allow her to make any submissions and made an interim care order. On the mother's appeal, *held*, the Magistrates' Courts Rules 1981, SI 1981/552, r 14 entitled the mother to address the court at the conclusion of the evidence. Under the Family Proceedings Courts (Children Act 1989) Rules 1991, SI 1991/1395, r 21(2) the court was able to give directions as to the order of speeches and evidence. However, the discretion to give such directions had to be exercised judicially. The circumstances in which the court would be justified in refusing to hear an advocate for a party would be extremely rare. In the present case the circumstances were not exceptional and accordingly, the magistrates were in error in not permitting counsel for the mother to address them. However, having regard to the facts and circumstances, it was not appropriate to remit the case for rehearing. The court would exercise its powers under the Children Act 1989, s 94 and make an interim care order.

F v Kent County Council [1993] 1 FCR 217 (Family Division: Cazalet J).

324   Care order—interim order—order pending assessment in respect of residence order

A child was placed in voluntary care and went to live with foster parents. The local authority was granted an interim care order. The father applied for a residence order. While the authority was still assessing him as a full-time carer, the authority's application for a care order came before the family proceedings court. The justices granted the authority a care order but the order was silent as to the father's application. On his appeal against the care order, *held*, a residence order and a care order were incompatible so that when the justices made the care order in the authority's favour, they must be deemed to have dismissed the father's application. However, the justices were required to adjudicate on the father's application instead of in effect leaving it to the discretion of the authority. As the authority had not completed its assessment of the father as a carer, the justices should have made an interim care order and adjourned both applications until evidence was forthcoming on the completion of the assessment. The court should always be slow to make a full care order which placed the responsibility for a child with the local authority. An interim care order would be made and the applications remitted to the family proceedings court for its determination.

Hounslow London Borough Council v A [1993] 1 WLR 291 (Family Division: Booth J).

325   Care order—interim order—powers of family proceedings court when making interim order

The local authority obtained an interim care order in relation to child A, following disturbances with her violent father. A further order was made in the family proceedings court, terminating contact between A and her mother until the final hearing. The magistrates concluded that the mother was unable to provide the level of care that could reasonably be expected from a parent and that if A resumed a relationship with the father, she would be put at severe risk of significant harm. A's mother appealed against that order. *Held*, the magistrates had effectively decided the case, whereas all they needed to decide was whether there should be contact pending the final hearing. This was not a case where matters were so exceptional, and the risk so severe that contact should be stopped. The mother would have hoped to persuade the court that a programme for rehabilitation should be started but the family proceedings court had precluded that possibility. That court was not the right court to deal with this matter; the question of whether rehabilitation was to be ruled out was to be decided at the final hearing, and pending that decision there ought to be reasonable contact between the mother and A. The access would have to be supervised to make sure that the risks of contact with the father were minimised. The local authority had leave to suspend contact if there was a danger from the father to the child. Accordingly, the appeal would be allowed.

A v M and Walsall Metropolitan Borough Council [1993] 2 FLR 244 (Family Division: Ewbank J).

326 Care order—interim order—risk of significant harm to child

The parents of a child were both schizophrenics. The local authority, concerned for the child's welfare, placed her on the child protection register. Subsequently, bruising was discovered on the child which, in the view of one paediatrician, had not been incurred accidentally. The local authority sought an interim care order. It had been agreed between the parties that the local authority would pursue an interim supervision order, not an interim care order, but during an adjournment to hear oral evidence, further evidence had come to light and the local authority successfully sought an interim care order. The child appealed through her guardian ad litem. *Held*, in the case of an interim order, the court had to be satisfied only that there were reasonable grounds for believing that the circumstances with respect to the child were as mentioned in the significant harm test contained in the Children Act 1989, s 31(2). The justices could have been satisfied that there were reasonable grounds that the child would be likely to suffer significant harm attributable to the care of the parents if she were to be returned to them. However, the justices had confused the welfare considerations under the 1989 Act, s 1 with their findings relating to the likelihood of significant harm, which was a matter of factual proof. The principles of s 1 had not been applied in relation to the question whether or not to make an order. The appeal would accordingly be allowed.

Humberside County Council v B [1993] 1 FLR 257 (Family Division: Booth J).

327 Care order—interim order—threshold criteria—placement with harmful parent

Three children were living with their mother and the father of the eldest child. Due to the stormy relationship between the mother and father, the children were placed upon the child protection register because of their "exposure to domestic conflict". The mother took the children to the applicant who was the father of the two youngest, and asked him to look after them. Later that day, she attempted to commit suicide. The local authority made an application for a care order to be made in its favour although it intended to allow the children to remain with the applicant. The applicant appealed against the interim care order on the ground that the court must be satisfied that the children were suffering, or were likely to suffer, significant harm. He argued that it was illogical for the court to conclude that the children were likely to suffer significant harm if left with him when the proposal of the local authority was to leave the children with him. He also submitted that the findings and reasons announced by the justices in making their order were inadequate to support the making of an interim care order. The applicant therefore applied for an interim residence order to be made in his favour which would confer parental responsibility upon him. *Held*, there would be many cases in which it would be appropriate for a court to make a care order on the basis that a child was suffering significant harm with its parent but where it was also proposed that the child should continue to live with that parent. It was not necessary for the court to be satisfied of the existence of the threshold criteria, but merely to be satisfied that there were reasonable grounds for believing that the threshold criteria would be satisfied. The court had to avoid prejudging issues of fact before the substantive hearing whilst ensuring the findings they had made were adequate to sustain their decision. The justices in the present case had succeeded in keeping this balance. Accordingly, the appeal would be dismissed.

Re S (Children: Interim Care Order) [1993] 2 FCR 475 (Family Division: Johnson J).

328 Care order—mandatory direction—direction requiring local authority to commence child's assessment by certain date—jurisdiction

A local authority removed a one-year-old child from her family home and commenced care proceedings. An interim care order was made and a guardian ad litem was appointed. At a further hearing a direction was given for the child to be assessed by a qualified social worker. A month later when the matter again came before the court, the local authority stated that the assessment could not yet start because of a lack of resources. The court therefore amended the original direction for assessment by requiring that the assessment commence on or before a specified date. On appeal by the local authority against the specified date, *held*, under the Children Act 1989, s 38(6), the court had the power to make a mandatory direction. Where a party to care proceedings sought a direction under s 38(6) that might affect a resource, be it financial or otherwise, then due account was to be taken of that information. Since the direction was not plainly wrong and since the practical problems of the local authority had been taken into account the matter was clearly within the court's jurisdiction. Accordingly, the appeal would be dismissed.

Berkshire County Council v C [1993] 2 WLR 475 (Family Division: Johnson J).

329 Care order—oral application for withdrawal of proceedings—application made in absence of guardian ad litem

A local authority applied for a care order in respect of a child who had been sexually abused by her father. A guardian ad litem was appointed and interim care orders were made in respect of the child, who was placed with foster parents. When the matter came to court again the local authority made an oral application for the care proceedings to be withdrawn. The guardian ad litem was unable to attend but was represented by counsel who opposed the local authority's application, but the application was granted by the magistrates after the child's mother gave assurances that she would allow the child to be accommodated by the local authority. On the guardian ad litem's appeal, *held*, under the Family Proceedings Courts (Children Act 1989) Rules 1991, SI 1991/1395, r 5, a request to withdraw an application could only be made orally if all the parties were present when the request was made. That meant the guardian ad litem should have been present personally, and the magistrates had erred in granting the application in the guardian ad litem's absence. Accordingly, the appeal would be allowed and the matter remitted to the county court for rehearing.

Re F (A Minor) (Care Proceedings: Withdrawal) [1993] 1 FCR 389 (Family Division: Hollings J).

330 Care order—parties to application—wishes of child

Following an allegation that a child, aged seven, was being sexually abused, the local authority commenced care proceedings joining the father, the mother, and the paternal grandparents as parties. The child's paternal aunt made an unsuccessful application for leave to apply for a residence order in respect of the child and also to be joined as a party to the care proceedings. The magistrates held that she had no significant contact with the child and that the child's father and paternal grandmother were already parties and the aunt had sufficient connection and a good relationship with them. In arriving at their decision the magistrates also had regard to the views of the child. On appeal by the aunt, *held*, the Children Act 1989, s 10(9) required the court to consider any risk there might be of a successful application disrupting the child's life to such an extent that he would be harmed by it. Under the Family Proceedings Courts (Children Act 1989) Rules 1991, SI 1991/1395, an application to be joined as a party could be heard in the absence of other parties. However, this did not preclude the court from taking into account the views of other parties. Whether the court would be assisted by the views of the parties in the case was essentially a matter of judgment for the court. Accordingly, the appeal would be dismissed.

A v A [1993] 1 FCR 870 (Family Division: Hollings J).

331 Care order—placement of child—placement in hospital for mentally ill

The behaviour of a 12-year-old girl in the care of a local authority had been disruptive and unco-operative at her placement centre. The local authority decided to place the girl for assessment in a hospital for adults providing psychiatric treatment. On the girl's appeal against the dismissal of her application for judicial review of the local authority's decision, *held*, the Mental Health Act 1983, s 131 did not cover admissions for assessment. With regard to the position at common law, the question was not whether there was a power to admit voluntarily but whether there was anything to prevent such admission. An adult could be admitted voluntarily to a mental hospital for assessment in the same way as he could be admitted to any other hospital. The fact that the girl in the present case was a minor made no difference provided that the local authority was capable of giving consent and did in fact give such consent. The local authority had all the powers and duties of the girl's parents and the girl was not herself capable of giving or withholding consent. The authority's decision was not therefore unlawful and the appeal would be dismissed.

R v Kirklees Metropolitan Council, ex p C (A Minor) [1993] 2 FLR 187 (Court of Appeal: Lloyd, Stuart-Smith and Farquharson LJJ). Decision of Kennedy J [1992] 2 FLR 117 (1992 Abr para 293) affirmed.

332   Care order—proceedings—appointment of guardian ad litem

See *Devon County Council v S*, para 338.

333   Care order—threshold conditions

The Children Act 1989, s 31(2) provides that a court can only make a care order if it is satisfied that the child concerned is suffering, or is likely to suffer, significant harm which is attributable to the care given, or likely to be given, to the child if the order was not made, not being what it would be reasonable to expect a parent to give him.

A father was sentenced to life imprisonment for murdering his child's mother and the child was placed with a short-term foster parent. The mother's cousin applied, with local authority support, for a residence order in respect of the child. However, the father and the guardian ad litem supported a care order with a view to adoption outside the natural family. The trial judge made a care order having found that the threshold condition in the 1989 Act, s 31(2) was satisfied: first, the child was suffering significant harm in that he had suffered ill treatment by being permanently deprived of his mother's love, and second, in the absence of an order the child was likely to suffer harm in having no permanent home. On appeal, *held*, a care order was not available on the grounds that a child was suffering significant harm if the child was no longer suffering such harm at the date of the hearing. The threshold condition was not fulfilled unless the court was satisfied, at the date of the hearing, that (1) the child was then suffering significant harm, and (2) that harm was attributable to the care given to him not being what it would be reasonable to expect a parent to provide. The trial judge's finding was incorrect in respect of both limbs since each was based on the past event of the father's murder of the mother and the second overlooked the care currently given by the child's foster parent. On the facts the trial judge had not been entitled to find that, at the date of the hearing, the child was suffering significant harm, nor that he would be likely to suffer significant harm if the cousin's application were allowed. Accordingly, the appeal would be allowed and a residence order made in favour of the cousin.

Re M (A Minor) [1994] 1 All ER 424 (Court of Appeal: Balcombe, Rose and Peter Gibson LJJ). Dicta of Lord Goff of Chievely in *Re D (A Minor)* [1987] AC 317, CA applied. *Northamptonshire County Council v S* [1992] 3 WLR 1010 overruled.

334   Care order—transfer of complex cases—refusal of magistrate to transfer

See *Re L (Care Proceedings: Transfer)*, para 393.

335   Care proceedings—application for interim order—procedure

A mother had three sons, two of whom lived with her and the third with another relative. One of the children who lived with the mother suffered a non-accidental injury, allegedly at the hands of the mother's partner, and the local authority obtained emergency protection orders in respect of both those children. The local authority subsequently sought interim care orders in respect of all three children, but the magistrates only granted an interim care order in respect of the child who had been injured and made a prohibited steps order preventing the mother from allowing her partner into her house. The magistrates gave no reasons for their decision, saying it was not necessary for them to give reasons in respect of interim care orders. On the local authority's appeal, *held*, the decision-making process was laid out in the Family Proceedings Courts (Children Act 1989) Rules 1991, SI 1991/1395, which required the justices' clerk to make a written record of the reasons for the court's decision and any findings of fact, and the magistrates to give the reasons for their decision at the time their decision was made. Those provisions applied to interim decisions as well as to final decisions, and the magistrates' failure to apply them had rendered their decision unsafe. Accordingly, the appeal would be allowed and the matter transferred to the county court and remitted for rehearing.

Hertfordshire County Council v W [1992] 2 FCR 885 (Family Division: Booth J).

336 Care proceedings—application for leave to be joined as a party—procedure

A local authority placed a homeless 15-year-old mother and her child with the mother's aunt as a foster parent. After three months the placement broke down and the mother and baby moved to new foster parents, but that placement also broke down and the local authority commenced care proceedings. The aunt applied for leave to be joined as a party to the care proceedings under the Children Act 1989, s 8 so she could seek a residence or contact order, but the magistrates rejected her application on the ground that granting it would not be in the best interests of the child. On the aunt's appeal, *held*, on applications under the 1989 Act, s 8 the child's welfare was not the paramount consideration. The magistrates should have considered the criteria set out in the 1989 Act, s 10(9), which included the applicant's connection with the child and the extent to which the child's life might be disrupted if the application was made. However, the person seeking leave had to establish a case which was reasonably likely to succeed, and as the local authority and the guardian ad litem had both expressed concerns about the aunt's family and her lifestyle there was no prospect of her obtaining a residence or contact order. In the circumstances it would be futile to grant the application, and, accordingly, the appeal would be dismissed.

G v Kirklees Metropolitan Borough Council [1993] 1 FCR 357 (Family Division: Booth J).

337 Care proceedings—appropriate order—duty of court to protect child

A father had three children by his first marriage. The children were repeatedly injured and one baby was killed whilst in his care, leading to the father being convicted of wilful cruelty to that child. He subsequently cohabited with another woman and they had a child. The local authority was concerned about the child's safety and, by agreement with all parties, the court made an interim supervision order and appointed a guardian ad litem. He made a report and concluded that a care order was necessary to protect the child. Four consultant psychiatrists reported that, given the father's previous history of abuse, the child was at risk, but they differed in their assessments of the degree of risk. At the hearing, the local authority sought a supervision order and stated that a care order might undermine the co-operation they were receiving from the parents. *Held*, a supervision order was limited to a one-year term and directions made under it were not directly enforceable. A care order, however, was of unlimited duration, was revocable only by an application to the court, gave the local authority parental responsibility for the child, and required it to make regular visits to the child and be satisfied as to the child's welfare. The local authority, the professionals involved, and the court had all approached the case on the basis that it was likely that the father had killed his baby. Therefore, the primary consideration was the protection of the child, and the local authority's emphasis on parental co-operation was misplaced. The decisive point in deciding between a care order and a supervision order was that any future decision to lift the child's safeguards was a matter for the court, and was not the responsibility of individuals. Accordingly, a care order would be made.

Re D (Care Proceedings: Appropriate Order) [1993] 2 FCR 88 (Family Division: Ewbank J).

338 Care proceedings—contact with mother—discontinuance of contact—duty to give reasons

A local authority made care orders in respect of four-year-old twin girls. It planned a programme of rehabilitation to the mother and arranged weekly contact with her. The local authority later decided that the planned rehabilitation had failed and, at a child protection conference, that contact would remain unchanged. However, an adoption planning meeting immediately followed where it was decided that contact was not in the interests of either of the twins and should be terminated. The local authority successfully applied for leave to discontinue contact and the mother appealed. She contended that the reappointment of the court welfare officer who acted as guardian ad litem in the original care proceedings was erroneous, that the local authority had belatedly disclosed documents relating to the decisions as to contact, and that the magistrates' reasons were flawed. *Held*, (1) the Family Proceedings Courts (Children Act 1989) Rules 1991, SI 1991/1395, r 10(7)(c) provided that a guardian ad litem should not be a serving probation officer, which included court welfare officers, and thus the appointment was incorrect. (2) In relation to the contradictory decisions as to contact, it was clearly unsatisfactory that relevant documents were not disclosed until the morning of the hearing. (3) The magistrates' typed reasons did not indicate whether due consideration was given to the Children Act 1989, s 1 and did not deal with the central issue of whether there should be contact between the mother and the children. Whilst neither of the first two errors were sufficient to allow the appeal, the magistrates' reasons were fundamentally flawed. Accordingly, the appeal would be allowed and a rehearing ordered.

Devon County Council v S [1993] 2 FCR 36 (Family Division: Ewbank J).

339 Care proceedings—costs—high cost of litigation

A child was committed to the care of his local authority. In his judgment the judge made adverse comments on the costs incurred during the litigation. Those costs were: (1) legal costs of approximately £1 million, borne in part by the Legal Aid Fund and in part by the local authority, and (2) in house costs of the local authority's social security and legal departments amounting to approximately £1 million. On the father's appeal, *held*, it was right that those figures ought to be disclosed to the public who funded the expense, and especially so bearing in mind the present pressure on the legal aid budget with its serious implications for the reduced eligibility of individual citizens to obtain legal aid. It was a matter of acute public concern that the present system of conducting such cases could result in such apparently profligate expenditure of public funds. Accordingly, the appeal would be dismissed.

Re W (A Minor) (1993) Times, 23 March (Court of Appeal: Butler-Sloss and Hirst LJJ).

340 Care proceedings—medical report—power of court to order disclosure of privileged documents

During directions in preparation for care proceedings, the mother's medical records were ordered by the court to be filed and served. A further application was made to order disclosure by consent of records from six hospitals. Counsel argued that the reports were governed by legal and professional privilege and that the mother could not be forced to disclose them against her will. *Held*, medical reports made on behalf of a party to litigation on the advice of a legal adviser were privileged documents and in the absence of waiver, no order for disclosure could be made. There was however an unrestricted jurisdiction to do whatever was best for the welfare of the ward in wardship proceedings that included the power in appropriate cases to override legal professional privilege. However as this case was primarily concerned with proceedings under the Children Act 1989, there was no power, as there might be in wardship proceedings, to override the privilege attaching to a medical report on which a party did not intend to rely. Accordingly, the directions in preparation for care proceedings would be amended.

Re B (Minors) (Disclosure of Medical Reports) [1993] FCR 241 (Family Division: Douglas Brown J).

341 Care proceedings—risk of serious harm to child—appropriate order

The parents were unmarried and had two boys. A care order was made in respect of the elder son and he was placed with foster parents with a view to adoption after repeatedly suffering non-accidental injuries. The younger son also suffered non-accidental injuries resulting from the father's use of inappropriate physical means to handle him. The local authority applied for a supervision order in respect of the younger child but the Official Solicitor contended that the concerns for the child's safety were so great that a care order was necessary. *Held*, the child was at very serious risk because the father had a deep-seated, and unacknowledged, problem in his personality of violence towards what he saw as a disobedient child. The child would always be at risk when the father was at home and the case thus required very detailed monitoring. Monitoring under a supervision order was not sufficiently adequate nor onerous to meet the present needs: parental responsibility and the obligation to safeguard and promote the child's welfare remained with the mother, and the local authority was only able to remove the child by applying for an emergency protection order. Under a care order, however, the local authority was given parental responsibility for the child, was under a duty to protect the child's welfare, and had the power and duty to remove the child if necessary. Given the risk of harm to the child and the possibility that the local authority might need to act swiftly to protect him, a care order was required. Accordingly, a care order would be made.

Re S (J) (A Minor) (Care or Supervision Order) [1993] 2 FCR 193 (Family Division: Judge Coningsby QC).

342 Care proceedings—termination of contact with natural parent—duty of court

A mother's two daughters were taken into care and placed for adoption. The mother continued to have frequent contact with them after they had been taken into care, but when prospective adopters were found the local authority applied for contact to be terminated. The mother, with the support of the guardian ad litem, opposed the application and sought an adjournment of three months so her ability to care for all her children (namely, the two girls and her newly-born son) could be assessed. The judge granted the local authority's application on the ground that there was an urgent need for the situation to be resolved so there would be a degree of stability in the girls' lives. On the mother's appeal, *held*, under the Children Act 1989, s 34 there was a presumption of continuing reasonable contact, but that presumption had to be balanced against the child's long-term welfare and the court could require the local authority to justify its long-term plans to ascertain whether it would be reasonable to exclude contact between parent and child. The judge had erred in not appreciating that under the 1989 Act he could give appropriate directions for the mother's suitability as a carer to be assessed, and it would be unfair to the children if the mother's potential was not investigated. The appeal would be allowed, and the judge's order would be set aside.

Re B (Children in Care: Contact) [1993] 1 FCR 363 (Court of Appeal: Butler-Sloss and Kennedy LJJ).

343 Child abduction and custody—access order made in foreign country—home proceedings—availability of legal aid

The Convention on the Civil Aspects of International Child Abduction, art 21 provides that "an application to make arrangements for organising or securing the effective exercise of rights of access may be presented to the central authorities of the contracting states".

In proceedings brought by the father under art 21 for an order that the mother take all the necessary steps to facilitate access to their three children, *held*, the Lord Chancellor's Department could receive applications properly sent by foreign central authorities for the enforcement of access rights in England. The issue of enforcement was to be decided under the Children Act 1989 and non-means-tested legal aid did not extend to applications under the 1989 Act. Article 21 conferred no jurisdiction on a court to determine matters relating to access or to recognise and enforce foreign access orders. The role of the central authority was limited to one of executive cooperation. The duty of the central authority on receiving an application under art 21 was to make appropriate arrangements to provide English solicitors to act on the applicant's behalf for the purposes of instituting an application under the 1989 Act, s 8. By reason of the international element which was usually involved in such proceedings, serious consideration was in most cases to be given to commencing proceedings in the High Court. Accordingly, the application would be allowed.

Re T (Minors) (Hague Convention: Access) [1993] 3 All ER 127n (Family Division: Bracewell J).

344 Child abduction and custody—habitual residence of child—access order made in different country—application of international convention

A couple married in England and subsequently lived in Canada where their child was born several years later. Following the break up of the marriage a Canadian court granted the mother a consent order allowing her to return with the child and live in England but nevertheless directed specific access in the father's favour to take place in Canada. Following the mother's refusal to comply with the access agreements the father initiated proceedings under the Convention on Civil Aspects of International Child Abduction, for the protection of his rights in England where it was held that although weight was to be given to a consent order made in the Canadian Court, the English court was to give paramount consideration to the welfare of the child. The English court therefore ordered specific access arrangements in the father's favour to take place in England. On appeal by the father, *held*, a child who was habitually resident with her mother in England and whose father had access rights granted by the Canadian court, was a child to whom the Convention applied. Any breach of access rights would be considered by the English court under its domestic law. The Convention had administrative effect but imposed no direct obligation on judicial authorities and required the Lord Chancellor's department, as the central authority for the purposes of the Convention, to assist the father by introducing him to local legal services and where necessary providing him with legal aid. The Convention focussed both on cooperation between central authorities and the enforcement of the return of the child wrongfully removed or retained outside the state of his habitual residence. The Convention did not envisage that orders from a state which was not the state of habitual residence would continue to govern the affairs and welfare of a child living permanently elsewhere. Although the existence of the earlier order, where the child was then habitually resident, was crucially important and a factor to be given the greatest weight, the court's discretion had been exercised impeccably and accordingly the appeal would be dismissed.

Re G (a Minor) (Hague Convention: Access) [1993] 3 All ER 657 (Court of Appeal: Sir Thomas Bingham MR, Butler-Sloss and Hoffmann LJJ).

345 Child abduction and custody—illegal abduction—enrolment of child at school—duty of school to inform parent of enrolment

See *Re S (A Minor) (Parental Rights)*, para 1096.

346 Child abduction and custody—Lord Chancellor's Department—Central Authority for England and Wales—duties

The Central Authority for England and Wales has issued the following *Practice Note* ([1993] 1 FLR 804).

1. In *Re G (A Minor) (Hague Convention: Access)* [1993] 1 FLR 669 (para 344), the Court of Appeal considered the duties of the Central Authority for England and Wales on an application in respect of rights of access under the Hague Convention on the Civil Aspects of International Child Abduction, art 21. The court took the view that art 21 conferred no jurisdiction to determine matters relating to access, or to recognise or enforce foreign access orders. Article 21 provides, however, for executive co-operation in the enforcement of such recognition as national law allows.

2. The duty of the Central Authority is to make appropriate arrangements for an applicant by providing solicitors to act on his behalf in applying for legal aid and instituting proceedings in the High Court under the Children Act 1989, s 8.

3. If, in the course of proceedings under art 12 of the Convention, an applicant decides to seek access instead of the return of the child, but no agreement can be reached and the provisions of the European Convention on the Recognition and Enforcement of Decisions Concerning Custody of Children are not available, a separate application under the 1989 Act, s 8 must be made.

347 Child abduction and custody—parties to conventions

The Child Abduction and Custody (Parties to Conventions) (Amendment) Order 1993, SI 1993/1243 (in force on 1 July 1993), amends the 1986 Order, SI 1986/1159 by adding Greece to the list of contracting states to the European Convention on Recognition and Enforcement of Decisions concerning Custody of Children and on the Restoration of Custody of Children 1980. The 1992 Order, SI 1992/1299, is revoked.

The Child Abduction and Custody (Parties to Conventions) (Amendment) (No 2) Order 1993, SI 1993/1573 (in force on 23 June 1993), amends the 1986 Order, SI 1986/1159, by adding Mauritius and Greece the the list of contracting states to the Hague Convention on the Civil Aspects of Child Abduction 1980. SI 1992/3199 is revoked.

The Child Abduction and Custody (Parties to Conventions) Order 1993, SI 1993/3144 (in force on 16 December 1993), supplements the 1986 Order, SI 1986/1159, as amended, and specifies, for the purpose of the Child Abduction and Custody Act 1985, The Bahamas, Bosnia-Hercegovina, Croatia and Macedonia as contracting states to the Hague Convention on the Civil Aspects of Child Abduction 1980.

348 Child abduction and custody—rights of access—access order made in different country—application of international convention

A married couple lived in America and had one child. The mother was British and the father American. Following their divorce an American court granted the mother a consent order allowing her to live in England with the child. The father was given access, initially in England but then, when the child was capable of going on an aeroplane alone, in the United States. When the child was seven the father sought access in the United States. Following the mother's refusal to allow access he applied to an American court to enforce the order. The mother opposed the application contending that the father was a homosexual, had Aids and a diminished life expectancy. Medical evidence showed that the father's illness posed no risk to the child and the court ordered the mother to co-operate in a four-week visit of the child to the United States. The mother failed to comply and the father issued an originating summons under the Child Abduction and Custody Act 1985. *Held,* the Hague Convention on the Civil Aspects of International Child Abduction, art 7(f) required the court, in a proper case, to make arrangements for organising or securing the effective exercise of rights of access and gave the court a discretion to ensure compliance with a foreign access order. The court would respect the decision of a foreign court unless it was contrary to the welfare of the child. In this case the American court had considered the mother's objections, decided that visits to the father posed no risk to the child and correctly ordered a visit to take place. Accordingly, the order of the American court would be confirmed.

Re C (Minors) (Enforcing Foreign Access Order) [1993] 1 FCR 770 (Family Division: Eastham J).

349 Child abduction and custody—rights of access—access order made in foreign country—application of convention

A Belgian girl aged 13 was resident in Wales with her mother. The father, who lived in Belgium, obtained an order from the Belgian court that he could receive his daughter for staying access and registered it in the High Court. The High Court made an enforcement order, despite the court welfare officer's report that the girl did not want any contact with the father. On appeal, *held*, the judge had erred in holding that, since the Belgian court's order had been registered, he was not entitled to refuse to enforce the order. In the European Convention on Recognition and Enforcement of Decisions concerning Custody of Children and on the Restoration of Custody of Children, the words "recognition and enforcement" were to be read disjunctively. Thus the European Convention, art 10(1) was applicable, and it provided that the court could refuse to enforce an order if it was found that by reason of a change in circumstances the effect of the original decision were manifestly no longer in accordance with the welfare of the child. Accordingly, the appeal would be allowed.

Re H (A Minor) [1994] 1 All ER 812 (Court of Appeal: Sir Stephen Brown P, Steyn and Kennedy LJJ).

350 Child abduction and custody—wrongful removal—acquiescence

The parties were unmarried parents of two children. They lived in France and separated in 1991. The mother who had twice attempted suicide, agreed that the father should look after the children. The father applied to a French court for parental authority but in the meantime went to work in England, taking the children with him. At the inter partes hearing in France the court refused the father's application, finding that he had taken the children to England without the permission of the mother, and ordered the return of the children to their mother. The father appealed and the mother then applied for return of the children under the Hague Convention. An ex parte order was made in England preventing the father from removing the children from the jurisdiction and there was a dispute between the parties as to the documentary evidence, in particular a letter from the mother purporting to allow the father to take the children to England if she had access. The letter was claimed by the mother to be a forgery. *Held*, the initial removal of the children from France was a wrongful removal within the Convention, arts 3 and 5. The mother was the only person with parental responsibility, and the father had merely delegated responsibility for temporary care. The mother therefore had a right to determine the children's place of residence. The conclusive factor was the decision by the French court that the children had been wrongfully removed without the mother's consent, and the fact that this had not been challenged in the father's grounds of appeal. Acquiescence could be established by a single act or communication, even though that might be at variance with the general conduct of the parent. Acquiescence was not established by the mother's visits to the children, which were necessary to maintain her relationship with them and were not to be taken as concurrence with the situation. If the legal status of a retention was equivocal pending a determination of a court in proceedings which originated before the abduction, then a clear finding of the court requiring the return of the children was sufficient to convert the equivocal retention into an unlawful one. This was therefore a case where the court was obliged to order the return of the children under art 12. If the court was wrong in that conclusion an order could be granted for the children's return in exercise of the discretion under art 13, on the basis that the person having care of the child was not actually exercising the custody rights at the time of removal. It was clear that the mother's capacity to care for the children was doubtful and that the father had looked after the children for the last 18 months. However his motives for taking the children from France were questionable and the children themselves had expressed a desire to live with their mother. The children should be returned to the country in which they had been born and there was nothing in the assessment of the welfare officer which would render that action manifestly inappropriate, or contrary to the welfare of the children. Any further investigations into welfare should be for the French court. The order would be granted accordingly.

Re R (Minors) (Abduction) [1993] 2 FCR 461 (Family Division: Thorpe J).

The parties who were married in England, had four children and later moved to Australia. After a brief period in Australia the mother returned to England with the children. Notwithstanding the fact that his solicitor advised him of his rights under the Hague Convention on the Civil Aspects of International Child Abduction the father wrote to the mother and the eldest child, on a number of occasions, and wished them luck for their new beginning. In none of the letters did he indicate a wish to make them return to Australia. The father then made an application under the Convention for the return of the children. *Held*, the mother had initially intended to take up long-term residence in Australia which meant that the children were habitually resident there immediately before the mother brought them to England. As a result their removal was prima facie wrongful within the terms of the Convention, art 3. However, under the Convention, art 13 a court was not bound to order the return of a child wrongfully removed from a country if the person having custody subsequently acquiesced in the removal. The father, in the writing and timing of the letters, had clearly acquiesced in the removal of the children, and therefore it was in the court's discretion whether or not to order the return of the children. In doing so the court had to balance its findings as to the interests of the children against the fundamental purpose of the Convention which was to ensure the prompt return of the children to the country from which they had been removed. The mother had suffered violence in the marriage and the children were now happily settled in this country. In all the circumstances, it would be wrong to order the return of the children to Australia, and accordingly, the application would be refused.

A v A (Child Abduction) [1993] 1 FCR 829 (Family Division: Rattee J).

A married couple lived in Australia with their son. The mother and child came to England for a holiday and, after their arrival, the mother's solicitors informed the father's solicitors that she did not intend to return to Australia. He expressed a wish to have access to the child but took no further action and was out of communication for seven months. He then wrote to the mother's solicitors requesting access and one month later applied for the child's immediate return to Australia, stating that he had only then become aware of the provisions of the Hague Convention on the Civil Aspects of International Child Abduction 1980. The issues were: was the child wrongfully retained in England; if so, had the father acquiesced in such wrongful retention; and, if so, should the court in its discretion make an order for the child's return. *Held*, (1) the father's agreement to the child visiting England for a holiday was an exercise of his custody rights, and his agreement ceased when the mother retained the child in England beyond the agreed length of the holiday without his authority. (2) acquiescence could be active or passive, arising by inference from silence or inactivity, and had to be real in the sense that the parent had to be informed of his general right of objection although knowledge of specific legal rights was not necessary. It had to be ascertained on consideration of all relevant circumstances. Here, the father had acquiesced through inactivity since, for ten months after learning of his wife's decision not to return, he took no steps towards having his son brought back, conduct wholly inconsistent with his subsequent request for a summary order under the Convention. (3) since the father had acquiesced in the child's retention in England, the court was not bound to return the child but could exercise its discretion, having regard to all relevant considerations. In particular, the child's welfare was an important, but not paramount, consideration and a balance had to be struck between the need to fulfil the purpose of the Convention through the child's return and any countervailing factors pointing to the child's retention in England. Whilst the considerations for choice of forum were evenly balanced, it was probable that the mother would be granted a residence order, and succeed in her request to live in England, in either jurisdiction. The child had attended school in England for almost a year and expected to remain there, the father had made no financial provision for their return, and the emotional effect of return would be significant. In considering the Convention, it was relevant to consider how far the father's conduct had been consistent with the Convention's underlying aims and the fact that he could not be contacted for seven months showed a lack of commitment to securing his child's return. In all the circumstances, a refusal of an order to return the child would run less risk than in most cases of conflicting with the spirit of the Convention. Considerations of public policy and child welfare outweighed the demands of loyalty to the Convention and, accordingly, the application would be dismissed.

W v W (Child Abduction) [1993] 2 FCR 644 (Family Division: Waite J). *Re A (Minors) (Abduction: Custody Rights)* [1992] 2 FCR 97 (1992 Abr para 299) and *Re A (Z) (Child Abduction)* [1993] 1 FCR 733 followed.

351 Child abduction and custody—wrongful removal—discretion of court not to order return

A married couple and their three children left England to live in Germany. The mother and children returned to England with the father's consent, but when the mother started divorce proceedings the father applied under the Hague Convention on the Civil Aspects of International Child Abduction 1980 for the children to be returned to Germany. The mother opposed the application on the ground that the father's consent to her taking the children meant there had not been a breach of custody rights. She also contended that the two elder children, aged 9 and 7, had indicated that they did not wish to return to Germany, and that bearing in mind their ages and understanding their views ought to be taken into account. *Held*, the 1980 Convention provided that any decision relating to the custody of children was best decided in the jurisdiction in which they had been normally resident. However, the elder children were sufficiently old and mature for their views to be considered, and the court would exercise its discretion under the 1980 Convention, art 13 not to order their return to Germany. The other child was too young to have his views considered, but he would remain in England with the others because returning him to Germany without his siblings would place him in an intolerable situation. Accordingly, the father's application would be dismissed, and questions relating to custody and access would be resolved in the High Court rather than in Germany.

B v K (Child Abduction) [1993] 1 FCR 382 (Family Division: Johnson J).

352 Child abduction and custody—wrongful removal—discretion to consider views of children

The parties and their nine-year-old daughter settled in France after living in various parts of the world. The daughter had behavioural problems caused by language confusion, and various psychologists advised she should be taught in English, which was her mother's native tongue. The marriage ran into difficulties and the mother and daughter moved to England, where the daughter's behaviour improved. The father applied for his daughter's return to France under the Hague Convention on the Civil Aspects of International Child Abduction 1980, and the mother argued the application should be refused because the daughter would be exposed to psychological harm if she returned to France. She also said her daughter objected to being returned, and argued she was of an age where it was appropriate to take her views into account. The application was dismissed, and, on the father's appeal, *held*, the purpose of the Hague Convention was to ensure the swift return of children who had been wrongfully removed, and bearing that in mind the court's discretion not to return them should only be exercised in exceptional cases. However, there were valid reasons for the daughter's objections to being returned, and her views were not merely the result of a wish to remain with her mother. The judge had considered all the issues before exercising his discretion, and there were no grounds for overturning the decision. Accordingly, the appeal would be dismissed.

Re S (A Minor) (Child Abduction) (Child's Views) [1992] 2 FLR 492 (Court of Appeal: Glidewell and Balcombe LJJ and Boreham J).

353 Child abduction and custody—wrongful removal—habitual residence

Scotland

A child of unmarried parents lived with her father in England after her parents separated. She occasionally spent a few days with her mother who, after the separation, had moved from Wales to Scotland. A year after the separation, the mother, with whom the child was going to spend two or three weeks, informed the father that the child was going to remain with her. The father obtained first an order requiring the mother to return the child to him and then a residence order which included the same requirement. He sought an order for delivery of the child. The mother contended that, as the child was illegitimate, only she had parental rights and that, therefore, the child had lost her English habitual residence when removed by her mother to Scotland. *Held*, habitual residence was a question of fact, not of legal right. There had been no agreement that the child should remain in Scotland either permanently or for an extended period. Accordingly, she had retained her habitual residence in England until at least the date of the first order. The order sought would be granted.

Rellis v Hart 1993 SLT 738 (Outer House).

354 Child abduction and custody—wrongful removal—jurisdiction

The unmarried parents of a child lived together in England. The mother took the child to Canada, having apparently made arrangements to stay there permanently. The father successfully sought an order in wardship and he was granted care and control of the child subject to a provision stating that the mother should have care and control provided she returned to the country within 28 days. In the wardship summons, notice was given that both parties should attend the wardship hearing. The mother, who did not return, sought to discharge the summons. Her application was granted on the basis that she had formed a settled intention to reside in Canada before the originating application was made, so that, since neither she nor the child were habitually resident in England on that date, the court had no jurisdiction in wardship relating to the child. The mother issued custody proceedings in Canada. A few days before, the father's appeal from the decision to discharge the summons was allowed and the wardship summons was reinstated. The Canadian court granted interim custody to the mother, with access to the father, and ordered that neither party should remove the child from the jurisdiction. The father took the child back to England. The mother issued an originating summons under the Child Abduction and Custody Act 1985, contending that the father's removal of the child from Canada had been wrongful within the terms of the Hague Convention, art 3. *Held*, the jurisdiction of the English court had to take precedence, as the minor was a ward of the English court where wardship proceedings were part heard. The mother had allowed the child to remain in Canada in breach of an order of the English court. It was therefore wholly wrong for the mother to seek to rely on the provisions of the 1985 Act to overcome her own disobedience of the order of the English court. In addition, as the mother had been under a duty imposed by the English court to return the child, it could not be said that the habitual residence of the child was in Canada at the date when the father removed her. The court would therefore not order the return of the child to Canada and wardship proceedings would continue.

Re EW (No 2) [1993] 1 FCR 710 (Family Division: Sir Stephen Brown P). For earlier related proceedings see [1992] 2 FLR 481, CA (para 435).

355 Child abduction and custody—wrongful removal—order for return of child—risk of psychological harm

A child lived in Texas with his father, an American citizen and his mother, a British citizen. His mother wrongfully removed him to England and filed a petition for divorce. The father applied for an order for the child's return under the Hague Convention on the Civil Aspects of International Child Abduction 1980. The mother claimed that the court did not have to order the child's return, as his return would expose him to physical or psychological harm or otherwise place him in an intolerable situation within the terms of the 1980 Convention, art 13(b). Evidence of this was the fact that she had been refused a visa to visit the United States and therefore if the child were forced to return he would not be with his mother and would therefore suffer psychological harm. *Held*, the evidence suggested that a properly made application for a visa backed up by a court order, would not be refused. Even if it were refused, the fact that the child would be looked after by his father and paternal grandmother suggested that he would not suffer the degree of psychological harm necessary for the 1980 Convention, art 13(b) to apply. Accordingly, the father's application would be allowed.

Re L (Child Abduction) (Psychological Harm) [1993] 2 FLR 401 (Family Division: Hollis J).

356 Child abduction and custody—wrongful removal—recognition and enforcement of orders made outside the jurisdiction

A married couple lived in the Irish Republic with their three children. Following the breakdown of their marriage the mother moved to England with two of the children, which contravened the terms of an Irish court order vesting custody of the children in the father. The European Convention on Recognition and Enforcement of Decisions concerning Custody of Children ("the Convention") had been ratified by the United Kingdom and the Irish Republic after the mother and children had moved to England, and the father applied for the order of the Irish court to be registered and enforced in the United Kingdom in accordance with the terms of the Convention. The mother applied for the Irish order to be set aside, contending the children had settled quickly in their new home and their interests would be best served if they were allowed to remain in England. *Held*, although the order had been made before the Convention had been ratified it was still a subsisting order within the terms of the Convention, and as such the court was obliged to uphold it. The court had a discretionary power to overturn an order which was manifestly not in a child's best interests, but the mother had failed to show sufficient grounds to justify the court invoking that power and the father's application should be allowed. Accordingly, the order would be registered and enforced in the United Kingdom.

L v L [1992] 2 FCR 821 (Family Division: Booth J).

357 Child abduction and custody—wrongful retention—habitual residence

The parents of an illegitimate child separated after the birth. The father was British and the mother and child were German citizens but their residence was in England. The father applied for orders relating to contact and parental responsibility under the Children Act 1989 but before the orders were obtained, interim access was agreed between the parties. The mother then took the child to Germany and on an ex parte application by the father the child was made a ward of court. The mother was also ordered to return the child to England. The father issued a summons which was served on the mother, seeking an order under the Hague Convention, art 3, that the retention of the child was unlawful. The question then arose as to whether the court had jurisdiction to make the order relating to wardship and the declaration that the child was wrongfully retained. *Held*, the English wardship court had jurisdiction over an alien child providing England or Wales was his habitual residence. The father in this case had to satisfy the court of the fact that the child was habitually resident in England and the mother had the burden of establishing that at the date the court exercised its wardship jurisdiction her habitual residence, and therefore the child's habitual residence, had changed to Germany. In the present case, the mother usually spoke to the child in English, and she had enrolled on a course in this country. These factors indicated that at the date of the wardship order she had not yet changed her habitual residence despite the fact that she was physically present in Germany at that time. The court therefore had jurisdiction to make the wardship order and the mother had no right to change the child's habitual residence. The child was removed before that order was made therefore the removal itself was not unlawful. However, keeping the child in Germany and failing to return her amounted to wrongfully retaining the child out of the jurisdiction. The fact that the father had not yet obtained the orders relating to custody and access did not prevent him from obtaining a declaration under the Hague Convention, as the court itself had custody. Accordingly the declaration would be granted.

Re BM (A Minor) (Wardship: Jurisdiction) [1993] 2 FCR 388 (Family Division: Eastham J).

358 Child abduction and custody—wrongful retention—habitual residence— application of international convention

An unmarried couple living in Sweden had a daughter. They separated when she was two and she lived principally with the mother, but spent substantial time with the father. Two years later the father applied for custody in the Swedish courts. The mother was granted interim custody and leave to take the child to England. An appellate court reversed that decision, granting interim custody to the father, and the mother then refused to return the child to Sweden. The father applied for the child's return under the Hague Convention on the Civil Aspects of International Child Abduction 1980. At the hearing, a preliminary point was taken as to the child's habitual place of residence immediately before the mother retained her in England contrary to the Swedish court's order. The mother had given evidence that, until learning of that order, she had intended to return, and on that basis the child was habitually resident in Sweden and was thus wrongly retained in England. However, the father stated that the mother left Sweden with no intention of returning, raising the inference that Sweden ceased to be the child's habitual place of residence from the date of departure and thus that there had been no wrongful retention. The judge held that, since the father was seeking an order based on a state of facts denied by him in his own case, it was inappropriate to grant the application and dismissed the originating summons. On appeal, *held*, the judge had misconceived the function of the courts in applications under the Hague Convention. The court was bound to order the return of a child who was wrongfully removed or retained unless one of the exceptions under the Convention was established. Further the litigation was sui generis, not adversarial nor inquisitorial. The evidence of the mother was consistent with surrounding circumstances, notably her purchase of return tickets to England. Until the appellate court order, she had no intention of remaining in England permanently and thus she and the child had remained habitually resident in Sweden. The fact that the father may not have believed her was irrelevant. Accordingly, the appeal would be allowed, the judge's order discharged and the case remitted.

Re N (Child Abduction: Habitual Residence) [1993] 2 FLR 124 (Court of Appeal: Balcombe, Mann and Leggatt LJJ).

359 Child abduction and custody—wrongful retention—habitual residence— parental agreement

Two children had been brought to England by their parents, who intended to reside in England for a year. The parents separated before the year had expired. The father returned to Israel and applied, under the Convention on the Civil Aspects of International Child Abduction 1980 (as enacted by the Child Abduction and Custody Act 1985) for the immediate return of his children on the ground that there had been unlawful retention of the children. The mother claimed that she and her children had become habitually resident in England, and argued that owing to the agreement between her and the father, she was protected under the Convention until the agreed period had elapsed. *Held*, where a parent announced that she did not intend to return the children at the end of a fixed period, she could not rely on the father's agreement to the limited period of retention as protecting her under the Convention, and there was a wrongful retention under the Convention, art 3, as at the date that intention was either formed or when it was communicated to the father. Where both parents had equal rights of custody, unilateral action by one of them could not change the habitual residence of the children except with the agreement or the acquiescence over time of the other parent or a court order determining custody and residence rights. The father's application would therefore be granted.

    Re S (Minors) [1994] 1 All ER 237 (Family Division: Wall J).

360   Child abuse—sexual abuse—interview

The daughter enjoyed regular untroubled access visits to her father from the date of her parent's separation. On the last access visit, her father told her that her grandfather had died but did not tell the mother that he had told the child. Due to her disturbed behaviour, her mother feared that inappropriate sexual behaviour had taken place. The child was interviewed by Social Services and anatomically correct dolls were introduced at the end of the lengthy interview. No record of the interview was made and the father was ultimately arrested following a medical examination of his daughter. The local authority convened a case conference, the conclusion of which was that the child was placed on the "at risk" register and access to the father terminated. The father was not interviewed at any stage. The father applied for restoration of the access pattern before the breakdown. *Held*, the dolls had been badly used in the interview. They were not recommended for use as a first-stage diagnostic aid and should only have been used with an understanding of child development, play, fantasising and psychopathology. Furthermore a video recording should have been taken of the interview. In cases where no facilities for video recording existed, the next best record was an audio recording or prepared manuscript. Social Services had rushed to the conclusion not just that access should be suspended but terminated, without any attempt to ascertain the father's point of view. Their conclusion had been imposed upon the family under the open or veiled threat that if the family did not accept it, there might be intervention. Insufficient attention had been paid to established procedure and guidelines and accordingly, the application would be granted.

    KS v GS (a Minor: Sexual Abuse) [1992] 2 FLR 361 (Family Division: Thorpe J).

361   Child abuse—sexual abuse—standard of proof

See *Re W (Minors) (Sexual Abuse: Standard of Proof)*, para 695.

362   Child care—care proceedings—failure to notify natural parents or appoint guardian ad litem

A child, aged 12 at the date of hearing, had suffered severe sexual abuse at the hands of her natural parents and no longer had contact with them. She had settled very well with long-term foster parents and had a strong desire to use her foster parents' surname, and the local authority applied under the Children Act 1989, s 33(7) for leave to change the child's name for specific purposes set out in the application. The application was made ex parte, and no guardian ad litem was appointed to act for the child. *Held*, the 1989 Act, s 41 required the appointment of a guardian ad litem in specified proceedings unless the court was satisfied that the child's interests could be safeguarded without that appointment being made. Although the application fell within the definition of "specified proceedings" for the purposes of the 1989 Act, s 41 the application was manifestly in the child's best interests and the appointment of a guardian ad litem could be dispensed with. An application for a change in the child's surname should be made ex parte only in exceptional circumstances, but the potential damage to the child justified the decision not to inform the natural parents and, accordingly, the application would be allowed.

    Re J (A Minor) (Change of Name) [1993] 1 FCR 74 (Family Division: Booth J).

363   Child care—representations, placements and reviews

The Children (Homes, Arrangements for Placement, Reviews and Representations) (Miscellaneous Amendments) Regulations 1993, SI 1993/3069 (in force on 1 January 1994), amend the

1991 Regulations, SI 1991/1506, so as to provide that certain requirements of the 1991 Regulations will not apply to independent schools which are children's homes within the meaning of the Children Act 1989, s 63. The regulations exempts from the definitions of "voluntary home" and "children's home" in the Children Act 1989 so as to remove the requirement to register premises used only for the purpose of providing holiday accommodation, or as approved probation hostels and approved bail hostels, or as hostels run by football clubs for professional footballers or trainee professional footballers who are under 18 years old, or as colleges of further education. Further minor amendments are made to the Arrangements for Placement of Children (General) Regulations 1991, SI 1991/890, the Review of Children's Cases Regulations 1991, SI 1991/895, and the Representations Procedure (Children) Regulations 1991, SI 1991/894, respectively so as to disapply these regulations in the case of placements, otherwise than by a local authority or voluntary organisation, in those independent schools that are children's homes and in special schools.

364 Child care legislation—duty of local authority—right of action against local authority

It has been held that a person has no right to claim damages for breach of statutory duty nor a cause of action in negligence against a local authority under the legislation relating to child care, in particular the Children Act 1989. Parliament did not intend to create a private law right of action with the 1989 Act because the duties imposed were similar to those in the housing legislation which can only be challenged by judicial review. If a local authority might be liable under the 1989 Act, then so might all the other agencies involved in the child care process, which is an unlikely aim of Parliament. The duty a local authority is called on to discharge is one imposed on it by law and is not voluntarily assumed. It would be neither just nor reasonable to allow a private law action to be brought and it is contrary to the public interest as local authorities would have to disclose their records which could lead to guarded or defensive record-keeping that disadvantages others.

X (Minors) v Bedfordshire County Council [1993] NLJR 1783 (Queen's Bench Division: Turner J).

365 Child support—appeals—jurisdiction of courts

The Child Support Appeals (Jurisdiction of Courts) Order 1993, SI 1993/961 (in force on 5 April 1993), provides that appeals against decisions of child support officers on reviews under the Child Support Act 1991, s 18 must be made to a court where an issue of disputed parentage is raised, notwithstanding the provision in the 1991 Act, s 20 that such appeals must be made to a child support appeal tribunal.

366 Child support—family proceedings courts—procedure

The Family Proceedings Courts (Child Support Act 1991) Rules 1993, SI 1993/627 (in force on 5 April 1993), deal with proceedings in family proceedings courts under the Child Support Act 1991. In particular, the 1993 Rules (1) prescribe the procedure under the 1991 Act, ss 20 (appeals against decisions of child support officers) and 27 (applications in respect of parentage issues); (2) remove the restrictions on disclosure of relevant information relating to court proceedings to the Secretary of State in connection with certain of his functions under the 1991 Act; (3) prescribe the procedure in relation to applications for relief which is precluded by the 1991 Act; and (4) amend a number of forms so as to obtain information about maintenance assessments made under the 1991 Act.

367 Child support—High Court proceedings—allocation—Family Division

See para 2042.

368 Child support—magistrates' court proceedings—hearsay evidence

See para 1242.

369 Child support—maintenance—increased periodical payments—effect on prior divorce settlement

See *Crozier v Crozier*, para 1011.

370 Child support—maintenance assessment—calculation

The Child Support (Maintenance Assessments and Special Cases) Amendment Regulations 1993, SI 1993/925 (in force on 26 April 1993), amend the 1992 Regulations, SI 1992/1815, by changing the way in which payments in place of payments of child support maintenance under the Child Support Act 1991, s 43 are apportioned where there is more than one person with care of the child. Provision is also made for the effective date of a decision given on a review of a decision relating to such payments.

371 Child support—maintenance order—backdating

The Maintenance Orders (Backdating) Order 1993, SI 1993/623 (in force on 5 April 1993), amends the Matrimonial Causes Act 1973, the Domestic Proceedings and Magistrates' Courts Act 1978 and the Children Act 1989 so as to permit maintenance orders to be backdated to the effective date of a maintenance assessment made under the Child Support Act 1991. The application for the maintenance order must be made within six months of the date of assessment. The 1993 Order also extends the definition of family proceedings in the Magistrates' Courts Act 1980, s 65 to cover certain proceedings under the 1991 Act.

372 Child support—maintenance order—written agreement

The Child Maintenance (Written Agreements) Order 1993, SI 1993/620 (in force on 5 April 1993), preserves the jurisdiction of courts to make a maintenance order in relation to a child, notwithstanding that a child support officer has jurisdiction to make a maintenance assessment under the Child Support Act 1991 in respect of the child, where the order is in the same terms as a prior written agreement as to maintenance for the child.

373 Child support—reciprocal arrangements—Northern Ireland

The Child Support (Northern Ireland Reciprocal Arrangements) Regulations 1993, SI 1993/584 (in force on 5 April 1993), give effect in Great Britain to reciprocal arrangements relating to matters for which provision is made in Great Britain by the Child Support Act 1991. The arrangements are contained in the Memorandum set out in the regulations and have been made between the Secretary of State for Social Security and the Department of Health and Social Services for Northern Ireland. The regulations provide that certain matters to which the provisions of the Northern Ireland legislation relate have a corresponding effect in respect of the provisions of the Child Support Act 1991.

374 Child support—recovery of maintenance—members of royal forces and merchant seamen

The Child Support Act 1991 (Consequential Amendments) Order 1993, SI 1993/785 (in force on 12 April 1993), amends the Army Act 1955, the Air Force Act 1955, the Naval Forces (Enforcement of Maintenance Liabilities) Act 1947 and the Merchant Shipping Act 1970 by making provision for the recovery of child support maintenance by deductions from the pay of members of the royal forces and merchant seamen.

375 Child support—regulations—miscellaneous amendments

The Child Support (Miscellaneous Amendments) Regulations 1993, SI 1993/913 (in force on 5 April 1993), make various miscellaneous amendments to the following regulations made under the Child Support Act 1991: the Child Support (Maintenance Assessment Procedure) Regulations 1992, SI 1992/1813, the Child Support (Maintenance Assessment and Special Cases) Regulations 1992, SI 1992/1815, the Child Support (Arrears, Interest and Adjustment of Maintenance Assessments) Regulations 1992, SI 1992/1816, the Child Support (Collection and Enforcement) Regulations 1992, SI 1992/1989, the Child Support (Collection and Enforcement of Other Forms of Maintenance) Regulations 1992, SI 1992/2643, and the Child Support (Maintenance Arrangements and Jurisdiction) Regulations 1992, SI 1992/2645.

376 Child Support Act 1991—commencement

The Child Support Act 1991 (Commencement No 3 and Transitional Provisions) Amendment Order 1993, SI 1993/966, amends the transitional provisions contained in the Schedule to the 1992 Order, SI 1992/2644. For a summary of the Act, see 1991 Abr para 254. For details of commencement, see the commencement table in the *Current Service* Noter-up binder.

377 Childminders—registration—cancellation

A local authority made a successful ex parte application under the Children Act 1989, s 75(3) to cancel the applicant's registration as a childminder. The magistrates refused her request for an inter partes hearing to challenge the order. She then applied for an order of mandamus requiring the magistrates to give her a hearing. *Held*, the correctness of an ex parte decision was open to challenge, particularly if, as here, it was made by a single justice. Accordingly, the application would be allowed.

R v St Albans Magistrates' Court, ex p J [1993] Fam Law 518 (Queen's Bench Division: Hutchison J).

378 Contact—conditions of contact—progress reports

A father of a three-year-old child was sentenced to three years' imprisonment. He applied for and was granted an order for indirect contact under the Children Act 1989, s 8. Conditions were attached under the 1989 Act, s 11(7) ordering the mother to write progress reports on the child and to send them to the father. The mother appealed against the imposition of the conditions. *Held*, the court was correct to order contact by post but it did not have the jurisdiction by way of a contact order pursuant to the 1989 Act, s 8 to impose a condition under s 11(7) for the mother to write progress reports on the child. However, there was the power under the 1989 Act, s 11(7) to direct a residential parent to keep the other parent informed of the child's whereabouts as a necessary condition of contact. Accordingly, the appeal would be allowed.

Re M (A Minor) (1993) Times, 10 November (Family Division: Wall J).

379 Contact order—adopted child—application for leave—guidelines

A child was living with her adoptive parents and had had no contact with her natural mother for over three years. An application was made by the natural mother for contact with the child. *Held*, the natural mother was not a parent within the meaning of the Children Act 1989, s 10 and therefore, before making an application for contact with the adopted child the mother would require the leave of the court. Guidelines were given on the conduct of applications for leave before seeking contact: (1) such applications should not be made ex parte, (2) the local authority concerned in the adoption arrangements ought to be informed, (3) the Official Solicitor ought to be joined as a party, (4) it would not be appropriate for the adoptive parents to be joined or informed about the application unless the Official Solicitor was of the view that they ought to be informed, (5) where the adoptive parents were joined in the action the notice of application ought to be served by the Official Solicitor and not by the court and (6) such applications ought to be transferred to the Family Division of the High Court. An adoption order was intended to be final and as such a natural parent would have to make out an extremely strong case and therefore, to reopen the issue of contact there would have to be a fundamental change of circumstances. In the present case the child had only lived with the mother for the first month of her life and had had no contact with her since the age of one. Accordingly, the application would be dismissed.

Re S (A Minor) [1993] 2 FCR 234 (Family Division: Thorpe J). *Re O (a Minor) (Wardship: Adopted Child)* [1978] Fam 196 applied.

380 Contact order—application for contact order—application by natural father—child believing step-father to be natural father

A father had had no contact with his five-year-old daughter for four years. She had been brought up to believe that her mother's cohabitee was her father and was not aware of her natural father. The mother requested that she be given time to defer the moment of telling until her daughter was eight. An order was made forbidding the father to have any contact with his daughter and on appeal by the father against the order, *held*, whilst the father's application was sincere it was unrealistic and dangerous to try to reintroduce him to the child without the child having received prior information which at this stage the mother was incapable of giving. Nevertheless to wait until the age of eight was not sensible as it would allow the mother to put an unwelcome duty to one side. The mother, stepfather and the child needed skilled help, best provided by a child psychiatrist who could get to know the family, give them reassurance and preferably enable the mother to tell the child herself. The next stage would be an evaluation of the best way to introduce the father and daughter. A great deal of patience was required of the father and he had to remember that going slowly at this stage made the prospect of a genuine long term relationship with his daughter more likely. Accordingly the appeal would be allowed.

Re R (A Minor) (Access) [1993] 1 FCR 954 (Court of Appeal: Nourse and Butler-Sloss LJJ).

381 Contact order—application for contact order—challenge to decision in wardship proceedings

A father had a three-year-old son and acted as de facto step-father to a seven-year-old girl. The children, who had been the subject of wardship proceedings, were committed to the care of the local authority with leave to place them with long term foster parents with a view to adoption. It was further ordered that parental contact would be at the authority's discretion and the authority was given leave to terminate such contact. The authority subsequently gave notice that it intended to terminate parental contact. The father applied for a parental responsibility order and contact with the boy and for leave to apply for contact with the girl. The authority successfully applied for his applications to be dismissed. The judge, applying the test in *Cheshire County Council v M* [1992] 2 FCR 817, found that the father's applications were fundamentally inconsistent with the wardship order and had little chance of succeeding, that it was not in the children's interest to further delay planning their future and that no relevant new material had been placed before the court. On appeal, *held, Cheshire County Council v M* was correctly decided and rightly followed by the judge. It applied to a limited class of cases, where the advent of the Children Act 1989 provided an opportunity to seek to undermine orders made in wardship to secure the welfare of children after full investigation and which had not been challenged on appeal. This was not a summary dismissal of the father's applications since the judge considered the substantive applications made at a preliminary hearing. The principles for parental responsibility applications were clearly established: (1) the court should have regard to the degree of commitment which the father had shown to the child, the degree of attachment which existed between them, and the father's reasons for applying for the order; and (2) the fact that the parental rights might not currently be exercisable in practice did not preclude the making of an order. The father had no good reason for making the application, particularly since he was entitled to apply to be joined as a party to the adoption proceedings. The judge was justified in dismissing the father's applications and, accordingly, the appeal would be dismissed.

Re W (Children in Care) (Contact and Parental Responsibility Orders) [1993] 2 FCR 427 (Court of Appeal: Sir Stephen Brown P, Simon Brown and Gibson LJJ). *Cheshire County Council v M* [1992] 2 FCR 817 (1992 Abr para 310) applied.

382 Contact order—application for contact order—denial of contact with one parent

The parties were unmarried and separated before the birth of their son. The father was very violent towards the mother during the course of the relationship. Because of his past behaviour the parents of the mother, with whom she returned to live, formed a very adverse view of the father. The father applied for access to the son and a recorder ordered interim supervised access for three trial periods. Interim access was later suspended and at the full hearing the father's application was dismissed. On appeal, *held*, the approach to access by a parent had not changed following the Children Act 1989. The starting point was that the child's right was to know both his parents, but there might be cases where there were cogent reasons why the child should be denied that opportunity. It was well settled that hostility of a mother towards access or contact was capable of supplying a cogent reason for departing from the general principle that a child should grow up in the knowledge of both his parents. The decision of the judge was well within the "generous ambit within which reasonable disagreement is possible", following the decision in *G v G (Minors: Custody Appeal)* [1985] 2 FLR 894 (1985 Abr para 1744). Accordingly, the appeal would be dismissed.

Re D (A Minor) (Contact: Mother's Hostility) [1993] 2 FLR 1 (Court of Appeal: Balcombe and Waite LJJ).

383 Contact order—long-term foster care—reasonable contact

The father of two children in the care of the local authority, was allowed access once a month for one hour. The eldest child expressed a wish to maintain contact with her father so the local authority sought to place the children in a long-term foster home with continued contact. The father applied for the discharge of the care order but, after the evidence was heard, conceded that there was insufficient support for his application. He therefore confined himself to an application for increased contact. At the time of the hearing, an applicant for foster care was being considered and a change of placement seemed likely in the foreseeable future. *Held*, the Children Act 1989, s 34 provided that a local authority must ensure there was reasonable contact between a child in its care and the child's parents. Reasonable contact was not the same as access at the discretion of the local authority but implied access which was agreed between the local authority and the parents or, if there was no such agreement, access which was objectively reasonable. It was not appropriate to order a change in frequency of access given the probable change of care within the near future. Accordingly, an order would be made allowing the father not less than $2\frac{1}{2}$ hours once a month.

Re P (Minors) (Contact with Children in Care) [1993] 2 FLR 156 (Family Division: Ewbank J).

384 Contact order—mother and son both children—priority between children

The Children Act 1989, s 34(1) provides that where a child is in the care of a local authority, the authority must allow that child reasonable contact with categorised persons, including the child's parents. Under the 1989 Act, s 34(2), on the application of the child or the authority, the court can make an order in respect of contact as it considers appropriate between the child and any named person. The 1989 Act, s 34(3) provides that on an application for contact by any person specified in s 34(1), the court can make such order as it finds appropriate. Under the 1989 Act, s 34(4), on the application of the child or the authority, the court can make an order authorising the authority to refuse to allow contact between the child and the persons specified in s 34(1).

A mother, aged 16 and in the care of a local authority, had a two-year-old son who was also in care. The authority successfully sought leave to terminate contact between the mother and the child. On the mother's appeal, the Court of Appeal held that the 1989 Act, s 34 did not indicate that, where both parent and child were children, the latter's interests were to prevail. Rather, the court had to approach the question of their respective welfare without giving either priority over the other. Having conducted that balancing exercise, the court held that, since properly monitored contact would be beneficial to the mother and not detrimental to the child, the judge's order should be set aside. The child, proceeding through his guardian ad litem, appealed and the authority supported his appeal. *Held*, correctly construed, the child referred to in the 1989 Act, s 34(4) was the child in care in respect of whom an order was sought by the persons categorised in s 34(1). That child was the subject of the application and his welfare had to be the court's paramount consideration. The fact that the parent was also a child did not require a balancing exercise to be carried out since no question fell to be determined about the parent's upbringing. The judge had correctly considered that the child's welfare was the court's paramount consideration and it was impossible to say that he erred in the exercise of his discretion by prohibiting contact. Accordingly, the appeal would be allowed.

Birmingham City Council v H (A Minor) [1994] 1 All ER 12 (House of Lords: Lords Keith of Kinkel, Jauncey of Tullichettle, Browne-Wilkinson, Slynn of Hadley and Woolf). Decision of Court of Appeal [1993] 1 FLR 883 reversed.

385 Contact order—procedure in magistrates' court

Following the breakdown of her relationship with the father of her child, the mother married another man and the child's surname was changed to that of her mother's married name. The child continued to have contact with her natural father, who subsequently applied for a parental responsibility order and a specific issue order requiring the child's surname to be changed back to that of the natural father. The court made an order as to contact with her natural father but made neither a specific issue order nor a parental responsibility order, and no written order was drawn up. On the father's appeal, *held*, in order to decide the issue of parental responsibility, the magistrates had to give express consideration to the degree of commitment which the father had shown towards the child, the degree of attachment which existed between them, and the father's reasons for applying for the order. The magistrates had not given sufficient consideration to those matters, and as a result the exercise of their discretion had been imperfectly completed and there would have to be a further hearing on the question of contact. Accordingly, the appeal would be allowed and the case remitted for rehearing.

S v R (Parental Responsibility) [1993] 1 FCR 331 (Family Division: Thorpe J).

386 Contact order—reasons for decision—duty to record reasons

The parents, who were not married to each other, had one child. The father and the paternal grandmother both applied for contact orders. A welfare officer's report concluded that although he had not had the opportunity to see the father, it appeared appropriate to grant contact to the father in tandem with the grandmother. At the hearing, contact with the grandmother was agreed but contact to the father was contested. After the hearing, the magistrates ordered that the child should have contact with the father. The chairman of the magistrates stated that contact with the father be shared with the grandmother but this was not recorded in the magistrates' reasons nor in the order which was drawn up. On appeal by the father, *held*, the court had failed to carry out its duty under the Family Proceedings Courts (Children Act 1989) Rules 1991, SI 1991/1395, r 21(5) and (6). The justices' clerk was required, in consultation with the magistrates, to record the reasons for the court's decision and any findings of fact. Furthermore, the court was required to state orally any findings of fact and the reasons for the decision when making an order or refusing an application. In giving reasons for the decision no reference was made to the welfare officer's report, the quantity of access and its effect on the child and the possibility of shared contact. Accordingly, the appeal would be allowed, and the case would be remitted to the family proceedings court for rehearing by different magistrates

W v L [1993] 1 FCR 591 (Family Division: Douglas Brown J).

A father sought a contact order. His application was opposed by the mother. An interim contact hearing took place, and after hearing the evidence and submissions, the justices retired. They returned approximately 1½ hours later and indicated that they had not finished writing down their reasons, but would give their decision that day. They refused to grant the application for interim contact, and stated that they would complete the writing of the reasons the next day. The father appealed, contending that there had been a breach of the Family Proceedings Court (Children Act 1989) Rules 1991, SI 1991/1395, r 21(5), as the clerk had not recorded in writing the reasons for the justices' decision and their findings of fact before they had refused to grant the application. It was also submitted that there had also been a breach of r 21(6), as the justices, in refusing the order, had not stated any findings of fact and the reasons for their decision. *Held*, there had been an innocent failure to comply with r 21(5), (6). The chairman, in his anxiety to assist the parties, had not complied with the rules, and in the light of the existing authorities, the appeal would be allowed.

Re K (Minors) (13 May 1993, unreported) (Family Division: Sir Stephen Brown P) (Ruth Blair, Messrs Hornby & Levy, for the father; Mark Maitland-James, Messrs Hugnell & Co, for the mother) (Kindly submitted for publication by Ruth Blair, Barrister) This case has now been reported at [1993] Fam Law 615.

387 Contact order—refusal—religious beliefs of father

The parties were married and had two children. The father was convicted of fraudulent trading as managing director of a finance house and sentenced to prison. Though the mother was an atheist the children were raised as Roman Catholics, ostensibly by the father, described by the court as having extreme religious views that were ultimately counter-productive to the children's development. Following his release from prison the father made numerous applications seeking legal custody of the children and various orders regarding the children's upbringing and education. At the final hearing the judge dismissed the father's applications, made no order as to access and granted custody, care and control of the children to the mother. On appeal by the father, *held*, the welfare of the children was paramount and active steps were to be taken to promote future access with the father. As to the father's insistence on a strict religious upbringing and education, someone other than the parents, such as the Official Solicitor, could assist the children in separating their own thoughts about religion from their own thoughts about their father. In the future the father was not to make religion the basis of renewed applications for access. In this case the Official Solicitor would be invited to act for the children as guardian ad litem to promote renewed access between the children and the non-custodial parent. Accordingly, the appeal would be allowed in part.

Re S (Minors) (Access: Religious Upbringing) [1992] 2 FLR 313 (Court of Appeal: Butler-Sloss and Mann LJJ).

388 Emergency protection order—magistrates' refusal of application—right of appeal

A local authority commenced proceedings for an inter partes application for an emergency protection order in relation to a child with special needs who had been taken into local authority care at the mother's request. They considered that the child was at risk of significant harm if she was returned to the immediate care of her mother without preparation or safeguards. A notice of the application was posted to the mother but the magistrates found that she had not received one clear day's notice of the proceedings and were minded to adjourn. The local authority then unsuccessfully made an alternative application that the magistrates deal with the application on an ex parte basis. The local authority appealed, contending that the magistrates failed to give reasons for their decision and that it was thus unreasonable. *Held*, the Children Act 1989, s 45(10) provided that no appeal might be made against the making of, or refusal to make, an emergency protection order. The 1989 Act, s 45(10) was clear in its terms and so the court was compelled to find that there was no scope for the appellate process. If the magistrates had acted unreasonably, the only remedy was by way of judicial review. Accordingly, the appeal would be dismissed.

Essex County Council v F [1993] 2 FCR 289 (Family Division: Douglas Brown J).

389   Family proceedings—application by minor—removal of guardian ad litem—factors to be considered by court

Following the breakdown of their relationship, the parents of an 11-year old boy were involved in acrimonious and persistent litigation about how the boy should be brought up and with which parent he should reside. The boy, who supported the father's contention that he should live with him, had been made a party to the proceedings and the Official Solicitor was appointed as his guardian ad litem. The Official Solicitor advised the court that the boy should live with his mother with reduced access to the father, and on the basis of that divergence of view the boy applied for leave to conduct the remaining proceedings without a guardian ad litem. His application was refused, and the boy appealed. *Held,* the Family Proceedings Rules 1991, SI 1991/1247, r 9.2A allowed a minor who wished to continue without the representation of a next friend or guardian ad litem to do so if the court considered that the minor had sufficient understanding to participate in the proceedings without being represented by either of those persons. Save in a relatively straightforward matter or in the case of an older child the court would be unlikely to grant leave unless the child proposed to be legally represented, in which case the application would turn on whether the child had sufficient understanding to give coherent instructions. The level of a child's understanding had to be assessed on the basis of the issues in the proceedings, and the judge's conclusion that the boy lacked sufficient understanding to participate as a party in emotionally complex and highly fraught proceedings was not open to criticism. Accordingly, the appeal would be dismissed.

Re S (A Minor) (Independent Representation) [1993] 3 All ER 36 (Court of Appeal: Sir Thomas Bingham MR, Rose and Waite LJJ).

390   Family proceedings—application by minor for independent representation—removal of guardian ad litem—appointment of Official Solicitor as amicus curiae

The family of H, who was 15 years old, went to live in France. H, who wished to remain in England, then went to live with S, a teacher. S was arrested and charged with serious sexual offences and H's parents commenced wardship proceedings. An injunction was granted restraining contact between H and S, and the Official Solicitor was appointed as guardian ad litem in relation to the proceedings. H applied to continue to defend the proceedings without the Official Solicitor, pursuant to the Family Proceedings Rules 1991, SI 1991/1247, r 9(2)(a)(iv). *Held,* the test to be applied was whether the child had sufficient understanding to participate as a party in the proceedings. The test had to be considered in the light of all the circumstances of the case and in the light of what had happened, as well as what was likely to happen in the course of the proceedings in the future. In this case H was not so strongly influenced by S that he was not able to present his views as his own. In the circumstances therefore, H had sufficient understanding to participate as a party in the proceedings. It was not for the court in applying the test to take into account what the court might or might not consider to be in the best interests of the child. The Official Solicitor should continue in the role of amicus curiae and not guardian ad litem. The role of amicus curiae would be extended to cover the wide range of assistance which would be appropriate in the circumstances. He did not represent the child but would be subject to the direction of the court and was in a position of independent adviser to the court. It was not therefore appropriate for the Official Solicitor to be joined as a party to the proceedings. The Official Solicitor would only be requested to act as amicus curiae where the court needed such independent assistance and it would be for him to decide whether to give his consent to act. The form of order appointing the Official Solicitor as amicus curiae was approved. Accordingly, the application would be granted.

Re H (A Minor) (Independent Representation) [1993] 2 FCR 437 (Family Division: Booth J). *Re S (A Minor) (Independent Representation)* [1993] 3 All ER 36, applied.

391   Family proceedings—applications for leave—written request

The Family Proceedings Courts (Children Act 1989) Rules 1991, SI 1991/1395, r 3 provides that where a person makes an application for leave of the court to bring proceedings under the Children Act 1989, the person seeking leave must file a written request and on considering that request the court may either grant the request or direct a date for the hearing of the request, with notice to the other party involved.

It has been held that although the 1989 Rules, r 3 provides that a written request must be filed, where a magistrate is dealing with a matter of some urgency and the addition of a written request would actually add nothing to the situation in a particular case, the fact that the magistrate makes an order without such a written request does not automatically invalidate the order.The validity of the order must be decided after taking into account all the facts and circumstances of the case.

Re O (Residence Order) (Application for Leave) [1993] 2 FCR 482 (Family Division: Ewbank J).

392   Family proceedings—courts—duty to give reasons—inadequate reasons

An unmarried couple had a baby girl and separated when she was nine months old. They agreed that the child would spend equal time with each of them on a half-weekly basis. About two years later the arrangement broke down due to parental animosity. It had proved stressful for the girl, who had learnt to play her parents off against each other. The mother, who had married, applied for a residence order and the father cross-applied. The magistrates made an order granting residence to the father and contact to the mother at weekends, giving the sole reason that they were impressed by the father's stimulation of the girl's educational needs. The mother promptly lodged a notice of appeal and the matter was listed for a hearing, the date of which was subsequently brought forward. A day before the hearing, the father successfully applied to have the matter removed from the list because he had not yet obtained an extension of his legal aid certificate and the appeal was relisted. The mother was informed that any attempt to apply for a stay or expedited hearing to the High Court would probably result in a vacating of the new hearing date. *Held*, the written reasons that the magistrates gave were defective and did not support their decision. They failed to state what the issues and material facts were, they did not refer to the evidence nor any findings on it, and they failed to provide a cogent explanation of how and why they reached the decision. Thus, from the record, it was impossible to assess whether their conclusion was right or wrong. Accordingly, the appeal would be allowed.

Re J (A Minor) (Residence) [1993] 2 FCR 636 (Family Division: Singer J).

393   Family proceedings—courts—transfer of proceedings

A girl made serious allegations of sexual abuse against her father. At a directions hearing for care proceedings the substantive hearing was set down for two days duration although in the interim the complexity of the case became apparent to the local authority and it applied to transfer the case to the appropriate county court. The magistrate refused, stating that the case was not one of exceptional complexity and that a transfer would not reduce delay. The local authority did not seek a review of the refusal because it was told by a clerk of the county court that if the transfer was successful, the earliest date for a two-day hearing by a judge would be in several months' time. On the question of whether the local authority felt it would be better to accept the jurisdiction of the magistrates at an earlier date, *held*, there were some issues that were not suitable for magistrates to determine and which required the attention of a professional judge. When the local authority sought to challenge the magistrate's refusal to transfer the case it was wrong for the court administration at the county court to deal with the request for court time. The local authority should have sought a review from a district judge who would have taken steps to ensure the availability of a judge to hear the case. Judgement would be given accordingly.

Re L (Care Proceedings: Transfer) [1993] 1 FCR 689 (Family Division: Bracewell J).

394   Family proceedings—evidence—contempt

Following a divorce, the mother was granted custody of her children, with supervised access to the father. At the hearing to determine custody, it was found that the father had sexually abused at least one of the children. A non-molestation injunction was obtained, and a second injunction was obtained restraining the father from approaching within 100 yards of the former matrimonial home. Neither injunction referred specifically to the children. The mother then began proceedings against the father for contempt, alleging breach of both injunctions. At the hearing, the mother sought to admit the children's evidence contained in a court welfare officer's report and an affidavit sworn by the minister of her church. The judge was asked to rule on the admissibility of the children's evidence, which apparently demonstrated breaches of the second injunction. The judge held that the hearsay evidence of the children was inadmissible in the contempt proceedings and the evidence of the minister was to be excluded on the grounds that contempt proceedings were not proceedings within the Children (Admissibility of Hearsay

Evidence) Order 1991, SI 1991/1115, art 2. On the mother's appeal, *held*, for the order to apply, the applicant who sought to rely on children's hearsay evidence should be required to demonstrate that the proposed evidence showed a substantial connection with the upbringing, maintenance or welfare of a child. The admission of hearsay evidence would depend on the facts in each case. The injunctions in this case were not granted for the children's protection, nor did the children appear to have been the objects of or to have been seriously affected by the alleged actions of the father. Although the judge correctly excluded the hearsay evidence, he went too far in ruling that hearsay evidence was always to be excluded in contempt proceedings. The appeal would accordingly be dismissed.

Re C (Minors) (Contempt: Evidence) [1993] 4 All ER 690 (Court of Appeal: Butler-Sloss and Simon Brown LJJ).

395   Family proceedings—evidence—disclosure

The mother was married to F. They had a son, and the mother had a daughter from a previous marriage. F left the matrimonial home and divorce proceedings were commenced. Joint custody of the son was given, with care and control to the mother and reasonable access to F. F's stepdaughter complained that she had been sexually abused by F and that she feared that he would kill her if he learned of the complaints. The mother, on the advice of the social services, terminated the son's access to F fearing that he would learn of the allegations and applied for an order prohibiting F from communicating with the son, preventing her affidavit evidence setting out the stepdaughter's allegations from being disclosed to him pending the completion of the investigations, and directing his solicitors not to disclose to him the nature of the matters under investigation or the evidence produced. The judge granted the order and suspended access. The application form was served on F with parts of it deleted and without the affidavit. F successfully sought a discharge of that order, requiring the mother to supply him with a copy of her affidavit and the completed application form. The mother appealed. *Held*, before making an order for non-disclosure of any evidence, the court had to satisfy itself that the disclosure of the evidence would be so detrimental to the child's welfare as to outweigh the normal requirements of a fair trial. The jurisdiction should only be exercised in exceptional circumstances and then only for the shortest period possible consonant with preserving the child's welfare. On the facts, an order would be made for the mother's affidavit and the materials contained in the application form to be disclosed to F, allowing for a short delay for one of the children to be informed of the step to be taken. The appeal would accordingly be dismissed.

Re B (A Minor) [1993] 1 All ER 931 (Court of Appeal: Glidewell and Balcombe LJJ and Boreham J).

See *Re D (Minors) (Conciliation: Disclosure of Information)*, para 996.

396   Family proceedings—jurisdiction—stay of proceedings

The mother lived with the father and their child in England. The mother took the baby to Scotland and informed the father that their relationship was over and that she was taking the child to Iceland. The father began proceedings in England for residence, contact and parental responsibility orders. The mother was granted, in a Scottish court, an interim interdict prohibiting the father from removing the child from Scotland without her written consent. Proceedings were stayed in England pending a decision in the Scottish court on the question of contact. The father's appeal against the stay of proceedings was dismissed, and a stay of proceedings under the Family Law Act 1986, s 5(2) was granted, although the judge refused a stay of the father's application for parental responsibility. Subsequently, proceedings were continued in England. On a further appeal by the father from the stay of proceedings and on a cross-appeal by the mother against the refusal to stay the application for a parental resposibility order, *held*, it would be the worst of both worlds for proceedings relating to contact or access to be dealt with in different jurisdictions at the same time, and the subsequent proceedings in the English court should not have been maintained. In respect of the mother's cross-appeal, all matters in the dispute had to be dealt with in the same forum, but there was nothing illogical in making a parental responsibility order even though the father had no immediate prospect of exercising parental rights. Therefore, there was nothing illogical in granting a stay of his residence and contact applications while refusing a stay of his application for a parental responsibility order. The father's appeal and the mother's cross-appeal would therefore be dismissed.

Re S (A Minor) (1993) Independent, 8 September (Court of Appeal: Lloyd, Butler-Sloss and Roch LJJ).

397 Family proceedings—legal aid—remuneration

See para 1667.

398 Family proceedings—legal aid—scope

See para 1660.

399 Family proceedings—Official Solicitor—appointment as guardian ad litem

The Official Solicitor and the Children Act Advisory Committee have issued the following *Practice Note* ([1993] 2 FLR 641) to assist the courts and the profession in securing the services of the Official Solicitor in cases where his appointment is considered appropriate and to avoid delay in undertaking his investigations.

1. In specified (public law) proceedings under the Children Act 1989, the Official Solicitor may only be appointed to act as a child's guardian ad litem (guardian) in the High Court. In private law proceedings under the 1989 Act, he may act as a child's guardian in the High Court and county court, but not the family proceedings court. The criteria for the appointment of the Official Solicitor as the guardian of a subject child include cases in which there is disputed medical evidence or medical opinion is at variance, where there is a substantial foreign element, where there are special or exceptional points of law, or where he is already acting for the child in other proceedings. Subject to the Family Proceedings Rules 1991, SI 1991/1247, r 9.2A (proceedings by minor without guardian or next friend) the Official Solicitor may also act as the next friend of a child seeking leave to make an application under the 1989 Act or making an application in other family proceedings. The Official Solicitor can also be appointed to act as the child's guardian in adoption and freeing proceedings in the High Court and as the guardian of a child who is the subject of wardship proceedings under the inherent jurisdiction of the High Court.

2. In the absence of any other suitable or willing person, the Official Solicitor is available to be appointed in the High Court or the county court as the guardian or next friend of: (a) an adult party who is suffering from mental disorder within the meaning of the Mental Health Act 1983 to an extent that renders him incapable of managing his property and affairs (medical evidence confirming this must be obtained by the Official Solicitor before he can accept the appointment); or (b) subject to the 1991 Rules, r 9.2A above, a minor party other than the child who is the subject of the proceedings.

3. Orders appointing the Official Solicitor must be expressed as being subject to his consent. To ensure that he is allowed sufficient time to undertake the investigations he considers necessary in any particular matters, a substantive hearing date must not be fixed without prior consultation between the court listing officer and the Official Solicitor's caseworker.

4. Where the circumstances of the case justify seeking the involvement of the Official Solicitor, the questionnaire below, and a copy of the order appointing him, must be sent with the court file to the Official Solicitor.

5. The questionnaire referred to in 4 above is as follows:
(a) name, address and telephone/fax number of court;
(b) title of case;
(c) case reference number;
(d) nature of proceedings, ie specified or private law;
(e) name of person(s) for whom the Official Solicitor is invited to act;
(f) state whether this person is a child or mentally incapacitated adult;
(g) is this person a party to the case?; if so, as what?;
(h) state briefly (having regard to the criteria for the Official Solicitor's involvement) the special circumstances that are thought to make the Official Solicitor's involvement appropriate;
(i) has the case been transferred, or is it proposed to transfer it? give details;
(j) what is the date of the next court appointment, where is it and in front of whom?

6. The Official Solicitor operates a help line on which he must be told of any invitation to act about to be sent by fax, and on which general advice can be obtained.

400 Family proceedings—orders—applications—applications by children concerned

The President of the Family Division, with the concurrence of the Lord Chancellor, has given the following *Practice Direction* ([1993] 1 All ER 820).

Under the Children Act 1989, s 10 the prior leave of the court is required in respect of applications by the child concerned for s 8 orders (contact, prohibited steps, residence and specific issue orders). The Family Proceedings Rules 1991, SI 1991/1247, r 4.3 and the Family Proceedings Courts (Children Act 1989) Rules 1991, SI 1991/1395, r 3 set out the procedure to be followed when applying for leave.

Such applications raise issues which are more appropriate for determination in the High Court and should be transferred there for hearing.

401 Family proceedings—proceedings before magistrates—acting stipendiary magistrate—jurisdiction

Following the separation of the parents, their three children stayed with the mother. The local authority commenced care proceedings under the Children and Young Persons Act 1969 and obtained an interim care order placing the children with the father who then applied for residence orders under the Children Act 1989, s 8. An acting stipendiary magistrate made residence orders in favour of the father under the 1989 Act and a supervision order under the 1969 Act. He also directed that the mother's contact be supervised by the local authority, under the 1989 Act, s 11(7). The mother then applied for judicial review on the ground that the acting stipendiary magistrate had acted without jurisdiction. The local authority appealed against the order that they supervise the mother's contact. *Held*, under the Family Proceedings Courts (Constitution) Rules 1991, SI 1991/1405, r 2(1), a "stipendiary magistrate" was a person who had been nominated by the Lord Chancellor and did not include an acting stipendiary magistrate, consequently the acting stipendiary magistrate did not have the appropriate jurisdiction to hear family cases. It was undesirable and unnecessary to make orders under both the 1969 and the 1989 Acts. Having made substantive orders under the 1989 Act, the court ought to have looked to see what orders under that Act were necessary for any further relief. Furthermore, it was not possible to require a local authority to supervise contact under the 1989 Act, s 11(7)(d) as the section did not enable the court to impose those obligations. Accordingly, the application would be granted, and the appeal allowed.

Leeds City Council v C [1993] 1 FCR 585 (Family Division: Booth J).

402 Family proceedings—proceedings before magistrates—interim order

A care order with staying contact was made by a family proceedings court in respect of a boy aged five. Soon after the staying contact started the local authority made an application for the amount of contact to be reduced. At a directions hearing a date was fixed for an interim hearing but no directions were given. The local authority filed statements of the evidence they proposed to adduce but the parents did not file any statements. At the beginning of the hearing the magistrates, explaining that they had not read any of the statements, decided to determine the question of interim contact on the basis of representations by the parties. Submissions were made on behalf of the parties and the guardian ad litem summarised the content of a report made by her. The court clerk made a short note of the proceedings, omitting reference to a number of the main submissions and making no reference to the submissions made by the guardian ad litem. The magistrates then made an interim order reducing the amount of contact, stating that their reasons would be given at a later date. On appeal by the parents, *held*, at the directions hearing the court ought to have directed the parents to file written statements prior to the interim hearing. In neglecting to read the documents filed, the magistrates failed to comply with the requirements of the Family Proceedings Courts (Children Act 1989) Rules 1991, SI 1991/1395, r 21(1). Further, the clerk did not take adequate notes of the oral submissions and the court failed to comply with the 1991 Rules, r 21(5), (6) in that the reasons and findings of fact were not recorded in writing before the order was made and were not stated when the court announced its decision. Accordingly, the appeal would be allowed.

Hampshire County Council v S [1993] 1 All ER 944 (Family Division: Cazalet J).

403 Family proceedings—proceedings before magistrates—reasons for decision—guidelines

A mother with care of her four children asked their father to look after them for a short period. The father refused to return the children to her care and the mother applied for residence orders and specific issue orders in a family proceedings court. The court made an ex parte specific issue order requiring the children to be returned to the mother. At the substantive hearing the magistrates, contrary to the recommendations of a welfare officer, made residence orders in favour of the father. On the mother's appeal, *held*, the findings of fact recorded by the justices were a recital of uncontroversial history and they made no findings as to matters that were in issue before them. The justices' reasons were also inadequate in that they represented conclusions rather than the reasons that led them to those conclusions, and were not expressed sufficiently for the parties and the appellate court to see how they had approached their task. Although courts were free to exercise their discretion contrary to the recommendation of a welfare officer, it was a well-settled practice that they had to give a sufficiently detailed explanation for doing so. The justices in the present case had failed to do so. Accordingly, the mother's appeal would be allowed.

Johnson J expressed the view that orders which have the consequence of moving children from one home to another should not be granted ex parte except in the most compelling of circumstances. He also stated that every effort should be made to enable courts at all levels to have the opportunity of reading the necessary papers in advance of the hearing.

M v C (Children Orders: Reasons) [1993] 1 FCR 264 (Family Division: Johnson J).

404 Family proceedings—prohibited steps order—application by guardian ad litem after expiry of emergency protection order

A local authority which had been granted an emergency protection order in respect of a teenage child subsequently decided not to initiate care proceedings. When the emergency protection order expired the guardian ad litem, purporting to act in a professional capacity, applied ex parte for leave to apply for a prohibited steps order preventing contact between the child and the father. The magistrates granted the application, and the local authority appealed. *Held*, when an emergency protection order had expired and no care proceedings were pending a guardian ad litem could not continue to act in a professional capacity, and although the guardian ad litem could have applied for a prohibited steps order under the Children Act 1989, s 8 with the leave on the court she would have been acting in a personal capacity only. The court had a discretion to deal with such applications ex parte, but unless the matter was particularly urgent the interests of justice normally required the application to be dealt with on notice so that other interested parties might be able to make submissions. The local authority should not have been denied that opportunity and, accordingly, the appeal would be allowed. The matter would be remitted to the magistrates to be dealt with on notice to the local authority and, if the magistrates thought fit, the parents.

Re M (Prohibited Steps Order: Application for Leave) [1993] 1 FCR 78 (Family Division: Johnson J).

405 Family proceedings—representation of children—joining children as parties to action

An application was made by a father for a residence order in relation to his three children who he wished to take back to Australia. The judge at first instance ruled that the children should be represented separately. It was decided that asking the Official Solicitor to act would create a substantial delay and therefore, a solicitor from the child care panel was ordered to represent the children although they were not added as parties to the proceedings. The father appealed against the order for separate representation. *Held*, there had been insufficient argument for the court to reach a clear conclusion on this point. However, the present view of the court was that the Family Proceedings Rules 1991, SI 1991/1247, which governed private law applications, did not alter the general procedural rules set out in RSC Ord 80, r 2 which stated that children were to be parties to an action by their guardian ad litem. Children intervening in family applications in the High Court ought for practical reasons to be made parties in order to be clear about their position and to obviate any difficulties over who represented them. Accordingly, the appeal would not be allowed in substance, but would be allowed for the technicality of joining the children as parties, and the existing guardian ad litem would be confirmed.

Re L (Minors: Parties) (1993) Times, Independent, 11 November (Court of Appeal: Balcombe and Butler-Sloss LJJ and Sir Christopher Slade).

406 Family proceedings—transfer of proceedings from magistrates' court to county court—criteria relevant to transfer

A mother of four children had been convicted of causing actual bodily harm to one of her children and her three eldest children were taken into care. She subsequently swore an affidavit that the father of the two elder children was responsible for the child's injuries. The local authority applied for a care order in respect of the mother's youngest child. She then unsuccessfully applied, with the father of the two younger children, for the care proceedings to be transferred to the county court because of their probable complexity and duration. The justices heard evidence for four days, deliberated for another day and delivered their judgment, that a care order be made and parental contact limited, three days later. On appeal, *held*, applications for upward transfer on the grounds of duration had to be made at the earliest possible stage. The relevance of the authority that the likelihood of a case running for more than three days might itself be a reason for an upward transfer had been evidenced in the present case because one of the justices fell asleep on two successive days during the hearing and consequently was unable to take any part in the decision. The appeal would, however, be dismissed on other grounds.

Re A (A Minor) (Procedure) [1993] Fam Law 619 (Family Division: Thorpe J).

407 Family Proceedings Rules

The Family Proceedings (Amendment) Rules 1993, SI 1993/295 (in force on 5 April 1993), amend the 1991 Rules, SI 1991/1247, consequent upon changes introduced by the Child Support Act 1991. The 1993 Rules set out the procedure for applications for a declaration of parentage under the 1991 Act, ss 20, 27 and for appeals to the Court of Appeal from decisions of Child Support Commissioners under the 1991 Act, s 25. They also deal with the disclosure of information about court proceedings to the Secretary of State and establish a procedure for dealing with cases where there is a dispute as to whether a court or the Child Support Agency has jurisdiction to deal with child maintenance. The requirements of a divorce petition and certain forms are also amended to elicit information about maintenance assessments made under the 1991 Act.

408 Guardian—dissolution or annulment of marriage—revocation of appointment of former spouse as guardian

See para 2668.

409 Local authority—duty to provide for children in need—provision of day care—closure of nursery—judicial review

The council provided a nursery for children pursuant to its obligations under the Children Act 1989, ss 17 and 18, to provide day care for young children in need. The council initially recommended the closure of the nursery but revised its opinion following a review of day care provided, which was carried out under ss 17 and 18. The council then proposed to close the nursery for financial reasons and decided to reduce the capacity of the nursery until a final decision was made. After consultation the council finally decided to close the nursery as there were only 11 children attending. On an application for judicial review of the decision to close the nursery, *held*, the question to be considered was whether the consultation was genuine and fair. In this case the council had been willing to reconsider its proposal and had given the applicants an adequate opportunity to make representations. This was a genuine consultation in which the applicants had participated and they were not therefore able to maintain that it was a charade because of what had happened before. The council owed a general duty under s 17 to promote the welfare of the children in need in its area. The question of whether it had fulfilled that duty by providing day care under s 18 could not be tested on a child by child basis. The circumstances of any individual child should be examined in the context of the general range and level of services provided. It was for the local authority concerned and not the court to decide what weight should be given to the circumstances of any individual child when his needs might conflict with the appropriate provision overall. The authority also had a duty to balance the weight given to the general circumstances of children, against its financial and budgetary constraints, and this would be a matter for the judgement and experience of the authority. The court would rarely be competent to intervene on the ground of irrationality and the fact that the decision of the authority was made by majority and as a result of voting on party lines would not per se amount to irrationality. Any breach by the council of its duty under s 19, to review day care provided under s 18, did not of itself place the council in breach of its duty to provide appropriate day care. In any event there was a statutory remedy available under s 26(3) of the 1989 Act which should have been pursued, therefore no remedy would be granted in the present case. Accordingly, the applications would be dismissed.

R v Barnet London Borough Council, ex p B (1993) Independent, 17 November (Queen's Bench Division: Auld J).

410 Medical treatment—consent to treatment—need to apply to the court

A hospital which specialised in handling cases of highly disturbed adolescents was often invoved in the emergency use of medication. Before admitting patients for treatment the hospital required written consent from the relevant parent or local authority or both. It was proposed that a child who was in the care of the local authority be admitted; his parents had given their consent to treatment. However, an application was made by the local authority for an order under the Children Act 1989, s 8. *Held*, the application was misconceived and unnecessary. If a child were *Gillick* competent he could consent to treatment. If the child declined to consent to treatment, consent could be given by someone else who had parental responsibility. In the present case, the child was not *Gillick* competent. Even if he had been *Gillick* competent, his refusal of consent to treatment would not expose the doctor to criminal or civil proceedings if he proceeded to administer medication in an emergency since he had parental consent. Therefore, no order was necessary and accordingly, the application would be dismissed.

Re K, W and H (Minors) (Consent to Treatment) [1993] 1 FCR 240 (Family Division: Thorpe J). *Gillick v West Norfolk and Wisbech Area Health Authority* [1986] AC 112, HL (1985 Abr para 1758) and *Re R (A Minor) (Wardship: Consent to Treatment)* [1992] 2 FCR 229 followed.

411 Medical treatment—power to order treatment—jurisdiction

An emergency protection order was made in relation to a child on the ground that the child was suffering or was likely to suffer from significant harm because the parents were withholding their permission to give urgent medical treatment. The local authority then applied for a care order on the basis that there was an urgent and continuing need for medical treatment to which the parents were refusing to give their consent. *Held*, the court's duty to the child required directions that would ensure that whenever the medical need arose she would receive the transfusion of blood or blood products that medical advice dictated. In cases where the court was asked to override the views of parents, it was imperative that justice was seen and felt to be done by all parties and that therefore the inherent jurisdiction of the High Court was the most appropriate legal framework within which to consider a contested issue of this nature. Accordingly, the application would be allowed.

Re O (A Minor) (Medical Treatment) [1993] 2 FLR 149 (Family Division: Johnson J).

An application was made by a local authority under the Children Act 1989, s 8 for a specific issue order to enable a child to receive blood transfusions. The child's parents refused to consent to the treatment for religious reasons. The parents submitted that in a case of such gravity, where the court was asked to override the parents' wishes, the local authority should have instead applied to invoke the inherent jurisdiction of the High Court. *Held*, in applications of this type strenuous efforts should always be made to achieve an inter partes hearing. Such issues should also be determined wherever possible by a High Court judge. An application under the Children Act 1989, s 8 could, and in such circumstances should, be made to the High Court. The welfare of the child was the court's paramount consideration and so overwhelming was her need for blood that the parents' wishes were bound to be overridden and the use of blood products authorised. In a life-threatening emergency situation doctors clearly could not consult with parents, but in the normal course of events it was reasonable that they should do so. In any situation which was less than imminently life-threatening, those medically responsible for the child were to consult with the parents and consider at every opportunity all alternative forms of management suggested by the parents. In the event that those medically responsible for the child concluded, after such consultation, that there was no reasonable alternative to the administration of blood products, they should be at liberty to administer blood products without the consent of the parents. Judgment would be given accordingly.

Re R (A Minor) (Blood Transfusion) [1993] 2 FCR 544 (Family Division: Booth J).

412 Parental home—interference with right of occupation—mode of application

An unmarried couple, with twins aged two, had lived together as joint tenants. When their relationship ended, the mother moved to her parents and took the children with her and the father remained in their home. She unsuccessfully applied to be allowed to reside at the home with the children in the absence of the father. On appeal, she contended that, given the paramountcy of the children's welfare under the Children Act 1989, s 1(1) and the fact that she had sole parental responsibility, the required order could be granted by way of a specific issue order under the 1989 Act, s 8. Alternatively, she contended that she was entitled to an injunction under the court's inherent jurisdiction. *Held*, it was in the children's best interests that they should return to live in the home with the mother in the absence of the father. However, although the issue of where a child should live was usually amenable to determination on an application for a specific issue order, that was not the case where a right of occupation would be interfered with. The mother was effectively seeking an ouster order and Parliament had not intended that such orders be available under the guise of a specific issue order. The court was also bound by authority to refuse to grant an injunction. However, the mother did have a potential remedy under the 1989 Act, s 15 and Sch 1, para 1(2)(e). She could apply for an order requiring the father to transfer his interest in the joint tenancy of the home to her for the benefit of the children and that would give her an exclusive right to occupy the home. Accordingly, the appeal would be dismissed.

Re F (Minors) (Parental home: Ouster) (1993) Times, 1 December (Court of Appeal: Nourse LJ and Thorpe J).

413 Parental responsibility order—application by unmarried father—factors for consideration

The parents were unmarried and had one child. For the first four years of her life she was brought up by both parents. The parents then separated and the child went to live with the mother. The child suffered a non-accidental injury caused by the mother, as a result of which the council commenced care proceedings. Under interim orders the child was placed with the father. The father filed applications for a residence order and for a parental responsibility order. At the hearing the magistrates made a care order and orders for contact to both parents. In giving their reasons the magistrates observed that the child had lived with the mother all her life and that, although she appeared to have settled well with the father, the change of circumstances ought not to be regarded as permanent and that the child ought to be gradually rehabilitated with the mother. The magistrates concluded that if a residence order was made in favour of the father it could result in the child losing contact with the mother. Therefore, they found that it was not appropriate to make a residence order or give the father parental responsibility. The father appealed against the refusal of the magistrates to make a parental responsibility order. *Held*, the magistrates had failed to consider the father's application for a parental responsibility order as an independent consideration in its own right. The important factors were the father's degree of commitment at the time of the hearing, the extent of the mutual attachment between him and the child at that time, and his motives for seeking parental responsibility. Had the magistrates considered these factors they would have properly conferred parental responsibility on the father. Accordingly, the appeal would be allowed and the magistrates' order would be varied to include a parental responsibility order.

Re CB (A Minor) (Parental Responsibility Order) [1993] 1 FCR 440 (Family Division: Waite J).

414 Parental responsibility order—application by unmarried father—prohibition against future applications

The parents were unmarried. The mother left the father three months before the child was born after he assaulted her. After the child's birth, the father made numerous applications to the court relating to contact and parental responsibility. An access order was made but was terminated after he repeatedly failed to comply with its terms, notably by retaining the child for nine days, rather than two hours, and disobeying an order to return her. He then unsuccessfully applied for parental responsibility under the Children Act 1989. The judge held that the order was contrary to the child's welfare: the father had never had any family life with the child, had a hostile and violent attitude to the mother, had failed to provided any financial support, and had treated the child without concern for her welfare. In a separate hearing, the father unsuccessfully appealed against the refusal of access and the judge ordered that there should be no further applications by the father for three years because they caused distress to the mother and that distress was being transmitted to the child. The father appealed against both orders. *Held*, with regard to the application for parental responsibility, the judge had considered the degree of commitment the father had displayed to the child, the degree of attachment between the father and child and the father's reasons for making the application. These were the correct criteria and the judge's decision to refuse to make the order was correct. The decisions to strike out the father's application for a contact order and to prohibit further applications were unusual and should be used sparingly. However, in the circumstances there was no prospect of the father successfully obtaining a contact order and the child's welfare required that the mother have a period free from the distress of further applications by the father. Accordingly, both appeals would be refused.

Re T (A Minor) (Parental Responsibility and Contact) [1993] 1 FCR 973 (Court of Appeal: Neill, Butler-Sloss and Scott LJJ).

415 Paternity—proof of paternity—blood tests—presumption of legitimacy

A mother was having sexual relations with her husband and another man at the time of her child's conception. She maintained the child was her husband's and that the moment she became pregnant she had broken off relations with the third party. The third party then applied for the taking and use of blood tests for DNA profiling from the child. On an appeal by the third party from his dismissed application, *held*, in general the court ought to permit a blood test of a young child unless satisfied that it would be against the child's interests. Although it might well be true that it must inevitably be in the child's interests to know the truth about her parentage, the child's physical and emotional welfare were inextricably bound up with the welfare of the family unit of which she presently formed a part and any harm to the welfare of that unit, as might be caused by an order for the taking of blood tests, would be damaging to the child. The court was disinclined to order a blood test against the will of the parent who had had since birth sole parental responsibility for the child. The child's welfare in the foreseeable future depended primarily on her relationship with her mother and given that the third party had expressly conceded that he did not dispute the right of the mother to have the child living with her, anything that might have disturbed that relationship or the stability of the family unit was likely to be detrimental to the child's welfare. Accordingly, the appeal would be dismissed.

Re F (A Minor) [1993] 3 All ER 596 (Court of Appeal: Balcombe, Nolan and Kennedy LJJ). Decision of Callman J (1992) Times, 31 July affirmed. *S v S, W v Official Solicitor* [1970] 3 All ER 107, HL applied.

416 Proceedings concerning children—allocation of proceedings

The Children (Allocation of Proceedings) (Amendment) Order 1993, SI 1993/624 (in force on 5 April 1993), amends the 1991 Order, SI 1991/1677, by adding proceedings under the Child Support Act 1991, s 27(1) (declaration of parentage) and on an appeal under s 20 where the appeal is to be dealt with in accordance with the Child Support Appeals (Jurisdiction of Courts) Order 1993, SI 1993/961, (para 365) to the list of proceedings which must be commenced in a magistrates' court and providing for them to be transferred to other courts in certain circumstances.

417 Prohibited steps order—application for order in same terms as residence or contact order

One of three daughters alleged she and her sisters had been sexually abused by their father over a number of years. An assessment by a specialist clinic indicated that the father would benefit from spending a year in the clinic, but the local authority stated it had no resources to pay for the treatment and said it was unwilling to seek a care order in respect of the girls. The local authority applied, having obtained ex parte the leave of a single justice of the family proceedings court, for a prohibited steps order under the Children Act 1989, s 8 that the father should not reside in the same household as his daughters and any contact should be supervised by the social services department. The judge having regard to the 1989 Act, s 9(2) which prohibits a local authority from seeking residence and contact orders, decided that the application sought to determine the residence of the children and the degree of contact with the father and therefore, under the restrictions in s 9(5), a prohibited steps order could not be made. As the father had also sought a residence order the court would grant a residence order in the same terms as that sought by the local authority, and a contact order preventing unsupervised contact with two of the three girls would also be made. On appeal by the local authority from the court's refusal to make a prohibited steps order, *held*, it was clear that the judge had no power to make a prohibited steps order. The local authority's application for a prohibited steps order was made with a view to achieving a result which would have been achieved by the making of a residence or contact order. In cases where children were found to be at risk of suffering significant harm within the meaning of the 1989 Act, s 31 a clear duty arose on the part of local authorities to protect them, and Part IV of the Act provided them with wide powers and a wide discretion. A prohibited steps order would not afford the local authority any authority as to how it might deal with the children. Further, it was inappropriate for the local authority to apply for leave to issue its application ex parte before the single justice. Such applications if made to a family proceedings court ought to be transferred to the county court and not dealt with ex-parte. Accordingly, the appeal would be dismissed.

Nottinghamshire CC v P [1993] 3 All ER 815 (Court of Appeal: Sir Stephen Brown P, Hirst and Waite LJJ).

418 Prohibited steps order—procedure in magistrates' court

Following the separation of her parents, a child lived with her mother but saw her father regularly. The mother subsequently began a relationship with an Australian citizen, and she wanted to remove the child from the jurisdiction so they could live with her new partner in

117

Australia. The father applied for, and was granted, a prohibited steps order to prevent the mother from removing the child from the jurisdiction. The case was heard over five non-consecutive days, and a number of other orders relating to custody and access were also made. On the mother's appeal, *held*, magistrates ought not to hear cases brought under the Children Act 1989 which had an estimated duration of more than two or three days, and the appeal would have been allowed for that reason but for the fact that the father had subsequently indicated in writing that he no longer objected to the child being removed from the jurisdiction. Accordingly, the appeal would be allowed by consent.

Re L (A Minor) (Removal from Jurisdiction) [1993] 1 FCR 325 (Family Division: Thorpe J).

419   Residence order—application by a minor—factors to be considered by court

A 14-year-old girl who had been in care for eight years sought leave to apply for a residence order to live with a family friend. The mother opposed the application. *Held*, although the Family Proceedings Rules 1991, SI 1991/1247, r 4.3 provided that an application for leave to commence proceedings could be made ex parte, if the applicant was a minor it was desirable that notice of the application be given to those with parental responsibility. The court was satisfied that the girl had sufficient understanding to bring the application, as required by the Children Act 1989, s 10(8) and therefore the court had a discretion whether to grant leave. In the absence of statutory guidelines, recent authorities indicated that relevant considerations for the court were the likelihood of the application succeeding, that no distinction be drawn between an application for leave by a child or by another person, and that the 1989 Act, s 1(1) welfare test was not applicable. Further, if, as in the present case, the application was brought by the child, the court had to consider the reasons why the person in whose favour the application was sought had not brought the application.

Re SC (A Minor) (Leave to Seek Residence Order) [1994] 1 FLR 96 (Family Division: Booth J). *F v S (Adoption: Ward)* [1973] Fam 203, CA and *Re A and W (Minors) (Residence Order: Leave to Apply)* [1992] 2 FLR 154 (1992 Abr para 363) followed.

420   Residence order—application by a minor—relevance of wardship proceedings

The appellant, a minor, and her sister were placed in long term foster care with a couple who later formally adopted them. The appellant wished to live with her maternal grandparents and aunt. She consulted a solicitor who was satisfied that she was capable of giving instructions. She applied to the county court for a residence order directing her to reside with her aunt. Leave for the application was granted. On an application for further directions the adoptive parents indicated they wished to start wardship proceedings. The court ordered that the aunt and the appellant be joined as defendants, that the Official Solicitor appear on the appellant's behalf as her guardian ad litem and that the appellant's application for a residence order be consolidated with the wardship proceedings. On appeal against the order by the minor, *held*, it was possible for a minor to engage in wardship proceedings without a guardian ad litem and the court would have no power in those circumstances to impose one on her against her will. It was at the court's discretion to decide whether a child, who came before it as a party without a next friend or guardian, had the necessary ability to instruct her solicitor. Wardship proceedings could not be invoked in order to introduce a guardian ad litem in an application for a residence order initiated by a minor who in her own right had instructed a solicitor. Accordingly, the appeal would be allowed.

Re T (A Minor) [1993] 4 All ER 518 (Court of Appeal: Sir Thomas Bingham MR, Staughton and Waite LJJ).

421   Residence order—application by grandparent

A child, who had lived with her mother and grandmother, continued to live with her grandmother after her mother left home. The grandmother applied for a residence order, supported by the mother and a recommendation from the welfare officer. The magistrates found that there was no risk of the child being taken away from the grandmother, and held that the application would be refused on the ground that the Children Act 1989, s 1(5) provided that the court should not make an order unless it considered that doing so would be better for the child than making no order at all. On appeal by the grandmother, *held*, where both separated parents had parental responsibility and agreed that the child should live with one of them, the court would usually decline to make an order. However where the applicant did not have parental responsibility and could only obtain it if a residence order was made, different considerations applied. It would be better for the child in this case if the order was made than if it was not made. The child was happy with the grandmother and accordingly the appeal would be allowed and a residence order made in favour of the grandmother.

B v B (Grandparent: Residence Order) [1993] 1 FCR 211 (Family Division: Johnson J).

A mother had an eight-year-old daughter. The mother had a history of depression and had attempted suicide. The maternal grandmother, concerned that the mother and child were living in accommodation for the homeless, wrote to the mother and offered to bring up the child. A few days later the mother telephoned the grandmother in a distressed and drunken state and asked her to collect the child. The grandmother did so and the next day was granted leave to make an ex parte application for a residence order. The justices ordered that the child should live with the grandmother until a further hearing in three months. On the mother's appeal, *held*, the justices were wrong to have made a residence order for three months ex parte without any provision for an earlier hearing and the appeal would be allowed to that extent. However, there were substantial reasons for concern about the mother's ability to provide a home for the child and these required further investigation. In the short term, it was important to establish stability for the child and, accordingly, a residence order would be made in favour of the grandmother.

Re Y (A Minor) (ex p Residence Order) [1993] 2 FCR 422 (Family Division: Johnson J).

422   Residence order—application by religious sect

A father and his ten-year-old son were members of a religious sect. The father offended against certain tenets of the fellowship and was punished by being "withdrawn from", entailing total ostracism from members of the fellowship and virtually no contact with his son. Members secured the father's voluntary consent to their care of his son, with his proviso that his son be allowed to return to him if he so desired. The fellowship applied, with leave, for a residence order and the father lodged an answer, applying for his son's return and for contact. An order for visiting and staying contact was made in favour of the father but his attempts at contact failed. An order was then made providing for the boy to spend a fortnight with his father and the court welfare officer reported on their warm and positive relationship. The father and son moved to another address following harassment by members of the fellowship. The judge found that the boy had suffered considerable emotional harm during the dispute over residence and that, whilst expressing a deep and sincere desire to stay within the fellowship, he had also expressed the wish to be with his father. There were two exclusive options: to commit the boy to a life with the fellowship at the exclusion of the father or to rehabilitate the child with his father outside the fellowship. The judge made a residence order in the father's favour and provided for supervised visits to an aunt, leading to staying access, upon her undertaking not to speak to the boy about the fellowship. He further ordered that a local authority officer be available to advise and befriend the father and son. On appeal by members of the fellowship, *held*, it was not part of the judicial function to comment on the beliefs and doctrines of a particular Christian sect, but their impact upon a child's future welfare was a relevant circumstance for consideration under the Children Act 1989, s 1. It was not the judge's task to assess the depth of the boy's religious convictions or desire to live within the fellowship, but those feelings were relevant when he considered the expressed views and feelings of the boy. A judge's decision whether or not personally to interview a child was a matter of judicial discretion and since the judge was aware of the boy's views, his decision not to interview him could not be criticised. The judgment was one of discretion and assessment of all the evidence. The decision was clearly correct and should not be interfered with. Accordingly, the appeal would be dismissed.

Re R (A Minor) (Residence: Religion) [1993] 2 FLR 163 (Court of Appeal: Purchas and Balcombe LJJ).

423   Residence order—county court—jurisdiction

The father, although absent from the matrimonial home, had contact with his children. The mother sought a residence order. Following a subsequent matrimonial dispute, police and social services were called in by the father. The judge at the hearing of the mother's application, ordered that neither the police nor the social services were to take any further step in relation to the welfare of the children without first consulting the court, and that all documents held by the police and the social services should be disclosed to the court and to the solicitors acting for the parents. On appeal against the orders, *held*, the Children Act 1989 did not give the court any power to interfere with the exercise by the police or a local authority of their statutory or common law powers in relation to children. The county court's lack of jurisdiction was even more apparent in the judge's order for discovery. If a party wished to adduce in law documents in the possession of a non-party then the procedure was by subpoena duces tecum in the High

Court or by witness summons in the county court. The appeals would accordingly be allowed.

D v D (1993) Times, 29 July (Court of Appeal: Balcombe and Leggatt LJJ and Sir Francis Purchas).

424 Residence order—disclosure of evidence—private letter from welfare officer

A court welfare officer incorporated certain allegations against an applicant for a residence order into a private letter as an addendum to her report, giving undertakings to the persons who made the allegations that their confidentiality would be respected. The child's mother applied for disclosure of the court welfare officer's letter, but her application was refused and the judge ordered that only the substance of the allegations should be disclosed to the parties. On the mother's appeal, held, the court welfare officer should not have given assurances of confidentiality, because only the court had the power to grant what amounted to an immunity for certain informants. The judge had been wrong in law to uphold the welfare officer's decision, and the case was not one for the exercise of the discretion not to disclose the informants' letter. Accordingly, the appeal would be allowed.

Re G (Minors) (Welfare Report: Disclosure) [1993] 2 FLR 293 (Court of Appeal: Balcombe LJ and Sir Francis Purchas).

425 Residence order—ex parte order—challenge—procedure

A child, aged two, lived with her mother. The mother recognised her shortcomings in caring for the child, was in touch with the social services, and had made moves towards the child's permanent placement with a family. She was estranged from her family, and had refused the support of her mother and sister. The sister made a successful ex parte application for a residence order, supported by an affidavit which gave a biased and highly critical portrait of the mother. The mother then made an ex parte application to have the order set aside and the judge adjourned for an inter partes meeting. On the mother's appeal, held, firstly, since the child was clearly under the scrutiny of the social services, she was in no immediate danger and thus the judge was not justified in making an ex parte residence order. Secondly, where a party challenged an ex parte order, the appropriate course was to apply to the judge who made the order and ask him to rescind or vary it. The application should be made on short notice, not ex parte, to enable the judge to weigh up the competing cases. Accordingly, the appeal would be allowed.

Re P (A Minor) (Ex p Residence Order) [1993] 2 FCR 417 (Court of Appeal: Purchas and Leggatt LJJ). Re G (Minors) (Ex p Residence Order) [1992] FCR 720, CA followed.

426 Residence order—joint residence order

The parties had separated and the two children of the marriage were living with the father in the matrimonial home. He worked on a shift basis and the mother cared for the children for the three days each week when he was at work. Her application for a joint residence order was opposed by the father on the grounds that the children required a settled base. The court welfare officer gave evidence that the children were so used to dividing their time between two homes that it was not disruptive. Held, the children coped well with the shared care arrangements. They had given evidence that they wanted a joint residence order and were sufficiently mature to have their views taken into account. Although a joint residence order was unusual, it was appropriate in the particular circumstances and, accordingly, such an order would be made.

G v G (Joint Residence Order) [1993] Fam Law 615 (Aldershot County Court: Judge Lauriston QC).

427 Residence order—possible need for care or supervision order—investigation of child's circumstances

A child's natural mother placed her with the applicants, a lesbian couple, who applied to the court for a residence order under the Children Act 1989, s 8. At the hearing, the local authority stated that at present the child was well cared for and that it had no grounds to apply for a care or supervision order, but that there might be a likelihood of significant future harm if the applicants lacked the capacity to respond to the child's emotional needs as they became more complex. Held, under the 1989 Act, s 31(2) the court could only make a care or supervision order if a child was suffering, or was likely to suffer, significant harm. When considering this, the court was not limited to looking only at the present and the immediate future, but could consider the likely position years hence. The 1989 Act, s 37 provided that where it appeared to the court that a care or supervision order might be appropriate, the court could direct the local authority to make an investigation into the child's circumstances. That provision was sufficiently wide to include any situation which might have a bearing on the likelihood of the child suffering significant future harm, and thus covered the obtaining of further psychiatric evidence. Here there was concern about the mental health of one of the applicants and her ability to care for the child, the stability of the applicants' relationship, the proximity of the natural mother and uncertainty as to the role she wished to play in the child's future. Accordingly, an interim residence order would be made in favour of the applicants and the local authority would be directed to make an investigation into the child's circumstances under the 1989 Act, s 37 focusing on: (1) the emotional and other difficulties the child was likely to face, (2) the consequences to the child of any such difficulties that could not be overcome with help and how this should weigh against removing her from the applicants, and (3) what help of a psychiatric or counselling nature was available to assist the applicants.

Re H (Child's Circumstances: Direction to Investigate) [1993] 2 FCR 277 (Family Division: Scott Baker J).

428 Residence order—shared residence order

The applicant had lived with the respondent for 10 years. During their cohabitation the respondent had given birth to two children, one aged 11 and the other 8. They had treated the applicant as their father. The applicant applied for a shared residence order under the Children Act 1989, s 11(4) and a prohibited steps order preventing the removal of the children from the jurisdiction. A welfare report was ordered and blood tests taken at the instance of the applicant. The results showed that the applicant was not the children's father. The magistrates made a residence order in favour of the respondent and ordered that the applicant should have defined access. A prohibited steps order was not made. On appeal by the applicant, *held*, the magistrates had correctly concluded that it was important for the welfare of the children that their primary home ought to be with their mother. However, the issue of the mother leaving the jurisdiction had not been raised in the welfare officer's report and the magistrates had decided the issue without a full report or without full argument and had not applied the appropriate test established in the case of *Poel v Poel* [1970] 1 WLR 1469. In finding that the status quo ought to continue, with regards the current weekly staying contact, it would have been appropriate to make a prohibited steps order to prevent the removal of the children from the jurisdiction. Accordingly, the appeal would be allowed in part.

N v B (Children: Orders as to Residence) [1993] 1 FCR 231 (Family Division: Thorpe J).

429 Residence order—welfare of child—shared order

The parents who were not married to each other, had a teenage child. For several years the child lived with the mother and spent alternate weekends with the father. The mother's mother died and the father became very concerned about the mother's state of mind, the highly unsatisfactory state of her home, and the child's failure to attend school regularly. The mother terminated the child's contact with the father. The father made an application for a shared residence order and the court made the order in favour of the mother with weekly visiting contacts with the father. On appeal by the father against the court's refusal to make a shared residence order, *held*, it was inappropriate to make a shared residence order except in exceptional circumstances. It was vital that a child make his settled home with one of the parents. The home of the other parent should be a place for visiting and accordingly the appeal would be dismissed.

Re H (A Minor) (Residence Order) [1993] 1 FCR 671 (Court of Appeal: Purchas LJ and Cazalet J).

430 Secure accommodation order—application to renew secure accommodation order—interim order made

The Children (Secure Accommodation) Regulations 1991, SI 1991/1505, reg 5 provides that the Children Act 1989, s 25 does not apply to a child detained under any provision of the Mental Health Act 1983.

A 16-year-old girl was the subject of a full care order. She had spent several periods in secure accommodation and her repeated absconding and self-injury prevented her rehabilitation into the community. She was subsequently placed in a teenage placement but whilst there she was arrested and charged on several counts of burglary and criminal damage, and was placed on remand in relation to a charge of arson. She was then hospitalised after injuring herself, prompting the local authority to place her in a secure unit under emergency powers in the 1991 Regulations, reg 10. The justices made further orders to detain her in secure accommodation. During that period the girl injured herself and was briefly detained under the 1983 Act, s 2 before apparently being released under the 1983 Act, s 17. The local authority applied for another secure accommodation order under the 1989 Act, s 25 but the justices, decided they could not hear the application since the girl was detained under the 1983 Act. The local authority appealed and also invoked its emergency powers under the 1991 Regulations, reg 10 to apply for a secure accommodation order for three months. The justices made an interim order for one month and adjourned the proceedings. The local authority appealed. *Held*, the justices wrongly decided that they had no power to make the order sought whilst the girl was detained under the 1983 Act. First, it was not clear whether she was so detained since she had been granted leave under the 1983 Act, s 17. Second, the justices misconstrued the 1991 Regulations, reg 5, the purpose of which was to ensure that where other statutory criteria were considered and were satisfied so as to affect the child's liberty, it was not necessary also to satisfy the 1989 Act, s 25. Thus applications under the 1989 Act, s 25 were to be considered in the normal way even if other statutory provisions applied. In respect of the interim order, the justices had correctly considered the duty of the court under the 1989 Act, s 25, they had had regard to the relevant considerations, and had given full reasons for their decision. The length of the order was a matter for the justices' discretion, as was the decision to adjourn proceedings and make an interim order under the 1989 Act, s 25(5). Accordingly, the appeal would be dismissed and a further interim order would be made until the matter was reconsidered by the same bench.

Hereford and Worcester County Council v S [1993] 2 FLR 360 (Family Division: Connell J).

431 Secure accommodation order—length of order—obligation of magistrates to give adequate reasons

A local authority had sought a secure accommodation order, in accordance with the Children Act 1989, s 25, allowing it to keep a minor in secure accommodation for the maximum period of three months. There was no dispute that the grounds for making the order had been established and the guardian ad litem had supported the application, but he considered the appropriate period was one of five weeks. The magistrates did not accept the guardian ad litem's recommendation and granted the order in the terms sought by the local authority, but the minor appealed on the ground that the magistrates should have given more consideration to the question of the length of time for which the order was necessary and unavoidable. The minor also contended the local authority had not made any findings of fact or given any adequate reasons for making an order for the maximum period. *Held*, when making an order under the 1989 Act, s 25, the court had carefully to consider the purposes which the order sought to achieve and to assess as best it could the length of time it would take to achieve that purpose. The justices should have explained why they considered the minor should be detained for the maximum period and why they were not following the guardian ad litem's recommendation, and their failure to give those explanations had been a serious oversight. Accordingly, the appeal against the accommodation order would be allowed.

Re W (Minor: Secure Accommodation Order) (1993) Times, 8 February (Family Division: Booth J).

432 Sterilisation—consent of High Court—declaration—procedure

The Official Solicitor has issued the following *Practice Note* ([1993] 3 All ER 222).

1. All cases require the prior sanction of a High Court judge.

2. Applications with regard to a minor should be made to the Family Division within proceedings either under the inherent jurisdiction of the court or under the Children Act 1989, s 8(1). The preferred course is to apply within the inherent jurisdiction, wherein applications should be in the following form: "It is ordered that there be leave to perform an operation of sterilisation on the minor (X) [if it is desired to specify the precise method of carrying out the operation add, eg by the occlusion of her fallopian tubes] and to carry out such post-operative treatment and care as may be necessary in her best interests". In proceedings under the 1989 Act, applications should be in the following form: "The court orders, in determining the specific question which has arisen in connection with the exercise of parental responsibility by (A and B) in respect of the minor (X) as to whether it is in the minor's best interests to perform an operation of sterilisation on her [if it is desired to specify the precise method of carrying out the operation add, eg by the occlusion of her fallopian tubes], that such an operation is in her best interests and can lawfully be performed on her [and that (A and B) can give a valid consent thereto]".

3. Applications with regard to an adult should be by way of originating summons issued out of the Family Division for an order in the following form: "It is declared that the operation of sterilisation proposed to be performed on (X) [if it is desired to specify the precise method of carrying out the operation add, eg by the occlusion of her fallopian tubes] being in the existing

circumstances in her best interests can lawfully be performed on her despite her inability to consent to it. It is ordered that in the event of a material change in the existing circumstances occurring before the said operation has been performed, any party shall have liberty to apply for such further or other declaration or order as may be just".

4. The plaintiff or applicant ought normally be a parent or one of those responsible for the care of the patient or those intending to carry out the proposed operation. The patient must always be a party and should be a defendant or respondent. In cases in which the patient is a defendant or respondent, the Official Solicitor should be the guardian ad litem. In any case in which the Official Solicitor is neither next friend nor guardian ad litem of the patient, or a plaintiff or an applicant, he should be the defendant or respondent.

5. Prior to the substantive hearing of the application, there must in every case be a summons for directions to be heard by a High Court judge. The principal registry must fix a date for directions before a judge of the Family Division on the first open day after the passage of eight weeks when asked to do so at the issue of the originating summons.

6. The note also deals with guidelines on the role of the Official Solicitor and evidence. It replaces the notes contained in [1990] 1 WLR 1248, [1989] 2 FLR 447 and [1990] 2 FLR 530.

433 Support for children—local authorities—power to request help—homelessness

See *R v Northavon District Council, ex p Smith*, para 1383.

434 Wardship—jurisdiction

The Children Act 1989, s 100(2)(d) provides that no court may exercise the High Court's inherent jurisdiction with respect to children for the purpose of conferring on any local authority power to determine any question which has arisen, or which may arise, in connection with any aspect of parental responsibility for a child.

A mother of nine children had a male friend, with three previous convictions for sexual offences against children, who was a welcome visitor to her family home. The local authority applied for leave to apply for the exercise of the court's inherent jurisdiction to protect the three youngest children. The district judge refused leave on the grounds that the authority was seeking to exercise restraining powers which the mother held but chose not to exercise, thus breaching the 1989 Act, s 100(2)(d). On appeal, *held*, on a correct construction of the 1989 Act, s 100(2)(d), the local authority had intended to invite the court to exercise its inherent jurisdiction to protect the children rather than to have protective powers conferred on itself. The authority's wish to prevent the children from coming into contact with the mother's male friend could not be achieved by care or supervision orders since it came within the wardship jurisdiction. No member of the family had exercised the right to apply to the court to exercise its inherent power to protect the children and a restrictive construction of the 1989 Act, s 100(2)(d) would wrongly exclude the authority from protecting them. Accordingly, notwithstanding the 1989 Act, s 100(2)(d), the appeal would be allowed and the authority would be granted leave to institute wardship proceedings.

Devon County Council v S (Wardship) (1993) Times, 7 December (Family Division: Thorpe J).

435 Wardship—jurisdiction—habitual residence of child

The Family Law Act 1986, ss 2, 3 provide that the court only has jurisdiction in wardship proceedings if the child was habitually resident within the jurisdiction on the date when the originating summons was issued.

A child was born to parents who cohabited in England. When the relationship deteriorated the mother decided to emigrate to Canada with the child, and the father wrote to the relevant immigration authority stating he was aware of the plan and had no objections. The mother and child subsequently returned to Canada for another holiday, and when they failed to return the father commenced wardship proceedings. In accordance with the 1986 Act, ss 2, 3 it fell to be determined whether the mother had formed a settled intention to reside permanently in Canada on the date when the originating summons had been issued. The judge found she had formed that intention, and consequently ruled the court had no jurisdiction to hear the wardship application. On the father's appeal, *held*, much of the mother's property had not been sent to Canada, and in addition to leaving a number of personal and financial matters unresolved she had made inquiries about buying a house in England shortly before leaving the country. Such matters had required more detailed consideration than the judge had given them, and bearing in mind that the mother had refused to come to England to give evidence it was impossible to say that she had discharged the evidential burden upon her. Accordingly, the appeal would be allowed and wardship reinstated pending the hearing of the father's summons.

Re EW (Wardship: Child Abduction) [1992] 2 FCR 441 (Court of Appeal: Balcombe and Leggatt LJJ).

See *Re BM (A Minor) (Wardship: Jurisdiction)*, para 357.

436　Wardship proceedings—Official Solicitor appointed as guardian ad litem—Official Solicitor's costs—liability of local authority

Three children, the subject of wardship proceedings, were represented by the Official Solicitor who had been appointed by the court to act as their guardian ad litem. At a subsequent interlocutory hearing, the judge ordered the local authority to undertake an investigation of the circumstances of the children's placement pursuant to the Children Act 1989, s 37. At a later hearing, the local authority was joined as a party to the proceedings and directed to carry out further investigations, and the children were committed to its interim care. Eventually care orders were made in respect of the children. The Official Solicitor then applied for an order that one half of his costs be paid by the local authority. The local authority resisted, relying on *Re G (Minors) (Wardship: Costs)* [1982] 1 WLR 438, and contending that since the Official Solicitor was in place before the authority was involved or joined as a party, it would be unfair to require a contribution. *Held*, the significance to be attached to the means by which the Official Solicitor was appointed in any case had to be considered in the light of the 1989 Act, s 41 which imposed a duty upon the court to appoint a guardian ad litem in specified proceedings. In such proceedings, the court had to provide for a child's representation, irrespective of an application for it to do so, and the court had a discretion to appoint the Official Solicitor if, on the facts, that was more appropriate. The position had thus changed since the Court of Appeal's decision in *Re G*. At the conclusion of any case the court had to look at all the circumstances before exercising its discretion in relation to costs. In this case the exceptional facts made it inevitable that both the local authority and the Official Solicitor would be involved. It was mere chance that the matter came before the court in such a way that it was appropriate for the latter to be involved before the former and that was not to be regarded as a significant fact in reaching a decision as to costs. In the absence of the Official Solicitor, the local authority would have had to appoint a panel guardian ad litem and it would have been bound to meet his reasonable expenses. It was, therefore, right that the local authority should contribute to the Official Solicitor's costs and the extent of that liability was a matter for the court's discretion. Accordingly, the application would be allowed.

Re P (Minors) (Official Solicitor's Costs) [1993] 2 FLR 411 (Family Division: Booth J).

CHOSES IN ACTION

Halsbury's Laws of England (4th edn) Vol 6 (reissue), paras 1–200

437　Assignment—statutory assignment—part of bankrupt's estate—right to appeal against tax assessment—vesting of property in trustee in bankruptcy

See *Hunt v Customs and Excise Comrs*, para 2594.

CLUBS

Halsbury's Laws of England (4th edn) Vol 6 (reissue), paras 201–500

438　Bingo duty—exemptions

The Bingo Duty (Exemptions) Order 1993, SI 1993/752 (in force on 6 April 1993), amends the 1989 Order, SI 1989/1357, by raising the monetary limit which must be observed to qualify for exemption for bingo duty. The maximum card money per game for small scale non-dutiable bingo played at fairgrounds and other non-commercial entertainments is increased from £20 to £25.

COMMONS

Halsbury's Laws of England (4th edn) Vol 6 (reissue), paras 501–800

439   Common land—compulsory purchase—notice to commoners
See *Mid-Glamorgan County Council v Ogwr Borough Council*, para 523.

440   Common land—exchange of open space land—determination of advantage to users of land
The applicants challenged the decisions of the Secretary of State for the Environment and the Secretary of State for Transport under the Acquisition of Land Act 1981, that there would be given in exchange for open space land, other land which was equally beneficial and not less in area, to people who were entitled to rights of common over that open space land and to the public. *Held*, the first issue was the contention by the Secretaries of State that the court had no jurisdiction in these matters. The court could find no reason to construe the Acquisition of Land Act 1981, as applying to procedural matters only. It was repugnant to common sense to attribute to Parliament an intention to confine a challenge on this issue on purely procedural grounds. In coming to his decision regarding the exchange of land, the Secretary of State had to be satisfied that at that date, the land exchanged was of the same advantage to its users and the general public. It was permissible to have regard to future developments which would affect either piece of land but it was not permissible to assume that future development would result in the exchanged land, not equally advantageous at the date of exchange, eventually becoming equally advantageous at some future date. Equal advantage was to be assessed by the nature of the public enjoyment of the land although there was no requirement for precise correspondence between the advantages attaching to each parcel. Accordingly, the applications would be dismissed.

Greenwich London Borough Council v Secretary of State for the Environment, Yates v Secretary of State for the Environment, (1993) Times, 2 March (Queen's Bench Division: Hutchison J).

441   Common land—gated or stinted pasture—rights of stintholder
The plaintiffs claimed to be entitled to the freehold of a moor. The defendants, who had registered stintage rights, opposed the claim. At first instance, it was held that the stints, which had been awarded by commissioners under a private enclosure Act of 1799, were incorporeal and that the plaintiffs had possessory title. On appeal by the defendants, *held*, the effect of the award of stints was that the defendants were awarded proprietary status and became tenants in common of the moor. On the proper construction of the award the stint was a right to graze on land held in common with other stintholders. The appeal would accordingly be allowed.

Brackenbank Lodge Ltd v Peart (1993) Times, 4 June (Court of Appeal: Russell and Simon Brown LJJ and Sir Michael Fox).

442   Common land—register—objection to registration of private land for public use—application for rectification
The Common Land (Rectification of Registers) Act 1989, s 1 provides that any person may object to the registration of land as common land if it is part of a garden ancillary to a dwelling house, used and enjoyed with a dwelling house at all times since 5 August 1945.

The applicant objected to the registration of an orchard as common land. He claimed that he had purchased it from the tenant of a nearby property and that it was part of his garden. The commons commissioner dismissed the objection on the grounds that the orchard was a considerable distance from the applicant's dwelling house as well as the dwelling house of the tenant and was therefore not ancillary to either under the 1989 Act, s 1. In addition, the orchard had not devolved with one single dwelling house to which it was at all times ancillary and there was insufficient evidence that the orchard was used and enjoyed as a garden. On appeal from the commissioner's decision, *held*, the question whether a garden was used and enjoyed with a dwelling house was a question of fact. If the garden was some distance from the dwelling house, this was a factor, but not a conclusive factor, in deciding that question. The land which was said to be ancillary to a dwelling house did not need to be held under the same title as the dwelling house nor did either need to be occupied by an owner-occupier. There was also no reason why the land had to be used and enjoyed as ancillary to one single dwelling house for the whole period after 5 August 1945. Accordingly, the appeal would be allowed.

Storey v Commons Comr (1993) 66 P & CR 206 (Chancery Division: Vinelott J). *Cresstock Ltd v Commons Comr* [1992] 1 WLR 1088 (1992 Abr para 381) applied.

443   Common land—register—rectification

The Common Land (Rectification of Registers) Act 1989 aims to rectify injustices suffered by homeowners under the Commons Registration Act 1965, under which land could become registered as common land without a person who purported to be the owner of the land being aware that an application for registration had been made.

A house and large area of garden owned by the applicant adjoined another area of land (the objection land) which had been registered as common land under the 1965 Act. The applicant claimed some of the objection land was part of his garden, and he applied to the Commons Commissioner to rectify the register under the 1989 Act. His application was refused on the ground that he had failed to show that the land had been used and enjoyed as a garden. He appealed by way of case stated, contending the commissioner's decision had been erroneous. *Held*, in order to satisfy the requirements of the 1989 Act the land must have been used and enjoyed as a garden with a dwellinghouse at all times since 1945. The land in question consisted of fields of pasture which had been for grazing cattle and growing hay, and as such it could not be described as being a "garden" within the meaning of the 1989 Act. The commissioner's decision had not been erroneous and, accordingly, the appeal would be dismissed.

Re Land at Freshfields (1993) 66 P & CR 9 (Chancery Division: Warner J).

444   Common land—registration—disposal of disputed registrations

The Commons Registration (Disposal of Disputed Registrations) (Amendment) Regulations 1993, SI 1993/1771 (in force on 13 August 1993), amend the 1972 Regulations, SI 1972/437, which provide for the indication of the disposal of disputed registrations in the registers maintained under the Commons Registration Act 1965. The 1993 Regulations prescribe a new model entry on the register to indicate when a registration has become final with modifications by setting out the registration in its modified form.

COMMONWEALTH AND DEPENDENCIES

Halsbury's Laws of England (4th edn) Vol 6 (reissue), paras 801–1108

445   Articles

The Future of the Judicial Committee of the Privy Council, Graham Hall and Douglas Martin: 143 NLJ 1652.

446   Antigua and Barbuda—appeals to Privy Council—appeals as of right— industrial proceedings

Antigua and Barbuda

The Antigua Industrial Court ruled that a number of employees had been unfairly dismissed. Their employers successfully appealed to the Court of Appeal against the decision. The employees sought leave to appeal to the Privy Council under the Industrial Court Act 1976, s 17(1). The Court of Appeal held that appeals to the Privy Council did not lie as of right under the Constitution of Antigua and Barbuda, s 122(1)(a) in respect of matters originating in the Industrial Court. The Privy Council having granted special leave to appeal, *held*, final decisions of the Court of Appeal on appeals from the Industrial Court under the 1976 Act, s 17 were "civil proceedings" within the meaning of s 122(1)(a) of the Constitution. An appeal to the Privy Council lay as of right in such proceedings provided the sum in dispute exceeded a prescribed value. Accordingly, the employees were entitled to an appeal as of right and their appeal would be allowed.

Sundry Workers (Represented by the Antigua Workers Union) v Antigua Hotel and Tourist Association [1993] 1 WLR 1250 (Privy Council: Lords Templeman, Bridge of Harwich, Oliver of Aylmerton, Jauncey of Tullichettle and Woolf).

447   Bahamas—constitution—right to trial by jury

See *Comr of Police v Davis*, para 556.

448   Cayman Islands—constitution

The Cayman Islands (Constitution) (Amendment) Order 1993, SI 1993/3143 (in force on a day to be appointed), makes further changes to the Constitution of the Cayman Islands. The amendments include providing for an increase in the number of members elected to the Executive Council by the Legislative Assembly and making more specific provision for the offices of speaker and deputy speaker. In addition, provision is made for a Commissioner for Complaints, for a Register of Interests and for referenda.

449   Hong Kong—Bill of Rights—repeal of legislation inconsistent with Bill of Rights

The first respondent was charged in Hong Kong with possessing suspected stolen goods without giving a satisfactory explanation as to innocent possession of them. The second respondents were charged with being involved in a transaction involving drug trafficking proceeds knowing, or having reasonable grounds to believe, that the proceeds were from drug trafficking. A magistrate dismissed the information preferred against the first respondent and a judge quashed the indictment against the second respondents. In both cases the rulings were made on the grounds that the respective statutory offences were inconsistent with the provision in the Hong Kong Bill of Rights that a defendant had the right to be presumed innocent until proved guilty, and, under the Bill of Rights, any legislation inconsistent with that provision was repealed to the extent of the inconsistency. The Attorney General's appeals in respect of both cases were dismissed. On further appeal, *held*, in the case of the first respondent the substantive effect of the statutory provision was to place the onus on the defendant to establish that he could give a reasonable explanation as to his innocent possession of the property. That was the most significant element of the offence, reducing the burden of proof on the prosecution and thus contravening the Bill of Rights. However, with regard to the second respondents, the onus of proving the substance of the offence lay with the prosecution and thus the offence did not contravene the Bill of Rights. Accordingly, the Attorney General's appeal in respect of the first respondent would be refused, but his appeal in respect of the second respondents would be allowed.

A-G of Hong Kong v Lee Kwong-kut; A-G of Hong Kong v Lo Chak-man [1993] 3 All ER 939 (Privy Council: Lords Keith of Kinkel, Lane, Bridge of Harwich, Browne-Wilkinson and Woolf).

450   Hong Kong—legislative powers

The Hong Kong (Legislative Powers) (Amendment) Order 1993, SI 1993/3145 (in force on 31 January 1994), amends the 1986 Order, SI 1986/1298, empowers the Hong Kong legislature to repeal or amend enactments of the United Kingdom, relating to fugitive offenders, intellectual property, protection of trading interests and outer space, which are part of the law of Hong Kong. The legislature of Hong Kong has power conferred on it to make laws having extra-territorial operation in these fields.

451   Turks and Caicos Islands—constitution

The Turks and Caicos Islands Constitution (Amendment) Order 1993, SI 1993/1248 (in force on a day or days to be appointed), amends the Constitution of the Turks and Caicos Islands. It provides for the increase of the number of elected members of the Executive Council from five to six and the establishment of single seat constituencies for elections to the Legislative Council. Further provision is made for an Electoral District Boundary Commission and for a Register of Interests.

COMPANIES

Halsbury's Laws of England (4th edn) Vol 7(1) (reissue), paras 1–1069, Vol 7(2) (reissue), paras 1070–2441

452   Articles

A Restriction on Statutory Powers, Stephen Griffin: 143 NLJ 589
Acquisition Financing in Europe, Julian Harris: 143 NLJ 1653

Administration Orders: White Knight or White Elephant, Andrew Campbell: 137 SJ 562
Company Charge Registration and Overseas Companies, Gerard McCormack: 137 SJ 1110
Corporate Liability, Geoff Holgate: 137 SJ 826
Creating a Compliance Burden, Ben Staveley: Tax Journal, Issue 232, p 6
Events of Default, Stephen Lear: LS Gaz, 21 April 1993, p 31
Execution of Documents by Foreign Companies, Kaz Stepien: 137 SJ 566
Fiduciary Duties and the Regulatory Rules, Harry McVea: 14 BLR 151
Illegality Under the Companies Act, Craig Eadie (on the rules governing loans to directors): Estates Gazette, 24 July 1993, p 90
Incorporating An Unincorporated Association, Francis Fitzpatrick: Tax Journal, Issue 230, p 16
Interest Relief—Loans to Buy Shares in Close Companies, Francis Sandison: Tax Journal, Issue 242, p 9
Looking for Direct Results, Andrew Hutchinson (on the reform of company law): LS Gaz, 8 December 1993, p 19
Non-Executive Directors, Janette Charley: 138 SJ 66
One-man Service Companies: a Gentleman's Agreement? David Southern: 143 NLJ 444
Options and Contracts After the Law of Property (Miscellaneous Provisions) Act 1989, Paul Jenkins (on the Law of Property (Miscellaneous Provisions) Act 1989, s 2(1)): [1993] Conv 13
Problems Surrounding Use of the Single Objects Clause, Sarah de Gay: 137 SJ 146
Protecting Yourself as Director of a Company in Difficulties, Richard Whitehouse and Tim Arnold: 137 SJ 218
Rescued From Oblivion, John Pennells (on the working of the company voluntary arrangement): 137 SJ 824
Restricted Plant and Machinery Allowances, Sean Moriarty: Tax Journal, Issue 244, p 8
Romalpa Clauses and Fiduciary Obligations, Simon Fisher: (1993) 8 JIBFL 505, 538
Small Company Legislation, Len Sealy: LS Gaz, 8 December 1993, p 16
The Juggernaut Comes to Grief, Andrew Hutchison and Ian Smedley: LS Gaz, 17 February 1993, p 21
Time is Running Out! Mark Baines: Tax Journal, Issue 229, p 24
Timing of Deduction for Bank Interest, David Martin (on the withdrawal of concessionary treatment for non-trading companies): Tax Journal, Issue 225, p 8
What Did Russell v Northern Bank Development Corporation Limited Decide? Brian Davenport (on *Russell v Northern Bank Development Corpn Ltd* [1992] 1 WLR 588, HL (1992 Abr para 400)): (1993) 8 JIBFL 469
What's in a Business Name? Tony Morris (on the registration of business names): 137 SJ 385
Whose Solvency Is It Anyway? Sujata Sharma: 137 SJ 318

453 Accounts—insurance companies

See para 1539.

454 Administration order—application by creditor to set aside order—duty to make full and honest disclosure on making application

Company A acted as agent for Company B then terminated their relationship because it wanted to act as agent for another company. Company B obtained judgment against Company A, which then claimed that it had a counterclaim against Company B, although this was rejected by the court. Company A presented a petition for an administration order which was granted by the court. Company B applied as creditor to rescind the administration order on the ground that administration would not achieve the survival of the company, which was the purpose of the procedure, and also applied to be made a party to the proceedings. Company A argued that the court could not discharge the administration order except under the Insolvency Act 1986, s 18 or 27. It was held at first instance that the court had jurisdiction to deal with applications for review and recission of administration orders which should not have been made. Under RSC Ord 15, r 6(2)(b)(ii), the court had jurisdiction to make an order joining Company B to the proceedings. As full disclosure had not been made on the application for the administration order, the order would be rescinded. On appeal by Company B, *held*, Company B was entitled to apply under the Insolvency Rules 1986, SI 1986/1925, r 7.47 to have the oppressive administration order discharged. In the present case there was no non-disclosure since the judge had all the information he needed. The making of the administration order was highly prejudicial to the interests of Company B and should not have been made. Accordingly, the appeal against the administration order would be allowed.

Cornhill Insurance plc v Cornhill Financial Services Ltd [1993] BCLC 914 (Court of Appeal: Dillon, Russell and Farquharson LJJ).

455   Administration order—costs—directors' personal liability for costs

The directors of a company presented an administration petition together with 29 other petitions in respect of the company's 29 subsidiaries. The directors' petition was opposed by a creditor which had presented a winding-up petition supported by a number of other creditors. The petition sought an administration order for the statutory purposes of the approval of a voluntary arrangement and a more advantageous realisation of the assets than would be achieved in a winding up. At the hearing the petitions in respect of the core subsidiaries were abandoned. The remaining administration petition was dismissed on the ground that none of the statutory purposes for which an administration order could be made was likely to be achieved. The directors were ordered to pay the costs personally of a number of the opposing creditors. The directors appealed against the costs order. *Held,* the judge had erred in principle in making the order for costs on the evidence before him. The directors had observed all the requirements of the Insolvency Rules 1986. The directors had acted throughout in good faith in the interests of the company and in the circumstances there was no ground on which they could properly be ordered to pay the costs personally and accordingly, the appeal would be allowed.

Re Land and Property Trust Co plc (No 2) [1993] EGCS 19 (Court of Appeal: Nourse, Beldam LJJ and Sir John Megaw).

456   Administration order—leave to commence proceedings—guidelines on granting leave

Scotland

The Insolvency Act 1986, s 11(3) provides that during the period for which an administration order is in force in relation to a company, no other proceedings may be commenced against that company except with the consent of the administrator or leave of the court.

The applicant landlords leased business premises to a company which subsequently went into administration. The landlords sought leave to terminate the lease on the grounds that the appointment of administrators breached a forfeiture clause in the lease. The landlords contended that a refusal of leave would be a denial of their proprietorial rights and that they would suffer loss by being prevented from regaining their property and by being tied to a financially parlous tenant. Further, there was authority that an administration order was intended to be an interim and temporary regime and the respondent administrators had already had sufficient time to dispose of the business as a going concern. The administrators argued that the company had met its obligations to pay rent, that more time was necessary to dispose of the business as a going concern, that they disputed the validity of the forfeiture clause, and that it was not reasonable for the landlords to rely on the clause. *Held,* in respect of the forfeiture clause, it was inappropriate at this stage to express an opinion on an issue in respect of which a party was seeking leave to commence proceedings unless that issue raised a short point of law which could be conveniently determined. The landlords had a seriously arguable case and, given that administration was intended to be a temporary regime and that the administrators had failed to dispose of the business as a going concern over a period of 18 months, nothing would be achieved by granting a further period of time. Accordingly, the application would be allowed.

Scottish Exhibition Centre Ltd v Mirestop Ltd (in administration) [1993] BCLC 1459 (Outer House). *Re Atlantic Computer Systems plc (No 1)* [1992] 2 WLR 367, CA (1990 Abr paras 284, 285) applied.

457   Administration order—overseas company—jurisdiction

The Insolvency Act 1986, s 426 (4), (5) provides that the courts having jurisdiction in relation to insolvency law in any part of the United Kingdom must assist the courts having the corresponding jurisdiction in another relevant country. For these purposes, a request made to a United Kingdom court by a court in a relevant country is authority for the court to which the request is made to apply, in relation to any matters specified in the request, the insolvency law which is applicable by either court in relation to comparable matters falling within its jurisdiction.

An Australian company was placed in liquidation and the liquidator made demands on a subsidiary company, incorporated under Australian law, with assets in England. These were not met and so the liquidator applied for an order to wind up the subsidiary. A provisional liquidator was appointed, who decided that a winding-up order was not the best method of realising the subsidiary assets. The liquidator of the parent company asked the Australian court to issue a letter of request to the English court seeking an administration order for the subsidiary. Following the Australian court's authorisation, the provisional liquidator presented a petition for an administration order in respect of the company. The request was opposed by creditors on the grounds that the English courts only had jurisdiction to grant an administration order in relation to a company formed and registered under the Companies Act 1985 or former United Kingdom Acts, and not a company incorporated overseas. The provisional liquidator however, contended that where a letter of request from a foreign court was made to an English court, jurisdiction was conferred by the 1986 Act, s 426. *Held,* a request made under the 1986 Act, s 426 did confer jurisdiction on an English court to make an administration order against an overseas company under the 1986 Act, s 8. Further, the mandatory wording of s 426 meant that, if the requirements of s 8 were satisfied, the court must make the requested order. An administration order would achieve a more advantageous realisation of the company's assets than winding up. Accordingly, the petition would be allowed.

Re Dallhold Estates (UK) Pty Ltd [1992] BCLC 621 (Chancery Division: Chadwick J).

458   Administration order—service of contractual notices—service without consent of administrator

The Insolvency Act 1986, s 11(3)(d) provides that during the period that an administration order is in force no proceedings or legal process may be commenced or continued against the company except with the consent of the administrator or the leave of the court.

The applicants served a contractual notice upon the respondent, a company in administration, purporting to make time of the essence. They also intended to serve a notice electing to treat a contract with the company as terminated by reason of the company's repudiatory breach. An application was made to determine whether s 11(3)(d) applied to service of the notices. *Held,* the words "proceedings" and "legal process" in s 11(3)(d) referred to all the steps involved in bringing legal proceedings. They did not refer to the taking of non-judicial steps such as the service of a contractual notice. Neither the consent of the administrators nor the leave of the court would therefore be required.

Re Olympia & York Canary Wharf Ltd [1993] BCLC 453 (Chancery Division: Millett J).

459   Administrative receivers—retention of title clause—application of clause to receivers

See *Compaq Computer v Abercorn Group Ltd*, para 467.

460   Administrator—vacation of office—contracts of employment adopted while in office—contracting out of adoption

By virtue of the Insolvency Act 1986, s 19(5), any sums payable in respect of debts or liabilities incurred, while a person was administrator of a company, under contracts of employment adopted by him in the carrying out of his functions are charged on company property in his custody or under his control in priority to his own remuneration and expenses.

The joint administrators of a company wrote to the company's employees advising them that they had been appointed as administrators of the company and that they would continue to pay their monthly salaries pursuant to their contracts of employment while a buyer for the business as a going concern was sought. The letter stated that, although the administrators acted as agents of the company and without personal liability, they would not assume personal liability in respect of the employees' contracts of employment. The employees were paid for the next few months until the company's operations were suspended when they were made redundant. It fell to be determined whether, in spite of the letter, the administrators had adopted the contracts so that the employees were entitled to amounts owing under their contracts in priority to the administrators' entitlement to remuneration. *Held,* the word "adopted" in s 19(5) meant "has procured the company to carry out". That meant that administrators had procured the company to continue to carry out the contracts of employment; it imposed no personal liability on them. The provisions of s 19(5) did not prevent an administrator from contracting out of the effect of adoption of contracts of employment. The administrators' letter, in order to be effective as a contracting out, would have had to be drafted specifically with s 19(5) in mind and to have made plain to the employees which of the employees' rights the administrators were purporting to contract out of. The letter had only excluded personal liability and, accordingly, the contracts had been adopted. The liabilities incurred under the contracts while the joint administrators were in office would be charged on the company's assets in priority to the administrators' remuneration and expenses.

Re Paramount Airways Ltd (in administration) (1993) Times, 14 September (Chancery Division: Evans-Lombe J).
This decision has been affirmed on appeal: (1994) Times, 1 March, Independent, 22 March.

461 Auditors—eligibility for appointment—recognised supervisory bodies—fees

The Companies Act 1989 (Recognised Supervisory Bodies) (Periodical Fees) Regulations 1993, SI 1993/1881 (in force on 16 August 1993), prescribe the fees payable by a body recognised by the Secretary of State for the purposes of the Companies Act 1989, Pt II (eligibility for appointment as a company auditor).

462 Capital—increase of capital—unilateral increase

See *Kerafina v The Republic (Greece)*, para 2706.

463 Capital duty—exempt transaction—conditions for exemption

Capital duty was payable under the Finance Act 1973, s 47 on a company's chargeable transactions, which included an issue of shares for a consideration. Shares issued on a takeover were exempt from duty where at least 75 per cent of the target company's shares were acquired, provided that any cash consideration on the takeover did not exceed ten per cent of the nominal value of the shares: Sch 19, para 10(2)(b). Capital duty was abolished by the Finance Act 1988, s 141.
The first company, a public limited company, offered to acquire all the issued share capital of the target company, another public limited company. Shareholders of the latter company who accepted the offer could take new stock units and cash, all cash or all stock units or a mixture of stock units and preference shares. In an attempt to gain the benefit of the exemption from capital duty under Sch 19, para 10(2)(b), the first company reserved to itself apportionment powers by virtue of which it treated shareholders who accepted a mixed share and cash offer as if they had transferred some of their shares wholly for shares in the first company and the rest of their shares exclusively for cash. On the first company's appeal against an assessment to capital duty under s 47, *held*, the contract constituted by the offer and its acceptance was an indivisible contract for the transfer of all the target company's shares held by the accepting shareholders for a composite consideration unless an accepting shareholder exercised an option to take all cash or all stock units or a mixture of stock units and preference shares. In spite of the apportionment provisions, the contract was a contract to acquire all the accepting shareholders' shares in the target company for the consideration expressed in the offer document. The consideration given by the first company for all the shares acquired from a shareholder of the target company who had not elected to take all stock or preference shares was a consideration which included a cash element in excess of the maximum ten per cent of the nominal value of the shares included in the consideration permitted in Sch 19, para 10(2)(b). The condition for exemption, therefore, was not satisfied and the appeal would be dismissed.
Guinness plc v IRC [1994] STC 86 (Chancery Division: Rattee J).

464 Charge—fixed charge over policy of assurance—interchangeability of terms "assurance" with "insurance"—validity of fixed charge

A company gave a debenture to a bank which provided that the bank would have a fixed charge over all of the company's polices of assurance. The debenture included a clause whereby the bank could also direct that any money recovered under a contract of insurance be used to reinstate the property or alternatively be used to repay the amount secured by the debenture. The company's premises were damaged by a fire and the company then went into voluntary liquidation. The liquidator had certain funds which were part of the proceeds from an insurance policy. The question arose as to whether the terms "insurance" and "assurance" were interchangeable, and whether the fixed charge over all policies of assurance was sufficient to cover the proceeds of the company's recovery from insurers for fire losses. The applicant, who was a former director and guarantor of the company, sought an order that the money should be paid directly to the bank in discharge of the debenture. The liquidator claimed the funds should first be used to meet proper liquidation expenses and the claims of the preferential creditors. *Held*, a charge on policies of assurance related to policies which either had or included death as a part of the triggering event entitling the policy to be enforced, therefore the bank's fixed charge did not apply to the insurance policy against fire. However, by virtue of the clause entitling the bank to direct reinstatement of the property or repayment of the sum secured, there was a fixed charge and not a floating charge over the proceeds of the insurance policy since the money was not at the free disposal of the company. Accordingly, the order would be granted and the money would be paid to the bank.

Re CCG International Enterprises Ltd [1993] BCLC 1428 (Chancery Division: Lindsay J).

465 Charge—floating charge—crystallisation—priority between preferential creditors and floating chargees

A company granted (1) a first debenture to a bank, creating fixed and floating charges over all its property, as security for all money and liabilities then or at any time thereafter owing by the company to the bank, (2) a second debenture to two directors, secured by a floating charge, in respect of a loan by them, and (3) a third debenture, creating fixed and floating charges similar to those under (1), to the trustees of its parent company's pension fund, in respect of a loan for the purpose of reducing its indebtedness to the bank. The bank, the two directors, the other trustees and the company executed a deed of priority providing for the postponement of the first and second debentures to the third. In the course of the winding up of the company, it fell to be determined (1) whether the trustees' debenture created a fixed charge over book and other debts, (2) in view of the deed of priority and the provisions of the Insolvency Act 1986, s 175(2)(b), whether the claims of the preferential creditors to be paid out of the proceeds of the realised book and other debts had priority to the claims of the trustees and the receiver, (3) whether the costs and expenses of the winding up were to be paid out of the proceeds of realised book and other debts in priority to the claims of the preferential creditors, pursuant to s 115. *Held*, by virtue of the deed of priority, the fixed charge in the bank's debenture became subject to the floating charge in the trustees' debenture and, as a result, upon crystallisation of the trustees' floating charge, the book and other debts of the company had to be applied in satisfaction of the debt secured by the trustees' charge before they could be applied in satisfaction of the bank's debt. The rule that where, by reason of the existence of a prior fixed charge, company assets were not payable to a floating chargee so that the assets were unavailable to satisfy preferential debts, did not apply, and the book and other debts were property comprised in or subject to the floating charge for the purpose of s 175(2)(b). Accordingly, the claims of the preferential creditors had priority over those of the trustees and their receiver. For the purposes of s 115, the company's assets included property comprised in or subject to a charge which as created was a floating charge but which had crystallised prior to the commencement of the liquidation, so that the expenses properly incurred in the winding up were payable out of the proceeds of the realisation of such property in priority to the claims of the preferential creditors.

Re Portbase Clothing Ltd [1993] 3 WLR 14 (Chancery Division: Chadwick J). *Re Woodroffes (Musical Instruments) Ltd* [1985] 2 All ER 908 (1985 Abr para 332) distinguished. *Re Christonette International Ltd* [1982] 3 All ER 225 (1982 Abr para 423) not followed.

466 Charge—retention of title clause—products from process and proceeds of sale—registration of charge—priorities

The plaintiff company supplied the defendant company with a number of goods on terms that the goods were to remain the property of the seller until payment of the price. The defendant acknowledged that until payment it was in possession of the goods as bailee, that the defendant was licenced to process the goods in its possession provided that the product of the process became the sole property of the plaintiff and that the proceeds of sale of the products made from the goods were held in trust for the plaintiff. The defendant had charged its stock and executed a debenture in favour of the bank to secure sums owing, which was then registered under the Companies Act 1985, s 395. The defendant then went into liquidation and the question arose as a preliminary issue, whether the agreement between the plaintiff and the defendant relating to the products from processing the goods, and the proceeds of sale of those products, had created a charge which was void for non-registration under the 1985 Act, s 395, and whether the bank's debenture had priority over the plaintiff's interest. *Held*, there was a distinction in the contract between the position in relation to the original goods and the processed product. At some point in the process the plaintiff's retained property in the original goods effectively disappeared and was replaced by a title in the finished product which was expressly conferred by the agreement between the parties. The property in the new product originated with the defendant but became or was deemed to be the property of the plaintiff pending the discharge by the defendant of its obligation to pay the price of the original goods. Accordingly, the plaintiff's interest in the new product was created by way of security in respect of that obligation and this constituted an interest by way of charge which would be void for non-registration.

Modelboard Ltd v Outer Box Ltd (in liquidation) [1993] BCLC 623 (Chancery Division: Michael Hart QC).

467   Charge—retention of title clause—registration—priorities

The plaintiff company appointed the defendant, Company A, as a dealer for its computers. The dealer agreement contained a retention of title clause. Company A then entered into an invoice-discounting agreement with the second defendant, Company B, under which debts due from the sub-purchasers of the computers were assigned from Company A to Company B. Company A then executed fixed and floating charges in favour of Company B which were duly registered under the Companies Act 1985, s 395. Receivers were appointed to carry on Company A's business and Company B notified the debtors of Company A of the discounting agreement. Company A was then put into creditors' voluntary winding up and in the plaintiff's action against the two companies and the receivers the question arose as a preliminary issue whether the plaintiff or Company B was entitled to the proceeds of sale of the plaintiff's computers. The plaintiff claimed that there was a fiduciary duty to account for the sale proceeds and the defendants argued that: (1) the retention of title clause constituted a registrable charge over the proceeds of sale under s 395 and as such was void for non-registration, and (2) Company B had priority over the plaintiff's claim by virtue of the assignment of debts under the discounting agreement and the registered charges. *Held*, (1) the plaintiff's interest in the proceeds ended when the debts were paid; it could not retain more money than the outstanding debt and if there were insufficient proceeds it should sue for the balance. Company A was able to sell the computers to sub-purchasers and pass full title without paying the plaintiff. It did not sell the computers as a bailee or fiduciary, and was entitled to retain the proceeds of sale from the sub-purchasers. There was a contractual obligation to account which did not operate as a retention. The plaintiff's claim in the proceeds of sale consisted of security for debts rather than a trust. These factors were more consistent with a charge than a fiduciary obligation and the charge was therefore void for non-registration against Company B, who had priority. (2) In any event, the plaintiff and Company A had agreed that the debts would be paid from a specific fund, namely the proceeds of the sub-sales. This amounted to an equitable assignment of the proceeds. Under the rule in *Dearle v Hall* (1928) 3 Russ 1, the priority of equitable assignments of debt depended on when notice of the interest created by the dealing was given to the debtors. Company B gave notice to the sub-purchasers first, therefore even if there were not a charge, Company B would still have priority. (3) If the rule in *Dearle v Hall* were not applicable, any legal assignment for value without notice of a prior equity, would take effect as an equitable assignment and priority would be determined by order of creation, pursuant to the Law of Property Act 1925, s 136(1). Accordingly all points of law on the preliminary issues were decided against the plaintiff.

Compaq Computer Ltd v Abercorn Group Ltd [1993] BCLC 602 (Chancery Division: Mummery J).

468   Community eco-management and audit scheme—companies in the industrial sector—environmental performance

See para 2698.

469   Company officers—misrepresentation—liability of company

Canada

The president and chief financial officer of the defendant company falsified company records and issued a press release which gave a false and misleading picture of the company's financial condition. The appellant, in reliance on the press report, purchased shares in the company. When the misconduct was discovered, amended financial statements were prepared which revealed a marked change in the company's financial position and caused a sharp fall in the share price. The appellant sold his shares at a significant loss. He claimed damages for economic loss resulting from fraud and misrepresentation. The trial judge held that whilst the company was guilty of negligent, but not fraudulent, misrepresentation, the appellant had failed to prove his damages. On appeal, *held*, since the president and chief financial officer were still the operating minds of the company at the time the press release was published, the fraudulent intent of the officers was also the fraudulent intent of the company. The company was thus guilty of fraudulent, as well as of negligent, misrepresentation which the appellant had relied on. He had proved the market price of the shares at the dates of purchase and sale, and was entitled to the difference in value. The judge erred in concluding that the appellant had not proved his damages and ought to have fixed the quantum on the basis that the market value of the shares was the best evidence on which to assess damages. The company failed to rebut the evidence of market value to show that the appellant had received value for his money and, accordingly, the appeal would be allowed.

Dixon v Deacon Morgan McEwan Easson (1993) 102 DLR (4th) 1 (British Columbia Court of Appeal).

470 Criminal liability—directing mind of company—nominee director

The plaintiff was the victim of a serious fraud. Some of the money he lost as a result of the fraud was received by the defendant company and invested by one of the company's nominee directors in a property development. The plaintiff brought an action to recover the money received by the company, which was dismissed at first instance because it was held that the investment was made by a nominee director with non-executive responsibility who had no authority to take business decisions and who therefore was not the company's directing mind and will in relation to receipt of assets. *Held*, it was not the management and control of the company in general that was important, but the management and control of the transaction in issue. In this case, the director had made all the arrangements for the receipt and investment of the money and had signed the relevant papers. He was therefore the company's directing mind and will which meant that the company had the requisite knowledge at the time and was consequently liable. Accordingly, the appeal would be allowed.

El Ajou v Dollar Land Holdings plc (1994) Times, 3 January (Court of Appeal: Nourse, Rose and Hoffmann LJJ). Decision of Millett J [1993] 3 All ER 717 reversed.

471 Director—disqualification—allotment of shares

It has been held that the allotment of shares by a director to himself and his supporter in order to maintain his control of the company constitutes evidence of unfitness and good grounds for making a disqualification order against him under the Company Directors Disqualification Act 1986, s 8.

Re Looe Fish Ltd [1993] BCLC 1160 (Chancery Division: Parker J).

472 Director—disqualification—application for disqualification order

Following the making of an administration order in respect of a company, the Secretary of State issued an originating summons seeking disqualification orders against two of the company's directors. The directors sought an order for the affidavit evidence filed in support of that application to be struck out because most of its contents were hearsay. They also sought a direction enabling them to give their evidence before the examining officer orally because they wished to preserve their right to submit that there was no case to answer, and an order staying the disqualification applications until a civil action brought by the company against one of the directors had been disposed of. *Held*, a director who wished to oppose a disqualification order had to present his evidence in the form of affidavits so the Secretary of State could consider that evidence before the effective hearing of the summons, and even if the director wished to make a submission of no case to answer that procedure had to be followed. The public interest required disqualification orders to be made in respect of unfit directors, and the applications for those orders were not an abuse of the court because the public should not have to wait for the outcome of parallel private litigation before those orders could be made. The examining officer had been acting in a statutory capacity in accordance with the Companies Act 1985, s 447, so the ordinary rules relating to hearsay evidence did not apply and there were no grounds for striking out the affidavit evidence. The directors' applications would be dismissed.

Re Rex Williams Leisure plc [1993] 2 All ER 741 (Chancery Division: Sir Donald Nicholls V-C).

473 Director—disqualification—application for disqualification order—summary procedure

The respondents were directors of five connected companies all of which were insolvent. The Official Receiver sought disqualification orders against the respondents under the Company Directors Disqualification Act 1986, s 6. The respondents agreed that their conduct made them unfit to be concerned in the management of a company and stated that they were prepared to accept an immediate disqualification order for the minimum period of two years if certain matters still in dispute were not proceeded with. It fell to be determined whether the court could make an order against them without a full hearing. *Held*, before making an order under s 6, the court had to be satisfied that the conduct of a director in relation to a particular company or companies made him unfit to be concerned in the management of a company. Accordingly, the parties in disqualification proceedings could not reach an agreement and then request the court to embody their agreement in a consent order. However, the court could not control the way in which either party conducted its case whether in respect of the scope and definition of the charges made or disputed or in respect of the evidence presented to support or rebut the charges. The court had jurisdiction to deal with an application under s 6 summarily without requiring a full trial and without requiring the parties to contest every point provided that some evidence, not merely an assertion of no evidential value or an admission which was unsupported by evidence was presented to the court which established unfitness. If the court considered that the disputed evidence substantially affected the seriousness of the unfitness it could in its discretion decline to deal with the matter summarily and direct a full hearing. The undisputed evidence put before the court contained all the facts necessary to establish that the conduct of the respondents made them unfit to be concerned in the management of a company but even if the disputed evidence was proved it was not such as to have a significant impact on the seriousness of the respondents' conduct. A relatively short period of disqualification would be appropriate. A two year period of disqualification would be imposed.

Re Carecraft Construction Co Ltd [1993] 4 All ER 499 (Chancery Division: Ferris J). *Re Net Book Agreement 1957* (No 2) (1964) LR 4 RP 484 applied.

474 Director—disqualification—insider dealing—offence having some relevant factual connection with management of company

Shortly before the announcement of a substantial loss in the affairs of a public company, the defendant, the company chairman, sought to dispose of his substantial shareholding and to resign as chairman. The purchasers of the shares were unaware of these facts. The defendant was convicted of insider dealing. He appealed against that part of his sentence disqualifying him from acting as the director of a company for ten years on the grounds that a disqualification order could not be made in respect of the offence of which he had been convicted and that the order would debar him from being a director not only of a public company but also of a private company whose shares were not traded on the Stock Exchange. *Held*, although the power to disqualify was not limited to offences which consisted of breaking some law relating to the management of a company, it was limited to cases where the offence was committed in the course of managing the company. In order for disqualification to be ordered, the offence had to have some relevant factual connection with the management of the company. The disqualification extended to private companies. The Company Directors (Disqualification) Act 1986, in conferring on courts power to make disqualification orders, made no distinction between different types of companies. Although the company's creditors had lost nothing in the present case because the defendant's attempted sale of shares had been set aside, the disqualification was not too long and the appeal would be dismissed.

R v Goodman [1993] 2 All ER 789 (Court of Appeal: Staughton LJ, McKinnon and Potter JJ).

475 Director—disqualification—length of ban—right of Secretary of State to appeal

An order for disqualification for a period of three years was made against the director of a company, following persistent breaches of the filing requirements. The Secretary of State appealed against the order on the grounds that the period was too short. *Held*, although there was no express power of appeal under the Company Directors Disqualification Act 1986, the Secretary of State did have a right of appeal. The court would only interfere with the exercise of the judge's discretion in deciding the length of the sentence on the well established principles as to the basis on which an appellate court would interfere with the exercise of the discretion of a judge. Whilst an isolated lapse in the filing of documents might be excusable, persistent lapses which showed a blatant disregard for the important aspects of accountability was not. Such lapses were serious and could not be condoned even in the absence of a dishonest intention. Those who persistently failed as in this case, to discharge their statutory obligations in that regard could be expected to be disqualified for an appropriate period of time. On the facts, the judge had misdirected himself and the appropriate period of disqualification was five years. Accordingly, the appeal would be allowed.

Secretary of State for Trade and Industry v Ettinger, Re Swift 736 Ltd [1993] BCLC 896 (Court of Appeal: Sir Donald Nicholls V-C, Farquharson and Steyn LJJ).

476 Director—disqualification—undischarged bankrupt—knowledge of discharge—defence

The defendant was charged with acting as a director of a company whilst being an undischarged bankrupt contrary to the Company Directors Disqualification Act 1986, s 11(1). He had been discharged pursuant to the provisions of the Insolvency Act 1986, but had been involved in running a hotel company before the discharge, without leave of the court. The defendant believed that he had been genuinely discharged during this time, but had failed to make enquiries of the Official Receiver which would have revealed that he was not in fact discharged. The defendant appealed against his conviction and the question arose as to whether the defendant had a defence in law and whether the offence under the Company Directors Disqualification Act 1986, s 11(1) was an absolute offence. On appeal, *held*, strict liability in relation to s 11 would prevent bankrupts from involving themselves in any of the prohibited activities, before being properly discharged. The mischief the section was intended to cure was therefore of social concern. Accordingly, the appeal would be dismissed.

R v Brockley (1993) Times, 25 November (Court of Appeal: Henry LJ, Otton and Garland JJ).

477 Director—fiduciary duty—share transfer

The plaintiff company was trustee of the assets of pension schemes for employees of companies controlled by another company. The defendant, a director of the plaintiff company, signed stock transfer forms transferring shares held by the plaintiff to another company, which were never paid for. The transfers had not been authorised by the board and no grounds had been put forward upon which it could honestly have been thought that the transactions were for the benefit of the plaintiff as trustee of the pension funds. The plaintiff's application for summary judgment under RSC Ord 14 was granted, and an order for an interim payment was made against the defendant. On appeal, *held*, it was clear that a company director owed a duty to act in the interests of the company and therefore the exercise of his power for any other purpose was a breach of his fiduciary duty. In signing the share transfer forms and giving away the plaintiff's assets for no consideration to a private family company of which he was a director the defendant was in breach of his fiduciary duty. The correct approach had been followed in ordering the interim payment, notwithstanding there was a high likelihood that the defendant would be made bankrupt, the court would be given the opportunity to discover exactly what assets the defendant held, and although the defendant's level of means was a consideration his lack of means was in no way a bar to making such an order. Accordingly, the appeal would be dismissed.

Bishopsgate Investment Management Ltd (in Liquidation) v Maxwell (No 2) [1994] 1 All ER 261 (Court of Appeal: Ralph Gibson, Leggatt and Hoffmann LJJ). Decision of Chadwick J, (1993) Times, 12 January affirmed. For earlier related proceedings, see *Bishopsgate Investment Management Ltd (in provisional liquidation) v Maxwell; Cooper v Maxwell; Mirror Group Newspapers plc v Maxwell* [1992] 2 All ER 856, CA (1992 Abr para 429).

478 Director—liability—improperly obtained money—attribution of knowledge to company

See *El Ajou v Dollar Land Holdings plc*, para 470.

479 Director—liability—personal liability to creditors

See *Nordic Oil Services Ltd v Berman*, para 1864.

480 EC provisions

See EUROPEAN COMMUNITIES.

481 Inquiry into company's dealings—criminal proceedings—disclosure of information to defendant

It has been held that transcripts of examinations under the Insolvency Act 1986, s 236, by liquidators with a person who is later subject to criminal proceedings, need not be disclosed to the person charged at the same time as they are disclosed to the Serious Fraud Office.

Re Headington Investments Ltd [1993] 3 All ER 861 (Court of Appeal: Dillon, Steyn and Rose LJJ).

482 Inquiry into company's dealings—disclosure of information—action for negligence against directors—whether disclosure oppressive

The two respondents were the directors, sole shareholders and solicitors of a limited company incorporated on a nominee basis which had purchased a property, a transaction on which it later defaulted. Following the winding up of the company, the liquidator sought from the respondents files relating to the affairs of the company to ascertain whether the respondents had continued to incur liabilities when they should have appreciated the company was insolvent. The respondents refused to provide the information. The liquidator applied for an order under the Insolvency Act 1986, s 236 that the respondents produce all accounting records kept on behalf of the company and all documents relating to the transactions on which the company had defaulted. *Held*, whilst the liquidator may not have pursued his original request for information as diligently as he might have, he was nevertheless seeking information which belonged to the company, which the respondents ought to have retained and which would enable him to discharge his duties. The documents relating to the transactions on which the company had defaulted belonged prima facie to the company, even where the respondents had acted for a third party. Privilege only arose in relation to documents which came into existence when the respondents had acted solely for a third party and it was for the respondents to claim privilege in relation to those matters. Accordingly, the application would be granted.

Re Brook Martin & Co (Nominees) Ltd [1993] BCLC 328 (Chancery Division: Vinelott J).

483 Inquiry into company's dealings—disclosure of information—information mistakenly provided

In proceedings concerning the mistaken disclosure of confidential documents pursuant to an order under the Insolvency Act 1986, s 236, it has been held that there is an analogy between the provision of information under s 236 and information provided under discovery and that the court should follow the same principles in dealing with documents provided by way of mistake under s 236 as information provided under discovery. Accordingly, the court will not normally undo the consequences of the mistake unless the person receiving the information was aware of the mistake or there was fraud.

Re Polly Peck International plc [1992] BCLC 1025 (Chancery Division: Hoffmann J).

484 Inquiry into company's dealings—disclosure of information—non-compliance with notice to produce evidence

The liquidators of a company received a request from the Serious Fraud Office (SFO) under the Criminal Justice Act 1987, s 2(3) for access to the transcripts of an examination of an officer of the company which had been carried out in accordance with the Insolvency Act 1986, s 236. The officer had already been charged by the SFO in connection with matters arising from the company's affairs, and he opposed the production of the transcripts on the ground that the principle of public interest immunity applied. The SFO submitted it had an untrammelled right to require the production of the transcripts, and argued no conditions should be attached which restricted its right to use the transcripts as evidence. It was ordered that the liquidators release and disclose to the SFO the transcripts of the interviews on the director of the SFO undertaking not to use the transcripts save in the circumstances specified in the Criminal Justice Act 1987, s 2(8). On appeal by the SFO, *held*, the civil court had no power to decide to what extent evidence which would be by statute admissible in criminal proceedings would be allowed to be used. There was no basis on which the restrictions in the 1987 Act, s 2(8) ought to have been imposed. Further, the court had no relevant discretion to curtail the supply of information by liquidators, in performance of their regulatory obligations, under the heading of public interest immunity. Accordingly, the appeal would be allowed and the director of the SFO released from the undertakings required by the judge.

Re Arrows Ltd (No 4) [1993] 3 All ER 861 (Court of Appeal: Dillon, Steyn and Rose LJJ). Decision of Vinelott J in *Re Arrows Ltd (No 4)* (1992) Times, 11 November (1992 Abr para 425), reversed.

485 Inquiry into company's dealings—disclosure of information—transcripts of interviews

The applicant was a director of two companies which went into liquidation and receivership. The office holders obtained orders for the examination of the applicant under the Insolvency Act 1986, s 236, and the interviews took place shortly afterwards. The applicant was subsequently charged with offences including theft and fraud. Notices were served by the Serious Fraud Office (SFO) on the office holders under the Criminal Justice Act 1987, s 2(3), requiring them to produce the transcripts of the applicant's interviews. The applicant claimed that he had a reasonable excuse for not answering the questions of the SFO as he had already been charged with criminal offences. An order was made requiring the production to the SFO of transcripts of the examinations of the applicant. The applicant applied for leave to appeal against the order. *Held*, the examinations took place before the applicant was charged. Even if the applicant had a reasonable excuse for not answering questions put by the SFO after he had been charged, it did not follow that the liquidator should be prevented from handing over material which came into his hands before charges were preferred and at a time when no excuse would have been available to the applicant. Accordingly, the application for leave to appeal would be dismissed.

Re Bishopsgate Investment Management Ltd [1993] 3 All ER 861 (Court of Appeal: Dillon, Steyn and Rose LJJ). For earlier related proceedings, see *Bishopsgate Investment Management (in liquidation) v Maxwell* (1993) Times, 16 February (para 477).

486   Insider dealing—legislation

See para 679.

487   Insolvency—floating charge—avoidance

By virtue of the Insolvency Act 1986, s 245(2), a floating charge created on a company's undertaking or property at a relevant time is invalid except to the extent of the value of so much of the consideration for the creation of the charge as consists of money paid to the company at the same time as, or after, the creation of the charge.

It has been held that, where there is an agreement to create a debenture which does not create a present equitable right, money paid to a company before the execution of the debenture does not fall within the invalidity exemption in s 245(2) unless the interval between payment and the execution is de minimis, for example a coffee break, so that the two acts can be regarded as contemporaneous. The words "at the same time as, or after, the creation of the charge" in s 245(2) are clearly included for the purpose of excluding from the exemption the amount of money paid to the company before the creation of the charge even though they are paid in consideration for that charge.

Power v Sharp Investments Ltd [1994] BCLC 111 (Court of Appeal: Ralph Gibson and Nolan LJJ and Sir Christopher Slade). Decision of Hoffmann J sub nom *Re Shoe Lace Ltd* [1992] BCLC 636 (1992 Abr para 402) affirmed.

488   Insolvency—proceedings—co-operation between courts—jurisdiction of High Court

Following an application by the liquidators of a company incorporated in the Cayman Islands, which had never been registered in the United Kingdom, the Grand Court of the Cayman Islands ordered a letter of request to be addressed to the High Court, asking the court to exercise its jurisdiction under the Insolvency Act 1986, s 426 by making declarations relating to the alleged participation of senior management of the company in allegedly wrongful activities. On the question of whether the English court had jurisdiction to entertain the liquidator's claims and if so, whether it had a discretion as to how that jurisdiction should be exercised, *held*, the effect of s 426 was to give the court discretion as to whether it should apply English insolvency law, or the law of the requesting court, to matters specified in the relevant request from the foreign court. The Grand Court would not ask the English Court to make declarations that could be made under Cayman law. The court could decide to apply Cayman law, in which case it had to refuse to make the declarations sought, or English law, and go on to consider whether the declarations ought to be made under English law. The court had jurisdiction to investigate the relevant facts and the assistance sought would accordingly be given.

Re Bank of Credit and Commerce International SA; Re Bank of Credit and Commerce International (Overseas) Ltd [1993] LS Gaz R 42 (Chancery Division: Rattee J).

489   Insolvency—proceedings—disclosure of evidence—disclosure by liquidator to creditor

Scotland

The plaintiffs were liquidators of a company who had obtained documents which they intended to use in proceedings against the defendants in relation to dealings with shares of the company. A creditor bank, which was the sole source of funding for the proceedings, requested that the documents be disclosed to it so that it could be satisfied that there were grounds to bring an action. The plaintiffs applied to the court for authority to disclose the documents. *Held*, the plaintiffs could not disclose the documents to the creditor. The court's power to order disclosure of evidence was to enable a liquidator to carry out his functions effectively and not to aid a prospective litigant in the preparation of his case by giving him rights not available to other litigants. Accordingly, the application would be dismissed.

Liquidators of First Tokyo Index Trust Ltd v Morgan Stanley Trust Co (1993) Times, 1 December (Outer House).

490 Partnerships of companies—accounts
See para 1908.

491 Receivership
See RECEIVERS.

492 Register of members—rectification—costs of rectification
The applicant held over 75 per cent of the shares in a company and the remainder were held by ten shareholders, nine of whom were also directors of the company. There was a dispute between the applicant and the other shareholders and as he was unable by himself to requisition a meeting of the company despite being the largest shareholder, he transferred one share to his daughter. The directors refused to register the transfer on the advice of their solicitor, notwithstanding that this refusal was not permitted by the articles. The applicant sought to rectify the register of members and it was then agreed that the transfer should be registered. The applicant sought an order for costs of the rectification against all of the directors personally. The directors claimed that the costs should be paid by the company. *Held*, on the correct interpretation of RSC Ord 102, r 3, and the statement in *The Supreme Court Practice 1991*, p 1479 (now *The Supreme Court Practice 1993*, p 1506), the proper respondents to an application to rectify the register were the company and the holder of the shares whose registration was disputed, if it was not the applicant. The other shareholders were represented by the company. The applicant should only apply to join the directors where he sought an order for costs as in the present case. Even though the directors had acted in good faith, they had acted beyond their powers, and it was therefore unfair for the applicant indirectly to bear three-quarters of the costs of the action. The applicant did not need to establish bad faith on the part of the directors. Accordingly the costs would be paid by the individual directors.

Morgan v Morgan Insurance Brokers Ltd [1993] BCLC 676 (Chancery Division: Millett J).

493 Security for costs—company as plaintiff—actions for which security for costs can be awarded
The Companies Act 1985, s 726 provides that where a limited company is the plaintiff in an action or other legal proceedings and there is reason to believe that it will be unable to pay the defendant's costs if successful in his defence, the court may require sufficient security to be given for those costs, and may stay all proceedings until such security is given.

A company presented a petition against the respondents under the 1985 Act, s 459 and the respondents were granted an order for security for costs. On appeal against that order, the petitioner unsuccessfully contended that the phrase "other legal proceedings" did not include a petition under s 459, particularly since the wording referred to a plaintiff rather than a petitioner. The judge held that "other legal proceedings" included originating summonses, originating notices and also petitions, and that "plaintiff" referred to the person who invoked the jurisdiction of the court irrespective of the form of originating process chosen. On further appeal, it was contended that the jurisdiction did not permit security for costs to be ordered in respect of any proceedings commenced under the Companies Act 1985. *Held*, there was no justification for reading into s 726 some such words as would be apt to exclude any proceedings brought under the 1985 Act. The phrase "other legal proceedings" in s 726 referred to any matter where the jurisdiction of the court was invoked by any originating process other than a writ, "plaintiff" embraced any person who had invoked the court's jurisdiction by whatever originating process he had selected, and thus s 726 covered proceedings commenced by petition. It logically followed that s 726 also applied to winding-up petitions under the Insolvency Act 1986, s 124. The judge had taken a correct view of the scope of the 1985 Act, s 726 and, accordingly, the appeal would be dismissed.

Re Unisoft Group Ltd (No 1); Saunderson Holdings Ltd v Unisoft Group Ltd [1993] BCLC 1292 (Court of Appeal: Parker, Scott LJJ and Sir Michael Kerr). Decision of Morritt J [1993] BCLC 528 affirmed.

494 Security for costs—company as plaintiff—relevance of defendants' indemnity insurance
The plaintiff company, which was in liquidation with a substantial deficiency, brought an action against a firm of auditors and accountants. The defendants successfully applied for a consent order requiring the plaintiff to give security for costs. The plaintiff then set the action down for trial and the defendants issued a summons for further security. The summons was dismissed and

the defendants appealed, contending that the judge had wrongly taken into account, and attached significant weight to, the fact that the defendants had professional indemnity insurance. *Held*, the judge was wrong to regard the defendants' insurance position as in any way determinative of the application. In an exceptional case, a defendant's means might be of minor relevance, but his insurance position was never a relevant factor in any circumstances. The judge erred in the exercise of his discretion and, accordingly, the appeal would be allowed and an order for further security would be made

Croft Leisure Ltd v Gravestock [1993] BCLC 1273 (Court of Appeal: Sir Donald Nicholas V-C, Staughton and Hirst LJJ).

495 Shares—disclosure of interests in shares—exemptions

The Disclosure of Interests in Shares (Amendment) Regulations 1993, SI 1993/1819 (in force on 18 September 1993), amend the Companies Act 1985, Pt VI (disclosure of interests in shares) by amending or replacing exemptions from the obligation to disclose contained in the 1985 Act and in regulations made thereunder. In particular, the 1993 Regulations amend the 1985 Act, s 199 to make special provision for certain interests in relation to the percentage level of interest constituting a notifiable interest. Section 209 (interests to be disregarded for the purposes of the obligation to disclose) is substituted so as to make some exemptions subject to certain conditions. The Public Company (Disclosure of Interests in Shares) (Exclusions) Regulations 1982, SI 1982/677, and the Public Company (Disclosure of Interests in Shares) (Investment Management Exclusion) Regulations 1988, SI 1988/706, are revoked.

The Disclosure of Interests in Shares (Amendment) (No 2) Regulations 1993, SI 1993/2689 (in force on 29 October 1993), amend the Companies Act 1985, s 209(2) (disregard of certain interests held by way of security for the purposes of the obligation to disclose interests in shares comprised in certain issued share capital of public companies). The amendment makes provision for the disregard of interests held by way of security by stock exchanges situated or operating in a member state and by persons who deal in securities and derivatives on an exchange situated or operating in a member state. The regulations also contain transitional provisions.

496 Shares—financial assistance given by company to purchase own shares—assistance by foreign subsidiary

The Companies Act 1985, s 151 states that where a person is acquiring or is proposing to acquire shares in a company, it is not lawful for the company or any of its subsidiaries to give financial assistance directly or indirectly for the purpose of that acquisition before or at the same time as the acquisition takes place.

The plaintiff bank loaned money to a British subsidiary company, the second defendant, so that it could purchase the whole share capital of its parent company. The parent company also had a subsidiary incorporated in Gibraltar, the first defendant. The Gibraltarian subsidiary charged a property that it owned to the plaintiff, and also assigned the rental income of the property to the plaintiff, as security for the plaintiff's loan to the British subsidiary. The plaintiff wished to realise its security by selling the property, but the defendants claimed that no power of sale had arisen or was exercisable and that the security was void as it was in breach of the 1985 Act, s 151. The potential purchasers of the property refused to enter into the contract of purchase until the plaintiff had obtained a declaration from the court. On the plaintiff's application for a declaration, *held*, the words "any of its subsidiaries" in the 1985 Act, s 151 referred only to English "subsidiary companies" and not foreign subsidiaries. A literal reading of the 1985 Act would make it unlawful for a foreign subsidiary to give financial assistance for the purchase of shares in its parent company. However, such a conclusion would be contrary to the principles of private international law whereby companies incorporated abroad were governed by the laws of the place of incorporation. Unless the contrary was expressed or implied, United Kingdom legislation was not intended to apply to persons or corporations who performed acts outside the United Kingdom. A limited interpretation of the 1985 Act, s 151 was therefore necessary to avoid imputing such an intention to Parliament. Accordingly, a declaration would be made that s 151 did not prohibit a foreign subsidiary from giving financial assistance for acquisition of shares in its parent company.

Arab Bank plc v Mercantile Holdings Ltd [1994] 2 WLR 307 (Chancery Division: Millett J).

497 Shares—issue of shares—date of issue

See *National Westminster Bank plc v IRC*, para 1481.

**498 Shares—sale—purchaser defaulting—agreement obliging vendor to vote
shares according to instructions of purchaser**

Shares in a company were sold to a purchaser (E). The contract of sale gave the vendor (H) an
option to repurchase the shares and H exercised the option. Completion did not take place on
the agreed date because H was unable to pay the option price. E however did not treat this as
repudiation of the repurchase agreement and sought completion. The agreement provided that
all rights attaching to the shares would accrue to H. It fell to be determined whether E was
obliged to vote the shares in accordance with H's directions. *Held*, an unpaid vendor of shares in
general had the right to vote the shares which remained registered in his name and was free
from any obligation to comply with the directions of the purchaser. If the agreement were to
be construed literally it would result in E being deprived of valuable rights, the right to dividend
and the right to vote, even where H had failed to make payment by or before the option
completion date. The agreement should not take effect so as to deprive E of his rights as an
unpaid vendor after the option completion date if the reason that actual completion had not
taken place was because of the default of H. Judgment would be given accordingly.

JRRT (Investments) Ltd v Haycraft; Haycraft v JRRT (Investments) Ltd [1993] BCLC 401
(Chancery Division: Chadwick J).

499 Shares—settlement of shares—treatment as income or capital

See *Re Lee; Sinclair v Lee*, para 2304.

500 Shares—transfer—failure to comply with transfer procedure

Scotland

A company's articles of association provided that shares in the company could only be transferred
in accordance with the procedure laid down in the articles, which required the transferee to sign
the form of transfer. Following the transfer of shares to certain individuals a company member
petitioned under the Companies Act 1985, s 359(1) for rectification of the company's register
by deletion of the entries of those individuals on the ground that the transferee had failed to sign
the form, and consequently the transfer had been unlawful under the 1985 Act, s 183(1). *Held*,
the absence of the transferee's signature on the form of transfer was a substantive matter and not
merely a matter of form, and as such there was a prima facie case for rectification. However, as
beneficial ownership of the shares had passed as a matter of contract, the new owners were
entitled to use and control of them despite the defect in the form of transfer. The companies
register would not be rectified and, accordingly, the petition would be dismissed.

Dempsey v Celtic Football and Athletic Co Ltd 1993 SLT 382 (Outer House).

501 Shares—transfer—instrument of transfer—omission

It is not lawful for a company to register a transfer of shares unless a proper instrument of
transfer has been delivered to it: Companies Act 1985, s 183(1).

One of the two members of a company sold to the other member all his shares in the company
by purporting to execute a stock transfer. The instrument of transfer was undated, did not state
the consideration given, omitted the addresses of the transferor and transferee, was not signed
by the transferee and was not stamped. Nevertheless, the company registered the transfer. In
proceedings by the company's liquidator for a declaration that the transferee was personally
liable jointly and severally with the company for all its debts after the date of the transfer of the
shares, the transferee contended that, as the instrument of transfer had been defective, it had not
been a "proper instrument" of transfer so that he was not the sole shareholder because the transfer
of the shares had been void. *Held*, a "proper instrument" was one which was "appropriate or
suitable", in this case suitable, for stamping. The omission from the instrument of transfer of the
amount of consideration given for the transfer was a mere irregularity and did not prevent it
being a proper instrument of transfer. Although the instrument was not stamped, which was an
omission of the transferee, it was an instrument which sufficiently recorded the transaction to be
chargeable with stamp duty, so that it was a proper instrument. The registration of the transfer
was lawful so that the transferee was the sole shareholder. Accordingly, the declaration would
be granted.

Nisbet v Shepherd (1993) Times, 1 July (Court of Appeal: Balcombe, Leggatt and Hoffmann
LJJ).

502 Unfair prejudice to members—costs—payment of costs from company assets

The petitioner, a member of the company, applied for a winding-up order on the just and
equitable ground under the Insolvency Act 1986, s 122(g). He also sought an order against the

respondent directors under the Companies Act 1985, s 459 on the ground that the company's affairs had been conducted in a manner unfairly prejudicial to the interests of some of the members. At an interlocutory hearing, the petitioner sought: (1) an injunction to prevent the respondents using company funds in the defence of the s 459 proceedings, and (2) an order that the respondents repay company moneys already expended for that purpose. *Held*, (1) in a petition under the 1985 Act, s 459 the company was purely a nominal party because the substantive dispute was between the shareholders. Therefore, the directors committed a misfeasance by using the company's money to pay the legal expenses in such proceedings. (2) The jurisdiction to order the respondents to reimburse the company would not arise unless and until the court found that the s 459 petition was satisfied. Further, the petitioner lacked the locus standi to make this application since he was acting in his capacity as a shareholder and did not represent the company. Accordingly, the injunction would be granted but the order for the repayment of company moneys would be refused.

Re a company (No 004502 of 1988), ex p Johnson [1992] BCLC 701 (Chancery Division: Harman J).

503 Unfair prejudice to members—petition—hearing—application for Mareva injunction

See *Re All Starr Video Ltd*, para 1531.

504 Winding up—company incorporated in Northern Ireland—presentation of petition to wind up in England—application of Insolvency Act 1986

The Insolvency Act 1986, s 441(2) provides that subject to any provision expressly relating to companies incorporated elsewhere than in Great Britain, nothing in the Act applies to companies registered or incorporated in Northern Ireland. Section 220 of the 1986 Act contains the definition of an unregistered company.

The company was incorporated in Northern Ireland and the Secretary of State presented a petition for the compulsory winding up of the company on just and equitable grounds. The company applied to strike out the petition as disclosing no cause of action because the company was incorporated in Northern Ireland and there was no such express provision as mentioned in s 441(2). The Secretary of State argued that there was such a provision in s 220. *Held*, the case depended on the proper construction of the words "expressly relating to" in s 441(2). The words "relating to" included but were not the same as, the words "referring to". It was possible however to have express relation without an express reference. Section 220 referred to "any company" as part of the definition of an unregistered company and these words were unlimited and therefore expressly included companies incorporated elsewhere than in Great Britain, notwithstanding the fact that there was no express reference to such a company. The effect of the 1986 Act, s 221, was that only companies incorporated in Northern Ireland which also had a principal place of business in England and Wales were liable to be wound up in England, and this dealt with the company's argument that all companies incorporated in Northern Ireland would be subject to all the provisions of the 1986 Act, if the view of the Secretary of State was allowed to prevail. The wording of s 441 suggested that this would be the exception rather than the rule. Section 220 was therefore a provision within the meaning of s 441(2) with the result that the Secretary of State was authorised by s 124 to present the petition and the company could be wound up under s 221 in due course, provided that it had a principal place of business in England or Wales. Accordingly, the application would be dismissed.

Re a Company (No 007946 of 1993) (1993) Times, 18 November (Chancery Division: Morritt J).

505 Winding up—creditors' claims—subordinated debts

Creditors of a company were guarantee creditors by reason of holding convertible bonds in another company under which payment of principal and interest was unconditionally and irrevocably guaranteed on a subordinated basis. The first company had guaranteed that, in the event of a distribution of its assets in a winding up, creditors of unsubordinated indebtedness would be entitled to be paid in full before any payment would be made on account of payments under the bonds. The administrators of the first company sought a declaration that they were entitled to exclude the guarantee creditors from a scheme of arrangement under the Companies Act 1985, s 425. *Held*, there was no principle of public policy precluding the postponement or subordination, by agreement, of a creditor's own claim to those of other creditors. As a creditor could waive his own debt, once a bankruptcy or winding up had commenced, simply by declining to submit a proof, he was even more entitled to agree that payment of the debt be postponed to the payment of the debts of other persons; on the assumption that such an agreement was binding, other persons who were aware of it might even have given the debtor company credit. A contract between a company and a creditor providing for the subordination, in the event of a winding up, of that creditor's debt to those of other unsecured creditors, was not rendered void by the insolvency legislation. The administrators were entitled to exclude the guarantee creditors from the scheme of arrangement and, accordingly, the declaration sought would be granted.

Re Maxwell Communications Corpn plc (No 2) [1993] 1 WLR 1402 (Chancery Division: Vinelott J). Dicta of Lord Denning MR in *Rolls Razor Ltd v Cox* [1967] 1 QB 552 at 570, CA, not followed. *Halesowen Presswork & Assemblies Ltd v National Westminster Bank Ltd* [1972] AC 785, HL, and *British Eagle International Airlines Ltd v Compagnie Nationale Air France* [1975] 1 WLR 758, HL (1975 Abr para 395), distinguished.

506 Winding up—grounds for winding up—just and equitable grounds—quasi-partnership

Scotland
The members of Company A held shares in Company B and the two companies were operated as one entity, without complying with the requirements of company law. Company A had made interest free loans to Company B, and Company B had lent surplus funds to Company A. Company A and also granted security to the bank for Company B's overdraft, and this security replaced a previous one which had been paid off. The granting of security was not authorised by Company A's memorandum and articles. Members of Company A purported to pass a special resolution altering its memorandum, but it was accepted that no meeting had been held. There had also been a threat to use Company A's assets to pay off Company B's liabilities. Two minority shareholders of Company A applied for an order under the Companies Company Act 1985, s 459 for the purchase of their shares, or alternatively, an order under the Insolvency Act 1986, s 122(1)(g) that Company A be wound up on just and equitable grounds. At first instance the court refused the orders on the grounds that: (1) it was necessary to look at the whole background between the two companies, and that the respondents had run the two companies together in what they considered was the benefit of the whole family; and (2) in the circumstances there had been no unfair prejudice and it was not just and equitable that Company A be wound up. On appeal, *held*, the court had been justified in considering the whole background between the two companies. Company A was however a quasi-partnership company in which there was mutual trust between the members. The loans, security and threats had broken that trust. Even though there had been no unfair prejudice, it was just and equitable that Company A be wound up. Accordingly, the appeal would be allowed.

Jesner v Jarrad Properties Ltd [1993] BCLC 1032 (Court of Session).

507 Winding up—liquidator—defunct company—compensation—distribution

A company had been incorporated, but had never commenced trading. Most of its assets had been seized by a foreign government, who had rejected compensation claims. The company was later wound up, and the creditors were paid out of the remaining assets. Some years later, an agreement was made with the foreign government for the payment of the claims and a liquidator was appointed under the Insolvency Act 1986. The liquidator applied under s 112 for directions as to the manner in which the compensation fund should be distributed. *Held*, the register of members was not conclusive in deciding who were the members of the company and rectification of the register could be ordered after, as well as before, the winding up. The liquidator would be directed to distribute the fund among the following: (1) the traceable registered members, and their executors and administrators, under an English grant of probate; (2) the executors and administrators of registered members under a foreign grant of probate; (3) beneficiaries under a will, whether English or foreign, where there was no English grant of probate; and (4) persons who had a company share certificate, where they were beneficially entitled to the shares. However, directions would be given not to distribute any part of the fund to a person whose only claim was that they were in possession of a share certificate, as a number of claimants were simply collectors of share certificates. The persons had not been intended to and did not become beneficially entitled to the shares to which their certificates related.

Re Baku Consolidated Oilfields Ltd [1994] BCLC 173 (Chancery Division: Chadwick J).

508 Winding up—mutual credit and set-off—enforcement of right of set-off

The directors of two companies guaranteed loans to the companies from a bank. The bank also took deposits of money from the directors. The bank subsequently became insolvent. The directors successfully applied for declarations that the indebtedness of the companies to the bank had been extinguished at the date of the winding-up order by the amount which at that date stood to the credit of the directors in their deposit accounts at the bank. On appeal by the bank against the declarations, *held*, where in an insolvency there was to be a set-off of mutual credits, mutual debts or other mutual dealings, the set-off was mandatory and could not be excluded by any contract between the parties. If there were mutual credits or mutual debts or mutual dealings between a company and a creditor, the set-off applied notwithstanding that one or other of the debts or credits was secured. The liabilities of the principal debtors to the bank were at all times enforceable by the bank without the need for a demand. In the case of the first company, the director expressly agreed that his liabilities would be those of a principal debtor, and thereby dispensed with the need for a demand. In the case of the second company, the director accepted that the liabilities of the company would be recoverable from him as principal debtor, and thereby there was immediate liability. On the winding up of the bank, all rights relevant to the question of set-off were immediately enforceable. There were debts presently due from each of the companies to the bank, and equally due from the directors as principal debtors, and there was liability from the bank to the directors on their deposits. This satisfied the requirements for statutory set-off and the Insolvency Rules 1986, SI 1986/1925, r 4.90 had effect. If there was set-off between the directors and the bank, the indebtedness of the companies to the bank was automatically reduced or extinguished. Accordingly, the appeals would be dismissed.

MS Fashions Ltd v Bank of Credit and Commerce International SA (in liquidation); High Street Services Ltd v Same; Impexbond Ltd v Same [1993] 3 WLR 220 (Court of Appeal: Dillon, Nolan and Steyn LJJ). Decision of Hoffmann LJ (1992) Times, 24 December (1992 Abr para 167) affirmed.

509 Winding up—petition—non-payment of debt—abuse of process

A company disputed its liability to pay a supplementary charge for certain goods and services invoiced to it. Without any statutory demand or formal or informal warning of intention, the petitioner presented a winding-up petition. No evidence specifically on the company's solvency or insolvency was before the court. The company sought an order restraining further proceedings upon the petition. *Held*, there was a bona fide dispute as to whether the debt was payable. It was a serious abuse of the process of the court to present a winding-up petition in the present circumstances. An injunction would be granted to restrain advertisement of the petition and an order would be made that costs be taxed on an indemnity basis even though the court had not been required to investigate the question of the company's solvency.

Re a company (No 00751 of 1992), ex p Avocet Aviation Ltd [1992] BCLC 869 (Chancery Division: Mummery J).

510 Winding up—petition—presentation of petition after judgment in default

See *Re Druce & Co*, para 1565.

511 Winding up—petition—retrospective effect—validation of transaction made after presentation of petition

A company carrying on business as hauliers was required to pay for deliveries to it of fuel oils before the suppliers would make further deliveries. After a petition had been presented for the winding up, the company paid for supplies delivered to it before presentation of the petition. On the liquidator's appeal against an order validating the payment under the Companies Act 1985, s 522, *held*, in receiving payment, the suppliers were acting in good faith because they were unaware that a winding-up petition had been presented against the company. The parties were acting in the normal course of business and the payment for the deliveries of fuel oils was for the benefit of creditors because it ensured that the suppliers would continue to make supplies to the company. Accordingly, the payment had been rightly validated and the appeal would be dismissed.

The court set out the following principles as those on which it would validate a transaction under s 522: (1) its discretion under s 522 was at large subject to the general principles that applied to any type of discretion and to the limitations on the discretion which flowed from general principles of insolvency law, (2) the basic principle was that the assets of an insolvent company existing at the time of the commencement of the liquidation should be distributed pari passu among the company's unsecured creditors, (3) there might be occasions where it was beneficial to the company and also the unsecured creditors that the company should be able to dispose of some of its assets after a winding-up petition had been presented but before an order had been made, (4) in determining whether an order should be made under s 522, the court should ensure that the interests of the unsecured creditors were not prejudiced, (5) the desirability of the company carrying on its business was often speculative and the court had to carry out a balancing exercise, (6) the court should not, except in special circumstances where it was in the interests of creditors generally, validate a transaction which would result in one or more pre-liquidation creditors being paid in full where other such creditors would only receive a dividend, (7) a disposition carried out by the parties in good faith at a time when they were unaware that a petition had been presented would normally be validated unless there were grounds for thinking that the transaction was an attempt to prefer the disponee, (8) the pari passu principle had no application to post-liquidation creditors because such a transaction at full, market value involved no dissipation of the company's assets.

Denney v John Hudson & Co Ltd [1992] BCLC 901 (Court of Appeal: Fox, Russell and Staughton LJJ).

1985 Act, s 522 now Insolvency Act 1986, s 127.

512 Winding up—petition—undisputed debt—abuse of process

The respondent served a statutory demand on a company for an undisputed sum due and owing by the company. The latter sought an injunction to restrain the presentation of a winding-up petition on the ground that, as the debt in question was not in dispute, the petition was an abuse of the process of the court. *Held*, the petition was not presented for an improper purpose such as to put pressure on the company to pay a disputed debt; it was presented for the entirely proper purpose of putting pressure on it to pay an undisputed debt. Any cross-claim of the company, which would be relevant to the exercise of the court's discretion on the hearing of the winding-up petition but which had not been established by litigation, was not a good reason for the company's failure to pay the properly made demand. The injunction sought would be refused.

Re a company (No 006273 of 1992) [1993] BCLC 131 (Chancery Division: Millett J).

513 Winding up—petition—unregistered company—meaning

The Insolvency Act 1986, s 220 provides that the expression "unregistered company" includes any association and any company, with specified exceptions. Rule 2 of the rules of a football club provided that it was to exist solely as a body for the purpose of professional association football, and that it would provide various social amenities for its players. Rule 13 provided that the management committee was to have the power to elect ordinary day members and that honorary day membership was to be open to officials, members and supporters of visiting clubs for the day of their visit only. Rule 17 provided that the club was only to be wound up by a resolution passed at a special general meeting called for that purpose and the assets of the club were to be disposed of, after repayment of outstanding loans and dues, in accordance with the resolutions passed at such meetings, and that on dissolution of the club, all net assets were to be devoted to association football and not to be distributed between the members.

The petitioners, who were all creditors of the club, sought an order that it be wound up. The club contended that it was not an unregistered company within the meaning of the 1986 Act, s 220 because (1) it was not formed to operate as a members' club but was set up for the purposes of professional football; (2) its activities and facilities were not restricted or intended to be restricted to the benefit of members only, but instead provided access to its grounds for non-members by payment of a fee for the purposes of watching football matches; (3) by participation in professional football, it was engaging in an activity not restricted to the club's members and as such it was commercially minded and not a social club. The club contended that the winding-up provisions of the 1986 Act did not therefore apply to it. At first instance, the petition for the winding-up order was dismissed. On appeal, *held*, the apparently unlimited word "any" in the 1986 Act, s 220 could not be given its literal meaning. The purpose expressed in rule 2 did not have the effect that the football club was not a club within the ordinary meaning of the term, and none of the rules justified an implication that Parliament intended that type of club to be capable of being wound up under the 1986 Act. The creditors' remedy lay against the individuals with whom their contracts had been made, and the appeal would accordingly be dismissed.

Western Counties Construction Ltd v Witney Town Football and Social Club (1993) Times, 19 November (Chancery Division: Morritt J).

514 Winding up—provident society—duty to pay preferential debts

The Insolvency Act 1986, s 40 provides that, in the case of a company, where a receiver is appointed on behalf of the holders of any debentures of the company secured by a charge which, as created, was a floating charge, if the company is not at the time in the course of being wound up, its preferential debts must be paid out of assets coming to the hands of the receiver in priority to any claims for principal interest in respect of the debentures.

By virtue of a debenture, a society registered under the Industrial and Provident Societies Act 1985 created fixed and floating charges over its assets in favour of a bank. Some years later, the society appointed receivers under the debenture. The society was later put into creditor's voluntary liquidation and a liquidator was appointed. The society's assets had been realised, and the receivers had a surplus after discharging the society's debt to the bank. However, there were insufficient funds to meet the demands of all the creditors. It fell to be determined whether the receivers had a duty, by virtue of the 1986 Act, s 40, to pay preferential creditors of the society, before handing over the balance to the liquidator. The liquidator argued that s 40 did not apply to a society registered under the Industrial and Provident Societies Act 1985; the receivers contended that it did. *Held*, since there was no definition of company in the 1986 Act, Pt III, in relation to administrative receivers, then by virtue of s 251, the definition in the Companies Act 1985, s 735 applied. In this case, the word "company" could not be interpreted as including industrial and provident societies. As such societies had their own legislation, including provisions regarding receivers, it was impossible to find that they were included within the definition of "company". A declaration would therefore be made stating that the society was not a company for the purposes of the 1986 Act, s 40 and that the receivers were entitled to distribute the assets of the society in their hands to the liquidator of the society without regard to the provisions of s 40.

Re Devon and Somerset Farmers Ltd [1994] 1 All ER 717 (Chancery Division: Nigel Hague QC).

515 Winding up—public examination—jurisdiction

Following an inquiry under the Companies Act 1985, s 447, a compulsory winding-up order was made in respect of an English company. The winding-up petition made several serious allegations against the appellant, who was a director of the company and who had been resident out of the jurisdiction for some years. The Official Receiver applied ex parte to the registrar for an order under the Insolvency Act 1986, s 133 for the public examination of the appellant. The registrar made the order, giving the Official Receiver leave to serve the appellant out of the jurisdiction. The order was set aside by another registrar but, on appeal by the Official Receiver, the judge reinstated the order. On appeal to the Court of Appeal, the appellant contended that the court had no jurisdiction to order the public examination of an officer of a company who was outside the jurisdiction. *Held*, on its true construction, s 133 was not limited by any territoriality principle and applied to the class of persons set out in s 133(1) irrespective of whether or not they were British subjects or within the jurisdiction of the court at the relevant time, since where a company had been wound up by the court, the purpose of s 133 was that those responsible for the company's state of affairs should be liable to be subjected to a process of public examination and Parliament could not have intended that a person who had had responsibility could escape liability by not being within the jurisdiction. Section 133 had to be construed in the light of the circumstances prevailing when the legislation was enacted, namely that it was possible for persons to manage companies using modern technology without ever setting foot in the jurisdiction. Furthermore, there was no requirement that an officer of an English company had to live in England. The court accordingly had jurisdiction under s 133 to order the public examination of the appellant. The appeal would be dismissed.

Re Seagull Manufacturing Co Ltd (in liquidation) [1993] 2 All ER 980 (Court of Appeal: Lloyd and Hirst LJJ, Peter Gibson J). Decision of Mummery J [1991] 4 All ER 257 (1991 Abr para 383) affirmed. Dictum of Lord Scarman in *Clark (Inspector of Taxes) v Oceanic Contractors Inc* [1983] 1 All ER 133 at 135, HL (1982 Abr para 1664) applied. *Re Tucker (a bankrupt), ex p Tucker* [1988] 1 All ER 603, CA (1987 Abr para 174) distinguished.

516 Winding up—transaction defrauding creditors—letter of instruction to bank

A company contracted with a foreign government ministry to carry out various works. The contract was financed by a bank, which required the company to assign all moneys becoming due under the contract and to agree to the payment of the moneys by the ministry directly into the company's account with the bank. No particulars of any charge that may have been created by the agreement were registered under the Companies Act 1985, s 395. The company got into financial difficulties and payment of the final account was delayed. By a letter of instruction, the company irrevocably instructed the bank to credit part of the funds to be received from the ministry to its local agent's account with the bank, and to apply a further part in paying off the company's overdraft with the bank. A winding up petition was presented against the company and a final settlement was negotiated between the company and the ministry. However, a creditor of the company obtained an injunction restraining the company from signing the agreement. The injunction was replaced by a consent order under which the company was to instruct the bank not to pay any more moneys to the agent until documents proving that the agent was a secured creditor were produced. The instructions were given to the bank, but the bank took the view that it was bound by the letter of instruction. The company was wound up shortly afterwards. On the creditor's application for relief against the bank, *held*, in proceedings to recover property or obtain reimbursement for the benefit of a company in liquidation, the proper plaintiff was the company itself, acting through its liquidator. Unless the creditor could point to a statutory provision which gave him the right to proceed by way of application in the winding up, the bank was entitled to have the proceedings struck out. Although a creditor was entitled to make an application under the 1986 Act, s 212 to challenge the application of the final settlement moneys, there was nothing in the creditor's claim to ground an allegation that, in dealing with the final settlement moneys in the way it did, the bank took part in the management of the company within the meaning of s 212. The creditor, as the creditor of an insolvent company, was capable of being prejudiced by the letter of instruction and was therefore a victim of the transaction who could apply for an order under the 1986 Act, s 423. On the facts alleged, the statutory requirements of s 423 were satisfied. Nor was it inconceivable that a court might make an order against the bank since, although a court could not, save in the most exceptional circumstances, make a repayment order against a bank which had carried out the debtor's payment instructions in good faith and without notice of the relevant facts, the allegations made by the creditor against the bank included several unusual features. Accordingly, the creditor would be given leave to pursue an application under s 423.

Re Ayala Holdings Ltd [1993] BCLC 256 (Chancery Division: Chadwick J).

517   Winding up—unenforceability of liens—documents giving title to property—solicitor's lien

The Insolvency Act 1986, s 246 contains provisions relating to the liquidation of companies and provides that a liquidator is an "office holder" for the purposes of the section. Section 246(2) states that a lien over any papers of the company is unenforceable to the extent that its enforcement would deny possession of those papers to the office holder, however under s 246(3) this does not apply to a lien on documents which give a title to property and are held as such.

Solicitors had acted for a company in connection with the recovery of debts and had obtained security for these debts in the form of debentures, charges on land, a counterpart lease and share certificates. The company went into liquidation and the liquidators of the company obtained an ex parte order for delivery to them of all company papers including the documents relating to the security. The solicitors applied to discharge the order in respect of all papers which gave title to property of the company and the question arose as to whether the papers were held by them "as such" within the meaning of s 246(3) and whether they were entitled to a lien. *Held*, the security documents gave title to property; the debentures and charges gave title to the benefit of the various charges, the counterpart lease entitled the landlord to the rent and the benefit of the covenants, and the share certificates were prima facie evidence of title pursuant to the Companies Act 1985, s 186. It was not a necessary ingredient of a lien that it should confer on the holder of the document a proprietary interest in the underlying property. The words "as such" in the 1986 Act, s 246(3) connoted a manner or capacity in which the documents were held not the description of the documents themselves. Thus "as such" referred to the circumstances in which the documents were held which gave rise to the lien, as contrasted with a case where the documents were held by someone entitled to assert a lien in circumstances where a lien did not arise. The conditions set down in s 246(3) were therefore satisfied and accordingly the solicitors were entitled to the order sought.

Brereton v Nicholls [1993] BCLC 593 (Chancery Division: Morritt J).

COMPULSORY ACQUISITION OF LAND

Halsbury's Laws of England (4th edn) Vol 8, paras 1–400

518   Compensation—assessment—basis of valuation

See *Aquilina and Carberry v London Borough of Havering*, para 50.

519   Compensation—disturbance—company ceasing trading on land to be compulsorily acquired

A local authority served on the plaintiff company a compulsory purchase order. At the date of the notice to treat, the majority of the issued shares in the company were held by P, who was over 60 years of age. The company ceased to trade before possession was required. It fell to be determined, on a preliminary question, whether a company could seek compensation under the Land Compensation Act 1973, s 46 (compensation for disturbance where business carried on by person over 60) where it had ceased to trade on land which was being compulsorily acquired, after the date of the notice to treat but prior to the date at which it was required to give up possession. The compensating authority argued that the Lands Tribunal had no jurisdiction to make an award under s 46 as the company had ceased to trade before possession was required, although it was conceded that had this not been the case, the company would have been entitled to compensation. *Held*, there was an entitlement to compensation for disturbance under s 46 as the requirement to give up possession was causal and not simply temporal. All that was required was that the claimant should not have disposed of the goodwill of the company and that he should have been prepared to give the statutory undertakings required. In this case, neither the company nor P had disposed of any part of the goodwill of the trade or business and they were both prepared to give the required undertakings to the authority. An order would be made accordingly.

Glossop Sectional Buildings Ltd v Sheffield Development Corpn (1993) 66 P & CR 106 (Lands Tribunal: Judge O'Donoghue).

520   Compensation—disturbance—"lawful possession"

A local authority made a compulsory purchase order in respect of office premises over which the respondents had leasehold interests. The respondents successfully claimed they were entitled to disturbance payments under the Land Compensation Act 1973, s 37 because they had been in lawful possession of the property at the time the order was made, although they had not had exclusive possession. On the local authority's appeal, *held*, "lawful possession" in s 37 only meant that the possession should not be unlawful, so it was possible for the respondents to have lawful possession of the land even if they did not have exclusive occupation of it. Consequently, a person who was not given exclusive occupation could still be entitled to a payment under s 37, although the fact that the owner had the power to terminate possession would be relevant to the amount of disturbance payment which the respondents would receive. Accordingly, the appeal would be dismissed.

MacDougall v Wrexham Maelor Borough Council [1993] RVR 141 (Court of Appeal: Ralph Gibson, Mann and Nolan LJJ).

521   Compensation—public works—immunity from actions for nuisance

Under its powers under the Road Traffic Regulation Act 1984, s 32, a district council acquired land for use as a public car park. The claimant, a tenant in a block of flats nearby, sought compensation for nuisance caused by the use of the car park. The council contended that, by virtue of the Land Compensation Act 1973, s 1(6), it had power to pay compensation only if the 1984 Act, s 32 conferred immunity on it from actions for nuisance in respect of the use of the car park. On a preliminary issue, it fell to be determined whether s 32 conferred such immunity on it. *Held*, s 32 did not require the council to provide the car park but gave it power to provide it if it so wished; s 32 was entirely permissive. If the power of providing a car park under that provision was exercised, it had to be exercised in strict conformity with private rights. Section 32, neither expressly nor by implication, conferred on the council immunity from actions for nuisance and, accordingly, the council had no power to pay compensation.

Vickers v Dover District Council [1993] RVR 35 (Lands Tribunal: VG Wellings QC).

522   Compensation—restrictive covenant—effect on reward

The claimants were owners of an estate. By a conveyance the claimants' predecessors in title sold part of the land subject to a covenant for the benefit of the estate not to develop the said land for building purposes except in strict accordance with the layout plan to be first submitted to and approved in writing by the vendor or his agent. The local council started to develop part of the restricted land for housing. An injunction to restrain the development was refused on the ground that the council was exercising statutory powers. The claimants sought compensation under the Compulsory Purchase Act 1965, s 10 for injurious affection to the benefited land. The Lands Tribunal held that compensation was payable under the 1965 Act, s 10 to be assessed by reference to the diminution in value of the benefited land consequent upon the carrying out of the authorised works on the restricted land. The claimants appealed on the ground that the measure of compensation ought to include the price that they could have exacted for allowing the development for which, under the covenant, they could have properly withheld their consent. *Held*, the tribunal's findings were based on reasoning that was sound, persuasive and based on a comprehensive review of the authorities. Accordingly, the appeal would be dismissed.

Wrotham Park Settled Estates v Hertsmere Borough Council [1993] RVR 56 (Court of Appeal: Sir Thomas Bingham MR, Beldam and Kennedy LJJ).

523 Compulsory purchase order—common land—notice to commoners

The defendant water authority had compulsorily acquired common land under the Compulsory Purchase Act 1965, Sch 4. In accordance with the terms of that schedule, the authority convened a meeting of the commoners by placing notices in local newspapers and on the door of the parish church. The plaintiffs claimed that the acquisition was invalid because mandatory notices to treat had not been served on each commoner under the 1965 Act, s 5. On appeal by the water authority, *held*, the 1965 Act, s 5 was only mandatory where an acquiring authority wished to make use of the provisions which applied upon service of notices to treat, for example the right to have compensation assessed by the Lands Tribunal. Where an alternative procedure was provided, such as the one set out in the 1965 Act, Sch 4, individual notices were not needed. In the present case, serving a notice on every single commoner would be impractical, and the notices placed in the local papers were adequate for word to get around. Accordingly, the appeal would be allowed.

Mid-Glamorgan County Council v Ogwr Borough Council (1993) Times, 8 November (Court of Appeal: Nourse, Rose and Hoffmann LJJ).

524 Compulsory purchase order—general vesting declaration—notice

The plaintiff acquired the lease of a parade of shops which formed part of the perimeter of a cricket ground. The defendant local authority made a compulsory purchase order in respect of the parade and, after the order had been confirmed by the Secretary of State, sent notice of confirmation to the plaintiff. The notice contained the statement of particulars prescribed by the Compulsory Purchase (Vesting Declarations) Act 1981, s 3. On the question of whether the inclusion of the statement constituted an exercise of the defendant's powers of compulsory purchase of the land under the Compulsory Purchase Act 1965, s 4 or whether it was only a necessary preliminary step to the acquisition of the land by means of a vesting declaration under the 1981 Act, s 4, if the defendant chose to do so, *held*, the notice containing the particulars prescribed by the 1981 Act, s 3 did nothing more than warn all those concerned that the defendant might proceed to complete the authorised purchase by a vesting declaration. However, the notice did not bind the defendant to complete and did not give those affected by it any rights. It had remained open to the defendant to proceed instead by way of a notice to treat. Accordingly, there had been no exercise by the defendant of its powers under the compulsory purchase order to acquire the plaintiff's land.

Co-operative Insurance Society Ltd v Hastings Borough Council [1993] 37 EG 151 (Chancery Division: Vinelott J). *Westminster City Council v Quereshi* (1990) 88 LGR 826 (1990 Abr para 358) not followed.

525 Compulsory purchase order—notice to treat—counter-notice—service of counter-notice prior to entry onto land

The Compulsory Purchase Act 1965, s 8 provides that no person is required to sell part of his property if he is willing and able to sell the whole of the property, unless the Lands Tribunal determines that the part can be taken without material detriment to the whole of the property.

The plaintiff owned an office block which contained a large car park within its curtilage. The defendant wished to purchase part of the plaintiff's land in order to carry out road improvements and served a notice to treat to that effect on the plaintiff under the 1965 Act, s 5. The defendant entered on the land and the plaintiff subsequently applied to the Lands Tribunal for a determination under s 8, claiming that no notice of the application needed to be served on the defendant and that, in any event an oral notice had been given prior to entry by the defendant. *Held*, although there was no express provision in s 8 for service of a notice of application under that section, the established position was that such a notice must be served prior to the acquiring authority entering the land. In this case, there was no documentary or oral evidence to suggest that notice had been given by the plaintiff prior to entry of the defendant on the land nor that the plaintiff was willing and able to sell the whole of its property. Accordingly, the claim would be dismissed.

Glasshouse Properties Ltd v Secretary of State for Transport (1993) 66 P & CR 285 (Lands Tribunal: Mr T Hoyes FRICS).

526   Lands Tribunal—decision—appeal—appeal to Court of Appeal

See *Practice Note*, para 2046.

CONFLICT OF LAWS

Halsbury's Laws of England (4th edn) Vol 8, paras 401–800

527   Articles

New Law in Jurisdiction Clauses, Brian Dye: 137 SJ 658

528   Contract—contract with foreign government—conflict between governing law of contract and governing law of indemnity clause

The defendants entered into a contract to supply plant to the government of Kuwait. At the request of the defendants an advance payment guarantee was issued by the plaintiff bank to the government and a letter of counter-indemnity was given by the defendants to the plaintiff in consideration of the plaintiff issuing the guarantee. The supply contract was governed by the law of Kuwait. However, by a governing law and jurisdiction clause the indemnity was to be governed by English law. Following the invasion of Kuwait by Iraq the government of Kuwait adopted a resolution by which public works contracts with the government were declared void and automatically terminated. The defendants maintained there could be no subsisting liability under the counter-indemnity and that it did not come within the jurisdiction of the English courts. The plaintiff claimed a declaration that it was still capable of giving rise to a liability to indemnify them. The defendants submitted that the relief sought by the plaintiff did not come within the terms of RSC Ord 11, r 1(1)(d) because such a claim was not a claim brought to enforce, rescind, dissolve or annul or otherwise affect a contract. *Held*, the claim made was properly characterised as a claim to enforce a contract. An indemnity clause made subject to English law within a contract entered into between foreign companies which was subject to foreign law would still constitute a matter concerning a contract, notwithstanding the fact that the contract was declared void under the governing law of the contract. Therefore it would still be subject to RSC Ord 11. Accordingly, the application would be dismissed.

Gulf Bank KSC v Mitsubishi Heavy Industries Ltd (1993) Times, 24 August (Queen's Bench Division: Hobhouse J).

529   Contract—exclusive jurisdiction clause—commencement of proceedings in foreign jurisdiction—enforcement of contract

The 1968 Convention on Jurisdiction and the Enforcement of Judgments in Civil and Commercial Matters, art 17, as set out in the Civil Jurisdiction and Judgments Act 1982, Sch 1, states that where parties, one or more of whom is domiciled in a contracting state, make an agreement as to the jurisdiction of the courts of the contracting state, that court is to have exclusive jurisdiction. Article 21 provides that where proceedings are brought involving the same cause of action and the same parties in courts of different contracting states, then any court which is not the court "first seised" must stay those proceedings until the jurisdiction of the court first seised is established. Article 22 contains similar provisions with regard to related actions.

The bank had granted the appellants, who were a group of borrowers and guarantors, a loan facility and the bank argued that certain sums were still owing after the last instalment date. The bank then commenced proceedings in England against the appellants. The appellants issued proceedings in Athens claiming damages from the bank and seeking a declaration that the guarantors should be released, on the grounds that the exercise of the bank's rights under the loan agreement was contrary to business morality. The bank then attempted to prevent the appellants from proceeding with the case in Greece, contending that the appellants were in breach of an agreement which gave exclusive jurisdiction to try disputes to the English court. At first instance the court found in favour of the bank. On appeal, *held*, the jurisdiction clause placed an obligation on the appellants, but not the bank, to refer any disputes to the English court. The Greek proceedings had in fact been started before the English proceedings and it had been submitted that the Greek court was "first seised" within arts 21 and 22. However the exclusive jurisdiction agreement was in conformity with art 17 which therefore took precedence over arts 21 and 22. Nothing in the Brussels Convention was inconsistent with the power of the English court to grant an injunction for the purpose of enforcing an exclusive jurisdiction agreement. Continuing with the proceedings in Greece was vexatious and oppressive conduct and accordingly, the appeal would be dismissed.

Continental Bank NA v Akakos Compania Naviera SA (1993) Times, 26 November (Court of Appeal: Sir Stephen Brown P, Steyn and Kennedy LJJ).

530 Contract—foreign judgment—bar to English proceedings

Part of a cargo of munitions affected by fire while in transit was jettisoned. The cargo owners brought a successful action in India against the shipowners for the loss of the jettisoned cargo prior to which the parties had agreed that a claim for the loss of the whole cargo would be subject to English law. It fell to be determined whether a subsequent English claim should be struck out on the grounds that the cause of action was the same as that in India and that the Civil Jurisdiction and Judgments Act 1982, s 34 was an absolute bar to the English proceedings. *Held*, the contract of carriage under which the goods were shipped regulated the respective rights and obligations of the parties in respect of the ship's seaworthiness and the care of the goods. Accordingly, the cause of action arose under the contract. The factual basis relied on by the cargo owners, ie the fire during transit resulting in the damage to, and loss of, the consignment, as giving rise to the two breaches of contract was the same in both actions; accordingly, there was identity of the causes of action in the two proceedings and s 34 applied. On its true construction, s 34 provided no more than a bar against proceedings by a plaintiff; it did not exclude the jurisdiction of the court. Its function was to give effect to the policy underlying the principle of res judicata in the circumstances specified in s 34. It was open to the cargo owners to raise the plea of waiver or estoppel. In the circumstances, the plea of waiver or estoppel should not be rejected summarily; whether the respondents were estopped from raising the plea of res judicata was a matter to be decided on the evidence.

Republic of India v India Steamship Co Ltd, The Indian Endurance [1993] 1 All ER 998 (House of Lords: Lords Templeman, Goff of Chieveley, Jauncey of Tullichettle, Mustill and Slynn of Hadley). Decision of Court of Appeal sub nom *The Indian Endurance, Republic of India v India Steamship Co Ltd* [1992] 1 Lloyd's Rep 124 (1991 Abr para 415) reversed.

531 Foreign judgment—access order—application of international convention to child resident in United Kingdom

See *Re G (a Minor) (Convention on the Civil Aspects of International Child Abduction: Access)*, para 344.

532 Foreign judgment—recognition and enforcement of judgment—allegation of fraud

Following the trial of an action in France judgment was obtained by the plaintiff against the defendant. While the defendant's appeal against the decision was pending, the plaintiff successfully applied for the judgment to be registered in England. The defendant appealed against the order under the Brussels Convention, art 27 (contained in the Civil Jurisdiction and Judgments Act 1982) on the grounds that the French judgment was obtained by fraud and forgery, that the recognition was contrary to public policy and that the issue of public policy was so important that the alleged fraud had to be tried in England before the judgment could be enforced here. *Held*, in following *Interdesco v Nullifire* [1992] 1 Lloyd's Rep 180, where a foreign judgment was alleged to have been obtained by fraud and means of redress were available in the court of judgment, there would be no breach of English public policy in recognising and registering the judgment which was subject to those means of redress. Accordingly, the appeal would be dismissed.

Société d'Informatique Service Réalisation Organisation v Ampersand Software BV (1993) Times, 27 July (Court of Appeal: Dillon, Staughton and Waite LJJ).

533 Jurisdiction—civil jurisdiction and judgments

The Civil Jurisdiction and Judgments Act 1982 (Amendment) Order 1993, SI 1993/603 (in force on 1 April 1993), amends the Civil Jurisdiction and Judgments Act 1982, Schs 4 and 8, which set out rules concerning the allocation of jurisdiction between the courts of England and

Wales, Scotland and Northern Ireland in civil and commercial proceedings, in order to accommodate 1989 revisions made to the Brussels Convention 1968.

534 Jurisdiction—civil jurisdiction and judgments—authentic instruments and court settlements

The Civil Jurisdiction and Judgments (Authentic Instruments and Court Settlements) Order 1993, SI 1993/604 (in force on 1 April 1993), applies specified provisions in the Civil Jurisdiction and Judgments Act 1982, as amended, to authentic instruments and court settlements from contracting states other than the United Kingdom which are enforceable in the same manner as judgments.

535 Jurisdiction—overseas divorce—financial provision

The parties were married citizens of Jordan with no children. There was a proposed separation and both parties signed an agreement listing assets acquired by the wife from the husband during the marriage, including two flats in London. The parties resumed living together and shortly afterwards the wife committed adultery and left London for Bahrain. While she was away the husband went to the Bahrain court, pronounced talaq and obtained a divorce. The wife returned to England and filed a petition for divorce and an application for financial relief. The divorce petition was dismissed on the ground that the marriage had already been dissolved by talaq. On her second application for relief, *held*, in establishing that it would be appropriate for an English court to make an order, the burden rested on the person seeking the order. Although there was a connection with England prior to the divorce, the connection with Bahrain was stronger. The wife had not established that it would be appropriate for an order to be made by the English court and accordingly the application would be refused.

Z v Z (Financial Provision: Overseas Divorce) [1992] 2 FLR 291 (Family Division: Ewbank J).

536 Jurisdiction—related proceedings in different states—court first seised of proceedings

The Lugano Convention 1988, art 21 provides that where proceedings involving the same cause of action between the same parties are brought in the courts of different contracting states, any court other than the first seised must of its own motion stay its proceedings until the jurisdiction of the court first seised is established, after which such other courts must decline jurisdiction in favour of the court first seised.

The plaintiffs brought an action for relief in respect of sums allegedly diverted by the defendants. The plaintiffs' solicitors sent a draft statement of claim to the defendants and invited them to discuss a compromise. A meeting ensued, and it was agreed that, in the absence of compromise, the plaintiffs would serve proceedings on 10 February 1993. On 8 February 1993, the first defendants made a submission to a Swiss Court that the plaintiffs' allegations were unfounded and requested a certificate of non-conciliation (a necessary precursor to legal proceedings) which was issued the following day. On 9 February, the plaintiffs' solicitors served their writ, and, the following day, their statement of claim. The defendants subsequently lodged the requisite documents with the court in Switzerland. The defendants applied for an adjournment of the action in England, pending a determination by the court in Switzerland of the date on which the defendants' action there had become definitively pending. The plaintiffs contended that under the 1988 Convention, art 21, the court first seised was the one before which the requirements for proceedings to become definitively pending were first fulfilled, and thus the English court had been first seised. *Held*, the court was unable to determine, merely on the basis of rival written opinions, precisely when the defendants' proceedings in Switzerland had become definitively pending under Swiss law. That was an issue for the Swiss court to determine and the English proceedings would be adjourned until such determination. Accordingly, the application would be granted.

Polly Peck International Ltd v Citibank NA (1993) Times, 20 October (Chancery Division: Vinelott J).

537 Reciprocal enforcement—maintenance orders—Hague Convention countries

The Reciprocal Enforcement of Maintenance Orders (Hague Convention Countries) Order 1993, SI 1993/593 (in force on 5 April 1993), implements the Convention on the Recognition and Enforcement of Decisions Relating to Maintenance Obligations concluded at the Hague on 2 October 1973. The Order replaces and revokes the Reciprocal Enforcement of Maintenance

Orders (Hague Convention Countries) Order 1979, SI 1979/1317, as amended. The differences between the 1993 Order and the 1979 Order, as amended, reflect changes made in the domestic law in England and Wales and Northern Ireland on maintenance as introduced by the Children Act 1989, the Maintenance Enforcement Act 1991 and the Maintenance Orders (Reciprocal Enforcement) Act 1992. The 1993 Order applies the provisions of the Maintenance Orders (Reciprocal Enforcement) Act 1972, Pt 1 as amended, in relation to the Hague Convention Countries listed in Sch 1 as they apply in relation to a reciprocating country, subject to the exceptions, adaptations and modifications set out in Sch 2 to the 1993 Order. The 1972 Act, Pt 1 is to have effect as set out in Sch 3 to the 1993 Order.

538 Reciprocal enforcement—maintenance orders—magistrates' courts

The Magistrates' Courts (Reciprocal Enforcement of Maintenance Orders) (Miscellaneous Amendments) Rules 1993, SI 1993/617 (in force on 5 April 1993), amend the Maintenance Orders (Facilities for Enforcement) Rules 1922, SI 1922/1355, the Magistrates' Courts (Reciprocal Enforcement of Maintenance Orders) Rules 1974, SI 1974/688, the Magistrates' Courts (Reciprocal Enforcement of Maintenance Orders) (Republic of Ireland) Rules 1975, SI 1975/286, the Magistrates' Courts (Recovery Abroad of Maintenance) Rules 1975, SI 1975/488, the Magistrates' Courts (Reciprocal Enforcement of Maintenance Orders (Hague Convention Countries) Rules 1980, SI 1980/108, and the Magistrates' Courts (Civil Jurisdiction and Judgements Act 1982) Rules 1986, SI 1986/1962, in consequence of the introduction of Maintenance Orders (Reciprocal Enforcement) Act 1992. New provisions relating to the service of documents, the procedure to be followed at hearings, evidence, and the confidentiality of documents are added to the instruments. The 1975 Rules, SI 1975/488, are amended to require the clerk to the justices notify payers of maintenance of the method by which they should pay.

539 Reciprocal enforcement—maintenance orders—Republic of Ireland

The Reciprocal Enforcement of Maintenance Orders (Republic of Ireland) Order 1993, SI 1993/594 (in force on 5 April 1993), replaces the 1974 Order, SI 1974/2140. The order applies the provisions of the Maintenance Orders (Reciprocal Enforcement) Act 1972, Pt I to the Republic of Ireland, with certain exceptions. The amendments made by the order include the introduction of a requirement that a maintenance order made by a court in the Republic of Ireland may not be varied or revoked by a court in the United Kingdom and only a United Kingdom court may vary or revoke a maintenance order made in the United Kingdom.

540 Reciprocal enforcement—maintenance orders—United States

The Recovery of Maintenance (United States of America) Order 1993, SI 1993/591 (in force on 5 April 1993), applies the provisions of the Maintenance Orders (Reciprocal Enforcement) Act 1972, Part II to specified American States and amends the 1972 Act, s 26(3) so that certain applications pursuant to the Order must be registered in the prescribed manner. The Recovery of Maintenance (United States of America) Order 1979, SI 1979/1314, the Recovery Abroad of Maintenance (United States of America) Order 1981, SI 1981/606, and the Recovery of Maintenance (United States of America) Variation Order 1984, SI 1984/1824, are revoked.

CONSTITUTIONAL LAW

Halsbury's Laws of England (4th edn) Vol 8, paras 801–1647

541 Articles

A Workable Bill of Rights, Alastair Hudson: 144 NLJ 25
Beyond the Sovereign State, Neil MacCormick: 56 MLR 1
Doing Justice to Women's Rights, Barbara Hewson (on whether bills of rights can advance gender equality): LS Gaz, 29 September 1993, p 19
Ministers, Government Departments and the Courts, Anthony Bradley (on *M v Home Office* [1993] 3 All ER 537, HL (para 583)): 137 SJ 1048

542 Citizens' charter—access to information

The Chancellor of the Duchy of Lancaster has published a white paper *Open Government* (Cm 2290). This refers to the government's intention to issue a code of practice setting out the circumstances in which it will volunteer information and those in which it will make information available on application. Areas where information will remain confidential are also indicated. A draft code is appended (Annex A). Allegations of a failure to comply with the code will fall within the investigative jurisdiction of the Parliamentary Commissioner for Administration. It is intended that similar codes should also be introduced for the national health service and for local government. A new and comprehensive statutory right of access to personal records held by government and by other public sector authorities, subject to safeguards and exemptions, is proposed. Similarly, there is a proposal for a statutory public right of access to information concerning human health and safety, subject to exemptions, held by public authorities; this right is intended to extend to such matters as the safety of public places, transport systems, food, consumer goods and environmental health risks. It is suggested that, in principle, charges for information should cover the reasonable cost of providing it; but the possibility is suggested that additional charges may be made for supplying information if a request is complex and requires extensive searching, processing or collating. The white paper lists (Annex B) some 200 statutes which currently restrict disclosure of information; the proposed rights of access to information will override statutory disclosure provisions which are more restrictive than the proposed rights. The criminal law is seen as the most effective sanction against unlawful disclosure, but consideration will be given to the inclusion of "harm tests" (ie no penalty for disclosing information which is not genuinely confidential) in all future legislation on disclosure and to review existing provisions as opportunities to do so occur. It is not proposed to change the 30-year rule on the disclosure of public records, but stricter criteria are proposed for records which remain confidential after the 30-year period.

543   Civil Service—pensions—pensionable emoluments—language allowances

See *R v Minister for the Civil Service, ex p Lane*, para 1925.

544   European Communities (Amendment) Act 1993

The European Communities (Amendment) Act 1993 makes provision consequential on the Treaty on European Union signed at Maastricht on 7 February 1992. The Act received the royal assent on 20 July 1993 and came into force on 23 July 1993. The Treaty itself entered into force on 1 November 1993 (by virtue of art R, para 2), that being the date on which the last of the member states ratified the Treaty.

Section 1 amends the European Communities Act 1972, s 1, by providing that those parts of the Treaty which relate to the European Communities, with the exception of the Protocol on Social Policy, are included among the list of "Community Treaties". Under the 1993 Act, s 2, an Act of Parliament and a report to Parliament by the government is required before the United Kingdom may notify the Council of the European Communities of the United Kingdom's intention to move to the third stage of economic and monetary union. Section 3 requires the government, in implementing the EC Treaty, art 108, to make provision for an annual report to Parliament by the Governor of the Bank of England. Certain information must be submitted to the Commission by the United Kingdom under s 4 for the implementation of the EC Treaty, art 103(3). Under s 5, the government must report to Parliament for its approval an assessment of the medium term economic and budgetary position in relation to specified matters; this report is to form the basis of any submission to the Council and Commission under the EC Treaty, arts 103 and 104c. United Kingdom representatives to the Committee of the Regions must be elected members of a local authority at the time of their nomination: 1993 Act, s 6. Sections 7 and 8 deal with commencement and short title.

545   Finance Act 1993—commencement

The Finance Act 1993, section 211, (Appointed Day) Order 1993, SI 1993/2831, appoints 9 December 1993 for the coming into force of s 211, by virtue of which the National Debt Commissioners may, with a view to facilitating the raising of money by means of the issue of securities under the National Loans Act 1968, s 12, acquire securities issued under s 12 and transfer such securities.

546   Foreign compensation—financial provision

The Foreign Compensation (Financial Provisions) Order 1993, SI 1993/224 (in force on 30 March 1993), directs the Foreign Compensation Commission to pay into the Consolidated Fund, out of funds paid to the Commission for the purpose of being distributed under the

Foreign Compensation Act 1950, an amount in respect of the Commission's expenses in relation to those funds during the period 1 October 1991 to 30 September 1992.

The Foreign Compensation (Financial Provisions) (No 2) Order 1993, SI 1993/2806 (in force on 31 December 1993), directs the Foreign Compensation Commission to pay into the Consolidated Fund, out of funds paid to the Commission for the purpose of being distributed under the Foreign Compensation Act 1950, an amount in respect of the Commission's expenses in relation to those funds during the period 1 October 1992 to 31 March 1993.

547 Foreign Compensation (Amendment) Act 1993

The Foreign Compensation (Amendment) Act 1993, amends the Foreign Compensation Act 1950 so as to extend the powers to make Orders in Council under the 1950 Act, s 3. The Act received the royal assent on 27 May 1993, and came into force on 27 July 1993.

Section 1 substitutes the 1950 Act, s 3 regarding compensation payable by governments of other countries under future agreements. The extended powers under the new s 3 enable Her Majesty by Order in Council to provide for certain specified matters either in contemplation of the Government receiving, or, where the Government has received, compensation paid by another country, an international organisation or an international tribunal. Section 2 makes financial provision and repeals the Foreign Compensation Act 1969, s 2(1) and (3). Section 3 deals with short title and commencement.

548 Judicial pensions

See PENSIONS AND SUPERANNUATION.

549 Legislation—General Synod measures—submission to Ecclesiastical Committee

See *R v Ecclesiastical Committee of the Houses of Parliament, ex p The Church Society*, para 1043.

550 Ministers—designation order

The European Communities (Designation) Order 1993, SI 1993/595 (in force on 12 April 1993), designates certain Ministers who, and departments which, may exercise powers to make regulations pursuant to the European Communities Act 1972, s 2(2) in relation to measures concerning (1) the protection of animals used for experimental and other scientific purposes, (2) batteries and accumulators containing dangerous substances, (3) copyright (other than those relating to the protection by copyright of computer programs) and to rights in performances, (4) the limitation of aircraft noise, (5) the allocation of take off and landing slots for aircraft at airports and (6) the safety of ships and the health and safety of persons on them. The order also designates any Northern Ireland department for the purpose of exercising the aforementioned powers to make regulations under s 2(2) in relation to measures under (1) and (2) supra.

The European Communities (Designation) (No 2) Order 1993, SI 1993/1571 (in force on 16 July 1993), designates certain ministers who, and departments which, may exercise powers to make regulations pursuant to the European Communities Act 1972, s 2(2) in relation to matters concerning (1) the equal treatment of men and women in relation to severe disablement and invalid care allowances and (2) access to the occupation of carrier of goods by waterways in national and international transport and the mutual recognition of diplomas, certificates and other evidence of formal qualification of this occupation. The order also designates any Northern Ireland department for the purpose of exercising the aforementioned powers to make regulations under s 2(2) in relation to measures under (1) supra. In addition severe disablement and invalid care allowances, are designated social security benefits payable in Great Britain under the Social Security Contributions and Benefits Act 1992, ss 68 and 70, and in Northern Ireland under the Social Security Contributions and Benefits (Northern Ireland) Act 1992, ss 68 and 70.

The European Communities (Designation) (No 3) Order 1993, SI 1993/2661 (in force on 1 November 1993), designates further Ministers who, and departments which, may exercise powers to make regulations conferred by the European Communities Act 1972, s 2(2) in relation to specified matters.

551 Ministers—Prime Minister—authority to enter into contract

See *Quintessence Co-Ordinators Ltd v Government of the Republic of Transkei*, para 3.

552 Ministers—salaries

The Ministerial and other Salaries Order 1993, SI 1993/3166 (in force on 1 January 1994), replaces the 1991 Order, SI 1991/2886, and increases the maximum salaries payable to ministers, to salaried Members of the Opposition, the Speaker of the House of Commons and other paid office holders.

553 Ministry of Defence—Defence Research Agency—funding

See para 2161.

554 Northern Ireland

See NORTHERN IRELAND.

555 Public service pensions

See PENSIONS AND SUPERANNUATION.

556 Rights of the subject—trial by jury—summary conviction—committal to superior court for sentence

The Bahamas

The respondents were summarily convicted of offences involving drugs over a specified limit, the maximum sentence in respect of which had been increased to life imprisonment and a substantial fine. They were, accordingly, committed to the Supreme Court for sentence. It fell to be determined whether the statutory provisions by virtue of which they were so committed were unconstitutional because the respondents had thereby been deprived of their right to trial by jury. *Held*, where the penalties that magistrates' courts could impose for offences within their jurisdiction were so increased as to confer on them jurisdiction which was appropriate only to the Supreme Court, that was in effect a transfer of jurisdiction, unconstitutional both in itself and because, under the Constitution, an accused charged with offences on information in the Supreme Court had the right to be tried by jury. Therefore, the vesting in magistrates' courts of a jurisdiction to try offences which under the Constitution were properly triable only in the Supreme Court, would inevitably deprive the accused of that right. A provision which increased the maximum sentence that could be imposed on summary conviction to life imprisonment was unconstitutional and void. However, applying the test of substantial severability (by virtue of which the court could modify the text of legislation in order to achieve severance only when it was satisfied that it was effecting no change in the substantial purpose and effect of the impugned provision), such a provision was only void in so far as it related to summary convictions, since the application of the provision to convictions on information effected no change in its substantial purpose and effect. There was no constitutional infringement in a magistrates' court having power to impose a substantial financial penalty as the power to impose very substantial fines could be conferred on courts of summary jurisdiction. Although magistrates' courts in The Bahamas could not exert the jurisdiction characteristic of a Supreme Court, they were courts of law and were lawfully entitled, consistently with the Constitution, to exercise the jurisdiction of inferior courts. In so far as the provisions in question related to summary convictions, they were unconstitutional and void as purporting to vest in inferior courts part of the jurisdiction which was reserved for the Supreme Court.

Comr of Police v Davis [1993] 4 All ER 476 (Privy Council: Lords Goff of Chieveley, Jauncey of Tullichettle, Lowry and Mustill, and Zacca CJ). *Hinds v R* [1976] 1 All ER 353, PC (1976 Abr para 328) and *DPP v Hutchinson* [1990] 2 All ER 836, HL (1990 Abr para 32) applied.

557 Treaty—ratification—legality of ratification

An application was made for judicial review of the decision of the Secretary of State for Foreign and Commonwealth Affairs to ratify the Maastricht Treaty on European Union on the grounds that (1) by ratifying the Protocol on Social Policy, the United Kingdom government would be in breach of the European Parliamentary Elections Act 1978, s 6, by virtue of which treaties which increased the powers of the European Parliament had to be approved by an Act of Parliament, because the European Communities (Amendment) Act 1993 which, by s 1(2), approved the Maastricht Treaty, specifically excluded in s 1(1) the Protocol on Social Policy; (2) by ratifying that Protocol, the government would be altering Community law under the EC Treaty without parliamentary approval, contrary to the European Communities Act 1972, s 2(1), which curtailed the prerogative power to amend or add to that Treaty; and (3) by ratifying the Maastricht Treaty, Title V, which established a common foreign and security policy among member states, the government would be transferring part of the royal prerogative to Community institutions without statutory authority. *Held,* (1) the 1993 Act, s 1(1) was intended to incorporate certain parts of the Maastricht Treaty in English domestic law; s 1(2) was intended to ensure that the Treaty as a whole, including the Protocols, could be ratified by the United Kingdom without breach of the 1978 Act. "Treaty" in the 1993 Act, s 1(2) included all the Titles, Protocols and Declarations. (2) The Protocol on Social Policy was not intended to apply to the United Kingdom. It was not one of the treaties covered under the 1972 Act, s 2(1). The United Kingdom's obligation under the Protocol was on the international plane, not the domestic plane. (3) Assuming the court had jurisdiction to consider the questions raised and assuming the government could not lawfully transfer any part of the Crown's prerogative powers in relation to foreign affairs without statutory enactment, the Maastricht Treaty, Title V, could not be regarded as a transfer of prerogative powers. It did not entail an abandonment or transfer of prerogative powers but an exercise of those powers. For those reasons, the application would be dismissed.

R v Secretary of State for Foreign and Commonwealth Affairs, ex p Rees-Mogg [1993] 3 CMLR 101 (Queen's Bench Division: Lloyd and Mann LJJ and Auld J).

CONSUMER CREDIT

Halsbury's Laws of England (4th edn) Vol 22, paras 1–400

558 Articles

An Update on the Consumer Credit Act, RG Lawson: 157 JP Jo 645

559 Advertisements—secured loans—credit rate

Under the Consumer Credit (Total Charge for Credit) Regulations 1980, SI 1980/52, reg 2(1)(d), a calculation under a transaction providing for variation of the rate or amount of any item included in the total charge for credit in consequence of the occurrence after the relevant date of any event must be made on the assumption that the event will not occur.

A bank offered a 25-year fixed rate mortgage providing for variation of the rate of interest after the initial fixed rate period. It calculated the annual percentage rate (APR) by reference to a fixed rate assuming that a change in interest rates would not occur at the end of the initial fixed rate period. A building society similarly offered a fixed rate mortgage until a specified time when its variable rate mortgage would apply. It calculated its APR on the basis of the initial fixed rate. In proceedings against both the bank and the building society for offences under the consumer credit legislation of conveying misleading information in an advertisement, it fell to be determined whether the APR rate was correctly calculated. *Held,* the offer by the bank was for a transaction which provided for variation of the rate of interest after the initial fixed rate period. In view of the possibility, however remote, that at the end of the fixed rate period the borrower would continue to pay interest at the same rate, the offer did not provide for variation in consequence of the occurrence after the date of the making of the agreement of any event which was certain to occur and of which the date of occurrence or the earliest date of occurrence could be ascertained at the date of the agreement. The bank had not assumed for the purpose of its calculation that there would be any change in the rate of interest at the end of the fixed rate period. It was correct in its interpretation of the 1980 Regulations, reg 2(1)(d) in assuming that a change in interest rates would not occur. The building society had adopted the same approach. The defendants were entitled to calculate the APR as they had done on the assumption that the interest rate throughout the whole of the term of the mortgage would be the fixed rate, not the fluctuating rate offered by them at the outset.

National Westminster Bank v Devon County Council; Devon County Council v Abbey National plc (1993) Times, 16 July (Queen's Bench Division: Kennedy LJ and Macpherson J).

560 Credit agreement—unlicensed trader—private or one-off loan

The plaintiff, a motor vehicle dealer, agreed to put a hire purchase agreement in his name on behalf of the plaintiff who wished to purchase a vehicle from the defendant but was unable to obtain credit. The agreement between them was contained in a used car sales invoice. The defendant made only the first six monthly payments under the agreement. The plaintiff sought to recover the remaining 30 instalments. It was held at first instance that the agreement was not a non-commercial agreement and was unenforceable because there was no licence to cover it. On appeal by the plaintiff, *held*, the agreement between the parties was purely private or, alternatively, if it was made in the course of business, it was an isolated transaction falling within the Consumer Credit Act 1974, s 189(2). It did not amount to a business activity within the Act so that no licence under s 40 was required. The appeal would be allowed. As there were no findings of fact as to whether the agreement was private or a one-off transaction, the case remitted for a rehearing.

Hare v Schurek (1993) Times, 28 May (Court of Appeal: Dillon, Mann and Steyn LJJ).

561 Exempt agreements

The Consumer Credit (Exempt Agreements) (Amendment) Order 1993, SI 1993/346 (in force on 18 March 1993), further amends the principal order, SI 1989/869, by adding the names of four friendly societies to the list of specified bodies certain of whose agreements are exempt from the provisions of the Consumer Credit Act 1974. The names of three friendly societies are removed from that list, and the names of three others are amended.

The Consumer Credit (Exempt Agreements) (Amendment) (No 2) Order 1993, SI 1993/2922 (in force on 21 December 1993), further amends the 1989 Order, SI 1989/869, by replacing references to certain revoked legislation, and making other minor amendments.

CONSUMER PROTECTION

562 Articles

A Thing of Danger, James Tipler (on US product liability rules): 137 SJ 1081
Advertising and Marketing Pharmaceutical Products, Richard Lawson: 137 SJ 1053
Deception on the Dotted Line, Elizabeth Palmer (on the sales representatives of finance companies): 143 NLJ 1400
Due Diligence Defence: Recent Precedents, Richard Lawson: 156 JP Jo 121
Food Hygiene Law: the Key Issues, Jeremy Stranks: 137 SJ 452
Good for You? Christine Clayson (on *Cheshire CC v Mornflake Oats* (1993) 157 JP 1011 (para 1289)): 137 SJ 1158
Indicating Prices, RG Lawson: 157 JP Jo 814
Regulating the Advertising Regulators, Richard Lawson: 137 SJ 366
Sunday Trading, Dr Richard Lawson: 137 SJ 1264
When is a Restrictive Trade Practice a Crime? Susan Singleton: Criminal Lawyer, Issue 38, p 5

563 Consumer contract—terms—unfair terms

See para 2691.

564 Consumer credit

See CONSUMER CREDIT.

565 Consumer information—Community Eco-label

See para 2689.

566 Consumer safety—cosmetic products

The Cosmetic Products (Safety) (Amendment) Regulations 1993, SI 1993/1539 (in force, with certain exceptions, on 21 June 1993), further amend the 1989 Regulations, SI 1989/2233. The amendments include an extension of the list of substances which may not be used in cosmetic products. In addition, some warning labelling requirements are deleted in respect of certain Phenylenediamines, Methylphenylenediames and their N-substituted derivatives and salts, and Diaminophenols. The use of hydrogen peroxide, with restrictions, is permitted in oral hygiene products. Subject to restrictions, the use of Strontium chloride hexahydrate and Strontium acetate hemihydrate in toothpaste is permitted, and labelling requirements are imposed in respect of talcum powders intended to be used by children.

567 Consumer safety—defence of due diligence—furniture not match resistant

The appellant laid an information alleging that the respondent had exposed for sale chairs which were not match resistant contrary to the Furniture and Furnishings (Fire) (Safety) Regulations 1988, SI 1988/1324 and the Consumer Protection Act 1987, s 12(1). The magistrates dismissed the information on the grounds that the respondent had made out the statutory defence of due diligence, under the 1987 Act, s 39. On appeal, *held,* one of the respondent's employees failed to notice a label on the chairs stating that they were not match resistant and this would have put the respondent on notice that the chairs contravened the 1988 Regulations. The failure to take this reasonable step meant that the respondent had not exercised due diligence and thus could not rely on the statutory defence. Accordingly, the appeal would be allowed.

Turtington v United Co-operatives Ltd [1993] Crim LR 376 (Queen's Bench Division: Leggatt LJ and Popplewell J).

568 Consumer safety—furniture and furnishings

The Furniture and Furnishings (Fire) (Safety) (Amendment) Regulations 1993, SI 1993/207 (in force on 1 March 1993), further amend SI 1988/1324 in order to disapply, until 31 December 1996, provisions imposing requirements with respect to second-hand furniture hired out at the same time as and in connection with the letting of accommodation.

569 Consumer safety—imitation dummies

The Imitation Dummies (Safety) Regulations 1993, SI 1993/2923 (in force on 21 December 1993), prohibit the supply of certain goods which may by their form, colour, appearance, packaging or labelling, be mistaken by persons (particularly by children) for dummies, and as a result, be placed in their mouths, sucked or swallowed with the consequence that they may suffer death or personal injury. This prohibition does not apply to certain goods complying with specified regulations.

570 Consumer safety—motor vehicles—tyres

See para 2210.

571 Consumer safety—products which may jeopardise health or safety—exchange of information

See para 2694.

572 Consumer safety—tobacco products—labelling

The Tobacco Products Labelling (Safety) Amendment Regulations 1993, SI 1993/1947 (in force on 1 January 1994), amend the 1991 Regulations, SI 1991/1530. The amendments partially implement Council Directive (EC) 92/41, and require producers of rolling tobacco to ensure that each packet of the product carries one of six specified additional health warnings. The warnings should appear on an equal number of packets over the course of a year, allowing for a five per cent variation. Producers, in relation to cigars, cigarillos, pipe tobacco and other tobacco products except cigarettes, rolling tobacco and smokeless tobacco products, must ensure that each packet carries one of four additional specified health warnings. These warnings should appear in rotation on the packets produced. An additional warning must be carried on all smokeless products. New provisions relating to the visibility and position of warnings are introduced. Other minor amendments are made.

See *R v Secretary of State for Health, ex p Gallagher*, para 2690.

573 Consumer safety—tour operator—duty of care

See para 598.

574 Consumer safety—toys

The Toys (Safety) (Amendment) Regulations 1993, SI 1993/1547 (in force in part on 16 July 1993 and in part on 1 October 1996), amend the 1989 Regulations, SI 1989/1275, by disapplying certain provisions relating to the requirement for the EC mark to be put on every applicable toy, or on the packaging of the toy. Other information, subject to certain exceptions, in respect of a toy which has been previously been supplied to any person who acquired it for private use or consumption. Certain limited savings of the 1974 Regulations, SI 1974/1367, which relate to certain toys first supplied in the Community before 1 January 1990, are also removed.

575 Monopolies and mergers

See TRADE AND INDUSTRY.

576 Price marking—price label—position of label on goods

A pharmaceutical chemist stocked perfumes in a locked glass cabinet. The price labels were on the reverse of the boxes containing the perfumes. A customer could only ascertain the price by asking the chemist or a member of his staff to unlock the cabinet to facilitate closer examination of the goods. The chemist was charged with failing to indicate the selling price of goods in accordance with the Price Marking Order 1991, SI 1991/1382, arts 3, 8, contrary to the Prices Act 1974, s 7, Schedule. The local authority contended that although it was not necessary for every price label to appear on the front of an item it was essential that a prospective purchaser should be able to see the price without assistance from anyone else. On appeal against conviction, *held*, in the absence of any additional instructions, the 1991 Order was fully complied with provided that there was, upon the article, clearly stated, some indicator which unmistakably related to that article, showing the price. A retailer was not obliged to put the price label on the front of the article or to put the article in a position where it could be handled by a prospective purchaser. It was sufficient that assistance from the retailer enabled the prospective purchaser to see the price on the article. Accordingly, the appeal would be allowed.

Allen v Redbridge London Borough Council [1994] 1 All ER 728 (Queen's Bench Division: Watkins LJ and Leonard J).

577 Restrictive trade practices

See TRADE AND INDUSTRY.

578 Trade descriptions

See TRADE DESCRIPTIONS.

CONTEMPT OF COURT

Halsbury's Laws of England (4th edn) Vol 9, paras 1–200

579 Breach of court order—committal order—appropriate fine for company director

Undertakings had been given to protect the plaintiffs from passing off by the defendants, one the company the other a director, pending trial of the action. It was later held that the defendants had by acts of omission committed serious breaches of the undertakings. The judge imposed a fine on them jointly and severally and committed the director to imprisonment for three months in default of payment. The defendants appealed against the judge's order. *Held*, in cases of contempt of court the imposition of a fine on two defendants jointly and severally was wrong in principle. In the circumstances it would cause considerable problems because of the different procedures for enforcement against a corporation and against an individual. The judge ought to have considered the means of each defendant separately, imposing a fine on the company and then going on to consider what was an appropriate fine to impose on the director and whether to impose a period of imprisonment against him in default. Accordingly, the appeal would be granted.

McMillan Graham Printers Ltd v RR (UK) Ltd [1993] 21 LS Gaz R 40 (Court of Appeal: Nourse, Stuart-Smith and Waite LJJ).

580 Breach of court order—committal order—criminal charge on same facts—application for an adjournment

The applicant obtained an order that the respondent should not use violence, threaten or harass her. Following an incident which led to the respondent being charged with rape the applicant sought a committal order. An application by the respondent's solicitor that the committal proceedings be adjourned until after the criminal trial was rejected and the respondent appealed. *Held*, contempt proceedings were quite separate from any criminal proceedings arising from the same facts, they were to be dealt with swiftly and decisively. However, if there was a real risk of serious prejudice which would lead to an injustice a judge would have a discretion to decline to proceed with contempt proceedings. Accordingly, the appeal would be dismissed.

H v C [1993] 1 FCR 1 (Court of Appeal: Neill, Butler-Sloss and Mann, LJJ).

581 Breach of court order—committal order—unintentional disobedience

The defendants were gipsies living on a site in breach of planning controls. The plaintiff borough council was granted an injunction restraining the defendants from stationing caravans or mobile homes on the land. The defendants remained on the land and the plaintiff sought a committal order. The defendants contended that they had nowhere else to go and that they had made every reasonable endeavour to find an alternative site. It was established that the county council had been, for the past 25 years, in breach of its duty under the Caravan Sites Act 1968, s 6 to provide adequate accommodation for gipsies. The judge found that the defendants were in contempt but that the court had no power of committal when, as in this case, the defendants had not intentionally disobeyed the order but had done so for good reason. On appeal by the plaintiff, *held*, there was strict liability to comply with a court order and "intentionally" meant non-accidentally. Therefore, the defendants were in contempt. The High Court had jurisdiction to commit for contempt whenever contempt involved a degree of fault or misconduct. The fact that the court was dealing with gipsies as opposed to another type of trespasser was a material consideration as it went to the genuineness of their efforts to find alternative accommodation. The right to have an injunction enforced by imprisonment was not automatic but subject to the discretion of the judge who, in this particular case, had decided to show compassion and dismiss the application. He was entitled to do so and accordingly the appeal would be dismissed.

Guildford Borough Council v Valler (1993) Times, 15 October (Court of Appeal: Russell, Staughton and Steyn LJJ). Decision of Sedley J (1993) Times, 18 May affirmed.

582 Breach of court order—non-molestation order

See *A v D (Contempt: Committal)*, para 1446.

583 Breach of court order—undertakings given by or on behalf of the Crown— enforcement

The applicant sought judicial review of a deportation order that was to take effect the same day. The judge ruled that the order should not be implemented until the application had been considered. Contrary to the ruling the Home Office failed to prevent the applicant being flown out of the country. The judge was informed of this and issued a mandatory order that the Home Secretary arrange for the immediate return of the applicant. On receiving legal advice that that order was made without jurisdiction, the Home Secretary cancelled arrangements for the applicant's return. The applicant subsequently brought contempt proceedings against the Home Secretary which were dismissed at first instance. On appeal, the court held that whilst a finding of contempt could not be made against the Crown, a government department or a minister of the Crown in his official capacity, the Home Secretary had taken the decision not to comply with the court order and was thus personally in contempt of court. The respondent appealed on the grounds that the court did not have jurisdiction to make coercive orders, such as an injunction, or findings of contempt against the Crown or its ministers. *Held*, on a true construction of the Supreme Court Act 1981, s 31 the court had jurisdiction during judicial review proceedings to grant an injunction against a minister in his official capacity. Further, RSC Ord 53, r 3(10), read in conjunction with the 1981 Act, provided that the court could make interim injunctions against ministers. The purpose of the court's power to make a finding of contempt was to ensure that orders of the court were obeyed. Thus, where an order was made against a government department or minister in his official capacity and that order was disregarded, the court had jurisdiction to find the appropriate body guilty of contempt. However, since the Crown's relationship with the courts did not depend on coercion, contempt proceedings should not be punitive: a finding of contempt sufficed to demonstrate that a government department had interfered with the administration of justice and it was then for Parliament to determine the consequences of that finding. Whilst there were circumstances where it would be appropriate to find a minister to have been personally in contempt, in the present case the Home Secretary had acted on department advice and so the finding should have been made against the minister in his official capacity. Accordingly, subject to that variation, the appeal would be dismissed.

M v Home Office [1993] 3 All ER 537 (House of Lords: Lords Keith of Kinkel, Templeman, Griffiths, Browne-Wilkinson and Woolf). Decision of Court of Appeal [1992] 2 WLR 73 (1991 Abr para 472) affirmed. *Factortame Ltd v Secretary of State for Transport (No 2)* [1991] 1 All ER 70, HL (1990 Abr parta 1354) distinguished.

584 Interference with the administration of justice—contempt in the face of the court—insulting behaviour

While in the public gallery during a trial, the appellant wolf-whistled at a juror. The judge found that the appellant's conduct was on the face of it contempt of court and the appellant was sentenced to 14 days' imprisonment. On appeal against conviction and sentence, *held*, when a wolf-whistle was addressed to a juror when she was returning with others to deliver a verdict, it was potentially insulting, offensive and a serious interference with the administration of justice and the courts. It was not a case of abuse or an insult directed at the judge. The judge's decision would be upheld and the appeal against conviction dismissed. The penalty imposed was inappropriate, however, and his appeal against the sentence would be allowed. As the appellant had already spent a day in custody, no further penalty would be imposed.

R v Powell (1993) Times, 3 June (Court of Appeal: Staughton LJ, Popplewell and Laws JJ).

585 Interference with the administration of justice—criminal trial—fully bound witness—failure to attend trial

The appellant, a police officer, forgot to appear at a criminal trial in which he was a fully bound witness. He was subsequently found to be in contempt of court on the ground that disobeying a witness order which had been issued in compliance with the requirements of the Criminal Procedure (Attendance of Witnesses) Act 1965 was an absolute offence, subject only to the words "without just excuse" in the 1965 Act, s 3(1). On appeal, *held*, the officer's forgetfulness could not amount to a just excuse within the terms of the 1965 Act, s 3(1). The purpose of the legislation was to ensure the attendance of witnesses in court, and that purpose would be destroyed if the "just excuse" proviso was interpreted in a way which prevented behaviour such as the officer's culpable forgetfulness from being treated as contempt of court. Accordingly, the appeal would be dismissed.

R v Lennock [1993] LS Gaz R 40 (Court of Appeal: Russell LJ, Morland and Mantell JJ).

586 Interference with the administration of justice—no criminal proceedings pending—risk of contempt of court at common law

The defendant television company was engaged in an investigation into allegations of a growing trade in the distribution of computer pornography. The plaintiff transmitted material to the defendants' computer, which then reproduced it in a permanent form and supplied it to the police. The police acquired a search warrant for the plaintiff's property. When executing the warrant the police were accompanied by an employee of the defendants and a television camera crew. They filmed the police entry into the flat, the plaintiff in bed, and parts of the flat's interior. The plaintiff successfully applied for an injunction to stop the defendants using the film in a programme on the subject on the basis of restraint of an anticipated contempt of court. The defendants appealed against the order. *Held*, at the date of the hearing no active steps had been taken in any prosecution against the plaintiff, therefore the strict liability rule under the Contempt of Court Act 1981, ss 1 and 2 did not apply. However, by virtue of the 1981 Act, s 6(c) a publication might still constitute contempt of court at common law. To uphold an injunction on that basis would require the court to be satisfied that publication of the film and other material obtained by the defendants at the plaintiff's flat would create a real risk of prejudice to the administration of justice and that the defendants were going to publish that material with the specific intention of causing that risk. In the circumstances there was no risk of that happening and accordingly, the appeal would be allowed.

Coe v Central Television (1993) Independent, 11 August (Court of Appeal: Glidewell, Butler-Sloss and Kennedy LJJ).

587 Interference with the administration of justice—prohibition of disclosure of name of person with notifiable disease—reasonableness of order

See *Birmingham Post and Mail Ltd v Birmingham City Council*, para 2097.

588   Interference with the administration of justice—restrictions on reporting trial—risk of prejudice to subsequent proceedings

See *Ex p The Telegraph plc*, para 2071.

CONTRACT

Halsbury's Laws of England (4th edn) Vol 9, paras 201–750

589   Articles

Contract Litigation in England and Wales 1975–1991—A Transformation in Business Disputing? Peter Vincent-Jones: (1993) 12 CJQ 337

Fair Dealing Between Creditor and Surety, Reziya Harrison (on *Barclays Bank v O'Brien* [1993] 4 All ER 417, HL (para 1826)): 137 SJ 1126

Lessons From New Zealand, Michael Whincup (on the developments in the law of contract in New Zealand): LS Gaz, 29 September 1993, p 22

Locking on to Lock-out Agreements, Roger Halson (on *Walford v Miles* [1992] 1 All ER 453 (1992 Abr para 544)): 137 SJ 594

Making More Use of the Unfair Contract Terms Act 1977, Edwin Peel (on *Stewart Gill Ltd v Horatio Myer & Co Ltd* [1992] 2 All ER 257 (1992 Abr para 556)): 56 MLR 98

Mental Distress—Damages in Contract, David James: 137 SJ 1108

Misdirected Funds—Problems of Uncertainty and Inconsistency, Steven Fennell (on the law of restitution): 57 MLR 38

NHS Contracts, Restitution and the Internal Market, Kit Barker: 56 MLR 832

One-man Service Companies: a Gentleman's Agreement? David Southern: 143 NLJ 444

Players and Their Promises, Michael Nash (on footballers' contracts): 143 NLJ 1449

Privity of Contract—That Pestilential Nuisance, John Adams and Roger Brownsword: 56 MLR 722

Restitution of Payments Made Under Swap Transactions, Andrew Burrows: 143 NLJ 480

590   Accord and satisfaction—cheque—effect of cashing a cheque

The plaintiff sent the defendant an invoice for works he had done for the defendant. The defendant considered it too high and offered the plaintiff a cheque for less than the amount requested "in full and final settlement". The plaintiff kept and cashed the cheque but informed the defendant that the cheque would not be accepted in full and final settlement. At first instance the court held that there was no agreement between the parties to accept the cheque in full and final settlement of the claim, and the defendant appealed. *Held*, accord and satisfaction depended on the debtor establishing an agreement between the parties whereby the creditor undertook for valuable consideration to accept a sum less than the amount of his claim. As such it was not what the plaintiff himself intended but what by his words and conduct he had led the defendant as a reasonable person to believe. Therefore, the keeping and cashing by the plaintiff of a cheque sent by the defendant in full and final settlement of a larger claim, was not conclusive evidence of accord and satisfaction, it was a question of fact whether the cheque was accepted in full and final settlement. Accordingly, the appeal would be dismissed.

Stour Valley Builders (a firm) v Stuart (1993) Times, 22 February (Court of Appeal: Lloyd LJ and Connell J).

591   Applicable law

See CONFLICT OF LAWS.

592   Breach of contract—derivation of advantage by party in breach—disadvantage suffered by innocent party

Under an agreement, the defendants were required to provide the plaintiff with a replacement motor car at intervals of no more than 30 months. They replaced the vehicle outside that period. In proceedings by the plaintiff for breach of contract, his contention that he was entitled to the next replacement vehicle within 30 months of the date when it should have been provided, not within 30 months of the date when it was in fact provided, succeeded. On appeal by the defendants, *held*, the words "at intervals of no more than 30 months" did not mean that a vehicle was to be provided on specific dates. The intervals referred to the periods of time between the provision of one car and its replacement by the next. Even though such a construction of the agreement allowed the defendants to derive an advantage from their own breach of contract, they were not debarred from relying on that construction if the plaintiff thereby suffered no disadvantage. The presumption that a party could not rely on his own wrong to secure an advantage did not apply in the present circumstances. The appeal would be allowed.

Thornton v Abbey National plc (1993) Times, 4 March (Court of Appeal: Neill and Beldam LJJ).

593 Building contracts

See BUILDING CONTRACTS, ARCHITECTS, ENGINEERS AND SURVEYORS.

594 Champerty—champertous agreement—car hire

The plaintiff was involved in a car accident damaging his vehicle. He was subsequently provided with a free replacement vehicle by a hire company, owing to the fact that under his comprehensive insurance policy, he was unable to claim for car hire charges while his vehicle was being repaired. The agreement was on the terms that the hiring company pursued the claim against the defendant at its own expense and employing solicitors of its choice, a charge was then made by the company for the loan of the replacement car, which was reimbursed from the damages recovered and until that happened the motorist was under no obligation to pay for the use of the replacement vehicle. At first instance the defendant's assertion that the agreement was champertous was rejected and following an unsuccessful appeal the defendant appealed to the House of Lords. *Held*, it was essential to the hirer's scheme that they selected only cases which they considered would succeed, they did not receive money which was due to the plaintiff and so did not share in the spoils of litigation and therefore, the car hire scheme was not contrary to public policy. The plaintiff had not assigned his claim to the hirers, the loss incurred in hiring a replacement car was a validly constituted action and accordingly, the defence of champerty would fail. Furthermore, the hire company was not wantonly or officiously interfering in the litigation, nor was it doing so in order to share in the profits. Accordingly, the appeal would be dismissed.

Giles v Thompson; Devlin v Baslington [1993] 3 All ER 321 (House of Lords: Lords Keith of Kinkel, Ackner, Jauncey of Tullichettle, Lowry and Mustill).

595 Collateral contract—agreement not to negotiate for fixed period— enforceability

The plaintiff was one of two parties interested in purchasing the defendant's property. He made two offers which were at first accepted by the defendant's agent but were withdrawn when the other party made higher offers. The plaintiff informed the agent that he would seek an injunction to prevent the sale to the other party and that if he told that party that he was withdrawing, any future offer would be lower in the absence of a rival. The defendant then agreed that it would stay with the plaintiff's offer, subject to contract, and would consider no further offers on the basis that contracts would be exchanged within two weeks of receipt of draft contracts. Before the end of that period, the defendant increased the price and sold the property to the other party. The plaintiff brought proceedings for breach of contract. *Held*, the agreement by virtue of which the defendant undertook not to negotiate with other prospective purchasers for a limited period was not part of the continuing negotiations between the plaintiff and defendant, subject to contract like the negotiations for the sale of the property, because there was nothing further to agree. The consideration given for the agreement by the plaintiff was the removal of the threats of an injunction and of causing trouble with the rival potential purchaser and his promise to limit himself to two weeks for the exchange of contracts was of some value to the defendant. Those three items constituted valuable consideration sufficient to support the lock out agreement by virtue of which the defendant undertook not to negotiate for a fixed period with a third party. It was not a contract for the sale of land or an option for the sale of land but was a lock out agreement the characteristic of which was its negative element. The defendant did not have to proffer a contract but, once it had done so, it was bound by the terms of the lock out agreement for the following two-week period. The agreement was not a contract for the sale of any interest in land and, therefore, the Law of Property (Miscellaneous Provisions) Act 1989, s 2, which required such a contract to be in writing, did not apply. The plaintiff's claim would succeed.

Pitt v PHH Asset Management Ltd [1993] 4 All ER 961 (Court of Appeal: Sir Thomas Bingham MR, Mann and Gibson LJJ).

596 Contract entered into by the Crown—Prime Minister's authority—contract for the construction of government building

See *Quintessence Co-Ordinators Ltd v Government of the Republic of Transkei*, para 3.

597 Contractual term—construction—reasonable expectations of parties

It has been held that, as a principle moulding force of the law of contract, the reasonable expectations of honest men ought to be protected. A ruling that a bank's senior manager did not have apparent authority to communicate that the bank's head office had approved financing facilities would have defeated the parties' expectations and would be contrary to the way in which negotiations were conducted between trading banks and customers who were seeking loans.

First Energy (UK) Ltd v Hungarian International Bank Ltd [1993] BCLC 1409 (Court of Appeal: Steyn, Nourse and Evans LJJ).

598 Contractual term—implied term—contract for services

The plaintiff, who was holidaying in Greece, fell through a glass patio door at his hotel and suffered injuries. The doors complied with Greek but not British safety standards. The plaintiff sought damages against the tour operator, contending that the characteristics of the glass fitted to the patio doors were such that the hotel was not reasonably safe for use by the tour operator's customers and that they were in breach of the duty of care arising out of the term implied by the Supply of Goods and Services Act 1982, s 13 that in a contract for the supply of services the supplier of services would carry out the service with reasonable care and skill. *Held*, the duty of care owed by a tour operator to its customers in accordance with the 1982 Act, s 13 was a duty to exercise reasonable care to exclude from the accommodation offered any hotel the characteristics of which were such that guests could not spend a holiday there in reasonable safety. The duty was discharged if the tour operator checked that local safety regulations had been complied with. The duty did not extend to excluding a hotel whose safety characteristics failed to satisfy the current standards applying in Great Britain, provided that the absence of a relevant safety feature would not make a reasonable holidaymaker decline to take a holiday at the hotel. As the defendants had inspected the accommodation offered as part of their services, and since the patio doors complied with Greek safety regulations and the danger posed by the absence of safety glass in the patio doors was not such that the plaintiff would have declined to stay at the hotel, the defendants had discharged the duty of care owed to the plaintiff. The plaintiff's claim would accordingly fail.

Wilson v Best Travel Ltd [1993] 1 All ER 353 (Queen's Bench Division: Phillips J). For proceedings dealing with quantum of damages, see 1991 Abr para 831.

599 Contractual term—unfair contract term—exclusion clause

Scotland

The plaintiffs applied for a loan from a building society in order to buy a house. They signed an application form in which the building society undertook to provide a copy of the report and mortgage valuation of the property. The form also included a declaration purporting to exclude liability for the mortgage valuation survey. The survey estimated no essential repairs were required to the property and the plaintiffs proceeded with the purchase. Defects were subsequently discovered and the plaintiffs sued the surveyors. The surveyors, relying on the exclusion clause, claimed that they owed no duty of care to the plaintiffs. The question arose whether the exclusion clause was a term of a contract within the meaning of the Unfair Contract Terms Act 1977. *Held*, there was a contract in relation to the provision and payment for a copy of the report and valuation of the property. The 1977 Act was not restricted in its application to cases where the exclusion clause was in favour of one of the parties to the contract. It followed that the 1977 Act applied to the contract and accordingly, the exclusion clause was of no effect.

Melrose v Davidson 1993 SLT 611 (Inner House: First Division).

600 Damages—breach of contract

See DAMAGES AND COMPENSATION.

601 Exclusion clause—breach of warranty

Canada

The buyer, a commercial vegetable grower, purchased cabbage seeds from the vendor who advertised the seeds as being his most popular and versatile apple green coloured storage cabbage.

The contract between them limited the vendor's liability to the purchase price of such seeds, and stated that the vendor made no warranties or guarantees of the merchantability or fitness for a particular purpose of the seed sold by it. The crop was disappointing and the buyer sought damages from the vendor on the ground that there had been a fundamental breach of contract which precluded the vendor from relying on the exclusion clauses in the contract. The trial judge held that there had been a fundamental breach of contract in that other types of cabbage were superior and that the plaintiff was entitled to recover damages. On appeal, *held*, there was no duty on the defendant to point out the comparative advantages of other kinds of cabbage. Even if the statement in the catalogue amounted to a warranty, it did not go to the root of the contract. The contract was not unconscionable and the appeal would accordingly be allowed.

Kordas v Stokes Seeds Ltd (1992) 96 DLR (4th) 129 (Ontario Court of Appeal).

602   Foreign jurisdiction clause

See CONFLICT OF LAWS.

603   Form of contract—written contract—parol evidence rule

See *W F Trustees v Expo Safety Systems Ltd*, para 482.

604   Indemnity clause—construction—extent of liability—negligence and breach of statutory duty

The plaintiffs were the joint owners and operators of a North Sea oil drilling platform. They employed the services of a service engineer supplied by the defendants under a contract that included an indemnity clause. The indemnity clause provided that each party would indemnify the other in the event of any claim being brought because of the death of any employee of the indemnifying party resulting from the performance of the contract. The engineer died in a fire on the platform, which the plaintiffs admitted was due to the negligence of their employees. His family settled a claim for damages against the plaintiffs who claimed the sum from the defendants under the indemnity clause. The defendants refused to pay. On the hearing of the plaintiffs' claim, *held*, the clause was subject to established rules of construction that indemnity and exemption clauses only applied to a party's own negligence where there was express provision to that effect. The words used in the contract in issue were wide enough to cover negligence but were also capable of applying to a breach of statutory duty. The indemnity clause would therefore not be construed as being wide enough to cover the negligence of the plaintiffs or their employees as there was no express provision to cover the consequences of such negligence. The plaintiffs were liable for the engineer's death because of their breaches of statutory duty and the negligence of their employees. Where the negligence of the plaintiffs' employees was one, but not the only, cause of liability and where the parties were not to be taken, in the absence of express words in the contract, to have intended an indemnity clause in the contract to cover the negligence of the party seeking the indemnity, the indemnity clause did not cover a loss or liability the negligence of the plaintiffs. Accordingly, the claim would be dismissed.

Hobhouse J stated that parties to commercial contracts had to be taken to know the established principles of construction of contracts. Where a particular result could have been easily obtained by an appropriate use of language but the parties instead only used general language, the result of the general principles of construction was that the parties would not be taken to have intended to include the consequences of a party's negligence in an exemption or indemnity clause.

EE Caledonia Ltd v Orbit Valve Co Europe [1993] 4 All ER 165 (Queen's Bench Division; Hobhouse J). For earlier related proceedings, see *McFarlane v EE Caledonia* [1993] PIQR P241.

605   Interest rate swap contracts—contracts between financial institutions— avoidance as wagering contracts

See *Morgan Grenfell and Co Ltd v Welwyn Hatfield District Council, Islington London Borough Council (Third Party)*, para 212.

606   Misrepresentation

See MISREPRESENTATION.

607   Quasi contract—unjust enrichment—money paid under ultra vires contract

Under an interest rate swap contract between a bank and a council, the latter received a number of payments from the bank. The contract was ultra vires the council's powers and, therefore, void. The bank sought to recover the sums outstanding under the contract. The council contended that, as it had made four "interest" payments to the bank, the consideration had not wholly failed so that the bank could not recover the sums outstanding. *Held*, as the interest rate swap transactions and the contract for them were ultra vires, there was no consideration for the payments made by the bank. On the basis of early cases decided under the Annuities Act 1777, the balance of the money paid by the bank and not so far repaid by the council could be recovered by the bank in quasi contract as money had and received or on the grounds of unjust enrichment. By virtue of that Act and cases decided under it, if there had been non-compliance, the grantor of an annuity was entitled to have it set aside and the grantee was entitled to have his capital premium repaid to him with interest subject to giving credit for the instalments of the annuity which he had received. The payments were not to be regarded as purely voluntary because they had been intended to be made for the consideration expressed in the annuity deed. The payments made by the bank and the council were to be treated in the same way. The bank was entitled to recover the balance of the sum paid to the council as money had and received or unjust enrichment at the expense of the owner of the money. The same result could be achieved on equitable grounds: as, contrary to the parties' expectations, the swap transactions and contract were ultra vires and void, the purpose for which the sums paid by the bank to the council had wholly failed, and those sums had, from the time the council received them, been held on a resulting trust for the bank. Interest was due from the date the council had the use of the bank's money, all of which it spent; it would be charged compound interest on the balance from time to time outstanding of the money it had received from the bank.

Westdeutsche Landesbank Girozentrale v Islington London Borough Council (1993) Times, 30 December (Court of Appeal: Dillon, Leggatt and Kennedy LJJ). Decision of Hobhouse J (1993) Times, 22 February, affirmed.

608 Repudiation—anticipatory repudiation—acceptance

The plaintiffs entered a contract to buy a cargo of propane from the defendants. The contract provided dates when the vessel should arrive, berth and leave. The plaintiffs repudiated the contract on the ground that loading would not be completed until after delivery was due to be made. Once loading had been completed neither party made any attempt to perform the contract. The defendants eventually sold the cargo at a much lower price than that which had been specified in the contract with the plaintiffs. An arbitrator, in deciding in favour of the plaintiffs, held that the repudiation by the plaintiffs was an anticipatory breach of contract, and that the breach had to be accepted by the defendants otherwise it was of no effect. The breach had not been remedied, however, and the nature of the repudiation was such that the failure of the defendants to take further steps to perform the contract was sufficient communication of acceptance. On appeal by the defendants, *held*, where an innocent party did not respond to a repudiation by affirmation, but took action incompatible with his own continued performance of the contract, it might be clear that he was responding to the repudiation by treating the contract as at an end. Whether an innocent party could demonstrate acceptance of a repudiation simply by failing further to perform contractual obligations depended on the circumstances. In this case it had been sufficiently demonstrated and the appeal would accordingly be dismissed.

Vitol SA v Norelf Ltd (1993) Times, 20 May (Queen's Bench Division: Phillips J).

609 Sale of goods

See SALE OF GOODS.

CONVEYANCING

Halsbury's Laws of England (4th edn) Vol 39, paras 301–800, Vol 42, paras 1–400

610 Articles

Contaminated Land—Issues for Conveyancers, Stephen Tromans: [1993] Conv 425
Cut-Price Chaos, Evlynne Gilvarry (on cut-price conveyancing): LS Gaz, 15 September 1993, p 9
Dishonest Conveyances, Touchstone: 137 SJ 750
Lock-Out Agreements—The New Legal Landscape, Derek Sendrove (on *Pitt v PHH Asset Management Ltd* (1993) Independent, 6 August, CA (para 595)): Estates Gazette, 25 September 1993, p 139

Plain Language and Conveyancing, Peter Butt: [1993] Conv 256

Stamp Duty—New Buildings, Kaz Stepien: 137 SJ 1003

The Cost of Default, HW Wilkinson (on conveyancing fraud): 143 NLJ 1344

The Protocol in Practice, Robert Abbey (on the Law Society's national conveyancing protocol): 137 SJ 1166

The Rate for the Job, Lesley Palmer (on economies provided by cut-price conveyancing): LS Gaz, 7 July 1993, p 25

611 Co-ownership—trust for sale—collateral purpose—right of mortgagee to sell property

The Law of Property Act 1925, s 30 states that if trustees for sale refuse to sell land or any requisite consent cannot be obtained, any interested person may apply to the court for a vesting order to give effect to the proposed transaction, and the court may make such order as it thinks fit.

The first defendant had transferred a property solely owned by her, into joint names with the second and third defendants, on terms that the house would not be sold whilst the first defendant was living. The transfer was effected in order to facilitate the passing of the property on the death of the first defendant. The second defendant then mortgaged the property without the knowledge of the first defendant and subsequently left the country. She stopped paying the mortgage and the plaintiff building society sued the defendants for the money due, and possession of the property. Judgment was given for the plaintiff and it was held that the plaintiff was a person "interested" within the meaning of s 30, and could therefore apply for an order to sell the property. On appeal, *held*, when the property was transferred into joint names a trust for sale was created which could not be implemented without the permission of the first defendant. Except for s 30, the requirement of consent could not be overlooked especially in a case where the property was passed to facilitate transfer on death and the transfer was made with certain conditions attached. Where the collateral purpose of the transfer was still in existence the court would not allow the enforcement of the trust for sale to defeat that purpose, even where the property had been assigned by one of the original parties to the purpose. However once the collateral purpose had come to an end, one beneficial owner could not insist on retaining the property when the other owner wanted to sell. In the present case the collateral purpose of the first defendant being able to reside in the property until death had not been affected by the second defendant losing her beneficial interest in the property through the mortgage, although it might have been different if the collateral purpose had been that the first and second defendants should live in the property together. The court's discretion should be exercised against ordering a sale. Accordingly, the appeal would be allowed.

Abbey National plc v Moss (1993) Times, 30 November (Court of Appeal: Ralph Gibson, Hirst and Peter Gibson LJJ).

612 Contract for sale—collateral contract—agreement not to negotiate for fixed period

See *Pitt v PHH Asset Management Ltd*, para·595.

613 Contract for sale—damages for breach of contract—entitlement to damages

The defendants owned two properties which were offered for sale. The plaintiffs were interested in purchasing the properties for the purpose of a quick resale at a profit and found a sub-purchaser willing to purchase at a higher price, but kept to themselves their intention to sell on. It was only after the contracts for sale between the plaintiffs and the defendants and between the plaintiffs and the sub-purchaser had been signed that the defendants learnt of the resale contract. The defendants believed they had agreed to sell at an undervalue and refused to complete. The plaintiffs were unable to complete the resale contract. The sub-purchaser considered that it was discharged from further performance of its contract by the plaintiffs' breach in failing to complete and brought an action claiming damages from the plaintiffs, who in turn brought an action against the defendants for specific performance. An order for specific performance was made in the plaintiffs' action and an inquiry as to damages was directed. The sale by the defendants to the plaintiffs was then completed and on the same day the plaintiffs sold the property to the sub-purchaser for a lower price than the plaintiffs had bought from the defendants. On the inquiry as to damages the plaintiffs claimed both their loss of profit (less certain deductions) under the original contract for resale and the loss made under the contract for resale as finally concluded. *Held*, a plaintiff was entitled to recover by way of damages all loss for a breach of contract which at the date of the contract the defaulting party was on notice might be occasioned by the breach such that he might fairly be held, in entering into the contract, to have accepted the risk. However, the defaulting party would only be held to have accepted the risk if he was on notice of the purpose and intent of the plaintiff in entering into the contract with him and the consequent exposure of the plaintiff to the risk of damage of the character in question in the event of the defaulting party's breach. A plaintiff claiming to recover from the defaulting party losses arising under a subcontract had to establish that the defendant was on notice of the existence, at the date of the contract, of the plaintiff's purpose and intent to enter into a further contract which was dependent for its fulfilment on the due performance by the defendant of the first contract. It was not sufficient for the plaintiff to establish that the making of a subcontract was an available option. In order for the defendants to be liable to the plaintiffs for the loss incurred by the plaintiffs it was necessary for the defendants to have been aware of the plaintiffs' contract to sell the property at a profit. Since the plaintiffs had deliberately withheld from the defendants the fact that they intended to sell on, the loss suffered by the plaintiffs in respect of the contract for resale was not within the contemplation of the parties. The plaintiffs' claim for damages arising out of the resale would therefore be dismissed.

Seven Seas Properties Ltd v Al-Essa (No 2) [1993] 3 All ER 577 (Chancery Division: Gavin Lightman QC). *Hadley v Baxendale* [1843–60] All ER Rep 461 and dictum of Lord Upjohn in *The Heron II, Koufos v C Czarnikow Ltd* [1967] 3 All ER 686, HL at 715 applied.

614   Contract for sale—failure to complete—forfeiture of deposit

Jamaica
A bank sold premises at an auction to the purchaser. The contract provided for a deposit of 25 per cent of the purchase price with payment of the balance within 14 days and that the deposit would be forfeited to the bank if the purchaser failed to comply. Following the failure of the purchaser to complete in time the bank rescinded the contract and forfeited the deposit. The purchaser then instituted proceedings claiming relief from forfeiture of the deposit. At first instance the court refused to grant the relief sought. The decision was reversed on appeal, the court granting relief from forfeiture to the extent of 15 per cent of the purchase price. On the bank's appeal and the purchaser's cross-appeal to the Judicial Committee, *held*, a vendor seeking to obtain a sum greater than 10 per cent of the purchase price as a forfeitable deposit had to establish special circumstances justifying it, and since the bank had failed to show that the deposit of 25 per cent was to encourage performance of the contract or that a deposit exceeding 10 per cent was reasonable, the provision for its forfeiture was a penalty. The deposit was repayable, together with interest from the date of rescission until the date of actual repayment and accordingly, the appeal would be dismissed and the cross-appeal allowed.

Workers Trust and Merchant Bank Ltd v Dojap Investments Ltd [1993] 2 All ER 370 (Privy Council: Lords Keith of Kinkel, Jauncey of Tullichettle, Donaldson of Lymington, Browne-Wilkinson and Sir Christopher Slade).

615   Contract for sale—rescission—undisclosed easement—easement unknown to purchaser

A builder bought part of the playing fields of a school, under the National Conditions of Sale (20th Edition), with the intention of constructing houses on the land. The value of the land subsequently fell to half the original purchase price. It was then discovered that, unknown to anyone concerned in the sale, a sewer was buried on the land and the land was subject to an easement of drainage. The builder decided that the sewer could not be re-routed, rescinded the contract for misrepresentation and common mistake and claimed repayment of the purchase price. The builder's claim was successful. On appeal by the vendor, *held*, the sewer was a defect in title but not a serious practical problem. Under the National Conditions of Sale, condition 14 the vendor was undertaking to disclose all easements and encumbrances of which it had knowledge. Subject to this, condition 14 required the purchaser to take the risk of encumbrances which might affect his ability to use the land. In answer to a pre-contract inquiry, the vendor had replied that it was not aware of any undisclosed easements affecting the land. This was a representation that it had no actual knowledge of a defect, but also that it had made such investigations as could reasonably be expected to be made by a prudent conveyancer. Although the sewer was recorded in documents held by the planning department of the vendor, it was not noted against the title deeds of the land. In these circumstances, there was no claim on the grounds of misrepresentation or mistake and the vendor's appeal would be allowed.

Although it was unnecessary to decide whether the judge had correctly exercised his discretion not to award damages in lieu of rescission, Hoffmann and Evans LJJ observed that they would have awarded such damages. Evans LJ observed that those damages ought not to include the decline in the market value of the land since the contract was made.

William Sindall plc v Cambridgeshire County Council [1993] EGCS 105 (Court of Appeal: Russell, Evans and Hoffmann LJJ).

616 Restrictive covenants
See EQUITY.

COPYRIGHT

Halsbury's Laws of England (4th edn) Vol 9, paras 801–1000

617 Articles
Databases and the Law, Susan Singleton: 137 SJ 122
Design Right—A Recipe for Complex Litigation? Heidi Stanley (on the Copyright Designs and Patents Act 1988): 137 SJ 587
Forgery and Signatures on Paintings, Caroline Fry: 143 NLJ 1233

618 Copyright protection—application of Community legislation
See *Collins v Imtrat Handelsgesellschaft mbH; Patricia Im-und Export Verwaltungsgesellschaft mbH v EMI Electrola mbH*, para 2720.

619 Copyright protection—application to other countries
The Copyright (Application to Other Countries) Order 1993, SI 1993/942 (in force 4 May 1993), applies the provisions of the Copyright, Designs and Patents Act 1988, Pt I, Sch I to works of different types originating in specified countries which are parties to the Berne Copyright Convention, the Universal Copyright Convention, and, in certain cases, the Rome Convention for the Protection of Performers, Producers of Phonograms and Broadcasting Organisation. Those works effectively receive copyright protection in the United Kingdom. Protection is provided for literary, dramatic, musical and artistic works, films, published editions, sound recordings and broadcasts. The 1989 Orders, SI 1989/1293, 1989/2415, and the 1990 Order, SI 1990/2153 are revoked.

620 Copyright protection—satellite broadcasting and cable retransmission
See para 2737.

621 Infringement—copyright subsisting in design documents—jurisdiction of Patents County Court
See *PSM International plc v Specialised Fastener Products (Southern) Ltd*, para 1920.

622 Infringement—investigator—conduct of interview
See *Joy v Federation Against Copyright Theft Ltd*, para 718.

623 Recording of broadcasts and cable programmes—educational establishments—certification of licensing scheme
The Copyright (Certification of Licensing Scheme for Educational Recording of Broadcasts and Cable Programmes) (Educational Recording Agency Limited) (Amendment) Order 1993, SI 1993/193 (in force on 1 April 1993), amends the 1990 Order, SI 1990/879, to reflect the increase in the annual tariff for licences under the licensing scheme operated for the purposes of the Copyright, Designs and Patents Act 1988, s 35 by the Educational Recording Agency Ltd.

The Copyright (Certification of Licensing Scheme for Educational Recording of Broadcasts) (Open University Educational Enterprises Limited) Order 1993, SI 1993/2755 (in force on 1 January 1994), replaces the 1990 Order, SI 1990/2008, so as to certify a new licensing scheme to be operated for the purposes of the Copyright, Designs and Patents Act 1988, s 35 by Open University Educational Enterprises Ltd.

624 Recording of broadcasts and cable programmes—recording for archives—designated bodies

The Copyright (Recording for Archives of Designated Class of Broadcasts and Cable Programmes) (Designated Bodies) Order 1993, SI 1993/74 (in force on 12 February 1993), replaces the 1991 Order, SI 1991/1116. The 1993 Order designates the British Medical Association, the British Music Information Centre and the Imperial War Museum as further bodies for the purposes of the Copyright, Designs and Patents Act 1988, s 75 (making of copies of broadcasts and cable programmes of a designated class for placement in an archive maintained by a designated body without infringement of copyright).

625 Rights in performances—reciprocal protection

The Performances (Reciprocal Protection) (Convention Countries) Order 1993, SI 1993/943 (in force on 4 May 1993), designates various countries which enjoy reciprocal protection under the Copyright, Designs and Patents Act 1988, Pt II relating to rights in performances. They are all parties to the International Convention for the Protection of Performers, Producers of Phonograms and Broadcasting Organisations (the Rome Convention). This order revokes SI 1989/1296.

CORONERS

Halsbury's Laws of England (4th edn) Vol 9, paras 1001–1200

626 Articles

Death and the Coroner, Paul Matthews: LS Gaz, 3 March 1993, p 28
The Coroner and the Quantum of Proof, Paul Matthews: (1993) 12 CJQ 279

627 Inquest—conduct of coroner—appearance of bias

Following a collision between a dredger and a pleasure cruiser, which resulted in fifty one deaths, an inquest was held. At the hearing the coroner decided to adjourn the hearing pending criminal proceedings and other inquiries. Three years later, following the inquiries, the coroner decided not to resume the inquests. The applicant, a relative of one of the dead, applied for judicial review of the decision on the basis that the coroner had shown apparent bias in his decision. The application was made on the grounds that the coroner, in a meeting with journalists, had described the applicant as being unhinged and had shown the journalists photographs of the applicant's son's body without seeking her permission. *Held*, the coroner denied all recollection of using the word "unhinged" and stated that he had great sympathy for the applicant. In applying the test laid down in *R v Gough* (1993) Times, 24 May (para 779) the question was whether there was a real danger that, in deciding not to resume the inquests, the coroner was influenced, consciously or unconsciously, to a material degree by his views about the applicant's psychological state. It was unfortunate that the coroner had expressed himself as he did but there was no real danger that any apparent bias by the coroner towards the applicant created injustice or materially influenced his decision. Accordingly, the application would be dismissed.

R v HM Coroner for Inner West London, ex p Perks (1993) Independent, 13 July (Queen's Bench Division: Neill J and Mantell LJ).

628 Inquest—duty to summon jury—judicial review

The Coroners Act 1988, s 8(3)(d) sets out the circumstances in which a coroner should summon a jury. Section 8(2)(a) of the 1988 Act and the Coroners Rules 1984 (SI 1984/552), r 44 state that jurors in those circumstances must be summoned by warrant. Rules 45 and 46 require written summonses to be sent to the jurors.

The applicant was the widow of the deceased, who had died shortly after returning home from hospital treatment. An inquest into the death was adjourned and resumed several months later without a jury. After submissions from the deceased's family, the coroner obtained a jury of nine from the pool of jurors at a nearby Crown Court. After a further adjournment one of the jurors was unable to continue. The family of the deceased claimed that the original jury had not been lawfully summoned and therefore the previous proceedings were a nullity, and that the coroner had no power to continue with only eight jurors. On a application for judicial review of the decision by the coroner to reject their submission, *held*, the procedures set out in the 1988 Act and the 1984 Rules were mandatory. Rule 48 included provisions to cover the informal summoning of jurors where a jury was incomplete and this made it impossible to construe an implied power permitting the coroner to summon a jury informally under common law. The jury had not been summoned lawfully and the inquest proceedings were a nullity. Accordingly, an order of certiorari would issue quashing the coroner's decision to carry on with the inquest and a declaration would be granted that the proceedings were a nullity.

R v Merseyside Coroner, ex p Carr [1993] 4 All ER 65 (Queen's Bench Division: Neill LJ and Mantell J).

629   Inquest—evidence—attendance of witnesses—coroner's discretion

The applicant's 26-year-old son hanged himself while in police custody. That year there had been a similar incident involving an attempted hanging and the applicant's solicitor sought to call that prisoner as a witness in order to establish want of care by the police. The coroner refused to call the witness or to allow any questions about the incident on the grounds that it was irrelevant. In proceedings for judicial review of the coroner's conduct of the inquest, *held*, the previous incident did not relate to any distinct act or omission which was closely and directly associated with the death of the applicant's son. In any event, the Coroners' Act 1988, s 11(2) gave the coroner a discretion to examine persons having knowledge of the facts of the death if he considered such an examination to be expedient. On the facts, the coroner was entitled to exclude the evidence as being irrelevant. Accordingly, the application would be dismissed.

R v HM Coroner for West Yorkshire (Eastern District), ex p Clements (1993) 158 JP 17 (Queen's Bench Division: Neill LJ and Mantell J).

630   Inquest—verdict—verdict withdrawn from jury

See *R v Coroner for Inner North London, ex p Diesa Koto*, para 9.

631   Treasure trove—duty of coroner—votive offerings

The applicant, whilst using a metal detector, discovered a gold torque. An inquest was held to determine whether the torque was treasure trove. The applicant submitted that the torque had at all material times been deliberately abandoned as a votive offering and was therefore not treasure trove. A verdict was returned that the torque was treasure trove and therefore the property of the Crown. The applicant applied for judicial review under the Coroners Act 1988, s 13 for the inquest to be quashed and a new inquest held, on the grounds that the coroner was wrong not to await the availability of a witness requested by the applicant and that his summing up was biased against the votive offering argument presented to the court. *Held*, the Coroners Act 1988, s 13 applied equally to inquests into treasure trove as well as into deaths. In his opening remarks to the jury the coroner had misdirected himself on the appropriate law and had erred in not allowing the obtaining of further evidence on the votive offerings. There had been insufficiency of inquiry and accordingly, the application would be granted and another inquest would be held.

R v HM Coroner for Wiltshire, ex p Chaddock (1992) 157 JP 209 (Queen's Bench Division: Mann LJ and Leonard J).

COUNTY COURTS

Halsbury's Laws of England (4th edn) Vol 10, paras 1–700

632   Articles

County Court Striking Out—A Nation Divided, Irvine Marr and Paul Coppin (on the varying interpretation of CCR, Ord 17, r 11(9)): 137 SJ 814

Order of the Day, Neil Hickman (on CCR Ord 17, r 11): LS Gaz, 30 June 1993, p 26

Summing Up Interest, James Pyke (on calculating interest pursuant to the County Courts Act 1984, s 69): 137 SJ 1029

633 Appeal—appeal with leave—prescribed classes of proceedings

The County Court Appeals (Amendment) Order 1993, SI 1993/2131 (in force on 1 October 1993), amends the 1991 Order, SI 1991/1877, which prescribes the classes of county court proceedings in which an appeal to the Court of Appeal lies only with the leave of a county court judge or of the Court of Appeal. The 1993 Order provides that the value of an appeal is to be the value of the claim or the value of the counterclaim, according to which is the subject of the appeal and not according to which is the greater. The order also provides that where a party wishes to appeal against two or more parts of a determination, and leave to appeal would be required in respect of any of those parts, leave is required for the whole of the appeal.

The County Court Appeals (Amendment) (Transitional Provisions) Order 1993, SI 1993/2789 (in force on 8 December 1993), provides that the County Court Appeals Order 1991, SI 1991/1877, art 2 (as amended by SI 1993/2131 supra) (circumstances in which leave to appeal to Court of Appeal from county court judgments is needed) applies to all proceedings in which an appeal is set down or an application is lodged with the Court of Appeal on or after 8 December 1993.

634 Appeal—scope of appeal—fresh evidence

The plaintiff was granted an injunction and awarded damages against the defendant for unlawful eviction. The defendant subsequently discovered fresh evidence which had not been available at the date of the trial and appealed to the Court of Appeal that there ought to be a new trial in the county court. The plaintiff contended that the court had no jurisdiction to entertain the appeal in view of CCR Order 37, r 1 and the case of *Weinbaum v Klein* [1950] 1 All ER 353 where it was held that under the County Courts Act 1934, s 105 fresh evidence could not be adduced at the hearing of an appeal in a county court case. The defendant contended that in view of the wording of the County Courts Act 1984, s 77 the case no longer applied. *Held*, the powers and scope of appeal were now considerably wider under the 1984 Act and applied to any party in any proceedings in the county court with a right of appeal. The case of *Weinbaum* no longer precluded in principle an appeal to the Court of Appeal when confined to one relating to the introduction of new evidence. However, the normal and proper route was to apply to the county court judge himself under Ord 37, r 1 rather than by making an application to the Court of Appeal. It would be inappropriate to decline to hear the appeal and leave it to the defendant to apply to the county court judge under Ord 37, r 1. Accordingly, the appeal would be granted.

O'Connor v Din (1993) Times, 15 February (Court of Appeal: Hirst LJ and Peter Gibson J).

635 Costs—taxation of costs—indemnity basis—appropriate county court scale

The plaintiff, a builder, carried out work for the defendant. The plaintiff claimed a sum of money in respect of the work. The parties came to a compromise in respect of the amount owed, the defendant undertaking to pay the plaintiff's costs of the action on an indemnity basis to be taxed if not agreed. On taxation of the costs the district judge had rejected the defendant's argument that the bill fell to be taxed under scale 2. The defendant applied for a review of the taxation and the judge held that as taxation was on an indemnity basis it was at large. On appeal by the defendant, *held*, when taxing county court costs payable on an indemnity basis, regard ought to be had to the county court scale appropriate to the sum recovered. The judge had failed to recognise the distinction between the scale at which costs were to be taxed and the basis of taxation. However, it would be open to the judge, in exercise of his discretion under CCR, Ord 38, r 9, to allow an increased sum if he was satisfied that the maximum amount allowable on scale 2 was inadequate. Accordingly, the appeal would be allowed.

Tucker v Woodroof (1993) Times, 18 March (Court of Appeal: Lloyd LJ and Thorpe J).

636 County Court Rules

The County Court (Amendment) Rules 1993, SI 1993/711 (in force on 31 March 1993), further amend the 1981 Rules, SI 1981/1687, by providing for certain functions in respect of the making and review of administration orders under the County Courts Act 1984, s 112 to be carried out by court staff.

The County Court (Amendment No 2) Rules 1993, SI 1993/2150 (in force on 1 September 1993), further amend the 1981 Rules, by inserting Ord 48B, which applies for the recovery of increased penalty charges provided for in parking charge certificates issued under the Road Traffic Act 1991, Sch 6, para 6, and amounts payable by a person other than the London authority which served the charge certificate under an adjudication of a parking adjudicator pursuant to s 73.

The County Court (Amendment No 3) Rules 1993, SI 1993/2175 (in force on 1 November 1993), further amend the 1981 Rules, so that (1) in actions for the recovery of land, additional information concerning the tenancy or mortgage agreement and the defendant's circumstances is now required; (2) the rent action is abolished; and (3) district judges may now make possession orders without a hearing in respect of property let under certain assured and assured shorthold tenancies and may provide fixed costs in cases where such an order is made.

The County Court (Amendment No 4) Rules 1993, SI 1993/3278 (in force on 17 January 1994 and 7 February 1994), further amend the 1981 Rules, by (1) amending provision for the making of a certificate of service where service is effected by the Summons Production Centre; (2) providing that leave to serve an originating process out of the jurisdiction may be given in proceedings under the Immigration (Carriers' Liability) Act 1987; (3) providing that the procedure for applying for a charging order under the Charging Orders Act 1979 is to apply to applications to enforce a liability to pay council tax under the Local Government Finance Act 1992; and (4) making specific provision for proceedings under the Leasehold Reform, Housing and Urban Development Act 1993.

637   County Court Rules—forms

The County Court (Forms) (Amendment) Rules 1993, SI 1993/712 (in force in part on 31 March 1993 and in part on 1 April 1993), amend the 1982 Rules, SI 1982/586, by substituting references to the council tax for references to the community charge, revoking a defence form used by the summons production centre (N9(SPC)), adjusting the computerised form of warrant (N42(c)), substituting a new form of administration order and related forms (N92, N94, N95, N95A), and amending the committal order (N79).

The County Court (Forms) (Amendment No 2) Rules 1993, SI 1993/2174 (in force on 1 November 1993), substitute forms N2, N5, N6, N26, N27, N27(1), N27(2), N28, N29 and N31 (possession summons and possession orders), and insert new forms, N5A, N11A, N11M, N11R, N26A, N119, N120, prescribing particulars of claim, with reply forms for the tenant, for use in cases involving residential property and prescribing forms for the accelerated possession procedure. Form N7 (summons for arrears of rent) is omitted.

638   Districts—delimitation of districts

The Civil Courts (Amendment No 2) Order 1993, SI 1993/3120 (in force on 4 January 1994), amends the 1983 Order, SI 1983/713, so as to close the East Grinstead, Hexham, Malton, Thorne and Whitby County Courts.

639   Divorce county courts

See DIVORCE.   •

640   Jurisdiction—distribution of business between High Court and county courts

The High Court and County Courts Jurisdiction (Amendment) Order 1993, SI 1993/1407 (in force on 8 June 1993), amends the 1991 Order, SI 1991/724, by providing that (1) appeals against decisions of auditors under the Local Government Finance Act 1982, s 19(4) are to be commenced in the High Court; (2) a county court judgment or order for the payment of a sum of money arising out of an agreement regulated by the Consumer Credit Act 1974, and which it is sought to enforce by execution against goods, must be enforced in a county court; and (3) proceedings to enforce certain road traffic debts arising under the Road Traffic Act 1991 are to be taken in Cardiff County Court.

641   Jurisdiction—order for possession—suspension of execution—time limit for application

It has been held that it is arguable that a solicitor who attends a county court in order to make an application for an emergency suspension of the execution of a possession warrant, and who is sent away and told to make his application the next day because the judge had finished his day's list, is to be treated as having made such an application pursuant to the Housing Act 1985, s 85(2).

Islington London Borough Council v Harridge (1993) Times, 30 June (Court of Appeal: Staughton and Farquharson LJJ).

642 Jurisdiction—residence order—jurisdiction to interfere with powers of other bodies

See *D v D (County Court Jurisdiction: Injunction)*, para 423.

643 Officer of the court—assault on officer of the court—defence—defendant's belief

The County Courts Act 1984, s 14(1)(b) contains provisions relating to the offence of assaulting a court officer in the course of his duty or rescuing any goods seized in execution.

A committal order was made against the defendant, a judgment debtor, who had consistently failed to respond to an order requiring him to appear at court for oral examination. An incident took place between the defendant and the bailiffs in the street and the defendant was charged with assault under the 1984 Act, s 14(1)(b). At first instance it was held that the offence was absolute and that it was not a good defence to show that the defendant did not know that the bailiffs were such, or that they were acting in the course of their duty. On appeal, *held*, it was clear that in a prosecution under the 1984 Act, s 14(1)(b), or the Police Act 1964, s 51, which provided for a similar offence in relation to the police, the prosecution or the complainant did not have to establish that the defendant knew or believed that the victim was a court officer or member of the police. The following steps in relation to the construction of s 14(1)(b) were approved: (1) not every contact between people amounted to an assault. To be criminal the force had to be unlawful; (2) when deciding whether a defendant had used reasonable force to defend himself the court had to judge him on the basis of what he believed the facts to be, not what the facts actually were; (3) if the force applied by the defendant would be reasonable if the person concerned was not a court officer, then if the defendant believed the person was not an officer, he would have a plea of self- defence even if his belief was unreasonable; and (4) the state of belief was therefore important, but the mistake had to be one of fact particularly as to the victim's capacity, and not a mistake of law as to the authority of a person acting in that capacity. That approach to the construction of s 14(1)(b) brought it into line with the law of contempt in that it was not contemptuous to do something which breached a court order if the contemnor had no knowledge of the order. The protection given to police and court officers would not be reduced by this construction because such people would identify themselves at the outset and the more unreasonable the belief the defendant claimed to have, the less likely it would be that the court would uphold that belief. Accordingly, the appeal would be allowed.

Blackburn v Bowering (1993) Times, 5 November (Court of Appeal: Sir Thomas Bingham MR, Leggatt and Roch LJJ).

644 Register of county court judgments

The Register of County Court Judgments (Amendment) Regulations 1993, SI 1993/710 (in force on 5 April 1993), further amend the 1985 Regulations, SI 1985/1807, by providing for the registration of administration orders made on applications issued on or after 31 March 1993; and by exempting from registration orders made to recover an increased penalty charge provided for in a parking charge certificate issued under the Road Traffic Act 1991, Sch 6, para 6, or an amount payable by a person other than a London authority under an adjudication of a parking adjudicator pursuant to s 73.

The Register of County Court Judgments (Amendment No 2) Regulations 1993, SI 1993/2173 (in force on 1 November 1993), further amend the 1985 Regulations supra, by providing that, where in proceedings to recover possession of land an order is made for the payment of money (whether for costs, payments due under a mortgage, arrears of rent or otherwise), the order is exempt from registration until the judgment creditor takes steps to enforce it.

645 Service of process—extension of time limits—discretion

The tenant had made an application under the Landlord and Tenant Act 1954, s 24. The county court failed to serve the application within the time prescribed for service under CCR Ord 7, r 20 and Ord 43, r 6(3) for extension of time for service. The tenant's application for an extension of time was rejected and she appealed. *Held*, the court had discretion to extend the time for service under CCR Ord 13, r 4 and to treat the failure to extend and serve as an irregularity and order the action to proceed under CCR Ord 37, r 5. It was clear that the tenant had discharged the burden of showing good reason for the court to exercise its power to extend and had provided a satisfactory explanation for the failure to apply for an extension before the validity of the proceedings expired. Although it was incumbent on parties to comply with the time limits and the discretion to extend ought only to be used sparingly, in the circumstances it would be unjust for the tenant to pay for the court's error. The judge had wrongly exercised his discretion and accordingly, the appeal would be allowed.

Ward-Lee v Lineham [1993] 2 All ER 1006 (Court of Appeal: Sir Thomas Bingham MR, McCowan and Hirst LJJ).

646 Service of process—service within jurisdiction—service by post—address

CCR Ord 7, r 10(1) provides that service of a summons is effected by an officer of the court sending it by first class post to the defendant at the address stated in the request for the summons.

A flat was demised to the defendant and his mother. A clause in the lease provided that any demands on the tenant would be sufficiently given if sent by post and addressed to the tenant by name or left for the tenant at the premises. After the mother's death, it was agreed that the defendant's stepfather would continue to live in the flat and pay all the outgoings. The defendant did not see the stepfather or visit the flat for several years, and at some time during that period the stepfather disappeared leaving others in occupation. In the interim, the landlord filed a request for the issue of a summons for possession of the land on a practice form approved by the Lord Chancellor but not prescribed by the County Court Rules. The address of the flat was stated in the appropriate boxes. The court then sent a summons to the defendant's flat in accordance with Ord 7, r 10(1), which never came to his notice, and judgment was subsequently entered for the landlord. The defendant's appeal was dismissed on the grounds that the rule simply obliged the landlord to state an address which had a direct and immediate connection with the defendant in the request for a summons and that, in view of the clause in the lease, the summons had been properly served. On further appeal, *held*, the judge's interpretation was incorrect. CCR Ord 7, r 10(1), referred to the defendant's address and "address" was to be construed in accordance with its ordinary meaning. It meant a place at which written communications could be delivered to him and where he was present to receive them. Whilst the extent to which his presence was necessary to make it his address might vary, if he was never there it could not be called his address notwithstanding the fact that he had a direct and immediate connection with it. Accordingly, the appeal would be allowed and the judgment would be set aside.

Willowgreen Ltd v Smithers (1993) Times, 14 December (Court of Appeal: Nourse and Thorpe LJJ).

647 Service of process—summons—service by post—summons forwarded abroad

The plaintiff issued proceedings against the defendant and the court posted the summons to the defendant's last known address. The defendant had emigrated some time earlier and the summons was posted on to him. The defendant did not act on the summons, and the plaintiff obtained judgment in default and subsequently a charging order on the defendant's house. The judgment was set aside on the ground that the summons had not been served on the defendant. On the plaintiff's appeal, the judge extended the time for service, purportedly under CCR Ord 7, r 20(3), and gave the defendant leave to defend on the payment of a sum into court. On the appeal of the defendant and the cross-appeal of the plaintiff, *held*, the judge had no power to grant an extension of the time for service under r 20(3) as the defendant's application had been made out of time. The scope of CCR Ord 7, rr 1, 10(2) (which dealt with postal service) was not limited by analogy with RSC Ord 10, r 1 to service only on a defendant within the jurisdiction. Further, the scope of rr 1, 10(2) could not be limited by the County Courts Act 1984, s 76 as that provision applied only where the County Court Rules 1981 made no express provision. The summons had therefore been properly served. Accordingly, the defendant's appeal would be dismissed and the plaintiff's cross-appeal would be allowed.

Rolph v Zolan [1993] 4 All ER 202 (Court of Appeal: Dillon and Butler-Sloss LJJ).

648 Small claims—jurisdiction—unliquidated claims

The Lord Chancellor's Department has published a consultation paper (October 1993) on proposals for changes to the treatment of small unliquidated claims in the County Court. This proposes that in future, all unliquidated claims should be automatically referred to the small claims arbitration procedure, in the absence of a specific statement that the amount involved exceeds £1,000.

In order to reduce the complexity of the procedure, a new expanded particulars of claim form and new forms of reply are recommended. It is proposed that the new form of particulars of claim will be accompanied by a standard letter from the plaintiff's medical advisor. If, on giving directions, the district judge requires more detailed medical evidence, this will be given by way of a new standard medical report form. There will be a preliminary hearing but with judicial discretion to dispense with it where the judge considers from the papers that a case has been fully and appropriately prepared. In response to concerns expressed within the legal profession in relation to introducing a no-costs procedure, a fixed sum for legal advice and preparation will be recoverable, with a separate fixed sum for attendance at a preliminary hearing. It is proposed that the levels for expenses recoverable in the new scheme will be the same as those that apply in the existing no-costs small claims scheme. Where a particular action is exceptionally complex or peculiar, or is a test case, or involves fraud, it can be dealt with by a provision similar to CCR Ord 19, r 3(2) which provides that a judge may order the trial of a case automatically referred to the no-costs procedure. Where the amount involved in an action is above the £1,000 threshold, both parties may consent to refer the action to the new scheme, in which case the costs recoverable will be limited to the fixed sums mentioned above. The new scheme is specifically tailored to the needs of small personal injury claims but applies to all unliquidated claims below £1,000. Where a claim involves both personal injury and non-personal injury elements it will automatically be referred to the new procedure, but no costs will be allowed in respect of the non personal injury element. As with the standard small claims arbitration procedure, an arbitration award is final, subject to it being set aside on one of the established, limited grounds.

649   Transfer of proceedings—transfer from High Court—striking out by High Court

See *Restick v Crickmore; Nisbet v Granada Entertainment Ltd; Reed v Department of Employment; Warren v Hinchcliffe*, para 2067.

COURTS

Halsbury's Laws of England (4th edn) Vol 10, paras 701–1000

650   County courts

See COUNTY COURTS.

651   Court of Appeal—Civil Division—annual review 1992–93

Sir Thomas Bingham MR has delivered a review of the administration of the Civil Division of the Court of Appeal for the period 1992–93.

Although the Civil Division of the Court of Appeal disposed of more cases in the legal year 1992–93 than in the previous year, the backlog of appeals and applications waiting to be heard was longer than at the end of the previous year: the total number of appeals set down for hearing was 1,838, of which 1,625 had been disposed of. Although, ideally, appeals should be heard as soon as they were ready for hearing, the current backlog made that impossible. Priority would have to be given to those appeals considered to be the most urgent: those were pre-eminently appeals concerning children and the liberty of the subject, and claims for interlocutory injunctions when justice might be denied if not done at once. Most appeals were unsuccessful; only 27·8 per cent were successful. In cases where leave was not required and unsuccessful litigants could appeal as of right, only 24 per cent were successful. Measures had now been taken to extend the requirement of leave to appeal to certain classes of case in which leave to appeal had not previously been required.

The court had adopted the practice of fixing "hear-by dates" for the following various types of appeal; most appeals were not in practice heard much earlier or later than these dates and these dates ought to be more generally known. (1) Matrimonial: child cases, three months; other cases, four months, but if very heavy, six months. (2) Crown Office cases: immigration appeals and Crown Office interlocutory, three months; Crown Office finals, nine months, but if very heavy, 12 months. (3) High Court interlocutory: Commercial Court and Official Referees, six months; Order 14, three months; other Queen's Bench, four months; Chancery, six months. (4) High Court final: Patents Court, Commercial Court and Official Referees, 16 months; personal injury, eight months; other Queen's Bench and Chancery, 14 months. (5) County Court: possession and interlocutory, three months; personal injury, eight months; other County Court finals, 12 months. (6) Tribunals: nine months.

See further (1993) Independent, 29 October.

652 Court of Appeal—Criminal Division—unresolved grounds of appeal—powers in respect of unresolved grounds

See *R v Berry*, para 682.

653 Court of Appeal—judges—maximum number

The Maximum Number of Judges Order 1993, SI 1993/605 (in force on 11 March 1993), amends the Supreme Court Act 1981 by increasing the maximum number of ordinary judges of the Court of Appeal from 28 to 29.

654 Employment Appeal Tribunal

See EMPLOYMENT.

655 European Court of Human Rights

See HUMAN RIGHTS.

656 European Court of Justice

See EUROPEAN COMMUNITIES.

657 High Court—Family Division—allocation of proceedings—child support proceedings

See para 2042.

658 High Court—judges—maximum number

The Maximum Number of Judges (No 2) Order 1993, SI 1993/1255 (in force on 13 May 1993), increases the maximum number of puisne judges of the High Court from 85 to 98.

659 High Court—jurisdiction—insolvency proceedings—co-operation with foreign court

See *Re Bank of Credit and Commerce International SA; Re Bank of Credit and Commerce International (Overseas) Ltd*, para 488.

660 House of Lords—practice directions

See PRACTICE AND PROCEDURE.

661 Judicial Committee of the Privy Council—criminal appeals—order for costs— recommendation

Jamaica

Following the defendant's conviction for murder he appealed to the Privy Council. The appeal was granted and an order for costs was made against the Crown. The Crown appealed against the costs order. *Held*, a successful defendant ought to ask the court to make a recommendation that he ought to receive assistance in relation to the costs of the appeal. If for any reason the defendant did not ask for a recommendation he would be prompted to do so by the Crown. The practice in criminal cases would not be to award a successful defendant costs against the Crown and accordingly, the appeal would be allowed.

R v Beckford (1993) Times, 30 June (Privy Council: Lords Griffiths, Bridge of Harwich, Lowry, Slynn of Hadley and Woolf).

662 Judicial pensions

See PENSIONS AND SUPERANNUATION.

663 Judicicial Pensions and Retirement Act 1993
See para 1926.

664 Magistrates' courts
See MAGISTRATES.

665 Practice and procedure directions
See CRIMINAL EVIDENCE AND PROCEDURE; PRACTICE AND PROCEDURE.

CREMATION AND BURIAL

Halsbury's Laws of England (4th edn) Vol 10, paras 1001–1243

666 Disinterment of dead body—faculty for removal from one churchyard to another
See *Re St Peter's Churchyard, Oughtrington*, para 1035.

667 Disposal of ashes—failure to follow instructions for disposal—damages for distress and anxiety
See *Griffiths v Ronald P Sherry & Son and The General Cemetery Co*, para 890.

CRIMINAL EVIDENCE AND PROCEDURE

Halsbury's Laws of England (4th edn) Vol 11(1) (reissue), paras 1–800, Vol 11(2) (reissue), paras 801–1592

668 Articles
Conceptual Versus Pragmatic Approaches to Hearsay, Rosemary Pattenden: 57 MLR 138
Confessions, Recording Rules and Miscarriages of Justice: a Mistaken Emphasis? Helen Fenwick: [1993] Crim LR 174
Contesting Bail, Alec Samuels: 37 SJ 1000
Corporate Liability, Geoff Holgate: 137 SJ 826
Crime Reporter, Stephen Gilchrist: 137 SJ 126
Defence Costs out of Central Funds—Expenses Properly Incurred, JN Spencer: 158 JP Jo 19
Draconian powers? John Lyons (SFO's power to compel disclosure of documents): 137 SJ 446
Ending Juvenile Remands in Custody, Declan Kerr: 157 JP Jo 73
Hearsay and the European Court of Human Rights, Craig Osborne: [1993] Crim LR 255
Investigating Fraud, Rakesh Kapila (on the role of the forensic accountant in the investigation of fraud cases): 137 SJ 878
Management of Fraud Trials, Leonard Leigh and Lucia Zedner: 137 SJ 116
Obtaining Defence Experts in Criminal Proceedings—Pragmatism and the Impossible Dream, Paul Roberts: Criminal Lawyer, Issue 42, p 1
On Close Inspection, Jeffrey Bayes (on the disclosure of unused material in criminal prosecutions): LS Gaz, 26 January 1994, p 25
On the Record, Anthony Heaton-Armstrong and David Wolchover (on the recording of statements made by prosecution witnesses): LS Gaz, 16 June 1993, p 25
On the Record, Bryan Gibson (on the Criminal Justice Act 1991, s 29): LS Gaz, 21 July 1993, p 28
Power and Police Interviews, John Baldwin: 143 NLJ 1194
Probation Orders After the Criminal Justice Act, Nick Shelley: 157 JP Jo 583
Propensity and the Police, Suzanne McKie (on similar fact evidence in police misconduct cases): LS Gaz, 9 June 1993, p 26
Qualified to Prosecute? Stephen Hall-Jones (on the prosecuting of serious fraud trials): LS Gaz, 23 June 1993, p 17

Recent Developments in Pace, Nicholas Paul: 137 SJ 249
Reform of Evidence Law in Australia, Andrew L-T Choo: [1993] Crim LR 268
Remanding Juveniles, Tony Wilkinson: 138 SJ 70
Right to Silence: An Update, Peter Thornton: 137 SJ 142
Serious Offences, Bryan Gibson (on the Criminal Justice Act 1991): LS Gaz, 30 June 1993, p 23
Similar Fact Evidence, Simon Cooper (on *DPP v P* [1991] 3 All ER 337, HL (1991 Abr para 627)): 137 SJ 344
Similar Fact Evidence and the Standard of Proof, R Mahoney: [1993] Crim LR 185
Spent Convictions: 157 JP Jo 597
Suspect Devices, Eric Shepherd (on police interviewing): LS Gaz, 1 December 1993, p 12
Ten Years of *Newton* Hearings—Whither the Magistrates' Court, Stephen Johns (on *R v Newton* [1983] Crim LR 198): 157 JP 467
The Benefit of a Good Character, JN Spencer: 157 JP Jo 627
The Civil-isation of the Serious Fraud Trial, Michael Levi: 143 NLJ 516
The Custodial Interrogation—Fitness to be Interviewed, Dr David Jenkins: Criminal Lawyer, Issue 38, p 1
The Proof of Fear, Roderick Munday (on protecting frightened witnesses): 143 NLJ 542, 587
The Right to Silence—A Case for Review, Leslie James: 157 JP 471
The Tainted Witness, (the evidence of accomplices): (1993) 157 JP Jo 707

669   Appeal—appeal to House of Lords—leave to appeal—petition—supporting documents

See para 2043.

670   Appeal—Court of Appeal—death of appellant prior to hearing

It has been held that in criminal cases where an appeal is made to the Court of Appeal or a case has been remitted to the Court of Appeal from the House of Lords, and the appellant dies before it is heard, the appeal abates as a result of his death. It is still open for relatives of the deceased to apply to the Secretary of State for him to refer the case to the House of Lords.

R v Kearley; R v Harris (1993) Times, 29 November (Court of Appeal: Lord Taylor of Gosforth CJ, Schiemann and Wright JJ).

671   Appeal—Crown Court—judicial review by High Court—jurisdiction

The Supreme Court Act, 1981, s 29(3) provides that in relation to the jurisdiction of the Crown Court, other than its jurisdiction in relation to matters relating to trial on indictment, the High Court has all such jurisdiction to make prerogative orders as it possesses in relation to the jurisdiction of an inferior court.

The defendant, a former member of the European Parliament, was charged on indictment with two counts of dishonestly obtaining by deception cheques in respect of expenses. He successfully applied to quash the indictment. The Crown Court held that it had no jurisdiction to hear the proceedings on the grounds that, because it would have to interpret the rules of the Parliament, it would infringe the Parliament's sovereignty and, because the Parliament had its own procedure for dealing with improper payment of expenses, it would offend the principle of comity. A Divisional Court of the Queen's Bench Division quashed the judgment of the Crown Court. It held that it was entitled to do so under the 1981 act, s 29 as the trial judge's decision to decline jurisdiction was not a matter relating to trial on indictment and the Parliament was autonomous but not sovereign, and therefore interpretation of its rules came within the Crown Court's jurisdiction. On appeal by the defendant, *held*, the decision of the Crown Court was made as part of its "jurisdiction in matters relating to trial on indictment". It was generally forbidden to conduct judicial review of such decisions, in order to avoid delay. The only Crown Court decisions which had been found judicially reviewable in the past were those where the order had been made in a wholly different jurisdiction or against someone other than the accused. This case fell into neither category and accordingly, the appeal would be allowed and neither the decision of the Crown Court nor the Divisional Court in relation to the sovereignty of the European Parliament would be binding on future consideration of the point.

R v Crown Court at Manchester, ex p DPP [1993] 4 All ER 928 (House of Lords: Lords Keith of Kinkel, Templeman, Jauncey of Tullichettle, Browne-Wilkinson and Mustill).

672 Appeal—dismissal of appeal—duty to give reasons

The applicant was convicted of assault occasioning actual bodily harm. Her appeal was dismissed, without reasons, by the Crown Court and she sought an order for certiorari to quash that decision. *Held*, a Crown Court judge, sitting in an appellate capacity, had a duty to give reasons for his decision and a failure to do so might amount to a denial of natural justice. An appellant had a right to know the basis upon which the court had accepted the prosecution case and, accordingly, the application would be allowed.

R v Crown Court at Harrow, ex p Dave [1994] 1 All ER 315 (Queen's Bench Division: Kennedy LJ and Pill J).

673 Arrest—lawfulness of arrest—arrest for likely breach of the peace—hunt saboteur

The plaintiff, a hunt saboteur, was involved in an altercation at a meeting of a hunt which resulted in his being assaulted by a hunt member. The plaintiff was then arrested by a police officer for conduct likely to cause a breach of the peace. He claimed damages for false imprisonment against the police. The judge dismissed the claim, holding that the police officer concerned had reasonable cause to arrest the plaintiff and had detained him for good cause in the circumstances. The plaintiff appealed, arguing that the judge ought to have put to the jury the question of whether the arresting officer was aware at the time of the plaintiff's arrest that the plaintiff had been assaulted. *Held*, the rule in *Dallison v Caffrey* was of general application, and it was a question for the judge alone whether, at the time of the arrest, the officer had reasonable cause to believe that a breach of the peace was likely to occur. The officer was required to act promptly and was not obliged to inquire into the circumstances of the altercation. The officer's knowledge of whether or not the plaintiff had been assaulted was irrelevant in deciding if the officer had acted reasonably in arresting him. Accordingly, the plaintiff's appeal would be dismissed.

Kelly v Chief Constable of Hampshire (1993) Independent, 25 March (Court of Appeal: Lloyd LJ and Sir David Croom-Johnson). *Dallison v Caffrey* [1965] 1 QB 348 applied.

674 Arrest—lawfulness of arrest—intervention by third party to prevent unlawful arrest—subsequent arrest of third party for wilful obstruction

Plain clothed police officers on duty in the late evening saw three men in the street and reasonably suspecting that they were in possession of cannabis, exercised their powers of search under the Misuse of Drugs Act 1971. The officers produced their warrant cards and said to one man, seeing a substance in his hand, that he was going to be searched. There was a struggle in which the man was told "you are nicked for obstruction". The appellant then intervened to release the man from the police officer's grip. The appellant was also subsequently arrested and convicted of obstructing a police officer. On appeal against conviction, *held*, the issue facing the court was whether the officer had been acting in the execution of his duty when he had arrested the first man and whether or not it had been a lawful arrest. The prosecution conceded that there was no power to arrest for obstruction under the 1971 Act, as it had been repealed by the Police and Criminal Evidence Act 1984, s 26. Therefore the question turned on the test as to the lawfulness of an arrest under the Police and Criminal Evidence Act 1984, s 25. The test included the state of mind of the officer making the arrest, whether he suspected the person arrested was guilty of an offence and a determination by the court as to whether there was reasonable cause for that suspicion. Even if it was permissible for the court to infer what was the arresting officer's state of mind, the express finding of a reference to obstruction made it impossible to infer he had something else in mind at the time. In the present case, the officer had given a reason for the arrest which was invalid and therefore the arrest had been unlawful. It followed that the appellant intervener who sought to assist the prevention of an arrest which, in the circumstances, was not a lawful arrest within the Police and Criminal Evidence Act 1984, s 25, could not be charged with wilful obstruction of a police officer in the execution of his duty. Accordingly, the appeal would be allowed.

Edwards v DPP (1993) Times, 29 March (Queen's Bench Division: Evans LJ and Morland J).

675 Bail—bail pending appeal—breach of bail—failure to pursue appeal

The appellant, who had been sentenced to four years' imprisonment and had a confiscation order made against her on her conviction of illegal possession of drugs with intent to supply, had been released on bail pending her appeal against conviction. She left the jurisdiction in breach of bail conditions without having instructed solicitors or counsel to act in the appeal. The Crown sought to have the appeal dismissed. *Held*, the appeal had already been adjourned once and the appellant had been informed that she would have to surrender to bail if she wished to pursue the appeal. She was not present in court either by herself or by counsel to pursue the appeal. Accordingly, the appeal would be dismissed.

R v Carter (1993) Times, 1 June (Court of Appeal: Lord Taylor of Gosforth CJ, Owen and Blofeld JJ).

676 Bail (Amendment) Act 1993

The Bail (Amendment) Act 1993, s 1 confers upon the prosecution a right of appeal against the decision of a magistrates' court to grant bail. Section 2 deals with short title, commencement and extent. The Act received the royal assent on 20 July 1993 and comes into force on a day to be appointed.

677 Committal proceedings

See MAGISTRATES.

678 Conviction—summary conviction—committal for sentence— constitutionality

See *Comr of Police v Davis*, para 556.

679 Costs—award of costs against one defendant—co-defendant

The defendant was charged with six counts of supplying goods to which a false trade description had been applied. The defendant, who was the proprietor of a car centre at which his sons were employed, allegedly sold a number of cars whose odometer readings had been falsified. He pleaded guilty and was sentenced to four months' imprisonment, suspended for two years, and ordered to pay compensation and costs. One of his sons pleaded guilty to four offences and was sentenced to 28 days' imprisonment suspended for two years, with no order to pay costs. On appeal against the costs order, *held*, it was accepted that where there were several defendants it would usually be appropriate when making an order for costs to look to see what would be a reasonable estimate of costs if each defendant were tried alone. The defendant was the principal defendant, he was the proprietor of the business and stood to gain financially from the offences, and therefore had the means to pay the amount ordered. Accordingly, the appeal would dismissed.

R v Harrison (1993) 14 Cr App Rep (S) 419 (Court of Appeal: Steyn LJ, Pill and Wright JJ).

680 Costs—payment out of central funds—successful appeals against wasted costs orders

The Supreme Court Act 1981, s 51(1) provides that the costs of and incidental to all proceedings in the Court of Appeal, Civil Division, and in the High Court are in the discretion of the court, and the court has full power to determine by whom and to what extent the costs are to be paid.

A number of firms of solicitors were subject to orders made by the Crown Court that they pay all or part of the prosecution costs in criminal trials in which they had represented defendants. They successfully appealed against the orders and their costs in the appeals were subsequently ordered by the Court of Appeal to be paid out of central funds. The order was made by the Court of Appeal, Civil Division, in exercise of a power to do so that the court had held to be implied in the 1981 Act, s 51(1). On appeal by the Lord Chancellor's Department, *held*, s 51(1) covered the making of an order for the payment of costs by the Crown in those categories of proceedings in which the Crown as a party was amenable by statute to such an order, and did not apply to the Crown as a party to any other category of proceedings nor to civil litigation to which the Crown was not a party. In relation to the Court of Appeal, jurisdiction to make such orders had only been conferred on the Criminal Division. The Prosecution of Offences Act 1985, s 19A (which came into force after the present proceedings had begun) now governed wasted costs orders made against solicitors in criminal proceedings, but nothing in s 19A(2) permitted, let alone required, the Lord Chancellor to make regulations authorising awards of costs out of central funds. The Court of Appeal, Civil Division, therefore had no power to make the order for the solicitors' costs to be paid out of central funds and the appeal would be allowed.

Steele Ford & Newton (a firm) v Crown Prosecution Service [1993] 2 All ER 769 (House of Lords: Lords Griffiths, Bridge of Harwich, Jauncey of Tullichettle, Slynn of Hadley and Woolf).

Decision of Court of Appeal, sub nom *Holden & Co v Crown Prosecution Service (No 2)*, [1992] 1 WLR 407 (1991 Abr para 1883) reversed. *R v Bow Street Metropolitan Stipendiary Magistrate, ex p Mirror Group Newspapers Ltd* [1992] 1 WLR 412 (1992 Abr para 1978) and *Ex p Central Television plc* [1992] 1 WLR 4, CA overruled in so far as they relate to costs.

681 Costs—witnesses' allowances

Allowances for witnesses payable out of central funds are specified by the Lord Chancellor under the Costs in Criminal Cases (General) Regulations 1986, SI 1986/1335, in respect of witnesses attending at the instance of the accused, a private prosecutor or the court. Similarly, costs and expenses to which witnesses and others attending court at the instance of the Crown Prosecution Service are entitled are specified by the Attorney General under the Crown Prosecution Service (Witnesses' etc Allowances) Regulations 1988, SI 1988/1862. The allowances specified are the maximum amounts normally payable and the requirements subject to which payment is made are set out in the regulations and in circulars. In the table below, the principal regulations are identified by years only and the amounts set out in the table were those payable on 1 November 1993.

Witnesses other than Professional or Expert

	Hours	Amount	Current provision
Expenditure allowance			
1986, reg 18(1)(a)		*not specified*	
1988, reg 8(1)(a)		£43·90	CPS(19)
Loss of earnings or benefits			
1986, reg 18(1)(a)	up to 4 hours	£21·95	
	exceeding 4 hours	£43·90	JC(93)5
1988, reg 8(1)(b)	*as above*		CPS(19)
Subsistence allowance			
1986, reg 18(1)(b)	up to 5 hours	£2·10	
	5 to 10 hours	£4·25	
	exceeding 10 hours	£9·30	JC(93)5
1988, reg 9(1)	*as above*		CPS(19)
Overnight subsistence			
1986, reg 18(1)(b)	Inner London	£68·50	
	elsewhere	£63·15	JC(91)3
1988, reg 9(1)	*as above*		CPS(13)
Seaman missing ship			
1986, reg 22	loss allowance	£29·70	JC(88)2
	discretionary sum for maintenance		

Professional Witnesses

	Hours	Amount	Current provision
Locum allowance			
1986, reg 19	up to 4 hours	£78·30	
	exceeding 4 hours	£156·50	JC(93)4
1988, reg 6(1)(a)	*as above*		CPS(18)
Compensatory allowance			
1986, reg 19	up to 2 hours	£52·20	
	2 to 4 hours	£78·30	
	4 to 6 hours	£117·40	
	exceeding 6 hours	£156·50	JC(93)4
1988, reg 6(1)(b)	*as above*		CPS(18)
Overnight allowance			
1986, reg 21	Inner London	£59·90	
	elsewhere	£54·55	JC(91)3
1988, reg 7(1)	*as above*		CPS(8)
Written medical reports			
1986, reg 25(1)	(i) report in pursuance of request to which the Criminal Justice Act 1967, s 32(2) applies:		
	consultant	£55·30	
	other medical practitioner	£39·10	

		Amount	Current provision
(ii) higher fees (more than 2 hours work) daily maximum:			
consultant		£220·70	
other medical practitioner		£156·50	
(iii) examination and report on fitness for detention centre training		£26·30	JC(93)4

Medical practitioners' car mileage
1986, reg 25(2) *as "Standard rate mileage allowance" (see below)* JC(92)8

Expert Witnesses

Attendance allowance
1986, reg 20

(i) consultant medical practitioner, psychiatrist, pathologist:

| preparation | £52 to £75 per hour | |
| attendance at court | £255 to £369 per day | JC(92)1 |

(ii) fire expert (assessor), explosives:

| preparation | £41 to £58 per hour | |
| attendance in court | £207 to £296 per day | JC(92)1 |

(iii) forensic scientist (including questioned document examiner, eg handwriting expert), surveyor, accountant, engineer, medical practitioner, architect, veterinary surgeon:

| preparation | £33 to £673 per hour | |
| attendance in court | £166 to £365 per day | JC(92)1 |

(iv) fingerprint expert:

| preparation | £24 to £41 per hour | |
| attendance at court | £123 to £207 per day | JC(92)1 |

| (v) interpreter: | £14 to £24 per hour | |

| (minimum 3 hours for those regularly so employed) | | JC(92)1 |

Overnight allowance
1986, reg 21 *as for professional witnesses (see above)*
1988, reg 7 *as for professional witnesses (see above)*

Travel Expenses

Public transport rate mileage allowance

1986, reg 24	motor cycles	22·3p	JC(92)6
	motor cars	22·3p	JC(92)6
1988, reg 10(5)(b)	*as above*		CPS(17)

Standard rate mileage allowance
1986, reg 24

motor cycles up to	up to 5,000 miles	15·4p	
125 cc:	over 5,000 miles	5·5p	JC(91)2
motor cycles over	up to 5,000 miles	24·7p	
125 cc:	over 5,000 miles	8·1p	JC(91)2

motor cars:	up to 1,500 cc	1,501 cc 2,000 cc	over 2,000 cc	
up to 7,000 miles				
over 7,000 miles	35·7p	40p	43p	
	17p	21p	27p	JC(92)6

		Amount	Current provision
1988, reg 10(5)(a), (6)			
motor cycles:	up to 125 cc	15·4p	
	over 125 cc	24·7p	CPS(12)
motor cars:	35·7p		CPS(9)
Mileage allowance for passengers			
	first passenger	+2p	JC(87)3,
	other passengers	+1p	CPS(2)
Solicitors and counsel			
	travelling rates for solicitors and counsel conducting criminal legal aid work follow the rates allowed to medical practitioners		JC(87)3

CPS(2)	=	scales and costs determined by the Attorney General, effective from 5 December 1988
CPS(8)	=	scales and costs determined by the Attorney General, effective from 27 August 1990
CPS(9)	=	scales and costs determined by the Attorney General, effective from 26 November 1990
CPS(12)	=	scales and costs determined by the Attorney General, effective from 15 July 1991
CPS(13)	=	scales and costs determined by the Attorney General, effective from 1 September 1991
CPS(17)	=	scales and costs determined by the Attorney General, effective from 1 October 1992
CPS(18)	=	scales and costs determined by the Attorney General, effective from 19 July 1993
CPS(19)	=	scales and costs determined by the Attorney General, effective from 1 November 1993
JC(87)3	=	Lord Chancellor's Department circular JC(87)3, effective from 1 July 1987
JC(88)2	=	Lord Chancellor's Department circular JC(88)2, effective from 23 May 1988
JC(91)1	=	Lord Chancellor's Department circular JC(91)1, effective from 15 April 1991
JC(91)2	=	Lord Chancellor's Department circular JC(91)2, effective from 15 July 1991
JC(91)3	=	Lord Chancellor's Department circular JC(91)3, effective from 1 September 1991
JC(92)1	=	Lord Chancellor's Department circular JC(92)1, effective from 1 May 1992
JC(92)5	=	Lord Chancellor's Department circular JC(92)5, effective from 1 September 1992
JC(92)6	=	Lord Chancellor's Department circular JC(92)6, effective from 1 October 1992
JC(92)8	=	Lord Chancellor's Department circular JC(92)8, effective from 1 November 1992
JC(93)4	=	Lord Chancellor's Department circular JC(93)4, effective from 19 July 1993
JC(93)5	=	Lord Chancellor's Department circular JC(93)4, effective from 1 November 1993

682 Court of Appeal—Criminal Division—appeal allowed on one ground— unresolved grounds

The appellant was convicted of making an explosive substance contrary to the Explosive Substances Act 1883, s 4. He appealed on a number of grounds. The Court of Appeal quashed his appeal on a point of jurisdiction but did not consider the other grounds. The House of Lords allowed an appeal by the Crown and restored the appellant's conviction. The appellant then applied to the Court of Appeal to adjudicate on the unresolved grounds of appeal. The Court of Appeal stated that it had no power to hear the case, but subsequently did so on a reference by the Home Secretary. *Held,* as the judge had failed to deal adequately with certain matters in his summing up, and in the light of fresh evidence, the appellant's conviction was unsafe and unsatisfactory and the appeal would be allowed.

Where the Court of Appeal was prepared to allow an appeal on one ground, leaving others unresolved, the Crown ought to inform it before judgment whether it might wish to certify the point at issue for consideration by the House of Lords. The Court of Appeal could then decide whether to consider the other grounds at the same time, as a precaution. Parliament ought to grant the House of Lords the power either to consider unresolved grounds in addition to the certified point of law or to refer them to the Court of Appeal. Also, consideration ought to be given to granting the Court of Appeal power to reserve argument on unresolved grounds with liberty to apply.

R v Berry (1993) Times, 19 October, Independent, 6 October (Court of Appeal: Lord Taylor of Gosforth CJ, Otton and Kay JJ).

683   Criminal justice—Royal Commission proposals

The Royal Commission on Criminal Justice, under the chairmanship of Viscount Runciman, has published its report (Cm 2263) on the effectiveness of the criminal justice system in England and Wales. Chapter one contains the introduction to the report, which recommends the amendment of the Contempt of Court Act 1981, s 8 to permit research into the reasons juries give for their verdicts and the introduction of ethnic monitoring of the criminal justice system. Chapter two contains recommendations relating to identification evidence, the interviewing of witnesses and suspects, the powers of the police to request or require samples, police questioning after a suspect has been charged, the supervision of investigations and the investigation of serious and complex fraud cases. The recommendations include requiring the police to make a record of the description of a suspect as first given to them by a potential witness and disclosing this to the defence as soon as possible; giving the police power to take without consent non-intimate samples (with saliva being reclassified as a non-intimate sample) for the purposes of DNA analysis from all those arrested for serious crimes, whether or not DNA evidence is relevant to the particular offence; permitting the relevant DNA data to be retained for subsequent use if the person concerned is convicted and permitting the retention of any DNA samples obtained in the course of police investigations for the purposes of frequency data bases kept by an independent body (with appropriate safeguards to protect persons acquitted or not proceeded against).

Chapter three deals with safeguards for suspects, both inside and outside police stations. In relation to safeguards inside police stations, recommendations are made concerning the establishment of proper grounds for detention, detention time limits, the role of the custody officer, interpreters, the provision of legal advice, the recording of interviews, interview records, the role of appropriate adults, police surgeons and police discipline. Among these recommendations are the introduction of continuous video recording of all activities in custody offices and the areas surrounding police cells; the requirement that police ask a suspect to give reasons for waiving the right to legal advice; and the removal of the bar to disciplinary proceedings on the same facts where a police officer has been acquitted of criminal charges.

Chapter four deals with the right to silence, in particular silence in the face of police questioning, silence in investigations of serious and complex fraud, existing safeguards against unreliable confessions, the admissibility of confession evidence and the corroboration of confessions. It is recommended that when the prosecution case has been fully disclosed, defendants should be required to offer an answer to the charges made against them at the risk of adverse comment at trial on any new defence they then disclose or any departure from evidence they previously disclosed. There should also be a judicial warning in cases where confession evidence is involved. The role of the prosecution is examined in chapter five, especially the current performance of the Crown Prosecution Service, its relationship with the police at the investigative stage, its power to require the police to make further inquiries, the giving of power to the CPS to discontinue proceedings, its relationship with prosecution counsel, victims and other witnesses, and its role in the cautioning of offenders by the police.

Chapter six deals with mode of trial, committal proceedings and disclosure by the prosecution and the defence. In cases involving offences triable either way, it is recommended that the defendant should no longer have the right to insist on trial by jury. It is also recommended that committal hearings in their present form should be abolished; that the prosecution should generally supply to the defence copies of all material relevant to the offence or to the offender, whether or not they intend to rely on the material, and inform the defence of any other material obtained during the course of the inquiry into the offence; and that the substance of a defence should be disclosed in advance of the trial. Chapter seven makes recommendations concerning pre-trial reviews and preparatory hearings, and various aspects of sentencing. In particular, it is recommended that preparatory hearings take place in more complex cases; that the system of sentence discounts should be clearer; that judges should be able to indicate the highest sentence they would impose, at the point in the proceedings when they are asked to do so, on the basis of the facts put before them; and that discussions on the level of charge should take place as early as possible.

Chapter eight deals with trials and includes recommendations concerning the examination and cross-examination of witnesses, evidence as to previous convictions, the treatment of victims and witnesses, the selection of juries, the training of barristers, solicitors and judges, the management of courts and cases and court design. The admissibility of evidence relating to a defendant's previous convictions should not be restricted to cases where there is a striking similarity in the evidence; defence barristers should be allowed to meet witnesses before the trial; and in exceptional cases the prosecution or the defence should be able to apply for the selection of a jury containing up to three people from ethnic minority communities. Forensic science and other expert evidence is covered by chapter nine, in particular the organisation of forensic science facilities, the role of the prosecution and defence, and the use of scientific evidence both prior to and during the trial. The setting up of an advisory council to monitor the performance of forensic science laboratories is recommended, as is pre-trial discussion between the prosecution and defence in all cases where scientific evidence is being lead; if the defence intend to dispute the prosecution's scientific evidence, they must give advance notice of the grounds on which they wish to do so.

Chapter ten deals with the Court of Appeal and includes recommendations on applications for leave to appeal against convictions, the reconsideration of the jury's verdict where there is no fresh evidence and appeals to the House of Lords. It recommends that the present grounds of appeal should be replaced by a single ground under which the court is asked to decide whether the conviction is or may be unsafe, and that the Court of Appeal should be entitled to reconsider the verdict of a jury where there is no fresh evidence. Chapter eleven recommends the setting up of a new independent body to consider allegations of miscarriages of justice and, where appropriate, refer any such cases to the Court of Appeal. Chapter twelve contains a summary of the report's recommendations, and the report also contains a note of dissent by Professor Michael Zander concerning defence disclosure, pre-trial procedures and the powers of the Court of Appeal.

684 Criminal law

See CRIMINAL LAW.

685 Criminal record—disclosure for employment vetting purposes

The Home Office has published a consultation paper, *Disclosure of Criminal Records for Employment Vetting Purposes* (Cm 2319), in which it seeks views on the present practice of disclosing information held by the police for employment vetting purposes. The possibility of a public agency concerned with handling applications for vetting is canvassed, and also the possibility of such an agency being run privately. Views are also sought on the disclosure of "non-conviction" information and the disclosure of convictions for minor offences and cautions. At present, the police meet the cost of vetting checks, but a system of charging would be needed by any agency handling applications for vetting and the consultation paper views the possible effect of charging and seeks views on whether checks should be sought by prospective employers or the prospective employee. Comments are sought on the possible enactment of legislation relating to checks of criminal records and on the information that might be made available in different circumstances. The consultation paper also considers whether the exceptions under the Rehabilitation of Offenders Act 1974 are so extensive as to undermine the effectiveness of the Act and whether those exceptions should correspond to the areas of employment subject to vetting. Finally, consideration is given to the possibility of reciprocal arrangements with other countries relating to vetting checks.

686 Crown Prosecution Service—disclosure of unused material

See *R v Crown Prosecution Service, ex p Warby*, para 13.

687 Custody—time limit—expiry—re-arrest

The defendants appeared before magistrates on charges of attempted murder and were remanded in custody pending their appearance in the Crown Court. The charges of attempted murder were later withdrawn, and charges under the Offences Against the Persons Act 1861, s 18 were preferred. The defendants wished to have an old-style committal. The committal proceedings were fixed for a date outside the custody time limit laid down by the Prosecution of Offences (Custody Time Limits) Regulations 1987, SI 1987/299, reg 4. An unsuccessful application for an extension of the time limit was made, but the justices held that the s 18 offences attracted a new set of custody limits. The defendants sought judicial review of the decision. *Held*, as a matter of construction of the regulations and as a matter of principle, the 1987 Regulations applied so as to permit the running of a new custody time limit from the date of preferment of a charge of a new offence. The application would accordingly be dismissed.

R v Waltham Forest Justices, ex p Lee (1993) 97 Cr App Rep 287 (Queen's Bench Division: Rose LJ and Pill J). *R v Great Yarmouth Magistrates, ex p Thomas, Davis and Darlington* [1992] Crim LR 116, CA (1992 Abr para 639) applied.

688 Custody—time limit—extension

The applicants had been charged with conspiracy to import drugs and were in custody awaiting trial. Prior to the expiry of the custody time limit, the prosecution made an application to the Crown Court for the custody time limit to be extended until the trial although it was established that the earliest trial date available was three months away. The judge exercised his powers under the Prosecution of Offences Act 1985, s 22(3) to grant a 14-day extension on the ground that further effort should be made to fix an earlier trial date. On an application for judicial review of the judge's decision, *held*, the court might grant an extension under s 22(3) where it was satisfied that there was good and sufficient cause for doing so. In the present case, to extend the custody time limit for 14 days for the possibility that an earlier date might be found, when the information before the court was that no date for trial was available for another three months, could not be regarded as "good and sufficient cause". The judge's order was unreasonable and the application would be allowed.

R v Crown Court at Maidstone, ex p Schulz (1992) 157 JP 601 (Queen's Bench Division: Beldam LJ and Tudor Evans J).

689 Drug trafficking—agreement with Ecuador

An agreement between the United Kingdom and the Republic of Ecuador on mutual assistance in relation to drug trafficking was signed in Quito in May 1992 and entered into force on 1 March 1993 (Cm 2162). Both countries have agreed to assist each other in their investigations and proceedings in relation to illicit drug trafficking, including the tracing, restraining and confiscation of the proceeds and instruments of drug trafficking. The agreement sets out the contents of requests for assistance. So far as domestic law permits, any request will be complied with by the requested party. Assistance under the agreement may include the production of information and documents, taking evidence, and searching for, seizing and delivering relevant materials. The parties may request the restraint or seizure of property in order to ensure that it is available for enforcing a confiscation order. Assistance may, however, be refused if compliance would seriously impair the requested party's sovereignty, security, national interest or other essential interest; or where it would prejudice an investigation or proceedings within the territory of the requested party, prejudice the safety of any person or impose an excessive burden on resources; or where the action sought is contrary to the principles of its domestic law; or where the request relates to an offence in respect of which the person concerned has been finally acquitted or pardoned, or has served any sentence imposed and any order made as a result of the conviction has been satisfied. Confidentiality may be imposed on either party to the agreement at the request of the other party.

690 Drug trafficking offences—recovery of proceeds—jurisdiction of High Court

See SENTENCING.

691 Evidence—case statements—Serious Fraud Office inquiry

The defendant was charged with theft and false accounting. Following the serving of case statements by both parties, the judge ruled that the prosecution, the Serious Fraud Office (SFO), ought not to serve more notices of further evidence without leave of the court. At a hearing for leave to serve a substantial quantity of further evidence, it became apparent that a number of witnesses whose statements had already been served had been re-interviewed following delivery of the defence case statement. The judge ruled that the SFO were not entitled to make use of a defence case statement by re-interviewing prosecution witnesses and asking further questions arising out of the case statement unless the SFO had drawn up a list of questions and obtained leave to ask those questions. The SFO appealed, submitting that the judge had no powers to curtail or circumscribe the powers of the director of the SFO. *Held*, the Criminal Justice Act 1987 did not give the judge the power to limit or supervise the director's access to witnesses. His powers related to the admission of evidence and conduct of the trial, not to the investigation process. The director of the SFO was responsible to the Attorney General. If he were to err in his conduct of an investigation, the Attorney General would be answerable to Parliament for such an error and the trial judge would have power to exclude evidence. Accordingly, the appeal would be allowed.

R v Nadir [1993] 4 All ER 513 (Court of Appeal: Lord Taylor of Gosforth CJ, Ognall and Sedley JJ).

692   Evidence—evidence of good character—accused's spent convictions

On an appeal against conviction of a drug offence, it has been held that although a judge has a discretion to allow a defendant who has spent convictions to be put forward to the jury as a person of good character, the jury must not be misled and, in particular, it must not be told that the defendant has no previous convictions.

R v O'Shea (1993) Times, 8 June (Court of Appeal: Staughton LJ, Popplewell and Laws JJ).

693   Evidence—evidence of good character—direction to jury

The defendant, in breach of an undertaking not to assault, molest or communicate with the mother of his child, attacked her with a knife, cutting her face. He was convicted of wounding with intent but appealed on the ground that the judge had failed to mention his good character in the summing up to the jury. *Held*, unless the trial judge reached the clear conclusion that the defendant was not a man of good character the standard direction should be given. If necessary, the direction could be tailored to present a fair and balanced picture to the jury by including information such as, in this case, the fact that the defendant was in breach of an undertaking. Provided the difference between good and bad character was adequately explained, it should then be left to the jury to weigh up the evidence. In the present case, it was not certain that the jury would have reached the verdict it did if an adequate explanation of the relevance of good character had been made. Accordingly, the appeal would be allowed.

R v Micallef (1993) Times, 26 November (Court of Appeal: Neill LJ, Buckley J and Sir Michael Davies).

694   Evidence—child abuse—evidence of child—reliability

At the defendant's trial for indecent assault, evidence of the victim, an eight-year-old girl, was admitted. On his appeal against conviction, the defendant contended that such evidence should not have been admitted because an interview with the child, in which she made statements to a police officer, had been conducted oppressively and in breach of the guidelines in the Report of the Inquiry into Child Abuse in Cleveland. *Held*, although there had been pressure on the child, it was not pressure requiring her to give a particular answer. The guidelines set out in the report, even though they had not been given statutory effect, should be regarded as expert advice as to the best practice to be followed for the purpose of ensuring that a child's evidence was reliable. If those guidelines were not observed, a judge or jury might have grounds for considering with particular care whether the child was reliable. The jury had not seen the video recording of the interview but had formed its view of the child's reliability from observing her through the video link at the trial. Defence counsel had not requested that the jury see the recording of the interview doubtless because he did not believe the child's evidence to be tainted by the way the interview was conducted. The appeal would be dismissed.

R v Dunphy (1993) Times, 2 June (Court of Appeal: Staughton LJ, Popplewell and Laws JJ).

695   Evidence—child abuse—sexual abuse—standard of proof—only one possible abuser

It has been held that although the standard of proof when deciding whether a child has been sexually abused may be less than the balance of probabilities used when establishing the identity of the perpetrator, this does not apply when there is only one possible perpetrator. In that case, a finding that there has been sexual abuse will automatically establish the perpetrator's guilt and the higher burden of proof must therefore apply.

Re W (Minors) (Sexual Abuse: Standard of Proof) (1993) Times, 1 December (Court of Appeal: Balcombe and Beldam LJJ).

696 Evidence—co-accused—evidence against accused—evidence before sentence

The appellant was convicted of aggravated burglary, kidnapping, burglary and arson. He appealed against his conviction on the ground that it had been improper to call the co-accused to give evidence against him at his committal proceedings and trial before the co-accused had been sentenced. *Held*, provided that the committal proceedings of the appellant and the co-accused were held separately, the Crown was entitled to call one to give evidence against the other. Whether a particular co-accused ought to be sentenced before giving evidence against another was a matter for the discretion of the judge. In the present case, the judge had been manifestly right in his exercise of that discretion. Accordingly, the appeal would be dismissed.

R v Palmer (1993) Times, 5 October (Court of Appeal: Russell LJ, Waterhouse and Potts JJ).

697 Evidence—complainant's previous inconsistent statement—defendant's right to call rebuttal evidence

The defendant was convicted of rape. At the trial, the victim, a schoolgirl, said that she delayed in reporting the rape because she was frightened of the boys involved. However, when interviewed by a teacher on the afternoon of the incident she had denied that she was frightened of any repercussions. During cross-examination, the victim denied making that statement. The judge refused to allow the defence to call the teacher. He ruled that the evidence would be inadmissible because it would go only to credit and in cross-examination as to credit the answer had to be accepted and no rebuttal evidence could be called. On appeal, *held*, there was authority that in sexual cases the distinction between what went to an issue and what went only to credit was quite fine. Although the victim's reason for delaying her complaint went only to her credit on the main issue, this was the first time that the element of fear was introduced in the case. The judge ought to have granted an adjournment to allow the teacher to give evidence. Although that evidence would have contradicted the victim, it was of doubtful benefit to the defendant as the jury might have decided that the victim's initial reluctance to report the incident was due to embarrassment. Whilst this complaint alone was not sufficient to interfere with the conviction, the defence had raised other questions and, taken together, these raised doubts as to whether the conviction was safe and satisfactory. Accordingly, the appeal would be allowed.

R v Gibson [1993] Crim LR 453 (Court of Appeal: Staughton LJ, Waterhouse and McCullough JJ).

698 Evidence—confession—breach of police code of practice

Police officers failed to take a contemporaneous note of an interview with the appellant at his home. They produced a lengthy note of confession, compiled from their pooled recollections, two hours later and gave the appellant a brief opportunity to read it. On his appeal against conviction of possession of drugs and a shotgun, the appellant contended that the confession should not have been admitted. *Held*, contradictory reasons for the police officers' failure to record a contemporaneous note of the interview had been advanced at the voir dire and subsequently. A contemporaneous note was required in order to provide the court with the most cogent version of events. There had been a significant and substantial breach of the Code of Practice, Code C, para 10.5, providing for a situation where there was a break in questioning of a person under caution. The appellant had not even been asked whether he agreed with the note. The confession should have been excluded. Accordingly, the appeal would be allowed and the convictions quashed.

R v Joseph [1993] Crim LR 206 (Court of Appeal: McCowan LJ, Waterhouse and Brooke JJ).

699 Evidence—confession—confession of mentally handicapped person

The defendant was charged with burglary. At the trial, a dispute arose as to whether the defendant was mentally handicapped within the meaning of the Police and Criminal Evidence Act 1984, s 77(3). Comparisons were made between the mental capacity of the defendant in the instant case and that of a defendant in another unconnected case. Following his conviction the defendant appealed. *Held*, it was inappropriate to attempt to take figures produced by intelligence tests in one case and to apply them to another in order to decide whether to exclude confession evidence. Each case had to be looked at on its own facts. Accordingly, the appeal would be allowed.

R v Kenny (1993) Times, 27 July (Court of Appeal: Hirst LJ, Ian Kennedy and Hidden JJ).

700 Evidence—confession—dishonesty in confession—directions to jury

The defendant was a bankrupt who continued his business under the name of another company. At his trial on charges of obtaining property by deception, it was alleged that he had obtained money by making a series of false representations. Although he did not give evidence at the trial, he told the jury through his counsel that he had told lies during an interview with the police. On appeal against his conviction, *held*, except in cases where lies have been relied upon as corroboration or as confirmation of identification evidence, it was not as a matter of law incumbent upon a judge to give a direction as to the significance of lies told by the accused. Such a direction was, however, commonly given and its effect was that the defendant had admitted that he had told lies to the police and the jury were entitled to ask themselves why he did so. The mere fact that a defendant told lies was not to be taken as evidence of his guilt; it depended on the motive for the lies. If the jury thought that there was, or might be, some innocent explanation for the lies, then they should pay no attention to them. If they were sure the lies were relevant to the allegation made against the defendant, but the lies had not been prompted by an innocent motive, then those lies would be evidence going to proof of his guilt. Where a direction was not given the judge had to be careful not to suggest that dishonesty either to the police or in court was tantamount to establishing the element of dishonesty which had to be proved in the case. In the present circumstances, it would undoubtedly have been better if the judge had explained to the jury the significance of lies told at the interview. Accordingly, the appeal would be allowed.

R v Sharp [1993] 3 All ER 225 (Court of Appeal: Stuart-Smith LJ, Ward and May JJ).

701 Evidence—confession—recorded confession of co-accused

The defendants, A and B, were convicted of robbery and their co-accused, C, of handling. During the trial, C led the evidence of her father and he was allowed to produce a tape recording of a conversation in which A admitted that he and B fought with the victim, ended up in possession of the victim's rings, and that B gave the rings to C when he thought the police were going to detain them. Despite defence objections, the trial judge ruled that the evidence could be led because it was a confession admissible against A and its admission was not adverse to the fairness of the proceedings. In summing up, the judge told the jury that the tape was only evidence against A and was to be disregarded in relation to B. The defendants appealed, contending that the admission of the evidence amounted to a material irregularity. *Held*, the defence had not challenged the truth of the evidence, nor had they contended that A's confession was involuntary. The alleged irregularity was that the evidence was inadmissible hearsay merely because it was adduced by C. At issue was whether it was permissible for a defendant to adduce confession evidence against a co-defendant which had not been adduced by the prosecution. A defendant was entitled to lead admissible evidence relevant to the proving of the case against a co-defendant if this strengthened his own case and thus A's allegation of material irregularity was unsound. Since an admission was only evidence against the maker and did not become part of the general evidence, it followed that there was no material irregularity in respect of B either. Accordingly, the appeal would be dismissed.

R v Campbell [1993] Crim LR 448 (Court of Appeal: Stuart-Smith LJ, Hobhouse and Sedley JJ).

702 Evidence—confession—remand in police custody—secretly taped confession

Two defendants were charged with robbery. The police requested that they be remanded in police custody so that they could take part in an identification parade. After allaying the defendants' suspicions, the police placed them in a cell together. The cell contained bugging equipment and the police recorded a series of conversations in which the defendants admitted the offences. The tape recordings were admitted in evidence at the trial and the defendants were convicted. On their appeals against conviction, *held*, the justices had not been misled by the police giving only one reason for the remand and making no reference to their intention to put the defendants together in a bugged cell. The Magistrates' Courts Act 1980, s 128(8)(a) required that the justices be told only whatever was directly pertinent to the existence of a need for the defendants to be detained at the police station for the purpose of inquiries into other offences. The police were not under a duty to inform the defendants' solicitors of their plan to bug the cell. In co-operating with the investigating officers, the custody officer was not allowing those officers to usurp his functions so as to be in breach of the Police and Criminal Evidence Act 1984, s 36(5). Neither was there a breach of the Code of Practice, Code C, para 8.1, which provides that so far as practicable no more than one person should be detained in each cell. As the plan was not otherwise unlawful, it was undoubtedly necessary for the defendants to be placed in the same cell. The right of silence did not extend to the defendants being protected from any opportunity to speak incriminatingly to each other if they chose to do so. The tactics employed by the police ought only to be used in serious cases and nothing was to be done oppressively or so as to render unreliable any admissions made. However, the confessions in the present case were reliable and the appeals would be dismissed.

R v Bailey [1993] 3 All ER 513 (Court of Appeal: Simon Brown LJ, Popplewell and Rattee JJ). *R v Ali* (1991) Times, 19 February, CA followed.

703 Evidence—corroboration—co-defendant's evidence—direction to jury

The appellant was convicted of murder and attempted murder together with her son, a co-defendant. She appealed against her conviction on the ground that, in relation to the evidence of her son, the judge had not given the jury a full corroboration warning appropriate to the evidence of an accomplice. *Held*, English law did not recognise a rule requiring a full corroboration direction in respect of a co-defendant's evidence. A witness was treated as an accomplice if called by the Crown but not if he gave like evidence as a co-defendant. There were three practical reasons for maintaining this distinction: (1) the prosecution had the burden of proof and therefore, if they called a witness of doubtful reliability, it was necessary that the jury be warned of the danger of convicting on that witness's evidence if it was uncorroborated; (2) where one defendant gave evidence that implicated another, it would be unfair for the jury to be given a full corroboration direction as it would devalue that defendant's evidence on his own behalf. A milder form of warning to the jury to have in mind that the defendant might have an axe to grind steered a middle course of fairness; (3) the complication involved in requiring a judge to give full corroboration directions in respect of co-defendants implicating each other would be likely to confuse and bewilder a jury. Since the son was not to be treated as an accomplice, his evidence was capable of corroborating the evidence of a prosecution witness who had been convicted of the same crime. Accordingly, the appeal would be dismissed.

The court recommended that there be a review of the law of corroboration which had become arcane, technical and difficult to convey to juries.

R v Cheema (1993) Times, Independent, 6 October (Court of Appeal: Lord Taylor of Gosforth CJ, Buckley and Hidden JJ).

704 Evidence—corroboration—risk of contamination in mutually corroborative evidence

The appellant was charged with five counts of indecent assault, allegedly committed on four women with whom he worked. The trial judge directed the jury that the complainants' evidence was capable of offering mutual corroboration, and the appellant was convicted on all counts. He appealed against conviction on the ground that the direction had been erroneous, contending there was a real risk that any one of the complainants' accounts might have been contaminated by any of the others. *Held*, the appellant had based his submission on the fact that, with one exception, the women's complaints had all been made at the same time, and that, except for one case, the complaints were made a considerable time after the incidents had allegedly taken place. Those circumstances gave rise to a real possibility that the complaints which formed the basis of the prosecution case were not truly independent of one another, and as the value of potentially corroborative evidence depended upon its being independent of the complaint which needed to be corroborated the judge had not had a discretion to let that evidence go before the jury. The convictions could not stand and, accordingly, the appeal would be allowed.

R v Ananthanarayanan (1993) 156 JP 1081 (Court of Appeal: Steyn LJ, Rougier and Laws JJ).

705 Evidence—cross-examination—character of accused—evidence adduced by co-accused

At the trial of the appellant and his co-defendant for aggravated burglary, neither of them gave evidence but both called alibi witnesses. They were both convicted. On his appeal against conviction, the appellant contended that his co-defendant should not have been permitted to cross-examine a prosecution witness for the purpose of eliciting the appellant's previous convictions. *Held*, questions tending to show that a defendant had previously committed criminal offences were, in general, inadmissible not primarily for the reason that they were prejudicial but because they were irrelevant. One defendant was not allowed to adduce evidence of the bad character of a co-defendant except by asking him about his previous convictions in the circumstances expressly provided for by the Criminal Evidence Act 1898, s 1(f) (ie where the defendant had asked questions of the prosecution witnesses with a view to establishing his own good character, or had given evidence of his own good character, or the nature or conduct of his defence was such as to involve imputations on the character of the prosecutor or witness for the prosecution, or he had given evidence against a co-defendant), or by leading or eliciting evidence of his co-defendant's previous convictions when they were relevant to the defendant's defence. At the stage of the trial at which the prosecution witness was cross-examined, no evidence had been given against the co-defendant, the appellant had not been called as a witness and the questions asked by his counsel had not been directed against the co-defendant; they were calculated only to establish that the latter shared any motive the appellant might have had for committing the offence, and that each of the prosecution witnesses had wrongly accused the appellant of participation in the offence either because the co-defendant was there and the witness associated the appellant with him or because the witness had a motive for accusing the appellant. The evidence of the appellant's previous convictions should not have been admitted and, accordingly, the appeal would be allowed and the conviction quashed.

R v Knutton (1992) 97 Cr App Rep 115 (Court of Appeal: Leggatt LJ, Rougier and Sedley JJ). Dictum of Devlin J in *R v Miller* [1952] 2 All ER 667 at 668 applied; *R v Neale* (1977) 65 Cr App Rep 304, CA, and *R v Douglass* (1989) 89 Cr App Rep 264, CA (1989 Abr para 532) considered.

706 Evidence—defendant—decision not to enter witness box

A police officer was convicted of unlawful wounding. At his trial, he did not give evidence and only one witness was called for the defence. He appealed against conviction on the grounds that he had been badly advised and poorly represented. He contended that he was unaware of the adverse consequences of his failure to give evidence on his own behalf and that a number of witnesses for the defence were not called. *Held,* the appellant's allegations were unfounded and the conduct of his counsel and solicitors was not defective. However, where a defendant decided not to enter the witness box, counsel should have that decision recorded and cause the defendant to sign the record and indicate that he made the decision of his own will bearing in mind the advice, if any, of his counsel.

R v Bevan (1993) 157 JP 1121 (Court of Appeal: Watkins LJ, Macpherson and Turner JJ).

707 Evidence—disclosure—duty of prosecution—guidelines

The defendant was charged with assault with intent to rob. The charge was based on identification evidence. The prosecution failed to disclose to the defence before the trial a photograph taken by the police of the defendant after his arrest and a crime report containing the first details given to the police by the victim. Following his conviction the defendant appealed. *Held,* in identification cases such photographs and crime reports were disclosable under the general common law duty of disclosure as explained in *R v Ward* [1993] 1 WLR 619, CA (1992 Abr para 662). There was no public interest immunity attached to such photographs and crime reports and therefore, they ought to be forwarded routinely by the police to the Crown Prosecution Service. Further, both prosecution and defence counsel ought to be aware of the duty to disclose and if necessary the trial judge ought to be asked for an appropriate order. Accordingly, the appeal would be allowed.

R v Fergus (1993) Times, 6 June (Court of Appeal: Steyn LJ, Hutchison and Rougier JJ).

708 Evidence—disclosure—prosecution evidence—advance disclosure to defence

Jamaica

The defendants were tried separately on charges relating to drugs and the receiving of stolen property in the resident magistrate's court. The Jamaican constitution made provision relating to a fair hearing and the right to adequate facilities for the preparation of a defence. However, in accordance with general practice, the statements of prosecution witnesses were not disclosed to the defence and, although at the beginning of each trial prosecution counsel outlined their case, the defence did not know the detail of the prosecution evidence. The defendants were convicted and their appeals against conviction were dismissed. On the question of the validity of the practice as to disclosure of prosecution evidence, *held,* it was desirable for copies of prosecution statements to be provided to the defence prior to the commencement of a trial where practicable, particularly in serious and complex proceedings. Where the offence was a trivial summary offence and where the issues were simple, the provision of statements prior to trial was less important. Although the constitution did not require a defendant to be provided with copies of prosecution statements in every case, in the light of the seriousness of the offences tried by the resident magistrate a defendant ought to be provided with copies of those statements reasonably necessary for the preparation of his defence. The established practice was therefore inappropriate. Where a request was made for the disclosure of the statements in a case, if it was not a case involving only petty offences, the request had to be carefully considered. If there were no circumstances making it undesirable to do so, the preferable course in the interests of justice was to disclose the statement.

Vincent v The Queen; Franklyn v The Queen [1993] 1 WLR 862 (Privy Council: Lords Templeman, Lane, Ackner, Goff of Chieveley and Woolf).

709 Evidence—disclosure—public interest immunity

In the course of applications for leave to appeal against convictions of murder in which the prosecution sought a ruling about disclosing a document, the Court of Appeal gave the following guidance on the approach to be adopted when the prosecution wished to rely on public interest immunity or sensitivity to justify non-disclosure of evidence. (1) Subject to certain discretionary exceptions, the prosecution had a duty to make available to the defence all unused material if it had some bearing on the offence or offences charged and the surrounding circumstances of the case. (2) If the prosecution wished to rely on public interest immunity or sensitivity to justify non-disclosure, it had, whenever possible, to give notice to the defence that it was applying for a ruling by the court and to indicate to the defence at least the category of material it held, and the defence had to have the opportunity to make representations to the court. (3) If the disclosure of the category of the material in question would in effect reveal that which the prosecution contended should not in the public interest be revealed, the prosecution should still notify the defence that an application to the court was to be made but the category of the material need not be specified and the application would be ex parte. If the court, on hearing the application, considered that the normal procedure under (2) above ought to have been followed, it would so order. If not, it would rule on the ex parte application. (4) In a highly exceptional case, where even to reveal the fact that an ex parte application was to be made might stultify the application, the prosecution had to apply to the court ex parte without notice to the defence. If the court, on hearing the application, considered that at least notice of the application should have been given to the defence or even that the normal inter partes procedure should have been adopted, it would so order. The court had the role of monitoring the views of the prosecution and deciding whether sensitive material should be disclosed.

R v Davis; R v Rowe; R v Johnson [1993] 2 All ER 643 (Court of Appeal: Lord Taylor of Gosforth CJ, Owen and Curtis JJ).

Certain documentary evidence had been covered by a ministerial certificate, signed by the Home Secretary who had objected to the use of the documents in question, in trial. The Divisional Court had given guidance to the Crown Prosecution Service on the voluntary disclosure of documents which were subject to public interest immunity. In the present situation the documents would have enabled the court to resolve a dispute thereby ending the case against the applicant. On an application by the applicant for discovery, the question arose as to whether the Crown Prosecution Service could take a decision to disclose documents covered by the immunity without referring to the court for a ruling on the matter. *Held*, the public interest in not disclosing the documents was that any information which might be useful to criminals should not be revealed, and that co-operation between authorities in different jurisdictions should not be inhibited. The public interest in such cases should be weighed against any public interest in the administration of justice. In criminal cases the public interest was subject to special considerations since the liberty of individuals was at stake. The public interest in the use of documents by the prosecution would never have the same weight as the defendant's right to establish his innocence, or of furthering his defence, as it was more important that an innocent man be acquitted than a guilty man be convicted. The prosecution had the ability to withdraw the case rather than disclose the documents. However, although disclosure could be refused on the basis that the documents belonged to a class to which there were no exceptions, disclosure in this case would be ordered on the basis that the claim of risk to co-operation between different jurisdictions had been weakened by prior voluntary disclosures. The Crown Prosecution Service was not obliged to seek the court's ruling in every criminal case where documents would normally be disclosed, except for the public interest immunity, however the express written approval of the Treasury Solicitor should be obtained prior to voluntary disclosure. When applying for approval, copies of the documents intended to be disclosed should be submitted, and the public interest immunity class into which they fell should be identified. The Crown Prosecution Service should also indicate the relevance of the documents to the proceedings in which it was proposed to disclose them. The Treasury Solicitor should consult other government departments, if relevant, and be satisfied that the balance fell clearly in favour of disclosure. Factors to be taken into account included; the class of documents, their materiality to the proceedings and the extent to which disclosure would affect the public interest in the integrity of the class claim. The Treasury Solicitor should keep a record of all approvals given in relation to voluntary disclosures so that the integrity of the class claim was not weakened by repeated disclosures. Accordingly, the application would be allowed.

R v Horseferry Road Magistrates Court, ex p Bennett (No 2) [1994] 1 All ER 289 (Queen's Bench Division: Simon Brown LJ and Buckley J).

710 Evidence—documentary evidence—computer printouts

A building society inadvertently credited the defendant's account with a sum greater than that which he had paid in. A number of withdrawals were subsequently made in quick succession from different towns leading to the defendant's conviction of theft by fraudulent use of his cash card. The issue on appeal was whether evidence in the form of computer printouts or till rolls should have been admitted. *Held*, on the information available the evidence was that two computers, the local branch computer and the mainframe computer, were involved in the withdrawal and debiting process, though to the surprise of the court, none of the prosecution witnesses had demonstrated an understanding of how the mainframe computer worked. To assist in the court's understanding of the charge, evidence had been required to explain how each of the relevant pieces of information on the till roll had come into existence including a description of the function and operation of the mainframe computer which included the information stored within it in order to validate a transaction and to enable an appropriate record to be made on the till roll. None of those matters had been covered competently by any of the witnesses and the judge had had to grapple with possibly incorrect information. There had been a failure to adduce adequate evidence to allow the court to properly rule that the till rolls were admissible evidence and in the absence of the till rolls the charge could not be proved. Accordingly, the appeal would be allowed.

R v Cochrane [1993] Crim LR 48 (Court of Appeal: McCowan LJ, Waterhouse and Brooke JJ).

711 Evidence—documentary evidence—construction of document— representations

The defendant was charged with obtaining services and pecuniary advantage by deception. The central issue was whether a driver's declaration form, completed by the defendant for the purposes of obtaining insurance, contained a false representation, express or implied, that he had never been disqualified, and whether this was a question of fact for the jury or whether the construction of the document was a question of law for the judge. The trial judge ruled that the construction of the form was a question of law for him. Consequently counsel for the defendant was denied the opportunity to address the jury on the construction of the document. Following his conviction the defendant appealed. *Held*, where the central question was whether a defendant had made a representation or not and if so whether it was false then both aspects of that question were questions of fact for the jury. Counsel for the defendant was entitled to address the jury on the question whether the document contained a representation, express or implied that the defendant had never been disqualified and as such the failure to allow counsel to do so was a material irregularity. However, the meaning of the document was transparently clear, the defendant had suffered no injustice and the proviso to the Criminal Appeal Act 1968, s 2(1) would apply. Accordingly, the appeal would be dismissed.

R v Adams [1993] Crim LR 525 (Court of Appeal: Lloyd LJ, Potter and Buckley JJ). *R v Spens* [1991] 1 WLR 624 (1991 Abr para 604) considered.

712 Evidence—documentary evidence—excluded material

The Police and Criminal Evidence Act 1984, s 11 provides that subject to certain provisions, "excluded material" means personal records which a person has acquired or created in the course of any trade, business, profession and which he holds in confidence. Section 12 defines "personal records" as documentary and other records concerning an individual (whether living or dead) who can be identified from them and relating to his physical or mental health.

Following a murder in the proximity of a mental hospital, police believed that they should interview a person who was an in-patient at the hospital at the time of the murder. They sought to inspect the records kept of patients' movements. A consultant psychiatrist at the hospital opposed the application on the ground that those records constituted excluded material within ss 11, 12, as they consisted of personal records relating to the mental health of individuals who could be identified. At first instance, an order was made granting the police access to the records. The consultant sought judicial review, by way of certiorari, of the decision. *Held*, the issue turned upon the meaning of "relating to his physical and mental health". In the analogous context of discovery in civil cases, "relating to any matter in question" had been given a wide meaning. The records relating to physical or mental health were not confined to clinical, nursing or surgical notes of treatment. The definition was expressly directed to the identifiability of the patient from the records. The records in question did relate to the mental health of the person or persons who could be identified, and were therefore excluded material within ss 11, 12. The application would accordingly be allowed.

R v Crown Court at Cardiff, ex p Kellam (1993) Times, 3 May (Queen's Bench Division: Evans LJ and Morland J).

713 Evidence—documentary evidence—refreshing memory from notes—unverified note

The defendants were charged with being knowingly concerned in the fraudulent evasion of value added tax at their restaurant and take-away food business. The case against them was based on observations by customs officers of the number of customers using the business. The officers worked in pairs, one observing and calling out what he saw and the other writing it down. The writer did not see what the observer saw and the observer did not see what the writer wrote down, although one of the officers testified that when observing he looked up from time to time and noted his colleague recording a large number of matters. At the defendants' trial, the judge ruled that the officers were entitled to refresh their memories from their written logs. The officers did not refer to the logs themselves, but did refer to schedules drawn from the logs. The defendants were convicted. On appeal, *held*, the judge had gone too far in holding that the officer's observation of entries being recorded amounted to verification of the logs. There was no verification by the observer of what the writer had written down, and therefore the use by the officers of the schedules drawn from the logs to refresh their memories was a material irregularity in the trial. Accordingly, the appeals would be allowed.

R v Eleftheriou (1993) Independent, 26 February, Times, 2 March (Court of Appeal: Nolan LJ, Swinton Thomas and Colman JJ). *R v Kelsey* (1981) 74 Cr App Rep 213, CA (1982 Abr para 779) followed.

714 Evidence—documentary evidence—supplier of statement outside United Kingdom—consular official

The defendant, a consular official, was charged with unlawfully importing cocaine into the United Kingdom. At her trial, she contended that she thought she had been smuggling emeralds, and she sought to introduce in evidence a letter from another consular official which supported her contention. When objection was taken to the production of the letter, the defendant contended that it was admissible as, because of the writer's diplomatic status, she was immune to process and therefore at all times "outside the United Kingdom" for the purposes of the Criminal Justice Act 1988, s 23(2)(b)(i). *Held*, the requirements of s 23(2)(b)(i) were clear: they required the physical presence of the person outside the United Kingdom and the difficulty of securing attendance. The witness was at all times within the United Kingdom: to contend that she was outside did not give any effect to what Parliament intended. The appeal would accordingly be refused.

R v Jiminez-Paez [1993] Crim LR 596 (Court of Appeal: Russell LJ, Morland and Mantell JJ).

715 Evidence—effect of offence on victim—disclosure to court—duty of Crown

The appellant pleaded guilty to three counts of indecently assaulting two young girls and was sentenced to four years' imprisonment on each count to run concurrently. He appealed against sentence on the ground that Crown counsel had given evidence as to the effect of the appellant's conduct on the victims without calling proper evidence, and that the judge had wrongly allowed himself to be influenced by that evidence. *Held*, counsel for the Crown had acted improperly in making emotive statements as to the effects of the assaults without informing defence counsel that such submissions were to be made. If such evidence was admissible, it had to be made available in a proper form such as a witness statement, thereby allowing defence counsel to deal with that evidence in a manner which ensured the judge would be fully informed and not influenced by the Crown's evidence alone. Accordingly, the appeal would be allowed to the extent that the sentence would be reduced to three years' imprisonment.

R v Hobstaff (1993) 14 Cr App Rep (S) 605 (Court of Appeal: McCowan LJ and Ognall J).

716 Evidence—evidence irregularly obtained—witness statements

See *Sharpe v DPP*, para 2179.

717 Evidence—evidence of interview—breach of code of practice—interview by customs officers—irregularly obtained evidence

The defendant was a Nigerian national whose bags were searched by customs officers upon his arrival at an airport. The officers discovered packets of cocaine hidden in his luggage although the defendant was not informed of the officers' discovery as it was hoped he would lead them to others involved in drug trafficking. The defendant gave his consent to undergo a body search, during which he was asked a number of questions. At no point was he cautioned or made aware of his entitlement to legal advice and the conversation was not recorded contemporaneously. A short while afterwards, the defendant was formally arrested and interviewed in accordance with the procedural code for interviewing suspects. The judge at first instance ruled that although there had been breaches of the procedural code in the conduct of the initial conversation, the defendant would not be unfairly prejudiced by the admission of the conversation in evidence. On appeal it was held that the case was analogous to *R v Christou* in which conversations held by undercover police officers were found admissible. On further appeal, *held*, the present case was distinguishable from *Christou* in that the customs officers were in uniform and conducted the conversation whilst performing a body search and had therefore not conversed with the defendant on equal terms. Customs officers had to either follow the codes of procedure and issue a caution, or avoid asking questions in relation to an offence. The conversation was therefore inadmissible evidence. Nevertheless, if the conversation had been excluded the jury could have come to no other verdict than the one they did. Accordingly, the appeal would be dismissed.

   R v Okafor (1993) Times, 10 November (Court of Appeal: Lord Taylor of Gosforth CJ, Turner and Dyson JJ). *R v Christou* [1992] 4 All ER 559, CA (1992 Abr para 670) distinguished.

718 Evidence—evidence of interview—breach of code of practice—person charged with duty to investigate

A warrant was issued and the plaintiff's house was searched by police officers looking for pornographic material. An investigator employed by the defendants accompanied the police officers in accordance with a second search warrant issued under the Copyright, Design and Patents Act 1988, s 109 which authorised him to accompany the police and to search for possible infringements of the 1988 Act. The investigator discovered a number of cassettes and then proceeded to interview the plaintiff. He told the plaintiff he was not a police officer but employed by the defendants, however he failed to administer a formal caution before the interview and failed to time it. The investigator made a note of the interview but it was not timed or witnessed and the plaintiff refused to sign it. The plaintiff contended that the interview ought not to be admitted as it was not obtained in accordance with the Police and Criminal Evidence Act 1984 Codes of Practice. However the evidence was admitted and following his conviction for possession of video cassettes which he knew or had reason to believe were infringing copies of copyright works and with a view to committing an act infringing that copyright, contrary to the Copyright, Design and Patents Act 1988, s 107(c) the plaintiff appealed. *Held*, it was a question of fact as to whether the investigator was a person charged with the duty of investigating offences. It was clear that he was employed by the defendant for that purpose. Once that was established the court ought to have considered, in accordance with the provisions of the 1984 Act, s 78, whether the admission of the evidence would have had such an adverse effect on the fairness of the proceedings that it ought not to be admitted. Accordingly, the appeal would be allowed and the matter would be remitted to a differently constituted court.

   Joy v Federation Against Copyright Theft Ltd [1993] Crim LR 588 (Queen's Bench Division: Kennedy LJ and Clarke J).

719 Evidence—evidence of interview—current code of practice

The appellant was found hiding near an empty stolen car which was being chased by police when it crashed. Evidence of a conversation between him and the two police officers who found and arrested him was admitted at his trial for reckless driving and taking a conveyance without authority on the ground that it did not constitute an interview within the meaning of the 1985 Code of Practice. On his appeal against conviction, the appellant contended that such evidence had been admitted in breach of the 1991 Code of Practice, Code C, para 11.13, which required the making of a written record of any comments made by a suspected person, including unsolicited comments, which were outside the context of an interview but which might be relevant to the offence. The Crown contended that the 1991 Code should be disregarded because it had not been in force at the time of the offence. *Held*, the existence of the new code might well be relevant when considering, under the Police and Criminal Evidence Act 1984, s 78, whether it was fair that the answers of a suspect should be admitted in evidence. In considering the meaning of the word "interview" within the context of the 1985 Code, the purpose of, and the objective sought to be achieved by the code were all-important and should be kept clearly in mind. Although only one question was put to the appellant when arrested and one answer made by him, that constituted an interview. The nature rather than the length of the questions would primarily determine whether there was an interview although the motive of the interviewing officer might be relevant when the judge exercised his discretion as to whether it was fair or not to admit the evidence under the 1984 Act, s 78. There had been no material irregularity and, accordingly, the appeal would be dismissed.

R v Ward (1993) Times, 29 July (Court of Appeal: Kennedy LJ, Morland and Cresswell JJ).

720 Evidence—evidence of interview—police questioning amounting to interview

On his appeal against conviction of burglary, the appellant contended that evidence of exploratory questions by police officers which had given rise to a well-founded suspicion that an offence had been committed should have been excluded because no contemporaneous note of the interview had been made. *Held*, what started out as an inquiry might become an interview. Where that was the case, in accordance with the spirit of the Police and Criminal Evidence Act 1984 and the codes made under it, the proper procedure was to follow the requirements of the relevant code so far as it was practicable to do so. Accordingly, although it was no longer possible to make a contemporaneous note, a record of the earlier questions and answers should be made as soon as practicable, the reason why there was no contemporaneous note should be recorded and the suspect should be given the opportunity to read the record. The question whether an inquiry by police officers amounted to an interview for the purposes of the 1984 Act had to be decided using a purposive construction. In the present case, there had been no significant breach of the code causing substantial prejudice to the appellant and, accordingly, his appeal would be dismissed.

R v Park (1993) Times, 30 July (Court of Appeal: Kennedy LJ, Morland and Cresswell JJ).

721 Evidence—exclusion of evidence—evidence of undercover police

The Police and Criminal Evidence Act 1984, s 78 provides that the court may refuse to admit prosecution evidence if it appears that, having regard to all the circumstances, including those in which the evidence was obtained, it would have such an adverse effect on the fairness of the proceedings that the court ought not to admit it. Section 8(3) states that nothing in the 1984 Act, Pt VIII will prejudice any power of the court to exclude evidence at its discretion.

The appellants were convicted of soliciting to murder their spouses. In both cases the person solicited was an undercover police officer posing as a contract killer. On appeal against the convictions, the appellants argued that as s 8(3) maintained the common law discretion to exclude evidence for the purposes of ensuring a fair trial, s 78 extended that power to exclude evidence which included an element of entrapment, came from an agent provocateur, or was obtained by a trick. *Held*, s 78 had not amended the rule of law that entrapment was not per se a defence to a criminal charge. The correct approach to the 1984 Act was that the natural meaning of the appropriate section should be considered and that the court should not strain to reach a meaning that would either alter or restate existing law. The judge was not therefore obliged to exclude the evidence merely because it was obtained by an undercover officer, although he could exclude it if to admit it would adversely affect the fairness of the proceedings. Some of the factors to be considered by the judge in exercising his discretion under s 78 as to whether to admit the evidence of an undercover officer were as follows: (1) whether the defendant was being enticed to commit an offence he would not otherwise have committed; (2) whether the evidence consisted of admissions to a completed offence or consisted of the actual commission of an offence; and (3) the extent of the officer's role in obtaining the evidence. Discussions between undercover officers and suspects were not within the Police and Criminal Evidence Act 1984 Codes of Practice and so the officer should not abuse his position by asking questions in his undercover role which he should have asked as a police officer in accordance with the Codes. However, each case had to be considered on its own facts. Accordingly, on the application of the above principles to the present case, the appeals would be dismissed.

R v Smurthwaite; R v Gill (1993) Times, 5 October (Court of Appeal: Lord Taylor of Gosforth CJ, Alliott LJ and Buckley J).

722 Evidence—exclusion of evidence—exclusion on grounds of public policy—details of premises used for police surveillance

The defendants were convicted of an offence of indecent behaviour in a churchyard. The principal evidence had come from police officers who claimed that they had been watching the activities of the defendants from an observation post in a neighbouring house. In accepting their evidence, the judge had ruled that it was right to protect the occupier and that the position of the observation post should not be disclosed on the ground that the owner would be in danger of harassment from people such as the defendants. The defendants contended on appeal that it was unreasonable for the judge to reach such a conclusion and that the relevant guidelines relating to the disclosure of information set out in *R v Johnson* [1989] 1 All ER 121, CA did not cover the circumstances of this case, as those guidelines related to an actual threat of violence or severe violence, and not to the danger of harassment. *Held*, it was untenable to suggest that harassment, as opposed to violence, was not something contemplated by the guidelines laid down in *Johnson*. The appeal would accordingly be dismissed.

Blake v DPP; Austin v DPP (1993) 97 Cr App Rep 169 (Queen's Bench Division: Watkins LJ and Roch J).

723 Evidence—exclusion of evidence—police acting as agents provocateurs

Police officers left an insecure and unattended vehicle with a visibly valuable load, which in fact consisted of dummy cigarettes, parked in a busy shopping area. The police had then kept the vehicle under observation. The defendant removed some cartons and was arrested. He made a full admission attributing his conduct to the temptation placed in his way by the police. He was charged and found guilty of interfering with a motor vehicle contrary to the Criminal Attempts Act 1981, s 9. The defendant appealed by way of case stated on the ground that the police had acted as agents provocateurs. *Held*, the police had merely had an expectation or hope that somebody, no particular individual, might act dishonestly and be apprehended. The defendant had incriminated himself through his own dishonesty, and as such the conduct of the police had not been unduly unfair. It was clear that the police had not been acting as agents provocateurs as they had done nothing to force, coerce or persuade the defendant to act as he did. Accordingly, the appeal would be dismissed.

Williams v DPP [1993] 3 All ER 365 (Queen's Bench Division: Farquharson LJ and Wright J).

724 Evidence—expert evidence—DNA typing—statistical evidence

Canada

The accused was charged with sexual assault. A DNA analysis showed that DNA from semen removed from the victim was matched on four probes to DNA taken from the accused's blood sample. At the trial the Crown called the biologist who carried out the DNA analysis as an expert witness and sought to admit his testimony on DNA typing and on the statistical probability that the particular DNA came from a person other than the accused. The defence contended that: (1) the reliability of this novel scientific technique remained unproven, (2) that the DNA evidence in this case was unreliable because there was no DNA database for the accused's native community, and (3) that the opinions on statistical probabilities would outweigh other evidence. *Held*, (1) novel scientific evidence, such as DNA typing, was subject to the same admissibility test as other expert evidence, namely that it be relevant and reliable. The DNA evidence satisfied such criteria. (2) The absence of the particular database was not crucial since evidence showed that it would be rare to find four matching probes at random in any population group. (3) The statistical evidence, and opinions on it, satisfied the admissibility tests and it was for the trial judge to give appropriate warnings and instructions on the uses that could be made of such evidence. Accordingly, the evidence would be admissible.

R v Lafferty (1993) 80 CCC 150 (Northwest Territories Supreme Court).

725 Evidence—expert evidence—identification—facial mapping expert

Whilst a man robbed a building society, a video film taken by a security camera recorded the crime. Several months later another building society was robbed and a similar video was taken. The appellant denied involvement in either crime and at his trial the judge ruled that the evidence of a facial mapping expert could be adduced by the prosecution to assist in determining whether the appellant appeared in both videos. On appeal against conviction and the admissibility of the evidence of the facial mapping expert, *held*, in cases where identification was an issue and where it was suggested that the accused might have been in disguise, identification was not always straightforward. There was no reason in these cases why expert evidence, if it could provide a jury with information and assistance, should not be given. In each case it was for the court to decide whether a jury could be assisted by expert evidence and whether the expert was able to provide assistance. In this case the expert evidence had been put in its proper perspective and accordingly the appeal would be dismissed.

R v Stockwell (1993) Times, 11 March (Court of Appeal: Lord Taylor of Gosforth CJ, Henry and Blofeld JJ).

726 Evidence—expert evidence—oath-helping

The appellant had been convicted of the rape of a 15-year-old mentally retarded girl. At the trial an educational psychologist gave evidence as to whether the girl was vulnerable to suggestion and whether she was a competent witness. The judge decided that she was competent to give evidence and she did so. On appeal against conviction, *held*, it was clear from the decision in *R v Turner* [1975] QB 834, CA (1975 Abr para 698) that evidence from an expert might be admissible in certain cases to provide the court with scientific information which might be outside the experience or knowledge of a judge or jury. However, that opinion might be unnecessary where the judge and jury were able to form their own opinion without help. Evidence from a psychiatrist or psychologist could be admissible to show that a confession was unreliable, but there was no authority for admitting evidence to enhance the evidence of a Crown witness. The Crown could not call a witness of fact and then call a psychologist to give reasons why the jury should consider that witness as reliable. It was accepted that if the defence wanted to call an expert witness to give evidence that a Crown witness was unreliable on account of some mental abnormality, then the Crown might be able to call an expert in rebuttal. In those situations, care should be taken so that the evidence of the expert did not extend to oath-helping. In the present case it was not put in cross-examination that the girl was particularly vulnerable to suggestion as a result of her mental abnormality, therefore no evidence was to be given attacking the reliability of the girl. In the circumstances the evidence of the psychologist should not have been admitted and the court could not be sure that the jury would have reached the same conclusion without that evidence. Accordingly, the appeal would be allowed.

R v Robinson (1993) Times, 25 November (Court of Appeal: Lord Taylor of Gosforth CJ, Schiemann and Wright JJ).

727 Evidence—failure of accused to give evidence—inference of guilt

Northern Ireland

The appellant was charged with attempted murder and possession of a firearm with intent to endanger life. At the trial, the prosecution's case was based on circumstantial evidence and the appellant gave no evidence in his own defence. The judge, sitting without a jury, inferred that he was guilty because there was strong prima facie evidence demanding an explanation and none was given. On his appeal against conviction, the appellant contended that a judge sitting alone was not entitled to draw adverse inferences from an accused's refusal to give evidence unless the evidence adduced was uncontested or clearly established facts which pointed so strongly to guilt as to call for an explanation from the accused. *Held*, as the prosecution had established a prima facie case, the judge was entitled to infer that there was no innocent explanation to that case and that the appellant was guilty. The appeal would be dismissed.

Murray v DPP [1994] 1 WLR 1 (House of Lords: Lords Templeman, Oliver of Aylmerton, Jauncey of Tullichettle, Mustill and Slynn of Hadley).

728 Evidence—hearsay—conspiracy—taped conversation—direction to jury

The defendant was charged with conspiracy to cause grievous bodily harm with intent. It was alleged that the defendant's two co-accused plotted to buy a gun intending to cause the victim serious harm, and that the three of them met a man, who was secretly taping their conversations, about buying a gun. This man later informed the police. From the tape the defendant appeared to be taking a great deal of interest in the conversations. The Crown, amongst other factors, relied on the defendant's presence at the meeting between the two co-accused and the informer. The defendant was convicted and appealed on the ground that the judge failed to direct the jury that the conversations at the meeting were not evidence against the defendant. *Held*, although the conversations themselves were admissible to establish the existence and purpose of the conspiracy, in so far as they pointed to the defendant they were hearsay. The judge failed to direct the jury that the contents of the tape were not evidence of any part by the defendant in the conspiracy. Accordingly, the appeal would be allowed and the conviction quashed.

R v Blake [1993] Crim LR 133 (Court of Appeal: Staughton LJ, Waterhouse and McCullough JJ).

729 Evidence—hearsay—first-hand hearsay—mentally disordered witness

The appellants were charged with theft and handling. At their trial, a prosecution witness, who had been admitted to a psychiatric hospital as an in-patient the day before he had made his first statement to the police, was unable to recall any of the relevant events due to mental illness. The prosecution applied for his previous statements to be read to the jury. Psychiatric evidence indicated that, due to mental disorder, the witness could have difficulty recalling the events sequentially and coherently. The judge ruled that the witness was unfit to attend as a witness within the Criminal Justice Act 1988, s 23(2)(a), but exercised his discretion to admit the witness's statements under s 25. On their appeal against conviction, the appellants contended that the statements should not have been admitted. *Held*, the principles which had to be followed in deciding whether or not the statements ought to be admitted were those set out in s 26, because the statements were prepared for the purpose of contemplated criminal proceedings. There was a difference in approach under s 25 and s 26. Under s 25, the court exercised its discretion by holding that the statement ought not to be admitted in the interests of justice, while under s 26, the court was required to start from the position that the statement could not be given unless the interests of justice required admission of the statement. Regard had to be given under s 26 to (1) the contents of the statement; (2) the risk that the admission of the statement would result in unfairness to the accused if the person making the statement did not give evidence; (3) other circumstances which appeared relevant. The judge had erred in failing to consider the requirements of s 26 and in this case the admission of the statements was a material irregularity. The appeal would accordingly be allowed.

R v Setz-Dempsey (1993) Times, 20 July (Court of Appeal: Beldam LJ, Auld and Scott-Baker JJ).

730 Evidence—hearsay—refusal of witness to testify—admission of written statement—guidance to jury

A witness in a criminal trial refused to give evidence because she was too frightened. The judge ruled that the witness's statement ought to be admitted under the Criminal Justice Act 1988, s 23. The defendant cast doubt on the witness's evidence and suggested that the witness might have been an accomplice to the crime. After the jury had retired, they sent a note to the judge asking why the witness had not been called in evidence. Without inviting comments from counsel, the judge answered that although the reason for the witness not being called was not a matter for the jury, that reason involved nothing to the witness's detriment. On the question of the judge's treatment of the question from the jury, *held*, the way in which the judge had dealt with the jury's question had been unfair to the defendant. The judge's explanation amounted to a compliment to the witness, whose testimony had been disputed but had not been tested in cross-examination. The way the matter was put before the jury might have suggested that the witness's failure to testify could have been a matter of discredit to the defendant. It was also calculated to erode the judge's directions requiring the jury to consider whether the witness was an accomplice. The judge ought simply have said that he could not answer the jury's question.

R v Churchill [1993] Crim LR 285 (Court of Appeal: Steyn LJ, Pill and Wright JJ).

731 Evidence—hearsay—supply of controlled drugs—assertion that recipient a known drug user

The defendant was charged with supplying and possessing heroin. The prosecution case was based on police surveillance. The defendant was allegedly observed passing small packages to various people. At the trial a police officer gave evidence that four of the recipients were known to him as users of heroin. Following his conviction the defendant appealed on the ground that it was clear that the officer was relying upon information given to him by others. *Held*, the judge ought to have inquired into the basis of the prosecution witness's evidence. The police officer did not have direct personal knowledge of matters which could justify his conclusion that those four persons were heroin users, therefore the admission of the evidence constituted an irregularity. However, on the strength of other evidence the Criminal Appeal Act 1968, s 2(1) proviso would apply, and the appeal would be dismissed.

R v Rothwell (1993) Times, 27 April (Court of Appeal: Roch, McCullough and Alliott JJ).

732 Evidence—identification—confrontation at insistence of accused

At the defendant's trial for assault occasioning actual bodily harm, the prosecution intended to proceed without any evidence of identification. However, in disregard of the trial judge's warnings, the defendant insisted on a confrontation in the cells by three witnesses two of whom identified the defendant. On his appeal against conviction, the defendant contended that such identification evidence should not have been admitted. *Held*, the fact that the defendant had insisted on the confrontation taking place was a relevant circumstance that the judge was entitled to take into consideration when deciding whether to exclude such evidence. However, it was only one factor, not a decisive factor, to be weighed against the many other circumstances of the confrontation. Although the defendant had insisted on the confrontation taking place in spite of warnings from the judge, the evidence of identification should have been excluded. However, there had been no miscarriage of justice and the Criminal Appeal Act 1968, s 2(1) proviso would be applied so that the appeal would be dismissed.

R v Joseph [1993] Crim LR 206 (Court of Appeal: Waite LJ, Waterhouse and Dyson JJ).

733 Evidence—identification—disputed identity—court's duty to give warning

The defendant was convicted of different offences at two separate trials. (1) On charges of robbery and unlawful wounding, he based his defence on alibi evidence. A police officer, who knew the defendant, stated that he saw him commit the offence. The trial judge did not warn the jury about the special need for caution before convicting on the identification evidence, nor of the reason for such a warning. The defendant was convicted and appealed, contending that the judge had failed to follow the guidelines laid down in *R v Turnbull* [1976] 3 All ER 549, CA (1976 Abr para 601). (2) On the charge of wounding with intent his defence was based on lack of intent due to the effects of alcohol. He was convicted and appealed on the grounds that the judge had misdirected the jury as to the meaning of intent because he had referred to "probability" rather than "virtual certainty". *Held*, (1) The case involved disputed identity and therefore *Turnbull* applied. The failure to give the requisite warnings was a material misdirection. (2) The judge's direction was misleading. It should have been framed so that the question facing the jury was whether they felt sure that the defendant had the requisite intent at the material time. The judge's references to "probability" reversed the burden of proof and meant that the defence case was not put to the jury correctly. Accordingly, both appeals would be allowed.

R v Bowden [1993] Crim LR 379 (Court of Appeal: Nolan LJ, Owen and Ward JJ).

734 Evidence—identification—identification in moving vehicle

The defendant was charged with two counts of theft, reckless driving, driving without a licence and driving without insurance. An issue arose as to whether the defendant was the driver of the vehicle in question. The prosecution case was that a policeman had seen the driver from a police car while travelling alongside at a speed of 60 mph on the motorway. As soon as the driver looked back the policeman accelerated and moved in front. The driver had been pursued for only a matter of seconds. The car later went out of control and was found abandoned. The defendant was arrested nearly three hours later. The policeman then caused the defendant to be brought from his cell and positively identified him as the driver of the car. Following his conviction the defendant appealed on the ground that the identification evidence ought to have been excluded under the Police and Criminal Evidence Act 1984, s 78. *Held*, the opportunity for identification on the motorway was restricted, and therefore there was a high risk of mistaken identification. The breaches of the Codes of Practice as to identification had led to considerable unfairness, and as such the evidence ought to have been excluded under the 1984 Act, s 78. Accordingly, the appeal would be allowed and the convictions quashed.

Powell v DPP (1993) 157 JP 700 (Queen's Bench Division: Leggatt LJ and Owen J).

735 Evidence—identification—identification of informer

Police officers seized a quantity of drugs which the appellant claimed had been planted on him. The appellant made a successful application that he be permitted to ask the relevant police officer whether there had been an informer in the case and if so, his identity. The police officers declined to disclose the identity of the informer and without hearing further submissions, the court reconsidered its earlier decision and ruled that the existence of the informer was to be disclosed but not his identity. The appellant was convicted of possession of drugs with intent to supply and appealed on the grounds that the court had been wrong to change its decision when confronted with non co-operation by the police. On appeal against conviction, *held*, it was open to the court to change its decision and the question of whether or not there should be an invitation for further submissions before a change in ruling depended upon the particular circumstances of each case. In the present case nothing new had emerged thereafter except the refusal of the police to co-operate. It was wrong of the judge to announce his change of ruling without asking for further submissions and accordingly the appeal would be allowed.

R v Vaillencourt [1993] Crim LR 311 (Court of Appeal: McCowan LJ, Waterhouse and Brooke JJ).

736 Evidence—identification—intimate samples

The Police and Criminal Evidence Act 1984, s 62 provides that an intimate sample can be taken from a person in police detention only if a police officer of at least the rank of superintendent authorises it to be taken and if the appropriate consent is given and that an officer can only give an authorisation if he has reasonable grounds for suspecting the involvement of the person from whom the same is to be taken in a serious arrestable offence and for believing that the sample will tend to confirm or disprove his involvement.

The appellant was convicted of robbery and possessing a firearm with intent to endanger life and was sentenced to concurrent terms of fifteen and ten years' imprisonment respectively. A police informer identified him as a participant in the robbery and alleged that he had been injured during a struggle with a guard. At the scene, there was sufficient blood on a money bag for analysis. The appellant was subsequently arrested in relation to a murder inquiry and gave a blood sample for the purposes of that inquiry which was then tested and found to match the sample taken at the scene of the robbery. At the trial, the defendant unsuccessfully sought to have the scientific evidence excluded. On appeal, it was contended that the judge was wrong to have admitted that evidence since the 1984 Act, s 62 inferred that the serious arrestable offence in the mind of the police officer was that which both he and the suspect knew to be under investigation. *Held*, it was not in the public interest to prevent samples lawfully obtained in connection with one investigation from being compared with blood left at the scene of another serious crime. If Parliament had intended that a sample obtained in connection with one inquiry could only be used in evidence in connection with that inquiry, and not generally, it could have said so but it had not. The words of the statute were not amenable to the appellant's construction and, accordingly, the appeal would be dismissed.

R v Kelt (1993) Times, 15 December (Court of Appeal: Kennedy, Waterhouse LJJ and Ebsworth J).

737 Evidence—identification—photographs

It has been held that, although identification of a defendant from photographs should not generally be admitted on the ground that it tends to show that he has a criminal record, if the defence has been conducted in such a way that the admission of such evidence is justified, the judge then has a discretion as to whether to admit it. In exercising that discretion, he must weigh the prejudicial effect of admitting it with the interests of justice.

R v Bleakley [1993] Crim LR 203 (Court of Appeal: Beldam LJ, Ian Kennedy and Morland JJ).

738 Evidence—identification—uncorroborated identification—withdrawal from jury

Jamaica
The appellant was charged with murder in Jamaica. The identification evidence was uncorroborated and it was not clear whether the appellant had been identified on the occasion of the crime. The judge at first instance directed the jury that identification was "very, very necessary", that there were serious weaknesses in the prosecution case as to identification, but that this was a matter for the jury. The appellant was convicted and his appeal to the Court of Appeal of Jamaica was dismissed. He then appealed to the Privy Council on the basis that the case should have been withdrawn from the jury because of the weakness of the identification evidence. *Held*, it was the jury's function to assess the credibility of witnesses and the judge should only withdraw the case if the identification evidence, even if honest, was so slender that it was unreliable and therefore not sufficient to found a conviction. In this case the evidence was so weak it should have been withdrawn from the jury. Accordingly the appeal would be allowed.

Daley v R [1993] 4 All ER 86 (Privy Council: Lords Mackay of Clashfern, Goff of Chieveley, Slynn of Hadley, Mustill and Zacca CJ).

739 Evidence—identification of prohibited substances—drugs

The appellant had been under police surveillance on the suspicion that he was involved in drug dealing and had been observed on three occasions handing over to another for cash something which was described by the witnesses as a "dark substance". He was subsequently charged and convicted with supplying cannabis resin and on appeal against conviction he contended that no evidence had been submitted identifying the drug alleged to have been supplied. *Held*, whilst scientific evidence was not required in every case to identify a drug, the prosecution was obliged to establish the identity of the drug with sufficient certainty to achieve the standard of proof required in a criminal case. In the present case, the descriptions give by police witnesses of what had changed hands was insufficient to justify an inference that it was cannabis resin. The prosecution had failed to prove the charge as laid and accordingly the appeal would be allowed.

R v Hill (1993) 96 Cr App Rep 456 (Court of Appeal: Staughton LJ, Waterhouse and McCullough JJ).

740 Evidence—mixed statement—direction to jury

The defendants were convicted of murder and applied for leave to appeal. They contended that the judge misdirected the jury in respect of their statements to the police. *Held*, a mixed statement, which was partly incriminating and partly exculpatory, did constitute evidence but did not have the same weight as evidence given on oath. A judge should thus direct the jury not to attach equal weight to sworn evidence, which was given in their presence and tested in cross-examination, and to what was said out of court. That should be followed by the usual directions about a defendant's right not to give evidence and, in respect of mixed statements, that more weight should be attached to the incriminating rather than the exculpatory parts. The application would be dismissed.

R v Downes; R v Rawlinson (1993) Times, 10 December (Court of Appeal: Stuart-Smith and McCullogh LJJ and Sir Gervase Sheldon).

741 Evidence—perjury—evidence of more than one witness

The Perjury Act 1911, s 13 states that a person must not be convicted of perjury solely on the evidence of one witness as to the falsity of any statement alleged to be false. The Criminal Appeal Act 1968, s 2(1) sets out the circumstances in which an appeal against conviction must be allowed.

The appellants were convicted with two co-accused of doing acts tending and intended to pervert the course of public justice and on individual counts of perjury. One of the co-accused had been on bail and confined to his house by curfew. The police tried to arrest someone whom they believed was the co-accused but he escaped. On an application to revoke his bail, the appellants alleged that appellant A was the man the police had attempted to arrest and that the co-accused had been at home. Appellant A gave evidence that the police had not given the co-accused's name when they sought to arrest him. However, according to a note of the magistrate's clerk, appellant A had referred to the name of the co-accused in cross-examination. The truth of the note was disputed by two of the appellants but accepted by one. The appellants argued that when the judge had directed the jury in relation to the 1911 Act, he had failed to refer to s 13. *Held*, it was a prerequisite to the summing up of the judge under the 1911 Act, that the judge should refer to s 13 and that the jury should have the accepted evidence of more than one witness. The correct test in determining whether s 2(1) of the 1968 Act applied was whether the court was satisfied that if the correct direction had been given to the jury they would inevitably have reached the same conclusion. In the present case, the witnesses who had identified the co-accused had no association with him and had no motive for making false statements. The circumstances of the case effectively pointed to the appellants being untruthful and the jury had in fact convicted the appellants on the charge of doing acts tending and intended to pervert the course of justice and these involved the same circumstances as those relied upon to support the counts of perjury. Accordingly, the appeals would be dismissed.

R v Carroll [1993] Crim LR 613 (Court of Appeal: Lord Taylor of Gosforth CJ, Auld and Curtis JJ). *R v Hamid* (1979) 69 Cr App R 324 applied.

742 Evidence—perjury—warning given to defence witnesses only

At his trial on a charge of criminal damage, the applicant and a witness appearing on his behalf had been warned by the justices' clerk about the significance of giving perjured evidence. The warning had not been given to the Crown's witnesses, and following his conviction the applicant sought judicial review and the quashing of his conviction on the ground that the failure to give the same warning to the other witnesses had been unfair. *Held*, the fact that the warning had only been given to the applicant and his witness gave the appearance that justice had not been applied equally to all parties. In any event if a warning about perjured evidence had been necessary it should have been given by the justices rather than by the clerk. The application should be allowed and, accordingly, the conviction would be quashed.

R v Richmond and Gilling West Magistrates, ex p Steel [1993] Crim LR 711 (Queen's Bench Division: Mann LJ and Tuckey J).

743   Evidence—previous convictions—handling stolen goods

The Theft Act 1968, s 27(3)(b) provides that where a person is charged with handling stolen goods, evidence that he has previously been convicted of theft or handling is admissible for the purpose of proving that he knew or believed the goods to be stolen.

The defendant was charged with handling stolen goods. At his trial, he admitted that he knew or believed the goods to be stolen and the only issue was whether he had acted dishonestly. He was convicted and appealed, contending that the judge erred in admitting evidence of his previous convictions for handling and directing the jury that it was relevant to his credibility and general disposition to handle stolen goods dishonestly. *Held*, the evidence was inadmissible in relation to the issue of the defendant's dishonesty. The trial judge had erred and, accordingly, the appeal would be allowed.

R v Duffas (1993) Times, 19 October (Court of Appeal: Stuart-Smith LJ, McCullough J and Sir Gervase Sheldon).

744   Evidence—previous inconsistent statement—non-disclosure—adverse press coverage

The defendants, who were sisters, were charged with murder. It was alleged that the defendants had stabbed the victim to death because one of the defendants was jealous, having had a sexual relationship with the victim's husband, and the other defendant was said to have disliked the way her sister had been treated. The defendants were found guilty and appealed. The prime ground of appeal was that material had come to light which indicated that a witness who provided the main identification evidence at the trial had made a previous inconsistent statement which was not disclosed to the defence. Further, it had not been revealed at the trial that shortly after making the statement the witness had telephoned the victim's employers seeking the reward which they had offered for information about the murder. The defendants also expressed concern as to the way the trial had been reported in the press, a matter which had been raised by defence counsel during the trial. *Held*, the failure to disclose the previous inconsistent statement was a material irregularity. It was clear that the press coverage of the trial was unremitting, extensive, sensational, inaccurate and misleading. Notwithstanding that the judge gave the jury several warnings that they ought to decide the case on the evidence before them, it was quite impossible to state that the jury was not influenced in their decision by what they had read. The coverage of the trial had created a real risk of prejudice against the defendants, and therefore the convictions were unsafe and unsatisfactory and would be quashed. The papers in the case would be sent to the Attorney General for him to consider whether any proceedings ought to be taken against the newspapers in question.

R v Taylor (1993) Times, 15 June (Court of Appeal: McCowan LJ, Douglas Brown and Tuckey JJ).

745   Evidence—previous unrelated conviction—relevance to accused's credibility

A solicitor and his assistant allegedly submitted legal aid claims for work which had not been done. They were jointly charged with conspiracy to obtain property by deception, and the solicitor was also charged with obtaining or attempting to obtain property by deception. They claimed they had acted honestly, contending the work had always been done and any confusion had arisen from problems in the office caused by the solicitor's drinking habits. The assistant did not give evidence, but the solicitor gave evidence of his own good character and admitted that he had been fined and disqualified for driving with excess alcohol. The defendants were convicted on all counts and appealed on the grounds that the judge had misdirected the jury on character and dishonesty. *Held*, the judge had referred to the assistant's previous good character but had not addressed the question of his credibility because he had not given evidence, and that direction was not open to criticism. The judge had rightly said the solicitor's conviction was serious while pointing out that he had not been convicted of an offence of dishonesty, but the direction had been flawed because the judge should have explained the relevance of character to the credibility of a defendant who had given evidence. It would have been desirable to treat the solicitor as a man of effectively good character and to have invited the jury to regard his conviction as irrelevant to the issue of dishonesty, but despite those flaws the evidence against both defendants was so overwhelming that the proviso to the Criminal Appeal Act 1968, s 2(1) should be applied. Accordingly, the appeals would be dismissed.

R v Timson, R v Hales [1993] Crim LR 58 (Court of Appeal: Staughton LJ, McKinnon and Potter JJ).

746 Evidence—prosecution evidence—duty to call witnesses

The defendant was charged with murder. It was alleged that the deceased had been a regular attender at a local casino. There was evidence in the Crown's possession to the effect that some witnesses stated that the deceased had not been at the casino on the night of her death while others said she was there that evening. All the evidence was correctly served on the defence as unused material. At the first trial none of that evidence was called or relied on by the defence as it was considered to be irrelevant. Following a successful appeal, a retrial was ordered. At the retrial counsel for the defendant sought an order that the Crown call the witnesses who spoke of seeing the deceased at the casino during that evening, the Crown declined to call them and the judge then declined either to require or invite the Crown to do so. Following his conviction the defendant appealed on the grounds that the judge ought to have invited the Crown to call the witnesses and that the Crown ought to have done so in any event. *Held*, in the circumstances the judge was correct not to accede to the application. To have pressed the prosecution to call the witnesses would, in effect, have required them to act as both prosecution and defence. Accordingly, the appeal would be dismissed.

R v Richardson (1993) Times, 9 June (Court of Appeal: Lord Taylor of Gosforth CJ, Owen and Blofeld JJ).

747 Evidence—recognition—video tape recording

At the defendants' trial on charges of robbery, evidence of the purported recognition of them by police officers who had viewed a video tape recording of the robbery was admitted. On their appeals against conviction, the defendants contended that such evidence should not have been admitted because its prejudicial effect outweighed its probative value. *Held*, although recognition evidence was quite different from identification evidence, some of the considerations underlying the safeguards built into the regulatory procedures laid down for identification parades and the showing of photographs applied also to the showing of video tapes. Where the quality of a video was poor or it provided only a limited opportunity for recognition, the analogy with showing photographs and identification was closest; the showing of the video should be regulated in order to maximise the prospects of any recognition evidence being truly spontaneous and independent and to minimise the risk of anything being said which might infect that independence and spontaneity and instead prompt the recognition of some particular person. Where known suspects existed, it was desirable that procedures should be instituted for regulating the showing of video recordings. Where a video was shown with a view to finding a suspect, regulation was less necessary. The trial judge had taken all the proper considerations into account and had been entitled to admit the evidence in question. Accordingly, the appeals would be dismissed.

R v Caldwell; R v Dixon (1993) Times, 8 June (Court of Appeal: Simon Brown LJ, Henry and Potts JJ).

748 Evidence—service courts—evidence through live television link

See para 2234.

749 Evidence—similar fact evidence—effect of collusion

The defendant was convicted of offences, including rape and attempted buggery, against several prostitutes. Two of the prostitutes were from one town, and two from another. The defendant's application to sever the indictment was dismissed, and the evidence of A, a fifth prostitute from the second town was admitted on the basis of similar fact evidence. The defendant appealed, contending (1) that the counts relating to one town should have been severed from the counts relating to the second town; and (2) that the evidence should not have been treated as similar fact evidence, as there might have been collusion between each group of prostitutes. *Held*, there were four possibilities: (1) where a real possibility of collusion was apparent on the face of the documents, the judge should not allow the similar fact evidence to be led; (2) if a submission was made raising the suggestion of a voir dire, the judge might find it necessary to hold a voir dire; (3) if the evidence was admitted but at the end of the case the judge thought that there was a real possibility of collusion, he should tell the jury in summing up not to use the evidence as corroboration; (4) if the judge was of the view that there was no real possibility of collusion, but the matter had been argued, he should leave the issue to the jury. In the circumstances, however, it could not be concluded that the judge should have severed the indictment or excluded the similar fact evidence on the ground of any perceived possibility of collusion. The appeal would be allowed in part.

R v Ryder (1993) 156 JP 1095 (Court of Appeal: Lord Taylor of Gosforth CJ, Popplewell and Laws JJ).

750   Evidence—telephone conversation—unlawful interception

The Interception of Communications Act 1985, s 2 provides that the Secretary of State may issue a warrant requiring the person to whom it is addressed to intercept, in the course of their transmission by post or public telecommunication system, communications. Section 9 provides that in any proceedings before any court or tribunal, no evidence is to be adduced and no question asked in cross examination which tends to suggest that an offence under s 1 (prohibition on unlawful interception of communications) has been or is to be committed. Section 6 provides that any intercepted material ought to be destroyed as soon as its retention is no longer necessary for the purpose of preventing or detecting serious crime.

The defendant, with others, was charged with conspiracy to evade the prohibition on the importation of cannabis resin. The defendant denied any part in the conspiracy and raised the defence of duress. The prosecution relied on telephone calls passing between the defendants. On discovering, during evidence, that telephone communications had been intercepted by the authorities, the defendant contended that the intercepted material ought to be disclosed. Prosecuting counsel was instructed by the Attorney General that it was not counsel's duty to acquaint himself with any material relating to any interception, since nothing which might be disclosed to him could be put in evidence under the 1985 Act, s 9. Following his conviction the defendant appealed, contending that during his trial, the prosecution had failed to disclose details of telephone communications intercepted by the authorities and that part of the proceedings had been held in camera with the defendant and his solicitor excluded. The appeal was dismissed, and on further appeal, *held*, the Attorney General's instruction to prosecuting counsel was unsustainable. The essential function of the investigating and prosecuting authority was to ensure that the prosecution of a suspected offender was conducted fairly, and therefore there was no sound reason for refusing disclosure to prosecuting counsel. It was the prosecution's duty to give complete disclosure of unused material to the defence. On a narrow interpretation of the 1985, s 2 the purposes for which the grant of a warrant was necessary did not extend to the prosecution of suspected offenders and therefore the destruction of material was an act which those responsible were bound by the 1985 Act, s 6 to perform. However, the proviso to the Criminal Appeal Act 1968, s 2(1) would be applied, and accordingly, the appeal would be dismissed.

R v Preston [1993] 4 All ER 638 (House of Lords: Lords Keith of Kinkel, Templeman, Jauncey of Tullichettle, Browne-Wilkinson and Mustill). Decision of Court of Appeal (1992) 95 Cr App Rep 355, CA (1992 Abr para 697) affirmed. *R v Effik* (1992) 95 Cr App Rep 427, CA (1992 Abr para 697) overruled.

751   Evidence—witness—pre-trial discussion of evidence

It has been held that although the practice of a pre-trial discussion of evidence between potential witnesses should be strongly discouraged, it would not always render the evidence of such witnesses unsafe. In each case it was a matter for the trial judge to decide.

R v Arif [1993] Crim LR 713 (Court of Appeal: Nolan LJ, Swinton-Thomas and Colman JJ).

752   Evidence—witness—screening of witness from accused

The defendants were convicted of rape and sentenced to five years' detention in a young offender institute and five years' imprisonment respectively. They appealed on the grounds that the complainant should not have been allowed to give evidence from behind a witness screen and that the judge had incorrectly answered a question by the jury after they had retired. The question was based on a factual premise of the complainant initially consenting to intercourse and then withdrawing her consent and the issue had not been canvassed during the trial. *Held*, whether a witness screen should be used was a matter of discretion for the trial judge. The use of screens had generally been confined to child witnesses and was only appropriate in relation to adults in exceptional cases. They had a prejudicial effect, even if a jury was properly warned not to make adverse assumptions from its use, by raising the suggestion that a witness needed to be protected from any contact, even visual, with an accused. However, it was the judge's duty to ensure that justice was done and if that required that a witness be afforded some form of protection, he should make the necessary order. In the present case, since the complainant had to give exceptionally unpleasant evidence relating to her multiple rape and the judge had properly warned the jury, it was impossible to say that he had exercised his discretion unreasonably and thus that ground of appeal would fail. However, in relation to the judge's answer to the jury's question, he should have directed them that since the issue had not been raised by either side they should ignore it and concentrate solely on whether the complainant was a consenting party from the outset. Accordingly, the appeals would be allowed and the convictions would be quashed.

R v Schaub, R v Cooper (1993) Times, 3 December (Court of Appeal: Farquharson LJ, Owen and Latham JJ).

The applicants were charged with violent disorder after four people were attacked by a gang of youths. They were identified at identification parades by witnesses who, fearing for their personal safety, wished to remain anonymous. At the committal proceedings the prosecution applied for permission for the witnesses to give evidence from behind screens using voice distortion techniques. The applicants contended that this breached the common law right of an accused to see and hear any witness who gave evidence in court. The magistrate ruled that the witnesses' anonymity would be preserved subject to the applicants' legal representatives having an opportunity to see them. The applicants requested a review of the decision. Held, the trial judge was under a duty to ensure that justice was done so that the system operated fairly to the defence, the prosecution and the witnesses. Sometimes the judge had to decide where the balance of fairness lay. In this case the magistrate decided that the need to ensure that the witnesses testified outweighed any possible prejudice to the applicants by the erection of the screen. It could not be said that the decision was so unreasonable that no magistrate could reasonably have reached it. Accordingly, the application was dismissed.

R v Watford Magistrates' Court, ex p Lenman [1993] Crim LR 388 (Queen's Bench Division: Beldam LJ and Laws J). R v DJX, SCY, GCZ (1989) 91 Cr App Rev 36, CA followed.

753 Evidence—witness outside jurisdiction—written statements—reasonable practicability of witness's attendance

The defendants were charged with robbery of a Mexican student. The student came back from Mexico to give evidence at the trial, which ended inconclusively. The student did not attend the re-trial, in spite of a number of attempts by the prosecution to secure his attendance. Leave was given for his statements to be admitted in evidence under the Criminal Justice Act 1988, s 23(2)(b) on the ground that it was not reasonably practicable to secure his attendance. The defendants were convicted. On their appeal against conviction, held, an application under the 1988 Act, s 23(2)(b) had to be considered as at the date of the application and it was not necessary for the judge to have regard to the future. In this respect, the judge's decision had been correct. However, the judge had exercised his discretion under the 1988 Act, s 26 incorrectly. Accordingly, the defendants' appeals would be allowed.

R v French; R v Gowhar (1993) Times, 25 March (Court of Appeal: McCowan LJ, Jowitt and Waller JJ). R v Bray (1988) Cr App Rep 354, CA (1988 Abr para 535) considered.

754 Indictment—additional counts

By virtue of the Administration of Justice (Miscellaneous Provisions) Act 1933, s 2(2)(i), where the person charged with an offence has been committed for trial, the bill of indictment against him may include any counts founded on facts or evidence disclosed in any examination or deposition taken before a justice in his presence.

One of the two perpetrators of a robbery had in his possession a sawn-off shotgun and the other had a handgun. During a search of a hotel room occupied by the appellants, the police found the handgun. The shotgun, loaded with live cartridges, was discovered by police the next day in the same room. The first appellant attempted to grab the shotgun when a police officer was retrieving it from under a bed. The appellants were originally committed for trial on a charge of robbery. On the first day of the trial, the prosecution was permitted to add two further counts, the first of possessing a firearm and the second of possessing a firearm with intent to endanger life. On their appeals against conviction of robbery and possessing a firearm and, in the case of the first appellant, of possessing a firearm and ammunition with intent to endanger life, the appellants contended that the two further counts should not have been added. Held, s 2(2)(i) did not demand that the evidence on the committal statements should be conclusive; there merely had to be some evidence to support the charges sought to be added. The evidence of the police officer that he had found the loaded shotgun in the hotel room was sufficient evidence from which a jury could reasonably infer that the gun was an effective weapon. The fact that it had been loaded, presumably by one of the appellants, was evidence from which the jury could reasonably have inferred that it was an effective weapon. The evidence that the first appellant had attempted to grab the weapon was sufficient to support the count of possessing a firearm with intent to endanger life. Further, there had been expert evidence before the jury as to the effectiveness of the shotgun and its status as a firearm. The appeals would be dismissed.

R v Biddis [1993] Crim LR 392 (Court of Appeal: Lord Taylor of Gosforth CJ, Potts and Judge JJ).

755 Indictment—amendment of indictment—amendment at close of defendant's case

The defendant was charged with rape. The prosecution had put its case on the basis that the defendant was charged with the full offence. However, during the trial, after the close of the defendant's case but before closing speeches, the prosecution made an application to put an alternative offence of attempted rape. The application was granted and following his conviction the defendant appealed. *Held*, although the judge had a discretion to allow alternative offences to be put, it was a matter of timing which would only be appropriate if it would cause no risk to the defendant and allow him a full opportunity to deal with it. The counsel for the defendant was unable to say that had the alternative charge been put at an earlier stage he would not have run his examination-in-chief or his re-examination differently. He would have discussed the charge with the defendant, and as such the court was not satisfied that putting the alternative charge at that late stage had not affected the way defence counsel had put his case. Accordingly, the appeal would be allowed and the conviction quashed.

R v Harris (1993) Times, 22 March (Court of Appeal: Steyn LJ, Rougier and Laws JJ).

756 Indictment—counts—evidence in respect of one count to support evidence on other counts

It has been held that evidence in respect of a count in an indictment which is statute-barred and in respect of which a defendant has been acquitted is admissible to prove other counts in the indictment provided that such evidence has probative value in respect of those other counts.

R v Adams [1993] Crim LR 72 (Court of Appeal: McCowan LJ, Jowitt and Waller JJ).

757 Indictment—single count—direction to jury

The defendant was charged with an offence of unlawful harassment of an occupier contrary to the Protection from Eviction Act 1977, s 1(3)(a). It was alleged, in a single count of the indictment, that the defendant had committed a number of different acts which would each amount to unlawful eviction. The defendant was convicted and appealed. The defendant contended that the judge did not direct the jury that, to reach a unanimous verdict, they must all be satisfied that a particular act complained of was proved and that all 12 jurors were sure in respect of that particular act. *Held*, it was clear that a number of separate and different acts were alleged against the defendant, each amounting to unlawful harassment. There was a real risk that, unless otherwise directed, the jury might have thought that so long as all 12 were agreed the defendant had committed one of the acts alleged, even though they were not all agreed as to which act, they could and ought to convict. The correct direction would have been that the jury ought to be unanimous as to proof of the particular act relied upon to find their verdict of guilty. Accordingly, the appeal would be allowed.

R v Mitchell (1993) Independent, 2 June (Court of Appeal: Simon Brown LJ, McCullough and Swinton Thomas JJ).

758 Indictment—sufficient nexus

It has been held that where two or more counts alleged against a defendant were of a broadly similar character and there was but one victim of the alleged offences, it would not generally be permissible to join the counts in a single indictment in accordance with the Indictment Rules 1971, SI 1971/1253, r 9. However, if the offences had been joined it would seldom be appropriate for the judge to exercise his discretion to order severance of the indictment under the Indictment Act 1915, s 5(3).

R v C (1993) Times, 4 February (Court of Appeal: Simon Brown LJ, Popplewell and Rattee JJ).

The defendant was charged with two counts of indecent assault on one boy "A" and one count of indecent assault on another boy "B". He was found guilty and appealed on the ground that the offences upon A were alleged to have occurred some nine years before the alleged offence upon B and as such could not be said to form a series of offences of the same or similar character within the terms of the Indictment Rules 1971, SI 1971/1253, r 9. *Held*, whether counts were properly joined depended on the circumstances of the case. In the present case the similarities between the sets of offences was truly remarkable. In considering whether two sets of alleged offences could be described as a series for the purposes of the 1971 Rules, r 9 it was inappropriate to consider the dictionary definition of the word "series", the correct approach was to discover whether the alleged offences were linked by a sufficiently close nexus to bring them within the rule and if there was such a nexus even offences separated by a period of nine years could be said to form a series of offences of the same or similar character within the terms of the 1971 Rules. Accordingly, the appeal would be dismissed.

R v Baird [1993] Crim LR 778 (Court of Appeal: Nolan LJ, Owen and Ward JJ).

759 Informations

See MAGISTRATES.

760 Investigation of offence—duty to investigate—store detective

It has been held that the Police and Criminal Evidence Act 1984, s 67(9), which provides that persons other than police officers who are charged with the duty of investigating offences or charging offenders must in the discharge of that duty have regard to the relevant provision of any codes of practice, may also apply to a store detective. The duty of investigating offences was not restricted to the officers of central government or other persons acting under statutory powers.

R v Bayliss (1993) 157 JP 1062 (Court of Appeal: Neill and Tudor LJJ and Clark J).

761 Legal aid

See LEGAL AID AND ADVICE.

762 Magistrates' courts

See MAGISTRATES.

763 Miscarriage of justice—compensation—reversal of conviction—meaning of "new or newly discovered fact"

The Criminal Justice Act 1988, s 133(1) provides that the Secretary of State must pay compensation to a person who has been convicted of a criminal offence where his conviction has subsequently been reversed or he has been pardoned on the ground that a new or newly discovered fact shows beyond reasonable doubt that there has been a miscarriage of justice.

It has been held that a reversal of conviction can only be relied on for the purposes of s 133 when based on a "new or newly discovered fact"; those words govern both pardons and reversed convictions on a proper construction of s 133(1). Accordingly, the Home Secretary was not wrong to refuse to grant compensation in one case where a conviction was reversed following a reference by him to the Court of Appeal, under the Criminal Appeal Act 1968, s 17, and in another case where a conviction was reversed following a decision of the House of Lords that the byelaw under which the conviction was obtained was invalid.

R v Secretary of State for the Home Department, ex p Bateman (1993) Times, 10 May (Queen's Bench Division: Leggatt LJ and McCullough J).

764 Preparatory hearing—refusal to grant application for severance—leave to appeal

The Criminal Justice Act 1987, s 7(1) provides that where it appears to a judge of the Crown Court that the evidence reveals a case of fraud of such seriousness and complexity that substantial benefits may accrue from a preparatory hearing before the jury is sworn for the purpose of (a) identifying issues which are likely to be material to the verdict; (b) assisting their comprehension of such issues; (c) expediting the proceedings before the jury; or (d) assisting the judge's management of the trial, then the judge may order that a hearing be held. The 1987 Act, s 9(1) provides that the judge at the preparatory hearing may exercise any of the powers specified in the section and s 9(11) provides for an appeal with the leave of the judge or the Court of Appeal.

The first two defendants applied for leave to appeal against the decision of the Crown Court judge to refuse their applications to sever two counts in the indictment against the third defendant. The question arose as to whether the Court of Appeal had jurisdiction to hear the appeal against the refusal to sever counts, which was made at a preparatory hearing under s 7. *Held*, if there was an application to sever in order to reduce complexity then this might be allowed under s 7(1)(a), but only if it related to the exercise of the judge's discretion, and it would only be successful where his discretion was fundamentally flawed. In the present situation, however, the basis of the application was prejudice, not complexity. Applications for leave to appeal from decisions made at preparatory hearings had to be attended to urgently. There was a duty on barristers and solicitors to scrutinise anxiously to see whether the court had jurisdiction to hear the appeal, and whether there was a real likelihood of success in the argument that the judge's exercise of his discretion was fundamentally flawed. If there was no such anxious scrutiny the court would be hesitant about awarding costs. The court had no jurisdiction to hear the application, but even if the court was wrong, the applications had no merit. Accordingly, the applications would be dismissed.

R v Jennings; R v Johnson; R v Mullins (1993) Times, 29 October (Court of Appeal: Rose LJ, Turner and Judge JJ).

765 Prosecution of offences—defendant acquitted of murder—retrial—same offence charged

Scotland
The defendant had been acquitted of murder but convicted of culpable homicide, but on appeal his conviction was quashed. The Crown was granted authority under the Criminal Procedure (Scotland) Act 1975 to bring a new prosecution, and the defendant was charged with murder notwithstanding his earlier acquittal of that charge. The defendant successfully applied for the murder charge to be dismissed on the ground that it was oppressive, and the Crown appealed. *Held*, the 1975 Act did not contain a similar provision to the Criminal Appeal Act 1968, s 7(2), which prevented courts in England and Wales from ordering a defendant to be retried for any offence other than the offence of which he had been convicted at the original trial, or an offence of which he could have been convicted at the original trial on an indictment for that offence. In setting aside the original verdict the Court of Appeal had been aware that the defendant was liable to be tried again for murder, but they had held that it was in the public interest for the Crown to be granted authority to bring that charge, and in those circumstances it could not be said that the new charge was oppressive. The court could not substitute its own views of what was fair or unfair for that of the Court of Appeal, and accordingly the appeal would be allowed and the murder charge reinstated.

HM Advocate v Boyle (1993) Times, 14 January (High Court of Justiciary).

766 Prosecution of offences—delay—stay of proceedings

The defendant was charged in connection with a conspiracy designed to defraud an international bank. The judge, in ordering that the proceedings be permanently stayed, held that the defendant had been seriously prejudiced by excessive delay. On an appeal by the Attorney General of Hong Kong against the order, *held*, the general rule that delay contributed to by the actions of a defendant was never to be the foundation of an order for the stay of criminal proceedings against him did not refer to acts or conduct which were to be issues at the trial. The judge had to bear in mind the nature of the prosecution's case as part of the factual background against which the alleged delay had to be considered and not regard it necessarily as a bar to the application succeeding. In the present circumstances, the judge had been well aware of that and there was nothing in his judgment to indicate that he had not given due consideration to the nature of the prosecution in reaching his decision to grant a stay. Accordingly, the appeal would be dismissed.

A-G of Hong Kong v Wai-Bun [1993] 3 WLR 242 (Privy Council: Lords Griffiths, Bridge of Harwich, Lowry, Slynn of Hadley and Woolf).

767 Prosecution of offences—private prosecution—unreliable complainant— abuse of process

The complainant alleged that while he was detained in a prison he was assaulted on three occasions by five prison officers. He initiated a private prosecution against the prison officers. At the committal proceedings, following the complainant giving his evidence-in-chief and being cross-examined, the magistrate interposed a witness who was only available on that day. Once she had finished her evidence, which did not assist the complainant, the magistrate stated that he did not wish to hear any more evidence. He decided that there was not sufficient evidence to put the prison officers on trial by jury and that the proceedings were an abuse of the process of the court. He discharged the prison officers and ordered the complainant to pay costs. The complainant applied for judicial review on the grounds that the magistrate acted prematurely in that he had not heard all the evidence which included six other witnesses. *Held*, as the magistrate was under the misapprehension that there were no other witnesses who were able to give relevant evidence he undoubtedly made the wrong decision. Further, the fact that the complainant was an unreliable witness, obsessive about his cause and behaved in an aggressive and abusive manner did not justify the magistrate's decision to discharge the prison officers on the basis that the proceedings were an abuse of process. Accordingly, the application would be granted and a fresh committal ordered to be heard before another magistrate.

R v Durham Magistrates' Court, ex p Davies (1993) Independent, 12 May (Queen's Bench Division: Stuart-Smith LJ and Judge J).

768 Restrictions on reporting—proceedings held in camera—appeal—use of written submissions

During the course of a criminal trial the judge made an order that part of the trial be heard in camera. The plaintiff, a newspaper, gave notice of an application for leave to appeal against the order under the Criminal Justice Act 1988, s 159 on the ground that the Criminal Appeal Rules 1968, SI 1968/1262, r 16B(6) and (7) which provide for the determination of the application for leave and the appeal itself without a hearing, was ultra vires. The application was refused and the matter came before the Court of Appeal pursuant to the Criminal Appeal Act 1968, s 31(3) so that the issue of leave could be determined by the full court. *Held*, where the issue before the Court of Appeal was whether certain material ought to be in the public domain the 1988 Act, s 159(6) provided for rules to be created making special provisions for such a situation. Rule 16B (6) and (7) provided for the application for leave, and for the appeal if leave was granted, to be determined without a hearing, and it was therefore not ultra vires. There was nothing in the statute or the rules to prevent an applicant putting written submissions before the Court of Appeal either at the leave stage or, if leave were granted, at the stage when the matter was to be determined. Accordingly, the application would be refused.

Ex p Guardian Newspapers (1993) Times, 26 October (Court of Appeal: Kennedy LJ, Ognall and Curtis JJ).

769 Restrictions on reporting—risk of prejudice to other proceedings

See *Ex p The Telegraph*, para 2071.

770 Search and seizure—intimate search—meaning of intimate body search

The Police and Criminal Evidence Act 1984, s 118 defines an intimate search as a search which consists of the physical examination of a person's body orifices.

A policeman informed the defendant that he wished to search him. The defendant then put something in his mouth which he refused to spit out. The policeman grabbed the defendant and held his nose, forcing him to open his mouth and spit out a bag of cannabis. The defendant claimed he had been subjected to an intimate search as defined by the 1984 Act and that the code of procedure for such searches had not been followed. The judge ruled that the policeman's actions did not constitute an intimate search but were merely intended to prevent incriminating evidence being destroyed. On appeal, *held*, the definition in the 1984 Act, s 118 involved some form of physical intrusion. Mere visual examination or an attempt to force someone to extrude something from one of his orifices were not intimate searches. Although there had been an ordinary search in this case, which had been improperly carried out, it did not render the evidence inadmissible as it was insufficiently prejudicial to the fairness of the proceedings. Accordingly, the appeal would be dismissed.

R v Hughes (1993) Times, 12 November (Court of Appeal: Lord Taylor of Gosforth CJ, Schiemann and Wright JJ).

771 Search and seizure—special procedure material—application for order—duty of disclosure

The appellant was alleged to have engaged a third party to acquire information relating to a business rival's affairs. He was charged with conspiracy to defraud the rival. On an inter partes application by the police, a Crown Court judge granted an order that the appellant produce to the police special procedure material. The appellant appealed against the order and also sought judicial review of a similar order that the third party's solicitors produce documents held on behalf of the third party, contending that the police had failed to make full disclosure in the applications before the judge and that the conditions for the obtaining of access to special procedure material set out in the Police and Criminal Evidence Act 1984, s 9, Sch 1, had not been fulfilled. *Held*, in order to fulfil those conditions, the applications for an order had to set out all the material in the hands of the police whether or not it assisted the applications. It was for the prosecution to make a clear revelation to the court of all appropriate material in its possession so that the judge could reach a safe conclusion as to whether the access conditions were fulfilled. Where, on an inter partes application, both parties had all the material before them, even though it was the prosecution's responsibility to ensure that the judge was provided with such information, a respondent could not complain if he had the material also but chose not to reveal it to the court. The main consideration for a judge in determining whether the first set of access conditions had been fulfilled was whether there were reasonable grounds for believing a serious arrestable offence had been committed. The judge had so concluded and his decision could not be faulted. The appeal would be dismissed and the application for judicial review would not be granted.

    R v Crown Court at Acton, ex p Layton [1993] Crim LR 458 (Queen's Bench Division: Watkins LJ and Roch J).

772   Stay of proceedings—abuse of process—jurisdiction of High Court

The Supreme Court Act 1981, s 29(3) provides that in relation to the jurisdiction of the Crown Court other than its jurisdiction in matters relating to trial on indictment, the High Court has all such jurisdiction to make orders of mandamus, prohibition or certiorari as it has in relation to the jurisdiction of an inferior court.

    The defendant was charged with a number of offences and committed for trial. The judge at first instance stayed two of the counts on the indictment on the basis that to proceed on those counts would amount to an abuse of process. The prosecution was granted judicial review of the judge's decision and the defendant appealed. The issue was the meaning of the words "relating to trial on indictment" in the 1981 Act, s 29(3) and whether an order by the Crown Court that a trial on indictment ought to be stayed as an abuse of process was a decision "relating to trial on indictment" and therefore not amenable to judicial review. *Held*, an order made on an application to stay proceedings for abuse of process was clearly an order affecting the conduct of the trial and therefore, it was an order in a matter "relating to trial on indictment" within the meaning of the 1981 Act, s 29(3). It did not make any difference whether the order was made on the day the trial was due to start, or at the beginning of the trial, or at an earlier date on a special hearing. Accordingly, the appeal would be allowed.

    Lord Slynn of Hadley was of the view that the cases of *R v Crown Court at Norwich, ex p Belsham* [1992] 1 WLR 54 (1992 Abr para 729) and *R v Central Criminal Court, ex p Randle* [1992] 1 All ER 370 (1990 Abr para 596) had been wrongly decided.

    R v Crown Court at Manchester, ex p DPP [1993] 2 All ER 663 (House of Lords: Lords Keith of Kinkel, Bridge of Harwich, Ackner, Browne-Wilkinson and Slynn of Hadley).

773   Stay of proceedings—abuse of process—promise of immunity from prosecution

The defendant was arrested on suspicion of murder and subsequently charged with doing acts with the intent to impede the apprehension of another. At committal proceedings the court rejected a submission that the proposed trial was an abuse of process as the applicant had received an undertaking from the police that he would not be prosecuted. In an application by the defendant for judicial review of the decision to prosecute, *held*, the police had no authority or right to tell the applicant that he would not be prosecuted for any offence connected with the murder investigation. The effect of the undertaking, promise or representation by the police was likely to have been the same whether or not it had been authorised by the Crown Prosecution Service and if the Crown Prosecution Service found that its powers had been usurped by the police then a greater degree of liaison between the two bodies at an earlier stage was required. The prosecution of a person who had received a promise, undertaking or representation from the police that he would not be prosecuted was capable of being an abuse of process. In this case an affidavit stated that the police had told the applicant that he would not be prosecuted for offences associated with the murder. Having regard to the fact that the applicant was only 17 at the time, it was clearly an abuse of process for him to be prosecuted. Accordingly, the application would be allowed.

    R v Croydon Justices, ex p Dean [1993] 3 All ER 129 (Queen's Bench Division: Staughton LJ and Buckley J).

774 Stay of proceedings—impossibility of fair trial—adverse publicity

The defendants were policemen who had interviewed the "Birmingham Six", who were convicted of murder following a terrorist bombing campaignn. During their imprisonment, the Six maintained that their confessions had been involuntary and therefore inadmissible, and that the defendants were guilty of violence and perjury. Similar claims were made by the media throughout the same period. Eighteen years later, the Six had their convictions quashed by the Court of Appeal when it was found that at least one of their confessions had been improperly obtained. The defendants were charged with conspiracy to pervert the course of justice. The defence claimed that it was impossible to give the defendants a fair trial. *Held*, the jurisdiction to grant a stay ought to be regarded as exceptional and used sparingly and only for compelling reasons. In this case, the volume, intensity and continuity of coverage given to the Birmingham Six had made them a synonym for forced confessions. The publicity attending their successful appeal gave the impression that the court was finding the defendants guilty of conspiracy and perjury. However the coverage should not have been restricted or moderated to avoid prejudicing future criminal proceedings as the law provided the means to determine what it was permissible to report and comment upon. Publicity was a powerful factor in deciding whether to stay this case but it was not the only one. Re-examining the events of nineteen years ago, together with difficulties as regards witnesses and evidence, put the defence at a substantial disadvantage. It would be impossible in practice to isolate the Crown case, relying on interviews with one of the Six, from the whole matrix of events that took place from the Six's original trial to the present, about which there were strong public perceptions. The defendants' application would be granted and the proceedings would accordingly be stayed.

R v Reade (1993) Independent, 19 October (Central Criminal Court: Garland J).

775 Trial—adjournment—delay—prejudice to the defendant

The defendant was convicted of rape. The complainant gave her evidence on the first day of trial. The trial was then adjourned for 14 days because the defendant was admitted to hospital suffering from angina. In summing up, the judge expressly stated that it would be a full summing up in relation to the evidence because of the 14-day gap during the trial. The defendant appealed, contending that the delay was prejudicial because it had made it impossible for the jury to accurately recall the complainant's evidence and demeanour, especially under cross-examination. *Held*, delays between parts of the evidence occurred in many circumstances and did not necessarily give rise to prejudice amounting to injustice or material irregularity. Indeed, in the present case, the delay resulted in the defendant's evidence being most fresh in the minds of the jury. Whether it was appropriate to discharge a jury was a matter of discretion for the trial judge. There was no evidence that the judge had given undue weight to the complainant's interest in not being called to give evidence again, and that was a material consideration in such cases, nor was there any suggestion that he had ignored other matters relevant to the exercise of his discretion. Accordingly, the appeal would be dismissed.

R v Dodson [1993] Crim LR 461 (Court of Appeal: Lloyd LJ, Latham and Smith JJ).

776 Trial—conduct of counsel—failure to call defendant

At the defendant's trial on charges of kidnapping and indecent assault, the court was of the view that he should give evidence in order to underline discrepancies regarding the complainant's identification of the defendant. The defendant did not give evidence at trial, and his counsel did not try to persuade him to give evidence. The defendant was convicted and appealed against his conviction. *Held*, cases where the conduct of counsel would afford a basis for appeal had to be regarded as wholly exceptional. However, where a decision had been taken either in defiance of or without proper instructions, or when all the promptings of reason and good sense had pointed the other way, it would be open to an appellate court to set aside the verdict by reason of the terms of the Criminal Appeal Act 1968, s 2(1)(a). In the circumstances the conviction was unsafe and unsatisfactory and accordingly, the appeal would be allowed.

R v Clinton [1993] WLR 1181 (Court of Appeal: Steyn LJ, Garland and Rougier JJ).

777 Trial—conduct of trial judge—continuous interruptions

The defendant was charged with being knowingly concerned in the fraudulent evasion of the prohibition on importation of a controlled drug. Following his conviction the defendant appealed on the ground that the judge had continually interrupted defence counsel during the trial and, in particular, the defendant during his evidence. *Held*, in following *R v Hulusi* (1973) 58 Cr App R 378, it was most undesirable for judges to interrupt witnesses, particularly a defendant, when giving evidence-in-chief or being cross-examined. It was for counsel on each side to conduct examination and cross-examination and for the judge to see that they did it fairly. However, the judge's direction and summing up had put the defence and prosecution cases fairly and accordingly, the appeal would be dismissed.

R v Marsh (1993) Times, 6 July (Court of Appeal: Lord Taylor of Gosforth CJ, Ognall and Sedley JJ).

778 Trial—conduct of trial judge—failure to secure services of interpreter

Mauritius
A trial was conducted in the English language, which the defendant did not understand. The trial judge knew that an interpreter was present and that he was not translating to the defendant the evidence of the prosecution witnesses. In his statement from the dock, the defendant stated that he had not understood what the witnesses had said. On appeal against conviction, *held*, an accused who had not understood the conduct of proceedings against him could not, in the absence of express consent, be said to have had a fair trial. The defendant in the present case had been deprived of the opportunity of a fair trial and a substantial miscarriage of justice had occurred. Accordingly, the appeal would be allowed and the conviction quashed.

Kunnath v The State [1993] 4 All ER 30 (Privy Council: Lords Goff of Chieveley, Jauncey of Tullichettle, Lowry, Slynn of Hadley and Gault J).

779 Trial—jury—bias

The appellant was convicted of conspiracy to commit robbery with D, his brother (against whom proceedings had been discontinued due to lack of evidence), and was sentenced to 15 years' imprisonment. One of the jurors was D's neighbour, and although D's name was mentioned frequently during the trial it was not until D started shouting from the public gallery after sentence had been passed that she recognised him as her neighbour. The appellant contended that the conviction should be quashed because the presence of the juror constituted a serious irregularity in the conduct of the trial. His first appeal was dismissed and he further appealed to the House of Lords. *Held*, in all cases of alleged bias the test to be applied was whether there was real danger of injustice having occurred as a result of the alleged bias. That test was applicable whether the allegation concerned jurors, justices, members of other inferior tribunals or arbitrators. In cases concerned with jurors, it would be applied by a judge to whose attention the possibility of bias on the part of the juror had been drawn in the course of a trial and by the Court of Appeal when it considered such a question on appeal. The test ought to be stated in terms of real danger rather than real likelihood, to ensure that the court was thinking in terms of possibility rather than probability of bias. Accordingly, the appeal would be dismissed.

R v Gough [1993] 2 All ER 724, (House of Lords: Lords Goff of Chieveley, Ackner, Mustill, Slynn of Hadley and Woolf). Decision of the Court of Appeal [1992] 4 All ER 481 (1992 Abr para 736) affirmed. *R v Liverpool City Justices, ex p Topping* [1983] 1 All ER 490, DC distinguished.

780 Trial—jury—examination of evidence after retiring

The applicant was convicted of possessing a firearm without a certificate and of causing grievous bodily harm with intent. At the trial, the victim alleged that the applicant concealed a gun in his overcoat before attacking her, and the jury heard evidence that the victim's injuries were consistent with being beaten with a gun muzzle. The applicant's defence was that he did not have the gun with him and that it was subsequently produced by the victim's son. The jury retired and the judge acceded to their request to examine the gun in the jury room. On his appeal against conviction, the applicant contended that the judge erred in allowing the examination, arguing that the evidence was complete and that there was a risk that the jury would experiment to see if the gun could be concealed in the manner alleged by the victim and that this would constitute further evidence. *Held*, subject to the judge's discretion, the jury was entitled to have access to any exhibit which would help them reach an informed decision. Unsupervised scientific experimentation was not permissible, but examination of the gun was a legitimate exercise. Accordingly, the appeal would be dismissed.

R v Wright [1993] Crim LR 607 (Court of Appeal: Nolan LJ, Owen and Kay JJ). *R v Maggs* (1990) 91 Cr App R 243, CA (1990 Abr para 605) applied.

781   Trial—jury—tape-recording given in evidence—provision of tape to jury on retirement

The defendant was convicted of murder. Shortly before her death the victim made a 999 call and, although she was unable to speak to the operator, the tape-recorder in the telephone exchange recorded the conversation that ensued between her and the defendant and the victim. At the trial, the tape-recording was played to the jury and a transcript exhibited. After retiring, the jury asked to hear the tape again. The judge directed that they must not try to decipher certain passages shown in the transcript as indecipherable and asked whether they wished to hear the tape in open court or in the jury room. The jury elected to retire with the tape. The defendant applied for leave to appeal, on the grounds that the judge should only have allowed the jury to hear the tape in open court as there was a risk that they might have embarked on a voyage of discovery and tried to decipher the indecipherable passages. *Held*, where a judge acceded to a jury's request, after retiring, to hear a tape, he should normally require it to be played in open court. However, if the tape had already been played in open court, and an agreed transcript had been made containing no inadmissible passages, he had a discretion to allow the jury to play it in their room if that was more convenient. That was what occurred in the present case. There was no irregularity and the judge had correctly exercised his discretion. Accordingly, the application would be refused.

R v Tonge (1993) 157 JP 1137 (Court of Appeal: Leggatt LJ, Tucker and Blofeld JJ).

782   Trial—late attendance of prosecution witness—re-opening of prosecution case

The defendant was charged with supplying a car in an unroadworthy condition. The main prosecution witness, who was the person to whom the car had been supplied, failed to arrive for the hearing. Following the closure of the prosecution case and whilst the defendant was giving evidence, the witness arrived. His excuse was accepted and the justices exercised their discretion in allowing the prosecution to reopen the case. The defendant was convicted and appealed by way of case stated on the ground that the justices had wrongly exercised their discretion. *Held*, in considering *R v Pilcher* (1974) 60 Cr App R 1, the prosecution ought only to be allowed to reopen the case in exceptional circumstances where the matter was one of substance. In the instant case the circumstances were exceptional, the evidence had not been available at the proper stage and as there was no unfairness to the defendant the discretion had been properly exercised. Accordingly, the appeal would be dismissed.

James v South Glamorgan County Council (1993) 157 JP 561 (Queen's Bench Division: Leggatt LJ and Owen J).

783   Trial—plea of guilty—divergence between prosecution and defence as to facts—duty of accused's legal representatives

The defendant pleaded guilty to wounding with intent. However, his version of the circumstances of the offence differed materially from the prosecution version. Without hearing any evidence, the judge decided that the defendant's version was manifestly false and sentenced him to eight years' imprisonment. On his appeal against sentence, *held*, it was the responsibility of the defendant's legal representatives to notify the prosecution that a plea of guilty was to be made on the basis that the defendant disputed the prosecution version of the circumstances of the offence so as to enable the prosecution to arrange for the necessary witnesses to be present in court to enable a *Newton* hearing to proceed. As no *Newton* hearing had been conducted, the defendant would be sentenced on the basis of his version of events. His appeal would be allowed and the sentence reduced to six years.

R v Mohun (1993) 14 Cr App Rep (S) 5 (Court of Appeal: Watkins LJ, Boreham and Cresswell JJ). *R v Newton* (1982) 77 Cr App Rep 13, CA (1983 Abr para 2994) considered.

784   Trial—plea of guilty—plea entered by mistake—jurisdiction

The first defendant was stopped by police while driving a vehicle belonging to the employer of the second defendant. When asked for his name and address, he gave the name in which the second defendant's licence was made out. The first defendant was required to produce his driving documents to the police, but it was the second defendant who actually produced the relevant documents. The defendants pleaded guilty to charges of using a licence with intent to deceive, using an insurance certificate with intent to deceive, and using a motor vehicle without insurance. In respect of the latter offence, the defendants were committed to the Crown Court for sentence under the Criminal Justice Act 1988, s 41. Charges of taking the vehicle without consent were not proceeded with by the prosecution. The defendants appealed on the ground that they had mistakenly entered pleas of guilty to the offences of using a motor vehicle without insurance. Both prosecution and defence counsel had proceeded on the basis that the employer's insurance policy covered only employees, but it was subsequently found that the policy applied to anyone driving with the policyholder's consent. On the question of whether the Court of Appeal had jurisdiction to hear the appeal, held, the statutory jurisdiction of the Court of Appeal under the Criminal Appeal Act 1968 was not available to the defendants as an offence referred to the Crown Court under the 1988 Act, s 41 was not an offence on indictment within the meaning of the 1968 Act, s 1(1). The defendants had appreciated the nature of the charge of using a motor vehicle without insurance, and had intended to admit it as part of the price of acquittal on the charges of taking the vehicle without consent. Conflicting pleas to the respective offences were not irreconcilable, as to prove the offence of taking a vehicle without consent required the negativing of the employer's consent beyond reasonable doubt, whereas in relation to the offence of using a vehicle without insurance it was for the defence to prove that the employer had consented. Accordingly, the court would not exercise its common law jurisdiction to hear the appeal.

R v Coniam [1993] Crim LR 272 (Court of Appeal: Leggatt LJ and Rougier and Sedley JJ).

785 Trial—summing up—direction on lies

The defendant was charged with murder. It was alleged that the defendant's brother had chased the victim from his house with a knife followed by the defendant. The victim had died of a wound through the heart. The brother escaped but the defendant was arrested and interviewed at length. The prosecution claimed that the interviews contained inconsistencies which amounted to lies. It was contended that there was a joint enterprise or that the defendant aided and abetted the brother in the commission of the crime. The defendant's case was that he acted as a peacemaker. Following his conviction the defendant appealed on the ground that the judge ought to have directed the jury in accordance with the specimen direction recommended by the Judicial Studies Board to consider whether there might be an innocent explanation for his lies. Held, the specimen direction ought to be given where a question arose whether: (1) lies could amount to corroboration, or (2) lies could amount to evidence supporting identification. However, outside the two recognised categories, a trial judge had a discretion whether to caution a jury about lies; that discretion should be exercised when fairness demanded it. In the present case fairness required a direction on lies and accordingly, the conviction would be quashed and a retrial ordered.

R v Bey [1993] 3 All ER 253 (Court of Appeal: Steyn LJ, Rougier and Laws JJ).

786 Trial—summing up—direction to jury—alternative verdict first mentioned in direction

At the defendant's trial for causing death by reckless driving, the judge of his own motion and without prior warning to counsel, directed the jury to consider the lesser and alternative offence, as provided by the Road Traffic Offenders Act 1988, s 24, of careless driving. Counsel was given the opportunity to address the jury further. The defendant was acquitted of causing death by reckless driving but was convicted of the alternative offence. On his appeal against conviction, held, although s 24 made clear the possibility of there being a conviction of careless driving on a charge of causing death by reckless driving, the raising of that matter in the direction to the jury was too late. When defence counsel was initially addressing the jury, he was not able to deal with the possibility of a conviction of the lesser offence. Although he had been able to address the jury further, his hands were tied in a way which could only be seen as having been grossly unfair to the defendant. The late introduction of the possibility of a conviction of the lesser offence was a material irregularity making the conviction unsatisfactory. Accordingly, the appeal would be allowed and the conviction quashed.

R v Hammett [1993] RTR 275 (Court of Appeal: Mann LJ, Owen and Kay JJ).

787 Trial—summing up—direction to jury—defence of manslaughter

The appellant was convicted of manslaughter. At the trial, the prosecution alleged that he had murdered the deceased by deliberately causing her to fall from a high-storey balcony whilst the defence case was that she had committed suicide. In summing up, the judge put the possibility of manslaughter to the jury. On appeal, held, the extent of a judge's duty in summing up varied according to the facts of the particular case and on the possible issues and inferences properly disclosed by the evidence. In the present case the judge had correctly left the hidden defence of manslaughter to the jury and, accordingly, the appeal would be dismissed.

R v Williams (1993) Times, 11 November (Court of Appeal: Neill LJ, Buckley J and Sir Michael Davies).

788 Trial—summing up—direction to jury—duty to give directions

The defendant was charged with indecent assault. Although the issue had arisen on the facts, the judge failed to give a direction as to the defendant's state of mind and its relevance to whether he had committed the offence. Following his conviction the defendant appealed. *Held*, where there was the slightest doubt about what issues ought to be left to the jury, it was incumbent upon the trial judge to raise the matter with counsel, at the latest before the commencement of final speeches, so that the matter could then be resolved. The jury had not had the opportunity of considering the issue, and therefore the conviction was unsafe and unsatisfactory. Accordingly, the appeal would be allowed.

R v Wren (1993) Times, 13 July (Court of Appeal: Watkins LJ, Auld and Scott Baker JJ).

789 Trial—summing up—direction to jury—evidence of police officer

During cross-examination, a police officer rejected allegations that he had fabricated his evidence and added that he would not jeopardise his family life and his home for the sake of securing the appellant's conviction. In closing, prosecuting counsel reminded the jury of the risk of imprisonment faced by a police officer who was found to have lied in evidence and reminded the jury of the officer's stated unwillingness to put his house, his wife and three young children at risk. Defence counsel applied for the jury to be discharged on the ground that the comments by the prosecuting counsel were improper and could not be negated effectively by any direction that the judge might give to the jury. The judge rejected the application and told the jury that police witnesses were not in a special category. He described prosecuting counsel's remarks as unfortunate and directed the jury that, as a matter of law, their verdict was not to be influenced by considerations of that kind. On appeal against conviction, *held*, prosecuting counsel should not comment to the jury on the potentially serious consequences to police officers of their evidence being disbelieved, even where a police officer had raised the matter in evidence himself. The judge's direction to the jury in this case had been correct and accordingly the appeal would be dismissed.

R v Gale (1993) Times, 2 June (Court of Appeal: Waite LJ, Waterhouse and Dyson JJ).

790 Trial—summing up—direction to jury—good character of defendant

In three appeals against convictions of different offences, questions arose as to (1) whether, where a defendant of good character had not given evidence but had made statements to the police or others, the "first limb" of a character direction (ie a direction about the relevance of good character to the defendant's credibility) needed to be given, (2) whether the "second limb" direction (ie a direction as to the possible relevance of good character to the question whether the defendant was likely to have behaved as alleged by the prosecution) should now be regarded as discretionary or obligatory, and (3) what course the judge should take in a joint trial where one defendant was of good character but another was not. *Held*, (1) a direction as to the relevance of his good character to the defendant's credibility was to be given where he had testified or made pre-trial answers or statements. (2) A direction as to the relevance of his good character to the likelihood of his having committed the offence charged was to be given, whether or not he had testified, or made pre-trial answers or statements. (3) Even where a defendant of good character was jointly tried with a defendant of bad character, the directions under (1) and (2) were to be given.

R v Vye; R v Wise; R v Stephenson [1993] 3 All ER 241 (Court of Appeal: Lord Taylor of Gosforth CJ, Judge and Hidden JJ). *R v Gibson* [1991] 93 Cr App Rep 9, CA (1991 Abr para 666) not followed.

It has been held that a judge, when summing up at the trial of a defendant of good character who has pleaded guilty to another offence in an indictment arising out of the same incident on the same occasion, ought to direct the jury as to the relevance of the defendant's good character to the credibility of his evidence. The plea of guilty to the other count may be an indication of propensity to commit such an offence but it is in no way probative of the defendant's guilt on the count to which he has pleaded not guilty.

R v Teasdale [1993] 4 All ER 290 (Court of Appeal: Farquharson LJ, Morland and Cresswell JJ). *R v Vye* [1993] 3 All ER 241, CA supra applied.

791 Trial—summing up—direction to jury—jury given choice as to when to retire

The defendant was charged with causing grievous bodily harm with intent, contrary to the Offences Against the Person Act 1861, s 18. At the trial the judge left it to the jury to decide whether they wished to retire and consider their verdicts late in the afternoon or to wait until the following morning. The judge made his inquiry of the jury in open court and left them to talk among themselves in the jury box. Following his conviction the defendant appealed. *Held*, the Court of Appeal expressed concern as to the way the matter had been left to the jury. As the jury had not yet begun their deliberations they were not qualified to exercise any sensible discretion on such an option, if it existed. However in the event no unfairness resulted from the matter but the conviction would be quashed owing to a misdirection on the issue of intent under the 1861 Act, s 18.

R v Hawkins (1993) Times, 29 June (Court of Appeal: Watkins LJ, Auld and Scott Baker JJ).

792 Trial—summing up—direction to jury—question from jury—dishonesty direction

The defendant attempted to purchase some items with a credit card which was in the name of someone else. He was charged with attempting to obtain goods by deception. Following the judge's summing up in which the *Ghosh* direction was given the jury asked, "Question of law: is ignorance of the law a defence?". The judge did not invite counsel to address him and answered the question saying "No, it is not". The defendant was convicted and appealed on the ground that in the light of his evidence, for the judge to have answered the jury's question with the simple negative effectively undermined his case. *Held*, there was a clear distinction between a defendant's knowledge of the law and his appreciation that he was doing something which, by the ordinary standards of reasonable and honest people, would be regarded as dishonest. As knowledge of the law was irrelevant, the judge ought to have explained to the jury the distinction. In answering the jury's question his failure to give the *Ghosh* direction amounted to a misdirection and accordingly, the appeal would be allowed.

R v Lightfoot (1993) 97 Cr App Rep 24 (Court of Appeal: Staughton LJ, Waterhouse and McCullough JJ). *R v Ghosh* [1982] QB 1053, CA applied.

793 Trial—summing up—direction to jury—rejection of defence case

The defendant was charged with supplying heroin. The defendant put forward a defence which was described by the prosecution as a "cock and bull" story, such that the jury could not only discount it but that it could support the evidence of his guilt. The judge in his summing up reminded the jury of the prosecution and defence cases and went through the evidence, but nowhere did he tell them that rejection of the defence version of events was not enough on which to convict. Following his conviction the defendant appealed. *Held*, the effect of the judge's direction was to invite the jury, if they rejected the defendant's account, to find him guilty. The jury still had to be sure guilt of the specific offence charged had been proved. The absence of a warning that rejection of the defence account was not enough and of the need to be sure that the specific charge had been established amounted to a material misdirection. Accordingly, the appeal would be allowed.

R v Fitzgibbon (1993) Independent, 3 September (Court of Appeal: Lord Taylor of Gosforth CJ, Ognall and Sedley JJ).

794 Trial—summing up—direction to jury—reliance on lies by defendant

The defendant was convicted on charges of murder and wounding with intent. The defendant appealed on the ground that the prosecution had relied on lies told by him as support for other evidence of his guilt and the judge had not given any direction as to how the jury should consider the lies. *Held*, where lies told by a defendant were relied upon by the prosecution or might be relied upon by the jury as corroboration, where that was required, or as support for identification evidence, the judge should give a direction along the lines of *R v Lucas* [1981] 2 All ER 1008, CA (1981 Abr para 720): the lie had to be deliberate and relate to a material issue. The jury had to be satisfied that there was no innocent motive for the lie and should be reminded that people sometimes lied in attempting to bolster up a just cause, or out of shame or out of a wish to conceal disgraceful behaviour. In relation to corroboration, the lie had to be established by evidence other than that of the witness who was to be corroborated. A *Lucas* direction should be given except where it was otiose because rejection of the explanation given by the defendant almost inevitably left the jury with no choice but to convict as a matter of logic. The appeal would accordingly be allowed, the conviction would be quashed and a retrial ordered.

Para 794   Halsbury's Abridgment 1993

R v Goodway [1993] 4 All ER 894 (Court of Appeal: Lord Taylor of Gosforth CJ, Alliott and Buckley JJ).

795 Trial—summing up—direction to jury—right to silence—guidelines

The following guidelines have been issued in regard to judges' directions where defendants fail to testify: (1) in giving directions to the jury on a defendant's failure to give evidence, the judge ought to follow the lines of the Judicial Studies Board specimen direction based on *R v Bathurst* [1968] 2 QB 99; (2) the essentials of that direction were that the defendant is under no obligation to testify and the jury ought not assume he is guilty because he has not given evidence; (3) provided those essentials are complied with, a stronger comment may be appropriate where the defence case involves alleged facts which (a) are at variance with the prosecution evidence or additional to it and exculpatory; and (b) are, if true, within the knowledge of the defendant; and (4) the nature and strength of such comment has to be a matter for the discretion of the judge and will depend upon the circumstances of the individual case. However, it must not be such as to contradict or nullify the essentials of the conventional direction.

R v Martinez-Tobon (1993) Times, 1 December (Court of Appeal: Lord Taylor of Gosforth CJ, Schiemann and Wright JJ).

796 Trial—summing up—direction to jury—self-induced drunkenness

The defendant was charged with causing grievous bodily harm with intent. At the trial in his summing up the judge referred to self-induced drunkenness stating that drunkenness could be such that a person was incapable of forming an intent and directed the jury that the evidence showed that the defendant was capable of forming an intent (to do grievous bodily harm). He added that the jury had to be satisfied that the defendant did form an intent but re-iterated that there was no suggestion that the defendant was so affected by alcohol as not to be able to form an intent. Following her conviction the defendant appealed on the ground that the judge had misdirected the jury. *Held*, the issue was whether the defendant had actually formed an intent, and not whether she was capable of forming the intent. The judge's direction concerning capacity to form an intent was incomplete and ought to have been followed by a direction that the jury must find that an intent had to be proved notwithstanding the consumption of alcohol. Accordingly, the appeal would be allowed, and the conviction for causing grievous bodily harm with intent would be quashed and a verdict of causing grievous bodily harm would be substituted.

R v Cole [1993] Crim LR 300 (Court of Appeal: Steyn LJ, Pill and Wright JJ).

797 Trial—summing up—direction to jury—use of specimen direction

The defendant was convicted of robbery from, and the rape of, a complainant who had numerous convictions for prostitution. The complainant's evidence was uncorroborated. The judge directed the jury that the complainant was a person of poor character. He told the jury that they should not assume that the complainant was not telling the truth just because she had numerous previous convictions, and that her convictions and bad character were not relevant to the likelihood of whether or not she had concocted her story. Finally, the judge said that the complainant's convictions were only relevant as to whether or not she could be believed and that it was for the jury to decide the extent to which, if at all, they were helped by the knowledge of those convictions. The defendant appealed on the ground that the judge had wrongly directed the jury. *Held*, it was agreed that the judge had taken and sought to adapt to the situation of the complainant the specimen direction in relation to a defendant's bad character published by the Judicial Studies Board. Parts of that direction were inappropriate and the effect was to create confusion. Specimen directions had to be used with the greatest care, particularly where the circumstances of a case required adaptation of a specimen direction. Specimen directions drafted for one purpose ought not to be used for a different purpose. The present case turned on the credibility of the complainant and her evidence was clearly incorrect in a number of respects. Accordingly, the appeal would be allowed.

R v Taylor (1993) Times, 15 June (Court of Appeal: Lord Taylor of Gosforth CJ, Otton and Sedley JJ).

CRIMINAL LAW

Halsbury's Laws of England (4th edn) Vol 11(1) (reissue), paras 1–800, Vol 11(2) (reissue), paras 801–1592

798 Articles

A Clear Concept of Intention—Elusive or Illusory? Nicola Lacey: 56 MLR 621
Alternative Verdicts to Affray and Violent Disorder, Kris Gledhill: Criminal Lawyer, Issue 40, p 4
Alternatives to Prosecution: The Public Interest Redefined: Jacqueline Tombs and Susan Moody: [1993] Crim LR 345
An Outsider's View of the Criminal Justice System, WG Runciman: 57 MLR 1
Assault and Psychological Injuries, David Kinchin: 157 JP Jo 200
Assaults—The Relationship Between Seriousness, Criminalisation and Punishment, Chris Clarkson et al: [1994] Crim LR 4
Balancing Acts and Constitutionalism, Mike McConville and Chester Mirsky (on the Royal Commission on Criminal Justice): 143 NLJ 1579
Bankruptcy—Its Associated Crimes, Andrew Campbell: 137 SJ 638
Battered Women and Provocation—The Implications of *R v Ahluwalia*, Donald Nicolson and Rohit Sanghvi (on *R v Ahluwalia* [1992] 4 All ER 889 (1992 Abr para 797)): [1993] Crim LR 728
Bringing Back the Verbal, Rowan Bosworth-Davies (on the Royal Commission on Criminal Justice): 143 NLJ 1231
Caldwell Recklessness Revisited, F Davies: 157 JP Jo 775
Cause and the Contemporaneity of *Actus Reus* and *Mens Rea*, GR Sullivan: [1993] 52 CLJ 487
Challenging the Validity of Byelaws by way of Defence to Prosecutions, Ian McLeod: [1994] Crim LR 35
Charge or Caution? Seàn Enright: 143 NLJ 446
Comparing Young Adult and Juvenile Cautioning in the Metropolitan Police District, Roger Evans: [1993] Crim LR 572
Complex Crimes, Alan Reed (on involuntary manslaughter, attempted rape and joint unlawful enterprise): 137 SJ 908
Consent and Appropriation: Has Gomez Settled the Dispute, Mark Florida-James (on *DPP v Gomez* [1993] 1 All ER 1 (1992 Abr para 828)): 157 JP Jo 403
Convicting Criminal Directors, Jessica Holroyd: 137 SJ 1218
Corporate Punishment, Gary Slapper: 144 NLJ 29
Corporations: Culture, Risk and Criminal Liability, Celia Wells: [1993] Crim LR 551
Cost Effective Criminal Justice, Seàn Enright (on the Royal Commission on Criminal Justice): 143 NLJ 1023
Crime and the Right of Prescription, Touchstone: 137 SJ 1161
Criminal Common Law Remedies Against the State for Breach of European Law, David Pedley: 158 JP Jo 3
Criminal Justice—a European Perspective, Heike Jung: [1993] Crim LR 237
Criminal Justice in the Dock, Mark Hinchliffe (on the Criminal Justice Act 1991): 137 SJ 582
Custodes Respondent, George Staple (on regulating the Serious Fraud Office): 143 NLJ 1560
Damp Squibs and Nasty Judges, Michael Beckman (on the Royal Commission on Criminal Justice): 143 NLJ 1196
Disclosure, Joanna Glynn (on the Royal Commission on Criminal Justice): [1993] Crim LR 841
Discretion to Prosecute and Judicial Review, Christopher Hilson: [1993] Crim LR 739
Drugs, Money and the Law, Christopher Sallon and David Bedingfield: [1993] Crim LR 161
EC Law Versus National Criminal Law, Susan Singleton: Criminal Lawyer, Issue 39, p 6
European Community Criminal Law? Janet Dine: [1993] Crim LR 246
Football and Racism a Legislative Solution? Neil Parpworth: 137 SJ 1016
How Will the Right of Silence be Abolished? Michael Zander: 143 NLJ 1710
International Mutual Assistance in Criminal Cases, David Kirk and Tony Woodcock: (1993) JIBFL 325
Intoxication and Defences in the Criminal Law, L M Clements (on *R v Egan* [1992] 4 All ER 470, CA): 157 JP Jo 55, 70
Investigative Powers and Safeguards for Suspects, Robert Reiner (on the Royal Commission on Criminal Justice): [1993] Crim LR 808

CHIEF EXECUTIVE

Involuntary Manslaughter—The Mental Element, Gill Korgaonkar and Diana Tribe: 137 SJ 639

Is Intoxication a Medical Reason for Failing to Provide a Specimen? Christine Clayson: 137 SJ 1027

Keeping Faith with their own Convictions—The Royal Commission on Criminal Justice, Lee Bridges and Mike McConville: 57 MLR 75

Keeping Terrorists Out, Fran Russell (on exclusion powers under the Prevention of Terrorism Act 1989): 137 SJ 732

Killing in Self-Defence—Is the Law an Ass? Leslie James: 157 JP Jo 691

Making Better Use of Bail Conditions, John Boyle: 137 SJ 151

Making Foul Play a Crime, Edward Grayson and Catherine Bond (on violence on the professional sporting field): 137 SJ 693

Making the Youth Court Work, Terence Moore: 157 JP Jo 503

Misadventures of Manslaughter, Glanville Williams: 143 NLJ 1413

Miscarriages of Criminal Justice Reconsidered, Steven Greer: 57 MLR 58

New Regime for Insider Dealing, Peter King: 137 SJ 1242

No Defence for a Sado-Masochistic Libido, Susan Edwards (on *R v Brown* [1993] NLJR 399, HL (para 800): 143 NLJ 406

Not Playing the Game—Is it a Crime? Simon Gardiner: 137 SJ 628

Plea, Sentence Discount and Cracked Trials, Paul Robertshaw: 143 NLJ 577

Plea, Venue and Discontinuance, Andrew Ashworth (on the Royal Commission on Criminal Justice): [1993] Crim LR 830

Plus Ça Change, Plus Nascetur Ridiculus Mus, Brian Block (on the Royal Commission on Criminal Justice): 157 JP Jo 580

Police Interrogation and Interruption, Ed Cape: 144 NLJ 120

Possession—Erotic Love in the Law of Rape, Ngaire Naffine: 57 MLR 10

Prosecuting Professionals for Manslaughter, Gary Slapper: 143 NLJ 897

Public Interest Immunity and Ministers' Responsibilities, T Allan: [1993] Crim LR 660

Putting a Price on Rape, Fiona Bawdon (on compensation awards for rape victims): 143 NLJ 371

Putting the Clock Back on Rape, Jennifer Temkin: 143 NLJ 1575

Quis Custodiet? Hugh Mainprice (on regulating the Serious Fraud Office): 143 NLJ 1483

R v Brown—Consensual Harm and the Public Interest, Marianne Giles (on *R v Brown* [1993] 2 All ER 75, HL (para 800)): 57 MLR 101

R v Savage, DPP v Parmenter—A Compelling Case for the Code (see [1991] All ER 698, HL (1991 Abr para 677)), Ivan Hare: (1993) 56 MLR 74

R v Savage, DPP v Parmenter and the Law of Assault (see [1991] All ER 698, HL (1991 Abr para 677)), Berni Bell and Kate Harrison: 56 MLR 83

"Second Helpings"—Taking a Conveyance Without Consent, When it has Already Been Previously Taken, JN Spencer (on *DPP v Spriggs* (1993) Times, 28 January (para 856)): [1993] 157 JP 675

Serious and Complex Fraud: A New Perspective, George Staple: 56 MLR 127

Silent Right, Paul Phippen (on the right to silence): LS Gaz, 29 September 1993, p 17

Soliciting for Immoral Purposes, Ronald Cottrell: 137 SJ 303

Spreading Disease and the Criminal Law, Simon Bronitt: [1994] Crim LR 21

Staying Silent, Julian Gibbons (on the Royal Commission on Criminal Justice): Criminal Lawyer, Issue 42, p 5

Summary of Recommendations, (on the Royal Commission on Criminal Justice): 143 NLJ 993, 143 NLJ 1028

The CPS—Fulcrum of the System of Piggy in the Middle? Brian Block: 157 JP Jo 792

The Criminalisation of the Squatter, Hugo Charlton: 143 NLJ 1721

The Disordering of Criminal Justice, Mike McConville and Chester Mirsky: 143 NLJ 1446

The Dissenting Voice, Nicola Padfield (on the Royal Commission on Criminal Justice): 143 NLJ 1002

The Evidence, Recommendations, John Jackson (on the Royal Commission on Criminal Justice): [1993] Crim LR 817

The Offence of Directing Terrorist Organisations, Clive Walker: [1993] Crim LR 669

The Problem of Causation, Simon Cooper: 143 NLJ 720

The Revised Custodial Sentencing Provisions of the Criminal Justice Act 1991, Leonard Jason-Lloyd: Criminal Lawyer, Issue 40, p 1

The Right to Jury Trial—How the Royal Commission got it Wrong, Lee Bridges: 143 NLJ 1542

The Royal Commission on Criminal Justice, George Carman QC: Counsel, July 1993, p 8

The Royal Commission on What? John Mackenzie (on the Royal Commission on Criminal Justice): 143 NLJ 1035

Theft, Appropriation and Consent, Michael Allen (on *R v Gomez* [1993] 1 All ER 1 (1992 Abr para 828)): 137 SJ 380

Unravelling Miscarriages of Justice, John Wadham (on the Criminal Cases Review Authority): 143 NLJ 1650

Variations on Conspiracy, David Fitzpatrick (on a new approach to organised crime): 143 NLJ 1180

What Constitutes Fitness to Plead? Dr Don Grubin: [1993] Crim LR 748

When is a Restrictive Trade Practice a Crime? Susan Singleton: Criminal Lawyer, Issue 38, p 5

What is Going On? Michael Zander (on the Royal Commission on Criminal Justice): 143 NLJ 1507

Where the Critics Got it Wrong, Michael Zander (on the Royal Commission on Criminal Justice): 143 NLJ 1338

Whither the "General Arrest Conditions"? Anna Lawson: [1993] Crim LR 567

Without Reasonable Excuse, Christine Clayson (on the failure to provide a specimen): 137 SJ 1260

799 Arson—recklessness—self-induced intoxication

The Criminal Damage Act 1971, s 1(2) provides that it is an offence if a person, without lawful excuse, destroys or damages any property intending to destroy or damage any property or being reckless as to whether any property would be destroyed or damaged, and intending by the destruction or damage to endanger the life of another or being reckless as to whether the life of another would thereby be endangered. Under the 1971 Act, s 1(3), where the damage is caused by fire, the offence is arson.

The respondents were charged with attempted aggravated arson, and the indictment particularised recklessness as to whether life would be endangered. They had thrown a lighted petrol bomb towards the complainants' occupied car which landed a pavement's width from the car. The trial judge held that they could only be convicted of attempt if it was proved that they intended, by the intended damage, to endanger the lives of others. She ruled that recklessness was insufficient, and directed the jury to return not guilty verdicts. On the Attorney General's referral on a point of law, *held*, the trial judge had erred in her direction. The substantive crime was committed if the defendants had a specific intent to cause damage by fire to property and were mentally reckless as to whether the life of another would thus be endangered. It followed that it was possible to convict for attempt if the prosecution proved that the defendants, in that state of mind, intended to damage the property by throwing a bomb at it.

Attorney-General's Reference (No 3 of 1992) [1994] RTR 122 (Court of Appeal: Lord Taylor of Gosforth CJ, Schiemann and Wright JJ).

The defendant, who shared a house with six others, had attempted to commit suicide by taking an overdose of pills and drink. He was discovered in his room surrounded by a number of cardboard boxes and magazines on fire which caused serious damage to the room and its contents. The defendant could not remember starting the fire but admitted that he must have caused it as the evidence showed a naked flame had been used to ignite the boxes. He was charged with arson but claimed that there was no case to answer as he had started the fire accidentally. At the trial, this argument was rejected and the jury was directed that the charge of arson was based on recklessness and that lack of awareness of the risk involved, due to self-induced intoxication, was not a valid defence. The defendant appealed on the ground that accident was a valid defence and that the judge had misdirected the jury in relation to recklessness and self-induced intoxication. *Held*, accident due to self-induced intoxication was not a defence to a crime as the defendant's actions must be viewed in the same light as if they had been carried out by a person who was sober. The defendant would therefore be guilty if he was aware of the risk of damage or the risk was such that a sober or ordinary prudent individual would have foreseen the damage. Although the judge had given a misdirection, it had not caused any injustice as the only issue was that of causation which was clearly established by the evidence. Accordingly, the appeal would be dismissed.

R v Cullen [1993] Crim LR 936 (Court of Appeal: Watkins LJ, Auld and Scott-Baker JJ).

800 Assault—indecent assault—sado-masochism—voluntary acceptance of risk of injury

The appellants had all been convicted of wounding or inflicting actual bodily harm upon one another, contrary to the Offences Against the Person Act 1861, ss 20 and 47. They had pleaded guilty after the trial judge ruled that consent on the part of the persons injured was not a defence because the injuries had been caused without good reason, namely in the course of participation in sado-masochistic acts of violence carried out for the sexual pleasure engendered in the giving and receiving of pain. Their convictions were upheld in the Court of Appeal, and, on their further appeal, *held*, Lords Mustill and Slynn of Hadley dissenting, the relevant authorities established that consent could be a defence to charges under the 1861 Act if the infliction of injury had been incidental to some other activity, but there was no authority for the appellants' proposition that the defence of consent ought to be extended so that it would be available where the violence had been inflicted in the course of an act of cruelty. The court would not invent a defence of consent to encounters which glorified cruelty and condoned pleasure which derived from the infliction of pain. Relaxing the prohibitions in the 1861 Act by withdrawing the legal penalty would only encourage sado-masochistic practices and the physical cruelty that it involved, and if such a radical change to the law was to be made it would have to be made by Parliament rather than by the courts. Accordingly, the appeal would be dismissed.

R v Brown [1993] 2 WLR 556 (House of Lords: Lords Templeman, Jauncey of Tullichettle, Lowry, Mustill and Slynn of Hadley). Decision of Court of Appeal [1992] 2 All ER 552 affirmed.

801　Assault—sexual assault—consent

Canada

The accused was charged with three counts of aggravated sexual assault. He knew he was infected with the human immuno-deficiency virus (HIV) but engaged in unprotected sexual intercourse without informing his partners of his infection and they subsequently contracted the virus. At the close of the Crown's case the defence moved for a directed verdict of acquittal, contending that the Crown had failed to vitiate consent. *Held*, the actus reus of the offence was the direct or indirect application of force without the consent of the person to whom the force was being applied. The criminal law was not based on the principle of informed consent and so whilst the victims may not have consented to the risk of the virus being transmitted, the evidence showed that the victims did consent to the application of the force inherent in the acts of sexual intercourse and that the force exerted was not excessive or dangerous. Further, no fraud sufficient to vitiate consent was committed. The victims were under no misapprehension as to the nature of the acts in which they were involved, they were fully aware that they were consenting to sexual intercourse with the accused and nothing he said or did induced them to believe otherwise. Finally, the consent could not be vitiated on public policy grounds. The purpose of the law of assault was to control the non-consensual application of force by one person to another, not to control the spread of HIV. Accordingly, the motion would be granted.

R v Ssenyonga (1993) 81 CCC (3d) 257 (Ontario Court (General Division)).

802　Child abduction—removal from lawful control—removal of control of child

It fell to be determined whether, in order for a person to be guilty of the offence of taking or attempting to take a child without lawful authority so as to remove him from lawful control, contrary to the Child Abduction Act 1984, s 2, the child had to be removed to some place outside the control of his parents. *Held*, it was relevant whether the child, without any lawful authority or reasonable excuse, was deflected by some action of the accused from what he would otherwise have been doing, with the consent of the person having lawful control, into some activity induced by the accused. In order for the offence to be committed, there was no requirement for the geographical removal of the child from lawful control but simply his removal from the control of his parent or other person having lawful control to the accused.

R v Leather [1993] Crim LR 516 (Court of Appeal: Watkins LJ, Owen and Kay JJ).

803　Complicity in crime—Law Commission consultation paper

The Law Commission has issued a consultation paper, *Assisting and Encouraging Crime* (consultation paper 131). It seeks views on its proposals to replace the existing law on aiding, abetting, counselling, procuring, and inciting crime and also on a suggestion to abolish the existing rules on joint enterprises. The Commission proposes the enactment of new offences of assisting crime and encouraging crime. The offence of assisting crime would be committed by a person who knew or believed that another ("the principal") was doing (or causing to be done, or would do or cause to be done) acts that involved (or would involve) the commission of an offence (as defined) by the principal; and knew or believed that the principal in so acting did (or would do) so with the "fault" required for the offence in question; and did any act that he knew or believed assisted (or would assist) the principal in committing the offence. For this purpose, the term "assistance" includes the giving to the principal of advice as to the commission of the offence, or as to the avoidance of detection or apprehension before or after the commission of the offence. The offence of assisting crime would not be committed, however, by a mere failure to prevent or impede the commission of an offence. The offence of assisting crime would be committed if the person knew or believed that the principal intended to commit one of a number of offences and did any act that he knew or believed would assist the principal in committing whichever of those offences the principal in fact intended. Special defences would be available to those charged with assisting crime. The offence of encouraging crime would be committed by any person who solicited, commanded or encouraged another ("the principal") to do (or cause to be done) an act or acts which, if done, would involve the commission of an offence by the principal; and intended that act or those acts should be done by the principal; and knew or believed that the principal, in so acting, would do so with the "fault" required for the offence in question. The bringing of the solicitation, command or encouragement to the attention of the principal would be an element of the offence of encouraging crime, but whether or not the principal reacted to it or was influenced by it would be irrelevant to the defendant's guilt. Provided that the defendant intended his communication to be acted upon by any person to whose attention it came, the defendant would neither need to know the identity of the principal nor have any particular principal or group of principals in mind. Comments are sought on these proposals and on related issues. In addition to the consultation paper, the Law Commission has published the gist of its proposals in the form of an "Overview".

804   Criminal Injuries Compensation Board—application—failure to report injury to police—discretion to make award

See *Re Taylor*, para 907.

805   Criminal Injuries Compensation Board—report

The Criminal Injuries Compensation Board has published its 28th report (Cm 2122) on the operation of the 1990 Scheme (see 1990 Abr para 530) up to 31 March 1992. The text of the scheme itself is appended to the report, together with a statistical analysis of applications for awards and guides to the scheme, to the level of awards, and to applications on behalf of children who have suffered physical or sexual abuse. The lower limit for compensation is unchanged at £1,000.

The board agreed to extend the time limit in respect of the Pan–Am aircraft bombing at Lockerbie and has received over two hundred applications from victims of the bombing and their dependants (para 7.2). The board again received an increased number of applications in respect of children who had suffered abuse (para 14.1). In one case, a teenage girl who was subjected to sexual abuse by her father and now suffers from behavioural problems received an interim award of £15,000 pending further reports on her condition (para 14.10). The report shows an increase in the number of decisions taken by staff to whom decision-making powers have been delegated (para 1.6) and gives examples of cases where the board has waived the three-year time limit for applications. The report gives two examples of train drivers awarded £1,000 and £815 for psychological injury suffered as a result of witnessing distressing incidents on the railway (para 19). Although compensation is not generally payable under the scheme for injuries caused as a result of road traffic offences, a cyclist was awarded £1,525 for injuries received in a fall from her cycle caused by a length of string having been deliberately stretched across the road (para 23.4). Among the examples of applications reopened on medical grounds, a woman raped by an assailant later found to be HIV positive received a sum of £2,500 in addition to an original award of £7,500 for the anxiety she suffered as a result of having to undergo hospital tests, even though these tests proved negative (para 24.9). Various examples of specimen awards are also given in paras 27.1–27.8, including the case of an applicant who received a net award of £389,368 for an attack by a burglar which left her paraplegic and incapable of managing her own affairs.

For examples of awards made by the board, see the title DAMAGES AND COMPENSATION.

806   Criminal Injuries Compensation Scheme—proposed changes

In a White Paper entitled *Compensating Victims of Violent Crime: Changes to the Criminal Injuries Compensation Scheme* (Cm 2434), the government has set out its plans for improving services to all victims of crime by the replacement, in respect of applications lodged on or after 1 April 1994, of the existing Criminal Injuries Compensation Scheme with a new, tariff-based, scheme. While it remains committed to providing a tangible measure of help to blameless victims of crimes of violence in recognition of the hurt which they have suffered, the government no longer believes that this is best achieved by attempting an individual assessment in each case.

Accordingly, under the new system, compensation will no longer be assessed on the basis of common law damages. Injuries of comparable severity will be grouped or banded together in a tariff of awards, each band attracting a single lump sum payment. There will be 25 tariff levels, with awards ranging from £1,000 to £250,000. Tariff levels will be based on the past award levels made by the Criminal Injuries Compensation Board which will have no role under the new tariff arrangements although claims lodged before 1 April 1994 will be cleared by the board under the present rules. It is believed that the average claimant will be no worse off under the new system than under the existing scheme. No separate payment will be made for loss of earnings or medical expenses but the government believes that the higher tariff awards will ameliorate the effects of the cessation of such payments. The basic rules for eligibility will remain much as before although the time limit for making an application will be reduced from three years to one year. There will still be a discretion, as under the present scheme, to waive the normal time limit in exceptional cases.

The territorial limits of the scheme are to be clarified in their application to British ships. An offence which has become spent under the Rehabilitation of Offenders Act 1974 will not in future be taken into account in determining whether an award should be reduced or withheld where the applicant has a criminal record.

New arrangements for dealing with appeals will enable an applicant who is dissatisfied with the initial decision to request a reconsideration of his case by the Criminal Injuries Compensation Authority from which he will be able to appeal, if he remains dissatisfied after such reconsideration, to a panel which is independent of both the authority and the Secretary of State. The panel will be able to confirm, set aside or change any earlier decision but its decision will be final and binding on the authority and will not be subject to review by ministers. In order to discourage or deter frivolous or vexatious appeals, the panel is to be empowered to reduce any award already offered by a notional amount to cover the administrative costs of a time-wasting appeal and to refuse to reimburse the appellant's expenses.

The new scheme will initially be non-statutory and payments will be made on an ex gratia basis. Although the provision made by the Criminal Justice Act 1988 for placing the existing scheme on a statutory basis, which has not been brought into effect, is to be repealed, consideration is to be given to putting the new scheme on a statutory basis.

807 Criminal Justice Act 1993

The Criminal Justice Act 1993 makes provision about the jurisdiction of courts in England and Wales in relation to certain offences of dishonesty and blackmail. It amends the law about drug trafficking offences and implements provisions of Council Directive (EC) 91/308 on the prevention of the use of the financial system for the purpose of money laundering. It amends the Criminal Justice Act 1988, Pt VI (ss 71–103: confiscation of the proceeds of an offence), and makes provision with respect to the financing of terrorism, the proceeds of terrorist-related activities and the investigation of terrorist activities. It amends the Criminal Justice Act 1991, Pt I (ss 1–31: powers of courts to deal with offenders). It implements provisions of Council Directive (EC) 89/592 on insider dealing, amends and restates the law about insider dealing in securities, provides for certain offences created by the Banking Co-ordination (Second Council Directive) Regulations 1992, SI 1992/3218, to be punishable in the same way as offences under the Banking Act 1987, ss 39–41 and enables regulations implementing Council Directive 89/646 (EC), art 15 (which requires the United Kingdom to make provision for the exercise in the United Kingdom by supervisory authorities of other member states of information and inspection powers in relation to institutions authorised by them) and Council Directive (EC) 92/30, arts 3, 6, 7 (which make similar provision in relation to the consolidated supervision of credit institutions) to create offences punishable in that way. It makes provision with respect to the penalty for causing death by dangerous driving or causing death by careless driving while under the influence of drink or drugs. It makes it an offence to assist in or induce certain conduct which for the purposes of, or in connection with, the provisions of Community law is unlawful in another member state and provides for the introduction of safeguards in connection with the return of persons under backing of warrants arrangements. The Act received the royal assent on 27 July 1993. Certain provisions came into force on that date, on 16 August, 20, 27 September and on 1 December 1993: SI 1993/1968, 2734. The remaining provisions come into force on days to be appointed. For details of commencement, see the commencement table in the title STATUTES.

Part I (ss 1–6) Jurisdiction
Section 1 identifies the offences to which the new jurisdictional rules introduced by Pt I apply and empowers the Secretary of State to amend the list of offences by order; s 2 sets out the test, based on the concept of the "relevant offence", which must be satisfied if the jurisdiction so extended is to be available in respect of any of the specified offences. Section 3 provides that certain questions are immaterial to jurisdiction in the case of certain offences to which Pt I applies. New rules concerning the obtaining of property and the transmission of communications between England and Wales and elsewhere are introduced by s 4. Section 5 amends the Criminal Law Act 1977 by providing that cases of conspiracy to commit elsewhere offences listed in the 1993 Act, s 1, are triable in England and Wales, provided that certain criteria are satisfied; similar provision is made in respect of the offence of conspiracy to defraud. The Criminal Attempts Act 1981 and the law relating to incitement are also amended by the 1993 Act, s 5 so as to extend jurisdiction to try cases of attempt and incitement to perform actions abroad which in England and Wales would involve an offence listed in s 1. By virtue of s 6, a person may be convicted of conspiracy, attempt or incitement to commit an offence listed in s 1 or of conspiracy to defraud only if the objective or some relevant course of conduct constitutes an offence under the law in force where it was intended to take place; this test is to be regarded as having been satisfied subject to procedural provisions enabling the defence to challenge the issue.

Part II (ss 7–26) Drug Trafficking Offences
Part II amends the confiscation provisions of the Drug Trafficking Act 1986 and existing legislation on money laundering so as to provide for the implementation of Council Directive 91/308 on prevention of the use of the financial system for the purpose of money laundering. Section 7 requires the court to proceed with a confiscation hearing if so requested by the prosecutor and provides the court with a discretion to proceed if no such request is made, and states that the standard of proof required to determine any question of benefit or the amount to be recovered arising under the Act is the civil standard; it also allows the court to make a confiscation order for a nominal amount where it appears that the amount that might be realised is nil. By virtue of s 8, the court may, when it considers that it requires further information or where the defendant has appealed against his conviction, postpone determining the question of benefit or the amount to be recovered, make more than one postponement and, where the defendant appeals against his conviction, extend an existing postponement; the court may proceed to sentence even though there has been a postponement or extension. Section 9 requires the court to make assumptions about property and expenditure unless they are shown to be incorrect in the defendant's case or it is satisfied that there would be a serious risk of injustice if they were to be made; the court must state its reasons if it decides not to make the assumptions. The court must be given a statement, or further statements, by the prosecutor of matters relevant to determining benefit or assessing the value of proceeds and it may order the defendant to provide it with such information, in such manner and before such date, as it may specify: s 10. A receiver may now apply to the High Court for the variation of a confiscation order: s 11. Section 12 enables the court to make a fresh determination, on the prosecutor's application, in respect of proceeds which were not known to the court when an earlier determination was made, and to vary an earlier confiscation order or, where no such order was made, make a new one. Where a defendant serves a term of imprisonment or detention in default of payment of a confiscation order, the debt is not expunged: s 13. By virtue of s 14, confiscation may be made where a drug trafficker dies or has absconded and, where an absconder subsequently returns to trial and is acquitted, compensation may be paid to any person who thereby suffers loss: s 15.

It is an offence to acquire, possess or use any property knowing that it is or represents another person's proceeds of drug trafficking: s 16. Section 17 applies to Scotland. By virtue of s 18, offences are created of failing to disclose to a constable, as soon as is reasonably practicable, knowledge or suspicion that another person is engaged in money laundering, where such knowledge or suspicion is gained in the course of a person's employment, and of disclosing information likely to prejudice an investigation into drug money laundering, knowing or suspecting that an investigation is being or is about to be carried out, or that a disclosure has been made to a constable. Section 19 applies to Scotland. The investigation and prosecution of offences under the 1986 Act are by the Commissioners of Customs and Excise: s 20.

Section 21 provides for the enforcement of overseas forfeiture orders in respect of items intended for use, in addition to those actually used, in drug trafficking, and s 22 extends the provision in respect of the enforcement of Northern Ireland orders. Section 23 transfers to the commissioners certain enforcement powers presently exercised by the Secretary of State under the Criminal Justice (International Co-operation) Act 1990, s 20, in relation to British ships and certain other ships used for illicit drug trafficking. A number of miscellaneous amendments are made to the 1986 Act, the Civil Jurisdiction and Judgments Act 1982 and the Police and

Criminal Evidence Act 1984 by the 1993 Act, s 24. Section 25 provides for appeals against orders forfeiting drug trafficking cash and s 26 provides that it is not an offence to disclose certain information received in privileged circumstances.

Part III (ss 27–35) Proceeds of Criminal Conduct
Section 27 states that the standard of proof to be used in determining certain questions arising under the Criminal Justice Act 1988, Pt VI is the civil standard. Under the 1993 Act, s 28, where a court considers that it requires further information or where the defendant has appealed against his conviction, the court may postpone determining certain questions; more than one postponement may be made and, where the defendant appeals against his conviction, an existing postponement may be extended; the court may proceed to sentence even though there has been a postponement or extension. It is an offence to assist another to retain the benefit or use another's proceeds of criminal conduct, knowing or suspecting that the other person is or has been engaged in or has benefited from criminal conduct (s 29) or to acquire, possess or use any property knowing that it is or represents another person's proceeds of criminal conduct: s 30. An offence of concealing or transferring the proceeds of criminal conduct, whether one's own or another person's, for the purpose of avoiding prosecution or the making or enforcing of a confiscation order is created: s 31. Section 32 creates an offence of disclosing information likely to prejudice an investigation into money laundering, knowing or suspecting that an investigation is being, or is about to be, carried out or that a disclosure has been made to a constable. Section 33 applies to Scotland. Section 34 extends the provision in respect of the enforcement of Northern Ireland orders, and s 35 provides that proceedings for specified offences may be instituted by order of the commissioners.

Part IV (ss 36–51) Financing etc of Terrorism
Sections 36–48 amend the Northern Ireland (Emergency Provisions) Act 1991. The 1993 Act, s 36 amends provisions relating to confiscation orders, s 37 adds provisions dealing with the reassessment of whether a defendant has benefited and with revised assessments, and s 38 amends the provision concerning statements, etc relevant to making confiscation orders. Section 39 enables the court to order the defendant to give it specified information for the purpose of obtaining information to assist it in carrying out its functions. Amendments are made by ss 40, 41, to provisions for the variation of confiscation orders and in respect of the availability of powers and satisfaction of orders. By virtue of s 42, the High Court is empowered to exercise the powers of the Crown Court to make a confiscation order against a defendant who has died or absconded. Section 43 adds provisions enabling compensation to be paid to any person who has suffered loss as a consequence of the making of a confiscation order in a case where the absconder subsequently returns to trial and is acquitted. Section 44 provides that property is not realisable property if an order under the Powers of Criminal Courts Act 1973, s 43 is in force in respect of it. The provisions concerning the making of orders and regulations under the 1991 Act are extended by the 1993 Act, s 45, and s 46 provides for the enforcement of orders outside Northern Ireland. Further amendments are made by s 47 to provisions in respect of offences relating to proceeds of terrorist-related activities and s 48 creates an offence of failing to disclose knowledge or suspicion relating to proceeds of such activities.

Sections 49–51 amend the Prevention of Terrorism (Temporary Provisions) Act 1989. Provisions concerning financial assistance for terrorism are amended by the 1993 Act, s 49 and s 50 amends the provision in respect of the investigation of terrorist activities. Section 51 creates an offence of failing to disclose knowledge or suspicion of financial assistance for terrorism.

Part V (ss 52–64) Insider Dealing
Section 52 sets out the offence of insider dealing. Section 53 sets out the defences to an offence, based on establishing lack of the necessary intent, and Sch 1 sets out special defences. Section 54, Sch 2 define the securities to which Pt V of the Act applies. Definitions of "dealing" in securities, "inside information", etc, "insiders", information "made public", "professional intermediary" are provided by ss 55–59 and s 60 sets out other interpretation provisions. Penalties for offences are set out in s 61, which provides for offences to be instituted by or with the consent of the Secretary of State or the Director of Public Prosecutions. Section 62 defines the territorial scope of the offence and s 63 excludes certain actions by persons acting on behalf of public sector bodies from the scope of the offence and prevents the existence of an offence from avoiding any contract. Section 64 provides for the making of orders under Pt V.

Part VI (ss 65–77) Miscellaneous
Section 65 substitutes the Criminal Justice Act 1991, s 18, concerning the fixing of certain fines by reference to units and repeals s 19, which provided for the fixing of fines in cases to which the unit fines system did not apply; the 1993 Act, Sch 3 makes further amendments in respect of financial penalties. Section 66 makes new provision in respect of the powers of courts to deal

with offenders. The penalty for causing death by dangerous driving or by careless driving while under the influence of drink or drugs is increased from five years to ten years: s 67. Sections 68, 69 apply to Scotland. Regulations under the European Communities Act 1972, s 2(2) for the purpose of implementing Council Directive 89/646 (the Second Banking Co-ordination Directive) and Council Directive 92/30 (the Supervision of Credit Institutions Directive) may apply the same level of penalties for new offences created under those regulations as are available for comparable offences under the Banking Act 1987, ss 39–41, by virtue of which the bank has power to obtain information from and mount investigations into authorised institutions and to impose maximum penalties which exceed the level which may be applied by regulations under the 1972 Act: 1993 Act, s 70. Offences under the law of the United Kingdom in relation to serious offences in other member states involving specified measures (ie taxes, duties, agricultural spending, and prohibitions and restrictions provided for by or under a Community instrument or regulation) with a Community character are created by s 71. Section 72 allows the inclusion of a rule of speciality in the arrangements under the Backing of Warrants (Republic of Ireland) Act 1965, and provides that the Secretary of State may by order provide that a person may not be delivered up to the Republic of Ireland unless his law contains provision corresponding to provision made, with respect to persons delivered up to the United Kingdom under arrangements in the Republic, by the 1965 Act. The 1993 Act, s 72 also empowers the Secretary of State to order that, except in specified cases, no person delivered up to the United Kingdom by the Republic may be dealt with in respect of any offence committed before his surrender, other than the offence for which he is delivered up and provided that, except in specified cases, no person delivered up to the United Kingdom by the Republic may then be delivered up to a territory other than the Republic to be dealt with in respect of any offence committed before his surrender to the United Kingdom. The Secretary of State may, with Treasury consent, make grants in relation to the combating of drug trafficking or the misuse of drugs or dealing with the consequences of such misuse: s 73. Section 74 adds to the Criminal Justice Act 1982, Sch 1, Pt II the offences created by the 1993 Act, ss 16, 29–31, so that, accordingly, persons who have committed any such offences will not be eligible for early release from prison. Sections 75, 76 apply to Scotland and s 77 gives effect to Sch 4, which empowers the Secretary of State to extend certain offences to Crown servants and to exempt persons from certain offences.

Part VII (ss 78, 79) Supplementary
Section 78 provides for commencement and s 79 for the short title and extent of the Act; s 79 also introduces Schs 5, 6, which deal with consequential amendments and repeals and revocations.

808 Defences—automatism—death by reckless driving

The defendant lorry driver was charged with two offences of causing death by reckless driving. The alleged offences occurred when the defendant, after driving for over six hours out of the preceding 12, drove onto the hard shoulder of a motorway and crashed into a stationary vehicle. At the trial the prosecution alleged that the respondent had been overcome by sleep at the wheel. The defendant adduced expert evidence contending that he was without awareness and in a state of automatism at the time of the accident and, therefore, not to be regarded as driving. The judge left the defence of automatism based on the expert's evidence as an issue properly open for the jury's consideration. The defendant was acquitted and the matter was referred to the Court of Appeal by the Attorney-General under the Criminal Justice Act 1972, s 36. *Held*, the defence of automatism required that there was a total destruction of voluntary control on the defendant's part. Impaired or reduced control was not enough. Driving without awareness did not involve total destruction of voluntary control as there still remained the ability to steer the vehicle straight and there was also the capacity to react to stimuli appearing in the road ahead. Accordingly, the judge ought not to have left the issue of automatism to the jury, and driving without awareness was not, as a matter of law, a state capable of founding a defence of automatism.

Attorney-General's Reference (No 2 of 1992) [1993] 4 All ER 683 (Court of Appeal: Lord Taylor of Gosforth CJ, Judge and Blofeld JJ).

809 Defences—automatism—insane or non-insane automatism

Canada
At his trial on a charge of murder, the defendant claimed he had been sleepwalking throughout the incident and raised a defence of automatism. The defence called expert evidence to establish that sleepwalking was a disorder of sleep rather than a disorder of the mind, that sleepwalkers had almost no ability to control their behaviour, and that there was no medical treatment for the condition. The jury acquitted the defendant after being directed that if they believed he had

been sleepwalking he was entitled to be acquitted on the basis of non-insane automatism. The Crown appealed on the ground that sleepwalking was a disease of the mind and the trial judge should have left the defence of insanity to the jury rather than the defence of automatism. That appeal was dismissed and, on the Crown's further appeal, *held*, the evidence that sleepwalking was not a disease of the mind had not been contradicted by the Crown, and on the basis of the evidence before him the judge had been right to place the defence of automatism before the jury. A defence of insanity could only have been placed before the jury if there had been evidence that the defendant's sleepwalking had been responsible for his state of mind at the time of the killing, but as there had been no evidence suggesting that was the case there were no grounds for interfering with the jury's verdict. Accordingly, the appeal would be dismissed and the defendant's acquittal upheld.

R v Parks (1992) 75 CCC 287 (Supreme Court of Canada). *R v Burgess* [1991] 2 All ER 769, CA (1991 Abr para 689) distinguished.

810 Defences—involuntary intoxication—direction to jury

The defendant was charged with indecent assault. Another man had arranged to blackmail the defendant by photographing and audio-taping him in a compromising situation with a 15 year-old-boy. He had lured the boy into his flat where he was given what seemed to be an innocuous drink and some cannabis. The boy fell asleep and remembered nothing. When invited to do so by the other man the defendant sexually abused the boy. The tape of the defendant contained a reference to him feeling sleepy and that he felt his drink had been drugged. Sedative drugs were found in the other man's flat. The trial judge directed the jury that if they found that the defendant was so intoxicated by drugs administered to him secretly, he did not intend to commit an indecent assault, and that it was open to them to find the defendant not guilty. However, he then directed the jury that a drugged intent was still an intent. Following his conviction the defendant appealed. *Held*, there was no doubt that the defendant had committed the actus reus of an indecent assault. If there was evidence capable of giving rise to the defence of involuntary intoxication, the jury ought to have been left to consider whether the defendant's intent to commit the criminal act was induced by involuntary intoxication and thereby negatived. That evidence did exist, and therefore the withdrawing of the issue from the jury by the judge amounted to a material misdirection. Accordingly, the conviction would be quashed and the appeal allowed.

R v Kingston [1993] 3 WLR 676 (Court of Appeal: Lord Taylor of Gosforth CJ, Pill and Sedley JJ).

811 Defences—religious beliefs

Following his arrest at a protest against the Gulf war, a vicar was convicted of causing criminal damage, contrary to the Criminal Damage Act 1971, s 1(1). He appealed by way of case stated, contending that he was carrying out God's instructions and as such had a lawful excuse for his actions. He submitted that all laws originated from God and the laws of the Church were the laws of the land. *Held*, a religious belief, however powerful and genuine, that God's instructions were being carried out did not amount to a lawful excuse under the domestic law of the land. Accordingly the appeal would be dismissed.

Blake v DPP [1993] Crim LR 586 (Queen's Bench Division: Evans LJ and Otton J).

812 Defences—voluntary intoxication—direction to jury

Canada

The accused was convicted of murder. He appealed, contending that the judge misdirected the jury on the defence of drunkenness. *Held*, the judge erred in directing the jury that if they were satisfied that the accused was not so drunk that he was incapable of forming the requisite intent they must reject the defence of drunkenness and not consider the offence of manslaughter. The jury should have been instructed that once satisfied that the accused had the capacity to form the necessary intent they then had to consider whether, taking into account the amount of alcohol consumed and all the other facts, the prosecution had proved beyond a reasonable doubt that he did in fact have the required intent. Accordingly, whilst the appeal would be dismissed, a conviction for manslaughter would be substituted.

R v Crane (1993) 81 CCC (3d) 276 (Manitoba Court of Appeal).

813 Defences—voluntary intoxication—Law Commission provisional proposals

The Law Commission has published *Intoxication and Criminal Liability* (consultation paper 127), in which it views the effect of voluntary intoxication on criminal liability in English law, as seen from the decision of the House of Lords in *DPP v Majewski* [1977] AC 443 (1976 Abr para 625). The commission provisionally recommends that the *Majewski* approach should be abolished. If it is abolished without any new provision to take its place, the effect would be to allow a defendant's intoxication to be taken into account, together with other relevant evidence, in determining whether or not he had the prescribed mens rea for the offence. Alternatively, the *Majewski* approach could be replaced by a new offence, provisionally named "criminal intoxication", which would be punishable if a person who was deliberately intoxicated committed any one of certain prescribed offences (eg homicide, bodily harm, rape). If the latter view should be favoured, comments are sought on which offences should be prescribed, the penalty for the offence of criminal intoxication, the criterion for deciding whether intoxication was deliberate, and the burden of proof, and the possible defence of mistake.

814 Drug offences—scheduled substances—manufacture and trade—Community provisions

The Controlled Drugs (Substances Useful for Manufacture) (Intra-Community Trade) Regulations 1993, SI 1993/2166 (in force on 6 October 1993), implement Council Directive (EC) 92/109 on the manufacture and placing on the market of certain substances used in the illicit manufacture of narcotic drugs and psychotropic substances. The directive applies only to manufacture and trade in scheduled substances occurring within the European Community. The 1993 Regulations treat the requirements in the directive on the documentation and labelling of scheduled substances as if they were requirements of regulations made under the Criminal Justice (International Co-operation) Act 1990, which provides rights of entry and search to investigate suspected breaches of regulations made under the Act and penalties for such breaches. The 1993 Regulations also provide for the grant of licences for manufacturers and suppliers in accordance with the directive.

815 Drug offences—supply—offer to supply—mens rea

The defendant was observed taking money from a customer for a bag containing pills. Following his arrest, the defendant claimed that he intended to cheat his customers by claiming that the pills were 'ecstasy' tablets when they were in fact vitamin C tablets. The defendant was convicted on charges of conspiracy to supply a controlled drug. He appealed, contending that a pretence to offer to supply a controlled drug did not constitute an offence and that it had to be proved, in the absence of evidence that the drugs were prohibited drugs, that the appellant believed that they were prohibited drugs. *Held*, the offence of offering to supply a controlled drug was complete when the offer was made whether or not the offeror intended to carry the offer into effect by supplying that drug. The fact that what was charged was a conspiracy rather than a substantive offence could not make any difference, and in those circumstances, the appeal would be dismissed.

R v Gill (1993) 97 CrApp Rep 215 (Court of Appeal: McCowan LJ, Schiemann and Curtis JJ). *R v Goodard* [1992] Crim LR 588, CA (1992 Abr para 779) applied.

816 Evidence and procedure

See CRIMINAL EVIDENCE AND PROCEDURE.

817 False trade descriptions

See TRADE DESCRIPTIONS.

818 Firearms—dangerous air weapons

The Firearms (Dangerous Air Weapons) (Amendment) Rules 1993, SI 1993/1490 (in force on 1 July 1993), amend the 1969 Rules, SI 1969/47, by adding to the category of air weapons declared to be specially dangerous by the 1969 Rules, an air weapon disguised as another object. Such a weapon now requires a firearm certificate by virtue of the Firearms Act 1968, s 1.

819 Firearms—Firearms Consultative Committee

The Firearms (Amendment) Act 1988 (Firearms Consultative Committee) Order 1993, SI 1993/2919 (in force on 27 November 1993), continues the existence of the Firearms Consultative Committee for a period of three years beginning on 1 February 1994.

820   Firearms—firearms dealer—registration—place of business

The Firearms Act 1968, s 8 provides that a person carrying on the business of a firearms dealer and registered as such under the Act may, without holding a certificate, have in his possession a firearm or ammunition in the ordinary course of that business. Section 33(3) provides that to be registered, the applicant must furnish the chief officer of police with the prescribed particulars, which should include particulars of every place at which he proposes to carry on business in the area as a firearms dealer.

The defendant was a registered firearms dealer, working from his principal place of business. Police officers seized ammunition stored in a renovated shed owned by the defendant. At his trial on charges of possession of ammunition contrary to the 1968 Act, s 1, it was held that lawful possession of ammunition in the ordinary course of business was limited to possession in the ordinary course of business at the registered place of business. The defendant was convicted and appealed, contending that the exemption offered by s 8 applied to a person, not to a place. *Held*, the words in s 33(3) should be given a wide construction. The defendant's place of business could include the place where he stored firearms and ammunition. The special exemption in s 8 applied to a person carrying on the business of a firearms dealer, registered as such under s 33, who in order to be registered under s 33 had furnished the chief of police with the prescribed particulars of every place of business at which he proposed to carry on business as a firearms dealer and who had in his possession or purchased or acquired a firearm or ammunition in the ordinary course of that business. The exemption therefore did not apply to the possession of a firearm or ammunition at a place of business whose address had not been furnished in accordance with s 33, as the possession was not in the ordinary course of business registered as such under the Act. The appeal would accordingly be dismissed.

R v Bull (1993) Times, 18 August (Court of Appeal: Kennedy LJ, Morland and Cresswell JJ).

821   Football Spectators Act 1989—commencement

The Football Spectators Act 1989 (Commencement No 4) Order 1993, SI 1993/1690, brings into force on 1 August 1993 s 9 which makes it an offence to admit spectators to premises to watch a football match designated under the Act unless the premises are licensed by the Football Licensing Authority. For a summary of the Act, see 1989 Abr para 460. For details of commencement, see the commencement table in the *Current Service* Noter-up binder.

822   Football spectators—designation of football matches

The Football Spectators (Designation of Football Matches in England and Wales) Order 1993, SI 1993/1691 (in force on 1 August 1993), revokes the 1990 Order, SI 1990/731, as amended. The Order designates football matches for the purposes of the Football Spectators Act 1989, Pt I.

823   Handling stolen goods—knowledge or belief that goods stolen—test to be applied

The defendant was convicted of handling stolen goods. He appealed, contending that the judge misdirected the jury by stating that they had to be certain that the defendant believed the goods were stolen at the time he took possession, whenever that was, and that the test for determining his belief was an objective one. *Held*, a person was guilty of handling only if he believed that the goods were stolen at the time he received them; subsequent belief was insufficient. Thus the direction as to the time of the defendant's belief was crucial and the judge's reference to possession "whenever that was" was incorrect. Further, the judge misdirected the jury as to the test for determining belief. Belief was a subjective matter and so the defendant's actual state of mind was at issue, not whether it was reasonable to conclude that the goods were not stolen. Accordingly, the appeal would be allowed.

R v Brook [1993] Crim LR 455 (Court of Appeal: Watkins LJ, Auld and Curtis JJ).

824   Illegal immigration

See BRITISH NATIONALITY, IMMIGRATION AND RACE RELATIONS.

825   Investigation and prosecution of crime—international co-operation

An agreement on co-operation in the investigation and prosecution of crime and the tracing, restraint and confiscation of the proceeds and instruments of crime and terrorist funds was signed between the United Kingdom and India in London on 22 September 1992 (Cm 2131).

Under the agreement, the governments agreed to assist each other in these matters on receipt of a written request, or an oral request in an urgent case, followed by confirmation in writing: arts 3, 4(1). The contents of requests are specified in arts 4(2), 9(2) and 10(2). Requests are to be executed in accordance with the domestic law of the requested party (art 5) and may only be refused if (1) the requested party suspects that the request, if granted, would seriously impair its sovereignty, security, national or other essential interest, (2) the provision of assistance might prejudice an investigation or proceedings, or constitute a substantial risk to the physical safety of any person, (3) the action sought is contrary to the domestic law of that party, (4) the request concerns a matter of restraint or confiscation which would not have been available in similar circumstances under the domestic law of that party, or (5) the request concerns an offence in respect of which the accused person has been finally acquitted or pardoned: art 6(2). The requested party will be under a duty of confidentiality in respect of any request, except so far as disclosure is necessary to execute the request (art 7(1)); the requesting party will also be under a duty of confidentiality in respect of evidence and information supplied, except so far as disclosure is necessary for the investigation or proceedings, and may not without permission use the evidence or information for any purpose other than that for which it was requested (art 7(2), (3)). Information and evidence may be sought for identifying or tracing the proceeds and instruments of crime, including crimes involving currency transfers, and terrorist funds which may become liable to restraint or confiscation: art 8(1). Requests may be made for the restraint of property in order to ensure that it will be available for the purpose of enforcing any confiscation order which may be made: art 9(1). Requests for assistance in the enforcement of a confiscation order may be made in respect of the proceeds or instruments of crime, including crimes involving currency transfers, and terrorist funds: art 10(1), (2). The parties undertake to assist each other in respect of the service of judicial documents, the search for and seizure of evidence, the taking of evidence and statements, and the transfer of persons for the purpose of assisting in investigations or giving evidence: art 11. Subject to any specific agreement in relation to extraordinary costs, each requested party will bear its own costs: art 12. The agreement is subject to ratification and is not yet in force.

826   Manslaughter—causation—series of events—continuing transaction—concurrence of mens rea and actus reus

Canada
The appellant was convicted of manslaughter. He administered drugs to the deceased, knowing that this could be fatal, and when the deceased was subsequently found apparently dead he disposed of the body by dumping it at sea. An autopsy indicated that death may have been caused by drowning, although the deceased was unconscious at the time and would have died from the overdose. At trial, the Crown contended that the appellant committed two wrongful acts with the intention of causing the deceased's death: first, he administered a noxious thing with the intention of endangering life and, second, he committed an assault by causing the deceased's body to be weighed down and thrown into the sea. The judge charged the jury that it was open to them to regard the events that led to the deceased's death as one continuing transaction and he declined to put the defence of honest but mistaken belief in relation to the alleged assault to the jury. On appeal, *held*, there was authority to support the judge's direction to the jury that if the entire episode was one continuing transaction, then at some point the requisite mens rea coincided with the continuing series of acts that constituted the transaction. It followed that it was not open to the appellant to subdivide the transaction and rely on the defence of honest but mistaken belief in relation to the alleged assault. The judge did not err in declining to put that defence to the jury and, accordingly, the appeal would be dismissed.
R v Frizzel (1993) 81 CCC (3d) 463 (British Columbia Court of Appeal).

827   Manslaughter—involuntary manslaughter—defence—mistake—excessive force

The defendant was the licensee of a public house. After closing time, a man demanded a drink and refused to leave. The defendant grabbed him and pushed him out the door. The man fell down some steps and sustained fatal injuries. At the defendant's trial on a charge of manslaughter, the judge directed the jury that if they concluded that the defendant used more force than was necessary in the circumstances and they were satisfied that the defendant had caused the man's death, then the defendant was guilty of manslaughter. The defendant was convicted and appealed. *Held*, in *R v Williams* [1987] 3 All ER 411, CA (1984 Abr para 536) it had been held that an accused person could be acquitted if he mistakenly believed that he was justified in using force, even if the mistake was unreasonable. There was no logical basis for distinguishing between a person objectively unjustified in using force, but who mistakenly believed he was justified, and a person who was justified in using force, but mistakenly believed that the circumstances called for a degree of force objectively regarded as unnecessary. The directions to the jury were inadequate, and their verdict was unsafe and unsatisfactory. The appeal would accordingly be allowed and the conviction quashed.

R v Scarlett [1993] 4 All ER 629 (Court of Appeal: Beldam LJ, Ebsworth and Tuckey JJ).

828 Manslaughter—involuntary manslaughter—gross negligence

In three separate cases heard together on appeal, two of which involved doctors administering treatment which resulted in the death of patients and the third involving an electrician incorrectly wiring an electrical heating system which delivered a fatal shock, the question arose as to the degree of negligence required to support a charge of involuntary manslaughter by breach of duty. *Held*, the essential ingredients of involuntary manslaughter by breach of duty were: (1) proof of the existence of the duty; (2) the breach of that duty causing death and (3) gross negligence which the jury considered justified a criminal conviction. Whilst it was not possible to prescribe a standard jury direction in all cases, a jury might be led to make a finding of gross negligence in cases where there was proof of any of the following states of mind in the defendant: (a) an indifference to an obvious risk of injury to health; (b) actual foresight of the risk coupled with the determination nevertheless to run it; (c) an appreciation of the risk coupled with an intention to avoid it, but also coupled with such a high degree of negligence in the attempted avoidance as the jury considered justified conviction; (d) an inattention or failure to advert to a serious risk which went beyond mere inadvertence in relation to an obvious and important matter which the defendant's duty demanded he should address. Having considered all the authorities, and in view of the different meanings which had in various contexts been attached to the words "reckless" and "recklessness", it was preferable that those words should be avoided when directing juries as to involuntary manslaughter by breach of duty. Judgment would be given in the three appeals accordingly.

The court also expressed the view that the Law Commission should examine, as a matter of urgency, the state of the law of manslaughter.

R v Prentice, R v Adomako, R v Holloway [1993] 4 All ER 935 (Court of Appeal: Lord Taylor of Gosforth CJ, Henry and Blofeld JJ). *Andrews v DPP* [1937] 2 All ER 552, HL, and *R v Stone* [1977] 2 All ER 341, CA (1976 Abr para 632) followed. *R v Caldwell* [1981] 1 All ER 961, HL (1981 Abr para 643), *R v Lawrence* [1981] 1 All ER 974, HL (1981 Abr para 2482) not followed.

829 Murder—defence—provocation—reasonable man

The Homicide Act 1957, s 3 provides that where on a charge of murder there is evidence on which the jury can find that the person charged was either provoked (whether by things done or by things said or by both together) to lose his self-control, the question whether the provocation was enough to make a reasonable man do as he did, must be left to the jury; and in determining that question, the jury must take into account everything, both done and said, according to the effect which, in their opinion, it would have on the reasonable man.

The deceased had an argument with the defendant over the defendant's addiction to glue-sniffing. A fight broke out, which was halted by a third party. The deceased wished to continue the argument and following another struggle, the deceased was fatally wounded by the defendant. At his trial on a charge of murder, the defendant contended that there was an absence of any intent due to intoxication by glue-sniffing. Following his conviction, the defendant appealed on the ground that addiction should have been left to the jury as a characteristic which they could take into account as affecting the gravity of the provocation to the defendant. The prosecution submitted that characteristics that were repugnant to the concept of a reasonable man did not qualify for consideration. *Held*, s 3 referred to a reasonable man, not just to a person with the self-control of a reasonable man. It was a matter for the judge as to whether any suggested characteristic was capable of being considered by the jury to be consistent with the concept of affecting the gravity of the provocation to the defendant. A self-induced addiction to glue-sniffing brought on by voluntary and persistent abuse of solvents was wholly inconsistent with the concept of a reasonable man. The appeal would accordingly be dismissed.

R v Morhall [1993] 4 All ER 888 (Court of Appeal: Lord Taylor of Gosforth CJ, Owen and Blofeld LJJ).

830 Murder—joint enterprise—absence from scene of crime

A taxi driver agreed to pay the appellant and his two co-defendants to murder his wife. The taxi driver drove his wife to an appointed place, but the appellant did not turn up as arranged and the killing was carried out by the co-defendants. On his own evidence at the trial it was clear that the appellant had taken a leading part in the planning of the murder, having foreseen that murder would, or at least might, have taken place. Though for a time during the preparations he had stalled the others, he had done nothing to prevent the murder and, apart from his absence on the appointed day, he had done nothing to indicate to his co-conspirators that he had changed his mind. On appeal against conviction, *held*, (1) it was now well established that in cases of joint enterprise, where both parties were present at the scene of the crime, it was not necessary for the prosecution to show that the secondary party had intended the victim to be killed or to suffer serious injury. It was enough that the secondary party should have foreseen the event as a real or substantial risk. Thus a secondary party might be liable for the unintended consequences of the principal's acts, provided the principal did not go outside the scope of the joint enterprise. There was no reason why the same reasoning should not apply in the case of a secondary party who lent assistance or encouragement before the commission of the crime but was absent from the actual scene of the crime. (2) A person who changed his mind about participating in the commission of an offence, but failed to communicate his intention to his co-conspirators, was liable as a secondary party. The appellant's absence from the scene of the crime did not amount to unequivocal communication of his withdrawal from the murder. Accordingly, the appeal would be dismissed.

R v Rook [1993] 2 All ER 955 (Court of Appeal: Lloyd LJ, Potter and Buckley JJ). *DPP for Northern Ireland v Maxwell* [1978] 3 All ER 1140, HL and *R v Whitefield* (1983) 79 Cr App Rep 36 applied.

831 Obtaining property by deception—deception—relationship with customer

The defendant, a milkman, was charged with five counts of deception contrary to the Theft Act 1968, s 15(1). The defendant had supplied the customer with milk for over 20 years and the customer would pay the amount asked for by the defendant without checking the bill. The customer found himself in financial difficulties and, on checking his bill, realised that he had been substantially overcharged and stated that he had never considered the amount he was paying for the milk because he trusted the defendant. The indictment alleged that the defendant had falsely represented to the customer that he had received goods to the value of a certain amount. The defendant initially pleaded not guilty but changed his plea following a rejection by the court of a submission of no case to answer on the ground that he had not deceived the customer. He appealed on a point of law. *Held*, the defendant had falsely represented to the customer that he had received goods to the value of a certain amount when in fact the defendant had only delivered goods to the value of one-half of that amount. The defendant was fully aware that the customer had been very careless in his financial affairs and he took advantage of this and therefore, the fact that the customer had looked upon the defendant as a friend did not mean that it was not a deception within the meaning of the 1968 Act, s 15(1). Accordingly, the appeal would be dismissed.

R v Jones (1993) Times, 15 February (Court of Appeal: Lord Taylor of Gosforth CJ, Auld and Curtis JJ).

832 Obtaining property by deception—other intangible property—transaction effected by electronic means

The defendants were convicted of conspiracy to obtain property by deception. At their appeal, *held*, the phrase "other intangible property" in the Theft Act 1968, s 4(1), included a sum of money represented by a figure in an account. Accordingly, a transaction effected by electronic means, rather than a cheque, was an obtaining of property. The appeal would, however, be allowed on other grounds.

R v Crick (1993) Times, 18 August (Court of Appeal: Roch LJ, Macpherson of Cluny and Sachs JJ).

833 Obtaining property by deception—valuable security—meaning of valuable security

The defendants had represented that they were free from debts and liabilities, but two properties jointly owned by them had been charged as security for loans totalling £120,000. As a result of those misrepresentations the defendants were advanced another loan, and when their deception came to light they were charged with dishonestly procuring the execution of a valuable security by deception, contrary to the Theft Act 1968, s 20. They appealed against their subsequent convictions of that offence on the ground that there had been no execution of a valuable security. *Held*, to succeed on an indictment under the 1968 Act, s 20 the Crown had to prove that the document in question was a valuable security which had been executed. The evidence as to how the money had been transferred was sparse because the bank had been dissolved, but the transfer procedure had consisted of the bank's instructions to make the advance, a telegraphic transfer to the defendants' solicitor, an entry in the bank's computerised ledger and the receipt of the further loan signed by the defendants. None of those methods could be characterised as a valuable security, notwithstanding the broad language of the 1968 Act, s 20, nor could any of them be said to have been executed. Accordingly, the appeals would be allowed and the convictions quashed.

R v Manjdadria [1993] Crim LR 73 (Court of Appeal: Farquharson LJ, Tudor Evans and Rougier JJ).

834 Offences against the person—actual bodily harm—psychiatric injury

The defendant was charged with an offence of causing actual bodily harm, contrary to the Offences against the Person Act 1861, s 47. At his trial, the prosecution contended that the victim had felt abused, humiliated and frightened, and alleged that even if the victim had suffered no physical injury as a result of the assault by the defendant, he had nevertheless been reduced to a mental state which in itself, without more, amounted to actual bodily harm. Following the judge's direction that an assault causing an hysterical and nervous condition was an assault occasioning actual bodily harm, the defendant was convicted. On his appeal, *held*, the word "harm" was a synonym for injury. The word "actual" indicated that the injury should not be so trivial as to be wholly insignificant. The body of the victim included all parts of his body, including his organs, his nervous system and his brain. Bodily injury therefore might include injury to any of those parts of his body responsible for his mental and other faculties; the term "actual bodily harm" was capable of including psychiatric injury. However, it did not include such emotions as fear or distress or panic. Juries could not be directed that an assault which caused an hysterical and nervous condition was an assault occasioning actual bodily harm. In any case where psychiatric injury was relied upon as the basis of an allegation of bodily harm, and the matter had not been admitted by the defence, expert evidence should be called by the prosecution. In the absence of appropriate expert evidence, a question whether or not the assault occasioned psychiatric injury should not be left to the jury. The appeal would accordingly be allowed.

R v Chan-Fook (1993) Times, 19 November (Court of Appeal: Hobhouse LJ, Judge and Bell JJ).

835 Offences against the person—draft Criminal Law Bill—Law Commission

The Law Commission published a draft Criminal Code in 1989 (HC 299, Law Com No 177); see 1989 Abr para 446. The commission regards the draft code as providing a framework within which it can draft Bills covering discrete areas of the criminal law which are suitable for immediate enactment. In the longer term it envisages combining all the different parts of the criminal law into a single unified code. The first step in the process is the drafting of a Bill dealing with non-fatal offences against the person, and also with certain general principles (eg transferred fault) and defences of general application (eg duress and self-defence). This Bill is appended to the commission's report, *Legislating the Criminal Code: Offences Against the Person and General Principles* (Cm 2370; Law Com No 218). The offences covered by the Bill are those of causing injury, assault, etc, and offences of detention and abduction. The Bill is accompanied by explanatory notes. It would also effect minor and consequential changes in certain other legislation, eg the Offences against the Person Act 1861.

836 Offences against the person—grievous bodily harm—offence unknown to law

The defendant was charged with causing grievous bodily harm contrary to the Offences Against the Person Act 1861, s 20, after he threw sulphuric acid in his wife's face. On appeal, *held*, the 1861 Act, s 18 deals with causing grievous bodily harm with intent but section 20 of the Act specified "inflicting" as opposed to "causing" grievous bodily harm. As a consequence, the defendant had been charged with an offence that did not exist. It would not be possible to substitute a verdict of guilty under section 20 as the defendant had not been legally convicted of any offence and accordingly, the appeal would be allowed.

R v Mandair [1993] Crim LR 679 (Court of Appeal: Nolan LJ, Swinton Thomas and Colman JJ).

837 Official secrets—prescribed persons and bodies

The Official Secrets Act 1989 (Prescription) (Amendment) Order 1993, SI 1993/847 (in force on 23 March 1993), amends the 1990 Order, SI 1990/200, by adding to the prescribed bodies and persons for the purposes of the Official Secrets Act 1989. Prescribed persons become Crown servants for all purposes of the 1989 Act, and the information which they hold by virtue of their position becomes information to which the 1989 Act applies.

838 Official secrets—prohibited places

The Official Secrets (Prohibited Places) (Amendment) Order 1993, SI 1993/863 (in force on 26 March 1993), amends the Official Secrets (Prohibited Places) Order 1975, SI 1975/182, by adding the place specified in the Schedule to those declared to be prohibited places for the purposes of the Official Secrets Act 1911.

839 Perverting the course of justice—impeding police investigation—acts prior to investigation

The defendants accompanied a man who wished to test a shotgun that he had recently acquired. The gun was discharged accidentally by one of the defendants and the owner of the gun suffered fatal injuries. The defendants took the gun and ran back to their car. After taking home another man who was with them, they unloaded the gun and threw it away. At their trial, the defendants gave evidence that they had acted in panic and had not thought about a police investigation. They were convicted of perverting the course of justice by intentionally impeding police investigations into the death. On their appeal against conviction, *held*, an act was not beyond the ambit of acts tending to pervert the course of justice because it was performed after the alleged crime but before investigations into the crime had begun. In the circumstances, it was open to the jury to conclude that the possibility of judicial proceedings must have been in the contemplation of the defendants. An act had occurred which was likely to bring a specific charge in judicial proceedings, and at the very least there would have been an inquest. The disposal of the gun and ammunition therefore had a tendency to pervert the course of justice. The judge's direction had to express the intention expressed in the charge. However, in the present circumstances, it had to follow from a finding that there was an intention to impede police investigations that there was an intention to pervert the course of public justice. Accordingly, the appeals would be dismissed.

R v Rafique; R v Sajid; R v Rajah [1993] Crim LR 761 (Court of Appeal: Lord Taylor of Gosforth CJ, Pill and Sedley JJ).

840 Perverting the course of justice—interference with witness—distinction between bribery and pressure by bribery

The defendant had been charged with assault. The victim of the assault indicated that he would accept payment in return for dropping his complaint. On the defendant's appeal against conviction of perverting the course of justice, he contended that the offer by him of money or money's worth made to the victim in exchange for the latter's agreement not to give evidence against him was not, without further pressure, an improper means of interfering with a witness amounting to an act tending to pervert the course of justice. *Held*, there was no distinction between bribery and pressure by bribery. Although there might be cases of pressure falling short of bribery, there was no form of bribery which did not constitute pressure. Once bribery was established, that constituted unlawful means. The appeal would be dismissed.

R v Ali [1993] 2 All ER 409 (Court of Appeal: Lloyd LJ, Latham and Smith JJ).

841 Prevention of terrorism—temporary provisions—continuance

The Prevention of Terrorism (Temporary Provisions) Act 1989 (Continuance) Order 1993, SI 1993/747 (in force on 22 March 1993), continues in force the provisions of the 1989 Act, Pts I–V and s 27(6)(c) (with the exception of Pts III and V so far as they have effect in Northern Ireland and relate to proscribed organisations for the purposes of the Northern Ireland (Emergency Provisions) Act 1991, s 28 or offences or orders thereunder) for a period of 12 months commencing on 22 March 1993.

842 Prostitution—living wholly or in part on the earnings of prostitution—meaning of prostitution

The defendant was convicted of living wholly or in part on the earnings of prostitution, contrary to the Sexual Offences Act 1956, s 30, and sentenced to four months' imprisonment.

On appeal, he contended that the woman with whom he lived was not a prostitute but a "clipper", a person who offered sexual services for reward and took payment before reneging on the offer. It was submitted that, to be a prostitute, a woman had to provide or be prepared to provide the services offered. Here, the woman had merely obtained money by false pretences and thus whilst the defendant could have been proceeded against for conspiring with her to do so, or aiding and abetting her, the offence of living off immoral earnings had not been made out. *Held*, the words "prostitute" and "prostitution" were not defined by statute but both the dictionary definition and case-law emphasised that the crucial element was the making of an offer of sexual services for reward. Since the mischief was the harassment and nuisance to members of the public on the streets, the distinction between a clipper and a hooker was immaterial. A man who lived on the earnings of a woman who offered sexual services, took the money in advance and then reneged on the offer, was no different from one who lived off the earnings of prostitution. Accordingly, the appeal would be dismissed.

R v McFarlane (1993) Times, 27 December (Court of Appeal: Lord Taylor of Gosforth CJ, Popplewell and Scott JJ).

843   Public order—affray—use of words as threat

The Public Order Act 1986, s 3 provides that a person is guilty of affray if he uses or threatens unlawful violence towards another and his conduct is such as would cause a person of reasonable fitness present at the scene to fear for his personal safety. For the purposes of the section a threat cannot be made by the use of words alone.

The defendant was fleeing the police accompanied by his dog. Upon being approached by two policemen, he ordered the dog, which was in an excitable state, to "go on, go on" and "go on, kill". The dog bit both policemen. The defendant was convicted of affray and appealed on the ground that the prosecution's case depended on words alone and was therefore contrary to the 1986 Act, s 3. He also claimed that there was no evidence that the dog had responded to his words when it attacked the policemen, and that the judge had failed to define the actus reus of the offence in his summing up to the jury. *Held*, the defendant had used the dog as a weapon and uttered threatening words at the same time, causing the policemen to fear for their safety. He was therefore just as guilty of an affray as any other person with a weapon, loaded or unloaded. Although there was no evidence that the dog had responded to commands, the words uttered by the defendant were highly relevant in considering the defendant's intent. The threats were uttered while the dog was excitable in order to use the dog as a weapon to make the policemen fearful. The judge could have given a better indication of what constituted the actus reus of the offence, namely "setting the dog at the police officers" but it was clear that the jury were aware of the nature of the prosecution's case. Accordingly, the appeal would be dismissed.

R v Dixon [1993] Crim LR 579 (Court of Appeal: Staughton LJ, Waterhouse and McCullough JJ).

The defendant, with another, asked a driver for a lift and threatened to take his car if he did not so. The plaintiff was arrested and charged with affray under the Public Order Act 1986, s 3. It was submitted that there was no case to answer because there was no conduct beyond words, which could not constitute a threat for the purposes of the 1986 Act. The defendant also complained that the judge had erred in his summing up when he stated that words were "probably" not enough to create an affray. The Crown contended that the threat came from the combination of a joint enterprise and conduct which created an aura of menace. On appeal, *held*, words alone could not constitute affray. The judge had given a misdirection in not making this clear to the jury. Although being subjected to oral threats in an aggressive tone was no doubt frightening in the middle of the night, this did not raise a sufficient case of affray. Accordingly, the appeal would be allowed.

R v Robinson [1993] Crim LR 581 (Court of Appeal: Stuart-Smith LJ, Ward and May JJ).

844   Public order—offensive conduct—defence—reasonable conduct

The appellant was approached by a police officer as it was suspected that he was trading without a licence. He confirmed that he did not have a street trader's licence and was told by the police officer that his vehicle would be seized. The appellant became agitated and was later convicted of using threatening behaviour. On appeal against conviction, *held*, whenever police officers threatened to confiscate property in excess of their powers it was likely that the owner of the property would object. If the police officer had said that the van might have been required to be used in evidence then he would have been within his confiscatory powers. If that explanation had been given to the appellant he might have appreciated that he would get the van back and would therefore have been less likely to act in the way he did. Accordingly, the appeal would be allowed.

Poku v DPP [1993] Crim LR 705 (Queen's Bench Division: Kennedy LJ and Clarke J).

845   Public order—riot—violent disorder—aiding and abetting—interview— appropriate adult

The defendants were charged with riot contrary to the Public Order Act 1986, s 1(1) and violent disorder contrary to the 1986 Act, s 2(1). The case against the defendants was that, in the absence of any evidence of specific acts of violence by them, their presence at the incidents of disturbance demonstrated a willing and persistent involvement in the disorder and an intention to encourage others to use violence and that each had, in effect, aided and abetted the violence. During the police interviews of one of the defendants, who was a juvenile, his father intervened robustly, and sometimes joined in the questioning of his son. An unsuccessful application was made for the trial judge to exclude the interviews under the Police and Criminal Evidence Act 1984, s 76(2) and or s 78 on the basis that the father was not an appropriate adult, as defined by the Police and Criminal Evidence Act 1984 (s 66) Codes of Practice, 1985 Edition, Code C, para 1.7. Following their conviction the defendants appealed against the judge's ruling and on the ground that the 1986 Act, s 2 created an offence for principals only by virtue of the 1986 Act, s 6. *Held*, the offence of aiding and abetting was a common law offence and was applicable to all Acts unless specifically excluded by statute. Therefore, offences created by the 1986 Act were committed by aiders and abettors as well as by principals. An appropriate adult who gave encouragement to a juvenile who was being fairly interviewed by police officers to tell the truth did not fail in his duty to advise under the 1986 Act, Codes of Practice nor did it make him an inappropriate adult. Accordingly, the appeal would be dismissed.

R v Jefferson; R v Skerritt; R v Readman; R v Keogh [1994] 1 All ER 270 (Court of Appeal: Watkins LJ, Auld and Scott JJ).

846   Road traffic offences

See ROAD TRAFFIC.

847   Sentencing

See SENTENCING.

848   Sexual Offences Act 1993

The Sexual Offences Act 1993, s 1 abolishes the presumption of criminal law that a boy under the age of 14 is incapable of sexual intercourse. Section 2 deals with short title, commencement and extent. The Act received the royal assent on 20 July 1993 and came into force on 20 September 1993.

849   Suicide—suicide pact

Canada

A couple decided to commit suicide together and the accused made the preparations. The next day, on her return from work, the victim lay on top of the accused, he called the police, confirmed their decision and then fired a gun in such a way that the bullet would pass through both their bodies. The shot was fatal to the victim and left the accused with serious injuries. He was charged with the first degree murder of the victim. The trial judge instructed the jury that suicide and attempted suicide were not offences and that if they concluded that, because of his mental state, the accused did not commit first or second degree murder but had made a suicide pact then they should acquit him. The accused was acquitted and the Crown appealed. *Held*, the survivor of a genuine suicide pact had a defence to murder. The defence was only available where the two individuals formed a common and irrevocable intent to commit suicide together in a simultaneous manner, through the same event and by the same instrumentality, where the risk of death was equal for both of them. On the evidence, the couple had identical intent and the acts done by the accused were merely components of a single act of suicide for both of them. The verdict was not unreasonable and, accordingly, the appeal would be dismissed.

R v Gagnon (1993) CCC 143 (Quebec Court of Appeal).

850   Theft—appropriation—assumption of owner's rights—relevance of dishonest motive

The defendant was a nurse responsible for patients' finances. Each patient had a trust account at a building society and she was the sole signatory. She was convicted on two counts of theft, the first relating to the transfer of money from a patient's account into her own account, and the second of opening a separate cash account for the patient and the paying of a cheque into it. At trial, the defendant made an unsuccessful submission of no case to answer in respect of the second count, contending that the paying-in was not evidence of appropriation. On appeal, *held*, a dishonest motive could not turn into an appropriation an act which was not an appropriation. Although the purpose in opening a second account might have been to facilitate unauthorised withdrawals, the act of paying the cheque into the patient's cash account was an affirmation, rather than an assumption, of the patient's rights and could not be regarded as an appropriation. Accordingly, the appeal would be allowed and the conviction on the second count quashed.

R v Gallasso [1993] Crim LR 459 (Court of Appeal: Lloyd LJ, Latham and Smith JJ).

851   Theft—appropriation—intention permanently to deprive owner—directions to jury

The defendant was charged with theft contrary to the Theft Act 1968, s 6(1). It was alleged that his co-accused took a newspaper from a package of newspapers which had been left outside a newsagent's shop. They then walked along the street where the defendant dropped the newspaper. When interviewed the co-accused said that he and the defendant, believing the package to be lost, were taking it to a police station. The defendant stated, in his interview, that as a joke he had suggested that he would pick up the package and drop it on a friend's door step and, in evidence, that because he had been drinking his recollection was very patchy. The co-accused did not give evidence. In summing up the judge made the following reference to the 1968 Act, s 6(1) "if you have an intention to treat property as your own regardless of the rights of the true owner, then that is an intention permanently to deprive". The judge reminded the jury as to the police interviews but did not summarise the defendant's evidence. The defendant was convicted and on appeal, *held*, in omitting from his direction the words "to dispose of" before the word "regardless" the judge had materially altered the meaning of the 1968 Act, s 6(1). Further, the judge had equated the evidential position of the defendant with that of the co-accused and therefore, placed the defendant's evidence on the same footing as that which the co-accused had given to the police. The judge ought to have reminded the jury of the defendant's evidence on the issue of his state of mind at the material time. Accordingly, the appeal would be allowed.

R v Cahill [1993] Crim LR 141 (Court of Appeal: Russell LJ, Waterhouse and Potts JJ).

852   Theft—appropriation—intention permanently to deprive owner—transfer of fixtures from one council house to another

Under the Theft Act 1968, s 6(1), a person appropriating property belonging to another without meaning the other permanently to lose the thing itself is nevertheless to be regarded as having the intention of permanently depriving the other of it if his intention is to treat the thing as his own to dispose of regardless of the other's rights.

A council refused to replace damaged doors at one of its properties on the grounds that the damage was the tenant's responsibility. The defendant, who lived at the property in question with the tenant, replaced the damaged doors by taking the doors from another council house nearby which was unoccupied. Justices dismissed an information charging the defendant with theft and the prosecution appealed. *Held*, the question was whether the defendant intended to treat the doors as his own regardless of the council's rights. The council's rights included the right not to have the doors from the unoccupied property removed and the right to require the tenant who was responsible for the damage in the first place to replace or pay for the damaged doors. In dealing with the doors from the unoccupied property regardless of those rights, the defendant manifested an intention to treat them as his own. Accordingly, the appeal would be allowed.

DPP v Lavender (1993) Times, 2 June, Independent, 4 June (Queen's Bench Division: Watkins LJ and Tuckey J).

853   Theft—appropriation—investment funds

The defendants operated a company marketing investment schemes. Under the terms of the investments, the companies were authorised to use investors' funds to deal in government stock on a fully discretionary basis and to place uninvested funds on such terms and conditions as they saw fit. Money obtained from investors was not invested as claimed, but used by the defendants for their own purposes. The defendants were convicted of theft. On their appeal against conviction, the issue was whether the company was a trustee of the funds invested with it. *Held*, the company received the investors' funds on trust to invest them in government stock and was only authorised to place them elsewhere temporarily pending their investment in gilts or their return to the investors. As such, the funds remained the investors' property by virtue of the Theft Act 1968, s 5 and the defendants, in diverting the funds for their own use, had appropriated property belonging to another contrary to the 1968 Act, s 1. Accordingly, their appeal would be dismissed.

R v Naylor (1993) Independent, 10 August (Court of Appeal: Watkins, Auld and Scott Baker LJJ).

854 Theft—appropriation—several appropriations—continuance of offence

The appellants hired expensive motor cars abroad and had them driven to the United Kingdom where, after making various changes to the vehicles, they sold them. They appealed against conviction of conspiracy to steal on the ground that, as they had stolen the vehicles abroad, they could not steal them again in England. *Held*, if a person acquired property by stealing it, his later dealing with it was, by implication, not among the assumptions of the right of an owner referred to in the Theft Act 1968, s 3(1) as amounting to an appropriation. Section 3(1) applied whether the stealing occurred in England and Wales or elsewhere. It was immaterial that an indictment in respect of the theft would not lie abroad. Goods once stolen could not be stolen again by the same thief exercising the same or other rights of ownership over them. The theft of the vehicles had been completed abroad so that the appellants could not again steal in the United Kingdom. Their appeals would be allowed.

R v Atakpu [1993] 4 All ER 215 (Court of Appeal: Stuart-Smith LJ, Ward and May JJ).

855 Theft—property received on account of another—financial consultant

The Theft Act 1968, s 5(3) provides that where a person receives property from or on account of another, and is under an obligation to the other to retain and deal with that property or its proceeds in a particular way, the property or proceeds will be regarded (as against him) as belonging to the other.

The appellant was a financial consultant and intermediary. He was suspended from carrying on investment business when a deficiency in clients' money was revealed. He was charged with theft and several offences of dishonesty, the prosecution contending that he had failed to keep his clients' money separate from the general trading account of his business. It was further alleged that in relation to two counts of theft, the clients had entrusted money to the appellant on the understanding that it was to be kept separate and distinct. The appellant contended that so long as he accounted for the money to the clients in the end, he was entitled to use it as he wished. The judge directed the jury to consider, in order to determine whether the 1968 Act, s 5(3) applied, what the parties would have told an officious bystander if at the time they entered into the contracts he had asked them what they intended to happen to the money, so as to ascertain whether there was an implied term that the clients' money was to be kept separate. The appellant was convicted. It was contended on appeal that no such term could be implied into the contracts. *Held*, the judge should have directed that s 5(3) would only apply if the jury were sure that the appellant and his clients had clearly understood that the clients' investments or their proceeds were to be kept separate from the appellant's own money and that of his business. However, for practical purposes the judge's direction was to that effect. Accordingly, there was no misdirection and the appeal against conviction would be dismissed.

R v McHugh (1993) 97 Cr App Rep 335 (Court of Appeal: Lord Taylor of Gosforth CJ, Auld and Curtis JJ). *R v Golechha* (1990) 90 Cr App Rep 241, CA (1989 Abr para 457) distinguished.

856 Theft—taking conveyance without authority—conveyance already unlawfully taken and abandoned

The appellant was seen driving a car which had earlier been taken from a car park. He ran away when he was stopped by the police. He contended that he was moving the car before informing police of its whereabouts, but he was convicted at trial of taking a vehicle without consent. He successfully appealed, the court holding that the moving was for the appellant's own use, but he was not the original taker and he could not be convicted on the basis of the subsequent removal. On appeal, *held*, where the vehicle was taken and then abandoned, if it was subsequently retaken without authority, there was a fresh assumption of possession. The taker of a conveyance without authority was guilty under the Theft Act 1968, s 12(1) even if that vehicle had already been unlawfully taken and then abandoned. The offences under the 1968 Act were not limited to facts where there had been only one taking either by a single person or by his acting jointly with another. The applicable test was that the defendant had to have taken control of the vehicle and have caused it to be moved and he must have done so for his or another's use. The appeal would accordingly be allowed.

DPP v Spriggs [1994] RTR 1 (Queen's Bench Division: Mann LJ and Tudor Evans J).

CROWN PROCEEDINGS AND CROWN PRACTICE

Halsbury's Laws of England (4th edn) Vol 11, Supp paras 1–37

857 Crown proceedings—Prime Minister's authority—conclusion of contract
See *Quintessence Co-Ordinators Ltd v Government of the Republic of Transkei*, para 3.

CUSTOMS AND EXCISE

Halsbury's Laws of England (4th edn) Vol 12, paras 501–1100

858 Articles
Excise Appeals and Civil Penalties, Gavin McFarlane: Tax Journal, Issue 234, p 14
Search Warrants in Commercial Customs Cases, Gavin McFarlane: Criminal Lawyer, Issue 39,
   p 2

859 Common commercial policy
See EUROPEAN COMMUNITIES.

860 Common customs tariff
See EUROPEAN COMMUNITIES.

861 Community Customs Code—consequential amendment of references
The Community Customs Code (Consequential Amendment of References) Regulations 1993, SI 1993/3014 (in force on 1 January 1994), amend the Customs and Excise Management Act 1979, the Free Zone Regulations 1991, SI 1991/2727, the Customs Controls on Importation of Goods Regulations 1991, SI 1991/2724, the Customs and Excise (Transit) Regulations 1993, SI 1993/1353, para 885, and the Customs Warehousing Regulations 1991, SI 1991/2725, in order to substitute for references to repealed Community instruments references to Council Regulation (EC) 2913/92, which established the Community Customs Code, and to Commission Regulation (EC) 2454/93, which implemented the code.

862 Customs duty—relief—quota reliefs
The Customs Duties (ECSC) (Quota and Other Reliefs) Order 1993, SI 1993/3254 (in force on 1 January 1994), provides for relief from customs duty, in so far as it is charged, on certain iron and steel products originating in specified developing countries. The reliefs apply until 30 June 1994.

863 Customs officers—procedure on interview—evidence improperly obtained
See *R v Okafor*, para 717.

864 European Economic Area Act 1993
The European Economic Area Act 1993 makes provision in relation to the European Economic Area (EEA) established under the Agreement signed at Oporto on 2 May 1992 as adjusted by the Protocol signed at Brussels on 17 March 1993. The Act received the royal assent on 5 November 1993 and came into force on that date.

By virtue of s 1, the 1992 Agreement, as adjusted, is added to the Community Treaties listed in the European Communities Act 1972, s 1(2). The 1993 Act, s 2 and the Schedule provide for the consistent application of United Kingdom law to the whole of the EEA and s 3 for the general implementation of the Agreement. Section 4 amends the 1972 Act by extending the provisions on evidence and judicial notice so that they also have effect in relation to the European Free Trade Association Court and the European Free Trade Association Surveillance Authority. The 1993 Act, s 5 provides for the parliamentary procedure to apply to regulations made under ss 2, 3; s 6 deals with interpretation and s 7 with the short title.

865 Excise duty—beer

See para 1557.

866 Excise duty—tobacco products

The Tobacco Products (Amendment) Regulations 1993, SI 1993/2167 (in force on 30 September 1993), further amend the 1979 Regulations, SI 1979/804, by making provision for the electronic removal of tobacco products from suitably approved registered stores (ie stores in respect of which the records relating to removal are kept by means of a computer or other electronic system approved by the Commissioners of Customs and Excise). Accordingly, where tobacco products are held in any such store, they may be cleared to home use on payment of tobacco products duty notwithstanding that they have not left the store, and such duty paid tobacco products may continue to be stored within the store.

867 Excise duty—vehicle excise duty—mitigated penalty

A vehicle was seen to have been used without a vehicle excise licence. The vehicle registration office wrote to the registered keeper of the vehicle requiring notice of the person who had used the vehicle on the day in question. The husband of the registered keeper of the vehicle replied to the effect that he had used the vehicle on that day. The office gave the husband the opportunity to settle the matter by payment of a mitigated penalty out of court in respect of the unlicensed use of the vehicle. The offer was declined. The office wrote a further letter to the husband and, after consideration of factors which he had mentioned, offered settlement by the payment of a smaller mitigated penalty. Nothing was heard from the husband and, as the six-month period for instituting proceedings was drawing to a close, a summons was issued against the registered keeper of the vehicle in respect of keeping an unlicensed vehicle on a public road. The registered keeper of the vehicle was found guilty, was fined, ordered to pay a penalty and also ordered to pay costs. She complained to the Parliamentary Commissioner for Administration that she had been treated unfairly over the matter. The commissioner upheld her complaint. The failure to offer her the opportunity to settle the matter out of court by a mitigated penalty, as had been offered to her husband, had caused injustice. The Driver and Vehicle Licensing Agency offered her an ex gratia payment representing the difference between the amount required to be paid by the court and the settlement offered to her husband by way of mitigated penalty. The agency also undertook to review its systems.

Case C135/92, Parliamentary Commissioner for Administration, Selected Cases 1993, Vol 2 (HC 673), p 65.

868 Excise duty—vehicle excise duty—simplification of goods vehicles rates

The Vehicles Excise Duty (Simplification of Goods Vehicles Rates) Order 1993, SI 1993/2452 (in force on 8 November 1993), makes modifications to the Vehicles (Excise) Act 1971, Sch 4. The annual rates of vehicles excise duty on goods vehicles are now specified by reference to fewer tables. The rates of duty on a farmer's goods vehicle and a showman's goods vehicle are now to be calculated by applying multipliers to the rates for other goods vehicles, so as to avoid the need for separate tables. In order to ensure that there is no change in the amount of duty payable in respect of any vehicle, the order provides for rounding and certain exceptions from the new approach.

869 Excise duty—vehicle excise duty—vehicle used for conveyance of goods— tractor used for towing

See *Booth v DPP*, para 2195.

870 Export of goods—control—Bosnia-Herzegovina

The Export of Goods (Control) (Bosnia-Herzegovina) (ECSC) (Revocation) Order 1993, SI 1993/1200 (in force on 30 April 1993), revokes the ealier order, SI 1993/719, which prohibited the export to Bosnia-Herzegovina of goods covered by the ECSC Treaty, unless an exemption to the prohibition had been granted by the Secretary of State. The order did not apply to the export of goods intended for essential humanitarian need or for activities related to peacekeeping efforts in the former Yugoslavia, or to goods which had an individual value of less than 1000 ECU.

871 Export of goods—control—Croatia and Bosnia

The Export of Goods (Control) (Croatian and Bosnian Territories) Order 1993, SI 1993/1189 (in force on 26 April 1993), prohibits the export to the United Nations protected areas of Croatia and those areas of the Republic of Bosnia-Herzegovina under the control of Bosnian Serb forces of any goods except under the authority of a licence granted by the Secretary of State.

872 Export of goods—control—export licence no bar to prosecution

A company and one of its employees were convicted of being knowingly concerned in the attempted export to Iran of tyres for combat aircraft, contrary to the Customs and Excise Management Act 1976, s 68(2) and the Export of Goods (Control) Order 1987, SI 1987/2070. The employee appealed, contending there had been no offence because the export had been licensed by the Secretary of State, and he said he had not known that the company named as the purchaser on the export licence was an attempt to disguise the fact that the goods were destined for Iran. The company appealed on the ground that the employee did not have enough power within the company to render it criminally liable for his actions. Held, the 1987 Order only concerned unlawful activity in the period preceding the application for a licence, but the 1976 Act covered the period up to the unlawful exportation or the attempt. Consequently, the jury could convict the employee if they felt he had knowingly attempted to avoid the prohibition on export at any time up to the date of seizure, and the fact that a licence had been granted did not protect him. The delegation of functions to an employee did not render the company liable for the employee's actions unless those functions gave him real managerial power, and as the judge had failed to make that sufficiently clear the jury may have felt the delegation of any executive or administrative function was enough to render the company liable for an abuse of that power by an employee. The company's appeal would be allowed, but there were no grounds for disturbing the employee's conviction.

R v Redfern and Dunlop Ltd (Aircraft Tyres Division) (1992) 13 Cr App Rep (S) 709 (Court of Appeal: Taylor LJ, Waterhouse and Kennedy JJ).

1987 Order replaced by 1989 Order, SI 1989/2376.

873 Export of goods—control—general orders

The Export of Goods (Control) (Amendment) Order 1993, SI 1993/1020 (in force on 3 April 1993), further amends the 1992 Order, SI 1992/3092, by (1) relaxing export control in respect of certain personalised smart cards using cryptography; (2) clarifying the scope of the prohibition on the export of aircraft and components to Libya, Iran, Iraq, Syria and South Africa; (3) extending the control on technology relating to the development or use of certain goods to nuclear power generating or propulsion equipment, including nuclear reactors, specially designed for military use, to certain sensors, lasers and related equipment and to certain navigation and avionics equipment; and (5) correcting an error in the definition of "personalised smart card".

The Export of Goods (Control) (Amendment No 2) Order 1993, SI 1993/1692 (in force on 24 July 1993), further amends the 1992 Order supra, by (1) removing most vaccines and fluorine from export control; (2) extending the control on certain acceloremeters designed for use in inertial navigation systems or in guidance systems to include specially designed components; (3) extending the control on certain gyros usable in missiles to include specially designed components; and (4) extending the control on certain solid and liquid fuelled rocket engines and rocket stages including specially designed production equipment, production facilities and technology required for their development, production or use.

The Export of Goods (Control) (Amendment No 4) Order 1993, SI 1993/1825 (in force on 15 July 1993), revokes the Export of Goods (Control) (Amendment No 3) Order 1993, SI

1993/1824, and further amends the 1992 Order by introducing controls on the export of certain vehicles to Croatia, Bosnia-Herzegovina, and the former Yugoslav Republic of Macedonia.

The Export of Goods (Control) (Amendment No 5) Order 1993, SI 1993/2515 (in force on 21 October 1993), further amends the 1992 Order by relaxing control in relation to specified duel-use goods and removing control on certain other duel-use goods, extending controls on specified goods and introducing control on certain other goods. Definitions for "isolated live cultures" and "focal plane arrays" are added.

The Export of Goods (Control) (Amendment No 6) Order 1993, SI 1993/3264 (in force on 1 January 1994), further amends the 1992 Order by removing the Czech and Slovak Republics from the countries listed in Sch 2.

874 Export of goods—control—Haiti

The Export of Goods (Control) (Haiti) (Revocation) Order 1993/2232 (in force on 1 September 1993) revokes the Export of Goods (Control) (Haiti) Order 1993, SI 1993/1677 (in force on 26 June 1993), which prohibited the export to Haiti of police equipment, spare parts for such equipment, and specified petroleum and petroleum products except under the authority of a licence granted by the Secretary of State.

875 Export of goods—cultural objects—unlawful removal

See para 2711.

876 Finance Act 1991—commencement

The Finance Act 1991 (Commencement and Transitional Provisions) Order 1993, SI 1993/1152 brings into force (1) on 1 May 1993 s 7(2), (3), (5), Sch 2, paras 3(1), (2), 5(1), (3), (4), 13, 14 (registration of persons who may hold and premises where beer may be held without payment of duty; registration of producers of beer; and amendment of enactments and instruments relating to beer duty); and (2) on 1 June 1993 s 7(1), (4), (6), (7), Sch 2, paras 1, 2, 3(3), 4, 5(2), 6–12, 15–20, 22 (beer duty and further amendment of enactments and instruments relating to beer duty). Transitional provision is also made. For a summary of the Act, see 1991 Abr para 2056. For details of commencement, see the commencement table in the title STATUTES.

877 Finance (No 2) Act 1992—commencement

The Finance (No 2) Act 1992 (Commencement No 5) Order 1993, SI 1993/1341 brings into force on 1 June 1993 s 1(5), Sch 1 (powers to fix excise duty point) and s 3(1), Sch 2 (protection of revenues derived from excise duties). For a summary of the Act, see 1992 Abr para 2157. For details of commencement, see the commencement table in the title STATUTES.

878 Finance Act 1993—commencement

See para 2160.

879 Hydrocarbon oil—claim for duty relief

The Hydrocarbon Oil (Amendment) Regulations 1993, SI 1993/2267 (in force on 15 October 1993), further amend the 1973 Regulations, SI 1973/1311, in order to comply with a provision of Council Directive (EC) 92/81 which requires the volume of certain hydrocarbon oils to be measured at a temperature of 15°C. Requirements of the 1973 Rules concerning the keeping of certain records and the making of certain returns are omitted.

880 Import of goods—goods from other member states—principle of free movement of goods

See *Criminal proceedings against Keck*, para 2712.

881 Import of goods—illegal import—customs duty

See *Witzemann v Hauptzollamt München-Mitte*, para 2710.

882　Import of goods—quantitative restrictions and equivalent measures—duty to provide information to consumers

See *CMC Motorradcenter GmbH v Baskiciogullari*, para 2713.

883　Import of goods—quantitative restrictions and equivalent measures— prohibition of eye-catching price comparisons

See *Schutzverband gegen Unwesen in der Wirtschaft v Yves Rocher GmbH*, para 2714.

884　Statistics of trade

The Statistics of Trade (Customs and Excise) (Amendment) Regulations 1993, SI 1993/541 (in force on 1 April 1993), amend the 1992 Regulations, SI 1992/2790, by permitting the Commissioners of Customs and Excise to conduct ancillary cost sample surveys in accordance with Commission Regulation (EC) 3046/92.

The Statistics of Trade (Customs and Excise) (Amendment No 2) Regulations 1993, SI 1993/3015 (in force on 1 January 1994), increase the assimilation thresholds set out in the 1992 Regulations, SI 1992/2790, to £140,000. They also apply the Customs and Excise Management Act 1979, ss 145–148 and 150–154 to the 1992 Regulations.

885　Transit of goods

The Customs and Excise (Transit) Regulations 1993, SI 1993/1353 (in force on 23 June 1993), replace the Customs and Excise (Community Transit) (No 2) Regulations 1987, SI 1987/2105 and the Customs and Excise (Common Transit) Regulations 1988, SI 1988/1476 in order to take account of amendments of Community Regulations concerning Community transit and of the EC-EFTA Convention on common transit. The regulations create penalties and provide for forfeiture for contravention of the transit procedures and make transitional provision for the changes in such procedures.

886　Value added tax

See VALUE ADDED TAX.

DAMAGES AND COMPENSATION

Halsbury's Laws of England (4th edn) Vol 12, paras 1101–1300

Contributors
Our thanks to the following, who have contributed items to this title:
Alexander Harris, Solicitors, Sale.
Julie Barratt, Pupil Barrister.
Jacqueline Beech, Barrister.
Bevan Ashford, Solicitors, Bristol.
Ruth Blair, Barrister.
Charles Bourne, Barrister.
Brindley Twist Tafft & James, Solicitors, Coventry.
John Brooke-Smith, Barrister.
Brutton & Co, Solicitors, Fareham.
Gary Burrell, Barrister.
James R Candlin, Barrister.
Canter Levin & Berg, Solicitors, St Helens.
Charles, Crookes & Jones, Solicitors, Caerphilly.
G & I Chisholm, Solicitors, Bodmin.
Jonathan Clarke, Barrister.
Clarke Willmott & Clarke, Solicitors, Bridgwater.
Clarkson Wright & James, Solicitors, Orpington.
Mariam Cohen, Lambert Hale & Proctor, Solicitors, London.
Susan Cooper, Barrister.

Paul Corben, Barrister.
Emma Cornah, Pupil Barrister.
Cornish & Birtill, Solicitors, Penzance.
Dakers Green Brett, Solicitors, Rochester.
Alasdair M Davidson, Barrister.
Douglas, Solicitors, Redhill.
Marion Egan, Barrister.
Richard Egleton, Barrister.
Sarah Evans-Lombe, Pupil Barrister.
Charles Foster, Barrister.
David Gallagher, Pupil Barrister.
Antonis Georges, Barrister.
Allan Gore, Barrister.
Richard Gregory, Solicitor, Andover.
Tim Grover, Barrister.
Ms E A Gumbel, Barrister.
Hodge Jones & Allen, Solicitors, London.
Andrew Hogarth, Barrister.
Jon Holbrook, Barrister.
Mr M A Hollidge, Solicitor, Tamworth.
Philip Holmes, Barrister.
Howe & Co, Solicitors, Ealing.
Leighton Alexander Hughes, Barrister.
Ingham Clegg & Crowther, Solicitors, Fleetwood.
Adrian Jackson, Barrister.
Geraint E Jones, Solicitor, Powys.
Joseph Aaron & Co, Solicitors, Ilford.
Peter William Keer-Keer, Solicitor, Hemel Hempstead.
Kelly & Anderson, Solicitors, Chesterfield.
Philip Kolvin, Barrister.
Howard Lederman, Barrister.
K J Martin & Co, Solicitors, Coventry.
Martin Smith & Co, Solicitors, Borehamwood.
David Mason, Barrister.
Andrew McDonald, Barrister.
Colin McEachran, QC.
Andrew Menary, Barrister.
Mendelsons, Solicitors, Manchester.
Colin Mendoza, Barrister.
Neil Mercer, Barrister.
Hugh Merry, Barrister.
Keith S H Miller, Barrister.
Vincent Moran, Barrister.
Penny Nagle, Pupil Barrister.
Miranda Napper, Pupil Barrister.
Kaiser Nazir, Barrister.
John Nivison & Co, Solicitors, Stockport.
David Owusu-Yianoma, Pupil Barrister.
Pattinson & Brewer, Solicitors, London.
Edward Pepperall, Barrister.
R H Perks, Barrister.
Martin Picton, Barrister.
Derek S Reed, Solicitor, Devon.
Rhodes Thain & Collinson, Solicitors, Halifax.
Graham Thrussell, Barrister.
Mr S Robinson, Frank Allen Pennington, Solicitors, Doncaster.
Stewart Room, Barrister.
Rowe & Cohen, Solicitors, Hyde.
Martin Russell, Barrister.
Russell Jones & Walker, Solicitors, London.
Sanjiv Sachdeva, Barrister.
Sarjeant & Sheppard, Solicitors, Reading.
Charles E Scott, Barrister.

Seldon, Ward & Nuttall, Solicitors, Bideford.
Shoosmiths & Harrison, Solicitors, Reading.
Paul Simpson, Barrister.
Peter R Smith, Barrister.
W F Smith & Co, Solicitors, Brandon.
Anthony Snelson, Barrister.
Jonathan Sofer, Barrister.
Paul M Statham, Pattinson & Brewer, Solicitors, London.
Stephens & Scown, Solicitors, Exeter.
Stuchbery Stone, Solicitors, Windsor.
Keith Thomas, Barrister.
Neil Thompson, Barrister.
Robin Thompson & Partners, Solicitors, Cardiff and London.
Graham Thrussell, Barrister.
Union of Shop, Distributive and Allied Workers, Manchester.
Laurence Vick, Solicitor.
Patrick Vincent, Pupil Barrister.
Charles Welchman, Barrister.
Simon Wheatley, Barrister.
Timothy White, Barrister.
Richard Wilkinson, Barrister.
Gerald O Wood, J P Hall & Co, Solicitors, Spennymoor.
Nicholas J Worsley, QC.

887 Articles

A Tax on Injury: Charles Taylor (on the Social Security Act 1989): 143 NLJ 1074
Dispensation with Undertaking in Damages—An Elementary Injustice, AAS Zuckerman: (1993) 12 CJQ 268
Fair Damages, Andrew Ritchie (on personal injury claims by unemployed plaintiffs): LS Gaz, 8 September 1993, p 25
Future Pecuniary Loss—A Better System, David Kemp (on the use of structured settlements): 137 SJ (Personal Injury Supplement) 8
Is Roberts v Johnstone Still Fair to Plaintiffs and Defendants? Charles Cooper and Cathie Illidge (on *Roberts v Johnstone* [1988] 3 WLR 1247, CA (1988 Abr para 623): 137 SJ 767
Lawyer's Comment Defiance or Compliance? RSC Ord 18, r 12 and CCR Ord 6, r 1, Richard Vallance (on the use of medical reports and Statements of Special Damages in medical negligence cases): (1993) 2 AVMA 6
Legal Limits on the Structured Settlement of Damages, Richard Lewis: [1993] 52 CLJ 470
Limitation and Intentional Torts, W V H Rogers: 143 NLJ 258
Multiplication Tables, Bill Braithwaite: 137 SJ 1154
Personal Injury Litigation 1992, Roderick L Denyer: LS Gaz, 19 May 1993, p 35
Post Traumatic Stress Disorder, Richard Hoare: 138 SJ 61
Post Traumatic Stress Disorder, Malcolm Weller: 143 NLJ 878
Recoupment of Benefits, Tess Gill: 137 SJ 918
RSI—Can You Claim? Simon Allen: 137 SJ 1152
Structured Settlements and Interim and Provisional Damages—The Law Commission's Consultation Paper, Iain Goldrein and Margaret de Haas: (1993) 2 AVMA 7
The Abused Child and the Quantum of Damages/Compensation, Roderick L Denyer: [1993] Fam Law 297
The End of the Line for Exemplary Damages? Alan Reed: 143 NLJ 929
The Reasonable Child Defined, Roderick Denyer QC (on the Contributory Negligence Act 1945, s 1): LS Gaz, 17 February 1993, p 25

888 Aggravated, exemplary and restitutionary damages—Law Commission consultation

The Law Commission has issued a consultation paper on certain aspects of the law of damages, *Aggravated, Exemplary and Restitutionary Damages* (Law Com consultation paper 132). The commission suggests, provisionally, that exemplary damages should be retained on a "principled" basis but asks whether such damages are justified on the basis of punishment and deterrence or on the need to provide redress for breach of intangible personality interests. A view is expressed, provisionally, in favour of codification, but it is asked whether the codification should be of a broad principle, leaving the courts to develop the law, or whether it should closely define the circumstances in which an award of exemplary damages might be made. Other matters relating to exemplary damages on which views are sought include the possible method of sharing exemplary awards between a class of victims, the possible renaming of the award to shift the focus away from retributory aspects, whether the judges should take over the role of juries in assessing damages, the standard of proof for exemplary awards, whether insurance should be acceptable in this area, vicarious liability, joint liability for such awards, and the possibility of adducing evidence as to the defendant's wealth. The commission provisionally suggests that aggravated damages should be abolished, and seeks views on the consequences of abolition. It further seeks views on the availability of restitutionary damages for all gains made by reason of a wrong where the gains are attributable to the interest infringed and asks whether such damages should only be available in respect of "proprietary torts" and infringements of interests analogous to property interests. Views are also sought on whether the development of the law in relation to restitutionary damages should be left to the courts or be the subject of legislation.

889 Assessment of damages—bereavement—prospect of divorce

The plaintiff claimed damages under the Fatal Accidents Act 1976 in respect of her loss of dependency arising from the death of her husband eleven months after their marriage. The plaintiff had been divorced by her previous husband on the grounds of adultery, and shortly after the deceased's death she had started a relationship with a married man who had worked with the deceased. He divorced and married the plaintiff. In calculating the plaintiff's dependency the judge took $\frac{2}{3}$ of the likely net earnings of the deceased in each of the 15 years following his death as the value of dependency in that year, resulting in an award of over £460,000. The defendants appealed on the basis that the multiplier of 15 and the calculation of the value of the dependency had been erroneous. *Held*, the 1976 Act, s 3(3) prevented remarriage from being taken into account when assessing a widow's dependency, but it did not prevent the prospect of divorce from being considered. The appropriate multiplier to apply was one which took account of whatever uncertainties the facts of the case revealed, and in the circumstances a multiplier of 11 was more appropriate. There was no rule that in the absence of striking evidence to the contrary the two-thirds rule should be applied, and the circumstances of the case required the value of dependency to be assessed on the basis of multiplicands of £8,000 for the five years preceding trial and £15,000 for each of the six years following trial, resulting in a total award of £150,000. To that extent, the appeal would be allowed.

Owen v Martin [1992] PIQR Q151 (Court of Appeal: Parker, Stuart-Smith and Beldam LJJ).

890 Assessment of damages—cremation—disposal of ashes—failure to follow instructions for disposal

After the death of her husband, the plaintiff engaged the first defendant for £989, to arrange cremation and for the ashes to be returned to her for interment in the family plot. The second defendant managed the crematorium and negligently scattered the ashes in the grounds of the crematorium. After initial efforts to make amends, the second defendant reacted in an extraordinary and unreasonable way to the instruction of solicitors by the plaintiff which aggravated her feelings of distress caused by the error. On the plaintiff's claim for damages, *held*, in assessing the amount of damages for the distress and anxiety caused to the plaintiff, the present case involved continuing pain and could therefore be distinguished from those cases where disappointment was experienced through the spoilt enjoyment of a holiday. A more appropriate starting point was the statutory bereavement award of £7,500 under the Fatal Accidents Act 1976, s 1A and the correct figure was one third of that amount. Accordingly, the total damages awarded were £2,870 comprising £350 for breach of contract (and interest at 12 per cent); £2,500 for distress and anxiety (and interest at 2 per cent); and £20 agreed special damages (and interest at 12 per cent).

Griffiths v Ronald P Sherry & Son (18 February 1993, unreported) (Central London County Court: Quentin Edwards QC) (Martin Russell, Messrs Moss Beachley and Mullem for the plaintiff; A Miller, Messrs Badhams Thompson for the defendants) (Kindly submitted for publication by Martin Russell, Barrister).

891 Assessment of damages—deductions—benefits—widow's pension

The Fatal Accidents Act 1976, s 4(1) provides that in assessing damages in respect of a person's death, benefits which have accrued or will or may accrue to any person from his estate as a result of his death are to be disregarded.

The deceased died as the result of his exposure to asbestos during his employment with the defendants. His widow sued on behalf of his estate pursuant to the Law Reform (Miscellaneous Provisions) Act 1934 and on her own behalf as his dependant under the 1976 Act. The defendants had admitted liability for his death and the parties had agreed all heads of damages except the widow's claim for loss of dependency. At the time of his death, the deceased had been receiving a Category A, and his wife a Category B, state retirement pension. However, after his death the widow's state pension was paid at a higher rate than during his lifetime under the provisions of the Social Security Contributions and Benefits Act 1992, s 50. The issue was whether that increase in the rate of pension was a benefit under the 1976 Act, s 4(1). The defendants submitted that no benefit accrued to the widow as a result of her husband's death: the benefit in question was her entitlement to her Category B pension which had accrued on her husband's 65th birthday and had simply increased as a result of his death. *Held*, the loss relied upon was the extent to which the widow would have benefited from the deceased's financial support. The increase in the rate of her pension which resulted from his death was incidental to that loss. Whilst the widow's entitlement to retirement pension accrued on her husband's 65th birthday, her right to the increase in question accrued on his death. That increase benefited her and was payable as a result of his death, and thus fell within the 1976 Act, s 4(2). Accordingly, judgment would be given for the plaintiff.

Brown v Rover Group Holdings plc (26 July 1993, unreported) (Queen's Bench Division: McCullough J) (Kindly submitted for publication by Andrew Hogarth, Barrister).

892   Assessment of damages—libel—reduction of excessive award

The plaintiff, a well-known television personality, was the founder and chairperson of a charity for sexually abused children. A national Sunday newspaper alleged the plaintiff had known that a teacher who had provided the charity with information about child abusers was himself an abuser, and said the plaintiff had been insincere and hypocritical because she had not informed the teacher's employer of that fact. In the plaintiff's subsequent action for defamation, a jury awarded her £250,000, and the defendants appealed against the award on the ground that it had been excessive. They also contended that the trial judge had erred in referring the jury to awards made by juries in other defamation cases. *Held*, although the jury in defamation actions could be referred to awards made by the Court of Appeal in defamation cases under the Courts and Legal Services Act 1990, s 8, it could not be referred to jury awards in other defamation cases or to conventional awards in personal injuries actions. Previous awards could not be regarded as establishing a standard to which reference could be made in the future, and the fact that the jury had been given the opportunity to consider such awards had resulted in an amount being awarded which was manifestly excessive. The court would exercise its power under the 1990 Act, s 8 to substitute the original award for a more appropriate one. Accordingly, the appeal would be allowed and the sum of £110,000 would be awarded.

Rantzen v Mirror Group Newspapers (1986) Ltd [1993] 4 All ER 975 (Court of Appeal: Neill, Staughton and Roch LJJ). *Sutcliffe v Pressdram Ltd* [1990] 1 All ER 269, CA (1989 Abr para 622) considered.

893   Assessment of damages—loss of use of car—diminution of value of car for insurance purposes

The plaintiff was involved in a road traffic accident in which his car sustained damage to its boot so that it would not close. The plaintiff took the view that, notwithstanding that the boot could be held down by string, the car was too dangerous to drive and borrowed another car. Two weeks later the plaintiff used a hammer to fix the boot so that it would close and thereafter he used his car. The car was stolen, never having been repaired. The plaintiff's insurers paid a reduced sum of money in respect of the theft because of the damage caused to the car's boot. The plaintiff claimed a sum of damages from the defendant driver in respect of loss of use of the car for two weeks and for the diminution in value of his car by reason of the damage caused by the defendant's negligent driving. *Held*, the plaintiff was entitled damages under both heads claimed plus interest.

Maynard v Loveday (6 January 1994, unreported) (Bow County Court: Judge Sich). (Kindly submitted for publication by Ruth Blair, counsel for plaintiff, instructed by Coleman & Tilley, Solicitors).

894   Assessment of damages—loss of use of caravan

The plaintiff's car and caravan were damaged in a road traffic accident in July 1992 and the defendant admitted liability. The plaintiff had uninsured losses in respect of the caravan damage, loss of use of the caravan, storage charges and excess on his insurance policy. These matters were to be agreed at an assessment of damages hearing. The defendant insurers delayed in authorising payment for the repairs until September 1993 and a bill for storage charges was presented by the garage, who had initially indicated that storage would be free. The garage refused to release the caravan until the charges were paid. The defendant argued that the plaintiff was not entitled to damages for loss of use of the caravan because under the terms of the hire purchase agreement the caravan should have been comprehensively insured and kept in good repair. The plaintiff submitted that he only used the caravan on one weekend a month and for his annual two week holiday, and could not afford to have the caravan comprehensively insured. *Held*, even if the caravan had been fully insured the plaintiff might have elected not to claim on the insurance as the accident was not his fault, so the terms of the hire purchase agreement were irrelevant in relation to that point. There must have been an implied term that the garage would not charge for storage if the repairs were authorised within a reasonable time, which was not done, and they were entitled to claim £393.75 for storage in view of the delay. The plaintiff could therefore claim for the storage charges. The plaintiff was not entitled to claim sums of £137.50 per month, for loss of use of the caravan, which were represented by instalments paid under the hire purchase agreement. The defendant submitted that loss of use of the caravan should be looked at in the same way as loss of use of a car and that £70 per week should be allowed. This would have resulted in 12 weekends (24 days) at £10 (£240), and 14 days annual holiday (£140), making a total of £380. The plaintiff was awarded a sum of £500 for loss of use and a split costs order was made.

Hawkins v Warren (2 November 1993, unreported) (Reading County Court: District Judge Catlin). (Kindly submitted for publication by Ruth Blair, counsel for plaintiff, instructed by Coleman & Tilley, Solicitors).

895 Assessment of damages—loss of use of motor vehicle—inconvenience of alternative means of transport

The plaintiff's vehicle was damaged in a road traffic accident in May 1992. The damage was such that the vehicle could not be driven without repairs. It took the plaintiff 12 weeks to save enough money to pay for these repairs, and during that time she was without a vehicle for 11 weeks in total. She had used the car to convey her two small children and her mother, and having to go to work by public transport instead of by car added 20 minutes each way to the plaintiff's journey. Damages were assessed for loss of use and inconvenience at the rate of £75 per week for the 11 week period, making a total of £825.

Caldow v Jones (3 June 1993, unreported) (Birkenhead County Court: Judge Bernstein) (Kindly submitted for publication by Tim Grover, Barrister).

896 Assessment of damages—wrongful dismissal—deduction of benefits received—company's pension payments

See *Norcros plc v Hopkins*, para 1203.

897 Assured tenancy—breach of covenant of quiet enjoyment—quantum of damages

The plaintiff was an assured tenant of the defendant's flat, which was repossessed by the defendant's building society after non-payment of the mortgage. The plaintiff left the flat because she faced imminent eviction by the building society, and was awarded damages from the defendant for breach of the implied covenant that she would have quiet enjoyment of her tenancy. Damages were assessed at £2,500 general damages to compensate the plaintiff for loss of an assured tenancy, and £800 special damages to cover the costs arising from the plaintiff's occupation of the repossessed flat, including the supply of new carpets, fitting an aerial, installing a gas cooker and connection of a telephone, together with the costs incurred in moving, which included a deposit for a new flat, removal expenses, gas connection and telephone connection. *Kirkham v Mason* (13 July 1993, unreported) (Bow County Court: Judge Butter) (Kindly submitted for publication by Jon Holbrook, Barrister).

898 Breach of contract—claim for loss of profit—nominal damages

The plaintiff sued the company and three of its directors for breach of a contract, which required the defendants to apply for planning permission in respect of certain land. The plaintiff had the option under the contract to purchase half of the land for a certain sum in addition to paying one half of the expenses incurred by the defendants in obtaining the permission. The plaintiff claimed damages for loss of profit equivalent to the difference between the value of one half of the land and the price he would have paid for it under the contract. *Held*, the plaintiff had not established that the probability of the defendants obtaining the planning permission was substantial, rather than merely speculative. Accordingly, the plaintiff would be entitled to nominal damages only and was ordered to pay the defendants' costs.

Obagi v Stanborough (Developments) Ltd (1993) Times, 15 December (Chancery Division: Blackburne J).

899 Breach of contract—failure of consideration—restitution

Australia

The respondent paid the appellant in advance for a 14-day cruise in the South Pacific. The ship sank during the cruise and the respondent lost her possessions and suffered personal injuries. She was given a partial refund of her fare. In proceedings for breach of contract she was awarded damages including a sum in restitution of the balance of the fare and a sum for disappointment and distress. On appeal from the award, by the cruise owner, *held*, the respondent was not entitled to recover the whole of the cruise fare on the ground of total failure of consideration, since the respondent had enjoyed the benefits of the first eight full days of the cruise. The advance payment of the fare was not conditional upon the appellant's complete performance of its entire obligations under the contract. The respondent was however entitled to an award of damages for disappointment and distress flowing from breach of contract, since the object of the contract had been to provide enjoyment, relaxation and freedom from molestation. Accordingly, the appeal would be allowed.

Baltic Shipping Co v Dillon (1993) 111 ALR 289 (High Court of Australia).

900 Breach of contract—remedial work—onus of proof that claim did not include profit

Scotland

The plaintiffs were nominated sub-contractors under a building contract. They in turn appointed sub-contractors, the defendants, whose defective work had to be rectified by another company. The plaintiffs sought to recover from the defendants a sum which included the cost of the remedial work together with the plaintiffs' standard markup of 15 per cent on sub-contracts. The defendants contended that the plaintiffs were not entitled to the whole amount claimed as the markup would include profit to the plaintiffs. *Held*, there was no evidence that if a different company had been engaged to carry out the remedial work, the cost would have been less. While there was evidence that the plaintiffs applied a markup to the prices charged to them, a markup, being intended to cover a variety of cost items, was not the same thing as a profit. The defendants had failed to prove that the plaintiffs made a profit on the original contract and, accordingly, the plaintiffs' claim would succeed.

Rotary Services Ltd v Honeywell Control Systems Ltd (note) 1993 SLT 781 (Outer House).

901 Breach of contract—remoteness of damage—reasonable foreseeability of loss

Scotland

The defendant electricity board contracted with a construction company, engaged in the construction of a roadway and aqueduct, to supply electricity to the company's batching plant for cement mixing. During the building of the aqueduct, the batching plant ceased to operate due to an electricity failure and, as the operation required a continuous pour of cement, the stoppage meant that the work so far accomplished had to be demolished. The company claimed that the stoppage was caused by the defendants' breach of contract and claimed damages for the cost of the remedial work. The Lord Ordinary found that although the defendants were in breach of contract, the need to demolish the whole operation had not been within their reasonable contemplation. The company appealed. *Held*, the evidence showed that it was within the defendants' reasonable contemplation that an interruption in the supply of electricity, and thus of concrete, would stop operations and might necessitate remedial work. It was not necessary for the defendants to have been able to foresee the precise consequences which flowed from their breach of contract and, provided that they could reasonably foresee the type of consequence which occurred, it did not matter that damage of the type that occurred was more expensive than they could have reasonably contemplated. Thus the company's loss, although of a greater degree than the defendants reasonably contemplated, was of a kind within their contemplation. Accordingly, the appeal would be allowed.

Balfour Beatty Construction (Scotland) Ltd v Scottish Power plc 1993 SLT 1005 (Inner House). *Hadley v Baxendale* (1854) 9 Ex 341, and *Parsons (H) (Livestock) Ltd v Uttley Ingham & Co Ltd* [1978] 1 QB 791, applied.

902 Breach of contract—sale of property—measure of damages

See *Seven Seas Property Ltd v Al-Essa (No 2)*, para 613.

903 Breach of contract—unauthorised cash withdrawals—worry and distress

The plaintiffs were account holders at the defendants' banks. They began actions against the defendants for wrongfully allowing debits from their bank accounts through automatic telling machines which the plaintiffs alleged were unauthorised. The plaintiffs applied for directions on how the actions would proceed and a preliminary ruling on whether damages were recoverable for worry and distress caused to them arising from the allegedly unauthorised debits from their accounts. *Held*, leave was given under RSC Ord 15, r 4(1) for the present plaintiffs and defendants to be joined together in one action until further order. In considering *Rae v The Yorkshire Bank* [1988] FLR 1 and *Watts v Morrow* [1991] 1 WLR 1421 the facts of the instant cases did not come within the exceptions to the rule that damages for worry and distress were not recoverable for breach of contract. Further, an application by the plaintiffs that the defendants be required at their own expense to circulate a memorandum to their personal customers asking if they had suffered from unauthorised withdrawals from their accounts by means of automatic telling machines and informing them of their entitlement to seek leave to join the action was misconceived and was dismissed.

McConville v Barclays Bank (1993) Times, 30 June (Official Referee's Court: Judge John Hicks QC).

904 Breach of covenant—basis of assessment—extent of loss

The plaintiff local authority offered a site for development as a housing estate, and accepted an offer by the defendant developers. The developers obtained planning permission in accordance with the plaintiffs' development scheme for the site. The plaintiff contracted to sell the land to the developers, who covenanted to build the estate in accordance with the terms of the planning permission. Fresh planning permission was later obtained. The developers built more houses on the land than was specified in the plaintiff's scheme and completed the estate without seeking modification of the covenants. The plaintiff had not sought an injunction or specific performance to compel the developers to develop the estate in accordance with the covenants. After disposal of the houses, an action for damages for breach of covenant was brought against the developers, for an amount equal to the payment that might have been extracted from the developers in return for agreed modifications to the covenants so as to authorise the more profitable development which had actually been carried out. At first instance it was held that the plaintiff was only entitled to recover nominal damages. On appeal, *held*, the plaintiff's only possible claim from the outset was for damages at common law only. Although damages might in an appropriate case, cover profit which the defendant had gained for himself by his breach of contract when the plaintiff had suffered no loss. As the plaintiff had not suffered any loss, the damages awarded had to be nominal. The appeal would accordingly be dismissed.

Surrey County Council v Bredero Homes Ltd [1993] 3 All ER 705 (Court of Appeal: Dillon, Steyn and Rose LJJ). Decision of Ferris J [1992] 3 All ER 302 (1992 Abr para 870) affirmed.

905 Criminal compensation order

See SENTENCING.

906 Criminal injuries—compensation—deductions in respect of insurance
benefits—awards to children

The applicant sought compensation for the murder of his wife on behalf of himself and their two children. In its decision the Criminal Injuries Compensation Board stated that the insurance moneys accruing to the father were deductible from the compensation award except from that part of the award made to the children since no benefit accrued to them. However, the Board only isolated the sum of £5,500 awarded to the children in respect of loss of love and affection as being part of the children's claim and thus immune from deduction. Consequently, the global sum was substantially reduced by the amount of insurance monies received by the father, impinging upon the amounts attributable to the children in their own right. The father applied for judicial review of the Board's decision. *Held*, the claims for compensation in respect of child dependants were to be calculated and treated as distinct from those of an affected parent, thus avoiding depletion resulting from any insurance benefit which was personal to the parent. Accordingly, the application would be granted and the decision of the Board would be quashed to the extent that it related to the children.

R v Criminal Injuries Compensation Board, ex p Barrett (1993) Times, 19 December (Queen's Bench Division: Latham J).

907 Criminal injuries—compensation—failure to report injury to police—discretion to make award

The applicant, a director of photography, was struck on the head by a scaffolding pole while filming a violent demonstration. He suffered no loss of consciousness and did not see his assailant nor appreciate the severity of his injury. No wound was caused by the assault. A week later, the applicant attended his general practitioner suffering from violent headaches, and was subsequently forced to curtail a trip abroad. He was admitted to a specialist neurological unit with a 24-hour history of headache and a 3-week history of irritability and poor concentration. His application to the Criminal Injuries Compensation Board was refused on the ground that he had failed to inform the police of the circumstances of the injury as required by the Criminal Injuries Compensation Scheme, para 6(a). The applicant requested an oral appeal hearing, and wrote to the police to formally record the incident, thereafter providing them with a detailed statement. On the hearing of the appeal, at which evidence was given by the applicant and a detective chief inspector of police, *held*, an order for a full award would be made, with quantum to be assessed. An interim payment of £2,000 would be granted and the appeal would be allowed.

Re Taylor [1993] 4 Med LR 34 (Criminal Injuries Compensation Board, London).

908 Criminal injuries—compensation—qualifying injuries—sexual abuse—date of injury

The applicant alleged that she had been sexually abused by her father between 1967 and 1976. She claimed that she had suppressed her recollection of this until 1988, and in 1989 her father pleaded guilty to criminal charges relating to three girls. The applicant sought compensation through the criminal injuries compensation scheme. Compensation was refused on the grounds of the applicant's delay in making the claim and because before 1 October 1979, no compensation was payable where the victim and the offender lived together as a family. The applicant sought judicial review of the decision to refuse compensation, contending that as the scheme had been amended and the restriction had not been retained with effect from 1 October 1979, the rule excluding compensation to victims whose injuries occurred before that date was arbitrary, irrational and unfair. *Held*, the scheme was not irrational at its inception and it had not been made so by later amendments. The making of a claim was not a right but a privilege, and the only legitimate expectation that a claimant could have was of recovering an award in accordance with the scheme in force for the time being. It was not demonstrated as, or rendered, perverse by the fact that some claimants were or continued to be excluded from the scheme by amendments. The application would accordingly be dismissed.

R v Criminal Injuries Compensation Board, ex p P [1994] 1 All ER 80 (Queen's Bench Division: Leggatt LJ and McCullough J).

909 Interest—date of calculation—compromise of Admiralty action

In an Admiralty action for damages arising from the collision of two vessels, it was agreed that each vessel was 50 per cent to blame. Their claims were agreed but a dispute arose as to when interest should be added. *Held*, it was unrealistic to strike a balance at the date of collision. The loss of each party should be assessed at the date the balance was struck. Accordingly, interest should be calculated on both claims up to the date of agreement, or otherwise the date of assessment. Such an approach would reflect the fact that time had passed between the collision and the assessment.

The Lu Shan (1993) Times, 15 June (Queen's Bench Division: Clarke J).

910 Interim payment—application for interim payment of damages—consideration by court of use to which sums are put

See *Stringman v McArdle*, para 2044.

911 Loss of reputation—business reputation—conspiracy to injure by lawful means—right to damages

The plaintiff started an action against the defendants for conspiracy to injure by lawful means and sought damages for loss of general or business reputation. The action arose following a dispute between the parties regarding the acquisition by the defendants of a department store. It was alleged that the defendants sent scurrilous letters to businesses worldwide where the plaintiff did business or hoped to do business. The defendants successfully applied for the action to be struck out. On appeal by the plaintiff, *held*, the particulars of loss claimed by the plaintiff failed to show loss of orders and loss of trade which was recognisable pecuniary damage. If the plaintiff wanted to claim damages for injury to reputation or injury to feelings, he ought to have commenced a defamation action. A claim for damages for loss of reputation or loss of business reputation was not sufficient to establish a cause of action in conspiracy nor could such damages be recovered by attaching them as an addition to damages for pecuniary loss. Accordingly, the appeal would be dismissed.

Lonrho plc v Fayed (No 5) [1994] 1 All ER 188 (Court of Appeal: Dillon, Stuart-Smith and Evans LJJ).

912 Measure of damages—loss of earnings—compensation for services provided—double recovery

The plaintiff was awarded damages on her claim for negligence against a doctor and a health authority in respect of the birth of her handicapped child. The award included a sum for the past and future care of the child but the plaintiff's claim for loss of earnings was refused. On her appeal, *held*, the plaintiff could not recover both her loss of earnings and compensation for the services which she had provided, and was providing, in caring for her child because that would constitute double recovery. She could neither make a profit out of her claim nor be compensated for doing two jobs. Her appeal would be dismissed.

Fish v Wilcox (1993) 13 BMLR 134 (Court of Appeal: Nourse, Stuart-Smith and Mann LJJ).

913 Measure of damages—services provided by third party—services voluntarily rendered by tortfeasor

In 1985, a pillion passenger (aged 30 at the date of appeal) was injured in a motor cycle accident driven by her husband. She was awarded total damages of £617,000 which included £4,429 for travelling expenses incurred by her husband and £77,000 for past and future services rendered by her husband in caring for her. On appeal by her husband against the award for services rendered, *held*, where services were voluntarily rendered by a tortfeasor in caring for the plaintiff from motives of affection or duty they should be regarded as in the same category as services rendered voluntarily by a third party, or charitable gifts, or insurance payments. They were adventitious benefits which, for policy reasons, were not to be regarded as diminishing the plaintiff's loss. In a case such as the present, it did not seem realistic to regard the defendant as paying twice, once in kind and once in damages, nor the plaintiff as making double recovery. Accordingly, the appeal would be dismissed.

Hunt v Severs [1993] 4 All ER 180 (Court of Appeal: Sir Thomas Bingham MR, Staughton and Waite LJJ).

914 Mental distress—injury to reputation—conviction due to negligence of solicitors—entitlement to damages

The defendants were solicitors who had acted for the plaintiff in criminal proceedings in which the plaintiff was found guilty and convicted. His conviction was later quashed by the Court of Appeal and the defendants admitted that, had they not acted negligently in the conduct of the plaintiff's defence, the overwhelming probability was that the plaintiff would have been acquitted. On an application by the plaintiff for an assessment of damages under the heads of mental distress and injury to reputation, *held*, the plaintiff could claim for mental distress as it was foreseeable that he would suffer from it if the defendants prepared his defence negligently. Damages were recoverable for loss of reputation in some torts but not negligence actions. It was difficult to draw a clear line between mental distress and injury to reputation but, in so far as any loss of reputation was an integral part of the plaintiff's distress, it was a matter that should be taken into account. The period of mental distress ran from the start of the trial, when it became apparent that the defendants were conducting the plaintiff's defence negligently, until the quashing of the conviction. In fixing the amount of the award the court considered the nature of the offences for which the plaintiff had been convicted, the penalty imposed, the length of time the conviction had stood and the particular effect on the plaintiff. The plaintiff was awarded general damages of £6,000.

McLeish v Amoo-Gottfried & Co (1993) Times, 13 October (Queen's Bench Division: Scott Baker J).

915 Nuisance and negligence—cockroach infestation—quantum of damages

The plaintiff was awarded damages in nuisance and negligence against a local authority for an acute, severe and persistent infestation of cockroaches in her four bedroom flat. The infestation had caused the plaintiff distress, anxiety and embarrassment and the local authority had failed to respond to her repeated complaints. General damages were awarded at a rate of £1,500 per year for a period of 7 years, making a total of £10,500. This sum was however reduced by £1,850 on account of a compensation order made by a magistrates court in proceedings based on the same facts under the Environmental Protection Act 1990. Special damages were awarded at a rate of £91 per year for the cost of insecticide sprays and the cost of regular redecoration. An amount of £700 interest was awarded on the special damages. *Hodder v London Borough of Tower Hamlets* (3 September 1993, unreported) (Shoreditch County Court: District Judge Silverman) (Kindly submitted for publication by Jon Holbrook, Barrister).

916 Personal injury—action—estoppel—res judicata

See *Talbot v Berkshire County Council*, para 1234.

917 Personal injury—action—procedure—debarring order

RSC Ord 38, r 36(1) provides that except with the leave of the court or where all parties agree, no expert evidence may be adduced at the trial or hearing of any cause or matter unless the party seeking to adduce the evidence . . . has complied with automatic directions taking effect under Ord 35, r 8(1)(b). Rule 8(1)(b) provides that where any party intends to place reliance at the trial on expert evidence, he must, within 10 weeks, disclose the substance of that evidence to the other parties in the form of a written report, which must be agreed if possible. Rule 37(1) provides that where in any cause or matter an application is made under r 36(1) in respect of oral expert evidence, then, unless the court considers that there are special reasons for not doing so, it must direct that the substance of the evidence be disclosed in the form of a written report or reports to such other parties and within such period as the court may specify.

In an action for damages, neither party disclosed any expert evidence in accordance with r 8(1)(b). The plaintiff's solicitors subsequently wrote to the defendant's solicitors, suggesting exchange of experts' reports. The defendant's solicitors indicated that they were still waiting for a report and the plaintiff issued a summons. At a preliminary hearing, an order was made debarring the parties from producing expert evidence at the trial of the action without leave of the trial judge unless the evidence was disclosed within 28 days. On appeal, the defendant contended that the judge had no power to make such an order. *Held*, r 37 made it clear that in the absence of any special reason for not doing so, the court would ordinarily order disclosure of the substance of expert evidence to other parties within a specified period. The purpose of that rule was to avoid trial by ambush, encourage settlement and ensure that as far as possible the issues between the parties were isolated in good time before the trial. It was unsatisfactory that one party should proceed to trial in personal injury litigation not knowing whether the other was going to apply to adduce expert evidence or if he was, when the application was going to be made and whether it was going to be successful. The rules should not be construed so as to leave the court without judicial control of litigation in circumstances such as this case. The order that the district judge made expedited the case in a manner fair to both sides and gave the best chance of an early settlement. It prevented last minute disclosure and ambush. The court had a residuary power to permit expert evidence, and the district judge had power to make the order that he did. The appeal would accordingly be dismissed.

Lowe v British Steel plc (14 July 1993, unreported) (Queen's Bench Division: Scott-Baker J). (Kindly submitted by Robin Thompson & Partners, Solicitors, Cardiff).

918 Personal injury—injury to foetus—injury sustained by a "person"

Scotland

The appellant's child showed symptoms of asphyxia at birth and died three days later. It was admitted that the cause of death had resulted from certain forceps procedures carried out at the respondents' hospital. It was agreed that the allegedly negligent acts occurred at a time prior to birth. At first instance, it was held that a child dying in consequence of injuries sustained when he was a foetus as a result of the fault of another person was not a "person dying in consequence of personal injuries sustained by him" within the meaning of the Damages (Scotland) Act 1976, s 1 as a foetus did not have the status of a person. On appeal, *held*, the appellant's child died as a "person" and consequently had a right of action in respect of the impairment of his physical health. "Sustained" was broadly synonymous with such words as "endured", "borne" or "experienced". It was therefore appropriate to treat the personal injuries as being sustained from the time they were inflicted until the time when the injured person died. The whole phrase "personal injuries sustained by him" included injuries inflicted to the person of a child immediately before his birth and continuing to have their effects on him by impairing his physical condition at and after the time of his birth. The person responsible for the child's injuries was therefore liable to pay damages to the appellant under the 1976 Act, s 1. The appeal would be allowed.

Hamilton v Fife Health Board [1993] 13 BMLR 156 (Inner House). Decision of the Outer House 1992 SLT 1026 (1992 Abr para 891) reversed.

919 Personal injury—measure of damages—claim for management advice

The plaintiff, aged 46 at the time of the accident, was a senior lecturer who also carried out work with his wife at a private physiotherapy practice. The plaintiff was involved in a road traffic accident in which he suffered certain physical injuries and also psychological damage comprising nervous shock, post-traumatic stress disorder, endogenous depression and reactive depression. The plaintiff alleged that the damage caused him to retire four years later and cease private practice three years after retirement. It was further alleged that his pension entitlement had suffered. He also claimed for the reasonable cost of management advice in relation to the fund of damages. *Held*, due to the plaintiff having a genetic predisposition to manic depressive illness the amount of damages for future loss of earnings and pension would be reduced by 15 per cent. He would be entitled to recover all the loss to the private practice as the practice was a joint venture for his benefit. In relation to the sum claimed for the cost of professional advice concerning the management of the sum of damages awarded, there was no difference in principle, between an expense which was necessary under the Rules of the Supreme Court or pursuant to a direction of the judge and an expense enforced by circumstance, save that Court of Protection fees were bound to be judged to be reasonable, whereas other management fees might or might not be so judged. Where a plaintiff sensibly incurred management fees to use his fund to provide true compensation, it would be part of the economic loss which the court was enabling him to recover. If such advice was not taken, at a cost to him, the award would not compensate him as the court intended it to. Accordingly, damages were awarded.

Anderson v Davis [1993] 5 PIQR Q87 (Queen's Bench Division: R Bell QC). As to quantum, see para 928.

920 Personal injury—measure of damages—future motor expenses

The plaintiff, a motor cycle courier, was involved in a motor accident in which he suffered a fractured spine leaving him permanently paralysed. Damages were awarded, and included sums in respect of future motoring expenses and future medical expenses. In relation to the future motoring expenses the court was required to achieve a capital figure which if properly invested would finance the plaintiff in the purchase of a motor car that would have to be replaced every four years by a new motor vehicle. This required the court to know the value of the new car and a notional trade-in value of the car at the end of every period in which the car deteriorated. The defendant appealed against the level of damages awarded for future motoring expenses and future medical expenses. *Held*, a motor car was a wasting asset, and therefore the figure to be achieved was a matter to be proved by actuarial evidence. Further, a plaintiff could not recover the cost of future medical treatment if, on the balance of probabilities, private facilities were not going to be used. Accordingly, the appeal would be allowed.

Woodrup v Nicol [1993] 5 PIQR Q104 (Court of Appeal: Fox, Russell and Taylor LJJ).

921 Personal injury—medical examination by defendant—reasonable refusal by plaintiff—late application to stay proceedings

The plaintiff, a male aged 26, suffered a whiplash injury in a road traffic accident in December 1991. The defendant's insurers requested a medical examination of the plaintiff in July 1992. Conditions of examination were agreed by September 1992, proceedings were issued and judgment was entered on liability in February 1993 with damages to be assessed. The assessment hearing was set down for May 1993. The plaintiff's medical reports were dated June 1992 and April 1993. The defendant's solicitor mistakenly believed that the defendant's insurers had arranged a medical examination of the plaintiff in October 1992. On 1 April 1993 the defendant's solicitor requested a medical examination of the plaintiff. This was six weeks before the assessment hearing. The plaintiff refused. The defendant issued a summons to stay the proceedings pending an examination by his expert. The summons was heard on 23 April 1993. The defendant argued that the plaintiff could be examined and the report produced and served in good time for the hearing on 11 May 1993. *Held*, the defendant's application was too late and would be dismissed. The case involved a moderate whiplash and damages were to be assessed only on the plaintiff's medical evidence. The defendant had paid £2,000 into court. After the application to stay failed, the case settled for £5,290 (with general damages of £5,000) with the plaintiff's agreed costs in full.

Maloney v Regan (23 April 1993, unreported) (Central London County Court: District Judge Lichfield) (Kindly submitted for publication by Howe & Co, Solicitors, Ealing, solicitors for the plaintiff).

Personal injury—quantum of damages

Examples of awards of damages in personal injury or fatal accident cases are arranged in the following order. Cases involving more than one injury are classified according to the major injury suffered.

Death	Internal injuries	Back, chest and
Brain damage and paralysis	Burns	abdomen
Multiple injuries	Scarring	Arm and hand
Psychological damage and	Head	Leg and foot
emotional stress	Neck and shoulder	Minor injuries

DEATH

922 *Death*

Total damages: **£130,000** (agreed damages). The plaintiff's husband was **fatally injured** when a car, overtaking along the inside lane of a dual carriageway, swerved on to the pavement and struck him. He suffered horrific injuries and was **killed instantly**. *Sandham v Pettipher* (8 June 1993, unreported) (Family Division: Smith J) (C Bloom QC for the plaintiff; J Priest QC and S Grime QC for the defendants).

Total damages: **£63,000** (agreed damages). The plaintiff's husband, aged 42, drove a staff bus for a bus company. He stumbled on a dark morning, while engaged in collecting passengers, because of a hole or depression in a footpath and sustained a twisting injury. His injury led to a **pulmonary embolism which caused his death** some days later. *Jones v Liverpool City Council* (28 January 1993, unreported) (Queen's Bench Division, Liverpool: Judge Kershaw QC) (A Lyon, Messrs John A Behn Twyford & Co, for the plaintiff; J Roberts, Messrs Weightman Rutherfords, for the defendant).

Total damages: **£45,000**. Plaintiff and deceased both aged 30 at time of accident in July 1990, plaintiff aged 33 at time of trial. Plaintiff and deceased were **not married** but had **lived together** for **four years** and had one **son aged one month**. Plaintiff also had a son aged eight dependent on her. Approving a settlement of £45,000 the judge accepted counsel's submission that other reported cases tended to indicate an apportionment of no more than about **ten per cent of the total** to a young infant dependant, but nevertheless felt that this was **too low** to provide an adequate sum of damages where, as here, the child was very young and the **period of the dependancy therefore very long**. He apportioned £7,500 to the deceased's infant son (ie approximately 16½ per cent of the total award). The plaintiff's elder son was not within the statutory categories of dependants and his needs fell to be considered as part of the plaintiff's own dependancy. *Heap v W E Ford & Sons* (4 February 1993, unreported) (Queen's Bench Division, Manchester: Morland J) (Mr P Holmes for the plaintiff; Mr J Lasker for the defendant) (Kindly submitted for publication by Mr Philip Holmes, Barrister).

Total damages: **£15,424**. The plaintiff's daughter, a self-employed fitness instructor aged 20 was **killed in the Marchioness disaster**. Liability had been admitted by the owners of the vessels some months after the disaster. The plaintiff brought a claim on behalf of the deceased's estate under the Law Reform (Miscellaneous Provisions) Act 1934 and on behalf of herself and the deceased's maternal and paternal grandparents as dependants under the Fatal Accidents Act 1976. The funeral expenses were disputed as to the sum of £400 spent on a reception for about 300 people who attended the deceased's funeral. Following the service, guests went to the plaintiff's home and were given wine and canapés. The Master decided that in this case the plaintiff could not ignore the social obligation attendant on a funeral service to provide some refreshment to guests on a warm day. The social decencies had to be observed and the amount was allowed in full. The Master found that the deceased was earning £240 per week or £11,520 per annum for a 48-week year. After deduction of the expenses of running her business, the cost of a car, tax and insurance, the Master decided that she had a net income of £6,500 per annum at the time of her death and would have been earning £7,500 per annum now if she had lived. The deceased made contributions to the weekly shopping and household chores. The master found that the plaintiff had lost a contribution to the household worth £25 per week for shopping and £5 per week for chores, a total of £30 per week which came to £5,360 for the period up to trial. Further loss was assessed at £30 per week. As to the multiplier, the deceased had no marriage plans and found it cheap living at home. However, she was making friends and her social circumstances were fluid. The Master allowed two years at £30 per week making £3,120 per annum. It was claimed that the deceased had a loving and close relationship to her maternal grandmother and her paternal grandmother and grandfather and gave them presents on birthdays and Christmas valued at £300 for each grandmother. It was accepted that she received gifts from her grandparents in the region of £30 per annum making a net claim of £270 per annum for each grandmother. The Master decided that the deceased's resources were stretched but that he should allow some sum and awarded £750 for each grandmother, making a total of £1,500. The total award was comprised as follows: £5,360 for the plaintiff's past dependency; £3,120 for future dependency; £2,177 for funeral expenses; £1,500 for the grandparents' claim; £167 for the deceased's clothing and personal effects; £3,100 agreed interest. *Smith v "Marchioness"/"Bowbelle"* (27 January 1993, unreported) (Queen's Bench Division: Master Topley) (Kindly submitted for publication by Hodge Jones & Allen, Solicitors, London).

Scotland
Total damages: **£10,000** (liability not proved; opinion of court as to quantum). The plaintiffs were the mother and stepfather of a 14-year-old boy who died in a fall from the roof of a school of which he was a former pupil. The judge suggested an award of £5,000 for each plaintiff and commented that as the boy was very close to his stepfather and treated him as a father, it was not appropriate to make any distinction between the plaintiffs in deciding the amount to be awarded. *Devlin v Strathclyde Regional Council* 1993 SLT 699 (Outer House).

BRAIN DAMAGE AND PARALYSIS

923 *Brain damage*

Total damages: **£916,750**. Plaintiff, male, suffered **severe asphyxiation and brain damage** at birth in 1982 by reason of defendant's **negligent obstetric care**. As a result the plaintiff has **severe cerebral palsy, moderately severe intellectual impairment** and **epilepsy**. Plaintiff **cannot walk** any useful distance unaided and his **speech is very indistinct**. He **requires assistance with self care**, will **remain dependent on others** and cannot manage his own affairs. Plaintiff's **life expectancy 40–50 years. Liability admitted** prior to trial. Plaintiff's claim valued by his advisors at £1,073,569 as follows: general damages £110,000 (interest £11,000); loss of earnings £149,530 (using a multiplier of 10); special damages £106,073 (including interest); accommodation £102,108; care £369,960 (using a multiplier of 16, net of benefit); transport £22,336; aids and equipment £37,655; therapy £99,680; holidays £20,100; extra household and clothing costs £10,128; Court of Protection £35,000. Agreed and approved in principle at 88·5 per cent of valuation (ie £950,000), but court adjourned for consideration of structured settlement. After taking into account £129,073 already paid out and £242,971 for immediate needs including purchase of suitable home for plaintiff and mother, and adaptations to father's accommodation to enable visits, £577,956 remained available. Proposals for structure as follows: £33,250 discount; £475,000 to fund annual payments by defendants in self-funded structure, starting at £21,500 per annum and linked to RPI; £69,706 plus £24,198 interest on moneys in court to be invested in a contingency fund. Plaintiff's accountants advised structured settlement would meet 57 per cent of plaintiff's needs over his projected life span, whereas conventional settlement would meet 37 per cent. Jointly instructed accountants advised that if conventionally invested sum required to match receipts from structured settlement, it would be exhausted by age 45. Judge approved proposed structured settlement on the grounds that plaintiff's needs in later life, when provision of care by family would be more difficult, would be more adequately catered for. *Bould v Wakefield Health Authority* (18 October 1993, unreported) (Queen's Bench Division, Leeds: Judge Herrod QC) (Robert Nelson QC, Marion Egan, Messrs Nelson & Co for the plaintiff; James Badenoch QC, John Cockroft, Mr Lovell, Yorkshire Health Legal Services for the defendant) (Kindly submitted for publication by Marion Egan, Barrister).

Total damages: £612,773. The plaintiff **received injuries at birth**, and was aged six at date of trial. As a result of **admitted negligence** the plaintiff's mother suffered an inter-uterine infection and the plaintiff was **asphyxiated** at birth; consequently the plaintiff was born with **severe disabilities**. Plaintiff suffers from **spastic quadriplegia and cerebral palsy** and is **severely subnormal**, and has a **very limited capacity to crawl** and might have very **limited insight**. Life expectancy is 30 years. A "whole life" multiplier of 13·75 was calculated using the 4·5 per cent discount tables with no basis for further discount for any element of contingency. Future care costs: multiplier of 13·75 divided into three periods: to age seven agreed multiplier of one and agreed multiplicand of £9,209; age 7-11 multiplier of 8·5 and agreed multiplicand of £22,914; age 19-30 multiplier of 4·25, multiplicand of £31,000 taken as mid-point between cost of residential care at £27,500 taking into account "domestic element" of £2,000, since plaintiff could possibly require residential care towards end of life, and cost of providing system of two carers at £34,000. Loss of earnings: assessed for a period of 12 years from age 18. Multiplicand corresponding with new earnings survey, average for all occupations. Multiplier of 3⅔ assessed using the 4·5 per cent discount tables and calculated on basis of considerable discount for contingencies such as risk that plaintiff will at no time achieve average earnings; suffer periods of unemployment; suffer periods of illness; suffer accident. No claim for "lost years". Housing: damages calculated on the basis of the formula in *Roberts v Johnstone* [1988] 3 WLR 1247, CA, except that the provision of second bedroom (valued at £4,700) to be treated as capital value of the property; discounted by ½ because second bedroom not required until some time in future. Multiplier of 12 applied, discounted from "whole life" multiplier of 13·75 on basis that house will not be required for whole period of years since part would be spent in residential care (12 represented discount of six years). In absence of medical evidence cost of swimming pool not allowed but on basis that the house was of a suitable nature bought at a reasonable price within reasonable limits total purchase price allowed in calculating loss under this head. The above award comprised £105,000 general damages, past and future care total £335,978, loss of earnings £39,000, housing £67,073, miscellaneous equipment and aids (partially agreed) £73,852, court of protection costs £21,525, interest agreed on general damages only because of interim payments £6,200, credit for DSS benefits using multiplier of 14 agreed £53,617. *Willett v North Bedfordshire Health Authority* (13 November 1992, unreported) (Queen's Bench Division: Hobhouse J) (Ian Karsten QC and Sarah Edwards for the plaintiff; Roger Bell QC and John Leslie for the defendant) (Kindly submitted for publication by Sarah Evans-Lombe, Pupil Barrister).

Total damages: £450,768. The plaintiff, aged 44 at the date of his accident, suffered severe injuries when he was hit by the defendant's car while repairing a cordoned-off section of a motorway. His injuries included a **fractured skull**, a number of **comminuted fractures to his ribs and the left hand side of his body** and a **severed artery** which required a massive blood transfusion. He spent five months in hospital and continued to have outpatient and specialist rehabilitative treatment. The accident had left him with **impaired memory and cognitive functions**, which made ordinary employment impossible and he now worked in a sheltered workshop, carrying out mundane packaging and labelling tasks. The trial judge described the plaintiff's injuries as being "at the top end of moderate brain damage", and he required a **great deal of supervision** at home and at work. The above award included £60,000 for pain, suffering and loss of amenity, £20,000 to cover the cost of past care, provided by his wife, and £95,000 to cover the cost of future care, based on a figure of £5,500 with a multiplier of 10, but also including an award of £10,000 per annum with a multiplier of 4 to take account of the possibility that at some stage in the future his wife would be unable to care for him and a professional carer would be needed. £15,000 was awarded to cover the cost of installing a bath lift in the plaintiff's home. Other awards included a total of £13,000 to cover his past and future travel and motoring expenses and £4,680 to cover the future cost of DIY work around the home which the plaintiff would have carried out himself but for his injuries. Certain other matters, including figures for the plaintiff's past and future loss of earnings, had been agreed by the parties before the hearing, and the judge did not address those matters in his judgment. *Potts v Buckley* (21 December 1992, unreported) (Queen's Bench Division, London: Tuckey J) (Mr J Cherry QC and Ms V Gray, Messrs Brian Thompson & Partners, for the plaintiff; Mr J Hooper, Messrs Hextall Irskine, for the defendant).

Total damages: £344,007. Male applicant, aged 29 when assaulted in 1984, was rendered **unconscious** and suffered a **large acute extradural blood clot**, which was **surgically removed**, and **bruising** to the brain. He later developed **hydrocephalus** and underwent surgery again, first for a shunt and then for a **cranioplasty**. The applicant sustained the following **continuing effects** of the assault: **personality change** leaving him **irritable**, aggressive, sometimes **violent**, emotionally **unstable, depressed**, with a **loss of confidence and initiative**; he was physically less able and was **unable to look after himself**; incontinence; **epilepsy**, having fits several times a week; **agoraphobia**; loss of **sense of smell**; **retrograde** and **post-traumatic amnesia**; longer-term loss of **memory** and of **concentration**, failure to absorb information; loss of the **ability to read** English; **psychological overlay** resulting from the trauma; sexual problems; and a **loss of social and family life**. The applicant's wife had given up her job and taken on the burden of **complete care** for her husband, treating him much as one would a very young child. As a result the applicant became **totally dependant** upon her and **failed** to become at all **rehabilitated**. He had a genuinely **low perception** of his own abilities and as a result would require a period of **six months' residence** in a rehabilitation centre. The applicant would **never** be able to work again. The above award comprised general damages of £279,250, comprising £55,000 for pain, suffering and loss of amenity; £22,250 for the cost of the rehabilitation centre; £132,000 for future care (using a multiplier of 16); and £70,000 for future loss of earnings. Special damages, awarded at £64,757 comprised £34,757 for past care (being largely the wife's loss of earnings, and which the Board directed should be paid directly to her); and £30,000 for the applicant's loss of earnings. Deducted from the award, under paragraph 19 of the CICB scheme, was the total value of past and future state benefits, the latter calculated using 16 as the multiplier (the same as for future care) and the current payments as the multiplicand (in this case £13,385 per annum). Added back to the total sum was an assessment of the benefits (income support) which would cease to be payable upon receipt of the award. *Criminal Injuries Compensation Board* (25 March 1993, unreported) (Susan Cooper, Messrs Brindley Twist Tafft & James for the applicant) (Kindly submitted for publication by Susan Cooper, Barrister, and Laurence Vick, Solicitor, Brindley Twist Tafft & James, Solicitors, Coventry).

Total damages: **£263,972** (the plaintiff received 75 per cent of this sum on account of contributory negligence and an additional £10,000 for Court of Protection costs). The plaintiff, a handyman aged 19 at the date of the accident, was involved in a road accident in which he sustained **frontal lobe brain damage as a result of fractures to the tempero–parietal skull region. Unconscious for three weeks** and in hospital for six weeks. Injuries to teeth and jaw. **Risk of epilepsy** between 5 and 10 per cent. Memory and concentration significantly impaired. **Unable to manage own affairs**. More aggressive than before accident. Needs to be advised when to wash, shave and change clothes. Unlikely to be fit for any employment. The above award comprised the following agreed damages: £37,500 for general damages for pain, suffering and loss of amenity; £3,187 for interest thereon; £20,000 for the cost of past care; £6,600 for interest thereon; £62,758 for the cost of future care; £26,604 for past loss of earnings; £8,779 for interest thereon; and £98,544 for future loss of earnings (calculated on the basis of 8 years at a full multiplicand of £8,791 and 8 years at a reduced multiplicand of £3,527). *Boulton v Brammer* (1 December 1992, unreported) (Queen's Bench Division, Sheffield: Blofeld J) (Kindly submitted for publication by Gary Burrell, Barrister).

Total damages: **£112,628**. The plaintiff, aged 46 at the date of the accident, was injured in an accident at work when a number of wooden boxes fell onto her. The accident made her agitated and nervous but did not cause any apparent injury, but the following day she suffered a **stroke**, resulting in **immediate loss of speech and partial paralysis**. The court found the plaintiff had been vulnerable to anxiety and high blood pressure, and held that on the balance of probability the anxiety she suffered after the accident had caused her blood pressure to rise, resulting in the closure of an artery and subsequent deprivation of oxygen to the brain. The plaintiff's **speech remained slightly slurred** and she was **prone to periods of depression**, but she had made an **excellent recovery** and was trying to become less dependent on anti-depressant drugs. She hoped to find new employment, but accepted that most employers would be unwilling to employ her once they knew she had suffered a stroke. The above award included £10,000 for pain, suffering and loss of amenity, £53,187 agreed special damages and £31,326 for future loss of earnings (calculated on the basis of one full year's salary of £11,326, and £5,000 with a multiplier of 4 thereafter), plus interest. *Clark v Austin Rover Group Ltd* (19 January 1993, unreported) (Queen's Bench Division: Birmingham: Mr H Wolton QC) (Mr N Worsley for the plaintiff; Mr W Wood for the defendants).

924 *Quadriplegia*

Total damages: **£1,270,000**. Plaintiff, born in 1983 by **emergency caesarean** section after trial of scar to the point that his mother's uterus ruptured, was severely asphyxiated and as a result of brain damage sustained at the time of his birth has **cerebral palsy** which is a mixture of **dyskinetic cerebral palsy** and **spastic quadriplegia**. Plaintiff has **involuntary movements of all four limbs** and head coupled with generally increased muscle tone. **Severely physically handicapped**. No mental impairment with vision, hearing and intelligence normal. Able to make some sounds but no words. **Total dependence for feeding, toileting, dressing and mobility**. Plaintiff needs **constant care and attention** together with specialist help from paediatric physiotherapist, occupational therapist and speech therapist as well as appropriate electronic learning and communication aids. **Life expectancy 40–50 years from trial**. Multiplier of 17 agreed. Liability admitted prior to trial. Value of plaintiff's claim agreed, and approved at £1,270,000, case then adjourned in order to explore possibility of a structured settlement. Proposed structure: after payment out of sums due to plaintiff's mother and purchase of a suitable home and certain other incidental expenses sum remaining for a possible structured settlement was approximately £900,000. Health Authority sought a discount of between £60,000 and £95,000 leaving approximately £800,000 of which it was proposed £150,000 should be invested in a contingency fund leaving £650,000 to purchase an annuity which would have produced an annual tax free index-linked income of £27,795 for life. Conventional lump sum award: on basis of a model portfolio obtained from Public Trustee, a fund of £900,000 invested 15 per cent in gilts, 5 per cent on deposit and 80 per cent in equities would be expected to produce an annual income of £42,392 gross and £30,768 net. The plaintiff's solicitors' in-house chartered accountant and external accountants advised that on past performance it was reasonable to assume that an appropriately invested portfolio of equities would produce a net return after inflation of between one and two per cent per annum over a life time and that the plaintiff would be better placed financially with a conventional award than a structured settlement and that provided the fund was managed appropriately it would not be exhausted before the plaintiff's death. Otton J approved an order making a conventional award, saying that the "case was a model of its kind". The plaintiff's claim was valued by his advisers as follows: general damages £130,000; interest on general damages £4,212; special damages and interest £136,723; future care to 19 years of age £257,000; future care from 19–life £400,000; occupational therapy £15,000; dietician £3,400; physiotherapy £37,500; speech therapy £16,325; educational therapist £53,214; communication aids and equipment £31,354; equipment £45,000; oral hygiene £510; accommodation £60,000; miscellaneous items £9,565; transport £50,000; loss of earnings £114,000; receivership fee £35,000 (plaintiff's entitlement disputed as a matter of principle); less future benefits of £65,106. The settlement figure represents 95·2 per cent of valuation. *Pimpalkhare v North West Hertfordshire Health Authority* (8 March 1993, unreported) (Queen's Bench Division, London: Otton J) (Michael Brent QC and Charles Welchman, Messrs Leigh Day & Co for the plaintiff) (Kindly submitted for publication by Charles Welchman, Barrister).

925   *Paraplegia*

Total damages: **£784,197**. Applicant, male aged 33 at time of assault and 39 at the date of hearing, was **stabbed in the back** resulting in **complete paraplegia** below T12. The applicant suffered from all the usual problems associated with a disability of this type; in addition he suffered **very frequent** episodes of **severe pain** radiating from his feet to his thighs. Each episode of pain lasted from **8–12 hours**. All forms of pain relief had failed and the prospect of any improvement was **negligible**. The applicant also suffered from **recurrent urinary tract infection** and from **pressure sores** which caused him to be confined to bed for long periods. He **required permanent live-in care** which had been provided by his wife and would continue to be provided by her in the foreseeable future. Commercial cost of past care reduced by 25 per cent to reflect the fact that care was provided by the applicant's wife. No discount made as to future care (the applicant's wife would have returned to work in the future if he had not suffered his injury). The applicant's **life expectancy** was **reduced** to 35 years from the date of the injury. A multiplier of 14 years was applied to future loss save for loss of earnings where a multiplier of 10 years was applied (the applicant was not in regular employment at the date of injury). The above award comprised general damages for pain, suffering and loss of amenity at £90,000; loss of past earnings £44,690; loss of future earnings £62,451; equipment purchased/needed £21,615; future replacement of equipment £38,570; past care £72,507; future care £242,412; future surgery £8,350; future physiotherapy £6,001; capital cost of transport £7,750; future cost of transport £38,842; accommodation £60,353; extra house insurance premium £1,656; future household expenditure (including cost of extra heating, cost of employing a gardener and DIY handyman) £75,000; and future holidays £14,000. *Criminal Injuries Compensation Board* (15 April 1993, unreported) (Mr Nicholas Davies, Messrs Stephens & Scown as Agent for Messrs Cornish & Birtill for the applicant) (Kindly submitted for publication by Stephens & Scown, Solicitors, Exeter; Cornish & Birtill, Solicitors, Penzance).

Total damages: **£750,000.** Plaintiff, male graduate physicist aged 23 at time of accident in December 1986, was knocked off motorcycle on dual carriageway when defendant's vehicle pulled out in front of the plaintiff whilst plaintiff was overtaking. Plaintiff suffered **complete paraplegia, fracture/dislocation of thoracic spine** at T8/9 and T11/12, **fracture of left distal humerus, left radial nerve palsy, fracture of several ribs** and **bilateral haemothoraces.** Plaintiff **forced to give up employment** as a result of injuries. Sexual function **severely impaired,** bowel and bladder function **impaired.** Plaintiff **confined to a wheelchair** with all resulting consequences, and **continued to suffer from pain, hypersensitivity and spasms.** Developed **severe reactive depression** as a result of his situation. Plaintiff's relationship with fiancée then wife **severely affected.** Social activities **severely affected.** Plaintiff could **still drive an adapted car** but suffered from a **loss of independence.** Promising career as a physicist was ruined. **Life expectancy reduced**: 55 to 60 years in total. *Hall v Witherspoon* (26 November 1992, unreported) (Queen's Bench Division: Kay J) (Daniel Serota QC, Colin Manning for the plaintiff; Nigel Gilmour QC for the defendant) (Kindly submitted for publication by Gerald O Wood, J P Hall & Co, Solicitors, Spennymoor).

Total damages: **£518,625.** Plaintiff, male inshore fisherman aged 26 at time of accident in September 1986, was a front seat passenger in a car being driven by the defendant when it overturned as the defendant lost control. Plaintiff **suffered serious injuries** to his **dorsal spine** and is now **paralysed.** He has **suffered complete paraplegia** from the level of the sixth and seventh dorsal vertebrae. Plaintiff **suffered from recurrent neurogenic pain** in the buttocks, backs of his legs and around his ribs. Plaintiff also suffered from a **reactive depression** and was **expected to continue suffering from fluctuations of mood, anger and frustration.** The above award comprised £80,000 general damages; £66,505 special damages, which included £35,000 for past earnings, £8,113 out-of-pocket expenses, £11,883 past care, £2,709 transport costs, £4,300 travel costs, and £4,500 for alterations to property; £372,120 for future losses, which included £135,000 for future loss of earnings, £58,875 for aids and equipment, £144,575 care costs (using a multiplier of 15), £22,750 provision of and further alterations to accommodation (including additional council tax), and £10,920 for physiotherapy. The defendant had made two payments into court: one of £298,000 in June 1991, the other of £137,000 in September 1992. In October 1991 the plaintiff had been awarded an interim payment of £150,000 out of the monies in court. Counsel for the plaintiff submitted that interest at two per cent on the general damages and at half the appropriate rate for the special damages should be awarded from the date of the writ's issue to the date of the interim payment (the interim payment was greater than the sum awarded for special and general damages). The judge refused, accepting the defendant's submissions, that the proper approach was to (1) calculate normal interest on the general and special damages to date, and then (2) set off interest on the £150,000 interim payment, from the time of its payment at the full short term investment rate. This created a negative figure. Therefore no interest was awarded. *Brignall v Kelly* (20 January 1993, unreported) (Queen's Bench Division, Teesside: Wright J) (Kindly submitted for publication by Vincent Moran, Barrister).

Total damages: **£216,426.** Plaintiff, male aged 59 at time of accident and 65 at time of trial, was knocked off his motorcycle when it was **hit from behind** by a taxi. He suffered a **burst fracture** of the body of the **first lumbar vertebra** with a **large fragment forced backwards** into the **spinal canal. Cuts** on scalp, right eyelid and left index finger. **Permanent damage** to the **spinal cord and nerve roots**. The plaintiff was in hospital for **six months**. On discharge he was suffering from **complete** loss of power in his right leg and **partial** lack of power in his left leg. He was described by a neurologist as an "**incomplete paraplegic**". The condition was **permanent.** The plaintiff used a **wheelchair,** wore a **brace** on his right leg, and even with the assistance of **sticks** he could walk a **maximum of 25 yards** and could not manage stairs. Sometimes he fell, and he suffered **constant back and leg pain. Bladder and bowel** control had been **impaired** and he was **incontinent** on occasions. He had lost **all sexual function,** causing **distress** to himself and to his wife. In the weeks following the accident he had suffered from **severely painful urinary infections,** he also developed **asthma** and **agoraphobia** as a result of his injuries. He was **unable to continue with his job,** which he had enjoyed. Because of his disabilities the plaintiff was unable to participate fully in the upbringing of his teenage son and had suffered a great loss of **self esteem.** His **life expectancy** had been reduced by five years. It was hoped that the agoraphobia and the bowel and bladder problems would improve with **counselling.** The judge held that the plaintiff's injuries were slightly less than complete paraplegia but considerably worse than the loss of one leg: he was **severely disabled and suffered great pain.** However, since most reported cases of paraplegia involved significantly

younger plaintiffs, he awarded general damages for pain, suffering and loss of amenity of
£35,000; £45,000 for past care and attendance provided by the plaintiff's wife in the 51 months
between his discharge from hospital and trial (she had given up her part time job so that she
could spend all her time at home); £76,000 for future care and attendance, using a multiplier of
6½; £19,979 for loss of earnings; £14,305 for pre-trial expenses, and £26,142 for future
expenses. *Michalski v Martin Stabin Ltd and another* (18 January 1993, unreported) (Queen's
Bench Division: Sir Michael Ogden QC) (Mr Paul Norris for the plaintiff; Mr Jonathan Barnes
and Mr Aiden Christie for the defendants) (Kindly submitted for publication by David
Gallagher, Pupil Barrister).

MULTIPLE INJURIES

926   Multiple injuries

Total damages: **£223,674·98**. Plaintiff, male aged 18 at time of accident in September 1988,
was involved in a **road traffic accident**, suffering **severe** multiple injuries which were initially
life threatening. The injuries comprised **head injury** with **fracture** to base of skull, CT scan
indicating collection of blood in left middle fossa and **petechial haemorrhages** in both
frontal lobes; damage to **facial skeleton** including to olfactory and glossopharyngeal nerves,
contusion to right optic nerve, Le Fort grade III facial **fracture**, comminuted fracture to upper
and lower **jaw**, loss of five **teeth**; severe **chest injury** with left sided pneumothorax and right
sided haemothorax requiring **drainage and tracheostomy**; fracture of pedicle of second
cervical **vertebra**; injuries to **legs and feet** involving fracture of left patella, comminuted
fracture of left ankle and of talus on left side, Lisfranc fracture of right foot. Plaintiff required
ventilator for a day and remained in **coma** for **three weeks**, treatment included pins inserted
into both supraorbital ridges and mandible. Extraoral craniomandibular fixation (Boxframe
technique) applied. He underwent **corrective osteotomy** to top and lower jaws in January
1990, maxillary and mandibular plate removed in July 1990. Rigid collar applied to neck and
substituted with soft collar after eight weeks. **Patellectomy** performed to remove left kneecap
and following **orthopaedic surgery** his left leg and right foot were **immobilised** in plaster
for approximately one month. **Internal fixation** secured his ankle until October 1989. In
patient at hospital for approximately **two and a half months**. Over four years after the
accident, the plaintiff had made **significant recovery**. The head injury had caused **retrograde
amnesia** of 12 hours and **post traumatic amnesia** of 9 weeks. He was left with mild
impairment of memory described as "social nuisance", **reduced concentration and
intelligence**, in addition to **loss of confidence**. The facial injuries resulted in almost **total loss
of smell** via the right nostril, very little sense of smell in left nostril, **substantial** permanent
impairment to sense of **taste**, sensory loss in both sides of lower lip, **no central vision in right
eye** to extent plaintiff's sight was that of a "one eyed man", change in **shape** of face and metal
based denture replacing lost teeth. Plaintiff also suffered **instability** in left knee with wasting of
quadriceps muscle, 20 per cent likelihood of developing some form of **degenerative arthritis**
over a 10–15 year period, the ankle and subtalar joints were subject to **deteriorating stiffness**,
limitation of movement, and **progressive degenerative arthritis**. Plaintiff will require
fusion surgery of subtalar joints in both feet within next five years and 20 per cent chance that
he will require **knee replacement** within 15–20 years. If such surgery was to result there
would be a need for **revision surgery** 10–15 years thereafter. Both operations will cause 4–6
months **total disability**. Tracheostomy caused unsightly **scarring** and **contour deformity**
on base of the throat. Further surgical scarring on right and left anterior chest wall, left and right
axilla, over front of left knee, left ankle, either side of lower jaw, forehead and on base of head.
Conscious that exposure of scars frightens people. Plaintiff will undergo **plastic surgery** to
improve tracheostomy scar and treatment may include operation to **improve airway** of right
nostril and **dental surgery**. He is no longer able to pursue pre-accident hobby of playing
football, as he can only stand or walk for up to **two hours**. He requires **special fitted shoes**
and due to **inability to stand** for long periods is **limited** to certain types of **employment**.
Despite his attempts to secure work the plaintiff has been unemployed since April 1991. Since
accident he married and now has family with two children. The above comprised £37,500 for
general damages; £25,910·28 for special damages; £122,619 for future loss of earnings based
on diminution of plaintiff's earning capacity (multiplier of 17); £11,000 for future medical
expenses; £18,150 for handicap on labour market in respect of plaintiff's prospects in obtaining
and/or retaining employment at his reduced earning capacity (multiplier of 2½); and £8,495·70
interest. *Ward v Holness* (11 February 1993, unreported) (Queen's Bench Division: J Hutchison
QC) (Paul Corben, Messrs Shoosmiths & Harrison for the plaintiff) (Kindly submitted for
publication by Paul Corben).

Total damages: **£196,457**. Plaintiff, male aged 28 at time of accident and 34 at date of trial, fell from scaffold and sustained various injuries in September 1988. **Minor head injury** with **amnesia** and chipped teeth, of which two capped. **Full recovery** from these injuries. **Comminuted fracture** proximal ulna and **comminuted intra-articular fracture** of head of radius with **displacement** of **right elbow**. **Comminuted intra-articular fracture** of lower end of radius and **fracture of ulnar styloid** of right wrist, the wrist being **dislocated** dorsally. Slightly **displaced intra-articular fracture** of head of radius of **left elbow**. **Comminuted intra-articular fracture** of lower end of radius with **dorsal displacement** of **left wrist**. Wrist fractures treated with wires and pinning, right elbow with plate and screws. **Fracture of lower articular surface of patella** of **left knee**. Knee tended to give way and cause falls. Advised by hospital to try and return to work with change of job in June 1989, though plaintiff had no memory of such advice. By trial date, the **pain**, exacerbated by inclement weather, **was continuing in both wrists and right elbow** with **intermittent discomfort in knee and left elbow**, however medical evidence was that right arm had recovered reasonable function except for use in heavy work. Right elbow **would not straighten** and lacked 20 degrees flexion (35 to 130 degrees), **both wrists lacked full movement** in both flexion and were **deviated**. Slight risk of arthritis in both elbows and wrists but not likely to increase pain or disability seriously. **Unfit to return to work as rigger** in which plaintiff had worked with father and uncle. Judge found plaintiff fit to return to work before trial and deducted one year's net earnings at agreed rate. Plaintiff had had to give up skilled work in the open air which he enjoyed. The above award comprised £25,000 general damages for pain and suffering; £500 DIY to date; £17,686 loss of earnings to date net of one year's earnings in unskilled work; £134,816 for future loss of earnings on basis that plaintiff had found work at £5,500 (£15,500 for two years whilst he worked his way up new employment ladder and £12,977 for eight years as judge found plaintiff would have stopped work as rigger at age 60); £1,500 future DIY (£100 for 15 years); £10,000 loss of employability; £1,665 interest on general damages and £5,290 interest on special damages. *Cord v Technico Site Services Ltd* (16 July 1993, unreported) (Queen's Bench Division, Birmingham: Tudor Evans J) (Nicholas J Worsley QC, Messrs Robin Thompson for the plaintiff; Lawrence West, Messrs Buller Jeffries for the defendant) (Kindly submitted for publication by Nicholas J Worsley, QC).

Total damages: **£173,479·11**. Plaintiff, male factory worker aged 18 at time of assault in December 1984, and 26 at date of hearing, was **assaulted by three men, knocked to the ground** and **kicked in the head**. While lying in the road he was **hit by a passing car**. He sustained multiple injuries, including an **unstable fracture of the body of the second lumbar vertebra, fracture of the left petrous temporal bone**, a **bilateral orbital haematoma and csf otorrhoea, injury to the left eardrum, fracture of the distal phalanx** of the index finger, **multiple soft tissue injuries to the face**, and **abrasions** to the left side of his chest. Plaintiff was admitted as an inpatient and treated on a stryker frame (where the bed is rotated either face up or face down every two hours, night and day) for **four weeks**. He was given **pain killers**, and a **urinary catheter and IV infusion** were inserted. He was **gradually mobilised in a plaster jacket** which he retained for six weeks. By March 1985 he was fitted with a **light weight corset** and was having **gentle therapy**. By January 1992 the radiographs showed a **collapse of the disc** space at L2/3 and a **significant kyphosis** measuring 25 degrees. There was also **marked tenderness** in the mid line and in the para-spinal region. A **scoliosis concave** existed to the right when he stood straight. The devastating injury to the spine had left him with a **permanent ugly deformity** with **loss of lumbar lordosis** and **persistent shooting pains** in the lower part of his back and thigh for which he had to take distalgesics at least twice a day. The **pain was present when sitting** for long periods and his spine felt stiff in the mornings and evenings. The **level of pain was likely to continue** and would probably deteriorate in the future. He also suffered from **bilateral high tone sensori and neural deafness** most marked in the right ear. Refused to undergo a spinal fusion because of the risks involved. The **excessive pain** which literally **governed his life** made him **irritable and bitter**. He was **unable to enjoy activities** such as the theatre, sports or other social events due to his inability to sit or stand for long periods. His **agility had been greatly impaired** and he was **unable to return to his pre-accident work** as he was unfit to bend, kneel, lift or carry heavy weights. He had difficulty in undertaking even sedentary occupation and was **virtually unemployable**. Described by his mother as leading the life of a languid "middle aged" man. The above award comprised £32,500 general damages for pain, suffering and loss of amenity; loss of future earnings £55,602 (based on a multiplier of 15 and a multiplicand of £6,000, less £2,293·20 invalidity benefit); recurring future losses £53,000; agreed special damages £25,455·11 (special damages sought but not awarded £6,922). *Criminal*

Injuries Compensation Board, London (3 December 1992, unreported) (Kindly submitted for publication by David Owusu-Yianoma, Pupil Barrister).

Total damages: £86,399. Plaintiff, male aged 46 at time of assessment, suffered multiple injuries as the result of an attack. Pain and shock, blood loss, **head injury** with **concussion, severe fracture** of left orbit and upper jaw, damage to **muscles of left eye**, orbital tissues, floor of orbit, **severe loss of skin and tissue** at left eyelid, cheek and base of nose, **fracture** of lower jaw, **tracheostomy required** due to onset of **pneumonia, severe contusion** of left shoulder, **fracture** of left shoulder blade, severe contusion left chest and **four rib fractures, severe abdominal contusions** with blood in abdomen, **requiring laparotomy**, bruising of caecum, **part de–gloving of right hand**, ruptured extensor tendon to middle finger of right hand, bruising and abrasion of left knuckles, **severe contusion left hip and thigh**, severe comminuted fracture upper left thigh and base of trochanter. Plaintiff has had **24 operations** to date and two more contemplated. Critical for a time, intensive care for 24 days. In-patient initially for 102 days, but also on many other occasions since. **Constant pain**, exacerbation of previously controlled **nocturnal epileptic fits**, which became daytime for a time, and now continue more **frequently** than before, **severe physical disability**, walks with crutches, hip and leg and left shoulder restriction of movement, **severe and embarrassing facial**, abdominal and leg **scarring**, and **facial asymmetry. Personality change**, temper, irritability, frustration, contributing to **breakdown of marriage** and straining relationships with children. **Permanent visual disturbance** (diplopia) due to structural damage around left eye, slight future risk of retinal detachment, and of abdominal obstruction due to adhesions. Severe disability, disintegration of home life, loss of pre–accident satisfying manual work but retains (less satisfying) clerical work, ability to maintain home and garden diminished, domestic assistance and physical aids would be needed, and plaintiff now requires car for work and shopping. The above award comprised £60,000 for pain and suffering; disability on labour market £10,000; past and future partial loss £113,947; motor expenses past and future £20,000; loss of pension rights £12,500; future home and garden maintenance £10,000; future domestic assistance £7,500; loss of subsidy to accommodation past and future £9,262; future cost of aids £3,000; past help (gratuitous) £1,000; travel expenses and other specials £2,308. Wage loss based on multiplier of 11, other future losses based on multipliers of 14. The amount was reduced by £163,118, for deductible past and future benefits. *Criminal Injuries Compensation Board, London* (26 March 1993, unreported) (Allan Gore, Messrs Brian Thompson & Partners for the plaintiff) (Kindly submitted for publication by Allan Gore, Barrister).

Total damages: £62,630·04. Plaintiff, male aged 27 at time of accident and 33 at date of trial, was employed by the defendants as driver of a road sweeper vehicle. The **vehicle collided with another due to faulty pedals** and **tipped over into a three foot deep stream.** Plaintiff was **trapped upside down in the vehicle by his legs and lower abdomen for 40 minutes** until he was rescued. Throughout this time his **head was held above water** by colleagues. Plaintiff sustained a **closed fracture of the right tibia requiring a fibulotomy** and an **intra medullary nail.** As a consequence of the crushing injuries to his lower abdomen (resulting in a **comminuted fracture of the sacrum** and a **fracture to the right pubic ramus**), the plaintiff suffered **scarring, indentation and numbness** of the left thigh still present at trial, **permanent low back pain** and **hesitancy of micturition unlikely to improve** beyond trial. Plaintiff was released from hospital after **two months** although he was still in a wheelchair and required about **three months of physiotherapy before he was able to walk, dress or bathe himself unaided.** Plaintiff was also diagnosed as suffering from **post traumatic stress disorder** especially during the first two months after the accident, characterised by **nightmares** and **personality changes** of mild degree, such that he became introverted and anxious. Plaintiff returned to work on a lighter, mainly sedentary job as a machinist approximately 18 months after the accident. Plaintiff will suffer **permanent low central back pain** which is **exacerbated by bending and lifting.** He **will require a further operation** on his right leg to remove the intra medullary nail as at the time of trial it was **causing shooting pains** throughout the leg. He has been assessed at **15 per cent disablement for life.** The above award comprised £20,000 for pain, suffering and loss of amenity and a separate award of £1,500 in respect of the post traumatic stress disorder; £6,463·04 special damages (net of benefits); £22,792 for future loss of earnings (days off and lost chance), using a multiplier of 14; future DIY etc, global sum of £5,000; future medical costs £1,875 (operation and painkillers); and a *Smith v Manchester* award of £5,000. *Cummings v W Lucy & Co* (19 October 1993, unreported) (Queen's Bench Division: Wright J) (Alan Jeffreys for the plaintiff; Ian Ashford-Thom for the defendant) (Kindly submitted for publication by Miranda Napper, Pupil Barrister). *Smith v Manchester Corpn* (1974) 118 SJ 597, CA applied.

Total damages: £50,799·97. Plaintiff, male farm worker aged 61 at time of accident on 3 May 1990, sustained injuries in a **road traffic accident**. The most serious injury being a **brachial plexus injury** as well as injuries to the neck, head and lower back, he also received **lacerations in the head** requiring four sutures and there was an **aggravation** of a pre-existing lower back condition. Plaintiff has not worked since the accident, and after two and a half years suffers **severe and permanent reduction of movement** in the left arm, loss of strength and grip in the left arm, and his activities are further restricted by the aggravation of the back condition. His walking distance is limited and he can now only carry out the lightest of duties. It was found that, but for the accident, the plaintiff would have worked to the date of normal retirement at least, possibly two years longer. The above award comprised £17,110·10 for loss of earnings to date of trial, £9,277·23 for loss of earnings to retirement, £5,000·00 for loss of earnings after retirement, £1,938·01, for loss of pension, £1,250·00 for loss of services, £1,224·63 for miscellaneous items, and £15,000·00 general damages for pain, suffering and loss of amenity. *Rogers v A & D Walter Ltd* (11 November 1992, unreported) (Portsmouth County Court: Judge Wroath) (Messrs Coffin, Mew & Clover for the plaintiff; Messrs Brutton & Co for the defendant) (Kindly submitted for publication by Brutton & Co, Solicitors, Fareham).

Total damages: £33,750. Applicant, female aged 17 at time of accident, was attacked with a "Stanley Knife" blade outside a nightclub. She suffered **multiple deep lacerations** to the **face, forehead and neck**, including a **laceration through the right upper eyelid. Minor laceration to the cornea of the left eye. Substantial lacerations** to the greater part of the **left leg**. Extensive **loss of blood**. Nine days in-patient treatment in hospital, during which time, under general anaesthetic, the lacerations were closed in layers by **internal and external sutures**. Thereafter regular and substantial out-patient treatment. Sixteen months after the attack the applicant required a **further operation** to assist in the healing of the facial wounds and, at the date of the hearing, three years after the attack, a "face-lift" type procedure was envisaged in the near future to further improve the scarring. She was left with **permanent and disfiguring facial and leg scarring**, of which she was **highly conscious**. There was a **loss of sensation** over the scars, but **pain and discomfort** when yawning, eating, talking and brushing teeth. **Ongoing pain in leg and knee**, with a degree of **restriction of movement**. The victim suffered **serious psychological effects** as a result of the attack and the resultant scarring. **Severe post-operative depression, intense self consciousness, nervousness** and **poor self image**. Before the attack she had been a pretty, normal and outgoing person. Previously an active and sporting girl she **lacked motivation**, was unable to continue horseriding or play netball, for **fear of further injury**, and was **too self conscious** of her scarring to swim or sun-bathe. Problems were envisaged regarding the victim's career development as her self-consciousness **effectively precluded presentation-type jobs** or any job where she was directly in the public eye. The victim was slowly rebuilding her life and regaining confidence but **psychological support** would be required for the foreseeable future. General damages were assessed at £45,000 but award reduced by 25 per cent by reason of conduct. *Criminal Injuries Compensation Board, Cardiff* (7 July 1993, unreported) (Kindly submitted for publication by Leighton Alexander Hughes, Barrister).

Total damages: £32,335. Plaintiff, male aged 21 at time of accident, was riding a motor cycle which was involved in a collision with a car driven by the defendant. Plaintiff suffered multiple injuries including a **fractured right wrist, compound fracture of the left tibia and fibula** and had a **haemothrosis of the left knee**. Left leg was in plaster for nearly **six months** and **bones** in his left arm were fixed with a plate. Plaintiff **off work for eight months**. Before the accident plaintiff worked as a self-employed brick layer, and returned to that occupation for four years, but returned to college in order to take an OND course with a view to employment as a site agent or building foreman, in view of the **likelihood of osteo-arthritis in the knee** within the next ten years (ie by the age of 40). Plaintiff was **able to resume** his pre-accident hobbies of tennis and football albeit with some lack of confidence because of **restricted movement** in the left knee. The above award included £18,000 general damages (plus £375 interest); £10,500 special damages including loss of earnings to date (plus £3,529 interest); £12,339 future loss of earnings (including a £5,000 *Smith v Manchester* award). The award was subjected to a 30 per cent reduction for contributory negligence. *Thorogood v Barron* (23 June 1993, unreported) (Wandsworth County Court: Judge Sumner) (Messrs Joseph Aaron & Co for the plaintiff; Mr J Bate-Williams for the defendant) (Kindly submitted for publication by Joseph Aaron & Co, Solicitors, Ilford). *Smith v Manchester Corpn* (1974) 118 SJ 597, CA applied.

Total damages: £9,160. Plaintiff, male aged 32 at date of accident and 36 at time of hearing, sustained various injuries as a result of a vicious and unprovoked assault by gang of 14 youths.

Plaintiff sustained **widespread bruising and lacerations, tri-malleolar fracture of left ankle**, and **lacerations of right eyelid** when his spectacles were kicked into his face. Admitted to hospital for one week, in plaster six weeks, but was able to return to employment five weeks thereafter. **Expected to recover reasonably well**. Second fracture of the same ankle some one and a half years later, **unclear whether directly linked to original fracture** although plaintiff believed leg spontaneously gave way and refractured. At date of hearing plaintiff suffering from **residual pain** and **intermittent swelling** of ankle. **Obscured vision** in right eye although unable to specifically attribute extent due to attack. **Scarring** around eye causing significant cosmetic effect and **near constant irritation of scars and eye** itself. **Tenderness** in affected area. **Unable to drive for more than an hour** at a time or lift heavy weights such as, for example, heavy bags of shopping. Plaintiff **unable to run, play football** with his children, and **can no longer garden or decorate**. Has been **discharged from Territorial Army due to his injuries** after nine years of regular service, which previously played a large part in his life. Plaintiff **no longer goes out socially due to fear of further assault**. **Handicapped on labour market** as unable to climb ladders or undertake heavy work. Has to wear special mask in his occupation as welder due to effect of ultra-violet light on his eye and scars. The above award comprised £8,000 for pain, suffering and loss of amenity; special damages £1,160; and also the Board expressed that there was a *Smith v Manchester* element to the award, although this was not specified. *Criminal Injuries Compensation Board, Birmingham* (11 October 1993, unreported) (Kindly submitted for publication by Alasdair M Davidson, Barrister).

Total damages: **£6,648·75.** Plaintiff, female aged 40 at time of accident in March 1988, suffered a **series of injuries** as a result of a road traffic accident. She sustained **fractures of several ribs**, an **injury to her abdomen**, which formed an **organised haematoma** in her pelvis, and an **injury to her back** which involved the **wrenching of an already vulnerable spine**, to which she had received operative attention six months prior to the accident. Plaintiff was initially in hospital for **six days** as a result of the accident, and three of these days she spent with a catheter fitted and a drip. Plaintiff off work for **five weeks** after the accident. She also **suffered pain** in her groin, on both sides of her body, and a **burning sensation** in her toes, and she had to lie on the floor to relieve these symptoms. Earlier back troubles had necessitated a **laminectomy** six months prior to the accident. Due to the pain the plaintiff was suffering in her groin, her doctor undertook a **scan** of her pelvis which found that there was a **mass** which had formed as a result of **internal bleeding** caused by the accident. **Employment was terminated** as a result of her ongoing injuries. A second scan later in the year found that the mass was still present in plaintiff's groin; a **laparotomy** was performed under general anaesthetic to **remove a haematoma**. Plaintiff has a permanent **scar** as a result of this operation. As a result of the laparotomy the symptoms in the plaintiff's pelvis resolved, however **sciatica** returned to her back and this became **more intense**. The doctors at the trial said that the plaintiff should not have returned to work after the laminectomy on her original back injuries as her back troubles would have returned at some future stage. However, there was a dispute as to how long the symptoms attributable to the road traffic accident would have lasted, and the acceleration of the plaintiff's injury as a result of the accident. The above award comprised £5,500 for general damages; £1,148·75 for special damages and interest. *Pitman v Clarke* (20 May 1993, unreported) (Court of Appeal: Roche LJ and Hurst LJJ) (D Eccles, Messrs Rowe & Cohen for the plaintiff; P Butler, Messrs Lace Mawer for the defendant) (Kindly submitted for publication by Rowe & Cohen, Solicitors, Hyde).

PSYCHOLOGICAL DAMAGE AND EMOTIONAL STRESS

927 *Physical and emotional stress*

Total damages: **£147,405·12.** The plaintiff, aged 50, had been afflicted by **Chronic Fatigue Syndrome** (CFS) for a substantial period of his life **prior to a motor accident**. He sustained no injury in the accident, described as one of moderate severity, but it **caused or materially contributed to or materially increased the risk of the development or prolongation of the symptoms** of CFS which the plaintiff had **suffered for 20 years since the accident**, converting the illness from a mild and sporadic **state to one of chronic intensity and permanency**. Prima facie multiplier of ten reduced to six, to take account of plaintiff's previous medical history, his innate vulnerability to episodes before the accident, the limited fields of activity in which he could have sought employment and the stresses that would have been imposed upon him had he continued in his employment as a teacher. The award comprised: £23,663 for past loss of earnings; £86,040 for loss of future earning capacity; £10,430 for loss of pension; £6,375 special damages for do-it-yourself and other miscellaneous items; £897·12 for car hire charges and policy excess; £20,000 general damages for pain and suffering and loss of amenity. *Page v Smith* [1993] PIQR Q55 (Queen's Bench Division: Otton J).

Total damages: **£31,500**. Plaintiffs, three sisters now aged 24, 25 and 28, suffered **physical and indecent assaults**, aggravated in some cases by sexual intercourse and buggery, **inflicted by their father** during their **childhood and adolescence**. Plaintiffs also claimed **frequent beatings** by cane and belt and **sexual abuse**. They claimed damages for **pain and mental suffering** and for future medical treatment, such as **counselling**. The above award comprised £3,500 for each of the three plaintiffs, to cover future medical treatment; and general damages of £7,000, £8,000 and £13,000 respectively. *P v Keleman* (1993) Independent, 11 November (Queen's Bench Division: Sir Gervase Sheldon).

Total damages: **£3,500**. Plaintiff, female aged 28 at time of assault, suffered **swelling** and **tenderness** to her right cheek bone together with **marks** and **grazing** around her neck when her husband **attempted to strangle her** with a three foot chain link dog lead. Her physical injuries healed quickly but there was evidence from her doctor of some **depression** following the accident and approximately five months after the assault she was placed on a course of anti-depressants. The initial award of £2,500 was made, which was increased at a hearing to the above amount. *Criminal Injuries Compensation Board, Leeds* (29 January 1993, unreported) (Kindly submitted for publication by Rhodes Thain & Collinson, Solicitors, Halifax).

928   *Post-traumatic stress disorder*

Total damages: **£271,725** (excluding interest). Plaintiff, male senior lecturer aged 46, was involved in a road traffic accident in which he **suffered bruising and injury to the tissues of his left shoulder**, right **lower ribs** and patella region of the right knee, **fracture of the eighth thoracic vertebra** but more significantly psychological damage comprising **nervous shock, post-traumatic stress disorder, endogenous depression** and **reactive depression**. Plaintiff took voluntary retirement from his post as a senior lecturer in physiotherapy four years after the accident and ceased private practice three years after that. Plaintiff was a keen weight lifter and runner. Strong likelihood that **degenerative changes to his vertebra will occur shortly**. Plaintiff treated with **anti-depressants** for post-traumatic stress disorder. Condition declined to a state of **manic depressive illness** which caused him to have only intermittent periods of work. A year after the accident he was **suicidal and ill enough to be admitted to hospital for a week**. Plaintiff then lectured for a year and then stopped to concentrate on his private practice. At that stage plaintiff suffering from **reactive depression triggered by stress**. He attended hospital as a psychiatric out patient for six months. There was a two-thirds prospect of the plaintiff being promoted to principal lecturer had he stayed in employment. Plaintiff suffered a genetic predisposition to manic depressive illness. The above award comprised £155 medical and other expenses in the immediate aftermath of the accident; £70,674 loss of earnings as a senior lecturer to date as a result of early retirement; £9,010 loss of earnings to date arising from loss of promotion opportunity; £19,313 loss of earnings to date from private practice; £88,162 loss of future earnings as a senior lecturer with a multiplier of 6·5 less 15 per cent for specific possibility of disabling illness; £10,011 loss of earnings from failure to achieve promotion to principal lecturer, also discounted by 15 per cent; £22,277 loss of future earnings from private practice, also discounted by 15 per cent; £4,000 cost of professional advice for management of the sum of damages awarded; £23,123 for loss of pension; and £25,000 pain, suffering and loss of amenity. *Anderson v Davis* [1993] 5 PIQR Q87 (Queens Bench Division: R Bell QC). As to the question of liability, see para 919.

Total damages: **£147,683·58**. Plaintiff, then aged 39, was a professional fire fighter in which capacity he was one of the first to attend the fire at the Kings Cross Underground Railway Station in November 1987, where he undertook fire fighting and rescue duties. He sustained **no physical injury** but suffered the development of **post-traumatic stress disorder** and **depression** as a result of what he saw. The role he played on the night of the fire led the judge to describe him as "probably one of the most courageous men I have had or shall ever have the privilege of meeting" who "showed devotion to duty to a level not only expected by the London Fire Brigade, his superior officers, his colleagues and the public but well beyond it". Although identified within days as **psychologically disturbed**, the full extent of the plaintiff's injury was **not self-recognised** until nearly two years after the incident as it became more and more difficult for the plaintiff to cope with the symptoms from which he was suffering. He **became** and **remained difficult, irritable, bad tempered**, his relationships with members of his family **deteriorated** to the point that his wife and one of his children nearly left home, he suffered **anxiety, depression, headaches, nightmares, disturbed sleep, introversion** and in summary a **profound change of personality**. Eventually, he was treated as an in-patient and an out-patient by way of **counselling** and **therapy** which continues and is likely to continue on an intermittent level in the future. **As a result** of his symptoms and disabilities, the plaintiff was **dismissed** from employment as an operational fire fighter on the grounds of ill-health in January 1991 and took up employment as a **non-operational** fireman undertaking fire prevention duties. This occupation **continued** to **cause him anxiety and distress** and he was unlikely to be able to continue for more than a further six months, whereafter the field of likely employment that he would be fit to undertake would be **limited** and he would be at **considerable disadvantage**. The above award comprised general damages of £27,500 for pain, suffering and loss of amenity; loss of congenial employment £5,000; loss of earnings to trial £980·70; future loss of earnings to reflect two years' total loss of earnings after ceasing to work in a non-operational capacity, eight and a half years partial loss of earnings based on reduced earning capacity in limited range of alternative employment, and an addition for handicap on the labour market beyond the age of 55, being the normal retirement age of fire fighters, £77,500; loss of employment protection rights £436; past and future loss of earnings of the plaintiff's wife who reduced her hours of work to take over a large range of family tasks previously undertaken by the plaintiff personally £8,503·25; loss of pensions rights £17,261; past and future cost of medical treatment £5,225; cost of future employment assistance in the form of counselling and rehabilitation £1,984; and interest at £3,298·03. *Hale v London Underground Limited* (4 November 1992, unreported) (Queen's Bench Division, London: Otton J) (Kindly submitted for publication by Allan Gore, Barrister).

Total damages: **£12,500**. (Case settled before trial). Female plaintiff aged 28 began suffering from **lower abdominal pain and nausea** three days after a positive pregnancy test, and a diagnosis of suspected appendicitis or ectopic pregnancy was made. Plaintiff was admitted to hospital for a **laparoscopy** possibly proceeding to a laparotomy. The laparoscopy findings were **suggestive of acute appendicitis** and the surgeon proceeded to a **laparotomy and appendectomy**. Plaintiff recalls losing consciousness after the pre-medication, but shortly thereafter **regaining consciousness**. She was **paralysed** by the action of the muscle relaxant drugs and thus unable to communicate her condition to the theatre staff, but recalled **hearing machinery noises** and conversations and a **feeling of being punched and kicked, suffocation and violent pain**. Following the experience, the plaintiff suffered from a **depressive illness** which manifested itself in the immediate post-operative period and lasted in its acute stage for some **six months** although she did not require psychiatric treatment. She experienced symptoms of **anxiety, appetite and weight loss, sleep disturbance, indecisiveness, lack of concentration** and **poor motivation** with **social withdrawal**. Her depressive illness remitted spontaneously after about six months leaving **low grade intermittent** symptoms of **anxiety** and **depression** although she is not expected to suffer significant long term sequelae. Counsel had advised the claim to have a potential of £7,500–£10,000 by way of general damages. The action was listed for trial. The defendant continued to deny liability, but discussions on settlement took place and settlement was eventually agreed on a payment of £12,500 by way of general damages plus all costs but **without admission of liability**. The plaintiff was not working before her operation and did not pursue any claim for special damages. *Barnaby v North Tees Health Authority* (unreported) (Manchester District Registry) (Ann Alexander, Messrs Alexander Harris for the plaintiff; Messrs Darling Hodgsons for the defendant) (Kindly submitted for publication by Alexander Harris, Solicitors, Sale).

Total damages: **£10,000**. Plaintiff, male aged 21 at time of injury and 25 at time of trial, was injured when involved in the Hillsborough Disaster in April 1989. He was initially **trapped in the crush** at Leppings Lane End, pulled to side by a friend and thereafter escaped from pen. **Saw his brother trapped** in gateway and pulled the brother free and assisted brother to ambulance. **Returned and assisted friends** to carry approximately 12 people from the scene onto the field **some of whom were dead**. Unable to find one of his friends but subsequently discovered friend uninjured. Plaintiff **suffered slight bruising**, no serious physical injury and no separate award for that aspect. Plaintiff became **very distressed** and when invited to television studio to appear on programme attended at studio but **unable to appear due to distress**. Thereafter took **excessive quantity of Valium and admitted to hospital**. Plaintiff changed from a 'happy-go-lucky' individual to a snappy and irritable individual. Tends to 'moon' around, has **withdrawn from friends, suffers nightmares and flashbacks**. Ended relationship with girlfriend, rarely goes out, **profound change in life-style**. Plaintiff often agreed to seek help but thereafter refused as **unwilling to discuss incidents experienced**. For a period of between six and twelve months in the year after the disaster, plaintiff took amphetamines but judge inclined to the view that he took them due to psychiatric illness of **post traumatic stress disorder**. Judge accepted that it was **likely to continue for the foreseeable future**. No physical degeneration in plaintiff. Judge found that plaintiff suffering from post traumatic stress disorder with symptoms similar to those found in *Re Inkersole*. The above award was for general damages. *Fendwick v Chief Constable South Yorkshire Police* (26 July 1993, unreported) (Liverpool County Court: Judge McKay) (Antonis Georges for the plaintiff; John Phipps for the defendant) (Kindly submitted for publication by Antonis Georges, Barrister). *Re Inkersole, Criminal Injuries Compensation Board, London* (8 May 1990, unreported) applied.

Total damages: **£3,800**. Plaintiff, male off-licence manager aged 37 at time of hearing, was **assaulted during a robbery** at the off-licence at which he worked. Two men burst into the shop, one carrying a **shotgun**. Plaintiff was **grabbed** by his clothing and **forced** to open the safe while the shotgun was pointed at him. **No physical injuries** were sustained. The plaintiff was **shaken** by the robbery, and for three to four weeks after the incident he **could not sleep properly, felt extremely tense** and had **lost his appetite**. Psychiatric evidence said that he had suffered from a degree of **post-traumatic stress disorder** which continued for up to six months, following which he made a **complete recovery**. The above award comprised £800 initial award and £3,000 general damages. *Criminal Injuries Compensation Board, London* (6 May 1993, unreported) (Kindly submitted for publication by the Union of Shop, Distributive and Allied Workers, Manchester).

929   *Post-traumatic stress disorder/legs*

Total damages: **£1,616**. Plaintiff, female aged 27 at time of injury in November 1990, was passing the defendant's house when the **defendant's dog ran into the street and attacked** her. There was **injury to the plaintiff's hips**. Although the defendant released the dog's grip on the plaintiff, it broke free and **attacked again**, causing **severe injury to the plaintiff's hips and legs**. Plaintiff sustained **two bite wounds** to the right thigh, one an **elongated tear of skin** two inches long, and **two bite marks** to the left thigh. Seven months later the wounds had healed, left thigh **painful at all times** with a slight **swelling**, and two **permanent discoloured scars**. Plaintiff suffers from a **phobia of dogs and cannot walk along her road**, or the next road (where attacked) out of **fear of a further attack**. The above award comprised £1,600 general damages and £16 interest. *Bhudia v Newman* (17 November 1993, unreported) (Willesden County Court: Judge Sich) (Anthony Snelson, Messrs Ved & Co for the plaintiff) (Kindly submitted for publication by Anthony Snelson, Barrister).

930   *Psychological damage*

Total damages: **£27,500**. Applicant, male aged 39 at date of injury in November 1985, was attacked by a gang of youths when he went to the aid of a neighbour who was under attack in the car park of a public house. The applicant sustained multiple injuries including a **punctured lung, fractured ribs** and an **eye injury**. He was in intensive care on the night following the attack and remained in hospital for a further six days. He appeared to make a good recovery from his injuries and returned to work in January 1986. His eye required treatment until April 1986 by which time it was fully healed. The applicant was, however, **unable to concentrate** on his pre-accident job as director of a small cooling equipment company. His personality had undergone changes and he became **irritable, lacked motivation, was prone to aggressive outbursts**, and he suffered **some degree of memory loss**. He left the company and attempted to start a similar operation but his personality changes lead to its failure and the applicant fell into debt. Medical evidence confirmed that the applicant was suffering from **post-traumatic syndrome** and that his **memory had been impaired**. His family and social life were also affected by his personality change. The applicant has worked sporadically since February 1991 and the Board found that he was fit to work from April 1992 and his unemployment at the date of the hearing was no longer connected to his injuries. Prior to the attack the applicant's earnings were £600 per month net, and the award for special damages was based on this figure. The above award comprised £12,500 general damages for pain, suffering and loss of amenity, and £25,000 special damages for loss of earnings. *Criminal Injuries Compensation Board, London* (15 January 1993, unreported) (Miss E A Gumbel, Messrs Marshall Harvey for the applicant) (Kindly submitted for publication by Miss E A Gumbel, Barrister).

Total damages: **£15,000**. Applicant, female aged 18 at time of hearing, was the subject of **sexual abuse** from her stepfather commencing at the age of **eight** and continuing until she was

thirteen. The abuse started with **digital interference** but from the age of ten until thirteen involved full sexual **intercourse against the child's will**, the intercourse taking place at least **two or three times per week**. The applicant suffered considerable **emotional trauma** and had been left a **vulnerable personality** who had difficulty in forming stable relationships and was prone to become involved in relationships based on sex, the other parties acting in a semi-abusive manner. She had been given some **therapy** but had difficulties facing up to what had taken place and exhibited some reluctance to pursue treatment. Applicant had also resorted to the use of **illegal drugs** to relieve the symptoms of the trauma. The single member offered £10,000 and at the hearing the sum was increased to an award of £15,000. *Criminal Injuries Compensation Board, Bristol* (17 March 1993, unreported) (Kindly submitted for publication by Martin Picton, Barrister).

Total damages: **£7,500**. Applicant, female aged 10–21 at time of injuries and 28 at date of hearing, was **sexually abused** by her father during the years 1969 to 1978. He encouraged her to masturbate him and fondled her. The worst instances occurred from 1975 to 1978. From 1972 to 1986 applicant was **abused in a similar manner by her uncle**, and this conduct continued even when **she was married and pregnant**. In 1973 she was **abused by a family friend** (a babysitter) over a 12 month period. Applicant's father and uncle **both violent men**. Father sentenced to three years' imprisonment in respect of the above. **Applicant gave evidence** at his trial. Applicant **attended a psychologist** to whom she described episodes involving jealousy and possessiveness towards her husband. **Incidents of self-harm** including cutting herself with razor blades, head banging, pulling her hair out, and drug overdoses. **Feelings of anxiety, insecurity and low self-esteem**. Applicant **requires psychological support** at a fairly low level. *Criminal Injuries Compensation Board, Liverpool* (29 July 1993, unreported) (Kindly submitted for publication by Andrew McDonald, Barrister).

Total damages: **£2,500**. Plaintiff, female aged 3½ at time of incident, was playing on staircase of mother's council block with older friend. Plaintiff **approached by male, knickers pulled down, vagina touched** (although no digital penetration) and **mouth kissed**. Friend ran away to get help. Plaintiff **hysterical**, suffered **increased night-time enuresis** (from once a week to 2–3 times per night) for two years, along with **nightmares**, and **sleeptalking**. Received **psychiatric treatment** (with mother) for three years. Injuries **exacerbated by publicity**, graffiti drawn outside flat by other children on estate. Also, attacker sentenced to twelve months' imprisonment with psychiatric treatment, but returned to live on same estate. Mother offered alternative accommodation but could not afford to move. Plaintiff's mother unable to carry out the full treatment, and prognosis for the future uncertain. Child on the whole happy and well balanced except when reminded of the incident or at night-time. Board referred by counsel to *Re T*, CICB Nottingham (12 February 1993), which received £5,000 (with more severe distinguishing features). Judicial studies guidelines also referred to for moderate psychiatric damage. Board rejected argument that mother's increased neurosis and inability to continue treatment would affect family life and plaintiff's future prognosis. Nonetheless increased award. The above award comprised £2,000 general damages and £500 special damages. *Criminal Injuries Compensation Board* (25 November 1993, unreported) (Kindly submitted for publication by Penny Nagle, Pupil Barrister).

931　Pain and suffering

Total damages: **£3,000**. Plaintiff, female aged 47 when her general practitioner prescribed tablets consisting of **two different drugs** for her **severe asthmatic condition**, suffered an **excessive dose** equivalent to **five to six times over the prescribed amount**. The pharmacist mixed up the labels on the bottles of drugs; the plaintiff took the drugs as instructed on the labels. As a result she suffered the **toxic side effects** later that evening. She became unwell, with **vomiting** which continued all night, four episodes of loose watery **diarrhoea**, **cramping pains** in the epigastrium, **headache** and some **pain in the chest and back**. The next morning she was taken to hospital where medical examination revealed a heart rate of 100/min, **widespread rhonchi, poor air entry, crepitations in the upper lobe area**, and **tenderness** in the abdomen, especially in the epigastric area. She remained in hospital where her condition improved after the third day. The plaintiff remained there for another four days before being discharged, however she was unable to resume work until **three months** after discharge. In addition to the above general damages, a sum of £3·50 per hour was awarded for the time spent by her husband and others travelling from door to door to and from the hospital and for their attendance of the plaintiff in hospital. *Patel v Patel* (3 March 1993, unreported) (Brentford

County Court: Judge Edwards) (Mr Jonathan Sofer for the plaintiff) (Kindly submitted for publication by Jonathan Sofer, Barrister).

INTERNAL INJURIES

932 *Internal injuries*

Total damages: **£260,588.** Plaintiff, male aged 40 at the date of diagnosis, was exposed to asbestos whilst working for the defendant shipbuilders. He was later diagnosed as having **mesothelioma, an asbestos-related cancer.** It was concluded by the judge that on the balance of probabilities the plaintiff's **life expectancy from trial would be 18 months,** a total of **2½ years from diagnosis.** The disease was particularly **painful and debilitating** and meant that the plaintiff's wife had had to give up work to provide nursing care for the plaintiff. The plaintiff was **unable to perform household tasks** and his **mobility was severely damaged** by the disease. The above award was comprised as follows: general damages, £40,000; loss of past earnings, £3,750; loss of future earnings, £172,250; care to the date of trial, £7,511 (actual loss of wife's earnings, £2,631, additional care by wife, £4,880); future care, £12,123; loss of subsidised canteen food, £1,000 (past loss, £400, future loss, £600); prescriptions, £127; additional travelling costs (at 20p per mile), £2,000 (past loss, £800, future loss, £1,200); additional holiday costs, £1,350 (past loss, £450, future loss, £900); special clothing, £180; loss of ability to perform DIY and gardening tasks, £5,600; telephone, laundry and heating, £300; electric golf caddy, £1,250; lost pension, £12,000; interest on general damages, £567; interest on special damages, £580. The plaintiff's claim for £2,000 in respect of funeral expenses was not allowed. *Bliman v Appledore Shipbuilders Ltd* (26 November 1992, unreported) (Exeter District Registry: Bracewell J) (Kindly submitted by Seldon, Ward & Nuttall, Solicitors, Bideford).

Total damages: **£17,778·72.** Plaintiff, male aged 12 at time of accident in 1990, was injured at a scout camp when a climbing tower collapsed. **He fell 20 feet and three 15-foot logs landed on him.** Plaintiff was treated in **hospital overnight** for a **small laceration** to the head, **abdominal pain** and **nausea.** Discharged but **returned to hospital the following day because of constant pain and vomiting.** A **laparotomy** was performed which revealed a **complete traumatic transection of the upper small bowel.** He was discharged after nine days and was absent from school for 22 days. Thereafter plaintiff **suffered bouts of colicky pain** about **twice a month.** He was treated conservatively in hospital a further **three times** with nasogastric tubes and an intravenous drip. Eighteen months post accident he suffered a **severe attack of pain** whilst on a walking holiday with the scouts and underwent a **second laparotomy.** The **small bowel loops were distended, adhesions had formed** causing a **blockage** of the bowel. These adhesions were removed and the blockage cleared. Plaintiff was discharged after 11 days in hospital. Plaintiff had been a keen sportsman but was **now nervous of returning to any contact sports.** His schooling and holidays had been **disrupted,** and his parents remain reluctant to allow him to travel abroad. Plaintiff was a keen sailor and the judge accepted that prior to the accident the plaintiff had expressed an interest in following his father into the Royal Navy. This **career was no longer open** to him. Currently (three years post accident) the plaintiff **suffers occasional bouts of dull intermittent aching** about twice a month that last for around two hours. **This will continue into the future.** He was left with an **unsightly abdominal scar** of which he was slightly aware. He was described as being an intelligent boy of strong character, who had made the best of his injuries. The threat of strangulation of the bowel meant there was a **small risk of major complications** in the future and a **significant risk of plaintiff requiring one or more laparotomies** during his lifetime. The above award comprised £17,500 general damages and £278·72 special damages. *Irwin v The Scout Association* (27 July 1993, unreported) (Watford County Court: Judge Green) (Martin Bailey for the plaintiff; Ian Burnett for the defendant) (Kindly submitted for publication by Richard Wilkinson, Barrister).

Total damages: **£16,816.** Plaintiff, female aged 45 at time of injury, underwent in February 1990 a **total abdominal hysterectomy,** bilateral salpingo-oophorectoy, colpo-suspension and hormonal implant. Following the operation plaintiff **felt ill and did not recover as expected.** She was discharged from hospital and had cause to consult her doctor having developed **high fever, pain, and diarrhoea.** She felt generally unwell and suspected she might have a **terminal illness.** A **haematoma** was drained. After further problems she was admitted as an **emergency** in June 1990 with abdominal pain, diarrhoea and fevers. A **laparotomy** was performed in July 1990 and **two large abdominal packs were found in the abdominal cavity and removed.** After the second operation plaintiff recovered well but there is a **future risk of the**

development of adhesions within the abdominal cavity. The above award comprised £15,000 general damages and £1,816 special damages. *A v Torbay Health Authority* (settled out of court) (Kindly submitted for publication by Derek S Reed, Solicitor, Devon).

Scotland

Total damages: **£16,000**. Plaintiff, male former shipyard electrician aged 73 contracted **asbestosis** as a result of exposure to asbestos at work. Doctors do not expect him to live beyond **five years**. The disease causes the plaintiff to suffer from **breathlessness**, which in turn creates difficulty in moving. He also suffers from **coughing and incontinence** and the chance of him **contracting respiratory infections or malignant lesions** has been significantly increased. The plaintiff's claim was complicated by the fact that he already suffered from **chronic bronchitis**. Consequently, the defendant's medical expert assessed the effect of the asbestosis on the plaintiff's respiratory function at only about 10 per cent whereas the plaintiff's medical expert estimated it at more like 50 per cent. The judge considered the plaintiff's medical expert to be a more experienced and reliable witness and therefore accepted that the asbestosis made a substantial contribution to the plaintiff's condition. The above award included £12,000 by way of solatium and £4,000 for services to the plaintiff being the extra work of a domestic and nursing character undertaken and to be undertaken in the future by the plaintiff's wife. *Campbell v Campbell & Isherwood Ltd* 1993 SLT 1095 (Outer House).

Total damages: **£4,980**. Plaintiff, female aged 44 at the time of injury, underwent an operation in 1988 for the removal of an ovarian cyst, surgeons undertaking a total abdominal hysterectomy and a bilateral salpingo-oophorectomy (removal of ovaries and fallopian tubes). On the seventh day after the operation the plaintiff found herself **wholly incontinent** of urine through the vagina. On review after two months, **diagnosis of vesico-vaginal fistula** made. **Surgical repair undertaken under a general anaesthetic** after further delay. **Considerable discomfort and inconvenience before repair** including **one month's continuous catheterisation, abstinence from sexual intercourse** and **social embarrassment. Further discomfort and irritation for a few weeks after repair. Post-operative scarring** greater due to the second operation. The judge found the most likely cause of fistula was **accidental surgical stitching on the bladder into the vaginal vault**. The above award comprised £4,500 general damages and special damages of £480. *Winterbone v West Suffolk Health Authority* (1 November 1993, unreported) (Cambridge County Court: Judge Bromley QC) (Kindly submitted for publication by Messrs W F Smith & Co, Solicitors, Brandon).

BURNS

933 *Burns*

Total damages: **£10,286·61**. Plaintiff, male aged 29 and employed as a lorry driver at the time of the accident and aged 31 and a gymnasium owner at the date of trial, suffered **first degree scalds** to his **face, neck and right side of his chest and abdomen** and **secondary degree scalds** to his **right arm extending from his wrist to above his elbow**, when the radiator of a lorry which he was driving exploded, **covering him in boiling water**. The scalds took **six months** to heal, after which time the plaintiff made a **good physical recovery**, however he suffered from **pigmentary changes** to his arm. Prior to the accident the plaintiff was a **champion bodybuilder**, holding both the United Kingdom and Welsh Championships. Owing to the pigmentary changes to the plaintiff's arm he was **unable to resume his former sport** as a bodybuilder, though he **was able to participate** on the judging side of bodybuilding competitions. The above award comprised £8,000 for general damages; £1,654·94 special damages; and £631·67 interest. *Day v South Wales Upholstery Ltd (in liquidation)* (29 April 1993, unreported) (Caerphilly County Court: Judge Hywel ap Robert) (Kindly submitted for publication by Charles, Crookes & Jones, Solicitors, Caerphilly).

Total damages: **£6,000**. Plaintiff, male aged 11 at date of accident and 13 at time of hearing, walked through a **nature reserve** onto property owned/occupied by British Coal which was an unused but **live colliery spoil heap**. The ground underneath the plaintiff gave way and he became **submerged** to his **waist** in colliery spoil that had been subject to **heat and combustion**. He sustained **burns** to his left hand and wrist and a **circumferential burn** to the lower part of the left leg. **Skin grafting** was performed to an area of 7cm on the left calf and 12cm by 10cm on the left thigh, and **scarring** of 5cm by 4cm on the right wrist also occured. Plaintiff remained an in-patient at the hospital for **26 days**. Plaintiff can experience **pain** in the grafted area on the left leg if kicked whilst playing sports, and the area is subject to periods of **itching**. The scar on the volar aspect of right wrist is white and completely flat, the donor site from left thigh is flat and difficult to see. The plaintiff is **not conscious** of the grafted area's cosmetic appearance. Grafting on the left leg matured and settled in well and does not constitute anything other than a fairly minor cosmetic defect on the plaintiff's leg. *Whorton (A Minor) v British Coal Corpn* (25 March 1993, unreported) (Doncaster County Court: Deputy District Judge Taylor) (Kindly submitted for publication by Mr S Robinson, Frank Allen Pennington, Solicitors, Doncaster).

SCARRING

934 *Scarring*
Total damages: £14,225. Plaintiff, female aged 23 at time of injury and 25 at date of trial, was involved in a road traffic accident. Sustained **disfiguring injuries** to her legs, which necessitated a period of **two weeks in-patient treatment**, away from work for a period of **six weeks**. **Residual scarring**. These included a 4 x 3 centimetre scar on the right leg below the knee, parts lighter and other parts redder than adjacent skin; an area of **discolouration** on the dorsum of the right foot of 3 x 2 centimetres, which was the area of a **skin graft**; an area of discolouration on the inside of the left thigh of 14 x 11 centimetres in size, which was a skin graft donor site; two scars just above the patella of 4 and 5 centimetres in length and ½ centimetre in width, pink and papery thin; an area of discolouration below the patella of 7 x 14 centimetres in area, representing a skin graft site; and on the antero-lateral aspect of the leg at the same level, a scar 8 centimetres by 4 millimetres, pink and of good contour. There was also a **lack of ten degrees flexion** in the left knee which is likely to be **permanent** and will **limit plaintiff's ability** to squat stably and symmetrically. **Surgery is unlikely to improve** the scarring and time will not change the scars. Plaintiff at time of trial continues to be **self-conscious** about her injuries, and has been advised to avoid sunbathing. The above award comprised £11,000 general damages and £3,225 special damages to include interest calculated at the full court special account rate applying *Prokop v Department of Health and Social Security* [1985] CLY 1037. *Goodall v Hall* (16 June 1993, unreported) (Brentford County Court: District Judge Karet) (Jonathan Sofer, Messrs Lambert Hale & Proctor for the plaintiff) (Kindly submitted for publication by Mariam Cohen, Lambert Hale & Proctor, Solicitors, London).

Total damages: £8,000. Plaintiff, male aged 24 at time of accident and 26 at hearing, was **forcibly thrust** through a glass door at a nightclub, sustaining quite **extensive scarring** to his forehead - **three vertical scars** measuring approximately **five centimetres each** with slight breaks in two of them. The first is at or about the middle of the forehead with the second towards the left and the third at the left temple running into the hairline. The latter at the left temple is **slightly raised**. In addition, there is a scar to the bottom part of his nose. The plaintiff's **recollections** of the incident were **vivid**. He is **embarrassed socially** when introduced to new people. The scar to the middle of his forehead is **numb** in part, and depending upon the weather, the **scars change colour**; this is expected to **settle** in the future. The scars are **beyond cosmetic repair**, are **permanent** and can be said to be **severe**. They cannot be covered or disguised. The above award was for general damages only. *Criminal Injuries Compensation Board, Manchester* (16 April 1993, unreported) (Mr Peter R Smith for the applicant) (Kindly submitted for publication by Peter R Smith, Barrister).

Total damages: £8,000. Plaintiff, female aged 9 at time of accident and 10 at date of trial, suffered **severe laceration of left arm leaving severe and ugly permanent scarring** above elbow when she fell into boating lake in public park and onto serrated metal inlet valve fence. Plaintiff suffered **severe laceration on inside of left arm, sutured** at hospital. Plaintiff left with **unsightly raised and lumpy scar** with **prominent adjacent suture scars**, measuring eight centimetres by one centimetre. In addition, **permanent loss of sensation for distance of nine centimetres below scar**. Plaintiff **embarrassed** by scar in public, and particularly during sporting activities. **Scar visible** when wearing short sleeved clothes or bathing costume. **Revision of scar possible by operation** to improve appearance of scar, **but loss of sensation will be permanent**. Scar will always amount to significant cosmetic disability. The above award was for general damages. *Maloney v Liverpool City Council* (21 October 1993, unreported) (Liverpool County Court: District Judge Knopf) (Paul Simpson, Messrs Burke Edwards for the plaintiff; Tania Griffiths, Liverpool City Council for the defendant) (Kindly submitted for publication by Paul Simpson, Barrister).

Total damages: £4,529.38. Plaintiff, female aged 23 at time of injury, had small red "thread veins" on both legs at knee and thigh level. The defendants operated a hair and beauty clinic which offered treatment of the veins by means of electrolysis. Plaintiff was **given no warning** of the possibility of failure or scarring consequent upon the treatment. Once a fortnight the plaintiff received up to 20 treatments; namely a **needle applied to the skin vertically** which **penetrated** then caused **acute discomfort** when it was activated by the therapist operating a foot switch. **Multiple punctures** were made during each session and occasionally there was **bleeding**. At least 30 needle pricks were received in a 20 minute session. Plaintiff subsequently developed **thick scars** at a few of the treated areas which were at first **purplish red and itchy**, and which have **slowly become pale, flatter and more comfortable**. These areas have left **noticeable scars**. Plaintiff is left with **white, slightly shiny, scarred areas** that can be seen quite easily at a distance of normal conversation with the legs uncovered. The scars are no longer itchy or tender. They do not restrict the function of the legs. The scars were **unlikely to tan** in sunlight so may be more obvious in summer. Cosmetic camouflage is impracticable because it is easily removed. The **scars are not amenable to surgery**. **No improvement is expected**. In addition the plaintiff sustained a **psychological** reaction. She was disappointed in the failure of the procedure and was unwilling to tell her boyfriend what had occurred. This was reflected in the award. Plaintiff wore trousers now rather than skirts and was self-conscious on the beach. Plaintiff was not absent from work as a result of the injury. The above award comprised £3,750 general damages; £621 special damages; and £158·38 interest. *Greensides v Bath Hair & Beauty Clinic* (20 October 1993, unreported) (Bath County Court: District Judge Rutherford) (Kindly submitted for publication by Bevan Ashford, Solicitors, Bristol).

HEAD

935 *Head*

Total damages: **£639,386·90**. Plaintiff, female aged three and a half years old at time of accident and 15 at date of trial, was involved in an accident that resulted in her head being **compressed** between a car bumper and a reversing coach. She was taken to hospital **unconscious** and **bleeding from the left ear**, and found to have sustained a **fractured skull and fractured humerus**. Plaintiff regained consciousness after **three months**, but exhibited **loss of vision** in the left eye, **near complete left facial nerve palsy** with an **inability to open the left eye**, **deafness** in the left ear, **partial right hemiparesis, emotional instability, learning difficulty** and **speech difficulty**. Plaintiff attended a normal primary school, where she exhibited **slow and erratic reading and writing, poor memory, poor verbal and performance IQ, behavioural and emotional instability** and **night-time incontinence**. At date of trial plaintiff was boarding at a special school, her physical and mental disabilities had not improved. She was **mostly independent** for dressing and toilet activities, but was still incontinent at night. Her physical awkwardness meant she could undertake basic household tasks, but only with supervision. Her poor concentration, erratic mood swings and inability to read social situations left her **unable effectively to interact** with her peers. Her inappropriate social behaviour had become a particular problem with peers of the opposite sex, to the extent that she was, unknown to her, receiving contraceptive injections. The only real area of possible improvement in her condition was the facial palsy. An operation could be performed to reactivate part of the left side of her face. This was important to the plaintiff as she was well aware of the obtrusiveness of her facial palsy. She would be able to remain at her special school for another four years. Thereafter she would need constant supervision and guidance from carers experienced with head injury patients, mainly because of her behavioural and emotional problems rather than her physical disabilities. The plaintiff would **never be capable of employment**. Her life expectancy was not shortened by her condition. The above award comprised £85,000 general damages for pain, suffering and loss of amenity; £40,122 for past care; £1,100 past extra travel expenses; £9,143 past accommodation; £2,000 past sundry expenses; £4,887 past bedwetting expenses (extra sheets and laundry); £2,500 for costs of maintaining extra car for four years; £329,750 for future care, being £9,750 for plaintiff to remain at special school for next four years (using a multiplier of 3 and a multiplicand of £3,250) and £320,000 for suitable residential accommodation thereafter (using a multiplier of 16 and a multiplicand of £20,000); £1,263 future accommodation expenses; £3,920 future transport; £959·90 future bedwetting expenses; £143,542 future loss of earnings (using a multiplier of 14 and a multiplicand of £10,253); and £15,200 for future medical treatment. *Feltham v Seaview Services Ltd* (10 June 1993, unreported) (Winchester District Registry: McKinnon J) (Nigel Wilkinson QC, Michael Kent for the plaintiff; Ronald Walker QC, Jonathan Howard for the defendant) (Kindly submitted for publication by Patrick Vincent, Pupil Barrister).

Total damages: **£125,000**. Plaintiff, male infant at time of injury in February 1979 and aged 14 at hearing, was struck by car and **thrown out of his pushchair**. Fractures of the skull causing damage to right frontal lobe of brain and pulsatile swelling overlying a growing fracture. Bone grafting and cranio-plasty carried out. Some shortening of left hand and leg with a little weakness in co-ordination. Some impairment of cognitive skills. Developed minor epilepsy with first seizure in 1984. Treated and controlled with sodium valproate. Further two convulsions in 1985. Since then number of minor seizures in the form of "spasms" leaving him confused, sickly and with headaches. Major fit with loss of consciousness in April 1990. Put back on medication which had previously been withdrawn. The view was that generalised epilepsy had probably developed but was capable of being controlled entirely by medication. Remote risk of an enlarging granuloma and a porencephatic cyst in right damaged frontal lobe of brain. Tendancy for partial or generalised epilepsy would always be present. He would suffer a disadvantage in the future with respect to employment as some occupations would be permanently closed to him. He would tire easily and would have difficulty with jobs requiring lifting or carrying of heavy objects or requiring dexterity of the left hand. Ability to organise and concentrate affected so restricting initiative, becoming easily distracted, but no outward signs of brain damage and any weakness/shortening of left limbs conspicuous only to those who know and observe him. His average net weekly income in adult employment would have been about £8,000 per annum but there was some chance he would get work and even had he been healthy, the unemployment problem for a boy of his background was severe in any event. Multiplier of 15 reduced to ten to represent accelerated receipt in respect of lost earnings which would not begin for a further two to four years. The above award comprised £45,000 for pain suffering and loss of amenity; £8,775 for interest; loss of earning capacity was put at between £50,000 and £80,000; and special damages plus interest £2,429·80. *Rhodes v Watson* (1 December 1992, unreported) (Queen's Bench Division: Ognall J) (Kindly submitted for publication by Gary Burrell, Barrister).

Total damages: £57,244. Plaintiff, male aged 40 at time of hearing, suffered head injuries including a fracture of the skull when involved in a road traffic accident whilst a passenger in his employers' van. He was rendered unconscious and had to stay in hospital for five days. The fracture was diagnosed immediately but he was only later diagnosed as having suffered a total loss of sense of smell and an extremely high degree of loss of taste (being only able to taste the extremes of exceptionally spicy or sweet foods). The above award included £19,000 general damages for pain, suffering and loss of amenity; and £29,951 special damages for loss of income for the period following the accident, and for the period between giving up his subsequent career as a self-employed plumbing and heating engineer for lack of insurance (the plaintiff experienced difficulties obtaining insurance due to the loss of sense of smell) and taking up alternative lower paid work. *Williams v Mound-Evans* (16 January 1993, unreported) (Queen's Bench Division, Stafford: B R Escott-Cox QC) (Mr S Hawkesworth QC and Mr K Walmsley, Messrs Burrowes & Co for the plaintiff; Mr I J Goldrein, Messrs Silverbeck Rymer for the defendant) (Kindly submitted for publication by Geraint E Jones, Solicitor, Powys).

Total damages: £5,000. Applicant, male aged 15 at time of injury, was struck over the head with a house brick and sustained a 15 centimetre laceration of his scalp above the hairline and an underlying fracture of the skull. Risk of developing epilepsy was regarded as less than one per cent by the date of hearing. Prior to the incident the applicant had been a difficult pupil at school who was described by his teachers as disruptive, abusive and a bully. He had also been in trouble with the police and had committed offences of assault and theft only months before he was attacked. The board held that if the applicant had experienced any personality change as a result of the blow to his head, having regard to his background history, it was so mild as to be of no significance in assessing damages. The above award was made for general damages. *Criminal Injuries Compensation Board, Liverpool* (24 August 1993, unreported) (Kindly submitted for publication by Tim Grover, Barrister).

Total damages: £700. The plaintiff, male in his forties, underwent hair replacement treatment whereby a hair piece was placed over the receding area on his head. His own hair was tied to the edges of the hair piece and knotted to secure it. Any of the plaintiff's own hair remaining under the hair piece was then pulled through and blended with the hair piece. The hair at the front of the plaintiff's head was shaved off to allow a better fit. The defendant was held, inter alia, to have misrepresented the process used and to have failed to fit the hair piece with reasonable skill and care. It had caused the plaintiff considerable pain for three days at the anchor points and when it was removed it could be seen that his scalp was inflamed. This inflammation was fully resolved within four days of the hair piece being removed. It took a further six weeks for the shaved area of hair to grow back and during this time the plaintiff altered his hair style and took to wearing a hat. The award was made for pain and suffering, disappointment and embarrassment. *Dickinson v Growth Hair Clinic* (19 January 1993, unreported) (Southport County Court: District Judge Humphreys-Roberts) (Kindly submitted for publication by Tim Grover, Barrister).

Total damages: £250. Plaintiff, female aged 11, was injured when the car in which she was a passenger was hit from the rear by another vehicle. She **banged her head** on the seat in front of her which caused **mild pain and tenderness** to her forehead but **no bruising**. Plaintiff felt **dizzy** with **nausea** and was shaken by the accident. Physical injuries fully resolved within two days, plaintiff still nervous of sitting in back seat of car and prefers to sit in the front. The above award was for general damages. *Caplin v Parkinson* (5 October 1993, unreported) (Birkenhead County Court: Judge Crowe QC) (Kindly submitted for publication by Tim Grover, Barrister).

936 *Face*

Total damages: £67,241·47. Panel beater, 53 at time of accident, suffered a **whiplash-type injury** when a chute from the machine sprang into his face while he was loosening a bolt on it. He suffered a **deep laceration** 6 cm long to the right side of his nose, and there was considerable damage to the underlying bones. The plaintiff also suffered from **soreness of the inner eyelid** and **recurrent pain** in upper right nasal region. He suffered acceleration of **cervical spondylosis** by some seven years and the aggravation of pre-existing **lower back pain**. The above award comprised £10,000 general damages for pain, suffering and loss of amenity, £57,241·47 (including interest) for special damages. *Woodburn v Liverpool City Council* (22 January 1993, unreported) (Queen's Bench Division, Liverpool: McKinnon J) (Mr Hinchcliffe, Messrs Brian Thompson, for the plaintiff; Miss Griffiths, City Solicitor for Liverpool City Council, for the defendant).

Total damages: £11,250. Plaintiff, male aged 26 at date of assault and 32 at time of hearing, was **struck on the left side of the face by a beer glass which caused a large deep laceration of the face**. The wound was initially explored, with **two pieces of glass being removed** and the laceration being **sutured**. It then transpired that one of the **main branches of the facial nerve** had been **severed** and was **surrounded by scar tissue**. A surgical operation took place, resulting in the scar tissue being dissected free and the two ends of the cut nerve being approximated and sutured. At the date of the hearing, there was a **very obvious two inch scar** lying horizontally in the left mid-face. There was also a **less obvious scar** in front of the left ear and extending into the neck, this latter scar being caused by the surgical operation. There was still a **partial left facial paralysis** so that, for example, the left eye could not close as tightly as the right in bright light and the left eye blinked slower than the right. There was **also a degree of numbness of the face and of the adjacent ear**. The situation was static with no improvement or deterioration being likely. The above award comprised £8,500 general damages and special damages of £2,750. *Criminal Injuries Compensation Board, Manchester* (27 August 1993, unreported) (Kindly submitted for publication by Messrs Ingham Clegg & Crowther, Solicitors, Fleetwood).

937 *Eye*

Total damages: £81,290. Plaintiff, male aged 34 at time of injury, was attacked by a neighbour who struck him on the **left cheek** and in the **left eye** with a large brick. On examination x-rays showed a **comminuted fracture of the floor of the left orbit** and a **comminuted fracture of the left zygoma** with some **opacification of the left maxillary antrum**. At operation the left eye was **enucleated** and the **fractured zygoma was reduced and fixed with internal wires** and the **lacerations repaired**. A pathology report on the eye showed a **severely traumatised** eye with **extensive haemorrhage** into the vitreous and **detachment of the retina**. Plaintiff was given a **false eye**. Residual complaints were **headaches, left facial pain** and **impaired sensation** over the left side of the face and nose. In addition, plaintiff suffered **anxiety, depression and post traumatic stress**. Plaintiff had previously worked as a plumber and heating engineer, and his **ability to work was now impaired**. The above award comprised £40,000 general damages; £31,935 special damages to date of hearing including loss of earnings; £50,000 further loss of earnings; this total figure of £121,935 reduced by one third by virtue of character, previous convictions and way of life. *Criminal Injuries Compensation Board* (10 November 1992; unreported) (Kindly submitted for publication by Derek S Reed, Solicitor, Devon).

Total damages: £25,076. Applicant, female aged 15 at date of accident, sustained a **severe perforating wound to the right eye** caused by an air rifle lead pellet which struck the right eye directly, having first penetrated the right upper eye lid. It **lodged within the right orbital tissues** but was not locatable at the time of surgery and **remains within the orbit**. Because of the severity of the injury, the right eye was rendered **blind** and despite surgical intervention on the day of admission, **no return of vision ensued** and the right eye has shrunk markedly. The applicant was detained in hospital for seven days. There is an **obvious cosmetic blemish** and the applicant has **worn an artificial eye** since 1990. This is not a good colour match and has been altered and replaced on a number of occasions. The applicant still **suffers difficulty of judgement, depth and distance**. Activities such as pouring a cup of tea and parking a car by the kerb-side are difficult. The applicant has **lost a large measure of confidence** following the accident and felt she was unable to pursue her chosen career in medicine as she would be unable to cope with the responsibility. The left eye is healthy with excellent vision, but a **small risk of sympathetic ophthalmia** to the left eye exists, although at well under one per cent. In time the **right eye could become inflamed** and **produce pain** and **may have to be removed completely**. At present it forms a useful base for the artificial eye. The applicant still experiences **discomfort** in the right eye occasionally. The above award comprised £25,000 general damages for pain, suffering and loss of amenity, and £76 special damages. *Criminal Injuries Compensation Board, London* (23 June 1993, unreported) (Messrs Barker Son & Isherwood for the plaintiff) (Kindly submitted for publication by Richard Gregory, Solicitor, Andover).

Total damages: £22,782. Plaintiff, female aged 17 at time of accident and 20 at time of award, was injured by a **flying glass** in a public house. As a result of this incident the plaintiff sustained a **deep laceration of the eyebrow, upper and lower eyelids** and **the eye itself**. She was taken to hospital and later that day under **general anaesthetic** two wounds were sutured. She remained in hospital for a **few days** and the wound healed without any problems. There is **residual scarring** over the right eye, a vertical scar approximately **two centimetres long** and approximately **three millimetres wide**, extending vertically through the mid point of the right upper eyelid. There is no loss of hairs as the scar crosses the eyebrow. There is a scar on the lower lid approximately **two and a half centimetres long**. There is a **smaller oblique scar** approximately **two centimetres** lying across the lower eyelid. The eyelid closes **without distortion**. The scarring is not in any way disfiguring and is only discernible on close examination but the plaintiff is understandably acutely aware of it. The more serious injury is the **loss of vision** in the **right eye**. The ophthalmic surgeon did repair a **lacerated corneal wound** with sutures and a **prolapsed iris** was excised. After the operation the right eye slowly regained vision but the plaintiff has lost about **50 per cent of the useful vision** in the right eye and even if she was to wear contact lenses there will **not be a full restoration of vision** in that eye. Because of the nature of this injury there is always a risk of a **cataract** developing in the right eye and a further risk of **inflammation** occuring in the left eye which is known as **sympathetic ophthalmia**. It is thought that the risk of both these conditions is **less than one per cent**. Plaintiff was absent from work for **four months** and was fortunately **paid in full** and there was no claim made in respect of loss of earnings. As well as a claim for compensation for personal injuries there was a claim for cost of **contact lenses** and the maintenance of her contact lenses which is now required. It is not thought that there will be any great loss for future employment prospects. The above award comprised £22,500 for general damages and £282 for specials. *Criminal Injuries Compensation Board, Glasgow* (4 November 1992, unreported) (Kindly submitted for publication by Canter Levin & Berg, Solicitors, St Helens).

938 *Ear*

Scotland
Total damages: £1,750. Plaintiff, male welder aged 24 at date of accident and 26 at date of trial, suffered injuries when a drop of **molten slag fell into his left ear**. Plaintiff off work for three or four days and then on light duties for a period thereafter. **Unable to hear in his left ear for three days. Suffered from tinnitus significantly for six months**, but cleared up within a year. Plaintiff has been **left with a minor hearing deficit and no longer has symmetrical hearing**. Of the above award, £1,250 was for pain and suffering. *Moffat v Babcock Thorn Ltd* 1993 SLT 1993 (Outer House).

939 *Nose*

Total damages: £5,810. Applicant, male aged 15 at date of injury in 1987, was playing football when **punched in the mouth** by a member of the opposing team, in an unprovoked attack. Applicant's **teeth were knocked through each lip** but the main damage was to the **nose**, which was **broken**. The **nasal septum was deviated to the right** hand side and the **lining of the nose was congested and oedematous**. A **submucus resection of the nasal septum** was carried out in July 1988. Applicant **continued to complain of a blocked sensation** on the right side of the nose and there was still some **deviation** in the nose. He subsequently was treated with various nasal sprays and also had some submucus diathermy to his inferior turbinates and a sinus wash out. By the middle of 1991 it was apparent that there was going to be **no further improvement** without further surgical intervention as far as the right sided nasal obstruction was concerned. There was a further operation, therefore, in April 1992 when a **revision of the submucus resection** of the nasal cartilage took place. The surgeon excised a further fracture line from the anterior nasal septum and repositioned the septum in the collumella pocket anteriorally. In spite of this, the applicant found that there had been **little or no improvement** to his symptoms of nasal obstruction on the right side. He still has some deviation of the nasal septum. It has been decided that there is **nothing further that can be done** to assist in relation to the obstruction in the right nostril. Applicant suffers from **colds more regularly** than he did before the assault and they **tend to be heavier and of longer duration**. Prior to the assault he also suffered from **hay fever** and these **symptoms are now made worse** than they were before the assault. The above award comprised £5,500, plus £310 special damages. *Criminal Injuries Compensation Board, Birmingham* (28 July 1993, unreported) (Kindly submitted for publication by Mr M A Hollidge, Solicitor, Tamworth).

940 *Jaw*

Total damages: **£1,000**. Plaintiff, male aged 28 at time of accident and 31 at date of hearing, was punched on the right side of his face, causing **swelling to jaw** and **damage to the muscles** associated with the **temporomandibular joint**. No bone injury. Plaintiff experienced **difficulty in eating, talking and sleeping** for a period of no more than seven weeks. Still suffers from **occasional discomfort** when yawning or tired, which is likely to be **permanent**. Residual symptoms described as being similar to cramp. The above award was made for general damages. *Criminal Injuries Compensation Board, Liverpool* (11 October 1993, unreported) (Kindly submitted for publication by Tim Grover, Barrister).

NECK AND SHOULDER

941 *Neck*

Total damages: **£181,432·13**. Plaintiff, female district nurse aged 41 at time of accident in February 1988 and 46 at date of trial, suffered symptoms of **soft tissue injury** to **muscles** and **ligaments** of her **neck** when involved in road traffic accident. She was prescribed **physiotherapy** and a **cervical collar** which she wore for a few weeks. Plaintiff off work for **seven months** although she managed to do some course work. One year after the accident, movement to the neck was still **very restricted**. In December 1989 plaintiff was still experiencing some slight pain in the right shoulder and some pain in her neck, which was present **virtually all the time**. In March 1992, she still complained of getting episodes of neck pain which could last for three weeks but which were becoming less frequent. Further improvement had taken place by the date of trial. In addition to the above, the plaintiff developed **psoriasis** which became apparent about six months after the accident and which had been **triggered off by the stress caused**. Initially it affected only her **palms**, but in July 1991 her condition began to **deteriorate** spreading over her **feet** and with an outbreak of lesions in **all areas of the skin**. Plaintiff's palms remained most seriously affected and it was noted that when seen for medical examination in February 1992, she could **only move her hands with difficulty**. The prognosis was that she would continue to develop exacerbations for many years, the condition would be difficult to treat and she might require **potentially dangerous** cytotoxic drugs which could lead to **bone marrow depression** or **acute liver failure**. Twenty per cent of patients taking such drugs have to stop because of side effects. Despite medical opinion, going back to December 1988, to the effect that most other people with such symptoms would have given up work, the plaintiff continued as a district nurse until the date of trial. This was in part because of her love for her job but also because of uncertainty over the level of damages she would receive. Before the accident plaintiff had led a normal happy family and social life; she swam, went dancing and to keep-fit classes. She had been **forced to give up** such activities; she **no longer went out**, and she could **not engage in household duties**. She was **unable even to enjoy reading** because of the pain involved in turning pages, she suffered from **insomnia**, and could **not bear to be cuddled** by her husband. In 1992 she had gone on a foreign holiday with her family but found it an ordeal because she could not bear the heat, could not swim and had to keep her hands and feet covered. The judge accepted that the prospects of the plaintiff **ever finding any alternative work** were **bleak**. The above award comprised £28,000 for pain, suffering and loss of amenity; loss of congenial employment £5,000; past earnings £5,805·97; future earnings (multiplier of 8 applied) £115,516·40; loss of car benefit provided by employer (multiplier of 8 applied) £10,109·76; past and future decorating costs (multiplier of 10 applied) £5,700; future housework, ironing and window cleaning (multiplier of 10 applied) £9,460; future medication (multiplier of 10 applied) £160; and agreed interest £1,680. *Jones v Pandis* (28 May 1993, unreported) (Middlesborough County Court: Judge Paling) (Keith S H Miller, Messrs Appleby, Hope & Matthews for the plaintiff; Jeremy Freedman, Messrs Downs Ashley for the defendant) (Kindly submitted for publication by Keith S H Miller, Barrister).

Total damages: **£97,370·20**. Plaintiff, male aged 45 at time of accident, was a driver/operator whose bus was **struck from behind** by another bus on 30 July 1989. The plaintiff was thrown forwards over the wheel of the bus and then thrown backwards **striking his head** on the rear bulk head of the bus and **losing consciousness**. He attended the hospital where x-rays revealed no bony injury and he was later discharged with a **soft collar**. He later attended hospital as an out-patient and for **physiotherapy**. He returned to work in January 1990 on light duties as a counter clerk but was **unable to return to driving duties** and was **dismissed** by his employers on 9 November 1990. The plaintiff's injuries were recorded firstly as a **soft tissue injury to the head** which resulted in momentary loss of consciousness (**concussion**) which caused or contributed to a continuing **headache** that the plaintiff suffered from up to the date of trial. The second injury was a **whiplash injury to the neck** which the judge categorised as a **serious** whiplash. The plaintiff also suffered from **dizzy spells** which, it was accepted, on the basis of a neuro-otological report, reflected a **dysfunction** of the vestibular mechanism sustained during the head injury and exacerbated by features of **post-traumatic stress disorder** where the plaintiff had a past history of underlying worries and depression. Although he had been actively seeking alternative employment, he had at the date of trial been **unable to find any alternative employment**, and the judge took the view that in the present economic climate the plaintiff's prospects were bleak. The above award comprised £10,000 for pain, suffering and loss of amenity, special damages £6,535·31, future loss of earnings £72,734·48 being a multiplier of seven and a multiplicand of £10,390·64, loss of pension £6,478·45 and interest of general and special damages £1,149·96. *Loughran v London Buses Ltd* (11 March 1993, unreported) (Clerkenwell County Court: Judge Owen) (Mr Robert Glancy, Messrs Pattinson & Brewer, Solicitors, for the plaintiff; Mr Cairns, Mr I E King, Solicitor, for the defendant) (Kindly submitted for publication by Pattinson & Brewer, Solicitors, London).

Total damages: **£42,631·99**. Plaintiff, male aged 33 at date of injury in September 1989, was involved in a car accident in which he was a passenger and was being driven by the defendant. On admission to hospital plaintiff complained of neck pain, and it was confirmed that his principle injury was a **fracture** at C7/T1 of the **cervical spine** for which **postural fixation** was carried out in June 1989. The major consequences of this were **substantial impairment of mobility of neck** and **diminution of the flexion of the fingers and thumb** of the right hand and the right wrist. There was some gradual improvement during 1989. Three medical reports were made and all concluded that plaintiff's **injury would cause further problems** in the future. Also it could cause plaintiff to suffer from a **depressive illness** as his injuries had changed his lifestyle and reduced his quality of life quite considerably. Upon leaving hospital, plaintiff went to live with his parent who had to look after him and assist him in his day-to-day habits, before returning to his own home in Plymouth. At the time of the accident the plaintiff was employed at the Land Registry in Plymouth as an Executive Officer where he had been employed for 16 years. At first he returned to part time work but by September 1990 he had resumed full time work. As the plaintiff's work is spent 95 per cent of the time at a desk, it means that his work is physically demanding and he frequently has to leave his desk in order to ease the ache in his neck and back which begin within an hour of commencing work and makes concentration difficult. In addition to the pain in his back the plaintiff's work is also impeded by the wasting and weakness in his right hand. He will be unable to take part in the new computer operative skills being introduced at his place of employment. Such a disadvantage could have serious implications for the plaintiff's future employment at the Land Registry. Also, if the plaintiff were to lose his present employment, he would find it extremely difficult and probably impossible to find any other suitable alternative employment. Before the accident the plaintiff was a very active member of the Civil Service Sports Club and was particularly keen on football, cricket, badminton, tennis and snooker. He can no longer pursue any of these sports. Likewise he used to be an enthusiastic walker and now is unable to participate in that. His other interests included DIY and home maintenance which he will no longer be able to do. Since the accident the plaintiff's social life has deteriorated, partly because he cannot participate in spontaneous suggestions for social evenings, and also at the end of the day he is too tired and in too much pain. Also, he is extremely self conscious of his change of posture which, for example, has deterred him from swimming at a beach or at public swimming baths. Plaintiff is aware of his change of posture and suffers embarrassment because of it and because of his lack of dexterity in the right hand. The above award comprised £21,000 general damages (taking into account all of the above factors and especially the pain which plaintiff has experienced and will continue to experience, and the disabling wasting of the right hand); £6,631·99 special damages; and a *Smith v Manchester* award of £15,000. *Willis v Reeby* (21 September 1993, unreported) (Plymouth County Court: Judge Previte QC) (Kindly submitted for publication by Bond Pearce, Solicitors, Plymouth). *Smith v Manchester Corpn* (1974) 118 SJ 597, CA applied.

Total damages: **£16,017·68**. Plaintiff, female aged 37 at time of injury, suffered a **whiplash** injury in a road traffic collision. She sustained a **soft tissue injury** to her neck and was referred to the accident and emergency department and placed in a **cervical collar**. Two days later the plaintiff attended a horse trials meeting whilst still in her collar, and had to keep her neck elevated whilst walking. Because of this she **lost her footing and fell**, sustaining a **fracture to her left ankle**. The leg was **plastered** from the toes to below the knee. The medical evidence was agreed to the extent of showing that the plaintiff would **not be fit again** for her previous activity of horseriding for **some three years** from the accident date. Plaintiff was a keen horsewoman who had previously had her horse in half livery but had to place the horse in full livery as a result of the accident. She recovered special damages for the extra costs of the livery from the date of the accident to the anticipated date when she would be fit again to take up the care of her horse. The above award comprised £7,375 general damages; £136·18 interest on damages; £4,080 special damages; £382·50 interest on special damages; and £4,044 future loss. *Baker v Keshwala* (14 May 1993, unreported) (Watford County Court: Recorder Lloyd) (Mr Simon Michael for the plaintiff; Mr Tan for the defendant) (Kindly submitted for publication by Peter William Keer-Keer, Solicitor, Hemel Hempstead).

Total damages: **£15,944·48**. Plaintiff, female aged 65 at date of accident and 67 at date of trial, was involved in a road traffic accident as a result of which she suffered a **whiplash injury to her neck** and **subsequent psychiatric damage**. She was taken to hospital and discharged two hours later, having been given some pain killers. She started to develop **severe pain in her head and neck** and a feeling of numbness over the left side of her face with tingling in the left arm and the little and ring fingers of her left hand. She was **x-rayed and a cervical collar was supplied** which she wore in bed and whenever she was in one position for any length of time. For the next three months she underwent physiotherapy. A year later she underwent **manipulation of her cervical spine under anaesthetic** and a further course of physiotherapy for another month. Prior to the accident the plaintiff was relatively **physically active**. She frequently went swimming and walking. These activities ceased almost completely until the manipulation, after which she resumed her physical activities fully. She suffers **residual discomfort in the neck posteriorly** on the right hand side, it is very intermittent and **not a major limitation or disability** in either domestic or leisure activities. The need for further treatment remains a possibility, however **progressive deterioration is not expected**. The plaintiff also experienced a **post-concussional state for four months** following the collision, during which time she was very anxious, depressed, irritable, emotional and forgetful. She remains anxious about and tries to avoid travelling and experiences intrusive thoughts about the collision. It is hoped that these **post-traumatic stress disorder symptoms** would respond to emotional support, however it was clear that it was by no means sure that the plaintiff would fully recover her previous "sunny" personality. The above award comprised £9,000 for pain, suffering and loss of amenity; £6,000 in respect of the post-traumatic stress disorder; and £944·48 for special damages. *Holland v Wood* (2 July 1993, unreported) (Torquay County Court: District Judge Meredith) (Graham Thrussell for the plaintiff; Bevan Ashford for the defendant) (Kindly submitted for publication by Graham Thrussell, Barrister).

Total damages: **£11,718·50**. Plaintiff, male part-time filling station attendant aged 68 at time of accident, suffered a **whiplash injury** when a car drove into the rear of his own stationary car at speed in December 1990. Plaintiff experienced **immediate pain** in the **neck**, taken to hospital where he was given a **cervical collar** and discharged with **pain killers**. The **pain and stiffness** grew worse overnight, mainly around the **right hand side and the base of the neck**. Pain also radiated out to the **right shoulder**, and plaintiff also suffered from **headaches**. The **pain** in the neck and shoulder and the **headaches persisted** right up until the trial; the symptoms caused problems virtually every day although some days were worse than others. Plaintiff still took **pain killers every day**, and his **sleep** was sometimes **disturbed**. There had been a **marked improvement** after seven sessions of **physiotherapy** in the summer of 1991, however in the months after the course the **symptoms returned**. At the time of the trial the plaintiff was in the middle of a second course of physiotherapy. He **wore his collar** for most of the first year, thereafter he used it occasionally. Plaintiff had **never returned to work**. The judge found that he would probably have worked for a further 18 months after his accident. Plaintiff had been a keen fisherman and virtually "lived on the river". He had tried **unsuccessfully** to return to fishing. He suffered from a **pre-existing** cervical spondylosis and a co-incidental abnormality in the cervical spine (fusion of the neural arches at C2/3). Both were **symptom-free before the accident**. The accident had **not aggravated** either pre-existing condition nor led to any greater restriction in movement. The accident had caused the previously asymptomatic conditions to **become painful some five years** before they would otherwise have done. The **symptoms suffered would never abate** but would after this period become more related to the pre-existing condition than to the accident. He was without his car for 20 weeks and had to take the bus into town during this time. The above award comprised £4,000 general damages for pain, suffering and loss of amenity; £7,018·50 special damages, and £700 for loss of use of car. *Edwards v GKN Chep Ltd* (7 June 1993, unreported) (Coventry County Court: Judge Harrison-Hall) (Kindly submitted for publication by Edward Pepperall, Barrister).

Total damages: **£10,500**. Plaintiff, male police officer aged 22 at date of accident and 24 at date of trial, was sitting in a stationary police car when it was hit by the defendant vehicle. Plaintiff suffered **moderate severe hyperextension whiplash injury to his cervical spine**. Off work **two months**, wore a **hard collar** only at night for **one month**. Severe neck pain gradually subsided but even after returning to work he **experienced severe discomfort**. At date of trial the neck pain had improved and had changed to **intermittent pain of varying degrees**. He may go a week without pain and spend another week continuously in pain. In addition, plaintiff also **developed headaches** which were decreasing in frequency at trial date. Plaintiff was **likely to suffer cervical spondylosis** in about ten year's time. Now more **vulnerable to neck injury** which would probably make him **unfit for duty** in the short-term and may in the long term **affect his employability**. The above award comprised general damages for pain, suffering and loss of amenity £6,5000, and a *Smith v Manchester* award of £4,000. *Nelson v Ellis* (8 June 1993, unreported) (Clerkenwell County Court: Judge Marr-Johnson) (Kindly submitted for publication by Russell Jones & Walker, Solicitors, London). *Smith v Manchester Corpn* (1974) 118 SJ 597, CA applied.

Total damages: **£8,000**. Plaintiff, female aged 72 at time of accident in January 1992, suffered a **whiplash injury** in a road traffic accident (rear end collision). **Significant pain and stiffness** in early stages, prescribed **painkillers, cervical collar** and **physiotherapy**. At date of examination in June 1992, **extension rotation** and **lateral flexion** of cervical spine **reduced by 50** per cent and **flexion** by **25 per cent**. All movements **painful**. Occasional **severe episodes of pain** radiating down left arm. **Long term symptoms** of aching and **restriction of movement** expected. Long standing disc degeneration **no bearing** on current symptoms. At date of hearing **no significant improvement**. Pre-accident activities of voluntary helper at local hospital, gardening, housework and so on **severely curtailed**. The above award was for pain, suffering and loss of amenity. *Farmborough v Davies* (12 February 1993, unreported) (Trowbridge County Court: Assistant Recorder Fullthorpe) (Messrs Bevan Ashford for the plaintiff; Messrs Fladgate Fielder for the defendant) (Kindly submitted for publication by Bevan Ashford, Solicitors, Bristol).

Total damages: **£7,000**. Plaintiff, female aged 53 at date of accident and 56 at time of trial, sustained a **mild to moderate whiplash injury**. She was advised to wear a **collar** for 48 hours and thereafter gradually decrease its use. Plaintiff experienced an improvement over a **three month** period, however **no further great improvement** after this time. At the date of the trial the plaintiff was still suffering from **discomfort** to the **neck and left trapezius**. There was evidence that this could return to normal, but this was **optimistic** and she may experience **episodic periods of pain**. The plaintiff also suffered from **depression** falling short of clinical depression which was due to an **irrational grief reaction** due to the loss of her car. However, this was not to be under valued. Accordingly the plaintiff was awarded the above amount for general damages. *Calvert v Greenfield* (9 March 1993, unreported) (Watford County Court: Judge Green) (Simon Livesey, Messrs Shoosmiths & Harrison for the plaintiff) (Kindly submitted for publication by Shoosmiths & Harrison, Solicitors, Reading).

Total damages: £6,810. Four plaintiffs, three of whom were university students in their early twenties at the time of accident in May 1991, were involved in a **road traffic accident**. First plaintiff was the owner of the car, which was **written off** in the accident, and was awarded 26 weeks at £60 per week for loss of use of the car and inconvenience. Second plaintiff, driver of the car, sustained a **whiplash injury**. Pain in neck for **four months** at most, during which time he could not play squash. On assessment of damages hearing **no symptoms remained**. Third plaintiff sustained **whiplash** injury and wore **neck collar** for about a week. Symptoms cleared up within another **two months**, during which time plaintiff experienced **discomfort** in neck. Fourth plaintiff sustained **whiplash** injury, and his injuries cleared up within **four months**. Could not play badminton during that period. First, second and third plaintiffs' injuries of **roughly equal severity**. The above award comprised £1,560 for first plaintiff's loss of use of car and inconvenience; and three awards of £1,750 general damages for pain, suffering and loss of amenity for second, third and fourth plaintiff. *Nakrani, Nakrani, Mandavia, Bajaj v Gajjar* (26 April 1993, unreported) (Reading County Court: District Judge Lamden) (Kindly submitted for publication by Stewart Room, Barrister).

Total damages: £5,250. Plaintiff, male aged 18 at time of accident in April 1991 and 21 at time of trial, sustained **whiplash injury** to **neck** and **lower thoracic spine**, together with **bruising** to knees, chest and face. Plaintiff had previously sustained whiplash to neck and upper thoracic spine in road accident in 1988. Undergoing treatment for continuing pain from that injury at time of accident in 1991 which aggravated the neck symptoms and caused pain in lower thoracic spine. Those symptoms continued and were continuing at trial, and consisted of intermittent **pain and crepitus in the neck**, and **pain** in the **lower thoracic and lumbar spine**, made worse by sitting for long periods, driving, lifting and repeated bending. Interfered with enjoyment of squash. Stretching and heavy breathing caused pain in the chest. Recovery anticipated but no improvement in symptoms between accident and trial. Recovery period delayed by imposition of injury on previously injured neck. Case said to fall at lower end of category (d) in Judicial Guidelines. The above award was made for general damages. *Norrington v Struth* (24 November 1993, unreported) (Colchester & Clacton County Court: Judge Bradbury) (Kindly submitted for publication by John Brooke-Smith, Barrister).

Scotland
Total damages: £4,446·18. Plaintiff, male aged 42 and employed as a van salesman at time of accident in July 1990, was injured when a cage containing **boxes of fruit and vegetables** fell from the tailgate of a lorry while being unloaded and **struck the plaintiff on the side of the head and neck**. He was rendered **unconscious** and taken to hospital. He suffered **severe pain** in his **head and neck**, no bones were found to have been fractured, and he was discharged from hospital the same day. He was advised to take **painkillers** and not to drive for 48 hours. The pain in his neck **continued** so that he could **not freely rotate his head** to the right **nor bend it forward**. He was **unable to sleep** on his left side because of the pain in his neck, and even when sleeping on his right side, was woken two to three times during the night because of the pain. Plaintiff underwent **physiotherapy**, was prescribed **analgesic** and **anti-inflammatory drugs**, and was **off work for some seven weeks**. Plaintiff had physiotherapy for five weeks and wore a surgical collar during the daytime. Plaintiff returned to work in September 1990 and managed to resume his work satisfactorily. The pain was less by the time he returned to work and had reduced to a **dull ache** some six months after the accident. He was unable to manage his hobbies of golf and bowls for some eight months after the accident. A degree of **muscle spasm** was still present in July 1991 and was diagnosed as continuing effects of a soft tissue injury. By January 1993 the plaintiff was still suffering from a constant dull ache, giving rise to some **restriction of free movement** in turning his head to the right, difficulty in sleeping, particularly on the left side, and plaintiff was taking painkillers three to four times a week. Plaintiff's symptoms had improved and were expected to continue to do so, if slowly. His condition was expected to settle in time, but he would probably continue to suffer minor discomfort which would not cause him much trouble. The above award included £3,000 general damages. *Murphy v MRS (Distribution) Ltd (note)* 1993 SLT 786 (Outer House).

Total damages: £4,384·50. Plaintiff, female aged 21 at time of accident and 23 at date of trial, was involved in a collision when her stationary vehicle was waiting to turn right and was struck from behind, causing a **moderately severe whiplash injury**. Plaintiff suffered **headaches and stiffness and pain in her neck** within 24 hours of the accident and was treated with **pain killers**. Because of **continuing symptoms** two and a half weeks later, she sought help from a local hospital and was issued with a soft cervical collar. X-rays showed a **severe muscle spasm**. Although by two months after the accident 90 per cent of the symptoms had improved, **damage to the rhomoidis major and minor muscles to her spine** took a further six months before there was any significant degree of improvement and the area was still tender a year later. Plaintiff was still not symptom-free by the time of trial. At the time of the accident the plaintiff was a drama student and there was some evidence that the final degree classification had been affected by the inability to take part in practical exercises, such as dance, stage fighting etc, as a result of the injury. The above award comprised £3,500 general damages; £775·50 special damages and £109 interest. *Santi v Rothesay* (7 December 1993, unreported) (Barnet County Court: Judge Green QC) (Kindly submitted for publication by Martin Smith & Co, Solicitors, Borehamwood).

Total damages: **£4,008.** Plaintiff, male engineer aged 25 at time of accident in January 1990, sustained a **whiplash injury to his cervical spine** in a road traffic accident. **Off work** for one week, wore a **collar for two weeks**, suffered **constant pain between shoulder blades** for four weeks, and **prolonged headaches** for two months. Since then, **intermittent burning sensation** and **aching between shoulder blades**, aggravated by driving, using visual display unit and strenuous physical activity. **Alleviated by anti-inflammatory pills.** Hobbies of cycling and motor repairs affected, but not seriously so. Symptoms **still lingering** by date of trial. Cervical spine **remains vulnerable** and injury may contribute to very late development of cervical spine degeneration. The above award comprised £4,000 general damages and £8 agreed special interest. *Deeley v Western National Ltd* (4 June 1993, unreported) (Aldershot & Farnham County Court: Judge Lauriston QC) (Kindly submitted for publication by Philip Kolvin, Barrister).

Total damages: **£3,712·23.** Plaintiff, male aged 20 at time of accident, sustained **flexion hypertension injury to cervical spine, jarring and jolting of lumbar spine** and **emotional distress** when involved in a road traffic accident. **Fully recovered** within five months. Plaintiff was a family man working shifts, the car was **written off** in the accident and plaintiff could not afford to repair it until he received money from third party's insurers after the accident. The above award included general damages for pain, suffering and loss of amenity at £1,250, and £750 (being ten weeks at £75) for loss of use of car. *Callaway v Charles* (24 June 1993, unreported) (Birkenhead County Court: Judge Crowe QC) (Kindly submitted for publication by Andrew Menary, Barrister).

Total damages: **£3,500.** Plaintiff, female aged 38 at date of accident and 39 at time of assessment, was a passenger in a vehicle travelling along a major road when defendant turned right across her path. Plaintiff suffered **pain to neck, back** and **suffered from headaches**. At date of assessment plaintiff was **still suffering from pain in neck and back**, and from headaches two or three times a week, these being described as due to **referred pain** from her neck. **Requires pain killers daily.** Able to continue with domestic chores although slower than normal, hobby of knitting restricted since accident, and apprehensive when driving. Plaintiff **recovering slowly** and full recovery is anticipated two years from date of accident. The above award was for general damages. *Lowe v Kapadia* (18 August 1993, unreported) (Bury County Court: District Judge Duerdon) (Kindly submitted for publication by Mendelsons, Solicitors, Manchester).

Total damages: **£3,017·32.** Plaintiff, male aged 26 at time of accident and 27 at date of assessment, sustained a **whiplash injury, jarred knee** and **emotional distress** when he was involved in an accident. Experienced whiplash symptoms for approximately **five months** after the accident, after which he was **fully recovered** apart from occasional awareness of **muscle spasm** in region of thoracic spine which persisted a little longer. The above award included £1,200 general damages for pain and suffering. *Brown v Walker* (24 June 1993, unreported) (Birkenhead County Court: Judge Crowe QC) (Kindly submitted for publication by Andrew Menary, Barrister).

Total damages: **£2,807·57.** Plaintiff, female office worker aged 23 at time of accident and 25 at date of trial, was involved in a **road traffic accident** in which her car was struck broadside by another. Plaintiff **suffered a soft tissue injury to the muscles and ligaments of her neck and back**. She was initially treated at hospital on the day of the accident and prescribed a **cervical collar** which she **wore continuously** for approximately two weeks and occasionally when driven by car, and at night for three further weeks. Plaintiff was also **prescribed analgesics for pain** which was initially considerable but which gradually lessened, ceasing altogether after approximately six weeks. Two days after the accident plaintiff fainted on her way to her only **physiotherapy** appointment, where she was treated by manipulation. She required **two days off work**, upon returning there was some **difficulty in looking down at** her computer screen for several weeks. Plaintiff had **trouble driving comfortably** for six to eight weeks and avoided doing so. A complete recovery appeared to have been achieved thereafter. The above award comprised general damages £1,250 and special damages £1,557·57. *Lyon v Chambers* (1 November 1993, unreported) (Mayor's and City of London County Court: Judge Byrt QC) (Kindly submitted for publication by James R Candlin, Barrister). *Ball v Genge* [1992] CLY 1757 cited in judgment with approval.

Total damages: **£2,592·64.** Plaintiff, female aged 31 at time of accident and 32 at date of assessment, sustained **whiplash injury,** a **blow to the posterior aspect of the skull, jarring to right calf** and **emotional distress.** Fully recovered in just over one year, except **very occasional twinges** in neck when tired. The above award included £2,000 general damages for pain and suffering. *Rhodes v James* (24 June 1993, unreported) (Birkenhead County Court: Judge Crowe QC) (Kindly submitted for publication by Andrew Menary, Barrister).

Total damages: **£2,044·87.** Plaintiff, female aged 44 at time of accident and 45 at date of trial, was **driver of a vehicle which collided** with car driven by the defendant, which was emerging from blind car-park entrance on her left. Plaintiff **shaken** by the accident. Next day she **experienced pains to back of neck and felt sick.** Symptoms persisted for **two weeks.** For the first week the plaintiff, a supply teacher, mostly stayed at home and so unable to utilise her half term. Second week she returned to work, thus no 'time off'. Plaintiff **did not seek medical attention, apprehensive** about the litigation. The above award included £500 for pain, suffering and loss of amenity. *Shipley v Street* (28 October 1993, unreported) (Bristol County Court: District Judge Stuart-Brown) (Jonathan Clarke, Messrs Judge & Priestly for the plaintiff; Julian Ironside, Messrs Clarke Wilmott & Clarke for the defendant) (Kindly submitted for publication by Jonathan Clarke, Barrister).

Total damages: **£1,558·23.** Plaintiff, male aged 18 at date of accident, was injured in a road traffic accident. Plaintiff was **not rendered unconscious,** was taken to hospital, but discharged on the same day. He had suffered a **whiplash** injury of his **cervical spine,** for which he was prescribed a **soft collar,** and **analgesics.** He had also sustained **non specific soft tissue injuries** of his **right foot** (from violent contact with the car brake) and his **chest** (from the seat-belt). He was prescribed a tubigrip bandage for his knee, and was off work for **three weeks.** For this period he wore the cervical collar all the time. He had **fairly severe pain** in his neck for **three weeks,** after which it settled. Six months after the accident he still had some **discomfort** in the **base of his neck** and the **upper part of his back** after sitting on a stool for long periods (as he had to do for his work) or when lying in bed. He had **no further pain** in his chest or his right knee **after three months** had elapsed. The **pain in his right foot** persisted for about **12 months,** and caused the plaintiff to absent himself from the Duke of Edinburgh's Award Scheme, which was his **principal source of recreation.** He missed 12 or 14 weekends of out door activities as a result, and was **frustrated** by this. Clinical examination of the foot six months after the accident showed little except **uncomfortable plantar flexion** and **tenderness and slight thickening** over the **proximal joint** of the second toe. The plaintiff had **recovered completely** two years after the accident. No long term sequelae were expected. The above award comprised £1,500 for pain, suffering and loss of amenity, and special damages of £58·23. *Gregory v Hale (t/a Hale Construction)* (9 July 1993, unreported) (Leeds County Court: Judge Hoffmann) (William Hanbury, Messrs Lupton Fawcett & Co for the plaintiff; Charles Foster, Messrs Firth Lindsay & Co for the defendant) (Kindly submitted for publication by Charles Foster, Barrister).

Total damages: **£1,500.** Plaintiff, female in her mid twenties at time of accident, sustained a **whiplash** injury in a **road traffic accident.** She attended hospital later in the day and was given a **cervical collar** to wear. Wore collar for **two weeks** and took **pain killers every day** for two weeks. Throughout that period she **experienced aches** in **neck** and **discomfort** when sitting at VDU at work. **No time off work.** Vast majority of symptoms **resolved** within **two weeks.** A few weeks before assessment of damages (hearing 15 months after accident), plaintiff felt a "**twinge**" in her neck which lasted for a **few seconds.** The above award was general damages for pain, suffering and loss of amenity. *Walsh v Clarke* (16 March 1993, unreported) (Kingston upon Thames County Court: District Judge Coni) (Kindly submitted for publication by Stewart Room, Barrister).

Total damages: **£200.** Plaintiff, male aged 39 at time of injury, sustained a **whiplash** injury to his **neck** when involved in a road traffic accident. Plaintiff **did not receive any medical treatment.** Plaintiff was **not employed** at the time of accident, and **injury did not impinge** upon his lifestyle at all. Plaintiff **fully recovered** within two days. The above award reflects the bare minimum for pain, suffering and loss of amenity. *Galtrees v Patten* (25 May 1993, unreported) (Birkenhead County Court: District Judge McCullagh) (Kindly submitted for publication by Tim Grover, Barrister).

942   *Neck and shoulder*

Total damages: £**100,000**. Plaintiff, male aged 52 at time of injury in November 1989, is a practising dentist with his own practice specialising in orthodontics. While sitting in his motor vehicle waiting to turn right, he was **struck from behind** by the first defendant driving a lorry **in the course of his employment**. As a result the plaintiff sustained **whiplash** injuries to his neck; a **jarring** injury to his left shoulder; **bruising** to his right knee and a degree of **shock**. The plaintiff has a previous history of back problems which had **largely stabilised** at the date of the accident. The plaintiff was **unable to practise** orthodontics for four months being forced to employ locums. Upon his return to work the plaintiff was **unable to maintain a work rate** equal to his pre-accident work rate and remained so to the date of trial, although to a lesser degree. A settlement was reached immediately prior to the trial of this action, the defendants' insurers agreeing to pay the plaintiff a gross sum of £100,000. This award comprised of £8,000 for general damages; £3,000 for direct expenditure; £12,000 for future loss of earnings; and £77,000 for past loss of earnings including interest. *Huston v Homewood and Mayne Nickless Finance plc* (11 January 1993, unreported) (Queen's Bench Division: Sir Gervase Sheldon) (Messrs Douglas for the plaintiff; Messrs Hall & Clark for the defendants) (Kindly submitted for publication by Messrs Douglas, Solicitors, Redhill).

Total damages: £**5,302**. Plaintiff, female aged 68 at time of accident and 70 at date of trial, wrenched her neck as a result of a **whiplash injury**. Plaintiff had **pain in her neck and shoulder**, and hoped the pain would go away, but it actually worsened. At the time of trial she experienced **pain on the right side of her neck radiating on to the shoulder and up her arm** which was very painful. Plaintiff's **sleep was often interrupted**, various household tasks such as ironing and hoovering took much longer. **Pain radiated** on to the back of the **right side of her head** from time to time. She was **terrified in the car** and is somewhat of a nuisance to the driver. She **cannot carry laden shopping bags** and has **not ridden her bicycle** since the accident. Plaintiff is **nervous and irritable**. X-rays indicated that the plaintiff had asymptomatic cervical spondylosis. The accident had **precipitated the cervical spondylitic symptoms** which would likely be **present for the rest of her life**. Prior to the accident the plaintiff had never suffered any neck or back trouble. It was considered that there had been an **acceleration of spondylitic symptoms of three to four years**. The above award comprised £5,250 general damages and £52 interest. *Young v Costello* (2 November 1993, unreported) (Oldham County Court: District Judge Needham) (Nigel Poole, Messrs Row & Cohen for the plaintiff; T J Willits, Messrs Moss Mooneram for the defendant) (Kindly submitted for publication by Rowe & Cohen, Solicitors, Cheshire).

Total damages: £**2,452·54**. The plaintiff, male aged 26 at time of injury and 29 and date of trial, was attacked by an unrestrained guard dog sitting next to its owner on the premises it guarded, while the plaintiff's friend chatted to the dog's owner during non-working hours. **No contributory negligence was found**. The injuries included **laceration to the left shoulder**, two **lacerations to the left forearm**, and two **lacerations to the left thigh**. The plaintiff made substantial recovery within two weeks. The scarring is **permanent** but does not trouble the plaintiff. The worst scar is on the left shoulder, the upper part of the **10cm scar** being **1cm broad** and **4cm long**. This injury has resulted in current aching of the shoulder at the end of a day's work as a polisher. The plaintiff is right-handed. The above award comprised £2,250 for pain, suffering and loss of amenity, £155·80 for special damages, and £46·74 for interest at 15 per cent over two years. *Foster v Appleton* (14 January 1993, unreported) (Oldham County Court: Judge Caulfield) (Kindly submitted for publication by John Nivison & Co, Solicitors, Stockport).

943   *Shoulder*

Total damages: £**22,300**. Plaintiff, female dancer aged 37 at date of accident in December 1987 and 43 at trial, was performing on rollerskates in Japan when another performer negligently collided into her, knocking her over on stage. Plaintiff struck her (dominant) **right shoulder** forcibly on the ground when she fell. She underwent **prolonged physiotherapy, arthroscopy** and had **pain killing injections** for pain in shoulder. Unable to perform in the show for 2–3

287

weeks due to **severe pain**, although continued in supervisory (non-dancing) duties after a few days. Right **arm in sling for three weeks**. Plaintiff then resumed dancing in performances when the production moved to Australia in mid-January 1988 until about May 1988, but only in alternate performances and despite suffering **intense pain and discomfort**. Plaintiff underwent further physiotherapy, osteopathy and similar treatment. From May 1988 to December 1988 only able to work as dance teacher and **unable to perform as dancer**. Unable to carry out activities such as hoovering, or lifting weights such as kettle or dressing herself, because of **problems in reaching behind her back**. Sexual relations adversely affected. Plaintiff suffered **constant pain** originating in the right shoulder and the pain was "pulling her down". Plaintiff returned to England in 1989 where she continued to suffer from these symptoms and was only able to carry out stylist work and not work properly as a dancer or assistant choreographer. She attended many kinds of alternative therapists for pain relief. Eventually she was referred to orthopaedic surgeon who diagnosed a **fracture of the front of the right acromion** and a **subluxation of the acromio-clavicular joint**. Plaintiff underwent yet further physiotherapy which did not relieve symptoms. In May 1991 a **decompression acromioplasty operation** was carried out which **relieved many of the symptoms**. She was left with **minor irritating symptoms** such as **discomfort** when reaching across her body with her right arm, **inability to sleep on her right side**, **aching** in the right shoulder **occasionally radiating to the neck**, all causing discomfort when performing household activities such as ironing and hoovering, and driving a car. Plaintiff was at the point in her career at the time of the injury when she was just making the transition from dancer to assistant choreographer, and the award of special damages reflected her **inability to work** as such until some six months after the operation in May 1991. The above award comprised £9,000 for general damages; special damages of £13,000 for loss of earnings, and £300 for physiotherapy fees. *Bryg v Fuji Television Network Inc* (2 June 1993, unreported) (Central London County Court: Judge Smith QC) (Howard Lederman and Christopher Donnison, Messrs Douglas-Mann & Co for the plaintiff) (Kindly submitted for publication by Howard Lederman, Barrister).

Total damages: **£15,650·18**. Plaintiff, male aged 41 at time of accident, was a bus driver who was travelling home from work on his **motor cycle** when it skidded, due to the presence of **builders' sand on the road** which had been left uncovered, **unlit** and **without warning signs**. This had been spread across a third of the carriageway. Plaintiff was thrown from his motor cycle and **lost consciousness** for a few minutes. He was **shocked** and **dazed**, the police took him home, he then noticed his right shoulder to be **very painful and stiff**. The next day he attended the casualty department where he was x-rayed, and was told that he had suffered a **fracture** of his right **clavicle** and a **soft tissue injury** to his right shoulder. His arm was placed in a sling and he was prevented from working for **two months**. The medical report recorded that "right shoulder **abduction** was **limited** to 150 degrees, and **extension** and **internal rotation** was limited to **two-thirds** of normal range, that there was a **lump** over the **clavicle** on the right side, but **no tenderness**". Examination of x-rays showed a fracture of the shaft of the clavicle, which had healed well, but with the usual deformity of a **callous formation**. The doctor agreed that the lack of movement in the shoulder had **improved** when he was examined just before the trial and abduction was now practically full, but there was some **crepitus**, particularly in the region of the acromio-clavicula joint and there was also some limitation of movement with **discomfort** when he tried to move his hand behind his back. Plaintiff had residual **stiffness** in his right shoulder. The doctor assessed his loss of function at 20 per cent in total, which was a **permanent disability** resulting from the fracture to the clavicle. The doctor accepted that the plaintiff would **not be able to drive buses again** because of this disability, and plaintiff had also **given up his hobby** of playing golf. Since the plaintiff had been promoted to Inspector and then Bus Controller he no longer had to drive buses. The judge accepted evidence as to the insecurity of employment with London Buses with privatisation and the compulsory tendering of routes, and awarded damages for his handicap on the open labour market. The above award comprised £6,500 for general damages; £1,744·40 special damages; damages for handicap on the open labour market (being one-third of the plaintiff's net salary) £6,500; interest on general damages £388·05; and interest on special damages £517·73. *Creedon v Rainor* (24 March 1993, unreported) (Brentford County Court: Judge Edwards) (Mr Matthias Kelly, Messrs Pattinson & Brewer for the plaintiff) (Kindly submitted for publication by Paul M Statham, Pattinson & Brewer, Solicitors, London).

Total damages: **£4,000**. Applicant, male shop manager aged 61, **slipped when about to apprehend a suspected shoplifter**, said to be taking an exceptional risk. He **suffered undisplaced fracture to neck of right humerus** with associated **fracture to greater**

tuberosity. Collar and cuff worn for **three weeks**, physiotherapy for **three months**. Absent from work for **six weeks**. One year after incident applicant complained of **pain when sleeping on his right side** and of an **ache if he did not exercise**. There was **slight restriction of internal and external rotation** though it was said that the function of the shoulder was satisfactory and that there would be further improvement over the next twelve months. The above award was made for general damages. *Criminal Injuries Compensation Board, Leicester* (15 October 1993, unreported) (Kindly submitted for publication by Union of Shop, Distributive and Allied Workers, Manchester).

Total damages: £3,533·69. Plaintiff, male police officer aged 30 at time of accident in August 1992, sustained **strain to left shoulder, spraining of neck** and **contusional injury** to right lower leg when involved in a road traffic accident. Plaintiff wore a **cervical collar for several days** and took **analgesics**. Plaintiff had seven sessions of **physiotherapy** over a period of three to four weeks. Off work for seven weeks and on returning to work was given light duties for four weeks. The **symptoms** in the neck and lower limb **settled** after a couple of weeks and plaintiff **continued to suffer pain** in his left shoulder which prevented him from his hobby of weight lifting for seven months and at the time of the assessment of damages the plaintiff was **still unable to lift** the heavier weights which he had been able to lift prior to the accident. By the time of the assessment of damages hearing, the plaintiff was **still experiencing aching** in the left shoulder after physical exercise. The prognosis was that the current aches and pains in the left shoulder joint **would resolve over the next three months** and a full recovery was to be expected. The above award comprised £3,000 general damages and £533·69 special damages plus interest. *Berry v Roe* (10 September 1993, unreported) (Bromley County Court: Judge Conningsby QC) (Kindly submitted for publication by Clarkson Wright & James, Solicitors, Orpington).

BACK, CHEST AND ABDOMEN

944 *Trunk*

Total damages: £1,850. Applicant, male police officer aged 34 at date of the incident and 36 at time of hearing, suffered a **fracture** of the 12th rib when he **fell in the pursuit of a suspect**. In **considerable pain for first four weeks** and was **off work** for a total of **eight weeks**. At date of hearing still experienced **occasional dull ache** at the site of the injury after strenuous exercise. **Residual symptoms may not resolve**. The above award was made for general damages. *Criminal Injuries Compensation Board, Liverpool* (25 August 1993, unreported) (Kindly submitted for publication by Tim Grover, Barrister).

945 *Stomach*

Total damages: £1,250. Appellant, male **police officer**, was **bitten by a dog** during the hot pursuit of a criminal. *Held*, whilst another officer held back and the appellant flung aside a dog which was **gripping him by the stomach** and **continued with a chase** only to be bitten in the **buttocks**, he was taking an exceptional risk within the Criminal Injuries Compensation Scheme. The appellant eventually arrested the criminal. **Puncture wounds** to the stomach and buttocks, on painkillers for two days, **disturbed sleep** pattern for one week and general upset thereafter. *Criminal Injuries Compensation Board* (1 February 1993, unreported) (Kindly submitted for publication by Andrew McDonald, Barrister).

946 *Back*

Total damages: £28,070. The plaintiff, a male aged 39 at time of accident and 45 at date of trial, suffered an **injury to his back and chest** when a mock building fell on him whilst taking part in a police exercise in public order. After the accident he suffered a **sore back with bruising** to his chest and shoulders. The soreness of the back developed into an ache, which was concentrated in his left buttock. As time went on there was pain in the back of the leg which became worse and was present eventually in both legs. The plaintiff was employed driving a panda patrol car, and after the accident he **found sitting in the car very difficult** and had trouble using the clutch. He bought himself an automatic car for his own use. On the advice of his employers the plaintiff was referred to a surgeon who diagnosed that he had a **prolapsed intervertebral disc at the L5 S1 level**. Two manipulations under general anaesthetic were carried out but were unsuccessful. His condition continued to deteriorate and the disc was removed and the **two vertebrae were fused** using the **bone grafts from the left iliac crest**. The operation resulted in **some scars**. At the time of the trial the plaintiff was **still suffering**

pain. He finds **sleeping difficult,** is now unable to tend to his garden and has difficulty playing with his children. After the operation the plaintiff was off work for five months and on return to work he was **confined to light work in the office,** he was then put onto neighbourhood watch. His tenure for that work has now expired and he is unsure as to whether it will be renewed (he is at present still engaged in that work). The plaintiff has three years to run to the completion of his 30 years service, and there is a risk that he will not be able to complete that period. The above award comprised £17,000 general damages for pain and suffering; £50 special damages; £10,000 for future loss of earnings; £1,020 interest on damages. *Vickers v Chief Constable of West Midlands* (29 July 1993, unreported) (Queen's Bench Division, Birmingham: Tudor Evans J) (R Lewis for the plaintiff; A Khangure for the defendant).

Total damages: **£23,430.** Plaintiffs, male and female aged 48 and 45 at time of accident and aged 52 and 49 respectively at date of trial, sustained injuries when the car which they were driving **hit an open manhole cover** at 60 miles per hour. Male plaintiff sustained **soft tissue injury** with damage occurring to **ligaments and discs in low back.** Prior to accident plaintiff had asymptomatic degenerative changes in lumbar. Off work five weeks, has continued to **suffer pain and discomfort** in back. Affects him throughout the day, and plaintiff has to break off work and walk around from time to time as he has a sedentary job. **Any activity exacerbates back ache.** Plaintiff has learnt to live with stiffness and limitations. Female plaintiff sustained **likely crush fracture** at T12. **One year in extreme pain,** now continues to **suffer pain in lumbar** which is more or less **constant.** Pain is aggravated by standing for more than 20–30 minutes. **Symptoms unlikely to improve and may deteriorate.** No longer capable of previous employment as part-time hairdresser, but capable of light employment which does not involve repetitive lifting, bending or prolonged standing. The above award comprised £5,000 general damages, £500 for powered lawn mower and £1,500 for future assistance in the garden for male plaintiff; £12,000 general damages and £4,430 special damages for female plaintiff. *Mochan v Paterson Candy Holst Ltd* (29 October 1993, unreported) (Lincoln County Court: Judge Brunning) (Kindly submitted for publication by Simon Wheatley, Barrister).

Total damages: **£19,631·25.** Plaintiff, male aged 41 at date of accident in September 1986 and 48 at time of trial, was employed by the defendants as a HGV driver. He sustained **injury to lower back attempting to catch central heating radiator** weighing 112 pounds, which fell from the back of his lorry. **Acute symptoms lasted four weeks,** during which time plaintiff was in **very severe pain. Unable to return to work and dismissed** on grounds of ill health in June 1987. At trial there was **conflict of medical evidence** but judge found injury had caused **mild to moderate prolapsed intervertebral disc.** The accident **aggravated pre-existing injury** to back which was sustained in similar accident in 1981. Before accident only very occasional discomfort in back and plaintiff able to work normally. Judge held this accident had caused aggravation of pre-existing back condition for a period of **five years** during which time plaintiff had **endured severe spasmodic pain in the back with pain in left buttock and leg.** Plaintiff **unable to lift, carry or stand** for prolonged periods. Symptoms worse in cold or damp weather. Marked **restriction of movement** in lumbar spine with virtually **no forward flexion.** No formal treatment undertaken apart from use of a heat lamp and group therapy. Judge referred specifically to *Hamer v North West Water* and also *Sheil v Chamberlain* during the course of the judgement. The above award comprised £8,000 general damages for pain and suffering; £780 interest on general damages; £7,641·73 special damages; and £3,209·52 interest on special damages. *Maslin v Sankey Jonchu Ltd* (21 October 1993, unreported) (Blackpool County Court: Judge Appleton) (Timothy White, Messrs Dickson Child & Green for the plaintiff; Philip Butler, Messrs Peter Rickson & Co for the defendant) (Kindly submitted for publication by Timothy White, Barrister). *Hamer v North West Water* (22 September 1992, unreported) (1992 Abr para 907) and *Sheil v Chamberlain* (3 April 1991, unreported) [1991] CLY 1405 applied.

Total damages: **£14,229·30** (including interest). Plaintiff, male labourer aged 28 at date of accident and 32 at time of trial, was in a trench, the sides of which collapsed onto him **striking him on the right side of the head** and **right shoulder** forcing him down into a flexed position. Thereafter a heavy weight of **soil fell onto him burying him.** He sustained a **fractured sternum, injury to the back** (compression fracture of T9 with minor damage to the upper border of T12), and to the **neck** (minor twisting injury). Plaintiff an in-patient for four days. **Sternum painful** for about two months, then pain gradually eased off. A little **tenderness** after six months, though resolved soon after. **Neck uncomfortable and stiff** for two to three weeks, then **complete resolution. Discomfort in lumbosacral spine** which should resolve completely. Major problem was **continuing discomfort in the thoracic spine** due to compression fracture. Unable to work involving heavy lifting for about **nine months** after the accident. Improved to the level of discomfiture but **no further improvement**. Will have **permanent discomfiture aggravated** when working with heavy weights. Plaintiff **takes pain killers regularly**. The above award comprised £9,500 general damages and £3,418·69 special damages. *Hyland v George* (12 August 1993, unreported) (Liverpool County Court: District Judge Harris) (Kindly submitted for publication by Antonis Georges, Barrister).

Scotland
Total damages: **£12,000** (negligence not proved; opinion of court on assumption that plaintiff would have been entitled to damages for all problems arising out of alleged negligence). Plaintiff, aged 30 at time of incident, sustained **spinal injury during childbirth. Fracture through fourth sacral segment** leading to **nerve damage**. Branches from segment innervating pubo-rectalis muscle damaged, causing whole of pelvic floor gradually to descend as normal resting tone of muscle lost. Over time continuation of pubo-rectalis muscle in more relaxed position led to secondary stretching of pudendal nerve causing secondary pudendal neuropathy and deficient muscle tissue in external anal sphincter. Suffered severe pain and became demoralised. Continued severe pain opening bowels, difficulty controlling bowels and episodes of faecal incontinence. Regularly experienced faecal urgency. Court also gave opinion on basis that sacral fracture was culpable but did not give rise to plaintiff's problems; £1,500 adjudged on that basis. *Bradnock v Liston* 1993 SLT 554 (Outer House).

Total damages: **£9,000**. Plaintiff, female aged 36 at time of accident and 40 at date of trial, **slipped and fell** when a defective shower squirted scalding water on her, sustaining a **twisting injury to her back**. For 11 months plaintiff suffered **pain in her right knee, calf, in the coccyx and radiating into her buttock, with right-sided sciatica**. Lumbar radiculogram revealed a **large prolapsed intervertebral disc**. Eleven months after the accident plaintiff had an **operation** under general anaesthetic to **remove a sequestrated disc**. This left a six inch scar. The operation cured the sciatic pain, but at trial she still had **back pain** brought on by prolonged sitting and exertion, plus **intermittent pain in her leg and buttocks** from 'muscle spasm'. The prognosis was that this **pain would probably continue all her life**. Plaintiff had undergone **physiotherapy** from soon after the accident until three months after the operation, and she was still wearing a **protective corset** four years after the accident. Plaintiff also had a long-term very serious hearing problem, unrelated to the accident. The effect of this plus her injury was that she had been unemployed since the time of the accident (she had previously worked intermittently in various jobs, usually earning no more than £100 per week), and her social life was non-existent. The above award comprised £7,500 general damages; and £1,500 damages for handicap on the labour market. *Coonan v Rashid & Rashid* (7 October 1993, unreported) (Brentford County Court: Deputy District Judge Dowling) (Kindly submitted for publication by Charles Bourne, Barrister).

Total damages: **£6,050**. Plaintiff, male aged 25 at time of accident and 27 at date of assessment, was driving along main road when the defendant drove out of side road into collision with plaintiff's car. Plaintiff suffered from a **stiff and painful neck** for two weeks and **pain to lower back**. Plaintiff was unemployed at time of accident, and tried two jobs as warehouseman since then, but left both after two days **due to pain on lifting**. At date of trial he was unemployed and continued to complain of **pain in lower back** lasting for **two to three hours** in the morning, which could recur later in the day. Plaintiff still taking three **painkillers** a day. Prognosis was for **full recovery two years** from date of accident. Plaintiff's car was written off in the accident, and he had the use of his mother's car two or three times a week, other than that he had **no transport**. Unable to take children for outings and had to walk children to and from school. The above award comprised £4,000 general damages for pain, suffering and loss of amenity, and £2,050 for loss of use of car and inconvenience for 41 weeks (taking into account 4 weeks post assessment). *Mattinson v Ullah* (18 August 1993, unreported) (Bury County Court: District Judge Duerden) (Kindly submitted for publication by Mendelsons, Solicitors, Manchester).

Scotland
Total damages: **£5,000** (liability not proved; opinion of court given as to quantum). Plaintiff, nursing auxiliary aged 42 at time of accident, slipped and fell on recently washed floor during course of her employment. Suffered from **back pain** since accident which increased with passage of time. **Pain radiates into right leg** and causes **paraesthesiae in right foot**. Plaintiff had history of back pain after number of accidents at work. X-ray after accident in question showed **minor degenerative changes** in lumbar spine indicating probability that at time of

accident degenerative changes of lumbar spine present for some time prior thereto. Plaintiff suffered another accident nearly one year later in which she twisted her back as she went down. Forced to cease working as nursing auxiliary three months after latest accident and presently employed as home support worker on shorter hours and lower rate of pay. Latest accident exacerbated lesion caused by accident in question. Plaintiff's present condition also affected by past history. On balance of evidence, plaintiff would have been required to give up employment as nurse within two or three years after latest fall, even if she had not suffered accident in question. The above award comprised £2,500 for solatium to date of trial; £500 for future solatium; and £2,000 for future loss of earnings. *Young v Greater Glasgow Health Board* 1993 SLT 721n (Outer House).

Total damages: **£3,300.** Plaintiff, male gardener aged 30 at date of accident and 33 at time of trial, **slipped** on moss-covered ramp and **twisted** his back. Judge found that plaintiff had suffered some **structural injury** to the **lumbar spine**, probably some **damage** to the disc, and a **prolapse** to a disc (described by the judge as a minor kind of disc prolapse). Plaintiff was **off work for 11 weeks** and had some medication (ie pain killers and anti-inflammatory medication). Plaintiff had flare up in November 1991, ten months after the accident, and again in February 1993, when he had a further 11 weeks off work but absence on this occasion had a dual causation as there were unrelated neck pains. **Minor symptoms** of **discomfiture** continued in the back at the time of trial. Judge accepted that three or four years after the accident the plaintiff would be in the same position in relation to the vulnerability of his back as any other gardener doing heavy work. The above award comprised £3,250 general damages and £50 for minor services rendered during first period of 11 weeks off work. *Jones v Liverpool City Council* (30 November 1993, unreported) (Liverpool County Court: Recorder Hand QC) (A Georges for the plaintiff; T Griffiths for the defendant) (Kindly submitted for publication by Antonis Georges, Barrister).

Total damages: **£3,000.** Plaintiff, female aged 57 at time of accident and 63 at trial, was entering a taxi cab when it suddenly moved away, **dragging her along the pavement. Driver failed to check** that plaintiff was safely inside and he **ignored shouts of warning** from two passengers already inside. Plaintiff sustained **severe twisting injury to back, grazed left knee, bruising** and **was shaken. Frightening** experience. Treatment from doctor included **anti-depressants** and **painkillers,** latter still taken as required. Plaintiff had symptomatic **pre-existing osteoarthritis,** and this complicated the assessment of damages as her arthritis had **worsened** since the accident. First three months following the accident **especially painful** and **stiff back,** thereafter continued to lesser degree. Lower left ribs area of chest **very tender** to touch, **aching and tenderness** can suddenly flare up, as it did week before trial. **Depression** for first three months after accident. **Difficulty in sleeping** ever since accident, **cannot sleep in a bed** (having to use a chair). This is part of the reason for **cessation** of sexual relations, but **marriage also broken down** due to other factors, including **worsening arthritic condition** generally, necessitating **walking sticks** and **installation of stair lift** at home. Accident did not help yet did not exacerbate arthritis, which is now primary problem. Medical opinion was that left rib area's tenderness would slowly diminish, but judge doubted this having heard from the plaintiff. (He found accident **70 per cent responsible for ongoing back pain**.) The above award was made for pain, suffering and loss of amenity. *Weeks v WJ & SD Williams (t/a Barum Cabs) and Gerald Lucas-Farley* (22 January 1993, unreported) (Barnstaple County Court: District Judge Turner) (Mr Graham Thrussell, Messrs Crosse, Wyatt Samuel for the plaintiff) (Kindly submitted for publication by Graham Thrussell, Barrister).

Total damages: **£2,000** (less 25 per cent for contributory negligence). Plaintiff, male fork lift truck driver, **injured his back** in an accident at work in January 1986, when **leaning over to lift** a heavy length of timber. He was in **hospital** for a period of three weeks, rested at home in bed for three further weeks and was able to return to work in May 1986. It was decided that the plaintiff was **contributorily negligent** to the extent of 25 per cent. In August a further incident occurred after which the plaintiff **never returned to work**. He continued to complain of **back pain** and in January 1989 a **discogram** was taken which showed injury at the level of L4. This was confirmed at **surgery** when a two centimetre **tear in the annulus** was discovered. The **disc was removed subtotally** and a **bone graft** was done. There were no complications except for a **trapped nerve** and this was excised in a **subsequent operation.** Plaintiff had a history of back trouble, and the judge found that the incident in January 1986 was responsible for **minor back injury only** and was unlikely to have caused the annular tear. The back injury suffered was not serious although the plaintiff was in a **considerable amount of pain** for a short time. The injury had resolved completely by May 1986. Therefore, having regard to the period of extreme pain and the reduced but continuing pain until plaintiff returned to work in May 1986, by which time he had made a full recovery, general damages for pain, suffering and loss of amenity were assessed at £2,000, before reduction on the basis of contributory negligence. *Ellaway v Bambergers Transportation Ltd* (30 November 1993, unreported) (Queen's Bench Division: Deputy Judge Griffith-Williams QC) (Kindly submitted for publication by Deborah Ball, Barrister).

Total damages: **£2,000.** Plaintiff, male aged 52 at date of accident and 53 when damages assessed, sustained injuries when he **slipped on an area of plastic sheeting** in the defendant's pet shop. Plaintiff **landed heavily on the base of his spine** and his **right leg** and **banged his head** on the ground in the course of the fall. Plaintiff **suffered severe immediate pain** and went home immediately. At home the plaintiff was obliged to **lie on the floor for three days,** suffering **considerable pain** to the lower back. Plaintiff developed **significant bruising** to the right leg and lower back and suffered **occasional occipital headaches** related to the pain in the lower back, for a **number of weeks** following the accident. There was an **exacerbation** of pre-existing **osteo-arthritis** at the **cervical spine** and the plaintiff suffered **sciatic pain** in the right leg, walking with a **slight limp,** a **restriction of back movement** at the right sacro-iliac joint, and a degree of **limitation of flexion and external rotation** of the right hip, following the accident. Plaintiff's symptoms resolved themselves almost completely within three to four months of the accident, with **no significant long term problems.** *Williams v Parry (t/a Animal Lovers)* (9 June 1993, unreported) (Cardiff County Court: District Judge Evans) (Kindly submitted for publication by Leighton Alexander Hughes, Barrister).

Total damages: **£1,200.** Plaintiff, male aged 59 at date of accident and 61 at time of trial, sustained a **jarring injury to his axial skeleton,** particularly his **lumbar spine.** His pre-accident back problem was **exacerbated** by the accident. Plaintiff **confined to bed** for three days and **unable to drive** for six weeks. He received **analgesics** and was given a **pain relieving injection.** His hobby of shooting was **interrupted.** After five months plaintiff had recovered to his pre-accident level of mobility but still had **some persistent lumbar pain.** The above award was for general damages. *Hornigold v Taylor (t/a Hesketh Shooting Club)* (23 June 1993, unreported) (Preston County Court: Deputy District Judge Lambert) (Kindly submitted for publication by Keith Thomas, Barrister).

Total damages: **£1,000.** Plaintiff, male, was involved in an accident at the defendants' foundry, dealing with molten metal. In order to avoid being splashed by metal he **jumped down from a platform,** a height of some **two to three feet. No pain experienced at the time,** some **twinges of pain experienced** two to three days later, no major symptoms until three months later when plaintiff was **immobilised** by pain in the **lower back,** and had to be rescued from him home by neighbours. Detained in hospital for **three weeks. Surgery for extruded spinal disc** four months later, followed by **extensive physiotherapy. Further surgical intervention** after six months, providing only **limited relief.** Plaintiff **now unable to work.** Medical evidence adduced that the plaintiff suffered from a (previously asymptomatic) pre-existing degenerative back condition which had been accelerated by six months by the jarring associated with the jump. The above award was for general damages. *Russell v John Williams Foundries Ltd* (25 November 1993, unreported) (Cardiff County Court: Recorder Gaskell) (Kindly submitted for publication by Julie Barratt, Pupil Barrister).

ARM AND HAND

947 *Arm*

Total damages: **£301,861.** The plaintiff, a welder aged 34 at the date of the accident, sustained a major **neuro-vascular injury** to the **left arm** with a **clinically apparent brachial plexus lesion** and circulatory compromise, a **fracture of the mid-shaft of the left femur,** an undisplaced but **comminuted fracture of the upper and lower shaft of the left fibula,** a **grossly comminuted and displaced fracture of the right distal radius, a fracture of the left upper humerus,** intra abdominal bleeding, and cuts and bruises. **Left arm almost completely paralysed.** Constant pain in hand and forearm. Likely to develop osteoarthritis in right wrist. Fractured left leg healed with 1 cm shortening and reduction in flexion. Sexual relations difficult. Depressed and irritable. **Disability permanent** and further improvement unlikely. The above award comprised £45,000 for pain, suffering and loss of amenity; £149,092 for future loss of earnings (calculated on the basis of 8 years at a full multiplicand of £14,091 and 4 years at a reduced multiplicand of £9,091 to reflect the possibility of the plaintiff obtaining some low paid work); £1,500 for cost of help with personal tasks to date of hearing;

£3,000 for cost of help with DIY tasks to date of hearing; £1,232 for cost of necessary aids and appliances; £3,750 for future cost of help with personal tasks; £7,762 for future cost of DIY and transport; and £330 for miscellaneous aids and appliances. The award also comprised the following agreed sums: £57,000 for loss of past earnings; £3,000 for loss of pension rights and £30,195 for interest. *Wright v Ramsden* (8 January 1993, unreported) (Queen's Bench Division, Sheffield: Judge Bentley QC) (Kindly submitted for publication by Gary Burrell, Barrister).

Total damages: **£5,137**. Plaintiff, female actress aged 30 at time of accident in June 1991, suffered **tenosynovitis** of the biceps tendon of the right (dominant) arm, and secondary to this, **inflammation** of the tendons of the rotator cuff of the same shoulder, as a result of lifting heavy and bulky scenery in an awkward manner and with poor posture. Defendants' doctor's contention that this injury had been caused by resumption of intermittent cello playing during and before each performance of the play, after along period of absence from the cello, was rejected by the court as unlikely. Initially the plaintiff developed **pain in the right upper arm** and later more **severe stiffness of the shoulder and neck**. Initially dressing, reaching behind her back, writing, washing and drying her hair, and leaning on her right hand were difficult. Plaintiff had dropped objects with her right hand, suffered some **interference with her sleep**, and underwent two **steroid injections** to the shoulder. By the date of trial the plaintiff still had to **avoid heavy lifting or violent activity** with her right arm and had adapted to using her left arm for tasks such as hoovering and carrying shopping. She still **suffered pain and discomfort** if she slept upon her right side and when the right arm was brought down from the abducted position there was a 'clunk' which was slightly uncomfortable. She had avoided applying for acting parts which involved strenuous activity. It was common ground that there were **excellent prospects of a full recovery**. The above award comprised £4,500 for pain, suffering and loss of amenity and £637 special damages. *Wickens v Red Shift Theatre Company* (25 November 1993, unreported) (Central London County Court: Recorder Knowles) (Kindly submitted for publication by Howard Lederman, Barrister).

948 *Arm and hand*

Total damages: **£189,502**. Plaintiff, aged 34 at date of hearing, employed as a rigger, fell from ladder, suffering serious injuries to **wrists** and **elbows**. **Comminuted fracture dislocation** of one elbow and **comminuted intra-articular fracture of the head of radius** in other elbow. **Comminuted intra-articular fracture of the head of radius** in both **wrists** and **fracture of ulnar styloid** in right wrist. Sustained **fracture of articular surface of left patella**, undisplaced **fracture of right transverse process of the fifth cervical vertebra**. Plaintiff suffered **considerable degree of pain**, especially in cold or damp weather. **Increased risk of post-traumatic osteoarthritis** in both elbows and wrists. Plaintiff only fit for **light work** in future. The above award comprised £25,000 general damages; £17,686 for loss of earnings; £500 for cost of gardening and decorating; £134,816 for future loss of earnings; £1500 for loss due to an inability to decorate in the future; £10,000 for future restriction in field of employment. *Cord v Technico* (16 July 1993, unreported) (Queen's Bench Division, Birmingham: Tudor Evans J) (N Worsley QC for the plaintiff; L West for the defendant).

Total damages: **£2,047·04**. The plaintiff, female aged 34 at time of injury and 38 at date of trial, was attacked by a dog as she walked down the street. She suffered one bite which made a **deep puncture wound to the palm of her left hand** and the back of the hand was **badly swollen and bruised**. She was treated by her doctor with **anti-tetanus vaccine and antibiotics**. For about six weeks following the bites she suffered from **interference of sensation in the hand** with severe pins and needles, and with a **weak and painful grip**. She also had **nightmares**. During this period the plaintiff, who lives with her parents, had to be helped by her mother to wash her hair and cut up her food. The plaintiff is a piano teacher, and it was **some six months after the bites** before she could play the piano properly again. It then took her some time to regain her previous standard of playing. She was able to carry on with her teaching work but for about six months **she could not play for her own enjoyment**, as she previously had done for at least 1½ hours per day, and her job satisfaction was much diminished. **She continues to be nervous of dogs**. In the summer following the accident she was afraid to go out without a coat and gloves because she felt unprotected. At the date of hearing (four years after the injury) the plaintiff was left with two tiny marks on her palm but had **effectively recovered**. The above award comprised £2,000 for pain, suffering and loss of amenity, and £47·04 for special damages. *Beal v Turner* (19 August 1992, unreported) (Slough County Court: District Judge Sonnex) (Kindly submitted for publication by Stuchbery Stone, Solicitors, Windsor).

949 *Elbows*

Total damages: £104,398·47. Plaintiff, male machine tool setter aged 39 at time of accident, tripped over a metal table top left on a factory floor. He sustained **dislocations** and **fractures** to **both elbows**. On the right side he sustained a **fracture of the coronoid process** which required **repeated manipulation** and two K-wires to fix the elbow in its position resulting in considerable **stiffness** of the joints which was dealt with by the **excision** of the head of the right radius. The range of flexion and extension in the right arm is **limited to 20 degrees** between the arc of 80 degrees to 100 degrees flexion range. This range of movement is **painful** and will not take his weight. The **limitation of movement and pain** may be cured by the insertion of an **artificial joint**; such a joint would **not** be sufficiently strong to allow the plaintiff to engage in heavy manual work and is likely to **wear out** within the plaintiff's life and his condition would then be irremediable. On the left side he sustained a **Monteggia fracture** of the upper third of the ulna. This was treated by **manipulation** and an above elbow plaster. He then had open reduction and **internal fixation** with plate and screws were fitted to the left ulna. Degenerative changes will develop over the course of next 20 years. The plaintiff has also suffered **acute reactive depression**. He finds it **very difficult to reach** out for items and has difficulty in putting on a jumper and performing twisting actions. He **cannot wash and comb** his hair. He **cannot lift** his daughter nor perform some of his pre-accident social hobbies of darts, pool and cricket. He was a keen photographer but has to use an automatic camera since he had **difficulty** in adjusting the focus and other functions of a non-automatic camera. The **pain** in his right elbow is exacerbated if he writes more than one page. His wife suffers from rheumatoid arthritis and he cannot assist her as he had pre-accident. The above award comprised £22,500 for pain, suffering and loss of amenity; £42,000 for future loss of earnings; and £39,898·47 for special damages and loss of earnings. The plaintiff was awarded three quarters of this total due to contributory negligence. *Fry v Double A Hydraulics* (17 December 1992, unreported) (Queen's Bench Division, Plymouth: Judge Sean Overend) (Kindly submitted for publication by G & I Chisholm, Solicitors, Bodmin).

950 *Elbow*

Scotland

Total damages: £193,080. Plaintiff, male farmer aged 38 at time of accident, an international clay target shooter having won the European Championship in 1988 and a Commonwealth Games Bronze Medal, was injured in a **road traffic accident** in 1989. Plaintiff suffered **lacerations to head and knee** and **very serious multiple fractures of the right arm and elbow**. An **operation** and **insertion of a pin** was required. Pin removed after two years when the movement of the arm had **stiffened almost entirely**. Plaintiff now left with **permanent disability** and **limited range of flexion**. Cannot bring a cup to his lips with right hand, and cannot tie his tie or do up shirt buttons. Plaintiff's wife helps him with driving and around the farm. He has **continuing pain** in the arm which is worse in wet weather. Plaintiff wakes at night and takes painkillers. He cannot take part in clay target competition where he used to win cash and other prizes. The above jury award comprised £120,000 general damages for pain, suffering and loss of amenity and loss of opportunity of competing at international level; £2,700 for past farming losses, £16,000 future farming losses; loss of prizes and prize money £10,000 for past losses and £18,000 future loss; services provided by wife £5,150 for past and £2,000 for the future; services which he is unable to render £2,500 for past and £15,000 for future; £1,680 for travelling costs and £50 for damage to clothing. *Girvan v Inverness Farmers Dairy* (8 December 1993, unreported) (Court of Session) (C N McEachran QC and Raymond Docherty, Messrs Dundas & Wilson for the plaintiff) (Kindly submitted for publication by Colin McEachran, QC).

951 *Elbow, wrist and hand*

Total damages: £5,000 (excluding interest). Plaintiff, male aged 43 at the time of the accident and 47 at time of trial, was **injured in an assault** when he was thrown to the ground. Plaintiff sustained a **crack fracture of his right scaphoid**, which has healed without further symptom; **severe contusion of soft tissues of wrist and carpel tunnel**, causing **carpel tunnel syndrome** in three fingers; and **severe contusions in right elbow** causing restriction and pain. Immediately after the accident plaintiff worked for approximately three days and was then away from work for eight weeks at first and then a further three weeks later on after an operation (nine months after the accident). **Persistent pain** in his elbow made worse by movement, **tingling of fingers and loss of grip** in the fingers, and **restriction** in his wrist flexion. Described as '**slight but permanent**' disability, **no risk of arthritis**, plaintiff presently takes pain killers twice a day. Plaintiff can't drive long distances without pain and can't hold a paint roller for DIY. The above award was for general damages, with three and a half per cent interest since date of issue (December 1991). *Radford v Giovanni* (24 September 1993, unreported) (Reading County Court: Judge Morton Jack) (Kindly submitted for publication by Sarjeant & Sheppard, Solicitors, Reading).

952 *Wrist*

Total damages: £26,923·73. The plaintiff, female aged 27 at date of judgment and employed by the defendants as a computer operator at the time of the accident, slipped on some liquid which had been left lying on a toilet floor and injured her right wrist (dominant hand). Plaintiff suffered some bruising and redness of the wrist. However, after increased pain, an x-ray showed that she had suffered a compression fracture of the lunate bone in the wrist. The plaintiff had a pre-existing abnormality of her right lunar, with the result that it was shorter than normal. A bone graft operation was carried out which resulted in the plaintiff being in plaster for 15 weeks and causing a scar four inches by four inches. Eight months later she suffered a second minor accident involving a small blow to the wrist but because consolidation of the bone had not occurred, there was a refracture. As a result a third operation was carried out and an artificial implant was inserted into the lunate space. She still suffers pain which improves if she straps the wrist up but the wrist is painful in cold and damp weather. She finds lifting painful and finds driving intolerable. She has clearly visible scars which are painful and which she finds embarrassing. Dorsiflexion on the right is 35 degrees, as opposed to 40 on the left. Palmarflexion is 25 degrees as opposed to 65 degrees on the left. There is a very low risk that osteoarthritis and silastic synovitis may develop. The plaintiff was made redundant and as a result is restricted on the labour market as she finds work as a computer operator very painful. The above award comprised a *Smith v Manchester* award of £9,000; £1,423·73 special damages; and £16,500 general damages. *Reynolds v Barratts & Baird* (1 July 1993, unreported) (Queen's Bench Division, Birmingham: Tudor Evans J) (Mr Glancy for the plaintiff and Mr Bleasdale for the defendants). *Smith v Manchester Corpn* (1974) 118 SJ 597, CA applied.

Total damages: £6,355. Plaintiff, male boiler house stoker aged 58 at time of the accident and 65 at the time of hearing, injured his right wrist whilst using a long handled shovel. The accident was caused when the plaintiff struck a hidden object with the shovel causing a jarring injury of the right wrist which was already the site of an old un-united scaphoid fracture and related osteo-arthritis. A plaster cast was applied from below the elbow to the knuckles, which was worn by the plaintiff for one month. Plaintiff off work for six months. Plaintiff experienced pain over the right radial side of the wrist, especially the scaphoid which was progressively increasing. On examination there was a moderate restriction of wrist movement, dorsiflexion 20 degrees, palmar flexion 30 degrees compared with 70 degrees on the opposite side, suppination lacked 10 degrees and his grip was impaired. Plaintiff used to do maintenance, decorating work and gardening work himself but has been unable to do so since the accident. Plaintiff has since given up driving because he felt that the wrist made him an unsafe driver. The above award comprised £5,500 for pain and suffering; £250 special damages; £505 interest on general damages; and £100 interest on special damages. *Murphy v West Midlands Regional Health Authority* (14 October 1993, unreported) (Queen's Bench Division, Birmingham: May J) (Mr T Bates for the plaintiff; Mr N Worsley QC for the defendant).

Total damages: £695. Plaintiff, male aged 33 and employed by a printing firm at time of injury, was tightening a bolt on a trimming machine when his wrist struck an unguarded blade. Plaintiff sustained a laceration of right wrist, requiring three stitches under local anaesthetic at hospital. Returned to work same day, off work next day only, and resumed work thereafter. Pain wore off after five days. Scar, barely visible, of 1·5 centimetres. Altered sensation over dorsum of first web space of right hand. Completely free of pain after two weeks, during which period his hobbies of cycling and weight training greatly affected. Residual tingling sensation whilst holding a pen, shaking hands and so on. Plaintiff finds this a "nuisance". If the pain has not gone within a four-year period, it is not likely to do so. This does not affect his work or other activities. General damages assessed at £650; special damages agreed at £45. *Chesham v R K Donnelley Ltd* (13 August 1993, unreported) (Wakefield County Court: District Judge Higgins) (S A Norcross for the plaintiff; Kaiser Nazir for the defendant) (Kindly submitted for publication by Kaiser Nazir, Barrister).

953 *Hand and wrist*

Total damages: £3,679. Applicant, male police officer aged 37 at date of assault in 1988 and 42 at time of hearing, was on **uniformed duty** at a football ground as part of a specialist unit dealing with football violence. A disturbance broke out between home crowd and visiting supporters. The **applicant felt in immediate danger of being assaulted** by the apparent leader of the home supporters, who was approaching him with a clenched fist. The **applicant struck the first blow** with his right fist at home supporter. **Sustained fractured bones in right hand, fractured dislocation** at the junction of his **right wrist** (carpus) **and hand** at the base of the fourth and fifth metacarpals. Applicant **off work for two months**. For **two years** he suffered **discomfort** in his hand, particularly when putting pressure on it, for example when shaking hands. **Slight swelling** in his hand but not particularly noticeable. **Small risk** of post traumatic **osteo-arthritis** which could cause aching later in life. Assailant was arrested and successfully prosecuted for threatening words and behaviour. Applicant's application to CICB turned down on grounds that it did not fall within paragraph 4a of the scheme (he had not been a victim of violence). On appeal, incident held to be an assault, therefore applicant had been a victim of violence. Board agreed he came within paragraph 4a as there had been an immediate threat of violence. The above award comprised £3,500 general damages and £179 special damages. *Criminal Injuries Compensation Board, London* (4 August 1993, unreported) (Kindly submitted for publication by Russell Jones & Walker, Solicitors, London).

Total damages: £1,912·50. Plaintiff, male A level student aged 16 at time of accident, was on the platform awaiting a train. He was walking and talking to his friend ahead of him while **gesticulating** with his arms stretched out either side of his body. A through train approaching from behind and travelling at **90 miles per hour** hit the plaintiff's right hand and the force of **impact threw him across the platform** and into the waiting room. He suffered **several broken bones** in his hand and wrist and **was in plaster and immobilised** for **six to eight** weeks. He was **unable to write** for several months and **did not finish** his A level course. He was also **unable to drive** for six months. He has made an almost complete recovery; the limited symptoms he still suffers should eventually settle down. Agreed damages of £3,750, reduced by 50 per cent for contributory negligence; the above award was made for general damages, including interest. *May v British Railways Board* (3 February 1993, unreported) (Coventry County Court: Judge Nicholl) (Mrs Carmel Wall, Messrs K J Martin & Co, for the plaintiff; Mr Griffiths, The Solicitor's Department, British Railways Board, for the defendant) (Kindly submitted for publication by K J Martin & Co, Solicitors, Coventry).

954 *Hands*

Total damages: £24,750 (excluding interest). Plaintiff, male aged 48 at date of trial, was employed full time by the defendant as a fettler since 1966. Plaintiff **exposed to vibration** during occupation, and developed **cold induced episodic blanching** to **all digits of both hands,** diagnosed as hand arm vibration syndrome (**Raynaud's Phenomenon**). Regular attacks of **blanching in winter** months and occasionally during summer months. **Loss of sensation** in digits until heat applied, causing 'pins and needles' sensation. Stage 2 on the Taylor and Pelmear Scale, 2R(5)/2L(5) vascular and 1SN neurological on Stockholm Scale. Vibration exposure continues, and plaintiff's symptoms likely to continue and **increase in severity**. The above award comprised £4,000 general damages for pain and suffering; £750 for future cost of electrically heated hand warmers (using a multiplier of ten years); and a *Smith v Manchester* award of £20,000. *Bir v A L Dunn & Co Ltd* (17 June 1993, unreported) (Coventry County Court: Judge Nichol) (Neil Thompson, Messrs Ward & Rider for the plaintiff) (Kindly submitted for publication by Neil Thompson, Barrister). *Smith v Manchester Corpn* (1974) 118 SJ 597, CA applied.

955 *Hand*

Total damages: £34,000. The plaintiff, a male machine operator aged 30 at the date of the accident, was working with a cutting machine at his place of employment. The plaintiff's hand came into contact with a rotating cutting blade which was still moving, causing extensive injuries to his dominant right hand. **One of his fingers had to be amputated, another was considerably shortened and the back of his hand was badly scarred.** The plaintiff spent two months in hospital and was unable to work for eight months in total, but he returned to work for his former employers on a machine which required less manual dexterity. The above figure consisted of £18,000 for pain, suffering and loss of amenity and £16,000 for loss of future earning capacity, based on a multiplicand of £8,000 and a multiplier of two.

Compensation was reduced by 25 per cent on account of the plaintiff's contributory negligence in failing to check whether the cutter had stopped rotating before he put his hand on it. On appeal by the employers, contributory negligence was increased to 66 per cent. *Gunter v Nicholas & Sons* [1993] PIQR P67 (Court of Appeal: Mann and McCowan LJJ).

Total damages: £33,564·29. Plaintiff, male aged 32 at time of injury and 34 at trial, sustained a **Bennett's fracture** of the **first metacarpal bone** involving the carpo-metacarpal joint of the **thumb of the dominant right hand** in a tripping accident. Plaintiff underwent an **operation** to **reduce the fracture** and **insert wires** under general anaesthetic. The hand was **in plaster for six to seven weeks** and the **pins were subsequently removed** three weeks after the first operation. He was **absent from work** despite one abortive attempt to return, for **six months** following the accident. At the time of trial, the plaintiff's right hand did not have its pre-accident **dexterity** and he suffered from **difficulty** in counting money, difficulty with handwriting, inability to fully tighten spanners, difficulty in handling weapons in the course of his activities in the Territorial Army and inability to fly-fish with the right hand. He needed to **wear an inner glove** for the right hand to stop it becoming excessively cold and **stiff** at work. He was **unable to train by lifting weights** or **carry out fitness training** as he had done before the accident. He was **unable to lift and balance heavy and lengthy scaffolding poles** with his right arm as he had done previously. The injured joint tended to become **stiff** and **sore** in cold conditions. The expert medical evidence was that the plaintiff would manage his work as a scaffolder without difficulty for **ten or twelve years** from June 1991, but the **probability** was that at that time he would **develop osteoarthritic change** in the joint at the base of the thumb. He would then have to go on to lighter work as the climbing of the scaffolding would become **dangerous** to himself and to fellow work mates. The medical evidence was that **probably further treatment** would have to be undertaken, but that the plaintiff would be able to continue working provided light work was available for him. The only light work which would have been available to him at the age of 45 was that of a foreman, who himself might have to climb scaffolding or carry out some scaffolding work. The plaintiff had obtained a class 2 HGV licence previously. The above award comprised £5,250 for pain, suffering and loss of amenity; a *Smith v Manchester* award of £27,000 (being 18 months' loss of net earnings as at the date of the trial); and £1,314·29 special damages (agreed). *Martin v Press Offshore* (24 March 1993, unreported) (Newcastle upon Tyne County Court: Judge Cartledge) (Mr Howard Lederman, Messrs Marrons for the plaintiff) (Kindly submitted for publication by Howard Lederman, Barrister).

Total damages: £9,869·31 (excluding interest). Plaintiff, male aged 27 at the time of accident and 32 at date of trial, sustained a **fracture of the scaphoid of the right wrist** (dominant hand) when steel bollard weighing 42 kilograms **fell on the dorsum** of his right hand. Treated with **scaphoid plaster** for 12 weeks. Due to non-union of fracture, plaintiff underwent **operation to insert bone graft**. Further period of plaster for three months. **Fracture united.** At time of trial plaintiff continued to suffer **slight restriction of wrist movement, weakened grip and aching** when heavy lifting. Unable to carry out heavy manual work involving repeated power gripping. Unable to return to hobbies of tennis, boxing and weight lifting. Chances of early osteo-arthritic deterioration assessed at 20 per cent over the next five to ten years. The above award comprised £7,500 general damages; special damages of £869·31; and a *Smith v Manchester* award of £1,500. *Albrighton v Townscape Products Ltd* (16 June 1993, unreported) (Mansfield County Court: Judge Davidson QC) (Simon Wheatley for the plaintiff; Jeremy Cahill for the defendant) (Kindly submitted for publication by Simon Wheatley, Barrister). *Smith v Manchester Corpn* (1974) 118 SJ 597, CA applied.

956 *Finger*

Total damages: £10,196·02. Plaintiff, male CNC (computer numerical controlled) turner aged 38 at time of injury and 43 at date of trial, suffered a **severe compound fracture** of the left non-dominant little finger when his hand became trapped in a vice. The fracture was **reduced under anaesthetic** but was found to be unviable upon review. An **amputation** at the level of proximal interphalangeal joint was carried out. **Five months later** plaintiff was suffering from **constant pain** in the stump which disturbed his sleep and which resulted in a **further amputation at the volar crease**. Plaintiff was off work for 14 weeks. By the date of trial, he was suffering from a **five centimetre scar** affecting the ulnar border of the left hand which was **slightly tender, slight stiffness** in his hand, **aching** in the hand, particularly over the ulnar border at the scar, **swelling and itching** at the sight of the scar, **stiffness** of the ring finger at the distal interphalangeal joint which slightly limited the creation of a full fist. Plaintiff tended to drop things and had difficulty carrying heavy objects and bags, and was aware of the cosmetic effect of the loss of the finger. If he knocked the site of the amputation, he suffered excruciating pain which made him stop for a few moments. He was able to continue with his employment without difficulty but would be disadvantaged in certain types of work which involved using a keyboard regularly, lifting and carrying, handling small items and working in the cold and with cold water. The judge found that the plaintiff was a highly regarded, skilled employee who his employers would be reluctant to lose. No improvement or deterioration was expected in the plaintiff's condition. The above award comprised £5,500 general damages; a Smith v Manchester award of £2,500; £1,268·02 special damages; and £928 interest. Cox v GKN Axles (24 August 1993, unreported) (Leeds County Court: Judge Bush) (Jacqueline Beech, Brian Thompsons for the plaintiff; Michael Taylor for the defendant) (Kindly submitted for publication by Jacqueline Beech, Barrister). Smith v Manchester Corpn (1974) 118 SJ 597, CA applied.

Total damages: £4,376·26. Plaintiff, male aged 24 and employed as loader/stacker at time of injury, sustained crushing injury to non–dominant left hand middle finger when potato tipper mechanism lowered by fellow employee. Partial amputation just proximal to distal interphalangeal joint. Plaintiff lost end three centimetres of finger. One night in hospital, bandage for two weeks during which finger very painful, three centimetre scar left when sutures removed after six weeks. Plaintiff returned to work six weeks after accident, could use hand normally after six to eight weeks once swelling had subsided. Permanent numbness due to damage to distal nerves. Finger tends to "freeze" in cold conditions. Loss of strength in hand; hand therefore gets sore particularly when operating clutch on motorbike. Difficulty in playing snooker. Plaintiff liable to drop small things, particularly coins which slip through gap in fingers. Judge accepted a known risk of redundancy (although small), that certain jobs the plaintiff couldn't do, and that it would probably take plaintiff a little longer to find a job in these circumstances. The above award comprised £3,000 for pain, suffering and loss of amenity; Smith v Manchester award (risk of redundancy small and accelerated receipt) of £500; and £876·26 for agreed special damages. Scott v Higgins Potato Merchants (25 March 1993, unreported) (Doncaster County Court: Judge Fricker QC) (Sanjiv Sachdeva, Messrs Frank Allen Pennington & Co for the plaintiff) (Kindly submitted for publication by Sanjiv Sachdeva, Barrister). Smith v Manchester Corpn (1974) 118 SJ 367, CA applied.

Scotland
Total damages: £3,750 (liability not proved; opinion of court as to quantum). Plaintiff, aged 36 at time of the accident, trapped fingers of right hand between hooks and load while working with overhead transporter at factory. Accident resulted in traumatic amputation of ring finger of right hand immediately distal to the interphalangeal joint. Small lacerations to pulp of middle and little fingers. Wound toilet and terminalisation performed under general anaesthetic. Formal amputation through neck of middle phalanx of finger. Plaintiff returned to work three months later. Now very small, well healed scars over tips of pulps of right middle and little fingers. No related loss of sensation or sweating to these fingers and normal flexion and extension. Stump of middle phalanx of right ring finger well healed. Some diminution of sensation over tip. Subcutaneous tissues over bone very thin and painful sensation on tapping. Full flexion of interphalangeal joints of all fingers. Power grip full on index, middle and little fingers, weak over right ring finger. Pain on sharp tapping over tip of amputation stump will not improve in future. Consequent slight loss of power grip due to amputation. No further untoward consequences such as osteoarthritis. The above award comprised £3,250 for solatium and £500 for services performed by plaintiff's wife in months after accident. Stark v Nairn Floors Ltd 1993 SLT 717 (Outer House).

Total damages: £1,250. Plaintiff, male aged 51 at time of injury, was employed as a pipe assembler and required to fit flanges onto pipe. The system of fitting involves striking flange with a seven pound hammer. On occasion of the accident, plaintiff mis-hit the flange, the hammer entered into the pipe dragging his right hand, and trapping right middle finger between wall of pipe and handle of sledgehammer. Plaintiff sustained burst injuries to right middle finger, no fracture. Wound surgically toiletted and dressed, plaintiff off work for three weeks. Injury healed with three centimetre scarring and no embarrassment. Manual dexterity minimally decreased due to finger being slightly stiff. Plaintiff experiences aching in cold and/or damp weather conditions. Reduced sensation on radial aspect is permanent. Initial loss of grip, now normal. No long term degenerative symptoms. The above award was assessed for pain, suffering and loss of amenity, but not awarded due to failure to establish liability. Edge v Stanton plc (23 April 1993, unreported) (Nottingham County Court: Judge Heald) (Mr Richard Payne, Messrs Huntsmans for the plaintiff; Mr Robert

Holdsworth, Messrs William Hatton for the defendant) (Kindly submitted for publication by Sanjiv Sachdeva, Barrister).

Total damages: £648·05. Plaintiff, male aged 45 at time of accident and 47 at the date of trial, was closing a window in a portacabin utilised as a kitchen on the **defendant's premises**. Whilst closing the window the glass shattered with a **sliver** entering the **tip of the right little finger** to a depth of **four millimetres** involving the pulp of the finger. The wound was cleaned and **sutured** requiring **five stitches**. Paracetamol tablets taken for one week thereafter due to the **pain**, plaintiff off work for **four weeks**. Small **faint scar** to tip of little finger, no damage to nerve endings in finger tips, no permanent disability. The above award comprised £600 for general damages, and special damages agreed at £48·05. *Leech v South Yorkshire Transport* (25 March 1993, unreported) (Doncaster County Court: Deputy District Judge Taylor) (Kindly submitted for publication by Mr S Robinson, Frank Allen Pennington, Solicitors, Doncaster).

957   *Thumb*

Total damages: £47,260·67. Plaintiff, male aged 50, sustained a **crush injury** to thumb of dominant hand causing **laceration** as well as **comminuted fracture** and **rotational deformity** of the distal part of the **proximal phalanx**. Fracture reduced and fixed with wire. Off work for nearly **seven months** and then re-trained to do desk work. There was now an area of **altered sensation** on the back of the thumb due to damage to the radial nerve and **gross restriction of flexion**. There was also some lack of **hypertension**. The possibility of osteo-arthritic changes were assessed at 20–30 per cent and there was a "strong possibility" that he might end up with **fusion** of the inter-phalangeal joint. Plaintiff had to give up playing darts as a result of the injury, and had **experienced some difficulty** with such tasks as holding a pen, or knife when eating, fastening buttons or tying shoe laces. The above award comprised £5,000 for pain, suffering and loss of amenity; special damages including past loss of earnings £11,419; future partial loss of earnings £29,251·04 (multiplier of seven applied); and interest £1,590·63. *Cook v Containerships Ltd* (8 June 1993, unreported) (Middlesborough County Court: Judge Faulks) (Keith S H Miller, Messrs Atha Barton for the plaintiff; Messrs Montgomery & Owen for the defendant) (Kindly submitted for publication by Keith S H Miller, Barrister).

Total damages: £5,554·85. Plaintiff, male aged 50 at date of accident and 54 at date of trial, sustained a **compound comminuted fracture** of his right thumb when a bar feed push mechanism to a lathe crushed his **right thumb** as he repaired the clutch. Repair under general anaesthetic took place, plaintiff remaining in hospital for **two days**. There was a **laceration** to the base of the right thumb, palmer as well as dorsal aspects involving the web space. The fracture was **stabilised** by "k" wires. Tendon was repaired by suture with **avulsed digital nerve** also repaired as best as possible. A dressing and plaster was applied. Plaintiff complained of a **dull ache** and **impaired pinch grip** which is **permanent**. The right thumb is **deformed** compared to left, joint movements are **restricted** and there is a **loss of sensation** over the tip of the right thumb. The **scarring will remain**. He is unable to play snooker. His work is not affected. The above award comprised £5,250·00 for pain, suffering and loss of amenity, £112·00 for special damages (agreed), and £192·85 interest. *Sanderson v Precision Engineering Ltd* (2 February 1993, unreported) (Preston County Court: Judge Appleton) (Mr P Smith for the plaintiff; Mr N Grimshaw for the defendant) *Ellwood v Ward (Thomas W)* (25 April 1988, unreported) considered. (Kindly submitted for publication by Mr Peter R Smith, Barrister).

Total damages: £1,810. Plaintiff, male aged 28 and **employed by the defendant** at a paper mill at the time of accident, tripped and **caught his hand** in the paper cutting machinery. **Liability** was **not disputed**. The injuries were to the **thumb of the left hand**, being a **fracture** of the tip of the distal phalanx; the **nail** was hanging on by a **small distal skin bridge**; **deep oblique lacerations** through the nail bed which extended onto the skin on both sides. **Sutures** were used and a **sling** applied. There was **psychological** sequelae in that the plaintiff was **shaken and upset**. Off work for **three weeks**, **stiffness** in thumb thereafter, with **spasms** causing the thumb to extend. **Numbness and pain** for three months. Plaintiff has made a **full recovery** save for minor tissue wasting and scarring. The above award comprised £1,500 general damages, and £310 special damages, being £278 loss of earnings, £12 bus fares, and £20 shoes. *Cook v Ideal Waste Paper Co Ltd* (3 June 1993, unreported) (Slough County Court: District Judge Keough) (Neil Mercer, Messrs Hetherington & Co for the plaintiff) (Kindly submitted for publication by Neil Mercer, Barrister).

LEG AND FOOT

958 Hip

Total damages: £285,546·45. The plaintiff, a forklift truck driver aged 44 at the date of trial, suffered a **fracture of the left hip** when his bicycle was involved in a motor accident. The **position** was **complicated by** the fact that the plaintiff suffered **poliomyelitis** as a result of which his left leg was damaged. He underwent **six operations**, all of which were preceded and followed by severe pain. He **requires two further operations**. He is able to walk only 100 yards with the aid of sticks. The plaintiff also suffered **severe reactive depression** which required prolonged treatment with anti-depressant drugs. He continued to work until such time as he could not cope and his employment was terminated. His prospects of finding work are very poor. The above award comprised the following agreed sums: £30,000 for general damages; £3,600 for interest thereon; £72,571·47 for special damages; and £12,691·80 for interest thereon, together with £43,247 for loss of earnings to date of trial; £24,789·18 for interest thereon; £91,508 for future loss of earnings; and £7,139 for loss of pension. *Houghton v Drayton* (16 December 1992, unreported) (Queen's Bench Division, Birmingham: Judge Crawford QC) (J Hoggett QC and H Halliday, Messrs Brindley, Twist, Taft & James for the plaintiff; G Tyrell, Messrs M Putsman & Co for the defendant).

959 Hip, leg and foot

Total damages: £10,500. Plaintiff, female aged 23 at time of injury and 25 at date of trial, was walking in town centre when a blackboard menu outside a cafe toppled without warning and hit her on the **left foot**. Attended hospital that day and was told that her foot was **bruised**, was given tubigrip and told to rest, which she did for about a week. There was **no real improvement** after treatment with analgesic cream by doctor and was advised by consultant to have **physiotherapy**. This she did for **16 weeks** without any sign of improvement. The consultant's final opinion in January 1992 was that there was **significant injury to the metatarsophalangeal joint** of the left great toe with **early arthritis** (hallux rigidus). The plaintiff was in **considerable** pain but the consultant thought that with sensible footwear she could tolerate the discomfort in the shorter term but that the joint would become **increasingly painful and stiff** and there was a prospect of surgery to replace the arthritic joint in the longer term. The plaintiff, who had three young children and was fully occupied as a housewife, was managing domestic chores but found shopping difficult and was unable to walk more than two miles without **extreme discomfort**. Hills and cold, damp weather worsened the condition. The award was made for pain and suffering. *Polley v Alasti* (27 January 1993, unreported) (Sunderland County Court: Judge Paling) (David Mason, Messrs Gerald Armstrong, Sunderland for the plaintiff) (Kindly submitted for publication by David Mason, Barrister).

Total damages: £4,000. Appellant, serving male police officer aged 24, sustained a **slightly comminuted fracture** of the left tibia and fibula after vaulting over a five foot fence in hot pursuit of a burglar. He failed to look over the fence in advance and thus failed to see a drop in excess of eleven feet on the other side. In hospital a week, in plaster four months, off work for six months and only able to resume full duties **eight months** after the event. **Complete recovery** save for **slight impaired sensation** over a small area of the foot. On appeal, *held*, the appellant was taking an exceptional risk within the scheme. *Criminal Injuries Compensation Board* (1 February 1993, unreported) (Kindly submitted for publication by Andrew McDonald, Barrister).

960 Legs

Total damages: £4,800. Plaintiff, male lorry driver aged 24 at time of accident, was **trapped** for 10–15 minutes **beneath the wheel** of an articulated heavy goods vehicle in September 1988. He suffered **severe fractures** to the inferior and superior **pubic rami** on the left side and a **wound to the perineum. Immobilised** for ten weeks in a pelvic sling and legs supported in frame. Treatment complicated by **pelvic abscess, jaundice, urinary tract infection** and **deep vein thrombosis** affecting his left leg. Treated with **physiotherapy** for nine months. Suffered mild **depression**. Resumed work driving light commercial vehicles in July 1990, with no time off since. Continued to experience difficulty in **running, carrying** heavy weights, **climbing** ladders, and **walking** distances in excess of two miles. Experienced **discomfort** and **swelling** in left leg with an **increased risk** of developing deep vein thrombosis as a result of trauma or surgery in future years. At trial the plaintiff had a secure job with a net annual income of £6,000. He had to conceal his handicap in order to obtain his present position and remained unfit for heavy work. The judge additionally took into account the increased risk of thrombosis and the current economic climate in making a *Smith v Manchester* award of £9,000, equivalent to 1½ years of his net income. General damages were awarded at £15,000, but after deduction for contributory negligence the plaintiff in fact received 20 per cent of the above figures. *Friar v Pickup* (16 October 1992, unreported) (Bradford County Court: Judge Hoffman) (Kindly submitted for publication by Gary Burrell, Barrister). *Smith v Manchester Corpn* (1974) 118 SJ 597, CA applied.

Total damages: **£1,775**. Plaintiff, female aged 55 at time of accident, suffered **large lacerations** to both shins with raised skin flaps when she fell down a flight of stairs when leaving a night club. Flaps were reattached, plaintiff in hospital for **ten days**, then transferred to the Hospital at Home scheme. Plaintiff has a 12 centimetre **distally based flap**, with a 25 centimetre surrounding **scar on each leg**. Complains left shin **painful** and that her left foot tends to **swell** towards the end of the day; right shin uncomfortable, but not as bad as the left one. No long term complications expected, although the flaps remain slightly more vulnerable than they were previously. The award made for general damages was £3,500, reduced by 50 per cent for contributory negligence, and £50 for interest thereon. *Smith v Creedon & Yiasoumi* (1 March 1993, unreported) (Peterborough County Court: Judge Morrell) (N J Elcombe for the plaintiff; J Rich for the defendant) (Kindly submitted for publication by Dakers Green Brett, Solicitors, Rochester).

961 Leg

Total damages: **£258,640·90**. The plaintiff, a male chloride operator aged 44 at the time of the hearing, was mixing powder in a mixing machine when the platform plate on which he was standing gave way, so that his legs became caught in the blades of the adjacent mixing machine. He sustained a **traumatic amputation of the left leg at the knee** and **crush fractures of right tuboid bone, big toe and fifth metatarsal** with **extensive laceration of the foot**. Attempts were made to try and save the leg but it became apparent that to continue with the attempt was **life threatening**. Subsequently it became necessary to **remove some of the toes** from the foot. Prior to the accident the plaintiff drove a manual car and has had to **transfer to an automatic car** and also has to **drive extra mileage** of around 1,500 miles a year; and further, he is **no longer able to maintain his own car**. Although working at present there is a **distinct possibility** that the plaintiff will have to give up his work. He formerly lived in a small house and is now **having to move** to a bungalow. The above award comprised £52,000 for general damages; loss of earnings to date of trial £67,312·60; care and assistance £3,408·30; cost of maintenance and gardening £3,500; cost of having to buy a different car £2,050; cost of extra mileage £1,800; cost of maintenance on car £900; loss of future earnings £92,370 (calculated using a multiplicand of £74,360, a multiplier of 11 and one year's full loss at £18,010); a *Smith v Manchester* award of £4,000; future care and assistance £12,160 (multiplier of 16 and a multiplicand of £760); future transport costs of £12,800 (multiplier of 16 and a multiplicand of £800); difference between the cost of an equivalent house and a bungalow £5,100; cost of moving house £750; and additional costs of miscellaneous equipment £490. *Welch v Albright & Wilson* (28 May 1993, unreported) (Queen's Bench Division, Birmingham: Kay J) (D Stembridge QC for the plaintiff; R Walker for the defendants). *Smith v Manchester Corpn* (1974) 118 SJ 597, CA applied.

Total damages: **£175,644** (including interest). The plaintiff, a policeman aged 31 at the time of the accident, suffered **severe** injuries to the **lower left leg and knee**, including **multiple fractures** of the tibia and fibula leaving his leg **severely disfigured, shortened** with **restriction of movement** and an **unstable knee**. Future **osteo-arthritic changes** were **virtually certain**. He found intermittent employment as a lorry driver, but had decided to start his own business manufacturing garden furniture. But for the accident the plaintiff would have continued work as a policeman until retirement at the age of 55. The judge awarded £37,000 for pain and suffering, £3,000 for loss of chosen career, £31,119 for special damages, £96,000 for future loss of earnings (multiplier of 12), £10,000 for loss of earning capacity and £14,275 for loss of pension rights. On appeal by the defendant, *held*, the plaintiff did not disentitle himself from a significant award for loss of earning capacity by his decision to return to work in a self-employed capacity as a businessman. The judge had not reduced the estimate of the plaintiff's likely future earnings to allow for periods out of work or possible failure of his business. On the evidence he was entitled to find that the plaintiff did face a real risk of periods of unemployment, in which he would find it more difficult to obtain new work by reason of his reduced earning capacity. The award for general damages for pain and suffering would be reduced to £28,000 as it was not possible to compare the plaintiff's injuries with cases of below the knee amputation. The appropriate multiplier for the period of 18 years of earnings loss would be 10 rather than 12 as the facts of the case did not provide a convincing justification for a multiplier of more than 10. Accordingly, the appeal would be allowed in part. *Frost v Palmer* [1993] 2 PIQR Q14 (Court of Appeal: Lloyd, Ralph Gibson and Butler-Sloss LJJ).

Total damages: **£21,551**. Applicant, male aged 56 at time of attack in July 1989, was **attacked by an intruder when asleep** in his bed. Sustained **serious stab wound** to the right groin resulting in a **severance of the right femoral nerve**. The neighbouring artery and vein were not divided. At time of operation, a six centimetre gap between the ends of the divided femoral nerve was noted. This was bridged with a **muscle autograft**. There followed **six weeks in a hip spica**. A period of six months **intensive physiotherapy** followed. The **muscle autograft was a failure**. Residual disability includes **complete absence of power** of the right quadriceps; **no restoration of sensation** to the medial thigh or calf; **weak right leg**, prone to give way; and **post traumatic stress disorder**. The applicant's wife who was also asleep in bed at the time of attack suffered no direct attack but was, of course, affected by the trauma of the attack on her husband. She suffered panic attacks and was still suffering from post traumatic stress disorder twelve months after the incident. The award in her own case was for general damages of £10,000. The above award for the applicant comprised £20,000 general damages and £1,551 special damages. *Criminal Injuries Compensation Board, Plymouth* (10 November 1992, unreported) (Kindly submitted for publication by Derek S Reed, Solicitor, Devon).

Total damages: **£3,500**. Plaintiff, male aged 15 at time of accident, ran along a pavement where agents of the defendant were removing glass from the window of a derelict shop. One allowed a piece of glass in his hands to project across the pavement one or two feet; the plaintiff ran into it. Very **deep laceration to right lower leg**, half way between knee and ankle, approximately **nine inches** long, cut through skin, muscle, tendons and ligaments. Plaintiff was a semi-professional footballer. Injury required approximately **80 stitches under general anaesthetic**, ten weeks in plaster, ten weeks off school, and some suggestion of this causing a poor performance in school. Full recovery after 18 months save for **numbness** of skin below the scar, **sensitivity** at the scar site, and **aching** of ankle in cold weather. Not embarrassed by scar. Able to play football and pursue work as a gardener. The award was made for pain, suffering and loss of amenity, and £41·50 for specials. *Richardson v Ravoof* (5 March 1993, unreported) (Birmingham County Court: Judge Orme) (Kindly submitted for publication by Mr R H Perks, Barrister).

962 Knee

Total damages: **£152,165**. The plaintiff, aged 23, a qualified basic scaffolder, suffered an accident at work when aged 18. He was operated upon for the removal of a **damaged cartilage**. While off work because of the accident, he was made redundant. He would have qualified as an advanced scaffolder if the cartilage operation had been successful. Due to the onset of **septic arthritis**, he underwent **three separate operations** and spent about five months in hospital. He had become **very seriously permanently disabled following a great deal of pain which persisted**. He suffered **constant pain in his left knee**, which was also stiff. He **could not walk distances over 400 yards** because this caused increasing pain in his left knee. He had to use a walking stick and found difficulty in negotiating stairs. He was unable to kneel, run, squat or use step-ladders and ladders, symptoms wholly related to **post-infective osteoarthritis**. His arthritis was severe and would progress, attracting increasing discomfort, further restriction of mobility and would eventually lead to surgical treatment, probably in the next seven or eight years, taking the form of an **arthrodesis**, boney stiffening of the joint. If the operation were successful, the pain would be eradicated but the plaintiff would be left with a stiff left leg making it difficult for him to kneel, squat or run. In addition, he would only be able to drive motor vehicles with automatic transmission. His long-term employment prospects would be limited to sedentary jobs requiring no kneeling, squatting, negotiation of steps, stairs, ladders or inclines. His long-term enjoyment of leisure pursuits had also been significantly affected. The effect of the stiff knee in a man of the plaintiff's age was to place successive strain on both his hip and back and to cause wear and tear and degenerative change at an earlier stage than normal, that is somewhere in the region of 25 years. The period to be taken into account was 22 years, from the plaintiff's present age of 23 to his likely ending of scaffolding at the age of 45. The above award included £40,000 for the general damages for pain and suffering and loss of amenity, £110,665 for loss of future earnings (calculated on the basis of 9 years at a multiplicand of £11,185 and £10,000 to compensate the plaintiff for what would happen after the age of 45), and £1,500 to cover the cost of the plaintiff's claim as handyman/gardener. *Leadbetter v Blackpool, Wyre and Fylde Health Authority* (15 December 1992, unreported) (Queen's Bench Division, Preston: Hodgson J) (Mr S Armitage for the plaintiff; Mr S E Grime QC and Mrs Trippier for the defendant).

Total damages **£91,243·64**. Plaintiff, female aged 26 at date of accident and 30 at date of trial, worked as communications assistant for the police. She suffered injuries when she **tripped over a misplaced rug**. She twisted her left leg badly and sustained an **injury to her left knee and ankle**. Plaintiff recovered quickly from the injury to her ankle but the injury to the knee required a number of operations and the knee is still defective and will remain so. Plaintiff had **an operation for lateral release** and as a result was **in plaster for some time** after the accident. Six months after the fall she suffered another bad fall. A year later she had a second operation in the course of which the **patella was removed**. Two years later she had another bad fall and two years after that the plaintiff underwent her third operation, **an arthroscopy of the left knee**. It was found that there was no significant laxity of the collateral ligaments, but there was a **grade two sagittal laxity at 90 degrees of flexion**. Plaintiff is in **constant discomfort** and sometimes suffers pain, and the knee has a tendency to give way. There is a possibility that she will develop degenerative changes and takes analgesics for the pain. As a result of the operations there is some **minor scarring** and she occasionally wears a **knee brace** but she finds it unsightly. It has been recommended that she has a further operation. The plaintiff's **sexual relations with her husband have deteriorated** and she now has to drive an automatic car. The above award comprised £25,000 for pain and suffering; £24,121·42 loss of earnings to date; £7,440 loss of future earnings (on the basis that she will be able to return to work following the operation); *Smith v Manchester* award of £20,000; £2,000 future motor expenses; £3,000 loss of pension rights; £2,000 cost of household structural alterations; £6,318·76 cost of future care; and £1,363·46 special damages. *Newberry v Warwickshire County Council* (12 October 1993, unreported) (Queen's Bench Division, Birmingham: Crawford QC) (M Stephens, Messrs Penmans for the plaintiff; W Pusey, Messrs Shakespeares for the defendants). *Smith v Manchester Corpn* (1974) 118 SJ 597, CA applied.

Total damages: **£12,500**. Plaintiff, male aged 18 at date of accident in 1989, was involved in a **collision** when a car turned across the path of his motorcycle. Plaintiff sustained **lacerations** to **both knees**. Not detained in hospital initially, but after two weeks was admitted for **three days** because of **discharge** from wound. Off work for **six weeks**. Left knee recovered **without complication**. Right knee developed **patello-femoral crepitation** which supported diagnosis of **traumatic chondromalacia patellae**. Right knee had **scar** one inch by three quarters of an inch. **Constant awareness** of "something there" in right knee. Exertion caused **aching**, driving long distances caused **stiffness**. **Difficulty** in kneeling, and jumping and running caused "stabbing pain". Had to use knee pad at work. **Condition permanent**. Degenerative change expected but thought **unlikely** that plaintiff would need surgical intervention within 20 years. The above award was for general damages, including a £3,000 *Smith v Manchester* award. *Lambert v Walker* (26 February 1993, unreported) (Ipswich County Court: District Judge Lam) (Kindly submitted for publication by John Brooke-Smith, Barrister).

Total damages: **£4,000**. Plaintiff, male aged 9 at time of accident and 10 at date of hearing, slipped and fell against a gate in a school playground. Plaintiff suffered a **deep laceration** on the lateral aspect of his right knee. He was **admitted to hospital** and spent one night as an in-patient and attended the outpatients department until discharged five weeks later. Plaintiff was **absent from school** for a period of one week and was **unable to do any physical exercise** until some two and a half months after the accident. Some seven months after the accident plaintiff was **still suffering occasional pain** in the region of the scar about once a week for a period of about two hours. He made a full recovery but was left with an **eleven centimetre** inverted 'v' shaped **scar on the lateral aspect** of his knee. The above award was a settlement in respect of general damages and was agreed and approved by the court. *Southwell v Calderdale Metropolitan Borough Council* (23 August 1993, unreported) (Halifax County Court: District Judge Lamb) (Kindly submitted for publication by Rhodes Thain & Collinson, Solicitors, Halifax).

963 *Ankle*

Total damages: **£100,316·21**. Plaintiff, fireman aged 38 at time of accident, injured right foot in fall at fire station while answering a call. Sustained a **fracture of the fifth metatarsal** and **significant soft tissue injury to the right ankle**. In plaster for six weeks and received physiotherapy for a further six weeks. Assessed by the Department of Social Security as being 10 per cent disabled. **Discomfort brought on by walking** more than half a mile to one mile. **Uncomfortable standing still** for more than two or three minutes. Some **difficulty on stairs**. Avoids rough ground where possible. Uncomfortable driving for more than half an hour. **Aching sensation in** ankle region in **cold or damp weather**. Incapable of gardening and only capable of lightest home decorating. Unlikely to develop osteo-arthritis as result of accident. Plaintiff lived in Newcastle but worked in London on shift system of four days on and four days off, living in London during shifts and travelling to Newcastle to spend days off. Salary included London weighting allowance. Plaintiff unable to continue active work with fire brigade, and now employed as building society clerk. Current job secure and plaintiff likely to gain promotion. The above award comprised £6,500 for general damages; £5,000 for loss of congenial employment; £19,551·21 for loss of earnings (calculated on a basis including the London weighting allowance with no deduction made for the cost of travelling from Newcastle to London); £48,000 for future loss of earnings (calculated using a multiplicand of £6,000 per annum and a multiplier of eight and again on the basis that no deductions are to be made for travelling expenses); £360 for loss of employment protection; £11,000 for loss of pension; £3,000 for the *Smith v Manchester* award; £1,780 for past decorating work; and £5,125 for loss of future gardening and decorating services. Hidden J stated that he knew of no case in which travelling expenses to work were deducted from a weekly wage and, although the point did not fall to be decided, he did not encourage any insurer or employer to seek to do so. He could, however, envisage a case where travelling expenses loomed so large an element in the damage that further consideration of the question would be justified. *Swinburn v London Fire and Civil Defence Authority* (5 February 1993, unreported) (Queen's Bench Division: Hidden J) (GF Pulman QC and Miss R Howard, Messrs Robin Thompson & Partners, for the plaintiff; RP Croxen QC and MW Jones, Legal Services Department, London Fire and Civil Defence Authority, for the defendant) (Kindly submitted for publication by Robin Thompson and Partners, Solicitors, London).

Total damages: **£12,500**. Plaintiff, male aged 49 at date of accident and 52 at time of trial, was a **pedestrian** knocked down by a car. He sustained a **bi-malleolar fracture** to the left ankle (the major and substantial injury), with a 25–30 per cent risk of **osteoarthritis** and a 20–25 per cent risk of need for **surgery**. He also sustained an **undisplaced medial malleolar fracture** of the right ankle; **abrasion** to the frontal lobe of scalp causing a **scar**, now faded but apparent due to baldness; **laceration** to right elbow causing a **scar** of which plaintiff is aware; **comminuted fracture to distal phalanx** of right big toe; and **soft tissue injury** to neck. Plaintiff in hospital for **three weeks**, left leg in plaster for **two months**, right leg in plaster for **three months**. **Continuing pain** in the left ankle which **gives out** from time to time. Plaintiff appears in court to **shuffle** in an **uncontrollable** way which may or may not be an accurate picture. With both ankles affected, effect on mobility more **severe** and symptoms **continuing**. Scars are **minor**, and difficult to say whether neck injury causing any problems beyond the usual for a man of plaintiff's age. The above award was for general damages. *Thomson v Hailstone* (7 April 1993, unreported) (Southampton County Court: Judge Rudd) (Kindly submitted for publication by Hugh Merry, Barrister).

Total damages: **£9,319·74**. Plaintiff, female police officer aged 26 at date of accident in June 1989 and 30 at time of trial. Whilst alighting from a police van she **stepped onto the edge** of a large pothole. As a result she **sustained ligament damage to her ankle** for which she had to undergo **surgery**. Plaintiff's injury was such that her leg would **give way** on occasions **causing her enormous pain** and making it **impossible for her to work**. She had been off work for about one month immediately after the accident from June to July 1989 and again from December 1989 to February 1990. She **underwent surgery** in April 1991 and was off work again until September 1991. The operation left a four and a half inch **scar** on the lateral aspect of her ankle, causing a **minor cosmetic disability**. Plaintiff has not suffered any problems with her leg since the operation. The judge was satisfied that the injury and subsequent operation were a direct result of the accident. The above award comprised £7,250 general damages and £2,069·74 special damages. *Cooper v Salford City Council* (29 July 1993, unreported) (Manchester County Court: Judge Howarth) (Kindly submitted for publication by Russell Jones & Walker, Solicitors, London).

Total damages: **£6,500**. Plaintiff, female aged 51 at date of accident and 52 at time of trial, suffered a **crack fracture of the navicular bone** in her left ankle when it turned over at edge of stage. **Fracture united satisfactorily** but with some **irregularity** of the articular surface. Total of **eight months in plaster** and thereafter two months of **physiotherapy**. Developed

post-traumatic degenerative change and **disuse osteoporosis**. **Permanent** discomfort. Residual disability no more than five per cent. The above award was made for general damages. *Dinsdale v Urban Firm Ltd* (28 September 1993, unreported) (Liverpool County Court: District Judge Harris) (Kindly submitted for publication by Antonis Georges, Barrister).

Total damages: £1,858·21. Plaintiff, female ticket collector who was employed by the defendants, aged 36 at date of injury in September 1991, slipped and fell down a ramp leading from a railway station. The ramp was wet and was covered with leaves, pine needles and twigs, the area was also very poorly lit. As a result the plaintiff **sprained her left ankle** and was **absent from work for two weeks**. She had a **limp for a further four weeks**, and was left with **residual weakness in her ankle**. Treatment was given by means of tubigrip support and physiotherapy over the initial four weeks. Her ankle has given way on four occasions since the accident although this has not caused further injury. The medical report, which was agreed, suggested that the plaintiff would make a full recovery within a 26-month period from the date of the accident. She is also **unable to dance as much as she used to** and is **unable to wear high heeled shoes** as this causes pain in her ankle after half an hour of wear. The award comprised £1,850 general damages for pain, suffering and loss of amenity and £8·21 interest thereon. *Brelsford v British Railways Board* (18 January 1993, unreported) (Derby County Court: Recorder Benson) (Adrian Jackson, Messrs Pattinson & Brewer for the plaintiff; Miss Burns, Messrs Browne Jackson for the defendants) (Kindly submitted for publication by Adrian Jackson, Barrister and Pattinson & Brewer, Solicitors, London).

964 *Foot*

Total damages: £17,500. Plaintiff, female aged 17 at the date of the accident, sustained a **severe crushing injury to four toes of her right foot** when a stone pillar toppled and fell as she walked along the pathway through a disused cemetery. She suffered **extensive bruising** of the great toe with a **transverse fracture** of its proximal phalanx, **severe crushing** of the distal halves of the second and third toes with **compound fractures** and **exposed bone** in the region of the proximal phalanges of both toes and **extensive crushing** of the distal phalanx of the fourth toe with a **fracture** of the middle phalanx. Within four days of the accident, the **second and third toes were amputated** through the metatarso-phalangeal joint. Nine days later the plaintiff was mobilised non-weight bearing on crutches and discharged home. X-rays revealed **angulation and non-union** at the fracture site of the great toe. Surgical fixation of the proximal phalanx was undertaken but angulation had subsequently returned. The plaintiff continues to experience pain, she has **restricted movement of the great toe**, with significant **deformity of the foot**. Surgical **amputation of the great toe** is recommended medically as inevitable. The defendants denied liability, claiming the plaintiff was a trespasser to the cemetery and further that the falling of the pillar constituted a novus actus interveniens. Before trial, the plaintiff's general and special damages were agreed, subject to liability, at £17,500. At trial, the defendants were found in breach of their duty of care owed to the plaintiff under the Occupier's Liability Act 1984. The doctrine of novus actus interveniens was found not to apply on the facts. *Redding v Sedgemoor District Council* (21 October 1993, unreported) (Bridgwater County Court: Recorder Cottle) (Jeremy Griggs, Clarke Willmot & Clarke for the plaintiff; Sarah Vaughn-Jones, Porter Bartlett & Mayo for the defendants) (Kindly submitted for publication by Clarke Willmot & Clarke, Solicitors, Bridgwater).

Total damages: £2,000. Plaintiff, female aged 37 at time of accident and 40 at date of trial, sustained an injury to her right foot as a result of **falling from a pavement** due to a stepped kerb. There was **no injury to the bone** and she was treated by means of **analgesic tablets** and a **bandage** support. She was given **crutches** to use which she used for seven weeks and four days. At the trial she gave evidence that this had **disrupted her enjoyment** of the Christmas holiday. After the crutches were no longer required she continued to suffer **some pain** which gradually reduced. At the trial, plaintiff gave evidence that since the accident she had been **unable** to wear a closed shoe as these caused pain in the foot. There was no claim for special damages; general damages were £2,000, reduced by 65 per cent for contributory negligence. *Thorpe v Calderdale MBC* (29 April 1993, unreported) (Halifax County Court: District Judge Lamb) (Kindly submitted for publication by Rhodes Thain & Collinson, Solicitors, Halifax).

Total damages: £1,580·73. Plaintiff, male aged 16 at time of accident in July 1989, sustained injuries when he attempted to cross the road, unaware that a bus was turning left into that road. Plaintiff attempted to step back, but his **right foot was run over by the bus's back wheel**. Plaintiff **sustained fractures** through the **base of the proximal phalanges** of the **right** fourth and fifth toes and through the neck of the proximal phalanx of the right third toe. Heel skin partially degloved. Manipulation of fracture the day after the accident, inpatient at hospital for five days in July 1989, then discharged home with crutches. Partial weight bearing on 4 September 1989. Discharged from follow-up on 27 November 1989. No residual disability around heel. Complaints of residual symptoms of a feeling of no padding under foot and sharp pain on occasions. At trial only unpadded feeling persisted. No severe functional disability but mild functional disability of nuisance value. This would be permanent, but no risk of degenerative arthritis. Sporting activities of football and squash given up but this was found to be due to lack of interest rather than effects of injury. Plaintiff working as labourer at date of trial prior to going on a world holiday and thereafter to college. No loss of earning capacity found. The above award comprised £3,000 general damages; £55 special damages; and £53·23 interest. Damages reduced by 50 per cent for contributory negligence. *Phillips v Southern Vectis plc* (28 October 1993, unreported) (Southampton County Court: Judge Galpin) (Richard Egleton, Messrs Parker Bullen for the plaintiff; William Norris, Messrs Berrymans for the defendant) (Kindly submitted for publication by Richard Egleton, Barrister).

Total damages: £1,500. Plaintiff, female aged three at time of accident and five at date of trial, was struck on left foot by bricks falling from wall, from a height of about four feet. Grazing, crack fracture of the shaft of the first metatarsal of the left foot, complete plaster cast applied which allowed her to walk, removed after two weeks. Residual swelling for about two months after accident. Excellent recovery with no long term consequences. The above award was for general damages. *Harcourt v Harper* (6 August 1993, unreported) (Chesterfield County Court: District Judge Owen) (Kindly submitted for publication by Kelly & Anderson, Solicitors, Chesterfield).

MINOR INJURIES

965 *Minor injury with anxiety neurosis*

Scotland
Total damages: £9,847. Plaintiff, when aged 28, sustained an alarming but minor physical injury at work when her arm was trapped in a housing on a conveyor belt. The accident gave rise to an anxiety neurosis. She gave up work for a period not because of anxiety but because of alleged pain in her arm. She had and might continue to have some difficulty, unrelated to her physical condition, in coping with certain types of machinery which might prejudice her ability to undertake some kind of employment in the future. There would be no persisting psychological disability and no physical disability beyond the date of the award of damages which comprised £4,000 for injury to feelings; loss of earnings £978·80; loss of employability £4,000; and interest at £868·20. *McGunnigal v DB Marshall (Newbridge) Ltd (note)* 1993 SLT 769 (Outer House).

966 *Minor injuries*

Total damages: £5,821·32 (with a 30 per cent reduction for contributory negligence). Plaintiff, female aged 68 at date of accident and 70 at date of trial, was knocked over by a car while attempting to cross the road. She sustained lacerations to her face, nose, mouth and scalp, and lost a number of teeth. She also suffered injuries to her back and to both legs although no fractures were present. She remained in hospital overnight and thereafter was admitted to a rest home for a five-week period of convalescence. Her left thigh was swollen for a number of weeks and she experienced difficulties in walking on her left leg. Ulcerations of the leg developed and took several weeks to heal. At the date of the trial she complained of pain in her lower back for which she took paracetamol daily, and aching in her thighs and knees. She had been fitted with a denture but found herself unable to wear it, although the removal of her remaining teeth was not attributable to the accident. Her quality of life has been adversely affected by the accident making a previously independent woman dependent on assistance with shopping and housework. She was also "terrified" of crossing the road. In view of her age improvement in her residual symptoms and mobility was considered unlikely. The award comprised £4,500 general damages for pain, suffering and loss of amenity, £225 interest on general damages, £846·40 special damages, and £244·92 interest on special damages. *Littlefair v Turner* (12 January 1993, unreported) (Preston County Court: Judge Holt) (Timothy White, Messrs Dickson Child Green & Greensmith for the plaintiff; Mr Main, Messrs Keogh Ritson for the defendant) (Kindly submitted for publication by Emma Cornah, Pupil Barrister).

967 *Skin*

Total damages: £2,400. Plaintiff, infant aged four and a half weeks at time of injury, had been admitted to hospital for treatment requiring a pyloromyotomy, in which the **muscle at the lower end of the stomach is divided** to allow the stomach contents to pass freely into the duodenum, thereby preventing vomiting. A **drip was inserted into the dorsum of the patient's right foot** but, the infusion **site was not inspected** until the morning after admission when the foot was found to be **very swollen** and there was **blistering** around the foot and ankle and the swelling extended to the thigh. It was accepted that the drip infusion was allowed to run into the tissues for a prolonged period of time during the night when it should have been inspected. As a result the blood supplied to the skin was obstructed and an area of **skin necrosis occurred**. This healed slowly over a period of nine weeks when dressings were changed frequently. The only **residual disability** was a **small scar** approximately two centimetres square on the dorsum of the right foot. Liability was accepted and the Health Authority settled the claim for the above amount. *MLD v Torbay Health Authority* (settled out of court) (Kindly submitted for publication by Derek S Reed, Solicitor, Devon).

968   Personal injury—repetitive strain injury—lengthy use of visual display unit

The plaintiff, who worked as a journalist, sought damages for personal injury and consequential loss from his former employer. Within a month of starting work he complained that he was suffering from tingling and numbness in his fingers and hands, then in his forearms. These symptoms worsened and his doctor gave him national insurance certificates on the basis that he had repetitive strain injury (RSI) tenosynovitis. The plaintiff alleged that he had suffered pain in his fingers, hands, arms and shoulders due to the length of time he had to sit at his desk and the position he was obliged to sit in as he worked at his visual display unit. He further alleged that his former employer failed to provide him with adequate advice and equipment to enable him to carry out his work in safety. *Held*, the term RSI was meaningless and its use by doctors could only confuse. The mainstream view was that there was no pathology and no clinical symptoms that could be pointed to as confirming a patient as having RSI. The plaintiff had failed to convince the court that he had suffered any injury as had been alleged, and the evidence did not show any failure or breach by his former employer such as to establish causation. It was clear that his former employer had been a careful and prudent employer and, accordingly, the claim for damages would be dismissed.

Mughal v Reuters Ltd (1993) Independent, 2 November (Queen's Bench Division: John Prosser QC).

969   Personal injury—vocational assessment—proceedings stayed pending plaintiff's submission to assessment

See *Bird v Longridge*, para 2062.

970   Structured settlements—provisional view of Law Commission

In a consultation paper, *Structured Settlements and Interim and Provisional Damages* (consultation paper 125), the Law Commission has looked at awards of damages for personal injuries and has provisionally concluded that actuarial evidence should receive greater judicial recognition and that greater use should be made of information from the financial markets to determine the appropriate rate at which to discount multipliers. It suggests a possible change in the taxation of annuities bought with personal injuries damages and considers the taxation of structured settlements. It further recommends, provisionally, that the uncertainties surrounding the ability of the Criminal Injuries Compensation Board and the Motor Insurers' Bureau to offer structured settlements should be removed. It considers the reviewability of structured settlements, the monitoring of the negotiations and a judicial power to impose and to review settlements. In relation to interim awards of damages, consideration is given to the effect of the recoupment of social security benefits and it is suggested that the courts should have jurisdiction to order the Motor Insurers' Bureau to make interim awards. A provisional recommendation is made that provisional awards of damages should not be extended to include the gradual deterioration of a plaintiff's condition nor to the medical uncertainty of recovery and that provisional awards should remain within the courts' overriding discretion, although a further or second application might be appropriate. It is also recommended, provisionally, that provisional and interim awards should be structured.

971 Trespass—trespass to land—measure of damages—property let at concessionary rent

The respondents were a couple living in married quarters rented from the Royal Air Force (the appellants). The husband, a flight sergeant, had signed a certificate which provided that he and his family were entitled to occupy the property only so long as he remained a serving member of the Royal Air Force, living with his spouse. The husband moved out, leaving his wife and children in possession, and the appellants gave notice for his wife to vacate. She did not do so until she was able to obtain local authority accommodation, one year later. The court granted possession to the appellants and awarded them mesne profits calculated by taking the national average of local authority rents and deducting 42·5 per cent to reflect the disadvantage of service occupation. On appeal as to the damages awarded, *held*, the measure of damages where a tenant remained on residential property as a trespasser was usually the proper letting value of the property which was, in an ordinary case and in a free market, the value to the trespasser of its use. In the present case, the property was not normally let on the open market, and the wife only remained in possession because she was in no position to move anywhere else. Therefore, more assistance as to the proper value to the wife of the use of the property might have been gained by looking at what she would have had to pay for suitable local authority accommodation, rather than by focusing on evidence given on behalf of the appellants as to market rent. The appeal would be allowed and the matter returned to the county court for damages to be reassessed.

The court also held that a person entitled to possession of land could make a claim against a person who had been in occupation without his consent, for either damages for the loss that he had suffered because of the trespass, or restitution of the value of the benefit that the occupier had received, and that the present case was a claim for restitution. Lloyd LJ dissented on the ground that the restitutionary remedy was not available in the case of wrongful occupation of land. The damages ought to have been equal to the amount that the rent would have been if the appellants had let the property to another tenant. In the present circumstances this sum would in practice have been no more than the artificially low level of rent applicable in the case of married quarters occupied by members of Her Majesty's Services.

Ministry of Defence v Ashman (1993) 25 HLR 513 (Court of Appeal: Lloyd, Kennedy and Hoffmann LJJ). *Swordheath Properties v Tabet*.[1979] 1 All ER 240 applied.

The respondent was a deserted army wife who remained in occupation in married quarters after her husband's licence to occupy the premises had been terminated. On an application to determine mesne profits, the judge at first instance ruled that the mesne profits ought to be calculated by reference to the previous rent rather than the open market value. On appeal, *held*, the principles formulated in *Ministry of Defence v Ashman* (supra) were equally applicable to the present case. The value of the right of occupation to a former licensee who has occupied at a concessionary rent and who has remained in possession only because she could not be rehoused by the local authority until a possession order had been made, would ordinarily be whichever was the higher of the former concessionary rent and what she would have paid for local authority housing suitable for her needs if she had been rehoused at the time when the notice expired. The appeal would be dismissed.

Ministry of Defence v Thompson (1993) 25 HLR 552 (Court of Appeal: Glidewell and Hoffmann LJJ and Sir John Megaw). *Ministry of Defence v Ashman* (1993) 25 HLR 513 supra applied.

972 Unlawful eviction—exemplary damages

See *Ramdath v Daley*, para 1647.

973 Unlawful eviction—quantum

See *Sullman v Little*, para 1646.

DATA PROTECTION

Halsbury's Laws of England (4th edn) Vol 12, Supp paras 1300A–1300G

974 Citizens' charter—access to information

See para 542.

975   Registration—improper use of data—viewing of data

The Data Protection Act 1984, s 5(2)(b) provides that a person who is registered under the Act to hold data must not hold any such data, or use any such data held by him, for any purpose other than the purpose specified in the register.

A police officer and a debt collector were convicted under the 1984 Act, s 5(2)(b) of improper use of personal data stored in a police computer. On their appeal against conviction, a question arose as to the meaning of the word "use" in s 5(2)(b). *Held*, the purpose of the 1984 Act was to protect the interests of private individuals. There was a distinction between gaining access to a computer in order to view information contained in it and using that information. The word "use" in its ordinary meaning required the taking of steps, beyond merely looking at the information, to deploy it in some way. As the defendants in the present case had not taken such steps, their appeal would be allowed.

R v Brown (1993) Times, 4 June (Court of Appeal: Staughton LJ, Popplewell and Laws JJ).

DEEDS AND OTHER INSTRUMENTS

Halsbury's Laws of England (4th edn) Vol 12, paras 1301–1566

976   Construction—contractual term—construction to advantage of party in breach of contract

See *Thornton v Abbey National plc*, para 592.

977   Deed—construction—conveyance of property—identification of property transferred

See *Rhone v Stephens*, para 1228.

978   Deed—construction—omission making term of deed ineffective if construed literally—intention of parties

The residue of a testator's estate was left to his three sons absolutely. In order to reduce the amount of inheritance tax payable, his wife, one of the executors, and his three sons and the other two executors executed a deed, within two years of the testator's death, varying the terms of the will so as to increase the part of the estate which attracted the surviving spouse's exemption. Under the deed, a pecuniary legacy was to be held as to income for the testator's wife for life and thereafter to the three sons absolutely. Provision was also made to the effect that "notwithstanding the terms of this deed income of and from assets money or property the subject hereof shall devolve as if this deed had not been executed". It fell to be determined whether the deed of variation was effective to vary the terms of the testator's will and, if it was, whether, on the true construction of the will and the deed, the income arising after the date of the execution of the deed of the additional pecuniary legacy referred to in the deed was held on trust to pay the same to the testator's wife for life or, if it was not so effective, whether the deed might be rectified. *Held*, where it was clear from a deed itself that words had been omitted by inadvertence, in construing the deed words would only be supplied so as to give effect to the clear intentions of the parties. It had to be clear, therefore, not only that a mistake of omission had been made but also what correction was required in order to carry out the intentions of the parties. There was a blatant contradiction between the aforementioned terms of the deed which was clearly not intended. It was apparent that a mistake had been made in that the reference to "income" should be taken to be income of the period between the testator's death and the deed of variation. The court would make a declaration that the deed should be so construed.

Schnieder v Mills [1993] 3 All ER 377 (Chancery Division: Robert Walker QC).

979   Interpretation—extrinsic evidence—parol evidence rule

It has been held that the parol evidence rule still applies in relation to documents which record the exchanges between parties to a contract and has not been relaxed as a result of the decision in *Pepper v Hart* [1992] 3 WLR 1032, HL (1992 Abr para 2498). The exclusion of parol evidence serves a valuable purpose, particularly in relation to transfers of interests in land. Subsequent purchasers of an interest in land should be entitled to read and understand the conveyancing documents without the assistance of the parties' recollections.

W F Trustees v Expo Safety Systems Ltd (1993) Times, 24 May (Chancery Division: Jonathan Sumption QC).

DISCOVERY, INSPECTION AND INTERROGATORIES

Halsbury's Laws of England (4th edn) Vol 13, paras 1–200

980 Articles
Public Interest Immunity, Ian Saunders: Tax Journal, Issue 226, p 18

981 Anton Piller orders
See PRACTICE AND PROCEDURE.

982 Disclosure of documents—post-judgment disclosure—order against third party—jurisdiction
See *Mercantile Group (Europe) AG v Aiyela*, para 1529.

983 Discovery—damages for personal injuries—evidence casting doubt on one party's bona fides—surreptitiously made video
The plaintiff brought an action against the defendant for damages for personal injuries. There was an issue as to whether or not the effects of the injuries which the plaintiff suffered were being exaggerated by him. An inquiry agent employed by the defendant made a videotape film of the plaintiff without the plaintiff's knowledge. Leave was granted for the defendant to put the video film in evidence at the trial without the plaintiff being given an opportunity to view the same. The plaintiff appealed on the ground that there was a breach of the requirements of RSC Ord 38, r 5 in that the affidavit upon which the defendant had obtained the order did not identify any "special reasons" other than that the evidence was relevant to an issue in the action and to the plaintiff's bona fides. *Held*, it was a sufficient special reason to justify an order under Ord 38, r 5 that the purpose of the evidence concerned was to cast doubt upon the bona fides of the plaintiff's own case as opposed merely to its strength, therefore prior disclosure of the evidence concerned would give the plaintiff the opportunity to adjust his evidence and thereby increase the lack of bona fides. Accordingly, the appeal would be dismissed.

Rattee J observed that the Supreme Court Practice (1991), p 632 note requiring a party applying under it to specify other reasons, in addition to the bona fides of the other party, was in error.

Morris v British Coal Corpn [1992] PIQR P366 (Queen's Bench Division: Rattee J).

984 Discovery of documents—affidavit evidence—pre-trial cross-examination on affidavits
Following the acquisition of a company by the plaintiffs' the defendant, who also wished to bid for the company, brought an action against the plaintiffs alleging wrongful interference with the defendant's business and conspiracy. An order was made under RSC Ord 24, r 7 for specific discovery and the plaintiffs made affidavits listing the documents and verifying the facts about documents no longer in their possession. The defendant applied to strike out the defence under RSC Ord 24, r 16 alleging that the plaintiffs' discovery was deficient and that their evidence about documents not in their possession was untrue. Following an order by the court for the plaintiffs to be cross-examined on their affidavits of documents, the plaintiffs appealed. *Held*, in following *Jones v The Monte Video Gas Co* [1880] 5 QBD 556, cross-examination on affidavits of documents was prohibited and the oath or an affirmation pursuant to an order for specific discovery under RSC Ord 24, r 7 was conclusive. Where a party alleged that another party had suppressed documents, the issue would be crucially relevant to the issues in the trial and could only properly be determined after the trial judge had heard all the evidence. To try the issue at an interlocutory stage would involve injustice to both sides. The judge had erred in admitting cross-examination and accordingly, the appeal would be allowed.

Lonrho plc v Fayed (No 5) [1994] 1 All ER 188 (Court of Appeal: Stuart-Smith, McCowan and Kennedy LJJ).

985 Discovery of documents—foreign firm—liability to criminal proceedings

French law provides that, "without prejudice to international agreements or treaties and laws and regulations in force, all persons are prohibited from applying for, searching or communicating, in writing, verbally or in any other form, documents or information of an economic, commercial, industrial, financial or technical nature aimed at the establishment of evidence with a view to foreign administrative or legal proceedings or within the framework thereof."

In an action against the defendants an order was made for discovery and inspection of documents. The defendants applied to have the order set aside on the ground that compliance with the order would leave them open to prosecution under French law. It was argued that it would be contrary to public policy to force a defendant to commit a criminal act in a foreign state and that under the general principles of conflict of laws, performance of a contract was excused if the contract necessarily involved doing an act which was unlawful by the law of the place where it had to be done. *Held*, there was no English decision where it had been submitted that the court ought not to order discovery against a French party in view of the law in question and there was no evidence that any person had ever been prosecuted for breach of that particular provision. Further, all matters of procedure were governed by the domestic law of the country in which the court where any legal proceedings were taken was situated. Accordingly, the application would be dismissed.

Partenreederei M/S "Heidberg" v Grosvenor Grain and Feed Co Ltd, The Heidberg [1993] 2 Lloyd's Rep 324 (Queen's Bench Division: Cresswell J).

986 Discovery of documents—implied undertaking as to confidentiality of documents—libel proceedings brought in relation to disclosed document

RSC Ord 24, r 14A provides that any undertaking, express or implied, not to use a document for any purposes other than those of the proceedings in which it is disclosed, ceases to apply to such document after it has been read to or by the court, or referred to in open court, unless the court, for special reasons, has otherwise ordered on the application of a party, or of the person to whom the document belongs.

The plaintiff brought defamation proceedings against the defendant solicitors over an attendance note disclosed as part of the discovery process in another action and read out in open court during the hearing of that action. The judge at first instance struck out the defamation proceedings on the ground that the plaintiff was bound to an implied undertaking that he would only use the disclosed attendance note for the purposes of conducting his case in the action for which it was disclosed. In those circumstances, the plaintiff could not found another action upon it. On appeal by the plaintiff, *held*, the relevant issue was the extent of the application of RSC Ord 24, r 14A. If that rule applied to all documents read out in open court, it would be a great injustice to the defendant solicitors who had written the note but were not parties to the action in which it was disclosed, as they would have no way of applying to the court to have the implied undertaking by the plaintiff brought back into effect. This injustice would be avoided if the application of RSC Ord 24, r 14A was limited so that a person was only freed from his undertaking for the purposes of making known the contents of a document and not for using it for any other purpose, including bringing a libel action. The scope of the rule could not be such as to effect a fundamental change in the law which would create a substantial injustice to people in the same position as the defendant solicitors in this case. Accordingly, the appeal would be dismissed and the plaintiff would not be released from his implied undertaking.

Singh v Christie (1993) Times, 11 November (Queen's Bench Division: Drake J).

987 Discovery of documents—patent action—action involving multinational companies

In a patent action the plaintiff company, part of a multinational organisation, commenced proceedings for discovery against the defendants, who were part of a different multinational organisation. The defendants unsuccessfully applied to have the proceedings set aside on the ground that there was no evidence to link them with the alleged infringement and, on appeal, *held*, in patent actions it was standard practice to ask for discovery of the research and development which had gone into the defendant's product in order to demonstrate, by reference to the work of the defendant's own researchers, that the subject matter of the work could not have been obvious to them. That approach worked adequately when the research, manufacture and sale were all undertaken by the same company, but it was less useful in the case of a multinational organisation in which sale, research and manufacture could have been carried out by different companies in different countries. The plaintiff could only have obtained discovery against the defendants if it had been able to show that the defendants had arguably been a party to a common intention to commit the alleged infringement, but it had failed to do so. Accordingly, the appeal would be allowed and the summons set aside.

Hoffmann LJ observed that the rules of discovery in patent actions concerning multinational companies were unsatisfactory and ought to be amended so that discovery of research and development documents would be obtainable against a multinational on a group basis.

Unilever plc v Chefaro (1993) Times, 29 March (Court of Appeal: Glidewell, McCowan and Hoffmann LJJ). *Unilever plc v Gillette (UK) Ltd* [1989] RPC 583 (1989 Abr para 1707) considered.

988   Discovery of documents—personal injury action—disclosure of defendant's medical reports

The plaintiff had sustained a neck injury in the course of his employment. He was unable to resume work and sought damages for loss of earnings up to normal retirement age. His employers indicated they wanted him to be examined by their own consultant, and they also requested that all his hospital records, general practitioner's notes and the notes of the employers' own medical officer should be disclosed to their consultant. The judge restricted disclosure to material which related to a pre-existing neck injury, stating that the employers were not entitled to embark on an extensive search of the plaintiff's medical history in the hope of uncovering other information which might be relevant to the question of damages. On the employers' appeal, *held*, the question of the financial loss which resulted from the plaintiff's injury could be affected by whether there had been either a pre-existing condition relating to the plaintiff's neck, or an unrelated condition which might supervene to affect the plaintiff's working capacity before he reached normal retirement age. There was no doubt that the disputed evidence was relevant to those issues, so the employers would have been able to issue a subpoena for the production of those documents at the start of the trial if the plaintiff refused to disclose them earlier. However, early disclosure was desirable in the interests of justice and, accordingly, the appeal would be allowed.

Dunn v British Coal Corpn [1993] ICR 591 (Court of Appeal: Nourse, Stuart-Smith and Mann LJJ).

989   Discovery of documents—persons not parties to the proceedings—production of transcripts—whether necessary for fair disposal of action

During the plaintiff's cross-examination of a witness called on behalf of the second defendant in the trial of an action for the recovery of assets transferred to the defendants, the witness was asked to produce copies of transcripts of his private examination under the Insolvency Act 1986, s 236 by the liquidators of a company which was closely associated with the first defendant. The witness, who was not a party to the action, declined to produce the transcripts unless ordered to do so by the court. He claimed that the application for production was speculative, that the liquidators had imposed restrictions which prevented him from producing the transcripts and that he was entitled to rely on a public interest immunity which prevented disclosure of the transcripts to third parties, such as the plaintiff, without consent. The judge, who dealt with the matter on the assumption that a subpoena duces tecum had been served on the witness requiring him to produce the transcripts, refused to make an order for their production on the ground that production was not necessary for disposing fairly of the cause or matter. The plaintiff appealed. *Held*, an order for the production of documents should not be made unless the court was of the opinion that the order was necessary either for disposing fairly of the cause or matter or for saving costs. The mere fact that a document was wanted for the purposes of cross-examination did not automatically mean that it could not be obtained by the process of a subpoena duces tecum but the purpose of a subpoena was to obtain evidence and not merely to obtain discovery which might lead to something else in the course of the development of the party's case. Since the plaintiff's only purpose in obtaining the transcripts was to see if the witness had made statements to the liquidators which were inconsistent with his evidence under cross-examination, it had not been shown that the production of the documents was necessary for the fair disposal of the action. The appeal would accordingly be dismissed.

MacMillan Inc v Bishopsgate Investment Trust Ltd [1993] 4 All ER 998 (Court of Appeal: Dillon and Kennedy LJJ and Sir Roger Parker). Decision of Millett J [1993] 4 All ER 998 affirmed. *R v Clowes* [1992] 3 All ER 440 (1992 Abr para 644) distinguished.

990   Discovery of documents—Police Complaints Authority—documents—public interest immunity

See *R v Blackhouse*, para 1980; *R v Chief Constable of the West Midlands, ex p Wiley; R v Chief Constable of Nottinghamshire Police, ex p Sunderland*, para 1981.

991   Discovery of documents—privilege—documents from separate interlocutory proceedings

A dispute arose between the defendant, acting as a sub-agent to R the charterer, and the plaintiff ship owner. The matter was referred to arbitration and the solicitors for the defendant accepted instructions in relation to the arbitration from R. Following a disagreement between R and the defendant as to the conduct of the proceedings, R applied, ex parte, for an injunction against the defendant. The application was supported by affidavit documents which included opinions from solicitors and counsel. The ex parte application was settled and the solicitors for the defendant resumed the practice of taking instructions from R in relation to the arbitration. At the arbitration the defendant claimed that he was protected by common interest privilege from producing for inspection the injunction affidavits, the settlement agreement and correspondence between R and the defendant either directly or through their solicitors. The arbitrators found in favour of the defendant and the plaintiff appealed. *Held*, the defendant and R had at all times a common interest in the claim being advanced by the defendant in the arbitration. That common interest did not come to an end simply because a dispute arose as to the conduct of the proceedings. However, the object of the affidavits was to advance R's case in a dispute with the defendant, and the doctrine of common interest legal professional privilege did not extend to such a purpose. Accordingly, the appeal would be allowed.

Leif Hoegh & Co A/S Petrolsea Inc, The World Era (No 2) [1993] 1 Lloyds Rep 363 (Queen's Bench Division: Phillips J). For earlier related proceedings, see [1991] 1 Lloyds Rep 45 (1991 Abr para 100).

992   Discovery of documents—privilege—legal professional privilege—disclosure of medical reports

It has been held that in actions under the Children Act 1989, legal advisers, in the interests of the child, must disclose medical reports containing adverse statements relating to parties. In considering the welfare of the child, the court has the power to override claims of legal professional privilege.

Re R (A Minor) [1993] 4 All ER 702 (Family Division: Thorpe J).

993   Discovery of documents—trade mark proceedings—use of information disclosed against third parties

See *Levi Strauss & Co v Barclays Trading Corpn Inc*, para 2542.

994   Production of documents—analogy with order in inquiry into company's dealings—principles to be applied

See *Re Polly Peck International plc*, para 483.

995   Production of documents—privilege—legal professional privilege—inadvertent disclosure

The plaintiff had obtained two medical reports which were adverse to his claim for damages for personal injury. In response to an order for discovery made under the Supreme Court Act 1981, s 34(2), the plaintiff's solicitor inadvertently sent the two adverse reports to the defendants' solicitor, but the court refused to grant an application by the plaintiff for an injunction restraining the defendants from relying on those reports. On the plaintiff's appeal, *held*, the principle that a party should be able to rely on the discovery of his adversary would apply unless discovery had been obtained by fraud or mistake. There was no question of fraud, and if the plaintiff contended that a mistake had been made the onus was on him to satisfy the court that the defendants' solicitor ought to have realised that the reports had been sent erroneously. The defendants' solicitor had sworn that she genuinely believed the reports had been disclosed pursuant to the order for discovery, and the court had not been satisfied that in the circumstances a reasonable solicitor ought to have realised that the privilege had not been waived. There were no grounds for granting the injunction and, accordingly, the appeal would be dismissed.

Pizzey v Ford Motor Co Ltd (1993) Times, 8 March (Court of Appeal: Nourse, Stuart-Smith and Mann LJJ). *Guinness Peat Properties Ltd v Fitzroy Robinson Partnership* [1987] 2 All ER 716, CA (1987 Abr para 787) considered.

996 Production of documents—privilege—matrimonial matters—statements made in conciliation proceedings

The parties to a marriage had made statements in the course of meetings held for the purpose of conciliation. In proceedings under the Children Act 1989, the mother applied for those statements to be disclosed, but her application was rejected on the ground that the statements were privileged. The mother appealed, contending the husband had not made the statements in the course of a bona fide attempt to conciliate and privilege could not be claimed by a party who had not made such an attempt. *Held*, the court did not accept that evidence could be given of statements made by a party to a conciliation attempt who, in the judgment of the other party or a conciliator, had not shown a genuine willingness to compromise. Conciliation was an important means of resolving disputes which concerned children, and non-disclosure was vital if the value of conciliation was to be maintained. Such statements should not be disclosed in proceedings under the 1989 Act unless they clearly indicated that the maker had caused, or was likely to cause, serious harm to the well-being of the child, and even in those circumstances the trial judge would still have to exercise a discretion whether or not to admit that evidence. There had been no suggestion that the father's statement indicated that the child's interests had been, or would be, harmed, and, accordingly, the appeal would be dismissed.

Re D (Minors) (Conciliation: Disclosure of Information) [1993] 2 All ER 693 (Court of Appeal: Sir Thomas Bingham MR, Butler-Sloss and Rose LJJ).

997 Production of documents—privilege—public interest immunity—abortion records

As part of their campaign against abortion, the defendants targeted a clinic where abortions were carried out and obstructed entrances to the building. They were convicted of disorderly behaviour and on appeal against conviction they contended their conduct was reasonable and justified and served a witness summons on an officer of the clinic to produce documents relating to scheduled abortions. A court set aside the summons and upheld the convictions. The defendants appealed, contending the documents were relevant to their defence. *Held*, the restriction on the disclosure of abortion records was imposed to encourage the use of safe and legitimate procedures so that patients would give information and submit to treatment in the knowledge that indiscriminate disclosure of such matters was prohibited. The documents were neither relevant nor material to the defences. Even if the documents were relevant, balancing the two competing public interests, the public interest in disclosure had to give way. The witness summons had been correctly set aside. Furthermore, even allowing for the sincerity of the defendants' views and the importance of the issue of abortion, their conduct in the organised invasion of the grounds of the clinic and the distress thereby caused made it difficult to consider the behaviour of the defendants as directed to the prevention of crime, particularly when they were preventing others from exercising their lawful rights. Accordingly, the appeal would be dismissed.

DPP v Morrow (1993) Independent, 13 April (Queen's Bench Division: Farquharson LJ and Wright J).

998 Production of documents—privilege—public interest immunity—acceptance of ministerial certificate

The employee, in pursuance of his claim of unfair dismissal, sought disclosure of certain documents in the possession of his former employers which related to the security and intelligence services. The Foreign Secretary and the Home Secretary signed three certificates claiming public interest immunity in respect of those documents, and an industrial tribunal refused the employee's application without going behind the ministers' statements to assess the dangers of disclosure. On appeal by the employee, it was held that some claims for public interest immunity were capable of being weighed by judicial experience, but when immunity was claimed on the ground that disclosure might endanger national security it would be inappropriate for industrial tribunals to go behind the ministerial certificate to assess the dangers of disclosure because questions of national security were not generally suitable for judicial evaluation. On further appeal by the employee, *held*, the court was bound by the terms of the certificates. Although the court must always ensure that public interest immunity was properly exercised, once the need for such immunity had been proved by an appropriate certificate, the court had no power to inspect. Therefore, in this case, the uninhibited prosecution of the employee's claim for unfair dismissal could not prevail and accordingly, the appeal would be dismissed.

Balfour v Foreign and Commonwealth Office (1993) Times, 10 December (Court of Appeal: Russell, McCowan and Hirst LJJ). Decision of Knox J [1993] ICR 663 affirmed.

999 Production of documents—privilege—public interest immunity—police complaints authority

See *R v Blackhouse*, para 1980.

1000 Production of documents—privilege—public interest immunity—tax documents

The appellants were ordered to produce tax documents on the grounds that, although public interest immunity attached to the documents, the public interest in their disclosure outweighed that in their non-disclosure. On appeal, *held*, the first issue was whether documents in the Inland Revenue's possession which related to a taxpayer's affairs were subject to public interest immunity if the taxpayer did not consent to their disclosure. A claim by the Revenue to withhold such documents was properly to be regarded as a claim for public immunity. It was established in *Conway v Rimmer* [1968] AC 910, HL, that where the state insisted on disclosure for a particular purpose, it required a very strong case to justify that disclosure being used for other purposes. The courts gave great weight to preserving the confidentiality of such documents in the hands of the Revenue and overrode it only where an applicant showed that, on the particular facts, the public interest in the administration of justice outweighed that in preserving confidentiality. The second issue was whether public interest, once established on the first issue, automatically extended to documents held by the taxpayer and his agents. There were no grounds to support that argument: statute imposed obligations of confidentiality on the Revenue but made no provision for protection of documents in the taxpayer's possession; in a series of Scottish and Commonwealth cases production had been ordered against the taxpayer, and the decision in *Conway v Rimmer* related to the state and had no bearing on whether the taxpayer himself could be required to produce the documents. Thus, public interest immunity did not attach to documents held by a taxpayer. It was not necessary to consider the third issue of whether, balancing the public interest in disclosure against that in non-disclosure, production should be ordered (although on the facts the public interest in non-disclosure would have been outweighed). Accordingly, the appeal would be dismissed.

Lonrho plc v Fayed (No 4) [1994] STC 153 (Court of Appeal: Bingham MR, Leggatt and Roch LJJ). Dictum of Lord Reid in *Conway v Rimmer* [1968] AC 910 at 946, HL, applied. Decision of Popplewell J (1993) Times, 13 July affirmed.

1001 Public interest immunity—industrial tribunal—police grievance procedure

The plaintiff initiated industrial tribunal proceedings against the defendant police force, her employers, complaining of racial and sexual discrimination in relation to her application for a post as a CID officer. She also invoked the internal grievance procedure. The plaintiff made a further complaint alleging that she had been victimised following her earlier complaint. An industrial tribunal ordered discovery of statements made during the grievance procedure and the defendants appealed on the ground that the statements were subject to public interest immunity. *Held*, because part of the plaintiff's complaint was that the grievance procedure had not been properly pursued, the result of the grievance procudeure was a legitimate subject for inspection in relation to that complaint. In *Neilson v Laugharne* documents generated under the disciplinary and complaints procedures under the Police Act 1964, s 49 were held to be subject to public interest immunity. The grievance procedure differed from the disciplinary and complaints procedures sufficiently to distinguish the decision in the above case in that those procedures were statutory processes intended to punish and deter wrong-doers, whereas the grievance procedure was a purely internal procedure which was more concerned with promoting non-discriminatory practices and securing remedies for victims of discriminatory practices. Therefore, the industrial tribunal had succeeding in striking the balance between the public interest in the administration of justice in securing that all relevant material was before the tribunal and the public interest in the proper functioning of the police. Accordingly, the appeal would be dismissed.

Comr of Police of the Metropolis v Locker [1993] 3 All ER 584 (Employment Appeal Tribunal: Knox J presiding). *Neilson v Laugharne* [1981] 1 QB 736, CA, *Halford v Brooks* [1992] ICR 583, CA distinguished.

DISTRESS

Halsbury's Laws of England (4th edn) Vol 13, paras 201–500

1002   Distress for rates—injunctive relief for excessive distress

A local authority had levied distress against a company in respect of a liability order for unpaid non-domestic rates, in accordance with the Non-Domestic Rating (Collection and Enforcement) (Local Lists) Regulations 1989, SI 1989/1058. A firm of certified bailiffs involved in the distraint process allegedly damaged the company's property and caused personal injury to one of its directors. The company subsequently paid the arrears and sought an injunction in the county court to restrain the bailiffs from disposing of the goods on the ground that the bailiffs had acted unlawfully. The injunction was granted and the bailiffs appealed, contending the 1989 Regulations restricted an aggrieved ratepayer to his rights of appeal in the magistrates' court in respect of securing the return of seized goods. Held, distress for rates was a statutory remedy which authorised what would otherwise be trespass or interference with goods. The levying of excessive distress had not been authorised by statute and was now the tort of wrongful interference with goods under the Torts (Interference with Goods) Act 1977, and the county court's general jurisdiction in such matters had not been ousted by the operation of the 1989 Regulations. The judge below had acted within his discretion in granting the injunction and the court would not interfere with his decision. Accordingly, the appeal would be dismissed.

Steel Linings Ltd v Bibby & Co [1993] RA 27 (Court of Appeal: Balcombe and Simon Brown LJJ and Peter Gibson J).

1003   Distress for rent—insolvency of tenant—right of landlord to distrain

See McMullen & Sons Ltd v Cerrone, para 193.

1004   Distress for rent—refusal to pay service charge—legality of distress

The tenant leased industrial units from the landlord. The lease provided that at the end of each year, the tenant was to pay a sum for the following year's service charge equal to the amount of the previous year's service charge, with adjustments at the end of each year. In practice, this system was not operated and the tenant paid a sum each quarter, comprising rent and regular expenses which had been invoiced. The tenant was dissatisfied with an invoice and refused to pay the requested amount, substituting a lower amount. The landlord authorised bailiffs to distrain the goods, chattels and effects in the industrial units. The tenant's action for damages for trespass and illegal distress was dismissed on the ground that the distress was lawful. On appeal, held, the practice adopted by the landlord and tenant with regard to the collection of the service charge was not sufficient to enable the landlord to distrain the tenant's goods for failure to pay a service charge which had fallen due in accordance with the practice but which was different from the sums which would have been payable had the covenants in the lease been applied. Distress would only be an effective remedy if it were shown that it was part of the arrangement and was clearly understood and accepted by the tenant that failure to conform to the practice rendered him liable to have his goods distrained. The appeal would accordingly be allowed.

D'Jan v Bond Street Estates plc [1993] EGCS 43 (Court of Appeal: Neill, Staughton and Roch LJJ).

DIVORCE

Halsbury's Laws of England (4th edn) Vol 13, paras 501–1352

1005   Articles

A Marriage of Inconvenience, Linda Tyler (dissolving marriage on grounds of duress): 143 NLJ 1148

Between Scylla and Charybdis—How to Value, Very Broadly, Shares in the Family Company, Nicholas Wilson QC et al: [1993] Fam Law 113

Breaking Up is Easier to do, Evlynne Gilvarry (on the Cambridge Divorce Centre): LS Gaz, 29 September 1993, p 8

Challenging Ancillary Relief Orders—the Impact of the 1991 Rules, Martyn Bennett: [1993] Fam Law 84

Child Support Act 1991—The Implications for Divorce Solicitors, Imogen Clout: [1993] Fam Law 236

Divorce—Development Rather than Transition, Peter Grose-Hodge: [1993] Fam Law 418

Divorce Reform in England and Wales a Visitor's View, Christine Davies QC: [1993] Fam Law 331

Divorce Reform, Rhona Schuz: [1993] Fam Law 580

Fair Shares? Simon Bennett (on developments in ancillary relief): LS Gaz, 29 September 1993, p 25

Freezing Transatlantic Assets, Sean Stanton-Dunne (on the forms of relief available to legally aided clients): 143 NLJ 1562

Give and Take in the Family Home, John Dewar: [1993] Fam Law 231

Mediation: Where Do You Draw The Line?, Nicholas Francis and Miranda Baker (on the effect of *Re D (Minors) (Conciliation: Privilege)* [1993] 1 FLR 932 (para 996)): [1993] Fam Law 482

Pensions—A Scheme for Divorcing Couples, Judith Masson: [1993] Fam Law 479

Pension Rights on Divorce: The Implications of *Brooks v Brooks*, David Chatterton (see *Brooks v Brooks* (1993) Times, May 5 (para 1020)): [1993] Fam Law 423

Pre-trial Conferences in Ancillary Matters, John Epp: [1993] Fam Law 145

Property Adjustment Orders and Negative Equity, Nicholas Roberts: [1993] Fam Law 351

Questionnaires and Disclosure—The Role of the Court, Simon Bennett (on the Family Proceedings Rules 1991, r 2·63): [1993] Fam Law 689

The Mediation Solution? Evlynne Gilvarry (on no-fault divorces): LS Gaz, 22 September 1993, p 5

Who is in Charge? Rhetoric and Evidence in the Study of Mediation, Robert Dingwall and David Greatbatch: [1993] 6 JSWFL 367

Whose Teapot Is It Anyway? Sandra Davies and Maggie Rae (on in-house conciliation and counselling services): 143 NLJ 375

Wills After Divorce, Francis Nation-Dixon: 138 SJ 18

1006 Custody of children

See CHILDREN AND YOUNG PERSONS.

1007 Dissolution or annulment of marriage—effect on will

See para 2668.

1008 Divorce county courts—designation

The Civil Courts (Amendment) Order 1993, SI 1993/1809 (in force on 1 September 1993), amends the 1983 Order, SI 1983/713, in consequence of the designation of Morpeth County Court as a divorce county court.

1009 Family Proceedings Rules

See para 407.

1010 Financial provision—appeal—discretion to admit fresh evidence

Following a divorce, a district judge ordered the husband to transfer to his wife the matrimonial home subject to a charge in the husband's favour. In his notice of appeal the husband wished to call further evidence to show that the mortgage debt figure used by the district judge was incorrect and that he had further debts. He also wished to cross-examine his wife about her earnings. At the hearing of the appeal, the wife submitted that fresh evidence could not be adduced. The judge made a preliminary ruling that the appeal was not a rehearing and that fresh evidence was only admissible according to the criteria laid down by the Court of Appeal. On the husband's appeal against the preliminary ruling, *held*, an appeal from a district judge to a county court under the Family Proceedings Rules 1991, SI 1991/1247, r 8.1(2) in ancillary proceedings was not a hearing de novo with the parties having an unfettered right to adduce fresh evidence. However, the admissibility of fresh evidence was not restricted by the criteria laid down by the Court of Appeal and the judge could in his discretion admit further evidence and reopen matters already determined by the district judge. Accordingly, the appeal would be allowed and the case remitted to the judge.

Marsh v Marsh [1993] 2 All ER 794 (Court of Appeal: Sir Stephen Brown P, Glidewell and Staughton LJJ). *Lauerman v Lauerman (Practice Note)* [1992] 1 WLR 734 (1992 Abr para 958) applied.

1011   Financial provision—consent order—application to set aside—increased child support liability

A consent order in divorce proceedings provided that a husband transfer his half share in the former matrimonial home to his wife in full and final settlement of all her financial claims against him. Subsequently, on an application to the magistrates' court by the Secretary of State under the Social Security Administration Act 1992, the husband was required to contribute £4 per week towards the maintenance of the only child of the family. It was expected that his liability for the child's maintenance would increase to £29 per week under the Child Support Act 1991. The husband applied for leave out of time to set aside the consent order so as to recover his share in the former home in order to provide for the future maintenance of the child. *Held*, while spouses could achieve a clean break between themselves, they could not do so in respect of their child. The wife was in receipt of income support and the state was empowered to seek recovery of expenditure on benefit from a person liable for maintenance. The magistrates had exercised a judicial discretion when making an order for maintenance. In contrast, under the Child Support Act 1991, a straight mathematical computation assessed liability for child maintenance outside the jurisdiction of the courts. Parliament had chosen a new administrative method by which the state might intervene to compel a parent to contribute towards the maintenance of a child, bypassing the jurisdiction of the courts. However, this did not constitute a new event which invalidated the basis of the consent order. It was immaterial that parental liability would now be enforced through an agency outside the courts. That was a difference only in the means by which the state might relieve itself of the obligation which it was the duty of the parents to discharge. There were no grounds on which to set the consent order aside and accordingly the application for leave would be refused.

Crozier v Crozier [1994] 1 FLR 126 (Family Division: Booth J).

1012   Financial provision—lump sum payment—financial resources of parties—effect of bankruptcy

Following the granting of a decree nisi, in proceedings for ancillary relief the court held that the husband had been evasive about his financial position, had assets above those disclosed, and made an order for him to pay a lump sum to the wife even though no capital could be identified. The husband later filed his petition in bankruptcy and appealed against the lump sum order. In dismissing the appeal, the judge concluded on the balance of probabilities that the husband did have the ability to meet the order. The husband failed to pay the lump sum and the wife issued a summons for payment. At the hearing of the summons the judge held that the findings of the judge at the appeal hearing were binding upon him and that by virtue of the Insolvency Rules 1986, r 12(3) orders made in family proceedings did not give rise to debts provable in bankruptcy and made a suspended committal order. The husband appealed on the grounds that the judge in making his finding on the balance of probabilities had applied the wrong standard of proof, that the judge had failed properly to consider the effect of bankruptcy on the proceedings and that the judge had adopted the wrong approach in sentencing the husband. *Held*, contempt of court proceedings were criminal or quasi criminal in nature and had to be proved by the criminal standard of proof. The judge had erred in adopting the findings of the judge at the appeal hearing which were decided on the balance of probabilities. Despite the bankruptcy and the consequent vesting of assets in trustees the husband had refused or neglected to pay the debt. In sentencing the husband the judge was punishing him for lying to a judge of another court and this was an unjustifiable reason for sentencing him. The bankruptcy itself would be a reviewable disposition under the Matrimonial Clauses Act 1973, s 37 so that the High Court would be in a position to set aside the bankruptcy which vested the assets in trustees. Accordingly, the appeal would be allowed.

Woodley v Woodley [1993] 1 FCR 701 (Court of Appeal: Steyn LJ and Ewbank J).

The Debtors Act 1869, s 5 provides for the committal to prison of any person who makes default in payment of any debt where it is proved to the satisfaction of the court that the person making default either has or has had since the date of the order or judgment the means to pay the sum in respect of which he has made default, and has refused or neglected, or refuses or neglects, to pay that sum.

Following the breakdown of the marriage the husband failed to make a proper declaration of his financial resources and did everything possible to defeat his wife's financial claims. The husband was ordered to pay a lump sum and to make periodic payments to his wife and the following month when the divorce was made absolute, the husband petitioned for bankruptcy leading to a bankruptcy order being made against him. The wife issued a judgment summons but the court held that the husband was not entitled in law to use the assets which had since vested in the trustee in bankruptcy to discharge the judgment debt. On appeal, *held*, Simon Brown LJ dissenting, the debt had become due from the husband and had not ceased to be due merely because the enforcement procedure had been stayed pending the wife's appeal. The stay did not alter the fact that so long as the husband did not pay the debt, he was in default. A person who refused to pay a judgment debt even though he had available resources was in default of payment and therefore subject to the Debtors Act 1869, s 5 even though the procedure for the enforcement of the debt was stayed pending appeal. Though the existence of the stay was to be taken into account in deciding whether to punish the husband and though the husband had so far succeeded in his determination to prevent his wife from having any of his money, the court would conclude reluctantly that the husband might very well have thought that the existence of the stay had affected his liability to pay the lump sum. Accordingly, the appeal would be dismissed.

Woodley v Woodley (No 2) [1993] 4 All ER 1010 (Court of Appeal: Balcombe and Simon Brown LJJ and Peter Gibson J). For earlier related proceedings see [1992] 2 FLR 417, CA, supra.

1013 Financial provision—lump sum payment—payment into court

After the sale of the parties' matrimonial home, a cheque for £8,000, which represented the proceeds of sale, had been drawn by the parties' solicitors in favour of both the husband and the wife. The husband forged his wife's signature on the cheque and used it to open a building society account, and when the wife subsequently petitioned for divorce she obtained an order restraining the husband from spending her half of the sale proceeds. A penal notice was attached to the order, and the wife obtained a further order requiring the husband to pay half of the sale proceeds into court. The husband failed to comply and the wife applied for his committal, but the trial judge held that he was unable to commit him by virtue of the Debtors Act 1969, ss 4, 5. On the wife's appeal, *held*, by virtue of the Administration of Justice Act 1970, s 11 the jurisdiction to commit for default in payment of a debt under the 1869 Act, s 5 was exercisable only in respect of a High Court or county court maintenance order. "Maintenance order" included maintenance or other payments made under the Matrimonial Causes Act 1973, Pt II, and as the wife's application for payment of the lump sum into court had been made under the 1973 Act, Pt II the husband could be committed to prison for failing to comply. Accordingly, the appeal would be allowed.

Graham v Graham [1993] 1 FCR 339 (Court of Appeal: May and Purchas LJJ).

1014 Financial provision—overseas divorce—jurisdiction

See *Z v Z (Financial Provision: Overseas Divorce)*, para 535.

1015 Financial provision—periodical payments—enforcement

The parties were divorced. The financial structure providing for the wife after divorce was contained in an order preceded by recitals. These stated that the husband would make annual periodical payments and would provide the wife with a new car every three years and meet its running costs. He subsequently stopped meeting these obligations and issued a notice of application to terminate them. The proceedings took several years to come to trial and at the hearing the wife was granted leave to enforce arrears which had become due more than 12 months before the proceedings began. The district judge ordered the husband to make good the arrears in respect of the periodical payments and car and to resume the periodical payments. On his appeal, *held*, it would have been wasteful of costs if the parties had litigated by way of a de novo hearing and the appellate judge was entitled to apply his own discretionary conclusions to the facts as found. Although the district judge correctly enforced the arrears, the finding that the husband should continue to make the periodical payments would not be upheld. The wife had substantial capital and a potentially successful business, whereas the husband now had no capital and his liabilities significantly exceeded his assets, and in these circumstances a clean break was appropriate. Accordingly, the appeal would be allowed to the extent of terminating the husband's liability for future periodical payments.

Horsman v Horsman [1993] 2 FCR 357 (Family Division: Thorpe J).

1016   Financial provision—periodical payments—money stated to be paid for and direct to child

See *R v Sheffield City Council, ex p Parker*, para 1077.

1017   Financial provision—protection of respondent's financial position—solicitor's duty

A wife was being divorced after a long marriage to a man in pensionable employment. Although specific instructions had been given, the solicitor failed to apply under the Matrimonial Causes Act 1973, s 10 to protect the wife's interests. As a result, the divorce was made absolute and the wife lost her right to a widow's pension. She sought damages against her solicitors for negligence. *Held*, where a solicitor was consulted by a woman in middle age who had been married for many years to a man in pensionable employment and who was being divorced against her will the solicitor should take the following steps: (1) file an application under s 10 in order to delay proceedings and enable the circumstances to be investigated; (2) obtain the rules of the pension fund and find out the wife's rights. It was negligent of the solicitor not to have filed an application under s 10, unless he had instructions not to do so. Judgment would accordingly be given in the wife's favour.

Griffiths v Dawson & Co [1993] 2 FLR 315 (Queen's Bench Division: Ewbank J).

1018   Financial provision—undertaking—enforcement—judgment summons

An order was made requiring the husband to make periodical payments to the wife for herself and two children. The order also contained an undertaking that the husband would pay a monthly supplement and assume responsibility for the childrens' school fees and school clothing. The husband fell into arrears and the wife issued judgment summonses in respect of each set of arrears. Whilst there was no dispute that the periodical payments order could be so enforced, the husband contended that the undertaking could not be enforced by that procedure. *Held*, the Debtors Act 1869, s 5 provided that a debtor could be committed for default in payment of a debt due in pursuance of any order or judgment. The Administration of Justice Act 1970, s 11 provided that the jurisdiction to commit under the 1869 Act, s 5 was exercisable in relation to a High Court or county court maintenance order. Further, the 1970 Act, Sch 8, para 2A (as amended by the Matrimonial Causes Act 1973, Sch 2), provided that "maintenance order" included an order for periodical or other payments made, or having effect as if made, under the 1973 Act, Part II. In the present case, the undertaking was inseparable from the order, the monthly obligations to pay the supplement and school fees were analogous to periodical payments, and the undertaking was made as if under the 1973 Act, Part II. Accordingly, the undertaking would be enforceable by way of judgment summons and, since the husband had neglected to make the requisite payments, a suspended committal order would be made.

Symmons v Symmons [1993] 2 FCR 247 (Family Division: Hunter J).

1019   Financial provision—variation of order—death of spouse—basis on which court should reconsider ancillary relief order

Upon the parents' divorce the mother was given care and control of the two children of the marriage. The mother's application for ancillary relief was dealt with on the basis that she needed sufficient funds to buy a home large enough for the children to live with her. The judge ordered the sale of the matrimonial home (which the parents owned jointly) and the mother received a lump sum out of the proceeds of sale. The mother subsequently died intestate, and the father was granted leave to appeal out of time against the terms of the property adjustment order on the ground that her death had invalidated the basis on which the order had been made. *Held*, the correct approach was for the court to consider the position at the time the ancillary order was made but to proceed as if the judge had known that the mother would die shortly after the decree absolute was granted. In those circumstances the mother would have continued to live in the matrimonial home until her death, then, as had happened, the father and the children would have moved back into the matrimonial home with the father's new partner and her children. The judge would not have ordered payment of a capital sum to the mother, and bearing in mind that as a result of the mother's intestacy the two children would have inherited her half share of the matrimonial home the correct order would be to give each child a 20 per cent interest in the home with a proviso that there would be no sale without the father's consent until the younger child attained the age of majority or further order. Accordingly, the appeal would be allowed and a new order would be substituted in those terms.

Barber v Barber [1993] 1 FCR 65 (Court of Appeal: Neill and Glidewell LJJ). *Smith v Smith* [1991] 2 All ER 306, CA (1991 Abr para 888) considered.

1020　Financial provision—variation of order—pension fund

After the date of a couple's marriage, the husband's employer set up a pension fund which provided for a pension for the spouse of an employee. In divorce proceedings the wife applied for the pension fund to be declared a post-nuptial settlement and for it to be varied in her favour. At first instance it was varied to provide the wife with an immediate annuity and the pension to be paid on the husband's death. On appeal by the husband, *held*, under the Matrimonial Causes Act 1973, s 24(1)(c) the court could make an order varying, for the benefit of the parties of the marriage, any ante-nuptial or post-nuptial settlement made on the parties to the marriage. As the pension fund specifically provided for a pension for the spouse of the husband and since the fund comprised a settlement the tests set out by Denning LJ in *Lort-Williams v Lort-Williams* [1951] 2 All ER 241, CA were satisfied. Therefore, the pension fund fell within the definition of a post-nuptial settlement and was open to variation by the court. Accordingly, the appeal would be dismissed.

Brooks v Brooks [1993] 3 WLR 548 (Family Division: Ewbank J).

1021　Foreign proceedings—recognition

See CONFLICT OF LAWS.

1022　Ground for divorce—consultation paper

The Lord Chancellor has issued a consultation paper, *Looking to the future: mediation and the ground for divorce* (Cm 2424). The objectives of the law are set down as support for the institution of marriage, the provision of practical steps to prevent the irretrievable breakdown of marriages, ensuring that the parties understand the practical consequences of divorce before they take any irreversible decisions, minimising (in the event of a divorce) the bitterness and hostility between the parties and reducing the trauma for the children, and keeping to the minimum the cost to the parties and to the taxpayer. Drawing extensively on the experience of the Law Commission and the responses which it received to consultations on divorce (*Facing the Future* (Law Com No 170) (see 1988 Abr para 705) and *The Ground for Divorce* (Law Com No 192) (see 1990 Abr para 814)), the consultation paper seeks views on maintaining irretrievable breakdown as the sole ground for divorce (but establishing it by the passage of time, and not by any other means) with a period of 12 months for consideration and reflection; consideration to be given to the length of this period and to whether it should be capable of extension or abridgment. Further consideration should also be given to the possible maintenance of the existing hardship bar, either in its present form or in some modified form. The consultation paper stresses the importance of maintaining judicial separation as an alternative to divorce, but questions whether the law and practice should be aligned with a revised law of divorce. The role of the magistrates' courts in making orders for financial provision could be modified to remove the grounds of behaviour and desertion. Consultation is also sought on the possible removal of wilful refusal to consummate as a ground for nullity. Consideration is given to the possible role of mediation to enable couples to resolve disputes currently handled by legal advisers; views are sought as to whether mediation should be made compulsory and whether statements made in the course of mediation should be privileged. The possibility of making mandatory an initial interview for parties contemplating divorce is explored. The initial interview would enable the parties to be offered information about marriage guidance to see whether or not the marriage has irretrievably broken down; information would also be provided about the divorce process, the mediation services, the role of lawyers and the courts, the likely costs, and eligibility for state funding and the system of means testing. If the law on divorce were to be reformed broadly along the lines envisaged by the Law Commission, there would be a need to devise an appropriate procedural scheme. Such a scheme has been devised by the Law Commission and has been well received; an outline of the scheme is appended to the consultation paper.

1023　Maintenance order—consent—variation of order—interests of child

A husband and wife both consented to a limited period maintenance order. The wife then made an unsuccessful application under the Matrimonial Causes Act 1973, s 31 for a variation of that order so that it could be extended. On appeal, *held*, the judge was correct to rely on the principle laid down in *Edgar v Edgar* [1980] 1 WLR 1410 that other than in unusual circumstances, the court ought to uphold agreements freely entered into at arm's length by parties who were properly advised, and that substantial weight would be given to such an agreement. If, however, there was a child of the family who was still a minor, the 1973 Act, s 31(7) required the court to have regard to the welfare of the child and to decide whether as the first consideration the detriment to the child arising from refusal to vary the order was sufficient to tip the balance against the order being upheld. In the present circumstances, the appeal would be dismissed.

N v N (Consent Order: Variation) [1993] 2 FLR 868 (Court of Appeal: Lloyd, Butler-Sloss and Roch LJJ).

1024 Maintenance orders—enforcement abroad

See CONFLICT OF LAWS.

1025 Maintenance Orders (Reciprocal Enforcement) Act 1992—commencement

The Maintenance Orders (Reciprocal Enforcement) Act 1992 (Commencement) Order 1993, SI 1993/618 brings the Act into force on 5 April 1993. For a summary of the Act, see 1992 Abr para 964. For details of commencement, see the commencement table in the title STATUTES.

1026 Matrimonial home—exclusion order

See HUSBAND AND WIFE.

EASEMENTS AND PROFITS A PRENDRE

Halsbury's Laws of England (4th edn) Vol 14, paras 1–300

1027 Articles

Access to Neighbouring Land, Sandi Murdoch: Estates Gazette, 30 January 1993, p 125
A Developer's Problem, Ian Rowson: Estates Gazette, 9 October 1993, p 138
Crime and the Right of Prescription, Touchstone: 137 SJ 1161
Drafting Easements, HW Wilkinson: 143 NLJ 1544
Effect on Freehold Sites, Stephen Walter and Mark Gaffney (on easements which interfere with development): Estates Gazette, 29 January 1994, p 122
Registration, Notice and Confusion, G Morgan (on *London and Blenheim Estates Ltd v Ladbroke Retail Parks Ltd* [1993] 4 All ER 157 (para 1029)): 143 NLJ 1793

1028 Easements—easement of drainage—unknown easement—apportionment of risk between vendor and purchaser

See *William Sindall plc v Cambridgeshire County Council*, para 615.

1029 Easements—transfer of easements—rights over retained land

A company transferred the absolute title of part of its registered land to the plaintiffs together with easements and other rights over the retained land specified in a schedule to the transfer. The schedule defined "transferred land" as including any other land if such land was capable of being benefited by the rights granted, if notice was given to the transferor within five years of the date of the transfer that the rights were to be exercised in respect of such land and if at the date of the notice the transferee was the registered proprietor of or had contracted to purchase such land. Six months later another company became the registered proprietor of the retained land by succession. The plaintiffs, who had contracted to purchase leasehold land adjoining the retained land, gave notice to the new proprietor that they were seeking to exercise the scheduled rights in respect of the leasehold land. Later that year the proprietor transferred the retained land to the defendants and shortly after, the plaintiffs' purchase of the leasehold land was completed. The plaintiffs then applied for a declaration that they and their successors in title as the proprietors of the leasehold land were entitled to the benefit of the easements specified in the schedule of the first transfer to the plaintiffs. That application was rejected and on the plaintiffs' appeal, *held*, no interest in land had been created because before there was a dominant tenement the servient tenement had been deposed of by the grantor. Therefore, no interest in land was created which, when registered, bound successors in title to the servient tenement and no such interest in land binding any successor in title to the servient tenement arose on the acquisition by the plaintiffs of the additional land. Accordingly, the appeal would be dismissed.

London and Blenheim Estates v Ladbroke Retail Parks [1993] 4 All ER 157 (Court of Appeal: Ralph Gibson, Beldam and Peter Gibson LJJ). Decision of Judge Paul Baker QC [1993] 1 All ER 307 (1992 Abr para 971) affirmed.

1030   Profit à prendre—right to fish—bait-digging on foreshore
The defendant was convicted of an offence contrary to a byelaw which prohibited bait-digging on the foreshore. His appeal was dismissed. On further appeal by way of case stated, the defendant contended that the public right of sea fishing included the ancillary right to take bait from the foreshore. *Held,* although the taking of worms for commercial purposes was not justified, there was a public right to take worms from the foreshore, recognised by common law as ancillary to the right to fish, as long as the taking of the worms was related to the public right to fish. Whether or not bait was so taken was a question of fact and degree for the magistrates to decide. The appeal would be allowed.

Anderson v Alnwick District Council [1993] 3 All ER 613 (Queen's Bench Division: Evans LJ and Macpherson J).

1031   Right of way—claim that right of way extinguished—claim registered as pending land action
See *Willies-Williams v National Trust for Places of Historic Interest and Natural Beauty,* para 1574.

1032   Right of way—nature of right—physical characteristics
On purchasing certain agricultural land, the defendant became entitled under a deed of conveyance to the benefit of a right of way over the plaintiffs' land. The right entitled him "to pass and repass on foot and with or without motor vehicles" along a track lying within 9 feet of the plaintiffs' bungalow which faced the track. On his appeal against an injunction limiting his use of the right of way, he contended that he was entitled to use the track for all agricultural purposes carried out on his land. *Held,* the main question was whether the right of passage with motor vehicles was restricted by the physical characteristics of the track. There were good grounds for finding excessive user of the track and for making a declaration that its user was not to be such as unreasonably to interfere with the rights of any other person to use it. Its use was to be restricted to vehicles whose size and weight did not exceed those specified by the court so that its use by unauthorised vehicles or its excessive use by authorised vehicles would be unlawful. A right of use with motor vehicles included horse-drawn carriages and carts; it also included the use of the track by horses, whether ridden or led, and the right to lead, but not to drive, cows and other animals. The defendant's appeal would be allowed to a limited extent.

White v Richards [1993] RTR 318 (Court of Appeal: Nourse, Stuart-Smith and Mann LJJ).

1033   Right of way—prescription—illegal use
A lease was granted to the former trustees of a common. The defendants owned land which adjoined the common. There had been no use of the defendants' land until commercial use of it began. There were several tracks and paths forming part of the common and one of the tracks was used in connection with several properties in the area. The defendants used their own property for maintenance and repair of double decker buses. The buses came and left the farm via the track. It was agreed the common came under the Law of Property Act 1925, s 193 as amended, and though the trustees could have granted the defendants a right of way for commercial vehicles, they had not. The court concluded that the 1925 Act, did not prevent the defendant from acquiring an easement by a user of the track, albeit that the user was illegal. On appeal by the plaintiffs, *held,* an easement could not be acquired by conduct which was prohibited by a public statute. Accordingly, the appeal would be allowed.

Hanning v Top Deck Travel Group Ltd (1993) Times, 6 May (Court of Appeal: Dillon and Kennedy LJJ and Sir Roger Parker).

ECCLESIASTICAL LAW

Halsbury's Laws of England (4th edn) Vol 14, paras 301–1435

1034   Churches—redundant churches—payments to redundant churches fund
The Payments to Redundant Churches Fund Order 1993, SI 1993/2846 (in force on 31 March 1994), provides that sums up to a total of £3,100,000 may, for the period from 1 April 1994 to 31 March 1999, be paid to the Redundant Churches Fund, either out of net proceeds of sale of redundant churches or by way of grant from the Church Commissioners.

1035 Faculty—churchyard—exhumation of body

The petitioner sought a faculty to permit the exhumation of his late wife's body, which had been buried nine years earlier in one churchyard, for its re-interment in another. *Held*, a consistory court's primary duty was to protect the remains of a deceased person buried in consecrated ground in accordance with the rites of the Church of England. There must be strong and compelling circumstances for the court to grant a faculty for the exhumation of a deceased's remains for re-interment elsewhere rather than to uphold that duty. A particularly heavy burden of proof was placed on a petitioner seeking such a faculty nine years after the burial had taken place. The petition would be refused.

Re St Peter's Churchyard, Oughtrington [1993] 1 WLR 1440 (Chester Consistory Court: Harold Lomas Ch).

1036 Faculty—consecrated school chapel—lease by school governors

The Pastoral Measure 1983, s 56(2) provides that it is unlawful to sell, lease or otherwise dispose of any church or part of a church or site or part of the site of any church or any consecrated land belonging or annexed to a church. "Church" is defined in the 1983 Measure, s 87(1) as meaning a church or a chapel which has been consecrated for the purpose of public worship.

The governors of a school wished to grant a lease of the consecrated school chapel, in which they held the freehold title. The sentence of consecration of the chapel provided that the chapel was consecrated "to the service of almighty God and divine worship". On their application for a faculty permitting them to grant the proposed lease, *held*, common law did not prevent the leasing of a consecrated school chapel where the freehold was vested in the school governors. In assessing the effect of the 1983 Measure on the common law position, a distinction had to be drawn between a chapel consecrated for divine worship and a parish church which, whether consecrated or not, was inevitably made available for public worship. As the chapel belonged to the school and the public were entitled to attend by invitation only, it was not consecrated for the purposes of public worship and the 1983 Measure, s 56(2) did not apply. Accordingly, the faculty would be granted.

Re Tonbridge School Chapel (No 2) [1993] 2 All ER 338 (Rochester Consistory Court: Judge Goodman Ch).

1037 Faculty—gifts to church—ownership of gifts

It has been held that a vicar and churchwardens are owners and not trustees or custodians of gifts given to their church. However, the disposal of such gifts is at the discretion of the consistory court which can impose terms on any disposal it allows.

Re St Anne's Church, Wrenthorpe [1994] 2 WLR 338 (Wakefield Consistory Court: Peter Collier QC, Ch).

1038 Faculty—monument—lettering of monument

The petitioner proposed, in accordance with the wishes of his late wife, to erect a headstone with an inscription in gilded lettering. The part of the churchyard in which the petitioner's wife was buried contained 28 headstones with gilded lettering, but in the churchyard as a whole only a comparatively small number of headstones had such lettering. The regulations for the erection of monuments in churchyards that had been promulgated by the diocesan advisory committee stated that the gilding of lettering was undesirable, but it was not specifically proscribed. The incumbent refused to consent to the use of the lettering on the ground that if he made an exception in the case of the petitioner he would be breaking faith with others whom he had persuaded to comply with the regulations. On the petitioner's application for a faculty for the erection of a headstone with gilded lettering, *held*, those who were buried in churchyards were buried in consecrated ground and it was the church's responsibility to see that what was placed there was fitting and appropriate. Those who sought to exercise the right to place memorials on consecrated ground had to accept that they did so by licence and had to conform to conditions imposed by the church. An incumbent had no power to license a monument which was outside the regulations and anyone who sought to erect such a monument had to apply for a faculty. So long as such regulations existed it was important that they were adhered to, and the fairest system was one that was seen to apply to all. Where a monument breached the rules, a faculty would only be granted in exceptional circumstances. Accordingly, the petition would be refused.

Re St Chad's Churchyard, Bishop's Tachbrook [1993] 1 All ER 208 (Coventry Consistory Court: William M Gage QC Ch).

1039   Faculty—refurbishment of pipe organ—use of written procedure

The incumbent and the secretary of the parochial church council sought a faculty to refurbish and restore a pipe organ. A member of the congregation objected. Both parties had expressed a desire to use the written representation procedure under the Faculty Jurisdiction (Injunctions and Restoration Orders) Rules 1992, SI 1992/2884, r 25, which had been made under the Care of Churches and Ecclesiastical Jurisdiction Measure 1991. The parties petitioned for a faculty. *Held*, the circumstances when, within the particular diocese, the court would make such an order for a determination on the basis of written representations rather than in open court were the following: (1) no aesthetic ground was raised, (2) no proposal was made to alter an existing building, (3) the basic difference between the parties was one of firmly held opinion rather than a series of disputed facts, (4) oral evidence and cross-examination was unlikely to add anything to the written representations of the parties, (5) the written representations contained all the information necessary to a determination of the issues raised by the parties, and (6) the chancellor did not consider that any judge's witness was necessary under the 1992 Rules, r 24. Accordingly, in the circumstances of the present case, a conditional faculty would be granted.

Re St James's, Malden [1994] 1 All ER 85 (Southwark Consistory Court: RMK Gray QC, Ch).

1040   Faculty—resiting of war memorial—detriment to neighbouring property

The vicar and churchwardens of a parish petitioned for a faculty for the construction of a new chapel and the consequent resiting of a war memorial cross. The proposals were approved by the parochial church council and the diocesan advisory committee. However, the owners of flats overlooking the proposed site objected to the positioning of the memorial because they claimed it would detrimentally affect the value of the flats. Leave was granted for the petitioners to proceed with all the work except that affecting the memorial. The Council for the Care of Churches, at the invitation of the court, submitted evidence supporting the proposals. On the hearing of the petition, *held*, the opinions of the parish on the proposal had to be opinions formed in relation to the proposed alteration itself and its effect on the convenience or beauty of the church, and not upon the motives or objects of those who proposed it. The personal subjective reasons and the personal condition of the parties opposing a petition were irrelevant. The court had to be reluctant to grant faculties to the detriment of private property, and ought to do so only when compelled by necessity or duty. However, the detriment incurred had to be real and sensible, viewed objectively, and not something small or trifling. As there was no other suitable site for the memorial, as it was in the public interest that the memorial was re-erected and put on view, and as the detriment to the flats could not be termed extremely serious, necessity and duty required the grant of the faculty.

Re St Peter and St Paul, Upper Teddington and St Michael and St George, Fulwell [1993] 1 WLR 852 (London Consistory Court: Henty Dep Ch).

1041   Fees—ecclesiastical judges and legal officers

The Ecclesiastical Judges and Legal Officers (Fees) Order 1993, SI 1993/1842 (in force on 1 January 1994), revokes the 1992 Order, SI 1992/2883, and increases fees in relation to faculty and court proceedings.

The Legal Officers (Annual Fees) Order 1993, SI 1993/1843 (in force on 1 January 1994), revokes the 1992 Order, SI 1992/1749, and increases the annual fees for diocesan and provincial registrars.

1042   Fees—parochial fees

The Parochial Fees Order 1993, SI 1993/1844 (in force on 1 January 1994), revokes the 1992 Order, SI 1992/1747, and increases the fees payable for specified matters related to baptisms, marriages and burials, for the erection of monuments in churchyards and for certain other miscellaneous matters.

1043   General Synod—ordination of women priests—submission of measure to Ecclesiastical Committee

The Church of England Assembly (Powers) Act 1919, s 3 provides that measures passed by the General Synod must be submitted to the Ecclesiastical Committee of the Houses of Parliament for its consideration. Once the Ecclesiastical Committee has considered the measure it must prepare a report for Parliament stating the nature and legal effect of the measure and expressing views as to its expediency. A measure may relate to any matter concerning the Church of England and may extend to the amendment or repeal of any Act of Parliament.

The General Synod passed a draft measure allowing the ordination of women priests, which was declared to be expedient by the respondents under the 1919 Act, s 3. The applicants claimed that the measure was ultra vires the 1919 Act and sought an order quashing the decision of the respondent. On an application for judicial review, held, the 1919 Act, s 3 permitted the General Synod to pass a measure on any matter concerning the Church of England. There was nothing in the Act to exclude matters relating to the fundamental doctrines of the Church, such as the ordination of women. The measure was not, therefore, ultra vires the 1919 Act. The notion of "expediency" in the 1919 Act, s 3 did not refer to the lawfulness of a measure. Parliament had intended that the 1919 Act should allow the General Synod to debate and legislate on its own affairs, including those with a fundamental constitutional effect. Accordingly, the application would be dismissed.

R v Ecclesiastical Committee of the Houses of Parliament, ex p The Church Society (1993) Times, Independent, 4 November (Queen's Bench Division: McCowan LJ and Tuckey J).

The Priests (Ordination of Women) Measure 1993 received the royal assent on 5 November 1993. For a summary of the Act, see para 1049.

1044 Incumbents (Vacation of Benefices) (Amendment) Measure 1993

The Incumbents (Vacation of Benefices) (Amendment) Measure 1993 reforms legislation relating to the removal of rectors and vicars from their parishes and introduces structured reconciliation processes into the legal procedures. The Measure also introduces new provisions relating to compensation for vicars and rectors. The Measure received the royal assent on 27 July 1993 and comes into force on a day or days to be appointed. For details of commencement, see the commencement table in the title STATUTES.

Section 1 requires the House of Bishops to draw up a code of practice as to reconciliation, for use in particular where a request for an inquiry into the pastoral situation in a parish is made under the Incumbents (Vacation of Benefices) Measure 1977, s 1. Section 2 provides that before such a request is made, between six and twelve months' notice must be given to the bishop of the diocese. Section 2 also provides for the withdrawal of a request upon the giving of appropriate notice. Under s 3, the bishop is given a general power to direct the institution of an inquiry if he thinks fit, and provision is made for a direction to be deemed to have been given if after six months the bishop neither gives a direction nor gives notification that he will not give a direction. Section 4 abolishes diocesan committees of inquiry and provides that in all cases inquiries are to be conducted by provincial tribunals.

Under s 5, a tribunal conducting an inquiry may direct that the incumbent concerned undergoes a medical examination for the purposes of obtaining a report on his physical or mental condition. Section 6 provides that where, after an inquiry, a bishop considers it desirable to do so, he may serve a notice on the incumbent concerned inhibiting him from executing or performing, without the bishop's consent, such rights or duties of his office as the bishop may specify. Section 6 makes special provision where the incumbent concerned is unable by reason of age or infirmity to discharge his duties. The powers of a bishop in cases where the pastoral relationship has broken down are amended by s 7, while the determination of compensation payable to an incumbent who resigns or vacates his benefice before or after an inquiry is amended by s 8 and Sch 2.

Section 9 establishes a committee for the purpose of making rules under the 1977 Measure, and s 10 defines the meaning of a serious breakdown of the pastoral relationship between an incumbent and his parishioners as a situation where the relationship between an incumbent and the parishioners is such as to impede the promotion in the parish of the whole mission of the Church of England, pastoral, evangelistic, social and ecumenical. Section 11 provides for the extension of the 1977 Measure to the Isle of Man, while s 12 and Sch 1 deal with the constitution of provincial tribunals. Section 13 inserts Sch 2, which deals with the form and amount of compensation payable to an incumbent as mentioned above, and s 14 and Schs 3, 4 deal with minor and consequential amendments and repeals. Section 15 contains transitional provisions and s 16 deals with short title, commencement, extent and interpretation.

1045 Jurisdiction—consistory courts—diocesan chancellorship

The Diocesan Chancellorship Regulations 1993, SI 1993/1841 (in force on 1 October 1993), limit the number of diocesan chancellorships that may be held by one person to two. A person who at the date of the coming into force of the 1993 Regulations holds more than the maximum number of chancellorships may continue to do so.

1046   Legal aid

The Church of England (Legal Aid) Rules 1993, SI 1993/1840 (in force on 1 September 1993), amend the 1988 Rules, SI 1988/1175, by revoking the provisions exempting applicants for legal aid in cases under the Ecclesiastical Jurisdiction Measure 1963 from the requirement to show that they have reasonable grounds for taking, defending or being a party to the proceedings in question. The 1993 Rules also give the Legal Aid Commission power to carry out taxations of costs in such manner as it considers appropriate and extend the circumstances in which costs may be assessed rather than taxed.

1047   Ordination of Women (Financial Provisions) Measure 1993

The Ordination of Women (Financial Provisions) Measure 1993 makes provision for the relief of hardship incurred by persons resigning from ecclesiastical service by reason of opposition to the ordination of women as priests. The Measure received the royal assent on 5 November 1993 and came into force on that day.

Section 1, Schedule provide that clerks in Holy Orders, deaconesses and licensed lay workers who have resigned from ecclesiastical service as a result of their opposition to the ordination of women as priests (and who have made a declaration to that effect in the prescribed form) are entitled to participate in church housing schemes and to receive resettlement grants and periodical payments from the Church of England Pensions Board, provided that they meet the prescribed qualifying conditions. Section 2 extends the provisions of the Clergy Pensions Measure 1961, s 26 (provision of residences) to persons coming within s 1. Sections 3, 4 deal with the calculation of the amount of resettlement grants and periodical payments, and s 5 provides for the making of discretionary payments.

Under s 6, periodical payments may be reduced to take account of other employment. Section 7 sets out the procedure for the making of the declaration required on applications for benefits under the Measure. The finance and administration of the benefits scheme established by the Measure is dealt with by s 8, and s 9 provides for the augmentation of the pensions of persons who have received periodical payments under the scheme. Section 10 provides for appeals against determinations of the board, and s 11 deals with interpretation. Section 12 provides that any measure amending or repealing any provision of the 1993 Measure must be approved by a majority of not less than two-thirds in each House of the General Synod. Section 13 deals with short title and extent.

1048   Ordination of Women (Financial Provisions) Measure 1993—appeals

The Ordination of Women (Financial Provisions) (Appeals) Rules 1993, SI 1993/2847 (in force on a day to be appointed), make provision for the practice and procedure in proceedings on appeals under the Ordination of Women (Financial Provisions) Measure 1993, s 10 (appeals against determinations of the Church of England Pensions Board regarding the relief of hardship incurred by persons resigning from ecclesiastical service by reason of opposition to the ordination of women as priests).

1049   Priests (Ordination of Women) Measure 1993

The Priests (Ordination of Women) Measure 1993 makes provision for the ordination of women as priests. The Measure received the royal assent on 5 November 1993 and comes into force on a day or days to be appointed. For details of commencement, see the commencement table in the title STATUTES.

Section 1 makes it lawful for the General Synod to make provision enabling a woman to be ordained to the office of priest, with the proviso that it is not lawful for a woman to be consecrated to the office of bishop. Section 2 gives a bishop power to declare that a woman is not to be ordained within the diocese, that a woman is not to be instituted or licensed to the office of incumbent or priest-in-charge of a benefice within the diocese, and that a woman is not to be given a licence or permission to officiate as a priest within the diocese. Under s 3, Sch 1, a parochial church council may, in certain circumstances, resolve that it will not accept a woman as the minister who presides at or celebrates the Holy Communion or pronounces the Absolution in the parish, and that the administrative body of a parish church cathedral will not accept a woman as dean of the cathedral. Under s 4, Sch 2, the administrative body of a cathedral church other than a parish church cathedral may resolve that it will not accept a woman as a minister who presides at or celebrates the Holy Communion or pronounces the Absolution in the cathedral church at any service other than a service held on the direction of the bishop of the diocese, and that it will not accept a woman as the dean of the cathedral church.

Section 5 provides that it is an offence against the ecclesiastical laws for bishops, priests or deacons to contravene declarations and resolutions under ss 2–4. Section 6 provides that, without prejudice to the Sex Discrimination Act 1975, s 19 (disapplication of Pt II of the 1975 Act to employment for the purposes of an organised religion where employment limited to one sex to comply with the doctrines of the religion), the provisions of Pt II of the 1975 Act (discrimination in employment) do not render unlawful sex discrimination against a woman in respect of her ordination as a priest, the giving to her of a licence or permission to serve as such a priest, and her appointment as dean, incumbent, priest-in-charge or team vicar or (in the case of a woman ordained to the office of priest) as assistant curate.

Section 7 applies certain provisions of the Measure to benefices in the patronage of the Crown. Sections 8, 9 deal with interpretation. Section 10, Sch 3 contain minor and consequential amendments, and s 11 provides that any measure or canon amending or repealing any provision of the 1993 Measure or of any canon promulged under it must be approved by a majority of not less than two-thirds in each House of the General Synod. Section 12, Sch 4 deal with short title, commencement and extent.

1050 Religious courts—Beth Din—arbitration order for costs

See *Cohen v Baram*, para 145.

EDUCATION

Halsbury's Laws of England (4th edn) Vol 15 (reissue), paras 1–300

1051 Articles

Colleges in Court, Peter Kaye (on the liability of UK learning institutions): 137 SJ 816
Local Complaints Procedures under the Education Reform Act 1988, Neville Harris: [1993] 1 JSWFL 19
Reforming Education—Some Hope, No Glory, Jonathan Robinson (on the Education Act 1993): 143 NLJ 1306
School Governors—A 1994 Agenda, Jonathan Robinson: 144 NLJ 58
School Tests Boycott—Are the Governors Liable? Oliver Hyams: 137 SJ 718
Schools: Who's in Control? Celia Wells (on the implications of the Data Protection Act 1984): 143 NLJ 1071

1052 Council for National Academic Awards—dissolution

The Education (Dissolution of the Council for National Academic Awards) Order 1993, SI 1993/924 (in force on 20 April 1993), dissolves the Council for National Academic Awards and transfers the Council's property, rights and liabilities to the Secretary of State for Education.

1053 Education Act 1993

The Education Act 1993 amends the law relating to education, in particular in relation to the distribution of responsibility for, and the provision of education in schools. The Act received the royal assent on 27 July 1993, and certain provisions have been brought into force: SI 1993/1975, 3106. The remaining provisions come into force on a day or days to be appointed. For details of commencement, see the commencement table in the title STATUTES.

Part I (ss 1–21, Schs 1, 2) Responsibility for Education
A duty is imposed by s 1 on the Secretary of State to promote the education of the people, and s 2 imposes a duty on him in the case of primary, secondary and further education. His duties in respect of funding agencies for schools are set out in ss 3–9 and Sch 1. Section 10 extends the functions of the Audit Commission, and s 11 makes provision as to the compulsory purchase of land. The responsibility for providing sufficient school places is set out in s 12 and Sch 2. Section 13 empowers an appropriate authority to give a direction to admit a child to school, and s 14 deals with the procedure for giving such a direction. Section 15 sets out the procedure for preparing an agreed syllabus of religious education, and s 16 relates to standing advisory councils on religious education. Miscellaneous other functions relating to grant-maintained schools are set out in s 17. The Secretary of State may by order provide for funding authorities to exercise the function of making and receiving payments in respect of city technology colleges and city

colleges for the technology of the arts: s 18. Section 19 empowers the Secretary of State to impose on a funding authority certain functions in respect of grants for certain expenditure due to immigrants. Section 20 provides for the resolution of disputes, and s 21 imposes a duty on a funding authority to compile information and conduct research about provision of education.

Part II (ss 22–155, Schs 3–8) Grant–Maintained Schools
Section 22 contains introductory provisions. The procedure for acquisition of grant-maintained status is set out in ss 23–24. Sections 25, 26 deal with the initiation of procedure, and s 27 makes provision for information to be available to parents of registered pupils. Provision is made for the holding of ballots of parents: ss 28–31. Section 32, together with Sch 3, deals with publication of proposals. Provisions relating to the approval and implementation of proposals are contained in ss 33–35, together with Sch 4. Supplementary provisions are dealt with in ss 36, 37.

Provision is made for the transfer of property, staff and contracts from an existing governing body and local authority to the governing body of a grant-maintained school by ss 38–47. Section 38 provides for the transfer of property, rights and liabilities. Section 39 deals with the transfer of staff to the employment of the governing body of a grant-maintained school. Section 40 defines the pending period for the acquisition of grant-maintained status. Section 41 controls the disposal by a local authority of land used wholly or partly for the purposes of a school while the procedure for the acquisition of grant-maintained status is pending. Section 42 relates to wrongful disposal of land. Section 43 restricts the ability of a local authority to enter into contracts which would or might bind the new governing body of a grant-maintained school. Contracts contrary to s 43 may be repudiated by the Education Assets Board: s 44. Restrictions are imposed on changes of the purpose for which property is used or held while the procedure for acquisition of grant-maintained status is pending: s 45. Restrictions are also imposed on staff changes: s 46. Supplementary provisions relating to transfers are contained in s 47. A funding authority may establish grant-maintained schools for the purpose of providing relevant education and publish proposals for that purpose: s 48. Section 49 empowers persons other than a funding authority to publish proposals in certain circumstances. Supplementary provisions are contained in s 50 and Sch 3. Section 51 makes provision for the approval, adoption or rejection of proposals, and s 52 contains provisions relating to their implementation. Section 53 makes provision relating to the exercise of powers before the proposed date of implementation and the payment of grants. Section 54 makes supplementary provision about proposals for new grant-maintained schools.

Sections 55–77 deal with the government and conduct of grant-maintained schools. Section 55, together with Schs 5, 6, requires each grant-maintained school to have an instrument and articles of government. Section 56 requires the initial instrument and articles of government to be prescribed in regulations, and ss 57, 58 make provision relating to subsequent instruments and articles of government. Provision is made for different categories of governors: s 59, Sch 7. Sections 60, 61 make provision for the governing body to include parent governors and teacher governors. Provision is made for the head teacher to be an ex officio member of the governing body: s 62. Provision is also made under ss 63–66 for the governing body to include first governors, foundation governors and sponsor governors, and for the Secretary of State to replace first governors. Section 67 allows the Secretary of State to appoint two additional governors in specified circumstances. The powers of a governing body are dealt with in s 68. Sections 69, 70 provide for joint schemes between two or more grant-maintained schools and the making and variation of such schemes. Provision for determination of initial parent, teacher, first or foundation governors is made by ss 71–73. Sections 74, 75 provide for the replacement of proposed initial parent, teacher, first or foundation governors before incorporation. Supplementary provisions are contained in s 76. Provision is made under s 77 for initial sponsor governors. Determination of initial governors is provided for under s 78. General provisions are included in ss 79, 80.

Sections 81–95 make provision for the funding of grant-maintained schools. Section 81 deals with maintenance grants and s 82 deals with special purpose grants. Provisions relating to capital grants are dealt with under s 83. Section 84 imposes requirements on a governing body in receipt of a grant, and s 85 makes further provision as to grants. Section 86 applies the provisions of ss 87–91 to grant-maintained schools in Wales before the establishment of the Schools Funding Council for Wales. Section 87 provides for the making of maintenance grants to grant-maintained schools, ss 88, 89 provide for the making of special purpose and capital grants, and s 90 imposes certain requirements on governing bodies of schools in receipt of such grants. Further provisions in respect of grants are made by s 91. Section 92 allows an appropriate authority to make loans to governing bodies in respect of specified expenditure. Section 93 sets out the recoverability from local funds of sums in respect of maintenance grant, and s 94 determines the total amount recoverable under s 93. Consequential provisions are set out in s 95.

Sections 96–103 make provision for the alteration of grant-maintained schools. Section 96 makes provision for proposals by the governing body to make a significant change in the character of a school, or a significant enlargement of its premises. Section 97 makes provision for similar proposals by funding authorities. Provision for the approval, adoption or rejection of proposals made under ss 96, 97 are made under s 98. Provision for approval of school premises in connection with proposals made under ss 96, 97 is made by s 99. Provisions relating to the implementation of proposals are contained in s 100. The Secretary of State may transfer certain functions in respect of proposals made under the preceding provisions: s 101. Provisions for the implementation of proposals for a change of character approved before the school becomes grant-maintained are included in s 102, and interpretation provisions are contained in s 103.

Sections 104–116 contain proposals for the discontinuance of grant-maintained schools. Sections 104, 105 make provision for proposals by the governing body or the funding authority for discontinuance. Provisions relating to the Secretary of State's approval, adoption or rejection of such proposals are contained in s 106. Section 107 provides for the implementation of proposals approved or adopted. The Secretary of State may transfer to the funding authority functions under the preceding provisions: s 108. Sections 109,110 deal with the withdrawal of a grant where the school is unsuitable to continue as a grant-maintained school. Powers are given under ss 111, 112 to provide by order for winding up and disposal of property. The funding authority may make grants to a governing body in liquidation for certain purposes: s 113. Sections 114, 115 provide for the disposal of school property. The procedure for transferring surplus money and investments to the Secretary of State is set out in s 116.

Sections 117–127 make provision for groups of grant-maintained schools. Section 117 permits a group of grant-maintained schools to be conducted by a single governing body. Sections 118–124, together with Sch 8, make provision as to instruments and articles of government, parent governors, and teacher, head teacher, core and additional governors of such groups of schools. Section 125 makes provision as to the power of the governing body of a group of schools. For each financial year, the governing body of a group must apply for the purposes of each school in the group the share of the maintenance grant attributable to that school: s 126. The Secretary of State may specify, by regulations, the arrangements for schools to join and leave a group and for specified other purposes: s 127.

Sections 128–155 contain general and miscellaneous provisions relating to grant-maintained schools. Section 128 imposes a restriction on the provision of further education in grant-maintained schools. Section 129 requires education authorities to treat pupils at grant-maintained schools no less favourably than pupils at schools maintained by them when providing benefits for pupils in their area. Provision relating to the transfer of premises to trustees is made by s 130. The Secretary of State may require the repayment of sums in respect of capital grant from the proceeds of disposal of school premises where the school is transferred to a new site: s 131. Section 132 provides for the disposal of school property transferred to the governing body under s 38. Where trustees dispose of premises held by them, or the funding authority disposes of premises provided by them, the Secretary of State may require them to pay to such local authority as he may specify, the whole or any part of the proceeds of the disposal: ss 133, 134. Section 135 relates to the interpretation of ss 130–134. The Secretary of State may by order make modifications of any trust deed or other instrument relating to a school: s 136. Section 137 provides for the modification of certain instruments relating to land held for the purposes of voluntary schools. Sections 138–140 set out religious education and worship requirements in respect of certain schools. Section 141 makes provision for changes in religious education and worship, and s 142 contains a relevant definition. Sections 143, 144 make provision as to the religious opinions and beliefs of staff. Provision is made for changes in the religious character of schools: s 145. Where any agreed syllabus for religious education falls to be reconsidered, consultation must take place: s 146. Sections 147, 148 make amendments to the Education Reform Act 1988 in respect of standing advisory councils on religious education and cases where there is no requirement for Christian collective worship. Sections 149–151 make provisions relating to the approved admission number of a grant-maintained school and its alteration. Supplementary provisions relating to notification, provision of information and inspection of accounts and reports to Parliament are contained in ss 152–154. Section 155 deals with the interpretation of Pt II.

Part III (ss 156–191, Schs 9–11) Children with Special Educational Needs
Section 156 sets out the meaning of "special educational needs" and "special educational provision". The Secretary of State must issue, and may from time to time revise, a code of practice giving practical guidance for local authorities which they must have regard to in respect

of their functions under Pt III: ss 157, 158. Local education authorities must keep under review their arrangements for special educational provision: s 159. There is a qualified duty to secure the education of children with special educational needs in ordinary schools: s 160. The duties of governing bodies of county, voluntary and grant-maintained schools and of local education authorities in the case of maintained nursery schools in relation to children with special educational needs are set out in ss 161, 162. Section 163 makes provision for special educational provision otherwise than in schools. Local education authorities may make arrangements for children for whom they maintain statements of special educational needs to attend institutions outside England Wales: s 164. The children for whom a local education authority is responsible are set out in s 165. There is a duty under s 166 for the district health authority or local authority to help the local education authority. The procedure for assessing a child's educational needs is set out in s 167, Sch 9, and the procedure to be followed when making and maintaining a statement of a child's special educational needs is set out in s 168, Sch 10. The right of appeal against a decision not to issue a statement is contained within s 169, and the right of appeal against the contents of a statement is contained within s 170. Section 171 provides for access for a local education authority to certain schools. Section 172 deals with reviews of educational needs. Sections 173–175 relate to assessments of educational needs. A district health authority must notify a parent where the authority is of the opinion that the child has special educational needs: s 176. Section 177 establishes a Special Educational Needs Tribunal and prescribes its constitution. Section 178 sets out the qualifications of the President and members of the tribunal. Section 179 relates to remuneration and expenses of members of the tribunal. Tribunal procedure is set out in s 180. The tribunal is under the supervision of the Council on Tribunals: s 181. Section 182, together with Sch 11, defines special schools and makes provision for their government and conduct. Provision for the establishment of maintained or grant-maintained special schools is contained within s 183. The procedure for dealing with proposals for the establishment, alteration and discontinuance of such schools is set out in s 184. Section 185 provides for the approval of premises of such schools. Section 186 allows regulations to be made providing for maintained special schools to become grant-maintained special schools. Section 187 makes provision for groups of schools including grant-maintained special schools. Approval by the Secretary of State of special schools and independent schools suitable for the admission of children with statements of special educational needs is dealt with by ss 188, 189. Local authorities must pay fees incurred when they have placed a child in a non-maintained special school: s 190. The Secretary of State may make modifications to trust deeds relating to any school to meet the requirements of ss 188, 189: s 191.

Part IV (ss 192–203) School attendance
Section 192 provides for a local education authority to serve a school attendance order if it appears that a child of compulsory school age is not receiving suitable education. Sections 193, 194 provide for the choice, including choice by a parent, of the school to be specified in a school attendance order in the case of a child without a statement of special educational needs. The attendance order may be amended at the request of a parent: s 195. The choice of school should be specified in an attendance order relating to a child with special educational needs: s 196. Section 197 makes provision for the revocation of an order at the request of a parent. It is an offence for a parent to fail to comply with the requirements of a school attendance order, or fail to secure the regular attendance at school of a registered pupil: ss 198, 199. Section 200 makes provision for the presumption of age for the purposes of ss 198, 199. Section 201 relates to the institution of proceedings under ss 198, 199 and sets out the punishment for a person guilty of an offence. An application for an education supervision order with respect to a child who is the subject of proceedings may be made by the local education authority if it considers it appropriate: s 202. There is an exemption in certain circumstances where a child achieves the age of five years during a school term: s 203.

Part V (ss 204–228, Sch 12) Schools Failing to Give an Acceptable Standard of Education
Sections 204–212 extend the provisions of the Education (Schools) Act 1992 by specifying further arrangements where a person making an inspection reports that he is of the opinion that the school is failing or likely to fail to provide an adequate standard of education. Section 204 contains introductory provisions. Section 205 empowers Her Majesty's Chief Inspector to secure an inspection under the 1992 Act, s 9 by a member of the Inspectorate of Schools. Sections 206, 207 deal with reports of inspections by registered inspectors and by members of the Inspectorate of Schools, and set out the procedure where the inspector or member is of the opinion that special measures are required to be taken in relation to a school. Time limits for inspections are imposed by s 208. Section 209 deals with arrangements for the distribution of reports. The appropriate authority for the school must prepare a statement of the action they propose to take in the light of inspection reports: s 210. Where the local education authority receives a statement

under s 210, they must send to Her Majesty's Chief Inspector and the Secretary of State a statement of the action they propose to take in the light of the inspection report: s 211. Section 212 provides for monitoring special measures and further inspections.

Sections 213–228 relate to new powers over schools requiring special measures. Section 213 specifies the schools to which the provisions apply. Section 214 empowers the local authority to appoint additional governors to a relevant school. Section 215 empowers the local authority to suspend the right of the relevant schools to a delegated budget. The inclusion of relevant schools in a group under a single governing body is prohibited by s 216. Section 216 also empowers the Secretary of State to bring to an end any grouping of relevant schools. Section 217 prohibits the holding of a ballot for the acquisition of grant-maintained status in certain circumstances. Section 218, together with Sch 12, empowers the Secretary of State to establish an education association to conduct a school. An education association, in exercising their functions, must comply with any directions given by the Secretary of State: s 219. Section 220 empowers the Secretary of State to transfer the responsibility for conducting the school to an education association. Section 221 sets out the effect of an order under s 220. Section 222 sets out the functions of education associations in respect of the schools they conduct. Each school conducted by an education association must be conducted in accordance with an instrument to be known as the articles of government: s 223. Section 224 prescribes the arrangements for a school conducted by an education association to become a grant-maintained school. Section 225 provides for the discontinuance of a school conducted by an education association, and s 226 provides for its winding up. Section 227 prescribes the arrangements following an inspection of a school conducted by an education association where the inspector is of an opinion that the school no longer requires special measures to be taken. Section 228 empowers the Secretary of State, by regulations, to apply, with any appropriate modifications, enactments relating to grant-maintained schools for the purposes of the transfer of a school to, and its conduct by, an education association and its subsequent transfer to grant-maintained status.

Part VI (ss 229–308, Schs 13–21) Miscellaneous
Section 229 amends the Education Act 1980 in respect of the requirements for publication of proposals for the establishment, discontinuance and alteration of schools by local education authorities and in respect of who may object to the proposals. Section 230 amends the 1980 Act, s 13 in relation to proposals for the establishment of voluntary schools by promoters. Section 231 restricts proposals for nursery education in grant-maintained schools. The Secretary of State is empowered by s 232 to make directions bringing forward proposals to remedy excessive provision. He is also empowered by s 233 to make directions bringing forward additional provision in maintained schools. Section 234 empowers the Secretary of State, after the expiry of the time allowed, to publish his own proposals for the establishment, alteration or discontinuance of schools. He must, where he has published his own proposals and these have attracted objections, establish a local inquiry: s 235. Section 236 provides for the adoption of proposals following an inquiry. Section 237 makes supplementary provision. Section 238, together with Sch 13, provides for the incorporation of governing bodies of local education authority maintained schools, and s 239 sets out their powers. Section 240 amends provisions of the Education Reform Act 1988 in respect of the national curriculum and examinations. Section 241 makes provision for sex education in secondary schools. Sections 242, 243 set out a temporary procedure for making certain orders. Sections 244, 245, together with Sch 14, establish the School Curriculum and Assessment Authority and set out its functions. Section 246 dissolves the National Curriculum Council and School Examinations and Assessment Council. Sections 247, 248 make provision for the transfer of property and staff from the old councils to the new authority. Sections 249–251 empower the Secretary of State to make grants to the Curriculum Council for Wales, and make provision as to its proceedings and accounts. The Secretary of State is empowered to transfer any function of the School Curriculum and Assessment Authority in relation to Wales to the Curriculum Council for Wales: s 252. Section 253, together with Sch 15, amends the Education Reform Act 1988 in respect of the name of the Curriculum Council for Wales.

A duty under s 254 now exists in certain circumstances for a local education authority to reconvene a conference to review its agreed syllabus for religious education, and s 255 imposes a duty on the authority to constitute a new standing advisory council on religious education. Section 256 makes provision for the reconsideration of an agreed syllabus. Section 257 amends the Education Reform Act 1988 by adding a provision relating to the Secretary of State's power to direct an advisory council to revoke a determination. Section 258 relates to access to meetings and documents of a standing advisory council. Section 259 amends the Education (Schools) Act 1992 by imposing a duty on the governing body of certain voluntary or grant maintained schools to secure that denominational education is inspected. Sections 260–262 make provision for arrangements for admission to maintained and grant-maintained schools and exclusion from them.

Sections 263–265 require a proprietor of a city technology college or a city college for the technology of the arts to provide certain information, and make provision as to the distribution of information about certain schools.

Sections 266, 267, together with Sch 16, provide for the inclusion of lay members on admission appeals committees and impose a duty to advertise for lay members for appeal committees. Section 268 gives indemnity for legal costs and expenses of members of appeal committees. Section 269 makes provision as to the investigation by a Local Commissioner of decisions of certain appeal committees. Section 270 amends the Education Act 1980 in respect of admission arrangements for aided schools. Section 271 enables the governing bodies of aided schools to include sponsor governors at the direction of the Secretary of State. A governing body of a county school is required to publish proposals for a change of character or significant enlargement of a school: s 272. Section 273 deals with proposals in the case of schools eligible for grant-maintained status. Section 274 provides for revision of schemes for financing schools maintained by local education authorities, and s 275 provides for the publication and auditing of financial statements. Section 276 provides for the application of schemes to special schools. Section 277 specifies compulsory school ages. Section 278 amends certain legislation relating o grants for education support and training, while s 279 makes provision as to inter-authority recoupment. Section 280 amends existing legislation to allow charges to be made for musical instrument tuition in groups of up to four pupils. Section 281 empowers the Secretary of State to make grants to the governing bodies of all voluntary aided and special agreement schools in respect of the provision, alteration or repair of premises and equipment. Sections 282–284 amend existing legislation governing the powers of voluntary aided and special agreement schools. Section 285 relieves the education authority of the duty under the Local Government Act 1972, s 123, to obtain market value for land disposed of in the case of certain disposals. Section 286 repeals provisions in the Education Act 1968 relating to temporary accommodation at voluntary schools. Sections 287, 288, together with Sch 17, make provision as to religious educational trusts. Section 289 makes provision as to teachers' pay and conditions in voluntary and grant-maintained schools, while section 290 makes provision as to the employment of teachers in independent schools. Existing legislation is amended by s 291 in relation to training for unqualified teachers in city technology colleges or city colleges for the technology of the arts. Section 292 amends the Children Act 1989, s 63 so as to change the circumstances in which an independent school is to be a children's home.

Section 293 makes provision with respect to corporal punishment. Section 294 applies to Scotland. Section 295 deals with the provision of goods and services by local authorities. Sections 296, 297 abolish the requirement to establish education committees and give the Secretary of State power to direct the appointment of members of committees. Section 298, together with Sch 18, deals with exceptional provision of education in school or elsewhere. Sections 299–307 and Schs 19–21 contain supplementary provision concerning stamp duty, publication of guidance, the making of orders and regulations, finance, interpretation, consequential amendments and repeals, transitional provisions and savings. Section 308 deals with short title, commencement and extent.

1054 Education associations—articles of government

The Education (Schools Conducted by Education Associations) (Initial Articles of Government) Regulations 1993, SI 1993/3101 (in force on 1 January 1994), prescribe the initial articles of government for schools conducted by education associations. The articles, which make provison with regard to the general responsibilities of the education association and the head teacher, include provisions relating to the curriculum, admissions policy, discipline and reports to parents.

1055 Education associations—responsibility for conduct of schools

The Education (Schools Conducted by Education Associations) Regulations 1993, SI 1993/3103 (in force on 1 January 1994), provide for certain enactments of the Education Act 1993 to have effect in relation to the conduct of schools by education associations. Specified provisions of the 1993 Act, s 220 are to have effect in relation to the transfer of responsibility for the conduct of a school and its subsequent conduct to an educational association. In addition, transitional provisions relating to certain provisions of the Education Reform Act 1988 are to have effect where there is a transfer to an educational association of responsibility for the conduct of a school.

1056   Education Assets Board—transfer of assets
The Education Assets Board (Transfers under the Education Reform Act 1988) (Amendment) Regulations 1993, SI 1993/3114 (in force on 1 January 1994), amend SI 1992/1348 so as to (1) extend from three to six months the period within which agreement is required to be reached on any matter for the purposes of the Further and Higher Education Act 1992, Sch 8, para 62; and (2) require that copies of any written representations and supporting documents, which are to be provided by the transferor and transferee, are sent at the same time as the original written representations and supporting documents are submitted to the Education Assets Board.

1057   Education (Schools) Act 1992—commencement
The Education (Schools) Act 1992 (Commencement No 2 and Transitional Provision) Order 1993, SI 1993/1190, brings into force on 1 May 1993 ss 14 (provision of inspection services by local education authorities), 9(7), Sch 2, paras 1–3 (selection of registered inspectors, inspection teams) and Sch 4, para 4 (amendment of Education Act 1980, ss 8, 9). Transitional provision is also made.

The Education (Schools) Act 1992 (Commencement No 3) Order 1993, SI 1993/1491, brings into force on 12 June 1993, s 9, so far as it is not already in force (inspection of certain schools), s 13 (religious education), s 14, so far as it is not already in force (provision of inspection services by local education authorities), Sch 2, paras 6–15 (inspections under s 9), and certain repeals in Sch 5. The order also brings into force, on 1 September 1993 in relation to secondary schools and on 1 September 1994 in relation to other schools, s 15 (power of local education authority to inspect maintained schools for specific purpose) and certain repeals in Sch 5. For a summary of the Act, see 1992 Abr para 993. For details of commencement, see the commencement table in the title STATUTES.

1058   Funding Councils—decisions—reasons for decisions—appearance of fairness
See *R v Universities Funding Council, ex p Institute of Dental Surgery*, para 34.

1059   Further and higher education—designated institutions
The Education (Designated Institutions in Further and Higher Education) (Interpretation) Order 1993, SI 1993/563 (in force on 1 April 1993), provides that references in the Education Acts to the governing body of an institution which is a company designated under the Further and Higher Education Act 1992 are normally to be read as references to the governing body provided for in the instrument of government of the institution.

The Education (Designated Institutions in Further and Higher Education) (Interpretation) (Amendment) Order 1993, SI 1993/870 (in force on 19 April 1993), amends the 1993 Order supra, in so far as it applies to the inspection of the accounts of designated institutions by the Comptroller and Auditor General.

1060   Further and higher education—institutions—provision of information
The Education (Further Education Institutions Information) (England) Regulations 1993, SI 1993/1993 (in force on 1 September 1993), require the governing bodies of all institutions within the further education sector in England to publish information about the educational achievements of their students and their careers after completing their courses.

The Education (Further Education Institutions Information) (Wales) Regulations 1993, SI 1993/2169 (in force on 5 October 1993), require the governing bodies of all institutions within the further education sector in Wales to publish information about the educational achievements of their students and their careers after completing their courses.

1061   Further and higher education—presence of teachers
The Education (Further Education in Schools) Regulations 1993, SI 1993/1987 (in force on 1 September 1993), prescribe the circumstances in which the governing bodies of county, voluntary, maintained special or grant-maintained schools may provide further education in rooms where pupils are being taught.

1062   Further and higher education—sex discrimination—designated educational establishments

The Further and Higher Education Act (Consequential Amendments) Order 1993, SI 1993/560 (in force on 1 April 1993), makes amendments to the Sex Discrimination (Designated Educational Establishments) Order 1975, SI 1975/1902, which are consequential upon the Further and Higher Education Act 1992.

1063   Further and Higher Education Act 1992—consequential amendments

The Further and Higher Education Act 1992 (Consequential Amendments) Regulations 1993, SI 1993/559 (in force on 1 April 1993), amend a number of regulations so as to take account of changes to further and higher education made by the Further and Higher Education Act 1992. The following regulations, the provisions of which are superseded by the 1992 Act, are revoked: SI 1990/532, 1990/155 and 1992/1166.

1064   Further education—attribution of surpluses and deficits

The Further Education (Attribution of Surpluses and Deficits) Regulations 1993, SI 1993/609 (in force on 1 April 1993), prescribe certain matters concerning the attribution of surpluses and deficits for the purposes of the Further and Higher Education Act 1992, s 37, namely (1) the amount to be deducted from an institution's budget share in respect of earned income; (2) the amount to be added in respect of any surplus carried forward; (3) the amount of earned income to be deducted in calculating "net expenditure"; (4) the expenditure to be taken into account; (5) the instalments by which payments are to be made; and (6) interest payable.

1065   Further education—exclusion of land from transfer

The Further Education (Exclusion of Land from Transfer) Order 1993, SI 1993/901 and the Further Education (Exclusion of Land from Transfer) (No 2) Order 1993, SI 1993/937 (both in force on 31 March 1993), provide that certain interests of local authorities in land are are excluded from transferring to further education corporations under the Further and Higher Education Act 1992, s 23(2). The orders also confer certain rights and impose certain liabilities in such land.

1066   Grant-maintained schools—acquisition of grant-maintained status—annual consideration of ballot

The Education (Annual Consideration of Ballot on Grant-Maintained Status) (England) Order 1993, SI 1993/3115 (in force on 1 January 1994), provides that the Education Act 1993, s 24 applies to the governing bodies of all schools in England which are eligible for grant-maintained status. The 1993 Act, s 24(2) requires the governing bodies of all schools which are eligible for grant-maintained status and to whom the section applies, to consider, at least once in every school year, whether to hold a parent's ballot on the issue of whether grant-maintained status should be sought for the school. The order also makes transitional provision for schools holding ballots under the Education Reform Act 1988, s 61, before the 1993 Act, s 28 comes into force, and also where schools have considered whether to hold such a ballot before the order comes in to force.

1067   Grant-maintained schools—acquisition of grant-maintained status—ballot information

The Education (Acquisition of Grant-maintained Status) (Ballot information) Regulations 1993, SI 1993/3189 (in force on 1 January 1994), specify the information which must be given to every person eligible to vote in a ballot for the acquisition of grant-maintained status, where the governing body are under a duty to hold a ballot of parents by virtue of the Education Act 1993, s 25 or 26.

1068   Grant-maintained schools—acquisition of grant-maintained status—governing body

The Education (Acquisition of Grant-maintained Status) (Transitional Functions) Regulations 1993, SI 1993/3072 (in force on 1 January 1994), provide for the appointment of a prospective head teacher, deputy head teacher or other staff, by a new governing body of a grant-maintained school. The regulations also make provision with respect to information which may be requested by the new governing body.

1069   Grant-maintained schools—finance

The Education (Grant-maintained Schools) (Finance) Regulations 1993, SI 1993/568 (in force on 1 April 1993), as amended by SI 1993/843, replace the 1992 Regulations, SI 1992/555, as amended. The principal changes relate to the method of calculating a grant-maintained school's maintenance grant. The Secretary of State is given the power to adjust the maintenance grant if it appears that, by reason of any extraordinary circumstances, the amount of any maintenance grant is insufficient to enable the governing body of the school to carry out its functions properly.

1070   Grant-maintained schools—initial governing instruments

The Education Act 1993 (Grant-maintained Schools) (Initial Governing Instruments) Regulations 1993, SI 1993/3102 (in force on 1 January 1994), prescribe the initial instrument and articles of government for specified grant-maintained schools. The regulations include provisions relating to the election and appointment of parent and teacher governors, and the appointment of a chairman and vice-chairman of a governing body and a clerk to the governing body. The initial articles of government are set out. The general responsibilities of the governing body and head teacher with regard to the conduct of the school are also dealt with by the regulations. The regulations provide that the governing body must prepare an annual report and hold an annual parents' meeting and includes provisions with respect to the use of school premises and provisions relating to the appointment and dismissal of staff.

1071   Grant-maintained schools—initial sponsor governors

The Education (Grant-Maintained Schools) (Initial Sponsor Governors) Regulations 1993, SI 1993/3188 (in force on 1 January 1994), provide for the determination of initial sponsor governors of grant-maintained schools in pursuance of proposals which include the name of a proposed sponsor. The regulations also make provision relating to the publication of notice of a selection and the replacement of proposed initial sponsor governors.

1072   Grant-maintained schools—loans

The Education (Grant-maintained Schools) (Loans) Regulations 1993, SI 1993/3073 (in force in part on 1 January 1994, in part on 1 April 1994), specify the types of expenditure in respect of which the appropriate authority may make loans to the governing bodies of grant-maintained schools under the Education Act 1993, s 92 and the ways in which such loans may be made.

1073   Grants—grants of land for educational purposes—grants under Schools Sites Act—reverter

It has been held that land conveyed as a site for a school under the School Sites Act 1841, s 2 which was not part of a larger estate, reverted to the successors in title of the grantors of the conveyance when it ceased to be so used.

  Marchant v Onslow (1993) Times, 12 November (Chancery Division: Mr David Neuberger QC).

1074   Grants—music and ballet schools

The Education (Grants) (Music and Ballet Schools) (Amendment) Regulations 1993, SI 1993/1938 (in force on 27 August 1993), further amend the 1989 Regulations, SI 1989/1236, by relaxing the means tests for the remission of fees, uniform grants and school travel grants. Amendments are made to the lists of choir schools in the 1989 Regulations supra, and to the Aided Pupil Scheme updating the references to the legislation relating to the adoption and fostering of children.

1075   Grants—travellers and displaced persons

The Education (Grants) (Travellers and Displaced Persons) (Amendment) Regulations 1993, SI 1993/569 (in force on 1 April 1993), further amend the 1990 Regulations, SI 1990/306, so as to authorise payments to institutions within the further education sector in addition to payments to local education authorities.

1076   Higher education—awards—mandatory awards—European students

The Education (Mandatory Awards) Regulations 1993, SI 1993/1850 (in force on 1 September 1993), supersede the 1992 Regulations, SI 1992/1270. Changes of substance include the following: (1) changes are made in the rates of grant and allowances; (2) European students are now entitled to a fees only award from the authority in whose area the institution is situated; (3) European students who have been ordinarily resident in the British Islands for only part of the three years preceding the first year of the course may obtain a fees only award; (4) students who have been ordinarily resident in the British Islands throughout the three years preceding the first year of the course are now prevented from receiving a fees only award as European students when they are not entitled to a full award from the authority in the British Islands in whose area they are ordinarily resident; (5) an award may be transferred when a student who has commenced a first degree course transfers to an honours degree course in the same subject; (6) payment of maintenance grants to students who have disabilities may, on their written instruction, be made to third parties; and (7) amendments have been made to the provisions on sandwich courses so that in certain cases periods of unpaid service outside the United Kingdom can be taken into account as periods of experience.

The Education (Mandatory Awards) (No 2) Regulations 1993, SI 1993/2914 (in force on 1 September 1994), supersede the 1993 Regulations, SI 1993/1850, supra. Changes of substance include the following: (1) changes are made in the rates of grant and allowances; (2) various amendments have been made to the methods of payment of fees; (3) the discretion given to local education authorities to pay a student's travel or medical insurance expenses in relation to a period of study outside the United Kingdom which is not a necessary part of the student's course has been removed; and (4) provision is made to reflect the fact that nationals of countries within the European Economic Area, in addition to nationals of countries within the European Community, have rights arising under Council Regulation (EC) 1612/68 (see SI 1993/3183 infra).

The Education (European Economic Area) (Amendment) Regulations 1993, SI 1993/3183 (in force on 1 January 1994), amend the Education (Mandatory Awards) Regulations 1993, SI 1993/1850 (supra), the Education (Student Loans) Regulations 1993, SI 1993/1214 (repealed from 1 August 1994 by SI 1993/2915; see para 1080) and the Education (Fees and Awards) Regulations 1983, SI 1983/973 so as to reflect the fact that Council Regulation (EC) 1612/68 now extends to the European Economic Area and not only to the European Community. It is provided that persons having rights arising out of Council Regulation (EC) 1612/68 are entitled to a full mandatory award in respect of maintenance and tuition fees and to student loans for attendance on prescribed courses of higher education. In addition, they are eligible for local authority discretionary awards and awards from the research councils. Fees charged must be no higher than those charged to United Kingdom students. A mandatory award in respect of tuition and other fees continues to be available only to nationals of a member state of the European Community who are not entitled to a full mandatory award, and is not made available to nationals from other states within the European Economic Area who are not so entitled. The regulations also extend the residence requirement so that it applies to residence within the European Economic Area.

1077   Higher education—awards—mandatory awards—student's resources

By virtue of the Education (Mandatory Awards) Regulations 1990, SI 1990/1628, Sch 3, para 5(5), where, in pursuance of any trust deed or other instrument, any income is applied towards the education of a student in receipt of an award, that income is to be treated as part of the parent's gross income.

Under a court order made under the Matrimonial Causes Act 1973, s 23(1)(d), a father was stated to pay money to a mother "for and direct to" the applicant, their child. The order was so worded for tax purposes and, in reality, the money was paid to the mother for the applicant's education. The applicant sought judicial review of a decision revising the award made to her under the 1990 Regulations and withdrawing the maintenance element of sums made to her by way of provisional grants, contending that the money paid under the court order was to be treated as her mother's income. Held, the money paid to the mother was applied by her for or towards the maintenance, education or other benefit of the applicant by reason of, because of and in pursuance of the court order. Although the money was stated to be paid "for and direct to" the applicant, it could nevertheless be said to be paid in pursuance of the order for it was for the parties to carry out the terms of the order by whatever method was most expedient. The words "other instrument" in Sch 3, para 5(5) were wide enough to include a county court order made without the parties' consent. For the purposes of that provision, the money could be treated as the mother's income and, accordingly, the application would be allowed.

R v Sheffield City Council, ex p Parker [1993] 2 FLR 907 (Queen's Bench Division: Tucker J).

1990 Regulations replaced by Education (Mandatory Awards) Regulations 1993, SI 1993/1850 (para 1076).

1078 Higher education—European co-operation scheme

See para 2673.

1079 Higher education—prescribed courses

The Education (Prescribed Courses of Higher Education) (Wales) Regulations 1993, SI 1993/481 (in force on 1 April 1993), list those courses of higher education which are prescribed courses for the purposes of the Further and Higher Education Act 1992, s 65(2), and as such may attract financial support from the Higher Education Funding Council for Wales. The regulations only apply to courses provided by institutions in Wales.

1080 Higher education—student loans

The Education (Student Loans) Regulations 1993, SI 1993/1214 (in force on 1 August 1993), replace the 1992 Regulations, SI 1992/1211. The main changes include prescribing a new condition of eligibility that the student has agreed to notify the loans administrator in writing if he ceases to attend his course due to early completion of it; removing the requirement that where a borrower transfers to another loan-bearing course at the same institution he must commence repayment of his loan following his ceasing to attend the first course; substituting a new formula for determining the threshold applicable for establishing a borrower's entitlement to defer making loan repayments; and adding to the duties of the governing bodies of institutions in relation to loans.

The Education (Student Loans) (Amendment) Regulations 1993, SI 1993/1620 (in force on 1 August 1993), amend the 1993 Regulations, supra by substituting for certain references to the Social Security Act 1975 references to the Social Security Contributions and Benefits Act 1992.

The Education (Student Loans) (No 2) Regulations 1993, SI 1993/2915 (in force on 1 August 1994), supersede the 1993 Regulations, SI 1993/1214, as amended. Changes of substance include the following: (1) changes are made in relation to the maximum amounts of loans and rates of interest; (2) the increase in the retail price index (which determines the rate of interest charged on loans) is required to be measured from March to March as opposed to June to June; (3) deferment of a loan may now take effect not more than two months after the date on which the loans administrator notifies the borrower of his entitlement to deferment; (4) a new procedure for the certification of eligibility for loans where students have borrowed before is introduced; and (5) provision is made to reflect the fact that nationals of countries within the European Economic Area, in addition to nationals of countries within the European Community, have rights arising under Council Regulation (EC) 1612/68 (see further para 1076).

1081 Higher education—Wales

The Higher Education (Wales) (Revocation) Regulations 1993, SI 1993/89 (in force on 1 April 1993), revoke the 1990 Regulations, SI 1990/1278.

1082 Independent schools—assisted places scheme

The Education (Assisted Places) (Incidental Expenses) (Amendment) Regulations 1993, SI 1993/1937 (in force on 27 August 1993), further amend the 1989 Regulations, SI 1989/1237, by relaxing the means tests for uniform grants and school travel grants.

The Education (Assisted Places) (Amendment) Regulations 1993, SI 1993/1936 (in force on 27 August 1993), amend the 1989 Regulations, SI 1989/1235, by relaxing the means test for the remission of fees. Provision is made for payments made under arrangements made by the Child Support Agency to be deducted from the income of the person making the payments for the purposes of the regulations and included in the income of the person receiving them.

1083   Local education authority—articles of government—joint agreement with other local education authorities

The Education (No 2) Act 1986, s 42 provides that the articles of government for every county and maintained special school will provide for the use of the school premises at all times other than during any school session to be under the control of the governing body, for the governing body to exercise control subject to any direction given to it by the local education authority and in so doing to have regard to the desirability of the premises being made available for use by members of the community served by the school.

Prior to the coming into force of the 1986 Act, three councils made an agreement for the construction and funding of a leisure complex. The defendant council sought to opt out of the agreement and refused to pay part of the annual running costs of the leisure complex. It fell to be determined whether the agreement was terminable by reasonable notice given by one of the parties or whether it was one which would endure for the likely future life of the buildings and whether the agreement was frustrated by the coming into force of the Education (No 2) Act 1986. At first instance the judge declared that the defendant was not lawfully entitled to withdraw from participation in the joint leisure committee without the consent of the plaintiffs and to refuse to pay part of the annual running costs of the leisure complex. On appeal by the defendant, *held*, Hirst LJ dissenting, since articles of government which did comply with the 1986 Act, s 42(a) entrusted the management to the joint committee, and therefore enabling continued compliance with the terms of the memorandum of agreement, s 42 did not have the effect of putting it out of the power of the parties to perform it. Therefore, the coming into force of the 1986 Act, s 42 did not operate to frustrate the prior agreement between the parties. Accordingly, the appeal would be dismissed.

Islwyn Borough Council v Newport Borough Council (1993) Times, 28 June (Court of Appeal: Glidewell, Hirst and Roch LJJ).

1084   Local education authority—exercise of education function—closure of single sex school—sex discrimination

The Education Act 1944, s 8 provides that it is the duty of every local education authority to secure that there are available for their area sufficient schools to provide secondary education. The Sex Discrimination Act 1975, s 23 provides that it is unlawful for a local education authority, in carrying out its functions under the Education Act 1944 to do any act which constitutes sex discrimination.

A local education authority decided to close a boys' school. The decision, which was backed by the Secretary of State, was seen as the only viable option given the falling number of pupils attending the school. The only other single-sex school in the area admitted only girls and accordingly, the authority was aware that closure of the school would risk a breach of the 1975 Act. The applicant, a pupil at the school, submitted that because of the authority's awareness of the risk, the decision was improper or unlawful and could not therefore have been lawfully approved by the Secretary of State. The applicant sought judicial review of the local education authority's decision and the decision of the Secretary of State to back the authority. *Held*, the local education authority could not have performed its statutory duties under the 1944 Act, s 8 nor under the 1975 Act, s 23 because of the future lack of educational opportunities at the school, there was nothing which was repugnant or unlawful in the authority's approach. The recognition by the authority that it might be vulnerable to a charge of sex discrimination was not sufficient to invalidate its decision to cease to maintain the school. Further, it was clear that the Secretary of State had accepted that the duty of the authority under the 1975 Act had been an important factor for him to take into account in deciding whether to give his approval and therefore, his decision was also reasonable and valid and there was no ground for impugning it. Accordingly, the application would be dismissed.

R v Northamptonshire County Council, ex p K (1993) Times, 27 July (Queen's Bench Division: Hutchison J).

1085   Local education authority—exercise of education function—school admissions policy—placement according to catchment area

The respondent local education authority had a school placement policy whereby pupils were awarded places at schools where a sibling was already attending. The remainder of places were filled with pupils living within a catchment area which would be widened if the school attracted relatively few applications, and narrowed if it was over-subscribed. A neighbourhood came within a school's catchment area if it maintained traditional ties with that particular school. The applicant parent, whose son had failed to receive a place at his three choices of school, sought judicial review of the respondent's policy. He submitted that the policy was unreasonable as well as contrary to the Education Act 1980, s 6 because it restricted parental choice by favouring pupils in some areas and not others. He also claimed that, as Asian children were under-represented in the chosen areas, the policy amounted to direct and/or indirect discrimination under the Race Relations Act 1976, s 1(1)(a) and (b). His final submission was that the respondent provided parents with insufficient information for them to express their preferences effectively. *Held*, the policy was not unreasonable simply because applicants were forced to compete on unequal terms. Establishing traditional ties was important and local pupils would have to travel long distances if they were unable to attend the school nearest to them. The respondent was entitled to take all these factors into account. The policy was not contrary to the 1980 Act, s 6 as, where schools were over-subscribed, there had to be some system of selection unless places were awarded by lottery. The respondent did not need to ensure Asian children were included in a catchment area as it was not for an authority to exercise positive discrimination. The 1976 Act provided that discrimination occurred where one group was found to be unfairly treated when compared to another group where the relevant circumstances were the same, or not materially different. The applicant had therefore erred in comparing the percentage of Asian applicants who did not receive an offer at a preferred school, to non-Asians not living in the same town. The statistics comparing Asians and non-Asians in the same town showed there was no discrimination. The respondent's policy was clearly enough set out to enable parents to make an informed choice. In any event, even if a good claim had been made out, relief would have been refused on the ground of being detrimental to good administration. Accordingly, the application would be dismissed.

R v Bradford Metropolitan Borough Council, ex p Sikander Ali (1993) Times, 21 October (Queen's Bench Division: Jowitt J).

1086 Local education authority—failure to provide appropriate educational facilities—private proceedings

See *Holtom v Barnet London Borough Council*, para 2457.

1087 Local education authority—provision of transport for attendance at school—policy

A young child suffered from a medical syndrome which gave rise to special educational needs. Although the needs of the child could be met at a nearby school, his parents preferred to send him to a school 14 miles away from home. The authority agreed to the parents' request that the child should attend the school further away but maintained that it had no legal obligation under the Education Act 1944, s 55 to provide free transport as there was a school nearby. On an application for judicial review of the authority's decision not to provide free transport, it was held that the authority's duty under the 1944 Act applied when the child attended a school of the authority's choice and did not apply to a child who attended a school chosen by the parents where that involved a choice of school which would not ordinarily be nominated by the authority. On appeal by the parents, *held*, the 1944 Act allowed a local education authority to decide whether to provide free transport in a particular case. In this case, the local education authority had exercised this discretion in a way that was not unreasonable. It could not have been Parliament's intention that parents could always demand free transport to whichever school they had selected for their child, particularly where there were equally suitable schools nearer the child's home. Accordingly, the appeal would be dismissed.

R v Essex County Council, ex p C (1993) Times, 9 December (Court of Appeal: Russell, Staughton and Steyn LJJ).

The applicant parents, who were English-speaking, had a daughter who was experiencing learning difficulties because of the majority of her classes being conducted in Welsh. They therefore claimed that the local education authority were obliged to provide transport for their daughter under the Education Act 1944, s 55(1), to a school which was located 10 miles away but which conducted only 15 per cent of its classes in Welsh. The authority claimed it was not so obliged as the school the daughter was presently attending was a suitable alternative within walking distance of her home. On an application by the parents, *held*, there were many relevant factors to take into account when applying the 1944 Act, s 55(1), including parental preference, although this was not conclusive, as well as the inherent suitability of the preferred and alternative school, financial considerations, such as avoidance of unreasonable public expenditure, and policy considerations lawfully adopted by the education authority. In this case, the authority had taken all these factors into account and addressed them to this particular child and its decision could therefore not be said to be irrational or perverse. There was a clear basis for establishing that the nearer school was suitable and accordingly, the application would be dismissed.

R v Dyfed County Council, ex p S (Minors) (1993) Times, 21 December (Queen's Bench Division: May J).

1088 Local education authority—school finance—application of scheme to special schools

The Education (Application of Financing Schemes to Special Schools) Regulations 1993, SI 1993/3104 (in force on 1 January 1994), replace the 1992 Regulations, SI 1992/164. The main change which the regulations introduce is to require schemes to provide for financial delegation to the governing bodies (or temporary governing bodies) of such schools as the Secretary of State directs. This is to apply to all schools maintained by local education authorities in England as from the financial year beginning on 1 April 1996.

1089 Local education authority—school finance—publication of schemes

The Education (Publication of Schemes for Financing Schools) Regulations 1993, SI 1993/3070 (in force on 1 January 1994), replace the 1989 Regulations, SI 1989/2335. The requirements for publication by local education authorities of their schemes for financing schools maintained by them are extended so as to require copies to be furnished to the governing body and head teacher of each grant-maintained school in their area. Copies are also to be furnished (when the relevant provisions of the Education Act 1993 come into force) to the governing body and head teacher of each grant-maintained special school which is established in the authority's area or which, before becoming such a school, was a special school maintained by the authority. In addition, the regulations extend the requirement to publish a scheme, on the entry into force of a variation made by direction of the Secretary of State, to require publication on the entry into force of any revision of a scheme.

1090 National curriculum—assessment arrangements

The Education (National Curriculum) (Assessment Arrangements for the Core Subjects) (Key Stage 1) Order 1993, SI 1993/1983 (in force on 6 August 1993), specifies arrangements for English, mathematics, and science subjects of the National Curriculum in the final year of the first key stage, as they apply to maintained schools in England. The 1992 Order, SI 1992/1857, is revoked.

The Education (National Curriculum) (Assessment Arrangements for the Core Subjects) (Key Stage 3) Order 1993, SI 1993/1984 (in force on 6 August 1993), specifies arrangements for the core subjects in the final year of the third key stage, as they apply to maintained schools in England. The 1992 Order, SI 1992/1858, is revoked.

The Education (National Curriculum) (Assessment Arrangements for English, Welsh, Mathematics and Science) (Key Stage 1) (Wales) Order 1993, SI 1993/2190 (in force on 31 August 1993), specifies assessment arrangements for mathematics, science, Welsh (in relation to schools and classes which are Welsh speaking), and English (in relation to schools and classes which are not Welsh speaking) in the final year of the first key stage as they apply to maintained schools in Wales. The 1992 Order, SI 1992/1983, is revoked.

The Education (National Curriculum) (Assessment Arrangements for English, Welsh, Mathematics and Science) (Key Stage 3) (Wales) Order 1993, SI 1993/2191 (in force on 31 August 1993), specifies the assessment arrangements for English, Welsh, mathematics and science in the final year of the third key stage, as they apply to maintained schools in Wales. The 1992 Order, SI 1992/2042, is revoked.

1091 National curriculum—individual pupils' achievements—information

The Education (Individual Pupils' Achievements) (Information) Regulations 1993, SI 1993/3182 (in force on 10 January 1994), largely replace the 1992 Regulations, SI 1992/3168. Several changes are made, including the following: (1) except where considered appropriate to do so, the head teacher is required to send a report on adult pupils' progress and achievements to adult pupils only, and not to their parents; (2) the requirement to send a report to adult pupils who are leaving school has been removed; (3) the information required to be reported about a pupil's achievements and progress has been reduced; (4) the requirement to provide in the report the

National Curriculum levels of attainment and GCSE, GCE "A" level and GCE "AS" results of pupils at schools in England has been removed. However, the head teacher is required to include information regarding all other pupils at the school in the final year of the first and third key stages; (5) on a request, the head teacher is required to provide additional information to the parents of pupils in the final year of any key stage; and (6) provisions concerning the circumstances in which information is not to be made available are amended.

The Education (Individual Pupils' Achievements) (Information) (Wales) Regulations 1993, SI 1993/835 (in force on 20 April 1993), revoke and re-enact with amendments the 1992 Regulations, SI 1992/1205. Certain changes of substance are made, including the introduction of a requirement that headteachers must provide a report on a pupil's progress to pupils aged over 18 years as well as to parents, and that school leavers must be provided with a record of their school achievements and examination qualifications.

1092   School Curriculum and Assessment Authority—transfer of property and staff

The National Curriculum Council and School Examinations and Assessment Council (Transfer of Property) Order 1993, SI 1993/2195 (in force on 1 October 1993), transfers certain assets and liabilities from the National Curriculum Council and the School Examinations and Assessment Council to the School Curriculum Assessment Authority, which has been established under the Education Act 1993.

The Education (School Curriculum and Assessment Authority) (Orders for Transfer of Property and Staff) Order 1993, SI 1993/3105 (in force on 9 December 1993), substitutes the period of two months for the period of six months, which was specified in the Education Act 1993, during which orders may be made by the Secretary of State for the transfer of property and staff from the National Curriculum Council and the School Examinations and Assessment Council to the School Curriculum and Assessment Authority.

1093   Schools—consecrated school chapel—lease by school governors—application for faculty

See *Re Tonbridge School Chapel*, para 1036.

1094   Schools—curriculum and related information

The Education (School Curriculum and Related Information) (Amendment) (Wales) Regulations 1993, SI 1993/998 (in force on 6 May 1993), further amend the 1991 Regulations, SI 1991/1658, so as to require parents to be informed of the arrangements for appealing against a decision refusing a child admission to a school, including aided or special agreement schools.

1095   Schools—discipline—exclusion of pupils—appeals against exclusion

The Education (No 2) Act 1986, Sch 3 deals with appeals against school exclusions on grounds of discipline.
      The Education (No 2) Act 1986 (Amendment) Order 1993, SI 1993/2709 (in force on 10 December 1993), amends the Education (No 2) Act 1986, Sch 3, para 8 by substituting "and" for "or" in two places. Schedule 3 is concerned with appeals against school exclusions on grounds of discipline and the effect of the amendment is to give pupils, parents and local education authorities the right to make both written and oral representations to an appeal committee.
      The Education (No 2) Act 1986 (Amendment) (No 2) Order 1993, SI 1993/2827 (in force on 10 December 1993), amends the 1986 Act supra, Sch 3 so as to give governing bodies and local education authorities the right to make both written and oral representations to an appeal committee on an appeal by a pupil or parent.

1096   Schools—duty of care—pupil illegally abducted—duty to inform parent of enrolment

The applicant claimed his son's school had been in breach of a duty of care to inform him, as a custodial parent, that his son was enrolled even though it knew the child had been illegally abducted. He also brought an action for deceit and conspiracy due to the school allegedly denying his son was a pupil at the school. *Held*, there was no right of action in damages for interference with a parent's parental rights. There was no claim for deceit as the pleadings did not show how the applicant had suffered any loss. Likewise, there was no claim for conspiracy as there were no particulars as to the unlawful acts necessary to establish conspiracy or how the defendant was meant to have profited. Accordingly, the claims would be struck out on the ground that they were frivolous, vexatious and an abuse of the court's process.

Re S (A Minor) (Parental Rights) [1993] Fam Law 572 (Queen's Bench Division: Phelan J).

1097 Schools—financial statements—prescribed particulars

The Education (School Financial Statements) (Prescribed Particulars etc) Regulations 1993, SI 1993/113 (in force on 22 February 1993), replace the 1990 Regulations, SI 1990/353, for any financial year beginning on or after 1 April 1993. The regulations prescribe the form in which budget and outturn statements, made for the purposes of the Education Reform Act 1988, s 42, are to be prepared, the particulars and information to be contained in budget statements in addition to those specified by s 42, the information to be contained in outturn statements, and the manner in which and the times by which all such statements are to be published.

1098 Schools—information about further education—distribution

The Education (Distribution by Schools of Information about Further Education Institutions) (England) Regulations 1993, SI 1993/3197 (in force on 25 January 1994), require the governing body of every county, voluntary or grant-maintained school providing secondary education to provide specified categories of information to pupils with respect to institutions within the further education sector. The information which must be provided is that published by the governing body of a institution within the further education sector under the Further and Higher Education Act 1993. The copies are to be given by the governing body of the school to all pupils who are in the second year of the fourth key stage. The same provision is made in respect of city technology colleges and other specified educational establishments.

1099 Schools—information on school performance—details of examination results

The Education (School Performance Information) (England) (No 2) Regulations 1993, SI 1993/2077 (in force on 6 September 1993), relate to the collection and publication of information about the performance of schools and correct defects in the Education (School Performance Information) (England) Regulations 1993, SI 1993/1503, which are revoked.

The regulations provide for certain information about results of specified National Curriculum assessments, unauthorised absence, and general information concerning schools, to be provided to the Secretary of State. The regulations also contain provisions relating to the duty of certain schools to pass information to parents.

The Education (School Performance Information) (Wales) Regulations 1993, SI 1993/2194 (in force on 4 October 1993), are made under the Education Reform Act 1988, ss 22 and 232(5) and (6), and the Education (Schools) Act 1992, ss 16 and 19(3).

The Regulations describe the way in which certain examination results should be determined, and the method of calculating points for GCE 'A' and 'AS' level exams. Head teachers have a duty to provide specified information to governing bodies of maintained secondary schools. The governing bodies and proprietors of certain schools have an obligation to provide information relating to their schools, and examination results to the Secretary of State, and also have to provide certain information to parents on request and to publish certain information in the school prospectus. The Education (School Performance Information) (Wales) Regulations 1992, SI 1992/2274, are revoked.

The Education (School Information) (England) Regulations 1993, SI 1993/1502 (in force on 9 July 1993), as amended by SI 1993/2824, provide for school governors to publish school prospectuses containing specified information including the results of statutory assessment of pupils, the results of public examinations, the courses taken by pupils over the age of 16 and unauthorised absence. The 1981 Regulations, SI 1981/630 and the 1992 Regulations, SI 1992/70, are revoked.

1100 Schools—inspection of schools

The Education (School Inspection) (No 2) Regulations 1993, SI 1993/1986 (in force in part on 1 September 1993, in force in part on 1 October 1993), replace the 1993 Regulations, SI 1993/1492. The regulations extend the categories of persons to whom the appropriate authority must notify the time when an inspection is to take place by including the funding authority. Provision is made in the case of grant-maintained and voluntary grant-maintained schools.

Further provision is made pursuant to the Education Act 1993 and the Education (Schools) Act 1992 as to the time by which inspections are to be completed, the period within which the report of the inspection is to be made, the period within which the appropriate authority is to prepare an action plan following an inspection and the period within which, and the persons to whom, the appropriate authority must distribute copies of the action plan. The regulations have been amended by SI 1993/2973.

The Education (School Inspection) (Wales) (No. 2) Regulations 1993, SI 1993/1982 (in force in part on 1 September 1993, in part on 1 October 1993), as amended by SI 1993/2968, replace SI 1993/1529, and contain provisions under the Education (Schools) Act 1992, s 9, in relation to the inspection of schools. Provision is made for the first inspection of secondary schools which is to take place on or after 1 September 1993 but before 1 August 1998 and for subsequent inspections to take place within five school years from the end of the school year when the last inspection took place. Further provision is made for the conduct of inspections and of registered inspectors.

1101 Schools—proposals in relation to school—publication of proposals

The Education (Publication of School Proposals and Notices) Regulations 1993, SI 1993/3113 (in force in part on 1 January 1994, in part on 1 April 1994), replace the Education (Publication of School Proposals) (No 2) Regulations 1980, SI 1980/658, and the Education (Grant-Maintained Schools) (Publication of Proposals) Regulations 1989, SI 1989/1469, by prescribing the manner in which proposals for the establishment, discontinuance, alteration or transfer of schools maintained at the public expense and notice of the determination of initial governors are to be published.

Minor amendments are also made to the Education (Publication of proposals to change the status of a controlled school) Regulations 1987, SI 1987/34, and the Education (Publication of Proposals for Reduction in Standard Number) Regulations 1991, SI 1991/411.

1102 Schools—school government—meetings and resolutions of governing body

The Education (School Government) (Amendment) Regulations 1993, SI 1993/3107 (in force on 1 January 1994), further amend the 1989 Regulations, SI 1989/1503. They allow additional governors to schools requiring special measures to hold office without being disqualified under the 1989 Regulations, reg 2, because they are members of governing bodies of more than two schools. Provision is made to allow removal of the chairman of a governing body by resolution of the governing body and special provisions are made in the case of governors appointed under the Education Act 1993. Provision is also made for a secret vote to be held when deciding whether a ballot of parents ought to be called to determine whether grant-maintained status ought to be sought for the school. A meeting of the governing body of a school is prohibited from considering whether a ballot of parents ought to be held to determine whether grant-maintained status ought to be sought for the school unless consideration of that question is a specific item of business on the agenda and at least seven clear days' notice of such a meeting is required.

1103 Student—national of member state—vocational training—right of residence

See para 2718.

1104 Teachers—barring of teacher—reasons for decision—judicial review

The Secretary of State had barred the applicant teacher from teaching at certain categories of schools as a result of the applicant's possession or authorship of obscene material. This direction was made under the Education (Teachers) Regulations 1989, SI 1989/1319, reg 10. The applicant sought judicial review of the Secretary of State's decision and his refusal to give reasons. *Held*, the purpose of the 1989 Regulations, regs 9(1) and 10 was to permit the Secretary of State to bar a teacher who did not have the health or physical capacity for the relevant employment as a teacher. The teacher's health and the effect of the diagnosed condition on his fitness to teach had to be considered in relation to the regulations. The risk to the pupils from the identified condition was also relevant. In this case the decision had been reached without an express finding of the applicant's health and without identifying the grounds on which the conclusion was reached. It was assumed that the applicant was grossly disturbed and psycho-sexually oriented such as to constitute a risk to pupils. The fact of the retention of the obscene material was too insubstantial to base a decision to bar the teacher and the direction was therefore irrational and flawed. The Secretary of State should also provide a short statement setting out findings of facts and his conclusions, and should consider whether the regulations as presently drafted were appropriate in cases where the risk to the pupils was of paramount concern. Accordingly, the application would be granted.

R v Secretary of State for Education, ex p Standish (1993) Times, 15 November (Queen's Bench Division: Potts J).

1105 Teachers—employment

The Education (Teachers) Regulations 1993, SI 1993/543 (in force on 1 April 1993), replace the 1989 Regulations, SI 1989/1319, as amended. The regulations reflect the changes made by the Further and Higher Education Act 1992, and provide that recommendations for licences for licensed teachers and for authorisations for overseas trained teachers must now contain particulars of the post in which the teacher is to be employed.

The Education (Teachers) (Amendment) Regulations 1993, SI 1993/1969 (in force on 1 September 1993), amend the principal regulations, SI 1993/543 supra, Sch 3, para 2(1) (qualifications needed to become a qualified teacher) to cover courses at schools, including city technology colleges; a redundant reference to the Council for National Academic Awards is omitted in consequence.

1106 Teachers—head teacher—appointment—discrimination—religion

See *Board of Governors of St Matthias Church of England School v Crizzle*, para 256.

1107 Teachers—industrial action—refusal to carry out national curriculum tests— protection from liability in tort

See *Wandsworth London Borough Council v National Association of Schoolmasters and Union of Women Teachers*, para 2553.

1108 Teachers—pay and conditions

The Education (School Teachers' Pay and Conditions) (No 2) Order 1993, SI 1993/1755 (in force on 1 September 1993), provides that the provisions relating to remuneration and other conditions of employment set out in the document entitled "The School Teachers' Pay and Conditions Document 1993" published by HMSO, are to have effect for the purpose of determining the remuneration and allowances of school teachers in England and Wales.

1109 Teachers—superannuation

See PENSIONS AND SUPERANNUATION.

1110 Teachers—training—bursaries

The Education (Bursaries for Teacher Training) (Amendment) Regulations 1993, SI 1993/1775 (in force on 1 September 1993), further amend the 1988 Regulations, SI 1988/1397, so as to empower the Secretary of State to pay bursaries to students commencing a course on or after 1 September 1993 to the sum of £1,000. Students commencing a course on or after that date will not be entitled to the equipment allowance of £200 for students of craft, design and technology or to the allowance of £500 a year for intending teachers of physics which have been available up to that date.

1111 Teachers—training—grants

The Education (Training Grants) Regulations 1993, SI 1993/72 (in force on 15 February 1993), replace the 1990 Regulations, SI 1990/1857, as amended. The regulations now (1) authorise the Secretary of State to make grants to education authorities to facilitate and encourage the further training of qualified teachers, non-qualified teachers who are employed as teachers by an education authority, persons who are studying for the Postgraduate Certificate in Education, nursery nurses, foreign language assistants and persons employed in schools in administrative capacities; (2) make provision for the payment of grants and set out the amount and rate at which payment is to be made; and (3) require education authorities to whom a grant is paid to comply with any requests of the Secretary of State.

1112   University—commissioners—duties and powers—continuation

The Education (University Commissioners) Order 1993, SI 1993/3056 (in force on 30 December 1993), continues the powers and duties of the university commissioners, which would otherwise have ceased on 1 January 1994, until 1 January 1995.

1113   University—examinations board—decision—judicial review

See *R v Manchester Metropolitan University, ex p Nolan*, para 39.

1114   University—unconditional offer of place to student—mistaken offer— interlocutory relief

A student applied for a place on a university course and received an unconditional offer of acceptance from the university. He accepted the offer, and under the terms of the university entrance scheme he was thereby ineligible to apply for alternative places. The student terminated his employment, left his accommodation and did not attend a second interview for a job that he had applied for. The university subsequently informed him that it had never intended to accept him and that the offer had been made as a result of a clerical error. The university argued that the offer of a place was a mere invitation to the student to enter into discussions which might lead to an agreement to accept him on the course, and that it had not intended to create a contract until the student had enrolled and agreed to pay the fees. The student applied for a mandatory injunction compelling the university to admit him to the course pending the trial of an action against the university for damages. On appeal against the dismissal of the application, *held*, the unconditional offer was on the face of it intended to create a legal relationship and appeared to be an offer capable of acceptance. When the student accepted the offer, there was a strong case for holding that there was an agreement under which the university agreed to offer him a place if he sought to enrol on the due date. The fact that by accepting the offer the student gave up his eligibility to apply for an alternative place was consideration for the agreement. However, taking into account all the circumstances of the case, it was wrong to grant a mandatory order at an interlocutory stage. Accordingly, the appeal would be dismissed.

Moran v University College Salford (No 2) (1993) Times, 23 November, Independent, 26 November (Court of Appeal: Glidewell, Evans and Waite LJJ). For earlier related proceedings, see (1993) Times, 27 October (para 1997).

1115   Unrecognised degrees—listed bodies

The Education (Listed Bodies) Order 1993, SI 1993/625 (in force on 5 March 1993), replaces the 1991 Order, SI 1991/383, which lists bodies which are not recognised bodies within the Education Reform Act 1988, s 214(2)(a) but which appear to the Secretary of State to fall within s 216(3). Such bodies are ones which provide any course in preparation for a degree to be granted by a recognised body and approved by or on behalf of the recognised body or is a constituent college, school or hall or other institution of a university which is a recognised body. Section 214(1), under which it is an offence to grant, offer or issue an invitation relating to unrecognised degrees and awards, does not apply to such listed bodies.

1116   Unrecognised degrees—recognised bodies

The Education (Recognised Bodies) Order 1993, SI 1993/626 (in force on 5 March 1993), designates bodies appearing to the Secretary of State to be recognised bodies within the Education Reform Act 1988, s 214(2)(a) or (b). Accordingly, awards granted by such bodies are not of a kind referred to in s 214(1), under which it is an offence to grant, offer to grant or issue any invitation relating to certain unrecognised degrees and awards. The 1988 Order, SI 1988/2036, as amended, is revoked.

ELECTIONS

Halsbury's Laws of England (4th edn) Vol 15 (reissue), paras 301–883

1117   Articles

The Fading Prospect of a Petition, Piers Coleman (on how an election can be overturned): 143 NLJ 1487

1118 European Parliament—right to vote and stand as a candidate
See para 2678.

1119 European Parliamentary Elections Act 1993
The European Parliamentary Elections Act 1993 gives effect to a decision of the EC Council, 93/81/Euratom, ECSC, EC, of 1 February 1993 having the effect of increasing the number of United Kingdom representatives to be elected to the European Parliament. The Act received the royal assent on 5 November 1993 and ss 2, 3 and the Schedule came into force on that date. Section 1 is to come into force on a day to be appointed.

Section 1 amends the European Parliamentary Elections Act 1978 by increasing the number of United Kingdom representatives to the European Parliament from 66 to 71 in England and from four to five in Wales. By virtue of the 1993 Act, s 2 and Schedule, for the purpose of determining the European parliamentary constituencies into which England and Wales are to be initially divided to give effect to such increases, European parliamentary constituency committees for England and Wales are to submit to the Secretary of State reports showing the European parliamentary constituencies into which they recommend that England or, as the case may be, Wales should be divided. Such reports are to be laid before Parliament together with draft Orders in Council giving effect, with or without modifications, to the committees' recommendations. Section 3 deals with short title, a consequential amendment and commencement.

1120 Parliamentary constituencies
See PARLIAMENT.

1121 Representation of the People Act 1993
The Representation of the People Act 1993, s 1 amends the Representation of the People Act 1983, s 59 to secure that members of the regular army who, except for the purposes of training, are required to serve only in Northern Ireland are not regarded as members of the forces for the purposes of the 1983 Act, Pt I. Section 2 deals with short title, commencement and extent. The Act received the royal assent on 20 July 1993 and came into force on that date.

ELECTRICITY AND ATOMIC ENERGY

Halsbury's Laws of England (4th edn) Vol 16, paras 1–500

1122 Area boards—dissolution
The Area Boards (Dissolution) Order 1993, SI 1993/2825 (in force on 10 December 1993), dissolves the area boards, following the transfer of their property, rights and liabilities to nominated successor companies.

1123 Electricity Board—duty of care—duty owed to minor
See *Adams v Southern Electricity Board*, para 1867.

1124 Electricity supply—restrictive trade practices—exempt agreements
The Electricity (Restrictive Trade Practices Act 1976) (Exemption) Order 1993, SI 1993/912 (in force on 30 March 1993), specifies a description of agreements relating to the generation, transmission or supply of electricity to which the Restrictive Trade Practices Act 1976 is deemed not to apply and never to have applied. By virtue of the Electricity Act 1989, s 100(1) electricity is treated as goods for the purposes of the 1976 Act. The 1993 Order provides that agreements meeting the description set out in the order will fall outside the provisions of the 1976 Act.

1125 Electricity supply—standards of performance—compensation
The Electricity (Standards of Performance) Regulations 1993, SI 1993/1193 (in force on 8 June 1993), re-enact and amend the 1991 Regulations, SI 1991/1344. The regulations prescribe the sum which a public electricity supplier must pay to a customer by way of compensation for

failure to meet specified standards of performance in respect of the electricity supply services to be provided by such suppliers. The sum payable differs between domestic and non-domestic customers, and between standards.

1126 Nuclear energy—supply—safeguards

See *Advanced Nuclear Fuels GmbH v EC Commission*, para 2704.

1127 Nuclear installations—security provisions

The Nuclear Installations (Application of Security Provisions) Order 1993, SI 1993/687 (in force on 24 March 1993), applies to Urenco (Capenhurst) Ltd the security provisions of the Nuclear Installations Act 1965.

1128 Radioactive substances—disposal—authorisation—variation

A company had been granted authorisations, subject to specified conditions, permitting it to dispose of liquid and gaseous radioactive waste from its premises. The authorisations were varied to allow it to test its new thermal oxide processing plant which was in the process of completion. The applicant, an organisation which had about 400,000 supporters (2,500 of whom were in the region of the company's site) and which campaigned for the protection of the natural environment, sought judicial review of the decision to vary the authorisations. The company contended that the applicant did not have sufficient interest in the matter to bring the proceedings. *Held*, premises, as defined in the Radioactive Substances Act 1960, s 19(1), included the plant on site. Testing of the new plant was within the purpose of any undertaking carried on by the company at the premises. Under its nuclear site licence, it had a wide power to extend or contract its activities on site. Relevant waste was defined in each authorisation; it was a constant definition of waste arising from the company's operations at its premises as distinct from the identity of the plant or the substance producing it. The power to revoke or vary the authorisation was very wide but not unlimited. Although any variation to the conditions or limitations of the authorisation could not widen its general terms, they could be used to relax or make more stringent the conditions governing the disposal of relevant waste. The relevant gaseous waste was a constant both in the authorisation and in the variation. There was no increase in the disposal of relevant waste even though there was an added stack, ie the new stack, contributing to the relevant waste. Similarly, the variations to the liquid waste authorisations still only permitted the disposal of relevant waste as defined. They did not extend the description of radioactive waste; it was irrelevant that the waste would emanate from new plant. The applicant had sufficient interest in the issues raised for it to be granted locus standi but, nevertheless, its application would be refused.

R v Her Majesty's Inspectorate of Pollution, ex p Greenpeace Ltd (1993) Independent, 30 September (Queen's Bench Division: Otton J).

1960 Act, s 19(1) now Radioactive Substances Act 1993, s 47(1).

1129 Radioactive substances—transfrontier shipment of radioactive waste

The Transfrontier Shipment of Radioactive Waste Regulations 1993, SI 1993/3031 (in force on 1 January 1994), implement Council Directive (EC) 92/3 Euratom on the supervision and control of shipments of radioactive waste between Member States and into and out of the European Community. The regulations provide for a system of authorisation and approval for the shipment of radioactive waste.

1130 Radioactive Substances Act 1993

The Radioactive Substances Act 1993 consolidates certain enactments relating to radioactive substances, with corrections and minor improvements made under the Consolidation of Enactments (Procedure) Act 1949. The Act received the royal assent on 27 May 1993 and comes into force on 27 August 1993. A table showing the destination of enactments consolidated appears on the following page.

DESTINATION TABLE

This table shows in column (1) the enactments repealed by the Radioactive Substances Act 1993, Sch 6 ante, and in column (2) the provisions of that Act corresponding thereto.

In certain cases the enactment in column (1), though having a corresponding provision in column (2) is not, or not wholly, repealed as it is still required, or partly required, for the purposes of other legislation.

A dash adjacent to a repealed provision indicates that that provision is spent, unnecessary or for some other reason not reproduced.

A reference to "M" followed by a number is a reference to the the number in the Lord Chancellor's Memorandum of proposed corrections and minor improvements made under the Consolidation of Enactments (Procedure) Act 1949.

(1)	(2)	(1)	(2)
Radioactive Substances Act 1960 (c 34)	Radioactive Substances Act 1993 (c 12)	Radioactive Substances Act 1960 (c 34)	Radioactive Substances Act 1993 (c 12)
s 1(1)	s 6	s 8(4A)	s 16(6)
s 1(2)	s 7(1)–(3)	s 8(5)	s 16(9), M2
s 1(3)	s 7(4)	s 8(5A)	s 25(2), (3)
s 1(3A)	s 7(5)	s 8(6)	s 16(10)
s 1(4)–(6)	s 7(6)–(8)	s 8(7)	s 17(1), (2), (4)
s 1(7)	s 25(1), (3)	s 8(8)	s 17(3), M2
s 2(1)	Rep 1990 c 43, ss 103, 162(2), Sch 16, Pt V	s 8A	s 20
s 2(2)	s 8(1)	s 9(1)	s 40(1)
s 2(3)	s 8(2)	s 9(2)	s 40(2)
s 2(4)	s 8(3)	s 9(3)	s 18(1)
s 2(5)	s 8(4), (5)	s 9(4)	s 18(2)
s 2(6)	s 8(6)	s 9(5)	s 18(3)
s 2(7)	s 8(7)	s 9(6)	s 40(3)
s 3(1), (2)	s 9	s 10(1)–(3)	s 29(1)–(3)
s 3(3)	s 10(1)	s 10(4)	s 30(1)
s 3(4)	s 10(2)	s 10(5)	s 30(3)
s 3(4A), (4B)	s 10(3), (4)	s 11(1)	s 28(1)
s 3(5)	s 10(5)	s 11(2)	—
s 3(6)	s 25(1), (3)	s 11(3)	s 19
s 4(1)	Rep 1990 c 43, ss 103, 162(2), Sch 16, Pt V	s 11(4)	s 28(2)
s 4(2), (3)	s 11(1), (2)	s 11A	s 4(1)–(5)
s 5	s 12	s 11B	s 21
s 6(1)	s 13(1)	s 11C	s 22
s 6(2)	s 13(2)	s 11D(1)–(4), (12)	s 26(1)–(5)
s 6(3)	s 13(3), (4)	s 11D(5)–(11)	s 27(1)–(7)
s 6(4)	s 15(1)	s 11E	s 28(3)
s 6(5)	s 15(2)	s 12(1)	Rep 1990 c 43, s 162(2), Sch 16, Pt V
s 6(6)	s 13(5)	s 12(2)	s 31(1)
s 7(1)	s 14(1)	s 12(3)	s 31(2), (3)
s 7(2)	s 14(2)	s 12(4)	s 31(4)
s 7(3)(a)	Rep 1990 c 43, ss 103, 162(2), Sch 16, Pt V	s 12(5)	s 31(5)
s 7(3)(b), (c)	s 14(3)	s 12(6)	s 31(6)
s 7(4)	s 15(1), (2)	s 12(6A)	s 31(7)
s 7(5)	s 14(4)	s 12(7)(a)	s 5(1), (2)
s 8(1)	s 16(3)	s 12(7)(b)	s 31(8)
s 8(2)	s 16(5)	s 12(7A)	s 31(9)
s 8(3)	s 16(1), (2)	s 12(7B)	s 4(6)
s 8(3A)	s 16(4)	s 12(8), (9)	s 31(10), (11)
s 8(3B)	s 16(7)	s 12A	s 23(1)–(4)
s 8(4)	s 16(8)	s 12B	s 24(1)–(4)
		s 13(1), (2)	s 32
		s 13(3)	s 34(1), (3)

(1)	(2)	(1)	(2)
Radioactive Substances Act 1960 (c 34)	Radioactive Substances Act 1993 (c 12)	Radioactive Substances Act 1960 (c 34)	Radioactive Substances Act 1993 (c 12)
s 13(4)	s 34(2)	Sch 1, Pt I, paras 1, 2	Sch 3, Pt I, paras 3, 4
s 13(4A)	s 33(3)	para 3	Sch 3, Pt I, para 1
s 13(5)	ss 33(1), 35	para 4	Rep 1963 c 33, s 93(1), Sch 18, Pt II
s 13(6)	s 33(2)		
s 13(7)	s 38(1)	paras 5, 6	Rep 1991 c 60, s 3(1), Sch 3, Pt I
s 13(8)	s 36		
s 13(9)	s 37	para 7	Rep 1974 c 40, s 108, Sch 4
s 13A	s 39(1)–(6)		
s 14	s 42(1)–(8)	para 8	Sch 3, Pt I, para 2
s 15(1), (2)	ss 44(1), (2), 45(1), (2)	para 8A	Rep 1974 c 40, s 108, Sch 4
s 15(3)	—		
s 15(4)	s 44(3)	para 8AA	Sch 3, Pt I, para 6
s 15(5)	s 44(4)	para 8B	Rep 1991 c 60, s 3(1), Sch 3, Pt I
s 15A	s 43(1)–(5)		
s 16	—	para 8C	Sch 5, para 11
s 17	—	para 8D	Sch 3, Pt I, para 5
s 18(1)–(3)	s 1(1)–(3)	para 8E	Rep SI 1989/1150
s 18(3A)	s 1(4)	paras 8F, 8G	Rep 1991 c 60, s 3(1), Sch 3, Pt I
s 18(4)	s 2		
s 18(5)	s 3	para 9	Sch 3, Pt I, para 7
s 18(6)	s 1(5)	paras 10–12	Sch 3, Pt I, paras 8–10
s 19(1)	s 47(1)	Sch 1, Pt II	Applies to Scotland
s 19(1A)	s 47(2)	Sch 1, Pt III, para 17	Rep 1966 c 17, s 210, Sch 7
s 19(2)–(4)	s 47(3)–(5)		
s 19(5)	s 46	para 18	Rep SI 1978/1049, art 87(2), Sch 7
s 20	Applies to Scotland		
s 21(1)	s 51(3)	para 19	Rep 1966 c 17, s 210, Sch 7
s 21(2)(a)	ss 1(6), 4(7)(a), (b), 5(3), 8(8), 11(3), 15(3), 16(3), (8), (10), 17(1), (2), (4), 18(1), (2), 20(3), 21(3), (4), 22(5), 23(5), 24(5), 25(4), 26(4), (6), 27(8), 28(1), (3), (4), 29(4), 30(2), (3), 31(12), 34(4), 39(2), (7), 42(9), 43(6), 45(1), (2), 47(1), (6)	para 20	Rep 1972 c 5, s 31(1)
		para 21	Sch 3, Pt III, para 18
		para 22	Sch 3, Pt III, para 19
		para 23	Rep 1978/1049, art 87(2), Sch 7
		para 24	Sch 3, Pt III, para 20
		para 25	Rep 1978/1049, art 87(2), Sch 7
		para 26	Sch 3, Pt III, para 24
		para 27 (1st)	Sch 3, Pt III, para 25
		para 27 (2nd)	Sch 3, Pt III, para 21
s 21(2)(b), (c)	s 45(3), (4)	para 28	Sch 3, Pt III, para 22
s 21(2)(d), (e)	—	para 29	Sch 3, Pt III, para 23
s 21(2)(f), (g)	s 47(1)	Sch 2	Sch 2
s 21(2)(h)	Rep 1973/70, art 60(2), Sch 4	Sch 3	Sch 1
s 21(2)(i)	s 40(3)		
s 21(2)(j)	s 30(3)		
s 21(2)(k)	s 4(7)(c)		
s 21(2)(l)	s 4(7)(d)	Fisheries Act (Northern Ireland) 1966 (c 17)	Radioactive Substances Act 1993 (c 12)
s 21(2)(m)	s 24(3)		
s 21(2)(n)	s 43(6)	Sch 7*	s 47(1), Sch 3, Pt III, para 21
s 21(2)(o)	s 42(9)		
s 21(3)	s 38(2)		
s 21(4)	Rep 1990 c 43, ss 105, 162(2), Sch 5, Pt II, para 20, Sch 16, Pt V	Sewerage (Scotland) Act 1968 (c 47)	Radioactive Substances Act 1993 (c 12)
s 21(5)	Rep 1973 c 36, s 41(1), Sch 6, Pt I	Sch 1, para 4	Applies to Scotland
s 22			

* Repealed in part

(1)	(2)	(1)	(2)
Water (Northern Ireland) Act 1972 (c 5)	Radioactive Substances Act 1993 (c 12)	Planning (Consequential Provisions) Act 1990 (c 11)	Radioactive Substances Act 1993 (c 12)
s 31(1)	Sch 3, Pt III, para 22		
		Sch 2, para 7	Sch 3, Pt I, para 6
		Sch 4*	Cf Sch 5, para 10
Northern Ireland Constitution Act 1973 (c 36)	Radioactive Substances Act 1993 (c 12)	Environmental Protection Act 1990 (c 43)	Radioactive Substances Act 1993 (c 12)
Sch 5, para 1†	s 40(3)	s 100(1)	s 4(1)–(5)
Sch 5, para 7(1)†	s 38(2)	s 100(2)	ss 7(1), (4), (6)–(8), 8(2), (3), 10(2), (5), 12, 16(1)–(3), (5), 18(1), (2), 47(1)
Local Government (Scotland) Act 1973 (c 65)	Radioactive Substances Act 1993 (c 12)	s 100(3)	ss 1(5), 8(6), 11(1), 15(2), 29(1)–(3), 30(1), (3), 31(1), (5), 34(1), (3), 44(1), (2), 45(1), (2)
Sch 27, Pt II, para 144 .	Applies to Scotland	s 101	s 43(1)–(5)
		s 102	ss 21, 22
		s 103	—
Customs and Excise Management Act 1979 (c 2)	Radioactive Substances Act 1993 (c 12)	s 104	s 42(1)–(8)
		s 105	—
		s 160(2)–(6)†	s 41, M4
Sch 4, Pt I*	—	s 164(3)	Sch 5, Pt II, para 11
		Sch 5, Pt I, para 1(1) . .	—
		para 1(2)	s 16(3)
		para 1(3)	s 16(8)
Water (Scotland) Act 1980 (c 45)	Radioactive Substances Act 1993 (c 12)	para 1(4)	s 16(9), M2
		para 1(5)	ss 16(10), 17, M2
Sch 10, Pt II*	Applies to Scotland	para 2(1)	s 18(1), (2)
		para 2(2)	s 31(1)
		para 3	s 47(1)
		para 4(1)	s 7(1), (2)
Building Act 1984 (c 55)	Radioactive Substances Act 1993 (c 12)	para 4(2)	s 16(4)
		para 5	s 47(1)
Sch 6, para 7	Sch 3, Pt I, para 5	para 6(1)(a)	s 7(3)
		para 6(1)(b)	s 7(8)
		para 6(1)(c)	s 25(1), (3)
Housing and Planning Act 1986 (c 63)	Radioactive Substances Act 1993 (c 12	para 6(2)(a)	s 10(3)
		para 6(2)(b)	s 10(5)
Sch 7, Pt II, para 1 . . .	Applies to Scotland	para 6(2)(c)	s 25(1), (3)
		para 6(3)	s 12
		para 6(4)(a)	s 16(6)
		para 6(4)(b)	s 16(9), M2
Water Act 1989 (c 15)	Radioactive Substances Act 1993 (c 12)	para 6(4)(c)	s 25(2), (3)
		para 7(1)	ss 9, 10(1)
Sch 25, para 27(1) . . .	s 16(5)	para 7(2)	s 3
para 27(2)	ss 18(1), 40(2)	para 7(3)	s 13(2)
para 27(3)	s 47(1)	para 8	s 20
		para 9(1)	s 28(1)
		para 9(2)	s 28(2)
		para 10	ss 26(1)–(5), 27(1)–(7), 28(3)
		para 11(1)	s 7(5)
		para 11(2)	s 10(4)

† Not repealed
* Repealed in part

(1)	(2)	(1)	(2)
Environmental Protection Act 1990 (c 43)	Radioactive Substances Act 1993 (c 12)	Water Consolidation (Consequential Provisions) Act 1991 (c 60)	Radioactive Substances Act 1993 (c 12)
para 11(3)	s 16(7)		
para 11(4)	s 47(1), (2)	Sch 5, Pt II, para	
para 12	ss 23(1)–(4), 24(1)–(4)	20(a)(ii)	ss 4(7)(c), (d), 24(3), 42(9), 43(6)
para 13(1)	—		
para 13(2)	s 31(1)	para 20(b)	—
para 13(3)	s 31(6), (7)	Sch 15, para 8	Sch 3, Pt I, para 7
para 13(4)	ss 4(6), 31(9)		
para 14(1)	—	Atomic Weapons Establishment Act 1991 (c 46)	Radioactive Substances Act 1993 (c 12)
para 14(2)	s 32		
para 14(3)	s 32		
para 14(4)	s 34(2)		
para 14(5)	s 33(3)	Schedule, para 5	—
para 14(6)	s 35		
para 14(7)	ss 33(1), 35		
para 14(8)	s 33(2)	Water Consolidation (Consequential Provisions) Act 1991 (c 60)	Radioactive Substances Act 1993 (c 12)
para 14(9)	s 38(1)		
para 14(10)	s 37		
para 15	s 39(1)–(6)		
para 16	—	Sch 1, para 9(1)	Sch 3, Pt I, paras 8–10
para 17	s 1(4)	para 9(2)	s 40(4)
Sch 5 Pt II, paras 18, 19.	Apply to Scotland		
para 20(a)(i)	ss 1(6), 4(7)(a), (b), 5(3), 8(8), 11(3), 15(3), 16(3), (8), (10), 17(1), (2), (4), 18(1), (2), 20(3), 21(3), (4), 22(5), 23(5), 24(5), 25(4), 26(4), (6), 27(8), 28(1), (3), (4), 29(4), 30(2), (3), 31(12), 34(4), 39(2), (7), 42(9), 43(6), 45(1), (2), 47(1), (6)		

1131 Renewable energy sources—Altener programme
See para 2705.

EMPLOYMENT

Halsbury's Laws of England (4th edn) Vol 16 (reissue), paras 1–650

1132 Articles

A Change of Job, John Bowers and Paul Mee (on the variation of employee's contracts): 137 SJ 1102

A Pause Over Pregnancy, Brian Napier: LS Gaz, 3 February 1993, p 21

Age and Sex Discrimination at Work: Britain v New York, Joseph Kelly: 143 NLJ 466

Demergers and Employee Share Schemes, Heather Savage: Tax Journal, Issue 233, p 11

Dismissal Due To Pregnancy, Damian McCarthy: 137 SJ 1274

Discrimination and Equal Pay, Colin Bourn: 143 NLJ 1302

Employer's Liability and the Provision of Defective 'Equipment" (on *Knowles v Liverpool City Council* [1993] ICR 21, CA (1992 Abr para 1264)): (1993) 22 ILJ 214

Fighting the Kiss of Death, Louise Dunford (on *Spring v Guardian Assurance* (1993) Independent, January 26, CA (para 1992 Abr para 1846)): 143 NLJ 408

Further and Better Particulars, Gwyneth Pitt (on the Trade Union Reform and Employment Rights Act 1993): 144 NLJ 84

Immunity System, Gordon Hausmann, Gillian Howard and Nigel Rivers (on the role of diplomatic immunity in unfair dismissal proceedings): LS Gaz, 8 September 1993, p 23

Individualism Versus Collectivism—An Evaluation of the Trade Union Reform and Employment Rights Act 1993, s 14, Bob Simpson: (1993) 22 ILJ 181

Industrial Action—Public and Private Interests, Gillian Morris: (1993) 22 ILJ 194

Industrial Tribunals—Recent Developments, John Bowers and Geoffrey Mead (on the Industrial Tribunal (Constitution and Rules of Procedure) Regulations 1993, SI 1993/2687): 138 SJ 12

Justice in Dismissal—A Reply to Hugh Collins, Gwyneth Pitt: (1993) 22 ILJ 251

Legislating Equal Pay? Lessons From Canada, Aileen McColgan: (1993) 22 ILJ 269

Maternity Rights: The New European Directive, Tess Gill: 137 SJ 8

New Rules for Old, Stephen Levinson (on the effect of the Industrial Tribunals (Constitution and Rules of Procedure) Regulations 1993 (para 1160)): 143 NLJ 1744

Non-Statutory Redundancy Payments, Philip Harrison: Tax Journal, Issue 230, p 8

Out of Sight, Out of Mind? Geoff Holgate (on the non-delegable nature of an employer's duty of care): 137 SJ 1156

Playing Politics, Fraser Younson (on anti-union discrimination law): LS Gaz, 30 June 1993, p 12

Proving Equal Value—The European Court Lends a Hand, Brian Napier: 143 NLJ 1648

Recession Hits Women, Sean Webster (on redundancies in solicitors' firms): 137 SJ 242

Remedies for Breach of the Contract of Employment, KD Ewing: [1993] 52 CLJ 405

Taking the Lead from Europe, Melanie Tether (on the influence of EC law on UK employment rights): LS Gaz, 15 September 1993, p 27

The EC Pregnancy Directive—Principle or Pragmatism? Valerie Cromack: [1993] 4 SWFL 261

The Reasonable Employer, Douglas Brodie: [1993] 24 SLT 231

Time Runs Out, Martin Edwards (on time limits in unfair dismissal cases): LS Gaz, 28 October 1993, p 25

Transfer of Undertakings and Community Law, Brian Napier: 137 SJ 175

Transfer of Undertakings and Pre-transfer Dismissals, Michael Duggan: 137 SJ 88

Transfer Regulations in Turmoil, Charles Wynn-Evans: [1993] 14 BLR 237

TUPE—The Summer's Harvest, Brian Napier (on the interpretation of the Transfer of Undertakings (Protection of Employment) Regulations 1981, SI 1981/1794): 137 SJ 904

Swimming with the Tide—Employment Protection and the Implementation of European Labour Law, K Ewing: (1993) 22 ILJ 165

Unfair Dismissal—Ill Health, Consultation and Progress Reports, Christine Clayson: 137 SJ 1076

Working Abroad, Louise Jones: 137 SJ 998

1133 Continuity of employment—additional provisions

The Employment Protection (Continuity of Employment) Regulations 1993, SI 1993/2165 (in force on 4 October 1993), replace the 1976 Regulations, SI 1976/660. Certain additional provisions are added which preserve continuity of employment for the purposes of employment protection rights contained in the Employment Protection (Consolidation) Act 1978 and the Trade Union and Labour Relations Act 1992 where a dismissed employee is reinstated or re-engaged as a result of (1) the making of a compromise contract authorised by (i) the 1978 Act, s 140(2)(fb) and relating to a complaint of unfair dismissal; (ii) the Sex Discrimination Act 1975, s 74(4)(aa) and relating to a complaint arising out of a dismissal; (iii) the Race Relations Act 1976, s 72(4)(aa) and relating to a complaint arising out of a dismissal; (2) the presentation of a complaint under the 1975 Act, s 63, arising out of a dismissal or the presentation of a complaint under the 1976 Act, s 54 arising out of a dismissal; or (3) action taken by a conciliation officer under the 1975 Act, s 64(2) or the 1975 Act, s 55(2).

1134 Continuity of employment—EC directive—transfer of undertakings

See *Rask v ISS Kantineservice A/S*, para 2758.

1135 Continuity of employment—National Health Service trust—transfer of undertakings

The National Health Service and Community Care Act 1990, s 6 provides that the contract of employment between an applicable person and the health authority by whom he is employed has effect from the operational date as if originally made between him and the NHS Trust. Section 6(1) provides that an applicable person is one who "immediately before an NHS trust's operational date is employed by a health authority to work solely at, or for the purposes of, a hospital or other establishment that is to become the responsibility of the trust".

The employee was employed by a health authority in 1987, his contract providing that he would undertake clinical duties within his health district or in other areas as designated. From 1990, he was employed solely at one hospital. The following year, he applied for a permanent post. After the hospital became an NHS trust, the employee was offered a full-time contract. His contract of employment provided that for the purposes of the Employment Protection (Consolidation) Act 1978, continuous employment dated from 1987. The employee was dismissed in 1992. The employee sought to bring a claim of unfair dismissal. At first instance it was held that an industrial tribunal had jurisdiction to entertain the employee's claim on the ground that he had been employed for not less than two years as required by the 1978 Act, s 64. On appeal, *held*, the critical factor for the application of the 1990 Act, s 6(1) was whether an employee's contract of employment required him to work solely at the relevant hospital. The employee's contract in this case did not. The Act applied to those employed to work solely at the hospital immediately before the day trust status was acquired. The appeal would accordingly be allowed.

Northern General Hospital National Health Service Trust v Gale [1993] ICR 638 (Employment Appeal Tribunal: Judge Peppitt QC presiding).

1136 Contract of employment—collective agreement—incorporation of terms—written particulars

The defendant employers had negotiated a collective agreement to pay a significantly enhanced severance payment to employees who were made redundant. A statement of terms and conditions issued by the employers incorporated general instructions and notices and relevant collective agreements, including the agreement on severance payments, into individual contracts of employment. However, a new statement of terms and conditions made no reference to the incorporation of general instructions and notices or collective agreements into individual employment contracts. The employers subsequently issued a general instruction, purporting to withdraw the previously existing severance terms and replace them with less favourable terms. A writ was issued by the plaintiff employees. The unions and employers negotiated a settlement regarding pay increases and agreed that in future any enhanced redundancy terms would be the subject of negotiations. Additionally, the unions agreed to withdraw from any pending or proposed legal action against the employers. The employees applied to the court for a declaration that their contracts of employment included within them a term entitling each of them to enhanced severance payments upon redundancy. The employers claimed there was no consideration given by the employees for the introduction of the enhanced terms in their contracts and that they were therefore not binding upon them. They also claimed that they were entitled to unilaterally alter the terms of the contract and that the settlement was a collective agreement incorporated into the individual contracts. *Held*, the consideration by the employees was that they continued to work and had not continued with a pay claim, thereby allowing the employers to avoid industrial action and benefit from the continued services of a known employee. The employers were not entitled to alter the contracts unilaterally as, where terms of a collective agreement were incorporated into individual contracts, those terms would remain part of the contracts until they were removed by either agreement or under a special right found in the contracts. There was neither agreement nor a special contractual right in this case. The settlement between the employers and the unions did not extinguish the employees' right to bring the action because the unions were not authorised to act as agents for the employees in the negotiations and did not therefore do so. The settlement did not constitute a collective agreement incorporated into the individual contracts as the new statement of terms and conditions did not make provision for such incorporation. It was clear that the negotiations were collective bargaining and that the subsequent agreement had not been intended to be binding upon the individual employees. Accordingly, it was declared that the employees' contracts of employment included a term entitling them to enhanced severance payments upon redundancy.

Lee v GEC Plessey Telecommunications [1993] IRLR 383 (Queen's Bench Division: Connell J).

1137 Contract of employment—implied term—employers' obligation to allow employee to work overtime

The plaintiff was employed as a postman by the defendants which involved him working overtime. His contract provided that in the event of misconduct he could be suspended with or without pay. The plaintiff was involved in an incident and criminal proceedings followed. He was immediately suspended on full basic pay pending an inquiry by the defendants' personnel officer. That suspension was lifted six months later. The plaintiff commenced proceedings against the defendants for damages for loss of overtime payments on the grounds that it was an implied term that the defendant would provide the plaintiff with work and the opportunity to earn overtime. The plaintiff further sought a declaration that the manner and length of the suspension was in breach of his contract of employment in that it was unfair, he was not given an opportunity to make representations and was in breach of the rules of natural justice. *Held*, it was not obvious that the parties to the contract would imply terms that an employee would only be suspended after he was fully informed as to the reason for the suspension and given an opportunity to make representations. It was inappropriate to import the rules of natural justice into the employer/employee relationship, and as the contract of employment expressly provided for suspension of an employee there was no general obligation on the defendants to act fairly and reasonably. There was no term implied into the plaintiff's contract that he was entitled, whilst suspended, to be provided with work and the opportunity to earn overtime. Although the plaintiff had an obligation to work overtime he had no contractual right to be provided with overtime, and therefore even if he had succeeded on liability he would not have been able to prove that he had suffered any damage. Accordingly, the appeal would be dismissed.

Mclory v Post Office [1992] ICR 758 (Chancery Division: David Neuberger QC).

1138 Contract of employment—termination of contract—mobility clause—failure to invoke mobility clause

The respondents supplied labour to a company under a contract. That contract was put out to tender and awarded to another company. The appellants were employed by the respondents and their contract of employment contained a mobility clause which stated that, if it was in the interests of the company, employees might be required to change the location and nature of their employment. The respondents circulated to their employees details of positions available in other companies including the company who won the contract but at no stage did the respondents seek to invoke the mobility clause. The majority of the employees accepted offers of employment with the company who won the contract, however the appellants claimed redundancy payments from the respondents. The respondents refused their requests on the ground that suitable alternative employment had been offered. An industrial tribunal dismissed the appellants' claims for redundancy payments on the ground that none of the employees was dismissed in law. On appeal, *held*, the only basis upon which it would be said that the appellants remained employed by the respondents after the business had been closed down was if the respondents were entitled to and did require them as a result of the mobility clause to take up other jobs, that did not happen and therefore the appellants were dismissed by the respondents. It was clear that no offer of suitable alternative employment had been made, the appellants had merely been provided with details of job vacancies. Accordingly, the appeal would be allowed. *Curling v Securicor Ltd* [1992] IRLR 549 (Employment Appeal Tribunal: Knox J presiding).

1139 Contract of employment—terms of employment—offer of alternative employment—suitability

The plaintiff was employed as a butcher by the defendant company. For several years, he was the manager of a mobile butchery service. The butchery service was withdrawn by the defendant and the plaintiff was appointed manager of a butchery shop. The shop was closed some years later and as the defendant did not own any more individual butcher's shops, the plaintiff was asked to take charge of the butchery department in a supermarket owned by the defendant. The plaintiff no longer had a key to the store and was not responsible for collecting and banking money. He was also partially under the jurisdiction of the store manager. The plaintiff gave notice and claimed a redundancy payment. The defendant resisted his claim, contending that there was a mobility clause in the plaintiff's contract which provided that the plaintiff would be required to pursue his employment at any of the establishments comprising the food division. An industrial tribunal held that the mobility clause did not entitle the defendant to require the plaintiff to work as the department manager in the supermarket. On appeal by the defendant, *held*, under the Employment Protection (Consolidation) Act 1978, s 82(5), the question of the suitability of an offer of alternative employment was an objective matter. However, the reasonableness of an employee's refusal was a subjective matter to be considered from the employee's point of view, and there was nothing in s 82(5) to restrict the employee's reasons to factors not connected with the employment itself. It was possible for an employee reasonably to refuse an objectively suitable offer of alternative employment on the ground of his personal perception of the job offered. Accordingly, the appeal would be dismissed.

Cambridge and District Co-Operative Society Ltd v Ruse [1993] IRLR 156 (Employment Appeal Tribunal: Judge Hague QC presiding).

1140 Contract of employment—terms of employment—restraint of trade—notice period

The employee was an options broker on the foreign exchange desk of the employers. His contract of employment was determinable by either party giving twenty weeks' notice and one of its terms stated that the employee must not be engaged in any other trade or business whilst the contract was operational. The employee gave notice, together with two other employees, in order to work for a competitor. The employer obtained an order restraining the employee from working for anyone other than the employer for twenty weeks. On appeal by the employee, *held*, the employee had established valuable customer connections at the employer's expense which would be of great benefit to a rival company. However, the court would not grant more relief than was absolutely necessary to protect the employer. In this case, the court would have normally forced the employee to wait the twenty weeks specified in his contract, but as his fellow employees, who were on a four-week notice period, were already working for the rival company, the court would substitute a period of thirteen weeks and vary the order accordingly.

GFI Group Inc v Eaglestone (1993) Times, 29 October (Queen's Bench Division: Holland J).

1141 Contract of employment—terms of employment—restraint of trade—solicitation and competition

The plaintiff company, an insurance broker's business, invoked a restrictive covenant set out in the service contracts of four of the defendants, who were former employees, which provided that the defendants could not solicit any employees of the company to the intent or effect that they terminated their employment. The covenant also restrained the defendants from soliciting the company's customers or clients. The covenant was upheld by the court at first instance, which issued an injunction against the defendants, that was subsequently discharged on appeal. On cross-appeal by the company, *held*, an employee had the right to work for any employer who wanted him. This clause had to be invalid as it was wide enough to prevent the defendants from soliciting people who became employees of the company after the defendants had left. Employees of an insurance broker's business were part of its goodwill but this did not mean they could be treated as one of its assets, nor did it mean that the company was entitled to impose a covenant against competition on employees. Accordingly, the company's cross-appeal would be dismissed.

Hanover Insurance Brokers Ltd v Schapiro (1993) Times, 17 November (Court of Appeal: Dillon and Nolan LJJ).

1142   Contract of employment—time off for public duties—complaint to industrial tribunal—tribunal's duty to provide reasons

Scotland

The plaintiff was employed by the defendants as a school teacher. She also held an appointment as a member of a regional Social Security Appeals Tribunal. The defendants allowed her to take time off work to perform her public duties. However, concern was expressed by parents of children attending the school that she was away too often. Following the refusal by the defendants to allow the plaintiff to take time off to attend a training session she made a complaint to an industrial tribunal alleging that the refusal was a breach of the Employment Protection (Consolidation) Act 1978, s 29. The tribunal concluded that she ought to have been allowed to take the time off, stating that in granting her permission to serve on that body, there were concomitant responsibilities. Those were not carried out and the plaintiff was disadvantaged as a result. On appeal by the defendants, *held*, the tribunal had failed to make it clear that it had taken all considerations into account, or explain how the various considerations were balanced. Further, it failed to make reference to the needs of the school, or the concerns of the parents about the amount of time the plaintiff was away from her class. Accordingly, the appeal would be allowed and the case remitted to a differently constituted industrial tribunal.

Borders Regional Council v Maule [1993] IRLR 199 (Employment Appeal Tribunal: Lord Coulsfield presiding).

1143   Contract of employment—written particulars of terms of employment—holidays and holiday pay

At the time his employment ceased, the plaintiff had taken only two of his 15 days' holiday entitlement. He claimed that it was an implied term of his contract of employment that he would be paid for holiday accrued but not taken. The employer refused to pay him and a county court dismissed his claim. On his appeal, *held*, in order to satisfy the requirements of the Employment Protection (Consolidation) Act 1978, s 1(3)(d)(i), which required particulars of the terms and conditions relating to holiday entitlement and pay (including any entitlement to accrued holiday pay on the termination of employment) to be sufficient to enable the employee's entitlement to be precisely calculated, no term entitling the plaintiff to accrued holiday pay had to be implied into his contract. The words "any entitlement to accrued holiday pay on the termination of employment, to be precisely calculated" did no more than recognise that a contract could include such a provision and that, if it did, the written statement must contain particulars of it. Section 1 left it open to an employer to enter into a contract with an employee which contained no such provision at all. It could not be said that, in order to give business efficacy to the plaintiff's contract, a term entitling him to accrued holiday pay on termination had necessarily to be implied or that the term was one which the parties would have included in the contract if they had applied their minds to it. The appeal would be dismissed.

Morley v Heritage plc [1993] IRLR 400 (Court of Appeal: Rose LJ and Sir Christopher Slade).

1144   Employer—vicarious liability—acts done in course of employment—liability for contempt of employee

The plaintiff owned a company which was restrained by injunctions from enforcing agreements which were restrictive of competition in contravention of the Restrictive Trade Practices Act 1976, s 35(1). The plaintiff issued instructions to his employees not to make any arrangements contrary to the 1976 Act. Notwithstanding the plaintiff's instructions some employees ignored the instructions and attended meetings with representatives from two other companies also subject to the injunctions. The Director General of Fair Trading sought sequestration orders against the plaintiff and the two other companies for breach of the injunctions. The plaintiff, on the advice of leading counsel, did not resist the charges of contempt and was fined by the Restrictive Practices Court. However, the other two companies successfully contested the charges of contempt in the Court of Appeal. The plaintiff was then granted leave to appeal out of time. *Held*, an employer did not become party to an agreement or arrangement if he prohibited his employees from entering into it, provided that the prohibition was in clear and unequivocal terms. If an employee then chose to enter into an agreement contrary to the instruction the employer did not, in the absence of the employee being cloaked in ostensible authority, become a party to the agreement. There was no reason for the plaintiff to suspect that his employees were likely to disobey instructions and accordingly, the appeal would be allowed.

Re Supply of Ready Mixed Concrete (No 2) [1994] ICR 57 (Court of Appeal: Russell, Hirst and Rose LJJ). Decision of Lincoln J (1990) Times, 15 October (1990 Abr para 954) reversed.

1145 Employment Appeal Tribunal—rules

The Employment Appeal Tribunal Rules 1993, SI 1993/2854 (in force on 16 December 1993), consolidate the 1980 Rules, SI 1980/2035, as amended, and make provision for a procedure for the Attorney General to apply to the tribunal for a restriction of proceedings order under the Employment Protection (Consolidation) Act 1978, s 136A. Provision is also made for the tribunal to make a restricted reporting order in certain cases involving allegations of sexual misconduct. In cases appearing to involve allegation of the commission of a sexual offence, the Registrar may take steps so as to prevent the identification to members of the public of any person affected by or making the allegation. The appeal tribunal must sit in private by virtue of a direction on grounds of national security from a Minister of the Crown. The rules specify who may dispose of an interlocutory application for a restricted reporting order, and specify that the hearing of any interlocutory application must be by the president alone where a minister has so directed on the grounds of national security.

1146 Employment training—community action—treatment of payments

The Community Action (Miscellaneous Provisions) Order 1993, SI 1993/1621 (in force on 27 July 1993), provides that for the purposes of specified subordinate legislation, a person using facilities provided under the Community Action programme will be treated as not being employed but as participating in arrangements for training under the Employment and Training Act 1973, s 2. Accordingly, any payment made to such a person in connection with his use of those facilities will be treated in the same manner as a payment made in respect of such training. The order also provides that a payment made to a person in connection with his use of facilities provided under Community Action will not be treated as earnings for the purposes of the Social Security Contributions and Benefits Act 1992, Pt I.

1147 Employment training—learning for work programme—social security provision

See para 2410.

1148 Employment vetting—disclosure of criminal record

See para 685.

1149 Equal pay—work of equal value—material difference other than sex

Women canteen workers and cleaners employed by the respondents in the coal industry made a claim before an industrial tribunal that they carried out work of equal value with their male comparators who were surface workers or clerical workers. An interlocutory decision was made in their favour and on appeal by the respondents, *held*, the issue was whether the comparators who did not work at the same establishment as the applicants were in the same employment as the applicants and whether the respondents could succeed with a defence that there was a "genuine material factor" difference between the separate wage structures. The relevant test was that both the applicant and the comparator had to be typical of their respective groups with no personal factors affecting the terms and conditions of employment. Furthermore, the applicant's employment and the comparator's employment had to enjoy common terms and conditions. Only then was it fair to compare an applicant at one establishment with a comparator at another. The tribunal accepted that common terms and conditions of employment were observed at the relevant establishments as far as cleaners and clerical workers were concerned. The terms for mine workers however included benefits of bonus incentives and concessions which were derived from a national agreement covering the whole of the country. As these terms were common to both the applicants and the comparators, it followed that the applicant cleaners and canteen workers were both engaged in work of equal value. Accordingly, the appeal would be dismissed.

British Coal Corpn v Smith [1993] ICR 529 (Employment Appeal Tribunal: Wood J presiding).

1150 European Employment Service—Euro-vacancies

See para 2717.

1151 Health and safety at work

See HEALTH AND SAFETY AT WORK.

1152   Industrial training boards—construction industry—levy

The Industrial Training Levy (Construction Board) Order 1993, SI 1993/265 (in force on 12 February 1993), provides for the imposition of a levy on employers in the construction industry. The levy imposed on all employers is limited to 0·25 per cent of payroll in respect of employees employed by them under contracts of service or apprenticeship and 2 per cent of payments made by the employers to persons under labour-only agreements. The levy is in respect of the period commencing on 12 February 1993 and ending on 31 March 1993. Provision is made for the right of appeal against an assessment.

1153   Industrial training boards—engineering construction—levy

The Industrial Training Levy (Engineering Construction Board) Order 1993, SI 1993/266 (in force on 12 February 1993), provides for the imposition of a levy on employers in the engineering construction industry. The levy is in respect of the period commencing on 12 February 1993 and ending on 31 August 1993. Provision is made for the right of appeal against an assessment.

1154   Industrial tribunal—constitution—death of tribunal member

At an industrial tribunal hearing, the chairman and two lay members found that the applicant had been unfairly dismissed. The case was adjourned to give the parties the opportunity to reach a settlement on compensation. Two months later the tribunal reconvened but by then one of the lay members had died and the tribunal consisted of only a chairman and one lay member. The tribunal made the basic award but made no compensation award. At a later application for review of the award, the constitution of the earlier tribunal was questioned and the employer appealed against the award on the ground that no consent was given to continuing the hearing without a properly constituted tribunal. *Held*, the provisions of the Industrial Tribunals (England and Wales) Regulations 1965, SI 1965/1101, reg 5(1) provided that the absence of any member of the tribunal would mean that the tribunal would not be properly constituted unless both parties gave their consent. There was nothing to indicate that the employer had consented to the constitution of the tribunal when the compensation award was made and accordingly, the award would be set aside and the appeal allowed.

Quenchers Ltd v McShane (1993) Times, 8 February (Employment Appeal Tribunal: Wood J presiding).

1155   Industrial tribunal—oral and written decisions—inconsistency—re-hearing

The appellant was dismissed for gross misconduct following an allegation that he had struck his fellow employee. He applied to an industrial tribunal alleging unfair dismissal and complaining that he had been subjected to racial discrimination. The matter was heard by an industrial tribunal where it was announced orally that the employer had been in breach of the Race Relations Act 1976, in relation to work practices and awarded the appellant damages. The tribunal however found the employer's decision to dismiss had not amounted to unfair dismissal. Both sides asked the tribunal to give reasons in writing. A written decision was given to the parties which stated that the employer was not in breach of the 1976 Act in relation to race discrimination and that the dismissal had not been unfair. The appellant then requested a review and also lodged notice of an appeal. Subsequently, the Employment Appeal Tribunal, anxious about additional costs, dismissed the appeal on unfair dismissal and substituted the oral for the written decision on racial discrimination. The appellant lodged another appeal from that decision on the ground that the issue of racial discrimination was irrevocably linked with the issue of the fairness of his dismissal. *Held*, in the present case the written decision on racial discrimination could not stand despite the fact that it would not be fair to the employer to restore the oral finding. It would however also be inappropriate to send the matter back to the same tribunal. The Employment Appeal decision was a less than satisfactory way of determining the issues in the absence of full written reasons for the oral decision. The employer having asked for written decisions, the Employment Appeal Tribunal could not properly dispense with the requirement that they be provided and lodged. The Employment Appeal Tribunal should have remitted the racial discrimination issue to another tribunal for rehearing. The unfair dismissal issue should have been similarly remitted since the Employment Appeal Tribunal had already accepted that the two issues were irrevocably mixed and the whole case should be re-heard by a differently constituted tribunal. Accordingly, the appeal would be allowed.

Gutzmore v J Wardley (Holdings) Ltd [1993] ICR 581 (Court of Appeal: Balcombe, Simon Brown LJJ and Peter Gibson J).

1156   Industrial tribunal—procedure—adjournment of hearing—costs

Three weeks before his claim for unfair dismissal was due to be heard, the applicant employee instructed new solicitors. The day before the hearing the solicitors contacted the employers' solicitors and suggested an adjournment. A request was also faxed to the industrial tribunal but refused by the chairman. On the day of the hearing the employee was neither present nor represented. The tribunal adjourned the hearing and made an order requiring the applicant to pay by a specified date the employers' costs thrown away fixed in the sum of £4,000 and if that sum was not paid the employee would be deprived of the right to restore his application. On the employee's appeal, *held*, under the Industrial Tribunals (Rules of Procedure) Regulations 1985, SI 1985/16, r 12(2)(b) there was no provision for conditions to be attached either with regard to payment of costs or otherwise. Further, under the 1985 Rules, r 12(1) an industrial tribunal's power to regulate its own procedure did not extend to the imposition of a condition regarding the payment of costs. It was wrong in principle for an award of costs to be made on a punitive as opposed to a compensatory basis and as such £4,000 was an excessive figure to cover the costs or expenses resulting from the adjournment and therefore must have contained a punitive element. Accordingly, the appeal would be allowed and the matter would be remitted to a different tribunal for reconsideration.

Cooper v Weatherwise (Roofing and Walling) Ltd [1993] ICR 81 (Employment Appeal Tribunal: Knox J presiding).

1157   Industrial tribunal—procedure—application to strike out proceedings for want of prosecution

A husband alleged that the terms of his late wife's pension scheme breached the Sex Discrimination Act 1975, s 6 and the Equal Pay Act 1970, s 1. His application to an industrial tribunal was adjourned pending determination by the European Court of Justice of two cases concerning the provisions of EC Treaty, art 119, with liberty to any party to restore. Those judgments proved to be of no assistance, but six years after the adjournment the European Court of Justice made a ruling on the provisions of art 119 which was favourable to the husband, and he applied for the case to be relisted before the tribunal. The employer successfully applied for the case to be struck out for want of prosecution, and the husband's appeal to the Employment Appeal Tribunal was dismissed. On the husband's further appeal, *held*, unless an applicant's default had been intentional and contumelious, an industrial tribunal's power to strike out an application for want of prosecution under the Industrial Tribunals (Rules of Procedure) Regulations 1985, SI 1985/16, Sch 1, r 12(2)(f) could only be exercised if there had been an inordinate and inexcusable delay by an applicant which was likely to cause serious prejudice to a respondent. It could not be suggested that the delay had made a fair hearing impossible, and there was no material on which an industrial tribunal could properly have come to the conclusion that the delay had caused prejudice to the employer. The application should not have been struck out, and, accordingly, the appeal would be allowed and the case remitted to an industrial tribunal.

Evans v Comr of Police of the Metropolis [1993] ICR 151 (Court of Appeal: Balcombe, Steyn and Hoffmann LJJ). *Birkett v James* [1977] 2 All ER 801, HL applied.

1158   Industrial tribunal—procedure—discovery—striking out

The Industrial Tribunals (Rules of Procedure) Regulations 1985, Sch 1, r 4(4) provide that where a tribunal's order for discovery of documents is not complied with, the tribunal may dismiss the whole or part of the originating application, or as the case may be, strike out the whole or part of the notice of appearance, and, where appropriate, direct that a respondent shall be debarred from defending altogether.

In an application to an industrial tribunal under the Race Relations Act 1976, the plaintiff employee sought discovery of documents. The application for discovery included a request for any guidelines issued by the defendant company to managers regarding the conduct of interviews and the constitution of interviewing panels. The reply was that no such documents existed. During the first day of the tribunal hearing it materialised that such documents did exist and that they had not been disclosed as, when asked by the defendant's solicitor, the plaintiff's manager was of the opinion that they were not sufficiently significant. As soon as the defendant was aware of the error they were disclosed. The plaintiff then made an application under the 1985 Regulations, Sch 1, r 4(4) and an order was made striking out certain parts of the defendant's notice of appearance and directing that he would be debarred from defending the proceedings. On the defendant's appeal, *held*, the industrial tribunal had erred in law in making an order striking out part of the defendant's notice of appearance because of his failure to comply with an order for discovery. In the circumstances of the case a punitive order to strike out was not appropriate. The 1985 Regulations, Sch 1, r 4(4) ought only to be applied in the most serious cases where any judgment ultimately obtained could not be considered to be fair between the parties. There was no suggestion that the failure to disclose was a deliberate act and disclosure had been made as soon as the existence of the documents in question was known. Accordingly, the appeal would be allowed.

National Grid Co plc v Virdee [1992] IRLR 555 (Employment Appeal Tribunal: Wood J presiding).

1159   Industrial tribunal—procedure—proceedings brought against wrong party— amendment

The applicant was employed by a company as an assistant accounts controller at a hotel. She brought a complaint for constructive dismissal and named the respondent hotel manager as her employer. The tribunal held that the proceedings had been brought against the wrong party and made no award, but went on to conclude that the company had unfairly dismissed the applicant and calculated the award of compensation she would have been entitled to. An application for review and for leave to amend the party named as respondent was refused. On appeal, *held*, the tribunal's failure to inform the applicant at the end of the hearing that it was necessary formally to amend the respondent named was a procedural irregularity. The company knew that they were the applicant's employer and that she had brought a claim in the industrial tribunal and, since the merits of the case were investigated in such circumstances that both parties knew who was the correct employer, there was no injustice in allowing an amendment. Accordingly, the appeal would be allowed so as to allow by amendment the substitution of the correct respondent, substitute for the decision that the tribunal reached, the decision the tribunal would have reached had they felt able to do so, and grant an extension of time under the Employment Appeal Tribunal Rules 1980, SI 1980/2035, r 26 to enable the respondent to apply for a review of the order.

Linbourne v Constable [1993] ICR 698 (Employment Appeal Tribunal: May J presiding). *Cocking v Sandhurst (Stationers) Ltd* [1974] ICR 650, NIRC and *Watts v Seven Kings Motor Co Ltd* [1983] ICR 135, EAT applied.

1160   Industrial tribunal—procedure—rules of procedure

The Industrial Tribunals (Constitution and Rules of Procedure) Regulations 1993, SI 1993/2687 (in force on 16 December 1993), replace the Industrial Tribunals (England and Wales) Regulations 1965, SI 1965/1101, the Industrial Tribunals (England and Wales) (Amendment) Regulations 1967, SI 1967/301, the Industrial Tribunals (England and Wales) (Amendment) Regulations 1970, SI 1970/941, the Industrial Tribunals (Improvement and Prohibition Notices Appeals) Regulations 1974, SI 1974/1925, the Industrial Tribunals (Amendment) Regulations 1977, SI 1977/1473, the Industrial Tribunals (Non-Discrimination Notices Appeals) Regulations 1977, SI 1977/1094, the Industrial Tribunals (Rules of Procedure) Regulations 1985, SI 1985/16, relating to the establishment of tribunals and rules of procedure for proceedings before industrial tribunals. The rules apply to (1) proceedings involving an equal value claim; (2) levy appeals; (3) appeals against an improvement or prohibition notice; (4) appeals against a non-discrimination notice; and (5) certain other proceedings. The rules incorporate provisions implementing or taking account of certain recent primary legislation, and the rules have been updated to take into account improvements to the procedures contained in the superseded rules.

1161   Racial discrimination

See BRITISH NATIONALITY, IMMIGRATION AND RACE RELATIONS.

1162   Redundancy—additional payment—sex discrimination

See *EC Commission v Kingdom of Belgium*, para 2753.

1163   Redundancy—continuity of employment—local government service

The Redundancy Payments (Local Government) (Modification) (Amendment) Order 1993, SI 1993/784 (in force on 1 April 1993), amends the 1983 Order, SI 1983/1160, by adding to the list of employers whose employees are deemed to be in continuous employment for the purposes of certain redundancy payments provisions by virtue of the 1983 Order.

1164   Redundancy—procedural unfairness—duty to consult trade union

Scotland

Following a decision to make redundancies, the defendant employers lodged the form HR1 with the Department of Employment. Copies of the form, giving the total number of anticipated redundancies broken down into broad job categories, were given to the relevant unions. The employers contended that the statutory consultation period should run from that date. The union contended that the information contained in the form was insufficient to enable meaningful consultation to take place. The employers gave more detailed information at various later stages. The union later recorded a failure to agree for the purposes of the negotiating machinery and a meeting was held with a full-time official of the union, which discussed the adequacy of the information supplied. The union made a complaint alleging that the employers had failed to comply with the requirements of the Employment Protection Act 1975, s 99. An industrial tribunal upheld the complaint, and specified the date on which the meeting with the union official was held as the date from which the consultation period ran. On appeal, *held*, whether the information given by an employer was sufficient to enable the period of consultation to begin depended on the facts and circumstances. In the present case, although the information contained in the form indicated the broad divisions of the redundancies, there was no indication as to which of the defendant's divisions, or which of the sites were to be affected and there was uncertainty as to the number of redundancies. However, the decision of the tribunal was defective as the tribunal had not explained why the information given by the employers was inadequate, and there had been no justification of the date chosen to be the appropriate date from which the consultation period ran. The appeal would accordingly be allowed and the case remitted to a tribunal for rehearing.

GEC Ferranti Defence Systems Ltd v MSF [1993] IRLR 101 (Employment Appeal Tribunal: Lord Coulsfield presiding).

See *R v British Coal Corpn, ex p Price (No 3)*, para 15.

1165   Redundancy—procedural unfairness—lack of consultation

Scotland

The appellant employee was made redundant when his employer company was reorganised for financial reasons. The decision to make the appellant redundant had been taken before he was called to a meeting; he was simply informed of it at the meeting and had no opportunity to make any input. An industrial tribunal held that the employer had used reasonably objective criteria for the selection, that the criteria had been applied in a fair manner and that lack of consultation was not sufficient to make the dismissal unfair. On appeal, *held*, consultation was a very important requirement in redundancy dismissals, and should not be overlooked or allowed to go by default. Whatever the pressures, consultation was one of the points to be considered and if it did not do so, then it was likely that the employer would be held to have acted unfairly. In the present case, the employer had neither considered nor carried out a consultation. The circumstances were not so urgent that the appellant could not have been given some opportunity to make his contribution. The failure to consult made the dismissal unfair, even though the result would have been no different with consultation. Accordingly, the appeal would be allowed, although the appellant would not be entitled to any remedy.

Robertson v Magnet Ltd [1993] IRLR 512 (Employment Appeal Tribunal: Lord Coulsfield presiding). *Polkey v AE Dayton Services Ltd* [1987] IRLR 503 (1987 Abr para 2874) applied.

1166   Redundancy—procedural unfairness—lack of consultation—exceptional circumstances

Following the loss of a major contract, employers introduced certain measures to reduce the company's overheads. They closed a branch office and made over 60 staff redundant, then dismissed the claimant employee with immediate effect, paying him four weeks' wages in lieu of notice. They did not consult him. On his complaint of unfair dismissal, *held*, the company's financial position had been deteriorating since the loss of the contract, but nothing had occurred making it necessary for the employers to dismiss the claimant on the date he was dismissed and at no later date. There was no reason why he could not have been given at least a week to consider his future and to put forward any suggestion for ameliorating, if not preserving, his situation. The fact that the employers believed that only the claimant could be dismissed without impairing the efficiency of the remaining team of employees did not justify their failure to consult him. The requirement that an employer consult an employee before making him redundant was not rendered otiose because the employer believed he had no alternative but to make the employee redundant. There might be circumstances known to the employee but unknown to the employer, such as the employee's preparedness to accept a more junior post or a significantly reduced salary for the sake of remaining employed, which might cause the employer to change his mind. Even if redundancy was inevitable, there were other areas in which consultation would be of benefit to the employee. It would at least provide an opportunity for the parties to discuss what help the employer could provide to find the employee alternative employment. The claimant had been unfairly dismissed. His case would be remitted to a differently constituted tribunal for the assessment of compensation.

Heron v Citilink-Nottingham [1993] IRLR 372 (Employment Appeal Tribunal: Judge Peppitt QC presiding).

1167 Redundancy—procedural unfairness—lack of consultation—objective test

An employee had worked for his employers for 18 years prior to being made redundant. In selecting him for redundancy, the employers followed a redundancy policy which involved an appraisal of the employee of which he had no knowledge and which he had no opportunity to challenge. It fell to be determined whether the employers' failure to consult him rendered the dismissal unfair. *Held*, on the facts known to the employers at the time when, and in consequence of which, the employee was dismissed, consultation would have served no useful purpose. The test to be applied in deciding whether a redundancy dismissal without consultation was fair was a purely objective one: the question was whether a reasonable employer, in the light of the facts known to him at the time, could have dismissed the employee without consultation. The failure to consult the employee in the present case did not render the dismissal unfair.

Duffy v Yeomans & Partners Ltd [1993] ICR 862 (Employment Appeal Tribunal: Judge Peppitt QC presiding).

1168 Redundancy—redundancy payment—entitlement—time limit for claim

Scotland

The appellant was made redundant and was not entitled to a redundancy payment as she was over the age of 60, whereas men were entitled to statutory redundancy payments until they reached the age of 65. This difference in treatment was remedied by the Employment Act 1989, although the change was not made retrospectively. The appellant then claimed under the EC treaty, art 119 for the redundancy payment she would have received under United Kingdom law had she been a man. The industrial tribunal dismissed the application on the grounds that it was out of time. On appeal following a subsequent European Court decision in which it was established that statutory redundancy payments fell within the scope of the definition of "pay" in the EC Treaty, art 119, *held*, there was no time limit directly applicable under United Kingdom law to a free standing claim under art 119, nor any general time limit applying to all proceedings brought before an industrial tribunal. However, there had to be a balance between the principle of legal certainty and the requirement to protect rights conferred upon individuals by art 119. In the present case, a period for bringing claims in the region of three to six months was not unreasonable. Since the appellant's claim was presented within three months from the date on which the legislation came into force, the case would be remitted. Accordingly, the appeal would be allowed.

Rankin v British Coal Corpn [1993] IRLR 69 (Employment Appeal Tribunal: Lord Coulsfield presiding). *Barber v Guardian Royal Exchange Assurance Group* [1990] 2 All ER 660 (1990 Abr para 2706) considered.

1169 Redundancy—selection for redundancy—pool for selection

Scotland

The employee was made redundant. The pool of selection for redundancy consisted of members of the company who worked a certain shift, which the employers wanted to discontinue. An industrial tribunal found that the discontinuance of the particular shift was part of a wider reorganisation, but that a proper selection procedure would have been to consider the skills, achievements and service of the employee against those of the whole workforce. On appeal by the employers, *held*, in every case it was important to consider whether the unfairness could properly be classified as procedural rather than substantive, such as choice of pool or criteria for selection. In the present case it was clear that the unfairness related to substance. The employers created an artificially narrow pool from which to make the selection and the result of their doing so was to deprive the employee of something of substantive importance, namely the opportunity of being compared with the whole range of employees who were genuinely involved in the reorganisation. It was the duty of an industrial tribunal to apply the principle laid down in *Polkey v AE Dayton Services Ltd* [1987] IRLR 503 (1987 Abr para 2874), however, it was not a tribunal's duty to embark on an independent investigation of the facts and circumstances in order to see whether it could identify some other criterion of selection on which the dismissal might have been justified. Accordingly, the appeal would be dismissed.

Steel Stockholders (Birmingham) Ltd v Kirkwood [1993] IRLR 515 (Employment Appeal Tribunal: Lord Coulsfield presiding).

1170   Sex discrimination
See SEX DISCRIMINATION.

1171   Trade Union Reform and Employment Rights Act 1993
See para 2558.

1172   Trade unions
See TRADE UNIONS.

1173   Training for work—payments
See para 2411.

1174   Transfer of undertakings—continuity of employment—character of transfer
The plaintiffs were employed by a local authority in the education department of a young offender institution. However, from 1 April 1993, prison education services were to be provided by the defendant college. It fell to be determined whether the plaintiffs would automatically become employees of the defendant. *Held*, the character of the transfer of the services within the meaning of Council Directive (EC) 77/187, art 1, had to be assessed. On 1 April, prisoners and young offenders who attended any particular class would generally be likely to be those who had attended the same class in the same classroom on the previous day using the same equipment. There would be a transfer of responsibility for the education department from the authority to the defendant. The latter would be obliged to employ the staff, including the plaintiffs, previously employed by the authority on the same terms and conditions.

Kenny v South Manchester College [1993] ICR 934 (Queen's Bench Division: Sir Michael Ogden QC).

1175   Transfer of undertakings—continuity of employment—transfer of services
Under the Transfer of Undertakings (Protection of Employment) Regulations 1981, SI 1981/1794, reg 5(1), a relevant transfer does not operate so as to terminate the contract of employment of any person employed by the transferor in the undertaking (which includes any trade or business but does not include any undertaking which was not in the nature of a commercial venture) transferred but any such contract which would otherwise be terminated by the transfer has effect after the transfer as if originally made between the person so employed and the transferee.

The applicants were employed by a council as refuse collectors and street sweepers. They were made redundant when the council transferred refuse collecting and street sweeping services to a private company which did not employ the applicants. Their claim for compensation for unfair dismissal was rejected by an industrial tribunal on the ground that the transfer of services only was incapable of being a relevant transfer within the 1981 Regulations. On their appeal, *held*, when considering whether the transfer of the services in question was a relevant transfer of an undertaking within the regulations, an industrial tribunal should identify the undertaking alleged to have been transferred, consider whether it was in the nature of a commercial venture and whether there was a relevant transfer of it. It had to look at the substance, not the form, of what had occurred, taking into account all the surrounding circumstances, to see whether there was a recognisable economic entity, a going concern which was carried on by the transferor and which was being continued by the new employer. The transfer of services was capable of falling within the regulations; there did not have to be a transfer of assets. The fact that nothing concrete was transferred nor any goodwill or outstanding contracts did not of itself prevent there having been a transfer. "The nature of a commercial venture" was to be construed in accordance with United Kingdom law but in a way that did not conflict with Community law. No one factor was conclusive. The appeal would be allowed and remitted to an industrial tribunal for reconsideration.

Wren v Eastbourne Borough Council [1993] ICR 955 (Employment Appeal Tribunal: Wood J presiding).

1176 Transfer of undertakings—employee seeking to restrain transfer—injunctive relief

The defendants sought to transfer part of their business to a subsidiary company. On being notified, the plaintiff, an employee of the defendants, sought an injunction restraining the defendants from giving effect to the transfer of his contract of employment until after consultation had taken place in conformity with the Transfer of Undertakings Regulations 1981, SI 1981/1794, reg 5. At first instance the application was refused and the plaintiff applied for an injunction pending appeal. *Held*, the transfer of a contract of employment was not a repudiatory breach of contract by the employer, therefore the employee was not entitled to restrain the employer from making the transfer. There was no right under the contract of employment to restrain the transfer of an undertaking; the effect of the 1981 Regulations, reg 5 was merely to bring about a change in the identity of the employer and to provide for a statutory novation of the contract of employment with the transferee becoming the employer in place of the transferor. Accordingly, the application would be dismissed.

Newns v British Airways plc [1992] IRLR 575 (Court of Appeal: Scott and Steyn LJJ).

1177 Transfer of undertakings—employment relationship—application of Community directive

Council Directive (EC) 77/187, art 3(1) provides that the transferor's rights and obligations arising from a contract of employment or from an employment relationship existing on the date of transfer will, by reason of such a transfer, be transferred to the transferee. Article 7 provides that the Directive will not affect the right of member states to apply or introduce laws, regulations or administrative provisions which are more favourable to employees.

A was employed as a cook by B. Following the transfer of undertakings from B to a new owner, A was dismissed by B, allegedly in the name of the new owner, after A had refused to work for the new owner. A sought compensation for amounts alleged to be due in respect of the period prior to his dismissal. B contended that he was not the employer at the time of dismissal since he had transferred the employment relationship to the new owner. At the hearing of the action, the court referred the question as to whether art 3(1) permitted an employee employed by the transferor at the date of the transfer to object to the transfer of the rights and obligations to the transferee, if by doing so he prevented the transfer taking place, and if not whether the right to object in this way to a transfer constituted a provision more favourable to employees within the meaning of art 7. *Held*, (1) art 3(1) did not preclude an employee employed by the transferor at the transfer date from objecting to the transfer. The Directive could not be construed as obliging the employee to continue his employment relationship with the transferee; such an obligation would undermine the rights of the employee to choose his employer. However, the Directive did not oblige member states to provide that the contract of employment or employment relationship be continued with the transferor where an employee freely decided not to continue in employment with the transferee. It was for the member state to determine the fate of the employment relationship. (2) In the light of the ruling on art 3(1), it was unnecessary to determine whether recognition of an employee's right to object to the transfer of his contract of employment or employment relationship constituted a more favourable provision to employees within the meaning of art 7.

Cases C–132/91, C–138/91, C–139/91: Katsikas v Konstantinidis; Skreb v PCO Stauereibetreib Paetz & Co Nachfolger GmbH, Schroll v Same [1993] IRLR 179 (ECJ: Full Court).

The Trade Union Reform and Employment Rights Act 1993, s 33 clarifies the position in English law as a result of the decision in this case (see para 2558).

1178 Transfer of undertakings—pension rights—application of Community directive

The Transfer of Undertakings (Protection of Employment) Regulations 1981, SI 1981/1794, reg 7, provides that regs 5 and 6 do not apply to any part of a contract of employment relating to certain pension schemes or to any rights connected with such a scheme. Council Directive (EC) 77/187, art 3, which is implemented by the regulations, states that on a business transfer the transferor's rights and obligations arising from contracts of employment at the date of transfer will be transferred to the transferee, but any supplementary company pension scheme outside the state scheme is excluded.

The employee was a member of his company pension scheme which was contracted out of the state scheme. The business was then transferred to a new employer. The employees were notified that the transfer would not affect their terms of employment for the purposes of benefits relating to their service. After the transfer the pension scheme was withdrawn and the employer contracted back into the state scheme. An industrial tribunal declared that the employee's terms of employment should be no less beneficial after the transfer than before and should reflect the terms of the original pension scheme. It concluded that the scheme was additional to the state scheme not supplementary to it and that reg 7 did not comply with the directive. On appeal by the employer, *held*, the contracted-out company scheme complemented the state scheme; it was clear from decisions of the European Court of Justice that contracted-out pension schemes were supplementary schemes and were therefore excluded by the directive. The court's duty was to interpret the Regulations in accordance with EC law if alternative constructions were available, consequently the scheme also came within the exclusion contained in reg 7. Even if the directive did not apply, there was no fresh contract relating to the pension rights. The notices were sent by the transferor employer not the transferee and were simply notices giving information. They were not intended to create a contractual relationship. Accordingly the appeal would be allowed and the employee's application would be dismissed.

Walden Engineering Co Ltd v Warrener [1993] IRLR 420 (Employment Appeal Tribunal: Wood J presiding).

1179   Transfer of undertakings—pension rights—protection of pension rights— contracts of employment—implied provisions

The applicant's contract of employment provided that he was entitled to become a member of his company's superannuation scheme. He joined the scheme to which his employer contributed. Several months later the applicant was told his company was to be transferred to another group which would organise the pension arrangements. The applicant was told that the new group did not offer a company pension scheme and pension arrangements were not covered by the Transfer of Undertakings (Protection of Employment) Regulations 1981, SI 1981/1794. He brought a complaint to an industrial tribunal contending that his rights under the previous contract or equivalent rights were transferred under the 1981 Regulations and that while the actual right of a member of the pension scheme was not transferred, the regulations could be construed so that an equivalent right was transferred. *Held*, the existing statutory provisions protecting "early leavers" by conferring an entitlement to a deferred pension did not provide the protection which an employee would obtain if the benefits of an actual term of the contract relating to pensions were transferred. When the pension provision of a contract was not transferred, the employee lost both the enhancement of the pensions benefits already accrued and future pension benefits which would be gained from continuing membership of the scheme. The regulations were to be construed so as to imply an additional clause that the applicant's contract of employment with the respondents included such rights as were necessary to protect his interests in respect of immediate or prospective entitlement to old age benefits, including survivors' benefit under supplementary pension schemes. Accordingly, the application would be granted.

Perry v Intec Colleges Ltd [1993] IRLR 56 (Industrial tribunal, Bristol).

1180   Transfer of undertakings—relevant transfer

The applicants were employed by company A as ancillary health workers to provide cleaning services at a National Health Service hospital. When the company's contract with the hospital expired, the contract was put out to tender and the tender of company B was accepted. Company A declared the applicants redundant. Under the new contract, company B introduced its own management, equipment, stocks and supplies and offered new contracts of employment to the applicants. The applicants brought a complaint of unfair dismissal against company A on the ground that they had been dismissed because of a relevant transfer under the Transfer of Undertakings (Protection of Employment) Regulations 1981, SI 1981/1974, reg 8(1) and alleged, as against company B, that their new conditions of employment were less favourable. The industrial tribunal found that the provision of cleaning services at the hospital was a separate economic entity and constituted an undertaking under the 1981 Regulations, reg 2(1). However, since there was no contractual relationship between the two companies and no transfer of equipment, materials or goodwill, there had not been "a transfer of an undertaking from one person to another" for the purpose of the 1981 Regulations, reg 3(1). On appeal, the applicants contended that the tribunal had misdirected itself in applying the 1981 Regulations. *Held*, the 1981 Regulations, reg 3(1) had to be construed in accordance with the United Kingdom's obligations under Community law. In carrying out that exercise, the tribunal had to give consideration to all the relevant factors, without giving undue weight to any single factor, in order to determine whether there was an identifiable economic unit and a transfer of that unit such that the business retained its identity and was disposed of as a going concern. The tribunal had not misdirected itself: it had correctly considered, and weighed, the relevant factors and its decision would be upheld. Accordingly, the appeal would be dismissed.

Dines v Initial Healthcare Services [1993] ICR 978 (Employment Appeal Tribunal: Wood J presiding). *Spijkers v Gebroeders Benedik Abbatoir CV* [1986] ECR 1119, ECJ (1986 Abr para 3041) applied.

1181 Unfair dismissal—compensation—calculation of compensatory award—effect of ex gratia payment

An employee was made redundant and was given an ex gratia payment by his employers in addition to the redundancy pay to which he was entitled and pay in lieu of notice. An industrial tribunal found that the dismissal was unfair because the employers had not given the employee sufficient prior warning, but they held, pursuant to the Employment Protection (Consolidation) Act 1978, s 74(7) that no compensation was payable, as the basic award had been subsumed by the redundancy payment and the ex gratia payment exceeded the amount of any compensatory award the tribunal might have made. On the employee's appeal, *held*, the 1978 Act, s 74(7) clearly required that in the calculation of a compensatory award an employer ought to receive credit for any redundancy payment he made, its purpose being to encourage employers who found it necessary to dismiss for redundancy to be generous in making ex gratia payments. The industrial tribunal had been correct in giving credit to the employers for the ex gratia payment when determining the compensatory award, and accordingly, the appeal would be dismissed.

Rushton v Harcros Timber and Building Supplies [1993] ICR 230 (Employment Appeal Tribunal: Judge Hague QC presiding).

1182 Unfair dismissal—compensation—compensatory award—increase of limits

The Unfair Dismissal (Increase of Compensation Limit) Order 1993, SI 1993/1348 (in force on 1 June 1993), increases from £10,000 to £11,000 the limit on the amount of compensation which can be awarded by an industrial tribunal in claims for unfair dismissal as the compensatory award or as compensation for failure fully to comply with the terms of an order for reinstatement or re-engagement.

The 1991 Order, SI 1991/466, is revoked.

1183 Unfair dismissal—compensation—illness attributable to dismissal

Scotland

The employee was dismissed from her employment and as a result suffered from anxiety and depression. She was unable to look for work and made a claim for unfair dismissal. An industrial tribunal awarded compensation but did not include an amount for loss of earnings. On appeal by the employee, *held*, there were three possible situations concerning dismissal and ill health: (1) an employee might become ill after a dismissal, without there being any relationship between the dismissal and ill-health. In that case, she would not be entitled to claim compensation from her employer in respect of a period for which she was unfit for work, (2) as illustrated by the decision in *Fougère v Phoenix Motor Co Ltd* [1976] IRLR 259 (1976 Abr para 2656), an employee might be ill at the time of dismissal and as a result, suffer a longer period of unemployment than she would have done if fit. In that case, the employee was entitled to compensation for the period of unemployment, and (3) there was the present case in which the employee suffered ill health immediately after the dismissal and the ill-health was directly attributable to the dismissal. In that case the employee should be entitled to compensation for loss of earnings for a reasonable period following the dismissal, until she might have reasonably been expected to find other employment. The personal circumstances of the employee, including the effect of the dismissal on her health, could be taken into account in ascertaining the appropriate amount of compensation. The industrial tribunal had to have regard to the loss and consider how far it was attributable to action taken by the employer, and arrive at a sum which it considered to be just and equitable. However, the fact that the unfitness was attributable to the dismissal did not necessarily imply that the whole period of unfitness was attributable to the actions of the employer. Accordingly, the appeal would be allowed and the case would be remitted to the tribunal to reconsider the question of the compensatory award.

Devine v Designer Flowers Wholesale Florist Sundries Ltd [1993] IRLR 517 (Employment Appeal Tribunal: Lord Coulsfield presiding).

1184   Unfair dismissal—compensation—sex discrimination

See *Marshall v Southampton and South West Hampshire Area Health Authority (No 2)*, para 2754.

1185   Unfair dismissal—complaint to industrial tribunal—time limit—effective date of termination

Following the employee's dismissal, his solicitor and a member of staff at the central office for industrial tribunals both gave him incorrect advice as to the date on which his complaint of unfair dismissal could be submitted. He presented his claim on what he believed to be the last possible date, but it was actually one day after the required period of three months beginning with the effective date of termination, specified in the Employment Protection (Consolidation) Act 1978, s 67(2). It was held by an industrial tribunal that in view of the erroneous advice given by the member of the tribunal staff, it had not been reasonably practicable for the employee to present his case in time. The employers appealed, contending that once a solicitor had been consulted, it had become reasonably practicable for the complaint to be submitted in time. The Employment Appeal Tribunal dismissed the appeal, holding that merely consulting a solicitor did not necessarily render it reasonably practicable to present the application in time. On further appeal, *held*, a prospective claimant did not lose for all time his right to rely on the "not reasonably practicable" defence once he consulted a solicitor who was potentially liable for wrong advice if, as in the present case, he distrusted that advice and immediately proceeded to obtain further advice from a body such as an industrial tribunal which might not be so liable. The appeal would accordingly be dismissed.

London International College v Sen [1993] IRLR 333 (Court of Appeal: Sir Thomas Bingham MR, McCowan and Hirst LJJ).

The Employment Protection (Consolidation) Act 1978, s 67(2) provides that an industrial tribunal may not consider a complaint of unfair dismissal unless it is presented to the tribunal before the end of the period of three months beginning with the effective date of termination or within such further time as the tribunal considers reasonable in a case where it is satisfied that it was not reasonably practicable for the complaint to be presented before the end of the period of three months.

The plaintiff was dismissed on the last day in August. His complaint of unfair dismissal, submitted on the last day in November, was dismissed by an industrial tribunal as being out of time. The plaintiff contended, on appeal, that the statutory period for presenting an unfair dismissal claim was calculated by taking the day before the effective date of termination and then going forward three months. The complaint was therefore made in time. The employer argued that the proper way was to go forward three months and then back one day. *Held*, the correct way to calculate the period within which such an application must be presented was to find the effective date of termination, take the day and the date before it, and go forward three months. If there was no corresponding date in that month, the last day of the month was taken. In the present case, therefore, the period of three months expired on the last day in November. The appeal would accordingly be allowed and the case remitted to an industrial tribunal for consideration on its merits.

Pruden v Cunard Ellerman [1993] IRLR 317 (Employment Appeal Tribunal: Wood J presiding).

Following her dismissal on 30 April 1991, the employee presented a claim of unfair dismissal on 30 July 1991. On a preliminary point the industrial tribunal held that the employee's claim was not precluded by the 1978 Act, s 67(2). It accepted the employee's contention that since dismissal one day later on 1 May would have given her until 31 July to present the application and that as she was dismissed one day before 1 May she ought to have had until one day before 31 July (ie 30 July) to apply. The employers appealed contending that the complaint was out of time. *Held*, on a correct construction, the 1978 Act, s 67(2) required a complaint of unfair dismissal to be presented within a three-month limitation period, beginning with, and including, the effective date of termination. The three-month period was strictly computed: it began on the effective date of termination and ran to the day before that with the same number in the third month. In the present case, the three-month period "beginning with" 30 April ended on 29 July and thus the employee's application was one day too late. The employee's proposition was contrary to the authorities and could not be accepted. Furthermore, it was inevitable that since all months did not have the same number of days, anomalous situations would arise. Accordingly, the appeal would be allowed.

University of Cambridge v Murray [1993] ICR 460 (Employment Appeal Tribunal: Hicks J presiding). *Hare v Gocher* [1962] 2 All ER, DC and *Rybak v Jean Sorelle Ltd* [1991] ICR 127, EAT (1990 Abr para 1004) applied.

The Employment Protection (Consolidation) Act 1978, s 67(2) provides that a complaint of unfair dismissal must be presented to an industrial tribunal before the end of the period of three months beginning with the effective date of termination, or such further period as the tribunal considers reasonable in a case where it is satisfied that it was not reasonably practicable for the complaint to be presented before the end of that period.

An employee was given notice of redundancy. Two months after the statutory three-month period had expired he presented a claim of unfair dismissal, stating that he had only learnt of the matters which gave grounds for him to believe that he had been dismissed unfairly, rather than by reason of redundancy, in the last month ("the first ground"). Six months later the originating application was amended to add a new complaint based on facts acquired one month earlier ("the second ground"). The industrial tribunal held that the complaint based on the first ground was not presented within such further period as it considered reasonable, but that it had jurisdiction to consider the complaint in respect of the second ground. On appeal, the employers contended that since the employee's first complaint was presented out of time the subsequent discovery of another ground did not give him another bite at the cherry and thus the tribunal had no jurisdiction in respect of the second complaint. The employee cross-appealed against the decision in relation to the first ground. *Held*, in relation to the 1978 Act, s 67(2), a tribunal had to ask: (1) was it satisfied that it was not reasonably practicable for the complaint to be presented before the end of the period of three months beginning with the effective date of termination, and (2) if so, was the complaint presented within such further period as it considered reasonable. In respect of the first complaint, the tribunal wrongly thought that it was constrained by *James W Cook Ltd v Tipper* (1990) ICR 716 (1990 Abr para 1003) to regard a delay in excess of four weeks as longer than a reasonable period and had concentrated exclusively on the length of the delay rather than considering the circumstances that gave rise to the delay. Further, the tribunal was entitled to regard the second incident as a further ground for presenting a complaint and to conclude that it was not reasonably practicable to present a complaint on that ground before the end of the three-month period. Accordingly, the employers' appeal would be dismissed, the employee's cross-appeal would be allowed and the matter would be remitted for reconsideration by the tribunal.

Marley (UK) Ltd v Anderson (1993) Times, 16 December (Employment Appeal Tribunal: Mummery J presiding).

Scotland

An employee lodged an originating application complaining of unfair dismissal and sex discrimination, naming a company which had contracted out her services as the respondent. Subsequently, the tribunal chairman ordered that the respondent employers be added as second respondents. At a preliminary hearing, the employers successfully contended that the complaint against them was time-barred, since the application to add them as second respondents was made outside the statutory three-month time limit for presenting such complaints. The tribunal declined to follow *Cocking*, which disapproved the time-bar approach and provided that the decision whether to amend an originating application which had been presented within the statutory time limit was a matter for the tribunal's discretion. The tribunal ruled that *Cocking* only applied to cases where the original and new respondents were related as principal and subsidiary, or in a similar manner. On the employee's appeal, *held*, the tribunal erred in failing to follow the *Cocking* approach and in limiting its relevance to cases where the original and new respondents were related. Although the presence of a relationship between respondents might be a relevant consideration when the tribunal considered whether to exercise its discretion, such considerations were only relevant as matters to be taken into account in exercising that discretion and were not limitations on the circumstances in which the discretion was exercisable. No time limit applied to proposals to add or substitute a respondent to an originating application which was lodged within the time limit, and whether the amendment should be allowed was a matter of discretion for the industrial tribunal which would consider all the circumstances. Accordingly, the appeal would be allowed and the case remitted to the industrial tribunal.

Gillick v BP Chemicals Ltd [1993] IRLR 437 (Employment Appeal Tribunal: Lord Coulsfield presiding). *Cocking v Sandhurst (Stationers) Ltd* [1974] ICR 650, NIRC (1975 Abr para 1935) considered.

Scotland

The Employment Protection (Consolidation) Act 1978, s 67(2) provides that an industrial tribunal must not consider a claim for unfair dismissal unless it is presented before the end of three months beginning with the effective date of determination or within such further period as the tribunal considers reasonable in a case in which it is satisfied that it was not reasonably practicable for the complaint to be presented before the end of the three months.

An employee's solicitors prepared an application complaining of unfair dismissal and posted it to the Central Office of Industrial Tribunals at least five weeks within the three-month time limit for applications. A few months later it was discovered that no acknowledgement of receipt of the application had been received, nor had the application been returned as undelivered. The solicitors then submitted a copy of the original application and covering letter. The tribunal held that the application was not time-barred because there was a presumption that what was posted would be delivered and, in the circumstances, it was not reasonably practicable for the employee to have submitted her application within the statutory time limit and she had submitted it as soon as was reasonably practicable thereafter. On the employers' appeal, *held*, there was authority that a complaint was not presented simply by being posted addressed to the industrial tribunal and the tribunal erred in accepting the presumption that what was posted would be delivered without considering whether it was reasonable to rely on that presumption in the circumstances. The solicitors' duty to the applicant went beyond simply posting the application, they should have checked that it duly arrived and had almost five weeks in which to do so. In relying on the assumption that the application had been duly presented, they failed to take such steps as were reasonable in the circumstances and so failed to satisfy the requirements set out in the 1978 Act, s 67(2). Accordingly, the appeal would be allowed.

Capital Foods Retail Ltd v Corrigan [1993] IRLR 430 (Employment Appeal Tribunal: Lord Coulsfield presiding).

1186   Unfair dismissal—constructive dismissal—effective date of termination

The Employment Protection (Consolidation) Act 1978, s 55(4)(b) provides that the effective date of termination in respect of an employee whose contract of employment is terminated without notice, is the date on which the termination takes effect.

The applicant was the chairman, chief executive and principal shareholder of a company. He charged his shareholding to secure loans from a bank, which then became the controlling shareholder of the company and its subsidiary. Resolutions were passed removing the applicant as a director of both companies. His solicitors then wrote to the bank stating that the resolutions constituted a constructive dismissal. The following day the applicant received a fax stating that the resolutions had terminated his directorships with immediate effect and requesting the return of all company property. The applicant presented a claim for unfair dismissal and the industrial tribunal found that, as a preliminary jurisdictional issue, the effective date of termination was the day the fax was sent and accordingly, the complaint was within the three-month time limit imposed by the 1978 Act, s 67(2). On the companies' appeal, *held*, the 1978 Act, s 55(4)(b) applied to cases of constructive dismissal. The effective date of termination was the date on which the termination took effect and was thus determined by the actual state of the parties' legal relationship and not by the applicant's understanding of it. The relevant date was the date the resolutions were made removing the applicant's directorships, and therefore his chairmanship of the parent company, as these effectively terminated the parties' contractual relationship. The complaint was out of time and, accordingly, the appeal would be allowed.

BMK Ltd v Logue [1993] ICR 601 (Employment Appeal Tribunal: Knox J presiding).

1187   Unfair dismissal—constructive dismissal—removal of duties

The appellant was employed as a steward at a social club and was also charged with carrying out the duties of club secretary. A resolution was passed at the club's annual general meeting to remove his secretarial duties and on learning of that resolution the appellant claimed constructive dismissal. An industrial tribunal found that though removing the duties as club secretary amounted to a fundamental breach of contract which therefore entitled the appellant to resign and claim constructive dismissal, the resolution which purported to remove those duties was invalid under the club's rules. Under those circumstances the tribunal concluded that the resolution had not removed the appellant's secretarial duties and that therefore his claim of constructive dismissal could not succeed. On appeal, *held*, the tribunal had erred in finding that because the resolution was invalid under the club's rules, it did not have the effect of removing those duties from the appellant. The industrial tribunal had specifically found that if the appellant had had his secretarial duties taken away from him, there would have been a fundamental breach of contract entitling him to regard himself as constructively dismissed. Therefore, the fact that the resolution purporting to take away those duties was invalid did not prevent a finding of constructive dismissal. Accordingly, the appeal would be allowed.

Warnes v The Trustees of Cheriton Oddfellows Social Club [1993] IRLR 58 (Employment Appeal Tribunal: Knox J presiding).

1188 Unfair dismissal—disciplinary procedure—procedural unfairness

The defendant employee was dismissed for allegedly striking a fellow employee. He brought an action for unfair dismissal against his employers contending that the dismissal hearing was procedurally unfair because: (1) he did not see the witnesses' statements; (2) both employees were represented by the same shop steward; (3) notes taken during the hearing were inadequate, and (4) the appeals procedure was unfair since the right to appeal did not belong to the individual employee but was contingent on the assent of the trade union convenor. The tribunal upheld the employee's complaint and found that there was no contributory fault. The employers appealed. *Held*, (1) it was sufficient that the witnesses' statements were read out to the employee, and (2) the employee was responsible for his own representation, but (3) the notes taken were inadequate and this was a procedural defect, and (4) the right of appeal was the right of the individual employee and the convenor's decision was not an adequate substitute. Accordingly, the appeal would be granted and the case would be remitted to a new tribunal.

Vauxhall Motors Ltd v Ghafoor [1993] ICR 376 (Employment Appeal Tribunal: Judge Hargrove QC presiding).

1189 Unfair dismissal—excluded employment—age limit—normal retiring age

The employees' contracts of employment stipulated that there was an obligatory retirement age of 60 for employees of their particular job description, although employees could apply each year for an extension until they reached the age of 65. The employer amended the scheme, with the effect that employees would no longer be able to apply for an annual extension beyond the age of 60 unless they had attained the age of 55 by a certain date. The employees were subsequently dismissed for redundancy, and an industrial tribunal ruled they could bring a complaint of unfair dismissal on the ground that the normal retirement age for employees of their job description was 65. On the employer's appeal, *held*, the employer had introduced a policy under which the normal retirement age for persons of the employees' job description was 60, subject to some limited and temporary exceptions. That general statement of policy and the reasoning behind it had been clear, so the employees were prevented from pursuing their complaints by virtue of the Employment Protection (Consolidation) Act 1978, s 64(1)(b). Accordingly, the appeal would be allowed, and the unfair dismissal claim dismissed.

Barclays Bank plc v O'Brien [1993] ICR 347 (Employment Appeal Tribunal: Wood J presiding). *Brooks v British Telecommunications plc* [1992] ICR 414, CA applied.

1190 Unfair dismissal—illness—duty to indicate prospects of recovery

It has been held that an employee who is absent from work through ill health is not under a duty to indicate his prospects of recovery to his employer. The failure of an employer to inquire about an employee's condition is not to be placed on a par with the employee's failure to give any information.

Mitchell v Arkwood Plastics (Engineering) Ltd [1993] ICR 471 (Employment Appeal Tribunal: Judge Hargrove presiding).

1191 Unfair dismissal—industrial action—compensation—discriminatory factors

A company which was engaged in the business of express parcels delivery had a number of depots throughout the country. At one of the depots the employees took industrial action and all participating employees were dismissed. Subsequently, following advertisements in local newspapers, a number of the employees were reinstated. On complaints of unfair dismissal under the Employment Protection (Consolidation) Act 1978, s 62, it was conceded that the dismissals were unfair and the issue of compensation arose. An industrial tribunal awarded ten employees compensation and the employers appealed on the ground that the tribunal had wrongly interpreted the 1978 Act, s 62. *Held*, the concession made in *Courtaulds Northern Spinning Ltd v Moosa* [1984] ICR 218 that the general intention of Parliament behind the 1978 Act, s 62 was to prevent tribunals going into the merits or demerits of collective industrial disputes was unsound. In following *Power Packing Casemakers Ltd v Faust* [1983] ICR 292 the correct approach was that once it was established that an employee was at the date of his dismissal engaged in a strike or other industrial action, an industrial tribunal could only enter upon a consideration of the merits of the case if it could be shown that the employee had been subjected to discriminatory treatment in the matter of dismissal. If it was shown that a discriminating factor existed then a tribunal ought to consider fairness or unfairness just as in any other case. Accordingly, the appeal would be allowed and the case remitted to the same industrial tribunal for assessment of compensation with the guidance that the circumstances surrounding the industrial action were relevant.

TNT Express (UK) Ltd v Rigby (1993) Times, 28 July (Employment Appeal Tribunal: Wood J presiding).

1978 Act, s 62 now Trade Union and Labour Relations (Consolidation) Act 1992, ss 238, 239(3).

1192 Unfair dismissal—industrial action—re-engagement

The respondents were among employees of the appellants who went on strike over a pay claim. The following month all the employees were dismissed. The employers recruited replacement staff and all new employees were offered new terms and conditions of employment in line with the employers' final pay offer. The respondents, who were not among those re-engaged, claimed they had been unfairly dismissed. An industrial tribunal held that it had jurisdiction to entertain the complaints on the grounds that there had been selective re-engagement of the striking employees. The tribunal found that although all the employees knew that the employers were recruiting, only those who had applied had been offered re-engagement. On appeal by the employers, *held*, the industrial tribunal had correctly found that the respondents had not been "offered re-engagement" within the meaning of the Employment Protection (Consolidation) Act 1978, notwithstanding that they knew that the employers were recruiting and that offers of employment were being made. A general advertising campaign offering employment to those who applied did not in itself amount to an offer of employment to any particular individual. In the present case the press, radio and other general notices issued amounted to an offer to treat for re-engagement rather than an offer of re-engagement to the respondent employees. What was made available to the employees was the opportunity of having an offer made to them. Accordingly, the appeal would be dismissed.

Crosville Wales Ltd v Tracey [1993] IRLR 60 (Employment Appeal Tribunal: Knox J presiding).

1193 Unfair dismissal—reason for dismissal—dismissal for "some other substantial reason"—fairness

The employee was offered employment in Australia and informed his company that he was going to accept the offer and that he intended to resign from his present employment. At a later date, the management of the company sought to confirm the date of the employee's cessation of employment. The employee informed them that he no longer wished to accept the job. His employers treated the employee's employment as terminated. The employee complained that he had been unfairly dismissed. An industrial tribunal decided that the reason for the dismissal had been the employee's late notification of his change of mind and that that reason represented "some other substantial reason of a kind such as to justify the dismissal" for the purposes of the Employment Protection (Consolidation) Act 1978, s 57(1)(b). The employee appealed, contending that the employers were not purporting to dismiss him and so could not have any reason for the dismissal. *Held*, although it might be illogical to say that when s 57 was literally construed, any employer could have a reason for dismissal when accepting a resignation in the belief that no question of dismissal arose at all. It was more illogical to interpret s 57 in a way which would result in dismissals occurring through an erroneous insistence on a supposed resignation being placed in their own category in which every such dismissal would be rendered automatically unfair because the employer could not supply a reason for it. To outlaw such dismissals from the ordinary rules as to fairness would introduce an unnecessary complication into employment relations which would be more likely to confuse rather than clarify resignation procedures. The appeal would accordingly be dismissed.

Ely v YKK Fasteners (UK) Ltd [1993] IRLR 500 (Court of Appeal: Neill, Simon Brown and Waite LJJ).

1194 Unfair dismissal—reason for dismissal—gross misconduct

Scotland

The plaintiff was employed by the defendant health board as a member of a team who carried out respiratory and cardiac tests on patients. It was alleged that the plaintiff tore up a card from a doctor requesting a test on a patient without the test having been carried out. The board considered that the plaintiff's action was an act of gross misconduct and dismissed her. They later agreed, after representations from the plaintiff's union representative, to consider the plaintiff for alternative employment not involving patient care. Although the plaintiff was supplied with details of other posts, she was never re-employed. The plaintiff's complaint of unfair dismissal was dismissed at first instance. On appeal, she contended that gross misconduct must be such misconduct that the employee could no longer reasonably be retained in the employment of the employer in any capacity. It was argued that the fact that the board was willing to employ her in some other capacity indicated that there was no true gross misconduct. *Held,* there was nothing inconsistent in an employer being willing to offer re-employment in a suitable capacity and a conclusion that an employee had been guilty of gross misconduct. There was no necessary inference that because an employee had been guilty of something regarded as gross misconduct in their actual employment, they must necessarily be considered unsuitable for any employment with the employer. The appeal would accordingly be dismissed.

Hamilton v Argyll and Clyde Health Board [1993] IRLR 99 (Employment Appeal Tribunal: Lord Coulsfield presiding).

1195   Unfair dismissal—reason for dismissal—sufficiency of reason—conduct

The appellant was employed by a company which operated garages and filling stations. Following a complaint received by a corporate customer, allegations of fraudulent conduct were made against the appellant. He denied the allegations, but admitted post-dating fuel vouchers and was given a written warning. He was later charged with criminal offences by the police. Following the charges, the appellant was suspended without pay, pending the result of the trial. After the trial had been adjourned twice, the appellant was told that he had been dismissed for falsifying company records. He was not given an opportunity to explain his conduct or to say anything in his defence. On his complaint of unfair dismissal, it was held by an industrial tribunal that the company's failure to give the appellant an opportunity to offer an explanation before dismissing him did not render the dismissal unfair because the employee could have used the grievance procedure to put forward a defence. The tribunal also held that although there was a difference between the reason given by the company for the dismissal and the real reason, the fraud being investigated by the police, the appellant was aware of the real reason. On appeal by the appellant, *held,* (1) the existence of a grievance procedure was not an adequate substitute for, or the equivalent of, the opportunity to explain, which natural justice required an employee to be given before being dismissed; (2) the tribunal had held correctly that the dismissal was not unfair because the reason stated in the letter of dismissal was different from the real reason, as the dominant consideration was that the reason for the appellant's dismissal was obvious to him. The appeal would however be allowed and the case remitted to an industrial tribunal for reconsideration.

Clarke v Trimoco Group Ltd [1993] IRLR 148 (Employment Appeal Tribunal: Knox J presiding).

1196   Unfair dismissal—reason for dismissal—sufficiency of reason—evidence not placed before employer

Scotland

The appellants alleged that they had been unfairly dismissed. During investigations conducted by their employer and at a disciplinary hearing and a subsequent appeal, they raised no question as to what they had been wearing at the time of the incident which had given rise to their dismissal. They first raised the matter at the hearing before an industrial tribunal, which concluded that the employer had not carried out reasonable investigations before dismissing them. The employer's appeal against that decision was allowed. On appeal by the appellants, *held,* the tribunal should have considered the nature of the evidence which was before the employer when it made its decision to dismiss the appellants. The tribunal was not entitled to conclude that no reasonable investigations had been carried out because the employer had failed to have regard to material which had not been placed before it and which had first emerged at the hearing before the tribunal. The appeal would be dismissed.

Dick v University of Glasgow (1993) Times, 18 August (Inner House).

1197   Unfair dismissal—reason for dismissal—trade union membership

An employee was dismissed and successfully claimed that it was by reason of his membership of a trade union within the terms of the Employment Protection (Consolidation) Act 1978, s 58. The industrial tribunal found that if the employee had not been a trade union member he would not have been dismissed. The employer appealed, contending that the tribunal had incorrectly applied a "but for" test in reaching that decision. *Held*, the tribunal had misdirected itself. When establishing the reason for dismissal, the tribunal had to consider the set of beliefs held by the employer which caused him to dismiss the employee. The "but for" test was inadequate because it did not introduce any question as to the employer's state of mind and failed properly to address the question of causation. The case would be remitted to a different tribunal and, accordingly, the appeal would be allowed.

CGB Publishing v Killey [1993] IRLR 520 (Employment Appeal Tribunal: Hicks J presiding).

1198 Unfair dismissal—reinstatement—employers' failure to comply with order—practicability of reinstatement

Following their redundancy a number of employees claimed that they had been unfairly dismissed. An industrial tribunal held that the employee's dismissal had been unfair and ordered their employer to re-engage them. The tribunal also held that the employer had failed to show that it was not practicable for him to comply with the re-engagement orders, and directed that the employees were entitled to a basic award, a compensatory award and a special award. The employer successfully appealed against the remedies and practicability issues. The employees appealed against the decision of the Employment Appeal Tribunal. *Held*, the issue of practicability was a question of fact for an industrial tribunal to decide. A tribunal ought to give due weight to the commercial judgment of the employer and as such it would be a matter of what was practicable in the circumstances of the employer's business at the relevant time. The tribunal had failed to direct itself correctly, and on the evidence it would have been bound to find that it would not have been practicable to re-engage the employees. In considering what would be the appropriate remedy for unfair dismissal under the Employment Protection (Consolidation) Act 1978, s 69 a tribunal ought to approach the issue as to whether it would be practicable to order an employer to reinstate or re-engage an employee in two stages. The first stage would be before any order for reinstatement or re-engagement was made when a provisional decision on practicability based on the evidence before the tribunal could be made. The second stage would arise if such an order was made but not complied with, the tribunal would then have to make a final conclusion on practicability as there would be the possibility it may affect the size of the special award. Accordingly, the appeal on the practicability issues would be dismissed.

Port of London Authority v Payne (1993) Times, 25 November (Court of Appeal: Neill, Staughton and Nolan LJJ). Decision Employment Appeal Tribunal [1993] ICR 30 (1992 Abr para 1108) affirmed.

1199 Unfair dismissal—waiver of right to compensation—fixed-term contract—extension

Northern Ireland
The appellant was appointed as a training and development officer at a university, initially for a fixed term of two years. Her contract of employment stipulated that she waived her unfair dismissal rights consequent upon the expiry of the fixed term. The post was funded externally and when, towards the end of the initial two-year period, the university received confirmation that the funding would continue, they extended her contract on the original conditions for an additional four months. Her contract expired on the specified date and was not renewed. She made an unsuccessful complaint of unfair dismissal. On appeal by way of case stated, the issue for the appellate court was whether, during the four-month period, the employee was engaged on an extension of her fixed term contract or under a new short term contract. *Held*, the industrial tribunal correctly found that the appellant's waiver of unfair dismissal rights in her initial fixed-term contract was a bar to her making a complaint when, following the four-month extension, the contract expired and was not renewed. It was not appropriate to apply Lord Denning's test in *BBC v Ioannou* [1975] IRLR 184. In the present case, that test would produce an unfair and unreasonable result since it would mean that, by providing an additional four months' employment, the university had revived the appellant's right to claim compensation for unfair dismissal. That was clearly contrary to the parties' agreed contractual terms. Looking at the substance of the contractual documents, those relating to the second period were very much part and parcel of the original contractual arrangements. The appellant had been employed under a two-year fixed-term contract which was then extended or renewed for a further four months. The second period was thus an extension of the first and was not severable, and the exclusion clause operated throughout. Accordingly, the appeal would be dismissed.

Mulrine v University of Ulster [1993] IRLR 545 (Court of Appeal in Northern Ireland).

1200   Wages—deduction—industrial action

The Wages Act 1986, s 1(5)(e) provides that nothing in the provisions contained in s 1 of that Act restricting deductions from salaries applies to any deduction from a worker's wages made by his employer where the worker has taken part in a strike or other industrial action and the deduction is made by the employer on account of the worker's having taken part in that strike or other action.

A lecturer at a polytechnic took part in a half-day stoppage and subsequently had a full day's pay docked from her wages. She complained to an industrial tribunal that the deduction was unlawful under the 1986 Act, s 1. The polytechnic contended that by virtue of s 1(5)(e), the tribunal lacked the jurisdiction to decide whether the deduction was lawful. The tribunal held that it did have jurisdiction. On appeal, *held*, in *Home Office v Ayres* [1992] ICR 175, EAT (1991 Abr para 1059), it had been held that the word "lawful" should be read into s 1(5)(a) before the word "deduction". If that was correct then "lawful" had to be imported into s 1(5)(e). However, some of the reasoning in that case could no longer stand. The wording of s 1(5) was sufficiently clear on its face and alternatively extracts from Hansard put the intention of Parliament beyond doubt. The industrial tribunal had no jurisdiction to decide whether the deduction was lawful. The appeal would accordingly be allowed.

Sunderland Polytechnic v Evans [1993] IRLR 196 (Employment Appeal Tribunal: Wood J presiding).

1201   Wages—deduction—stocktaking shortages

Following the discovery of deficiencies in stocktaking at a retail store in which he was a manager, the employee signed an agreement to the effect that £20 per week would be deducted from his salary to reimburse the company for those losses. The employee was dismissed following the discovery of another stocktaking deficiency, and the money due to him for wages, holiday pay and pay in lieu of notice was withheld by the employers on the ground that their claim exceeded the amount due to the employee. An industrial tribunal upheld the employee's claim that the deduction from his wages contravened the Wages Act 1986, s 1(4) because such deductions could not be made in respect of conduct which had occurred before the employee's authority had been given. On the employer's appeal, *held*, the purpose of the 1986 Act, s 1(4) was to prevent employers from placing pressure on employees to agree deductions. Such pressure could only be obviated if the agreement, variation or consent relied upon was made before the happening of the event which was the cause of the disputed deduction, and the industrial tribunal had been correct to rule that the employers could not rely on the agreement of the employee in the present case. Accordingly, the appeal would be dismissed.

Discount Tobacco and Confectionary Ltd v Williamson [1993] ICR 371 (Employment Appeal Tribunal: Wood J presiding).

1202   Wrongful dismissal—damages—damages only remedy

The plaintiff was employed as the principal at a school maintained by a charitable society. His contract of employment provided that three months' written notice was required by either side to terminate the employment. The plaintiff's conduct in handling a series of incidents at the school was criticised and referred to a disciplinary panel. Although the panel found that the charges did not merit dismissal, the society gave the plaintiff notice terminating his contract of employment with immediate effect. The society subsequently accepted that it ought to have complied with the three-month contractual notice requirement and accordingly paid the plaintiff remuneration for that period, contending that this represented all the damages the plaintiff could recover for breach of contract. The plaintiff contended that the society's termination of his contract constituted a repudiatory breach of contract and that the contract continued unless and until he accepted that breach or received proper notice. He sought by motion: (1) an interlocutory injunction restraining the society from dismissing him except in accordance with the contract, and (2) an order that his remuneration be paid until then. *Held*, although the society had committed a repudiatory breach of contract, that did not entitle the plaintiff to remuneration as a matter of debt. The plaintiff's remedy was a claim for damages for breach of contract, and authority provided that if damages were an adequate remedy an injunction would not be granted. Accordingly, the motion would be dismissed.

Marsh v National Autistic Society [1993] ICR 453 (Chancery Division: Ferris J). *American Cyanamid Co v Ethicon Ltd* [1975] AC 396, [1975] 1 All ER 504, HL (1975 Abr para 1864) applied.

1203 Wrongful dismissal—damages—deduction from award—pension receipts
The respondent was the managing director of a company. He was a member of the company pension scheme, the rules of which provided that if he ceased to be employed for any reason he was entitled to an immediate pension. The company dismissed him in breach of contract and he immediately opted for his pension. The court held that he was entitled to recover damages for wrongful dismissal, and that the pension receipts were not deductible from the damages. The company appealed, contending that credit should have been given for the pension payments. *Held*, the aim of damages was to put the injured party in the same position he would have been in had the contract been performed. Although generally credit had to be given for any benefits received as a result of the breach of contract, certain collateral benefits, including money received through benevolence or insurance, were exempt from that requirement. There was authority that where a plaintiff effected insurance, he was not required to give credit if he had paid the premiums from his own money, even if this resulted in double recovery. A pension was analogous to insurance. Accordingly, the appeal would be dismissed.
    Norcros plc v Hopkins (1993) Times, 13 October (Court of Appeal: Russell, Staughton and Steyn LJJ). *Parry v Cleaver* [1970] AC 1, HL applied.

ENVIRONMENT

1204 Articles
A Right to Know: The Environmental Information Regulations 1992, William Birtles: [1993] JPL 615
A Rude Awakening, Mike Fordham (on net liability in the United States): 143 NLJ 750
Back From the Brink, Owen Lomas and Robert Hunter (on *Cambridge Water Co v Eastern Counties Leather plc* (1993) Times, 10 December, HL (para 1899)): 138 SJ 73
Contaminated Land, Giles Frost: 137 SJ 636
Contaminated Land Without Registers, Simon Payne (on the Environmental Protection Act 1990, s 143): 137 SJ 1020
Councils, Councillors and Costs, J Cameron Blackhall (on costs at planning enquiries): [1993] JPL 112
Environmental Issues—the Right to Know, William Birtles: 137 SJ 408
Environmental Protection and the Common Law, James Driscoll: 144 NLJ 64
Hazardous Waste Legislation—Will the UK follow the US? Susan Fink: 137 SJ 246
Lazarus Arises, PR Ghandhi (on *Cambridge Water Co v Eastern Counties Leather plc* [1992] EGCS 142 (para 1899)): 137 SJ 611
Liability of Environmental Consultants, Jacqui O'Keeffe: Estates Gazette, 4 September 1993, p 112
No Fault Liability: The *Cambridge Water* case (see *Cambridge Water Company v Eastern Counties Leather* [1992] EGCS 142, CA (para 1899)), Rosalind English: [1993] JPL 409
Oil Spillages at Sea, Michael Bundock: 137 SJ 97
Planning and Pollution Control, Gill Castorina: Estates Gazette, 2 October 1993, p 113
'Poisonous, Noxious or Polluting'—Contrasting Approaches to Environmental Regulations, William Howarth: 57 MLR 171
Sellafield Judgment, Tess Gill: 137 SJ 1184
The Extent of Listing, Charles Mynors: [1993] JPL 99
The Legal Protection of Whales—Time for a Re-Think? Steven Wheatley: 143 NLJ 855
The Profits of Pollution, Michael Fordham: 143 NLJ 230
The Right to Know, Simon Payne (on the Environmental Information Regulations 1992): 137 SJ 1216

1205 Biological diversity—international Convention
The Convention on Biological Diversity (Cm 2127) was signed in Rio de Janeiro on 5 June 1992. The term "biological diversity" is defined as the variability among living organisms from all sources, including terrestrial, marine and other aquatic ecosystems, and the ecological complexes of which they are part. The Convention recognises that states have the right to exploit their own resources pursuant to their environmental policies, and also the responsibility to ensure that activities within their jurisdiction or control do not damage the environment of other states or of areas beyond the limits of national jurisdiction: art 3. States are called upon to develop strategies, etc for the conservation and sustainable use of biological diversity (art 6), to

establish a system of protected areas to conserve biological diversity (art 8), and to adopt measures for the ex situ conservation of components of biological diversity and for the conservation of and research on plants, animals and micro-organisms: art 9. The Convention recognises that access to genetic resources should be subject to national legislation (art 15), but the contracting parties undertake to provide and/or facilitate access for and transfer to other contracting parties of technologies that are relevant to the conservation and sustainable use of biological diversity or that make use of genetic resources and do not cause significant damage to the environment: art 16. The contracting parties also undertake to take appropriate measures for the effective participation in biotechnological research by other contracting parties, especially developing countries, which provide the genetic resources for such research: art 19. The Convention provides for a conference of the parties (art 23), which can adopt rules of procedure and financial rules, and for the establishment of a secretariat: art 24. The Convention, which will come into force on the ninetieth day after the deposit of the thirteenth ratification, etc (art 36) has not been ratified by the United Kingdom.

1206 Clean Air Act 1993

The Clean Air Act 1993 consolidates the Clean Air Acts 1956 and 1968 and certain related enactments, with amendments to give effect to recommendations of the Law Commission. The Act received the royal assent on 27 May 1993 and came into force on 27 August 1993. A table showing the destination of enactments consolidated appears overleaf.

DESTINATION TABLE

This table shows in column (1) the enactments repealed by the Clean Air Act 1993 and in column (2) the provisions of that Act corresponding thereto.

In certain cases the enactment in column (1), though having a corresponding provision in column (2), is not, or not wholly, repealed as it is still required, or partly required, for the purposes of other legislation.

A "dash" adjacent to a repealed or revoked provision indicates that that provision is spent, unnecessary or for some other reason not specifically reproduced.

A reference to "LC rec" is a reference to one of the recommendations of the Law Commission in its Report on the Consolidation of Certain Enactments Relating to Clean Air (Law Com No 209; Cm 2085).

(1)	(2)	(1)	(2)
Public Health Act 1936 (c 49)	**Clean Air Act 1993** (c 11)	**Clean Air Act 1956** (c 52)	**Clean Air Act 1993** (c 11)
s 297*	s 50(3)	s 11(10)	ss 18(2), 20(2)
s 318*	s 59(1), (2)	s 12(1)	Sch 2, para 1(1)–(4)
s 343(1)*	s 64(1), LC rec 11	s 12(2)	s 24(1)–(3)
		s 12(3)	Applies to Scotland
Clean Air Act 1956 (c 52)	**Clean Air Act 1993** (c 11)	s 13(1)	Sch 2, para 4(1)
		s 13(2)	Sch 2, para 4(2)(a), (b)
s 1(1)	s 1(1), (6)	s 14(1)	s 27(1)–(3)
s 1(2), (3)	s 1(3), (4)	s 14(2)	s 28(1), (2)
s 1(4)	s 1(2)	s 15(1), (2)	s 26
s 2	Rep 1968 c 62, s 14(2), Sch 2	s 15(3)	ss 27(4), 28(3)
s 3(1)	s 4(2), (4), LC rec 1(i)	S 16(1), (2)	Rep 1990 c 43, s 162(2), Sch 16, Pt III
s 3(2)	s 4(3)	s 16(3)	Applies to Scotland
s 3(3)	s 4(1), (4)	s 16A	s 41
s 3(4), (5)	s 4(5), (6)	s 17(1), (2), (5), (6) . . .	Rep 1968 c 62, ss 11(8), 14(2), Sch 2
s 4	Rep 1980 c 65, ss 1(2), 194, Sch 2, para 1, Sch 34, Pt II	s 17(3)	Rep SI 1974/2170, reg 7
		s 17(4)	Cf s 66(1)(c)
s 5	Rep 1968 c 62, ss 2(6), 14(2), Sch 2	s 18(1)	s 42(1), (2)
s 6(1)	s 8, LC rec 1(ii)	s 18(2)	s 42(4)
s 6(2)	Sch 5, para 6(2), (3)	s 18(3)	Sch 5, para 10
s 6(3)	Rep 1980 c 65, ss 1(2), 194, Sch 2, para 1, Sch 34, Pt II	s 18(4)	s 42(6)
		s 18(5)	Applies to Scotland
s 6(4), (5)	s 9(2), (3)	s 19(1)	s 43(1), (2)
s 7(1)	s 10(1), (6)	s 19(2)	s 43(3)
s 7(2), (3)	s 10(2)	s 19(3)	s 43(5)
s 8	s 12	s 20(1)	s 44(1), (2)
s 9	s 13	s 20(2)	s 44(3)
s 10(1)	s 16(1), (2)	s 20(3)	s 44(4), (5)
s 10(2)	s 16(3)(a)	s 20(4)	s 44(6)
s 10(3)	s 16(3)(b), (4)	s 21	s 45
s 10(4)	Rep 1989 c 29, s 112(4), Sch 18	s 22(1)	s 46(1), (2)
		s 22(2), (3)	s 46(3), (4)
s 10(5)	Applies to Scotland	s 22(4)	s 46(5), (6)
s 11(1)	s 18(1)	s 22(5)	s 46(6)
s 11(2)	s 20(1), (2), (3)(a), (4)	s 23	Rep 1980 c 65, ss 189, 194, Sch 34, Pt XVI
s 11(3)	s 18(2)	s 24	Rep 1974 c 37, s 83(2), Sch 10
s 11(4)	s 21		
s 11(5), (6)	s 18(3), (4)	s 25(a), (b)	Rep 1974 c 40, ss 79(10), 108(2), Sch 4
s 11(7)	s 22(1), (2)	s 25(c)–(e)	s 34(1)(c)–(e)
s 11(8)	—	s 26	s 49, LC rec 3
s 11(9)	s 22(3)	s 27(1)	ss 1(5), 44(2)

*Not repealed

(1)	(2)
Clean Air Act 1956 (c 52)	**Clean Air Act 1993 (c 11)**
s 27(2)	ss 4(4)(a), 20(5)
s 27(3)	s 49(1)
s 27(4)	ss 4(4)(b), 8(2), 10(3), 12(2), 42(3), 43(4), 50(1), (2), LC rec 1
s 27(5)	Applies to Scotland
s 28(1)	s 54(1)
s 28(2)	Applies to Scotland
s 29(1)	s 55(1), Sch 3, para 6, LC rec 5
s 29(2)	s 55(2)
s 29(3)	Applies to Scotland
s 30(1)	s 51(1), (2)
s 30(2)	s 51(3)
s 31(1)	ss 50, 56, 57, 59(1), (2), 60, 61(1), 62(1), 64(1), LC recs 9, 11
s 31(2)	—
s 31(3), (4)	s 61(3), (4)
s 31(5)	Rep 1972 c 70, s 272(1), Sch 30
s 31(6)	s 61(5)
s 31(7)	Applies to Scotland
s 32	Rep 1963 c 33, s 93(1), Sch 18, Pt II
s 33(1)	s 63(2), (3)
s 33(2)	Rep 1981 c 19
s 34(1)	ss 20(6), 29, 64(1)
s 34(2)	s 3
s 34(3)	s 64(2)
s 34(4)	s 64(6), LC rec 12
s 34(5)	Rep 1964 c 56, s 108(2), Sch 5
s 34(6), (7)	s 64(5), (6)
s 34(8)	—
s 35(1)	Rep 1974 c 22
s 35(2), (3)	—
s 35(4)	Rep 1980 c 65, ss 1(2), 194, Sch 2, para 4, Sch 34, Pt II
s 36	s 68(3)
s 37	—
Sch 1	Sch 1
Sch 2	—
Sch 3, Pt I, para 1	s 56
para 2	s 50(3)
para 3	—
Pt II	Rep 1963 c 33, s 93(1), Sch 18, Pt II
Pt III	Applies to Scotland
Sch 4	Rep 1974 c 22

(1)	(2)
London Government Act 1963 (c 33)	**Clean Air Act 1993 (c 11)**
s 40(4)(e)	—
Sch 11, para 30	—

(1)	(2)
London Government Act 1963 (c 33)	**Clean Air Act 1993 (c 11)**
Sch 11, para 31	s 16(1)

(1)	(2)
Housing Act 1964 (c 56)	**Clean Air Act 1993 (c 11)**
s 95(1)	s 25(2)
s 95(2)	Sch 2, paras 2, 3(1), (2), (5)
s 95(2A)	Rep 1980 c 65, s 194, Sch 34, Pt II
s 95(3)	Sch 2, para 3(3), (5)
s 95(4)(a)	Sch 2, para 1(5), (6)
s 95(4)(b)	Sch 2, para 3(4)
s 95(5), (6)	—
s 95(7), (8)	Sch 2, para 4(2)(c), (3)
s 95(9)	s 27(1)(d), (2)
s 95(10)	Applies to Scotland

(1)	(2)
Clean Air Act 1968 (c 62)	**Clean Air Act 1993 (c 11)**
s 1(1)	s 2(1), (5)
s 1(1A)	s 2(3)
s 1(2), (3)	s 2(2)
s 1(4)	s 2(4)
s 1(5)	s 2(6)
s 2(1)	s 5(2)
s 2(2)	s 5(3), (6)
s 2(3)	s 5(4)
s 2(4)	s 5(5), (6)
s 2(5)	s 5(1)
s 2(6)	—
s 3(1)	s 6(1), (2)
s 3(2)	s 6(3)
s 3(3)	s 6(5)
s 3(4)	s 6(4), Sch 5, para 6(1)
s 3(5)	ss 8(1), 9(2), (3)
s 3(6)	s 9(1)
s 3(7)	s 9(2)
s 4(1), (2)	s 7(1), (2)
s 4(3)	Rep 1980 c 65, ss 1(2), 194, Sch 2, para 6(b), Sch 34, Pt II
s 4(4)–(7)	s 7(3)–(6)
s 5(1)	s 10(1)
s 5(2)	s 10(5)
s 5(3)	s 11(1), (2)
s 5(4), (5)	s 11(3)
s 5(6)	s 11(4)
s 5(7)	s 10(4)
s 6(1)	s 14(2), (3), (6)
s 6(2)	s 14(4)–(6)
s 6(3)	Rep 1980 c 65, ss 1(2), 194, Sch 2, para 6b, Sch 34, Pt II
s 6(4)–(6)	s 15(2)–(4)

(1)	(2)
Clean Air Act 1968 (c 62)	Clean Air Act 1993 (c 11)

s 6(7)	s 15(5), (6)
s 6(8), (9)	s 15(7), (8)
s 6(10)	s 14(1), Sch 5, para 7
s 6(11)	ss 14(7), 15(9)
s 6(12)	s 16(1)
s 7(1)	s 47(1)
s 7(2)	—
s 7(3)	s 47(2)
s 7A(1)	s 47(1)
s 7A(2)	—
s 7A(3)	s 47(2)
s 7A(4), (5)	s 47(3), (4)
s 8(1)–(6)	s 19
s 8(7)	s 60(7)
s 8(8)	—
s 9	s 23
s 10(1)–(4)	Rep 1980 c 65, s 194, Sch 34, Pt II
s 10(5)	Sch 2, para 3(1)(a)
s 11(1)	Sch 3, para 2
s 11(2)	Rep SI 1983/943, reg 7(1)(b)
s 11(3)	Sch 3, paras 3, 4
s 11(4)	Sch 3, para 5
s 11(5)	Rep SI 1974/2170, reg 9
s 11(6), (7)	Sch 3, para 1
s 11(8), (9)	—
s 11A	s 41
s 12(1)	ss 2(2), 63(1)
s 12(2)	s 63(2)
s 13(1)	ss 7(4), (5), 15(6), 19, 64(1)
s 13(2)	s 64(3)
s 13(3)	—
s 14(1), (2)	—
s 14(3)	Rep 1980 c 65, ss 1(2), 194, Sch 2, para 6(b), Sch 34, Pt II
s 15(1)–(5)	—
s 15(6)	s 68(3)
Sch 1, para 1	ss 42(4), 43(5), 44(6), 46(3)–(5), 49, 54(1), 55(1), 59(1), (2), 61(1), 62(1)
para 2	s 10(2)(a)
para 3	s 12(1)
para 4	s 13, LC rec 2
para 5	—
para 6	s 45(1)
para 7	—
para 8	s 55(2)
para 9	s 51
para 10	s 64(1)
para 11	s 3
para 12	s 64(6)
Sch 2	—

(1)	(2)
Local Government Act 1972 (c 70)	Clean Air Act 1993 (c 11)

s 180(3)(f)	s 64(1)

(1)	(2)
Consumer Credit Act 1974 (c 39)	Clean Air Act 1993 (c 11)

Sch 4, para 15	s 28(2)
para 16	s 29

(1)	(2)
Control of Pollution Act 1974 (c 40)	Clean Air Act 1993 (c 11)

s 30(1)*	s 64(1), LC rec 12
s 75(1), (2)	s 30(1), (2)
s 75(3)(a)	s 30(3)(a)
s 75(3)(b)	s 32(1)
s 75(4)	s 30(3)(b)
s 75(5), (6)	s 30(4), (5)
s 75(7)	Applies to Scotland
s 75(8)	s 30(7), (8)
s 75(9)	s 30(9)
s 76(1), (2)	s 31(1), (2)
s 76(3)(a), (b), (d)	s 31(3)
s 76(3)(c)	s 32(1)
s 76(4)	s 31(4), Sch 3, para 7
s 76(5)	s 31(5)
s 77(1)	s 32(2)
s 77(2)	s 32(3), (4)
s 78(1)	s 33(1), Sch 3, para 8
s 78(2)	s 33(2)
s 78(3)	Rep SI 1983/943, reg 7(1)(c)
s 79(1)	s 34(1)(a), (b)
s 79(2), (3)	s 35(1), (2)
s 79(4)	s 35(3), Sch 3, para 9
s 79(5)	s 34(2)
s 79(6), (7)	s 34(3), (4)
s 79(8)	s 35(4), (5)
s 79(9)	s 35(6)
s 79(10)	s 34(1)(c)
s 80(1), (2)	s 36(1), (2)
s 80(3)	s 36(3), Sch 3, para 10
s 80(4), (5)	s 36(4), (5)
s 80(6)	s 36(6), (7)
s 80(7), (8)	s 36(8), (9)
s 81(1), (2)	s 37(1), (2)
s 81(3)	s 37(3), (4)
s 82	s 38
s 83(1), (2)	s 39(1), (2)
s 83(3)	s 39(1), (3)
s 84(1)	ss 36(2), 64(1), Sch 3, para 11, LC rec 12
s 84(2), (3)	s 40
s 87(1)*	s 52, LC rec 4
s 87(2)*	s 53, LC rec 4
s 91(1)–(4)*	s 56(1), (3)–(5), LC rec 6

*Not repealed

(1)	(2)	(1)	(2)
Control of Pollution Act 1974 (c 40)	Clean Air Act 1993 (c 11)	Building Act 1984 (c 55)	Clean Air Act 1993 (c 11)
s 92*	s 57, LC rec 6	Sch 5, para 2	ss 16(1), 55(1)
s 93*	s 58	Sch 6, para 5	s 16(3)
s 94(1)*	s 49(1), LC rec 3		
s 94(2)(a)*	s 49(2)(a), LC rec 3		
s 96(1), (2)*	s 59(1), (2)		
s 97(1)–(8)*	s 60(1)–(6), (8), LC rec 8	Control of Smoke Pollution Act 1989 (c 17)	Clean Air Act 1993 (c 11)
s 102(1)*	s 48		
s 103	—		
s 104(1)(a)*	s 63(1)(a), (b), LC rec 10	s 1	Rep 1990 c 43, s 162(2), Sch 16, Pt III
s 105(1)*	s 64(1), Sch 3, para 11, LC rec 11	s 2(1)	s 2(1)
s 107*	s 65	s 2(2)	s 2(3)
s 109(3)†	s 68(3)	s 3(1), (2)	—
Sch 2, para 19(1)	ss 1(5), 44(2)	s 3(3)	s 68(3)
para 19(2)	ss 4(4)(a), 20(5)		
para 19(3)	s 49(1)		
para 19(4)	ss 4(4)(b), 8(2), 10(3), 12(2), 42(3), 43(4), 50(1), (2)	Environmental Protection Act 1990 (c 43)	Clean Air Act 1993 (c 11)
para 26(a)	s 2(5)	s 85	s 47
para 26(b), (c)	s 5(6)	Sch 15, para 6	s 41
para 26(d)	s 6(5)	para 7(1)	—
para 26(e)	s 7(6)	para 7(2)	s 42(4)
para 26(f)	s 14(6)	para 7(3)	s 45(1)
para 27	s 23(1)	para 12	s 41
Sch 3, para 16(1)	s 51(1)	para 15(6)	s 31(4)
para 16(2)	s 51(3)	para 15(7)	s 33(1)
para 16(3)	—	para 15(8)	s 35(3)
		para 15(9)	s 36(3)
Local Government, Planning and Land Act 1980 (c 65)	Clean Air Act 1993 (c 11)		
s 189*	—	Atomic Weapons Establishment Act 1991 (c 46)	Clean Air Act 1993 (c 11)
Sch 2, para 1	—		
para 2	s 26(1), Sch 2, para 1(1), Sch 5, paras 8, 9	Schedule paras 4, 8(1)	Sch 4, para 5
paras 3, 4	—		
para 5	Sch 1, Sch 5, paras 8, 9		
para 6(a)	s 9(2), (3)		
para 6(6)	—		
Sch 2, para 16	—		

*Not repealed   †Repealed in part

1207   Clean Air Act 1993—smoke control areas—exempted fireplaces
The Smoke Control Areas (Exempted Fireplaces) Order 1993, SI 1993/2277 (in force on 18 October 1993), exempts specified classes of fireplace from the provisions of the Clean Air Act 1993, s 20 (which prohibits the emission of smoke in smoke control areas) subject to certain conditions.

1208   Contaminated land—public registers of information—withdrawal of proposals for implementation
The Government has, after a consultation process, withdrawn its proposals for establishing registers of contaminative uses of land under the Environmental Protection Act 1990, s 143, and has announced a new wide-ranging review of the powers and duties of local authorities in this area. The responses which were received by the Government showed that the proposed registers would have reduced confidence in the value of sites placed on the register, thereby exacerbating blight without giving any clear indication as to how such sites could be brought back into good condition and confidence restored. The review will be conducted by an inter-departmental group of officials under the chairmanship of the Department of the Environment and will seek contributions from interested parties. See 544 HL Official Report written answers col 17.

1209   Controlled waste—scrap metal—duty of care
The Controlled Waste (Amendment) Regulations 1993, SI 1993/566 (in force on 1 April 1993), amend the 1992 Regulations, SI 1992/588, relating to scrap metal. The duty of care under the 1990 Environmental Protection Act 1990, s 34 will not apply in relation to scrap metal until the day on the which the disposal licensing provisions of the Control of Pollution Act 1974, Pt I relating to scrap metal are repealed.

1210   Environmental Protection Act 1990—commencement
The Environmental Protection Act 1990 (Commencement No 13) Order 1993, SI 1993/274 brings into force on 18 February 1993 ss 35(6), 36(1), 39(3), 40(3), 41(2), (4), (5), 43(8), 54(14), 63(1), 64(1), (4), (8), 74(6), enabling the Secretary of State to make regulations for various purposes in connection with the waste management licensing system under Pt II (ss 29–78), Sch 15, para 21, and certain repeals in Sch 16, and, in so far as they enable the Secretary of State to give directions, ss 37(3), 38(7), 42(8), 65(2), 66(7); and on 1 May 1993 Sch 16 in so far as it relates to a repeal in the Housing and Planning Act 1986, Sch 7, para 8. For a summary of the Act, see 1990 Abr para 1032. For details of commencement, see the commencement table in the title STATUTES.

1211   Genetically modified organisms—deliberate release—applications for consent
The Genetically Modified Organisms (Deliberate Release) Regulations 1993, SI 1993/152 (in force on 1 February 1993), correct an error in the Genetically Modified Organisms (Deliberate Release) Regulations 1992, SI 1992/3280.
    The regulations provide that the advice of the committee appointed under the Environmental Protection Act 1990, s 124, as to applications for consents to release or market genetically modified organisms must be placed on the public register of information kept under s 122 within fourteen days of it being received by the Secretary of State.

1212   Hazardous waste—control of transboundary movements—Basel Convention
See para 2700.

1213   Marine pollution
See SHIPPING AND NAVIGATION.

1214   Pollution control—discharge of waste—discharge into controlled waters by third party—liability of company
The Water Act 1989, s 107(1)(a) provides that a person is in contravention of the Act if he causes or knowingly permits any poisonous, noxious or polluting matter or any solid waste matter to enter any controlled waters.

Vandals damaged an oil tank owned by the defendant company, causing it to leak oil into a nearby stream. The plaintiff brought an information against the company alleging a breach of the 1989 Act, s 107(1)(a), which was dismissed by the court. On appeal by the plaintiff, *held*, the concept of foreseeability was relevant in determining whether somebody "knowingly permitted" polluting matter to enter controlled waters but was merely one factor to take into consideration when determining whether he "causes" it to do so. Past cases were of limited guidance as they were confined to their particular facts. In this case, the court at first instance had considered the fact that there had been acts of minor vandalism to the oil tank in the past, but had decided that these were not sufficient to alter their view that the vandals and not the company caused the pollution. They were entitled to make such a finding and accordingly, the appeal would be dismissed.

National Rivers Authority v Wright Engineering Co Ltd (1993) Independent, 19 November (Queen's Bench Division: Simon Brown LJ and Buckley J).

The defendant company owned a sewerage treatment works which was gravity operated. It had been granted consent to discharge effluent into controlled waters on condition that a harmful chemical, iso-octonal was not also discharged. One night, a discharge of iso-octanol was made by somebody without the knowledge of the company. The company was convicted of being in breach of the Water Act 1989, s 107 (1)(a). On appeal, *held*, once the facts had been established, whether a party had caused a certain result was a question of fact in each case, although past cases could provide guidance as to the meaning of "causes". In this case, it was unarguable that due to the treatment works utilising the flow of gravity, the company merely stood by and did not cause the outflow but, as the notion of "causes" in the 1989 Act, s 107(1)(a) did not import either knowledge or negligence, it was also clear that the company had caused the contents of the effluent, including the iso-octonal, to discharge into the controlled waters in breach of the 1989 Act. The fact that the person responsible for putting the iso-octonal in the sewers might also be regarded as causing the pollution did not change the situation. The 1989 Act, s 108(7) provided a defence but only to a charge of contravening the conditions of a consent. As the company had been charged with a breach of the 1989 Act, s 107(1)(a) it could not rely on this defence. The finding that the company could not reasonably have been expected to prevent the iso-octonal from entering the sewers or works and could not have known of its presence might have been material considerations to the question of penalties imposed but did not go to liability. Accordingly, the appeal would be allowed.

National Rivers Authority v Yorkshire Water Services Ltd (1993) Times, 24 November, Independent 19 November (Queen's Bench Division: Simon Brown LJ and Buckley J).

Water Act 1989, s 107(1)(a) replaced by Water Resources Act 1991, s 85(1).
See *Cambridge Water Co v Eastern Counties Leather plc*, para 1899.

1215 Pollution control—injurious substances—marketing and use

The Environmental Protection (Controls on Injurious Substances) Regulations 1993, SI 1993/1 (in force on 31 January 1993), implement part of Council Directive (EC) 91/173 on the approximation of the laws, regulations and administrative provisions of the member states relating to restriction on the marketing and use of certain dangerous substances and preparations. The Regulations prohibit the marketing of PCP other than its marketing, under certain conditions, for use in industrial installations for the impregnation of fibres or heavy duty textiles or as a synthesising and/or processing agent.

The Environmental Protection (Controls on Injurious Substances) (No 2) Regulations 1993, SI 1993/1643 (in force on 31 July 1993), give effect to EC Directive 91/338/EC on the approximation of the laws, regulations and administrative provisions of Member States relating to restriction on the marketing and use of certain dangerous substances and preparations. Restrictions are placed on the marketing and use of cadmium in relation to specified processes involving certain plastics. A person who contravenes or causes or permits another person to contravene a regulation will be guilty of an offence.

1216 Pollution control—nitrogen oxides—control of national annual emissions

See para 2696.

1217 Pollution control—prescribed processes and substances

The Environmental Protection (Prescribed Processes and Substances) (Amendment) Regulations 1993, SI 1993/1749 (in force on 30 July 1993), further amend the 1991 Regulations, SI

1991/472, by exempting the prescribed process relating to the treatment and processing of animal or vegetable matter the fleshing, cleaning and drying of pelts of fur-bearing mammals.

The Environmental Protection (Prescribed Processes and Substances) (Amendment) (No 2) Regulations 1993, SI 1993/2405 (in force on 26 October 1993), further amend the Environmental Protection (Prescribed Processes and Substances) Regulations 1991, SI 1991/472.
    The regulations set out provisions relating to the treatment of processes in the chemical industry and applications in respect of such processes.

1218   Pollution control—radiation—radioactive substances
See para 2702.

1219   Pollution control—water pollution—north-east Atlantic
See para 2701.

1220   Protection of environment—carbon dioxide emissions—energy efficiency
See para 2697.

1221   Protection of environment—financial assistance
The Financial Assistance for Environmental Purposes Order 1993, SI 1993/1062 (in force on 12 May 1993), varies the Environmental Protection Act 1990, s 153(1) to enable the Secretary of State, with the consent of the Treasury, to give financial assistance to or for the purposes of the environment.

The Financial Assistance for Environmental Purposes (No 2) Order 1993, SI 1993/1518 (in force on 15 July 1993), varies the Environmental Protection Act 1990, s 153(1). The order enables financial assistance to be given for the purposes of the Promotion of Positive Environmental Management in Industry Programme, which aims to help small and medium sized companies improve their environmental performance.

1222   Protection of environment—industrial activities—environmental performance—evaluation and improvement
See para 2698.

1223   Protection of environment—sea water—bathing water
See *EC Commission v United Kingdom of Great Britain and Northern Ireland*, para 2703.

1224   Waste—collection and disposal—arrangements—discrimination
It has been held that a waste disposal authority which has set up a waste disposal company under and for the purposes of the Environmental Protection Act 1990, should not, when tendering for contracts as required by the 1990 Act, s 51, discriminate unduly so as to avoid competition between different companies.
    R v Avon County Council, ex p Terry Adams Ltd (1994) Times, 20 January (Court of Appeal: Ralph, McCowan and Hobhouse LJJ). Decision of Jowitt J (1993) Times, 7 July, reversed.

1225   Waste—collection and disposal—recycling of waste
The Environmental Protection (Waste Recycling Payments) (Amendment) Regulations 1993, SI 1993/445 (in force on 1 April 1993), substitute the amounts for the determination of a waste disposal authority's net saving in waste disposal costs per tonne of expenditure for the purposes of the Environmental Protection Act 1990, s 52(1) or (3) as set out in the 1992 Regulations, SI 1992/462.

EQUITY

Halsbury's Laws of England (4th edn) Vol 16 (reissue), paras 651–950

1226 Articles

Clean Hands Need not be Spotless, Bron Council (on *Tinsley v Milligan* [1993] 3 All ER 65 (para 2583)): 143 NLJ 1577

1227 Equitable jurisdiction—remedies—restitution of property—depreciation in value

The plaintiff paid a sum of money to the defendant who obtained an additional sum of money by way of a building society loan. The defendant then purchased a house, in his sole name, in which the plaintiff was to live for the rest of his life; on his death the house was to pass to the defendant. When the plaintiff discovered that the defendant had failed to pay the mortgage instalments he decided to withdraw from the agreement and sought the return of his money. The house was sold for considerably less than the defendant had paid for it. At first instance, the agreement was set aside for undue influence; the loss brought about by the fall in the market value of the house was to be shared between the plaintiff and the defendant in the same proportions as they had contributed to the price. On appeal it was suggested that there was no authority for ordering the loss to be shared in that way and that it was a principle unknown to English law. *Held*, it was well established that a court of equity would set aside a transaction even when it could not restore the parties precisely to the state they had been in before the contract. When considering what had been the original position of the parties it was important to identify and properly characterise the transaction being set aside. The transaction in the present case involved both parties making a financial contribution to the acquisition of a new asset from which both were intended to benefit. Clearly, when reversing that transaction, the court was concerned to achieve practical justice for both parties, not the plaintiff alone. In order to achieve a practically just outcome, the court had to look at all the circumstances while bearing in mind the basic objective which was to restore the parties as near as possible to their original positions. In all the circumstances, it would not be just to require the defendant to bear the whole of the loss. Each party should receive a proportionate share of the net proceeds of the house. Accordingly, the appeal would be dismissed.

Cheese v Thomas [1994] 1 All ER 35 (Court of Appeal: Sir Donald Nicholls V-C and Butler-Sloss and Peter Gibson LJJ). Dictum of Lord Blackburn in *Erlanger v New Sombrero Phosphate Co* (1878) 3 App Cas 1218 at 1278, HL applied.

1228 Positive covenant—covenant to repair—wording of covenant—use of wording to ascertain ownership

The owner of a house conveyed as a separate dwelling part of his property and some land which became known as "the cottage". The effect of dividing the property was that part of the roof of the house, the disputed roof, overhung a part of the cottage. The deed of conveyance contained a clause whereby the vendor covenanted for himself and his successors in title to maintain to the reasonable satisfaction of the purchaser and his successors in title the disputed roof. The house and cottage changed hands and several years later leaks appeared in the disputed roof and the owners of the cottage, the plaintiffs, claimed the new owner of the house, the defendant, was under a duty to pay for repairs. The defendant's attempts at repairing the roof were inadequate and the plaintiffs initiated legal proceedings. The court held that the disputed roof was owned by the defendant and that the failure to maintain it constituted an actionable nuisance. On appeal by the defendant, *held*, the description of the cottage in the deed had to include the whole of the structure including the disputed roof. The deed together with the attached plan clearly conveyed the disputed roof to the owner of the cottage. It was not permissible as the court below had held, to take into account the wording of the covenant to demonstrate that the parties had intended that the property conveyed did not include that part of the roof. It was the plaintiffs and not the defendant who owned the disputed roof. That meant that the plaintiffs had no cause of action in nuisance or negligence and therefore the plaintiffs sought to enforce the covenant to repair against the defendant. However it was established law that although the benefits of positive covenants which touched and concerned other land could run with freehold land, the burden of them could not. It followed that the original vendor's covenant to maintain the disputed roof

was not enforceable against his successors in title. Accordingly, the appeal would be allowed.
Rhone v Stephens (1993) Times, 21 January (Court of Appeal: Nourse and Steyn LJJ).
Austerberry v Oldham Corp (1885) 29 Ch D 750, CA applied.

**1229   Principles of equitable jurisdiction—he who comes to equity must come
with clean hands—beneficial interest in house—fraudulent purpose of
registration of ownership**

See *Tinsley v Milligan*, para 2583.

1230   Restrictive covenant—building scheme—enforceability

Trinidad and Tobago
In 1938 a company subdivided its land into five lots which were then sold to four purchasers.
The purchasers of lots 1, 4 and 5 entered into covenants with the company and its assigns
including a covenant not to build more than one dwelling house each. In 1948 a deed was
executed by the company and the owners of the lots releasing the owner of lots 4 and 5 from
the restriction in the original conveyance which had previously prohibited all owners from
building more than one house. The 1948 deed specified that the other parties or their successors
in title were not however released from any of the obligations imposed on them under the
original conveyances. The plaintiff subsequently became the owner of lot 3 and the defendant
of lot 1. In 1983 the defendant commenced the construction of more than one house on his land.
The plaintiff initiated proceedings attempting to enforce against the defendant the restrictive
covenant in the 1938 conveyance. The court dismissed the action holding that a building scheme
had not been created in 1938 and so the covenants were not mutually enforceable between the
owners of the lots. On appeal, *held*, in order to establish a building scheme it was necessary to
prove that the original common vendor had laid out a defined portion of his land for sale in lots
subject to restrictions intended to be imposed on all the lots and consistent only with a general
scheme of development and that the purchasers of all the land within that area of the scheme
had known what the area was. The evidence in relation to the intention of the company and the
purchaser of the lots in 1938 was inconsistent with an intention to create a building scheme and
the 1948 deed, although admissible as evidence of what the parties had intended in 1938, was
too equivocal to prove the requisite intention. Therefore since no building scheme had been
created, the restriction imposed on the defendant's predecessor in title in 1938 was not
enforceable. Accordingly, the appeal would be dismissed.
Emile Elias & Co Ltd v Pine Groves Ltd [1993] 1 WLR 305 (Privy Council: Lords Keith of
Kinkel, Oliver of Aylmerton, Goff of Chieveley, Browne-Wilkinson and Woolf).

1231   Restrictive covenant—discharge or modification—restriction on building

The applicant bought a plot of land, aware that the previous owner had covenanted with the
local authority not to erect any buildings on part of the plot, although he had been granted
planning permission for the erection of garages on the rest of the plot. The applicant obtained
planning permission to erect a further block of garages and sought to discharge or modify the
covenant, contending that there could be no objection on environmental or highway safety
grounds, that no-one would be injured and no policy of the local authority would be contravened
or hindered, and that additional off-street parking was in the public interest. The local authority
objected to the application on the ground that the proposal would have an adverse impact on
adjoining residential occupiers. *Held*, there was no basis for regarding the restriction as obsolete
as the object of the covenant, to keep the restricted land open and to limit garage development
to that which could reasonably be related to the adjoining houses, could still be achieved.
Although the restrictions were an impediment to a reasonable user, they secured a practical
benefit of value to the local authority as custodian of the public interest and it gave the ability to
resist undesirable development, a benefit which was not capable of assessment in money terms.
Although the local authority possessed no land in the area, it was entitled to safeguard the
interests of the people it represented. The application would accordingly be dismissed.
Re Wallace & Co's Application (1993) 66 P & CR 124 (Lands Tribunal: Judge Marder QC).

1232   Restrictive covenant—discharge or modification—restriction on trade

The applicants had been granted planning permission to convert a private house into a
community care home for ten psychiatric patients. They applied under the Law of Property Act
1925, s 84 to discharge or modify restrictions on their property which provided that no trade
or business should be carried out on certain land or any building erected thereon. The use of the

premises as a school or boarding house was not forbidden. They contended that there had been a change in the residential character of the area as one neighbouring house was used commercially by a builder and another was used as a home for elderly people in breach of covenant. The applicants also argued that it was in the public interest that the proposed service should be provided by well qualified applicants in suitable premises. The objectors argued that although there was a potential demand for the proposed facilities, the applicants had not shown that the public interest required that the demand be met in that area, and contended that they would suffer substantial injury if the proposal was carried out. *Held*, the restrictions had not been rendered obsolete as they had preserved the essential character of the neighbourhood. However, the restrictions, in impeding what was a reasonable user of the property, were contrary to the public interest, as government policy relating to mental illness required the provision of care in the community. There was a desperate need for such a facility in the area and the premises were well located to answer that need. The owners were well qualified and able and willing to adapt the premises for that use. The restrictions did not confer a substantial benefit or advantage on the objectors, nor would the proposal cause injury. There was no evidence that the proposed use would be more or less objectionable than a school or boarding house, both of which were permitted. The restrictions would accordingly be modified to permit the proposed use.

Re Lloyd's and Lloyd's Application (1993) 66 P & CR 112 (Lands Tribunal: Judge Marder QC).

ESTOPPEL

Halsbury's Laws of England (4th edn) Vol 16 (reissue), paras 951–1091

1233 Estoppel by record—res judicata—foreign judgment—identity of causes of action in foreign and English proceedings

See *The Indian Endurance, Republic of India v India Steamship Co Ltd*, para 530.

1234 Estoppel by record—res judicata—issues available in former proceedings—personal injury action

The driver of a motor car and his passenger were injured in a road accident. The passenger sued the driver for damages, and the driver issued third party proceedings against the local highway authority claiming contribution to the passenger's claim but not claiming for his own injuries. The passenger also joined the highway authority as a defendant. Judgment was given in favour of the passenger against both the driver and the highway authority. The driver subsequently began proceedings against the highway authority in respect of his injuries. The judge at the hearing of a preliminary issue held that the driver was estopped from bringing his action but that there were special circumstances that took the case outside the doctrine of estoppel. On the appeal of the driver and the cross-appeal of the highway authority, *held*, the rule in *Henderson* that, except under special circumstances, a party may not in subsequent proceedings raise a ground of claim or defence which was open to him in the former proceedings, applied to personal injury actions. The driver's claim could have been included in the original third party notice issued against the highway authority or started by a separate writ and then consolidated. The third party proceedings could also have been amended to include the claim. The judge was therefore right to order that the claim be struck out unless there were special circumstances. However, he erred in finding that such special circumstances existed. Accordingly, the driver's appeal would be dismissed and the highway authority's cross-appeal would be allowed.

Talbot v Berkshire County Council [1993] 3 WLR 708 (Court of Appeal: Nourse, Stuart-Smith and Mann LJJ). *Henderson v Henderson* (1843) 3 Hare 100 applied.

1235 Issue estoppel—issues available in former action—demand for payment under guarantee not called in at date of original judgment

It has been held that the principle in *Henderson v Henderson* ((1843) 3 Hare 100), that a party to litigation will not be allowed after judgment, to re-open a point which should have been raised in the original proceedings, did not prevent a demand for payment being made under a guarantee which had not been called in at the date of the original judgment.

Duchess Theatre Co Ltd v Lord (1993) Times, 9 December (Court of Appeal: Balcombe, Stuart-Smith and Peter Gibson LJJ).

EUROPEAN COMMUNITIES

In conformity with the arrangement of titles in *Halsbury's Laws*, this title appears as the final title, on pages 767–790 post.

EVIDENCE [CIVIL]

Halsbury's Laws of England (4th edn) Vol 17, paras 1–400

1236 Articles
Evidence From Imagery, Geoffrey Oxlee (on the use of imagery derived evidence in court): 143 NLJ 915

1237 Criminal cases
See CRIMINAL EVIDENCE AND PROCEDURE.

1238 Expert evidence—application to adduce expert evidence—late application—refusal by court to grant leave
RSC Ord 38, r 36 provides that, except with the leave of the court or where all parties agree, no expert evidence may be adduced at a trial unless the party seeking to adduce the evidence has applied to the court to determine whether a direction ought to be given in respect of oral expert evidence or expert evidence contained in a statement.

The defendants to an action wished to adduce expert evidence and therefore took out a summons under Ord 38, r 36, three weeks before the trial date. The judge refused to grant the application and made an order debarring the defendants from calling experts in the forthcoming trial. On appeal, *held*, the hearing of the summons for directions was the appropriate time for considering expert evidence. Where an application for leave to adduce expert evidence was made at the last minute, so that no directions could be practicably made, the court had an inherent jurisdiction to dismiss the application. It was right to do so if, otherwise, an adjournment would have to be called to consider the evidence, thereby prejudicing the other party. In the present case, the defendants had to seek the leave of the trial judge to adduce their expert evidence, and it was then a matter for his discretion. Accordingly, the appeal would be dismissed.

Winchester Cigarette Machinery Ltd v Payne (1993) Times, 19 October (Court of Appeal: Rose and Hoffmann LJJ).

1239 Expert evidence—expert witnesses—duties and responsibilities
Cresswell J has set out the following guidelines for the duties and responsibilities of expert witnesses in civil cases: (1) expert evidence presented to the Court of Appeal should be, and should be seen to be, the independent product of the expert uninfluenced as to its form or content by the exigencies of litigation; (2) an expert witness should provide independent assistance to the court by way of objective unbiased opinion in relation to matters within his expertise, and an expert witness in the High Court should never assume the role of an advocate; (3) an expert witness should state the facts or assumption upon which his opinion is based, and should not omit to consider material facts which could detract from his concluded opinion; (4) an expert witness should make it clear when a particular question or issue falls outside his expertise; (5) if an expert's opinion is not properly researched because he considers that insufficient data is available, then this must be stated with an indication that the opinion is no more than a provisional one; (6) where an expert witness who has prepared a report could not assert that the report contained the truth, the whole truth and nothing but the truth without some qualification, that qualification should be stated in the report; (7) if, after the exchange of reports, an expert witness changes his view on a material matter having read the other party's expert report or for any other reason, such change of view should be communicated (through legal representatives) to the other party without delay and, when appropriate, to the court; (8) where expert evidence refers to photographs, plans, calculations, analyses, measurements, survey reports or other similar documents, these must be provided to the opposite party at the same time as the exchange of reports.

National Justice Compania Naviera SA v Prudential Assurance Co Ltd, The Ikarian Reefer [1993] 2 Lloyd's Rep 68 (Queen's Bench Division: Cresswell J).

1240 Expert evidence—opinion—handwriting—opinion based on photocopy of original document

A cheque, the proceeds of which were claimed by the appellant, was alleged by the appellant to have been wrongfully converted by the respondent. The respondent did not admit that he had signed and indorsed the cheque or that he had received the proceeds as alleged by the appellant. The latter wished to submit in evidence opinions of handwriting experts based on a comparison from a photocopy of the cheque which had been stolen from the safe in which it had been deposited by the appellant's solicitors. The respondent contended that such evidence should not be admitted because a photocopy would not reveal pressure marks, overwritten words or pen lifts. *Held,* the Criminal Procedure Act 1865, s 8, which allowed witnesses to make a comparison of a disputed writing with any writing proved to the judge's satisfaction to be genuine, and the submission to the court of the evidence of witnesses on such writings as evidence of the genuineness or otherwise of the writing in dispute, could accommodate an expression of opinion based on a facsimile of a disputed writing. The respondent's contentions related to the credibility of an opinion, not its admissiblity. The evidence in question, accordingly, would be admitted.

Lockheed-Arabia v Owen [1993] 3 All ER 641 (Court of Appeal: Ralph Gibson, Mann and Nolan LJJ).

1241 Expert evidence—personal injury action—employment consultant

See *Bird v Longridge,* para 2062.

1242 Hearsay—civil proceedings concerning upbringing, welfare and maintenance of children—abolition of hearsay rule

The Children (Admissibility of Hearsay Evidence) Order 1993, SI 1993/621 (in force on 5 April 1993), replaces the 1991 Order, SI 1991/1115. The 1993 Order reproduces the provisions of the earlier order, which dealt with the abolition of the hearsay rule in respect of evidence given in civil proceedings before the High Court, county courts and in certain magistrates' courts in connection with the upbringing, maintenance or welfare of a child, and extends those provisions to civil proceedings under the Child Support Act 1991 in magistrates' courts.

1243 Hearsay—Law Commission recommendations

The Law Commission has recommended the abolition of the rule excluding the admission of hearsay evidence in civil proceedings; see *The Hearsay Rule in Civil Proceedings* (Cm 2321; Law Com No 216). Except where rules of court otherwise state, parties intending to rely on hearsay evidence would be expected, where this was reasonable and appropriate, to give notice of the fact; but failure to give such notice would not render the evidence inadmissible although it might affect the weight to be given to it or be penalised in costs. There would be a power for a party whose evidence had been adduced as hearsay to be called and be cross-examined. Statutory guidelines would be provided to assist courts in assessing the weight to be given to hearsay evidence. Documents (including documents produced with the aid of computers) forming part of the records of a business would be admissible in evidence without the need for oral proof from a witness, provided that their authenticity was certified by an appropriate officer. The absence of an entry in the records of a business would be capable of proof by affidavit. A draft Bill which would give effect to the recommendations is appended to the report.

1244 Letter of request—request for production of documents—power to issue letter of request

The plaintiff recording artist entered into agreements in respect of his performances with a company which had subsequently been taken over by the defendant. The plaintiff later brought proceedings claiming that he was not bound by those agreements as they were an unlawful restraint of trade. In order to require a branch of the defendant's business in the United States to produce certain documents, the plaintiff applied to the court for the issue of a letter of request to a court in the United States seeking that court's assistance. The defendant contended that RSC Ord 39, r 2, while allowing an issue of a letter of request for the attendance of a person to be examined and to produce documents, it did not give jurisdiction for an English Court to issue a letter of request concerned only with the production of documents. *Held,* the court's power to issue a letter of request to the judicial authorities of a foreign company stemmed from the inherent jurisdiction of the court. When a letter of request was issued, the court was not making an order; it was doing no more than making a request to a foreign court for assistance. A direction would accordingly be made to issue a letter of request, although the letter of request

had to be confined to particular documents.
Panayiotou v Sony Music Entertainment (UK) Ltd [1993] 1 All ER 755 (Chancery Division:
Sir Donald Nicholls V-C).

1245   Oaths—fees

The Commissioners for Oaths (Fees) Order 1993, SI 1993/2297 (in force on 18 October 1993),
increases the fees chargeable by commissioners for oaths and practising solicitors for taking
affidavits and similar declarations from £3·50 to £5·00 and for marking exhibits from £1 to
£2. It replaces the Commissioner for Oaths (Fees) (No 2) Order 1988, SI 1988/998.

The Commissioners for Oaths (Authorised Persons) (Fees) Order 1993, SI 1993/2298 (in force
on 18 October 1993), prescribes the fees chargeable by authorised persons acting as commissioners
for oaths. The fees are £5 for taking affidavits and similar declarations, and £2 for marking
exhibits.

1246   "Without prejudice" negotiations—admission of impropriety

An exception to the general rule prohibiting admissions made in the course of negotiations for
a settlement being admitted in evidence, exists in cases where there has been an unambiguous
admission of impropriety during negotiations between the parties.
Alizadeh v Nibkin (1993) Times, 19 March (Court of Appeal: Balcombe and Simon Brown
LJJ and Peter Gibson J).

1247   "Without prejudice" negotiations—document outside scope of
negotiations—extent of privilege

The plaintiffs' solicitors wrote a letter before action to the defendants alleging that a television
programme broadcast by the defendants was defamatory. A writ was issued. Some months later
there was without prejudice correspondence between the parties with a view to settling the
action, but that proved inconclusive. The defendants' solicitors wrote to the plaintiffs' solicitors
two almost identical letters stating that the defendants wished to negotiate a compromise and
suggesting that the defendant make an apology and statement in open court. The first letter was
not headed, and made no reference to its being without prejudice, while the second was headed
'open letter', and both were clearly intended to be referred to by the defendants at trial. The
offer was not accepted by the plaintiffs and the matter came to trial in the course of which
counsel for the defendants sought to refer to the letters in cross-examination of one of the
plaintiffs' witnesses. The plaintiffs' counsel objected to the letters being admitted in evidence on
the ground that they were clearly written without prejudice as an offer to negotiate a settlement
and were therefore subject to privilege and were inadmissible without the consent of both
parties. On the defendants' application to put the letters in evidence, *held*, a party to an action
could write a letter containing an offer to settle the action without attracting to that letter any
privilege which could be claimed by the opposing party, provided the letter was not part of
continuing negotiations. However, if the letter was a reply to a letter written without prejudice
or was part of a continuing sequence of negotiations, whether by correspondence or orally, then
it would be privileged and could not be admitted in evidence without the consent of both
parties, it followed that since the letters were written after the negotiations and without prejudice
correspondence had finished and come to nothing, they were not subject to privilege and could
be used by the defendants in the course of the action without the consent of the plaintiffs. An
order would be granted accordingly
Dixons Stores Group Ltd v Thames Television plc [1993] 1 All ER 349 (Queen's Bench
Division: Drake J).

1248   "Without prejudice" negotiations—references to negotiations in statement
of claim—striking out

Canada
The plaintiff claimed against the defendant as the guarantor of a mortgage. The defendant
defaulted on the mortgage and the parties entered into a settlement agreement. Under the
agreement the defendant acknowledged his obligation under the guarantee and the plaintiff
agreed to release him from the claim upon payment of certain sums, but reserved the right to
pursue him if he defaulted under his covenants in the mortgage and "in this agreement". The
defendant defaulted and the plaintiff issued a statement of claim against him claiming the
amount owing under the terms of the mortgage. The defendant moved to strike out those

paragraphs in the statement of claim which referred to the settlement agreement, contending that they were subject to privilege under the "without prejudice" rule. *Held,* the "without prejudice" rule was founded on public policy. It precluded the admission into evidence of admissions made for the purpose, or during the course, of an attempt to reach a settlement, irrespective of whether a settlement was reached and of whether the admissions were contained in the pre-settlement negotiations or the settlement itself. Only where the parties expressly excluded the rule would it not apply and the reference to the defendant's covenants "in this agreement" was not sufficiently explicit to abrogate the operation of the rule. Privilege ceased to apply if the issue between the parties concerned either the existence, enforcement or interpretation of a settlement agreement, but here the plaintiff was merely relying on the agreement to assert rights under the original guarantee and so could not rely on one of the exceptions. The reference to the settlement agreement in the statement of claim would be struck out. Accordingly, the motion would be granted.

Sun Life Trust Co v Dewshi (1993) 99 DLR (4th) 232 (High Court of Ontario).

EXECUTION

Halsbury's Laws of England (4th edn) Vol 17, paras 401–700

1249   Stay of execution—stay pending appeal—appeal against determination of interim rent

See *Simonite v Sheffield City Council,* para 1621.

1250   Stay of execution—stay pending appeal—appeal against money judgment

A company was awarded a money judgment in their action against the defendants. The defendants applied for a stay of execution of the money judgment pending their appeal against it. *Held,* until recently, the practice of the court was based on the principle that the only ground for a stay of execution was the reasonable probability that damages and costs paid would not be repaid if the appeal succeeded. More recent cases had held that the court's approach was a matter of common sense and a balance of advantage. However, the court should give full and proper weight to the starting principle that there had to be a good reason to deprive a plaintiff from obtaining the fruits of a judgment. The applicants had not made out a good or sufficient reason and, accordingly, the application would be dismissed.

Winchester Cigarette Machinery Ltd v Payne (No 2) (1993) Times, 15 December (Court of Appeal: Ralph Gibson, McCowan and Hobhouse LJJ).

EXECUTORS AND ADMINISTRATORS

Halsbury's Laws of England (4th edn) Vol 17, paras 701–1591

1251   Family provision—application by widow—widow claiming reasonable financial provision not made by will

The plaintiff widow was the second wife of the deceased. They had no children, but the deceased had a son by his first marriage. A week before his death, the deceased gave his wife £15,000. In his will, he left two articles of furniture to his son, and the remainder of his chattels and a life interest in the residue of the estate to his wife. The trustees purchased a house for the wife's occupation, valued at £70,000. The total value of the estate in possession was £177,000 and there was an expectation valued at £90,000. The wife unsuccessfully sought the transfer to herself of the freehold of the house. The court rejected her contention that, under the Inheritance (Provision for Family and Dependants) Act 1975, the deceased had failed to make reasonable financial provision for her by the terms of his will. On appeal, *held,* by the provisions of the will and the actions of the trustees, the wife was rehoused and proper and adequate provision was made for her maintenance. She had accepted the adequacy of this maintenance and her case rested solely on the failure to provide an absolute interest in the house. The judge had clearly considered all the relevant circumstances set out in the 1975 Act, s 3 in reaching his decision. He had not made any error of principle in reaching his qualitative judgment and, accordingly, the appeal would be dismissed.

Re Davis (Deceased) [1993] 1 FCR 1002 (Court of Appeal: Sir Stephen Brown P, Stuart-Smith and Mann LJJ).

1252 Intestacy—surviving spouse's statutory legacy

The Family Provision (Intestate Succession) Order 1993, SI 1993/2906 (in force on 1 December 1993), replaces SI 1987/799 and increases the surviving spouse's statutory legacy on intestacy from £75,000 to £125,000 where the intestate is survived by issue and from £125,000 to £200,000 where there is no surviving issue but the intestate is survived by certain close relatives.

EXPLOSIVES

Halsbury's Laws of England (4th edn) Vol 18, paras 1–200

1253 Transfer of explosives—supervision

The Placing on the Market and Supervision of Transfers of Explosives Regulations 1993, SI 1993/2714 (in force on dates between 11 November 1993 and 1 January 1995), make provision with respect to the placing on the market and the supervision of transfers of explosives. The regulations prohibit any person from placing any explosives on the market unless they satisfy specified requirements. Provision is made in connection with the appointment by the Secretary of State of notified bodies for the purposes of the attestation procedure. A system for the supervision of the transfer of explosives is established, and provision is made with respect to the keeping of records in connection with transfers of explosives.

The regulations also make minor amendments to the Explosives Act 1875, and the Control of Explosives Regulations 1991, SI 1991/1531.

EXTRADITION AND FUGITIVE OFFENDERS

Halsbury's Laws of England (4th edn) Vol 18, paras 201–300

1254 European Convention on Extradition—fiscal offences

The European Convention on Extradition (Fiscal Offences) Order 1993, SI 1993/2663 (in force on a date to be notified in the London Gazette), gives effect to Chapter II of the Second Additional Protocol to the European Convention on Extradition, which removes the existing restriction on extradition under the Convention for fiscal offences. Extradition for a fiscal offence can take place between contracting parties which have accepted Chapter II, if the offence corresponds to an offence of the same nature under the law of the requested party.

1255 European Convention on Extradition—parties—Hungary and Poland

The European Convention on Extradition (Hungary and Poland) (Amendment) Order 1993, SI 1993/2667 (in force on 1 December 1993), amends the 1990 Order, SI 1990/1507, by adding Hungary and Poland to the list of parties to the European Convention on Extradition. It also has the effect of revoking the extradition treaties between the United Kingdom and Hungary and between the United Kingdom and Poland.

1256 Extradition crimes—committal order—evidence—jurisdiction of magistrate

The Extradition Act 1989, s 9(4) states that where an extradition request is made by a foreign state and an Order on Council is in force in relation to that state, there is no need to furnish a committal court with sufficient evidence to warrant the trial of the arrested person if the extradition crime took place within the jurisdiction of the court.

A magistrate had ruled that the applicant was not entitled to call evidence with regard to Swedish law and the applicant sought a discharge from a committal order and argued that the magistrate's ruling was wrong in law. *Held*, it was clear that the correct procedure under the Extradition act 1870, was for the magistrate to hear evidence if the arrested person wished to call such evidence. However under the 1989 Act, allowing a person to call evidence would frustrate the intention of Parliament because it would then be necessary for the foreign state which had requested the extradition to call evidence in rebuttal. The purpose of the European Convention on Extradition Order 1990, SI 1990/1507, was that the parties to the Convention accepted that the other states were capable of providing a fair trial for the person concerned with regard to resolving the issues of fact and applying the law of the state which requested the order. The functions of the committal court were: (1) to consider whether details of the conduct of the person in the foreign state amounted to an extradition crime. Conduct amounted to an extradition crime if, had it occurred in the United Kingdom, it would be an offence in the United Kingdom. The magistrate who had knowledge of the criminal law in England and Wales was the proper person to decide such a matter. (2) The magistrate had to be satisfied that the punishment for the offence was 12 months' imprisonment or some greater punishment. (3) The magistrate also had to be satisfied that the punishment under foreign law was 12 months' imprisonment or more and to decide this he would have the legal description of the alleged conduct, the relevant legal provisions and a copy of the relevant enactments, or a statement of the relevant law. In a case where the Convention applied, if the magistrate admitted evidence on behalf of the person, he would be examining the adequacy of the evidence and this would be beyond his powers. Accordingly, the application would be dismissed.

R v Governor of Brixton Prison, ex p Evans (1993) Times, 10 December (Queen's Bench Division: Roch LJ and Sedley J).

The applicant faced extradition proceedings relating to a murder allegedly committed by him in Hong Kong. He requested that the proceedings be adjourned so he could call expert evidence to the effect that, following the transfer of Hong Kong's sovereignty to the People's Republic of China, it was highly likely that he would face the death sentence if convicted. The magistrate refused, and the applicant sought a writ of habeas corpus under the Extradition Act 1989. He also made a renewed application for judicial review, contending that the magistrate's failure to take account of the expert evidence meant that the magistrate had merely applied a rubber stamp to the Hong Kong government's request for extradition. *Held*, the 1989 Act provided that the state requesting extradition was the sole arbiter of what material to put before the court and the Secretary of State in support of its application. That state therefore took the risk that its request for extradition would be refused if the material was inadequate, but if it did provide sufficient material the committing magistrate did not have the power to go beyond that material and consider extraneous matters. It had to be remembered that the magistrate committed the applicant to await the decision of the Secretary of State, who could consider any political dimensions to the extradition request, but the magistrate had no power to consider such matters and he had been correct to treat them as irrelevant to his decision. Accordingly, the appeal would be dismissed.

R v Governor of Pentonville Prison, ex p Lee; R v Bow Street Metropolitan Stipendiary Magistrate, ex p Lee [1993] 3 All ER 504 (Queen's Bench Division: Watkins LJ and Ognall J).

1257 Extradition proceedings—extradition—extension of categories

The Extradition (Hijacking) (Amendment) Order 1993, SI 1993/1574 (in force on 27 July 1993), amends the 1992 Order, SI 1992/3200, by substituting a reference to the Extradition Act 1989, s 22(4)(b) for a reference to the 1989 Act, s 22(4)(g) where it appears in the 1992 Order, Pt II, Sch 4, para 1(a).

1258 Extradition proceedings—extradition crime—specification of offences

The Extradition Act 1989, s 7(5) provides that an authority to proceed must specify the offence or offences under the law of the United Kingdom which it appears to the Secretary of State would be constituted by equivalent conduct in the United Kingdom.

The Norwegian government requested the extradition of the applicant from the United Kingdom in order to face charges alleging that he supplied cocaine to another while in Norway. The applicant challenged the request by way of habeus corpus. On the question of the requirements of an authority to proceed, *held*, the Extradition Act 1989, s 7(5) required only the specification of the offences and not the particular statutory provision creating the offences under United Kingdom law which in the Home Secretary's opinion would be constituted by equivalent conduct in the United Kingdom. The guidance given in *Government of the United States of America v Bowe* [1989] 3 All ER 315, PC (1989 Abr para 941) applied to the present

case. Accordingly the application would be dismissed.
Re Farinha (1993) Times, 3 May (Queen's Bench Division: Lloyd LJ and Blofeld J). For earlier related proceedings, see [1992] Imm AR 174, DC (1991 Abr para 1132).

1259   Suppression of terrorism—designated countries
The Suppression of Terrorism Act 1978 (Application of Provisions) (India) Order 1993, SI 1993/2533 (in force on a date to be notified in the London Gazette), applies the 1978 Act and the Extradition Act 1989, s 24(1)(a), (2)(a) in relation to India. The offences listed in the 1978 Act, Sch 1 are not to be regarded as offences of a political character in relation to a request for the extradition of a person to India made after the order comes into force.

FAMILY ARRANGEMENTS, UNDUE INFLUENCE AND VOIDABLE CONVEYANCES

Halsbury's Laws of England (4th edn) Vol 18, paras 301–400

1260   Articles
Housekeepers, Companions and Family Provision—A Comparative Interlude, Frank Bates: [1993] Conv 270
Matrimonial Homes and Guarantees, HW Wilkinson: 143 NLJ 1723
Victory Roles, Nigel Clayton and Paul Brimelow (on *CIBC Mortgages plc v Pitt* (1993) Times, 7 April (para 1827)): LS Gaz, 3 November 1993, p 19
Who Dares Loses, Nigel Clayton and Paul Brimelow (on *CIBC Mortgages plc v Pitt* (1993) Times, 7 April, CA (para 1827): LS Gaz, 15 September 1993, p 20

1261   Family arrangement—variation of disposition—identity of settlor
See *Marshall (inspector of Taxes) v Kerr*, para 284.

1262   Family provision—application under Inheritance (Provision for Family and Dependants) Act 1975
See EXECUTORS AND ADMINISTRATORS.

FINANCIAL SERVICES

1263   Articles
A Question of Status, Derek Wheatley (on the system of enquiries between bankers): 143 NLJ 1448
Auditors' Liability—Dangerously Exposed or Immune from Suit? Jonathan Davies: (1993) 8 JIBFL 311
City Comment, Nicholas Sayers (on the changes to the Yellow Book): LS Gaz, 8 September 1993, p 26
Deception on the Dotted Line, Elizabeth Palmer (on the sales representatives of finance companies): 143 NLJ 1400
Emergent Trends in Bank Supervision in the United Kingdom, Ken McGuire: 56 MLR 669
Financial Instruments—Into the Limelight, Roger Muray: Tax Journal, Issue 227, p 6
Jersey Finance Companies, Jon Bourne: Tax Journal, Issue 228, p 14
Managing Shares at Arm's Length, Gil Brazier (on the Financial Services Act 1986): LS Gaz, 28 July 1993, p 20
Rethinking Subordinated Debt, John R Powell: [1993] 3 LMCLQ 357
Taxation of Lloyd's Names, Rod Gautrey: Tax Journal, Issue 233, p 4
The New Insider Dealing Regime, Robert Finney: (1993) 11 JIBFL 525
United Kingdom Finance Companies, Jon Bourne: Tax Journal, Issue 233, p 7

1264 Disclosure of information—designated authorities

The Financial Services (Disclosure of Information) (Designated Authorities) (No 7) Order 1993, SI 1993/1826 (in force on 16 August 1993), designates a person authorised by the Secretary of State under the Companies Act 1985, s 245C (application by an authorised person to the court for a declaration that the annual accounts of a company do not comply with the requirements of the 1985 Act) as an authority in relation to his function in securing compliance by companies with the accounting requirements of the 1985 Act for the purposes of the 1985 Act, s 449(1B), the Financial Services Act 1986, s 180(3) and the Companies Act 1989, s 87. The designation permits the disclosure of information which would otherwise be restricted if the disclosure is for the purpose of enabling or assisting the designated authority to discharge the specified functions.

1265 Investment firms and credit institutions—capital adequacy

See para 2727.

1266 Investment services—securities—investment firms—authorisation

See para 2728.

1267 Investors' Compensation Scheme—claims for compensation—rights of personal representatives

As a result of entering into home income plans with investment brokers the applicants suffered losses. They had been persuaded to enter into the plans in contravention of the rules governing the conduct of financial advisers and thus the brokers were exposed to actions for damages under the Financial Services Act 1986. The brokers were worthless and in default. The applicants sought compensation under the Investors Compensation Scheme (ICS), set up under the 1986 Act. The applicants sought judicial review of the ICS board's decision relating to the quantification of compensation under the rules and its decision not to entertain claims made by the personal representatives of a deceased investor. *Held*, matters of judgment by the board of the ICS in respect of claims by investors who had entered into home income plans with authorised brokers would only be impugned if the judgment was clearly irrational. Since the scheme was designed for small investors who would have regarded their savings as a benefit for their family, their death ought not to adversely effect their inheritance. On the default of an authorised person, an eligible investor had, under the rules of the ICS, both the right or power to apply for compensation and a legitimate expectation that his application would be determined. On an investor's death his right or power and his expectation were a right and an expectation which were transferable to his personal representatives. Accordingly, a declaration to this effect would be granted.

    R v Investors' Compensation Scheme Ltd, ex p Bowden [1994] 1 All ER 525 (Queen's Bench Division: Mann LJ and Tuckey J).

1268 Investors' Compensation Scheme—right to compensation—operative date of scheme

The applicants were advised by financial brokers to take out home income plans. As a result the applicants incurred substantial losses and applied for compensation under the Investors' Compensation Scheme Ltd (ICS), enacted under the Financial Services Act 1986, s 54, on the ground that the brokers, in advising the applicants to enter into the plans, carrying out the necessary transactions and acting thereafter as discretionary fund managers, acted negligently and in breach of contract and of the Financial Intermediaries, Managers and Brokers' Regulatory Association Ltd (Fimbra) rules. The ICS accepted that the brokers were liable but it refused to compensate the applicants on the ground that they had entered into the plans before the brokers' participation date when the ICS came into being. Therefore the relevant breach of the rules, namely the bad advice to enter the plans, occurred before the compensation scheme took effect, so the claims were not scheme business claims within the Financial Services (Compensation of Investors) Rules 1990, r 2.02(2)(b). The applicants, two of whom were applying as personal representatives of their respective spouses, applied for judicial review of the decision. *Held*, the brokers' liability arose not only when the original bad advice was given but also when thereafter, the brokers failed to correct that bad advice, to manage the plans according to Fimbra rules or to warn the applicants of the inherent risks. Even though they had first entered into the plans before the compensation scheme came into effect the applicants would be entitled to compensation under the 1990 Rules. Further, the 1990 Rules, r 2.02 did not preclude an investor's right to claim being transmitted to his or her personal representative. Accordingly, the applications would be granted.

R v Investors' Compensation Scheme Ltd, ex p Weyell (1993) Independent, 22 July (Queen's Bench Division: Glidewell LJ and Cresswell J).

1269 Money laundering—prevention

See para 175.

1270 Overseas investment exchanges and clearing houses—fees

The Financial Services Act 1986 (Overseas Investment Exchanges and Overseas Clearing Houses) (Periodical Fees) Regulations 1993, SI 1993/954 (in force on 10 May 1993), prescribe that overseas investment exchanges and overseas clearing houses recognised under the Financial Services Act 1986 must pay periodical fees of £8,000. The first such fee is payable on the date the exchange or clearing house is recognised and each subsequent fee is payable at the end of each successive period of 12 months. The 1987 Regulations, SI 1987/2143, are revoked.

1271 Securities and Investments Board—enforcement functions—Mareva injunction—requirement for cross-undertaking

The Securities and Investments Board (SIB) sought to restrain various breaches of the Financial Services Act 1986 by the defendants. The provisions under which the alleged breaches occurred were enforceable by injunctions pursuant to the 1986 Act, ss 6 and 61 under powers granted to the Secretary of State and delegated by him to the SIB. A worldwide Mareva injunction was granted against the defendants. On the question of whether the SIB were required to give a cross-undertaking in damages to the defendants in respect of the injunction, *held*, the 1986 Act, ss 6 and 61 conferred jurisdiction to make monetary judgements to provide restitution for those who suffered losses or to obtain from persons who infringed the provisions of the 1986 Act the profits wrongfully made, in addition to the power to apply for injunctions. The former remedies were provided by statute for the benefit of the public at large or for those who had suffered from infringement of the Act, and were as much law enforcement as the grant of an interlocutory injunction. Although a worldwide Mareva injunction was a draconian remedy, this reflected the fact that the activities of the defendant were worldwide and did not prevent the grant of the injunction being law enforcement. The 1986 Act, s 187(3) did not prevent the court from requiring a cross-undertaking in damages, but it was a clear pointer in the exercise of the court's discretion that no such cross-undertaking would be required where the designated agency was seeking to discharge functions exercisable pursuant to a delegation under the 1986 Act. In the circumstances, a cross-undertaking from the SIB would not be required.

Securities and Investments Board v Lloyd-Wright [1993] 4 All ER 210 (Chancery Division: Morritt J).

FIRE SERVICES

Halsbury's Laws of England (4th edn) Vol 18, paras 401–600

1272 Appointment and promotion

The Fire Services (Appointments and Promotion) (Amendment) Regulations 1993, SI 1993/2946 (in force on 1 January 1994), amend the 1978 regulations, SI 1978/436 and introduce revised practical examinations for promotion in a fire brigade to the ranks of leading firefighter and sub-officer. The Regulations also make a transitional provision with regard to certain provisions relating to eligibility to enter a practical examination, which operate by reference to non-attendance at the examination in question in the previous year.

1273 Fire and civil defence authorities—transfer of functions

See para 2648.

1274 Pensions

See para 1928.

FISHERIES

Halsbury's Laws of England (4th edn) Vol 18, paras 601–1000

1275　Fish health—movement documents

The Fish Health (Amendment) Regulations 1993, SI 1993/2255 (in force on 11 October 1993), amend the 1992 Regulations, SI 1992/3300, so as to provide alternative movement documents for molluscs and require an additional movement document for species of carp. In addition, the regulations provide that a movement document which has been incorrectly issued is not a valid movement document.

1276　Fishing vessels—decommissioning grants

The Fishing Vessels (Decommissioning) Scheme 1993, SI 1993/1345 (in force on 27 May 1993), provides for the making of grants by the Minister of Agriculture, Fisheries and Food in respect of the decommissioning of fishing vessels registered in the United Kingdom. Applications for grants must be in accordance with certain conditions and provision is made for the recovery of grants in specified circumstances.

1277　Fishing vessels—safety improvements

The Fishing Vessels (Safety Improvements) (Grants) Scheme 1993, SI 1993/1325 (in force on 22 May 1993), enables grants towards expenditure, incurred in making essential safety improvements to vessels registered in the United Kingdom and engaged or to be engaged in catching sea fish, to be made by the Minister of Agriculture, Fisheries and Food and the Secretary of State concerned with the sea fish industry. The regulations specify the rates of grant and make provision for the recovery of grant paid in certain circumstances.

1278　Sea fishing—Community provisions—enforcement

The Sea Fishing (Enforcement of Community Control Measures) Order 1993, SI 1993/2016 (in force on 1 September 1993), consolidates the 1985 Order, SI 1985/487, as amended, which makes provision for the enforcement of certain of the enforceable Community restrictions and other obligations relating to sea fishing set out in Council Regulation (EC) 2241/87 establishing certain control measures for fishing activities and Commission Regulation (EC) 2807/83 laying down detailed rules for recording information on member states' catches of fish.

The Third Country Fishing (Enforcement) Order 1993, SI 1993/1197 (in force on 5 May 1993), makes breaches of certain specified articles of European Community regulations offences for the purposes of United Kingdom law where they occur within British fishery limits. The Community regulations in question lay down certain measures for the conservation and management of fishery resources applicable to vessels of third countries, namely Norway, Sweden and the Faroe Islands. The offences arise out of breaches of the regulations concerning methods of fishing, the holding of licences, the keeping of log books and the making of radio reports. Powers of enforcement are conferred on British sea-fishery officers. In addition, the order makes provision for the punishment of any person found guilty of obstructing or assaulting an officer. SI 1991/522 is revoked.

1279　Sea fishing—conservation measures—undersized lobsters

The Undersized Lobsters Order 1993, SI 1993/1178 (in force on 20 May 1993), (1) prescribes a minimum size for the landing of lobsters in Great Britain; (2) prescribes a minimum size for the sale of lobsters and for the carriage of lobsters on a British fishing boat; (3) provides for an exemption from the minimum landing size and the minimum sale size for lobsters which are landed from foreign boats; and (4) gives British sea-fishery officers further enforcement powers (in addition to the powers they already have by virtue of the Sea Fish (Conservation) Act 1967, s 15(2), as amended) in relation to fishing boats.

1280　Sea fishing—licensing

The Sea Fish Licensing (Variation) Order 1993, SI 1993/188 (in force on 1 May 1993), removes the exceptions in the 1992 Order, SI 1992/2633, which applied in the fishing by handline for mackerel and fishing by boats whose length did not exceed 10 metres. The order also extends the exception in the 1992 Order which applied to boats used for the purpose of conveying persons wishing to fish for pleasure with rod and line or by handline so that it applies regardless of the method of fishing.

The Sea Fish Licensing (Variation) (No 2) Order 1993, SI 1993/2291 (in force on 12 October 1993), further varies the 1992 Order supra, by adding two exceptions, in respect of fishing for common eels and fishing by a new boat which does not have an engine to power it, in the case of boats whose length does not exceed 12 metres.

The Sea Fish Licensing (Time at Sea) (Principles) Order 1993, SI 1993/1196 (in force on 5 May 1993), sets out principles on which the time that certain fishing boats may spend at sea is to be arrived at for the purpose of any condition included in a licence under the Sea Fish (Conservation) Act 1967, s 4 as amended. The order, which applies to fishing boats exceeding 10 metres in overall length, sets out the principles applicable in arriving at the initial allocation of time at sea in respect of a vessel in a period not exceeding 12 consecutive months. The minimum allocation for these purposes is 160 half-days. The order provides, subject to the minimum allocation, for a basic allocation based on half-days spent at sea by the vessel in a specified year. The basic allocation may be increased to take account of a variety of circumstances specified in the order. In addition, the order sets out the principles applicable in arriving at subsequent allocations of time at sea in respect of a vessel.

1281 Sea fishing—local fisheries committees—fees for copy of byelaws
The Local Fisheries Committees (Fees for Copy Byelaws) Order 1993, SI 1993/1116 (in force on 21 May 1993), amends the Sea Fisheries Regulation Act 1966, s 9(1) in order to dispense with the provision for payment of a sum not exceeding one penny to local fisheries committees for supplying a copy of their byelaws.

1282 Sea fishing—prohibition
The Cod (Irish Sea) (Prohibition of Fishing) Order 1993, SI 1993/1212 (in force on 7 May 1993), prohibits, until 1 January 1994, fishing for cod in a specified sea area by British boats which are registered in the United Kingdom. British boats which are registered in the Isle of Man or the Channel Islands, or which are British-owned, are prohibited from fishing within any part of that sea area which is within British fishery limits. The provisions do not normally apply to boats which are more than 10 metres in length. For enforcement purposes, British sea-fishery officers are given certain powers. The following orders are revoked: SI 1991/1163, 1473, 2085, 2593, 2806, 2849.

The Norway Lobsters (Prohibition of Method of Fishing) Order 1993, SI 1993/1887 (in force on 22 August 1993), prohibits, subject to exceptions, fishing for Norway lobsters anywhere, except on the Fladen Ground, by British fishing boats registered in the United Kingdom with any trawl other than a single trawl. The prohibition does not apply to beam trawlers or to fishing with a trawl having a specified minimum mesh size in certain specified areas. The order gives British sea-fishery officers certain enforcement powers. Offences and penalties are prescribed by the Sea Fish (Conservation) Act 1967.

The Sole (Specified Sea Areas) (Prohibition of Fishing) Order 1993, SI 1993/2459 (in force on 14 October 1993), prohibits, until 1 January 1994, fishing for sole in a specified sea area by British boats which are registered in the United Kingdom. British boats which are registered in the Isle of Man or the Channel Islands, or which are British-owned, are prohibited from fishing within any part of that sea area which is within British fishery limits. The provisions do not apply to fishing by boats registered in the United Kingdom within that part of the sea area ICES Statistical Division Vb which lies outside British sea fishery limits. For the purpose of the enforcement of the order, British sea-fishery officers are given certain enforcement powers.

The Sole (Specified Sea Areas) (Prohibition of Fishing) (No 2) Order 1993, SI 1993/2465 (in force on 14 October 1993), prohibits, until 1 January 1994, fishing for sole in a specified sea area by British boats which are registered in the United Kingdom. British boats which are registered in the Isle of Man or the Channel Islands, or which are British-owned, are prohibited from fishing within any part of that sea area which is within British fishery limits. The provisions do not normally apply to boats which are more than 10 metres in length. For the purpose of the enforcement of the order, British sea-fishery officers are given certain enforcement powers. The

Sole (Eastern English Channel) (Prohibition of Fishing) Order 1992, SI 1992/1756, the Haddock and Hake (Specified Sea Areas) (Prohibition of Fishing) Order 1992, SI 1992/3262, and the Sole (Specified Sea Areas) (Prohibition of Fishing) Order 1992, SI 1992/3266, are revoked.

The Herring (Specified Sea Areas) (Prohibition of Fishing) Order 1993, SI 1993/3063 (in force on 9 December 1993), prohibits until 1 January 1994, fishing for herring in a specified sea area by British boats which are registered in the United Kingdom. British boats which are registered in the Isle of Man or any of the Channel Islands, or which are British-owned, are prohibited from fishing within any part of the sea area which is within British fishery limits. The provisions do not apply to boats registered in the United Kingdom within that part of the sea area ICES Statistical Division IIa which lies outside British fishery limits.

The Haddock, Hake, Nephrops, Plaice and Sole (Specified Sea Areas) (Prohibition of Fishing) Order 1993, SI 1993/3193 (in force on 21 December 1993), prohibits, until 1 January 1994, fishing for haddock, hake, nephrops, plaice and sole in a specified sea area by British boats which are registered in the United Kingdom. British boats which are registered in the Isle of Man or the Channel Islands, or which are British-owned, are prohibited from fishing within any part of that sea area which is within British fishery limits. The provisions do not normally apply to boats which are more than 10 metres in length. For the purpose of the enforcement of the order, British sea-fishery officers are given certain enforcement powers.

The Cod and Saithe (Specified Sea Areas) (Prohibition of Fishing) Order 1993, SI 1993/3192 (in force on 21 December 1993), prohibits, until 1 January 1994, fishing for cod or saithe in a specified sea area by British boats which are registered in the United Kingdom. British boats which are registered in the Isle of Man or the Channel Islands, or which are British-owned, are prohibited from fishing within any part of that sea area which is within British fishery limits. The provisions do not normally apply to boats which are more than 10 metres in length. For the purpose of the enforcement of the order, British sea-fishery officers are given certain enforcement powers.

1283   Sea fishing—quotas—enforcement

The Sea Fishing (Enforcement of Community Quota Measures) Order 1993, SI 1993/387 (in force on 27 February 1993), revokes the 1992 Order, SI 1992/190. Provision is made for the enforcement of Council Regulation (EC) 3919/92, which lays down total allowable catches and quotas for 1993. Breaches of the provisions may result in the forfeiture of catches, nets and other fishing gear. Obstructing or assaulting an enforcing officer is punishable by the imposition of a fine.

1284   Seals—conservation

The Conservation of Seals (England) Order 1993, SI 1993/2876 (in force on 19 December 1993), replaces the 1990 Order, SI 1990/2500. The order prohibits for three years, with effect from 19 December 1993, the killing, injuring or taking of grey seals in counties of England bordering the North Sea and adjacent territorial waters.

FOOD, DAIRIES AND SLAUGHTERHOUSES

Halsbury's Laws of England (4th edn) Vol 18, paras 1001–1400

1285   Articles

A Matter of Prejudice, Julian Gibbons: 143 NLJ 575
Food Claims, Richard Lawson: 143 NLJ 520
Food Hygiene Law: the Key Issues, Jeremy Stranks: 137 SJ 452

1286   Dairy produce—quotas

The Dairy Produce Quotas Regulations 1993, SI 1993/923 (in force on 1 April 1993), revoke and replace the 1991 Regulations, SI 1991/2232. The regulations establish an additional levy in the milk and milk products sector and provide that a levy continues to be payable on dairy produce sold by direct sale by a producer or delivered by him wholesale to a dairy business. Other changes of substance include the introduction of a provision whereby member states can choose between collecting the levy through purchasers of dairy produce and calculating it by reference to individual purchasers, and producers who are in a position to make wholesale deliveries must be registered.

The Dairy Produce Quotas (Amendment) Regulations 1993, SI 1993/3234 (in force on 24 December 1993), amend the 1993 Regulations, SI 1993/923 and implement Council Regulation (EC) 2187/93. The regulations expand the definition of "Community legislation" and provide that the minister may withhold or recover compensation where a producer has made a false or misleading statement in his application for compensation or has failed to comply with relevant Community rules.

1287   Food—labelling

The Food Labelling (Amendment) Regulations 1993, SI 1993/2759 (in force on 29 November 1993), further amend the 1984 Regulations, 1984/1305 by removing from Schedule 7 the entries relating to shandy, shandygaff, ginger beer shandy, cider shandy, cider shandygaff and cider and ginger beer shandy.

1288   Food—labelling—emulsifiers and stabilisers

The Emulsifiers and Stabilisers in Food Regulations 1993, SI 1993/1161 (in force on 31 May 1993), further amend the 1989 Regulations, SI 1989/876, by introducing new purity criteria for sucrose esters of fatty acids.

1289   Food—labelling—medicinal claim

A company advertised their oat product in a national newspaper and claimed that it helped reduce excess cholesterol levels, cutting down the risk of heart disease. The advertisement also contained a book offer and invited readers to find out how the oats were a key to preventing heart disease. A council laid an information contending that the advertisement constituted a medicinal claim about a food and, since no product licence had been issued in respect of the product, breached the Food Labelling Regulations 1984, SI 1984/1305, reg 36(2). The company successfully contended that the advertisement was actually two in one, the main body of which merely suggested that heart disease could be reduced whilst the reference to prevention was confined to the book offer and was simply an invitation to find out more, and that any ambiguity should be resolved in their favour. On appeal, *held*, this was one advertisement. The book offer was a subsidiary part of the whole and the preventative claims related directly to the advertisement for the oats and were not merely part of an invitation to find out more. Further, the claim that the product cut down the risk of heart disease was an express or implied claim that the product prevented heart disease. The company had made medicinal claims contrary to the 1984 Regulations and, accordingly, the appeal would be allowed.

Cheshire County Council v Mornflake Oats Ltd (1993) 157 JP 1011 (Queen's Bench Division: Kennedy LJ and Clarke J).

1290   Food hygiene—enforcement—continuing offences

The council discovered offences contrary to the Food Hygiene (General) Regulations 1970, SI 1970/1172, at certain premises. The owners assured the council that they would comply with the regulations and undertake the necessary remedial works. At a later inspection, the council discovered further offences under the 1970 Regulations and laid an information against the owners in respect of the offences. The stipendiary magistrate found that the offences alleged in the information were discovered on the first inspection and had become statute-barred under the Food Act 1984, s 95(1)(b), replicated by the Food Safety Act 1990, s 34(b). The council applied for judicial review of his refusal to state a case for the High Court. *Held*, the stipendiary magistrate had misconstrued the 1984 Act, s 95(1)(b). The relevant offences were continuing offences, and were committed afresh each day that the 1970 Regulations were breached. Although the council had discovered offences on the date of the first inspection, the decision to prosecute was made in relation to the continuing offences discovered on the subsequent inspection. Thus the 1970 Regulations, reg 30, which penalised continuing offences against the 1970 Regulations applied. Accordingly, the application would be allowed.

R v Thames Metropolitan Stipendiary Magistrate, ex p Hackney London Borough Council (1993) Times, 10 November (Queen's Bench Division: Simon Brown LJ and Buckley J).

1291 Food hygiene—licensing of premises—farmed game meat—charges

The Farmed Game Meat (Hygiene and Inspection) (Charges) Regulations 1993, SI 1993/1359 (in force on 25 June 1993), provide for local authorities to make a charge for every health inspection and control exercise carried out by them in respect of farmed game meat at a slaughterhouse, cutting premises, cold store, farmed game handling facility or farmed game processing facility. Before making a charge for a health inspection and control exercise under the regulations, a local authority is required to notify the occupier of the premises to be charged and consider any representations made to it by the notified person. If the occupier considers that the authority has determined an amount which is excessively high the occupier may appeal to the appropriate minister who may recalculate the amount of the charge.

1292 Food hygiene—licensing of premises—poultry

The Poultry Meat (Hygiene) (Amendment) Regulations 1993, SI 1993/209 (in force on 5 March 1993), further amend SI 1976/1209 in order to correct a drafting error in the amending SI 1992/2036 (reference to a "local authority" not to a "food authority"), which is consequentially partially revoked.

1293 Food hygiene—measures necessary to secure safety and wholesomeness of foodstuffs—Community Directive

See para 2693.

1294 Food hygiene—registration of premises—exemption for child minders

The Food Premises (Registration) Amendment Regulations 1993, SI 1993/2022 (in force on 1 September 1993), amend the 1991 Regulations, SI 1991/2825, to exempt certain domestic premises used for child minding from the requirement in the 1991 Regulations to register food premises. An additional exception is created in relation to domestic premises used for the purposes of a food business, on which the proprietor of the business resides and on which the only commercial food operations are the sale of food ancillary to the proprietor's activities as a child minder.

1295 Food premises—registration—Welsh form of application

The Food Premises (Registration) (Welsh Form of Application) Regulations 1993, SI 1993/1270 (in force on 11 June 1993), prescribe, pursuant to the Food Premises (Registration) Regulations 1991, SI 1991/2825, a Welsh version of the form to be used in connection with an application for the registration of food premises. The Welsh version may only be used in respect of applications for the registration of food premises which are in Wales.

1296 Food production—extraction solvents—regulations

The Extraction Solvents in Food Regulations 1993, SI 1993/1658 (in force on 29 July 1993), implement the provisions of Council Directive EC 88/344, as amended, on the approximation of the laws of the member states on extraction solvents used in the production of foodstuffs and food ingredients.

1297 Food safety—contaminants in food—Community procedure

See para 2692.

1298 Food safety—egg products

The Egg Products Regulations 1993, SI 1993/1520 (in force on 14 June 1993), make provision for the preparation and manufacture of egg products used in food intended for sale for human consumption, including the process of pasteurisation, and prohibit the manufacture of egg products otherwise than in an approved establishment.

1299 Food Safety Act 1990—code of practice—food hazard warnings

The Ministry of Agriculture, Fisheries and Food, and the Secretaries of State for Scotland, for Wales and for Health have issued code of practice 16 under the Food Safety Act 1990, *Enforcement of the Food Safety Act 1990 in Relation to the Food Hazard Warning System*. The code advises food authorities of the action which should be taken if a potential national or regional problem arises in their area. It also describes the action to be taken by central government departments. The classification of notifications issued by the latter is described (category A, immediate action; category B, for information and suggested action; category C, for information and action as deemed necessary; and category D, for information only). Guidance is given in the code to food authorities on the action to be taken locally on receipt of a food hazard warning or an emergency control order.

1300 Meat—fresh meat and meat products—examination for residues

The Animals, Meat and Meat Products (Examination for Residues and Maximum Residue Limits) (Amendment) Regulations 1993, SI 1993/990 (in force on 5 May 1993), amend the 1991 Regulations, SI 1991/2843, by adding six substances to the list of substances in respect of which maximum residue limits are prescribed. The regulations also permit the administration to an animal of vaccines, toxins or serums for specified purposes, and require a record to be kept within 72 hours of the administration of a veterinary medicinal product to an animal or of the slaughter of an animal.

1301 Meat—inspection—charges

The Fresh Meat and Poultry Meat (Hygiene, Inspection and Examinations for Residues) (Charges) (Amendment) Regulations 1993, SI 1993/1360 (in force on 25 June 1993), further amend the 1990 Regulations, SI 1990/2494, by introducing an upper limit on the amount which a food authority may charge in relation to health inspection and control exercises carried out at a slaughterhouse. The regulations also define the term "livestock unit".

1302 Soft drinks

The Soft Drinks (Amendment) Regulations 1993, SI 1993/1240 (in force in part on 1 June 1993, and in part on 1 January 1994), amend the 1964 Regulations by removing the minimum sugar composition requirements. The higher maximum permitted quantities of saccharin for soft drinks for consumption after dilution other than semi-sweet soft drinks continue to apply, until 1 January 1994, provided that such soft drinks contain not less than 22·5 pounds of sugar per 10 gallons.

1303 Welfare foods

See SOCIAL SECURITY AND SOCIAL SERVICES.

FOREIGN RELATIONS LAW

Halsbury's Laws of England (4th edn) Vol 18, paras 1401–1908

1304 Asylum

See BRITISH NATIONALITY, IMMIGRATION AND RACE RELATIONS.

1305 Consular fees—entry visa

The Consular Fees (Amendment) Order 1993, SI 1993/1781 (in force on 22 July 1993), further amends the 1989 Order, SI 1989/152, by specifying a fee of £10 for persons under 25 years of age and £20 for persons 25 years of age and over for a visa for passing through the United Kingdom without entering it.

1306 European Communities

See EUROPEAN COMMUNITIES.

1307 Human rights

See HUMAN RIGHTS.

1308   International Court of Justice—jurisdiction—order against genocide

In a suit initiated by Bosnia-Herzegovina under the Convention on the Prevention and Punishment of the Crime of Genocide concluded by the United Nations in 1948, Bosnia-Herzegovina claimed that acts of genocide had been committed and would continue to be committed against in particular, its Muslim inhabitants. It was submitted that Yugoslavia was committing acts of genocide, both directly and by means of its agents and surrogates. Yugoslavia observed that the situation was not one of aggression by one state against another, but a civil war and that Yugoslavia had not committed any acts of genocide and requested that the responsibility of the authorities of Bosnia-Herzegovina for acts of genocide against the Serb people in Bosnia-Herzegovina be established. *Held,* whether or not any acts of genocide had been committed in the past, Yugoslavia and Bosnia-Herzegovina were under an obligation to do all in their power to prevent the commission of any such acts in the future. Taking into account the obligation imposed by the 1948 Convention, art 1, the court was satisfied that there was a grave risk of action being taken which might aggravate the existing dispute. The decision in these proceedings in no way prejudiced the question of the jurisdiction of the court to deal with the merits of the case or any questions relating to the merits themselves, and left unaffected the right of the governments of Bosnia-Herzegovina and Yugoslavia to submit arguments in respect of such jurisdiction. The government of the Federal Republic of Yugoslavia (Serbia and Montenegro) should immediately take all measures to prevent the commission of genocide; in particular it should ensure that any military, paramilitary or irregular armed units directed or supported by it and organisations and persons subject to its control, did not commit any acts of genocide against any national, ethnic or religious group.

Bosnia-Herzegovina v Yugoslavia (Serbia and Montenegro) (1993) Times, 3 May (International Court of Justice).

1309   International organisations—Asian Development Bank

The Asian Development Bank (Fifth Replenishment of the Asian Development Fund and Second Regularized Replenishment of the Technical Assistance Special Fund) Order 1993, SI 1993/1060 (in force on 24 March 1993), provides for the payment on behalf of the United Kingdom Government of a contribution to the Fifth Replenishment of the resources of the Asian Development Fund of the Asian Development Bank and to the Second Regularized Replenishment of the resources of the Technical Assistance Special Fund of the Bank. In addition, provision is made for the redemption of non-interest bearing and non-negotiable notes issued by the Secretary of State in respect of the payment. Any sums received by the United Kingdom Government in pursuance of the above arrangements are to be paid into the Consolidated Fund.

1310   International organisations—International Finance Corporation—capital increase

The International Finance Corporation (1991 General Capital Increase) Order 1993, SI 1993/1059 (in force on 24 March 1993), provides for payment on behalf of the government of the United Kingdom of a sum not exceeding US $52,615,000 as a further subscription to a capital stock of the International Finance Corporation. The Order further provides that any sums which may be received by the government of the United Kingdom in pursuance of the arrangements relating to the further subscription will be paid into the Consolidated Fund.

1311   Outer Space Act 1986—licence

The Outer Space Act 1986 (Fees) (Amendment) Regulations 1993, SI 1993/406 (in force on 1 April 1993), amend the Outer Space Act 1986 (Fees) Regulations 1989, SI 1989/1306, by providing a definition a new definition of "further education" so that exemption from the fee payable on an application for a licence under the Outer Space Act 1986 extends to a sixth form college.

1312   Privileges and immunities—arms control and disarmament—extension

The Arms Control and Disarmament (Privileges and Immunities) Act 1988 (Guernsey) Order 1993, SI 1993/2666 (in force on 27 October 1993), extends the Arms Control and Disarmament (Privileges and Immunities) Act 1988, subject to specified modifications, to the Bailiwick of Guernsey.

1313   Privileges and immunities—exemption from liability to pay community charge

See para 1717.

1314   Privileges and immunities—jurisdictional immunity—commercial transactions

The State Immunity Act 1978, s 14(2) provides that a separate entity is immune from the jurisdiction of the United Kingdom courts if the proceedings relate to anything done by it in exercise of sovereign authority and the circumstances are such that a state would have been so immune. Under the 1978 Act, s 3, a state is not immune in respect of proceedings relating to commercial transactions, which are any activities in which a state engages otherwise than in the exercise of sovereign authority.

Following the Iraqi invasion of Kuwait the defendant corporation, which was state-owned and acting on ministerial instructions, confiscated ten Kuwaiti civilian aircraft belonging to the plaintiffs and removed them to Iraq. The plaintiffs issued a writ in respect of that action, and their claim was held to be justiciable in the English courts. On appeal, *held*, the first issue was whether the corporation was a separate entity and immune under the 1978 Act, s 14(2) and thus the court had to consider whether the action related to acts done by the corporation in the exercise of sovereign authority. The alleged actions, namely wrongfully removing the aircraft from Kuwait and wrongfully retaining unlawful possession and control of them, were clearly committed sub judice and could only have been done by, or at the behest of, a sovereign state in the exercise of its sovereign authority. The second issue was whether, under the 1978 Act, s 2, the corporation had lost that immunity by submitting to the jurisdiction of the English courts. It had merely claimed immunity, which did not constitute taking a step in the proceedings, and thus it had not submitted to such jurisdiction. Accordingly, the appeal would be allowed.

Kuwait Airways Corpn v Iraqi Airways Co (1993) Times, 27 October (Court of Appeal: Nourse, Leggatt and Simon Brown LJJ).

1315   Privileges and immunities—state immunity

The State Immunity (Federal States) Order 1993, SI 1993/2809 (in force on 7 December 1993), applies the provisions of the State Immunity Act 1978 to the constituent territories of the Federal Republic of Germany, which made a declaration to the effect that its constituent territories may invoke the provisions of the European Convention on State Immunity applicable to contracting states and have the same obligations.

1316   Privileges and immunities—Treaty on Open Skies

The Treaty on Open Skies (Privileges and Immunities) Order 1993, SI 1993/1246 and the Treaty on Open Skies (Privileges and Immunities) (Overseas Territories) Order 1993, SI 1993/1247 (both in force on a date to be published in the London Gazette), confer privileges and immunities upon persons designated by States Parties to the Treaty on Open Skies, signed at Helsinki on 24 March 1992, while they are in prescribed dependent territories for the purpose of carrying out duties relating to the conduct of overflights pursuant to the treaty.

The Treaty on Open Skies (Privileges and Immunities) (Guernsey) Order 1993, SI 1993/2669 (in force on the date of entry into force of the Treaty on Open Skies, signed at Helsinki on 24 March 1992 "the Treaty", to be published in the London Gazette) confers privileges and immunities upon persons designated by States Parties to the Treaty, while they are in the Bailiwick of Guernsey for the purpose of carrying out duties relating to the conduct of overflights pursuant to the Treaty.

1317   Territory and jurisdiction—the sea bed—state boundaries—median line—adjustment—special circumstances

Under the Geneva Convention on the Continental Shelf 1958, art 6, para 1, where the same continental shelf is adjacent to the territories of two or more states whose coasts are opposite each other, the boundary line is, in the absence of agreement between them and unless another boundary line is justified by special circumstances, the median line.

The coast of Jan Mayen, an island which was part of Norway inhabited solely by technical and other staff of the island's meteorological station, was about nine times the length of the coast of East Greenland which lay 250 nautical miles away. The total population of Greenland, which was an integral part of Denmark, was about 55,000 of whom about 6 per cent lived in East Greenland. The fisheries sector of Greenland employed about one quarter of the labour force and accounted for about 80 per cent of total export earnings. A dispute having arisen between Norway and Denmark over access to fishery resources in the sea area between the territories described above, questions arose concerning the boundary lines of the continental shelf and the fishery zone. *Held*, in general, a median line delimitation between opposite coasts resulted in an equitable solution, particularly if the coasts in question were almost parallel. However, the striking difference in the length of the relevant coasts in the instant case constituted a special circumstance within the meaning of art 6, para 1 of the Convention requiring an adjustment or shifting of the line. In the light of the disparity in coastal lengths, the median line should be shifted so as to effect a delimitation closer to the coast of Jan Mayen. Taking account of the disparity of coastal lengths did not mean a direct and mathematical application of the relationship between the length of the coastal front of eastern Greenland and that of Jan Mayen nor a delimitation according to the 200-mile line calculated from the coast of eastern Greenland. Neither the limited nature of the population of Jan Mayen nor socio-economic factors were circumstances to be taken into account. Further, the delimitation so near to the coast of either party did not make security a relevant consideration. The delimitation line dividing the continental shelf and the fishery zones of the parties lay between the median line and the 200-mile line from the eastern coast of Greenland. The principal fishing area would be divided into two equal parts and the remaining disputed area would be divided roughly two to one in favour of Norway.

Maritime Delimitation in the Area between Greenland and Jan Mayen (Denmark v Norway) (1993) Times, 24 June (International Court of Justice).

1318   United Nations—arms embargoes—Liberia, Somalia and the former Yugoslavia

The United Nations Arms Embargoes (Liberia, Somalia and the Former Yugoslavia) Order 1993, SI 1993/1787 (in force on 22 July 1993), imposes restrictions pursuant to decisions of the Security Council of the United Nations (Resolution 713 of 25 September 1991, Resolution 733 of 23 January 1992 and Resolution 788 of 23 January 1992) which made provision for states to implement a general and complete embargo on all deliveries of weapons and military equipment to the former Yugoslavia, Somalia and Liberia.

1319   United Nations—sanctions—Angola

The Angola (United Nations) (Sanctions) Order 1993, SI 1993/2355 (in force on 1 October 1993), imposes restrictions pursuant to a decision of the Security Council of the United Nations (Resolution 864 of 15 September 1993), relating to the export to Angola and the supply to persons in Angola of arms and related goods, and petroleum and petroleum products. Certain related activities are also restricted.

The following orders have also been made under the United Nations Act 1946 in respect of specified territories in relation to Angola.

Specified area	SI 1993 No
Dependent Territories	2356
Channel Islands	2357
Isle of Man	2358

1320   United Nations—sanctions—Haiti

The Haiti (United Nations Sanctions) Order 1993, SI 1993/1784 (in force on 22 July 1993), imposes restrictions pursuant to a decision of the Security Council of the United Nations (Resolution 841 of 16 June 1993). The order restricts the export to Haiti of arms and related material, and petroleum and petroleum products. Further restrictions include those on certain actions making available or otherwise transferring funds or other financial or economic resources to or for the benefit of persons exercising public functions in Haiti.

The following orders have also been made under the United Nations Act 1946 in respect of specified territories in relation to Haiti.

Specified area	SI 1993 No
Dependent Territories	1785
Channel Islands	1793
Isle of Man	1794

1321   United Nations—sanctions—Libya

The Libya (United Nations Sanctions) Order 1993, SI 1993/2807 (in force on 1 December 1993), re-enacts, with certain modifications, the provisions of the 1992 Order, SI 1992/975, and imposes further restrictions, pursuant to a decision of the Security Council of the United Nations (Resolution No 883 of 1993). The order restricts the training of Libyan pilots and other aviation personnel and also restricts certain actions which make available or otherwise transfer certain funds or other financial resources to or for the benefit of certain persons connected with Libya.

The following orders have also been made under the United Nations Act 1946 in respect of specified territories in relation to Libya.

Specified area	SI 1993 No
Channel Islands	2811
Dependent Territories	2808
Isle of Man	2812

1322   United Nations—sanctions—Serbia and Montenegro

The Serbia and Montenegro (United Nations Sanctions) Order 1993, SI 1993/1188 (in force on 1 May 1993), gives effect to a decision of the Security Council of the United Nations (Resolution 820 of 17 April 1993). Provision is made for the impounding of ships, goods vehicles and aircraft which are majority owned or effectively controlled by persons connected with Serbia or Montenegro or which are determined to have been operated or used in violation of relevant Security Council Resolutions, and for the forfeiture of any such ships, vehicles, aircraft or their cargo. There is also a restriction on the provision of services for the purposes of any business carried on in Serbia or Montenegro and a prohibition on the entry of commercial ships registered in the dependent territories and certain other commercial ships into the territorial sea of Montenegro.

The following orders have also been made under the United Nations Act 1946 in respect of specified territories in relation to Serbia and Montenegro.

Specified area	SI 1993 No
Dependent Territories	1195
Channel Islands	1253
Isle of Man	1254

1323   United Nations—sanctions—Serbia and Montenegro—retrospective application

The United Nations Security Council issued a resolution prohibiting exports of goods to Serbia and Montenegro (Serbia) other than medical goods or foodstuffs. It also prohibited payment from Serbian funds held in other United Nations member states except for exports of medical goods or foodstuffs. The resolution was adopted by the United Kingdom under the United Nations Act 1946, s 1, as the Serbia and Montenegro (United Nations Sanctions) Order 1992, SI 1992/1302. Pursuant to art 10 of the order, which dealt with Serbian funds in the United Kingdom, the Bank of England adopted a policy whereby it would allow payment to be made from those funds only in respect of goods exported from the United Kingdom, and nowhere else, to Serbia. This policy was applied retrospectively to four applications made by a bank for the release of funds to be paid to an Italian pharmaceutical company, which had exported medical goods from Italy to Serbia. On an application for judicial review by the company, *held*, the policy was not ultra vires the 1992 Order, art 10 or the 1946 Act, both of which allowed, but did not oblige, the United Kingdom government to permit exceptions to the general prohibitions, as its object was to improve the effectiveness of the United Nations sanctions by reducing the scope for their evasion. Although Italy allowed exports of medical goods to Serbia, this did not establish a common commercial policy obliging other EC member states to permit payment for exported goods from Serbian funds within their jurisdiction. There was no discrimination on the ground of nationality between United Kingdom products and those of other member states under the EC Treaty, art 7 because restricting the application of Serbian funds to exports from the United Kingdom alone allowed the Bank of England to implement and monitor the required sanctions more effectively. To the extent that it influenced the pattern of trade at all, the policy was not in breach of the EC Treaty, art 30 as it encouraged rather than discouraged or hindered imports into the United Kingdom. In any event, the policy was justifiable under the EC Treaty, art 36 on the ground of public policy. The object of the 1946 Act, s 1 and the 1992 Order was that the United Kingdom should effectively apply the United Nations sanctions. The application of those sanctions affected partly completed transactions and thus operated retrospectively. Accordingly, the application would be dismissed.

R v HM Treasury, ex p Centro-Com Sarl (1993) Times, 7 October (Queen's Bench Division: Watkins LJ and Auld J).

1324   United Nations—sequestration of assets—Iraq

The Iraq (United Nations) (Sequestration of Assets) Order 1993, SI 1993/1244 (in force on 24 May 1993), gives effect in the United Kingdom to a decision of the Security Council of the United Nations (Resolution No 778 of 1992). The order requires that any funds, held in the United Kingdom to which specified Iraqi persons are entitled, representing the proceeds of sale of Iraqi petroleum or petroleum products on or after a specified date, are transferred to the escrow account established by the United Nations, following a procedure for ascertaining entitlement to relevant funds and to petroleum or petroleum products. Certain funds are exempt from the requirement. Provision is also made for the re-transfer of any monies received by the Secretary of State or the Treasury from the Secretary General of the United Nations representing monies transferred to the escrow account back to the persons entitled to them. The Secretary of State and the Treasury are empowered to obtain information and documents to secure compliance with it. The circumstances permitting the disclosure of such information and documents are limited by the order. In addition, certain obligations which would conflict with the requirements of the order are disapplied.

The following orders have also been made under the United Nations Act 1946 in respect of specified territories in relation to Iraq.

Specified area	SI 1993 No
Dependent Territories	1245
Guernsey	1798
Isle of Man	1575
Jersey	1799

FORESTRY

Halsbury's Laws of England (4th edn) Vol 19, paras 1–100

1325   Plant health—protective measures—Community requirements

The Plant Health (Forestry) (Great Britain) Order 1993, SI 1993/1283 (in force on 1 September 1993), replaces the 1989 Order, SI 1989/823, and implements Community legislation dealing with protective measures against the introduction into member states of organisms harmful to plants, including protected zones, registration of producers and importers of plants, and standardisation and issue of plant passports together with procedures for their replacement.

1326   Spruce wood—restriction on movement

The Treatment of Spruce Bark Order 1993, SI 1993/1282 (in force on 1 June 1993), controls the movement of spruce bark from trees grown in specified areas unless it has been treated against specified tree pests. The order permits movement of spruce bark in accordance with a licence or pursuant to a notice served by an inspector or instructions issued by an inspector, to serve a notice requiring the treatment or destruction of spruce bark and to carry out treatment or destruction in default of compliance with the order and provides that the contravention or failure to comply with a provision of the order will be punishable by a fine. The Restriction on Movement of Spruce Wood Order 1982, SI 1982/1457, as amended, is revoked.

FRIENDLY SOCIETIES

Halsbury's Laws of England (4th edn) Vol 19, paras 101–400

1327 Actuaries—qualifications

The Friendly Societies (Qualifications of Actuaries No 2) Regulations 1993, SI 1993/2518 (in force on 1 January 1994), provide that actuaries appointed by friendly societies under the Friendly Societies Act 1992, s 44 must (1) be Fellows of the Institute of Actuaries or of the Faculty of Actuaries and (2) must have attained the age of 30 (although an actuary who has not yet attained the age of 30 may be appointed as actuary to a registered society if he carried out the last valuation of the society under the Friendly Societies Act 1974, s 41 prior to the entry into force of the regulations). The regulations revoke the Friendly Societies (Qualifications of Actuaries) Regulations 1993, SI 1993/60, which applied only to incorporated societies, and re-enact the provisions of those earlier regulations in relation to incorporated and registered societies.

1328 Authorisation of business—application for authorisation—prescribed information

The Friendly Societies (Authorisation No 2) Regulations 1993, SI 1993/2521 (in force on 15 November 1993), prescribe the information which a friendly society is required to provide to the Friendly Societies Commission on an application under the Friendly Societies Act 1992, s 32 for authorisation to carry on business. The regulations do not apply to applications under the 1992 Act, s 33. The information required varies according to whether the society seeks authorisation to carry on long term, general or non-insurance business, whether the society is already authorised in respect of other classes of insurance business or whether the Commission already has the information. The regulations also implement the relevant requirements of Council Directive (EC) 79/267 and Council Directive (EC) 73/239 concerning life and non-life assurance and extend these requirements to all friendly societies seeking authorisation to carry on insurance business, notwithstanding that certain societies may not be within the scope of those directives. The regulations revoke the Friendly Societies (Authorisation) Regulations 1993, SI 1993/99, which applied only to incorporated societies, and re-enact the provisions of those earlier regulations in relation to incorporated and registered societies. The previous 1993 Regulations, SI 1993/99, are revoked.

1329 Authorisation of business—restrictions—Community provision

The Friendly Societies (Amendment) Regulations 1993, SI 1993/2519 (in force on 1 January 1994), amend the Contracts (Applicable Law) Act 1990 and the Friendly Societies Act 1992 so as to implement the relevant provisions of (1) Council Directive (EC) 90/619 (co-ordination of laws relating to direct life assurance), (2) Council Directive (EC) 88/357 (co-ordination of laws relating to direct insurance other than life assurance), and (3) Council Directive (EC) 92/96 (co-ordination of laws relating to direct life assurance). The 1993 Regulations introduce the above provisions for societies to which the 1992 Act supra, s 37(2), (3) (restrictions on combinations of business) applies.

1330 Corporation Tax Acts—modification

The Friendly Societies (Modification of the Corporation Tax Acts) (Amendment) Regulations 1993, SI 1993/3111 (in force on 31 December 1993), amend the 1992 Regulations, SI 1992/1655, by providing for a new classification of friendly societies into incorporated friendly societies and registered friendly societies in order to take account of changes made by the Friendly Societies Act 1992. The definitions of "directive society" and "non-directive society" are amended although no society is thereby reclassified. The scope of the regulations is reduced, the original modifications of the Corporation Tax Acts made by the 1992 Regulations no longer being appropriate in the case of all non-directive societies.

1331 Friendly Societies Act 1992—commencement

The Friendly Societies Act 1992 (Commencement No 4) Order 1993, SI 1993/197 brings into force on 5 February 1993 s 120(2) of the Act in respect of the repeal by Sch 22 of the Industrial Assurance Act 1923, s 8(1)(b) and the Friendly Societies Act 1974, Sch 5.

The Friendly Societies Act 1992 (Commencement No 5 and Savings) Order 1993, SI 1993/1186, brings into force on 28 April 1993 ss 51–54, 56 (powers of Friendly Societies Commission), 57 (covering of risks situated in another member state), 62–64 (information), 65–67 (inspections), 98 (to the extent specified) (financial services), 100 (to the extent specified) (industrial assurance), Sch 18, para 3 (amendment to Financial Services Act 1986), and Sch 19, paras 2(2), 3, 4, 5(1)(a), (b), (d), (e), (2)(a), 11 (with savings), 13, 15, 16 (amendments to Industrial Assurance Act 1923) for all remaining purposes. Schedule 16, paras 3, 34–36, 38(b), (c) (for certain purposes), 39–41 come into force generally on the same date and Sch 22 (repeals) comes into force on that date for the specified purposes.

The Friendly Societies Act 1992 (Commencement No 6 and Transitional Provisions) Order 1993, SI 1993/2213, brings into force (1) on 13 September 1993, for all remaining purposes, ss 27(5) (part), 30 (part), 32(1)–(6), (8), (9), 33–43, 44(8), 45, 46(1), (3), (8), 49(1), 50, 70(5)–(7), 72(2) (part), 95 (part), 100 (part), Sch 11, para 16, Sch 12, para 7, Sch 13, Sch 14, para 17, Sch 16, para 32 (part), Sch 19, para 14; (2) on 13 September 1993, generally, ss 72(2) (part), 85–92, 95 (part), 120(2) (part), Sch 14, para 7(4), Sch 15, Sch 16, paras 29, 31, 33, and certain repeals in Sch 22; (3) on 13 September 1993, for specified purposes, ss 48(1), (2), (6), (7), 71(1), (2); (4) on 1 January 1994, for all remaining purposes, ss 27–30 (part), 32(7), 44 (part), 46 (part), 47, 48, 49 (part), 55, 68–79 (part) (except for s 72(2) (part)), 98 (part), 120(2) (part), Sch 11 (part), Sch 12 (part), Sch 14 (except para 7(1)–(3), (5)–(7)) (part), 18 (except para 13), and certain repeals in Sch 22; and (5) on 1 January 1994, generally, ss 93(5)–(15), 95 (part), 100 (part), 120(2) (part), Sch 14, para 7 (part), Sch 16, paras 4(b), 8, 9, 11, 12, 15, 17, 18(1)(a), 22, 23, 43, 51, Sch 19, paras 5(1)(c), (2)(b), 7, and certain repeals in Sch 22. Section 31 is brought into force on 1 January 1994 and on 1 July 1994 for specified purposes.

The Friendly Societies Act 1992 (Commencement No 7 and Transitional Provisions and Savings) Order 1993, SI 1993/3226, brings into force on 1 January 1994, for all remaining purposes, s 98 (in part), Sch 18 (para 13); and on the same date, generally, ss 82(5), 95 (in part), 96, 100 (in part), 120 (in part), 124, Sch 16 (paras 1, 2(1)(b), (2), 13, 14, 18(1)(b), 20, 21, 27, 30, 32 (in part), 38(c) (in part), 42(b), (c), 44, 46, 48(a), (c), (d), 49, 50), Sch 19 (paras 17 (in part), 18–25, 27, 29–32), Sch 21 (paras 18, 19), and certain repeals in Sch 22. Notwithstanding SI 1993/2213, art 2(2), which brings the 1992 Act, s 31 into force on 1 January 1994 and on 1 July 1994 for the specified purposes, s 31 is to come into force on 1 January 1995 in relation to the carrying on of any insurance or non-insurance business by a friendly society to which s 96(2) applies. Transitional provision is also made. For a summary of the Act, see 1992 Abr para 1251. For details of commencement, see the commencement table in the title STATUTES.

1332 Friendly Societies Act 1992—transitional provisions

The Friendly Societies Act 1992 (Transitional and Consequential Provisions and Savings) Regulations 1993, SI 1993/932 (in force on 1 May 1993), provide for the continuation of any outstanding obligations to carry out annual, triennial or quinquennial actuarial investigations and to make valuation reports in relation to incorporated friendly societies which have not met the obligations at the date of incorporation. The 1993 Regulations also provide for the participation of incorporated friendly societies in voluntary indemnity schemes for registered or incorporated friendly societies and their members pending the coming into force of the Friendly Societies Act 1992, s 97 (extension of Policyholders Protection Act 1975 to contracts of insurance with friendly societies), for the treatment of the calendar year in which a registered friendly society is incorporated as a single financial year for the purpose of calculating its annual contribution income under the 1992 Act, s 37(2), (3), for the determination of disputes involving registered friendly societies, other societies registered under the Friendly Societies Act 1974 and industrial and provident societies by the courts instead of by the Chief Registrar or an assistant registrar where so provided under the rules of the society, and for the continuing validity of certificates of exemption granted to collecting societies under the Industrial Assurance Act 1923.

The Friendly Societies Act 1992 (Transitional and Consequential Provisions) Regulations 1993, SI 1993/3084 (in force on 1 January 1994), provide for a transitional period during which industrial assurance companies and collecting societies are to change the particulars in their premium receipt books. They also permit friendly societies, in the first financial year in which they are obliged to give details of related business, to elect to provide the details in banded form as prescribed by the Friendly Societies Commission after the start of the financial year. The regulations also contain a number of consequential repeals.

1333 Friendly Societies Commission—appeals—appeal tribunals—procedure

The Friendly Societies Appeal Tribunal Regulations 1993, SI 1993/2002 (in force on 1 September 1993), make provision as to the time and manner in which appeals under the Friendly Societies Act 1992, s 58 are to be brought, the evidence and procedure at the hearing of such appeals, the procedure after the hearing, and the payment of the costs of appeals.

1334 Friendly Societies Commission—appeals—appeal tribunals—supervision

See para 51.

1335 Friendly Societies Commission—expenses—general charge

The Friendly Societies (General Charge and Fees) Regulations 1993, SI 1993/547 (in force on 1 April 1993), require friendly societies to pay a general charge towards the expenses of the Friendly Societies Commission. The charge is levied with respect to each accounting year of the Commission. Societies are required to pay a sum equal to 0·22 per cent of their specified income, calculated on the basis of contributions from members and interest on investments reported in annual returns submitted for the previous year. This is subject to a minimum charge of £150 and a maximum charge of £14,000. The 1993 Regulations also revoke SI 1992/498 and, in part, SI 1975/205.

1336 Friendly Societies Commission—information—disclosure to commission

The Friendly Societies Act 1992 (Consequential Provisions) (No 2) Regulations 1993, SI 1993/1187 (in force on 24 May 1993), permit the disclosure of information furnished to the Chief Registrar, the central office or the Industrial Assurance Commissioner to the Friendly Societies Commission to enable it to discharge its statutory functions. The regulations also provide that an award by the Industrial Assurance Commissioner dissolving a collecting society under the Industrial Assurance Act 1923 is to have effect as if it were made under the Friendly Societies Act 1974, s 95A (dissolution of registered friendly societies and branches).

1337 Incorporated and registered friendly societies—insurance business

The Friendly Societies (Insurance Business No 2) Regulations 1993, SI 1993/2520 (in force on 1 January 1994), revoke the Friendly Societies (Insurance Business) Regulations 1993, SI 1993/98 (which applied to incorporated friendly societies), and the Friendly Societies (Long Term Insurance Business) Regulations 1987, SI 1987/2132 (which applied to certain registered friendly societies carrying on long term insurance business) and re-enact those provisions, with minor amendments, so as to apply to both incorporated friendly societies and registered friendly societies which carry on insurance business.

1338 Incorporated friendly societies—group insurance schemes

The Friendly Societies (Group Schemes) Regulations 1993, SI 1993/59 (in force on 19 February 1993), prescribe clubs formed for the promotion of lawful sports or games or for the provision of facilities for recreation (including physical exercise) or other leisure-time occupation as additional groups of persons in respect of which a friendly society may provide benefits under a group insurance scheme pursuant to the Friendly Societies Act 1992, s 11.

1339 Registered friendly societies—special resolutions—proxy voting

The Friendly Societies (Proxy Voting) Regulations 1993, SI 1993/2294 (in force on 1 November 1993), set out the requirements that must be complied with by registered friendly societies in respect of proxy voting on special resolutions.

GAS

Halsbury's Laws of England (4th edn) Vol 19, paras 401–600

1340 Boilers—efficiency

The Boiler (Efficiency) Regulations 1993, SI 1993/3083 (in force in part on 1 January 1994 and in part on 1 January 1995), implement Council Directive (EC) 92/42 (as amended by Council Directive (EC) 93/68) relating to efficiency requirements for new hot water boilers fired with liquid or gaseous fuels which are supplied within the European Economic Community. The regulations (1) specify the boilers and appliances to which the regulations do not apply; (2) prohibit the supply or putting into service of new boilers which do not satisfy the efficiency requirements; (3) provide that a boiler is deemed to satisfy the efficiency requirements if it complies with any relevant harmonised standard for boilers and also bears the EC mark and is accompanied by an EC declaration of conformity; (4) provide that gas boilers are to be assessed in accordance with the Gas Appliances (Safety) Regulations 1992, SI 1992/711; (5) make provision for the supply of appliances; (6) deal with the affixing of the EC mark; (7) make provision for the approval by the Secretary of State of notified bodies to perform specified functions and specify the powers which notified bodies will have after 1 January 1995 in relation to a failure to comply with the regulations; (8) provide for an optional marking of products by manufacturers to indicate energy performance; (9) require manufacturers to keep certain information about boilers available for a specified period; and (10) provide for the enforcement of the regulations, offences and defences.

1341 Gas (Exempt Supplies) Act 1993

The Gas (Exempt Supplies) Act 1993 amends the prohibition on supplying gas through pipes without authorisation by adding a new exception and providing for the grant of exemptions to certain persons. The Act received the royal assent on 19 January 1993 and comes into force on a day or days to be appointed.

Section 1 substitutes the Gas Act 1986, s 5 and provides that an offence under s 5 will not be committed by a person supplying, to any premises, gas which consists wholly or mainly of propane or butane. Exemptions to the prohibition on unauthorised supply are introduced by s 2 and may be granted to persons of a particular class or to a particular person. Section 3 substitutes the Gas Act 1986, s 36 by introducing a register, to be kept by the Director General of Gas Supply, of those exempted from the prohibition in the 1986 Act, s 5. Section 4 deals with short title, commencement and extent.

1342 Gas fittings and appliances—safe installation—work not done in a proper and workmanlike manner

Scotland

The Gas Safety (Installation and Use) Regulations 1984, SI 1984/1358, reg 3(1) provides that no person must carry out any work on a gas fitting unless he is competent to do so. No person must carry out work on a gas fitting other than in a proper and workmanlike manner: ibid, reg 4(3).

The appellants carried on a part-time plumbing business. They had installed an open gas flue central heating boiler which was unsafe because it was inadequately ventilated, causing carbon monoxide to escape into the property, and the manner in which it had been fitted contravened the relevant British Standard Code of Practice. They were convicted of offences under the 1984 Regulations, regs 3(1), 4(3), and appealed on the grounds that (1) although they may have been negligent they were not proved to have lacked competence, and (2) there had been no evidence upon which the court could have concluded they had not acted in a proper and workmanlike manner. *Held*, a person who was competent to carry out any work was a person who had the knowledge and ability to perform it, and having regard to the circumstances of the case the court had been entitled to infer that neither appellant had the knowledge and ability to do the job, and accordingly that neither had been competent to install the boiler. The court had also been entitled to conclude that the accused had failed to carry out the work competently, bearing in mind that their efforts had endangered the life of the property's owner, and there were no grounds for disturbing those findings. Accordingly, their appeal would be dismissed.

Paterson v Lees 1993 SLT 48 (High Court).

1343 Meters—fees

The Gas (Meters) (Amendment) Regulations 1993, SI 1993/1521 (in force on 12 July 1993), further amend the 1983 Regulations, SI 1983/684. The regulations prescribe standards for new designs of domestic gas meters and on the importation of gas meters manufactured in another member state. The provision exercises the power under the Gas Act 1986, s 17(1) to make arrangements for meters manufactured in other member states fit to be stamped by a person other than a meter examiner.

1344 Public gas supplier—application for authorisation

The Gas (Authorisation Application) (Amendment) Regulations 1993, SI 1993/2105 (in force on 20 September 1993), amend the 1986 Regulations, SI 1986/1355, reg 2 which prescribes the manner in which an application for an authorisation to supply gas under the Gas Act 1986, s 7 is to be made. The principle amendment alters the requirements imposed on applicants for authorisation under the 1986 Act to supply gas which consists wholly or mainly of propane or butane. Such applicants are relieved of the obligation to provide a description of the proposed supply including specified particulars, and the obligation to provide any business accounts.

GIFT AND ESTATE TAXATION

See INHERITANCE TAXATION.

GUARANTEE AND INDEMNITY

Halsbury's Laws of England (4th edn) Vol 20 (reissue), paras 101–400

1345 Guarantee—joint and several guarantee—contribution payable by co-guarantor

See *Leisureking Ltd v Cushing (Inspector of Taxes)*, para 278.

1346 Guarantee—surety—right to set-off and counterclaim—mortgage

See *National Westminster Bank plc v Skelton; Ashley Guarantee plc v Zacaria*, para 1828.

1347 Indemnity—indemnity clause—extent of liability—negligence and breaches of statutory duty

See *EE Caledonia Ltd v Orbit Valve Co Europe*, para 604.

HEALTH AND SAFETY AT WORK

Halsbury's Laws of England (4th edn) Vol 20 (reissue), paras 401–951

1348 Articles

A Cure for All Ills? Fraser Whitehead (on the deregulisation of health and safety): LS Gaz, 1 December 1993, p 11
Breaches of Safety Legislation—Commensurate penalties? Geoffrey Holgate: 157 JP Jo 485
Fire Precautions and Managers' Responsibilities, Michael Griffiths: 157 JP Jo 439
Hazardous Substances, Roger Peters: 137 SJ 746
Health and Safety at Work—Sentencing, Alec Samuels: 157 JP Jo 763, 745
Local Authority Contract Compliance Practices and the Imposition of Workplace Health and Safety Requirements, Geoff Holgate: [1993] 14 BLR 253
Personal Protective Equipment, Roger Peters: 137 SJ 119
Pressure on the Jubilee Line, Frank Wright (on safety regulations on work in compressed air): 143 NLJ 1708
Qualifications on the Employer's Duty of Care, Geoffrey Holgate (on employers duties under the Management of Health and Safety at Work Regulations 1992, SI 1992/2051): 143 NLJ 1328

Safety in Mines, Roger Peters: 137 SJ 1078
Train Door Accidents, Bill Braithwaite (on the technical problems facing claimants): 143 NLJ 1070
Work to Rule, Roger Peters (on the Workplace (Health, Safety and Welfare) Regulations 1992/3004 (1992 Abr para 1287): 137 SJ 372

1349 Dangerous substances—new substance—notification

The Notification of New Substances Regulations 1993, SI 1993/3050 (in force on 31 January 1994), replace the 1982 Regulations, SI 1982/1496. The regulations implement Council Directive (EC) 92/32 relating to the classification, packaging and labelling of dangerous substances insofar as the provisions relate to the placing on the market of new substances. Further provision is made for the importation of new substances into the United Kingdom.

1350 Employer—breach of statutory duty—duty to persons other than employees

By virtue of the Health and Safety at Work etc Act 1974, s 3(1), every employer must conduct his undertaking in such a way as to ensure, so far as is reasonably practicable, that persons not in his employment who may be affected thereby are not exposed to risks to their health or safety.

It was alleged that the defendant's air conditioning system had been inadequately maintained so that members of the public had been exposed to risks to their health from exposure to legionella pneumophilia. On its appeal against conviction of failing to discharge its duty under s 3(1) contrary to s 33(1)(a), the defendant contended that the prosecution had failed to prove that members of the public had actually inhaled the bacteria in question or that it had actually been there to be inhaled. *Held*, the broad purpose of s 3(1), together with ss 20–22 with which it was linked, was preventive. The word "risks" in s 3(1) conveyed the idea of a possibility of danger, not actual danger. Such an interpretation made those statutory provisions effective in their role of protecting public health and safety. Subject to the defence of reasonable practicability, s 3(1) was intended to be an absolute prohibition. It was sufficient to show that there had been a risk of the bacterium in question being there. The appeal would be dismissed.

R v Board of Trustees of the Science Museum [1993] 1 WLR 1171 (Court of Appeal: Steyn LJ, Garland and Rougier JJ).

1351 Employer—breach of statutory duty—duty to provide safe equipment

The Employers' Liability (Defective Equipment) Act 1969, s 1 provides that where an employee suffers personal injury in the course of his employment in consequence of a defect in equipment provided by his employer for the purposes of the employer's business, and the defect is attributable wholly or partly to the fault of a third party, the injury is deemed to be also attributable to negligence on the part of the employer.

An award of damages was made to an employee for injuries sustained in the course of employment when a flagstone he was handling broke. The employer's appeal was dismissed on the ground that a flagstone was "equipment" for the purposes of the 1969 Act. On further appeal, *held*, the definition of equipment set out in the 1969 Act, s 1(3) referred to "any plant or machinery". The key word in this subsection was "any" which had to be construed so as to embrace every article of whatever kind furnished by the employer for the purposes of his business. The definition of "equipment" was therefore wide enough to include a flagstone. Accordingly, the appeal would be dismissed.

Knowles v Liverpool City Council [1993] 4 All ER 321 (House of Lords: Lords Keith of Kinkel, Templeman, Jauncey of Tullichettle, Browne-Wilkinson and Mustill). Decision of Court of Appeal [1993] ICR 21 (1992 Abr para 1264) affirmed.

Scotland

The Woodworking Machines Regulations 1974, SI 1974/903, reg 14(1)(a) provides that every person employed must, whilst operating a woodworking machine, use and keep in proper adjustment the guards and devices provided in accordance with the regulations.

The plaintiff was an experienced sawyer. His foreman demonstrated how to use a mechanical circular saw with the blade and guard already set. The plaintiff continued the job without adjusting the saw and was injured when the blade touched his hand. He claimed damages in negligence and for the employers' breach of the 1974 Regulations relating to the protective guard which enclosed the machine's cutters. The employers alleged contributory negligence, contending that there was strict liability on the part of the plaintiff to comply with reg 14(1)(a). *Held*, an employee's duties under reg 14(1)(a) only arose when the employers had provided a saw with a guard that was properly adjusted. However, since the saw provided did not have such a guard, the accident could not be attributed to any breach of reg 14(1)(a) by the plaintiff. The employer clearly breached the regulations relating to the guard and, accordingly, the plaintiff's claim would be allowed.

Arbuckle v A H McIntosh & Co Ltd 1993 SLT 857n (Outer House).

1352 Employer—breach of statutory duty—duty to provide safe place of work—electricity—minimal risk

The defendant pleaded guilty to two offences of failing to prevent danger from electrical conductors contrary to the Electricity (Factories Act) Special Regulations 1944, SR & O 1944/729, reg 2 and the Health and Safety Act 1974, s 33 and was sentenced to a fine of £10,000 on each count. The defendant appealed against the sentence on the grounds that it was excessive, that no consideration had been taken by the court of the fact that the risk to his employees was minimal and that the court had over-emphasised the company's ability to pay a substantial fine. *Held*, the purpose of the regulations was to protect employees against the consequences of actions done by reason of inadvertence or inattention which they would not normally do. The court had in no way over-emphasised the possibility of an accident occurring and as such the fact that offences were committed in circumstances where the risk to employees was minimal was not a mitigating factor. Accordingly, the appeal would be dismissed.

R v Sanyo Electrical Manufacturing (UK) Ltd (1992) 156 JP 863 (Court of Appeal: Lord Lane, Rose and Potts JJ).

1353 Employer—breach of statutory duty—duty to provide safe place of work—meaning of "place"

Scotland
The Factories Act 1961, s 29(1), requires employers, so far as is reasonably practicable, to make and keep safe every place at which any person has to work.

An employee, a forklift truck driver, was injured when a truck which he was driving inside a factory collided with pallets stacked on the floor and the seat of the truck was dislodged. It fell to be determined whether his employer was in breach of s 29(1). *Held*, an article brought into a workshop might in certain circumstances properly be viewed as a "place" at which a person had to work. The lack of safety in the present case arose from the interaction between place and plant. The truck was a movable tool employed within the place to enable the employee to perform his duties there. Although he had to sit on the seat to use the truck and to perform his duties within the workplace, the truck itself was not a "place" within the meaning of s 29(1). Accordingly, there had been no breach of s 29(1).

McFaulds v Reed Corrugated Cases Ltd 1993 SLT 670n (Outer House).

1354 Employer—breach of statutory duty—duty to provide safe place of work—test of safety

The plaintiff was an experienced mechanical fitter who was injured whilst working on a heavy piece of equipment known by his defendant employers to be cracked. It fell and severely crushed his right leg. In a negligence claim, the plaintiff alleged that there had been a failure to inspect the structure sufficiently and a failure to give adequate warning of the fracture. The defendants denied liability but failed to plead that it was not reasonably practical to make the place of work safe. The court however concluded that the defendants had taken all reasonable and practical steps to keep the work place safe and dismissed the claim. On appeal, *held*, the court below appeared to have treated its conclusions on the plaintiff's allegation of negligence as determinative of the question of whether there had been a breach of statutory duty by the defendants under the Factories Act 1961, s 29(1) of keeping a place of work safe for any person working there. The way the duty was framed under the section, the employer was required to establish and plead that it was not reasonably practicable to make and keep the work place safe. The defendants' failure to plead and prove that meant the plaintiff's claim for breach of statutory duty had to succeed. The meaning of the word "safe" in the section contained no express reference to foreseeability, reasonable or otherwise and there was no reason why the question of whether a place of work was "safe" should not be decided purely as a question of fact. It was plain on the facts that the defendants had failed to make and keep safe for the plaintiff his place of work. Accordingly, the appeal would be allowed.

Larner v British Steel plc [1993] 4 All ER 102 (Court of Appeal: Hirst LJ and Peter Gibson J).

1355   Factories—safety—transitional provision

The Miscellaneous Factories (Transitional Provisions) Regulations 1993, SI 1993/2482 (in force on 17 November 1993), make provision for safety in specified factories. On 1 January 1997, when corresponding provision in respect of such factories comes into force by virtue of the Provision and Use of Work Equipment Regulations 1992, SI 1992/2932, these regulations will cease to have effect. The 1993 Regulations enact provisions to preserve the effect of specified regulations in workplaces in respect of which those regulations were inadvertently revoked without replacement by the Personal Protective Equipment at Work Regulations 1992, SI 1992/2966, and the Workplace (Health, Safety and Welfare) Regulations 1992, SI 1992/3004.

1356   Improvement notices—service of improvement notices—distinction between occupier and employer

It has been held that where there is a contravention of the Health and Safety at Work Act 1974 by a person or limited company as occupier of premises, then notice can be served on them under the 1974 Act, s 46(6). If the contravention is not as an occupier, but as an employer, that section cannot be invoked. The subsections of the 1974 Act, s 46 are permissive only and do not constitute a complete code of all the methods by which relevant notices may be served.

Health and Safety Executive v George Tancocks Garage (Exeter) Ltd [1993] Crim LR 605 (Queen's Bench Division: Kennedy LJ and Clarke J).

1357   Ionising radiations—outside workers

The Ionising Radiations (Outside Workers) Regulations 1993, SI 1993/2379 (in force on 1 January 1994), implement Council Directive 90/641/Euratom on the operational protection of outside workers employed by outside undertakings exposed to the risk of ionising radiation during their activities in controlled areas. The regulations (1) impose duties on the outside undertaking to obtain from the operator information about the risks which might arise in the controlled area and to ensure that the dose of ionising radiation received by an outside worker is estimated; (2) require the outside undertaking to provide the outside worker with a radiation passbook; (3) require the operator to provide suitable radiation monitoring and enter into the outside worker's radiation passbook an estimate of the dose of ionising radiation received by the outside worker; (4) require the outside worker to look after the passbook and take reasonable steps to ensure that it is completed by the operator for whom he undertakes activities; (5) provide for a defence against a breach of duty under the regulations; and (6) make provision in relation to enforcement and civil liability, exemption certificates, extension outside Great Britain and modifications relating to the Ministry of Defence.

1358   Mineral-extracting industry—protection of workers—minimum requirements

See para 2695.

1359   Mines—safety

See MINES, MINERALS AND QUARRIES.

1360   Offshore installations—safety

The Health and Safety (Fees) Regulations 1993, SI 1993/1321 (in force on 21 June 1993), update fees payable under the Offshore Installations (Life-saving Appliances) Regulations 1977, SI 1977/486 (as amended), the Offshore Installations (Fire-fighting Equipment) Regulations 1978, SI 1978/611 (as amended) and the Road Traffic (Training of Drivers of Vehicles Carrying Dangerous Goods) Regulations 1992, SI 1992/744.

The Offshore Installations (Life-Saving Appliances and Fire-fighting Equipment) (Amendment) Regulations 1990, SI 1990/707, are revoked.

The Offshore Safety (Repeals and Modifications) Regulations 1993, SI 1993/1823 (in force on 23 August 1993), which are made in consequence of the coming into force of the Offshore Safety Act 1992, ss 1 and 2 (see 1992 Abr para 1281), (1) repeal the power to appoint inspectors under the Mineral Workings (Offshore Installations) Act 1971, and power to make regulations under that Act, the Petroleum and Submarine Pipe-lines Act 1975 and the Petroleum Act 1987; those powers are now replaced by powers in the Health and Safety at Work etc Act 1974; (2) change various references to the Minister or the Secretary of State in certain provisions of the above Acts (and in certain statutory instruments) to, or to include, the Health and Safety

Executive; (3) insert a provision into the Petroleum Act 1987 requiring the Health and Safety Commission to submit proposals to the Secretary of State for the making of safety zones orders; (4) modify provisions relating to inspectors; and (5) revoke the Offshore Installations (Public Inquiries) Regulations 1974, SI 1974/338, and the Submarine Pipe-lines (Diving Operations) Regulations 1976, SI 1976/923. These have been superseded by provisions in and under the Health and Safety at Work etc Act 1974.

1361 Offshore Safety Act 1992—commencement

The Offshore Safety Act 1992 (Commencement No 1) Order 1993, SI 1993/2406, brings into force on 30 November 1993 s 3(1)(a), (e), (2), and s 7(2), Sch 2, relating to the repeal of the Continental Shelf Act 1964, s 1(4). For a summary of the Act, see 1992 Abr para 1281. For details of commencement, see the commencement table in the title STATUTES.

1362 Protective equipment—Community directive

The Personal Protective Equipment (EC Directive) (Amendment) Regulations 1993, SI 1993/3074 (in force on 1 January 1994), give effect to amendments made to Council Directive (EC) 89/686 as implemented by SI 1992/3139. Motor-cycle helmets and visors are excluded from the scope of the Directive (and accordingly from the scope of the 1992 Regulations). In addition, the 1992 Regulations are disapplied until 30 June 1995 in relation to personal protective equipment which complies with the law in force on 30 June 1992.

1363 Substances hazardous to health—control

The Health and Safety (Miscellaneous Modifications) Regulations 1993, SI 1993/745 (in force on 14 April 1993), modify the Anthrax Prevention Order 1971, SI 1971/1234, by revoking provisions in that order which imposed restrictions on the importation of certain goods into Great Britain where those provisions related to the importation of those goods into Great Britain from any member state of the European Community. The Control of Substance Hazardous to Health Regulations 1988, SI 1988/1657, are also modified by revoking similar provisions prohibiting the importation of certain substances and articles into the United Kingdom where those provisions related to the importation of those substances and articles into the United Kingdom from any member state of the European Community.

HIGHWAYS, STREETS AND BRIDGES

Halsbury's Laws of England (4th edn) Vol 21, paras 1–996

1364 Highway—adoption by local highway authority—adoption agreement—overriding interest

The defendants entered into an agreement with a city council under the Highways Act 1980, s 38 whereby the council agreed to adopt a road which was due to be built over land owned by the defendants as a highway maintainable at the public expense. The agreement was to take effect upon issue of a final certificate by the council but was never registered as a charge. The defendant's land was subsequently bought by the plaintiff. The council issued the final certificate and the plaintiff applied to the court to determine whether the s 38 agreement was an overriding interest under the Land Registration Act 1925, s 70(1)(a). *Held*, the s 38 agreement clearly came into effect not on the date it was made, but on the date of issue of the final certificate, although it did not deal with a change of owner of the land before the final certificate was issued. The Highways Act 1980, s 38(3) envisaged a situation where a highway has not yet come into existence, but did not make provision for a change of ownership prior to the highway being completed. The s 38 agreement was an overriding interest under the 1925 Act, s 70(1)(a), which was binding on the plaintiff. Accordingly, it was declared that a public highway, adopted by the city council, existed over the plaintiff's land.

Overseas Investment Services Ltd v Simcobuild Construction Ltd (1993) Times, 2 November (Chancery Division: Judge Colyer QC).

1365 Highway—injunction restraining obstruction—tort of wrongful interference with business

The Highways Act 1980, s 303 provides that a person who wilfully obstructs any person acting in the execution of the Act or any byelaw or order made under it is guilty of an offence and liable to a fine.

The defendants were protesters against the building of a motorway across an area of countryside, who had resorted to violence and obstructing or sabotaging the construction vehicles. Injunctions were obtained by the plaintiff against the defendants, preventing the defendants from trespassing upon the site. An injunction was also issued to restrain the plaintiffs from "preventing or interfering with the carrying out of works on the said land". The plaintiffs appealed against this last injunction, on the ground that there was no basis in law for granting it. They argued that the 1980 Act, s 303 only provided for a fine and not civil proceedings. *Held*, there was an established common law right to an injunction for wrongful interference with business so long as such interference was conducted by unlawful means. The 1980 Act, s 303 provided that any wilful obstruction or interference was unlawful. Therefore, such obstruction or interference could constitute the tort of wrongful interference with business, against which an injunction could be granted. Accordingly, the appeal would be dismissed.

Department of Transport v Williams (1993) Times, 7 December (Court of Appeal: Dillon, Staughton and Mann LJJ).

1366 Public paths—ascertainment—definitive maps

The Wildlife and Countryside (Definitive Maps and Statements) Regulations 1993, SI 1993/12 (in force on 31 January 1993), revoke the 1983 Regulations. The Regulations prescribe the scale of definitive maps, the notation to be used on them. Further provisions are made in relation to the making, submission and confirmation of modification and reclassification orders.

1367 Public paths—orders—costs

See para 1698.

1368 Public paths—orders—maps

The Public Path Orders Regulations 1993, SI 1993/11 (in force on 31 January 1993), revoke the Public Path Orders and Extinguishment of Public Rights of Way Orders Regulations 1983, SI 1983/23. Provision is made for new forms for public path creation orders, public path diversion orders and public path extinguishment orders made under the Highways Act 1980 and the Acquisition of Land Act 1981. Further provision is made for the orders to contain a map, and for the scale of all order maps.

1369 Public paths—orders—requirements

The Town and Country Planning (Public Path Orders) Regulations 1993, SI 1993/10 (in force on 31 January 1993), prescribe requirements for orders made by local planning authorities under the Town and Country Planning Act 1990, s 257(1), s 258. By authorising the stopping up or diversion of footpaths or bridleways to enable development to be carried out in accordance with planning permission or by a government department. Orders made by local planning authorities under the 1990 Act, s 258(1) extinguish public rights of way over footpaths or bridleways over land held by such local authorities for planning purposes. Further provision is made for orders to contain a map on a specified scale.

1370 Rail crossings—extinguishment and diversion orders—procedural requirements

The Rail Crossing Extinguishment and Diversion Orders Regulations 1993, SI 1993/9 (in force on 31 January 1993), prescribe the requirements for the making of rail crossing extinguishment orders and diversion orders under the Highways Act 1980, ss 118A and 119A (as added by the Transport and Works Act 1992). The regulations prescribe various forms and notices in relation to orders as well as setting out procedural requirements. In addition, the regulations prescribe requirements with regard to compensation claims for depreciation of land or loss caused by orders.

1371 Special road—procedure
The Special Road Schemes and Highways Orders (Procedure) Regulations 1993, SI 1993/169 (in force on 1 March 1993, prescribe the means of indicating the centre lines of a planned road on a plan available for public inspection, and set the limits of deviation. The existing provisions are replaced, except where the procedure has already started before the regulations came into force.

1372 Tolls—concession statements—prescribed information
The Concession Statements (Prescribed Information) Regulations 1993, SI 1993/1300 (in force on 14 June 1993), prescribe the information to be included in a statement to be published together with a toll order under the New Roads and Street Works Act 1991, s 6 where the toll order authorises the charging of tolls by a concessionaire.

1373 Traffic calming—prescribed works
The Highways (Traffic Calming) Regulations 1993, SI 1993/1849 (in force on 27 August 1993), prescribe the works which may be traffic calming works for specified purposes and the features which may be provided with them. Provisions are included relating to consultation about traffic calming proposals.

HIRE PURCHASE AND CONSUMER CREDIT

Halsbury's Laws of England (4th edn) Vol 22, paras 1–400

See CONSUMER CREDIT.

HOUSING

Halsbury's Laws of England (4th edn) Vol 22, paras 401–900

1374 Articles
"A Suitable Home" and the Housing Act 1985, Mark Watson-Gandy: 158 JP Jo 7
Decision and Determination, Nicholas Dobson (on the work of the Housing Benefit Review Board): 143 NLJ 518
Homelessness—Applications for Accommodation, Priority, Need and Eligibility, Geoffrey Holgate: [1993] Fam Law 487
Immigration and Homeless, Nicholas Dobson: 137 SJ 1436
New Angles on Homelessness, David Cowan and Julia Fionda: [1993] 6 JSWFL 403
No Children Need Apply, Paul Buggy (on whether children can apply for housing): 143 NLJ 1001
The Housing Act 1988—Four Years On, Neil Hickman: 143 NLJ 1271
The Public/Private Dichotomy and "Suitable Accommodation" under Section 69(1) of the Housing Act 1985, David Cowan: [1993] 4 SWFL 236
Want to Buy a 19th Floor Flat? Paul Harris (on the right to buy leaseholds): 137 SJ 244

1375 Community charge benefit
See para 2353.

1376 Community charge benefit subsidy
See SOCIAL SECURITY AND SOCIAL SERVICES.

1377 Council tax benefit
See SOCIAL SECURITY AND SOCIAL SERVICES.

1378 Home energy efficiency grants—regulations
The Home Energy Efficiency Grants (Amendment) Regulations 1993, SI 1993/2799 (in force on 9 December 1993) amend the 1992 Regulations, SI 1992/483, by increasing the maximum amounts of the grants for the improvement of energy efficiency in dwellings occupied by persons of low income. Contributions from applicants for grants are no longer specified.

1379 Homeless persons—duty of local authority to provide accommodation—accommodation officer—value judgment
It has been held that it is a breach of his duty under the codes of guidance for dealing with persons facing impending homelessness, issued under the Housing (Homeless Persons) Act 1977, for a local authority's homelessness officer to comment on an applicant's conduct.
   R v Tower Hamlets London Borough Council, ex p Hoque (1993) Times, 20 June (Queen's Bench Division: Sir Louis Blom-Cooper QC).
   1977 Act now Housing Act 1985, Pt III.

1380 Homeless persons—duty of local authority to provide accommodation—deferment of duty
The applicant refused an offer of accommodation on a housing estate from a local authority on the ground that to do so would exacerbate her mental condition. The authority indicated it was prepared to review the case following a psychiatrist's report, offered by her solicitors, and said it would withdraw the offer of accommodation in the interim. The applicant then accepted second stage temporary accommodation which was not secure as it was leased from a private landlord on a short lease and in so doing the authority deferred discharging its housing duty until it received the psychiatrist's report. In an application for judicial review of the authority's decision, *held*, the authority might discharge its statutory obligation by stages. If a stage could not itself qualify as secure, the deferment of the authority's statutory duty while the applicant lived in temporary accommodation, however suitable, was unlawful. Accordingly, the application would be granted.
   R v Brent London Borough Council, ex p Macwan (1993) Times, 24 May (Queen's Bench Division: Sir Louis Blom-Cooper QC).

1381 Homeless persons—duty of local authority to provide accommodation—illegal immigrant—responsibility for enforcement of immigration rules
The Housing Act 1985, s 71(1) states that a local authority shall have regard to guidance given by the Secretary of State in relation to homeless persons. A Code of Guidance was issued under that section in 1991, and paras 4.11 and 4.12 of the Code contain provisions relating to immigrants' housing rights.
   The appellant local authority applied for judicial review of paras 4.11 and 4.12, in particular the words 'Everyone admitted to this country is entitled to equal treatment under the law" in para 4.11. It was argued by the local authority that these words could include illegal immigrants, that the authority was entitled to investigate whether or not the applicant for housing had obtained leave to enter the country by deceit relating to housing accommodation, and that it was entitled to decide that question in the light of the investigation. If the decision was adverse to the applicant then the local housing authority had no duty to provide accommodation under the 1985 Act and the words in para 4.11 were therefore misleading. The Secretary of State submitted that it was for the immigration authorities and not the local housing authority to decide whether the applicant was an illegal immigrant. The application was unsuccessful at first instance and the local authority appealed. *Held*, it was agreed between the parties that: firstly, if the immigration authorities decided that an applicant for housing was an illegal immigrant then the local housing authority owed no duty to provide housing under the 1985 Act, pt III; secondly, that there was nothing in the 1985 Act, the Immigration Act 1971, or the Immigration Rules preventing the local housing authority concerned from making enquiries as to representations made by the applicant for accommodation, and in fact the authority had a duty to do so; and thirdly, that if as a result of the enquiries the local housing authority suspected the applicant was an illegal immigrant, not only was there nothing to prevent the authority from informing the immigration authority, but it would be under a duty to do so. It was not suggested that para 4.11 of the Code, which advised the local housing authority to treat information received relating to the applicant's immigration status as confidential, would prevent such action. There was nothing in the language of the 1971 Act, s 33 and the definition of "illegal immigrant" which imported into it the opinion of the Secretary of State, and there

was nothing in the Immigration Act or Rules which suggested that they were only enforceable by the immigration authorities. A person who was not a British citizen, who obtained leave to enter by deceit, was an illegal immigrant from the moment he obtained leave and the fact of being an illegal immigrant had nothing to do with the opinion of the immigration officer. If the local housing authority discovered deception by an applicant in relation to accommodation then it should not have to refer the case to the immigration authorities for a decision on the matter which might take some time, although the authority should report it. No criticism was made of para 4.12 but para 4.11 of the Code was incorrect in law for the reasons given. Accordingly, the appeal would be allowed.

R v Secretary of State for the Environment, ex p Tower Hamlets London Borough Council [1993] 3 All ER 439 (Court of Appeal: Sir Thomas Bingham MR, Stuart-Smith and Waite LJJ).

1382 Homeless persons—duty of local authority to provide accommodation—intentional homelessness—duty to consider all the circumstances

A council rejected the applicant's housing application on the grounds that she was intentionally homeless. She abandoned the premises following repeated subjection to domestic violence and sexual harassment by her partner. The council, however, decided that she lost her accommodation due to her failure to maintain rent payments or repay arrears and that the harassment was peripheral to the intentionality of homelessness. She applied for judicial review of that decision. *Held*, in considering the intentionality of homelessness, a council must consider all the applicant's relevant circumstances and conduct. Here, the applicant's unexplained failure to meet rent payments was the deliberate act that resulted in homelessness, but that failure could not be divorced from her abandonment of the accommodation due to harassment. However, even if the council had given due consideration to the harassment, it would still have concluded that the dominant cause of her cessation of occupation was non-payment of rent. Accordingly, although the council had misdirected itself, the decision would not be quashed and the application would be refused.

R v Newham London Borough Council, ex p Campbell [1993] NLJR 1295 (Queen's Bench Division: Sir Louis Blom-Cooper QC).

1383 Homeless persons—duty of local authority to provide accommodation—intentional homelessness—duty to reconsider finding of intentional homelessness

The Children Act 1989, s 27(1) provides that where it appears to a local authority that any authority could help in the exercise of any of the authority's functions under the Act, it may request the help of the other authority. Section 27(2) provides that an authority whose help is requested must comply with the request if it is compatible with its own duties and obligations and does not unduly prejudice the discharge of any of its functions.

A local housing authority refused an application for accommodation by a family with five young children on the ground that they were intentionally homeless. The social services department of the relevant county council made a request under the 1989 Act, s 27(1) that the housing authority should assist the family in finding accommodation. The housing authority refused to comply with the request on the ground that it had already considered the family's case and, having found that they were intentionally homeless, had fulfilled its duty to them. On the family's appeal against a refusal of their application for judicial review of the housing authority's decision, *held*, s 27(1) contained a condition which, if satisfied, gave the county council a discretion to request the housing authority to help in the exercise of its functions, including its duty to safeguard the welfare of children in need. A housing authority was obliged to comply with the request if the two conditions in s 27(2) were satisfied, even if compliance involved the exercise of powers which it had decided not to exercise and which in the absence of a request it could not be compelled to exercise. The request required the housing authority to consider the family's position afresh. In failing to do so, the housing authority was at fault and the appeal would be allowed.

Smith v Northavon District Council (1993) 25 HLR 663 (Court of Appeal: Sir Thomas Bingham MR, Steyn and Waite LJJ).

1384 Homeless persons—duty of local authority to provide accommodation—intentional homelessness—homelessness through fraud

The applicant, who was unemployed, obtained a sum of money for a business venture by mortgaging her property to a building society. She gave false information to the society stating that she was employed. The business venture failed and the society took possession of the property. The local authority deemed the applicant intentionally homeless and therefore refused to offer her permanent accommodation. The applicant appealed successfully against the decision and on a subsequent appeal by the authority, *held*, the authority was entitled to look at the whole course of conduct which led to the eventual dispossession, starting as it did with the application for a mortgage and the fraudulent statement as to earnings. The applicant's dishonesty related to the declaration of her earnings and it was not possible to hold that such an act was done in good faith. The applicant, dispossessed of her home as a result of having obtained a mortgage by deliberately giving false information to the society was, therefore, intentionally homeless. Accordingly, the appeal would be allowed.

R v London Borough of Barnet, ex p Rughooputh (1993) 25 HLR 607 (Court of Appeal: Nourse, Farquharson and Rose LJJ).

**1385 Homeless persons—duty of local authority to provide accommodation—
intentional homelessness—inquiries**

The Housing Act 1985, s 60(1) provides that a person becomes homeless intentionally if he deliberately does or fails to do anything in consequence of which he ceases to occupy accommodation which is available for his occupation and which it would have been reasonable for him to continue to occupy.

The applicant applied for a housing transfer on the grounds that he had been subjected to violence and harassment by neighbours. The council informed the applicant that the relevant officer was awaiting information from the police regarding the allegations, that the neighbours' counter allegations had to be considered, and that a transfer offer was unlikely given the applicant's rent arrears. After further complaints of harassment the applicant surrendered his tenancy and applied for accommodation to the homeless persons unit. He ignored advice to retract the termination. The council subsequently informed the applicant that he had been found to be intentionally homeless. The applicant sought judicial review contending that the council's decision was procedurally unfair. *Held*, (1) the council's failure to put the neighbours' counter allegations to the applicant did not amount to a breach of natural justice. (2) The 1985 Act, s 62(2) provided that where an applicant was homeless and in priority need the authority must make inquiries to satisfy itself that he was intentionally homeless. Here, the council was entitled to rely on the inquiries made in relation to the transfer application but, since these were still in progress, judgment ought to have been deferred until the investigation was completed. (3) Under the 1985 Act, s 71, the council was bound to have regard to any guidance by the Secretary of State, namely the third edition of the Code of Guidance. The council had breached statutory procedure by only considering an earlier edition, which differed substantially by placing less emphasis on the issue of harassment. Accordingly, the application would be allowed.

R v Newham London Borough Council, ex p Bones (1993) 25 HLR 357 (Queen's Bench Division: Robert Carnwath QC).

**1386 Homeless persons—duty of local authority to provide accommodation—
intentional homelessness—interim accommodation**

The applicant, who had entered the United Kingdom on a visitor's permit, later requested accommodation as a homeless person and was given temporary accommodation. Statutory inquiries were made under the Housing Act 1985, s 63(1), following which the housing authority decided that the applicant was intentionally homeless and informed her of its decision under the 1985 Act, s 64(1). The authority was granted a possession order. The applicant unsuccessfully sought judicial review of the authority's decision. She then sought an interim mandatory injunction requiring the housing authority to provide her with accommodation pending the outcome of her appeal against the dismissal of her application for judicial review. *Held*, a decision notified under s 64(1) adverse to an applicant would extinguish his right to interim accommodation under s 63(1). To justify granting a mandatory injunction on an appeal, the applicant had to show that there was a very strong case for allowing the appeal. The applicant had not come near to satisfying this burden. There had been no error on the part of the judge and the appeal would accordingly be dismissed.

R v Westminster City Council, ex p Augustin [1993] 1 WLR 730 (Court of Appeal: Sir Stephen Brown P, Mann and Nolan LJJ).

**1387 Homeless persons—duty of local authority to provide accommodation—
intentional homelessness—priority need—dependent children and disabled
person**

In three separate cases, it fell to be determined whether a local authority is under a duty to rehouse a dependent child or a mentally disabled person who makes an application for housing in his own right. In the first case the applicant, aged four, applied to the council claiming homelessness after his mother's application for accommodation had been refused. The council refused to entertain the child's application on the basis that it was intended to circumvent the provisions of the Housing Act 1985. In the second case, the applicant, aged four, applied to the council for housing after his parents had been refused accommodation because they were considered to have become intentionally homeless by their deliberate failure to make their mortgage repayments. The child appealed against the council's rejection of his application. In the third case, a woman who lacked hearing, speech and education applied for accommodation after the council refused her father's application for accommodation on the basis that the family were intentionally homeless, having left previous accommodation in Bangladesh. The council decided that she was so disabled that she could not have made an application for housing and that the application had also been devised to circumvent the 1985 Act. The three cases were heard together on appeal. Held, under the 1985 Act, a duty was imposed on local housing authorities to give the homeless and their families first priority in the housing queue. It was then up to the applicant to decide whether to accept the accommodation. Dependent children relied on their parents to decide where they were to live and consequently the offer of accommodation could only sensibly be made to those in charge of them. If a family lost its right to priority treatment through intentional homelessness, the parent could not achieve the same result by an application in the name of a dependent child. Accordingly, the first two appeals would be dismissed. The third appeal concerned the duty owed to a vulnerable adult. The court found that no duty was owed to a person so disabled that he had neither the capacity to make an application himself nor to authorise an agent to make it on his behalf. There was no purpose in making an offer of accommodation to a person so disabled that he was unable to comprehend or evaluate the offer and therefore no duty was owed to him. However the circumstances in this case were such that the authority wished to evaluate the evidence and reconsider the decision and therefore the appeal would be allowed.

R v Oldham Metropolitan Council, ex p G; R v London Borough of Bexley, ex p B; R v London Borough of Tower Hamlets, ex p Begum [1993] 2 All ER 65 (House of Lords: Lords Griffiths, Bridge of Harwich, Ackner, Slynn of Hadley and Woolf). Decision of Court of Appeal in first two cases sub nom *Re B; Re G* (1992) 24 HLR 726 (1992 Abr para 1316) affirmed; decision of Court of Appeal in third case [1993] 2 WLR 9 (1992 Abr para 1317) reversed.

1388 Homeless persons—duty of local authority to provide accommodation— intentional homelessness—priority need—further inquiries

The applicant, a single parent with a ten-year-old daughter, was the tenant of a flat on a council estate. Both the applicant and her daughter experienced problems arising from crime and drugs on the estate. The applicant's account was supported by letters from her doctor and letters from her daughter's school, which stated that the child showed signs of emotional disturbance. As a result, the daughter often lived at her grandparents' home. The applicant applied for a transfer of accommodation, but the local authority assessed her prospects of being rehoused as low. The applicant eventually left the flat. The authority decided that the applicant was homeless and in priority need, but that she was intentionally homeless. The judge found that consideration of the daughter's position was based on consideration of written reports from the authority's medical adviser, who had not seen the applicant or her daughter. The judge further found that the authority had given no indication of the process of reasoning of the medical adviser, and quashed the decision on the ground that the authority had failed to take proper account of the daughter's position. On the authority's application for judicial review of the judge's decision, held, the judge's decision was unassailable. Under the Housing Act 1985, s 75 the applicant's accommodation was to be regarded as available for occupation for the purposes of establishing intentional homelessness only if both she and her daughter could reasonably be expected to occupy it. The daughter's position was of great significance. If it was reasonable for her to live with her grandparents, it could not be held reasonable for the applicant to remain in occupation of the flat alone. There was no indication that the authority, except by its medical adviser, had ever addressed that matter. Although the authority had taken considerable care in the inquiries regarding many aspects of the case, in respect of the position of the applicant's daughter its approach was seriously flawed. Accordingly, its application would be dismissed.

R v Westminster City Council, ex p Bishop (1993) 25 HLR 459 (Court of Appeal: Nourse, Farquharson and Rose LJJ).

1389   Homeless persons—duty of local authority to provide accommodation—intentional homelessness—short-term accommodation

The applicant was living in temporary accommodation as a stage in the local authority's prospective fulfilment of its duty to secure that permanent accommodation was made available for her occupation. She was then offered permanent accommodation. The local authority interpreted her ambivalent response to its offer to be a refusal, and applied for a possession order in respect of the temporary accommodation. The applicant applied to a second authority for accommodation. The second authority decided that the applicant's temporary accommodation was settled as she held it for an indefinite period pending an offer of permanent accommodation, and found her disinclination to take up the first authority's offer had resulted in her becoming intentionally homeless. The applicant sought judicial review of the second authority's decision. *Held*, where a person was in intermediate accommodation, provided as a stage in the local authority's duty to house him under the Housing Act 1985, it was wrong to focus on the temporary accommodation in isolation from the overall provision of accommodation. As soon as an offer of suitable accommodation was made, the temporary accommodation was merged in the performance of the statutory duty and the fact that the temporary accommodation was not settled became irrelevant. The authority's duty had been performed, but the applicant's subsequent eviction from the intermediate accommodation was not capable of making her intentionally homeless. The application would accordingly be allowed.

  R v Brent London Borough Council, ex p Awua (1993) 25 HLR 626 (Queen's Bench Division: Sir Louis Blom-Cooper QC).

1390   Homelessness—duty of local authority to provide accommodation—intentional homelessness—surrender of interest

The Housing Act 1985, s 60(1) provides that a person becomes homeless intentionally if he deliberately does or fails to do anything in consequence of which he ceases to occupy accommodation which is available for his occupation and which it would have been reasonable for him to continue to occupy.

J moved out of the house she shared with others and applied to the local authority for accommodation. The authority were not satisfied that she was homeless, because she retained an interest in the shared house, and warned her that if she surrendered her interest, she was likely to be considered intentionally homeless. J transferred her interest in the property to her mother. The authority wrote to her that her homelessness was considered intentional by reason of her failing to protect her right to occupy the shared house. J appealed against this decision. *Held*, before the authority could be satisfied that J was intentionally homeless, four conditions had to be fulfilled: (1) she must have deliberately done something or failed to do something; (2) she must have ceased to occupy as a result of the deliberate act or omission; (3) the accommodation must have been available for her occupation; (4) it must have been reasonable for her to continue to occupy. The authority had relied on J's transfer of her legal interest in the house as her deliberate act, meaning that the condition that she had to have ceased to occupy as a result of the deliberate act or omission had not been satisfied. Section 60 could not be extended to cover a situation in which the applicant had ceased to occupy 12 months or so before the deliberate act on which the authority had relied. The appeal would accordingly be allowed and the case remitted to the authority for reconsideration.

  R v Wandsworth London Borough, ex p Oteng (1993) Times, 23 June (Court of Appeal: Lloyd, Butler-Sloss LJJ and Roch J).

1391   Homeless persons—duty of local authority to provide accommodation—interview with applicant—conduct of interview

In 1990 the applicant who had been resident in England went to live with her parents in Bangladesh. On her return in June 1992 she lived with her parents-in-law where she had lived previously. She then applied to the council for accommodation, stating that she had been asked to leave and was now homeless. The applicant sought judicial review of the council's decision that the applicant was intentionally homeless. *Held*, the conduct of the interviews was unsatisfactory and unfair. Applicants for accommodation as homeless persons should be treated sympathetically and any cross-examination, hostile questioning, adverse comment or indications of a likely adverse decision would be inappropriate at the interview. The applicant should be given the opportunity to have someone present to assist and advise them. Without this help there would be inequality and unfairness. Accordingly the council's decision would be quashed.

  R v Tower Hamlets London Borough Council, ex p Khatun (1993) Independent, 1 October (Queen's Bench Division: Sir Louis Blom-Cooper QC).

1392 Homeless persons—duty of local authority to provide accommodation—risk of domestic violence—extent of inquiries

The Housing Act 1985, s 67(2)(c) provides that before referring a homeless person's application for housing to another local housing authority, the referring authority must be satisfied that the applicant will not run the risk of domestic violence in that other district.

The applicant lived in temporary accommodation provided by the council. The council decided to refer her application for accommodation as a homeless person to another council and subsequently obtained a possession order against her. Its application to enforce the order was adjourned pending her application for judicial review of the council's earlier decision. The court held that although she had established grounds to set aside the council's decision, she was not entitled to relief because of her undue delay in seeking judicial review. On appeal, *held*, (1) the council was under a duty to make inquiries about the risk of domestic violence and its failure to do so entitled the applicant to have its referral decision set aside. (2) RSC Ord 53, r 4(1) provided that an application for judicial review must be made within three months from the date when grounds for it arose unless there was good reason to grant an extension. Any delay would also constitute undue delay under the Supreme Court Act 1981, s 31(6). In deciding whether to grant an extension for an application for judicial review the court had to apply the two statutory provisions separately. If there was a good reason an extension would be granted and the court then had a discretion to refuse relief if substantial hardship or prejudice would be caused to the rights of a third party or the interests of justice would be harmed. Here, there was a good reason under Ord 53, r 4(1) and no objection under the 1981 Act, s 31(6) was made out. Accordingly, the appeal would be allowed.

R v Greenwich London Borough Council, ex p Patterson (1993) Times, 20 July (Court of Appeal: Neill, Nolan and Evans LJJ).

1393 Homeless persons—duty of local authority to provide accommodation— suitability of accommodation for applicant—breach of duty

The applicant sought accommodation from a local authority in accordance with the Housing Act 1985, Pt III on the ground that she was unintentionally homeless and in priority need. The authority offered her accommodation which she rejected because it was unsuitable for her two young children who had behavioural problems. She submitted medical evidence in support of her application, but the authority decided that she had acted unreasonably and refused to offer her alternative accommodation. The applicant sought an order of mandamus requiring the authority to offer her alternative accommodation but the district judge refused to grant the order. On her appeal, *held*, the authority had known that the applicant's children had behavioural problems, and it should have considered the relevant medical evidence before making an offer of accommodation. The applicant had been placed in the unfair position of having to decide whether to accept or refuse the offer before the medical evidence had been considered, and as the authority had failed to consider the medical evidence earlier the offer of accommodation had not been a reasonable one. The appeal would be allowed, and the court would grant a declaration that the authority had failed to fulfil its statutory duty.

R v Wycombe District Council, ex p Hazeltine (1993) 25 HLR 313 (Court of Appeal: Lloyd and Hirst LJJ and Gibson J). *R v Ealing London Borough Council, ex p McBain* [1986] 1 All ER 13, CA (1985 Abr para 1145) considered.

1394 Homeless persons—duty of local authority to provide accommodation— suitability of accommodation for applicant—fairness of housing policy

A council's standard letting procedure provided that families containing children under ten and adults over 60 years of age would not be housed above the fourth floor and that families would be given one living room, one bedroom for parents and a further bedroom for every two children of the same sex, In addition, an applicant's choice of area would be met where possible. The council adopted new criteria for homeless families, offering properties irrespective of area preference, on any floor level and to the minimum legal space standards. Each individual council neighbourhood could decide for itself whether it applied the amended letting procedure. On an application for judicial review of the council's decision that they had made suitable offers of accommodation to homeless families, the applicants contended that the council had failed to adopt and apply any consistent standards or principles for the allocation of housing for the homeless and submitted that the only proper basis for allocation of accommodation was housing need and it was arbitrary and irrational to exclude the homeless from the list for transfer to accommodation satisfying the standard letting criteria. *Held*, the removal of the standard letting criteria for the homeless and the arbitrary and random way it was operated between neighbourhoods demonstrated unfairness and irrationality requiring intervention by the court. Accordingly, the decisions of the council would be quashed.

R v Tower Hamlets London Borough Council, ex p Ali, R v Tower Hamlets London Borough Council, ex p Uddin (1993) 25 HLR 218 (Queen's Bench Division: Rose LJ and Pill J).

1395 Homeless persons—duty of local authority to provide accommodation—suitability of accommodation for applicant—obligation to give reasons for decision

The applicant, who had a child with spina bifida, was granted temporary accommodation by her local authority pursuant to their obligations under the Housing Act 1985. The authority decided that she was unintentionally homeless and rehoused her in permanent accommodation. The applicant regarded the new accommodation as unsuitable for her child due to lack of appropriate heating and obtained a letter from her medical practitioner in support of her contention. The local authority stated that it had carried out an assessment of the child's medical condition and dismissed her appeal regarding the suitability of the permanent accommodation. As far as the applicant was aware the authority had not carried out an assessment, nor did they obtain any medical records relating to the child before the appeal was dismissed. In addition, the applicant was not informed of the reasons for the assertion that the accommodation was suitable. The applicant applied for judicial review of the decision to dismiss her appeal. *Held*, the local authority had acted unfairly in the way it dealt with the medical aspects of the case. The applicant should have been given every opportunity to assess the medical evidence against her and the authority should have obtained the child's medical records and provided the applicant with details of its own assessment. It could also be said that there was a general duty in English law to give reasons where a statute incorporated the concept of fair treatment to those affected by administrative actions. Without a general duty to give reasons for decisions in every aspect of the homelessness legislation, the administrative process would operate unfairly against the homeless applicant. Therefore in the present case, reasons should have been given sufficient to show that the authority had directed its mind to the medical assessments of the applicant's medical practitioner and to show indirectly whether the decision was lawful according to the principles of judicial review. Accordingly the application for judicial review would be allowed.

R v Lambeth London Borough Council, ex p Walters (1993) Times, 6 October (Queen's Bench Division: Sir Louis Blom-Cooper QC).

1396 Housing benefit

See SOCIAL SECURITY AND SOCIAL SERVICES.

1397 Housing renovation grants—grant limit

The Housing Renovation etc. Grants (Grant Limit) Order 1993, SI 1993/553 (in force on 5 April 1993), prescribes the formula for calculating the maximum amount of grant which a local housing authority may pay in respect of applications for grants which it must approve under the Local Government and Housing Act 1989, ss 112, 113 or 114 in Pt VIII.

The Housing Renovation etc. Grants (Grant Limit) (Amendment) Order 1993, SI 1993/2711 (in force on 14 January 1994), amends the 1993 Order, SI 1993/553, for calculating the maximum amount of grant which a local housing authority may pay under the Local Government and Housing Act 1989, Pt VIII.

1398 Housing renovation grants—prescribed forms and particulars

The Housing Renovation etc. Grants (Prescribed Forms and Particulars) (Amendment) Regulations 1993, SI 1993/552 (in force on 5 April 1993), amend the 1990 Regulations, SI 1990/1236. Provision is made for the amendment of Forms 1 to 4.

The Housing Renovation Grants (Prescribed Forms and Particulars) (Amendment) (No 2) Regulations 1993, SI 1993/1452 (in force on 6 July 1993), correct minor defects in the 1993 Regulations, SI 1993/552.

The Housing Renovation etc. Grants (Prescribed Forms and Particulars) (Welsh Forms and Particulars) (Amendment) Regulations 1993, SI 1993/715 (in force on 6 April 1993), amend the 1991 Regulations, SI 1991/80. The Regulations translate into Welsh the amendments made by the Housing Renovation etc. Grants (Prescribed Forms and Particulars) (Amendment) Regulations 1993, SI 1993/552 supra.

The Housing Renovation etc. Grants (Prescribed Forms and Particulars) (Welsh Forms and Particulars) (Amendment) (No 2) Regulations 1993, SI 1993/2078 (in force 16 September 1993), correct minor defects in the 1993 Regulations, SI 1993/715.

1399   Housing renovation grants—reduction of grant
The Housing Renovation etc. Grants (Reduction of Grant) (Amendment) Regulations 1993, SI 1993/551 (in force on 5 April 1993), further amend the principal Regulations, SI 1990/1189. The amendments take account of changes in legislation relating to social security, children and young persons, education and the introduction of the council tax.

1400   Housing renovation grants—specifications and directions
The Assistance for Minor Works to Dwellings (Amendment) Regulations 1993, SI 1993/554 (in force on 5 April 1993), amend the 1990 Regulations, SI 1990/338. Provision is made for the maximum amount or value of assistance which may be given under the Local Government and Housing Act 1989, s 131 on any one application for assistance to be increased from £1,000 to £1,080 and the maximum amount of assistance which may be given over a three year period in respect of the same dwelling to be increased from £3,000 to £3,240. Further, the reference to community charge benefit is substituted by a reference to council tax benefit and disability working allowance.

1401   Housing revenue account—subsidy—content
The appellants, a number of London borough councils, claimed that they were entitled to receive housing revenue account (HRA) subsidy in respect of the residual housing debt transferred to them in 1986 on the abolition of the Greater London Council (GLC). They contended that the debt was referable to HRA expenditure because it had qualified for housing subsidy prior to the abolition of the GLC and the reorganisation of local government could not have been intended to relieve central government of its obligation to subsidise debt charges associated with the provision of housing. *Held*, a local housing authority had a duty, under the Local Government and Housing Act 1989, s 74, to keep a HRA in respect of property held for the proper discharge of its housing function. HRA subsidy, payable by the Secretary of State under s 79, replaced housing subsidy. An authority could not include as a debit entry in its HRA a debt imposed on it by statute and bearing no relation to any property ever available to its housing committee. The "opening subsidy credit ceiling" in the Housing Revenue Accounts Subsidy (Consolidation) Determination 1990, in accordance with which the amount of the subsidy was to be calculated, referred simply to the HRA of the borough whose subsidy was under consideration. Such an interpretation excluded from subsidy any advance attributable to the residual housing debt because there were no relevant "houses or other property" within the appellants' housing revenue accounts. Advances relating to transferred housing could be included within the subsidy calculation but advances consequent on the deemed statutory debt, the residual housing debt, were excluded. Accordingly, the appellants' claim would fail.
   R v Secretary of State for the Environment, ex p London Borough of Enfield (1993) 26 HLR 51 (Court of Appeal: Nourse, Leggatt and Simon Brown LJJ).

1402   Leasehold Reform, Housing and Urban Development Act 1993
See para 1612.

1403   Local authority housing—right to buy
See LANDLORD AND TENANT.

1404   Local authority housing—secure tenancy
See LANDLORD AND TENANT.

HUMAN RIGHTS

Halsbury's Laws of England (4th edn) Vol 18, paras 1625–1722

1405 Articles

A Full-Time European Court of Human Rights in Strasbourg, Andrew Drzemczewski: 143 NLJ 1488
At Death's Door—Jamaica Executions, Barry Phillips (on *Pratt v A-G for Jamaica* (1993) Times, 4 November, Independent, 3 November (para 1415)): 137 SJ 1134
Death in Paradise, Saul Lehrfreund (on human rights abuse in Jamaica): 143 NLJ 397
Entrapments and Gay Rights, Helen Power: 143 NLJ 47
"If it were done when 'tis done, then 'twere well it were done quickly", PR Ghandhi (on *Pratt v AG for Jamaica* [1993] 3 WLR 995 (para 1415)): 144 NLJ 21
Paper Rights, Saul Lehrfreund (on the Covenant on Civil and Political Rights): 143 NLJ 918
Taking Sides: Religion, Law and Politics, Anthony Bradney: 143 NLJ 434
The Right to Die, Carol Brennan (on *Airedale NHS Trust v Bland* [1993] 2 WLR 316, HL (1992 Abr para 1770)): 143 NLJ 1041
The Right to Know, Saul Lehrfreund and Anthony Metzer (on death row prisoners in Jamaica): 143 NLJ 1330

1406 Data protection

See DATA PROTECTION.

1407 European Convention on Human Rights—application by individual—victim of a violation—risk of deportation

The applicants, two Sri Lankan citizens of Tamil origin who had been refused refugee status in France, remained unlawfully in the country after the expiry of the time limit specified in departure orders made against them. They complained that their unlawful residence in France and the risk that they would be returned to Sri Lanka with the danger that they would be exposed to a real risk of torture or inhuman or degrading treatment was a violation of the European Convention on Human Rights, art 3. The French government contended that, although the applicants were unlawfully in the country, as no expulsion orders had yet been made against them they were not victims within art 25(1) of the Convention and, accordingly, could not bring the present application. *Held*, if a deportation order was made, there was a right of appeal against the order with attendant safeguards. When an appeal against an order was lodged, the order was suspended. The applicants would then be in a position to raise before the administrative courts arguments based on the risks of ill-treatment in Sri Lanka. They were not 'victim[s] of a violation' within art 25(1) and, therefore, the court was unable to consider the merits of the case.

Vijayanathan and Pusparajah v France (Applications 17550/90 and 17825/91) (1992) 15 EHRR 62 (European Court of Human Rights).

1408 Criminal record—disclosure for employment vetting purposes

See para 685.

1409 Data protection

See DATA PROTECTION.

1410 Freedom of association—compulsory membership of trade union

The applicant, a taxi cab driver, complained that a statutory requirement that he join the relevant trade union as a condition of being granted a taxi cab licence was a violation of his right to freedom of association guaranteed by the European Convention on Human Rights, art 11. *Held*, art 11 had to be regarded as encompassing a negative right of association. The applicant held a licence prior to the coming into force of the law in question and had been compelled by ministerial regulation to join an association of professional taxi cab drivers. It was only when the new law came into force that it became clear that membership of the association was a licence condition. The fact that the applicant was compelled to remain a member of the association at the risk of losing his licence was a form of compulsion that struck at the very substance of the right guaranteed by art 11 and itself amounted to an interference. Further, the fact that the impugned compulsion was contrary to the applicant's beliefs constituted an interference with his right under art 11 as viewed in the light of arts 9, 10 (freedom of thought and speech). Although the association doubtless served the public interest, the imposition by law of compulsory membership was disproportionate to the aim pursued. The statutory membership obligation was incompatible with art 11 and, accordingly, the application would succeed.

Sigurjonsson v Iceland (Application 16130/90) (1993) 16 EHRR 462 (European Court of Human Rights).

An employee resigned from his trade union following a disciplinary dispute, and was ostracised and obstructed in his work by some of his fellow employees. A strike was threatened unless the employee either rejoined the union or was employed elsewhere. The employee declined to rejoin and refused an offer of employment at a nearby site in the belief that his conditions of employment would be less advantageous. Having been told by the employers that he would be sent home without pay if he reported for work at the original site, the employee resigned. A decision that the employee had been constructively dismissed and that the dismissal was unfair was reversed on the ground that the employers were justified in requiring him to change sites because there was an implied term in his contract that he could be directed to work anywhere within reasonable daily reach of his home. On the question of whether the employee's treatment amounted to a breach of the European Convention on Human Rights, art 11 (freedom of association), *held*, the employee did not object to rejoining the union because of any specific convictions regarding trade union membership, and in fact joined another trade union. There was no closed shop agreement in force, and the employee was not faced with a threat of dismissal involving loss of livelihood as he had the possibility of working at the nearby site whether or not he rejoined the union. Further, he had not established that his working conditions at the alternative site would have been significantly less favourable than at the original site. Accordingly, there had been no violation of art 11.

Sibson v United Kingdom (Case No 4/1992/349/422) (1993) Times, 17 May (European Court of Human Rights).

1411 Freedom of expression—advertising by medical practitioner

The applicant, a medical practitioner in private general practice, had sought the permission of the General Medical Council to advertise his practice in local newspapers. The council informed him that it would take disciplinary action against him if he did so. The applicant complained of a violation of his right, under the European Convention on Human Rights, art 10, to freedom of expression and that he had no effective remedy under English law in respect of his complaint, contrary to art 13. Following a report of the Monopolies and Mergers Commission to the effect that the council's rules in this respect were not in the public interest, the council revised its rules on advertising so as to permit the publication of factual information about doctors' services. A friendly settlement was concluded between the applicant and the United Kingdom government (without any admission by the latter that a breach of the Convention had occurred and on condition that the case was withdrawn from the court and that no further cases were instituted against the government in respect of this matter in any national or international court) under which the government paid the applicant £12,500. Accordingly, the European Court of Human Rights decided that the case be struck out of its list.

Colman v United Kingdom (Case No 2/1993/397/475) (1993) Times, 11 August (European Court of Human Rights).

1412 Freedom of expression—criminal defamation of police—matter of public concern

The applicant published articles in a newspaper in which he alleged police brutality. He was found guilty of criminal defamation of unspecified members of the police force and fined. He complained that, as the public prosecutor had been absent from a number of hearings of his case, his rights to a hearing by an impartial tribunal, guaranteed by the European Convention on Human Rights, art 6(1), and to freedom of expression, guaranteed by art 10, had been violated. *Held*, impartiality had to be assessed both subjectively and objectively. A judge's impartiality was presumed until the contrary was shown. There was no evidence that the trial judge was personally biased. As there were no hearings at which the merits were considered or evidence adduced in the public prosecutor's absence except for one at which videotaped evidence was shown, there was no objectively justified reason to fear that the court was not impartial. There had been no violation of art 6(1). The applicant's sentence for defamation interfered with his

429

right to freedom of expression. The conviction and sentence were for the legitimate aim of protecting the reputation of others. Freedom of expression was an essential foundation of a democratic society; it applied not only to information and ideas which were favourably received but also to those which offended, shocked or disturbed. The exceptions allowed by art 10(2) were to be interpreted narrowly and established convincingly. The pre-eminent role of the press in a state governed by the rule of law to impart information and ideas on matters of public interest, which the public had a right to know, had to be taken into account. Nevertheless, the press must not overstep the boundaries set by the protection of the reputation of others. The applicant's account of police brutality was based on rumours and information given by other persons and, therefore, it was unreasonable for the national authorities to require him to establish the truth of his statements. The applicant intended to encourage a public investigation into complaints of police brutality, not to defame the police force, so that this bore on a matter of public concern. The applicant's conviction was capable of discouraging open discussion of matters of public concern and, therefore, was disproportionate to the legitimate aim pursued. There had been a violation of art 10 and that part of the application would succeed.

Thorgeirson v Iceland (Application 13778/88) (1992) 14 EHRR 843 (European Court of Human Rights).

1413   Freedom of expression—public broadcasting monopoly—justification

The applicants were unable to set up radio or television stations because, under Austrian law, the right to do so was restricted to the national broadcasting corporation. They complained of a violation of their freedom of expression, guaranteed by the European Convention on Human Rights, art 10, contending that the Austrian authorities were seeking to retain their political control over broadcasting. *Held*, the question was whether the interference with the applicants' freedom to impart information and ideas was justified. The purpose of art 10(1), by virtue of which states were not prevented from requiring the licensing of broadcasting, television or cinema enterprises, was to make it clear that states were permitted to regulate by a licensing system the way in which broadcasting was organised in their territories, particularly in its technical aspects. The monopoly system operated in Austria was capable of contributing to the quality and balance of programmes through the supervisory powers over the media conferred on the authorities and was therefore consistent with art 10(1). Of all the means of ensuring that the principle of pluralism, of which the state was the ultimate guarantor, a public monopoly was the one which imposed the greatest restrictions on the freedom of expression, by preventing broadcasting otherwise than through a national station and, in some cases, to a very limited extent through a local cable station. Such far-reaching restrictions could only be justified where they corresponded to a pressing need. Technical progress made over the last decades meant that those restrictions could not be justified by considerations concerning the number of frequencies and channels available. In view of the multiplication of foreign programmes aimed at Austrian audiences and the national court's decision to recognise the lawfulness of their retransmission by cable, the restrictions in question had lost much of their raison d'être. There might be equivalent, less restrictive, solutions such as those of certain countries which either issued licences subject to specified conditions of variable content or provided for forms of private participation in the activities of the national corporation. The restrictions in question were disproportionate to the aim pursued and, therefore, not necessary in a democratic society. The applications would succeed.

Informationsverein Lentia v Austria (Applications 13914/88, 15041/89, 15717/89, 15779/89, 17207/90) (1993) 17 EHRR 93 (European Court of Human Rights).

1414   Freedom of religion—proselytism—improper proselytism

The applicant, a Jehovah's witness, called at the home of an orthodox Christian whom he attempted to convert to his faith. The applicant was convicted of proselytism, an offence under Greek law. He complained of a violation of his right to freedom of religion, guaranteed by the European Convention on Human Rights, art 9. *Held*, freedom of thought, conscience and religion was one of the foundations of a democratic society. Religious freedom implied freedom to manifest one's religion not only in community with others, in public and within the circle of those whose faith one shared, but also alone and in private; it included in principle the right to try to convince one's neighbour, for example through teaching. The Greek law was intended to protect the rights and freedoms of others and only to punish improper proselytism. A distinction had to be made between bearing Christian witness and improper proselytism. The former corresponded to true evangelism, of which the latter was a corruption or defamation and incompatible with respect for the freedom of thought, conscience and religion of others. In the criminal proceedings against the applicant, the facts on which the charge of proselytism was based had not been sufficiently specified. There had been a violation of art 9 and, accordingly, the application would succeed.

Kokkinakis v Greece (Case No 3/1992/348/421) (1993) Times, 11 June, Independent, 16 June (European Court of Human Rights).

1415   Inhuman or degrading treatment or punishment—capital punishment—delay in execution

Jamaica
The defendants were convicted of murder and were sentenced to death in 1979. Since then, they had been on "death row", awaiting execution. On the defendants' appeal against the dismissal of proceedings for redress for alleged infringments of their constitiutional rights, the defendants contended that to execute them after so many years would be inhuman and a breach of the Constitution of Jamaica, s 17(1), which provided that no person was to be subject to torture or to harsh or inhuman or degrading punishment or other treatment. *Held*, a state that wished to retain capital punishment must ensure execution followed as swiftly as practicable after sentence, allowing a reasonable time for appeal and consideration of reprieve. A condemned man would take every opportunity to save his life through the use of an appellate procedure. If he was able to prolong the appellate hearings over two years the fault lay with the appellate system and not with the prisoner who took advantage of it. Appellate procedures that echoed down the years were incompatible with capital punishment. In this case, the total period of delay amounted to almost 14 years. To execute the defendants after holding them in the agony of suspense for so many years would be an inhuman punishment under s 17(1). If execution was to take place more than five years after sentence there would be strong grounds for believing that the delay was such as to constitute inhuman or degrading punishment or other treatment. There would accordingly be a recommendation that the appeal should be allowed and the sentences commuted to life imprisonment.

Pratt v A-G for Jamaica [1993] 4 All ER 769 (Privy Council: Lords Griffiths, Lane, Ackner, Goff of Chievely, Lowry, Slynn of Hadley and Woolf).

Jamaica
The defendants were convicted of murder and were sentenced to death. Their applications for leave to appeal were dismissed on dates between 1984 and 1987. The defendants then sought to have the sentences set aside on constitutional grounds, based upon the delay that had occurred following the refusal of their applications, and that to hang them would be contrary to the Constitution of Jamaica, s 17, which prohibited subjecting prisoners to inhuman or degrading treatment. *Held*, the jurisdiction of the Privy Council was an appellate jurisdiction derived from the Judicial Committee Act 1833 and the Judicial Committee Act 1844, s 1, which superseded the royal prerogative. In the present case, there was no appeal against the sentences passed, and if there had been, there would have been no power to alter the mandatory death sentence. The jurisdiction of the Privy Council to enter upon the question of whether the execution would infringe the constitutional rights of the defendants, which had not yet been considered by a Jamaican court, would only arise when it had been considered and adjudicated on by a Jamaican court. The appeals would accordingly be dismissed.

Walker v R [1993] 4 All ER 789 (Privy Council: Lords Griffiths, Lane, Ackner, Goff of Chievely, Lowry, Slynn of Hadley and Woolf).

1416   Inhuman or degrading treatment or punishment—corporal punishment—private school

A seven-year-old pupil at a private boarding school was reprimanded by a teacher for talking in the corridor. Having already received four similar reprimands, it was decided that he should be corporally punished. Three days after the decision, the headmaster administered a "slippering", striking the pupil three times on his buttocks, through his shorts, with a rubber-soled gym shoe. No other persons were present. The pupil complained that the punishment was a violation of his rights under the European Convention on Human Rights, arts 3 (right not to be subjected to inhuman or degrading treatment), 8 (right to respect for private life), and 13 (right to an effective remedy). *Held* (by a majority of five votes to four on art 3), although the treatment complained of was the act of a headmaster of an independent school, it could still engage the responsibility of the state under the Convention if it was proved to be incompatible with art 3 or 8. In order for the punishment to be contrary to art 3, the humiliation or debasement involved had to reach a particular level of severity and had to be greater than the usual element of humiliation inherent in any punishment. This minimum level of severity depended on the particular circumstances of each case. While the court had misgivings as to the automatic nature of the punishment and the three-day wait before it was carried out, the minimum level of severity had not been attained in the present case. The notion of private life was not susceptible to exhaustive definition, and measures taken in the field of education could, in certain circumstances, interfere with the right to respect of private life. However, every act that might adversely affect a person's physical or moral integrity did not necessarily give rise to such an interference. Having regard to the purpose of the Convention, and to the fact that sending a child to school necessarily involved some degree of interference with his private life, the pupil's treatment did not sufficiently affect his physical or moral integrity to bring it within art 8. As it was open to the pupil to institute civil proceedings for assault, an effective remedy was available for his complaints under arts 3 and 8. The effectiveness of a remedy for the purposes of art 13 did not depend on the certainty of a favourable outcome, and the court could not speculate on what decision the English courts would have reached. Accordingly, there had been no breaches of the Convention.

Costello-Roberts v United Kingdom (Case No 89/1991/341/414) [1994] 1 FCR 65 (European Court of Human Rights).

1417 Prohibition of discrimination—assumption about mother—discrimination on ground of sex

The applicant, who paid invalidity insurance contributions while she was employed, was dismissed on account of illness and was granted a full pension. Following the birth of her son and a medical examination, her pension was cancelled on the ground that her health had improved and she was 60 to 70 per cent able to look after her home and her child. Her claim for a full or half-pension was dismissed. The insurance court, in determining whether she was in financial difficulties and, therefore, entitled to a half-pension, reached its conclusion on the assumption that, even if she had not had health problems, she would have given up work when her son was born. She complained that the assumption made by the court constituted sex discrimination contrary to the European Convention on Human Rights, art 14, taken together with art 6(1). *Held*, it was already established that art 6(1) applied in the field of social insurance, including welfare assistance. The insurance court had not questioned the validity of the assumption that women gave up work when they gave birth to a child. That assumption was the sole basis for the court's reasoning and was, therefore, decisive; it introduced a difference of treatment based on the ground of sex only. As the advancement of the equality of the sexes was a major goal in the member states of the Council of Europe, cogent reasons had to be advanced before such a difference of treatment could be regarded as compatible with the Convention. No such reasons had been advanced and, therefore, there had been a violation of art 14, taken together with art 6(1). Accordingly, the application would succeed.

Schuler-Zgraggen v Switzerland (Application 14518/89) (1993) 16 EHRR 405 (European Court of Human Rights).

1418 Right to fair and public hearing—civil and criminal proceedings—appellate court—denial of oral hearing

The applicant claimed that the report of a committee which had investigated his complaint of bias by the recruitment board which had failed to select him for appointment to a university lectureship contained matter defamatory of him. He brought private prosecutions for defamation against a member of the committee and his secretary, claiming nominal damages from each of them. The prosecutions were dismissed by the court at first instance. His appeal against that decision was dismissed on the basis of written evidence without an oral hearing. On his complaint of a violation of his right to a fair and public hearing contrary to the European Convention on Human Rights, art 6(1), *held*, as the proceedings were both civil and criminal in nature, art 6(1) applied. The applicant's right not to be defamed was a civil right within the meaning of art 6(1); the outcome of both the claim for damages and the private prosecutions depended on the same assessment of the merits of the applicant's case. Public oral hearings contributed to the achievement of fair trials which were fundamental to a democratic society. Provided that there had been an oral hearing at first instance, the absence of such a hearing at second or third instance might be justified by the special features of the proceedings at issue even where the appellate court had jurisdiction to review the case both as to the facts and as to the law. That court had interpreted the law differently from the first instance court which led it to make findings of fact at first instance. As a matter of fair trial, a proper assessment of the merits of the case could not have been made without the evidence of the applicant and the two accused in person. There were no special features justifying the appellate court's refusal of an oral hearing.

There had been a violation of art 6(1) and, accordingly, the application would succeed. *Helmers v Sweden (Application 11826/85)* (1991) 15 EHRR 285 (European Court of Human Rights).

1419 Right to fair and public hearing—civil proceedings—length of proceedings

The applicant, a consultant microbiologist employed by a regional health authority, was dismissed for failing to follow staff appointment procedures. He was suspended from duty two years before his dismissal while disciplinary procedures against him were being carried out. Proceedings brought by him for unfair dismissal lasted for nine years before his case was eventually dismissed. His allegation of a violation of his right to a hearing within a reasonable time, guaranteed by the European Convention on Human Rights, art 6(1), was not contested by the United Kingdom government but no friendly settlement had been secured. *Held*, the applicant's medical competence had not been challenged or criticised but he had nevertheless suffered serious damage to his career because of time lost from the practice of medicine. Although the government's representative had made a public apology at the present hearing, the applicant would also be awarded a sum of £5,000 in respect of non-pecuniary damage. He would also be awarded a sum for legal costs.

Darnell v United Kingdom (Case No 34/1992/379/453) (1993) Times, 24 November (European Court of Human Rights).

1420 Right to fair and public hearing—civil proceedings—public adversarial hearing

In an administrative, non-adversarial and closed procedure carried out in the absence of the applicant, a post office accountant, the post office authorities decided that she should reimburse the post office for a sum which had disappeared from a cashier's desk for which she was responsible. She complained of a violation of her right to a fair hearing guaranteed by the European Convention on Human Rights, art 6(1). *Held*, the Belgian government had entered into a private settlement with the applicant which included the payment of compensation to her. A draft Act, which had as its purpose the rectification of the offending procedure by the introduction of adversarial and public hearings in cases such as the applicant's, was before parliament. There was no longer any reason of public policy requiring a decision on the merits and, accordingly, the court would strike out the application.

Muyldermans v Belgium (Application 12217/86) (1991) 15 EHRR 204 (European Court of Human Rights).

1421 Right to fair and public hearing—criminal proceedings—appellate proceedings—publicity

The applicant's appeal against conviction of a traffic offence was decided without an oral hearing and on the basis of the case file. He complained of a violation of his right to a fair and public hearing guaranteed by the European Convention on Human Rights, art 6(1). *Held*, account had to be taken of the entirety of the proceedings in the domestic legal order and of the appellate court's role. The trial at first instance had been held in public. The applicant's appeal raised no questions of fact or law which could not adequately be resolved on the basis of the case file. The offence in question was a minor one and the appeal court had no jurisdiction to increase the applicant's sentence. His application would fail.

Andersson v Sweden (Application 11274/84) (1991) 15 EHRR 218 (European Court of Human Rights).

1422 Right to fair and public hearing—criminal proceedings—equality of arms

Following a successful appeal against his conviction of forgery offences, the applicant's case was remitted to a different court. He was convicted again. On his second appeal against conviction, the court heard submissions from the avocat général, a member of the procureur général's department, in his capacity as adviser to the court and to whose submissions the applicant had no right to reply. The appeal was dismissed. The applicant complained of a violation of his right to equality of arms under the European Convention on Human Rights, art 6(1). *Held*, although the objectivity of the procureur général's department was unquestionable, the avocat général could not be regarded as neutral in the proceedings in question and, by making legal submissions unfavourable to the applicant, he became the applicant's opponent. There was no justification for the statutory restriction preventing the defence from replying to the avocat général's unfavourable submissions. The avocat général had even taken part, in an advisory capacity, in the appeal court's deliberations prior to its decision so that the inequality between the defence and the prosecution had been increased. It was reasonable to believe that the avocat général thereby had an additional opportunity to promote his submissions without fear of contradiction. There had been a violation of art 6(1) and, accordingly, the application would succeed.

Borgers v Belgium (Application 12005/86) (1991) 15 EHRR 92 (European Court of Human Rights).

1423   Right to fair and public hearing—criminal proceedings—impartial tribunal—presumption of impartiality

See *Thorgeirson v Iceland*, para 1412.

1424   Right to fair and public hearing—criminal proceedings—impartial tribunal—pre-trial decisions

The applicant was arrested in connection with bomb attacks on police stations. He was charged with criminal conspiracy and unlawful possession of weapons and with criminal damage and was detained on remand on both charges. Both his appeals against detention were dismissed. He was convicted of criminal conspiracy and unlawful possession of weapons by a court two of the judges of which had previously heard his appeal against detention on remand in respect of the charge of criminal damage. He complained that this constituted a violation of his right to a fair trial by an impartial tribunal, guaranteed by the European Convention on Human Rights, art 6(1). *Held*, fears concerning the partiality of the judges could not be justified merely because two of the trial judges had already taken pre-trial decisions in the case, including decisions concerning the detention on remand of the applicant. Such fears could only be justified by special circumstances which did not exist in this case. In ruling on the question of detention, the two judges relied on the applicant's own statements and the uncontested physical evidence. They had made only a brief assessment of the case for the purpose of establishing whether there was a risk of the applicant absconding. The application would be dismissed.

Sainte-Marie v France (Application 12981/87) (1992) 16 EHRR 116 (European Court of Human Rights).

The first applicant, in the absence of counsel, waived his right under national law to have disqualified from presiding over criminal proceedings against him two judges who had sat as investigating judges prior to his detention on remand. On his appeal against conviction, his challenge of the qualifications of the trial judges was dismissed and his sentence of imprisonment was confirmed. His correspondence with the second applicant, also detained on remand in connection with separate criminal proceedings, was censored by prison authorities. The first applicant complained of a violation of his right to an impartial trial contrary to the European Convention on Human Rights, art 6(1). Both applicants complained of a violation of their right to respect for correspondence contrary to art 8. *Held*, the waiver of rights guaranteed by the Convention had to be established in an unequivocal manner. Where procedural rights were concerned, such waiver had to accord with minimum guarantees commensurate with the importance of such rights. There was no provision of national law allowing for a defendant expressly to waive his right to have disqualified investigating judges. Further, in the absence of counsel, the first applicant was unable fully to appreciate the nature of such waiver. Accordingly, the waiver was deprived of any validity under the Convention. While some measure of control over prisoners' correspondence was not of itself incompatible with the Convention, the censorship of letters which criticised prison conditions and the behaviour of certain prison officers were, in the circumstances, disproportionate to the aim of protecting the rights of others and the prevention of crime. There had been a violation of arts 6(1), 8, and, accordingly, the applications would succeed.

Pfeifer and Plankl v Austria (Application 10802/84) (1992) 14 EHRR 692 (European Court of Human Rights).

1425   Right to fair and public hearing—criminal proceedings—legal assistance

Following a series of cases of arson and attacks on buildings using explosives during political demonstrations, the applicant was arrested and charged with the use of explosives. He complained that the exercise of surveillance over his meetings with his lawyer while the applicant was remanded in custody and the interception of his communications with him was a violation of his right to defend himself by means of legal assistance contrary to the European Convention on Human Rights, art 6(3)(c). *Held*, one of the basic requirements of a fair trial in a democratic society was the ability to communicate in confidence with one's lawyer out of the hearing of third parties. Even though the charges against the applicant were serious, a risk that defence counsel might collaborate to co-ordinate their defence strategy was not sufficient to restrict the rights guaranteed by art 6(3)(c). Further, the fact that the applicant had not necessarily suffered injury did not affect a finding that there had been a violation of the Convention. The application would succeed.

S v Switzerland (Applications 12629/87 and 13965/88) (1991) 14 EHRR 670 (European Court of Human Rights).

1426 Right to fair and public hearing—criminal proceedings—non-disclosure of material evidence

The applicant was convicted and sentenced to imprisonment for offences of robbery and burglary. Following a police investigation which revealed that evidence by a number of police witnesses had been withheld during his trial, the applicant's case was referred to the Court of Appeal. It reviewed the shortcomings in the police evidence but concluded that his convictions were not unsafe or unsatisfactory. The applicant complained of a violation of his right to a fair trial contrary to the European Convention on Human Rights, art 6. *Held,* the failure of the prosecution authorities to disclose to the defence all the material evidence for or against the accused gave rise to a defect in the trial proceedings. However, following an independent police investigation, the case had been referred to the Court of Appeal which had examined the transcript of the trial. The applicant was represented at the proceedings before the Court of Appeal by senior and junior counsel who had failed to apply for the police witnesses to be called to give evidence. The defects in the original trial had been remedied by the subsequent procedure before the Court of Appeal. The proceedings before that court appeared to be fair. Accordingly, the application would fail.

Edwards v United Kingdom (Application 13071/87) (1992) 15 EHRR 417 (European Court of Human Rights).

1427 Right to fair and public hearing—criminal proceedings—preparation of defence—advance disclosure of prosecution evidence

See *Vincent v The Queen; Franklyn v The Queen,* para 708.

1428 Right to family and private life—child in public care—access by parent to child

A child was taken into public care and placed in a foster home for the protection of his health and development. The social welfare authorities, in accordance with domestic legislation, prevented almost all contact between the child and his mother for over a year in order to avoid harm to the child. On their complaint of a violation of their right to respect for their family and private life contrary to the European Convention on Human Rights, art 8, *held,* the taking of a child into public care constituted an interference with the mutual enjoyment by parent and child of each other's company, a fundamental element of family life. Interference, the consequences of which must be reasonably foreseeable by those concerned, must be based on domestic law, if necessary with the assistance of appropriate advice. Provided that the scope and manner of the exercise of a discretionary power granted by legislation did not violate the principle of respect for family life, arbitrary decisions could be avoided. Although the interference with the rights of the mother and her son was in accordance with the law, that law was to be applied restrictively and only for the purpose of fulfilling the care measures concerned. Those measures were designed to protect health and morals and the rights and freedom of children, both legitimate for the purposes of art 8(2). The right to respect for family life included measures for uniting a family. The authorities concerned had failed to show that the prevention of contact between the mother and her child were both necessary and aimed at unification of their family. The measures taken were disproportionate to the legitimate aims pursued and were not necessary in a democratic society. There had been a violation of art 8.

Andersson v Sweden (Application 12963/87) (1992) 14 EHRR 615 (European Court of Human Rights).

1429 Right to family and private life—custody of children—religious discrimination

The applicant and her husband were divorced and she was granted custody of the children. The applicant was a Jehovah's Witness and intended to bring the children up according to the principles of that group. The father's appeal was allowed by the Austrian Supreme Court on the grounds that the intended education of the children contravened a federal Act on the religious education of children, and that such an upbringing was detrimental to the childrens' best interests because the applicant would refuse to consent to their receiving blood transfusions and the group was socially marginalised. The applicant contended that the decision violated the European Convention on Human Rights, arts 8 (right to respect for private and family life), 9 (right to freedom of religion), and 14 (prohibition on religious discrimination). *Held*, the Supreme Court's judgment violated art 8 taken in conjunction with art 14: the applicant had been discriminated against on the grounds of religion in the enjoyment of her right to respect for her private and family life. Whilst the Supreme Court was legitimately concerned with protecting the childrens' best interests, the fact that the decision was based primarily on religious differences was not justifiable. No separate issue arose under art 9. Accordingly, the application would be allowed.

Hoffmann v Austria (Case No 15/1992/360/434) [1994] 1 FCR 193 (European Court of Human Rights).

1430   Right to family and private life—foreign national—deportation

The applicant was born in Morocco and came to the United Kingdom when about six or seven years of age with his mother and brothers and sisters to live with his father who had already settled there. The applicant acquired a long criminal record for minor offences of dishonesty and some offences of violence. Following his conviction of wounding when he was aged about 18, the Secretary of State decided to make a deportation order against him on the ground that this would be conducive to the public good. The applicant's appeal against the order on the ground that he spoke no Arabic and that all his family lived in the United Kingdom was rejected and he was taken to Morocco. He returned to the United Kingdom but was subsequently deported. He complained of a violation of his rights, under the European Convention on Human Rights, arts 8, 14, to respect for private and family life and to the securing of rights and freedoms under the Convention without discrimination. A friendly settlement was concluded between the applicant and the United Kingdom government (without any admission by the latter that a breach of the Convention had occurred and on condition that the case was withdrawn from the court and that no further cases were instituted against the government in respect of this matter in any national or international court) under which the government proposed to revoke the deportation order, allow the applicant to re-enter the United Kingdom, give him indefinite leave to remain, allow him to make an application for naturalisation and pay the costs actually and necessarily incurred by the applicant and which were reasonable. Accordingly, the European Court of Human Rights decided that the case be struck out of its list and that, therefore, it did not need to decide whether the decision to deport the applicant was in breach of the Convention.

Lamguindaz v United Kingdom (Application 16152/90) (1993) 17 EHRR 213 (European Court of Human Rights).

1431   Right to family and private life—homosexual conduct in private—prohibition

The applicant was a homosexual male adult involved in a sexual relationship with another male adult and was the president of an organisation for the freedom of homosexuals in Cyprus where male homosexual conduct in private between adults was a criminal offence. He complained that this law caused him great strain, apprehension and fear of prosecution in violation of his right to respect for his private life guaranteed by the European Convention on Human Rights, art 8. *Held*, the policy of the Attorney General of Cyprus not to bring prosecutions in respect of private homosexual conduct was not a guarantee against police investigation and private prosecutions, particularly in the light of statements made by some government ministers who were not in favour of amending the law in question. The existence of the statutory prohibition continuously and directly affected the applicant's private life. There was no justification for such interference with his private life. The application would be granted.

Modinos v Cyprus (Application 15070/89) (1993) 16 EHRR 485 (European Court of Human Rights).

1432   Right to family and private life—professional or business activities or premises—search of lawyer's premises

Police effected a search of the offices of the applicant, a lawyer, pursuant to a search warrant for the purpose of obtaining information that would reveal the identity and possible whereabouts of a third party who was the subject of a criminal investigation. The applicant complained of a violation of his right to respect for his home and correspondence, guaranteed by the European

Convention on Human Rights, art 8, and a breach of his rights, under Protocol 1, art 1, by the impairment of his reputation as a lawyer. *Held*, the right to respect for private life included the right to develop relationships with others. The interpretation of "private life" and "home" in art 8 so as to include certain professional or business activities or premises would be in accordance with the object and purpose of art 8. The terms of the warrant were wide and the police had carried out an extensive search which must have included examination of materials which constituted "correspondence" for the purposes of art 8 which, although the correspondence was of a professional nature, was applicable. Although the search was lawful under German law and its aims were legitimate under art 8(2), because they were intended to protect the rights of others and to prevent crime, the interference was not necessary in a democratic society. The search was not proportionate to the legitimate aims sought to be achieved; it had not been accompanied by any special procedural safeguards. Further and more importantly, the search impinged on the professional secrecy of the lawyer to a disporportionate extent. As the court had already considered the potential effects of the search on the applicant's professional reputation in the context of art 8, no separate issue arose under Protocol 1, art 1. There had been a violation of art 8 and, accordingly, the application would succeed.

Niemietz v Germany (Application 13710/88) (1992) 16 EHRR 97 (European Court of Human Rights).

1433   Right to family and private life—security surveillance—discretionary measures

The applicants complained that secret surveillance of their private lives, including indirect interception of communications with persons under direct telephone tapping and the maintenance of records classifying them as "communist sympathisers" and "subversives", by the national secret service constituted a violation of their right to respect for their private life contrary to the European Convention on Human Rights, art 8. *Held*, the storing of information concerning a person's private life in a secret police register interfered with the right to respect for private life so that the collection and retention of such information also violated that right. A complainant was not required to show that such information had actually been compiled and retained but had to show the existence of secret measures designed to collect and retain such information, and a reasonable likelihood that the secret service had compiled and retained information concerning his private life. That burden had been discharged by the evidence of an ex-intelligence officer. The interference with the applicants' private lives was based on a non-binding and unpublished directive from the British government to the Director General of the Secret Service; it did not constitute legally enforceable rules nor establish a framework indicating sufficiently clearly and with adequate foreseeability the scope and manner of the exercise of the authorities' discretion in carrying out secret surveillance activities. The applicants had no means of knowing when and on what basis their communications might be intercepted. Accordingly, the interference was not in accordance with the law within the exceptions in art 8(2). The applications would succeed.

Hewitt and Harman v United Kingdom (Application 12175/86) (1992) 14 EHRR 657 (European Court of Human Rights).

1434   Right to liberty—arrest without warrant and extended detention—public emergency

The applicants were arrested without warrant pursuant to the Prevention of Terrorism (Temporary Provisions) Act 1984 on suspicion of involvement in terrorist acts and detained for a period which was extended by order of the Secretary of State under his powers under the Act. They complained of a violation of their right, guaranteed by the European Convention on Human Rights, art 5(3), to be brought promptly before a judge. *Held*, in the light of the extent and impact of terrorist violence in Northern Ireland and elsewhere in the United Kingdom, a "public emergency" threatening the life of the nation within art 15, entitling the United Kingdom to derogate from its obligations under the Convention, existed at the relevant time. The power of arrest and extended detention had been considered necessary by the United Kingdom government since 1974 in dealing with the threat of terrorism. In the context of Northern Ireland, where the judiciary was small and vulnerable to terrorist attacks, public confidence in the independence of the judiciary was understandably a matter to which the government attached great importance. It could not be said that the government had exceeded the margin of appreciation in deciding, in the prevailing circumstances, against judicial control. The remedy of habeas corpus was available to test the lawfulness of the original arrest and detention of suspects under the 1984 Act; that remedy satisfied the requirements of the right to an effective remedy under art 13 of the Convention. The United Kingdom had not exceeded its margin of appreciation in considering that the derogation from the Convention was strictly required by the exigencies of the situation and, accordingly, the applications would be dismissed.

Brannigan and McBride v United Kingdom (Case No 5/1992/350/423–424) (1993) Times, 28 May, Independent, 28 May (European Court of Human Rights).

1435 Right to liberty—lawfulness of detention—detention pending trial

The applicant, a member of a political organisation which sought the independence of Corsica, was detained in custody while several serious criminal offences, including murder and the possession of firearms, in which he was believed to be implicated were investigated. He was eventually acquitted of all the offences. He complained that his detention, which had lasted for five years and seven months during which he had made numerous applications for his release, was a violation of his right, under the European Convention on Human Rights, art 5(3), to be released pending trial and that ill-treatment suffered by him while in police custody was a violation of his right, under art 3, not to be subjected to inhuman or degrading treatment. *Held*, national judicial authorities were required to ensure that the pre-trial detention of an accused person did not exceed a reasonable time. After a certain time, it was not sufficient that there was a reasonable suspicion that the accused had committed an offence, there had to be other sufficient and relevant grounds for his detention. The investigation of the offences was delayed by the judicial authorities and the public prosecutor for two periods of over a year each. Medical evidence showed that the applicant's injuries related to the time when he was in police custody and were sufficiently serious to render his treatment inhuman and degrading. The requirements and difficulties of investigating and fighting crime, particularly with respect to terrorism, could not result in limits being placed on the protection to be afforded in respect of the physical integrity of individuals. There had been a violation of arts 3, 5(3) and, therefore, the application would succeed.

Tomasi v France (Application 12850/87) (1992) 15 EHRR 1 (European Court of Human Rights).

The applicant, a suspect in a murder and arson case who had previous convictions for attempted aggravated theft and for desertion from the army, was detained in custody for three years and two months and then released with no case to answer. He complained that the period of his detention was unreasonable contrary to the European Convention on Human Rights, art 5(3). *Held*, although psychiatric reports showed the applicant to be dangerous but in need of therapy, neither the charges against him nor his psychiatric condition justified his continued detention without therapeutic treatment. The length of the detention was due in part to the complexity of the case, in which more than 200 people were questioned, reheard and confronted with one another, and in part to the conduct of the applicant who gave more than 20 different versions of the events in question and persistently changed his statements. Fears of the applicant absconding had become immaterial 31 months after his arrest. The length of his detention exceeded a reasonable time within art 5(3) and his application would succeed.

Clooth v Belgium (Application 12718/87) (1991) 14 EHRR 717 (European Court of Human Rights).

The applicant was detained for six weeks while serious currency offences alleged to have been committed by him were being investigated and, subsequently, for two years and nine months after his committal for trial. He complained of a violation of his right to a trial within a reasonable time or to be released pending trial, contrary to the European Convention on Human Rights, arts 5(3), 6(1), contending that, in view of the rapidity with which he had been released after the six-week detention, that detention had been unjustified and that the period of his detention pending trial had been unreasonable. *Held*, in view of the gravity of the offences and the requirements of the investigation, the first detention was justified: the investigating judge had only agreed to release the applicant subject to court supervision and after the payment of a substantial security. As to his detention pending trial, although the existence and persistence of serious indications of a detainee's guilt were relevant factors, they did not alone justify such a long period of pre-trial detention as in the applicant's case. Pre-trial detention on the ground of the requirements of public order was only justified if based on facts capable of showing that the detainee's release would actually disturb public order and his detention might continue as long as public order remained actually threatened. It was not sufficient that the detainee was expected to incur a custodial sentence. While the risk of pressure being brought to bear on witnesses and the applicant's co-accused might have justified his pre-trial detention, that detention could only continue if the risk remained. Once the offence had been investigated by the judge, that risk disappeared and the justification for the detention was no longer valid. A risk of the accused absconding might also justify pre-trial detention, but once there appeared to the court to be no such risk, he had to be released. There had been a violation of arts 5(3), 6(1) and the application would succeed.

Kemmache v France (1992) 14 EHRR 520 (European Court of Human Rights).

HUSBAND AND WIFE

Halsbury's Laws of England (4th edn) Vol 22, paras 901–1178

1436 Articles
Marital Rape: Justice at Last, Marianne Giles: 135 SJ 1210
The Policing of Domestic Violence, Valerie Cromack and Ada Kewley: [1993] Fam Law 594

1437 Consent to marriage—misrepresentation as to identity—vitiation of consent
The petitioner married the respondent, not knowing that he had no right to be in this country nor that he had assumed the identity of another man. She did not discover his true identity until he was deported. She applied for a decree of nullity. *Held*, there was authority that fraud as to the identity of the parties vitiated consent. Marriage must be by mutual consent and where one party married the other on the basis of a false representation, the marriage was void. Accordingly, the application would be allowed.

Militante v Ogunwomoju [1993] 2 FCR 355 (Family Division: Judge Owen).

1438 Dissolution of marriage—validity of Ghanaian dissolution
The parties were married in Ghana and came to live in England. The wife subsequently commenced divorce proceedings. Meanwhile, the husband returned to Ghana and, without the wife's knowledge or consent, successfully applied to the customary arbitration tribunal for the marriage to be dissolved. He contended that the dissolution was entitled to recognition in the United Kingdom by virtue of the Family Law Act 1986, s 46. *Held*, the court accepted evidence that the tribunal's decision would not be effective under Ghanaian law. The requirement for both parties to express their voluntary agreement to submit to arbitration had not been complied with, nor, given the wife's absence, had the tribunal fulfilled its duty to go into the merits. Further, even if the proceedings were effective under Ghanaian law, the court was entitled to exercise its discretion to refuse recognition under the 1986 Act, s 51 because there had been an unreasonable failure to notify the wife of the proceedings. The marriage was thus valid and subsisting and, accordingly, the husband's petition would be dismissed.

D v D (1993) Independent, 13 October (Family Division: Wall J).

1439 Divorce
See DIVORCE.

1440 Foreign marriage—validity of Ghanaian marriage
It has been held that a marriage conducted in Ghana between an Irishman and a Ghanaian according to local custom, which does not require the attendance of the parties to the marriage either in person or by proxy, could be recognised by an English court as a valid marriage.

McCabe v McCabe [1993] 1 FLR 257 (Court of Appeal: Butler-Sloss LJ and Bracewell J).

1441 Matrimonial home—application for injunction—order made subsequent to decree absolute—applicability of statute
The appellant and respondent, who were married, separated and occupied different rooms in the matrimonial home. The appellant subsequently purchased the property with her daughter and commenced divorce proceedings. The respondent then went to Jamaica and while he was there the decree nisi was pronounced. On his return he attempted to enter the property but was prevented by the appellant, so he obtained an ex parte order protecting his rights of occupation. After the decree absolute an injunction was granted requiring the appellant to permit the respondent to occupy the matrimonial home. The judge held that since the application for an

injunction was made while the marriage was still continuing, he had jurisdiction to make the order under the Matrimonial Homes Act 1983. On appeal, *held*, the 1983 Act did not apply to the rights of a former husband or wife; this was clearly indicated by the use of the word "spouse" throughout the Act. The Domestic Violence and Matrimonial Proceedings Act 1976 applied to a man or woman living in the same household, and was primarily designed to deal with urgent situations and to give short term relief. The judge had concerned himself with matters relevant to the 1983 Act and not the 1976 Act. Under the 1976 Act he should have considered such factors as the urgency of the situation, the quality of the relationship and the availability of alternative accommodation, which he clearly did not do. Even if the judge did have jurisdiction to make an order under the 1976 Act, he did not carry out any exercise of discretion under that Act and the decision could not therefore be supported on that ground. In addition, there was no inherent jurisdiction to grant an injunction after decree absolute in the absence of the involvement of children, or in the absence of a legal right to found the claim. It was also important in cases of this type that the orders for occupation were limited in time, so that parties should have a clear idea of what was expected of them in the future. Accordingly, the appeal would be allowed.

Hennie v Hennie [1993] 2 FLR 351 (Court of Appeal: Lloyd LJ and Connell J).

1442   Matrimonial home—charging order against husband's interest—order for sale

A husband was the legal owner of the matrimonial home and held it on trust for sale for himself and the wife in equal shares. He and another director signed a joint and several guarantee to the bank for the debts of their company. The bank obtained a default judgment for the principal and interest due and a charging order against the husband's interest in the matrimonial home. It then successfully applied for an order for sale of the property under the Law of Property Act 1925, s 30 and the wife appealed. *Held*, under the 1925 Act, s 30 the court had an unfettered discretion to make such order as it thought equitable and just. The court had to consider all the circumstances and weigh the competing equities. Where a spouse who had a beneficial interest in the matrimonial home became bankrupt and the debts could not be repaid without the realisation of that interest, the voice of the creditor would usually prevail over that of the other spouse and a sale of the property would be ordered. That principle equally applied where the applicant for an order for sale was a chargee. In the present case the voice of the bank would prevail. It had a mounting debt which would be satisfied by the sale proceeds, leaving a sufficient amount to rehouse the couple. Accordingly, the appeal would be dismissed.

Lloyds Bank plc v Byrne [1993] 2 FCR 41 (Court of Appeal: Parker and Taylor LJJ and Sir Roualeyn Cumming-Bruce).

1443   Matrimonial home—order relating to occupation of matrimonial home—matters to be taken into account

It has been held that courts making orders relating to the occupation of the matrimonial home ought to have regard to the factors contained in the Matrimonial Homes Act 1983, s 1(3) namely, the conduct of the parties in relation to each other, their respective needs and financial resources, the needs of any children and all the circumstances of the case. Of the aforementioned factors none would be paramount over any other, but the weight to be given to each depended on the facts of each case. Further the case of *Richards v Richards* [1984] AC 174 had not been abrogated by the provisions of the Children Act 1989.

Gibson v Austin [1992] 2 FLR 437 (Court of Appeal: Nourse and Balcombe LJJ).

1444   Matrimonial home—severance of joint tenancy—property vesting in trustee

See *Re Kumar (A Bankrupt), ex p Lewis v Kumar*, para 178.

1445   Matrimonial injunction—contempt—consideration of consequences of breach

It has been held that in cases involving injunctions where the potential consequences of a breach are important, courts ought only to use the power to amend orders made in inferior courts in exceptional cases. Further, it is inappropriate to use the county court slip rule under CCR Ord 15, to extend an injunction where a respondent is not represented.

Langley v Langley (1993) Times, 20 October (Court of Appeal: Russell, Staughton and Steyn LJJ).

1446   Matrimonial injunction—non-molestation injunction—breach—whether sentence of imprisonment appropriate

The contemnor breached a non-molestation order and was committed to prison for three months. He appealed on the grounds that it was his first breach of the order. *Held*, the contemnor had not pleaded guilty nor had he expressed remorse and it was no defence that this was the first breach. Accordingly, the appeal would be dismissed.

A v D (Contempt: Committal) [1993] Fam Law 519 (Court of Appeal: Russell, Leggatt and Rose LJJ).

1447   Matrimonial injunction—ouster order—breach—whether custodial sentence appropriate

The wife obtained an injunction which prohibited the husband from entering the matrimonial home. It warned that non-compliance would render him guilty of contempt and might result in a custodial sentence. The husband subsequently used a trick to enter the house whilst the wife was out, threatened the wife's sister and her boyfriend, and ransacked the house. He was committed to prison for six months. On appeal, he contended that the judge was wrong in principle to deal with the matter as he did since a committal order should be a last resort in matrimonial cases. *Held*, in matrimonial disputes, the order that had to be made following a breach of undertaking or injunction was dependent upon the circumstances of the case and varied accordingly. Here, there was a blatant and aggravated contempt by a man who had been repeatedly warned of the consequences of non-compliance. Such serious contempt was a defiance of the court's authority and prejudiced the wife's rights. It justified the imposition of an immediate custodial sentence, but six months was unnecessarily long in the circumstances. Accordingly, the appeal would be allowed to the extent of reducing the sentence to three months' imprisonment.

Jones v Jones [1993] 2 FCR 82 (Court of Appeal: Russell and Simon Brown, LJJ and Sir Michael Fox).

1448   Matrimonial injunction—ouster order—interests of child

The parties purchased a property in their joint names. They later had a child and when their relationship deteriorated the mother left the home and sought an ouster order against the father. At the hearing the judge found that both parties were equally to blame for the state of their relationship and whilst there might have been violence the mother had not left because of that but because she found it intolerable to live with the father as he was having an affair. It was equally inconvenient for the mother and the father to be removed from the matrimonial home. An order was granted in favour of the mother because she was caring for the child. On appeal by the father, *held*, the correct test was not what was in the best interests of the child, as this fell short of what was required to make an ouster order. The judge did not find any risk of continuing physical danger or violence and as such the housing of the child was irrelevant to an application under the Domestic Violence and Matrimonial Proceedings Act 1976. In exercising his discretion, the judge had failed to take into account the nature of an ouster order and the effect it would have on the party against whom it was made. Accordingly, the appeal would be allowed and the case remitted for a rehearing.

Grant v James [1993] 1 FCR 850 (Court of Appeal: Purchas LJ and Cazalet J).

1449   Matrimonial proceedings—marriage entered into under duress—proceedings to nullify marriage

Scotland

The applicant had, at the age of 21, entered into a marriage which had been arranged by her parents five years previously. She had protested against the marriage, but her parents had threatened to disown her, to desist supporting her financially and to send her to live in Pakistan if she failed to comply with their wishes. At a procedure roll hearing she gave evidence that her parents had already disowned her elder sister and brother for refusing to enter into arranged marriages, and she applied for the marriage to be annulled on the ground that her consent had been obtained by duress. Her husband accepted that lack of true consent could be a ground for nullifying marriage, but contended that the duress suffered by his wife would not have constituted threats of such gravity as would have swayed the mind of an ordinary person. *Held*, in every case it was a question of degree as to whether or not the threats offered were sufficient to overcome the will of the person concerned. The specific threats made to the applicant had gone beyond the limits of proper parental influence and were sufficient to overwhelm someone of her age and cultural background, and it was necessary to consider the matters which arose before her consent was given to determine whether or not her consent had been genuine. Judgment would be given accordingly.

Mahmood v Mahmood 1993 SLT 589 (Outer House).

IMMIGRATION

See BRITISH NATIONALITY, IMMIGRATION AND RACE RELATIONS.

INCOME TAXATION

Halsbury's Laws of England (4th edn) Vol 23 (reissue), paras 1–1747

1450 Articles

A Royal Taxing Problem? Adam Tomkins and Adrian Shipwright: 137 SJ 102

Away with the Schedules! George Horsman: Tax Journal, Issue 232, p 12

Credit Unions, David Harris (on the tax consequences of credit unions): Tax Journal, Issue 231, p 10

Current Developments with Thin Capitalisation, Andrew Wells: Tax Journal, Issue 203, p 9

Distributions: Not Just Dividends, Tim Good (on advance corporation tax): Tax Journal, Issue 219, p 18

Extending Share Schemes Overseas, Patrick Moon: Tax Journal, Issue 207, p 16

If At First You Don't Succeed, Martin Kaye (on the Finance Act 1993, s 108): Tax Journal, Issue 228, p 12

Income or Capital? James Savoury (on the distinction between income and capital for tax purposes): Tax Journal, Issue 219, p 10

Is it Allowable? Sylvia Elwes (on expenses incurred in the course of employment): 137 SJ 662

Newspapers and Periodicals, Hugh McKay (on journalists' expenditure on newspapers): Tax Journal, Issue 219, p 6

Partnerships and Parts of Businesses, Richard Holme and David Williams (on *Re Sutherland & Partners' Appeal* [1993] STC 399 (para 1452)): Tax Journal, Issue 224, p 15

Payments to Employees—To Tax or Not to Tax, Francis Fitzpatrick: Tax Journal, Issue 234, p 16

Questions of Cessation, David Harris (on *Maidment v Kibby* [1993] STC 494 (para 1496)): Tax Journal, Issue 227, p 13

Restitution of Taxes, Levies and Other Imposts—Defining the Extent of the *Woolwich* Principle, J Beatson (on *Woolwich Equitable Building Society v Inland Revenue Commissioners* [1993] 1 AC 70, HL (1992 Abr para 1398)): 109 LQR 401

Restitution of Unlawfully Demanded Tax, Ewan McKendrick: [1993] LMCLQ 88

Share Schemes and the Expatriate Participant, Patrick Moon: Tax Journal, Issue 205, p 15

SP3/91: A Nail in the Coffin? Mark Penney and Bruce Reeves-Dienes (on *Gallagher v Jones* [1993] STC 199 (para 1480)): Tax Journal, Issue 205, p 18

Tax Aspects for Overseas Investors, Malcolm Finney: Estates Gazette, 19 June 1993, p 92

Taxing Perks and Interpreting Statutes—*Pepper v Hart*, David Miers (on *Pepper v Hart* [1993] 1 All ER 42 (1992 Abr para 2498)): 56 MLR 695

Tax Law Versus Tax Practice, Ian Saunders (on *Gallagher v Jones* [1993] STC 199 (para 1480)): 137 SJ 680

Taxing Issues, David Williams (on taxation of the self-employed): LS Gaz, 21 July 1993, p 31

The Proposed New Regime, Francis Sanderson (on the tax treatment of foreign exchange gains and losses): Tax Journal, Issue 204, p 4

What Will the City Think, Stephen Edge (on the tax treatment of foreign exchange gains and losses): Tax Journal, Issue 204, p 9

Year-End Personal Tax Planning, Julie Clift: Tax Journal, Issue 205, p 12

1451 Appeal—appeal by way of case stated—remission to commissioners— further findings of fact

Following investigations by the Inland Revenue as a result of information received from informants, assessments to income tax, based on rentals from residential lettings, were made on the taxpayer. The hearing of his appeal against the assessments lasted for 15 days during which 19 witnesses were called and a substantial amount of documentary evidence was adduced. The Special Commissioners found that the taxpayer was not a witness of truth and that the weight of evidence supporting the assessments was overwhelming. Where the evidence of witnesses conflicted with the facts found, that evidence was rejected. On further appeal, the taxpayer contended that the case stated by the commissioners should be remitted for further findings of fact because they had refused to admit certain evidence. *Held*, on the basis of the facts set out in the case stated, the appeal was bound to fail. In view of the length of the hearing before the commissioners, the number of witnesses called and the amount of documentary evidence adduced, and the commissioners' finding that the taxpayer was not a witness of truth, it could not be said that they had erred in refusing to admit any evidence. The appeal would be dismissed.

Zielinski v Pickering (Inspector of Taxes) (note) [1993] STC 418 (Chancery Division: Vinelott J).

1452 Appeal—appeal by way of case stated—striking out—appeal by single partner

Six doctors who practised medicine in partnership appealed against tax assessments on the partnership. The main points of contention were the deductibility of each partner's personal expenses. Before the date of the hearing of the appeal, the partnership divided between five of the doctors. The partnership's accountants, acting only for the five doctors, negotiated their clients' expense claims with the Revenue. The sixth doctor unsuccessfully sought to have some of the expenses disallowed. In an application by the five doctors to strike out a case that had been stated by the General Commissioners at the request of the sixth doctor, to challenge the assessments, *held*, a single partner acting against the wishes of his co-partners could not bring an appeal by way of case stated against a determination by the commissioners as to the partnership's income tax liability. The sixth doctor was not to be described as an appellant who was dissatisfied with the commissioner's determination for the purposes of the Taxes Management Act 1970, s 56; he had expressed his dissatisfaction and had requested a case to be stated neither in the partnership name nor in any other manner showing an intention to bind the partnership. The commissioners and the Revenue knew that the sixth doctor was acting against the wishes and without the consent of the other doctors. Accordingly, the application would be allowed.

Re Sutherland & Partners' Appeal [1993] STC 399 (Chancery Division: Lindsay J).
This decision has been reversed: (1994) Times, 4 March, CA.

1453 Appeal—appeal by way of case stated—transmission to High Court—time limit

The provisions of the Taxes Management Act 1970, s 56 govern the jurisdiction of the High Court to entertain an appeal by way of case stated from either General or Special Commissioners. The 1970 Act, s 56(1) provides for either the appellant or inspector to declare dissatisfaction with the commissioner's decision. Section 56(2) requires a notice in writing addressed to the clerk to the commissioners, requesting the statement of case within 30 days of the determination and s 56(4) states that the case must contain the facts and the determination of the commissioner, and that the party requiring it should transmit it to the High Court within 30 days of receiving it.

The taxpayer appealed to a Special Commissioner in respect of two income tax assessments. One assessment was then reduced and the other was discharged. The taxpayer and the Crown were dissatisfied with the decision of the commisioner and both requested a case to be stated for the opinion of the High Court, pursuant to s 56. The taxpayer received the case after it had been stated and signed, and transmitted it to the High Court. The Crown applied for an order that the taxpayer's appeal be struck out on the grounds that it had not been transmitted within 30 days, as required by s 56(4). The taxpayer then sought to strike out the Crown's appeal against the commissioner's decision on the grounds that it disclosed no reasonable cause of action and that it was frivolous and vexatious under RSC Ord 18, r 19, and an order that the Crown's application to dismiss the appeal be struck out on the grounds that it disclosed no reasonable cause of action, was scandalous and vexatious, had delayed the fair trial of the action, and was otherwise an abuse of process. *Held*, the 30-day limit was imperative and mandatory. The taxpayers failure to comply with the terms of the provision deprived the court of its jurisdiction to entertain the appeal. The court's power to strike out proceedings under RSC Ord 18, r 19, or under its inherent jurisdiction to control any step of the proceedings before it, could only be exercised in plain and obvious cases. It was very unlikely to be plain and obvious that a case stated, under the 1970 Act, s 56, would be such as to disclose no reasonable cause of action or be frivolous or vexatious. The only way to determine whether the commissioner was correct was to have the matter argued, not by way of an application to strike out. Accordingly, the taxpayer's application to strike out the Crown's appeal and to strike out the Crown's application would be dismissed.

Petch v Gurney (Inspector of Taxes); Gurney (Inspector of Taxes) v Petch [1992] STC 892 (Chancery Division: Harman J).

1454 Appeal—pending appeal—liability to pay tax

The taxpayer appealed against a refusal to set aside a statutory demand in respect of income tax assessments. He contended that the statutory requirement that, where an appeal against assessment was pending, tax had to be paid, was unfair, and offered to provide his house as security. *Held*, the taxpayer's offer did not satisfy the Insolvency Rules 1986, SI 1986/1925, r 6.5(4)(c), by virtue of which an application to set aside a statutory demand might be granted if it appeared to the court that the creditor held some security in respect of the debt claimed by the demand. The Revenue did not hold security in respect of the debt which it claimed by the demand. The most there had been was a general offer from the taxpayer without any specific details of the value of his house or the incumbrances, in addition to the mortgage, on it. There were no grounds for setting aside the statutory demand. The appeal would be dismissed.

Re a Debtor (No 960/SD/1992), ex p the Debtor v IRC (note) [1993] STC 218 (Chancery Division: Mummery J).

1455 Assessment—agreement—further assessment

The Taxes Management Act 1970, s 54 provides that where a person gives notice of appeal and, before the appeal is determined by the General Commissioners, the inspector and the appellant come to an agreement that the assessment or decision under appeal should be treated as upheld without variation or as varied in a particular manner the like consequences will ensue for all purposes as would have ensued if, at the time when the agreement was reached, the commissioners had determined the appeal.

The taxpayer appealed against estimated assessments to tax which had been raised against him. Agreement was reached between the taxpayer and a tax inspector and the amounts of the assessments were determined in accordance with s 54. Subsequently these assessments were found to have been incorrectly made and further assessments were raised under the 1970 Act, s 29(3). The General Commissioners discharged the further assessments. On appeal on the question of whether the tax inspector was precluded from making further assessments, *held*, the trading profits shown in the taxpayer's accounts had been incorrect. The further assessments could not be barred by an agreement between the parties that was based on statements by the taxpayer as to his trading profits during the relevant period which although made innocently, were incorrect. Accordingly, the appeal would be allowed.

Gray (Inspector of Taxes) v Matheson [1993] STC 178 (Chancery Division: Vinelott J).

1456 Assessment—assessment made in accordance with practice generally prevailing—validity

Tax was deducted from payments made to the taxpayer's wife by the Home Office to sponsor her postgraduate training as a probation officer on the basis that the payments were subject to income tax under Schedule E. The taxpayer appealed against assessments made alternatively under Schedule E and Schedule D in respect of those payments for the years 1983–84 to 1985–1986 inclusive. The assessments made under Schedule E for 1983–84 and 1984–85 were made more than 12 months after the end of the relevant years of assessment, and were made in accordance with the practice generally prevailing at the time, pursuant to the Income and Corporation Taxes Act 1970, s 206, which was to treat sponsorship payments such as those received by the taxpayer's wife as income chargeable to tax under Schedule E and not as exempt under s 375. The Special Commissioner decided that the payments would be chargeable to tax under Schedule D but were exempt by virtue of s 375 as scholarship income and that, even though the assessments for 1983–84 and 1984–85 were made in accordance with s 206, he had jurisdiction to vary them. The Crown appealed against the latter decision contending that, since the assessments had been made in accordance with s 206, they were correct as a matter of law and could not be successfully appealed against. *Held*, only Parliament could authorise the levying of taxes and it had done so by way of the charging provisions of the Schedules. However, in s 206, it had expressly required the assessment to be made, not in accordance with the charging provisions of the Schedules, but in accordance with the practice generally prevailing at the relevant time. Section 206 gave the assessment a status which it would not otherwise command.

Although s 206 was ambiguous and obscure, s 375 was not. It conferred unqualified exemption on the sums received by the taxpayer's wife and could only be displaced by plain words to that effect in s 206. Section 206 contained no such words. Section 375 excluded the normal charging provisions and, accordingly, excluded the charge under s 206. The appeal would be dismissed.

Walters (Inspector of Taxes) v Tickner [1993] STC 624 (Court of Appeal: Lloyd, Mann and Nolan LJJ). Decision of Rattee J [1992] STC 343 (1992 Abr para 1381) affirmed.

1970 Act, ss 206, 375 now Income and Corporation Taxes Act 1988, ss 206, 331.

1457 Basic rate limit and personal reliefs—indexation

The Income Tax (Indexation) Order 1993, SI 1993/755 (made on 16 March 1993), prescribes the basic rate limit and the personal reliefs for 1993–94, increased in accordance with the percentage increase in the retail prices index for December 1992 over that for December 1991. The basic rate limit will be £24,400. The lower rate limit will be £2,100. The personal allowance will be £3,535, or £4,310 (for those aged 65–74), or £4,490 (for those aged 75 and over); the enhanced reliefs on account of age are reduced where a claimant's total income for the year of assessment exceeds £14,600. The married couple's allowance will be £1,770, or £2,535 (where either party is aged 65–74), or £2,575 (where either party is aged 75 and over); the enhanced reliefs on account of age are reduced where a claimant's total income for the year of assessment exceeds £14,600. The amounts have effect unless Parliament otherwise determines (see the Finance Act 1993, para 2160).

The Income Tax (Indexation) (No 2) Order 1993, SI 1993/2948 (made on 30 November 1993), prescribes the basic rate limit and the personal reliefs for 1994–95, increased in accordance with the percentage increase in the retail prices index for September 1993 over that for September 1992. The basic rate limit will be £24,200. The lower rate limit will be £2,600. The personal allowance will be £3,515, or £4,280 (for those aged 65–74), or £4,450 (for those aged 75 and over); the enhanced reliefs on account of age are reduced where a claimant's total income for the year of assessment exceeds £14,500. The married couple's allowance will be £1,760, or £2,515 (where either party is aged 65–74), or £2,555 (where either party is aged 75 and over); the enhanced reliefs on account of age are reduced where a claimant's total income for the year of assessment exceeds £14,500. The amounts have effect unless Parliament otherwise determines (see the Budget, para 2151).

1458 Capital allowances—expenditure on films, tapes and discs—options for writing off expenditure

The Inland Revenue has issued a Statement of Practice SP 1/93, incorporating and updating Statements of Practice SP 2/83 and SP 2/85, in which it gives guidance on certain procedural and other points arising from changes made by the Finance (No 2) Act 1992 to the Capital Allowances Act 1990, s 68, concerning the tax treatment of expenditure on films and audio products. The changes, which apply to films certified under the Films Act 1985 which have to meet certain criteria in respect of their Community and Commonwealth content, provide additional options for writing off expenditure on such films and, consequently, accelerate tax relief for such expenditure. See further *STI*, 14 January 1993.

1459 Capital allowances—expenditure on scientific research—grants—corresponding Northern Ireland grants

The Capital Allowances (Corresponding Northern Ireland Grants) Order 1993, SI 1993/2705 (in force on 23 November 1993), specifies certain grants the amounts of which are not to be deducted from the recipient's capital expenditure when his capital allowances are calculated. The order succeeds the 1991 Order, SI 1991/518, which applies to grants made under agreements entered into before 1 April 1993.

1460 Capital allowances—industrial buildings—buildings in enterprise zone—withdrawal of assurance

The applicants had sponsored a unit trust scheme which enabled higher rate taxpayers to purchase certain buildings in a designated enterprise zone. The solicitors for the applicants had received written assurance from a tax inspector that capital allowances would be available to the purchasers in respect of the purchase price of the buildings. They then took steps to proceed with the purchase in reliance on the assurance given by the tax inspector. Following adverse press comment the assurance was withdrawn. An application for judicial review of the withdrawal was refused at first instance. On appeal by the applicants, the question arose whether the withdrawal was unfair and whether there had been sufficient disclosure of material facts by the applicants' solicitors to the tax inspector. *Held*, Roch LJ dissenting, if a taxpayer sought assurances as to the taxation consequences of a course of action there had to be candid disclosure on his part. In certain cases it was merely necessary to set out the facts in full and then ask the question to which an answer was required from the inspector. However, in the present case the purchase involved many complex arrangements and it was impossible to distinguish the facts from the legal issues. The Revenue had to exercise great care to make sure that tax inspectors did not take on more than they were able to cope with. In this case the relationship of trust which existed between the Revenue and the solicitors, and on which the system depended, was probably damaged by the actions of the inspector. It was accepted that there had been no intention by the solicitors deliberately to mislead the Revenue, however, the court had an obligation to uphold the principle that reliance on informal advance assurance was dependant on the main issues being clearly stated in the application. This had not been established in the present case. Accordingly, the appeal would be dismissed.

R v IRC, ex p Matrix Securities Ltd [1993] STC 774 (Court of Appeal: Dillon, Nolan and Roch LJJ). Decision of Laws J [1993] STC 774 affirmed.

This decision has been affirmed: [1994] STC 272, HL.

1461 Capital allowances—machinery and plant—glasshouse at garden centre

The taxpayer garden centre incurred expenditure on the construction of a glasshouse in which plants could be maintained in a good condition until sold. It fell to be determined whether that expenditure qualified for first-year capital allowance on the ground that it was capital expenditure laid out on the provision of "plant" within the meaning of the Finance Act 1971, s 41. *Held*, the trees and flowers which were stored in the glasshouse were already in a saleable condition before being stored there, and the design of the structure was such that mini-climates could be created so that they could be stored in the best conditions possible. It was possible for members of the public to walk around the structure and choose from the varieties on offer. The glasshouse was simply the premises in which the final part of the taxpayer's trade as a garden centre, that is the display and sale of plants, was carried on; it was not "plant" within the meaning of s 41 and, accordingly, the expenditure incurred on its construction did not qualify for first-year capital allowance relief.

Gray (Inspector of Taxes) v Seymours Garden Centre (Horticulture) [1993] STC 354 (Chancery Division: Vinelott J). *Wimpey International Ltd v Warland* [1988] STC 149, CA (1988 Abr para 1182) applied.

1971 Act, s 41 now Capital Allowances Act 1990, s 22.

1462 Construction industry—sub-contractors—tax deduction scheme

The Income Tax (Sub-contractors in the Construction Industry) Regulations 1993, SI 1993/743 (in force on 6 April 1993), consolidate the regulations, including SI 1993/724, in respect of sub-contractors in the construction industry. The regulations now (1) specify the particulars which are to be contained in a deduction certificate, (2) contain provisions for a certificate to be used in connection with proceedings for recovery in a case where a contractor fails to pay amounts deducted to a collector of taxes, and (3) where records are maintained by computer, require the person required to make them available for inspection to provide the authorised officer with all facilities necessary for obtaining information from them.

1463 Corporation tax—advance corporation tax—groups of companies—arrangements

The Inland Revenue has issued a Statement of Practice SP 3/93, which replaces SP 5/80, giving general guidance on how it interprets "arrangements" in the Income and Corporation Taxes Act 1988, ss 240(11)(a) (surrender of advance corporation tax to a subsidiary company), 247(1A)(b) (group income elections in certain consortium cases), 410(1), (2) (group and consortium reliefs), and "option arrangements" in Sch 18, para 5B(1) (group and consortium reliefs). See further *STI*, 21 January 1993.

The Inland Revenue has also published a revised extra-statutory concession (see *STI*, 21 January 1993) concerning the treatment of certain kinds of commercial transaction which are not treated as being arrangements or option arrangements for the purposes of the statutory provisions referred to above.

1464   Corporation tax—group relief—requirements for holding company

The taxpayer was a public limited company forming part of a consortium which owned a holding company. That company had 23 subsidiary trading companies four of which were resident in the United Kingdom. One of those four subsidiaries had trading losses that it wished to surrender to the taxpayer to enable the latter to claim group relief, under the Income and Corporation Taxes Act 1970, s 258(2), in respect of the losses. It fell to be determined whether, as the holding company's business did not consist wholly or mainly of shareholdings of United Kingdom companies, the holding company was not a holding company within the meaning of s 258(5) (which defines "holding company" as a company the business of which consists wholly or mainly in the holding of shares or securities of companies which are its 90 per cent subsidiaries and which are trading companies) so that the taxpayer could not claim group relief. *Held*, the definition of "holding company" in s 258(5) and the opening words of s 258(7), which required companies to be resident in the United Kingdom, were independent qualifications. To require all or the majority of 90 per cent subsidiaries of a holding company to be resident in the United Kingdom seemed to be an irrational restriction. Group relief from corporation tax was, therefore, available to the taxpayer.

ICI plc v Colmer (Inspector of Taxes) [1993] STC 710 (Court of Appeal: Dillon, Stuart-Smith and Evans LJJ). Decision of Millett J [1992] STC 51 (1991 Abr para 1366) affirmed. *Davies (Inspector of Taxes) v Davies Jenkins & Co Ltd* (1965) 44 TC 273, HL, applied.

1970 Act, s 258 now Income and Corporation Taxes Act 1988, ss 402(1)–(3), (5), (6), 413(3)(b)–(d), (4), (5).

1465   Corporation tax—pay and file

The Inland Revenue has issued the following statements of practice concerning the procedure under pay and file for making and amending corporation tax returns and claims to group relief, and the circumstances under which late claims for capital allowances and group relief claims may be accepted. See further *STI*, 14 October 1993.

Statement of Practice SP 9/93 explains how the Board of Inland Revenue will exercise its powers, under the Taxes Management Act 1970, s 113(1), to require returns under the Income and Corporation Taxes Act 1988 to be made in a prescribed form, and under the 1970 Act, s 11(8A), to require amendments to corporation tax returns under pay and file to be made in a prescribed form.

Statement of Practice SP 10/93 describes a special arrangement for a group of companies which is dealt with mainly in one tax district by virtue of which claims to group relief may be made and revised, and notices of consent to surrender relief under pay and file may be given and revised.

Statement of Practice SP 11/93 explains the criteria the board adopts in exercising its power, under the Capital Allowances Act 1990, Sch A1, para 5 and the 1988 Act, Sch 17A, para 4, to admit claims to capital allowances or group relief which are made outside the normal time limit.

1466   Debts of overseas governments—determination of relevant percentage

The Debts of Overseas Governments (Determination of Relevant Percentage) (Amendment) Regulations 1993, SI 1993/1623 (in force on 30 June 1993), amend the 1990 Regulations, SI 1990/2529, by (1) omitting the provision previously made for an averaging process in determining the relevant percentage of a debt owed to a company which is owed or guaranteed by an overseas state authority; (2) replacing the existing tables which attribute numerical values to various factors relating to the overseas state and its ability to repay, or make payments of interest on, its debts; (3) removing certain factors contained in the replaced tables, merging others and introducing a new factor relating to a state's debt service/export ratio; (4) making changes to the numerical values attributable to certain factors and the scoring systems relating to those values; and (5) replacing the existing table of percentages corresponding to the aggregate of the numerical values attributed by provisions referred to under (2) supra in the case of the particular state or territory with which the debt is connected.

1467   Double taxation relief—arrangements

Double taxation relief arrangements have been made with the following countries:

447

Country	Relevant statutory instrument (SI 1993 No)
Ghana	1800
India	1801
Uganda	1802
Ukraine	1803

1468 Double taxation relief—manufactured overseas dividends

The Double Taxation Relief (Taxes on Income) (General) (Manufactured Overseas Dividends) Regulations 1993, SI 1993/1957 (in force on 1 October 1993), provide that the Commissioners of Inland Revenue may make arrangements with the payer of a manufactured overseas dividend enabling the payment to be made without deduction of tax if the person beneficially entitled to the dividend is resident in a territory with the government of which the United Kingdom has made arrangements, having effect under the Income and Corporation Taxes Act 1988, s 788, for the relief of double taxation which provide for exemption from United Kingdom tax in respect of such income and if a number of other conditions are fulfilled.

1469 Double taxation relief—unilateral relief—dividend income

The Inland Revenue has issued a Statement of Practice SP 12/93 concerning tax credit relief on dividend income. Hitherto, where dividends were received from companies resident in certain countries outside the United Kingdom by United Kingdom companies which directly or indirectly controlled 10 per cent or more of the voting power in the company paying the dividend, the Inland Revenue would allow a credit against the United Kingdom tax payable on the dividend of either the actual tax paid by the overseas company on the profits out of which the dividend was paid or tax calculated on the dividend at the standard rate applicable to company profits in the country concerned, whichever was the greater. If the tax ultimately payable by the company on the profits was less than the tax on the dividend, this meant that the tax credit relief would exceed the tax actually paid by the company. Under the new practice, a credit against United Kingdom tax due on dividends declared on or after 27 July 1993 by companies resident in specified countries will only be allowed for the amount of tax paid by the overseas company on the particular profits out of which the dividend is paid. Where those profits are not taxed in the other country, no tax credit relief will be available. See further *STI*, 5 August 1993.

1470 Exemptions—stock lending

The Income Tax (Stock Lending) (Amendment) Regulations 1993, SI 1993/2003 (in force on 30 September 1993), further amend the 1989 Regulations, SI 1989/1299, by (1) providing for the application of the Finance Act 1991, s 57 to transfers of securities made after 30 September 1993 under stock lending arrangements; (2) introducing the concepts of "approved agent" and "approved nominee" in relation to any person acting for an approved lender as an agent or nominee in connection with such an arrangement; and (3) specifying the conditions which must be satisfied in order for the reliefs from income tax, under the Income and Corporation Taxes Act 1988, s 129, and from capital gains tax, under the Taxation of Chargeable Gains Act 1992, s 271(9), to apply to transfers made in pursuance of certain extended arrangements.

1471 Finance Act 1989—commencement

The Finance Act 1989, section 178(1), (Appointed Day) Order 1993, SI 1993/754, appoints 6 April 1993 as the day for periods beginning on or after which the 1989 Act, s 178(1) is to have effect for the purposes of the Social Security Contributions and Benefits Act 1992, Sch 1, para 6 (which provides for the making of regulations providing for Class 1, Class 1A or Class 2 contributions to be paid, accounted for and recovered in the same manner as income tax deducted under the PAYE scheme, and that the regulations may require the payment of interest on sums due in respect of unpaid Class 1 or Class 1A contributions).

The Finance Act 1989, section 158(1) and (2), (Appointed Days) Order 1993, SI 1993/753, appoints (1) 19 April 1993 as the day on which s 158(1)(a) has effect in relation to income tax under Schedule E, where the demand for tax is made on or after that day and, in any other case, where the tax is charged by an assessment notice of which is issued on or after that day, and as the day on which s 158(1)(b) has effect where the tax is charged by an assessment relating to an accounting period beginning on or after that day; and (2) 6 April 1993 as the day on which s 158(2) has effect in relation to payments of tax made on or after that day. For a summary of the Act, see 1989 Abr para 1956. For details of commencement, see the commencement table in the title STATUTES.

1472 Finance (No 2) Act 1992—commencement

See para 2159.

1473 Friendly societies—provisional repayments for exempt business

The Friendly Societies (Provisional Repayments for Exempt Business) Regulations 1993, SI 1993/3112 (in force on 1 January 1994), provide for the Income and Corporation Taxes Act 1988, Sch 19AB (under which provisional repayments may be claimed on account of tax deducted from payments made to insurance companies and referable to their pension business, and tax credits in respect of distributions received by such companies which are so referable) to have effect, with modifications and exceptions, in relation to the tax exempt business of friendly societies.

1474 Lloyd's underwriters

The Lloyd's Underwriters (Tax) (1990–91) Regulations 1993, SI 1993/415 (in force on 23 March 1993 but having effect for the year of assessment 1990–91 only), provide for the assessment and collection of tax charged on underwriting members of Lloyd's under the Income and Corporation Taxes Act 1988, s 450, so far as not provided for by Sch 19A, and the Taxation of Chargeable Gains Act 1992, s 207. The regulations provide for the determination in certain circumstances of the person who is a managing agent in relation to a syndicate of underwriting members of Lloyd's, and a member's agent in relation to an underwriting member, for the purposes of the 1988 Act, Sch 19A and the 1993 Regulations; and for the extension of time limits for underwriting members of Lloyd's and their spouses to make claims, elections or applications under specified provisions of the Taxes Management Act 1970.

1475 Manufactured overseas dividends

The Income Tax (Manufactured Overseas Dividends) Regulations 1993, SI 1993/2004 (in force on 1 October 1993), which apply to manufactured overseas dividends in respect of overseas securities, (1) prescribe the rates of relevant withholding tax which are to apply in relation to such dividends; (2) provide for the tax treatment of approved manufactured overseas dividends paid to approved United Kingdom intermediaries or approved United Kingdom collecting agents and for the tax treatment of such dividends paid to persons resident outside the United Kingdom; (3) provide for the retention and record of notices given under (2) supra; (4) provide for the offsetting of tax by overseas dividend manufacturers; (5) set out rules for determining whether overseas dividends and manufactured overseas dividends fall to be matched against each other, and provide for the forwarding of tax vouchers relating to overseas dividends matched against manufactured overseas dividends; (6) provide for the payment of tax pursuant to the Income and Corporation Taxes Act 1988, Sch 23A, para 4(2) or (3), or under the 1993 Regulations, and for the making of returns, and for the assessment and recovery of tax due; (7) provide for the tax treatment of manufactured overseas dividends which are representative of foreign dividends, interest on quoted Eurobonds, or overseas public revenue dividends, and for accounting for tax in respect of such manufactured overseas dividends; (8) provide for the keeping of records by overseas dividend manufacturers and approved United Kingdom collecting agents in respect of certain manufactured overseas dividends paid without deduction of tax, and for the carrying out of an audit of such manufactured overseas dividends in the event of a failure to keep records as required; (9) provide for the furnishing of vouchers by overseas dividend manufacturers and approved United Kingdom collecting agents to the recipients of manufactured overseas dividends which are paid under deduction of tax in respect of which tax has been accounted for and paid; and (10) apply, with modifications, the information powers conferred on the Commissioners of Inland Revenue by the Taxes Management Act 1970, s 21 to businesses carried on by approved United Kingdom intermediaries and approved United Kingdom collecting agents.

See also para 1468.

1476   Occupational pension schemes

See PENSIONS AND SUPERANNUATION.

1477   Pay As You Earn—regulations

The Income Tax (Employments) Regulations 1993, SI 1993/744 (in force on 6 April 1993), consolidate the regulations in respect of income tax subject to Pay As You Earn, in particular the 1973 Regulations, SI 1973/334, as amended, and SI 1993/725–727. The Income Tax (Councillors' Attendance Allowances) Regulations 1974, SI 1974/340, the Income Tax (Reserve and Auxiliary Forces) Regulations 1975, SI 1975/91, the Income Tax (Repayment Supplement) Regulations 1975, SI 1975/1283 and the Income Tax (Holiday Pay) Regulations 1981, SI 1981/1648, are also consolidated.

The Income Tax (Employments) (Amendment) Regulations 1993, SI 1993/2276 (in force on 12 October 1993), amend SI 1993/744 supra, by providing that payments of emoluments which consist of qualifying removal expenses of an employee which are liable to tax under Schedule E as exceeding a qualifying limit need not be subject to Pay As You Earn, and by including in the particulars which have to be given in returns particulars of removal expenses and benefits within the Income and Corporation Taxes Act 1988, Sch 11A. The Profit-Related Pay (Shortfall Recovery) Regulations 1988, SI 1988/640, are also amended.

1478   Personal pension schemes

See PENSIONS AND SUPERANNUATION.

1479   Profits—profits of partnership—assignment of share in partnership—liability to tax

See *Hadlee v Comr of Inland Revenue*, para 1907.

1480   Profits—profits of trade—computation—set off of trading losses

The taxpayers traded in the hiring of narrow boats. They entered into a leasing agreement for the lease of the boats for a primary period of about 24 months involving a heavy outlay and thereafter for a secondary period of 21 years at a low annual rent. They sought to carry back trade losses incurred in the year 1989–90 for set off against taxable income for 1986–87. A Special Commissioner rejected the taxpayers' claims. The taxpayers successfully appealed, the judge holding that expenditure incurred by a taxpayer for the purposes of his trade fell to be deducted, for the purposes of computing the profits or losses of that trade, during the accounting period during which it was incurred under the relevant contract even though ordinary principles of commercial accounting would allocate the expenditure wholly or partly to other accounting periods. On further appeal, the Crown argued that the taxpayers' liability was to be calculated according to accepted accountancy principles, and thus the full sum of the initial payment and the monthly payments made under the lease agreements during the period were not correctly shown as a debit in the accounts. *Held*, the ordinary way to ascertain the profits or losses of a business was to apply accepted principles of commercial accounting, and so long as such principles remained current and generally accepted, they provided the surest answer to the question the legislation required to be answered. There was no rule requiring the expenditure under the agreement to be chargeable in the accounts in the year in which it fell due. The appeal would accordingly be allowed.

Gallagher v Jones (Inspector of Taxes); Threlfall v Jones (Inspector of Taxes) [1993] STC 537 (Court of Appeal: Sir Thomas Bingham MR, Nolan LJ and Sir Christopher Slade). Decision of Vinelott J [1993] STC 199 reversed. *Vallambrosa Rubber Co Ltd v Farmer (Surveyor of Taxes)* (1910) 5 TC 529 considered. *Ostime (Inspector of Taxes) v Duple Motor Bodies Ltd* [1961] 2 All ER 167, HL, distinguished. *Odeon Associated Theatres Ltd v Jones (Inspector of Taxes)* (1972) 1 All ER 681, CA, applied.

1481   Relief—business expansion scheme—issue of shares—date of issue

For the purposes of sponsorship by the plaintiff of a business expansion scheme (BES), five companies were incorporated. A prospectus was issued by those companies offering for subscription up to 25 million ordinary shares. The companies were 'qualifying companies' and the shares offered for subscription were 'eligible shares' for the purposes of BES tax relief under the Income and Corporation Taxes Act 1988, s 289. Annexed to the prospectus was an application form which provided that the applicant irrevocably offered to subscribe for a specified number of shares in one of the companies and that he irrevocably requested and authorised the company to accept any shares accepted in the name of his nominee. By 10 March 1993, the applications for the shares had been received and allocated. On 12 March 1993, the committee of the board of directors of the companies resolved to allot the shares to the successful applicants. The shares were to be held by a nominee company for and on behalf of the successful applicants. On the same date, letters were sent out to the successful applicants informing them that shares had been allotted to them. The nominee company was registered as the holder of all the shares in the relevant company's register of members after 16 March 1993, the day on which the 1988 Act, s 299A came into force.

The plaintiff sought a declaration that, for the purposes of the BES provisions under the 1988 Act, Pt VII, Chapter III, including s 299A, the shares were issued before 16 March. The plaintiff contended that the shares were issued as soon as the companies and the applicants became contractually bound and that an issue of shares was not dependent either on actual registration or the issue of a share certificate. The Crown submitted that the shares were issued on or after 16 March because they were not issued until the name of the nominee company was written in the relevant company's register of members, which in all cases took place after 16 March. At first instance it was held that in the context of the provisions of Pt VII, Chapter III, including s 299A, the time when shares in a company were issued was the time when a mutual obligation arose between the applicant and the company whereby the applicant was obliged to cause those shares to be registered in the applicant's name or that of his nominee. Therefore, the shares were issued before 16 March, and an order was made accordingly. On appeal by the Inland Revenue, *held*, the issue of shares occurred only when the allottee was registered or a certificate was issued. In this case, the shares had been entered in the register after 16 March 1993 and were therefore subject to the 1988 Act, s 299A. Accordingly, the appeal would be allowed and the plaintiff's business expansion scheme declared invalid.

National Westminster Bank plc v IRC [1994] STC 184 (Court of Appeal: Dillon, Mann and Hirst LJJ). Decision of Rattee J [1993] STC 639 reversed.

1482 Relief—charitable status—relief and exemption distinguished

The taxpayers and their sons owned all the shares in a company, and the taxpayers were also the trustees of a registered charity. They decided to finance the charity out of the company's profits by means of a bonus issue of new shares to the company's members, and the renunciation by those members of the new shares in favour of the taxpayers as trustees of the trust. The shareholders then waived their dividend rights in favour of the trust, and the taxpayers claimed repayment of the tax credit under the provisions of the Income and Corporation Taxes Act 1970, s 360, which exempted dividend income received by a charity which was applied to charitable purposes from tax. The commissioners refused the claim on the ground that the taxpayers had obtained a tax advantage, namely relief in the form of the nil rate of tax applicable to the charity, and the taxpayers appealed. *Held*, a person who had obtained relief from tax had gained a tax advantage for the purpose of the 1970 Act, s 466(1), so the issue turned on whether the position of charities under the 1970 Act, s 360 amounted to "relief", or whether it amounted to an exemption, under which the obligation to pay tax had been removed altogether. The taxpayers had possessed charitable status, which meant tax exemption had been conferred on them. They had not obtained a tax advantage, so they had not claimed relief in the sense that that word had been used in the 1970 Act, s 466, and the commissioners' decision had been erroneous. Accordingly, the appeal would be allowed.

Sheppard (Trustees of the Woodland Trust) v IRC (No 2); IRC v Sheppard (Trustees of the Woodland Trust) (No 2) [1993] STC 240 (Chancery Division: Aldous J). For earlier related proceedings, see *Sheppard (Trustees of the Woodland Trust) v IRC; IRC v Sheppard (Trustees of the Woodland Trust)* [1992] 3 All ER 58 (1992 Abr para 1951).

1970 Act, ss 360, 466(1) now Income and Corporation Taxes Act 1988, ss 505(1), 506(1), 709(1).

1483 Relief—gifts—designated educational establishments

The Taxes (Relief for Gifts) (Designated Educational Establishments) (Amendment) Regulations 1993, SI 1993/561 (in force on 1 April 1993), amend the 1992 Regulations, SI 1992/42, by altering the categories of establishment of further and higher education referred to in the Schedule, Pt III for the purposes of the Income and Corporation Taxes Act 1988, s 84, as a consequence of the Further and Higher Education Act 1992.

1484   Relief—mortgage or loan interest—loans made to acquire close company

The taxpayers arranged a management buy-out of P Ltd, a loss-making company that their employers owned. The taxpayers each borrowed money to buy shares in a new company, R Ltd, formed by the management team to acquire and carry on the business of P Ltd. The purchase of P Ltd was completed, and its business was transferred to R Ltd and thereafter carried on by that company. The taxpayers sought tax relief on the interest payable on the bank loans. Their claims were refused by a tax inspector on the ground that at the time when the taxpayers subscribed for shares in R Ltd, the company did not then exist wholly or mainly for the purpose of carrying on a trade, and the relief granted by the Income and Corporations Act 1988, ss 353, 360, Sch 19, para 7 only applied in respect of interest on a loan to an individual to defray money applied in acquiring any part of the ordinary share capital of a close company that was a company which exists wholly or mainly for the purpose of carrying on a trade. A special commissioner determined that the loans made to the taxpayers attracted relief. The crown appealed. *Held*, if a loan was made to obtain shares so as to allow a company to acquire a business and at a time when the company was a shell company it could reasonably be said that the company existed for the purpose of carrying on that business. The acquisition of the business was the means by which that purpose was achieved. In the present case, R Ltd existed for the purpose of carrying on a trade. The interest payments therefore came within the relieving provisions of ss 353, 360. The commissioner's decision was correct and the appeal would accordingly be dismissed.

Lord (Inspector of Taxes) v Tustain; Lord (Inspector of Taxes) v Chapple [1993] STC 755 (Chancery Division: Vinelott J).

1485   Relief—mortgage or loan interest—qualifying lenders

The following orders prescribe certain bodies as qualifying lenders so that interest on qualifying loans made by them may be paid to them under deduction of tax under the mortgage interest relief at source scheme (MIRAS). In addition, certain earlier orders are amended.

SI 1993 No	SI Nos of orders amended
949	1987/2127, 1991/2604
1821	1986/1440, 2191
2478	1983/1907, 1988/1962
3055	

1486   Relief—retirement annuity—premiums paid out of income—Lloyd's syndicates

The taxpayer was a member of a number of syndicates at Lloyd's. After becoming a "name", he spent three to four hours a week on Lloyd's affairs. The agency agreement between him and his agent at Lloyd's gave the agent sole control and management of the underwriting business; the taxpayer was to interfere in no way with the exercise of such control and management. He paid a premium under an annuity contract out of income which he had received from the syndicates to which he belonged and claimed retirement annuity relief, under the Income and Corporation Taxes Act 1988, s 619(1), on the ground that the income he received from Lloyd's was "immediately derived" by him from the carrying on or exercise by him of his trade as an individual" within s 623(2)(c) and was therefore "relevant earnings" for the purposes of s 619(1). *Held*, for income to qualify as "relevant earnings" within s 623(2)(c), it had to be earned by the taxpayer's "personal exertions, care, skill and work". Even if the taxpayer had by his exertions satisfied some of the requirements of the provision, there were intervening events occurring between his exertions and the derivation of the income, so that his income could not be said to be "immediately derived" by him from the carrying on of any trade by him. That income was not relevant earnings for the purposes of s 619(1) and, accordingly, his claim would fail.

Koenigsberger v Mellor (Inspector of Taxes) [1993] STC 408 (Chancery Division: Lindsay J).

1487   Relief—value of trading stock—transitional relief—period of account

A company made a claim for stock relief in relation to an annual accounting period but, although it was entitled to do so, failed to make an election for transitional relief pursuant to the Finance Act 1981, Sch 10, para 2, within the prescribed time. The company made a valid claim for relief in respect of the following accounting period. The company subsequently made a claim for relief for a 104-week period of account covering the two accounting periods in respect of which claims had already been made. The claim in relation to the 104-week account included an election for transitional relief. It was common ground that the 104-week account was prepared solely for the purpose of obtaining stock relief. The special commissioners determined that the 104-week period covered by the 104-week account was a "period of account" for the purposes of the 1981 Act, but concluded that the company was not entitled to make a claim for a period of account that encompassed periods covered by earlier claims. On appeal by the company, *held*, the period of account for stock relief purposes meant, in relation to a company, any period of account used by the company for assessing its trade profits for corporation tax purposes. Accordingly, the 104-week period was not a period of account within the meaning of the 1981 Act and the taxpayer company was not entitled to make a stock relief claim by reference to the 104-week period. Accordingly, the company's appeal would be dismissed.

Bass Holdings Ltd v Money (Inspector of Taxes) [1993] STC 300 (Chancery Division: Sir Mervyn Davies).

Stock relief was abolished by the Finance Act 1984, s 48.

1488 Relief—vocational training—entitlement to tax relief

The Vocational Training (Tax Relief) (Amendment) Regulations 1993, SI 1993/1082 (in force on 7 May 1993), amend the 1992 Regulations, SI 1992/746, so as to extend the definition of "approved auditor" to include auditors appointed by bodies in Scotland or Northern Ireland for the purpose of auditing accounts relating to a provider of vocational training.

The Vocational Training (Tax Relief) (Amendment No 2) Regulations 1993, SI 1993/3118 (in force on 1 January 1994), further amend the 1992 Regulations supra by inserting two additional requirements to the certificate to be given by the individual making the training payment.

1489 Relief—vocational training—public financial assistance and disentitlement to tax relief

The Vocational Training (Public Financial Assistance and Disentitlement to Tax Relief) (Amendment) Regulations 1993, SI 1993/1074 (in force on 7 May 1993), amend the 1992 Regulations, SI 1992/734, by replacing references to 'Employment Training" and 'Employment Action" with references to "Training for Work".

1490 Repayment of tax—insurance companies—pension business

The Insurance Companies (Pension Business) (Transitional Provisions) (Amendment) Regulations 1993, SI 1993/3109 (in force on 31 December 1993), amend the 1992 Regulations, SI 1992/2326, which make provision, for a transitional period, for the reduction by a prescribed percentage of provisional repayments of tax to insurance companies carrying on pension business. The 1993 Regulations prescribe 7·5 per cent as the percentage by which the amount of a provisional repayment is to be reduced where the accounting period of the company ends after 1 October 1992 and before 1 January 1994, and 12·5 per cent as the percentage in other cases.

1491 Repayment of tax—repayment supplement—individual resident within the Community

The Inland Revenue has published an extra-statutory concession concerning repayment supplement on repayments made to individuals resident within the Community. By virtue of the concession, supplement will be added to repayments made to an individual for a year of assessment in which he is resident in a member state other than the United Kingdom on the same basis as payments are made to individuals resident in the United Kingdom provided that the other conditions of the Income and Corporation Taxes Act 1988, s 824 are satisfied. Where a repayment has been made since 12 July 1987 in respect of a year of assessment for which the individual concerned was resident in a member state other than the United Kingdom, supplement will be added under the rules provided in s 824. The concession applies also to partnerships, the trustees of a settlement and personal representatives but does not apply to other non-resident taxpayers. See further *STI*, 30 September 1993.

1492 Repayment of tax—supplement—residence requirement—compatibility with Community law

See *R v IRC, ex p Commerzbank AG*, para 2721.

1493   Residence—visitor to United Kingdom—residence in United Kingdom—concessions

The Inland Revenue has published a revised text of concession A11 concerning persons who are treated as becoming resident or not resident during a tax year. As a consequence of the change in the rules of individual residence introduced by the Finance Act 1993, s 208 (by virtue of which, from 6 April 1993, the fact that a person has living accommodation available in the United Kingdom will not be taken into account when deciding whether his residence in the United Kingdom is merely temporary), it is no longer necessary to consider whether any duties of employment are performed in the United Kingdom.

Concession A78, concerning accompanying spouses of those taking up full-time employment abroad, is also revised as a consequence of the abolition of the "available accommodation" rule. The changes to both concessions take effect from 6 April 1993. See further *STI*, 23 September 1993.

1494   Return—notice to deliver return—failure to comply with notice

The taxpayer failed to deliver tax returns for two tax years, contrary to notices issued under the Taxes Management Act 1970, s 8. The General Commissioners found that this failure was wilful and, in the absence of any mitigating circumstances, imposed the maximum penalty available under the 1970 Act, s 93(1). The taxpayer unsuccessfully appealed on the grounds that, as certain information was outstanding, he could not have made a complete return at the requisite time without committing perjury. On further appeal, *held*, the 1970 Act, s 8(2) merely required the taxpayer to declare that the return was to the best of his knowledge correct and complete. It did not require that he be in possession of all conceivably relevant knowledge before making a return. Accordingly, the decision of the General Commissioners was correct and the appeal would be dismissed.

Alexander v Wallington General Comrs [1993] STC 588 (Court of Appeal: Lloyd, Butler-Sloss and Roch LJJ). Decision of Rattee J [1992] STC 314 (1992 Abr para 1437) affirmed.

1495   Schedule A—agricultural land—business use of farmhouse

The Inland Revenue has amended Concession B5, concerning maintenance expenses of owner-occupied farms which are not carried on on a commercial basis, so that, as from 19 February 1993, in determining the allowable proportion of the expenditure on a farmhouse for the purpose of the concession, regard will be had to all the particular facts and circumstances of an individual case instead of applying a one-third : two-thirds apportionment between business and private use. See further *STI*, 25 February 1993.

1496   Schedule D—assessment—change of ownership

The taxpayers owned a fish and chip shop business. They bought another such shop as a going concern and integrated it into their existing business. They paid income tax on their profits on a preceding year basis under Schedule D, Case 1. The Crown raised assessments on the taxpayers for the combined profits of both businesses and applied the 1970 Act, s 154(1) to the newly acquired shop, assessing the profits as if a new trade had been set up and commenced. However, the taxpayers contended that the acquisition was a continuation and expansion of their existing trade rather than a succession to a new one. The commissioners accepted the taxpayers' argument and the Crown appealed. *Held*, the 1970 Act, s 154(1) provided for a deemed commencement of a new trade where there was a change in the persons engaged in carrying on the trade. It was intended to apply to cases where the profits before and after the change arose from the same business. At issue was whether the business from which the taxpayers made profits was an expansion of their existing trade or a business to which they had succeeded on the acquisition of the second shop. The commissioners were entitled to find that the taxpayers had not succeeded to a new trade and accordingly, the appeal would be dismissed.

Maidment (Inspector of Taxes) v Kibby [1993] STC 494 (Chancery Division: Sir Donald Nicholls V-C).

1970 Act, s 154 now the Income and Corporation Taxes Act 1988, s 113.

1497   Schedule D—carrying on of business by individual—test

See *Hall (Inspector of Taxes) v Lorimer*, para 1504.

1498 Schedule D—profits—allowable deductions—annuity payments to charity—tax avoidance scheme

The taxpayers participated in a tax-saving scheme under which they sold a five-year annuity to a registered charity in consideration for a capital sum. That sum was invested by the taxpayers in promissory notes which were deposited with the charity as security, and out of which the five annual payments were made. The Court of Appeal ruled that the taxpayers were entitled to deduct such payments when computing their total income under the Income and Corporation Taxes Act 1970, s 52, on the ground that tax-saving plans such as the one in question were not to be regarded as a fiscal nullity. On appeal by the Commissioners, *held*, the plan was a self-cancelling tax avoidance scheme which had no object or effect except the manufacture for the taxpayers of claims that he had reduced his income. The taxpayers' income had not actually been reduced, and they had not been put to any capital expense other than the cost of the scheme. Despite the fact that a similar scheme had been accepted in *IRC v Plummer* it would be appropriate to declare such schemes to be a fiscal nullity so that justice between individual taxpayers and the general body of taxpayers would be restored. Accordingly, the appeal would be allowed.

Moodie v IRC, Sotnick v IRC [1993] STC 188 (House of Lords: Lords Keith of Kinkel, Templeman, Goff of Chieveley, Browne-Wilkinson and Mustill). Decision of the Court of Appeal [1991] STC 433 (1991 Abr para 1393) reversed. *Ramsay v IRC* [1981] 1 All ER 865, HL (1981 Abr para 360) applied, *IRC v Plummer* [1979] 3 All ER 775, HL (1979 Abr para 1552) not applied.

1499 Schedule D—profits—allowable deductions—remuneration to director

A company, on the advice of its accountant, paid the sole shareholder and director a sum as remuneration for services rendered. The General Commissioners permitted a deduction from the company profits of only five per cent of the sums paid as remuneration to the sole shareholder. The company appealed on the ground that the commissioners had overlooked the principle that it was for a company to decide what was remuneration for services rendered to it and that the court could not interfere unless it was shown that what was paid was not in truth remuneration. *Held*, the commissioners were entitled to conclude that the sum represented in part a diversification of the sole shareholder's husband's earnings to her for fiscal purposes, and were therefore not deductible in computing the company's tax liability, not being incurred wholly and exclusively for the purposes of the trade under the Income and Corporation Taxes Act 1970, s 130. Accordingly, the appeal would be dismissed.

Earlspring Properties Ltd v Guest (Inspector of Taxes) [1993] STC 473 (Chancery Division: Vinelott J).

1970 Act, s 130 now Income and Corporation Taxes Act 1988, s 74.

1500 Schedule D—profits—allowable deductions—subsistence and use of home

The Income and Corporation Taxes Act 1988, s 74(a) provides that in computing the amount of profits or gains to be charged under Schedule D, Cases I and II, no sum is deductible in respect of expenditure not wholly and exclusively incurred for the purposes of trade.

The taxpayer was self-employed and was engaged as a labour-only sub-contractor in London. He lived at various addresses in London whilst working and used his father's home in Bournemouth as a postal address. He kept his tools and business records at his London addresses and kept other equipment in a rented garage in Bournemouth. He appealed against assessments under Schedule D, Cases I and II, contending that at all material times he conducted his business from Bournemouth, that expenditure on travelling, subsistence and the use of his home was incurred wholly and exclusively for the purposes of his trade and that it therefore constituted allowable deductions under the 1988 Act, s 74(a). The General Commissioners allowed the deductions in part and the Crown appealed against their decision in respect of the expenditure on subsistence and use of home. *Held*, the General Commissioners erred in their application of the 1988 Act, s 74(a). The money spent on subsistence was not wholly and exclusively expended for the purposes of trade, and the expenditure claimed in relation to storage of tools was primarily incurred as rent for the taxpayer's accommodation and thus also fell outside the scope of allowable deductions. Accordingly, the appeal would be allowed.

Prior (Inspector of Taxes) v Saunders [1993] STC 562 (Chancery Division: Sir Mervyn Davies).

1501   Schedule E—emoluments from office or employment—duties performed abroad and in the United Kingdom

The taxpayer, an airline pilot who was resident and ordinarily resident in the United Kingdom, flew aircraft to destinations overseas and back to the United Kingdom. His income was apportioned between duties performed overseas and those performed in the Uunited Kingdom. The question arose whether his emoluments for the days when he was absent from his duties (such as for rest periods, holiday leave and sick leave) ought also to be apportioned. At first instance it was held that they would be and the taxpayer appealed. *Held*, the exception under the Income and Corporation Taxes Act 1970, s 184(1) would be given a narrow application and would not apply to the emoluments received by the taxpayer under the terms of his contract in respect of his non-working periods. For the purposes of calculating the taxpayer's overseas earnings relief for his intermittent absences from the United Kingdom under the provisions of the Finance Act 1977, Sch 7 his emoluments attributable to duties performed outside the United Kingdom would be calculated by apportioning his annual salary on a time basis with a denominator of 365. Further, his emoluments for the periods when he was not working would not by virtue of the 1970 Act, s 184(1) be treated as emoluments for duties performed outside the United Kingdom. Accordingly, the appeal would be dismissed.

Leonard v Blanchard (Inspector of Taxes) [1993] STC 259 (Court of Appeal: Nourse, Stuart-Smith and Mann LJJ). Decision of Hoffmann J [1992] STC 20 (1992 Abr para 1443) affirmed.

1970 Act, s 184 now Income and Corporation Taxes Act 1988, s 132.

1502   Schedule E—emoluments from office or employment—ex gratia payment in consideration of giving up contingent right to redundancy payment

Northern Ireland

The taxpayer accepted an offer of new employment as an alternative to redundancy, made by the company which had bought out the company by which he was formerly employed, under the terms of which he received an ex gratia payment consisting of a sum to which he would have been entitled under the enhanced redundancy scheme available to employees who accepted redundancy and a sum relating to his years of service with his former employer. It fell to be determined whether the payment was taxable under Schedule E as an emolument from the taxpayer's employment under the Income and Corporation Taxes Act 1988, s 19. *Held*, the payment consisted of two elements: the first was to be treated as compensation for the loss of contingent rights under the enhanced redundancy scheme and the second as consideration for the acceptance of the new terms and conditions of working. The payment was made for two separate identifiable considerations, one in consideration of the new terms and conditions of employment, and the other in consideration of the termination of the enhanced redundancy scheme. Although neither of the two elements of the payment was exclusively referable to either element of the consideration, if the payment had been paid for two considerations it could be apportioned between the separate considerations. A payment made to compensate for the loss of a contingent right to a payment derived its character from the nature of the payment it replaced; a significant characteristic of a payment under the enhanced redundancy scheme was that it was to compensate or to relieve an employee for his not being able to continue to earn a living in his former employment. Accordingly, such a non-statutory redundancy payment did not fall within the definition of emolument from employment. It was, instead, a payment to compensate the employee for not being able to receive emoluments from his employment. Since a redundancy payment would not be taxable under Schedule E as an emolument "from" employment, then that part of the payment which was received by the taxpayer as compensation for the loss of the contingent right to receive a redundancy payment, was not taxable as an emolument "from" employment and, therefore, was not taxable; that part received as consideration for the acceptance of the new terms and conditions of employment was taxable under Schedule E.

Mairs (Inspector of Taxes) v Haughey [1993] 3 WLR 393 (House of Lords: Lords Griffiths, Ackner, Browne-Wilkinson, Mustill and Woolf). Decision of Northern Ireland Court of Appeal [1992] STC 495 (1992 Abr para 1444) affirmed. *Tilley v Wales (Inspector of Taxes)* [1943] 1 All ER 280, *Hochstrasser (Inspector of Taxes) v Mayes* [1959] 3 All ER 817, HL, and *Shilton v Wilmshurst (Inspector of Taxes)* [1991] 3 All ER 148 (1991 Abr para 1402) applied.

1503   Schedule E—emoluments from office or employment—expenses— newspaper allowance

Each of the taxpayers was employed by a newspaper group and each received an allowance in reimbursement of the cost of newspapers and periodicals which they bought. The General

Commissioners found that the taxpayers' expenditure on those purchases was "wholly, exclusively and necessarily" incurred in the performance of their duties so that the amounts of the allowances they received were deductible as expenses under the Income and Corporation Taxes Act 1970, s 189(1). On appeal by the Crown, *held*, the taxpayers purchased and read the publications and the question was whether it formed part of the daily performance of the duties of employment. They were studying the news and the purpose of their reading was to assist in the production of the next edition of the newspaper. Therefore allowances paid to cover the costs of purchasing newspapers and magazines were deductible in computing tax liability under Schedule E as they were all required to read the publications in the actual performance of the duties of their employment and not just in the preparation of performing those duties. Accordingly, the appeals would be dismissed.

Smith (Inspector of Taxes) v Abbott [1993] 2 All ER 417 (Court of Appeal: Ralph Gibson, Mann and Nolan LJJ). Decision of Warner J [1992] 1 WLR 201 (1991 Abr para 1397) affirmed.

1970 Act, s 189(1) now Income and Corporation Taxes Act 1988, s 198(1). This decision has been reversed: [1994] STC 237, HL.

1504   Schedule E—emoluments from office or employment—freelance vision mixer

The taxpayer worked as a skilled freelance vision mixer with various television companies. He worked with equipment owned by the companies, who controlled the times and places where he worked, and received a lump sum payment for each engagement. He did not contribute to the cost of producing the programmes, but was registered for value added tax and had taken out a personal retirement policy and insurance against sickness. The Crown contended that he was not in business on his own and that he was liable to pay Schedule E income tax. A Special Commissioner determined that the contracts that the taxpayer entered into were not contracts of employment and that his activities indicated that he was a man in business on his own account. On appeal to the High Court, it was held that the commissioner had applied the right test and there was no reason to interfere with his conclusion. On further appeal by the Crown, *held*, the High Court judge had been correct in his statement of the test to be applied for determining whether a person was in business on his own account. It was necessary to consider many different aspects of that person's work activity and paint a picture from the accumulation of detail, which was not necessarily the same as the sum total of the individual situation. The commissioner had applied this test satisfactorily and accordingly, the appeal would be dismissed.

Hall (Inspector of Taxes) v Lorimer [1994] STC 23 (Court of Appeal: Dillon, Nolan and Roch LJJ). Decision of Mummery J [1992] STC 599 (1992 Abr para 1446) affirmed.

1505   Schedule E—emoluments from office or employment—loss of employment—compensation—legal costs

The Inland Revenue has published an extra-statutory concession concerning the tax treatment of legal costs, including disbursements and value added tax, incurred by an employee in legal proceedings to recover compensation for loss of employment. Under the concession, no charge will be imposed (1) where the dispute is settled without recourse to the courts, on payments of costs made by the former employer direct to the former employee's solicitor, in full or partial discharge of the solicitor's bill of costs incurred by the employee only in connection with the termination of his employment, under a specific term in the settlement agreement providing for the payment, or (2) where the dispute goes to court, on payments of costs made by the former employer, even where made direct to the employee, in accordance with a court order, whether made following judgment or compromise of the action. Documentary evidence that a payment by a former employer meets the above conditions may be required in support of a claim. See further *STI*, 9 September 1993.

1506   Schedule E—emoluments from office or employment—part only of payment assessable under Schedule E

Scotland

On his appointment as executive director of a subsidiary of a group of companies, the taxpayer acquired shares in the subsidiary. He resold the shares to the parent company for a consideration in excess of their market value. On his appeal against an additional assessment to income tax under Schedule E in respect of the sale of shares, the Inner House decided that the parent company should have deducted and accounted for tax. On appeal by the Crown, *held*, an employer's obligation under the Income and Corporation Taxes Act 1970, s 204 to deduct tax from an employee's emoluments arose on the "making of any payment of, or on account of, any income assessable to income tax under" Schedule E but there was no obligation under the 1970 Act or the Income Tax (Employments) Regulations 1973, SI 1973/334 on a payer to deduct tax from a payment of which only part was assessable to income tax under Schedule E. The liability under both the Finance Act 1972, s 79 and the Finance Act 1976, s 67 to tax under Schedule E arose on only part of the consideration paid and the charging mechanism in neither provision treated the whole payment as an emolument and then preserved a right to claim a deduction by way of allowance. The payment of the consideration was, instead, subject to two different provisions which provided for two different charges under Schedule E on sums which were in total less than the total of the payment. The consideration paid by the parent company for the shares was not a payment of income assessable to income tax under Schedule E. The taxpayer was liable to account for the tax in question. Accordingly, the Crown's appeal would be allowed.

IRC v Herd [1993] 3 All ER 56 (House of Lords: Lords Mackay of Clashfern LC, Keith of Kinkel, Jauncey of Tullichettle, Browne-Wilkinson and Slynn of Hadley). Decision of Inner House [1992] STC 264 reversed.

1970 Act, s 204 now Income and Corporation Taxes Act 1988, s 203. 1972 Act, s 79 now 1988 Act, s 138 (repealed in relation to acquisitions on or after 26 October 1987). 1976 Act, s 67 now 1988 Act, s 162. 1973 Regulations now Income Tax (Employments) Regulations 1993, SI 1993/744.

1507   Schedule E—emoluments from office or employment—sick pay

The taxpayer was an employee of the British Railways Board. The conditions of employment included arrangements for employees to receive sick pay, for periods up to a year, for absence due to illness or accidents. The conditions provided that sick pay would be calculated by reference to the employee's gross salary and that sick pay would be paid as a loan repayable to the board if the employee recovered any damages. The taxpayer was absent through illness for over a year. He received sick pay of £5,550 from the board, net of tax and national insurance contributions (NIC) of £1,079 which the board paid to the Revenue and the Department of Social Security (DSS). The board subsequently paid the taxpayer damages which included the sum of £5,550 for loss of net earnings and he duly repaid this to the board. The board claimed that the taxpayer was also liable to reimburse it for the sum of £1,079, contending that they had paid the tax and NIC to the government departments as the employee's agent. The board were awarded judgment. The taxpayer appealed, contending that the board should look to the two government departments for reimbursement since it would be more difficult for him, as a private individual, to pursue a repayment claim and it was not established, as a matter of law, that a taxpayer was entitled to such repayments. *Held,* although the references to "sick pay" were to the amount of gross salary, the sum repayable by the taxpayer was not necessarily the gross amount. Further, the sums handed over by the board to the Revenue and the DSS, in discharge of an accepted statutory duty, did not constitute a loan to the taxpayer which was repayable to the board. The only sum which could be described as repayable was the £5,550 which the taxpayer actually received and had already repaid. Accordingly, the appeal would be allowed.

British Railways Board v Franklin [1993] STC 487 (Court of Appeal: Sir Thomas Bingham MR, Nolan LJ and Sir Michael Fox).

1508   Unpaid tax—interest

The Taxes (Interest Rate) (Amendment) Regulations 1993, SI 1993/222 (in force on 6 March 1993), further amend the 1989 Regulations, SI 1989/1297, by decreasing the applicable rate of official rate of interest for the purposes of the Income and Corporation Taxes Act 1988, s 160 from 8·25 to 7·75 per cent.

The Taxes (Interest Rate) (Amendment No 2) Regulations 1993, SI 1993/758 (in force on 6 April 1993), further amend the 1989 Regulations, SI 1989/1297, by providing for the rate of interest applicable for the purposes of the Social Security Contributions and Benefits Act 1992, Sch 1, para 6 (which provides for the making of regulations providing for Class 1, Class 1A or Class 2 contributions to be paid, accounted for and recovered in the same manner as income tax deducted under the PAYE scheme, and that the regulations may require the payment of interest on sums due in respect of unpaid Class 1 or Class 1A contributions).

The Taxes (Interest Rate) (Amendment No 3) Regulations 1993, SI 1993/2212 (in force on 1 October 1993), amend the 1989 Regulations, SI 1989/1297, by inserting regulations which specify (1) 6·25 per cent per annum as the interest rate applicable under the Taxes Management Act 1970, s 178 in respect of overdue corporation tax (see s 87A), and (2) 3·25 per cent as the interest rate applicable under s 178 on tax overpaid (see the Income and Corporation Taxes Act 1988, s 826). The new regulations also make provision for changes in the interest rate applicable, and for the formula to be used in calculating the new rate.

The Taxes (Interest Rate) (Amendment No 4) Regulations 1993, SI 1993/3171 (in force on 6 January 1994), further amend the 1989 Regulations, SI 1989/1297, by decreasing the applicable rate of official rate of interest for the purposes of the Income and Corporation Taxes Act 1988, s 160 from 7·75 to 7·5 per cent.

INDUSTRIAL AND PROVIDENT SOCIETIES

Halsbury's Laws of England (4th edn) Vol 24 (reissue), paras 1–200

1509   Credit unions—authorised investments

The Credit Unions (Authorised Investments) Order 1993, SI 1993/3100 (in force on 31 December 1993) specifies the investments in which credit unions can invest their surplus funds and implements Council Directive (EC) 88/361. Certain classes of investment, in particular local authority securities, have been removed but provision is made to allow credit unions who invested in these classes of investment prior to the order coming into force to continue to hold these investments.

1510   Credit unions—fees

The Industrial and Provident Societies (Credit Unions) (Amendment of Fees) Regulations 1993, SI 1993/548 (in force on 1 April 1993), supersede the 1992 Regulations, SI 1992/500. They generally increase, by approximately 4 per cent, the fees payable for matters to be transacted and for the inspection of documents under the Industrial and Provident Societies Acts 1965 and 1967 and the Credit Unions Act 1979.

1511   Industrial and provident societies—fees

The Industrial and Provident Societies (Amendment of Fees) Regulations 1993, SI 1993/549 (in force on 1 April 1993), supersede the 1992 Regulations, SI 1992/499. They generally increase, by about 4 per cent, the fees to be paid for matters transacted and for the inspection of documents under the Industrial and Provident Societies Acts 1965 and 1967.

INDUSTRIAL ASSURANCE

Halsbury's Laws of England (4th edn) Vol 24 (reissue), paras 201–400

1512   Collecting societies—returns

The Collecting Societies (Returns) Regulations 1993, SI 1993/2826 (in force on 1 January 1994), replace the Industrial Assurance (Collecting Society Returns) Regulations 1968, SI 1968/1585. The provisions of the 1968 Regulations are repeated with minor amendments in addition to new provisions requiring collecting societies to submit annual returns relating to industrial assurance policies to the Friendly Societies Commission instead of the Industrial Assurance Commissioner. The date by which returns are to be made has been changed to the same date by which accounts must be submitted under the Friendly Societies Act 1992, s 78.

INHERITANCE TAXATION

Halsbury's Laws of England (4th edn) Vol 24 (reissue), paras 401–800

1513   Articles

A Castle in Spain? Maurice Thomas (on Spanish inheritance rules): 137 SJ 1046
Assessing Irish Inheritance Tax, John Costello: LS Gaz, 17 February 1993, p 31

Inheritance Law the French Way, Martin Scannall and John Venn: LS Gaz, 17 March 1993, p 25

1514   Payment—accounts—form of accounts

The Inland Revenue has issued a Statement of Practice SP 2/93 in which it states that an accurate facsimile of an official account or other document required under the Inheritance Tax Act 1984, s 257(1) will satisfy the requirements of that provision. A facsimile will be considered accurate if it (1) provides the same information as that on official forms, (2) is readily recognisable as an inheritance tax account or form, (3) has been approved by the Inland Revenue before its use, and (4) bears the correct reference number. See further *STI*, 21 January 1993.

1515   Rate of tax

The Inheritance Tax (Indexation) Order 1993, SI 1993/759 (made on 16 March 1993), prescribes a single rate of inheritance tax of 40 per cent on a person's chargeable transfers in excess of the nil rate threshold of £154,000. The order applies to chargeable transfers on or after 6 April 1993 unless Parliament determines otherwise. For a summary of the Finance Act 1993, see para 2160.

The Inheritance Tax (Indexation) (No 2) Order 1993, SI 1993/2949 (made on 30 November 1993), prescribes a single rate of inheritance tax of 40 per cent on a person's chargeable transfers in excess of the nil rate threshold of £153,000. The order applies to chargeable transfers on or after 6 April 1994 unless Parliament determines otherwise. For a summary of the November 1993 Budget proposals, see para 2151.

1516   Settled property—avoidance scheme—composite transaction— discretionary trust under will

In order to avoid a substantial charge to capital transfer tax, solicitors for a family trust devised a five-step scheme of elaborate and complicated transactions to take advantage of various provisions under the Finance Act 1975, Sch 5 and the Finance Act 1976. The trustees successfully appealed against a decision of the Special Commissioners upholding notices of determination on the trustees. The Crown then appealed to the Court of Appeal, contending that the transactions constituted the first steps leading to an avoidance scheme which satisfied the principles laid down in *Ramsay (W T) Ltd v Inland Revenue Comrs* [1982] AC 300, HL (1981 Abr para 360). However, the court held that there had to be a preordained series of transactions or one single composite transaction in order to satisfy the *Ramsay* test. It was an essential part of that test that when a step was entered into, there was no practical or real likelihood that the pre-planned events would not take place. In the present case, the beneficiaries each received independent legal advice which might have resulted in different proposals being put forward. Therefore, it could not be said that the steps taken by the trustees were pre-ordained nor that there was a single composite transaction and the appeal was dismissed. The Crown appealed, again on the basis of *Ramsay*. Whilst it accepted that the first step was not part of any preordained single composite transaction, it contended that the following four steps did constitute such a transaction. It further argued that step five, which dealt with a vested moiety, did not qualify for the reverter to settlor exemption under the 1975 Act, Sch 5. *Held*, (Lord Templeman dissenting), the court had to consider whether the last four steps formed a single interdependent whole, as the Crown contended, or whether each step could have independent effect. Since each had the fiscal effect of creating a charge to income tax, they could not be treated as a composite whole and thus were not caught by the anti-avoidance principles in *Ramsay*. Further, whilst the steps were preordained in that they constituted a pre-planned tax-avoidance scheme, they were not capable of being construed as inconsistent with the application of the tax liability exemptions which they were intended to create. The Crown's additional contention in relation to step five also failed. Accordingly, the appeal would be dismissed.

Countess Fitzwilliam v IRC [1993] STC 502 (House of Lords: Lords Keith of Kinkel, Templeman, Ackner, Browne-Wilkinson and Mustill). Decision of Court of Appeal [1992] STC 185 (1992 Abr para 1458) affirmed. *Craven v White* [1989] AC 398, HL (1988 Abr para 188) applied.

1517   Transfer on death—alteration of disposition—deed of variation—reduction of inheritance tax—construction of deed

See *Schnieder v Mills*, para 978.

INJUNCTIONS

Halsbury's Laws of England (4th edn) Vol 24 (reissue), paras 801–1100

1518 Articles
Anton Pillers after *Universal Thermosensors*, Ian Craig: 136 SJ 1078
Injunctive Orders Relating to Children, Judge Nigel Fricker QC: [1993] Fam Law 141, 226
Principle in Mind, Daniel Alexander and Delia Watson (on *Secretary of State for the Home Department v Central Broadcasting Ltd* (1993) Times, 28 January, CA (para 1523): 143 NLJ 156

1519 Anton Piller order—discharge of order—material non-disclosure
The plaintiff was a manufacturer of leisure wear which claimed that the defendant was passing off clothing as being that of the plaintiff. It obtained an Anton Piller order against the defendant. The defendant applied to have the Anton Piller order discharged on the grounds that there was insufficient evidence to justify the granting of the order and that there had been material non-disclosure. The defendant also claimed that the plaintiff ought to be injuncted from making use of the information it had obtained from the exercise of the order. *Held*, information such as the defendant's company accounts, description of its premises and the conduct of its business, which the plaintiff knew or would have been expected to inquire into, ought to have been disclosed to the judge on the application. It should also have been drawn to the judge's attention that as the clothing was not being sold behind closed doors or in a market, but displayed in a shop window, this did not constitute an exceptional circumstance that justified the granting of an Anton Piller order. An order restraining the plaintiff from using the information obtained as a result of the Anton Piller order was appropriate in the interest of justice to the defendant. Accordingly, the application would be granted and the Anton Piller order discharged.
Naf Naf SA v Dickens (London) Ltd [1993] FSR 424 (Chancery Division: Hoffmann J).

1520 Interlocutory injunction—grant of injunction—factors for consideration—conduct of parties
The plaintiff was the manufacturer of a snack product who applied for an interlocutory injunction restraining the defendant from selling, supplying or advertising its rival product in a container that was in the same shape or form as the plaintiff's product. *Held*, when determining whether to issue an injunction the court should take whichever course appears to carry the lower risk of injustice if it should turn out to be the wrong decision. An important factor to consider in such a determination was the behaviour of the parties. In this case, the defendant had informed the plaintiff by letter that it would be producing its product in a particular container, and had provided a sample container for reference. The plaintiff had not responded to the letter, other than by acknowledging its receipt, and had only brought an action one year later after the defendant had expended time and resources in developing its rival product. In such circumstances, there was less chance of an injustice being committed if the injunction was not granted and accordingly the application would be refused.
Dalgety Spillers Foods Ltd v Food Brokers Ltd (1993) Times, 2 December (Chancery Division: Blackburne J).

1521 Interlocutory injunction—injunction against minister of the Crown—judicial review proceedings
See *M v Home Office*, para 583.

1522 Interlocutory injunction—injunction to restrain action in furtherance of a trade dispute
See TRADE UNIONS.

1523 Interlocutory injunction—injunction to restrain broadcast of interview with serial killer
The Secretary of State made an application for an interlocutory injunction restraining the broadcasting of part of a film made by the defendant showing an interview with a convicted serial killer. The interlocutory relief was sought in the Secretary of State's action against the first

defendant for breach of copyright in the film and breach of an agreement that the defendant would not broadcast or use the film without the Secretary of State's consent. These claims were disputed by the defendant. The injunction was refused and the Secretary of State appealed on the ground that there was a risk of distress to the relatives of the serial killer's victims if the extract were shown. *Held*, the relatives of the victims of the serial killer would be spared distress since it was not necessary for them to watch the programme. In the instant case there were serious issues to be tried and the public interest did not require prohibition by interlocutory injunction of the publication of an extract from a film on murderers which showed an interview with a serial killer. Accordingly, the appeal would be dismissed.

Secretary of State for the Home Department v Central Broadcasting Ltd (1993) Times, 28 January (Court of Appeal: Sir Thomas Bingham MR, McCowan and Hirst LJJ). Decision of Aldous J (1993) Times, 27 January affirmed.

1524 Interlocutory injunction—injunction to restrain enforcement of domestic law—injunction pending ruling of European Court of Justice

Pornographic programmes were transmitted by a Dutch company by satellite from Denmark to subscribers in the United Kingdom who had purchased or hired special decoding equipment. The Secretary of State made an order under the Broadcasting Act 1990, s 177 proscribing the programmes and making it an offence to publish the programme times and other details of the programmes or to supply decoding equipment to enable them to be received. On the company's application for judicial review of the order, certain questions as to the effect of the order were referred to the European Court of Justice. The trial court also refused the company's request for an interim injunction restraining the Secretary of State from enforcing the order pending the decision of the European Court. On the company's appeal against the refusal of interim relief, *held*, the trial court, in exercising its discretion as to whether to grant an injunction, had considered the prospect of success or failure resulting from the European Court's eventual ruling and, finding the prospect evenly balanced, gave decisive weight to the public interest in upholding the Secretary of State's decision pending the ruling. There were no grounds for interfering with his decision and, even if the trial court had exercised its discretion improperly, the Court of Appeal, in exercising its own discretion, would have forecast a strong likelihood that the European Court's ruling would favour the Secretary of State. The injunction would be refused and the appeal dismissed.

R v Secretary of State for the National Heritage, ex p Continental Television BV [1993] 3 CMLR 387 (Court of Appeal: Glidewell, Kennedy and Hirst LJJ). Decision of Queen's Bench Divisional Court [1993] 2 CMLR 333 affirmed.

1525 Interlocutory injunction—undertaking as to damages—enforcement

The defendants had ex parte interlocutory injunctions made against them following an application by a building society, which was supported by an affidavit alleging that a possible fraud had been perpetrated by the defendants. The defendants' application to discharge the interlocutory injunctions and to enforce an undertaking as to damages was successful, and an inquiry into what damage, if any, the defendants had suffered was ordered. On appeal by the plaintiffs, *held*, on an application for the enforcement of an undertaking as to damages, made on the discharge before trial of an interlocutory injunction, the court must consider all the circumstances of the case when deciding whether to exercise its discretion as to the enforcement of the undertaking. A final determination could not be made if material matters were in dispute and the court should postpone the matter until the trial. The judge had erred in principle; he was bound to consider all the circumstances in exercising his discretion and he could not properly, in advance of the trial, treat the allegations of fraud as bound to fail. Accordingly, the court was free to exercise the discretion afresh. The application to enforce the undertaking would be adjourned to the trial judge, to be determined at the conclusion of the trial. The appeal would accordingly be allowed.

Cheltenham and Gloucester Building Society v Ricketts [1993] 4 All ER 276 (Court of Appeal: Neill, Mann and Peter Gibson LJJ).

1526 Interlocutory injunction—wrongful interference with business—obstruction of highway construction

See *Department of Transport v Williams*, para 1365.

1527   Mandatory injunction—interim injunction to disapply domestic law—injunction pending ruling of European Court of Justice

The plaintiff had brought judicial review proceedings to quash certain provisions of the Utilities Supply and Works Contracts Regulations 1992, SI 1992/3279, Sch 2, by virtue of which utilities were obliged to throw their procurement contracts open to international competition. It contended that the regulations, which were intended to implement Council Directives (EC) 90/531 and 92/13, failed correctly to give effect to the provision which relieved utilities of that obligation. Certain questions arising in the proceedings were referred to the European Court of Justice. The plaintiff sought an interim mandatory injunction to amend the 1992 Regulations so as to disapply the provisions in question pending the reference. On appeal against the refusal of its application, *held*, where the dispute between the parties involved a conflict between private and public interests and damages were not an adequate remedy for either party, the adequacy of damages as redress to the plaintiff, if injunctive relief were denied, or to the Treasury, if it were granted, had first to be considered. Next, the plaintiff's chances of success before the European Court had to be considered. In assessing the balance of convenience, the apparent strength of the plaintiff's case and the need to protect putative Community rights would weigh less heavily in a case where an issue of Community law not previously raised or explored was raised than in a case where the national court might be all but persuaded by the jurisprudence of the European Court that the plaintiff had the Community right he asserted but might entertain just sufficient doubt to lead the national court to make the reference to the European Court. Although the national court would never disapply any legislation without great circumspection, its reluctance would weigh more heavily in a case where the law to be disapplied was a major piece of primary legislation on which an election had been fought than in a case where the law to be disapplied was a minor piece of subordinate legislation affecting very few parties other than the plaintiff. In assessing the balance of convenience, the court would consider all the above matters and would not adopt a formulaic approach. While, in some cases, the apparent strength of a plaintiff's case might be a weighty factor, in most cases where the court decided to refer it would be able to conclude little more than that the plaintiff's case was arguable or strongly so. A national court should not consider in depth a question which, by referring, it declared itself unable to resolve, which the European Court was better placed to resolve and which the national court would never have to resolve. There were no compelling reasons for making the order sought by the plaintiff and, accordingly, the appeal would be dismissed.

R v HM Treasury, ex p British Telecommunications plc (1993) Times, 2 December (Court of Appeal: Sir Thomas Bingham MR, Beldam and Simon Brown LJJ). *American Cyanamid Co v Ethicon Ltd* [1975] 1 All ER 504, HL (1975 Abr para 1864) and *Factortame Ltd v Secretary of State for Transport (No 2)* [1991] 1 All ER 70, HL (1990 Abr para 1354) applied.

1528   Mareva injunction—assets abroad—plaintiffs' undertakings

The plaintiffs were the liquidators of an international banking company who believed that the defendants, who were senior executives of the company, were guilty of fraud. They were granted a world-wide Mareva injunction against the company subject to an undertaking that they would not seek to enforce the injunction in any country apart from England and Wales. The defendants appealed on the ground that the undertaking gave inadequate protection against a multiplicity of suits and sought a prohibition that the plaintiffs would not commence new proceedings based upon the same or similar subject matter "including, for the avoidance of doubt, the making of any new complaints, laying of any information or similar procedure to criminal authorities". *Held*, the English court could not decide in which foreign jurisdictions proceedings could be brought and it could not therefore prohibit the plaintiffs from co-operating with any criminal prosecutions brought in such jurisdictions. However, to avoid possible oppression it was reasonable in this case to order the plaintiffs to undertake not to commence civil proceedings based on the same or similar subject matter, in foreign courts. Accordingly, the appeal would be allowed to that extent.

Morris v Mahfouz [1993] NLJR 1748 (Court of Appeal: Dillon, Nolan and Roch LJJ).

1529   Mareva injunction—compromised proceedings—injunction against third party

The plaintiffs began proceedings against the defendant, his wife and a number of other persons in respect of moneys allegedly owing to them. The proceedings were then compromised, the defendant undertaking to pay a specified amount and the plaintiffs abandoning all causes of action against his wife and the other persons. When he failed to pay the agreed sum, judgment was entered against the defendant. The plaintiffs then attempted to enforce the judgment by obtaining a Mareva injunction against the defendant, an order requiring the wife to provide certain financial information about herself and the defendant, and a further Mareva injunction against her in respect of specified bank accounts. The defendant maintained that he had no assets within the jurisdiction and that the luxurious lifestyle which he and his wife continued to enjoy was financed by his wife. On appeal by the wife on the ground that the court did not have the jurisdiction to make the orders. *Held*, the issue was whether, ancillary to the post-judgment Mareva injunction made against the defendant, the court could order discovery from a person against whom there was no substantive cause of action. For the court to have the appropriate jurisdiction it had to be shown that the third party was mixed up in the transaction concerning which discovery was required and that it was just and convenient to make the order. Since there was prima facie evidence that the wife had become mixed up in the arrangements made by her husband to defeat execution of the judgment the court had the appropriate jurisdiction to make the disclosure order against her. The Mareva injunction against the wife was incidental to and in aid of the enforcement of that right and as such there was jurisdiction to grant it. Accordingly, the appeal would be dismissed.

Mercantile Group (Europe) AG v Aiyela [1994] 1 All ER 110 (Court of Appeal: Sir Thomas Bingham MR, Steyn and Hoffmann LJJ).

1530 Mareva injunction—cross-undertaking in damages—Securities and Investments Board

See *Securities and Investments Board v Lloyd-Wright*, para 1271.

1531 Mareva injunction—ex parte application—application during trial

The applicant brought proceedings against the respondent by means of a petition under the Companies Act 1985, s 459 (unfair prejudice to member or shareholder in the conduct of the affairs of a company). After the inter partes hearing had been in progress for ten days, the applicant sought an ex parte Mareva injunction against the respondent. The injunction was granted. On appeal by the respondent, *held*, it was wrong to make the application ex parte in the course of the trial as this resulted in counsel for the applicant obtaining an unfair advantage. If a Mareva injunction was necessary during a trial, it had to be made in open court in the presence of counsel for the respondent. Accordingly, the appeal would be allowed.

Re All Starr Video Ltd (1993) Times, 25 March (Court of Appeal: Dillon and Leggatt LJJ).

1532 Matrimonial injunctions

See HUSBAND AND WIFE.

1533 Perpetual restrictive injunction—violation of common law right—harassment

The plaintiff alleged harassment against his son-in-law, the defendant, and was granted an injunction restraining him from molesting or interfering with the plaintiff, and from trespassing on his property or approaching within 50 yards of it. The defendant breached this order and was fined £25. The injunction was discharged and replaced with one restraining the defendant from assaulting or molesting the plaintiff and from trespassing on his land. No order for costs was given against the defendant. The plaintiff contended that the fine was inappropriate and that an immediate or suspended prison term should have been given, together with an order for costs against the defendant. On appeal, *held*, at common law injunctions were only an appropriate remedy where an actual tortious act had been or was likely to be committed. The allegations of harassment by the plaintiff did not constitute a tort or give any reason for thinking a tort might be committed. The restriction of the order could not therefore be criticised. The defendant's conduct had not been as serious as the plaintiff had contended and it was largely a domestic matter. In these circumstances the fine was appropriate. In respect of the request to commit the defendant for conduct after the order, it would have been wrong to commit for breach of the order where the defendant had not been given notice of the allegations, or of the fact that the court had been asked to commit him. If there were serious breaches then the defendant could expect to be committed, however the present situation had been overstated and to return to court would only intensify the problem. No order for costs had originally been made because of the lack of seriousness of the allegations. The basic rule was that costs followed the event and the judge had no reason to exercise his discretion not to follow that rule. The scale on which costs were awarded could be adjusted to take into account the lack of seriousness of the allegations. Accordingly the appeal would be dismissed except for the order for costs which

would be substituted with an order for costs against the defendant.
Patel v Patel [1993] 1 FCR 1016 (Court of Appeal: May LJ and Waterhouse J).

INSURANCE

Halsbury's Laws of England (4th edn) Vol 25 (reissue), paras 1–907

1534 Articles

All or Nothing, Clive Boxer (on *Pan Atlantic Insurance Co v Pine Top Insurance Co* (1992) 1 Lloyd's Rep 101 (para 1549)): 137 SJ 713
Insolvency of Insurer—Are We Safe? Clive Boxer (on the Policyholder Protection Act 1975): 137 SJ 1060
Insurance Against Terrorism, William Gloyn: LS Gaz, 9 June 1993, p 20
Insurance Ombudsman's Report, Michael Wilson: 137 SJ 258
Insuring Investment Property, Kaz Stepien: 137 SJ 230, 330
Resolving Insurance Disputes without Going to Court, Ian Cadogan and Richard Lewis: 136 SJ 1104
Second Hand Life Policy Market, Michael Wilson: 137 SJ 1237
Subrogation and Insurance Law: Proprietary Claims and Excess Clauses, Charles Mitchell: [1993] 2 LMCLQ 192
Subrogation and the Insurer's Lien, JE Martin (on *Napier and Ettrick (Lord) v Hunter* [1993] 1 All ER 385 (1992 Abr para 1494)): 143 NLJ 1061
Terrorism and Leases, Steven Fogel and Sally Pinkerton: Estates Gazette, 20 February 1993, p 74

1535 Assurance policy—fixed charge over policy of assurance and policy of insurance—interchangeability of terms

See *Re CCG International Enterprises Ltd* , para 464.

1536 Insurance brokers—regulation—provision of life insurance—Lautro regulations—indebtedness of sale representative

The applicant was employed as an insurance salesman for a firm of life insurers which was a member of Lautro, the self-regulating body of the life insurance industry. The applicant was paid by commission and, under a scheme operated by his employers, obtained an advance on commission which was to be repaid by deductions from subsequent earnings. He left the firm while still owing a sum of money and later found work with another firm of life insurers who were also members of Lautro. His employment with the second firm was suspended when they learned of his outstanding debts, which he was unwilling or unable to reduce or discharge. One of the Lautro Rules stated that a member cannot appoint any person as a company representative unless the member is satisfied on reasonable grounds that the person is not indebted to any other member of Lautro or any other recognised self-regulating organisation. The applicant was told by Lautro that there could be no dispensation or relaxation of the rule. In applying to quash the rule he argued that the rule was anomalous and unjust, that the decision to make it was unreasonable and that it failed to take into account relevant considerations such as its effect on employees. *Held*, indebtedness on the part of an employee in an investment business might well reflect on his competence, and could encourage him to sell policies with a view to maximising commission, without having regard to the interests of the investor. In the circumstances the rule was neither unreasonable nor unlawful. Accordingly, the application would be dismissed.
   R v Lautro, ex p Kendall (1993) Independent, 16 December (Queen's Bench Division: Latham J).

1537 Insurance companies—accounts—actuary's certificate

The Insurance Companies (Accounts and Statements) (Amendment) Regulations 1993, SI 1993/946 (in force on 1 January 1994), amend the 1983 Regulations, SI 1983/1811, to provide that the certificate signed by the appointed actuary and annexed to the documents deposited with the Secretary of State in accordance with the Insurance Companies Act 1982, s 22(1) by companies which carry on long term business must contain a statement that (if such is the case) the prescribed guidance notes issued by the Institute of Actuaries have been complied with.

1538 Insurance companies—accounts—Community provision

The Insurance Accounts Directive (Miscellaneous Insurance Undertakings) Regulations 1993, SI 1993/3245 (in force on 19 December 1993), implement Council Directive (EC) 91/674 (annual accounts and consolidated accounts of insurance undertakings) as it applies to bodies corporate or unincorporate other than bodies corporate to which the Companies Act 1985, Pt VII (accounts and audit) applies and friendly societies. The 1993 Regulations also implement the directive as it applies to the Council of Lloyd's and amend legislation applicable to industrial and provident societies which prepare accounts under the regulations.

1539 Insurance companies—accounts—requirements

The Companies Act 1985 (Insurance Companies Accounts) Regulations 1993, SI 1993/3246 (in force on 19 December 1993), implement the relevant provisions of Council Directive (EC) 91/674 (annual accounts and consolidated accounts of insurance undertakings). The regulations, by substituting the Companies Act 1985, Sch 9A, require insurance companies to prepare accounts in accordance with new requirements as to form and content. The regulations also specify certain companies which may continue to prepare accounts under the existing requirements, and make transitional provision.

1540 Insurance companies—direct non-life insurance—Switzerland

The Insurance Companies (Switzerland) Regulations 1993, SI 1993/3127 (in force on 5 January 1994), amend the Insurance Companies Act 1982 and the Insurance Companies (Accounts and Statements) Regulations 1983, SI 1983/1811, in order to implement Council Directive (EC) 91/371 (compliance with the Agreement between the EEC and Swiss Confederation on direct insurance other than life assurance). The Agreement provides to companies with their head office in a member state or Switzerland and which carry on direct general insurance business a reciprocal right to establish branches or agencies in the territory of the other party to the Agreement.

1541 Insurance companies—fees

The Insurance (Fees) Regulations 1993, SI 1993/601 (in force on 1 April 1993), replace the 1992 Regulations, SI 1992/516, and prescribe the fees payable to the Secretary of State under the Insurance Companies Act 1982, s 94A. Such fees are payable by companies when depositing their accounts and other documents under the 1992 Act, s 22(1) and by the Council of Lloyd's when the statement in respect of Lloyd's is deposited under s 86(1). The level of fee for an insurance company is fixed according to the amount of its gross premiums receivable in respect of its global business or, in the case of a Community company or a Community deposit company, its United Kingdom business, for the financial year to which the accounts relate. Special provision is made for Swiss companies and companies which are part of a group. No fee is payable where a company is being wound up, whether in the United Kingdom or in another jurisdiction, or where a company is no longer authorised to effect, or is prohibited from effecting, contracts of insurance. Where a company carries on both long-term and general business, the amounts of premiums in respect of each type of business are aggregated for the purpose of determining the fee payable.

1542 Insurance companies—insurance business—regulation

The Insurance Companies (Amendment) Regulations 1993, SI 1993/174 (in force on 20 May 1993), implement Council Directive (EEC) 90/619 by amending the Insurance Companies Act 1982, the Financial Services Act 1986, the Insurance Companies (Amendment) Regulations 1992, SI 1992/2890, and the Contracts (Applicable Law) Act 1990. The 1990 Directive amends the supervisory procedures for direct life insurance business carried on by insurers through an establishment in a member state by making new provision to cover commitments in a member state otherwise than through an establishment in that state. The 1993 Regulations also limit the application of the 1986 Act, s 183 (reciprocal facilities for financial business).

1543 Insurance contracts—restrictions on promotion of contracts of insurance—designated countries and territories

The Financial Services Act 1986, s 130(1) provides that the issue of advertisements in the United Kingdom inviting persons to enter into a contract of insurance which constitutes an investment for the purposes of the 1986 Act, is prohibited. The restriction does not apply where the contract of insurance is to be with an insurance company authorised to effect or carry out such contracts of insurance in a designated country or territory.

The Financial Services (Designated Countries and Territories) (Overseas Insurance Companies) Order 1993, SI 1993/1237 (in force on 2 June 1993), designates, for the purposes of the Financial Services Act 1986, s 130, the State of Iowa, United States of America.

1544 Insurance contracts—undisclosed principal—validity of contract
See *Siu v Eastern Insurance Co Ltd,* para 65.

1545 Insurance policy—construction—risk of loss arising from accident to plant or machinery—meaning of accident
Malaysia
The defendant operated a plant refining edible palm oil. It insured its plant and machinery, including a steam boiler, with the plaintiff insurance company against the risk of loss arising from any accident. A rupture in the upper coil of the boiler caused a leakage of water which in turn resulted in the whole plant being shut down for approximately one month. The defendant claimed on its policy but the plaintiff repudiated liability. The court at first instance declared that the plaintiff was liable. The plaintiff appealed on the ground that the rupture occurred as a result of corrosion fatigue over time, which could therefore not be described as an accident. *Held,* although the onus was on the defendant to establish that it came under the peril insured against, it was the plaintiff who had the burden to prove that the rupture fell under the exceptions to the definition of "accident" in the policy, which did not include any damage that was caused deliberately or intentionally. The defendant had followed the manufacturer's operating manual when installing and running the boiler and the coil was manufactured to last for hundreds of years. Therefore, the defendant could not have expected or intended the rupture to occur and the damage could be said to have been caused by accident. The dominant cause of the accident was not corrosion fatigue but the lack of feed water in the boiler. The defendant did not intentionally or deliberately feed insufficient water into the boiler as it had followed the manufacturer's instruction manual to the letter and accordingly, the appeal would be dismissed.

American Home Assurance Co v Nalin Industries Sdn Bhd [1993] 2 MLJ 409 (Malaysian Supreme Court).

1546 Insurance policy—duty to give information—third parties
The plaintiff, an architect, sued for fees, damages and a quantum meruit. The defendants denied liability and counterclaimed, seeking damages which greatly exceeded the plaintiff's claim. The defendants were anxious to discover whether the plaintiff had appropriate insurance cover and what the limits of any cover were. The requests for this information were refused on the grounds that they were premature. Liability of the plaintiff to the defendant was not yet established. The defendants sought an order against the plaintiff pursuant to the Third Parties (Rights Against Insurers) Act 1930, s 2. *Held,* the 1930 Act, s 2 imposed a statutory duty to give information for specified purposes, namely of ascertaining whether any rights had been transferred and vested by the Act and of enforcing such rights. It was clear from the language of 1930 Act, s 1(1) that the rights to be transferred had to be in respect of the liability and not the insured's general rights under the contract of insurance. Further, the 1930 Act, s 1 did not transfer to a third party a contractual right to seek declaratory relief before specific liability had been established, nor did the section transfer to the third party a right to be indemnified contingent upon liability being established. Accordingly, the application would be dismissed.

Nigel Upchurch Associates v The Aldridge Estates Investment Co [1993] 1 Lloyd's Rep 535 (Queen's Bench Division: Barbara Dohmann QC).

1547 Insurance policy—individual life assurance contract—cross-border contract—cancellation
The Insurance Companies (Cancellation) Regulations 1993, SI 1993/1327 (in force on 20 May 1993), amend the Insurance Companies Act 1982 to implement Council Directive (EEC) 90/619, art 15 (as amended by Council Directive (EEC) 92/96). Article 15 gives a policy holder who has purchased an individual life assurance contract on a cross-border basis a period during which he may cancel the contract, although member states may remove the right of cancellation from contracts for six months or less. The right of cancellation is extended to any policy holder who purchases an individual life assurance contract from an insurance undertaking with a head

office in a member state, although the right may again be removed where the policy holder does not need protection because of his status or because of the circumstances in which the contract is made.

The Insurance Companies (Cancellation No 2) Regulations 1993, SI 1993/1092 (in force on 20 May 1993), amend the Insurance Companies Regulations 1981, SI 1981/1654, to further implement Council Directive (EEC) 90/619, art 15 supra by setting out the form of the statutory notice of the right of cancellation and providing exemptions from the requirement to give the right of cancellation.

1548   Insurance policy—protection of policyholders—insolvency
The Policyholders Protection Act 1975, s 4(2) provides that a policy of insurance is a United Kingdom policy at any time when the performance by the insurer of any of his obligations under the contract evidenced by the policy would constitute the carrying on by the insurer of insurance business of any class in the United Kingdom.
   The plaintiffs were professionals from the United States and Canada. They insured against professional liabilities under policies subscribed by United Kingdom insurance companies which had become insolvent. Declarations as to the liability of the Policyholders' Protection Board to indemnify the plaintiffs were sought. The Court of Appeal declined to make any declarations as to the right of the plaintiffs to be indemnified, but made declarations as to the effect of s 4(2), and considered that payment of claims under a policy of insurance effected in the United Kingdom would constitute the carrying on of insurance business within the United Kingdom, wherever the claim was paid. On appeal, *held*, an insurance policy was a United Kingdom policy if, had any of the obligations under the contract evidenced by the policy been performed at the relevant time, such performance would have formed part of an insurance business which the insurer was authorised to carry on in the United Kingdom, whether or not such obligations would have been performed in the United Kingdom. The appeal would therefore be dismissed and the declaration previously made to similar effect would be upheld.
   Scher v Policyholders' Protection Board, Ackman v Same [1993] 3 All ER 384 (House of Lords: Lords Templeman, Griffiths, Ackner, Goff of Chieveley and Mustill). Decision of Court of Appeal [1993] 3 All ER 384 (1992 Abr para 1495) affirmed.

The Insurance Companies Act 1982, s 96(1) defines a "policyholder" as "a person . . . to whom a sum is due or a periodic payment is payable". The Policyholders Protection Act 1975, s 8(2) provides that it is the duty of the Policyholders' Protection Board to secure that a sum equal to 90 per cent of the amount of any liability of a company in liquidation towards a private policyholder under the terms of any policy which was a United Kingdom policy at the beginning of the liquidation is paid to the policyholder as soon as reasonably practicable after the beginning of the liquidation.
   The plaintiffs were individual and professional partners in accountancy, legal and medical practices in the United States and Canada. They had taken out professional liability insurance under policies subscribed by United Kingdom insurance companies in respect of which liquidators had been appointed. The plaintiffs sought the determination of the court as to whether their policies fell within the scope of the Policyholders Protection Act 1975, s 8. Declarations were made at first instance as to the meaning of s 8(2), which were varied on appeal. The plaintiffs appealed against the variation. *Held*, the plaintiffs, who were not the legal holders of policies of insurance, but who had contingent claims under the policies on the companies' liquidation, were not persons "to whom a sum is due" within the meaning of the 1982 Act, s 96(1) so as to entitle them to compensation from the Policyholders' Protection Board by virtue of the 1975 Act, s 8. The words "to whom a sum is due" meant what they said and not "to whom a sum is afterwards deemed to have been due". Even if it was possible that a sum became due to a contingent plaintiff at the moment of the liquidation, it was no more due under the policy at that moment than it was immediately beforehand. The occurrence of the liquidation gave a new right, but it did not give a new right under the policy of insurance. In addition, the requirement under s 8(2) that the claimant had to be a "private" policyholder was intended to protect only certain partnerships. A partnership was to be treated as a partnership only if it consisted of private individuals, and a partnership loss was only to be recoverable if the partnership had no corporate member. The appeal would accordingly be dismissed.
   Scher v Policyholders Protection Board (No 2), Ackman v Same (No 2) [1993] 4 All ER 840 (House of Lords: Lords Templeman, Ackner, Goff of Chievely and Mustill). Decision of Court of Appeal [1993] 3 All ER 384 (1992 Abr para 1495) affirmed.

1549   Insurance policy—reinsurance—failure to disclose relevant information to reinsurer

The plaintiffs had entered into a reinsurance agreement in which the defendants were the reinsurers. The plaintiffs sought to rely on the reinsurance agreement, but the defendants successfully claimed that they had avoided liability under the agreement because the plaintiffs had failed to fully disclose all the relevant information to them before the reinsurance agreement was signed. The plaintiffs appealed on the ground that the defendants would still have insured the risk even if they had been aware of the undisclosed material. *Held*, in deciding whether the defendants were entitled to avoid the contract the court was only required to consider whether a prudent insurer would have regarded the undisclosed material as probably tending to increase the risk, and once the judge had answered that question in the affirmative he had been correct to rule that the reinsurers had avoided liability. The plaintiffs' contention that non-disclosure only allowed a reinsurer to avoid liability if the reinsurers would not have entered into the agreement if they had been aware of the non-disclosed material was an erroneous interpretation of the authorities and, accordingly, their appeal would be dismissed.

Pan Atlantic Insurance Co Ltd v Pine Top Insurance Co Ltd [1993] Lloyd's Rep 496 (Court of Appeal: Sir Donald Nicholls V-C, Farquharson and Steyn LJJ). *Container Transport International Inc v Oceanus Mutual Underwriting Association (Bermuda) Ltd* [1984] 1 Lloyd's Rep 476, CA considered.

1550   Liability insurance—contribution—co-insurers

The Bahamas

The plaintiff was injured as the result of negligent driving by the defendant who was driving a car lent to him by a car repairer. The defendant failed to meet the judgment obtained against him by the plaintiff. Accordingly, the plaintiff brought proceedings against the defendant's insurers and the repairer's insurers. The defendant's insurers had cancelled the policy taken out by the defendant before the accident but had failed to take steps to obtain the surrender of the policy and therefore remained statutorily liable for third party risks. The repairer's insurers would have been able to avoid liability to the defendant if he had made a claim on them because they had not been given notice of the accident within the time specified in the policy. The Court of Appeal of The Bahamas decided that, as both insurers were equally liable to the plaintiff both as judgment debtors and as statutory insurers and their obligation was in respect of the same loss, they were to be regarded as statutory co-insurers for the purpose of contribution and, since neither was under statute primarily liable, each was required to contribute one-half of the amount awarded to the plaintiff. The defendant's insurers appealed to the Privy Council. *Held*, where two insurers were under a statutory liability for the same third party risk the question of contribution between the two was to be determined in accordance with the extent of their respective liabilities to the person insured for the loss under the separate contracts of insurance rather than in accordance with their respective statutory liabilities, since the extent of their respective liabilities to the person insured would indicate the scale of the double insurance. If both insurers were under no liability to the person who was insured, they must share the statutory liability for loss equally irrespective of the date upon which they repudiated liability. In the present case, both insurers were in the same position: they were both under a statutory liability in relation to the plaintiff's claim but they both would have been entitled to repudiate liability to the defendant. No distinction was to be made in relation to their respective positions and, accordingly, they should each contribute equally to the amount payable to the plaintiff. The appeal would be dismissed.

Eagle Star Insurance Co Ltd v Provincial Insurance plc [1993] 3 All ER 1 (Privy Council: Lords Griffiths, Bridge of Harwich, Ackner, Goff of Chieveley and Woolf). *Monksfield v Vehicle and General Insurance Co Ltd* [1971] Lloyd's Rep 139 approved. *Legal and General Assurance Society Ltd v Drake Insurance Co Ltd* [1992] 1 All ER 283, CA (1990 Abr para 1374) doubted.

1551   Lloyd's—action by underwriting members—action for breach of contract against agents—outstanding cash calls

A number of Lloyd's "names" claimed damages for breach of contract by their agents in the conduct of underwriting for four syndicates. The agents claimed that a clause in a standard agreement between the "names" and the agents precluded a "name" from bringing an action relating to a cash call which had yet to be met. On the question of the construction of the agreement, *held*, the scheme of the clause was clear and sensible and stated clearly that a "name" had to pay any sums required without prevarication. This reflected the overriding need to ensure that funds are available for settlement of claims of those who are insured or re-insured at Lloyd's. Nevertheless, this did not prevent a "name" bringing a claim for negligent underwriting where there were still outstanding cash calls to be paid.

Arbuthnott v Feltrim; Deeny v Gooda Walker Ltd (1993) Independent, 1 October (Court of Appeal: Sir Thomas Bingham MR, Steyn and Hoffmann LJJ).

1552 Lloyd's—members' agents and managing agents—duty of care

It has been held that managing agents subject to agreements made prior to 1987 owe a duty ordinarily binding on any professional agent to exercise reasonable care and skill in relation to dealings with indirect names. Any claim for negligence against managing agents must therefore establish that there has been a failure to exercise a standard of skill and care reasonably to be expected of such an agent at the time and with the knowledge that he had or ought to have had. Managing agents also owe a tortious duty to take reasonable care not to cause economic loss. Where the managing agents are also members' agents, they also have a duty to carry out underwriting activities with reasonable care. Members' agents who are not also managing agents and who are governed by post-1987 forms of agreement are liable to names for the defaults of the managing agents in the conduct of the names' underwriting.

Arbuthnott v Feltrim; Deeny v Gooda Walker; Henderson v Merrett Syndicates (1993) Times, 30 December (Court of Appeal: Sir Thomas Bingham MR, Hoffmann and Henry LJJ). Decision of Saville J (1993) Times, 20 October affirmed.

1553 Motor insurance—insurance cover obtained by misrepresentation—whether policy void or voidable

Scotland
The appellant was convicted of using an uninsured motor vehicle contrary to the Road Traffic Act 1988, s 143(1). He obtained motor insurance cover after falsely representing that he had not been convicted of any motoring offences in the previous five years. The insurers subsequently wrote to him, asking him to sign a statement that his representation as to past convictions was false and that the policy was void from its inception. After taking legal advice, the appellant signed. The sheriff convicted him on the grounds that, since the insurance policy was void, he had driven without any motor insurance cover. He appealed, contending that the policy was voidable rather than void. *Held*, since it had been agreed by the appellant and the insurers that the policy was void, not voidable, the sheriff was entitled to arrive at the decision he made. Accordingly, the appeal would be dismissed.

Barr v Carmichael 1993 SLT 1030 (High Court of Justiciary).

1554 Personal accident insurance—exclusion clause—needless peril

The plaintiffs, the deceased's next of kin, claimed the death benefit payable under an insurance policy taken out with the defendants. The defendants relied on an exclusion clause which stated that no benefit was payable if the "death, injury or incapacity resulted directly or indirectly from or was accelerated by wilful exposure to needless peril". The deceased had died from a head injury when he fell from the back of a car driven by his fiancée. The accident occurred when the deceased jumped onto the rear bumper of the car and his fiancée, for a practical joke, started moving the car forward slowly but instead of stopping she accelerated. At first instance the defendants were allowed to rely on the exclusion clause and the plaintiffs appealed. *Held*, the issue was whether at the moment the deceased stepped onto the rear bumper he wilfully exposed himself to an unnecessary peril within the meaning of the policy. It was not enough to show an intentional act which resulted in peril, there had to be a conscious act of volition which included recklessness, directed to the running of the risk. Accordingly, it was necessary to have regard to all the circumstances including the likelihood of the insured injury being incurred if the risk was taken and the opportunity for reflection before the risk was taken. The deceased's action was a momentary act of stupidity, the peril was clearly unnecessary but the deceased had not wilfully exposed himself to unnecessary peril. As such the exclusion clause could only be relied on where it was shown that an insured injury was quite likely to occur or that the insured person clearly appreciated the risk of the injury occurring. Accordingly, the appeal would be allowed.

Morley v United Friendly Insurance plc [1993] 3 All ER 47 (Court of Appeal: Neill and Beldam LJJ).

1555 Reinsurance (Acts of Terrorism) Act 1993

The Reinsurance (Acts of Terrorism) Act 1993 provides for the payment out of money provided by Parliament or into the Consolidated Fund of sums referable to reinsurance liabilities entered into by the Secretary of State in respect of loss or damage to property resulting from or consequential upon acts of terrorism and losses consequential on such loss or damage. The Act, which does not extend to Northern Ireland, received the royal assent on 27 May 1993 and came into force on that date.

Section 1 provides for the financing of reinsurance obligations of the Secretary of State under any reinsurance agreement entered into pursuant to arrangements to which the Act applies, or any guarantee entered into pursuant to any such agreement, and for any receipts to be paid into the Consolidated Fund. The Secretary of State must lay before Parliament a copy of any such agreement or guarantee. The arrangements to which the Act applies are those under which the Secretary of State, with Treasury consent, undertakes to any extent the liability of reinsuring risks against loss of or damage to property in Great Britain resulting from or consequential upon acts of terrorism (that is, acts of persons acting on behalf of, or in connection with, any organisation which carries out activities directed towards the overthrowing or influencing, by force or violence, of Her Majesty's government in the United Kingdom or any other government de jure or de facto) and any loss which is consequential on such aforementioned loss or damage: s 2. Section 3 deals with citation and extent.

INTOXICATING LIQUOR

Halsbury's Laws of England (4th edn) Vol 26, paras 1–500

1556   Articles

Justices' On-Licences and the Imposition of Conditions, Christine Clayson: 157 JP Jo 633
Liquor Licensing—Linger Longer? Christine Clayson: 157 JP Jo 615

1557   Beer—regulations

The Beer Regulations 1993, SI 1993/1228 (in force on 1 June 1993), replace the 1985 Regulations, SI 1985/1627 and the Spoilt Beer (Remission and Repayment of Duty) Regulations 1987, SI 1987/314. They replace the beer duty system based on the volume and original gravity of the beer before fermentaion commences by a new system based on the alcoholic strength of the finished product. Provision is also made for (1) the revenue control of the production of beer liable to excise duty; (2) the holding and movement of beer in duty suspension; (3) the determination and payment of the duty; and (4) relief from excise duty on beer which has been returned to the brewer as spoilt or otherwise unfit for use.

1558   Licence—application—discretion to allow

It has been held that the power of licensing justices to exercise a discretion to allow a licence application containing technical errors or verbal inaccuracies does not apply where the statutory requirements have not been fulfilled.

R v Mid-Warwickshire Licensing Justices, ex p Patel (1993) Times, 15 December (Queen's Bench Division: May J).

1559   Licence—on-licence—prescribed categories—grant of licence falling outside prescribed categories

The appellant held a justices' on-licence, subject to a prohibition on the sale of beer, in respect of his wine bar. The licence was revoked on the grounds that the no beer condition was unlawful and rendered the whole licence invalid. The appellant contended that the unlawful condition was severable and the licence thus valid. *Held*, where an invalid condition was attached to a licence the relevant test was whether the licensing authority would have granted the permission without the offending condition. The court did not know whether the justices would have granted the appellant's licence without attaching the no beer condition and in those circumstances was forced to conclude that the entire licence was invalid. Accordingly, the appeal would be dismissed.

R v Inner London Crown Court, ex p Sitki (1993) Times, 26 October (Court of Appeal: Russell, Staughton and Steyn LJJ). Decision of Queen's Bench Divisional Court (1992) Times, 2 December (1992 Abr para 1513) affirmed.

1560   Licensed premises—closing time—patrons remaining on premises
The appellant was convicted of contravening a condition in his licence to keep a late night refreshment house, which required the closure of the premises between 3 am and 5 am, contrary to the Late Night Refreshment Houses Act 1969, s 7(2). On appeal against conviction, *held*, premises were not "kept open" if customers were not permitted to enter after hours for the purpose of purchasing refreshment and there were sufficient indications to the public that further customers were not welcome. It was not necessary however to lock the doors and patrons already inside the restaurant were permitted to complete their meals. Obviously if a "closed" sign was just a token and the premises were in reality open then the premises were being "kept open", but if the situation was that a customer who ignored the "closed" sign walked in and was refused service then they were not. Accordingly, the appeal would be allowed.
   Amin v DPP (1993) Times, 9 April (Queen's Bench Division: Rougier J).

1561   Licensed premises—security of tenure
See *Taylor v Courage Ltd*, para 1598.

1562   Licensed premises—tie provisions—severance
See *Inntrepreneur Estates (GL) Ltd v Boyes*, para 1616.

JUDGMENTS AND ORDERS

Halsbury's Laws of England (4th edn) Vol 26, paras 501–600

1563   Foreign judgments—reciprocal enforcement
See CONFLICT OF LAWS.

1564   Judgment debt—rate of interest
The Judgment Debts (Rate of Interest) Order 1993, SI 1993/564 (in force on 1 April 1993), reduces from 15 per cent to 8 per cent per annum the rate of interest on judgment debts under the Judgments Act 1838, s 17.

1565   Judgment in default—conditional order to set aside—creditors right to present winding-up petition—order as to costs
A writ was issued by Company A against the applicant company, and was ignored by the applicant. Judgment was then filed in default and a statutory demand was made for the judgment debt. On the same day as the statutory demand was made the applicant raised a potential defence to the claim. The solicitors for Company A admitted that the statutory demand was in the wrong form, but they refused to undertake not to present a petition for winding up based on the judgment debt. The applicant then sought to restrain Company A from presenting a petition. The master made a conditional order that judgment should be set aside if notice of intention to defend was given promptly, and an amount in respect of costs thrown away was paid within 14 days. The first condition was satisfied but not the second. Company A accepted that if the second condition was satisfied there would be no judgment and it would have to proceed with the action in the county court, where it would be transferred by the Queen's Bench Division. If that happened it would be wrong to seek a winding-up petition, and an undertaking was given that no petition would be presented until the expiry of 14 days from the date of the order and that if, within that time the judgment was set aside because the second condition was satisfied, no petition would be presented unless the debt was converted into a judgment in due course. *Held*, where a company was served with a writ and allowed judgment in default to be entered, there was a strong inference that the company was unable to pay its debts. It was proper in those circumstances for the judgment creditor to proceed by way of statutory demand and winding-up petition, and if an application was made to set aside the judgment, the creditor should refuse to give an undertaking not to present a petition until it had seen the full evidence in support of the application. Accordingly, Company A did not have to pay the costs of the application to restrain presentation of a winding-up petition. However, the master's order showed that the applicant had an arguable defence, and if the conditions were satisfied the judgment would be

set aside. The applicant should not therefore have to pay Company A's costs on the application. The court would accept the undertakings given by Company A, to cover the 14-day period relating to costs, and to cover the indefinite future from satisfaction of the condition down to judgment on the defended action. Each side would bear its own costs. The order would be granted accordingly.

Re Druce & Co [1993] BCLC 964 (Chancery Division: Harman J).

1566   Order for costs

See PRACTICE AND PROCEDURE.

1567   Summary judgment—director's fiduciary duty—share transfer

See Bishopsgate Investment Management Ltd (in liquidation) v Maxwell, para 477.

1568   Summary judgment—leave to defend—conditional leave—affidavit evidence

A bank claimed against the defendant on a guarantee. The bank applied for summary judgment under RSC Ord 14, but the defendant was given leave to defend upon the payment into court of the sum claimed. His appeal against that decision was allowed to the extent of reducing the amount he had to pay into court. On further appeal, he contended that he was unable to pay any sum at all, sought leave to adduce fresh evidence and unconditional leave to defend. The bank cross-appealed on the grounds that the defendant's evidence was inconsistent and failed to disclose a bona fide defence, and that the proper course was to enter judgment for the bank in the sum claimed. Held, the judge failed to adopt the correct test when faced with conflicting affidavits in an application for summary judgment under Ord 14. The relevant test was whether there was a fair or reasonable probability of the defendant having a real or bona fide defence. The defendant had produced two affidavits which were inconsistent, thus casting doubts on the correctness of each. Accordingly, since there was no fair or reasonable prospect of the defence succeeding, the order for conditional leave would be set aside and judgment entered for the bank.

National Westminster Bank Plc v Daniel [1993] 1 WLR 1453 (Court of Appeal: Glidewell and Butler-Sloss LJJ). Banque de Paris et des Pays-Bas (Suisse) SA v Costa de Naray [1984] 1 Lloyd's Rep 21, CA followed. Dictum of Webster J in Paclantic Financing Co Inc v Moscow Narodny Bank Ltd [1983] 1 WLR 1063 at 1067 disapproved.

JURIES

Halsbury's Laws of England (4th edn) Vol 26, paras 601–700

1569   Articles

Deaf Jurors, Douglas Silas (on the inequalities of jury service for deaf people): 143 NLJ 896

1570   Juror—misconduct—inquiry

After a jury retired, a juror was discovered to have a mobile telephone with him. In an appeal by the defendant against conviction on the basis of a material irregularity, held, as only one call had been made, concerning the juror's business, there was no material irregularity in this particular case. The prosecution had advised that the particulars of the juror be sought from the court administrator and that an independent officer be appointed to interview the juror. To allow such inquiries threatened the secrecy of the jury room. Such inquiries were only to be initiated with the consent of the court where the judge had officially discharged his duty, with the consent of the Court of Appeal. Accordingly, the appeal would be dismissed.

R v McCluskey (1993) Times, 4 June (Court of Appeal: Watkins LJ, Henry and Pill JJ).

1571   Jury—discharge—court's discretion—recall of jury

The jury forewoman was asked on two occasions whether the jury had come to a conclusion and on both occasions the answer was in the negative. The jury were then asked whether they were likely to reach a verdict upon which at least ten of them were agreed and again the answer was in the negative. The jury were discharged but after a disturbance in the public gallery and another disturbance in the jury box the judge sent the jury out to think again. The appellant was convicted and on appeal against conviction, *held*, even though the jury had not left the jury box before the judge had changed his mind, setting aside the order to discharge the jury was not to be lightly taken and only in very rare circumstances. Where a judge made an order discharging a jury from returning a verdict, there was no principle of law which prevented him from setting the order aside to allow the jury to deliberate further, but the circumstances in which that might occur were extremely rare. The present case did not come within that category and accordingly the appeal would be allowed.

R v Follen (1993) Times, 21 January (Court of Appeal: Watkins LJ, Auld and Kay JJ).

1572 Jury—dissension—procedure

During the defendants' trial, two members of the jury complained that due to the nature of the case, there was dissension among the jury which was affecting concentration. The complainant jurors were brought separately into open court and questioned as to whether they could continue to give proper consideration of the evidence in the case. Subsequently, the entire jury was brought back as a whole and asked whether they could as a whole carry on with their duties. The defendants were convicted and both appealed. *Held*, the procedure of initially questioning the two complainants in the absence of the rest of the jury was wrong so as to amount to an irregularity. Circumstances giving rise to an inference that a member of a jury might not be able to fulfil his duties were normally external to a jury; it was common in such cases to have the individual juror questioned in open court so that the trial judge might make inquiries without jeopardising the continued participation of the rest of the jury. Occasionally, as in this case, the circumstances were internal to the jury, and while a judge had a discretion enabling him to take the course best suited to the circumstances so as to ensure a fair trial, to separate one juror from the rest was unjustified. The whole jury should be asked in open court as to their capacity, as a whole, to continue. The appeals would accordingly be allowed.

R v Orgles [1993] 4 All ER 533 (Court of Appeal: Nolan LJ, Wright and Holland JJ).

LAND CHARGES

Halsbury's Laws of England (4th edn) Vol 26, paras 701–900

1573 Registration—estate contract—option to purchase—single registration

The first defendant granted the plaintiffs an option to purchase unregistered land on terms that if the option was exercised, the price was to be determined on the open market. The option was registered as an estate contract under the Land Charges Act 1972 and subsequently exercised by the plaintiffs. The defendant failed to co-operate in fixing a price for the land, and sold part of it to a third party, the sale being expressed to be subject to the option agreement. The land was then sold by the third party to the second defendant, and registered at the Land Registry in the second defendant's name. The plaintiffs successfully claimed specific performance against both defendants and damages against the first defendant. The second defendant appealed on the ground that the agreement resulting from the option had not been registered as an estate contract and so was unenforceable against him. *Held*, the purpose of the 1972 Act was to give notice of contracts creating interests in land. The original option created an equitable interest in land and that interest was not altered on the exercise of the option. A later potential purchaser from the grantor of the option was sufficiently warned by registration of the option and did not require further registration of the contract of sale resulting from the option. Accordingly, the appeal would be dismissed.

Armstrong and Holmes Ltd v Holmes [1994] 1 All ER 826 (Chancery Division: Judge Paul Baker QC).

1574 Registration—pending land action—claim that easement extinguished

The Land Charges Act 1972, s 5(1) provides that a pending action for trespass and abandonment of rights of way can be protected by lodging a caution in the proprietorship register.

The plaintiff's property was surrounded by common land over which three rights of way had been preserved. The defendants, who owned the common land, sought a declaration that two of the rights of way had been extinguished, and they lodged a caution in accordance with the 1972 Act, s 5(1). The caution was vacated on the ground that the rights of way had not been abandoned, and the plaintiff sought damages under the Land Registration Act 1925, s 56(3) on the ground that the caution had been lodged without reasonable cause because the action had not been a pending action within the meaning of the 1972 Act, s 17(1). That claim was rejected, and the plaintiff appealed. *Held*, for the purpose of the 1925 Act an easement was "land" which had been vested in the proprietor of the dominant tenement, and as such it was an interest against which a caution could be lodged even though an easement could not exist in gross. A pending action aimed at establishing that the easement no longer existed was an action relating to land within the meaning of the 1972 Act, s 17(1) and as such it could be registered. The defendants had not acted unreasonably and there were no grounds for awarding damages. Accordingly, the appeal would be dismissed.

Willies-Williams v The National Trust for Places of Historic Interest or Natural Beauty (1993) 65 P & CR 359 (Court of Appeal: Ralph Gibson, Leggatt and Hoffmann LJJ). *Selim Ltd v Bickenhall Engineering Ltd* [1981] 3 All ER 210 (1981 Abr para 1730) approved.

LAND REGISTRATION

Halsbury's Laws of England (4th edn) Vol 26, paras 901–1490

1575 Articles

Dancing on the Green, Robert Bryce (on the registration of new village greens): 137 SJ 370
Pinekerry v Needs—A Conflict Between Law and Practice, Jean Howell (on *Pinekerry Ltd v Needs (Kenneth) (Contractors) Ltd* (1992) 64 P & CR 245, CA): 57 MLR 121
When is a Legal Charge not a Legal Charge? Bron Council: 137 SJ 1113

1576 Charging order—failure to register

Two judgment debtors jointly owned land under a statutory trust for sale, subject only to a mortgage in favour of a bank. The plaintiffs, who were judgment creditors obtained a charging order on the debtors' interest in the property, which they protected by cautions. The second defendant advanced to the judgment debtors a sum of money secured by a legal charge on the property. The Land Registry failed to give notice to the plaintiffs as cautioners pursuant to the Land Registration Act 1925, s 55 thereby depriving them of an opportunity to object to the registration of the second defendant's charge, and registered the charge forthwith. Therefore, the second defendant's charge had effect subject only to the charge in favour of the bank. The plaintiffs then issued a summons for a declaration that they were entitled to an indemnity from the first defendant, the Chief Land Registrar, under the 1925 Act, s 83 and for determination of the issue whether their charge had priority over that of the second defendant. *Held*, although the procedural requirements for obtaining a charging order under the Charging Orders Act 1979, s 2(1)(b)(iii) had not been strictly complied with, any failure to comply had not been serious. Accordingly, the charging order created a charge under the 1979 Act, s 2(1)(b)(iii) over the legal estate in the land held under the statutory trust for sale rather than over the proceeds of sale. Although the second defendant's charge was subject to the plaintiffs' caution, a caution was merely a procedure whereby a cautioner was given the opportunity to object to the registration of subsequent charges and did not itself create an interest in land. Therefore, the second defendant's charge had priority over the plaintiffs' charging order, and since the first defendant's error in failing to give the plaintiffs the requisite notice under the 1925 Act, s 55 had caused the plaintiffs' loss which would not be remedied by rectification of the register the plaintiffs were entitled to an indemnity from the first defendant and the declaration sought. Accordingly, the application would be granted.

Clark v Chief Land Registrar [1993] 2 WLR 141 (Chancery Division: Ferris J).

1577 Charities—rules

The Land Registration (Charities) Rules 1993, SI 1993/1704 (in force on 1 August 1993), amend the Land Registration Rules 1925, SR & O 1925/1093, by substituting rr 60 (applications for first registration of land held by or in trust for a charity), 61 (statements to be contained in instruments effecting a disposition in favour of a charity), 62 (statements to be contained in instruments effecting a disposition by a charity), 122 (dispositions in favour of a charity), 123 (applications for the registration of dispositions or dealings with titles to be held by or in trust for a charity), 124 (duties of charity trustees to make applications where a registered title is held by or in trust for a charity) and 128 (dispositions and other dealings by a charity). Certain forms and definitions are also amended. All amendments are consequent on the Charities Act 1993.

1578 Fees

The Land Registration Fees Order 1993, SI 1993/3229 (in force on 1 March 1994), replaces the 1992 Order, SI 1992/2089. The principal changes are as follows: (1) the fixed fees of £8, £16 and £80 are reduced to £5, £10 and £50 respectively; (2) official searches of the register or of pending first registration applications which were exempt from any fee now attract a fee of £5; (3) the fee for taking an affidavit or declaration is increased from £3·50 to £5 and the fee for taking exhibits to an affidavit or declaration is increased from £1 to £2 per exhibit; and (4) the exemption for personal inspection of the register, the title plan and any document referred to in the register made by the registered proprietor is removed.

The Land Registration (Determination of Costs) Order 1993, SI 1993/939 (in force on 1 April 1993), specifies a requirement to secure a return on the resources employed in the working of the Land Registration Act 1925 as a matter to be taken into account in the determination of the costs which fall to be taken into account on the exercise of the power to fix fees under the 1925 Act, s 145.

1579 Land Registry—funding

See para 2161.

1580 Leasehold Reform, Housing and Urban Development Act 1993—prescribed forms

The Land Registration (Leasehold Reform) Rules 1993, SI 1993/3045 (in force on 1 January 1994), prescribe the forms of the statements required by the Leasehold Reform, Housing and Urban Development Act 1993, ss 34(10), 57(11). For a summary of the 1993 Act, see para 1612.

1581 Legal charges—prior caution—priority

A partnership was registered as proprietor of certain freehold land on which it was proposed to build a block of flats. The defendant, who had agreed to lease one of the flats, put a caution on the register. The partners then took a loan facility from the plaintiff on terms that the plaintiff would take a legal charge over the freehold. The defendant moved into the flat without a lease and obtained an order for specific performance of the lease contract against the partners who were now in financial difficulties. The plaintiff then attempted to enforce the charge. On the interpretation of the Land Registration Act 1925 and the Land Registration Rules 1925 (SR & O 1925 No 1093), the question arose as to whether the defendant's caution affected the plaintiff's dealings with the land as registered chargee. In the case of *Clark v Chief Land Registrar* [1993] 2 WLR 141 (see para 1576), it was held that a registered charge took priority over the caution although in that case the cautioner was not notified before registration of the charge, as in the present case. The defendant submitted that this decision was inconsistent with the earlier decision in *Parkash v Irani Finance Ltd* [1970] Ch 101, even though that case was fully considered by the judge in *Clark*. It was argued that the judge in the present case should follow the principle laid down in *Colchester Estates (Cardiff) v Carlton Industries plc* [1986] 1 Ch 80 (1984 Abr para 1440), where it was held that a judge should follow the later decision unless he was convinced that the judge in that case was wrong in not following the earlier decision. It was also argued that the defendant should be successful because he had given his consent to the registration of the charge by the plaintiff. *Held*, the reasoning in *Clark* would be applied to the present case and the plaintiff could deal with the land free of the rights of the defendant. However, following the decision in *Colchester*, no reasons for this conclusion would be given. If the plaintiff's charge took priority over the lease, following the principle in *Clark*, then the question had been dealt with and if not, then that was also the end of the matter. Accordingly, the plaintiff's charge would take priority over the caution.

    Chancery plc v Ketteringham (1993) Times, 25 November (Chancery Division: David Neuberger QC).

1582 Legal charges—unregistered charges—priority

The registered proprietors of a residential property executed a legal charge in favour of the plaintiffs (the plaintiffs' charge) to secure an advance. They then executed a further legal charge in favour of the defendants (the defendants' charge) to secure a smaller advance. A notice under the Land Registration Act 1925, s 49 was entered in the charges register of the title in respect of the defendants' charge. No application was made to register the plaintiffs' charge as a registered charge or to register any notice or any other protection of it. The plaintiffs subsequently obtained an order for possession against the registered proprietors and sold the property. Since the proceeds of sale were not sufficient to repay both the plaintiffs and the defendants in full, it was agreed that the defendants would withdraw their s 49 notice in order to enable the sale to be completed and that the question of priority between the plaintiffs' and the defendants' charges would be determined by an application to the court after completion. The judge held that the plaintiffs' charge had priority over the defendants' charge even though the defendants' charge was protected by notice in the charges register of the title to the land under s 49 and the plaintiffs' was not. The defendants appealed. *Held*, under the 1925 Act, s 106, a charge protected by notice under s 49 but not registered only took effect in equity until it became a registered charge, so that priority in time of creation gave the better equity. Further, under the 1925 Act, s 52(1), a disposition by the registered proprietor took effect subject to all interests protected by notice at the date of registration or entry of notice on the register of the disposition only if the interest protected by the notice was valid apart from the notice and if the interest protected by the notice would not, independently of the 1925 Act, be overridden by the rival disposition. Although the defendants' charge was undoubtedly valid it was overridden by the plaintiffs' charge by virtue of s 106 and, if considered independently of the Act, could only take effect as a legal charge on the equity of redemption in the property subject to the plaintiffs' charge. It followed that the plaintiffs' charge had priority over the defendants' charge. The appeal would therefore be dismissed.

Mortgage Corpn Ltd v Nationwide Credit Corpn Ltd [1993] 4 All ER 623 (Court of Appeal: Dillon and Kennedy LJJ and Sir Roger Parker). Decision of David Neuberger QC (1992) Times, 27 July (1992 Abr para 1534) affirmed.

1583   Register—search—refusal to permit search—appeal

The Land Registration Act 1925, s 112(2)(b) provides that documents in the custody of the Chief Land Registrar may be inspected at his discretion in cases where there is no right of inspection.

The appellant's application, under s 112(2)(b), to inspect certain documents in the registrar's custody and to search the proprietorship register was refused on the ground that his only interest therein was as a friend of a vexatious litigant. It fell to be determined whether there was a right of appeal against the registrar's exercise of his discretion under s 112(2)(b). *Held*, under the Land Registration Rules 1925, SR & O 1925/1093, r 299, any person aggrieved by a decision of the registrar might appeal to the court against the decision. The right of appeal under r 299 was restricted to appeals against orders or decisions made by the registrar at hearings under r 298; it did not confer a right of appeal against every decision of the registrar. The exercise of his administrative power by the registrar might, nevertheless, be subject to judicial review.

Quigly v Chief Land Registrar [1993] 4 All ER 82 (Court of Appeal: Balcombe, Leggatt and Hoffmann LJJ). Decision of Millett J [1992] 3 All ER 940 (1992 Abr para 1535) affirmed.

1584   Register—search—rules

The Land Registration (Official Searches) Rules 1993, SI 1993/3276 (in force on 28 March 1994), replace the 1990 Rules, SI 1990/1361. The principal changes are as follows: (1) searches with priority delivered by a purchaser, other than in documentary form or by facsimile transmission, are deemed to be delivered at the time notice of them is entered on the day list maintained by the Land Registry; and (2) the date to be specified in an application for a search in respect of a registered title as the date from which the search is to be made must be a "search from date" as defined in the 1993 Rules. The rules also provide for revised forms of application for searches and results of searches.

1585   Rules

The Land Registration Rules 1993, SI 1993/3275 (in force on 1 March 1994), amend the Land Registration Rules 1925, SR & O 1925/1093, and the Land Registration (Open Register) Rules 1991, SI 1992/122. The principal changes to the 1925 Rules are (1) the removal of the requirement that the result of a search of the index of proprietors' names must include a short description of the property comprised in each title number revealed and, in the case of a proprietor of a charge, the date of the charge; (2) the substitution of r 17 (new editions of the register); (3) the revocation of rr 92 (return of building society charges after registration) and

93 (endorsement of certificate of registration on building society charges); and (4) the amendment of r 262 to provide that either the original or an office copy of a charge must be contained in the charge certificate. The principal amendments to the 1991 Rules (1) prescribe conditions for access to the registrar's computer system, by means of a remote control terminal, for the purpose of inspection and the making of copies and extracts from entries on the register of a registered title held on that system; (2) enable a person authorised by the Inland Revenue Commissioners, and having the consent of a Special or General Commissioner, to apply in the prescribed form (in connection with the assessment, or the amount, of tax liability) to inspect and copy, and to obtain office copies of, leases and charges and documents in the custody of the registrar relating to any land or charge which is not referred to in the register and to apply for a search of the index of proprietors' names; and (3) provide for the making of applications in documentary form to the district land registry responsible for the land to which the application relates, and for the making of applications not in documentary form to the registrar.

LANDLORD AND TENANT

Halsbury's Laws of England (4th edn) Vol 27(1) (reissue), paras 1–986, Vol 27(2) (reissue), paras 987–1739

1586 Articles

Accelerated Possession, Philip Walter: LS Gaz, 17 November 1993, p 19

Admissibility, Confidentiality and Compulsion, Peter Jones (on procedure in rent review tribunals): Estates Gazette, 18 September 1993, p 132

A Fine Point—Premiums as Covenanted Rights, Letitia Crabb: [1993] Conv 215

A Question of Quality, Nic Madge (on lessees' liability to pay service charges): LS Gaz, 3 November 1993, p 28

Assumptions of Fitness for Immediate Occupation and Use, Martin Howe: Estates Gazette, 2 October 1993, p 118

Business Tenancies and the Law Commission—Proposals for Reform, Michael Haley: [1993] Conv 334

Can a Contract of Letting be Repudiated? Alan Reed: 137 SJ 410

Certainty of Leasehold Term, David Wilde (on *Prudential Assurance Co Ltd v London Residuary Board* [1992] 3 All ER 504, HL (1992 Abr para 1557)): 57 MLR 117

Collective Enfranchisement, Trevor Aldridge: 137 SJ 1180

Commercial Leases—Further Changes? Elizabeth McKibbin: Estates Gazette, 6 November 1993, p 109

Contested Rent Reviews, James Brown: Estates Gazette, 22 May 1993, p 118

Dilapidations—A Strategic Approach, Vivien King and Nigel Laing: Estates Gazette, 17 July 1993, p 112

Finding a Tenancy, Colin T McInerney (on the ending of periodic tenancies): 137 SJ 384

Forfeiture and Waiver, Martin Codd and Jonathan Cantor: Estates Gazette, 6 March 1993, p 104

Future of the Institutional Lease, Peter Baguley: Estates Gazette, 4 December 1993, p 125

Getting at the Truth, Kirk Reynolds (on the admissibility of evidence at rent review arbitrations): Estates Gazette, 11 September 1993, p 118

Getting Your Hands on the Money, Neil Murray (on income from rental agreements): Estates Gazette, 25 September 1993, p 145

Get Those s 25 Notices Right, John Hewitt: 137 SJ 154

Harassment and Eviction, Nic Madge: 143 NLJ 844, 880

Housing and Urban Development Bill, John Stephenson: Estates Gazette, 27 March 1993, p 120

Housing and Urban Development Bill, Victoria Mitchell: Estates Gazette, 10 July 1993, p 122

Invalid Contracts and Leases—What are the Remedies? J Midgley-Hunt and M Dawson: 137 SJ 704

Keep Paying the Rent, Michael Griffiths (on liability after the expiry of a lease): 137 SJ 890

Landlords' Continuing Liability, John Spencer-Silver: Estates Gazette, 14 August 1993, p 69

Law Commission Proposals for Reform, Sandi Murdoch: Estates Gazette, 23 January 1993, p 106

Leasehold Reform, Kenneth Caesar: Estates Gazette, 17 April 1993, p 42

Marriage Value and Flats, Michael Daiches (on leasehold enfranchisement): Estates Gazette, 30 October 1993, p 104
Mid-Term Rent Reductions Offer Hope for Tenants, Anthony Lorenz: 137 SJ 352
New Age Travellers, TA Glesson: 137 SJ 734
New Developments in the Right to Buy, Jonathan Manning and Susan Belgrave (on the Leasehold Reform, Housing and Urban Development Act 1993): 137 SJ 1082
Onerous Leases—Landlords Beware? Martin Codd (on *Whyfe v Michael Cullen & Partners* (1993) Times, 15 November, CA (para 1608)): 138 SJ 64
On the Flat Rate, James Driscoll (on the scope of collective enfranchisement): LS Gaz, 8 December, 1993, p26
Overseas Landlords and Their Agents: Watch Out! Christopher Cox: Estates Gazette, 22 May 1993, p 102
People Power, James Driscoll (on the scope of collective enfranchisement): LS Gaz, 3 November 1993, p 23
Pitfalls Under the 1993 Act, David Marcus and Gerald Sherriff (on the Leasehold Reform, Housing and Urban Development Act 1993): Estates Gazette, 27 November 1993, p 136
Privity of Contract and Estate, Kaz Stepien: 137 SJ 462
Quiet Revolution, Kerry Stephenson (on the implementation of Leasehold Reform, Housing and Urban Development Act 1993): 137 SJ 1136
Relief Against Forfeiture of Instalments, Mark Pawlowski: Estates Gazette, 27 March 1993, p 122
Rent a Room Scheme, Gordon Pickering (on tax relief for owner occupiers): 137 SJ 1032
Rent Review: Renewed Lease Terms, Del Williams: Estates Gazette, 30 January 1993, p 108
Residential Leasehold Reform, Jennifer Ellis: Estates Gazette, 7 August 1993, p 65
Residential Leases, Tony Blackburn and Sue Boyall: 137 SJ 883, 911
Right to Buy and Security of Tenure, Jonathan Manning and Andrew Dymond: 137 SJ 796
Safe as Houses, LM Clements (on the position of tenants of defective premises): 137 SJ 382
Statutory Nuisances and Abatement Notices, Naomi Cohen: Estates Gazette, 28 August 1993, p 106
Succeeding to a Secure Tenancy, Stephen Jones (on *Waltham Forest LBC v Thomas* [1992] 3 All ER 244, HL (1992 Abr para 1580)): 143 NLJ 1689
Tenants' Continuing Liability: A Two-Tier System, Elizabeth McKibbin: Estates Gazette, 22 May 1993, p 90
Tenant's Remedies for Condensation Dampness, Mark Pawlowski: Estates Gazette, 4 September 1993, p 108
Termination of Joint Tenancies in the Light of *Pilling*, Stephen Jones (on *Hounslow LBC v Pilling* (1993) Times, 4 March, CA (para 1617)): 143 NLJ 1236
The 1954 Act: The Changes in Tactics, Alan Langleben and Clive Newnham: Estates Gazette, 20 March 1993, p 120
The Cost of Prohibiting Upward-Only Rent Reviews, Richard Harrold: Estates Gazette, 20 November 1993, p 169
The Landlord's Right to Distress—How Distressing? Martin Codd: 137 SJ 1084, 1100
The Tenant, Landlords' Costs and VAT, Stuart Davidson: Tax Journal, Issue 219, p 15
"Touching the Time of the Beginning of a Lease for Yeares" Elizabeth Cooke: [1993] Conv 206
Voluntary Arrangement by Assignment of Lease, J Holroyd-Doveton: 137 SJ 1272

1587   Agricultural tenancies

See AGRICULTURE.

1588   Assignment—consent—refusal of landlord—reasons

It has been held that the Landlord and Tenant Act 1988 has not altered the existing law that where a landlord refuses consent to the assignment of a tenancy, it is not necessary for him to establish that the grounds for his doing so are not only reasonable but true.

Air India v Balabel [1993] 30 EG 90 (Court of Appeal: Stuart-Smith and Waite LJJ).

1589   Assignment—consent—statutory duties relating to consent

The plaintiff was the landlord of a flat which he let to the defendant at a fixed rent. The lease contained a covenant on the part of the defendant not to assign without the consent of the plaintiff. The defendant put his lease up for sale by auction where it was purchased by a company. The defendant unsuccessfully sought the plaintiff's consent. The defendant's rent then fell into arrears and the plaintiff issued a writ for the arrears. The defendant counter-claimed for damages for breach by the plaintiff of his statutory duty under the Landlord and Tenant Act 1988 in relation to his refusal to consent to the assignment. Shortly before the trial of the defendant's counterclaim the plaintiff applied to use, as part of his evidence, the accounts of the company and an order that the company be wound up. The documents were discovered on a search of the companies register just before the trial but subsequent to the plaintiff refusing his consent. The defendant contended that the documents were irrelevant and ought not to be admitted. *Held*, a landlord could not rely upon matters which had not influenced him at the time he refused to consent to the assignment. It was clear that the matters which the plaintiff sought to adduce in evidence did not influence him at the time of his refusal as he was not aware of those matters until just before the trial. The time at which the reasonableness of a landlord's refusal must be judged under the 1988 Act was the time at which a landlord refuses consent. Accordingly, the application would be dismissed.

CIN Properties v Gill [1993] 37 EG 152 (Queen's Bench Division: Sir Godfray Le Quesne QC).

1590   Assignment—obligation to pay rent—liability of assignee after further assignment

The plaintiff granted a tenancy of freehold land and premises for a term of twenty years. The lease provided that rent was payable quarterly and subject to provisions for review. By a deed signed by the plaintiff, the assignee and the assignee's surety, the plaintiff granted the existing tenant a licence to assign the premises to an assignee. The assignee covenanted to pay the rents reserved by the lease at the time and in the manner provided therein. The assignee later lawfully assigned the lease. Ten years later, the plaintiff claimed from both the assignee and the surety for unpaid rent. The assignee refused to pay and the plaintiff applied for summary judgement under RSC Ord 14. The master refused leave to defend the summons. On appeal, *held*, the assignee's covenant to pay rent did not contain an express covenant to make the assignee liable for breaches committed after further assignment by him. The sums claimed had fallen due after such further assignment, and so it followed that neither the assignee nor the surety was liable to pay the rent claimed by the plaintiff. Accordingly, the appeal would be allowed and the defendants would be granted unconditional leave to appeal.

Estates Gazette Ltd v Benjamin Restaurants Ltd [1993] 4 All ER 367 (Queen's Bench Division: Judge Zucker).

1591   Assured shorthold tenancy—unlawful termination—error in date of termination of earlier tenancy

In November 1990 a landlord granted a tenancy of a flat for a term of 12 months, but the notice of an assured shorthold tenancy served on the tenant prior to the grant erroneously stated that the date of termination was May 1991. In November 1991 a new assured shorthold tenancy came into being for a term of six months. When the tenant refused to give up possession in May 1992, the landlord sought, and was granted, a possession order. The tenant appealed against the order on the ground that the 1990 grant had not been of an assured shorthold tenancy but of an assured tenancy. *Held*, there was a statutory precondition that a notice should be served in the prescribed form contained in the Assured Tenancies and Agricultural Occupancies (Forms) Regulations 1988, SI 1988/2203, and that form had to include the date on which the tenancy commenced and ended. The writing of "May" rather than "November" had been a perplexity rather than an evident error, but the mistake meant that an assured shorthold tenancy had not been granted, and it was immaterial that the tenant had not actually been misled by the mistake. The tenant was an assured tenant enjoying the protection of that status and, accordingly, the appeal would be allowed.

Panayi v Roberts (1993) 25 HLR 421 (Court of Appeal: Ralph Gibson and Mann LJJ). *Tegerdine v Brooks* (1977) 36 P & CR 261, CA (1977 Abr para 1656) considered.

1592   Assured tenancies and agricultural occupancies—forms

The Assured Tenancies and Agricultural Occupancies (Forms) (Amendment) Regulations 1993, SI 1993/654 (in force 1 April 1993), amend the 1988 Regulations, SI 1988/2203, and are consequential on the introduction of the council tax. They amend Forms Nos 1, 2 and 5 to 8 and prescribe two new forms which relate to the transitional case under the Local Government Finance (Housing) (Consequential Amendments) Order 1993, SI 1993/651, in which rent under an assured tenancy or agricultural occupancy may be increased to take into account a tenant's liability to make payments to his landlord in respect of council tax.

1593 Assured tenancies and agricultural occupancies—rent information

The Assured Tenancies and Agricultural Occupancies (Rent Information) (Amendment) Order 1993, SI 1993/657 (in force on 1 April 1993), amends the 1988 Order, SI 1988/2199, by including a reference to the council tax in the information on rents of assured tenancies and agricultural occupancies which is to be made publicly available by the president of each rent assessment panel.

1594 Assured tenancies—notice of proceedings for possession—validity

A tenant with an assured monthly tenancy failed to pay the rent. The notice served on her by the landlord for possession of the premises did not set out the full text of each ground relied on as entitling him to possession nor was it in the prescribed form. On the tenant's appeal against a county court order for possession, *held*, although the ground on which possession was sought under the Housing Act 1988, Sch 2 might be specified in the notice in words different from those set out in Sch 2, the words used had to state fully the substance of the ground so that the notice was adequate to achieve the legislative purpose of Sch 2 which was to give the tenant the specified information in order to enable her to consider what she should do and to take steps to protect herself against the loss of her home. Section 8(2) required the ground on which possession was sought to be specified, not merely identified. In omitting certain required information, the landlord's notice, was not substantially to the same effect as that required by Sch 2 and, accordingly was invalid. The appeal would be allowed.

Mountain v Hastings (1993) 25 HLR 427 (Court of Appeal: Ralph Gibson, Mann and Nolan LJJ).

1595 Assured tenancies—rent assessment committees—council tax

See para 1623.

1596 Business tenancy—application for new tenancy—determination of rent

The applicants were tenants of offices located in Gray's Inn and administered by the respondents. A new lease was agreed except for a provision dealing with rent. The applicants and the respondents submitted conflicting proposals as to rent, and relied on comparables from outside and inside Gray's Inn respectively. It was claimed by the applicants that the respondents' proposed rent should be disregarded as Gray's Inn was not an open market and, therefore, the respondents' comparables were not open market lettings. On an application under the Landlord and Tenant Act 1954, s 34 for the court to determine the rent, *held*, Gray's Inn did operate open market principles in respect of lettings. "Open market" as a term in the 1954 Act, s 34 included a situation to create a market, a willing lessor and lessee, a reasonable period in which to negotiate the letting and the negotiations at arm's length, the property freely exposed to the market and account not being taken of any higher rent that might be paid by a potential lessee with a special interest. All these criteria were satisfied in the present case. A market could still be an open market, and did not cease to be such a market, even though most of the persons occupying premises in that market belonged to a particular profession or engaged in a particular trade. The rent would be set accordingly.

Baptist v Masters of the Bench and Trustees of the Honourable Society of Gray's Inn [1993] 42 EG 287 (Clerkenwell County Court: Judge Aron Owen).

1597 Business tenancy—assignment—liability of original lessee

The parties entered into a lease of business premises which the tenants later assigned with the landlord's consent. The assignee continued to occupy the premises after the expiry of the contractual term and became a protected tenant under the Landlord and Tenant Act 1954, Pt II. The assignee went into liquidation and the liquidator surrendered the term, with arrears of rent and outgoings still owing. The landlords unsuccessfully tried to recover the arrears from the tenants, contending that the tenants' obligation to pay rent continued after the end of the contractual term. On appeal, *held*, the tenants were under no contractual liability to pay rent after the expiry of the contractual term. Nor was there any statutory liability since the 1954 Act did not expressly impose liability on anybody except the landlords and the occupying tenants. It was intended to protect occupying tenants from landlords, not to impose liability on former tenants who had ceased to have an interest in the property. At common law, the benefit and burden of covenants that touched and concerned the land ran with the term granted by the lease on an assignment. That principle was necessary for the effective functioning of the law of landlord and tenant. Common law and statute created rights and obligations in a lease which were independent of, and parallel to, those of the original human covenantor by annexing them to the term and the reversion in so far as they touched and concerned the land. Although covenants were introduced when a lease was created, they were not necessary to sustain it. The landlord's submission was based on a confusion of contract and status. On an assignment, the original tenant's covenants continued to attach to the term because they touched and concerned the land, not because there continued to exist an original tenant who had ceased to own any interest in the demised land but remained liable in contract on his covenants. Accordingly, the appeal would be dismissed.

London City Corpn v Fell [1993] 4 All ER 968 (House of Lords: Lords Templeman, Goff of Chievely, Jauncey of Tullichettle, Browne-Wilkinson and Mustill). Decision of Court of Appeal [1993] 2 All ER 449 affirmed.

1598 Business tenancy—security of tenure—excluded tenancies—licensed premises

Tenancies of premises licensed for the sale of intoxicating liquor, other than premises adapted to be used, and bona fide used, for a business which comprises the carrying on of a restaurant, a substantial proportion of which business consists of transactions other than the sale of intoxicating liquor, are excluded from the Landlord and Tenant Act 1954, Pt II (ss 23–46) which gives security of tenure to business premises.

During his five-year lease of a public house, the tenant had carried out substantial extensions to the building which now included a dining room. Customers ordered food from a menu chalked up on a blackboard at the bar servery or from an à la carte menu. All such orders and drink were ordered from, and paid for at, the bar servery. Customers who had ordered food from the bar menu or groups of customers who had ordered only drinks might sit at empty tables in the dining room; customers who had ordered food from the à la carte menu might consume food either in the dining room or at tables in the bar. The tenant sought a new tenancy. In a preliminary issue, it fell to be determined whether he was entitled to the protection of the 1954 Act, Pt II. *Held*, the premises could not be said to be a restaurant only nor was the dining room a restaurant separate from the rest of the premises and only to be used by those eating meals and not by those merely consuming drinks. However, looking at the premises as a whole and taking account of the nature of the food provided and the extent to which the takings were provided by food as opposed to drink, the tenant provided the facilities of a restaurant and the activities comprised overall the carrying on of a restaurant. Accordingly, the tenant was entitled to the protection of the 1954 Act, Pt II.

Taylor v Courage Ltd [1993] 44 EG 116 (Court of Appeal: Dillon, Stuart-Smith and Evans LJJ).

1599 Covenant—covenant against use for business purposes—breach of covenant

The Landlord and Tenant Act 1954, s 23(4) provides that where a tenant carries on a business in a property in a tenancy in breach of a prohibition against use for business purposes in the terms of the tenancy, Pt II of that Act does not apply to the tenancy unless the landlord consents to the breach or acquiesces therein.

The respondent landlord demised a property to school trustees, who covenanted to use the property for the purposes of a private residence in single occupation only. Subsequently the school governors employed a resident caretaker and required him to live at the property on a service occupancy. In response to the landlord's service of a statutory notice of termination of the tenancy, the trustees served a statutory counter-notice stating that they would not be willing to surrender possession and applied for the grant of a new tenancy under the 1954 Act, Pt II. The landlord filed an answer contending that the 1954 Act, Pt II did not apply to this tenancy. The judge found that: (1) in law, occupation by a servant was deemed to be occupation by his master and therefore, the trustees occupied the property by virtue of the caretaker's residence, (2) since the caretaker's occupation was partly for the purposes of his employment, the trustees were deemed to occupy it partly for the purposes of business carried on by them, therefore, (3) the trustees were in breach of their user covenant, and (4) the landlord had neither consented to nor acquiesced in the breach. On appeal, *held*, (1) the caretaker used the property in part to fulfil his duties of employment and thus the judge had correctly found the trustees in breach of their covenant, and (2) since the landlord had no knowledge of the facts that gave rise to the breach, he could not be said to have acquiesced in its continuance. Accordingly, the appeal would be dismissed.

The Trustees of the Methodist Secondary Schools Trust Deed v O'Leary (1993) 25 HLR 364 (Court of Appeal: Glidewell and Rose LJJ and Sir Christopher Slade).

1600   Covenant—covenant to pay legal costs incurred by landlord—action brought by tenants—recovery of costs through service charge

The plaintiffs were tenants of a building who were subject to a covenant in their lease which stated that they would pay all legal and other costs that may be incurred by the defendant landlord in obtaining the payment of maintenance contributions from any tenant in the building. The tenants brought proceedings against the landlord for an order establishing the future management of the building and verifying past accounts. The proceedings were settled and under a consent order the landlord agreed to pay the tenants' costs. The landlord subsequently sought to recover both the tenants' costs and his own costs through the service charge by invoking the covenant. On an application by the tenants, *held*, the landlord could not claim the costs of the action through the service charge. The covenant only applied to actions for outstanding maintenance contributions. It did not apply where, as in this case, the tenants had obtained relief of a general and long term nature and the landlord himself sought no relief. Giving the covenant a restrictive rather than a wider effect did not result in any unfairness to the landlord as, in any dispute, the court would have the power to award costs in the normal way. The consent order for costs was a contract between the landlord and tenants, a proper construction of which was that the landlord could not claim costs through the service charge provision. Where the landlord had agreed to pay the whole of the tenants' costs, the onus was firmly on the landlord to establish that those costs, or some of them, had been reasonably and properly incurred and that they were fair and reasonable as service charges. There was insufficient evidence that these criteria had been fulfilled in this case and judgment would accordingly be given to the tenants.

Morgan v Stainer (1992) 25 HLR 467 (Chancery Division: David Neuberger QC).

1601   Covenant—covenant to repair—construction

The parties entered into a lease and the defendant landlord covenanted to maintain, repair, and otherwise keep the property in good and tenantable condition. Aluminium cladding on the outside of the building was not watertight and allowed water to leak into the interior. The tenant claimed the landlord was in breach of the covenant and was required to undertake the necessary works even though the property had not been watertight when the tenant took possession. *Held*, correctly construed, the covenant required the landlord to put the property into a condition reasonably fit for occupation by a reasonably minded tenant of the class likely to occupy it, and then to keep it in good and tenantable condition. The cladding had never been of, nor kept in, the required standard and were the landlord to undertake the necessary works the tenant would merely be getting that which was due to a reasonably minded tenant. Accordingly, judgment would be given for the tenant.

Credit Suisse v Beegas Nominees Ltd (1993) Independent, 15 September (Chancery Division: Lindsay J).

1602   Covenant—covenant to repair—replacement of roof—repair or improvement

The plaintiffs were the landlords of a commercial building and under its lease the tenant covenanted to pay a contribution towards the cost and expense of repairing and rebuilding "all things the use of which is common to the premises". The landlord became aware of cracks and a bulge in a gable wall and as a result of subsequent works, a different roof was built with a different pitch, proper restraints and more substantial timbering. As the roof structure was radically altered, the tenants resisted a claim for contribution claiming it did not fall within the general meaning of "repairs". The work was paid for by the landlord. In an application by the landlord to recover the cost of the works to the roof from the tenants. *Held*, the roof in the present case was an integral part of the building and the option to strengthen the roof was plainly within the repairing covenant. Whatever test was used by the court it was all ultimately a matter of degree. The fact that an inadequate roof had been replaced by an adequate roof did not cease to make it a matter of repair. If however that meant that the landlord got back a building radically altered then that might make it a borderline case. However in the present case and taking into account the original defects in design and the imminent danger of collapse, and by comparing the costs of either repairing or replacing the roof, it was not a matter which came under the category of "improvement". The court found the works carried out constituted a "repair" and accordingly the application would be granted.

New England Properties plc v Portsmouth News Shops Ltd [1993] 1 EGLR 84 (Chancery Division: Terence Cullen QC).

1603 Covenant—covenant to repair—replacement of roof—running repairs

The plaintiff was a tenant of a Grade 1 listed building. The defendant landlord brought possession proceedings against the plaintiff. The plaintiff counterclaimed contending that the defendant was in breach of his obligation to repair imposed on him by the Landlord and Tenant Act 1985, s 11, in that the roof of the building was in a state of disrepair. The defendant accepted that a new roof was required and stated that he had been attempting to obtain the necessary funding for a new one. Since he had become aware of the state of the roof he had been carrying out running repairs. An order was made dismissing the counterclaim and granting possession. On appeal by the plaintiff, *held*, notwithstanding the fact that it would have been desirable for the roof to be completely replaced, regard had to be given to the age and character of the dwelling. In the circumstances the defendant's obligation under the 1985 Act, s 11 was satisfied by the carrying out of running repairs as and when he was notified of a problem to the roof. Accordingly, the appeal would be dismissed.

Trustees of the Dame Margaret Hungerford Charity v Beazeley [1993] 29 EG 100 (Court of Appeal: Nourse and Roch LJJ).

1604 Covenant—covenant to use property for private residence—exclusion of tenant's family

The parties entered into a lease and the tenant agreed to use the premises as a private residence for the purpose of accommodating the tenant's staff or directors. The landlords had wished to let to a company but agreed to grant the tenancy to the defendant personally on his false representation that he carried on a business through several companies and it would be inconvenient to grant the tenancy to only one of them. The tenant did not have a company and used the property as a pied-a-terre when on business in London. He allowed his partner and her daughters to live at the property. The landlords successfully brought possession proceedings. The judge found that although the tenant's occupation was sufficient for statutory residence he had breached the user clause by allowing his partner and her daughters to live in the property. On the tenant's appeal, *held*, correctly construed, the user clause provided that the tenant or his staff had the right of occupation. A tenant of a residential property should naturally be allowed to have his family living with him, and clear words were necessary to exclude the family and there was no such provision in the lease, and therefore there was no breach by the tenant. Accordingly, the appeal would be allowed.

Blanway Investments Ltd v Lynch (1993) 25 HLR 378 (Court of Appeal: Dillon and Rose LJJ and Peter Gibson J).

1605 Distress for rent

See DISTRESS.

1606 Forfeiture—relief against forfeiture—application by mortgagee

The County Courts Act 1984, s 138(7) provides that if a lessee does not within the period specified in an order for possession pay into court all the rent in arrear, and the costs of the action, the order is enforceable in the prescribed manner and the lessee is barred from all relief.

A tenant acquired a long lease of a flat for a substantial premium, part of which was advanced by the mortgagee. The tenant defaulted on the payment of rent and the landlord obtained and executed an order for possession. The mortgagee sought relief from forfeiture in the High Court, having failed to apply to the county court within the six-month time limit contained in the 1984 Act, s 138(9A). On the landlord's appeal against a decision that the High Court had jurisdiction to grant the relief sought by the mortgagee, *held*, it was accepted by the mortgagee that if the case fell within s 138(7) its right to relief was barred both in the county court and in the High Court. It was further agreed that if the mortgagee was a lessee which could have paid rent arrears into court within the period specified in the possession order under s 138(5), it was also the lessee for the purposes of s 138(7). The mortgagee was, applying the decision in *Doe dem Wyatt v Byron* (1845) 1 CB 623, a lessee within the meaning of the 1984 Act, s 138(2) capable of paying off the arrears not less than five days before the return day. This interpretation applied equally to s 138(5) and meant that the mortgagee was a lessee within the meaning of that subsection, and therefore also within the meaning of s 138(7). As the mortgagee had not made an application for relief under s 138(9C) within the six-month time limit in s 138(9A), it was barred from all relief. Accordingly, the landlord's appeal would be allowed.

United Dominions Trust Ltd v Shellpoint Trustees Ltd [1993] 4 All ER 310 (Court of Appeal: Nourse and Butler-Sloss LJJ and Sir Christopher Slade). Decision of David Neuberger QC (1992) 64 P & CR 457 (1992 Abr para 1549) reversed.

1607   Forfeiture—relief against forfeiture—entitlement of landlord to forfeit without notice

Under the Law of Property Act 1925, s 146(9)(e), the statutory provisions as to the service of notices and the grant of relief against forfeiture do not apply to a condition for forfeiture on bankruptcy of the tenant, or on taking in execution of the tenant's interest, if contained in a lease of any property with respect to which the tenant's personal qualifications are of importance for the preservation of the value or character of the property or on the ground of neighbourhood to the landlord or any person holding under him.

The plaintiff held the lease of two units and the reversion was held by the first defendant. Shortly before going into liquidation the plaintiff entered into negotiations with the second defendant to sublet one of the units. Permission had been given to the second defendant by the plaintiff to store stock in the unit. That permission was given without the consent of the first defendant and was a breach of covenant. The liquidator was granted access to the premises only on request and with the assistance of the first defendant. The first defendant then re-entered the premises although no notice had been served on the plaintiff under the Law of Property Act 1925, s 146. The plaintiff claimed damages against the first defendant for trespass and for breach of the covenant for quiet enjoyment. The first defendant contended that re-entry was lawful under the 1925 Act, s 146(9)(e). *Held*, s 146(9)(e) was concerned with land that was both the subject of the lease to the lessee and also land of a particular type which had some particular quality. The court was obliged to determine whether the lessee, was a neighbour of the lessor or someone claiming through him. If he was, then the court was obliged to determine if there was something about the property, which made it of particular importance to the lessee. In this particular case there was nothing special about the land, the subject of the plaintiff's lease, which could bring it within s 146(9)(e). The first defendant acted unlawfully in re-entering the premises and accordingly the application would be allowed.

Hockley Engineering Co Ltd v V & P Midlands Ltd [1993] 18 EG 129 (Chancery Division: Judge Micklem).

1608   Lease—fraudulent misrepresentation—deliberately onerous terms

The plaintiff claimed that he had accepted a draft lease as a result of the fraudulent representation of the defendants. The lease contained clauses that were so unfair to the tenant that they rendered the whole lease uneconomic thereby forcing the plaintiff to surrender it. The plaintiff alleged a conspiracy but their action was struck out by the court at first instance. On appeal by the plaintiff against the striking out, *held*, assuming that the allegations were true, the defendants had submitted a draft lease which contained clauses so obscurely drafted as to escape detection and so onerous as to oblige the tenant to surrender and lose the substantial premium paid for the lease. In those circumstances, the plaintiff was able to establish a triable issue of misrepresentation. Accordingly, the appeal would be allowed and the action would be reinstated.

Whyfe v Michael Cullen & Partners (1993) Times, 15 November (Court of Appeal: Butler-Sloss, Stuart-Smith and Leggatt LJJ).

1609   Lease—negotiations for new lease—negotiations "subject to lease"—tenant's failure to apply to court—entitlement to new lease

A tenant held a lease on premises by assignment which had expired although the tenant remained in possession. The landlord served notice terminating the tenancy. By a letter marked "subject to lease" the tenant stated that he was prepared to enter into a new lease. The landlord accepted by a letter marked "subject to lease". The landlord subsequently enclosed the counterpart lease for signature but refused to complete because the tenant's cheque was not honoured. The landlord obtained a possession order for the premises. On appeal by the tenant, *held*, there was nothing in the case to justify a departure from the well-established rule that either party might withdraw from the negotiations before exchange of the lease and counterpart. Such negotiations did not give rise to a collateral contract or an estoppel preventing either party from withdrawing. There had been no physical exchange of lease and counterpart both of which were essential to the formation of a contract. There was no promise by the landlord to grant a lease in consideration of the tenant's forbearance in applying for a new tenancy. The tenant could not be said to rely on any representation by the landlord when all such representations were marked "subject to lease". Although the tenant had a right to apply to the court for the grant of a new tenancy but did not, that was not of itself sufficient to give rise to an estoppel. The appeal would be dismissed.

Akiens v Salomon (1993) 65 P & CR 364 (Court of Appeal: Dillon, Steyn and Evans LJJ).

1610   Lease or licence—purchase at undervalue—licence to vendors—rent-free licence for life

The defendants purchased a flat for one-third of its value and purported to grant a licence to the vendors to occupy the property for their joint lives and the life of the survivor. The agreement indemnified the vendors for outgoings under the lease of the flat, but expressly provided that exclusive possession should remain with the defendants. The defendants, acting dishonestly, subsequently obtained a mortgage from the plaintiff. Following the defendants' failure to keep up the repayments on the mortgage, the plaintiff began possession proceedings. On the plaintiff's appeal against a refusal to grant possession, *held*, the court at first instance had found that the defendants had acted dishonestly, that the purpose of the agreement was to avoid the law relating to the creation of a tenancy, and that in reality the vendors had exclusive possession. There was no basis on which to interfere with those findings. As the agreement granted a term of years to the vendors for their joint lives and the lives of the survivor and the premium for that grant was a discount of two-thirds of the value of the flat, the vendors had a tenancy under the Law of Property Act 1925, s 149(6). The tenancy was binding on the plaintiff and its appeal would be dismissed.

Skipton Building Society v Clayton (1993) 66 P & CR 223 (Court of Appeal: Nourse and Butler-Sloss LJJ and Sir Christopher Slade). *Street v Mountford* [1985] AC 809, HL (1985 Abr para 1454) applied.

1611   Leasehold enfranchisement—long tenancy—tenancy for a term certain

The applicants, tenants of premises who had purchased the leasehold by way of a deed of assignment, sought to purchase the freehold of the premises. They knew neither the terms of the original lease, which dated from 1563 but had been lost, nor the identity of the reversioner. A question arose as to whether their interest in the premises could be construed as a tenancy for a term certain and therefore a long tenancy for the purposes of the Leasehold Reform Act 1967. *Held*, there was evidence that every assignment since 1802 had recited that the premises were leased for the term or several terms of 500 years. No tenant of the premises within living memory had been required to pay rent because the identity of the freeholder was unknown. In those circumstances, and notwithstanding their ignorance of the identity of the reversioner and the exact terms of the lease, the applicants were entitled to purchase the freehold.

Re 51 Bennington Road, Aston (1993) Times, 21 July (Chancery Division: Vinelott J).

1612   Leasehold Reform, Housing and Urban Development Act 1993

The Leasehold Reform, Housing and Urban Development Act 1993 confers rights of collective enfranchisement and lease renewal on tenants of flats and makes further provision with respect to enfranchisement by tenants of houses. The Act received the royal assent on 20 July 1993 and certain provisions came into force on that day; most of the remaining provisions come into force on various dates in 1993 and 1994: see SI 1993/2134, 2762. For further details of commencement, see the commencement table in the title STATUTES.

Part I (ss 1–103) Landlord and Tenant
Sections 1–38 deal with collective enfranchisement in the case of tenants of flats. Section 1 confers the right to collective enfranchisement on qualifying tenants. Section 2 deals with the acquisition of leasehold interests where the right to collective enfranchisement is exercised. The premises to which the right to collective enfranchisement applies and the premises excluded from the right are defined in ss 3 and 4. Section 5 defines a qualifying tenant as a person who is the tenant of a flat under a long lease at a low rent, while s 6 specifies the residence condition for qualifying tenants. Sections 7 and 8 define the meaning of a long lease and a lease at a low rent, while s 9 and Schs 1 and 2 define the reversioner and other relevant landlords and s 10 defines premises with a resident landlord. Sections 11 and 12 confer on a qualifying tenant the right to obtain information about superior interests and other specified matters. Section 13 requires that initial notice of claim must be given by not less than two-thirds of the total number of qualifying tenants in the premises concerned and not less than half of the total number of flats. Not less than half of the qualifying tenants by whom notice is given must satisfy the residence condition. Schedule 3 contains supplementary provision regarding initial notices.

Section 14 defines the participating tenants in relation to any claim for collective enfranchisement and s 15 provides for the appointment of a nominee purchaser to conduct all proceedings arising out of the initial notice on behalf of the participating tenants, with a view to the eventual acquisition by him, on their behalf, of any freehold or other interests. Section 16 deals with the retirement or death of a nominee purchaser. Section 17 provides for access by relevant landlords for the purposes of valuation and s 18 imposes a duty on the nominee purchaser to disclose the existence of certain agreements affecting the premises. Under s 19, restrictions are placed on the freeholder's powers of disposition following the registration of an initial notice, and under s 20 a reversioner may require the nominee purchaser to deduce the title of any person claiming to be a qualifying tenant. Section 21 and Sch 4 provide for the service of a counter-notice by a reversioner stating whether or not he admits that the participating tenants are entitled to exercise the right to collective enfranchisement. Section 22 deals with applications to the court by the nominee purchaser, on which the court may declare that the participating tenants are entitled to exercise the right of collective enfranchisement and require the reversioner to give a further counter-notice. Under s 23, a tenants' claim may be defeated if the landlord establishes that he intends to redevelop the whole or a substantial part of the premises. Sections 24 and 25 and Sch 5 deal with applications to the court and the leasehold valuation tribunal where a reversioner has admitted the tenants' right to collective enfranchisement but where terms are in dispute or there has been a failure to enter into a binding contract, and where a reversioner fails to give a counter-notice. Sections 26 and 27 deal with applications where the relevant landlord cannot be ascertained, and s 28 gives tenants the opportunity to withdraw from an acquisition prior to the making of a binding contract. Section 29 provides for the deemed withdrawal of an initial notice in specified circumstances. Sections 30 and 31 concern the effect of compulsory acquisition and designation for inheritance tax purposes on initial notices and subsequent contracts.

Section 32 and Sch 6 deal with the determination of the price of interests acquired by a nominee purchaser, and s 33 makes the nominee purchaser liable for the reversioner's costs of enfranchisement. Section 34 and Sch 7 set out the requirements for the conveyance to a nominee purchaser and s 35 and Sch 8 deal with the discharge of existing mortgages on a transfer. Under s 36 and Sch 9, the nominee purchaser is required to grant leases back to a former freeholder in certain circumstances, while s 37 and Sch 10 make special provision for the acquisition of interests from a local authority. Section 38 deals with interpretation.

Sections 39–62 deal with the individual rights of tenants of flats to acquire new leases. Section 39 confers on a qualifying tenant of a flat who has occupied the flat as his only or principal home for the previous three years or for periods amounting to three years in the previous ten the right to acquire a new lease of the flat on payment of a premium. Section 40 and Sch 2 define a landlord for these purposes, Sch 11 deals with the procedure where the competent landlord is not the tenant's immediate landlord, and s 41 gives a tenant the right to obtain information regarding superior interests in the flat concerned. Sections 42 and 43 and Sch 12 deal with the tenant's notice of claim to exercise his right to acquire a new lease, and s 44 gives landlords the right of access to the property for the purposes of valuation. Landlords are required to give a counter-notice in accordance with s 45 and proceedings relating to the validity of a tenant's notice are dealt with in s 46. Under s 47, a tenants' claim may be defeated if the landlord establishes that he intends to redevelop any premises in which the tenant's flat is contained. Sections 48 and 49 deal with applications to the court and the leasehold valuation tribunal where a landlord has admitted the tenants' right to a new lease but where terms are in dispute or there has been a failure to enter into a new lease, and where a landlord fails to give a counter-notice. Sections 50 and 51 make provision for applications where the landlord cannot be ascertained and s 52 gives tenants the opportunity to withdraw from an acquisition prior to entering into a new lease. Section 53 provides for the deemed withdrawal of a notice in specified circumstances. Under s 54, a tenant's notice must be suspended where there is a current claim for collective enfranchisement with respect to any premises containing the tenant's flat. Section 55 provides for the effect of compulsory acquisition procedures on the tenant's notice.

Under s 56, a landlord is obliged (except in certain circumstances) to grant the tenant a new lease, which the tenant is obliged to accept. Schedule 13 provides for the calculation of the premium payable by the tenant on the grant of a new lease. Section 57 sets out the terms upon which a new lease is to be granted and s 58 deals with the grant of a new lease where the interest of the landlord or tenant is subject to a mortgage. Section 59 provides for a further renewal of a new lease granted under these provisions but excludes the application of the statutory provisions relating to security of tenure to a new lease. Under s 60, the tenant is liable for costs incurred in connection with a new lease and under s 61 and Sch 14 a landlord may terminate a new lease if he establishes an intention to redevelop the premises. Section 62 deals with interpretation.

Sections 63–68 deal with the extension of the right to enfranchisement under the Leasehold Reform Act 1967. Under s 63, the right of enfranchisement is extended to houses whose value or rent exceeds the limits specified in the 1967 Act. Section 64 deals with tenancies terminable by notice after a death or marriage, while s 65 imposes alternative rent limits for the purposes of the extensions introduced in s 63 above. Section 66 and Sch 15 amend the determination of the price payable on enfranchisement, s 67 excludes the right to enfranchise in the case of houses let by charitable housing trusts, and s 68 excludes that right in the case of property transferred for public benefit.

Sections 69–75 relate to estate management schemes. Section 69 defines an estate management scheme for the purposes of enfranchisement, and s 70 provides for the approval of such schemes by leasehold valuation tribunals. Section 71 deals with applications for approval by two or more landlords or by representative bodies, s 72 with late applications for approval, and s 73 with applications by certain public bodies. Section 74 sets out the effect of applications for approval on claims to acquire freeholds and s 75 deals with the variation of existing schemes.

Sections 76–84 deal with the right of tenants to a management audit. Section 76 confers on two or more qualifying tenants of dwellings held on leases from the same landlord the right to have an audit carried out on their behalf relating to the management of the premises. Section 77 defines qualifying tenants and s 78 sets out the purposes for which an audit is to be carried out. Section 79 confers certain rights on the auditor and ss 80 and 81 deal with the procedure to be followed by tenants in exercising their right to an audit. Under s 82, a landlord is required to supply the tenant with information held by a superior landlord. Section 83 contains various supplementary provisions and s 84 deals with interpretation.

Sections 85–103 contain miscellaneous and general provisions. Sections 85 and 86 make amendments to the Landlord and Tenant Act 1987 relating to the compulsory acquisition of a landlord's interest and the variation of leases. Section 87 gives the Secretary of State power to approve codes of practice for the management of residential property. Section 88 deals with the jurisdiction of leasehold valuation tribunals in relation to the enfranchisement of Crown land while s 89 renders void provisions prohibiting the occupation of leasehold property by persons with mental disorders. Section 90 confers on the county court jurisdiction in relation to the enfranchisement provisions of the Act. Section 91 provides for the exercise of the jurisdiction conferred on a leasehold valuation tribunal under the enfranchisement provisions of the Act by a rent assessment committee. Section 92 deals with the enforcement of certain obligations under ss 1–62 of the Act and s 93 provides that agreements are void in so far as they exclude or modify the rights of tenants under ss 1–62. Section 94 deals with Crown land, s 95 contains a saving in respect of the National Trust and s 96 makes special provision for property within the precinct of a cathedral. Section 97 deals with the registration of notices, applications and orders under ss 1–62 and s 98 gives the Secretary of State power to prescribe procedure for claims under those sections. Section 99 relates to the form and service of notices, s 100 concerns the exercise of the Secretary of State's power to make orders and regulations, s 101 deals with interpretation, and s 102 deals with matters relating to periodical tenancies. Section 103 applies the provisions of Pt I of the Act to the Isles of Scilly.

Part II (ss 104–157) Public Sector Housing
Sections 104–106 deal with the right to buy. Section 104 amends the content of the landlord's notice of purchase price and other matters. Section 105 requires the tenant to serve notice of intention to exercise the right to buy where the landlord has served a notice of purchase price and provides for the landlord to serve notice on the tenant's default. Section 106 amends the exceptions to the right to buy in respect of dwelling houses for pensioners. Section 107 provides for the abolition of certain rights ancillary to the right to buy.

Sections 108–120 deal with the right to acquire on rent to mortgage terms. Section 108 creates such a right and provides for exclusions. Section 109 deals with the tenant's notice claiming the right, s 110 with the landlord's notice admitting or denying the right, and s 111 with the tenant's notice of intention and the landlord's notice of default. Section 112 provides for the service of notice of the landlord's share and the amount of the initial discount, while s 113 deals with the calculation of these matters. Section 114 provides for the situation where a change of landlord occurs after the tenant has served notice claiming the right to buy, s 115 deals with the landlord's duty to convey the freehold or grant a lease, and s 116 provides for the terms and effect of the conveyance or grant. The redemption of the landlord's share is dealt with by ss 117 and 118 and Sch 16, landlords' notices to complete by s 119 and the repayment of the discount on an early disposal of the property by s 120.

Sections 121–125 deal with other rights of secure tenants. Section 121 empowers the Secretary of State to make regulations entitling secure tenants whose landlords are local housing authorities to have specified repairs carried out to their properties at their landlords' expense. Section 122 provides for certain secure tenants to receive compensation for home improvements and s 123 amends the right to information about tenancies. Section 124 amends existing rights relating to disposals by housing action trusts and s 125 creates new rights with respect to such disposals. Sections 126–128 deal with housing welfare services. Section 126 enables local housing authorities to provide housing welfare services, s 127 deals with accounting for housing welfare services, and s 128 gives the Secretary of State power to repeal provisions made by ss 126 and 127.

Sections 129–132 deal with the delegation of housing management. Sections 129 and 130 amend the provisions as to management agreements and consultation with respect to such agreements. Sections 131 and 132 introduce new provisions concerning compulsory competitive tendering in relation to management agreements and management agreements with tenant management organisations. Sections 133 and 134 deal with the priority of charges securing repayment of a discount in relation to voluntary disposals by local authorities and housing associations. Sections 135–137 deal with programmes for, and levies on, disposals of dwelling houses by local authorities and transitional provisions in relation to such disposals. Sections 138 and 139 deal with expenses on defective housing and s 140 with the calculation of the housing revenue account subsidy. Sections 141–157 make provision for Scotland.

Part III (ss 158–185) Development of Urban and Other Areas
Sections 158–165 deal with the Urban Regeneration Agency. Section 158 and Schs 17, 18 establish the agency and s 159 provides that its main object is to secure the regeneration of specified descriptions of land in England. Section 160 sets out the general powers of the agency, and s 161 and Sch 19 deal with the vesting of land in the agency by order of the Secretary of State. Section 162 makes provision for the acquisition of land by the agency and s 163 empowers persons authorised by the agency to enter and survey land. Under s 164, the agency may provide financial assistance in respect of certain expenditure on land and under s 165 the agency may, for the purpose of achieving its objects, require a local highway authority to connect a private street to an existing highway. Sections 166–169 and Sch 20 contain supplementary provisions relating to the agency.

Under s 170, the Secretary of State may make a designation order in respect of an urban area or an area suitable for urban development. Section 171 provides that under such an order the agency may, for specified purposes, become the local planning authority for the designated area. Section 172 deals with the adoption of private streets in a designated area and s 173 provides for the Secretary of State to make traffic regulation orders for private streets in such an area. Section 174 extends the Secretary of State's power to give financial assistance for urban regeneration, and under s 175 the Secretary of State has power to appoint the agency to act as his agent in connection with specified functions. Section 176 amends the Secretary of State's power to direct disposal of unused land held by public bodies. Under s 177, the agency may appoint an urban development corporation to act as its agent in connection with specified functions. Section 178 amends the powers of urban development corporations in relation to private streets and s 179 deals with the adjustment of the boundaries of urban development areas. Section 180 deals with the transfer of the property, rights and liabilities of urban development corporations. Sections 181–183 make miscellaneous and supplementary provisions, s 184 dissolves the English Industrial Estates Corporation and s 185 deals with interpretation.

Part IV (ss 186–188) Supplementary
Section 186 deals with financial provision, s 187 and Schs 21 and 22 contain amendments and repeals, and s 188 deals with short title, commencement and extent.

1613 Leasehold Reform, Housing and Urban Development Act 1993—collective enfranchisement and lease renewal

The Leasehold Reform (Collective Enfranchisement and Lease Renewal) Regulations 1993, SI 1993/2407 (in force on 1 November 1993), prescribe the procedure to be followed, in the absence of agreement to the contrary, by the nominee purchaser, reversioner and any relevant landlord in giving effect to an initial notice claiming to exercise the right of collective enfranchisement under the Leasehold Reform, Housing and Urban Development Act 1993. The regulations also prescribe the procedure to be followed, in the absence of agreement to the contrary, by a landlord and tenant in giving effect to a tenant's notice claiming the right to lease renewal under the 1993 Act.

1614 Leasehold Reform, Housing and Urban Development Act 1993—leasehold valuation tribunals—procedure

The Rent Assessment Committee (England and Wales) (Leasehold Valuation Tribunal) Regulations 1993, SI 1993/2408 (in force on 1 November 1993), revoke the 1981 Regulations, SI 1981/271, and prescribe the procedure to be followed by leasehold valuation tribunals in dealing with matters over which they have jurisdiction under the Leasehold, Housing and Urban Development Act 1993, the Leasehold Reform Act 1967 and the Landlord and Tenant

Act 1987. The regulations also prescribe the particulars to be included in applications to leasehold valuation tribunals under those Acts.

1615 Leasehold Reform, Housing and Urban Development Act 1993—notices

The Leasehold Reform (Notices) (Amendment) Regulations 1993, SI 1993/2409 (in force on 1 November 1993), amend the 1967 Regulations, SI 1967/2409, by making amendments, consequential on the changes made by the Leasehold Reform, Housing and Urban Development Act 1993 to the Leasehold Reform Act 1967, relating to forms of notice to be used by tenants of houses claiming the right to have the freehold or an extended lease under the 1967 Act.

1616 Licensed premises—lease—tie provisions—severance of provisions

The tenants acquired the 20-year term of a lease of a public house. The lease contained tie provisions by which the tenants were to purchase specified beers from the landlords. Following a partial release of the tie provisions, the annual rent was reviewed. Subsequently, the tenants failed to pay the rent due and the landlords issued proceedings claiming possession, arrears of rents and mesne profits. The tenants asserted that the tie provisions in the lease contravened art 85 of the Treaty of Rome, and that therefore the lease was void and the tenants held the premises under an implied periodic tenancy at a reasonable rent and not the rent payable under the lease. The main case for the landlords was that, as a matter of law, the tie provisions in the lease, if rendered void by art 85, were severable from the remaining provisions in the lease which remained valid, including the covenant to pay rent. *Held*, if the tie provisions were void, those provisions were clearly severable. The effect of the nullity upon the rest of the lease would then be a matter for the domestic law. Since the tenants had not adduced any evidence which could have given rise to an arguable case that the covenant to pay rent was itself void under art 85 as having as its object or effect the restriction or distortion of competition, full effect should be given to the covenant to pay rent.

Inntrepreneur Estates (GL) Ltd v Boyes [1993] 47 EG 140 (Court of Appeal: Glidewell, Ralph Gibson and Waite LJJ).

1617 Notice to quit—notice given by joint tenant of periodic tenancy—validity

A local authority granted a joint tenancy of residential premises to the defendant and another joint tenant. The tenancy agreement provided that a tenant who wished to determine the tenancy would give the local authority "four weeks' written notice, or such lesser period as the council may accept". After making allegations of domestic violence, the other joint tenant wrote to the local authority indicating that she wished "to terminate my tenancy . . . with immediate effect". On receipt of the letter, the local authority purported to determine the defendant's tenancy, and successfully instituted possession proceedings against him when he refused to move. The defendant appealed against the possession order on the ground that a joint tenant's unilateral decision to determine a secure tenancy did not entitle the landlord to a possession order against the other joint tenant. *Held*, the joint tenant's letter had not been a notice to quit in its true sense, but a notice which operated a break clause in the tenancy agreement so as to determine the tenancy in the middle of a period. The operation of a break clause was not something which could be done by one joint tenant unilaterally, and in any event the defendant was entitled to rely on the Protection from Eviction Act 1977, s 5(1), under which a notice to quit would not be valid unless it was given at least four weeks before the date on which it was due to take effect. The court had erred in granting the local authority's application for a possession order, and, accordingly, the defendant's appeal would be allowed.

London Borough of Hounslow v Pilling (1993) 25 HLR 305 (Court of Appeal: Nourse, Stuart-Smith and Waite LJJ). *Hammersmith & Fulham London Borough Council v Monk* [1992] 1 All ER 1, HL (1991 Abr para 1495) considered.

1618 Protected tenancy—possession—suitable alternative accommodation—environmental factors

The tenant held a protected tenancy. The landlord arranged alternative accommodation and sought a possession order under the Rent Act 1977, Sch 15, Pt IV, para 5(1)(a). The judge visited both properties and formed the view that it was not reasonable to make an order for possession. He found that if he could have ignored the neighbourhood, the second property was in many ways superior. The landlord appealed on the ground that the environmental considerations, although relevant, were to be given less weight when the landlord was putting the case under the 1977 Act, Sch 15, Pt IV, para 5(1)(a) than when under para 5(1)(b). *Held*, the weight to be given to environmental factors was essentially a matter for the trial judge and it was difficult to imagine a case where the Court of Appeal would interfere because a judge had given too much weight to one factor and not enough to another. That was especially so when the judge had seen both properties. Accordingly, the appeal would be dismissed.

Dawncar Investments v Plews (1993) 25 HLR 639 (Court of Appeal: Lloyd and Roch LJJ).

1619   Recovery of possession—closing order on property

The Housing Act 1985, s 317(1) provides that where premises in respect of which a closing order has become operative form the subject matter of a lease, the lessor or lessee may apply to the county court for an order determining or varying the lease.

A dwelling house was let in 1960 on a weekly tenancy. In 1972, the local authority made a closing order on the property but failed to enforce the order and, for the next 20 years, the tenant remained in occupation paying rent to the landlord. The contractual tenancy was terminated by notice to quit in 1992. On the landlord's claim for possession of the house, the tenant counterclaimed for an order under s 317, varying what she claimed was an existing statutory tenancy, under the Rent Act 1977, requiring the landlord to carry out works necessary to bring the house into a state of repair. *Held,* the power of the court under the 1985 Act, s 317 to determine or vary a lease of premises in respect of which a closing order had become operative did not extend to statutory tenancies under the 1977 Act. The 1985 Act, s 276 stated that nothing in the 1977 Act prevented possession being obtained by the owner of premises in respect of which a closing order was in force. The word "lease" in the 1985 Act, s 317 did not include a statutory tenancy under the 1977 Act, there being no reference to it in the definition of "lease" in the 1985 Act, s 621. The tenancy in the present case was concluded upon the expiration of the notice to quit. By virtue of s 277, once a closing order was operative, the premises could not lawfully be used or permitted to be used by persons who knew the order had become operative; in such circumstances, s 276 would render a statutory tenancy under the 1977 Act an illegal contract for illegal purposes and unenforceable. As the tenancy had been determined, there remained no tenancy to which the 1985 Act, s 317 could apply. Accordingly, an order for possession would be made.

Johnson v Felton (12 May 1993, unreported) (Stoke-on-Trent County Court: Judge Styler) (Kindly submitted for publication by Onions & Davies, Solicitors, Market Drayton).

1620   Rent—arrears—distress—insolvent tenant

See *McMullen & Sons Ltd v Cerrone,* para 193.

1621   Rent—interim rent—appeal—pending appeal

The applicant was a stallholder in a market run by the local authority. His tenancy under the Landlord and Tenant Act 1954, s 25 had been determined in March 1986, and after that date he continued to pay rent at pre-March 1986 levels. The local authority successfully applied for an interim rent to be fixed in accordance with the 1954 Act, s 25A, and the applicant sought a stay against any action the local authority might take to enforce payments of the interim rent pending the hearing of his appeal, contending (1) his appeal faced a reasonable prospect of success, and (2) without a stay of execution he faced financial ruin. *Held,* a competently drawn notice of appeal would usually offer a reasonable prospect of success, and in any event the financial problems which the applicant faced were due to his failure to put money aside against the possibility that he would face a demand for substantial arrears of rent. The spectre of imminent ruin was not a ground for denying the local authority the right to enforce payment of those arrears, and although the application would be allowed it would only be allowed on terms which required the applicant to pay off part of the arrears within 14 days, and to pay quarterly increases of rent in the future. Judgment would be entered accordingly.

Simonite v Sheffield City Council (1993) Times, 12 January (Chancery Division: Harman J). *Linotype-Hell Finance Ltd v Baker* [1992] 4 All ER 887 (1992 Abr para 2023) considered.

1622   Rent—property let at concessionary rent—trespass to property—measure of damages

See *Ministry of Defence v Ashman, Ministry of Defence v Thompson,* para 971.

1623   Rent—registration of rent—forms

The Rent Act 1977 (Forms etc) (Amendment) Regulations 1993, SI 1993/655 (in force on 1 April 1993), amend the 1980 Regulations, SI 1980/1697. The regulations prescribe the forms to be used where there is an application for an interim increase of rent on account of council tax under the Rent Act 1977, s 67A and for the rent officer to notify the other party that such an application has been made.

The Rent Act 1977 (Forms etc) (Welsh Forms and Particulars) Regulations 1993, SI 1993/1511 (in force on 13 July 1993), amend the 1980 Regulations, SI 1980/1697 by prescribing Welsh versions of Forms 5, 6, 7, 9A, 10, 11, 12 and 13.

1624   Rent—rent assessment committees—council tax

The Rent Assessment Committees (England and Wales) (Amendment) Regulations 1993, SI 1993/653 (in force on 1 April 1993), amend the 1971 Regulations, SI 1971/1065, to take account of the functions of rent assessment committees under the Housing Act 1988, s 14A in relation to increases in sums payable under assured tenancies and assured agricultural occupancies in respect of council tax.

1625   Rent—review clause—construction of review clause

A rent review clause in a lease provided that an arbitrator had to make an assumption "that the demised premises are fit for immediate occupation and use and in a state of good repair and condition and that all fitting out and other tenant's works required by a willing tenant have already been completed". On the construction of the clause, *held*, the clause did not require the arbitrator to make any determination as to hypothetical fitting out and other tenant's works. The actual tenant was precluded from arguing before the arbitrator that the hypothetical tenant would be entitled to a discount on the best open market rent on account of the actual state of repair and condition of the premises. He was also precluded from arguing for a discount on the ground that the hypothetical tenant would have required further or different works from those carried out by the actual tenant, the cost of which would necessarily be borne by the hypothetical tenant, with a corresponding reduction in the rent that he would be willing to pay. The clause could not be construed as containing a requirement for the arbitrator to determine what hypothetical works the hypothetical tenant would have required. If such a requirement was intended, express provision had to be made.

London and Leeds Estates Ltd v Paribas Ltd (1993) 66 P & CR 218 (Court of Appeal: Nourse, Stuart-Smith and Waite LJJ).

A lease contained a clause allowing a rent review on 1 April 1981 and on every fifth anniversary of that date. If the rent was still in dispute not later than three months before the review date it would be determined by a nominated surveyor on the application of either party made at any time before the "said next review date or the expiration of the term" as the case may be (time being of the essence). The landlord did not attempt to agree the new rent nor to apply for the appointment of a surveyor until after 1 April 1991. His claim that he had until 31 March 1996 to do so was upheld at first instance. The tenant contended that the landlord was too late and appealed. *Held*, since "the expiration of the term" meant the expiration of whatever proved to be the last rent review period, then it followed that in that period the landlord had until its end to apply for the appointment of a surveyor. By analogy, the landlord was intended to have until the end of each earlier rent review period, ie until the commencement date of the next one. The "next" rent review date meant the date immediately following the end of each rent review period other than the last (and the word "said" should be disregarded). Thus the landlord's contention that he had until 31 March 1996 to act was correct. Accordingly, the appeal would be dismissed.

Holicater Ltd v Grandred Ltd [1993] 23 EG 129 (Court of Appeal: Gibson, Leggatt and Hoffmann LJJ).

1626   Rent—review clause—counter-notice—validity of letter

The parties entered into an agreement whereby property was leased for a term of 20 years, with provisions for rent reviews at four-yearly intervals. The landlord was to specify in a notice in writing to the tenant the rent required. In the absence of agreement between the parties, the rent was to be determined at the election of the tenant by counter-notice in writing. The landlord stipulated a rent figure and in reply the tenant stated that he did not agree with the proposed figure and asked for the landlord to acknowledge the letter as a formal notice of disagreement to his rent proposal. An issue arose whether the letter by the tenant was sufficient to constitute counternotice for rent review purposes. *Held*, it was a matter of construction of the lease as to whether the communication made by the tenant satisfied the requirements of the lease. To be an effective counternotice a letter would have to make it clear that the tenant was exercising the relevant election. A notice ought to be in terms which were sufficiently clear, indicating to the ordinary landlord that the tenant was purporting to exercise his right under the relevant clause of the relevant lease. In response to the letter in question any reasonable landlord would have consulted his lease and have known that the relevant notice had been served upon him. It was clear that a valid counternotice had been given under the terms of the lease.

Prudential Property Services Ltd v Capital Land Holdings Ltd [1993] 1 EGLR 128 (Chancery Division: Judge Colyer QC).

1627 Rent—review clause—retail premises—damage to turnover

A large retail supermarket chain closed its premises in a shopping centre after making it generally known some two years previously that the shop would be closed. A tenant in the same complex sustained a 40 per cent loss in turnover following the supermarket's closure. However, the tenant had known when he took the assignment of the lease that the supermarket's closure would take place in the near future. In an appeal by the tenant against a determination of a new rent and an interim rent, *held*, a substantial reduction in turnover of a shop tenant caused by the closure of a large supermarket in the same retail complex was a relevant factor to be considered when determining an interim rent. A discount was required on account of the damage to his turnover, whatever it might have been beforehand and accordingly the appeal would be allowed.

French v Commercial Union Life Assurance Co plc [1992] 24 EG 115 (Court of Appeal: Nourse and Russell LJJ).

1628 Rent—review clause—service of notice—whether time of the essence

A lease provided for rent reviews every five years and contained stipulations as to the time for service of the rent review notice by the landlords. The lease also provided that time was to be of the essence. A separate paragraph of the rent review clause contained a provision for a reference of the matter to arbitration in accordance with the Arbitration Act 1950 at the election of the tenants. The landlords served their rent review notice out of time and the tenants acknowledged receipt of the notice. The landlords obtained an order granting them an extension of time for service of the notice pursuant to the 1950 Act, s 27. On the tenants' appeal against the order, *held*, as time was of the essence, the landlords' notice was invalid and the acknowledgement of receipt by the tenants did not constitute an agreement to extend the time. However, service of the landlords' notice under the appropriate paragraph of the rent review clause was separate and distinct from the paragraph containing the arbitration provisions as it was not referred to in the latter paragraph, was not subject to the same time limit and was to be put into effect by a different person. It was not therefore a step to commence arbitration proceedings within the meaning of the 1950 Act, s 27. In addition, as no valid rent review notice had been served by the landlords, no dispute had arisen to which the arbitration agreement applied. Accordingly, there was no jurisdiction to extend the time for service of the notice and the tenants' appeal would be allowed.

Richurst Ltd v Pimenta [1993] 1 WLR 159 (Chancery Division: David Neuberger QC). *Babanaft International Co SA v Avant Petroleum Inc, The Oltenia* [1982] 3 All ER 244, CA (1982 Abr para 232) applied.

1629 Rent—right of set-off—clause excluding deductions—whether right of set-off excluded

The parties entered into a lease in which the plaintiff tenants covenanted to pay rent "without any deductions". Following serious breaches of the landlords' covenants, the tenants stopped paying rent. The landlords successfully brought an action to recover the unpaid rent, the tenants successfully counterclaimed for damages for the landlords breach, and the two sets of costs were ordered to be set-off against each other. On the question of whether the tenants could exercise the equitable right of set-off, the court held that the phrase "without any deductions" excluded the tenants' right to set-off their claim for unliquidated damages against the rent due. The tenants appealed, contending that their right of set-off should not have been excluded and consequently they should have been awarded costs in both the landlords' action and on the tenants' counterclaim. *Held*, a tenant's equitable right of set-off could only be excluded by explicit wording and the phrase "without any deductions" was not sufficiently clear. Accordingly, the appeal would be allowed and the order for costs would be granted on the terms sought by the tenants.

Connaught Restaurants Ltd v Indoor Leisure Ltd [1993] 46 EG 184 (Court of Appeal: Neill, Simon Brown and Waite LJJ).

1630 Rent—right of set-off—clause excluding right of set-off—whether exclusion clause unfair

The Unfair Contract Terms Act 1977, Sch 1, para 1(b) provides that s 3 (liability arising in contract) does not apply to any contract in so far as it relates to the creation or transfer of an interest in land.

The parties entered into a lease in which the plaintiff landlord covenanted to keep the building in repair and the tenant covenanted to pay the rent and all other sums payable without any deduction or set-off. The landlord sued for unpaid service charges and interest on late payment of rent. The tenant counterclaimed, and sought a set-off, for breaches of the landlord's repairing covenant. The tenant contended that the purported anti-set-off clause in the lease was excluded by the 1977 Act, s 3. *Held*, the tenant's covenant was an integral part of the creation of the lease and thus related to the creation or transfer of an interest in land within the 1977 Act, Sch 1, para 1(b). It followed that the 1977 Act, s 3 did not apply to the anti-set-off clause. Accordingly, judgment would be granted in favour of the landlord.

Electricity Supply Nominees Ltd v IAF Group Ltd [1993] 1 WLR 1059 (Queen's Bench Division: Adrian Hamilton QC).

1631 Rent book—forms of notice

The Rent Book (Forms of Notice) (Amendment) Regulations 1993, SI 1993/656 (in force on 1 April 1993), amend the forms of notice prescribed by the 1982 Regulations, SI 1982/1474. The forms of notice relate to restricted contracts, regulated tenancies, tenancies under the Rent (Agriculture) Act 1976 and assured tenancies or assured agricultural occupancies. The amendments in the regulations are consequential on the introduction of the council tax.

1632 Secure tenancy—change of landlord

The Housing (Change of Landlord) (Payment of Disposal Cost by Instalments) (Amendment) Regulations 1993, SI 1993/581 (in force on 7 April 1993), replace the previous regulations, SI 1992/3176 and further amend the 1990 Regulations, SI 1990/2219, by decreasing the rate of interest on disposal costs paid by instalment from 8·55 per cent to 8·01 per cent.

1633 Secure tenancy—designated courses

The Secure Tenancies (Designated Courses) (Amendment) Regulations 1993, SI 1993/931 (in force on 1 April 1993), amend the 1980 Regulations, SI 1980/1407, by designating additional full-time courses at establishments within the higher or further education sectors. The amendments are consequential on the Further and Higher Education Act 1992.

1634 Secure tenancy—order for possession—suspension of execution—application to suspend

See *Islington London Borough Council v Harridge*, para 641.

1635 Secure tenancy—right to buy—advances secured by way of mortgage—indemnities for advances

The Mortgage Indemnities (Recognised Bodies) Order 1993, SI 1993/304 (in force on 10 March 1993), adds Derbyshire Home Loans Ltd, Derbyshire Mortgages Ltd, Norwich & Peterborough (AMC) Ltd, Portman Financial and Mortgage Services Ltd, Portman Land Services Ltd, Portman Loans Ltd and Portman Mortgage Services Ltd to the list of recognised bodies for the purposes of the Housing Act 1985, ss 442, 443.

The Mortgage Indemnities (Recognised Bodies) (No 2) Order 1993, SI 1993/2758 (in force on 23 November 1993), adds Alliance & Leicester Mortgage Loans Ltd, CIS Home Loans Ltd, CIS Mortgage Finance Ltd and CIS Residential Mortgages Ltd to the list of recognised bodies for the purposes of the Housing Act 1985, ss 442, 443.

1636 Secure tenancy—right to buy—charges on dwelling house—priority of charges

The Housing (Right to Buy) (Priority of Charges) Order 1993, SI 1993/303 (in force on 10 March 1993), adds to the bodies specified as approved lending institutions for the purposes of the Housing Act 1985, s 156 the following bodies: Derbyshire Home Loans Ltd, Derbyshire

Mortgages Ltd, Norwich & Peterborough (AMC) Ltd, Portman Financial and Mortgage Services Ltd, Portman Land Services Ltd, Portman Loans Ltd and Portman Mortgage Services Ltd.

The Housing (Right to Buy) (Priority of Charges) (No 2) Order 1993, SI 1993/2757 (in force on 23 November 1993), adds to the bodies specified as approved lending institutions for the purposes of the Housing Act 1985, s 156 the following bodies: Alliance & Leicester Mortgage Loans Ltd, CIS Mortgage Finance Ltd, CIS Home Loans Ltd and CIS Residential Mortgages Ltd.

1637   Secure tenancy—right to buy—completion—injunction to enforce completion

The plaintiff tenant applied for an injunction forcing the defendant council, as landlord, to complete the sale of a dwelling house by conveying the freehold to her. The plaintiff had exercised her right to buy the property under the Housing Act 1985 and had satisfied the relevant conditions under s 138(1). At first instance the injunction was granted and the defendant appealed on the ground that the court had the discretion to refuse the relief sought. *Held*, once the conditions of the 1985 Act, s 138(1) were satisfied the plaintiff was entitled as of right to an injunction enforcing the defendant's duty to convey the property to her and as such the court had no discretion to withhold the injunction. Accordingly, the appeal would be dismissed.

Taylor v Newham London Borough Council [1993] 2 All ER 649 (Court of Appeal: Sir Thomas Bingham MR, McCowan and Hirst LJJ).

1638   Secure tenancy—right to buy—death of tenant before completion

Following the death of a secure tenant the defendant local authority applied for possession of the property. Notice had been served by the tenant claiming the right to buy the property which had been admitted by the defendant and a price had been agreed. The plaintiff sought a declaration on her counterclaim on the ground that the right to buy was an equitable interest vested in and enforceable by her as the representative of the secure tenant's estate. At first instance the application was refused and the declaration granted. On appeal by the defendant, *held*, under the Housing Act 1985, five events had to take place before property could be vested in a secure tenant. Firstly, a secure tenant had to claim to exercise the right to buy by written notice. Secondly, the landlord had to state whether it accepted the right or denied it. Thirdly, the landlord then had to state a price at which the house ought to be sold and the terms to be included in the conveyance. Fourthly, those terms had to be agreed by the tenant. Finally, by the 1985 Act, s 138(1) where a secure tenant had claimed to exercise a right to buy and that right had been established, if the dwelling house was a house and the landlord owned the freehold, the landlord had to make to the tenant a grant of the dwelling house in fee simple absolute. At the time of the tenant's death only the first four steps had been completed. The provisions of the Housing Act 1985 dealing with a council tenant's right to purchase the property contained an implicit requirement that the tenant had to remain a secure tenant until the conveyance or grant of the property. Where a tenant died after the right to buy had been established and a price agreed between the parties but no conveyance had taken place, the right to buy disappeared and did not pass under the tenant's estate. Accordingly, the appeal would be allowed.

City of Bradford Metropolitan Council v McMahon (1993) 25 HLR 534 (Court of Appeal: Balcombe, Staughton and Waite LJJ).

1639   Secure tenancy—right to buy—delay procedure

The Housing (Right to Buy Delay Procedure) (Prescribed Forms) (Amendment) Regulations 1993, SI 1993/2245 (in force on 11 October 1993), amend the 1989 Regulations, SI 1989/240. The regulations repeal form RTB5 and amend other forms. The amendments are consequential on the introduction of the right to acquire on rent to mortgage terms and the abolition of the right to a shared ownership lease by the Leasehold Reform, Housing and Urban Development Act 1993.

1640   Secure tenancy—right to buy—extension

The Housing (Extension of Right to Buy) Order 1993, SI 1993/2240 (in force on 11 October 1993), modifies the Housing Act 1985, Pt V. The order extends the right of a secure tenant to buy the freehold of his dwelling house to cases where the dwelling house is a house, the secure tenant's landlord has a lease of the dwelling house, and the freeholder and each intermediate landlord is a specified authority or body. The 1987 Order, SI 1987/1732, and the 1990 Order, SI 1990/179, are revoked.

1641   Secure tenancy—right to buy—local authority employee—entitlement to free use of house

By virtue of the Housing Act 1985, Sch 1, para 2(1), a tenancy is not a secure tenancy if the tenant is an employee of a local authority and his contract of employment requires him to occupy the dwelling house for the better performance of his duties.

Under his contract of employment with a local authority, the plaintiff, the headmaster of a boarding school, was entitled to free board and lodging. Accommodation in the school grounds having become unsuitable for him, a new headmaster's house was built within the grounds but not within the curtilage of the school buildings. He and his family moved into the house although he was not obliged under his contract of employment to occupy the house. He sought to exercise the right to buy the house under the 1985 Act, s 188 which confers upon a secure tenant the right to buy his house. At first instance and on appeal it was held that the plaintiff was entitled to buy the property as he did not fall within the exception from the right to buy in Sch 1, para 2. On further appeal, *held*, there was no implied term in the plaintiff's contract that he was required to occupy the property for the better performance of his duties and further there was no compelling reason for such a term to form part of the contract as it was clear that the employer was providing a facility rather than imposing an obligation. Accordingly, the appeal would be dismissed.

Hughes v Greenwich London Borough Council [1993] 4 All ER 577 (House of Lords: Lords Templeman, Bridge of Harwich, Lowry, Browne-Wilkinson and Slynn of Hadley). Decision of Court of Appeal (1992) 24 HLR 605 (1992 Abr para 1574) affirmed.

1642   Secure tenancy—right to buy—local authority employee—variation of contract of employment to require occupation of premises for better performance of duties

The Housing Act 1985, Sch 1, para 2(1) provides that a tenancy is not a secure tenancy if the tenant is an employee of the landlord and his contract of employment requires him to occupy the dwelling house for the better performance of his duties.

The applicant was employed by a local authority at a park. He accepted a tenancy of a cottage in the park and agreed that his right to occupy the premises would cease if his employment ended. His contract of employment neither expressly nor impliedly required him to live in the cottage. The applicant was subsequently promoted and the terms of his contract of employment were varied so that it became a term that he should occupy the cottage for the better performance of his duties. The applicant later claimed to exercise the right to buy as a secure tenant. This claim was rejected by the local authority on the ground that his tenancy was not a secure tenancy within the meaning of the 1985 Act, Sch 1, para 2(1) as he was required to occupy the premises for the better performance of his duties. In county court proceedings, the judge concluded that the change in the applicant's terms of employment brought the tenancy within Sch 1, para 2(1) so that he was not a secure tenant at the relevant date. The applicant appealed. *Held*, there was a distinction between the use of the present tense in the formulation of the exception to a secure tenancy in para 2(1) and the use of the past tense in the formulation of other exceptions contained in that paragraph. Accordingly, the exception in para 2(1) applied, not once and for all at the commencement of the tenancy, but at any time when the employee's contract required him to occupy the cottage for the better performance of his duties. The exception operated to exclude the applicant's right to buy and the appeal would be dismissed.

Elvidge v Coventry City Council [1993] 3 WLR 976 (Court of Appeal: Steyn, Hoffmann and Peter Gibson LJJ).

1643   Secure tenancy—right to buy—prescribed forms

The Housing (Right to Buy) (Prescribed Forms) (Amendment) Regulations 1993, SI 1993/2246 (in force on 11 October 1993), amend the forms of notice to be used by secure tenants to claim the right to buy under the Housing Act 1985, Pt V and by the landlord in reply. The regulations also prescribe the form to be used by tenants claiming the right to acquire on rent to mortgage terms and the form of notice to be used by a landlord to admit or deny that claim. The amendments and the new forms are consequential on amendments made to the 1985 Act, Pt V by the Leasehold Reform, Housing and Urban Development Act 1993.

1644   Secure tenancy—right to buy—preservation

The Housing (Preservation of Right to Buy) Regulations 1993, SI 1993/2241 (in force on 11 October 1993), modify the Housing Act 1985, Pt V in cases where an authority or body disposes of a qualifying dwelling house let to a secure tenant and the tenant's right to buy is preserved by the 1985 Act, s 171A. The regulations take account of the amendments made by the Leasehold Reform, Housing and Urban Development Act 1993.

1645   Service charge—validity

The Housing Act 1985, Sch 6, para 16A provides that a lease may require a tenant to bear a reasonable part of the costs incurred by the landlord (1) in discharging or insuring against the obligations implied by virtue of para 14(2) (repairs, making good structural defects, provision of service etc), or (2) in insuring against the obligations imposed by the covenant implied by virtue of para 14(3) (rebuilding or reinstatement etc). Schedule 6, para 18(a) provides that a provision of the lease is void in so far as it purports to authorise the recovery of such a charge as is mentioned in para 16A otherwise than in accordance with that para and para 16B (restrictions in initial period of lease).

The defendants were secure tenants of a council-owned property. They exercised their right to buy, and the flat was demised to them on a long lease. By virtue of a clause in the lease, the defendants covenanted to pay such service charge as was specified in the lease. Another clause in the lease specified the charge as £208 per annum plus a sum calculated in accordance with the building cost information service tender price index. The defendants refused to pay the service charge and the council brought an action against the defendants. The case was dismissed at first instance on the ground that the council, by virtue of the provisions of the 1985 Act, were not entitled to recover the service charge. The council's appeal was allowed. On appeal by the defendants, the council submitted that the clause relating to the service charge in the lease was unaffected by para 18(a), as para 18(a) related to variable charges, and that neither paras 16A, 16B nor 18(a) were concerned with the fixed charges of the type specified in the clause in the lease. *Held*, the council's submissions were correct and Sch 6 and the protection it conferred on a tenant had to be looked at in the context of the statutory control relating to variable charges. The reasonableness of a fixed charge could be examined at a time when a long lease was under negotiation, and assuming that the fixed charge was reasonable the tenant was protected over the whole period of the lease from fluctuating and unpredictable costs. A tenant's only exposure to risk was due to a clause dependent on inflation. It was therefore correct to treat the service charge clause in the lease as falling outside para 16A and outside the scope of para 18. The appeal would accordingly be dismissed.

Coventry City Council v Cole (1993) Times, 3 June (Court of Appeal: Neill, Steyn and Rose LJJ).

1646   Unlawful eviction—damages—definition of landlord

The occupier was evicted from the annexe of the owner's property. The annexe had been let to him under an oral agreement with the owner's wife. In breach of the oral agreement the occupier kept his cats indoors, causing the premises to become filthy, and refused to vacate the premises at the end of the informally agreed period despite indicating that he would do so when he took up occupation. The owner and his wife thereupon removed the occupier's belongings from the premises and bolted the door against him. On the question of whether the occupier could recover damages for unlawful eviction against the owner's wife and on the issue of quantum, *held*, the wife fell within the definition of landlord in the Housing Act 1988, s 27(9)(c) as, although she had no legal interest in the property, her right of occupation as against the occupier was in the character of a landlord. Damages of £3,000 would be awarded under the 1988 Act and £250 would be awarded for trespass to goods. Section 27(7)(a) of the 1988 Act gave the judge a wide discretion to reduce the statutory damages. In the present case, the damages would be reduced by four-fifths to take account of the occupier's conduct in keeping cats in the premises and reneging on his agreement to leave. No award would be made for aggravated damages as there were no aggravating factors. No award of exemplary damages would be made because the owner and his wife had not acted with a view to a profit ands because any such award would duplicate the statutory award.

Sullman v Little (23 July 1993, unreported) (Canterbury County Court: Judge Peppitt) (Kindly submitted for publication by Michael Batey, Barrister).

1647 Unlawful eviction—damages—exemplary damages

The plaintiff was the sub-tenant of property owned by the first defendant. The second defendant, the first defendant's son, began to manage the property as his father's agent. He sought an increase in the plaintiff's rent and later evicted him. The plaintiff was awarded exemplary damages against both defendants for unlawful eviction. On their appeals against those awards, *held*, the first defendant had both authorised and encouraged the second defendant to evict the plaintiff. Exemplary damages were rightly awarded against him and, accordingly, his appeal would be dismissed. However, exemplary damages against the second defendant acting as the landlord's agent might not be awarded unless it was established that he himself stood to benefit from the eviction. In following the test laid down in *Rookes v Barnard* [1964] 1 All ER 367, HL, it had not been established that the second defendant's conduct had been calculated to make a profit for himself. His appeal would be allowed.

Ramdath v Daley (1993) 25 HLR 273 (Court of Appeal: Nourse and Steyn LJJ).

1648 Unlawful eviction—damages—right of set-off

It has been held that damages awarded at common law to a tenant for loss of the right to occupy premises must be set off against any damages awarded under the Housing Act 1988, ss 27, 28 in respect of the same loss.

Nwokorie v Mason (1993) 26 HLR 60 (Court of Appeal: Dillon LJ and Hollis J).

LEASEHOLD ENFRANCHISEMENT OR EXTENSION

See LANDLORD AND TENANT.

LEGAL AID AND ADVICE

Halsbury's Laws of England (4th edn) Vol 27(2) (reissue), paras 1851–2075

1649 Articles

Buying Time for the Debate over Criminal Legal Aid, David Wall and Adrian Wood: 143 NLJ 324

Civil Legal Aid—a Comparative Study, Mel Cousins: [1993] CJQ 154

Costs Orders Against Legally Aided Persons, Bullock DJ: [1993] Fam Law 389.

Early Cover and the Legal Aid Board, Alison McNair and George Ritchie: 137 NLJ 232

Enforcement of Contribution Orders During Currency of Criminal Legal Aid Orders, James Parry: 157 JP Jo 739

Immigration Law Threatened by Legal Aid Cuts, Penny Smith: 137 SJ 247

Legal Aid Eligibility Criteria: The Impact for Immigration Law Practitioners and their Clients, Penny Smith: [1993] CJQ 167

Legal Aid Franchising, Michael Simmons: 137 SJ 92

Legal Aid Round-up, Henry Hodge: LS Gaz, 24 March 1993, p 19

Reading the Small Print, Roger Smith: LS Gaz, 23 April 1993, p 23

The Price of Expert Advice, Simon Morgans (on the payment of experts in legal aid cases): LS Gaz, 7 July 1993, p 22

Ways of Making Legal Aid Pay, Rosslyne Dixon: LS Gaz, 17 February 1993, p 23

1650 Advice and assistance—eligibility

The Legal Advice and Assistance (Amendment) Regulations 1993, SI 1993/790 (in force on 12 April 1993), further amend the 1989 Regulations, SI 1989/340. Now, with the exception of ABWOR, contributory advice and assistance is abolished. The regulations increase, where applicable, the fraction of disposable income payable as contributions to ABWOR, and provide that there is a continuing liability to contribute throughout the period in which ABWOR is given. The free advice and assistance limit and the disregards of certain benefits are brought into line with those applying in civil legal aid. In addition, the regulations specify that the deduction made where an assisted person has a spouse is the difference between the couple's income support allowance and the allowance payable to a single person aged 25 or over.

1651   Advice and assistance—Green Form Scheme

The applicant was a member of a group which was petitioning the Visitors to the Inns of Court. They sought to challenge the Council of Legal Education's decision not to certify them as having passed the Bar examinations. Legal Aid was not available for those proceedings and so an application was made, under the Legal Advice and Assistance Regulations 1989, SI 1989/340, reg 21, for an extension of the financial limits of the Green Form scheme for the purpose of obtaining experts' reports. The Legal Aid Board refused and the applicant sought judicial review of that decision. *Held*, it was implicit in the 1989 Regulations, reg 21 that whether it was reasonable for advice and assistance to be given was a matter for the Legal Aid Board. When deciding whether to grant an extension of the Green Form, the board had to consider the simplicity and informality of the Green Form procedures, the low level of the financial limit and the need for more compelling reasons the greater the extension sought, particularly in relation to proceedings excluded from legal aid. However, the board also had to consider that it had the power to grant further funding for assistance short of actual representation. In the present case, the board should have considered the necessity of the applicant obtaining the experts' reports to facilitate a full and fair hearing of the merits of the petition. Accordingly, the application would be allowed.

R v Legal Aid Board, ex p Higgins (1993) Times, 19 November (Queen's Bench Division: Simon Brown LJ and Buckley J).

1652   Advice and assistance—remuneration—advisory service similar to duty solicitor scheme

A company contracted with individual solicitors to provide advisory services, the solicitors being paid commitment fees for shifts performed. Subscribing solicitors allowed telephone calls from detained clients to be diverted to one of the contracted solicitors, who would then carry out advisory work in a manner akin to the duty solicitor scheme for a fee not exceeding £90. The company and the advising solicitors wished to be funded under the legal aid scheme. The Legal Aid Board prohibited the company from paying the advising solicitors on the ground that the scheme was an artificial service which did not fall within the provisions of the Legal Aid Act 1988, and it also felt the advisory service would undermine the duty solicitor scheme. On the company's application for judicial review of that decision, *held*, the service had been arranged in such a way that it was, both in law and effect, a scheme to provide services, and it did not create a master/servant relationship between the company and the advising solicitors. Under the terms of the scheme, assistance would be available regardless of the client's means, as required by the Legal Advice and Assistance Regulations 1989, SI 1989/340, and there were no grounds for regarding it as an artificial arrangement which ought not to be allowed. The Law Society could act against its own members if it was unhappy with the existence of the service, but the Legal Aid Board did not have the power to withhold payment for work done under it. The application for judicial review would be allowed.

R v Legal Aid Board, ex p Gilchrist (1993) 137 Sol Jo LB 146 (Queen's Bench Division: Macpherson J).

1653   Civil proceedings—costs—taxation—practice

See *Practice Direction*, para 2023.

1654   Civil proceedings—costs—taxation—review of taxation

See *Brush v Bower Cotton & Bower*, para 2024.

1655   Civil proceedings—costs—unassisted successful defendant

The Legal Aid Act 1988, s 18 provides that in proceedings to which a legally-aided person is a party and which are decided in favour of an unassisted party the court can make an order requiring the Legal Aid Board to pay the unassisted person's costs, provided that the court is satisfied that the unassisted party would otherwise suffer severe financial hardship and that it is just and equitable to so order.

The assisted plaintiffs' claim against the unassisted defendant was dismissed. The defendant applied for an order of costs against the Legal Aid Board under the 1988 Act, s 18. The court adjourned the proceedings under the Civil Legal Aid (General) Regulations 1989, SI 1989/339, reg 138 and, under reg 142, required the defendant to file an affidavit of costs and resources which complied with the 1989 Regulations, Sch 2. The defendant's affidavit was faulty and, at the adjourned hearing, he tried to tender oral evidence to redress this. The court dismissed the application on the grounds that the defendant had not shown that he would suffer severe financial hardship if the order was not made. The defendant appealed. *Held*, the purpose of the 1989 Regulations was to ensure that the court could make a fully informed evaluation of the financial position of an applicant under the 1988 Act, s 18. The court could overlook minor errors in an affidavit, but it could not make an order in favour of an applicant whose affidavit contained substantial errors of which the board complained. Further, the applicant did not have the right to correct his faulty affidavit by oral testimony, although the court had a discretion to allow this if the board consented. The court could therefore have dismissed the defendant's application on the basis that his affidavit substantially failed to meet the statutory requirements; dismissal on the merits was also correct. Accordingly, the appeal would be dismissed.

Jones v Zahedi [1993] 4 All ER 909 (Court of Appeal: Sir Thomas Bingham MR, Mann and Gibson LJJ).

Prior to the hearing of a wife's application for variation of periodical payments, the unassisted husband wrote to the Legal Aid Board informing it that the application was without merit and would be dismissed. The wife's application was dismissed. The husband's application for costs was dismissed on the ground that his affidavit of costs and resources was not filed within the 21-day period prescribed by the Civil Legal Aid (General) Regulations 1989, SI 1989/339, reg 142. On his appeal, *held*, the court had an inherent power to control its own procedure and, accordingly, had power to extend time for the filing of the affidavit. The board was a party in the matter. Regulation 142 should not be construed so as to exclude the court which had to do justice between the parties. The appeal would be allowed and remitted to the district judge for rehearing.

Middleton v Middleton (1993) Times, 4 June (Family Division: Thorpe J).

1656 Civil proceedings—eligibility—assessment of resources

The Civil Legal Aid (Assessment of Resources) (Amendment) Regulations 1993, SI 1993/788 (in force on 12 April 1993), further amend the 1989 Regulations, SI 1989/338. The 1993 Regulations link more closely the personal allowances applicable for income support to the financial limits relating to eligibility of a person to receive free legal aid and the assessment of disposable income. An increase, from one quarter to one third, is made to the fraction of disposable income payable by way of contribution, and monthly contributions from income will be payable for as long as the legal aid certificate is in force. In addition, the deduction made where an assisted person has a spouse is specified as the difference between the income support allowance for a couple and the allowance which would have been payable to a person who has reached the age of 25.

1657 Civil proceedings—eligibility—dual applications

The applicant was the tenant of a property. The owner of the property defaulted on loans and as a result, two actions for possession were brought against the tenant. Her only substantial asset was an income bond realisable on three months' notice. She applied for legal aid for each possession action, requesting that her income bond capital should be disregarded under the Civil Legal Aid (Assessment of Resources) Regulations 1989, SI 1989/338, Sch 3, para 15, which conferred a discretion on the legal aid assessment office to disregard all or some of the applicant's capital having regard to the circumstances of the case. The assessment office decided that it was not entitled to consider, as part of the exercise of its discretion, the fact that she had made or was making two legal aid applications. The office assessed her capital separately for each application, and declined to disregard any of her capital. On appeal, *held*, the fact of the two applications and the effect of them was a highly relevant circumstance of the case, to which the assessment office should have had regard in the exercise of its discretion under para 15. The decisions of the assessment office in each case would accordingly be quashed and remitted for reconsideration.

R v Legal Aid Assessment Officer, ex p Crocker (1993) Independent, 23 July (Queen's Bench Division: Auld J).

1658 Civil proceedings—enforcement of statutory charge—rate of interest

The Civil Legal Aid (General) (Amendment) (No 2) Regulations 1993, SI 1993/1756 (in force on 1 September 1993), further amend the 1989 Regulations, SI 1989/339. The Regulations reduce, from 10·5 per cent to 8 per cent, the rate of interest chargeable where enforcement of the statutory charge is postponed.

1659   Civil proceedings—payments on account—proportion of fees payable

The Civil Legal Aid (General) (Amendment) Regulations 1993, SI 1993/565 (in force in part on 1 April 1993, in part on 12 April 1993), further amend the 1989 Regulations, SI 1989/339. An assisted person is now liable to pay monthly contributions from his disposable income for as long as the legal aid certificate is in force. In certain specified circumstances, the requirement to make further contributions may be waived, and subsequently revived. Amendments are made to the payment on account scheme, including changing the periods at which payments on account are to be made and delaying for one year the increase in the maximum proportion of the fees payable in a financial year; the maximum proportion which can be paid on account remains at 62 per cent for the year 1993–94.

1660   Civil proceedings—scope

The Civil Legal Aid (Scope) Regulations 1993, SI 1993/1354 (in force on 27 May 1993), extend the categories of proceedings for which civil legal aid is available so as to include magistrates' courts' proceedings under the Child Support Act 1991, s 20 (as modified), and applications for a declaration of parentage under s 27.

1661   Criminal proceedings—applications—documentary information

The Legal Aid in Criminal and Care Proceedings (General) (Amendment) (No 2) Regulations 1993, SI 1993/1895 (in force on 1 September 1993), amend the 1989 Regulations, SI 1989/344. The new regulations require applications for legal aid to be accompanied by supporting documentary evidence of the information contained in the statement of means, or an explanation why the applicant is unable to provide such documentary evidence. In addition, legal aid may be withdrawn or contribution orders made or amended as a consequence of documentary evidence provided after the legal aid order has been made. Legal representatives must now report abuse of legal aid by an applicant or legally assisted person who intentionally fails to comply with regulations requiring him to provide information, or who furnishes false information.

1662   Criminal proceedings—costs—Queen's Counsel's fees—comparison with fees of opposing counsel

The respondent, a Queen's Counsel, and his junior were instructed to defend a man who, with two others, faced a single count of conspiracy to rob. The trial ran for 18 days and, following a failure by the jury to agree a verdict, there was a re-trial which lasted six days. The respondent claimed a basic fee and refreshers which were subsequently reduced by the court. He then sought a re-determination under the Legal Aid in Criminal and Care Proceedings (Costs) Regulations 1989, SI 1989/343, Reg 14. The re-determining officer decided that the fee set was reasonable and on appeal to the taxing master the respondent's brief fee was increased in line with the brief fee received by the prosecution Queen's Counsel. The Lord Chancellor appealed against the taxing master's decision, *held*, the 1989 Regulations did not preclude an appropriate authority, determining officer or taxing master from looking at the fees paid to prosecuting counsel. Prosecuting counsel's fees were part of the material on which the exercise of judicial discretion was based in determining what was reasonable remuneration. Accordingly, the appeal would be dismissed.

Lord Chancellor v Wright [1993] 4 All ER 74 (Queen's Bench Division: Garland J).

1663   Criminal proceedings—costs—standard fees

The Legal Aid in Criminal and Care Proceedings (Costs) (Amendment) Regulations 1993, SI 1993/934 (in force in part on 26 April 1993, in part on 1 June 1993), further amend the 1989 Regulations, SI 1989/344. Provision is made for the introduction of standard fees for criminal proceedings in magistrates' court. The proceedings in which standard fees do and do not apply are specified, and the regulations also list the classes of work covered by the standard fee, additional costs and the allowance of standard fees. The regulations also allow a solicitor to seek interim payment of disbursements equal to or greater than a specified value in Crown Court cases for which he has obtained prior authority from an area committee. Forty per cent of a total claim for costs may now be paid as an interim payment pending determination of the bill where the claim is equal to or greater than a prescribed amount or is related to other claims of such amounts. Provision is made for the recovery by an appropriate authority of overpayments from a solicitor or barrister.

1664 Criminal proceedings—defence—witnesses—cross-examination

The Legal Aid Act 1988, s 22(2)(d) provides that a defence involving the tracing and interviewing of witnesses or expert cross-examination of a prosecution witness is a relevant factor in determining whether it is in the interests of justice that representation be granted for the purposes of trial proceedings.

The applicant was charged with driving whilst disqualified but contended that his girlfriend, not he, was driving. He applied for legal aid on the grounds that the defence needed to trace and interview witnesses, that police witnesses would be cross-examined and that he was likely to be sentenced to a community service order. The request was refused and the applicant sought judicial review of that decision. *Held,* the justices had misconstrued the 1988 Act, s 22(2)(d) as providing that the cross-examination had to be of expert witnesses, rather than expertly conducted. Accordingly, the decision would be quashed.

R v Liverpool City Magistrates, ex p McGhee [1993] Crim LR 609 (Queens Bench Division: Rose LJ and Waller J).

1665 Criminal proceedings—eligibility

The Legal Aid in Criminal and Care Proceedings (General) (Amendment) Regulations 1993, SI 1993/789 (in force on 12 April 1993), further amend the 1989 Regulations, SI 1989/344. The regulations link more closely the personal allowances for income support to the financial limits relating to the eligibility of a person to receive free legal aid and the assessment of disposable income. The deduction made where an assisted person has a spouse is specified as the difference between the income support allowance for a couple and the allowance which would otherwise be payable to a single person who has reached the age of 25. A deduction is also to be made where an allowance is paid for a dependant child or relative. The fraction of disposable income payable by way of contribution is increased.

1666 Criminal proceedings—revocation of aid—reapplication

The Legal Aid in Criminal and Care Proceedings (General) Regulations 1989, SI 1989/344, reg 10 provides that, subject to certain provisions, nothing affects the power of a court, a judge of the court or the registrar to make a legal aid order, whether an application has been made for a legal aid order or not, or the right of an applicant whose application has been refused or whose legal aid order has been revoked to apply to the court at trial or in other proceedings.

The defendant's legal aid certificate was revoked for non-payment of contributions. A magistrate at the defendant's subsequent remand hearing held that he had no power under reg 10 to grant the defendant legal aid following the revocation of the original certificate on the ground that there were "no other proceedings" before him. The defendant sought judicial review of the decision. *Held,* it would be straining the language of reg 10 to conclude that "other proceedings" referred to proceedings only after trial. To deny that "other proceedings" referred to pre-trial matters would be to deprive defendants who had been refused legal aid of the safeguard afforded by the general power in reg 10 to make a legal aid order. The application would accordingly be allowed.

R v Liverpool City Magistrates' Court, ex p Pender [1993] 2 All ER 929 (Queen's Bench Division: Watkins LJ and Leonard J). For earlier related proceedings, see *R v Liverpool Deputy Stipendiary Magistrate, ex p Shaklady, R v Clerk to Liverpool City Justices, ex p Pender* (1992) Times, 28 December, DC (1992 Abr para 1606).

1667 Family proceedings—remuneration

The Legal Aid in Family Proceedings (Remuneration) (Amendment) Regulations 1993, SI 1993/1117 (in force on 27 May 1993), further amend the 1991 Regulations, SI 1991/2038, to add (1) specified appeals under the Child Support Act 1991, s 20; and (2) references under s 27 to a court for a declaration of parentage, to those proceedings remunerated in accordance with the 1991 Regulations, Sch 2 where the client is legally aided.

1668 Lord Chancellor—power to make regulations—duty to consult Law Society

In accordance with the Legal Aid Act 1988 the Lord Chancellor introduced the following statutory instruments amending eligibility for legal aid: the Civil Legal Aid (General)

(Amendment) Regulations 1993, SI 1993/565, the Civil Legal Aid (Assessment of Resources) (Amendment) Regulations 1993, SI 1993/788, the Legal Aid in Criminal and Care Proceedings (General) (Amendment) Regulations 1993, SI 1993/789, and the Legal Advice and Assistance (Amendment) Regulations 1993, SI 1993/790. The Law Society applied for judicial review of the regulations on the grounds that they were unlawful, in that they frustrated rather than promoted the purposes of the 1988 Act, they were so unreasonable as to be irrational and they were made without proper consultation with the Law Society. *Held*, the purpose of the 1988 Act was to establish a framework for the provision of advice, assistance or representation which was publicly funded. Even though the Lord Chancellor failed to consult the Law Society before introducing the regulations, the court would not declare the regulations invalid since additional consultation would not have led to any different result. Accordingly, the application would be dismissed.

R v Lord Chancellor, ex p the Law Society (1993) Times, 25 June (Queen's Bench Division: Neill LJ and Mantell J).

1669   Lord Chancellor—power to make regulations—standard fees scheme

The Lord Chancellor introduced a scheme, under the Legal Aid in Criminal and Care Proceedings (Costs) (Amendment) Regulations 1993, SI 1993/934, pursuant to the powers conferred on him under the Legal Aid Act 1988, s 34, for the use of standard fees in remunerating solicitors for criminal legal aid work in magistrates' courts. The plaintiff sought judicial review on the ground that the regulations were outside the powers of the Lord Chancellor and that the scheme did not produce a standard fee in individual cases. *Held*, any system of standard fees necessarily meant that there would be some cases which were paid less than would be appropriate were they to be considered in isolation. In introducing the regulations the Lord Chancellor would be within his powers provided that he complied with the express limitations of the 1988 Act, s 34. Accordingly, the appeal would be dismissed.

R v Lord Chancellor, ex p the Law Society (1993) Times, 11 August (Court of Appeal: Balcombe, Farquharson and Rose LJJ). Decision of Queen's Bench Divisional Court (1993) Independent, 4 May affirmed.

1670   Report on legal aid—Home Affairs Committee

The Home Affairs Committee of the House of Commons has published a report following consideration of the reforms of the legal aid system proposed by the Lord Chancellor and after hearing evidence from him and also from the Bar Council and the Law Society (HC 517). The committee expressed its concern at the continued absence of management information on the cause for the increase in legal aid expenditure in recent years and called urgently for a study to establish why costs were rising so rapidly and for a complementary inquiry into the scope for savings and efficiency gains in the way legal services were delivered and the courts run. It further called for the government to undertake to restore cuts made in eligibility in real terms for legal aid as soon as compensatory savings were found. It further suggested that the government should set a long-term goal of ensuring that citizens had access to advice and assistance either free or at a price that they could afford. Particular concern was expressed at the ending of the contributory green form scheme in England and Wales when it was continued in Scotland; the committee called for the withdrawal of the proposals for eliminating the contributory taper for green form advice in England and Wales. The committee recommended the exemption of legal aid from value added tax; this would reduce costs and save pointless bureaucracy.

LIBEL AND SLANDER

Halsbury's Laws of England (4th edn) Vol 28, paras 1–300

1671   Articles

Libel and the Advertising Agency, R G Lawson: 143 NLJ 432
Libelling Public Figures, Ian Loveland: 143 NLJ 1755

1672   Defamation—meaning of defamatory words—natural and ordinary meaning

The defendant television company broadcast a programme which presented serious doubts about the convictions of six men convicted of causing death and injury by planting bombs in city centre public houses. Part of the programme dealt with the scientific evidence in the case where it was stated that the plaintiff, a forensic scientist who had presented evidence at the trial, used a test that did not prove that any particular substance was present on the convicted men, and that the test carried out on other substances gave identical results to explosives, something which the plaintiff had told the court could not happen. The plaintiff brought a libel action against the defendant contending that the words and visual images presented by the defendant meant that he had negligently misrepresented to the court the effect of the scientific tests carried out. In a preliminary ruling it was held that the words bore the meaning that there were reasonable grounds to suspect that the plaintiff was negligent as a forensic scientist because he based his conclusions on the test and that caused or contributed to the wrongful imprisonment of the convicted men. On appeal by the plaintiff, *held*, in determining the meaning of the words and their defamatory sense the court ought to give the material its natural and ordinary meaning. A statement would be taken to be defamatory if it would tend to lower the plaintiff in the estimation of right-thinking members of society generally or would be likely to affect a person adversely in the estimation of reasonable people. The natural and ordinary meaning of the material complained of was that the plaintiff in giving evidence at the trial of the convicted men had failed to show the skill, knowledge, care and thoroughness to be expected of him in his role as a forensic scientist. Accordingly, the appeal would be allowed.

Skuse v Granada Television (1993) Independent, 2 April (Court of Appeal: Sir Thomas Bingham MR, Beldam and Kennedy LJJ).

1673 Defamation—qualified privilege—malice

Scotland

A police officer claimed damages for defamation in respect of allegations contained in a letter written to his chief constable, the author of which had been charged by the officer with receiving two stolen television sets. The charges had later been found not proven. One of the allegations was that the police officer had laid the charges because the author was an Asian justice of the peace and in employment. It was accepted that the occasion was covered by qualified privilege and that the police officer was required to prove malice. At first instance it was held that the author was in effect stating that the police officer had had no evidence to justify the charges against him and therefore, malice was established by the fact that the author must have known this to be untrue. The author appealed, and it was held that the terms of the letter did not support the innuendo that the officer had had no evidence justifying the charges. On appeal by the police officer to the House of Lords, *held*, the absence of a belief in the truth of a defamatory allegation was conclusive evidence of improper motive amounting to express malice. Therefore, no valid reason existed for not holding that the same inference was necessarily to be drawn where the maker of the communication was proved to have intended by it to convey a defamatory allegation in the truth of which he did not believe, but which on a proper construction of the communication it was found not to bear. If the communication was found to bear some untrue defamatory allegation albeit not as serious as the maker of it intended, the qualified privilege was lost, because the occasion giving rise to it had been misused. Accordingly, the appeal would be dismissed.

Fraser v Mirza 1993 SLT 527 (House of Lords: Lords Keith of Kinkel, Goff of Chieveley, Jauncey of Tullichettle, Slynn of Hadley and Woolf).

1674 Defamation—settlement of action—statement in open court—nature of settlement

The plaintiff alleged that the defendants, newspaper owners and employees, had defamed her personally and in her business. The defendants pleaded justification. The defendants paid a sum into court, and wrote a letter on the same date stating that the payment in was made for commercial reasons only. The payment in was rejected. A further payment in was made, and the defendants again stated that it was made for commercial reasons. The plaintiff informed the defendants that she was going to set the action down for trial the next week. A further sum was paid into court, and the plaintiff accepted the payment in, which totalled £75,000. She then applied to the judge in pursuance of RSC Ord 82, r 5(1) to make a statement in open court. The defendants opposed the proposed terms of the statement, wishing to have included in the statement an explanation of their reasons for making the payment in. It fell to be determined whether the statement should refer only to the fact that the money paid into court was paid in without any admission of liability. *Held*, in order to make a decision, the nature of the allegations and the language in which they were expressed had to be considered along with the several other factors, including the fact that (1) the defendants' allegations were printed in seven articles over two months; (2) the newspaper had a large circulation where the plaintiff carried out her business; (3) the plaintiff contended that she had lost a large amount of business; (4) the defamatory meanings ascribed to the articles were meanings which the articles could be found to bear; (5) the defendants had maintained that the allegations were true and had supported that defence; (6) the defendants maintained that the plaintiff's claims for special damages and aggravated and exemplary damages were unsuitable; (7) a large enough sum had been paid into court to vindicate the plaintiff totally; (8) the defendants warned the plaintiff when they proposed to pay in £40,000, that it would put the plaintiff at risk with regard to the costs of her trial; (9) the payment in of £75,000 put the plaintiff seriously at risk with regard to the costs of trial; (10) the plaintiff had rejected earlier lower payments into court and established that until the payment reached £75,000, she was going to trial. In view of these factors, the plaintiff was entitled to a statement vindicating and exonerating her in every respect of all the allegations, and nothing said by the defendants detracted from the vindication. Judgment would accordingly be given for the plaintiff.

Charlton v EMAP plc (1993) Times, 11 June (Queen's Bench Division: Judge Previté).

LIBRARIES AND SCIENTIFIC AND CULTURAL INSTITUTIONS

Halsbury's Laws of England (4th edn) Vol 28, paras 301–500

1675 Public Lending Right Scheme—Central Fund—increase of limit

The Public Lending Right (Increase of Limit) Order 1993, SI 1993/799 (in force on 1 April 1993), increases from £4.75m to £5m the limit on sums to be paid into the Central Fund out of money provided by Parliament to satisfy liabilities of the fund in respect of the Public Lending Right in any financial year.

1676 Public Lending Right Scheme—variation

The Public Lending Right Scheme 1982 (Commencement of Variation) Order 1993, SI 1993/3049 (in force on 30 December 1993), varies the Public Lending Right Scheme 1982 by increasing the sum attributable to each qualifying loan from 1·86p to 2·00p.

LIMITATION OF ACTIONS

Halsbury's Laws of England (4th edn) Vol 28, paras 601–1000

1677 Articles

Limitation and Intentional Torts, W V H Rogers: 143 NLJ 258
Limitation of Actions—Where Are We Now? Nicholas Mullany: [1993] LMCLQ 34
Trespass to the Person and the Limitation Act 1980, Diana Tribe and Gill Korgaonkar (on *Stubbings v Webb* [1993] 1 All ER 322, HL (1992 Abr para 1629)): 137 SJ 157

1678 Limitation period—expiry—discretion to extend—abuse of process

The plaintiff suffered permanent brain damage during an operation. Solicitors acting on his behalf issued proceedings against the local health authority alleging negligence by the anaesthetist, but those proceedings were struck out for want of prosecution. After his retirement the anaesthetist destroyed all the records held by him in respect of the operation, but the plaintiff's new solicitors obtained the health authority's records in return for an assurance that the proceedings against them would not be resurrected. A new writ was issued against the anaesthetist, who subsequently joined the health authority as second defendant. Both defendants unsuccessfully applied to strike out the claim, but their subsequent appeal was successful. On appeal by the plaintiff, *held*, a litigant could be deprived of the statutory extension to a limitation period under the inherent jurisdiction of the court if there had been an abuse of process, even if the limitation period remained unexpired. The way in which the claim had initially been handled on the plaintiff's behalf, the years of inactivity before the matter had been resurrected, and the fact that the second defendants (with whom the anaesthetist had been closely associated) had been assured that action would not be taken against them if they provided information afforded sufficient evidence of an abuse of process to justify the decision to strike out the proceedings. The appeal would be dismissed.

Hogg v Hamilton [1992] PIQR P387 (Court of Appeal: Purchas and Mann LJJ and Sir Michael Kerr).

1679 Limitation period—expiry—discretion to extend—claim for lost income after death

The Limitation Act 1980, s 33 provides that the court may direct that the limitation provisions set out in the Act are waived in relation to a particular action if it appears to the court that it would be equitable to do so.

The plaintiffs were personal representatives claiming damages from the defendants as a result of a fatal accident. As well as a claim for damages for the estate, a claim was also made for the benefit of the dependent children under the Fatal Accidents Act 1976. The claim for damages for the estate was made outside the relevant limitation period but the court exercised its discretion under the 1980 Act, s 33 to allow the action to proceed. The defendants appealed on the ground that by making two separate claims the plaintiffs were seeking to give the children double damages which was unfair to the defendant and therefore it was inequitable to apply the 1980 Act, s 33. Although it came into force after the cause of the present action accrued, the Administration of Justice Act 1982 had abolished the right of a deceased's estate to claim damages for loss of income in respect of any period after the deceased's death (a "lost years" claim), which the defendant claimed was further evidence that to allow such a claim would be inequitable. *Held*, in the present case a claim for lost years would produce over-compensation. However, it was wrong to assume that because Parliament had legislated against lost years claims, an action containing such a claim was inequitable under the 1980 Act. The 1980 Act, s 33 was not concerned with whether the actual claim was equitable, but whether it was equitable to allow the action to proceed having regard to certain matters, which did not include the fairness of the laws of England at a given point of history. One of the matters for the court to take into account when deciding whether to exercise its discretion under the 1980 Act, s 33, was the prejudice to the defendant of the delay in bringing proceedings. In this case, insufficient prejudice to the defendant would be created by waiving the limitation period and, accordingly, the appeal would be dismissed.

Ward v Foss; Heathcote v Foss (1993) Times, 29 November (Court of Appeal: Sir Thomas Bingham MR, Simon Brown and Hobhouse LJJ).

1680 Limitation period—expiry—latent damage—knowledge of defects in respect of which damages are claimed

The plaintiff purchased a house in reliance upon a report of the defendant surveyors. He became aware of certain defects in the property, undetected by the defendants, but, in the belief that he had no cause of action against them, he had the defects repaired at his own expense. He subsequently became aware of further, more serious, defects in the property, similarly undetected, when a structural engineer's report was obtained. On the plaintiff's claim for damages for negligence, the defendants contended that the claim was statute-barred because time had begun to run against him when he first became aware of defects. *Held*, in the Limitation Act 1980, s 14A(6)(a), knowledge of "the damage in respect of which damages are claimed" meant knowledge of the particular head of damage in respect of which the plaintiff sought to claim damages, not damage in a general sense. Although the plaintiff was aware that the defendants had been negligent to some extent and decided to live with that situation, he was not thereby prevented from instituting proceedings in respect of the more serious example of their negligence of which he had earlier been unaware. The defendants' report was not so obviously defective as necessarily to alert the plaintiff to the desirability or necessity of obtaining a further report when he first became aware of defects in the property. The fact that claims in respect of heads of damage which were statute-barred were included in the plaintiff's claim did not vitiate the validity of his claim in respect of other heads of damage which were not statute-barred. Accordingly, his claim in respect of the more serious defects was not statute-barred.

Felton v Gaskill Osborne & Co [1993] 43 EG 118 (Liverpool County Court: Judge O'Donoghue).

1681 Limitation period—expiry—plaintiff's knowledge—personal injury arising from surgery

The appellant claimed against the defendant firm of solicitors for failing to prevent her claim in negligence against a surgeon from becoming statute-barred. The court found that she had no cause of action and she appealed. *Held*, the limitation period for an action in respect of personal injuries caused by medical negligence was three years from the date the cause of action accrued or (if later) the date of the appellant's knowledge that her injury was caused by damage following the act or omission of the surgeon. It was not necessary for knowledge sufficient for her solicitors to draft the statement of claim to have been accumulated before time began to run. Accordingly, the appeal would be dismissed.

Broadley v Guy Clapham & Co (1993) Times, 6 July (Court of Appeal: Balcombe, Leggatt and Hoffmann LJJ). *Bentley v Bristol and Western Health Authority* [1991] 2 Med LR 359 (1990 Abr para 1506) overruled.

1682 Limitation period—expiry—proceedings brought without authority— ratification

See *Presentaciones Musicales SA v Secunda*, para 64.

1683 Limitation period—time from which period runs—deliberate concealment of facts

The Limitation Act 1980, s 32(1) provides that where a fact which is relevant to the plaintiff's right of action has been deliberately concealed by the defendant, the period of limitation will not run until the plaintiff has discovered the concealment or could have discovered it by reasonable diligence.

The defendant applied to strike out the plaintiff's reply, based on s 32, to the defendant's plea of limitation. The defendant contended that s 32 applied to deliberate concealment which had occurred at the time when the cause of action arose, and not to any concealment which occurred later. *Held*, the provisions relating to concealment by fraud which were contained in the Limitation Act 1939, and which had been replaced by the 1980 Act, s 32, did apply to subsequent concealment. If there was deliberate concealment, the ordinary time limit would be extended so that the period would run from the time when the concealment was discovered or ought to be discovered. Deliberate concealment would only occur where the plaintiff was unaware of facts which were relevant to the right of action. At any point from the date at which the cause of action arose until the expiry of the ordinary limitation period, if there was unconscionable behaviour which concealed facts, that would discourage the plaintiff from pursuing the action. However, where a concealment took place after expiry of the limitation period, the plaintiff would have already lost the ability to sue so that the concealment had no detrimental effect and was not therefore unconscionable. Accordingly, the application would be dismissed.

Sheldon v R H M Outhwaite (Underwriting Agencies) Ltd (1993) Times, 8 December (Queen's Bench Division: Saville J).

LOCAL GOVERNMENT

Halsbury's Laws of England (4th edn) Vol 28, paras 1001–1403

1684 Articles

Care for the Elderly: Who Pays? Philip Spiers: 137 SJ 394
CCT and the Lawyers, Simon Carter and Ian Kinloch: 137 SJ 1025
CCT for Legal Services: Update, Stepen Cirell and John Bennett (on competitive tendering for legal services): 137 SJ 564, 584
Compulsory Competitive Tendering—An Appraisal, Alec Samuels: 157 LG Rev 581
Curbing Unauthorised Street Trading, Geoffrey Holgate: 157 JP Jo 634
Documenting CCT, Stephen Cirell and John Bennett (on the draft conditions of contract for CCT for legal services): 137 SJ 742
Local Authorities and Libel Again, Brian Bix and Adam Tomkins: 56 MLR 738
Reasons to be Cheerful, Alan Harrison (on competition in local authority legal services): 137 SJ

12

The Externalisation Option, John Bennett and Stephen Cirell (on competitive tendering for legal services): 137 SJ 514, 590
The Local Government Dimension, Alec Samuels: 157 LG Rev 521
Who is Subject to the Public Procurement Regime? John Bennett and Stephen Cirrell: 137 SJ 170
Who Needs to Know? Alan Harrison (on the public's right of access to information): 137 SJ 630

1685 Direct service organisations—competition

The Local Government (Direct Service Organisations) (Competition) Regulations 1993, SI 1993/848 (in force on 10 May 1993), provide for the conduct of competitive tendering for the carrying out of specified work by local authorities. Time limits are prescribed for the tendering procedure for work which does not fall within the Public Works Contracts Regulations 1991, SI 1991/2680, or Council Directive (EEC) 92/50, as are the maximum and minimum period which may elapse between announcing who will carry out work and the commencement of the work. The 1993 Regulations also prescribe conduct restricting, preventing or distorting competition, and matters which an authority is required to take into account in the course of evaluating tenders and its own bid for the work. Certain costs and other amounts must also be taken into account by local authorities. Provision is also made for the calculation and estimation of certain costs which authorities would incur as a result of accepting one of the tenders, for the issue of guidance as to how conduct restricting, distorting or preventing competition is to be avoided and for the extent of any contravention of such guidance to be taken into account in determining whether an authority has fulfilled the conditions for competition which apply in the case of any work.

1686 District auditor—statutory duty—duty owed to local authority and officers of local authority

A local council alleged that a number of its senior officers had procured payments to be made without proper authority and began proceedings against them for breach of contract and breach of fiduciary duty. The officers joined the employees of the Audit Commission responsible for auditing the accounts of the council during the relevant period as third parties, claiming contribution or indemnity from the auditors on the ground that the auditors had advised them in respect of matters relevant to the council's claim and that in reliance on that advice the officers performed their duties as servants or agents of the Audit Commission in accordance with the Local Government Finance Act 1982, Pt III. The auditors applied for the third party notices served by the officers to be set aside on the ground that they disclosed no reasonable cause of action. *Held*, the function of an audit was to scrutinise the actions of the servants or agents of the body whose accounts were being examined and not to protect those servants or agents. Thus, applying the test in *R v Deputy Governor of Parkhurst Prison, ex p Hague* [1990] 3 All ER 687 (1990 Abr para 1932), the officers had no cause of action against the auditor for damages for breach of statutory duty. As the object of an audit was to ensure that the money of the body in question had been properly spent and accounted for, the 1982 Act, Pt III was intended primarily to protect the council and the auditors owed a statutory duty to the council. However, the 1982 Act, Pt III did not expressly confer on the council any remedy for the enforcement of the statutory duty. In certain circumstances, the council could apply for judicial review, but that remedy afforded little protection against the negligent conduct of a statutory audit. Thus a claim by the council based on the breach of the statutory duty owed to it by the auditors was not bad in law. Accordingly, the application would be allowed in part.
West Wiltshire District Council v Garland, Cond (third party) [1993] 4 All ER 246 (Chancery Division: Morritt J).

1687 Employees—redundancy—continuity of employment

See para 1163.

1688 Finance—capital finance—credit arrangements

Capital finance of local authorities is dealt with in the Local Government and Housing Act 1989, Pt IV. Section 49(2) of the Act provides a formula for determining the value of consideration falling to be given by a local authority under a credit arrangement in any financial year after the one in which the arrangement comes into being. One of the factors referred to in the formula is the percentage rate of discount prescribed for a financial year. The Local

Authorities (Capital Finance) (Rate of Discount for 1993/94) Regulations 1993, SI 1993/312 (in force on 1 April 1993), prescribe 9·9 per cent for the financial year beginning on 1 April 1993.

1689 Finance—capital finance—credit liabilities

The Local Authorities (Capital Finance) (Amendment) (No 2) Regulations 1993, SI 1993/2014 (in force on 6 September 1993), amend the 1990 Regulations, SI 1990/432, in relation to the provisions for the use of amounts set aside to meet credit liabilities by enabling those provisions to apply to amounts set aside for the time being. The 1993 Regulations also delete a specified condition relating to the use of amounts set aside in consequence of housing disposals.

1690 Finance—capital finance—expenditure

The Local Authorities (Capital Finance) (Amendment) Regulations 1993, SI 1993/520 (in force on 1 April 1993), amend the 1990 Regulations, SI 1990/432, by providing (1) that a local authority's expenditure on the payment of interest included in the amount of a disposal cost attributable to a property acquired under the Housing Act 1988, Pt IV is expenditure for capital purposes; (2) that a sum in respect of the proceeds of disposal of premises which the Secretary of State has required the governing body of a grant-maintained school to pay to the local authority which is the former maintaining authority is a capital receipt; (3) for the reserved part of capital receipts derived from the disposal of mortgages or loans involving an advance to a housing association which was made for the purposes of expenditure in respect of which the association received a grant; and (4) in respect of financial years beginning on or after 1 April 1992, for the amount in respect of principal which is taken into account in determining an authority's minimum revenue provision for a year.

1691 Finance—capital finance—receipts

The Local Authorities (Capital Finance) (Amendment) (No 3) Regulations 1993, SI 1993/3054 (in force on 1 January 1994), further amend the 1990 Regulations, SI 1990/432. The regulations provide that certain sums received in respect of a disposal of a local authority on rent to mortgage terms will be capital receipts. Further provision has been made for reductions which an authority may make in its capital receipts before setting aside the reserved part as provision for credit liabilities.

1692 Finance—capital finance—transactions—bodies under local authority control public—airport companies

The Public Airport Companies (Capital Finance) (Fourth Amendment) Order 1993, SI 1993/2875 (in force on 17 December 1993), further amends the 1990 Order, SI 1990/719. The principal changes include (1) the exclusion of liabilities owed to a principal council which transfers all of its share in the equity share capital of a public airport company to a person which is not a local authority or a company or trust under the control or subject to the influence of a local authority, and (2) the exclusion of liabilities owed to such a person by reason of his holding a share in the equity share capital of a public airport company or of a subsidiary of such a company issued to such a person or transferred to such a person from the controlling authority or a constituent council of that authority.

1693 Finance—council tax—consequential amendments

The Local Government Finance (Housing) (Consequential Amendments) Order 1993, SI 1993/651 (in force on 1 April 1993) as amended by SI 1993/1120 (in force on 23 April 1993), makes amendments, consequential on the introduction of the council tax, to the Landlord and Tenant Act 1954, the Rent (Agriculture) Act 1976, the Rent Act 1977, the Housing Act 1985, the Landlord and Tenant Act 1985, the Housing Act 1988 and the Local Government and Housing Act 1989.

1694 Finance—council tax—parish councils

The Local Government Finance (Miscellaneous Provisions) (England) Order 1993, SI 1993/22 (in force on 1 February 1993), makes provision consequential upon and supplementary to the Local Government Finance Act 1992 in relation to billing authorities where a boundary order provides for the creation of a new parish or the transfer of a parish from the area of one billing authority to another.

1695   Finance—council tax—setting of amount—calculations to be made by billing authority

The Billing Authorities (Alteration of Requisite Calculations and Transitional Reduction Scheme) (England) Regulations 1993, SI 1993/401 (in force on 2 March 1993), amend the Local Government Finance Act 1992, ss 32(3), 33(3) to provide that the Common Council of the City of London, when calculating its budget requirement, is not to take into account sums which are to be transferred in respect of an amount calculated by reference to the provisional amount of its non-domestic rating contribution. The 1993 Regulations also amend SI 1993/175 (transitional reduction scheme) to provide for the special circumstances of the Common Council to be taken into account in calculating its council tax under the scheme.

1696   Finance—discretionary expenditure—annual limits

The Local Government Act 1972, s 137(4) provides that the annual limit on the amount of expenditure which a local authority may incur for purposes not otherwise authorised is to be determined by multiplying the relevant population of the authority's area by the sum appropriate to the authority.

The Local Authorities (Discretionary Expenditure) (Relevant Population) Regulations 1993, SI 1993/40 (in force on 1 April 1993), provide for the determination of the relevant population of local authority areas in England and Wales for the purposes of the 1972 Act, s 137(4).

The Local Authorities (Discretionary Expenditure Limits) Order 1993, SI 1993/41 (in force on 1 April 1993), specifies the sums appropriate to county and non-metropolitan district councils, London borough councils, the Common Council of the City of London and the Council of the Isles of Scilly for the purposes of the 1972 Act, s 137(4).

1697   Finance—payments—setting off of amounts

The Local Government Finance (Payments) (Welsh Authorities) Regulations 1993, SI 1993/613 (in force on 1 April 1993), replace the 1990 Regulations, SI 1990/609. The regulations make provision, where applicable, for the setting off of amounts, payable by the Secretary of State and a receiving authority under the Local Government Finance Act 1988, s 141(7) or (8), against each other.

1698   Finance—public path orders—recovery of costs

The Local Authorities (Recovery of Costs for Public Path Orders) Regulations 1993, SI 1993/407 (in force on 15 March 1993), provide for local authorities to impose charges for dealing with requests to make specified public path orders. The amount that may be charged cannot exceed the costs actually incurred, and there is a maximum of £400 for the making of an order relating to a path, plus £75 for each additional path included in the order, and the fee for one advertisement in a local newspaper on the making, confirmation and certification of the order.

1699   Finance—revenue support grant—payment to specified bodies

The Revenue Support Grant (Specified Bodies) (Amendment) Regulations 1993, SI 1993/139 (in force on 22 February 1993), amend the 1992 Regulations, SI 1992/89, in relation to any financial year beginning on or after 1 April 1993, so as to omit the entry relating to the Local Authorities' Race Relations Information Exchange and to amend the entry relating to the Local Authorities Co-ordinating Body on Trading Standards.

1700   Local authority—boundaries—alteration—judicial review

See *East Kilbride District Council v Secretary of State for Scotland*, para 28.

1701   Local authority—civil defence—functions

See para 2648.

1702   Local authority—discharge of functions—committees and political groups

The Local Government (Committees) (Amendment) Regulations 1993, SI 1993/1339 (in force 23 June 1993), amend the 1990 Regulations, SI 1990/1553, in respect of the circumstances in which the members of certain committees of local authorities may have voting rights. The 1993

Regulations enable the members of the Sussex Downs Conservation Board to vote in respect of the matters delegated to that body by the councils of the counties of East Sussex and West Sussex.

1703 Local authority—goods and services

The Local Authorities (Goods and Services) (Public Bodies) Order 1993, SI 1993/2097 (in force on 21 September 1993), designates eleven limited companies and two other bodies as public bodies under the Local Authorities (Goods and Services) Act 1970. A local authority may now provide goods and services to those bodies, but may only do so as long as the provision of goods and services relates to financial or other assistance to those bodies by any person for the purposes of regeneration of any part of the authority's area.

1704 Local authority—interest rate swap contracts—validity

See *Morgan Grenfell and Co Ltd v Welwyn Hatfield District Council (Islington London Borough Council, third party)*, para 212.

1705 Local authority—market licences

The Local Government Administration (Matters Subject to Investigation) Order 1993, SI 1993/940 (in force on 28 April 1993), amends the Local Government Act 1974, Sch 5 so that action taken in connection with transactions relating to either the grant, renewal or revocation of a licence to occupy a pitch or stall in a fair or market ceases to be excluded from investigation by a Commissioner for Local Administration.

1706 Local authority—meetings and proceedings—standing orders

The Local Authorities (Standing Orders) Regulations 1993, SI 1993/202 (in force on 1 April 1993), require local authorities to incorporate in standing orders provision relating to their staff, meetings and proceedings. Local authorities are also required to make provision in relation to chief officers, the recording of votes and the signing of minutes at extraordinary meetings.

1707 Local authority—members—allowances

The Local Authorities (Members' Allowances) (Amendment) Regulations 1993, SI 1993/545 (in force on 1 April 1993), amend the 1991 Regulations, SI 1991/351, by increasing the following allowances payable to local authority members by 1·5 per cent: (1) the amounts by reference to which a ceiling is imposed by the 1991 Regulations in relation to schemes for the payment of basic, special responsibility and attendance allowances; (2) the amount of special responsibility allowance under such a scheme which a member may be paid in any year; (3) the maximum amount of attendance allowance payable to parish and community councillors and the maximum financial loss allowance payable both to those councillors and to non-elected members of local authorities; and (4) the allowance payable for attendance at conferences and meetings.

1708 Local authority—powers—power to appropriate land

See *Sutton London Borough Council v Bolton*, para 2476.

1709 Local authority—powers—power to institute legal proceedings—defamation

A local authority instituted proceedings for defamation against a newspaper which had made allegations of financial impropriety on the part of the local authority and certain individual members. The local authority contended the allegations had resulted in loss and damage by injuring its credit and reputation, and at first instance it was held as a preliminary issue that the local authority could maintain a cause of action in defamation. The newspaper successfully appealed against that ruling, the Court of Appeal determining that the right to sue in defamation would enable the local authority to stifle legitimate public criticism of its activities. On appeal by the local authority, *held*, it was clearly established that trading corporations were entitled to sue in respect of defamatory matters which could be seen to have damaged their business dealings, but although a local authority could argue that defamatory statements could have an adverse affect on its ability to carry out its functions efficiently it was distinguished from other types of corporation in that it was a democratically-elected governmental body. It was highly important that such a body should be open to public criticism, and as the threat of a civil action for defamation would inevitably inhibit the freedom of speech it would be contrary to the public interest to allow the action to proceed. The decision of the Court of Appeal had been correct, and the appeal would be dismissed.

Derbyshire County Council v Times Newspapers Ltd [1993] 1 All ER 1011 (House of Lords: Lords Keith of Kinkel, Griffiths, Goff of Chieveley, Browne-Wilkinson and Woolf). Decision of Court of Appeal [1992] 3 All ER 65 (1992 Abr para 1664) affirmed.

1710 Local authority—public works contracts—competitive tendering—incorporated term

A local council invited tenders under the Local Government Act 1988 for the cleaning of public conveniences. The council issued instructions to tenderers that a specified performance bond would be required, and although no specific reference was made in the form of tender, a holding company guarantee incorporated by reference to a standard contract condition by which the tenderer agreed to be bound was also required. The plaintiff company, which was a wholly owned subsidiary, submitted a tender but did not offer either a performance bond or a holding company guarantee. The council accepted the tender but asked for the bond and guarantee. The plaintiff stated that it was company policy to offer either a bond or a guarantee but not both. However the council submitted that a contract existed between the parties and insisted that the plaintiff was bound by its tender to offer both the bond and the guarantee. The council's action for breach of contract was dismissed and the council appealed. *Held*, there was no contract in existence between the parties and therefore, by tendering for a council cleaning contract the plaintiff was not bound, in the absence of consideration, to provide a performance bond and a guarantee from its holding company as required by standard contract conditions incorporated into the form of tender. Accordingly, the appeal would be dismissed.

Southampton City Council v Academy Cleaning Services London Ltd (1993) Times, 11 June (Queen's Bench Division: Judge Zucker).

1711 Local authority—public works contracts—competitive tendering—position of employees

The employees were employed as building workers by a local authority. The authority had embarked on a programme of building work, and, after considering tenders from outside contractors, it had resolved to give the work to the employees. Owing to the economic climate, the authority subsequently sought fresh tenders for some of the work from the outside contractors. The employees contended that the authority had acted unfairly in going back on their previous resolutions, and that the authority had jeopardised their legitimate expectations that they would remain in secure employment for some time. They sought an order of certiorari to quash the authority's decision. At first instance, the employees' application was refused. On appeal, *held*, the employees were not entitled to expect or assume as a matter of public law that the council was committed to give all the work to the employees. The terms of the authority's resolution did not support such an assumption, and the authority could not reasonably be expected to have entered into an irrevocable commitment with the employees. The only legitimate expectation of the employees was that the council would not vary its resolutions except on rational grounds, and the authority had not failed to carry out its duty in this respect. The appeal would accordingly be dismissed.

R v Walsall Metropolitan Borough Council, ex p Yapp (1993) Times, 6 August (Court of Appeal: Nourse, Staughton and Nolan LJJ).

1712 Local authority—public works contracts—competitive tendering—restricted invitation procedure—refusal to invite to tender

The Public Works Contracts Regulations 1991, SI 1991/2680, reg 12 provides that a contracting authority may exclude a contractor from those persons from whom it will make the selection of persons to be invited to tender if the contractor fails to satisfy the minimum standards of economic and financial standing and technical capacity required.

A council invited tenders for the repair and maintenance of its housing stock. The adopted procedure had been the restricted invitation procedure under the 1991 Regulations, reg 12. The council had decided not to invite the defendants to tender for the contract because they had failed to meet three of the council's requirements of health and safety. The defendants then applied for an injunction restraining the council from awarding its housing maintenance contract until after the defendants had been allowed to tender for it. The application was on the grounds that it was not permissible under the 1991 Regulations for the council to take into account matters of health and safety when deciding whom to invite to tender. *Held*, matters of health and safety were within the ambit of the regulations. The phrase "technical capacity" meant the contractor's ability to carry out competently the operations of the contractor's trade, and as such that included the ability to carry it out with proper regard to the health and safety of their employees and the public. Accordingly, the application would be dismissed.

General Building and Maintenance plc v Greenwich London Borough Council [1993] IRLR 535 (Queen's Bench Division: Sir Godfray Le Quesne QC).

1713 Local authority—sole trustee of charity—conflicts of interests

The Charity Commissioners have stated that although they have hitherto been willing to appoint local authorities under schemes or orders as sole trustees of charities, they will in future carefully examine any proposal for such an appointment. There have been occasions when property held in trust by a local authority has been applied for other purposes, either because it was not realised that the property was held on trust or because it failed to appreciate the limitations on its use. The commissioners will now require to be satisfied that the appointment of a local authority is the most beneficial arrangement in the particular circumstances, and will have regard to possible conflicts of interests (see Decisions of the Charity Commissioners, Vol 1, p 29).

1714 Local authority—statutory duty—child in local authority care

See *Holtom v Barnet London Borough Council*, para 2457.

1715 Local Government Act 1992—commencement

The Local Government Act 1992 (Commencement No 3) Order 1993, SI 1993/3169, brings into force on 6 January 1994, s 11 (in part), and Sch 1, para 12 (which amends the Local Government Act 1988, s 6, concerning restrictions on functional work).

1716 Local Government (Amendment) Act 1993

The Local Government (Amendment) Act 1993, s 1 amends the Local Government Act 1966, s 11 to permit grants to be made to local authorities making special provisions in exercising their functions in consequence of the presence within their areas of persons belonging to ethnic minorities. Section 2 contains financial provisions and s 3 deals with short title, commencement and extent. The Act received the royal assent on 20 July 1993 and came into force on 20 September 1993.

1717 Local Government and Housing Act 1989—commencement

The Local Government and Housing Act 1989 (Commencement No 15) Order 1993, SI 1993/105 brings into force on 25 January 1993, Sch 11, para 14 (which adds to the privileges and immunities of representatives, members of subordinate bodies, high officers, experts and persons on missions listed in the International Organisations Act 1968, Sch 1, Pt II, the same exemption from being liable to pay a community charge or contribution to a collective community charge as is accorded to the head of a diplomatic mission) and so much of the 1989 Act, s 194(1) as relates to Sch 11, para 14.

The Local Government and Housing Act 1989 (Commencement No 16) Order 1993, SI 1993/2410, brings into force on 7 October 1993 ss 67–70, so far as not already in force, and s 73. Those provisions relate to companies in which local authorities have interests and trusts which are subject to local authority influence. For a summary of the Act, see 1989 Abr para 1464. For details of commencement, see the commencement table in the title STATUTES.

1718 Local Government (Overseas Assistance) Act 1993

The Local Government (Overseas Assistance) Act 1993, s 1 enables local authorities in Great Britain to provide advice and assistance as respects matters in which they have skill and experience to bodies engaged outside the United Kingdom in the carrying on of any of the activities of local government. Section 2 deals with short title, commencement and extent. The Act received the royal assent on 20 July 1993 and came into force on 20 September 1993.

1719 Local government reorganisation—distribution of capital receipts

The Local Government Reorganisation (Capital Money) (Greater London) (Amendment) Order 1993, SI 1993/2878 (in force on 22 December 1993), specifies money received by the

London Residuary Body as capital money for the purposes of the Local Government Act 1985, s 77 and provides for the distribution of some of it by the London Residuary Body to charging authorities in Greater London. The 1991 Order, SI 1991/439, has been amended by providing for a further distribution of capital money in accordance with specified proportions and by substituting new percentages for those specified in the 1991 Order.

1720 Local Government Staff Commission—establishment
The Local Government Staff Commission (England) Order 1993, SI 1993/1098 (in force on 12 May 1993), establishes the Local Government Staff Commission (England) and makes provision relating to the composition of the commission.

1721 Superannuation
See PENSIONS AND SUPERANNUATION.

LONDON GOVERNMENT

Halsbury's Laws of England (4th edn) Vol 29, paras 1–200

1722 Street trading—trading in unlicensed street—trading with permission of occupier
See O'Gorman v Brent London Borough Council, para 1752.

1723 Traffic regulation—parking
See paras 2212, 2213, 2214.

MAGISTRATES

Halsbury's Laws of England (4th edn) Vol 29, paras 201–600

1724 Articles
Alcohol-Server Training Schemes—A Pilot Study, Susan Light and Jane O'Brien: 157 JP Jo 423
Is it Reasonable to Commit for Poll Tax? Paul Russell: 157 JP Jo 697
Lay Justices or Stipendiaries? Michael O'Connor: 157 JP Jo 453
Reforming Magistrates' Courts—A Framework for Injustice? John Raine and Michael Willson: 157 JP Jo 661
Sentencing Guidelines for the Magistrates' Courts, Martin Wasik and Adrian Turner: [1993] Crim LR 345
Ten Years of Newton Hearings—Whither the Magistrates' Court, Stephen Johns (on R v Newton [1983] Crim LR 198 (1983 Abr para 2994)): 157 JP Jo 467, 483
The Abolition of Unit Fines—The Basic Implications, Leonard Jason-Lloyd: 157 JP Jo 679
The Merits of Legal Aid in the Magistrates' Courts, Richard Young: [1993] Crim LR 336

1725 Bail (Amendment) Act 1993
See para 676.

1726 Committal proceedings—justices hearing submission of abuse of process—adjournment of proceedings—subsequent hearing before stipendiary magistrate
Though the applicants appeared before justices at committal proceedings, the prosecution had no witnesses at court and could not proceed. The applicants submitted that the proceedings should be stayed as an abuse of process but the justices rejected that submission and adjourned the proceedings. Subsequently, a stipendiary magistrate ruled that he had the power to hear the committal proceedings. In an application to quash the decision of the stipendiary magistrate,

held, it was not true that when justices sat as examining justices they were necessarily inquiring into an offence. When justices sat as examining justices they did not embark on an inquiry into the offence until either the prosecution opened the case or witnesses were called or some step was taken pertinent to the committal of the case to trial. Examining justices had not commenced committal proceedings, despite having heard argument as to abuse of process, where the prosecution had not opened the case, no witness had been called and no other step pertinent to the committal of the case for trial had taken place. Accordingly, the application would be dismissed.

R v Worcester Magistrates' Court, ex p Leavesley (1993) Times, 14 January (Queen's Bench Division: Rose LJ and Pill J).

1727 Domestic proceedings—matrimonial injunctions
See HUSBAND AND WIFE.

1728 Family proceedings
See CHILDREN AND YOUNG PERSONS.

1729 Information—ambiguous information—remedy of defect
The Magistrates' Courts Rules 1981, SI 1981/552, r 100(1) states that an information must be in ordinary language avoiding as far as possible the use of technical terms and without necessarily stating all the elements of the offence. Rule 100(2) provides that in the case of a statutory offence the relevant provision must be referred to in the information.

The appellant was convicted under the Local Government Act 1963, Sch 12, paras 1 and 10 (1)(a) of being concerned in the management of public entertainment without a licence as required by the 1963 Act, Sch 12, para 1. His appeal was dismissed and he appealed by way of case stated against the dismissal on the basis that each information disclosed no offence known to law. It was argued on behalf of the appellant that: (1) there was a failure to aver that the entertainment was one for which a licence was required; and (2) the information was unclear and therefore defective under r 100(1) and the defect could not be corrected by the reference to the statute which was supposedly breached in accordance with r 100(2). *Held*, reference to a provision of a statute under r 100(2) could cure a defect in an information by clarifying something which was ambiguous. When looking at the information as a whole, the reference to the particular statutory provision could not be ignored. In the present case the ambiguities in the informations were cured by the reference to Sch 12, para 10(1) of the 1963 Act, which named the appellant as the person who was concerned in the entertainment without a licence as required by para 1. An offence known to law was therefore set down in each information. Accordingly, the appeal would be dismissed.

Karpinski v City of Westminster [1993] Crim LR 606 (Queen's Bench Division: Rose LJ and Waller J).

1730 Information—duplicity of information—circumstances
It has been held that there are five circumstances where informations can be duplicitous, being (1) where two or more separate offences are joined together in one information, for example dangerous driving and careless driving, (2) where two offences are charged separately or in the alternative in one information, (3) where an offence can be committed in more ways than one, for example driving under the influence of drink or drugs, (4) where a single offence is charged in respect of an activity involving two or more acts, for example stabbing somebody five times and (5) where a single activity is charged but several particulars go to prove the offence, for example a deception involving several misrepresentations.

Carrington Carr Ltd v Leicestershire County Council [1993] Crim LR 938 (Queen's Bench Division: Neill LJ and Mantell J).

1731 Justices—adjournment of hearing—factors to be considered—judicial review
It has held that the following factors should be taken into account in determining whether an adjournment should be granted to any of the parties to a matter arising in the magistrates' court, and whether fairness dictated that an adjournment should be granted, such that any refusal to grant that adjournment would lead to an application for judicial review: (1) the importance of the proceedings, (2) the likely adverse consequences for the person seeking the adjournment, (3)

the risk of prejudice if the application were not granted, (4) the convenience of the court and the interests of justice in ensuring that cases were dealt with efficiently so that future parties to litigation were not delayed, and (5) the extent to which the applicant had been responsible for the circumstances which led to the application for an adjournment.

R v Kingston upon Thames Justices, ex p Martin (1993) Times, 10 December (Queen's Bench Division: Simon Brown LJ and Buckley J).

1732 Justices—breach of natural justice—dismissal of information for want of prosecution

On the day the defendant's case was fixed for trial, an error in the court listing office resulted in the case being listed for hearing in a different court to that in which the prosecution had been informed that the case would be heard. When the prosecution were informed that no prosecutor had attended in the court where the case was listed, they made arrangements for a prosecutor to be available. The justices were informed about the listing error and the pending arrival of a prosecutor, but shortly afterwards in exercise of their powers under the Magistrates' Courts Act 1980, ss 10, 15, they acceded to an application by the defence to dismiss the information for want of prosecution. On an application for a declaration that the justices had acted in breach of the principles of natural justice, *held*, the exercise of justices' statutory powers should not contravene natural justice. Both the prosecution and the defence should be treated fairly and prosecutions which were properly brought and conducted should be allowed to be properly presented. The justices had acted unfairly and the application would accordingly be granted.

R v Dudley Magistrates' Court, ex p DPP (1993) 157 JP 177 (Queen's Bench Division: Mann LJ, French and Auld JJ).

1733 Justices—decision—costs—appeal

The Crown Court decided that it was entitled to determine that it had jurisdiction to hear an appeal against a costs decision of justices made under the Magistrates' Courts Act 1980, s 64 in civil proceedings brought under the Control of Pollution Act 1974, s 16 but that the terms of settlement of the proceedings before the justices had ousted that jurisdiction. On an application for judicial review of those decisions, *held*, within the statutory framework in magistrates' courts, there was no free-standing right of appeal against a costs order. The appeal provisions of the 1974 Act, s 85 did not provide for an appeal against the justices' decision on costs. The application would be refused.

R v Crown Court at Canterbury, ex p Kent County Council (1993) Times, 22 July (Queen's Bench Division: Kennedy LJ and Macpherson J).

1734 Justices—decision—duty to consider evidence—appearance of bias

The applicant was charged with being drunk and disorderly and assaulting a police officer in the exercise of his duty. At his trial, during his examination-in-chief, the magistrate looked at a law report to establish its relevancy to the case. The applicant was subsequently convicted. On appeal, the applicant sought to quash the decision. *Held*, the correct test was whether there was the appearance of bias, rather than whether there was actual bias. It was a judicial duty to give the case an undivided attention. When evidence was being given, particularly by a defendant-in-chief, it was not likely to be appropriate for a magistrate to study a law report without halting proceedings. The conclusion was that a reasonable and fair-minded person, knowing all the relevant facts, would rightly entertain a reasonable suspicion that the magistrate's attention had been divided and incomplete. The conviction would accordingly be quashed.

R v Marylebone Magistrates' Court, ex p Joseph [1993] NLJR 655n (Queen's Bench Division: Rose LJ and Waller J).

1735 Justices—decision—inference of improper participation by justices' clerk

The applicant was charged with four road traffic offences arising out of one incident of allegedly reckless driving. When the justices retired to consider their decision the court clerk left the court and did not return until the justices had re-assembled and were about to deliver their verdict. The clerk then spoke to the justices and went with them when they retired for a second time to reconsider their verdict, but she failed to give the parties an explanation for her actions. The applicant, who accepted that the clerk had being clarifying the law in order to ensure his interests were safeguarded, was granted leave to apply for judicial review of the justices' decision to convict him on three of the charges. *Held*, the clerk's conduct had been such that a reasonable defendant or bystander might have concluded that the clerk had been participating in the decision-making process. She should have explained her reasons for leaving the court to the parties, which would have rendered her conduct impeccable, but her failure to do so meant the application for judicial review had to be allowed. Accordingly, the convictions would be quashed.

R v Eccles Justices, ex p Farrelly (1992) 157 JP 77 (Queen's Bench Division: Mann LJ and French J).

1736 Justices—decision—sentence—challenge—appropriate mode of challenge

It has been held that applications for judicial review of sentences imposed by justices are to be discouraged where a defendant has a statutory right of appeal to the Crown Court and a statutory right of requesting a case stated from the justices.

R v Ealing Justices, ex p Scrafield (1993) Times, 29 March (Queen's Bench Division: Evans LJ and Morland J).

1737 Justices—decision—use of specialist knowledge

See *DPP v Curtis*, para 2180.

1738 Justices—decision—validity of repealed legislation

See *R v Folkestone Justices, ex p Kibble*, para 27.

1739 Justices—jurisdiction—issue of summons—exercise of discretion

The applicant's son died following a collision with the defendant's van. The Crown Prosecution Service (CPS) subsequently laid informations and issued summonses against the defendant, the most serious allegation being that he had driven without due care and attention. At the hearing, the applicant laid an information and requested that the magistrate issue a summons in respect of the offence of causing death by reckless driving. The magistrate refused and the applicant sought judicial review of the decision. *Held*, the Magistrates' Courts Act 1980, s 1 gave the magistrate a discretion to issue a summons. In exercising it the magistrate had a duty to consider all the relevant circumstances, particularly: (1) whether the incident had been investigated by a responsible prosecuting authority, and (2) that the CPS had a duty to charge the most serious offence available on the evidence with a view to gaining a conviction. Where the Crown had already laid one or more informations against a defendant, the magistrate should only accede to a private prosecutor's request that he issue another summons in respect of the same incident with great caution. The magistrate had exercised his discretion correctly and accordingly the application would be dismissed.

R v Tower Bridge Metropolitan Stipendiary Magistrate, ex p Chaudhry [1994] 1 All ER 44 (Queen's Bench Division: Kennedy LJ and Bell J).

1740 Magistrates' courts—fees

The Magistrates' Courts Fees (Amendment) Order 1993, SI 1993/1889 (in force on 1 August 1993), revokes the 1992 Order, SI 1992/842, and amends provisions relating to certain court fees for civil business in magistrates' courts. The order introduces new fees in respect of proceedings concerning the council tax and proceedings under the Child Support Act 1991, and clarifies the fees payable in respect of warrants of entry. The order also makes it clear that no fee is payable in relation to any stage of binding over proceedings, and breaks down the composite fee for "other civil proceedings" into separate fees for complaints or applications, summonses, orders, and warrants.

1741 Magistrates' courts—justices' clerk—consultation with magistrates—duty to hear legal submissions

It has been held that, where a clerk who is not present in court when legal submissions are made is asked to advise the magistrates on points of law, it is of the utmost importance that he hears in open court those submissions from the parties concerned in order to avoid the appearance of bias.

R v Chichester Magistrates' Court, ex p DPP (1993) 157 JP 1049 (Queen's Bench Division: Evans LJ and Morland J).

1742 Magistrates' courts—legal representation—eligibility

See *R v Liverpool City Magistrates, ex p McGhee*, para 1664.

1743   Magistrates' courts—rules

The Magistrates' Courts (Miscellaneous Amendments) Rules 1993, SI 1993/1183 (in force on 24 May 1993), amend the Justices' Clerks Rules 1970, SI 1970/231, and the Magistrates' Courts Rules 1981, SI 1981/552. The amendments to the 1970 Rules enable certain persons appointed as justices' clerks' assistants to deal with various matters authorised to be done by the clerk himself. A clerk (and a person assisting him) is now authorised to issue warrants for failure to surrender to the court and warrants of distress, and to adjourn criminal proceedings, where the prosecution does not object, in the absence of the accused. A clerk is also authorised to commit a person who is on bail under the Magistrates' Court Act 1980, s 6(2), to ask an accused if he pleads guilty or not guilty to a charge, to fix or set aside a date for the trial of an information, to apply for deductions to be made from an offender's income support, and to amend or vary probation orders, community service orders and attendance centre orders in certain circumstances. The amendments to the 1981 Rules require a court, where it appears in a trial that an information charges more than one offence, to ask the prosecution to decide on which offence it wishes to proceed. New procedures are introduced for informations where the accused is not legally represented and the clerk is now required to take a note of the arguments in bail hearings. Entries on the register of convictions may be certified as authentic rather than individually signed, and where a decision is appealed against, the clerk is required to send a copy of the relevant extract of the register to the Crown Court. New provision is made with regard to the issue of warrants out of hours and the requirement to prove that a summons came to the recipient's knowledge (where it was not delivered to him) in order to prove service of the summons is removed. The procedure for an application by a disqualified driver under the Road Traffic Offenders Act 1988, s 34B(6) or (7) for the review of a notice issued to him by the organiser of a road traffic rehabilitation course, or for a declaration of default in respect of that organiser, is also prescribed.

1744   Maintenance orders

See DIVORCE.

1745   Mode of trial—supply of advance information—power to order

Certain video tapes containing allegedly pornographic material were seized from the defendant by Customs and Excise officers. The question arose whether there was a power under the Magistrates' Courts (Advance Information) Rules 1985, SI 1985/601, to order the prosecution to provide the defence with copies of the seized tapes. *Held*, there was no such power but it was open to the justices to exercise the power of adjournment under the Magistrates' Courts Act 1980, s 10(1) in order to encourage the prosecution to make fuller disclosure of evidence for the purpose of enabling the defendant to determine the most appropriate mode of trial. However, in the present case, it would not have been reasonable to have adjourned since the content of the video tapes could be easily determined from the written evidence.

  R v Dunmow Justices, ex p Nash (1993) 156 JP 1153 (Queen's Bench Division: Watkins LJ and Tuckey J).

1746   Petty sessional divisions

Under the powers conferred by the Justices of the Peace Act 1979, ss 23(3), (5), the Secretary of State has made the following orders:

County or borough	SI 1993 No
City of Salford	2149
Cumbria	2352
Devon	1361
Dorset	2274
East Sussex	844
Kent	2148
Suffolk	2880

1747   Probation areas

The Combined Probation Areas Order 1986, SI 1986/1713, as amended, has been further amended by the following orders to take account of the reorganisation of certain petty sessions areas:

Probation area affected	SI 1993 No
Cornwall	71
Cumbria	2852
Devon	1364
Dorset	2512
East Sussex	2332
Greater Manchester	2853
Hertfordshire	2151
Kent	173, 3142
Northumbria	748
Powys	52
Staffordshire	749
Suffolk	3139
Surrey	750

The 1986 Order has also been amended by the Combined Probation Areas (Amendment) (No 2) Order 1993, SI 1993/716, so that a committee for a combined probation area may appoint as its secretary such person as it thinks fit.

The Combined Probation Areas (Amendment) Order 1993, SI 1993/92, amends the 1992 Order, SI 1992/2121, for the purpose of making it clear that the terms of appointment which are shortened by that order are those of persons who were, immediately before 31 March 1993, members of the Middlesex, North East London, South East London and South West London Probation Committees, as well as having been appointed in the specified circumstances.

1748 Probation order—breach—sentence

See *R v Ipswich Justices, ex p Best*, para 2287.

1749 Probation rules

The Probation (Amendment) Rules 1993, SI 1993/367 (in force on 1 April 1993), amend the 1984 Rules, SI 1984/647, by providing that co-opted members of a probation committee are now eligible to be the chairman or deputy chairman of the committee. The 1993 Rules also dispense with the requirement that the chief financial officer of the local authority liable for the expenses of a committee is to be its treasurer and provide that a committee may now appoint as treasurer such person as it thinks fit.

1750 Probation Service Act 1993

The Probation Service Act 1993 consolidates certain enactments relating to the probation service and its functions and to arrangements for persons on bail and the rehabilitation of offenders. The Act received the royal assent on 5 November 1993 and came into force on 5 February 1994. A table showing the destination of enactments consolidated appears overleaf.

DESTINATION TABLE

This table shows in column (1) the enactments repealed by the Probation Service Act 1993 and in column (2) the provisions of that Act corresponding thereto.

In certain cases the enactment in column (1), though having a corresponding provision in column (2), is not, or not wholly, repealed as it is still required, or partly required, for the purposes of other legislation.

A "dash" adjacent to a repealed provision indicates that that provision is spent, unnecessary or for some other reason not specifically reproduced.

A reference to "LC rec" is a reference to one of the recommendations of the Law Commission in its Report on the Consolidation of Certain Enactments Relating to the Probation Service (Cm 2256; Law Com No 214).

(1)	(2)	(1)	(2)
Children and Young Persons Act 1969 (c 54)	Probation Service Act 1993 (c 47)	Powers of Criminal Courts Act 1973 (c 62)	Probation Service Act 1993 (c 47)
s 13(3)*	s 4(1), (4)	para 2(5)	Cf Sch 2, para 6
		para 3(1)	s 4(1)–(3), (5), LC rec 4
Courts Act 1971	Probation Service Act 1993 (c 47)	para 3(2)	s 8(2)
		para 3(2A)	s 5
		para 3(3)	s 28(1), (2)
s 53(6)†, (7)(a)	—	para 3(4)	Cf Sch 2, para 7
		para 3(5)	—
Powers of Criminal Courts Act 1973 (c 62)	Probation Service Act 1993 (c 47)	para 4(1)	s 12(1), Sch 1, para 4(1)
		para 4(1A)	s 12(3), Sch 1, para 4(2)
		para 4(2)	s 13(1)
s 47	—	para 4(3)	s 12(2)
s 49(1)	s 27(1)	para 4(4)	s 28(3)
s 49(2)	s 27(2)	para 5(1)	s 12(4), Sch 1, para 5
s 49(3)	Rep 1982 c 48, ss 65, 78, Sch 11, para 1(b), Sch 16	para 5(2)	s 13(2)
		para 6	Sch 1, para 6
		para 6A	Sch 1, para 7
s 51(1)(a)	—	para 6B	Sch 1, para 8
s 51(2)	Rep 1982 c 48, s 78, Sch 16	para 7	Rep 1988 c 33, ss 132, 170(2), Sch 11, paras 1, 4, Sch 16
s 51(3)	s 20(1)–(3)	para 8(1)	s 14
s 51(3A)	s 21	para 8(2)	—
s 51(4), (5)	s 22(3)	para 9	s 4(1), (4), LC rec 3
s 51(6)	s 22(1)	Pt II, para 10(1) . .	s 6(1)
s 51(7)	ss 22(2), 30(1)	para 10(2)	Rep 1988 c 48, s 78, Sch 16
s 51(8)	—	para 10(3)	s 6(2)
s 54(1)*	s 31(1)	para 11	s 7
s 54(2)*, (3)†	s 31(2)	para 12(1)	s 8(1)
s 54(4)†	—	para 12(2)	s 8(2)
s 57(1)*	s 30(1)	para 12A	s 9
ss 58*, 59*	s 33(3)	Pt III, para 13(1) . .	Sch 1, para 10(1)
Sch 3, Pt I, para 1(1) .	s 2(1), (4), (5), LC rec 2	para 13(2)	Rep 1988 c 48, s 78, Sch 16
para 1(2)	s 2(2)	para 13(3)	Sch 1, para 10(2)
para 1(3)	s 2(3)	para 14(1)	s 16, LC rec 5
para 1(4)	—	para 14(2), (3) . . .	Rep 1988 c 48, s 78, Sch 16
para 1(5)	s 1(c)		
para 2(1)	s 3(1), (2)	para 15(1)	ss 17(2), (3), 19(1)
para 2(2)(a)	Sch 1, para 1(2), (3)	para 15(2)	s 17(2), (3), LC rec 6
para 2(2)(b)	Sch 1, para 2	para 15(3)	s 19(2)
para 2(3)	Sch 1, para 1(1)		
para 2(4)	Sch 1, para 3		

* Not repealed   † Repealed in part

(1)	(2)
Powers of Criminal Courts Act 1973 (c 62)	Probation Service Act 1993 (c 47)
para 15(4)	Rep 1985 c 51, s 102(2), Sch 17
para 16	s 18
para 16A	s 17(4), (5)
para 17(1)–(3) . . .	s 10
para 17(4)	—
para 18(1)	s 25(1), LC rec 7
para 18(2)	Sch 1, para 11
para 18(3)	s 25(2)
para 18A	s 15
para 19(1)	s 30(1)
para 19(2)	Rep 1985 c 51, s 102(2), Sch 17
Sch 4, para 2	—
Sch 5, para 10 . . .	Cf Sch 3, para 2(1), (2)(b)
para 14	—
para 35	Cf Sch 3, para 3(1), (2)(a)
para 36	Sch 3, para 3(1), (3)
para 37	—
para 38	Cf Sch 3, para 3(1), (4)
para 41	—

(1)	(2)
Juries Act 1974 (c 23)	Probation Service Act 1993 (c 47)
Sch 1, Pt I, Group B†	—

(1)	(2)
Criminal Law Act 1977 (c 45)	Probation Service Act 1993 (c 47)
Sch 12†, para 6	s 27
para 7	—
para 8	ss 20(2), 22(3)
para 9(a)	s 30(1)
para 9(b)	—
para 11(1)	—
para 11(2)	s 4(1)
para 11(3), (4) . . .	—
para 11(5)	s 15
para 11(6)	—

(1)	(2)
Criminal Justice Act 1982 (c 48)	Probation Service Act 1993 (c 47)
s 65(1)	Passim
s 65(2)	—
Sch 11, para 1(a) . . .	—
para 1(b)	s 27(3)
para 1(c)	—
paras 2–5	—
para 6(a)(i)	—
para 6(a)(ii)	s 8(2)
para 6(a)(iii)	s 5
para 6(a)(iv)	—

(1)	(2)
Criminal Justice Act 1982 (c 48)	Probation Service Act 1993 (c 47)
para 6(a)(v)	Rep 1991 c 58, s 101(2), Sch 13
para 6(b)	ss 12(1)–(4), 13, Sch 1, paras 4(1), (5)
para 6(c)	Sch 1, para 6
para 6(d)	s 6(1)
para 6(e)	s 25(1), Sch 1, para 10(1)
para 6(f)	—
Sch 17, paras 16, 17 . .	—

(1)	(2)
Local Government Act 1985 (c 51)	Probation Service Act 1993 (c 47)
s 15(1)	ss 10, 19
s 15(2)	s 30(3)
s 15(3)	Sch 1, para 9(1)
s 15(4)	Sch 1, para 9(2), (3)
s 15(5)	—
s 15(6)	LC rec 7

(1)	(2)
Criminal Justice Act 1988 (c 33)	Probation Service Act 1993 (c 47)
s 132	—
Sch 11, para 1	—
para 2(a)	s 12(1), Sch 1, para 4(1)
para 2(b)	s 12(3), Sch 1, para 4(2)
para 2(c)	s 28(3)
para 3	Sch 1, paras 7, 8
para 4	—
para 5	s 6(2)
para 6	s 25(1)
Sch 15, para 42	s 5
para 105	Sch 1, para 9(3)

(1)	(2)
Children Act 1989 (c 41)	Probation Service Act 1993 (c 47)
Sch 13, para 34	s 5

(1)	(2)
Criminal Justice Act 1991 (c 53)	Probation Service Act 1993 (c 47)
s 15(1)(a), (b)	s 26(1)
s 15(1)(d)★	s 26(2)
s 15(2)	s 26(3)
s 15(3)(a)★, (b)★	s 26(2)
s 15(4)	—
s 73(1)	s 23(1)
s 73(2)	s 23(2)
s 73(3)	s 24
s 73(4)	s 23(3)
s 74	s 11

★ Not repealed   † Repealed in part

(1)	(2)	(1)	(2)
Criminal Justice Act 1991 (c 53)	Probation Service Act 1993 (c 47)	Criminal Justice Act 1991 (c 53)	Probation Service Act 1993 (c 47)
s 75(1)	—	s 94(1)	s 21
s 75(2)	s 2(3)	s 94(2)(a)	s 4(1)–(3)
s 75(3)	ss 12(1)–(4), 13, 25(2), Sch 1, paras 1(1), 4, 5, 6, 10(2)	s 94(2)(b)	s 4(3)
		s 94(2)(c)	—
s 75(4)	Sch 1, para 1(1)(b)	s 96	s 20(2)(d)(ii)
s 75(5)	s 18	s 97	s 9
s 75(6)(a)	s 10	s 98(a)†	—
s 75(6)(b)	—	Sch 11, para 17(1) . .	—
s 75(7)	s 30(1)	para 17(2)	s 14
		para 41(2)(b)* . . .	Sch 1, para 1(1)(c)

* Not repealed   † Repealed in part

1751 Summary offence—substitution for offence triable either way—abuse of process
The defendant was charged with assault occasioning actual bodily harm and elected trial by jury. Nine weeks later that charge was substituted by a charge of common assault. Following the defendant's submission that the delay in preferring the latter charge would prejudice him and was an abuse of process, the magistrates' court stayed the proceedings. The prosecutor applied for judicial review of the magistrates' court's decision. *Held*, the defendant's solicitor was aware of the proposed substitution but at the time did not express any objection or refer to any prejudice. The reason given for the substitution of the lesser offence was the comparatively minor nature of the injuries sustained by the complainant. It was accepted that the prosecution were not bound to prefer the gravest charge possible on the facts, and as such the charge to be preferred was a matter for their discretion. In the absence of bad faith the prosecutor's motive was irrelevant and accordingly, orders of certiorari and mandamus would be granted.
R v Sheffield Justices, ex p DPP [1993] Crim LR 136 (Queen's Bench Division: McCowan LJ and Jowitt J).

MARKETS AND FAIRS

Halsbury's Laws of England (4th edn) Vol 29, paras 601–716

1752 Street trading—street trading in Greater London—trading in unlicensed street—trading with permission of occupier
The London Local Authorities Act 1990, s 38(1)(a) provides that a person who engages in street trading in London in an unlicensed street is guilty of an offence. The 1990 Act, s 21(2)(j) provides that the sale, exposure or offer for sale or offer or provision of services on any land comprised in a street by the owner or occupier of the land is not street trading for the purposes of the Act.
The appellant traded from tables set up in the forecourt of a store with the permission of the store manager. He was convicted of engaging in street trading in an unlicensed street contrary to the 1990 Act, s 38(1)(a). He appealed on the ground that he fell within the exception in s 21(2)(j) of the Act. *Held*, whether the appellant, as a licensee of the forecourt, was an occupier of the land was a question of fact and degree depending on the nature of the permission to trade given by the manager. The appellant had a licence for the limited purpose of setting up tables on the forecourt and trading from it. He did not acquire from the licence any right to trade, power, possession or control of the area. Accordingly, he was not an occupier within the meaning of s 21(2)(j) and the appeal would be dismissed.
O'Gorman v Brent London Borough Council (1993) Times, 20 May (Queen's Bench Division: Evans LJ and Morland J).

MEDICINE, PHARMACY, DRUGS AND MEDICINAL PRODUCTS

Halsbury's Laws of England (4th edn) Vol 30 (reissue), paras 1–1000

1753 Articles
Advertising and Marketing Pharmaceutical Products, Richard Lawson: 137 SJ 1053
Airedale NHS Trust v Bland, Michael Hinchcliffe and Dr Keith Andrews (see [1993] 1 All ER 821, HL (1992 Abr para 1770)): [1993] Fam Law 137
Informed Consent to Treatment, Rajeev Thacker (on doctors' duties in Australia): 143 NLJ 1342
Medical Treatment—The Mother's Rights, Jo Bridgeman: [1993] Fam Law 534
Sexual Fantasies, Anaesthesia and False Accusations, Malcolm Weller (on doctors being accused of sexual impropriety): 143 NLJ 1471
The Dilemma of Parental Choice, Claire Gilham (on withholding medical treatment): 143 NLJ 1219

The Right to Die, Carol Brennan (on *Airedale NHS Trust v Bland* [1993] 1 All ER 821, HL (1992 Abr para 1770)): 143 NLJ 1041

1754 Access to health records—control of access

The Access to Health Records (Control of Access) Regulations 1993, SI 1993/746 (in force on 13 April 1993), preclude access under the Access to Health Records Act 1990, s 3(2) to any part of a health record where the granting of access would disclose information showing that an identifiable individual was, or may have been, born as a consequence of treatment services provided in accordance with the Human Fertilisation and Embryology Act 1990.

1755 Clinical thermometers—EC requirements

The Clinical Thermometers (EEC Requirements) Regulations 1993, SI 1993/2360 (in force on 21 October 1993), implement Council Directive (EC) 76/764. The regulations make provisions relating to EC pattern approval and verification in respect of clinical thermometers and provide for powers of inspection.

1756 Consent to treatment—patient informed of associated risks—interruption of treatment—duty to re-inform patient

Canada

The patient suffered a brain haemorrhage. She consented to medical tests after being fully informed of the associated risks. During a test the patient became agitated and the test was stopped at her request. A doctor recommended that the test be completed and the patient consented to this. The patient suffered a severe reaction which left her a quadriplegic. The plaintiff brought an action against the doctor, contending that her consent to the resumption of the test was invalid because the doctor did not give another warning of the risks involved. The trial judge dismissed the action and that decision was upheld on appeal. On further appeal, *held*, where a patient consents to the continuation of a medical procedure, such consent must be fully informed. Whilst a patient must be informed of any material change in circumstances which affected risk-assessment, there had been no material change of circumstances in this case and so a repeat explanation was not necessary. Accordingly, the patient's consent to completion of the test was valid and the appeal would be dismissed.

    Ciarlariello v Keller (1993) 100 DLR (4th) 609 (Supreme Court of Canada). Decision of Ontario Court of Appeal (1991 Abr para 1640) affirmed.

1757 Consent to treatment—refusal of treatment—capacity of individual

See *Re C*, para 1791.

1758 Controlled drugs—drugs and drug addiction—European Monitoring Centre for Drugs and Drug Addiction

See para 2750.

1759 Controlled drugs—production and supply—licence fees

The Misuse of Drugs (License Fees) (Amendment) Regulations 1993, SI 1993/539 (in force on 1 April 1993), further amend the Misuse of Drugs (Licence Fees) Regulations 1986, SI 1986/416, so as to increase by approximately 4·5 per cent, the fee payable in relation to a licence to produce, supply or offer to supply or possess controlled drugs.

1760 Dangerous drugs—offences

See CRIMINAL LAW.

1761 General Medical Council—discrimination—jurisdiction of industrial tribunal

See *Khan v General Medical Council*, para 255.

1762 General Medical Council—professional conduct committee—procedure

Scotland

A Scottish doctor practising in Scotland was charged before the professional conduct committee of the General Medical Council with serious professional misconduct arising out of acts of dishonesty. The committee sat in Scotland for the first time, but the parties were represented by English counsel, the hearing was attended by an English legal assessor and English law was applied. The committee found the doctor guilty of professional misconduct and directed that his name be erased from the register of medical practitioners. The doctor appealed, arguing that Scottish law applied to the hearing before the committee and that the assessor's failure to advise on corroboration amounted to a material misdirection. *Held*, although the professional conduct committee could sit anywhere in the United Kingdom, English law applied to its proceedings wherever they took place. Even if Scottish law had applied, the civil law of evidence rendered corroboration unnecessary. Even in the event that corroboration was required, there was ample evidence to corroborate the evidence of the doctor's dishonesty. In charges brought against a doctor where the events giving rise to the charges would also found serious criminal charges, it might be appropriate for criminal standards of proof to apply. However, although it was of prime importance that the charge and the conduct of the proceedings before the committee was fair to the doctor in question in all respects, where the charges faced by a doctor could not be the subject of criminal proceedings, it was unnecessary for criminal standards of proof to be applied. Accordingly, the appeal would be dismissed.

McAllister v General Medical Council [1993] 2 WLR 308 (Privy Council: Lords Keith of Kinkel, Griffiths and Jauncey of Tullichettle). *Lanford v General Medical Council* [1989] 2 All ER 193, HL (1989 Abr para 1520) not applied.

1763   General Optical Council—registration and enrolment—fees

The General Optical Council (Registration and Enrolment (Amendment) Rules) Order of Council 1993, SI 1993/483 (made on 26 February 1993), approves rules which increase, with effect from 1 April 1993, the fees payable to the General Optical Council by ophthalmic and dispensing opticians and bodies corporate carrying on business as opticians for registration, enrolment, retention, restoration to, and transfer within the Register of Opticians. Previous rules effecting fee increases are revoked.

1764   Hearing Aid Council—disciplinary proceedings—monetary penalties

The Hearing Aid Council Monetary Penalty (Increase) Order 1993, SI 1993/3052 (in force on 31 December 1993) increases the maximum monetary penalty which may be imposed by the Disciplinary Committee of the Hearing Aid Council from £1000 to £5000.

1765   Medical practitioner—advertising of practice—restrictions on advertising

See *Colman v United Kingdom*, para 1411.

1766   Medical practitioner—disciplinary proceedings—length of proceedings

See *Darnell v United Kingdom*, para 1419.

1767   Medical practitioner—duty of care—artificial insemination—HIV infection

Canada
The plaintiff contracted HIV as a result of an artificial insemination procedure (AI) carried out by the defendant doctor using infected semen. Knowledge of the transmission of HIV via AI at that time, was not widespread. The defendant was found liable in negligence and appealed. *Held*, the jury ought to have been instructed to decide whether the doctor had conducted himself as a reasonable doctor would have done in similar circumstances. In so deciding, the jury had to confine itself to prevailing standards of practice. In the present case, the doctor had acted in accordance with the standards of AI practice current at the time of the plaintiff's insemination and was not therefore negligent in being unaware of the risk of HIV infection. The only issue was whether the doctor had taken reasonable steps to protect his patients against sexually transmitted diseases in general. If he failed to do so, he would be liable even if the specific disease of HIV was one which he did not actually foresee. Accordingly, the appeal would be allowed and a new trial would be ordered.

Ter Neuzen v Korn (1993) 103 DLR (4th) 473 (British Columbia Court of Appeal).

1768   Medical practitioner—duty of care—duty to inform of risks of surgery

Canada
The plaintiff had implants manufactured by the defendant company inserted surgically into her breasts. A few years later, one of the implants ruptured, causing pain and swelling that continued

after the implant was removed. The plaintiff brought an action for negligence against the company and the doctor who inserted the implant. The court at first instance found for the plaintiff against the company by applying the res ipsa loquitur maxim, but dismissed her claim against the doctor. On appeal by the company and cross-appeal by the plaintiff in relation to the dismissal of her claim against the doctor, *held*, in relation to the company's appeal, the plaintiff could not rely on the maxims of res ipsa loquitur or strict liability when dealing with the claim against the company as there had been no evidence of a defect in the implant and there were a number of other possible reasons for the rupture such as external trauma or surgical error. However, the company was liable for negligently failing to warn of the risk of rupture. There had been a significant amount of ruptures prior to the plaintiff's surgery, of which the company had been aware. It therefore had a duty to inform the medical profession of this because a reasonable woman, in the position of the plaintiff, would not have consented to the implant being performed if she had been given adequate warning of the risks involved. The company could not avoid liability by placing the burden of the duty to inform of risks onto the doctor. In relation to the plaintiff's cross- appeal, plastic surgeons were aware of the possibility of rupture at the time of the plaintiff's surgery and therefore the doctor had a duty to warn the plaintiff of this possibility even though it was comparatively rare. He had not fulfilled this duty and was therefore negligent. Accordingly, the company's appeal would be dismissed and the plaintiff's cross-appeal would be allowed.

Hollis v Dow Corning Corp (1993) 103 DLR (4th) 520 (British Columbia Court of Appeal)

1769 Medical practitioner—self-employed or employed Community nationals—mutual recognition of diplomas, etc

See para 2729.

1770 Medical records—access—common law right

A family health services authority refused the applicant access to his medical records concerning his early life. A health authority was prepared to consider access to such records on condition that the applicant did not have litigation in mind. Both authorities offered disclosure of the records to a medical adviser nominated by the applicant. He refused the offers and sought judicial review of their decisions contending that he had a common law right of unconditional access to the records. *Held*, as the records were made prior to 1 November 1991, the Access to Health Records Act 1990 did not apply. The Data Protection Act 1984 gave an individual a right of access to information held about him in computerised form and the Data Protection (Subject Access Modification) (Health) Order 1987, SI 1987/1903 provided that the 1984 Act did not apply where access to health records would be either likely to cause serious harm to the physical or mental health of the data subject or be likely to disclose the identity of another individual. The Acts seemed an almost insuperable obstacle to the applicant's contention that there was a common law right of access. They had come into existence in order to give a right of access to records which otherwise a patient did not have. The European Convention on Human Rights, art 8 on the right to respect for an individual's private and family life would not assist the applicant's case for the common law was quite clear. If he did have some right of access to his records, it was conditional. In offering sight of the records to an independent person, the authorities had complied with their duty to the applicant. Accordingly, his application would be dismissed.

R v Mid-Glamorgan Family Health Services Authority, ex p Martin (1993) Times, 2 June, Independent, 8 June (Queen's Bench Division: Popplewell J).

1771 Medical services—advertising specialist qualifications—restrictions on advertising

The applicant was a medical practitioner who specialised in rheumatology. He wished to advertise the fact that he was a specialist practitioner to the public in the United Kingdom and throughout the European Community, but he was unable to do so because of certain restrictions on advertising which prevented medical specialists in the United Kingdom from making their specialisations known. He sought a declaration that the United Kingdom had failed to implement the First and Second Medical Directives (Council Directives (EC) 75/362 and 75/363) properly, contending that proper implementation of the directives required publication in the medical register of a list signifying which persons held specialist qualifications, and the furnishing of that list to all other member states. *Held*, the directives were designed to facilitate rights of freedom of establishment and freedom to provide services in other member states in accordance with the EC Treaty, but they did not go so far as to harmonise all the provisions of member states on the training of specialists. In any case the matters which formed the basis of the applicant's complaint were purely internal, and the directives had no application in such situations. There were no grounds for granting the declaration sought and, accordingly, the application would be dismissed.

R v Secretary of State for Health, ex p Goldstein (1993) Times, 5 April (Queen's Bench Division: Schiemann J).

1772 Medicinal products—manufacturer's duty of care—duty to inform of risks involved in use of product

See para 1768.

1773 Medicinal products—Medicines Control Agency—funding

See para 2161.

1774 Medicinal products—products for human use—application for licence

The Medicines (Applications for Grant of Product Licences-Products for Human Use) Regulations 1993, SI 1993/2538 (in force on 29 November 1993), prescribe the information, documents and samples to be provided in or with an application for a product licence under the Medicines Act 1968, Pt II in relation to medicinal products for human use. The regulations replace, in relation to such applications, the requirements of the Medicines (Applications for Product Licences and Clinical Trial and Animal Test Certificates) Regulations 1971, SI 1971/973.

The Medicines (Standard Provisions for Licences and Certificates) Amendment (No 2) Regulations 1993, SI 1993/2539 (in force on 29 November 1993), further amend the 1971 Regulations, SI 1971/972, by imposing additional requirements to be incorporated into standard provisions for product licences relating to medicinal products.

1775 Medicines—manufacturer's and wholesale dealer's licences

The Medicines (Applications for Manufacturer's and Wholesale Dealer's Licences) Amendment Regulations 1993, SI 1993/832 (in force on 14 April 1993), further amend the 1971 Regulations, SI 1971/974, so as to implement in part Council Directive (EC) 92/25. The regulations require applicants for licences to give the name and address of a responsible person who is to oversee wholesaling operations, to submit details of an emergency plan to be instituted where products are recalled, and to submit details of arrangements for keeping records relating to products received or dispatched.

The Medicines Act 1968 (Amendment) Regulations 1993, SI 1993/834 (in force on 14 April 1993), amend the Medicines Act 1968 so as to implement in part Council Directive (EC) 92/25, which concerns the wholesale distribution of medicinal products for human use which are marketed within the European Community. The regulations provide that the distribution of such products by way of wholesale dealing is only authorised by a wholesale dealer's licence if distribution occurs in the course of a business which is carried on at a place specified in the licence, and provide that the holder of a manufacturer's licence for such a product who wishes to engage in the wholesale distribution of that product will not require a wholesale dealer's licence.

1776 Medicines—prescription only drugs

The Medicines (Products Other Than Veterinary Drugs) (Prescription Only) Amendment Order 1993, SI 1993/1890 (in force on 23 August 1993), amends the 1983 Order, SI 1983/1212, by exempting certain products containing Acrivastine, Cetirizine, Ketoprofen 2·5 per cent, Loratadine and Terfenadine from being prescription only medicines.

The Medicines (Products Other Than Veterinary Drugs) (Prescription Only) Amendment (No 2) Order 1993, SI 1993/3256 (in force on 21 January 1994), further amends the 1983 Order supra, by exempting certain products containing beclomethasone dipropionate, cimetidine, famotidine, mebendazole, and sodium cromoglycate from being prescription only medicines, and amending the list of substances, contained in the 1983 Order, which render medicinal products prescription only medicines except in specified circumstances.

1777　Medicines—standard provisions for licences and certificates

The Medicines (Standard Provisions for Licences and Certificates) Amendment Regulations 1993, SI 1993/833 (in force on 14 April 1993), further amend the 1971 Regulations, SI 1971/972, so as to implement in part Council Directive (EC) 92/25. Wholesale dealers of medicinal products for human use are required to institute an emergency plan to ensure the effectiveness of any recall of such products, to keep specified records of products received or dispatched, to specify the persons from whom such products may be obtained and to whom such products may be supplied, and to specify that the licence shall name a person as being responsible for ensuring that the conditions of the licence are being adhered to.

1778　Nurse—misconduct—disciplinary proceedings—procedure before professional conduct committee

The appellant, a nurse, had been convicted of eight road traffic offences. She appeared before the professional conduct committee to face charges of misconduct arising from those convictions. Her representative conducted her defence on the basis that because the charges did not relate to the appellant's work and conduct as a nurse the committee could not find her guilty of misconduct, but the committee decided that the representative's view was erroneous and found the appellant guilty of misconduct. After hearing evidence of the circumstances surrounding the commission of the offences and considering evidence of the appellant's competence and behaviour as a nurse, the committee decided to strike her name off the register. On her appeal, *held*, the committee should have informed the appellant's representative that his construction of the rules of professional conduct was wrong and, having done so, should have invited him to adduce evidence of the background to the commission of the offences before deciding whether the appellant's behaviour had amounted to misconduct. The committee had erred in treating the circumstances surrounding the offences as relevant only to the question of mitigation rather than to the question of whether the appellant's actions had amounted to misconduct, and the decision could not be upheld. Accordingly, the appeal would be allowed and the case remitted for rehearing both as to the finding of misconduct and the penalty imposed.

Dennis v United Kingdom Central Council for Nursing, Midwifery and Health Visiting (1993) Independent, 23 March (Queen's Bench Division: Watkins LJ and Ognall J).

1779　Nurses, midwives and health visitors—Central Council—term of office of members

The United Kingdom Central Council for Nursing, Midwifery and Health Visiting (Term of Office of Members) Order 1993, SI 1993/590 (in force on 1 April 1993), specifies the term of office of the members of the United Kingdom Central Council for Nursing, Midwifery and Health Visiting and revokes the Nurses, Midwives and Health Visitors Act 1979 (Membership of Central Council) Order 1982, SI 1982/961. Appointment as a member of the Council is for a period of five years.

1780　Nurses, midwives and health visitors—examinations and training

The Nurses, Midwives and Health Visitors (Entry to Examinations and Training Requirements) Amendment Rules Approval Order 1993, SI 1993/1901 (in force on 13 August 1993), further amend the 1983 Order, SI 1983/873, in respect to the maximum number of times student nurses may enter a training course for entry to any of parts 1–8 of the Register of Nurses, Midwives and Health Visitors. Further provision is made removing the maximum number of times a student nurse may enter for examinations. The Nurses, Midwives and Health Visitors (Midwives Training) Amendment Rules 1990, SI 1990/1624, are amended so as to remove the provision relating to the maximum number of times student midwives who commenced their training before 1 September 1990 may enter midwifery examinations.

1781　Nurses, midwives and health visitors—legal assessors

The United Kingdom Central Council for Nursing, Midwifery and Health Visiting (Legal Assessors) (Amendment) Order 1993, SI 1993/892 (in force on 1 April 1993), amends the 1983 Order, SI 1983/839, so as to provide that a Preliminary Proceedings Committee may sit without a legal assessor being present.

1782　Nurses, midwives and health visitors—midwives

The Nurses, Midwives and Health Visitors (Midwives Amendment) Rules Approval Order 1993, SI 1993/2106 (in force on 1 September 1993), amends the 1983 Order, SI 1983/873. The principal amendments include a requirement that local supervising authorities give monthly notice to the United Kingdom Central Council for Midwifery and Health Visiting about midwives who give them notices of their intention to practice. Further, any person appointed as a supervisor of midwives is required to complete an appropriate course of education before appointment.

1783 Nurses, midwives and health visitors—national board—constitution and administration

The National Board for Nursing, Midwifery and Health Visiting for Wales (Constitution and Administration) Order 1993, SI 1993/614 (in force on 1 April 1993), makes provisions relating to the constitution and administration of the National Board for Nursing, Midwifery and Health Visiting for Wales. In particular, the order provides for the appointment and replacement of senior officers of the board and the appointment of employees of the board. The 1982 Order, SI 1982/962, is revoked in so far as it applies to Wales.

The National Board for Nursing, Midwifery and Health Visiting for England (Constitution and Administration) Order 1993, SI 1993/629 (in force on 1 April 1993), makes provisions relating to the constitution and administration of the National Board for Nursing, Midwifery and Health Visiting for England. In particular, the order provides for the appointment and replacement of senior officers of the board and the appointment of employees of the board. The 1982 Order, SI 1982/962, is revoked in so far as it applies to England.

1784 Nurses, midwives and health visitors—professional conduct

The Nurses, Midwives and Health Visitors (Professional Conduct) Rules 1993 Approval Order 1993, SI 1993/893 (in force on 1 April 1993), approves rules which are made by the United Kingdom Central Council for Nursing, Midwives and Health Visiting and have effect throughout the United Kingdom. The rules provide for all circumstances in which, and the means by which, a nurse, midwife or health visitor may be removed from the register or restored to it. The main provisions are those concerned with removal from the register for misconduct or because the fitness of the practitioner to practise is seriously impaired by reason of the practitioner's physical or mental condition. The 1987 Order, SI 1987/2156, is revoked.

1785 Nurses, Midwives and Health Visitors Act 1992—commencement

The Nurses, Midwives and Health Visitors Act 1992 (Commencement No 1) Order 1993, SI 1993/588 brings into force on 1 April 1993 the whole of the Act so far as it is not already in force except for s 4, in so far as it relates to the Nurses, Midwives and Health Visitors Act 1979, s 5(8)(e), and the repeal, by the 1992 Act, Sch 3, of the 1979 Act, Sch 2, para 7. For details of commencement, see the commencement table in the title STATUTES.

1786 Nursing home—registration—cancellation of registration—urgent procedure

An area health authority was alleged to have acted carelessly in carrying out an investigation into a registered nursing home leading to an urgent application under the Registered Homes Act 1984, s 30 for cancellation of registration of the proprietor. It fell to be determined whether the authority owed the proprietor of the home a duty of care not to carry out the investigation negligently. *Held,* under the urgent procedure provided by s 30, the Secretary of State or the health authority acting on his behalf was intended to act properly in a judicial or quasi-judicial capacity. The task of a health authority deciding whether the urgent procedure under s 30 should be invoked would be impeded if it had to concern itself with the possibility of a claim for damages by the registered proprietor of the home. The authority owed the proprietor of the home no duty of care in carrying out its investigation to decide whether it was appropriate to invoke the urgent procedure.

Martine v South East Kent Health Authority (1993) Times, 8 March (Court of Appeal: Dillon, Leggatt and Hirst LJJ).

1787 Osteopaths Act 1993

The Osteopaths Act 1993 provides for the regulation of the profession of osteopathy and requires the registration of persons acting as osteopaths. The Act received the royal assent on 1 July 1993 and comes into force on a day or days to be appointed.

Section 1 together with the Schedule, Pts I, II provide for the establishment of the General Osteopathic Council ("the General Council"), which has the duty to develop, promote and regulate the profession of osteopathy. It also establishes four committees ("the statutory committees") of the General Council: the Education Committee; the Investigating Committee; the Professional Conduct Committee (PCC); and the Health Committee, and enables the General Council to establish other committees as necessary for the discharge of its functions. Section 2 provides for the appointment by the General Council of the Registrar of Osteopaths ("the Registrar") who has the duty of establishing and maintaining a register of osteopaths. Section 3 sets out the conditions which must be satisfied before a person is entitled to be registered as a fully registered osteopath.

The conditions which must be satisfied before a person is entitled to be registered as a conditionally registered osteopath are set out in s 4. Section 5 empowers the General Council to make rules providing for all applicants for registration who are entitled to be registered to be registered initially with provisional registration, for a period of one year, during which they may only practise under the supervision of a fully registered osteopath, and provides for the conversion, in prescribed circumstances, of provisional registration into full registration; the council is to maintain a list of those fully registered osteopaths approved to supervise. Supplementary provisions in relation to registration are set out in s 6. Section 7 provides for the Registrar to enter details of an osteopath's suspension into the register. Section 8 provides for those osteopaths whose entries as fully registered osteopaths have been removed as a result of findings against them by the PCC to apply for restoration to the register. The General Council is required to make the register available for public inspection, to publish it on an annual basis and to make copies available to the public: s 9. Provisions relating to fraud or error in relation to registration are contained in s 10.

Section 11 confers on the Education Committee the general duty of promoting high standards of education and training in osteopathy, and to keep this under review, and requires the General Council to consult the committee on matters relating to education, training, examinations or tests of competence. Provisions relating to visitors are contained in s 12. The General Council is required by virtue of s 13 to determine from time to time, and to publish, a statement of the standard of proficiency required for the safe and competent practice of osteopathy. Section 14 provides for the recognition of any qualifications by the General Council if it is satisfied that they reach the required standard of proficiency, and requires it to maintain and publish a list of those qualifications. Supplementary provisions in relation to the recognition of qualifications are made by s 15. Provision is made for withdrawal of the recognition of a qualification by the General Council as a result of any visitor's report or other information acquired by the Education Committee as to the standard of proficiency: s 16. Section 17 enables the General Council to make rules, after appropriate consultation, requiring registered osteopaths to undertake further courses of training. Information to be given by institutions is set out in s 18.

The General Council must prepare and publish, after consultation with the representatives of practising osteopaths, a Code of Practice laying down standards of conduct and practice expected of osteopaths, and giving advice in relation to the practise of osteopathy: s 19. Section 20 makes provisions relating to professional conduct and fitness to practise. The Investigating Committee may impose an interim suspension order on the osteopath's registration while it is investigating an allegation where the committee thinks it necessary to do so in order to protect members of the public: s 21. Provisions relating to the consideration of allegations by the PCC are set out in s 22. Under s 23, the Health Committee must consider any allegation referred to it; if the committee is satisfied the allegation is well-founded, it may impose conditions on the osteopath's right to practise (a "conditions of practice order"), or suspend his registration (a "suspension order"), ensuring that the conditions or period of suspension imposed are the minimum necessary for the protection of the public. Section 24 empowers the PCC or the Health Committee to impose an interim suspension order on the osteopath's registration when it is considering any allegation against a registered osteopath or has reached a relevant decision and considers it necessary in order to protect members of the public. The osteopath concerned may appeal against the order. Section 25 enables the PCC or the Health Committee, on the application of the osteopath concerned, to revoke an interim suspension order in a case falling within s 24(1)(a) on the grounds that a change in the circumstances of a case has made the order unnecessary. Where the application has been refused, the osteopath concerned may appeal against a decision. Section 26 requires the General Council to make rules as to the procedure to be followed by the PCC or the Health Committee in considering any allegation under ss 22, 23. Section 27 requires the General Council to appoint legal assessors to advise the Investigating Committee, the PCC, the Health Committee or any person appointed to give preliminary consideration to an allegation. The General Council may appoint registered medical practitioners to be medical assessors under s 28.

Section 29 provides for appeals against any decision of the Registrar, and s 30 provides for appeals against a decision of the Health Committee. Provision for appeals against a decision of the PCC is made under s 31. It is an offence for a person who is not a registered osteopath to describe himself as an osteopath of any kind: s 32.

Section 33 enables the Secretary of State to issue a competition order in respect of any regulatory provision made by the General Council, its committees or sub-committees. The Privy Council may direct the General Council to perform any functions which, in its opinion, it should have performed and, in default of the General Council complying, for the Privy Council to perform those functions: s 34. Under s 35, any rules made by the General Council are to be approved by the Privy Council, and certain rules are made to be subject to the negative resolution procedure in Parliament. Section 36 provides that, where the Privy Council is to approve any rules made by the General Council, it does so by order made by statutory instrument, and requires certain orders to be subject to the negative resolution procedure in Parliament. The General Council may make rules requiring registered osteopaths practising as osteopaths, and prescribed categories of registered osteopaths practising as osteopaths, to secure that they are properly insured against liability to, or in relation to, their patients: s 37. Section 38 makes minor amendments to the Access to Health Records Act 1990, and s 39 exempts osteopaths from specified provisions about rehabilitation of offenders. The General Council must keep proper accounts, and these must be audited, published and submitted to the Privy Council for laying before Parliament: s 40.

Sections 41, 42 deal with interpretation, short title, commencement and extent.

1788 Pharmacies—applications for registration and fees

The Medicines (Pharmacies) (Applications for Registration and Fees) Amendment Regulations 1993, SI 1993/2902 (in force on 1 January 1994), further amend the 1973 Regulations, 1973/1822, so as to increase the fees for registration of premises at which a retail pharmacy business is, or is to be, carried on, the subsequent annual, or retention, fees and the penalty for failure to pay retention fees. The 1992 Regulations, SI 1992/2939, are revoked.

1789 Veterinary drugs—licences—applications

The Medicines (Veterinary Drugs) (Renewal Applications for Licences and Animal Test Certificates) Regulations 1993, SI 1993/1227 (in force on 31 May 1993), replace the 1974 Regulations, SI 1974/832, in so far as they relate to veterinary drugs, to take account of Council Directive (EC) 81/851 (as amended by Council Directive (EC) 90/676) on the approximation of the laws of EC member states on veterinary medicinal products. The principal amendments are: (1) the 1993 Regulations do not apply to an application for the renewal of a product licence in consequence of a notice served on the licence holder under the Medicines Act 1968, s 24(1A); (2) a renewal of a licence or certificate may only be made where its terms are identical to the existing licence or certificate and the only additional particulars to be included are those pursuant to the 1993 Regulations; (3) the submission of additional prescribed particulars with applications for the renewal of certain product licences if never submitted before; and (4) the change of the period during which renewal applications can be submitted to at least three months and not more than five months before the expiry of the current licence or certificate.

The Medicines (Veterinary Medicinal Products) (Applications for Product Licences) Regulations 1993, SI 1993/2398 (in force 29 October 1993), apply to applications for product licences in relation to veterinary medicinal products to which Council Directive (EC) 81/851 applies. Such products are to be treated as medicinal products within the meaning of the Medicines Act 1968, s 130. The regulations revoke the Medicines (Applications for Product Licences and Clinical Trial and Animal Test Certificates) Regulations 1971, SI 1971/973.

The Medicines (Veterinary Medicinal Products) (Renewal Applications for Product Licences Subject to Review) Regulations 1993, SI 1993/2399 (in force 29 October 1993), make provision for renewal applications for product licences for veterinary drugs in consequence of notices of expiry served on the holders of such licences by the licensing authority under the Medicines Act 1968, s 24(1A). The notices are to be served on holders of licences which do not comply with the provisions of Council Directive (EC) 81/851.

MENTAL HEALTH

Halsbury's Laws of England (4th edn) Vol 30 (reissue), paras 1001–1305

1790   Articles

Applications For Secure Accommodation—A Further Twist in the Labyrinth, Peter Dawson and Robert Stevens: 157 JP Jo 761

Arrest or Injection, Phil Fennell (on the need for compulsory community supervision orders): 143 NLJ 395

Beyond Belief, Dr Terence Stephenson (on the legal ramifications of munchausen syndrome): LS Gaz, 23 June 1993, p 28

Competence and the Right to Die, Richard Gordon and Craig Barlow: 143 NLJ 1719

Detaining Mental Patients, Fenella Morris: 137 SJ 682

Disabling Progress—The Law Commission's Proposals on Mentally Incapacitated Adults' Decision-Making, David Carson: [1993] 5 JSWFL 304

Diversion from Custody, Phil Fennell (on alternatives to sending mentally disordered offenders into custody): LS Gaz, 30 June 1993, p 18

Incapacitated Clients, Phil Fennell: LS Gaz, 23 April 1993, p 27

Judicial Review and the Detained Patient, Richard Gordon: 137 SJ 43

Munchausen Syndrome by Proxy, Graham Lyons: 143 NLJ 988

Ripe for Reform? Dr Edward Munir (on the Mental Health Act 1983): LS Gaz, 7 April 1993, p 19

Wills Containing Provision for a Mentally Handicapped Child, District Judge Gordon Ashton: 143 NLJ 1190

1791   Medical treatment—consent to treatment—capacity—amputation

The patient, who was mentally ill, was diagnosed with gangrene. Although it was thought that he might die unless his leg was amputated, he refused amputation and was treated with alternative methods. The hospital refused to undertake that they would not amputate the leg in the future if the patient's life was at risk. The patient applied for an injunction to prevent an amputation without his consent. *Held,* the question to be considered when establishing the capacity of an individual to refuse treatment was whether his capacity was so reduced by chronic mental illness that he did not sufficiently understand the nature, purpose and effects of the amputation. There were three parts to the decision-making process: (1) understanding and retaining the information relating to the treatment; (2) believing it; and (3) assessing the information and comparing the risks in order to make a choice. In this case although the patient's general capacity was impaired by schizophrenia, he was able to understand the nature, purpose and effects of amputation. The presumption that the patient had the right of self-determination had not been displaced on the application of this test to the present facts. Accordingly the application would be allowed.

Re C [1993] NLJR 1642 (Family Division: Thorpe J).

1792   Medical treatment—consent to treatment—capacity—Law Commission provisional proposals

The Law Commission has published a consultation paper, *Mentally-Incapacitated Adults and Decision-Making: Medical Treatment and Research* (Law Commission consultation paper 129). The commission seeks views on its provisional proposals regarding the criteria for incapacity in relation to the acceptance, or otherwise, of medical treatment, the possible scope and effect of anticipatory decisions made by the patient, the provision of a range of orders which could be made by a court in relation to an incapacitated patient, the use of an enduring power of attorney giving another person the authority to give or refuse consent to medical treatment, the existence of special categories of treatment (eg sterilisation) which might call for the intervention of a particular authority or the court before being authorised, and the application of these proposals to mental disorders other than to the treatment of persons subject to the Mental Health Act 1983, Pt IV (ss 56–64).

1793   Medical treatment—consent to treatment—capacity—sterilisation

The plaintiff's daughter was a 20-year-old mentally handicapped epileptic with a mental age of seven. There was a risk that if she became pregnant there would be an increase in her epileptic fits and she would not be able to cope with the discomfort and distress of pregnancy. It was also clear that she could not be taught to protect herself from unwelcome advances and that the various methods of contraception were not appropriate. She was incapable of giving her consent to medical treatment. Following a proposal that she ought to be sterilised, the plaintiff issued an originating summons seeking a declaration that such an operation would not be lawful. *Held*, there was a responsible body of medical opinion in favour of sterilisation in cases such as the present case. Notwithstanding that there was only a small risk of the young woman becoming pregnant at the present time, in the circumstances sterilisation would be in her best interests. Accordingly, the application would be dismissed.

Re W (An Adult: Sterilisation) [1993] 2 FCR 187 (Family Division: Hollis J).

See also *Practice Note*, para 432.

1794   Medical treatment—consent to treatment—order to force-feed—interim declaratory relief—availability

A patient suffering from anorexia nervosa was detained in hospital under the Mental Health Act 1983, s 3. The hospital successfully applied for an ex parte order to force-feed her. Her solicitors were not present at the hearing as legal aid had not been granted and their subsequent appeal to set aside the order was refused. On further appeal, *held*, when granting the order, the judge had also directed that the proceedings be adjourned pending an inter partes hearing. The order thus constituted interim declaratory relief which was unknown to English law. Accordingly, the appeal would be allowed.

Riverside Mental Hospital NHS Trust v Fox (1993) Times, 28 October (Court of Appeal: Sir Stephen Brown P, Leggatt and Kennedy LJJ).

1795   Mentally-incapacitated and other vulnerable adults—public law protection—Law Commission provisional proposals

The Law Commission has published a consultation paper, *Mentally-Incapacitated and Other Vulnerable Adults: Public Law Protection* (Law Commission consultation paper 130). The commission provisionally suggests replacing the existing powers of intervention to protect incapacitated, mentally disordered and vulnerable persons by a clearer scheme giving more appropriate powers to local social services authorities in respect of those aged 16 years or more. Such authorities might be required to investigate the need for protection where they have reasonable cause to suspect that any such person is in danger of suffering significant harm or serious exploitation. Emergency protection orders might be available to such authorities enabling them to remove such persons to a place of safety. Guardianship under the Mental Health Act 1983 should be restricted to local authorities, and perhaps health authorities, who would be empowered to convey the person to specified premises. Such guardianship would not extend to include the incapacitated. The commission also considers the authorities, other than the local social services, and persons who might be empowered to apply to the court for an order relating to a mentally-incapacitated or vulnerable person, the appointment of personal and financial managers for such persons, and the criteria on which the court might act on making orders in respect of such persons and also to which the administrative authorities would have regard when making decisions.

1796   Nurses—classes of nurses

The Mental Health (Nurses) Amendment Order 1993, SI 1993/2155 (in force on 1 October 1993), amends the 1983 Order, SI 1983/891, by adding two further classes of nurses to the classes of nurses prescribed for the purposes of the Mental Health Act 1983, s 5(4).

1797   Nurses—register of qualified nurses

The Mental Health (Hospital, Guardianship and Consent to Treatment) Amendment Regulations 1993, SI 1993/2156 (in force on 1 October 1993), amend the 1983 Regulations, SI 1983/893, by adding additional parts to the Register of Qualified Nurses, Midwives and Health Visitors.

1798   Patient—admission to hospital—recommendation for compulsory admission—special experience of medical practitioner

The Mental Health Act 1983, s 12(2) provides that the medical recommendations given for the purposes of an application to compulsorily admit someone to a mental hospital must be given by a practitioner approved by the Secretary of State as having special experience in the diagnosis or treatment of mental disorder.

It has been held that "special experience" is a minimum threshold and that the Secretary of State is entitled to consider the fitness of the particular practitioner for the task in hand, before approving him under the 1983 Act, s 12(2).

R v Trent Regional Health Authority (1993) Times, 10 December (Queen's Bench Division: Potts J).

1799 Patient—discharge of patient—criteria

The Mental Health Act 1983, s 3(2)(a), (b) provides that an application may be made for admission for treatment in respect of a patient on the grounds that he is suffering from a psychopathic disorder of such nature or degree that it is appropriate for him to receive medical treatment in hospital and such a treatment is likely to alleviate or prevent a deterioration in his condition. The 1983 Act, s 72(1)(b)(i) provides that a mental health tribunal must discharge a patient detained under the Act if it is satisfied that he is not then suffering from a psychopathic disorder of a nature or degree which makes it appropriate for him to be liable to be detained for medical treatment.

The applicant had been detained under the 1983 Act, s 3 and continued to be detained under the 1983 Act, s 20, on the same criteria. She applied to be discharged under the 1983 Act, s 72(1)(b)(i). The mental health review tribunal found that group psychotherapy was the only treatment which might alleviate the applicant's disorder. Although the applicant was not amenable to such treatment and hospital treatment was unlikely to alleviate or prevent a deterioration in her condition, the tribunal refused her application on the grounds that continued detention might prompt her to assent to the group therapy. The applicant contended that the intention of the 1983 Act was that psychopaths only be detained if they were treatable, that the tribunal's decision was thus unlawful and should be quashed. *Held*, the 1983 Act, s 72(1)(b)(i) should be construed in the context of ss 3 and 20. These referred to the appropriateness of medical treatment and the likelihood of its success as criteria for determining liability for detention. The tribunal's contention that the 1983 Act, s 72 gave it a wider remit failed since it implied that the tribunal was a primary decision-making body which could determine liability to be detained on criteria outside the scope of the 1983 Act. The tribunal's decision was unlawful and, accordingly, the application would be allowed.

R v Cannons Park Mental Health Review Tribunal, ex p A [1994] 1 All ER 481 (Queen's Bench Division: Mann LJ and Sedley J).

1800 Patient—discharge of patient—subsequent application to readmit

The patient was admitted to hospital under the Mental Health Act 1983, s 4 (compulsory admission for assessment in an emergency) after she had started a number of small fires in her flat. The following day, after a medical review, her status was converted to that of a patient under the 1983 Act, s 2 (compulsory detention for assessment). She unsuccessfully appealed against her detention to the hospital managers, and then applied to a mental health review tribunal. The tribunal concluded that the patient was suffering from a mental disorder but not of a sufficient degree to warrant her detention in hospital. The consultant psychiatrist at the hospital, following receipt of the tribunal's decision, saw the patient and then recommended her readmission for treatment under the 1983 Act, s 3 (compulsory admission for treatment). The following day a second doctor made a s 3 recommendation and the case was referred to an approved social worker who interviewed the patient and completed an application for her admission for treatment under s 3. The patient's mother was also interviewed by a person other than the approved social worker as the patient's nearest relative in purported compliance with the 1983 Act, s 11(4). In an application by the patient for habeas corpus directed against the hospital managers and the consultant psychiatrist, *held*, (1) hospital managers were obliged to consider an application made by the approved social worker in pursuance of his statutory duty under the 1983 Act, s 13. The existence of a recent tribunal decision did not constitute a fetter on the social worker's duty and did not prevent a subsequent application under s 3 to detain the patient. The duty and discretion of the approved social worker to make the s 3 application, and the function of the hospital managers in considering it, were not impliedly limited or abrogated by the existence of an earlier tribunal decision. (2) The writ of habeas corpus only ran to the party having the applicant in his custody. The consultant psychiatrist was not an appropriate respondent in the habeas corpus application as he was not the party which had the detained patient in his custody. (3) Although it was desirable for consultation under s 11(4) with the person appearing to be the patient's nearest relative to be carried out by the approved social worker, such consultation could be delegated provided it was full and effective. Accordingly, the application would be dismissed.

R v Managers of South Western Hospital, ex p M [1993] 3 WLR 376 (Queen's Bench Division: Laws J).

1801 Patient—restricted patient—power of Secretary of State to recall

The defendant was convicted of indecent assault. Acting on medical evidence, the court made a restriction order without limit of time under the Mental Health Act 1959, s 69. Some years after his discharge, the conditions attaching to the discharge were allowed to lapse, but he was informed that his liability to be recalled to hospital continued. He was subsequently convicted on assault charges and sentenced to four years' imprisonment. Prior to the defendant's release from his term of imprisonment, a mental health tribunal decided that he was still in need of treatment and the Home Secretary accordingly issued a warrant of recall under the original restriction order. The defendant applied for an order of certiorari to quash this decision, contending that since the conditions had been allowed to lapse, he was in effect absolutely discharged so that the original restriction order was no longer in force. *Held*, the power to issue the warrant of recall could be exercised at any time while the original restriction order remained in force. Before a restriction order could be brought to an end, the Home Secretary had either to make a direction to that effect or discharge the patient absolutely. There was no room for the situation whereby a restriction order ceased to have effect by inference or implication. The issue of the warrant was accordingly intra vires and the application would be dismissed.

R v Secretary of State for the Home Department, ex p Didlick (1993) Times, 30 March, Independent, 9 April (Queen's Bench Division: Watkins LJ and Rougier J).

1959 Act, s 69 now Mental Health Act 1983, s 41.

MINES, MINERALS AND QUARRIES

Halsbury's Laws of England (4th edn) Vol 31, paras 1–1000

1802 British Coal and British Rail (Transfer Proposals) Act 1993

The British Coal and British Rail (Transfer Proposals) Act 1993 empowers the British Coal Corporation and the British Railways Board to act in relation to proposals for the transfer of their functions. The Act received the royal assent on 19 January 1993 and came into force on that date.

Section 1 empowers the British Coal Corporation and the British Railways Board or any subsidiary to take appropriate steps for facilitating the implementation of government proposals for, or in relation to, the transfer of their functions, property, rights or liabilities to other bodies or persons. Section 2 deals with the short title, financial provision and extent.

1803 Coal industry—closure of mines—review procedure

See *R v British Coal Corpn, ex p Price (No 2)*, para 40.

1804 Coal industry—equal pay

See *British Coal Corpn v Smith*, para 1149.

1805 Coal industry—redundancy—consultation procedure

See *R v British Coal Corpn, ex p Price (No 3)*, para 15.

1806 Coal industry—restructuring—grants

The Coal Industry (Restructuring Grants) Order 1993, SI 1993/1745 (in force on 12 July 1993), specifies, for the year ending March 1994, eligible expenditure for the purposes of the Coal Industry Act 1987, s 3, as amended, under which grants may be made by the Secretary of State to the British Coal Corporation.

1807 Coal Industry Act 1992—commencement

The Coal Industry Act 1992 (Commencement) Order 1993, SI 1993/2514 brings into force on 20 November 1993 ss 2, 3(3) (in part), Schedule, Pt II, which repeal the Coal Mines Regulation

Act 1908 and make certain other consequential repeals. For a summary of the Act which is now entirely in force, see 1992 Abr para 1776. For details of commencement, see the commencement table in the title STATUTES.

1808   Mines—health and safety—management and administration

The Management and Administration of Safety and Health at Mines Regulations 1993, SI 1993/1897 (in force on 1 October 1993), impose requirements relating to the management and administration of safety and health at mines, and amend the Mines and Quarries Act 1954.

The regulations (1) impose duties on the owner of a mine including a duty to ensure that the mine is managed and worked in accordance with the relevant statutory provisions and that adequate financial and other provisions are made; (2) make provision in relation to the structure of health and safety management, supervision and inspection of the mine; and (3) provide for the approval of qualifications and for the issue of certificates of qualification. The regulations also make provision with respect to training requirements, surveyors and plans, and records and information.

1809   Mines—owner's operating rules

The Coal Mines (Owner's Operating Rules) Regulations 1993, SI 1993/2331 (in force on 1 January 1994), prohibit the owners of coal mines from working the mine unless there are in force suitable written rules made by the owner, who must notify the rules to the Health and Safety Executive. The owner must also ensure that the rules are brought to the attention of persons at work at the mine whom they affect and that operations at the mine are carried out in accordance with them. The rules which relate to the ventilation of blind ends, mine fires and frictional ignition, may be modified by the owner at the request of the Health and Safety Executive. The rules must be kept and made available at the covered accommodation at the mine.

1810   Mines—safety-lamp mines—explosives

The Coal and Other Safety-Lamp Mines (Explosives) Regulations 1993, SI 1993/208 (in force on 1 April 1993), in imposing requirements and prohibitions in relation to the use of explosives and associated material and equipment in safety lamp mines, replace a number of regulations relating to the use of explosives in coal mines and in other mines where flammable gas is likely to be present. The regulations include provisions relating to (1) the appointment of shotfirers and trainee shotfirers; (2) the safety and security of explosives; (3) detonators and shotfiring procedures.

1811   Mines—shafts and winding

The Mines (Shafts and Winding) Regulations 1993, SI 1993/302 (in force in part on 1 April 1993 and in part on 1 January 1996), make provision with respect to health and safety of mine shafts and of winding and associated apparatus.

The regulations require the owner of a mine to ensure, so far as is reasonably practicable, that the sinking of a shaft for the purpose of working a mine is so specified, planned and designed as to be safe and without risk of injury. The regulations make requirements with respect to the equipment of a shaft and the safe use of a shaft or its fixtures, and with respect to the suitability of winding apparatus and its installation and modification. The manager of a mine must prepare specifications for ropes intended for use in a shaft, and the manager must ensure that no rope is used for winding after the expiry of the life so specified. Provision is also made with respect to signalling and communication and the use of winding apparatus. The regulations also impose a requirement on the manager with respect to the appointment of competent persons and with respect to the recording of hours worked by enginemen. The manager must ensure, so far as is reasonably practicable, that other persons at the mine comply with their obligations under the regulations.

1812   Mineworkers—pensions

See PENSIONS AND SUPERANNUATION.

MISREPRESENTATION

Halsbury's Laws of England (4th edn) Vol 31, paras 1001–1137

1813 Deceit—defence of contributory negligence—availability
The defendant company sought leave to amend its defence so as to plead contributory negligence as a defence to claims in deceit. Held, a person liable for deceit, whether personally or vicariously, was not entitled, either at common law or by virtue of the Law Reform (Contributory Negligence) Act 1945, to plead as a defence that his victim was guilty of contributory negligence. Accordingly, the defendant's application for leave to amend its defence would be refused.
   Alliance & Leicester Building Society v Edgestop Ltd; Same v Dhanoa; Same v Samra; Mercantile Credit Co Ltd v Lancaster [1993] 1 WLR 1462 (Chancery Division: Mummery J). *Redgrave v Hurd* (1881) 20 Ch D 1 applied.

1814 Fraudulent misrepresentation—company officers' fraudulent misrepresentations—liability of company
See *Dixon v Deacon Morgan McEwan Easson*, para 469.

MONEY

Halsbury's Laws of England (4th edn) Vol 32, paras 101–400

1815 Financial services
See FINANCIAL SERVICES.

1816 Interest—compound interest—right to compound interest
See *Westdeutsche Landesbank Girozentrale v Islington London Borough Council*, para 607.

1817 International Development Association—additional payments to resources
The International Development Association (Tenth Replenishment) Order 1993, SI 1993/2046 (in force on 26 July 1993), provides for the payment to the association of sums not exceeding £620m as an additional contribution to the resources of the association and for the redemption of non-interest-bearing and non-negotiable notes issued by the Secretary of State in payment of those additional contributions. It further provides that certain sums which may be received by the Government of the United Kingdom from the association are to be paid into the Consolidated Fund.

1818 Loans of money—offences in relation to minors—building society promotional leaflet
A minor, aged nine, had a savings account with a building society. With his annual statement he had received a mail-shot which purported to offer up to £7,500 by way of an unsecured personal loan. At the bottom of the leaflet were the words "loans are not available to applicants under 18 years of age". The building society's policy was not to make loans to persons under the age of 18. The building society was convicted of sending a minor a document inviting him to borrow money with a view to financial gain contrary to the Consumer Credit Act 1974, s 50(1)(a). On appeal by way of case stated, held, the document, read as a whole, operated to exclude those under 18. When sending out the leaflet the building society had no intention to obtain financial gain from any person who received it who was a minor. Although the leaflet had been sent to account holders regardless of their age, every invitation to borrow money had been subject to the building society's policy. Accordingly, the appeal would be allowed.
   Alliance & Leicester Building Society v Babbs (1993) 157 JP 706 (Queen's Bench Division: Farquharson LJ and Wright J).

1819 National savings—investment deposits—limits
The National Savings Bank (Investment Deposits) (Limits) (Amendment) Order 1993, SI 1993/1239 (in force on 10 May 1993), further amends the 1977 Order, SI 1977/1210. The limit

on the aggregate amount which can be accepted by the Director of Savings from any person by way of an investment deposit in the National Savings Bank is increased from £25,000 to £100,000.

1820   National savings—value of deceased's deposits—Inland Revenue statement regarding inheritance tax

The National Savings Bank (Amendment) Regulations 1993, SI 1993/3130 (in force on 5 January 1994), amend the 1972 Regulations, SI 1972/764, by increasing from £25,000 to £50,000, the aggregate value of a deceased's deposits which needs to be exceeded before a statement from the Commissioners of the Inland Revenue regarding payment of inheritance tax is required.

1821   National Savings Stock Register—nominal value of stock

The National Savings Stock Register (Amendment) Regulations 1993, SI 1993/783 (in force on 7 April 1993), further amend the 1976 Regulations, SI 1976/2012, to raise from £10,000 to £25,000 the two limits which relate to the nominal value of stock of any one issue which may be registered in the National Savings of Stock Register and the value of any stock of any one description which may be purchased on any one day.

1822   National Savings Stock Register—value of deceased's stock—Inland Revenue statement regarding inheritance tax

The National Savings Stock Register (Amendment) (No 2) Regulations 1993, SI 1993/3131 (in force on 5 January 1994) amend the 1976 Regulations, SI 1976/2012, so as to increase from £25,000 to £50,000, the figure for the value of a deceased's holding of stock which needs to be exceeded for the purposes of the production of a statement from the Commissioners of the Inland Revenue that inheritance tax has been paid in respect of that stock.

1823   Premium savings bonds—maximum permitted holding

The Premium Savings Bonds (Amendment) Regulations 1993, SI 1993/782 (in force on 13 April 1993), further amend the 1972 Regulations, SI 1972/765, by increasing the permitted holding of premium savings bonds from 10,000 to 20,000 bond units.

1824   Savings certificates—value of deceased's certificates—Inland Revenue statement regarding inheritance tax

The Savings Certificates (Yearly Plan) (Amendment) Regulations 1993, SI 1993/3132 (in force on 5 January 1994), amend the 1984 Regulations, SI 1984/779, by increasing from £25,000 to £50,000, the aggregate value of a deceased's certificates which needs to be exceeded before a statement from the Commissioners of the Inland Revenue regarding payment of inheritance tax is required.

The Savings Certificates (Amendment) Regulations 1993, SI 1993/3133 (in force on 5 January 1994), amend the 1991 Regulations, SI 1991/1013, by increasing from £25,000 to £50,000, the aggregate value of a deceased's certificates which needs to be exceeded before a statement from the Commissioners of the Inland Revenue regarding payment of inheritance tax is required.

MORTGAGE

Halsbury's Laws of England (4th edn) Vol 32, paras 401–1052

1825   Articles

Default Measures, Kerry Stephenson (on ways to prevent mortgage fraud): 137 SJ 667
Equitable Set-Off and Right of Possession, Geraldine Andrews (on sureties who mortgage their properties): 137 SJ 434
Lenders' Panels, Kerry Stephenson (on valuers qualifications): 137 SJ 798
Money Judgments for Mortgagees—An Own Goal? Katy Manley: 143 NLJ 1451

Mortgages and Ownership of the Family Home, Philip Wylie: [1993] Fam Law 176
Mortgages: Rights, Remedies and Reform, Robert Elliott: 1993 SLT 23
Never Trust a Man . . . Mark Lunney (on *Equity and Law Loans v Prestidge* [1992] 1 All ER 909,
   CA (1991 Abr para 1697)): 56 MLR 87
The Pitfalls of Mortgage Possession Actions, Rhys Jones: 143 NLJ 1762
The Priority of Dealings with Equitable Interests in Land—Section 137 of the Law of Property
Act 1925 or Registration? Jean Howell: [1993] Conv 23

1826   Equitable interest—priority—constructive notice

A wife agreed to execute a legal charge over the jointly owned matrimonial home as security
for the overdraft facility of a company in which the husband had an interest. The wife signed
the charge without reading it, in reliance on the husband's false representations as to the amount
and duration of the security. The company subsequently exceeded its overdraft and the creditor
attempted to enforce the legal charge. The Court of Appeal held that married women who
provided security for their husband's debts, and others in an analogous position, were to be
treated as a special class of sureties. The wife was entitled to set aside the legal charge because she
was induced to execute it by her husband's misrepresentation in circumstances which put the
creditor on enquiry. On the creditor's appeal, *held*, where the doctrine of notice was properly
applied there was no need, nor basis in principle, for affording a limited class of special rights in
equity in relation to surety transactions. A wife who had been induced to stand as surety for her
husband's debt by his undue influence, misrepresentation or other legal wrong had an equity
against him to set that transaction aside. Under the ordinary principles of equity, that right was
also enforceable against third parties for whom the husband acted as agent or who had actual or
constructive notice of the facts giving rise to her equity. Where a wife offered to stand surety
for her husband's debts, a creditor was put on enquiry since the transaction was on its face not to
her advantage and there was a substantial risk in such transactions that the husband procured the
wife's agreement by some legal or equitable wrong entitling her to set it aside. In such
circumstances, unless the creditor took reasonable steps to ascertain that the wife's agreement
was properly obtained, it would have constructive notice of her equitable rights. A creditor
would satisfy the reasonable steps requirement if it insisted that the wife attend a private meeting,
in the absence of the husband, with a representative of the creditor at which she was told of the
extent of her liability as surety, warned of the risk she was running and urged to take independent
legal advice. Further, since unmarried cohabitation was now widespread, these principles were
also applicable to other cases where a creditor was aware that the surety was cohabiting with the
principal debtor. In the present case, the creditor had constructive notice of the husband's
misrepresentation and the wife's consequent entitlement, as against the creditor, to set the legal
charge aside. Accordingly, the appeal would be dismissed.

   Barclays Bank plc v O'Brien [1993] 4 All ER 417 (House of Lords: Lords Templeman, Lowry,
Browne-Wilkinson, Slynn of Hadley and Woolf). Decision of Court of Appeal [1992] 3 WLR
593 (1992 Abr para 1790) affirmed on other grounds. *Avon Finance Co Ltd v Bridger* [1985] 2
All ER 281, CA approved. *Hoghton v Hoghton* (1852) 15 Beav 278 overruled.

1827   Legal charge—undue influence—constructive notice

The plaintiff company advanced £150,000 to a husband and wife on the security of the
matrimonial home. They fell into arrears when repaying the loan. In proceedings by the plaintiff
for possession of the property, the wife, who claimed that she had reluctantly signed the
documents for the loan (which, although stated to be for the purpose of purchasing a holiday
home was in fact to pay the husband's debts), contended that the security could not be enforced
against her because of her husband's undue influence. At first instance, it was held that a legal
charge on the matrimonial home in favour of the plaintiff was valid as against her. On appeal it
was held that the innocent lender was not affected by the undue influence exerted by the
husband over the wife. On further appeal by the wife, *held*, even though the wife was entitled to
set aside the transaction against the husband, she had to establish that the plaintiff was affected
by the wrongdoing of the husband so as to entitle her to set aside the legal charge as against the
plaintiff. Although the wife had established undue influence by the husband, the plaintiff would
not be affected by the undue influence unless the husband was acting as the plaintiff's agent in
procuring the wife's agreement or the plaintiff had actual or constructive notice of the undue
influence. In this case, the husband was not acting as the plaintiff's agent, and the plaintiff had no
actual notice of the undue influence. As far as the plaintiff was aware, there was nothing in the
transaction to indicate that it was anything other than a normal advance to husband and wife

for their joint benefit. The appeal would accordingly be dismissed.

CIBC Mortgages plc v Pitt [1993] 4 All ER 433 (House of Lords: Lords Templeman, Lowry, Browne-Wilkinson, Slynn of Hadley and Woolf). Decision of Court of Appeal (1993) P & CR 179 affirmed. *Bank of Credit and Commerce International SA v Aboody* (1988) [1992] 4 All ER 953, CA (1989 Abr para 947) overruled.

1828   Mortgagee—action for possession—counterclaim by mortgagor—effect on entitlement to possession

The defendant mortgagors charged their home to a bank as security in respect of debts owed by a company to the bank. The mortgage agreement provided that the defendants were deemed to stand charged with the liabilities secured "as if they were primarily due from the mortgagor". The bank subsequently began possession proceedings. The defendants alleged in their defence and counterclaim that the company was entitled to recover unliquidated damages against the bank for an alleged breach of duty and that, as the sum claimed would exceed the amount of the arrears, that claim could be set off against the sums owing by the company to the bank, thus extinguishing the company's debt and discharging the mortgage. The bank applied successfully to strike out the defence. On the defendants' appeal, *held*, the general rule that, subject to contractual or statutory limitations, the existence of a cross-claim, even if it exceeded the amount of the mortgage debt, would not itself defeat the right to possession of a mortgagee was applicable both where the cross-claim was a mere counterclaim and where it was a cross-claim for unliquidated damages which, if established, would give rise to a right by way of equitable set-off. Any potential right of set-off to which the defendants might be entitled as sureties was excluded by the mortgage agreement since the mortgage was deemed to be a primary security and the defendants were deemed to be in the position of primary debtors rather than guarantors. Accordingly, there was no defence to the bank's claim to possession and the defendants' appeal would be dismissed.

National Westminster Bank plc v Skelton [1993] 1 All ER 242 (Court of Appeal: Slade LJ and Anthony Lincoln J).

The defendant mortgagors charged their home to the plaintiffs as security in respect of debts owed by a company to which the plaintiffs had lent money. The mortgage agreement provided that the plaintiffs could enforce their rights against the mortgaged property "in the event that the company made default in any of its obligations to the lender". Having failed to obtain payment of amounts owing from the company and the defendants, the plaintiffs began possession proceedings. The defendants contended that the company had cross-claims against the plaintiffs which gave it the right of equitable set-off for an unliquidated sum exceeding the figure owed. The district judge ordered that the defendants were entitled to have their claim for an equitable set-off tried before a possession order was made. On the plaintiffs' application to vary or rescind the order, the judge dealt with the application as an appeal and granted the plaintiffs possession. On the defendants' appeal, *held*, the general rule that, subject to contractual or statutory limitations, a mortgagor could not defeat a legal mortgagee's right to possession by claiming an equitable set-off for an unliquidated sum exceeding the amount of the mortgage arrears applied irrespective of whether the mortgagor was the principal debtor of the mortgagee or was only a guarantor. In each case the mortgagee had, as an incident of his estate in the land, a right to possession of the mortgaged property and in each case the cross-claims could not be unilaterally appropriated in discharge of the mortgage debt. The mere fact that a guarantor was not primarily liable for payment of the debt was immaterial because when he came to be made liable his position in relation to the appropriation of cross-claims was at best no different from, and could not be better than, that of a mortgagor who was a primary debtor. Further, as the aggregate value of the company's cross-claims did not exceed the sums owed to the plaintiff, the company was in default of its obligations to the plaintiff under the terms of the mortgage agreement. Accordingly, the defendants' appeal would be dismissed.

Ashley Guarantee plc v Zacaria [1993] 1 All ER 254 (Court of Appeal: Nourse, Ralph Gibson and Woolf LJJ). *National Westminster Bank plc v Skelton* [1993] 1 All ER 242, CA supra applied.

1829   Mortgagee—order for possession and concurrent judgment for mortgage debt—suspension of orders

On a building society's application for an order for possession of mortgaged property and a concurrent money judgment for the whole balance of the mortgage debt, it has been held that there is no inconsistency between the grant to the society of an order for possession, suspended subject to conditions as to payment being met by the borrower, and a concurrent money judgment for the whole of the debt, suspended for as long as the possession order remains suspended.

Cheltenham and Gloucester Building Society v Grattidge (1993) 25 HLR 454 (Court of Appeal: Lloyd, Kennedy and Hoffmann LJJ).

NATIONAL HEALTH SERVICE

Halsbury's Laws of England (4th edn) Vol 33, paras 1–300

1830 Articles

Care for the Elderly—Who Pays? Philip Spiers: 137 SJ 394
Health Authorities and the Payment of Damages by Means of a Pension, Richard Lewis: 56 MLR 844
NHS Contracts, Restitution and the Internal Market, Kit Barker: 56 MLR 832

1831 Central Blood Laboratories Authority—abolition

The Central Blood Laboratories Authority (Revocation) Order 1993, SI 1993/587 (in force on 1 April 1993), abolishes the Central Blood Laboratories Authority. The 1982 Order, SI 1982/1515, is revoked. As to the national Blood Authority, see para 1849.

1832 Charges—dental charges

The National Health Service (Dental Charges) Amendment Regulations 1993, SI 1993/419 (in force on 1 April 1993), further amend the 1989 Regulations, SI 1989/394, by increasing the proportion of the charge for dental treatment and appliances which is payable by a patient to 80 per cent, and increasing the prescribed maximum charge payable by the patient to £250. The increases apply where the contract or arrangement leading to the provision of such treatment and the supply of such appliances is made on or after 1 April 1993. The 1992 Regulations, SI 1992/369, are revoked.

1833 Charges—drugs and appliances

The National Health Service (Charges for Drugs and Appliances) Amendment Regulations 1993, SI 1993/420 (in force on 1 April 1993), further amend the 1989 Regulations, SI 1989/419, by increasing the charge for items on prescription or supplied to out-patients to £4·25, and by increasing certain charges for drugs and appliances supplied by doctors and chemists providing pharmaceutical services. The regulations also specify that applications for repayment of charges are to be made within three months from the date on which the drug or appliance was supplied.

1834 Charges—optical services

The National Health Service (Optical Charges and Payments) Amendment Regulations 1993, SI 1993/418 (in force on 1 April 1993), further amend the 1989 Regulations, SI 1989/495, so as to increase by an average of 2·75 per cent the value of vouchers issued in respect of the cost of the repair, replacement and supply of glasses and contact lenses, and of the repair and replacement of optical appliances. In addition, the additional values of vouchers for prisms, tints, photocromic lenses and special categories of appliances are increased.

1835 Charges—remission and payment—travelling expenses

The National Health Service (Travelling Expenses and Remission of Charges) Amendment Regulations 1993, SI 1993/608 (in force on 1 April 1993), further amend the 1988 Regulations, SI 1988/551, by introducing new provisions for determining the manner in which a person's requirements are to be calculated following the replacement of the community charge by the council tax. The regulations also provide that claims for remission or payment of certain charges which would otherwise be payable under the National Health Service Act 1977 may be sent or delivered to the Secretary of State as well as to an office of the Department of Social Security.

1836 Community care—Isles of Scilly

The Isles of Scilly (Community Care) Order 1993, SI 1993/570 (in force on 1 April 1993), revokes the 1991 Order, SI 1991/552, and extends to the Isles of Scilly, with appropriate modifications, the provisions of the National Health Service and Community Care Act 1990, Pt III (relating to community care in England and Wales), and the Community Care (Residential Accommodation Act 1992, s 1 (relating to arrangements for provision of residential accommodation in premises managed by voluntary organisations).

1837 Dental services—general services

The National Health Service (General Dental Services) Amendment Regulations 1993, SI 1993/2209 (in force on 1 October 1993) as amended by SI 1993/3172 (in force on 22 December 1993), further amend the 1992 Regulations, SI 1992/661, by providing that a Family Health Services Authority (FHSA) may not include any dentist in its dental list unless satisfied that he has completed a period of vocational training, or has acquired dental experience or training which may be regarded as the equivalent of such training, or is within one of the specified categories of exemption from the vocational training requirements. The FHSA has the function of allocating a vocational training number to an applicant where it is so satisfied. The Regulations further provide for a right of appeal and for appeal procedures in cases where the FHSA determines not to allocate a vocational training number. The functions of FHSA's under these regulations are to be exercised by the Dental Vocational Training Authority.

1838 Dental Vocational Training Authority

The Dental Vocational Training Authority (Establishment and Constitution) and Appeal Body (Specification) Order 1993, SI 1993/2211 (in force on 1 October 1993), provides for the establishment and constitution of the Dental Vocational Training Authority. The authority will exercise certain functions on behalf of the Family Health Services Authorities in England and Wales in connection with general dental services under the National Health Service. Provision is also made for the setting up of an appeal body to deal with appeals from the authority.

The Dental Vocational Training Authority Regulations 1993, SI 1993/2210 (1 October 1993), provide rules to govern the membership and procedure of the Dental Vocational Training Authority.

1839 District health authorities—determination of districts

The National Health Service (Determination of Districts) Order 1993, SI 1993/574 (in force on 1 April 1993), abolishes certain districts and determines new districts for the purposes of the National Health Services Act 1977. Provision is made for officers to be transferred from the abolished authorities to the relevant new health authorities, and for the transfer of rights and liabilities to the new authorities.

The National Health Service (Determination of Districts) (No 2) Order 1993, SI 1993/2219 (in force on 1 October 1993), abolishes certain districts, determines new districts and varies other districts. Provision is made for the transfer of officers from the abolished health authorities to the relevant new authorities. In addition, provision is made for the transfer of rights and liabilities of the abolished authorities.

1840 District health authorities—duty to consult Community Health Council— failure to consult council

A district health authority decided to close the bone marrow treatment unit at a children's hospital and not to continue to provide the services and treatment offered by the unit at any other hospital within its area. In judicial review proceedings for certiorari or a declaration that the closure of the unit without providing its service elsewhere in the authority's area was unlawful, *held*, under the Community Health Council Regulations 1985, SI 1985/304, reg 19(1), a district health authority had a duty to consult the Community Health Council on any proposals for the substantial development or variation of the authority's service. The failure to continue to provide the service offered by the unit anywhere in the area amounted to a substantial variation in the provision of the service so that the failure to consult the council was unlawful. However, as a formal declaration to that effect would achieve nothing, the court would, in its discretion, refuse the orders sought.

R v North West Thames Regional Health Authority, ex p Daniels (1993) Independent, 18 June, Times, 22 June (Queen's Bench Division: Kennedy LJ and Macpherson J).

1841   District health authorities—establishment of new authorities

The National Health Service (District Health Authorities) Order 1993, SI 1993/572 (in force on 1 April 1993), and the National Health Service (District Health Authorities) (No 2) Order 1993, SI 1993/2218 (in force on 1 October 1993), amend the 1990 Order, SI 1990/1756, so as to abolish specified district health authorities and to establish a number of new district health authorities.

1842   District health authorities—residential accommodation

The Residential Accommodation (Determination of District Health Authority) (Amendment) Regulations 1993, SI 1993/582 (in force on 1 April 1993), amend the 1992 Regulations, SI 1992/3182, by clarifying the procedure to be followed in cases where there is a doubt as to the district health authority in which a person who requires treatment is usually resident.

1843   Employees—redundancy payments

The Redundancy Payments (National Health Service) (Modification) Order 1993, SI 1993/3167 (in force on 13 January 1994), modifies certain redundancy payments provisions of the Employment Protection (Consolidation) Act 1978 in their application to persons employed in relevant health services so that a change of employer does not break continuity for the purposes of the provisions of the 1978 Act.

1844   Family health services authority—employment—general practitioner— whether employment contractual or statutory

See *Ealing Hammersmith and Hounslow Family Health Services Authority v Shukla*, para 2308.

1845   Fund-holding practices—regulations

The National Health Service (Fund-holding Practices) Regulations 1993, SI 1993/567 (in force on 1 April 1993), consolidate, with amendments, the existing provisions relating to the operation and recognition of fund-holding practices. Changes of substance relate to the purchase of district nursing and health visiting services by fund-holding practices, and to the circumstances in which a fund-holding practice may use its allotted sum to make payments to one of the members of the practice. The position relating to the exercise of purchasing decisions by fund-holding practices is clarified, as are certain matters concerning the payment of employees' salaries out of a fund-holding practice's allotted sum.

1846   General medical services—regulations

The National Health Service (General Medical Services) Amendment Regulations 1993, SI 1993/540 (in force on 1 April 1993), further amend the 1992 Regulations, SI 1992/635, so as to enable family health service authorities to make payments to doctors in respect of health promotion programmes and disease management programmes. In addition, a provision is introduced which requires doctors to issue free of charge medical certificates which are required by patients to enable them to claim exemption from or a reduction in liability to pay the council tax.

The National Health Service (General Medical Services) Amendment (No 2) Regulations 1993, SI 1993/2421 (in force on 1 November 1993), further amend the 1992 Regulations supra. Certain substances are removed from the list of drugs and other substances which may not be prescribed for supply in the course of pharmaceutical services under the National Health Service Act 1977.

1847   Health Service Commissioners Act 1993

The Health Service Commissioners Act 1993 consolidates certain enactments relating to the Health Service Commissioners for England and Wales with amendments to give effect to recommendations of the Law Commission. The Act received the Royal assent on 5 November 1993 and came into force on 5 February 1994. A table showing the destination of enactments consolidated appears overleaf.

DESTINATION TABLE

This table shows in column (1) the enactments repealed by the Health Service Commissioners Act 1993 and in column (2) the provisions of that Act corresponding thereto.

In certain cases the enactment in column (1), though having a corresponding provision in column (2) is not, or not wholly, repealed as it is still required, or partly required, for the purposes of other legislation.

A "dash" in the right hand column means that the repealed provision to which it corresponds in the left hand column is spent, unnecessary or for some other reason not specifically reproduced.

A reference to "LC rec" is a reference to one of the recommendations of the Law Commission in its report on the consolidation of the Legislation relating to the Health Service Commissioners (Cm 2255; Law Com No 213).

(1)	(2)
Parliamentary Commissioner Act 1967 (c 13)	Health Service Commissioners Act 1993 (c 46)
s 1(1)†	s 19
s 7(1)†	s 11(1)
s 7(2)†	s 11(2), (3)
s 7(3)†	s 11(4)
s 7(4)†	s 11(5), (6)
s 8(1)†	s 12(1)
s 8(2)†	s 12(2)
s 8(3)†	s 12(3), (4)
s 8(4)†	s 12(5)
s 8(5)†	s 12(6)
s 9†	s 13
s 11(2)†	s 15
s 11(3)†	s 16
s 12(1)†	s 19

(1)	(2)
Local Government Act 1974 (c 7)	Health Service Commissioners Act 1993 (c 46)
s 33(3)*, (4)*	—

(1)	(2)
Local Government (Scotland) Act 1975 (c 30)	Health Service Commissioners Act 1993 (c 46)
s 31(3)*, (4)*	s 18(1), LC rec 4

(1)	(2)
National Health Service Act 1977 (c 49)	Health Service Commissioners Act 1993 (c 46)
s 106(1)	s 1(1)
s 106(2)	Sch 1, para 1(1)
s 106(3)	Sch 1, para 1(2)
s 106(3A)	Sch 1, para 1(3)
s 106(4)	Sch 1, para 3(1)
s 107(1)	Sch 1, para 4
s 107(2)	Sch 1, para 7
s 107(3)	Sch 1, para 5
s 107(4)	Sch 1, para 8
s 107(5)	Sch 1, para 6
s 107(6)	Sch 1, para 9(3)–(5)

(1)	(2)
National Health Service Act 1977 (c 49)	Health Service Commissioners Act 1993 (c 46)
s 107(7)	Sch 1, para 9(2)
s 107(8)	Sch 1, para 15
s 108(1), (2)	Sch 1, para 11
s 108(2)	Sch 1, para 12
s 108(3)	Sch 1, para 13
s 108(4)	Sch 1, para 14
s 108A(1)–(3)	Sch 1, para 2(1)–(3)
s 108A(4)	Sch 1, para 15
s 108A(5)	Sch 1, para 3
s 109(a), (bb), (da), (dd), (e), (f)	s 2(1)
s 109(b)	—
s 109(c)	s 2(1), (5)
s 109(d)	s 2(1), (5)
s 109(g)	Rep 1980 c 53, ss 9, 25(4), Sch 2, para 7, Sch 7
s 109 (remainder) . . .	—
s 110(a)	—
s 110(aa), (b), (ba), (c)	s 2(2)
s 110(d)	Rep 1980 c 53, ss 9, 25(4), Sch 2, para 8, Sch 7
s 111(1)	s 8
s 111(2)	s 9(3)
s 112(a)	s 9(5)
s 112(b)	s 9(6)
s 113(1)	s 3(2)
s 113(2)	ss 3(3), 10(4)
s 114(1)(a)	s 9(2), (4)
s 114(1)(b)	s 9(4)
s 114(2)	—
s 115	s 3(1)
s 116(1)	s 4(1)
s 116(2)(a)	passim
s 116(2)(b)	s 6(1)
s 116(3)	s 7(4)
s 117	s 10(1)–(3), (5)
s 118(1), (1A), (1B) . .	s 18(1)
s 118(2)	s 18(2)
s 118(3)	s 18(3)
s 119(1)(a)–(e)	s 14(1)
s 119(1)(f)	Rep SI 1985/39, art 7(21)

† Not repealed
* Repealed in part

(1)	(2)	(1)	(2)
National Health Service Act 1977 (c 49)	Health Service Commissioners Act 1993 (c 46)	Health Services Act 1980 (c 53)	Health Service Commissioners Act 1993 (c 46)
s 119(2)	s 14(2)	Sch 1, Pt I	
s 119(3)	s 14(3)	para 72	s 2(1)
s 119(4)	s 14(4)	para 73	s 2(2)
s 119(5)	s 14(5)	para 74	s 14(1)
s 120(1)	ss 1(1), (2), 19	Sch 2, para 7	s 2(1)
s 120(2)	s 3(4)	paras 8, 9	—
s 126(1)†	ss 2(6), 7(5), 22(3), Sch 1, para 9(7)	para 11(a)–(f) . . . Apply to Scotland	
s 126(4)†	Sch 1, para 9(6)		
s 128(1)†	ss 5(2), 19		
s 130(3)(c).	s 22(2)		
s 130(4)†	s 22(3)		
Sch 13, Pt I		Mental Health (Scotland) Act 1984 (c 36)	Health Service Commissioners Act 1993 (c 46)
para 1	s 11(1)		
para 2	s 11(2), (3)	Sch 3, para 42 . . . . . s 4(3), LC rec 2	
para 3	s 11(3)		
paras 4–6	s 11(4)–(6)		
para 7	s 12(1)		
para 8	ss 12(2), 19		
para 9	s 12(3), (4)		
para 10	s 12(5)	Parliamentary and Health Service Commissioners Act 1987 (c 39)	Health Service Commissioners Act 1993 (c 46)
para 11	s 12(6)		
para 12	s 13(1)		
para 13	s 13(2)	s 2(2)	Sch 1, para 1(1), (3)
para 14	s 13(3)	s 4(3)(a)	s 18(1), LC rec 4
para 15	Rep 1989 c 6, s 16(4), Sch 2	s 4(3)(b)	s 18(2)
para 16	s 15	s 4(4)	s 17
para 16A	s 17	s 4(5)	Applies to Scotland
para 17	s 16(1), (3)	s 5(1)	s 14(1)
para 18	s 16(2), (3)	s 5(2)	s 14(2)
Sch 13, Pt II		s 5(3)	Applies to Scotland
para 19(1)	s 5(1)	s 6(2)	Sch 1, paras 2, 3, 15
para 19(2)	s 6(3)	s 6(3)	Applies to Scotland
para 19(3)	s 7(1)	s 7	s 10(3)
para 19(4)	s 7(2), (3)	s 8	Applies to Scotland
para 19(5)	s 4(2)		
Sch 14, para 17	—		
Sch 15, paras 60, 61 . .	—		
National Health Service (Scotland) Act 1978 (c 29)	Health Service Commissioners Act 1993 (c 46)	Health and Medicines Act 1988 (c 49)	Health Service Commissioners Act 1993 (c 46)
s 90(1)–(4)	Apply to Scotland		
s 90(5)	Sch 1, para 3	s 12(4)	s 2(1)
ss 91, 92, 92A(1)–(4) .	Apply to Scotland	s 12(5)	Applies to Scotland
s 92A(5)	Sch 1, para 3		
ss 93–97	Apply to Scotland		
Sch 14		Official Secrets Act 1989 (c 6)	Health Service Commissioners Act 1993 (c 46)
para 1	s 6(2)		
para 2	Applies to Scotland		
para 3	s 6(4)		
paras 4–6	Apply to Scotland		
para 7	s 4(3), LC rec 2		
Sch 15, para 12	Applies to Scotland	Sch 1, para 1(h) . . . . s 15(1)	

† Not repealed

(1)	(2)	(1)	(2)
National Health Service and Community Care Act 1990 (c 19)	Health Service Commissioners Act 1993 (c 46)	Judicial Pensions and Retirement Act 1993 (c 8)	Health Service Commissioners Act 1993 (c 46)
		Sch 4, Pt III	
s 2(1)†	ss 2(1), (2), 6(2)	para 3(1)	—
Sch 9		para 3(2)	Sch 1, para 7
para 18(10), (11) . .	s 2(1), (2)	para 3(3)	Sch 1, para 9(3), (4)
para 19(18)	Applies to Scotland	para 3(4)	Sch 1, para 9(2)
		para 3(5)	Sch 1, para 10
		para 4	Applies to Scotland

† Not repealed

1848 Medical practices committee—composition

The National Health Service Act 1977 (Composition of Medical Practices Committee) Order 1993, SI 1993/887 (in force on 21 April 1993), amends the National Health Service Act 1977 so as to alter from six to five the number of members of the Medical Practices Committee (other than the chairman) who are to be registered medical practitioners, and from five to four the number of those members who are to be actively engaged in medical practice.

1849 National Blood Authority

The National Blood Authority (Establishment and Constitution) Order 1993, SI 1993/585 (in force on 1 April 1993), provides for the establishment and constitution of the National Blood Authority, which is required to oversee the preparation and supply of blood products. The authority is obliged to co-ordinate, monitor and publicise arrangements made for the collection and supply of blood by the regional health authorities.

The National Blood Authority Regulations 1993, SI 1993/586 (in force on 1 April 1993), provide for the appointment and tenure of office of members of the National Blood Authority, the termination of their employment and their eligibility for re-appointment. SI 1982/1516 is revoked.

As to the abolition of the Central Blood Laboratories Authority, see para 1831.

1850 National Health Service trusts—originating capital debt

The National Health Service Trusts (Originating Capital Debt) Order 1993, SI 1993/289 (in force on 11 March 1993), determines the amount of originating capital debt for NHS trusts, in accordance with the National Health Service and Community Care Act 1990, s 9. The order also provides for the splitting up of the originating capital debts into loan and public dividend capital.

1851 National Health Service trusts—transfer of undertakings

See *Northern General Hospital National Health Service Trust v Gale*, para 1135.

1852 Pharmaceutical services—regulations

The National Health Service (Pharmaceutical Services) Amendment Regulations 1993, SI 1993/2451 (in force on 11 November 1993), amend the 1992 Regulations, SI 1992/662, which govern the arrangements to be made by family health services authorities for the provision in their locality of pharmaceutical services under the National Health Service Act 1977. The principal change will enable chemists to provide "additional professional services" consisting of publishing a practice leaflet and displaying health promotion material.

1853 Regional and district health authorities—membership and procedure

The Regional and District Health Authorities (Membership and Procedure) Amendment Regulations 1993, SI 1993/573 (in force on 1 April 1993), further amend the 1990 Regulations, SI 1990/1331, in accordance with the provisions the National Health Service (District Health Authorities) Order 1993, SI 1993/572 (para 1841), which abolishes a number of health authorities and establishes a number of new ones.

1854 Regional health authorities—determination of regions

The National Health Service (Determination of Regions) Amendment Order 1993, SI 1993/571 (in force on 1 April 1993), further amends the 1981 Regulations, SI 1981/1836, by removing the borough of Spelthorne, Surrey from the North West Thames Regional Health Authority and including it in the South West Thames Regional Health Authority.

1855 Service committees and tribunals—regulations

The National Health Service (Service Committees and Tribunal) Amendment Regulations 1993, SI 1993/2972 (in force on 1 January 1994), amend the 1992 Regulations, SI 1992/664, so as to provide that where a complaint has been made about a doctor, dentist, optician or chemist providing services under the National Health Service Act 1977, Pt II that he is in breach of his terms of service, there is a right of appeal from the decision of the family health services authority dealing with the complaint, in specified cases. Those cases are (1) where the committee of the family health services authority dealing with the complaint has not held an oral hearing of the complaint, (2) where it has been decided initially that the complaint as received does not show any grounds for thinking that there has been a possible breach of terms of service by a practitioner, and (3) where the complaint is about the conduct of a doctor deputising for a patient's own doctor, and it has been decided initially that the complaint as received shows no grounds for believing that the doctor with whom the patient is registered was himself in breach of his terms of service.

1856 Social security
See SOCIAL SECURITY AND SOCIAL SERVICES.

1857 Superannuation
See PENSIONS AND SUPERANNUATION.

NEGLIGENCE

Halsbury's Laws of England (4th edn) Vol 34, paras 1–200

1858 Articles
Can Negligent Solicitors Hide Behind the Limitation Act? Hugh Brayne: 137 SJ 10
Failure to Warn: Establishing the Causal Link, Michael A Jones: (1993) 1 AVMA 6
Is a Doctor Negligent if His Patient Lapses From Follow-Up? Dr Walter Scott: (1993) 3 AVMA 7
Liability for References—*Spring v Guardian Assurance*, Thomas Allen (on *Spring v Guardian Assurance* [1993] 2 All ER 273, CA (1992 Abr para 1846)): 57 MLR 111
Osman v Metropolitan Police Commissioner—The Cost of Police Protectionism, Marcus Tregilgas-Davey (on *Osman v Ferguson* [1993] 4 All ER 344, CA (para 1880)): 56 MLR 732
Police Liability After *Ancell*, Steve Greenfield et al (see *Ancell v McDermot* [1993] 4 All ER 355, CA (para 1879)): 137 SJ 328
Scepticism and the Law of Negligence, Jenny Steele: 52 CLJ 437
Slippery Slopes, Paul Maxlow-Tomlinson (on Codes of Practice for Ski Resorts): LS Gaz, 10 March 1993, p 25
Unreliable Assumptions in the Modern Law of Negligence, Kit Barker: (1993) 109 LQR 461
Vehicle Accident Damage—Loss of Use and Hire Costs, Irvine Marr and Paul Coppin: 137 SJ 1072

1859 Damages
See DAMAGES AND COMPENSATION.

1860 Duty of care—auditor—duty to report
New Zealand
The respondent acted as trustee for unsecured depositors of a money market operating company and the appellant was the auditor of that company. The trustee was under a duty to exercise reasonable diligence to ascertain whether any breach of the trust deeds had occurred and whether the assets of the borrower were likely to be sufficient to repay the deposits as they became due. The auditor was under a statutory duty to send a written report to the company and to the trustee within seven working days of becoming aware of any matter that was, in its opinion, relevant to the performance of the trustee's duties. The company was insolvent at the end of 1985. In early 1986 the auditor prepared the audit for the previous year and was concerned about the collectability of certain associated company loans. However, it did not report the probable insolvency of the company to the company or to the trustee for several months. The company subsequently went into liquidation and the trustee incurred a liability to the company's depositors which it settled. The trustee sought to recover that money from the directors and the auditor. With regard to the auditor, the court held that the auditor had not breached its statutory duty because it had not formed the requisite opinion but, since a reasonably prudent auditor would have formed an opinion and reported much earlier, the auditor was in breach of its

common law duty to report the company's probable insolvency to the trustee. On the auditor's appeal, *held*, the only positive statutory duty imposed on the auditor was to send a report within the specified time to the company and trustee once it became aware of a certain matter and formed the opinion that it was relevant to the exercise of the trustee's powers. There was no statutory duty to form such an opinion and the superimposition of a positive common law duty to report which was of wider scope than the statutory duty was not justified. Further, given that the company was insolvent at the end of 1985, the trustee had not established that its loss was caused by the auditor's failure to report earlier in 1986. The auditor was not liable to the trustee and, accordingly, the appeal would be allowed.

Deloitte Haskins and Sells v National Mutual Life Nominees Ltd [1993] 3 WLR 347 (Privy Council: Lords Keith of Kinkel, Bridge of Harwich, Griffiths, Jauncey of Tullichettle and Mustill). *Hedley Byrne & Co Ltd v Heller & Partners Ltd* [1964] AC 465, HL, dicta of Lord Keith of Kinkel in *Yuen Kun Yeu v Attorney General of Hong Kong* [1988] AC 175 at 195, PC (1987 Abr para 1863) considered.

1861 Duty of care—building contractors—economic loss

Canada

The plaintiff became the owner of an apartment building eight years after it was constructed. At the time of construction, the original owner and developer retained an architect and the defendant company, which acted as general contractor and employed a subcontractor to do the exterior stone cladding. A section of the stone cladding collapsed and the plaintiff commenced an action in negligence against the defendant company, its subcontractor and the architect, alleging inadequacies in design and workmanship. The defendants unsuccessfully applied for summary dismissal. On appeal, *held*, in *D & F Estates Ltd v Church Comrs for England*, the court held that a remote purchaser could not recover for economic loss against a general contractor of an alleged defective building. The concept of caveat emptor applied as between purchaser and vendor, and negated any relationship of proximity between the plaintiff and defendant. The plaintiff could have protected itself by seeking a warranty from the vendor or taking out insurance. Accordingly, the appeal would be allowed.

Winnipeg Condominium Corpn No 36 v Bird Construction Co Ltd (1993) 101 DLR (4th) 699 (Manitoba Court of Appeal). *D & F Estates Ltd v Church Comrs for England* [1988] 2 All ER 992 (1988 Abr para 1704) applied.

1862 Duty of care—building engineer—economic loss

See *Kerajaan Malaysia lwn Cheah Foong Chiew dan Lain-lain*, para 262.

1863 Duty of care—company—liability for officers' negligent mis-statements

See *Dixon v Deacon Morgan McEwan Easson*, para 469.

1864 Duty of care—company directors—personal liability to creditors

Scotland

The plaintiffs leased an aircraft to a company, of which the defendants were directors. The company went into receivership and failed to pay certain charges to the Civil Aviation Authority and the British Airports Authority with the result that both authorities detained the aircraft under statutory powers of detention, until their charges had been met by the company. The plaintiff paid the charges in order to release the aircraft and prevent its statutory sale but claimed the sum back from the defendants as damages for breach of a duty of care. *Held*, the plaintiff's claim had to be for economic loss as the aircraft had not been physically destroyed or lost. In order to establish whether there was a duty of care as regards economic loss in particular circumstances, one had to look to past cases in which the same circumstances existed. Past decisions established that company directors were not liable in negligence to the company's creditors unless particular circumstances existed, for example, by way of agreement. In this case, there were nothing amounting to particular circumstances, such as contractual guarantees, and the defendants therefore did not owe the plaintiff any duty of care. Accordingly the action would be dismissed.

Nordic Oil Services Ltd v Berman 1993 SLT 1164 (Outer House).

1865 Duty of care—Crown Prosecution Service—failure to inform magistrates of state of proceedings

The plaintiff was on bail from the magistrates' court for two offences of theft. He later appeared before the Crown Court where he sought to have both offences taken into consideration, together with other charges. The court agreed to this and the police and the Crown Prosecution Service (CPS) assured him that the magistrates would be informed. However, the magistrates remained unaware that the theft charges had already been taken into consideration and when the plaintiff failed to appear before them a warrant was issued for his arrest. He was arrested and held in custody for three days. The plaintiff then brought an action against the police and the CPS alleging that he had suffered loss, damage and distress as the result of the defendants' negligent failure to ensure that the magistrates' court was aware that the offences had been taken into consideration. The CPS claimed immunity under the Crown Proceedings Act 1947, s 2(5) and the plaintiff's claim against them was struck out on the ground that the CPS did not owe the plaintiff any duty of care. The plaintiff appealed. *Held*, the 1947 Act, s 2(5) did not apply as the recording of the fact that an offence had been taken into consideration or communicating that fact to a particular court did not fall within the ambit of judicial functions but was an administrative act and therefore the CPS would not be able to claim immunity. Furthermore, the CPS had a general duty to carry out its general administrative responsibility to keep the court informed as to the state of an adjourned criminal case and a particular responsibility to do so in the plaintiff's case by virtue of having undertaken to do so. As such the relationship between the plaintiff and the CPS was sufficiently proximate for the CPS to owe a duty of care to the plaintiff to ensure that the magistrates' court was informed that the offences with which the plaintiff had been charged had already been taken into consideration by the Crown Court. Accordingly, the appeal would be allowed and the plaintiff's claim against the CPS would be reinstated.

Welsh v Chief Constable of the Merseyside Police [1993] 1 All ER 692 (Queen's Bench Division: Tudor Evans J).

1866   Duty of care—driver and passenger—defences—contributory negligence

Canada

The plaintiff and defendant both consumed beer at a party. They left in the defendant's car, parked it and drank more beer. The defendant then drove to a gravel road which was so rough that the car keys fell out of the ignition and the car stalled. The defendant decided on a rolling-start to restart his car. The plaintiff asked if he could drive and the defendant consented, knowing that the plaintiff had consumed a large amount of alcohol and that the particular road was dark, inclined and had an open gravel pit on one side. The plaintiff lost control and the car overturned into the gravel pit, leaving the plaintiff with significant head injuries. The plaintiff claimed against the defendant in negligence and was awarded damages, apportioned on the basis that the defendant was 75 per cent negligent. The defendant's appeal was allowed on the grounds that the plaintiff had not proved that the defendant owed him a duty of care. On further appeal, *held*, the defendant breached the duty of care he owed to the plaintiff by allowing him to drive his vehicle, knowing he was unfit to do so. The defendant could not rely on the defence of ex turpi causa non oritur actio since the plaintiff sought damages to compensate for his personal injuries and had not sought to profit from his own misconduct. Nor was the defence of volenti non fit injuria relevant, as it applied only where the plaintiff agreed to accept both the legal and physical risk of harm and surrendered any right to recover for any injuries incurred. However, in recognition of the plaintiff's contributory negligence the parties would be found equally to blame and liability divided equally. Accordingly, the appeal would be allowed.

Hall v Herbert (1993) 101 DLR (4th) 129 (Supreme Court of Canada).

1867   Duty of care—electricity board—duty owed to minor

The plaintiff, who was 14 years old, was electrocuted while playing on an electrical transformer installation. To prevent children playing on such structures electricity undertakers were required by statutory regulations to fit anti-climbing devices. However the device fitted to the transformer in the present case was defective at the time of the plaintiff's injury. It was held at first instance that the plaintiff knew his act was dangerous and was old enough to take responsibility for his actions. However the electricity board were held to have breached a common law duty of care to take reasonable care for the safety of the plaintiff. On appeal, *held*, if the device had been fitted properly it would have prevented the plaintiff from climbing the pole. He had been lulled into a false sense of security because he had climbed the pole on several occasions without injury and this contributed to his insensitivity to the danger. The judge had been correct in his conclusion that the board had breached their duty of care, however damages would be reduced by two-thirds because of substantial contributory negligence. Accordingly, the appeal would be dismissed.

Adams v Southern Electricity Board (1993) Times, 21 October (Court of Appeal: Neill, Beldam and Leggatt LJJ).

1868   Duty of care—employer—breach of statutory duty

See HEALTH AND SAFETY AT WORK.

1869   Duty of care—employer—information in respect of former employee—provision to third party

The plaintiff had been retired from the civil service on medical grounds. He claimed injury benefit under the Civil Service pension scheme on the ground that his mental breakdown and subsequent problems emanated from his work situation. In order to determine his claim, the trustees of the pension scheme sought information concerning the plaintiff's work record from the defendants, a department in which the plaintiff had been employed. It fell to be determined whether they owed him a duty of care in formulating the information so provided. *Held*, a reference given by an employer in respect of a former employee to a third party who was a prospective future employer was given on an occasion of qualified privilege; words written on such an occasion were protected by the privilege and were only actionable if malicious. The employer owed no duty of care to the ex-employee in the preparation of the reference. The law of negligence was not to be imported into that class of case. There was no distinction between giving such a reference and giving information in response to questions about the ex-employee's work record requested by pension scheme trustees from whom the ex-employee was seeking a financial benefit. Accordingly, the defendants owed no duty of care to the plaintiff.

Petch v Customs and Excise Comrs [1993] ICR 789 (Court of Appeal: Dillon, Beldam and Roch LJJ). *Spring v Guardian Assurance plc* (1992) Times, 22 December, CA, (1992 Abr para 1846) considered.

1870   Duty of care—existence of duty—parties in contractual relationship—liability for defects in building

The plaintiffs engaged the defendant architects to design and act as contractor in the construction of a new sanctuary for their church. The plaintiffs were dissatisfied with the completed building and issued a writ claiming damages for breach of contract and negligence. The plaintiffs accepted that their claim in contract was statute-barred but contended that the damage occurred within the tortious limitation period. The defendants contended that: (1) the existence of a duty of care was precluded by the existence of a contract between the parties, and (2) the plaintiffs' loss was purely economic and the defendants owed no duty of care to prevent such loss. *Held*, (1) since it was established that a duty of care existed for negligent statements where the parties were in a contractual professional relationship, it was logical to extend liability to negligent acts. However, where the parties to a contract had expressly defined their rights and obligations in that contract, the law would not impose a higher duty in tort and the extent of the duty would be determined by the implied and express terms of the particular contract. Here, the defendants submitted designs so that the plaintiffs could consider the appearance of the building and this did not constitute a representation as to the technical adequacy of the proposed work. (2) The plaintiffs did not suffer actual damage to the person or to property, any loss was purely economic (the cost of rectifying the defects), and the defendants owed no duty of care to prevent such loss. Accordingly, the plaintiffs' action would be dismissed.

Lancashire and Cheshire Association of Baptist Churches Inc v Howard & Seddon Partnership (a firm) [1993] 3 All ER 467 (Queen's Bench Division: Judge Michael Kershaw QC). *Midland Bank Trust Co Ltd v Hett Stubbs & Kemp (a firm)* [1978] 3 All ER 571 (1977 Abr para 1960) considered.

1871   Duty of care—health authority—investigation into registered nursing home

See *Martine v South East Kent Health Authority*, para 1786.

1872   Duty of care—Law Society—liability for solicitor's misconduct

A solicitor arranged a mortgage for the plaintiff, secured on her home, but did not disclose that her husband, a partner in the firm, was a proprietor of the lenders, nor that she was acting for both parties to the mortgage. The plaintiff failed to meet her repayments and the solicitor's firm, acting for the lenders, brought proceedings against her and successfully sought possession of her home. The plaintiff wrote a letter of complaint about the solicitor's conduct to the defendants who replied that the firm had a duty to act for their client, the lender, rather than a third party like the plaintiff. She pointed out that she was also a client but the defendants merely referred her to the courts for redress. In response to further letters the defendants stated that, in the absence of misconduct, it would not get involved. A report subsequently commissioned by the defendants concluded that, whilst there had been no professional misconduct, the solicitor's failure to reveal her husband's interest in the lender company was conduct unbefitting to a solicitor. The plaintiff brought an action for damages against the defendants for negligence and misfeasance in public office over its handling of the complaints. *Held*, the question was whether there was such a close and direct relationship between the parties as to place the defendants under a duty of care to the plaintiff. The plaintiff was a member of a wide and indeterminate class of complainants, it was impossible to ascertain which persons were owed a duty of care, and so the plaintiff could not make out the requisite special relationship. The fact that the defendants had no power to control and supervise the day-to-day conduct of solicitors also militated against a duty of care being found. The defendants only owed a duty of care to sanction conduct unbefitting to a solicitor, not to safeguard individuals, such as the plaintiff, from loss. Accordingly, the appeal was dismissed and the plaintiff was advised of alternative courses of action available to her.

Wood v The Law Society (1993) Times, 30 July, Independent, 29 July (Queens' Bench Division: Otton J).

1873 Duty of care—local authority—child care legislation

See *X (Minors) v Bedfordshire County Council*, para 364.

1874 Duty of care—manufacturer of medicinal products

See *Hollis v Dow Corning Corp*, para 1768.

1875 Duty of care—medical practitioner—artificial insemination—HIV

See *Ter Neuzen v Korn*, para 1767.

1876 Duty of care—medical practitioner—duty to inform of risks

See *Hollis v Dow Corning Corp*, para 1768.

1877 Duty of care—members' agents and managing agents—Lloyd's of London

See *Arbuthnott v Feltrim; Deeny v Gooda Walker; Henderson v Merrett Syndicates*, para 1552.

1878 Duty of care—nervous shock—proximity

The plaintiff's husband died in hospital of a heart attack. The defendants admitted that their negligence in failing to diagnose serious heart disease caused his death. Within an hour of the death the plaintiff went to the hospital, was informed of her husband's death and identified his body. The plaintiff suffered nervous shock from her involvement at the hospital and brought a claim for damages in negligence against the defendants. She claimed that her experience came within the "immediate aftermath" extension on the law of entitlement to damages for nervous shock caused by another's breach of duty. The defendants contended that the plaintiff's involvement did not meet the established criteria in respect of: (1) proximity to the incident, and (2) the means by which the shock was caused. On the question of whether the plaintiff was entitled to recover damages for nervous shock, *held*, (1) whereas the proximity test required an external, traumatic event causing immediate injury or death, the plaintiff's husband's death, whilst shocking to the plaintiff, was the natural result of heart disease. (2) The means by which the shock was caused lacked the requisite immediacy and directness, and it was established that the law did not compensate shock caused by communication from a third party. Accordingly, the plaintiff's claim would fail.

Taylor v Somerset Health Authority [1993] PIQR P262 (Queen's Bench Division: Auld J).

1879 Duty of care—police—highway hazards—duty to members of public

An accident involving a diesel lorry resulted in a spillage of fuel on the road. Police officers helped victims of the accident away, but did not return to the spillage. Shortly afterwards the plaintiffs' car was involved in an accident after skidding on the spilt fuel. They claimed damages for negligence against the police forces concerned. An application by the police for the claim to be struck out was refused. On appeal by the police, *held*, when it was contended that a special relationship arose out of duties carried out in the performance of a public office, the court was to have regard to the purpose and scope of the public duties and in particular whether they were intended to benefit a particular section of the public and whether reliance could be placed on the fulfilment of those duties. A duty of care in the present case would impose on the police potential liability of almost unlimited scope. The diversion of police resources would hamper the performance of ordinary police duties and create an unacceptable diversion of police manpower. The officers therefore did not owe the plaintiffs a duty of care. Accordingly, the appeal would be allowed.

Ancell v McDermott [1993] 4 All ER 355 (Court of Appeal: Nourse and Beldam LJJ and Sir John Megaw). Decision of Garland J (1992) Times, 17 February (1992 Abr para 1844) reversed.

1880 Duty of care—police—victim of crime—failure to apprehend criminal

A teacher repeatedly harassed one of his pupils. He changed his surname to that of the boy's, damaged property connected with the boy, and slashed the tyres of the boy's father's car. The teacher was dismissed from the school, but the harassment continued. The police were aware of these incidents and had been informed, by the teacher, that there was a danger he might do something criminally insane. The police laid an information against the teacher alleging driving without due care and attention following an incident in which he rammed a car in which the boy was a passenger, but they failed to serve it. Subsequently, the teacher broke into the boy's flat, shot and severely injured the boy, and killed his father. The mother, as administratrix of the father's estate, and the boy brought an action in negligence against the Police Commissioner, alleging that the police had failed to apprehend the teacher despite being aware of his activities. The commissioner's application to strike out the statement of claim as disclosing no reasonable cause of action was dismissed and he appealed. *Held*, since the boy and his family had been exposed to a risk from the teacher over and above that of the public, there was an arguable case that a very close degree of proximity, amounting to a special relationship, existed between the family and the investigating police officers. However, the existence of a general duty on the police to suppress crime did not entail liability to individuals for damage caused to them by criminals whom the police had failed to apprehend in circumstances where it had been possible to do so. It would be against public policy to impose such a duty and, accordingly, the appeal would be allowed and the action dismissed.

Osman v Ferguson [1993] 4 All ER 344 (Court of Appeal: McCowan, Beldam, and Simon Brown LJJ).

1881 Duty of care—psychiatric injury

The defendants were the owners and operators of the "Piper Alpha", an off-shore oil and gas platform. The plaintiff was employed on a support vessel by one of the defendants' sub-contractors. He was on board his vessel on the night that explosions and serious fires claimed the lives of 164 people on the platform and he witnessed the disaster. He sought damages for psychiatric injury which he suffered as a result of his experiences that night. On a preliminary issue, the judge ruled that the defendants owed a duty to exercise reasonable care to avoid causing the plaintiff psychiatric injury. On the defendants' appeal, *held*, the relevant test was whether a reasonable rig owner in the defendants' position would have foreseen that a person of ordinary fortitude in the plaintiff's position would reasonably be in such fear for his life and safety as to suffer psychiatric injury. The court had seen video films which recorded the horror of the disaster, but these did not provide evidence that a man of reasonable fortitude in the plaintiff's position would have reasonably feared for his life and safety. The court also refused to extend the duty of care to mere witnesses of a disaster, and the plaintiff's claim that he was entitled to succeed because he was a bystander in reasonable fear for the safety of others was rejected on the grounds of lack of proximity. Accordingly, the appeal would be allowed.

McFarlane v E E Caledonia Ltd [1993] NLJR 1367 (Court of Appeal: Ralph Gibson, Stuart-Smith, and McCowan LJJ). Decision of Smith J [1993] PIQR P241 reversed.

1882 Duty of care—Royal Navy—drunkenness

A naval airman died when he choked on his own vomit after drinking a large amount of alcohol at a naval base. His wife claimed damages under the Fatal Accidents Act 1976 and the Law Reform (Miscellaneous Provisions) Act 1934 from the defendant, alleging that it was in breach of its duty of care to the airman. The defendant pleaded the defence of volenti non fit injuria, contending that the airman had willingly consumed the alcohol. *Held*, it was only in exceptional cases that a duty arose to take positive steps to protect a person of full age and capacity from his own weakness. This case was such an exceptional circumstance, and it was reasonable to impose a legal duty to take reasonable steps to prevent the airman becoming unconscious through alcohol abuse. Strict requirements had now been imposed on the defence of volenti. The airman had to expressly or impliedly agree to waive any claim for injury arising from the defendant's failure to measure up to the standard of care required. In this case, the defendant's mind was clouded with alcohol and the evidence could not possibly justify a conclusion that he voluntarily assumed the risk of grave or fatal injury by carrying on drinking through the evening, despite the defendant's lack of control over excessive drinking. Damages would however be reduced by 25 per cent because of the airman's contributory negligence.

Barrett v Ministry of Defence (1993) Independent, 3 June (Queen's Bench Division: Phelan J).

1883   Duty of care—school—pupil illegally abducted—duty to inform parent of enrolment

See *Re S (a Minor) (Parental Rights)*, para 1096.

1884   Duty of care—soil engineer—duty to purchaser of dwelling house

A soil engineer was instructed by a local authority to advise it as to the ground conditions and requirements for adequate foundations of a dwelling house that the authority proposed to build. The plaintiff purchased the property from the authority, and later discovered that the soil engineer had failed to establish that the house was built on an infilled quarry. The plaintiff alleged that the soil engineer owed a duty of care to the ultimate purchasers of property for future economic loss if his advice to the local authority was negligent. The plaintiff's statement of claim was struck out and he appealed. *Held*, the soil engineer did not owe a duty of care to the first purchaser of the property from the local authority, nor to the owner occupier for the time being. Accordingly, the appeal would be dismissed.

Preston v Torfaen Borough Council (1993) Times, 21 July (Court of Appeal: Farquharson LJ and Sir Michael Fox).

1885   Duty of care—solicitor

See SOLICITORS.

1886   Duty of care—sport—participant in sport—standard of care towards other participants

Canada

During an amateur ice hockey game the plaintiff was checked from behind by the defendant. Although the check was deliberate, the defendant did not mean to cause injury. The plaintiff broke his neck. The rules of the relevant Hockey Association specifically prohibited checking from behind, and the action was known to be dangerous by the defendant. The plaintiff sought damages. *Held*, the defendant's action was intentional and the plaintiff had not assumed the risk of an illegal check from behind, and the defendant was therefore liable for negligence.

Unruh v Webber (1993) 98 DLR 294 (British Columbia Supreme Court).

1887   Duty of care—sport—sports coach—disabled athletes

A paraplegic sportswoman was injured during a disabled persons' sporting event organised by the British Les Autres Sports Association (BLASA). Discus and archery practice areas were set up in the same hall, divided by a fish net curtain. Discuses were being thrown against the net and whilst there was no possibility of a discus travelling over the top of the net, it was possible for a stray discus to pass down through the sides of the netting or to hit the netting and cause it to billow towards the archery section. The plaintiff, an archer, was hit by a stray discus which struck the netting and caused it to billow towards the archery section. She was left with permanent brain damage and brought a claim for damages for personal injury against the defendant members of BLASA. Her claim that she had not been informed of the nature or danger of the events at the other end of the hall was disputed. *Held*, the court accepted the plaintiff's account of events. The archers had not received safety instructions and the BLASA coaches had failed to take any special safety precautions. Both the misthrow and the accident were of an entirely foreseeable kind. Further, the BLASA coaches owed a greater duty of care to the participants than that owed by coaches to able-bodied athletes. In particular, they had a duty to instruct the participants in appropriate safety procedures, to provide for the safe passage of those moving into and out of the practice area and to watch over the movements of the disabled. Accordingly, judgment would be given in favour of the plaintiff.

Morrell v Owen (1993) Times, 14 December (Queen's Bench Division: Mitchell J).

1888   Duty of care—teacher—student injured during game
Canada
The plaintiff student was injured during an indoor baseball game which was supervised by a teacher. The person batting swung and missed the ball so that the bat flew from his hands and hit the plaintiff in the face causing serious injuries. In an action for damages, the trial judge found that the teacher was negligent for positioning the plaintiff in a dangerous position and for failing to warn of the danger, and found that the school board was vicariously liable. On appeal on the issue of liability, *held*, the plaintiff should have been positioned at a significantly greater distance from the person batting and at a position of much lesser risk of being in the projectile path of a bat which might slip from a that person's grip. Accordingly, the appeal would be dismissed.
   Peterson v School District No 36 (1993) DLR 334 (British Columbia Court of Appeal).

1889   Duty of care—unattended vehicle—liability of owner
The plaintiff's wife died after being knocked down by a minibus which had been stolen. The plaintiff claimed damages against the defendants, the owners of the minibus, for their negligence in leaving the vehicle parked and unlocked with the keys in the ignition, contending that they were in breach of duty in failing to collect the bus or to render it incapable of being driven away by unauthorised persons. *Held*, the defendants owed no duty of care to the plaintiff's wife because the parked minibus did not fall within a special category of risk as a source of danger on the highway since the acts of the wrongdoer were to be regarded as a novus actus interveniens which broke the chain of causation. Further, there was not sufficient proximity between the plaintiff's wife and the defendants such as to give rise to a duty of care. Accordingly, the plaintiff's claim would fail.
   Topp v London Country Bus (South West) Ltd [1993] 3 All ER 448 (Court of Appeal: Dillon and Rose LJJ and Peter Gibson J). Decision of May J affirmed (1991) Times, 3 December (1991 Abr para 1760).

NORTHERN IRELAND

Halsbury's Laws of England (4th edn) Vol 8, paras 1637–1647

1890   Articles
Race Relations in Northern Ireland, Ciaran White: 143 NLJ 337

1891   Emergency provisions—codes of practice
The Northern Ireland (Emergency Provisions) Act 1991 (Codes of Practice) (No 1) Order 1993, SI 1993/2761 (in force on 1 January 1994), appoints 1 January 1994 as the date on which the code of practice, made under the Northern Ireland (Emergency Provisions) Act 1991, Sch 5, and relating to the exercise by authorised by investigators of specified powers, comes into force.

The Northern Ireland (Emergency Provisions) Act 1991 (Codes of Practice) (No 2) Order 1993, SI 1993/2788 (in force on 1 January 1994), appoints 1 January 1994 as the date on which two codes of practice, made under the Northern Ireland (Emergency Provisions) Act 1991, s 61, and relating to (1) the detention, treatment and questioning of persons detained under the Prevention of Terrorism (Temporary Provisions) Act 1989; and (2) the identification of persons detained under the 1991 Act, come into force.

1892   Emergency provisions and prevention of terrorism—temporary provisions— continuance
The Northern Ireland (Emergency and Prevention of Terrorism Provisions) (Continuance) Order 1993, SI 1993/1522 (in force on 16 June 1993), continues in force, with certain exceptions, the provisions of the Northern Ireland (Emergency Provisions) Act 1991 and the provisions referred to in the Prevention of Terrorism (Temporary Provisions) Act 1989, s 27(11) for a period of 12 months from 16 June 1993.

1893   Government—extension of provisions

The Northern Ireland Act 1974 (Interim Period Extension) Order 1993, SI 1993/1753 (in force on 13 July 1993), extends, until 16 July 1994, the period specified in the 1974 Act, s 1(4) (as previously extended) for the operation of specified temporary provisions for the government of Northern Ireland.

NUISANCE

Halsbury's Laws of England (4th edn) Vol 34, paras 301–400

1894   Articles

A Noisy Dog Story, Alec Samuels: LS Gaz, 30 June 1993, p 29

1895   Noise and Statutory Nuisance Act 1993

The Noise and Statutory Nuisance Act 1993 makes provision in relation to street noise and expenses incurred by local authorities in abating or preventing the recurrence of a statutory nuisance. The Act received the royal assent on the 5 November 1993 and comes into force in part on 5 January 1994 and in part on a day or days to be appointed. For details of commencement, see the commencement table in the title STATUTES.

Section 1 makes provision for Scotland. Section 2 amends the Environmental Protection Act 1990, s 79 so as to provide that noise emitted from, or caused by, vehicles, machinery or equipment in a street falls within the definition of statutory nuisances contained in that section. Section 3(1)-(5) amends the 1990 Act, s 80 by bringing the new class of statutory nuisance within the ambit of that section. Section 3(6) inserts s 80A into the 1990 Act, allowing an abatement notice to be fixed to the machinery, vehicle or equipment from which the noise has been emitted or by which noise is likely to be caused. Section 80A also creates an offence of removing or interfering with such a notice. Section 4(1)-(4) amends the 1990 Act, s 81 by extending it to cases where more than one person is responsible either for noise in the street or for an unattended vehicle, machinery or equipment that is causing the noise. Section 4(5) inserts para 2A into the 1990 Act, Sch 3, enabling an environmental health officer to enter, open or remove a vehicle, or a piece of machinery or equipment, in order to abate a nuisance. Amendments consequential on the insertion of the 1990 Act, s 80A and Sch 3, para 2A are made by s 4(6), (7) which makes further amendments to the 1990 Act, Sch 3, paras 3(1), 4(1).

Section 5 amends the 1990 Act, s 82 to enable a person to take summary proceedings in respect of a nuisance caused by noise in the street. Section 6 makes provision for Scotland. Section 7 amends the Control of Pollution Act 1974, s 62 to enable the Secretary of State to alter the hours between which loudspeakers used for non-advertising purposes may be operated in a street. Section 8 allows a local authority to adopt certain provisions which enable it to grant consents, where appropriate, to those who wish to operate loudspeakers in the street outside the hours specified in the Control of Pollution Act 1974, s 62. Section 9 enable a local authority to resolve that certain provisions of Sch 3 are to have effect in its area. Schedule 3 provides that a local authority has the power to require installers of audible intruder alarms on premises in its area, and occupiers of such premises, to fit cut-off devices and to supply the names of key-holders to the police. Furthermore, where an alarm causes a nuisance, Sch 3 allows an environmental health officer to enter the premises in order to de-activate the alarm. If entry cannot be made without the use of force, the officer can enter the premises only when he has obtained a warrant from a Justice of the Peace. Consequential amendments to the 1990 Act, s 79(7), (11) are made by s 10. Section 10(2) inserts ss 81A, 81B into the 1990 Act. Section 81A empowers a local authority to recover costs reasonably incurred in abating a nuisance under the 1990 Act, Pt III by putting a charge on the premises where the owner is or was responsible for the nuisance. Section 81B provides that these costs may be paid in instalments Section 11 deals with expenses. Sections 11–14 relate to commencement, short title and extent.

1896   Private nuisance—invasion of privacy—harassment

The plaintiff and defendant met and developed a friendship which later broke down. Following threats of violence and abusive behaviour by the defendant, the plaintiff obtained an injunction restraining the defendant from molesting, harassing or otherwise interfering with her or entering or coming within a specified distance of her parents' home or any other address at which she might reside. The defendant appealed against the injunction. *Held* (Peter Gibson J dissenting), the court had jurisdiction to grant an injunction restraining the making of deliberately harassing and pestering telephone calls to a person notwithstanding that the parties were not married and had never cohabited or that the recipient of the calls had no freehold or leasehold interest in the premises in which he or she received the calls. The inconvenience and annoyance to the recipient caused by such calls constituted an actionable interference with the ordinary and reasonable use and enjoyment of property and could be restrained without further proof of damage. As there was an obvious risk that the cumulative effect of continued and unrestrained further harassment would cause the plaintiff physical or psychiatric illness, the court was entitled to look at the defendant's conduct as a whole and restrain those aspects of his behaviour that could not be classified as threats. The appeal would accordingly be dismissed.

Khorasandjian v Bush [1993] 3 All ER 669 (Court of Appeal: Dillon and Rose LJJ and Peter Gibson J).

1897   Private nuisance—remedy—abatement—availability

The defendants' predecessors in title built a garage and the plaintiff alleged that part of it was built on her land. She brought proceedings in trespass and nuisance and sought a mandatory injunction requiring the defendants to pull down that part of the garage which encroached on her land. The judge granted a declaration that half of the garage wall encroached on her property but refused to grant the mandatory injunction and adjourned the claim for damages pending valuation. The plaintiff's appeal was dismissed and she was refused leave to appeal to the House of Lords. She then built a wall on the defendants' land in front of the garage, in breach of an injunction and a suspended sentence of two years' imprisonment was imposed. On the plaintiff's appeal, the question arose whether she was entitled to exercise her common law right of abatement or was restricted to her right to damages. *Held*, self-redress was a summary remedy which was only justified in clear and simple cases or in an emergency. Here, the plaintiff had delayed too long before seeking to exercise the right of abatement, there was no emergency, difficult questions of law and fact had to be considered, and demolition of the garage wall would be disproportionate to the damage suffered. Further, where an application for a mandatory injunction had failed, there was no justification for self-redress. Since the court found that the plaintiff was not entitled to have the encroaching wall removed she had no right to remove it herself. The plaintiff was unwilling to give an undertaking that she would not interfere with the wall and, accordingly, the appeal would be dismissed.

Burton v Winters [1993] 3 All ER 847 (Court of Appeal: Lloyd LJ and Connell J).

1898   Public nuisance—criminal liability—knowledge of defendant—whether actual knowledge required

An "acid house party" took place on farm land owned by the appellant and the event caused a great deal of noise and disturbance. On appeal against his conviction for public nuisance, *held*, the appellant had agreed to hire out his land but claimed not to have known what type of event had been intended. The requirement as to the defendant's state of mind was the same whether criminal or civil proceedings were brought. Actual knowledge of the nuisance did not need to be established. A defendant was guilty of public nuisance if he knew or ought to have known (because the means of knowledge were available to him) that there was a real risk that the consequence of granting a licence to use his land would create the sort of nuisance that in fact occurred. It was sufficient for the prosecution to show that the defendant knew or ought to have known that as a result of his actions a public nuisance would be committed. Accordingly, the appeal would be dismissed.

R v Shorrock [1993] 3 All ER 917 (Court of Appeal: Simon Brown LJ, Popplewell and Rattee JJ). *Sedleigh-Denfield v O'Callagan* [1940] 3 All ER 349, HL applied.

1899   Rylands v Fletcher—extent of rule—storage of chemicals—contamination of water

The plaintiff discovered that water extracted from one of its boreholes was contaminated by a chemical from a tanning works owned by the defendant. The plaintiff brought an action against the defendant in negligence, nuisance and the rule in *Rylands v Fletcher* (1868) LR 3 HL 330. At first instance, the court dismissed the actions because the test of foreseeability had not been satisfied sufficiently to establish nuisance and negligence, and because the operations by the defendant were a natural use of the land and therefore *Rylands v Fletcher* did not apply. The plaintiff appealed relying only on the rule in *Rylands v Fletcher*. The Court of Appeal held that the contamination was an interference with a natural right and therefore the defendant was strictly liable. On further appeal by the defendant, *held*, it was established that foreseeability of damage was a pre-requisite of any liability under the *Rylands v Fletcher* rule. The court ought not to extend the rule to one of strict liability for any ultra-hazardous operations which cause injury to any persons. The appropriate forum for determining strict liability in such cases was Parliament. Already much well-informed and carefully structured legislation was being put in place, and it was therefore undesirable that the courts developed a common law principle to achieve the same end. In this case, the storage of chemicals in substantial quantities was a non-natural use but nobody could have foreseen that bringing the chemical into the tanning works would cause the damage that it did and therefore the pre-requisite of foreseeability under the *Rylands and Fletcher* rule was not satisfied. Accordingly, the appeal would be allowed.

Cambridge Water Co v Eastern Counties Leather plc [1994] 1 All ER 53 (House of Lords: Lords Templeman, Goff of Chieveley, Jauncey of Tullichettle, Lowry and Woolf). Decision of Court of Appeal [1992] EGCS 142 (1992 Abr para 1860) reversed.

OPEN SPACES AND HISTORIC BUILDINGS

Halsbury's Laws of England (4th edn) Vol 34, paras 401–1000

1900   Listed building—enforcement notice—non-compliance with notice—reasonable steps taken to comply with notice

It has been held that the offence of failing to comply with a listed building enforcement notice contrary to the Town and Country Planning Act 1971, s 98(1) is an absolute one so that it is no defence to a charge of failing to comply with a notice that all reasonable steps have been taken to comply with it. Accordingly, where a defendant, on receipt of a notice, took immediate steps to carry out the work specified in the notice by commissioning a firm of builders, but the work was not finished within the period specified in the notice, there was no defence to a charge of failing to comply with the notice.

Mid-Devon District Council v Avery (1992) 65 P & CR 47 (Queen's Bench Division: Beldam LJ and Tudor Evans J).

1971 Act, s 98(1)–(3) now Planning (Listed Buildings and Conservation Areas) Act 1990, s 43(1)–(3).

1901   National parks—protection—replacement of old buildings—planning permission

See *Bride Brick Co Ltd v Secretary of State for the Environment*, para 2502.

PARLIAMENT

Halsbury's Laws of England (4th edn) Vol 34, paras 1001–1506

1902   Articles

The Publication of Controversial Parliamentary Papers, Patricia Leopold: 56 MLR 690

1903   House of Commons—disqualification

The House of Commons Disqualification Order 1993, SI 1993/1572 (in force on 14 July 1993), amends the list of offices which disqualify holders from membership of the House of Commons contained in the House of Commons Disqualification Act 1975, Sch 1.

1904   Parliamentary constituencies—Wales

The Parliamentary Constituencies (Wales) (Miscellaneous Changes) Order 1993, SI 1993/227 (in force on 23 February 1993), give effect, without modification, to Boundary Commission for Wales proposals for changes to the areas of certain parliamentary constituencies where county boundary changes have resulted in inconsistencies between those boundaries. The coming into force of the order does not affect a parliamentary election until a proclamation is issued by Her Majesty summoning a new Parliament, or affect the constitution of the House of Commons until the dissolution of the Parliament then in being.

1905 Pensions

See PENSIONS AND SUPERANNUATION.

PARTNERSHIP

Halsbury's Laws of England (4th edn) Vol 35, paras 1–300

1906 Articles

Partnership Provision for Tax Liabilities, Colin Davies: 138 SJ 44
Rights Accruing to Professional Partners, Joanna Rasamalar Jeremiah (on *Hadlee v Comr of Inland Revenue* [1993] STC 294): 144 NLJ 86

1907 Partner—dealings with share of partnership—assignment of part of share

New Zealand
The taxpayer, a partner in a firm of chartered accountants, executed a deed of trust under which the trustees were empowered to pay the income to the primary beneficiaries, the taxpayer's wife and child who, under New Zealand law, were assessed to tax separately. He also assigned to the trustees 40 per cent of his share in the partnership. Under New Zealand law, a partnership was not a separate tax entity; returns in respect of partnership income were made for information purposes only so that each partner's income could be calculated separately. It fell to be determined whether the assignment effectively transferred the tax liability in respect of the income assigned from the taxpayer to the assignees. *Held*, the taxpayer assigned no revenue-producing interest of a capital nature nor was he in a position to do so since he had no proprietary interest in any such asset. Accordingly, the income which flowed to the assignees flowed not from capital but from the performance by the taxpayer of such obligations as he was required to perform under the partnership agreement. The assignment was ineffective to shift liability to income tax from the taxpayer to the assignees.
Hadlee v Comr of Inland Revenue [1993] STC 294 (Privy Council: Lords Keith of Kinkel, Templeman, Jauncey of Tullichettle, Browne-Wilkinson and Mustill).

1908 Partnerships—partnerships of companies—accounts

The Partnerships and Unlimited Companies (Accounts) Regulations 1993, SI 1993/1820 (in force on 21 July 1993), implement Council Directive (EC) 90/605 (amendment of scope of Community provisions on annual and consolidated accounts). The 1993 Regulations apply to partnerships, limited partnerships and unlimited companies all of whose members having unlimited liability are limited companies (qualifying partnerships). Members of a qualifying partnership are required to prepare accounts and a directors' report and to obtain an auditors' report on such accounts. The regulations also contain requirements as to the publication of accounts so prepared. A qualifying partnership which has been dealt with in consolidated group accounts prepared by a member of the partnership established under the law of a member state (or a parent of such a member), by the method of full or proportional consolidation or by the equity method, is exempt from the regulations. Criminal penalties are imposed for failure to comply with the requirements of the regulations. Unlimited companies that are qualifying companies are required to deliver their accounts to the registrar of companies, and the regulations impose additional disclosure requirements in the notes to the accounts of companies that are members of qualifying partnerships or qualifying companies.

PATENTS AND INVENTIONS

Halsbury's Laws of England (4th edn) Vol 35, paras 301–800

1909 Infringement—discovery—action involving multinational companies

See *Unilever plc v Chefaro*, para 987.

1910   Infringement—discovery—election for damages or account of profits—time for election

Australia

The plaintiffs in a patent infringement action were granted an injunction restraining the defendants from engaging in conduct involving an infringement of the patent. The plaintiffs then applied for an order for discovery against the defendants. The application was opposed by the defendants on the ground that the plaintiffs had not yet elected whether to seek damages or an account of profits. The plaintiffs argued that they could not make an election until they had access to the relevant documents in the possession of the defendants. *Held,* the plaintiffs sought to keep their options open notwithstanding that they had obtained the grant of injunctive relief by deferring making an election until they had access to the defendants' documents. Once they had inspected the documents, the plaintiffs would make their election. In consequence, the election would be made prior to the hearing of the claim for damages or an account of profits and before any other step was taken towards the preparation of the case for hearing. The order sought by the plaintiffs was not a general order for discovery in relation to an account of profits or a claim for damages, but was limited to certain documents. The discovery of the documents was likely to be necessary whether the plaintiffs elected to claim damages or an account of profits, and the documents were in the possession and knowledge of the defendants. In such circumstances, the plaintiffs' application would be granted.

Minnesota Mining & Manufacturing Co v C Jeffries Pty Ltd [1993] FSR 189 (Federal Court of Australia).

1911   Infringement—practice—pleadings

In a patent infringement action the defendants served their objections and later amended their pleading. It was agreed by the parties to allow the amendment of the particulars of objections and the remaining issue was which date was to be inserted into the pleading. The plaintiff in an application contended the relevant date was the date upon which the original particulars of objections had been served whilst the defendant submitted the date was the date upon which the amended particulars of objections were served. *Held,* the relevant date was the date upon which the original particulars of objections had been served and costs in the amendment proceedings were to follow those of the action and counterclaim. Accordingly, the application would be allowed.

Ecolab Inc v Reddish Savilles Ltd [1993] FSR 193 (Patents Court: Aldous J).

1912   Infringement—stay of injunction—entitlement to damages—joint plaintiffs

The plaintiffs, the registered proprietor and exclusive licensee of a patent, obtained judgment against the defendants for infringement of the patent which related to products used in the construction of solar panels for space satellites. The parties were the only suppliers of such products, so orders which did not go to one party went to the other. The defendants sought a stay of injunction pending appeal as substantial orders were expected in the period before the date of the appeal hearing. The plaintiffs opposed a stay contending that an injunction was necessary to protect their business prior to the appeal and they offered a cross-undertaking in damages should the appeal succeed. The defendants also argued that damages should only be assessed in relation to the second plaintiff's loss since, by granting the exclusive licence, the first plaintiff had become a bare proprietor with no right to damages. *Held,* (1) the Patents Act 1977, s 67(2), which dealt with the grant of relief to the exclusive licensee, did not remove the proprietor's right to sue and, if successful, to claim injunctive relief and damages. (2) The defendant's business was not expected to suffer in the long term from an injunction prior to the appeal hearing and, if successful, their damages would not be difficult to assess. Accordingly, the application would be dismissed.

Optical Coating Laboratory Inc v Pilkington Pe Ltd [1993] FSR 310 (Patents County Court: Judge Ford).

1913   Patents—disclosure of invention—sufficiency of disclosure

The plaintiff, who was the holder of a patent for a male incontinence device, alleged that the defendants had infringed the patent. At first instance it was held that the patent was valid and had been infringed by the defendants. On appeal, the defendants contended that the patent was invalid since it did not sufficiently disclose the invention. In particular the defendants argued that the plaintiff had failed to identify the particular silicone release system and adhesive used. *Held,* whether the specification disclosed the invention clearly and completely enough for it to be performed by a person skilled in the art involved a question of degree. In determining the required degree of clarity and completeness, it was impossible to lay down any precise rule. It was clear that sufficiency was a question of fact which depended on the nature of the invention. Accordingly, the appeal would be dismissed.

Mentor Corpn v Hollister Inc [1993] 1 RPC 7 (Court of Appeal: Lloyd, Stuart-Smith and Scott LJJ).

1914 Patents—medicinal products—supplementary protection certificates

The Patents (Supplementary Protection Certificate for Medicinal Products) (Amendment) Rules 1993, SI 1993/947 (in force on 21 April 1993), amend certain drafting errors in the 1992 Rules, SI 1992/3162.

1915 Patents—protection of industrial property—convention countries

See para 2547.

1916 Patents—revocation—service of petition—service outside jurisdiction

RSC Ord 11, r 1(2)(a) provides that service of a writ out of the jurisdiction is permissible without the leave of the court provided that each claim made by the writ is a claim which by virtue of the Civil Jurisdiction and Judgments Act 1982 the court has power to hear and determine, made in proceedings to which the following conditions apply: (i) no proceedings between the parties concerning the same cause of action are pending in the courts of any other part of the United Kingdom or of any other Convention territory, and (ii) the proceedings begun by the writ are proceedings to which the 1982 Act, Sch 1, art 16 refers.

The petitioner was granted leave to serve a petition for the revocation of a patent upon the respondent patentee outside the jurisdiction. On the respondent's application to set aside leave, *held*, modern rules contemplated that a revocation petition had to have a true respondent and that the petition had to be served personally on the respondent. The petition in the present case complied with these requirements. The petition also fell within the 1982 Act, Sch 1, art 16, case 4 (proceedings concerned with the registration or validity of patents) and could therefore be served outside the jurisdiction without leave under Ord 11, r 1(2)(a). Further, the petition was not subject to the requirement in RSC Ord 6, r 7 that it bear the appropriate indorsement as that requirement applied to writs but not to petitions. Accordingly, the respondent's application would be dismissed.

Napp Laboratories v Pfizer Inc [1993] FSR 150 (Chancery Division: Hoffmann J). *Re Drummond's Patent* (1889) 6 RPC 576 not followed.

1917 Patents—revocation—transfer of revocation petition from High Court to Patents County Court—relevant factors

The plaintiff started proceedings against the defendant for infringement of one of its United Kingdom patents. A year later the plaintiff was granted two European patents closely related to the subject matter of the United Kingdom patent. The defendant then issued a petition for the revocation of the two European patents in the High Court. The plaintiff started infringement proceedings in the Patents County Court against the defendant in respect of the two European patents. The plaintiff then applied to transfer the petition to the Patents County Court. *Held*, in exercise of its general discretion whether to order transfer to the Patents County Court, the court ought to consider the following factors: (1) the financial position of the parties, (2) the financial substance of the action, (3) the importance of the action generally, and in particular whether it would affect persons not party to the action, (4) the complexity of the matters raised, (5) the speed with which a trial would be heard, and (6) the proper administration of justice, which included the length of time the trial would take, and the purposes for which the Patents County Court was designed. A transfer ought only to be ordered if after considering all the relevant factors transfer on balance was appropriate. In the present case the administration of justice favoured retention of the petition in the High Court. Accordingly, the application would be dismissed.

Symbol Technologies Inc v Opticon Sensors Europe BV (No 2) [1993] RPC 232 (Patents Court: Aldous J).

1918 Patents—rules

The Patents (Amendment) Rules 1993, SI 1993/2423 (in force on 1 November 1993), amend the principal rules, SI 1990/2384, so as to (1) make revised provision for the furnishing of addresses by applicants for, and proprietors of, patents and persons concerned in patent proceedings; (2) make clear that the requirement that documents be translated into English does not apply where information relating to micro-organisms is added to an international application for a United Kingdom patent after the international filing date; (3) extend the circumstances in which an international application for a United Kingdom patent is not to be treated as withdrawn; (4) provide a restriction on the inspection of confidential documents issued by the Patent Office; (5) provide for any document sent by the Patent Office before 1 June 1978 to be one which the comptroller is under no duty to make available for public inspection; and (6) provide for a request to the comptroller for a document to be treated as confidential to be made in respect of a specified part of a document.

1919 Patents County Court—appeal—notice—extension of time for service

The plaintiff brought an action for alleged infringement of a patent and applied to amend the specification of the patent. The patent was held invalid and leave to amend was refused. The judgment concluded that the court would hear the parties on the form of the order and other outstanding matters on a date to be fixed. Prior to any further hearing, the plaintiff applied for an extension of the period for serving notice of appeal. *Held*, all that had happened was that reasons for the judgment had been given. No order for costs and no order to the Patent Office for revocation of the patent had been made. There was therefore nothing to appeal against, time was not running and an extension of time was not necessary. Time would start to run when the judge made orders for costs and for revocation.

Pavel v Sony Corpn [1993] FSR 177 (Patents County Court: Recorder Pumfrey QC).

1920 Patents County Court—jurisdiction—copyright subsisting in design documents

The plaintiff began proceedings against the defendant for infringement of design right in respect of designs recorded before the commencement of the Copyright Designs and Patents Act 1988. At the hearing of the defendant's application to strike out the proceedings, the plaintiff was given leave to amend his statement of claim. The amendments deleted all allegations of infringement of design right, particularised allegations of copyright infringement and maintained allegations of passing off. The defendant made a second application to strike out the proceedings, arguing that the Patents County Court had no jurisdiction in copyright law in respect of infringement of rights in a design drawing. *Held*, the court did not consider it appropriate on a striking out application to conduct a minute and protracted examination of the points raised. These could more suitably be considered at the preliminary consideration stage. The Patents County Court had the general jurisdiction of a county court, which included jurisdiction over any action founded in tort. As infringement of copyright had always been treated as a tortious invasion of a property right, county courts had jurisdiction in copyright actions. The court also had special jurisdiction in the case of copyright infringement in respect of a design document within the meaning of the 1988 Act, s 51(3), Sch 1, para 19(1). The purpose of giving the court special jurisdiction in actions relating to designs was to give litigants an alternative forum to that of the Chancery Division in which the parties could, if they wished, be represented by patent agents. There was no justification for restricting the special jurisdiction to design documents recorded after the commencement of the relevant part of the 1988 Act. Accordingly, as the action related to design within the meaning of the Patents County Court (Designation and Jurisdiction) Order 1990, SI 1990/1496, all the matters that were the subject of the action were within the jurisdiction of the court and the defendant's application would be dismissed.

PSM International plc v Specialised Fastener Products (Southern) Ltd [1993] FSR 113 (Patents County Court: Judge Ford).

PENSIONS AND SUPERANNUATION

Halsbury's Laws of England (4th edn) Vol 33, Supp paras 1078–1158

1921 Articles

Employers' Contributions to Pension Schemes, John Hayward: Tax Journal, Issue 203, p 12
Enforcing Judgments Against Pensions, Carole Broughton: 137 SJ 919

Enforcing Judgments Against Pension Rights, Michael Tennet and Paul Newman: 137 SJ 424, 458

Payments from Occupational Pension Schemes, John Hayward: Tax Journal, Issues 233, 237, pp 16, 18

Pension Trustees and Trading, John Hayward: Tax Journal, Issue 228, p 21

Pre-Emptive Costs Orders, Sean Hand: 137 SJ 760

Taking Stock of the Transitional VAT System, Peter Jenkins: Tax Journal, Issue 223, p 12 and Issue 224, p 9

1922   British Coal Corporation—superannuation scheme—obligation to pay additional contributions—set-off against surplus

The British Coal Corporation staff superannuation scheme, clause 5 provides that the Corporation must pay a sum equal to a certain percentage of employees' salaries into the fund. The rules also provide that additional contributions to the fund made by the Corporation in special cases shall be paid in such manner as the scheme committee shall direct. Clause 45 gives the Corporation power to amend the rules subject to a proviso which precludes making any of the money payable to the employers.

When the number of Corporation employees was reduced, an arrangement was made between the Corporation and the Government that the cost of providing the extra benefits for workers taking voluntary redundancy would be paid into the fund by the Corporation in instalments. The question then arose as to whether outstanding instalments of £100m, could be set off against an actuarial surplus of £983m. To achieve this it would be necessary to amend the scheme without breaching the proviso in clause 45. It had already been agreed that half of the surplus was to be used for the members' benefit. It was submitted that the sole method of using the other half for the benefit of the Corporation was to set it off against the instalments owed by the Corporation. *Held*, the obligation owed by the Corporation was to pay additional contributions which had been actuarially determined, to the fund. It was not contested that the Corporation would be prevented by clause 45 from taking an amount from the fund which was equal to the extra amounts paid in by it; the fact that the Corporation could pay those extra amounts by instalments did not relieve it of the obligation to pay actual sums into the fund. Accordingly the Corporation was not entitled to make the proposed set-off.

British Coal Corpn v British Coal Staff Superannuation Fund Scheme Trustees Ltd (1993) Times, 12 October (Chancery Division: Vinelott J).

1923   Children's pensions—earnings limit

The Superannuation (Children's Pensions) (Earnings Limit) Order 1993, SI 1993/220 (in force on 12 April 1993), increases the limit on emoluments for the purposes of the Judicial Pensions Act 1981, s 21 from £1,614 to £1,672 per year. The 1992 Order, SI 1992/360, is revoked.

1924   Civil service—early retirement pensions

The Pensions Increase (Civil Service Early Retirement Pension Scheme 1992) Regulations 1993, SI 1993/806 (in force on 12 April 1993), apply the Pensions (Increase) Act 1971 to pensions payable under the Civil Service Early Retirement Pension Scheme 1992, and allow increases to take effect from dates before the making of the 1993 Regulations.

1925   Civil service—pension scheme—pensionable emoluments—language allowances

The Principal Civil Service Pension Scheme 1974, Sch 1, App 1 provides that additional emoluments paid for extra responsibility and granted on a permanent basis are pensionable emoluments for the purposes of calculating civil service pensions.

A civil servant employed in the Diplomatic Service obtained a foreign language qualification in Turkish which entitled him to an operational language allowance (OLA) in addition to his salary. He maintained that entitlement by requalifying at appropriate intervals. On a subsequent posting to Italy, he obtained a second foreign language qualification in Italian. During his time in Italy he received the OLA for Italian and a language continuation allowance (LCA) for Turkish. On his retirement, he claimed that the allowances counted as part of his salary for the purpose of calculating his pension. His claim was disputed by the Treasury, which had taken over the functions of the Minister of the Civil Service under the 1974 Scheme. The civil servant obtained a declaration that the allowances were pensionable emoluments under the scheme. On appeal by the Treasury, *held*, payment of an OLA was based on the operational requirements of the job and a recipient of an OLA could be required to carry out tasks which a non-recipient could not carry out. An OLA was therefore paid for extra responsibility within the meaning of the 1974 Scheme. The fact that an OLA, once granted, remained payable while an officer held a post to which the language was relevant was sufficient to satisfy the requirement that it had to be "granted on a permanent basis". The OLA was therefore a pensionable emolument for the purposes of the scheme. However, the LCA failed to satisfy either of the relevant criteria and, to this extent, the Treasury's appeal would be allowed.

R v Minister for the Civil Service, ex p Lane (1993) Times, 23 March (Court of Appeal: Neill, Staughton and Roch LJJ). Decision of Kennedy J (1991) Times, 1 November (1991 Abr para 1800) reversed in part.

1926   Judicial Pensions and Retirement Act 1993

The Judicial Pensions and Retirement Act 1993 makes new arrangements with respect to the pensions payable in respect of certain judicial offices, and makes amendments to the date on which the holders of certain offices are required to retire from these offices. By establishing a common accrual period of 20 years, the Act creates uniformity in the pension arrangements for judges and brings them into line with requirements for occupational pension schemes generally. The Act received the royal assent on 29 March 1993 and comes into force on a day to be appointed.

Part I (ss 1–18) New Arrangements for Judicial Pensions
Section 1 specifies the persons to whom Pt I applies. Applicable persons are those who hold "qualifying judicial office" for the first time after a specified day and to certain persons who held such office before that day, but who after that day are appointed to another such office or re-appointed to their former office or who make an election under s 2. Section 2 provides for a pension to be payable to any person who retires with at least 5 years' service in qualifying judicial office and to certain other persons who leave office without that length of service. It makes provision for the pension to be actuarially reduced in certain circumstances where it comes into payment before that person has attained the age of 65. Provision is made under s 3 for the calculation of the rate of the pension. A lump sum of a specified amount must be paid where a judicial pension commences to be paid, and a specified lump sum must be paid in the event of the death of the judicial officer: s 4. Section 5 provides for the payment of a pension to the surviving spouse of a judicial officer at an annual rate equal to one-half of the annual rate of the deceased's judicial pension. In the event of the officer's death, a children's pension is to be granted and paid in favour of all those persons who satisfy certain conditions of eligibility: s 6. Section 7 defines "period of childhood and full-time education". Section 8 sets out the rates at which a children's pension is payable. Power is conferred by s 9 to make regulations prescribing the contributions to be made by officers towards the cost of the liability for providing for the surviving spouses' and children's pensions. Section 10 makes provision for additional benefits from voluntary contributions. Section 11 makes provision against the payment of pensions and other benefits under two or more judicial pension schemes, while s 12 allows a transfer of the rights of persons holding qualifying judicial office before commencement. An applicable person to elect for membership of a personal pension scheme instead of the judicial pension, and allows a person who has made such an election to be re-admitted to the judicial scheme in certain circumstances: s 13. Section 14 provides for the application of Pt I to holders of the office of Lord Chancellor. Section 15 preserves the arrangements under which the pensions and other benefits payable to a Circuit judge in respect of any service of his as Recorder of London or Common Serjeant are defrayed by the Common Council, and service as a Circuit judge by virtue of those appointments is not to be regarded as service in qualifying judicial office.

Section 16 provides for any abatement of a pension payable under the Social Security Act 1973, s 65 to be disregarded for the purpose of calculating the payment of any derivative benefits for the purposes of the 1993 Act, ss 4–8. The same results are to follow under Pt I from the annulment of a voidable marriage as would have followed from its dissolution, had it been a valid marriage: s 17. Section 18 relates to continuity of tax treatment.

Part II (ss 19–31) Miscellaneous, General and Supplementary Provisions
Section 19 makes provision for benefits in respect of earnings that are in excess of pension-capped salary. Section 20 makes provision for appeals to the appropriate Minister by any applicable judicial officer, or by the widow or widower or any surviving dependent of such a person aggrieved by certain decisions of the administrators of the schemes constituted under Pt I and s 19. An order may be made requiring local authorities in England and Wales to make payments to the Treasury for that part of a judicial officers salary payable by them before the

making of an order under s 1(8): s 21. Section 22 makes provision for the application of the Pensions (Increase) Act 1971 to the pensions schemes. Provision is made for the transfer of accrued rights into and out of the pension schemes: s 23, Sch 2. Section 24 and Sch 3 make corresponding amendments to other pension enactments. Section 25 and Sch 4 make provision with respect to the pensions of the Comptroller and Auditor General, the Parliamentary Commissioner for Administration and the Health Service Commissioners. Section 26, together with Schs 5–7, makes provision for the date by which specified judicial officers must retire from office. It also provides for the continuation of certain judicial officers in office beyond that date where it is desirable in the public interest, and for those persons appointed to tribunals, not for a term, but in a particular case, to be appointed beyond the age of 70. Section 27 provides for the completion of certain proceedings by allowing the office holder to continue to deal with, give judgment in, or deal with any ancillary matter relating to any case begun; this service is not to be regarded as service in qualifying judicial office. Section 28 makes general financial provisions. General provisions as the making of regulations and orders under the 1993 Act are contained in s 29. Section 30 contains provisions relating to the interpretation of the Act generally.

Section 31, together with Schs 8, 9, relates to the short title, commencement and extent, and makes minor and consequential amendments and consequential repeals and revocations.

1927 Local government—compensation for premature retirement

The Local Government (Compensation for Premature Retirement) (Amendment) Regulations 1993, SI 1993/2890 (in force on 23 December 1993) (as amended by SI 1993/3108), amend the 1982 Regulations, SI 1982/1009. The principal amendment provides that children of female beneficiaries have the same entitlement to children's compensation under the 1982 Regulations as the children of male beneficiaries. Specified regulations are made retrospective in effect.

1928 Local government—superannuation

The Local Government Superannuation (Amendment) Regulations 1993, SI 1993/366 (in force on 22 March 1993), amend the 1986 Regulations, SI 1986/24, so as to (1) allow up to 25 per cent of the value of a fund to be invested by means of a single contract in a managed fund with an insurance company or similar body; (2) allow for a greater concentration of investments by permitting up to 10 per cent of a fund to be invested in a single holding, and by permitting up to 25 per cent of a fund to be invested in unit trusts managed by a single body (subject to certain exceptions); (3) where an administering authority is required to obtain a certificate from an actuary specifying the common rate of employer's contribution to a superannuation fund, provide for the common rate to be set to ensure the fund's solvency; and (4) provide for a new method of calculating the standard rate of interest.

The Local Government Superannuation (Local Commissioners) Regulations 1993, SI 1993/1367 (in force on 28 June 1993), amend the 1986 Regulations supra by adding the Commission for Local Administration in England and the Commission for Local Administration in Wales to the list of bodies whose employees are pensionable employees for the purposes of the local government superannuation scheme.

The Local Government Superannuation (Part-time Employees) Regulations 1993, SI 1993/1814 (in force on 17 August 1993), amend the 1986 Regulations supra by (1) abolishing the requirement that part-time employees must work at least 15 hours per week in order to qualify for membership of the local government superannuation scheme; (2) providing for the exclusion of part-time firemen who would otherwise have been eligible for entry to the scheme as a result of the abolition of the minimum hours requirement; and (3) providing for a part-time employee's pension enhancement for ill health to include reckonable service purchased by additional contributions or a lump sum paid on or after 17 September 1990.

The Local Government Superannuation (Investments) Regulations 1993, SI 1993/1848 (in force on 20 August 1993), amend the 1986 Regulations supra so as to (1) allow local authorities, as part of the investment of fund moneys, to enter into stocklending arrangements subject to a limit of 25 per cent of the value of the fund and compliance with certain prescribed provisions; and (2) remove the limit on the amount of investments which may be held in the form of a deposit with certain European institutions and to widen the category of European institutions which may be investment managers of superannuation funds.

The Local Government Superannuation (Maternity Absence) Regulations 1993, SI 1993/2531 (in force on 16 November 1993), amend the 1986 Regulations supra so as to implement in respect of the local government superannuation scheme and maternity leave the requirements of Council Directive (EC) 86/378 (equal treatment for men and women in occupational social security schemes).

The Local Government Superannuation (Educational Institutions) Regulations 1993, SI 1993/3030 (in force on 31 December 1993), amend the 1986 Regulations supra by (1) making provision for the pensionable status of persons employed by further education corporations or institutions which are established or designated under the Further and Higher Education Act 1992, and for the appropriate superannuation fund for such persons; and (2) removing restrictions on the qualification for pensionable status of employees of a designated institution formerly assisted by a local education authority and of the governing body of a grant-maintained school which was formerly a voluntary school.

The Local Government Superannuation (Membership) Regulations 1993, SI 1993/3043 (in force on 1 January 1994), amend the 1986 Regulations supra so as to (1) prevent bodies which are authorised by statute to undertake the provision of certain transport services or energy or water supplies, or which provide such services or supplies and are approved by the Secretary of State for the purpose of admission to the local government superannuation scheme, from entering into admission agreements on or after 1 January 1994; and (2) provide for a new category of pensionable employee who is employed by a company which is under the control of a local authority and who, immediately before starting his employment with the company, was employed by such an authority.

1929 Occupational and personal pension schemes—miscellaneous amendments

The Occupational and Personal Pension Schemes (Miscellaneous Amendments) Regulations 1993, SI 1993/519 (in force on 6 April 1993), amend various regulations relating to occupational and personal pension schemes. The Occupational Pension Schemes (Contracting-out) Regulations 1984, SI 1984/380, are amended to provide that, where contracted-out employment ceases the fixed rate of revaluation of accrued rights to guaranteed minimum pension is to be a specified appropriate percentage. The Personal Pension Schemes (Disclosure of Information) Regulations 1987, SI 1987/1110, are amended to require the disclosure of the minimum contributions attributable to the 1 per cent addition under the Social Security Act 1986, s 3(1)(aa) as part of the information to be made available to individuals. The Personal and Occupational Pension Schemes (Modification of Enactments) Regulations 1987, SI 1987/1116, are amended to extend to Northern Ireland the power of the Occupational Pensions Board to disclose certain information obtained by the Inland Revenue Commissioners relating to the liability to pay personal pensions. The Personal Pension Schemes (Appropriate Schemes) Regulations 1988, SI 1988/137, are amended to provide for the calculation of earnings and the verification of age for the purposes of determining the amount of any payment under the 1986 Act supra, s 3(1)(aa).

1930 Occupational pension schemes—amalgamation of pension funds— employer's obligations

It has been held that where two pension funds are amalgamated into one, and a degree of latitude is given to the employer which puts him in a position where his duties and interests are likely to conflict, the court ought to be vigilant to see that his duty to have regard to pre-existing rights of the two funds' members is properly observed, and not taken away unless that was a proper incident of the amalgamation.

London Regional Transport Pension Fund Co Ltd v Hatt (1993) Times, 20 May (Chancery Division: Knox J).

1931 Occupational pension schemes—bridging pension—sex discrimination

See Birds Eye Walls Ltd v Roberts, para 2755.

1932 Occupational pension schemes—early retirement—retirement by reason of incapacity—meaning of incapacity

An employee was dismissed due to long absences which she claimed were due to medical grounds, namely cervical spondylosis and agoraphobia. She was entitled to a deferred pension under the rules of her employer's pension scheme, but she claimed that she was eligible for the full pension which was payable to anyone who had retired "by reason of incapacity" under the terms of the scheme. The employer's medical expert stated that the employee's illnesses were psychogenic in origin and not permanently disabling. The employer therefore decided that the employee was not incapacitated and so was not entitled to a full pension, and also claimed that termination of employment by dismissal did not constitute retirement. The court at first instance dismissed an action brought by the employee who subsequently appealed in relation to the meaning of the words "retirement from the [employer] . . . by reason of incapacity". *Held*, "incapacity" in the terms of the pension scheme meant that an employee had had to leave before reaching pensionable age due to physical or mental disability or ill health so serious that, at the time she left the employer's service, it was probable she would be unable to follow her present or similar employment, with either the present, or any other, employer, during any part of the period before reaching normal retiring age. As far as termination by dismissal was concerned, this was capable of being described as retirement and accordingly the appeal on this point would be allowed.

Harris v Lord Shuttleworth (1993) Independent, 26 November (Court of Appeal: Glidewell, Evans and Waite LJJ).

1933 Occupational pension schemes—guaranteed minimum pensions—increase

The Guaranteed Minimum Pensions Increase Order 1993, SI 1993/279 (in force on 6 April 1993), made following a review by the Secretary of State under the Social Security Pensions Act 1975, s 37A, specifies 3 per cent as the percentage by which that part of any guaranteed minimum pension attributable to earnings factors for the tax year 1988–89 and subsequent years and payable by occupational pension schemes is to be increased.

1934 Occupational pension schemes—liquidation of employer—surplus funds— application of funds—provision for price indexing

The Social Security Act 1990, s 11(3) provides that no payment is to be made out of the resources of an occupational pension scheme, constituted by a trust deed, to a person who is the employer of pensioners in the scheme until provision has been made for limited price indexing of pensions under the scheme.

It has been held that where, following the winding up of a company, a pension fund is in surplus, the employer is precluded from taking or receiving the surplus until the condition in the Social Security Act 1990, s 11(3) requiring provision to be made for the limited price indexing of pensions has been satisfied. The condition embraces prospective as well as current pensions. In the case of a scheme which is being wound up, the pensions which are to have the benefit of the limited price index increase before any payment of surplus to the employer can be made on a winding up are those payable under the scheme, either actually or prospectively, when the scheme goes into liquidation.

Thrells Ltd v Lomas [1993] 1 WLR 456 (Chancery Division: Sir Donald Nicholls V-C).

1935 Occupational pension schemes—preservation of benefit

The Occupational Pension Schemes (Preservation of Benefit) Amendment Regulations 1993, SI 1993/1822, amend the 1991 Regulations, SI 1991/167, by varying the condition subject to which an actuary may certify that there may be a bulk transfer of members from one scheme to another without the members' consent.

1936 Occupational pension schemes—public service pensions

The Occupational Pension Schemes (Public Service Pension Schemes) (Amendment) Regulations 1993, SI 1993/1888 (in force on 1 September 1993), amend the 1978 Regulations, SI 1978/289, by extending the purposes for which the schemes listed in the 1978 Regulations are to be treated as public service pension schemes and by adding further schemes to that list.

1937 Occupational pension schemes—revaluation

The Occupational Pensions (Revaluation) Order 1993, SI 1993/2904 (in force on 1 January 1994), specifies the revaluation percentage for each revaluation period for the purposes of the revaluation of benefits under occupational pension schemes.

1938 Occupational pension schemes—transfer of undertakings—implied provisions

See *Perry v Intec Colleges Ltd,* para 1179.

1939 Occupational pension schemes—transitional provisions

The Occupational Pension Schemes (Transitional Provisions) (Amendment) Regulations 1993, SI 1993/3219 (in force on 11 January 1994), amend the 1988 Regulations, SI 1988/1436, by providing further circumstances in which specified provisions set out in the Income and Corporation Taxes Act 1988, Sch 23, are applied with prescribed modifications to occupational pension schemes approved before 23 July 1987. An employee who takes early retirement as the result of physical incapacity may now be retired on the pension that could have been paid if service had continued up to the normal retirement date and, where the scheme rules so permit, on a pension which takes account of rises in the cost of living or the general level of earnings obtaining in Great Britain. In certain other circumstances and where the scheme rules so permit, a pension may now take account of rises in the cost of living or the general level of earnings. The amendments have effect as from 17 March 1987.

1940 Parliamentary pensions—additional voluntary contributions

The Parliamentary Pensions (Additional Voluntary Contributions Scheme) Regulations 1993, SI 1993/3252 (in force on 21 January 1994), allow additional voluntary contributions to be paid by participants in the Parliamentary Pension Scheme, which will secure additional benefits within limits established by the Board of Inland Revenue. The scheme will be administered by the Trustees of the Parliamentary Contributory Pension Fund.

1941 Parliamentary pensions—general

The Parliamentary Pensions (Consolidation and Amendment) Regulations 1993, SI 1993/3253 (in force on 21 January 1994), consolidate and amend a number of acts and statutory instruments relating to Parliamentary pensions. They also introduce new provisions relating to the right of members to opt out of the Parliamentary Pension Scheme, children's pension schemes, guarantees for a participant's survivors and an earnings cap for participants who joined the scheme after 1 June 1989.

1942 Parliamentary pensions—House of Commons Members' Fund

A resolution of the House of Commons dated 23 April 1993, SI 1993/1181 (in force on 1 April 1993), has been made varying (1) the maximum annual amounts of the periodical payments which may be made out of the House of Commons Members' Fund under the House of Commons Members' Fund Act 1939; and (2) the annual rate of payments under the Parliamentary Pensions Act 1981, s 1.

1943 Pension fund—trustees—action for breach of trust—action by employees

See *McDonald v Horn*, para 2579.

1944 Pension Schemes Act 1993

The Pension Schemes Act 1993 consolidates certain enactments relating to pension schemes with amendments to give effect to recommendations of the Law Commission. The Act received the Royal assent on 5 November 1993 and comes into force on a day or days to be appointed.

1945 Pensions Ombudsman—directions and determinations—enforcement

The County Court (Pensions Ombudsman) (Enforcement of Directions and Determinations) Rules 1993, SI 1993/1978 (in force on 1 September 1993), provide for the enforcement by a county court of directions by the Pensions Ombudsman for the payment of money and for taking, or refraining from taking, any step as if such directions were judgments or orders of that court.

1946 Personal equity plans—regulations

The Personal Equity Plan (Amendment) Regulations 1993, SI 1993/756 (in force on 6 April 1993), further amend the 1989 Regulations, SI 1989/469, by (1) substituting the reference in the definition of "authorised unit trust" to "an authorised securities scheme" by a reference to "a securities fund" and substituting the definition of "an authorised securities scheme" by a definition of "feeder fund"; (2) altering the rules by virtue of which a plan investor is able to hold units in unit trust schemes and funds of funds, and shares in investment trusts, which do not satisfy the requirement that 50 per cent of their holdings should be in ordinary shares and qualifying EC shares; (3) altering the conditions for application forms in cases where arrangements are made to subscribe on an annual basis; (4) specifying additional information to be given to the transferee plan manager when a plan is transferred from one plan manager to another; and (5) introducing requirements for plan managers to submit monthly statistical returns when making interim claims for repayment of tax and to make annual information returns.

1947 Personal pension schemes

See para 1929.

1948 Public service pensions—increased rates

The Pensions Increase (Review) Order 1993, SI 1993/779 (in force on 12 April 1993), increases the rates of public service pensions. For pensions which began before 6 April 1992, the increase is 3·6 per cent. For those which began on or after 6 April 1992, the increase is a proportion of 3·6 per cent calculated according to the number of complete months in the period between the beginning date of the pension and 6 April 1992. The same percentage increase applies to deferred lump sums beginning on or before 27 March 1993 which became payable after 11 April 1993. The 1993 Order also provides for increases of certain deferred lump sums payable on or after 6 April 1992 and before 12 April 1993, and for the amount by reference to which any increase in the rate of an official pension is calculated to be reduced by an amount equal to the rate of the guaranteed minimum pension entitlement deriving from the employment which gives rise to the official pension.

1949 Retirement benefits schemes—continuation of rights of members of approved schemes

The Retirement Benefits Schemes (Continuation of Rights of Members of Approved Schemes) (Amendment) Regulations 1993, SI 1993/3220 (in force on 11 January 1994 but taking effect as from 14 March 1989), amend the 1990 Regulations, SI 1990/2101, by prescribing further circumstances in which certain provisions of the Finance Act 1989, Sch 6, Pt II, are applied with prescribed modifications.

1950 Retirement benefits schemes—indexation of earnings cap

The Retirement Benefits Schemes (Indexation of Earnings Cap) Order 1993, SI 1993/757 (made on 16 March 1993), specifies £77,400 as the earnings cap for the year of assessment 1993–94.

The Retirement Benefits Schemes (Indexation of Earnings Cap) (No 2) Order 1993, SI 1993/2950 (made on 30 November 1993), specifies £76,800 as the earnings cap for the year of assessment 1994–95.

1951 Retirement benefits schemes—restriction on discretion to approve—additional voluntary contributions

The Retirement Benefits Schemes (Restriction on Discretion to Approve) (Additional Voluntary Contributions) Regulations 1993, SI 1993/3016 (in force on 27 December 1993), impose restrictions in respect of the repayment to an employee of surplus funds arising from the provision of benefits under retirement benefits schemes to which an employee pays additional voluntary contributions.

1952 Retirement benefits schemes—tax relief on contributions—earnings cap

The Retirement Benefits Schemes (Tax Relief on Contributions) (Disapplication of Earnings Cap) (Amendment) Regulations 1993, SI 1993/3221 (in force on 11 January 1994), amend the 1990 Regulations, SI 1990/586, by extending to the case where an employee is posted to the foreign branch of the employer the circumstances in which the earnings cap will be disapplied when calculating tax relief on contributions to exempt approved retirement benefits schemes.

1953 Retirement pension

See SOCIAL SECURITY AND SOCIAL SERVICES.

1954 Retirement pension—pensionable age—sex discrimination

See *Griffin v London Pension Authority*, para 2311.

1955 Teachers—superannuation

The Teachers' Superannuation (Amendment) Regulations 1993, SI 1993/114 (in force on 1 March 1993), further amend the 1988 Regulations, SI 1988/1652. A number of changes of substance are made, including (1) adding to the categories of part-time employment that may become pensionable on election; (2) enabling service in a reserve force to count as reckonable service if the teacher makes an appropriate election and pays certain contributions; (3) providing for payment of incapacity benefits to be made where pensionable employment continues beyond the age of 60 provided that incapacity occurred before that age and the date of retirement was deferred beyond that age because the teacher was absent on paid sick leave; (4) providing that where a deceased person is survived by more than one widow, a death grant or supplementary death grant is to be paid to the widows in equal shares; and (5) relaxing the prohibition on payment of a widower's pension where a family pension is payable to someone else as a nominated beneficiary.

1956 War—civilians' pensions

The Personal Injuries (Civilians) Amendment Scheme 1993, SI 1993/480 (in force in part on 1 April 1993 and in part on 12 April 1993), amends the 1983 Scheme, SI 1983/686, for the payment of pensions and allowances to or in respect of civilians killed or injured in the 1939–45 war. The maximum amount of annual earnings which may be received by a disabled person while he is deemed to be unemployable for the purposes of unemployability allowances under the 1983 Scheme is increased from £2,106 to £2,184, and the rates of pensions and allowances in respect of disablement and death are revised. The 1993 Scheme also provides for treatment allowance to be payable only where there has been a loss of earnings, for medical expenses to be defrayed where they arise wholly or mainly from disablement due to a qualifying injury, and for the abolition of the restoration of pension to women who remarry and of education allowances pensions to parents and other dependants.

1957 War—Home Guard

The Home Guard (Amendment) Order 1993, SI 1993/597 (in force on 1 April 1993), amends the previous instruments relating to the payment of pensions and other grants in respect of disablement and death due to service in the Home Guard in consequence of the introduction of the council tax and the abolition of the community charge.

1958 War—non-service pensions

The War Pensions (Miscellaneous Amendments) Order 1993, SI 1993/692 (in force on 1 April 1993), amends the War Pensions (Naval Auxiliary Personnel) Scheme 1964, SI 1964/1985, the War Pensions (Mercantile Marine) Scheme 1964, SI 1964/2058, and the War Pensions (Coastguards) Scheme 1944, SI 1944/500, in consequence of the abolition of the community charge and the introduction of the council tax.

1959 War—service pensions

The Naval, Military and Air Forces etc (Disablement and Death) Service Pensions Amendment Order 1993, SI 1993/598 (in force in part on 1 April 1993 and in part on 12 April 1993), amends the 1983 Order, SI 1983/883, by raising the maximum annual earnings which may be received by a disabled person while he is deemed to be unemployable for the purposes of unemployability allowance under the 1983 Order. The 1993 Order also provides for treatment allowance to be payable only where there has been a loss of earnings, and for medical expenses to be defrayed where they arise wholly or mainly from disablement due to service. The restoration of pensions to certain classes of widows on the death of their second husbands, education allowances, pensions to parents and other dependants, pensions to certain special classes of disabled servicemen and rank additions are abolished, rates of retired pay, pension, gratuities and allowance are revised, and provision is made to invalidate any assignment or charge on a pension.

1960 War—shore employments

The Injuries in War (Shore Employments) Compensation (Amendment) Scheme 1992, SI 1993/807 (deemed to come into effect on 6 April 1992), amends the 1914 Scheme by increasing the maximum weekly allowance payable under the scheme to £89 and by increasing other allowances proportionately.

The Injuries in War (Shore Employments) Compensation (Amendment) Scheme, SI 1993/1192, (in force on 10 May 1993) amends the 1914 Scheme by increasing the maximum weekly allowance payable under the scheme to £97 and by increasing other allowances proportionately.

PETROLEUM PRODUCTION

Halsbury's Laws of England (4th edn) Vol 35, paras 1201–1445

1961   Continental shelf—designation of areas

The Continental Shelf (Designation of Areas) Order 1993, SI 1993/599 (in force on 10 March 1993), defines a further area where the rights of the United Kingdom are exercisable with respect to the seabed and subsoil and their natural resources.

1962   Offshore installations—safety

See para 1360.

1963   Offshore Safety Act 1992—commencement

See para 1361.

1964   Petroleum revenue tax

See PETROLEUM REVENUE TAXATION.

PETROLEUM REVENUE TAXATION

Halsbury's Laws of England (4th edn) Vol 35, Supp paras 1446–1543

1965   Computation—oil disposed of other than at arm's length—market value

The Inland Revenue has issued a Statement of Practice SP 14/93 to the effect that, where it is not practicable or appropriate to determine, by the normal method of valuation in accordance with the Oil Taxation Act 1975, Sch 3, para 2, the market value of oil disposed of otherwise than at arm's length, it may set a different method of valuation under Sch 3, para 2(2D)(b). The normal basis of valuation is to be regarded as inappropriate in the case of companies which both habitually dispose of all their United Kingdom produced oil of the same kind otherwise than at arm's length, and price that oil on a consistent and reasonable arm's length basis. Companies that wish to avail themselves of the new practice are to apply to the Oil Taxation Office, setting out the method under which they regularly dispose of their oil on non arm's length terms and their proposals in respect of future valuation on an appropriate arm's length basis. Such arrangements will apply for deliveries of oil on or after 1 January 1994 or from such later time as may be agreed with the Oil Taxation Office. See further *STI*, 30 November 1993.

1966   Foreign fields—specification

The following areas have been designated by order as foreign fields for the purposes of the Oil Taxation Act 1983:

Foreign field	SI 1993 No
Lille Frigg Field	1408
Odin Field	1565 (amends errors in SI 1991/1982)
Froy Field	1566

1967   Nomination scheme for disposals and appropriations

The Petroleum Revenue Tax (Nomination Scheme for Disposals and Appropriations) (Amendment) Regulations 1993, SI 1993/2939 (in force on 22 December 1993), further amend

571

the 1987 Regulations, SI 1987/1338, by providing that, for chargeable periods ending after 31 December 1993, participators in oil fields will be able to notify the Inland Revenue in advance that they expect to satisfy the conditions for exclusion from the nomination scheme established by the Finance Act 1987, Sch 10. Oil which forms part of their equity production will then be excluded from the scheme in such chargeable periods unless they fail to satisfy those conditions or they withdraw the notification. Nominations may now be made by participators' agents.

PLEADING

Halsbury's Laws of England (4th edn) Vol 36, paras 1–100

1968   Amendment—defence—amendment where action not ready for trial

The plaintiff employee claimed an award under an employee suggestion scheme operated by the defendant company under which suggestions by employees which saved the company money were rewarded. The company refused to make an award and the employee began proceedings. In its defence, the company initially argued that the employee did not receive an award because his suggestion was not original. Following the service of lists of documents and interrogatories, and some five years after the issue of the writ, the company applied to amend its defence to argue that the employee's claim was barred because the scheme provided that the decision of the committee which scrutinised suggestions was final. On the company's appeal against the refusal of the application, *held*, the principles in *Ketteman v Hansel Properties Ltd* did not apply to the present case because the action was not ready for trial and the application to amend did not involve a limitation defence. In addition, the judge had misdirected himself as to the facts. Accordingly, as there would be no injustice in permitting the company to amend its defence, the appeal would be allowed.

Easton v Ford Motor Co Ltd [1993] 4 All ER 257 (Court of Appeal: Dillon and Butler-Sloss LJJ). *Ketteman v Hansel Properties Ltd* [1988] 1 All ER 38, HL (1987 Abr para 1953) distinguished.

1969   Amendment—statement of claim—adjournment

The plaintiff was the owner of a shed and the defendant was the owner of the adjoining premises. The defendant gave the plaintiff a notice of intention to carry out work on the defendant's premises but before the period for the giving of consent expired, the defendant's boundary wall collapsed and damaged the shed. Two surveyors appointed under the London Building Acts (Amendment) Act 1939 then appointed a third surveyor who determined that the prime cause of the collapse was the defendant's work. The plaintiff issued a summons for summary judgment and a week later sought leave to amend the statement of claim with a pleading that the defendant was estopped from denying he was responsible for the collapse of the wall. The court gave the plaintiff leave to amend the statement of claim and granted the defendant leave to defend on condition that a sum of money be paid into court. The defendant appealed contending that if the statement of claim were to be amended there should be an adjournment of the original summons. *Held*, in general, where an amendment to a statement of claim was allowed, the plaintiff should have formally taken out a fresh summons and an adjournment should have been granted. However, as the defendant had time to consider the amendments and had produced additional affidavit evidence, its appeal against the amendment would be dismissed and the court would hear the appeal as if a new summons had been issued. Under the 1939 Act, a third surveyor's jurisdiction for the resolution of disputes between owners of adjoining land was limited to whether one of them was permitted to carry out works which were the subject of a notice and did not authorise the surveyor to determine other disputes. The court was correct in giving leave to defend and, accordingly, the appeal would be dismissed.

Woodhouse v Consolidated Property Corpn Ltd (1993) 66 P & CR 234 (Court of Appeal: Glidewell and Simon Brown LJJ).

1970   Striking out—application to strike out—time for making application

It has been held that although an application to strike out pleadings, pursuant to RSC Ord 18, r 19, should be made as early as possible, when such an application is made after the action has been set down, it should not be refused where the refusal would result in even greater costs being wasted in a long trial of a hopeless action.

Goymer v Lombard North Central Wheelease Ltd (1993) Times, 1 April (Court of Appeal: Dillon, Leggatt and Hirst LJJ).

1971 Striking out—group action—consideration of defendants' costs versus benefit to plaintiffs

See *AB v John Wyeth & Brother Ltd (No 2)*, para 2041.

1972 Striking out—originating application under Insolvency Rules—definition of pleadings

The Insolvency Rules 1986, SI 1986/1925, r 7(2) defines an originating application as one not made in pending proceedings. Any other application is known as an ordinary application. RSC Ord 18, r 19(1) provides that the court may strike out any pleading or endorsement of writ on one of four grounds; Ord 18, r 19(3) provides that r 19(1) applies to an originating summons or petition as if it were a pleading.

The respondent trustee applied to strike out an "originating application" made by the applicant in bankruptcy proceedings and the question arose as to whether the application was a pleading covered by RSC Ord 18, r 19. *Held*, the document in this case, although described as an originating application, was clearly an ordinary application and therefore not a "pleading". Rule 19(3) stated that the rule should apply to an originating summons or petition as if they were pleadings, although they were not strictly within the definition of pleadings. The rule did not apply to ordinary interlocutory motions, summons or ordinary applications under the Insolvency Rules. The court did, however, have power to dismiss the action under its inherent jurisdiction, on the ground that the action was frivolous or vexatious. On the present facts there was no evidence of wrongdoing by the respondent trustee. Accordingly, the "originating" application would be dismissed.

Re Port (a Bankrupt) (No 516 of 1987); Port v Auger (1993) Times, 16 December (Chancery Division: Harman J).

PLEDGES AND PAWNS

Halsbury's Laws of England (4th edn) Vol 36, paras 101–200

1973 Consumer credit

See CONSUMER CREDIT.

POLICE

Halsbury's Laws of England (4th edn) Vol 36, paras 201–400

1974 Articles

A Question of Morale? Adam Crawford (on police moral): Criminal Lawyer, Issue 40, p 5
Dona Ferentis, Brian Hilliard (on the police response to the Royal Commission on Criminal Justice): 143 NLJ 1036
Police Discipline, John Harrison and Stephen Cragg: 137 NLJ 591
Privatisation and Protection—Spatial and Sectoral Ideologies in British Policing and Crime Prevention, Les Johnston: 56 MLR 771
Suspect Devices, Eric Shepherd (on police interviewing): LS Gaz, 1 December 1993, p 12
Time for a Full Review of the Authorities in Claims of Public Interest Immunity, MI Tregilgas-Davey: (1993) 157 JP Jo 659

1975 Assault on police officer—defence—defendant's belief

See *Blackburn v Bowering*, para 643.

1976 Conditions of service—pay and emoluments

The Police (Amendment) Regulations 1993, SI 1993/313 (in force on 22 March 1993), amend the 1987 Regulations, SI 1987/851, by (1) increasing the maximum amount of removal allowance payable in respect of incidental expenses (with effect from 1 April 1992), and (2) setting out new scales of police pay and increasing the dog handler's allowance (with effect from 1 September 1992).

The Police (Amendment) (No 2) Regulations 1993, SI 1993/1198 (in force on 14 June 1993), amend the 1987 Regulations supra by providing that (1) transitional rent allowance is not to be less than the amount of flat-rate rent allowance payable to officers of the appropriate rank and force on 31 March 1990; (2) where two police officers are married to each other and each is in receipt of transitional rent allowance and one of them retires, resigns or is discharged while a probationer, the other can thereafter receive such an allowance at an enhanced rate; and (3) where two police officers are married to each other and one is appointed to serve part-time, the other can receive a compensatory allowance to take account of the part-time officer's reduced housing or related allowances (with effect from 1 July 1992).

The Police (Amendment) (No 3) Regulations 1993, SI 1993/2047 (in force on 8 September 1993), amend the 1987 Regulations supra in order to make provision for variable shift arrangements. The amendments authorise a chief officer of police, with the consent of the Secretary of State, to bring into operation variable shift arrangements agreed with the Police Federation. The arrangements may be for all full-time officers below the rank of superintendent or a particular class, and must provide for hours of duty and annual leave equivalent to those of other full-time officers. The 1993 Regulations also increase annual leave entitlements by one day for leave years beginning after 31 December 1993.

The Police (Amendment) (No 4) Regulations 1993, SI 1993/2527 (in force on 22 November 1993), amend the 1987 Regulations supra by (1) increasing the maximum amount of removal allowance payable in respect of incidental expenses (with effect from 1 April 1993), and (2) setting out new scales of police pay and increasing the dog handler's allowance (with effect from 1 September 1993).

1977 Conditions of service—pay and emoluments—cadets

The Police Cadets (Amendment) Regulations 1993, SI 1993/2528 (in force on 22 November 1993), amend the 1979 Regulations, SI 1979/1727, by retrospectively increasing the pay of police cadets and increasing the charges payable by them for board and lodging provided by police authorities.

1978 Duty of care—duty to members of public—highway hazards

See *Ancell v McDermott*, para 1879.

1979 Pensions

See PENSIONS AND SUPERANNUATION.

1980 Police Complaints Authority—documents—disclosure—public interest immunity—appeal in criminal proceedings

The applicant following his conviction of murder, made a complaint to the Police Complaints Authority concerning the investigation that had led to his conviction. A reinvestigation of his case was completed culminating in a report which concluded that there was no evidence of a conspiracy among police officers to secure the applicant's conviction. Whilst the report conceded that there had been minor procedural irregularities relating to his detention, it concluded that the murder investigation had been carried out in a professional manner. The applicant sought an order requiring the disclosure of documents relating to his detention and documents that had come into existence in the course of the Police Complaints Authority's inquiry. *Held*, the material of which the disclosure was sought was subject to public interest immunity. The applicant was obliged to make out a clear prima facie case that the documents in question were likely to contain material of real relevance in relation to arguable grounds of appeal. In this case there was no prima facie case for disclosure. To have ordered disclosure would have set an undesirable and dangerous precedent. Accordingly, the application would be refused.

R v Blackhouse [1993] Crim LR 67 (Court of Appeal: Russell LJ, Roch and Wright JJ).

1981 Police Complaints Authority—documents—disclosure—public interest immunity—civil proceedings for damages

The applicants had made complaints against the police under the police complaints procedure. That procedure involved the accumulation of a file of documents. It was established that public interest immunity applied to those documents during civil proceedings. The applicants brought civil actions for damages against the police, or intended to do so, and had asked the chief constables to give an undertaking not to use the documents, nor to rely on any information contained therein, during the course of the proceedings. These requests were refused and the applicants successfully brought judicial review proceedings against the chief constables' decisions. Both chief constables appealed. *Held,* documents which were created and came into existence for the purpose of a police complaints investigation were not to be used for any purpose in civil proceedings except to allow a legal adviser to advise on discovery. Accordingly, the appeals would be refused.

R v Chief Constable of the West Midlands, ex p Wiley; R v Chief Constable of Nottinghamshire Police, ex p Sunderland [1993] NLJR 1403 (Court of Appeal: Nourse, Staughton and Nolan LJJ). Decision of Popplewell J (1992) Times, 29 December (1992 Abr para 1934) affirmed.

1982 Traffic wardens—functions

See para 2229.

PORTS AND HARBOURS

Halsbury's Laws of England (4th edn) Vol 36, paras 401–600

1983 Harbours—harbour authority—pilotage—negligence of pilot—liability of harbour authority

See *Oceangas (Gibraltar) Ltd v Port of London Authority, The Cavendish,* para 2345.

1984 Port health authorities

See PUBLIC HEALTH.

POST OFFICE

Halsbury's Laws of England (4th edn) Vol 36, paras 601–800

1985 Business—monopoly of conveying letters—legislation prohibiting infringement—compatibility with Community law

See *Criminal proceedings against Paul Corbeau,* para 2739.

1986 Import restrictions—abolition

The Post Office (Abolition of Import Restrictions) Regulations 1993, SI 1993/1324 (in force on 22 June 1993), amend the Post Office Act 1953, s 63(5), by no longer prohibiting the importation into the United Kingdom of fictitious postage stamps and specified articles involved in their manufacture, where such importation is from an EC member state.

1987 Letter post—inland—express packets

The Post Office Inland Letter Post Amendment (No 5) Scheme 1993, L1/1993 (coming into operation on 28 June 1993) further amends the 1989 Scheme, L1/1989, by making revisions to certain conditions in respect of express packets, recorded delivery packets and registered packets.

1988 Letter post—overseas—registration and insured letter facilities

The Post Office Overseas Letter Post (Amendment) (No 14) Scheme 1993, L2/1993 (in operation on 14 July 1993), further amends the 1982 Scheme, P2/1982, by introducing references to "International Recorded" and "International Registered", which are the trading names for the registered and insured letter facilities. Certain fees for ancillary services are revised.

1989   Parcel post—inland—postal facilities

The Post Office Inland Parcel Post Amendment (No 5) Scheme 1993, P2/1993 (in operation on 26 April 1993), amends the 1989 Scheme, P1/1989, by revising certain postal facilities and removing the Channel Islands and Datapost from the Scheme.

1990   Parcel post—inland—redirection charges

The Post Office Inland Parcel Post Amendment (No 4) Scheme 1983, P1/1993 (in operation on 25 January 1993), further amends the 1989 Scheme, P1/1989. The Scheme revises certain postal charges, redirection prices and provisions relating to the redirection of parcels by the public.

1991   Parcel post—overseas—postal charges

The Post Office Overseas Parcel Post Amendment (No 15) Scheme, OP1/1993 (in operation on 6 April 1993), amends the 1982 Scheme, P3/1982, by revising certain charges applicable to parcels to all countries and certain other fees. Express' and 'delivery free of charges' facilities no longer exist, and services to the Channel Islands are now included under the 1982 Scheme.

1992   Postal warrant for interception of communication—cancellation—delay in implementing cancellation—unauthorised interception

See para 2446.

PRACTICE AND PROCEDURE

Halsbury's Laws of England (4th edn) Vol 37, paras 1–1000

1993   Articles

Aids Anonymous, Michael Furminger (on whether legal proceedings involving HIV sufferers can be held in camera): 137 SJ 374
Asset Tracing, Mike Trigg: 137 SJ 716
Automatic Striking Out, Philip Tebbatt: 137 SJ 1208
Being Civil to Similar Fact Evidence, John Peysner: [1993] CJQ 188
Beyond the Court Office, James Pyke (on the effect of delays in the administration of justice): 137 SJ 692
Can Negligent Solicitors Hide Behind the Limitation Act? Hugh Brayne: 137 SJ 10
Civil Justice on Trial—The Case for Change: Counsel, July 1993, p 23
Civil Litigation Brief, Gordon Exall: 137 SJ 400
Compulsory Exchange of Witness Statements, James Pyke: 137 SJ 350
Costs Orders Against Legally Aided Persons, District Judge Bullock: [1993] Fam Law 389
Costs—Who Pays? Steven Fennell (on costs orders against non-parties): 137 SJ 744
Enforcement of Judgments and the Brussels Convention, Duncan Black: 137 SJ 225
Lawyer's Comment Defiance or Compliance? RSC Ord 18, r 12 and CCR Ord 6, r 1, Richard Vallance (on the use of medical reports and Statements of Special Damages in medical negligence cases): (1993) 2 AVMA 6
Mareva Injunctions and Security for Judgement in a Framework of Interlocutory Remedies, AAS Zuckerman: (1993) 109 LQR 432
Mistaken Disclosure of Medical Evidence, Diana Tribe and Gill Korgaonkar: 137 SJ 268
Order 14—Avoiding the Pitfalls, Gordon Exall: 137 SJ 788
Radical Surgery for Civil Procedure, Adrian Jack: 143 NLJ 891
Refinements on Non-suiting, Leslie Wise: LS Gaz, 24 March 1993, p 20
Security for Costs and Counterclaims, Andrew Keltie: 143 NLJ 1258
Security For Costs and Foreign Litigants, Paul Friedman: 137 SJ 1018
Striking Out for Want of Prosecution and Estoppel, Nicholas Yell: 143 NLJ 1759, 1782
Testing Times for Taxation, Michael Bacon: 137 SJ 316
The Doctrine of Abuse of Process, Andrew Shepstone: 143 NLJ 1757
Think Strategically, Stephen Mason: 137 SJ 300
What Price This Plaintiff? James Comyn (on payments into court): 137 SJ 773
When Cases Are Delayed, is Justice Denied? Saleem Ahmed: 137 SJ 1028

1994   Anton Piller order—discharge—non-disclosure on application

Prior to commencing an action for infringement of a registered trade mark and passing off, the plaintiffs were given information by an officer of the Health and Safety Executive which had been obtained from the defendant under powers conferred by the Food and Environment Protection Act 1985. The plaintiffs used this information to support a successful ex parte application for an Anton Piller order against the defendant. The defendant contended that the plaintiffs, in applying for the order, should have drawn the court's attention to the defendant's ability to prevent the information being tendered in evidence, and that if it had not been taken into account the order would not have been granted. In an application by the defendant to have the order discharged, *held*, there was no impropriety in disclosing information to a person for whom the information was of mutual interest and concern. A third party proposing to use such information was not to be restrained unless that party was aware of its confidentiality at the time of the proposed use. On an application to discharge an Anton Piller order the court had to consider whether an injustice had been caused to the defendant. The fact that the evidence before the judge was not as strong as it ultimately became did not provide a ground for challenging the order, unless the order had been obtained in bad faith or by the non-disclosure of material. In this case, the alleged non-disclosure had not been of a fact but of a matter of law which might have caused the judge to exclude part of the evidence. The alleged non-disclosure could therefore only have affected the strength of the case and the order was justified and correctly granted. Accordingly, the application would be refused.

   Hoechst UK Ltd v Chemiculture Ltd [1993] FSR 270 (Chancery Division: Morritt J).

1995   Anton Piller order—terms of employment—breach of confidence

The defendants were employed by the plaintiff as salesmen and in the course of their work had worked with a list of customer particulars, listed on customer management cards. Both defendants left the plaintiff and started a rival firm. They took with them the plaintiff's list of customers but not, they maintained, the customer management cards. An Anton Piller order was granted to the plaintiff leading to the recovery by the plaintiff of a number of documents including the list of customers. The defendants applied to discharge the order. The judge hearing the application to discharge ordered certain parts of the order to be varied and on appeal by the plaintiff against the variation, *held*, if the plaintiff had wished to control the activities of ex-employees, the correct way was to have taken appropriate covenants from the employees in their contracts of employment. In this case, the plaintiff was attempting to use the law and the courts to stop competition. Accordingly, the appeal would be dismissed.

   Roberts v Northwest Fixings (1980) [1993] FSR 281 (Court of Appeal: Lawton, Brandon and Templeman LJJ).

1996   Appeal—judge's finding—credibility of witness

Australia

In a personal injury action the trial judge, in accepting the plaintiff's evidence as to how the injury occurred, found that the plaintiff had been injured as the result of the defendants' negligence. The trial judge saw the plaintiff in the witness box for four days and accepted his evidence after taking into account the inconsistencies between his evidence and his out of court statements. The ruling was set aside and the plaintiff appealed. *Held*, where a judge's finding of fact depended on the credibility of a witness, the finding must stand unless it could be shown that the trial judge failed to use or palpably misused his or her advantage or acted on evidence which was inconsistent with facts incontrovertibly established by the evidence or which was glaringly improbable. There was no evidence that any of the above factors existed at the trial. The finding was not vitiated by some error of principle or mistake or misapprehension of fact, nor was the effect of the overall evidence such that it was not reasonably open to the trial judge to accept the plaintiff as a witness of truth. Even where it appeared that a challenged finding of fact had, to a significant extent, been based on the trial judge's observation of the demeanour of the witness, the appeal court could not excuse itself from the task of weighing the conflicting evidence and drawing its own inferences and conclusions. Accordingly, the appeal would be allowed.

   Devries v Australian National Railways Commission (1993) 4 ALR 641 (High Court of Australia).

1997   Appeal—leave to appeal—interlocutory orders

The applicant sought an interlocutory mandatory injunction compelling a university to admit him. The application was refused and he than sought leave to appeal against the decision. *Held*, it was necessary to clarify the rules concerning leave to appeal. The categories of cases where leave was necessary had been increased by the combined effect of: the Courts and Legal Services Act 1990, s 7, which amended the Supreme Court Act 1981, s 18, and the Rules of the Supreme Court (Amendment) 1993, SI 1993/2133, reg 6 (1), which amended RSC Ord 59. RSC Ord 59, r 1B, as added, provided, inter alia, that appeals against interlocutory orders of the High Court required leave, except in specified circumstances. In the present case, the application for leave to appeal would be allowed but the appeal would be dismissed.

Moran v University College, Salford (1993) Times, 27 October (Court of Appeal: Glidewell, Evans and Waite LJJ).

1998 Appeal—notice of appeal—single action—multiple orders—requirement of separate notices

The *Supreme Court Practice 1993*, Note 59/1/4, para 2 states that where two or more orders have been made by the court or tribunal below, separate notices of appeal are required in respect of each order.

It has been held that the practice of lodging separate notices of appeal in respect of each order of the court in respect of one action should not continue. There was nothing in RSC Ord 59, r 1 which required it, and it was hoped that Note 59/1/4 would be amended to read that in respect of two or more orders in one action it was only necessary to file one notice of appeal.

Hawes v Chief Constable of Avon and Somerset Constabulary (1993) Times, 20 May (Court of Appeal: Lloyd, Mann and Steyn LJJ).

1999 Appeal—time for appeal—date from which time for appeal runs

See *Pavel v Sony Corpn*, para 1919.

2000 Barristers

See BARRISTERS.

2001 Chancery Division—Chancery masters—ex parte and urgent applications

The Chief Chancery Master, by the direction of the Vice-Chancellor, has issued the following *Practice Direction* ([1993] 1 WLR 304).

1. It has been established practice for Chancery masters to be available at 2.15 pm on working days for ex parte applications, to advise on court procedure, and to deal with urgent applications.

2. Applicants have previously been required to bespeak the file from the Registry, 7th Floor, Thomas More Building by not later than 12 noon on the day of the application. In future, the file must be bespoken by 4.30 pm on the previous day, except in cases of real emergency.

3. In future, and except in cases of real emergency, masters will only deal with ex parte applications relating to cases allocated to them: see Chancery Division Practice Direction (13)(A)(*The Supreme Court Practice 1993*, Vol 2, p 210, para 853).

4. Chancery Division Practice Direction (5)(vi) (*The Supreme Court Practice 1993*, Vol 2, p 194, para 809) is now replaced by the following:

"(vi) Masters are normally available to hear ex parte applications at 2.15 pm on working days. Notice should be given to the master's clerk in Room TM709 or by telephone on 071 936 6146 or 7391 by 4.30 pm on the previous day, except in cases of real emergency when notice may be given at any time. If the allocated master (as shown in para (13)(A) below) is not available on any particular day, the applicant will be informed and (except in cases of emergency), asked to come when the master is next available. Applications will only be heard by another master in cases of emergency or when the allocated master is on vacation. Minutes of orders to be made by consent, signed by all relevant solicitors or parties, should, except in emergency, be left initially in Room TM709 and not with the master".

2002 Civil liability—contribution—notice—inconsistent facts—effect of foreign law

It has been held that in proceedings pursuant to a contribution notice under the Civil Liability (Contribution) Act 1978, s 1 where a fact pleaded by way of defence is inconsistent with a fact pleaded in the plaintiff's statement of claim the court has to assume that the former fact would not have been established. However where the defendant alleges a material fact which is not so inconsistent, the court is not obliged to treat the negation of that fact as forming part of the factual basis of the claim against him within the meaning of the proviso to the 1978 Act, s 1(4).

Propositions of foreign law which the plaintiff advances in order to succeed against the party claiming contribution do not form part of such factual basis so as to be incontrovertible by the defendant. It follows that the proviso will be construed in such a way that it is immaterial whether any issue relevant to a defendant's liability is determinable by English or by foreign law.

Arab Monetary Fund v Hashim (No 8) (1993) Times, 17 June (Chancery Division: Chadwick J).

2003   Costs—appeal as to costs only—judge's discretion

At the hearing of an action for possession the judge ordered that the defendants' solicitors be personally liable for part of the plaintiffs' costs of the proceedings and a proportion of the costs of the application. Leave to appeal in respect of the costs of the application was refused. On appeal by the defendants, *held*, an order that a defendant pay the costs of an application was an order relating only to the costs which were by law left to the discretion of the court within the meaning of the Supreme Court Act 1981, s 18(1)(f), and therefore, provided a judge exercised his discretion judicially, no appeal from that further order would lie to the Court of Appeal without leave of the judge. The judge had neither failed to exercise her discretion at all nor exercised it improperly and therefore the Court of Appeal had no jurisdiction. Accordingly, the appeal would be dismissed.

Wilkinson v Kenny [1993] 3 All ER 9 (Court of Appeal: Sir Thomas Bingham MR, Rose and Waite LJJ).

2004   Costs—costs on an indemnity basis—effect of legislation

It has been held that the fact that legislation has been promulgated by Parliament during the course of proceedings which render those proceedings abortive cannot be a factor which can lead to a party being made responsible for costs on an indemnity basis. Such costs can only be awarded after careful consideration and then only in exceptional circumstances.

R v IRC, ex p Leeds Permanent Building Society (1993) Times, 28 May (Queen's Bench Division: Neill LJ and Mantell J).

2005   Costs—costs on an indemnity basis—order against a non-party—closely associated company

A dispute arose between the plaintiffs and the defendants with regard the payment of a debt owed by the plaintiffs to the defendant. The plaintiffs brought an action against the defendants. In dismissing the action the judge found that the plaintiffs had brought the action in the expectation that they would be able to force the defendants to negotiate a settlement and that the plaintiffs' claim was a malicious fabrication and an abuse of process. He ordered the plaintiffs to pay the defendants' costs to be taxed on an indemnity basis. It became apparent that the plaintiffs would not be in a position to pay the costs and the defendants sought an order that a non-party and a company controlled by him be made jointly and severally liable for the costs together with the plaintiffs on the grounds that the non-party had conspired with or induced the plaintiffs to institute malicious proceedings against the defendants and had substantially funded the plaintiffs' action knowing that the case presented against the defendants was malicious fabrication. An affidavit showed that the company and one of its subsidiaries had paid a proportion of the plaintiffs' costs of the action. *Held*, in exercising its power under the Supreme Court Act 1981, s 51 to determine by whom and to what extent costs were to be paid the court could not make an order that the non-party pay the defendants' costs of the action brought against them by the plaintiffs on the grounds that he had conspired with or induced the plaintiffs to institute the proceedings. Since he was a non-party who had not been separately represented at the hearing, the claim against him had not been formulated until after the hearing and he had not been warned that there might be a claim that he should pay the costs of the action. No order could be made against the companies controlled by the non-party since there was no evidence that those companies had a direct interest in the outcome of the proceedings and they could not be said to have funded an action brought on their behalf. Accordingly, the application would be dismissed.

Shah v Karanjia [1993] 4 All ER 792 (Chancery Division: Vinelott J).

2006   Costs—criminal cases

See CRIMINAL EVIDENCE AND PROCEDURE.

2007 Costs—divorce cases

See DIVORCE.

2008 Costs—litigant in person—value added tax tribunal

See *Nader (trading as Try Us) v Customs and Excise Comrs*, para 2592.

2009 Costs—jurisdiction to award costs—costs of appeal—order to pay costs in absence

It has been held that where a Queen's Bench Divisional Court allows an appeal by way of case stated by the prosecution from the Crown Court and orders costs against the defendant, who was neither present nor represented at the hearing of the appeal and had not been asked whether she would consent to the appeal being allowed in her absence, it is unjust to require that she ought to pay the costs of the appeal.

Canterbury City Council v Cook (1992) Times, 12 December (Queen's Bench Division: Mann LJ and Leonard J).

2010 Costs—jurisdiction to award costs—costs out of central funds—successful appeals against wasted costs orders

See *Steele Ford & Newton v Crown Prosecution Service; Bradburys v Same; Robin Murray & Co v Same; McGoldrick & Co v Same*, para 680.

2011 Costs—jurisdiction to award costs—entitlement of successful party

The Secretary of State appealed from a refusal of the court to award him costs despite his successful challenge to an application for leave to appeal against an enforcement notice and a refusal of planning permission. *Held*, the general rule that an unsuccessful applicant should pay the respondent's costs was not usually varied just because the respondent was the Secretary of State. Sometimes different considerations might apply if there was more than one respondent or in some cases it might be inappropriate to order an unsuccessful applicant to bear more than one set of costs if the Secretary of State and the local planning authority both appeared and advanced duplicated arguments. A respondent who exercised his right to appear and be heard in an application for leave to appeal against an enforcement notice was normally entitled to his costs where his opposition to the grant of leave was successful. Accordingly, the appeal would be allowed.

Rozhon v Secretary of State for Wales (1993) Times, 29 April (Court of Appeal: Neill, Steyn and Rose LJJ).

2012 Costs—legal representative's personal liability for costs—wasted costs order—failure to apply for adjournment

A solicitor had been unable to resolve difficulties regarding his client with the Legal Aid Board. As a result, he had not applied for an adjournment until the day before the fixed hearing. He caused expense to the other side. He was ordered to pay the costs of the abortive hearing on the ground that he should have given a warning earlier that he might have to apply for an adjournment. On appeal, *held*, the failure to apply for an adjournment earlier was an error of judgment on the solicitor's part, but it was not a dereliction of duty, and did not warrant the making of a wasted costs order against him personally. The appeal would accordingly be allowed.

Re a Solicitor [1993] 2 FLR 6 (Court of Appeal: Nourse and Butler-Sloss LJJ).

2013 Costs—legal representative's personal liability for costs—wasted costs order—interlocutory order

Before the trial of an action for breach of contract and infringement of copyright, the plaintiffs sought a wasted costs order against counsel for the defendants on the ground that they had acted unreasonably or negligently in moving a motion for discovery before the time when an order for discovery would ordinarily be made and which had been dismissed by the judge as wholly misconceived. *Held*, what might seem to have been a misconceived application during the trial might, after trial, be seen to have been worth trying because of the saving of time and costs, had it succeeded. Wasted costs orders should not be sought before trial except in exceptional circumstances. The plaintiffs' application had persuaded counsel for the defendants to withdraw from the case, thereby effectively depriving the defendants of the counsel of their choice. Even though the motion for discovery had been considered to be misconceived when made, that did not mean that counsel had made an error that no competent counsel could make. It would not be possible until after the trial to look at the application in its context of the whole proceedings. The test of liability for a wasted costs order was the same whether the client for whom the lawyer acted was legally-aided or not. The plaintiffs' application would be dismissed.

Filmlab Systems International Ltd v Pennington [1993] NLJR 1405 (Chancery Division: Aldous J).

2014   Costs—legal representative's personal liability for costs—wasted costs order—judicial review proceedings

The applicants were gypsies who had obtained legal aid to bring judicial review proceedings against a district council. The application for judicial review had been dismissed. The district council applied for a wasted costs order to be made under the Supreme Court Act 1981, s 51 (as substituted by the Courts and Legal Services Act 1990, s 4) against the solicitors and the barrister who had acted for the applicants. *Held*, in judicial review proceedings, legal advisers should always reconsider the merits of their application once the respondents had served their evidence. This avoided the wasting of time and the incurring of expense in hopeless applications. The 1990 Act, s 4 indicated that Parliament must have intended to provide redress for all who incurred expense in civil and criminal cases which was caused by the negligence of lawyers. In this case there were no grounds for making a wasted costs order. The new jurisdiction under the 1990 Act had not come into effect in relation to barristers at the time the application for judicial review had been made, but the case had disclosed so many departures from good practice that the Bar Council ought to arrange for the preparation and publication of a statement of the professional standards to be expected of counsel having the conduct of judicial review proceedings. In such circumstances, it would be wrong to make a wasted costs order against the solicitors. Accordingly, the application would be dismissed.

R v Horsham District Council, ex p Wenman [1993] NLJR 1477 (Queen's Bench Division: Brooke J).

2015   Costs—legal representative's personal liability for costs—wasted costs order—liability for work prior to commencement of relevant provisions

It has been held that an order for wasted costs under the Supreme Court Act 1981, s 51(6), (7) as amended by the Courts and Legal Services Act 1990, s 4, can only be made against counsel in respect of acts done after 1 October 1991, when the amendment came into force.

Fozal v Gofur (1993) Times, 9 July (Court of Appeal: Sir Thomas Bingham MR, Peter Gibson LJ and Sir Francis Purchas).

2016   Costs—order against non-party—material considerations

The defendant entered into a contract of employment with the plaintiff, a term of which was that on termination of his employment he would not engage in similar work elsewhere for one year. On leaving the plaintiff's employment the defendant commenced work for a competitor of the plaintiff. The plaintiff brought an action against the defendant claiming damages. During the proceedings a director of the competitor company gave evidence for the defendant. Judgment was given for the plaintiff and he applied for an order for the competitor to pay the costs of the action. The matter was then referred to the Court of Appeal for a preliminary ruling. *Held*, in ordering the costs of the proceedings to be paid by some person other than a party to the proceedings the following factors ought to be considered: (1) such an order would always be exceptional; (2) it would be even more exceptional where the applicant had a cause of action against the non-party and could have joined him as a party to the original proceedings; (3) the applicant ought to warn the non-party at the earliest opportunity that he might apply for costs against him; (4) an application ought to be determined by the trial judge; (5) an order would only be justified if the connection of the non-party with the original proceedings was so close that he would not suffer any injustice by allowing a departure from the general rule that judicial findings were inadmissible as evidence of the facts upon which they were based in proceedings between one of the parties to the original proceedings and a non-party; (6) the fact that by being a witness in proceedings might lead to an application for the costs of those proceedings against the witness or his company was an exception to the principle that witnesses enjoyed immunity from any form of civil action in respect of evidence given during those proceedings, and (8) the judge ought to be alert to the possibility that an application for costs against a non-party was motivated by resentment of an inability to obtain an effective order for costs against a legally-aided litigant.

Symphony Group plc v Hodgson [1993] 4 All ER 143 (Court of Appeal: Balcombe, Staughton and Waite LJJ).

2017 Costs—pre-emptive costs order—pension fund trustees—action for breach of trust

See *McDonald v Horn*, para 2579.

2018 Costs—security for costs—ability to pay costs—financial hardship

The defendant applied for an order that the plaintiff provide security for costs with respect to two actions being brought by the plaintiff against the defendant. The plaintiff was a subcontractor and was seeking payments under a contract held with the defendant. The defendant's application was refused and on appeal by the defendant against the refusal, *held*, the court only had jurisdiction to make an order for security for costs if it appeared by testimony that there was reason to believe that the plaintiff would (and not merely might) be unable to pay the defendant's costs if successful. In this case the plaintiff was operating on a limited profit margin in a time of great recession. Having regard to the efforts the plaintiff had made to keep afloat during the long recession it was oppressive that the plaintiff be forced to abandon a genuine claim by an order for security for costs. The abandonment of the claim would almost certainly mean that the plaintiff would have to restart its business entirely afresh. Accordingly, the appeal would be dismissed.

Europa Holdings Ltd v Circle Industries (UK) plc [1993] BCLC 320 (Court of Appeal: Dillon and Bingham LJJ).

2019 Costs—security for costs—Community law—discrimination on the ground of nationality

See *Hubbard v Hamburger*, para 2725.

2020 Costs—security for costs—counterclaim—availability of security in respect of counterclaim by defendant

The plaintiff brought an action against the defendant claiming damages for the defendant's breach of a written agreement. The defendant counterclaimed and the plaintiff applied under the Companies Act 1985, s 726 for security for costs in respect of the defendant's counterclaim. An order for security was made and the defendant successfully appealed against the order. On subsequent appeal by the plaintiff, *held*, there was a discretion in the court to do what was fair and just and the court was wrong to limit its analysis to whether the claim and counterclaim turned on the same issue of fact. The defendant had pleaded an extensive counterclaim in which the damages claimed exceeded those claimed by the plaintiff and in which the ambit of the action was substantially enlarged. The defendant had clearly crossed the boundary which divided an aggressive defence from an independent counterclaim. The counterclaim raised far-reaching issues which were time consuming and expensive to explore and it was therefore just and equitable that the plaintiff be secured against the costs of exploring those issues in the event of being successful in defeating the counterclaim. Accordingly, the appeal would be allowed.

Hutchison Telephone (UK) Ltd v Ultimate Response Ltd [1993] BCLC 307 (Court of Appeal: Dillon and Bingham LJJ).

2021 Costs—security for costs—security for costs by company

See *Re Unisoft Group Ltd (No 1)*, para 493.

2022 Costs—taxation—interest—power to disallow—inordinate or inexcusable delay

After the trial and appeal of an action, the defendants were awarded costs against the plaintiffs. There was a delay of over ten months before they lodged their bill for taxation. The chief taxing master, purporting to exercise his power under RSC Ord 62, r 28(4)(b)(ii) to disallow part of a successful party's costs where prejudice had been suffered by another party as a result of delay in lodging a bill of costs for taxation, disallowed interest on the defendants' bill for the ten-month period on the grounds that the delay, although not inexcusable, bordered on the inordinate; the effect of this was to deprive the defendants of a large sum of money. The defendants appealed, contending that the master had no jurisdiction to disallow interest on the bill since Ord 62, r

28(4)(b)(ii) did not permit him to deprive a successful party of the statutory entitlement to interest on assessed costs under the Judgments Act 1838, s 17, and his decision amounted to an excessive and unjustifiable penalty. *Held*, although on the true construction of r 28(4)(b)(ii) the taxing master was only empowered to disallow the whole or part of a successful party's costs where he delayed lodging his bill for taxation and could not in terms disallow interest, that was merely a technical distinction since the master, having taken additional interest payable into account, could disallow part of the costs calculated by reference to some or all of the interest that was payable. However, before doing so the court had to be aware of the taxed costs on which that interest was accruing, otherwise the final result could not be known and the final sum could be either excessive or insufficient. Since the master had made his determination when the proceedings had reached the stage where although he had given his decision on various points of principle arising on the bill of costs, he had not yet applied those principles to the amounts in the bill, he could not have been aware of the final figures involved in the bill and could not therefore have been aware of the precise implications of the order; (2) the taxing master had jurisdiction to "fine" a successful party by disallowing costs under RSC Ord 62, r 28(4)(b)(ii) where the delay in lodging a bill for taxation had been inordinate or inexcusable or had been shown to be prejudicial to the unsuccessful party in the action, but where those conditions were not fulfilled it was inappropriate for the court to disallow costs. In this case the defendants were not guilty of inordinate or inexcusable delay. Accordingly, it was an inappropriate exercise of the power under r 28(4)(b)(ii) to deprive the defendants of a significant measure of their costs. The appeal would accordingly be allowed.

Pauls Agriculture Ltd v Smith [1993] 3 All ER 122 (Queen's Bench Division: Judge Peter Crawford).

2023 Costs—taxation—practice—legal aid taxation

The Chief Taxing Master, with the concurrence of the Lord Chief Justice and, in so far as it is relevant to proceedings in the Family Division, with the concurrence of the Senior District Judge of the Family Division, has issued the following *Practice Direction* ([1993] 1 All ER 263). Paragraphs 1.20, 2.1, 2.2 and 2.6 do not apply to the Family Division.

Introduction

This Direction will apply to all taxation proceedings in the Supreme Court Taxing Office under RSC Ord 62 with effect from 1 December 1992. It introduces a system of identifying before taxation the items in dispute.

The Practice Notes are designed to enable complex bills to be taxed expeditiously and without loss of fairness, and have been compiled in the light of the experience of the taxing masters and taxing officers since RSC Ord 62 was comprehensively amended in 1986.

Direction 1: Taxation practice

1.1 Items which are properly part of a solicitor's normal overhead costs, and as such provided for in his expense rate, are wholly to be excluded. Each chargeable item is the subject of a discretionary allowance which should be shown in two parts, the first representing the direct cost of the work, properly itemised, and the second the appropriate allowance for care and conduct.

1.2 The allowance for care and conduct is intended to reflect all the relevant circumstances of the case and in particular the matters set out in para 1(2) of Pt I of App 2 to Ord 62. It also intended to reflect those imponderable factors, for example general supervision of subordinate staff, for which no direct time charge can be substantiated, and the element of commercial profit. Accordingly the allowances to be made for different items may, in the discretion of the taxing officer, be allowed at different rates. In particular it is anticipated that, save in unusual circumstances, the rate appropriate to items 1, 2, 3 and 5 in Pt II of App 2 for care and conduct will be less than the rate appropriate to item 4 for general care and conduct.

1.3 The bill should commence with a short and succinct narrative indicating the issues, the relevant circumstances, when instructions were received and when the matter ended. The assessment of allowances which depend partly on arithmetical computation and partly on judgments of value is not assisted by prolixity. This narrative should be followed by a statement showing the status of the fee-earners concerned and the expense rates claimed for each.

1.4 The bill should then set out in chronological order, with dates, all the relevant events, whether or not any such event constitutes a chargeable item. Where the event in question is one which does constitute a chargeable item the allowance claimed should be shown against it. Where any event, whether a chargeable item or not, has occasioned a disbursement, the amount claimed for that disbursement should be inserted alongside that event. Item 4, which comprises the general work of preparation, is to be placed after all the other items save only item 5, which is to be the last item. Attention is particularly drawn to r 29(7)(c)(iii), which requires that every bill which is lodged for taxation must be signed by the solicitor whose bill it is or, if costs are due to a firm, by a partner of that firm.

1.5 Items 1, 2 and 3 should show separately the time engaged and the allowances claimed for care and conduct and for the time engaged in travelling and waiting. In the case of an interlocutory hearing, a note should be made of any order for costs made thereon and any certificate for counsel granted. If an order is drawn up a copy should be among the papers lodged in its appropriate chronological order.

1.6 Item 4. This item should be divided into three parts.

Part A. In this part the work done and the amount claimed for it should be set out in separate sections as indicated in App 2, Pt II, para 4. If necessary (as for example where in sub-para (ii) there is more than one witness) these sections should be subdivided. Each section or subsection should contain a breakdown of the work comprised in it and should have its own separate subtotal. At the foot of the last of these sections there should be shown a total Pt A figure. Where a charge is included in item 4, Pt A for correspondence and telephone attendances with counsel or his clerk, the work should only relate to such communications as are proper to be made by a fee-earner. Instructions by letter must be charged for under 'Preparation of documents'. Telephone discussions should be charged as conferences under item 2. Communications which may be included in item 4 are those which are properly fee-earner's work and deal with such matters as agreeing a brief fee, or arranging conferences, or reserving counsel for a trial or hearing.

Part B. The amount claimed for general care and conduct on the basis of the guidance given in para 3 of these notes should be claimed as a separate monetary amount which should also be expressed as a percentage of the total Pt A figure. This part should include a statement identifying those factors in para 1(2) of Pt I of App 2 to Ord 62 which are relied on in relation to the assessment of the claim for general care and conduct.

Part C. In this part an amount should be claimed for time engaged in travelling and waiting without uplift in connection with the work comprised in Pt A only. Details should be given showing to which part of that work the claim or claims relate.

The section subtotals and the totals of Pts A, B and C figures referred to above should be shown in the narrative column of the bill. The aggregate of those figures should be shown in the profit costs column.

1.7 Travelling time will be allowed in respect of each item at the full amount of the appropriate expense rate. Waiting time will be similarly allowed but neither travelling nor waiting time will attract any allowance for care and conduct.

1.8 Letters and telephone calls will in general be allowed on a unit basis of six minutes each, the charge being calculated by reference to the appropriate expense rate. The unit charge for letters will include perusing and considering the relevant letters in and no separate charge should be made for incoming letters. The taxing officer may allow an actual time charge for letters of substance and for telephone calls which properly amount to an attendance, providing details of the work done are provided and the time taken has been recorded.

1.9 If it is proper for service of process to be effected by a fee-earner in the employment of the solicitor a relevant chargeable item should be shown in sub-para (xiii) of item 4. If service is effected by an inquiry agent or solicitor agent the agent's charges should there be shown as a disbursement. This paragraph does not relate to subpoenas, which are dealt with in para 1.10.

1.10 Conduct money paid to witnesses who attend a trial or hearing should be shown as part of the expenses claimed at the trial or hearing and not included in the bill at the date of the service of a subpoena. Where the witness does not attend the trial or hearing conduct money paid and (despite reasonable efforts) not recovered should be shown at the date of service of subpoena. Work properly done by a fee-earner in connection with the issue of a subpoena should be shown in sub-para (ii) of item 4.

1.11 Properly kept and detailed time records are helpful in support of a bill provided they explain the nature of the work as well as recording the time involved. The absence of such records may result in the disallowance or diminution of the charges claimed. They cannot be accepted as conclusive evidence that the time recorded either has been spent or, if spent, is 'reasonably' chargeable.

1.12 Accounts must accompany the bill for all payments claimed (other than court fees or minor out-of-pocket disbursements) whether or not these payments have later to be vouched. In the case of substantial witness expenses and professional fees including counsel's fees (but not those of medical experts) the account should be accompanied by details showing the work done, the time spent, by whom and when, and the computation of the charge. Copies of those details should be annexed to the copy bill served on the paying party. The importance of this rule of practice is stressed: failure to comply with it invariably delays the taxation and may result in a reduction in or the disallowance of item 5. Counsel's fees should continue to be charged for each separate piece of work undertaken. A 'composite fee' must be broken down into its component parts.

1.13 Where travelling expenses are claimed they should be shown as a disbursement and details supplied. Local travelling expenses will not be allowed. The definition of 'local' is a matter for the discretion of the taxing officer. While no absolute rule can be laid down, as a matter of guidance in cases proceeding in the High Court in London 'local' will, in general, be taken to mean within a radius of ten miles from the Royal Courts of Justice.

1.14 The cost of postage, couriers, outgoing telephone calls, fax and telex messages is in general part of the solicitor's normal overhead expense, but the taxing officer may in his discretion allow such a disbursement in unusual circumstances or where the cost is unusually heavy, if the solicitor could not reasonably be supposed to have taken it into account when estimating his normal overheads for the purpose of calculating his expense rate.

1.15 The making of copies of documents is part of the solicitor's normal overhead expense. The taxing officer may in his discretion make an allowance for copying in unusual circumstances or when the documents copied are unusually numerous in relation to the nature of the case: for example, they may be allowed in proceedings in the Court of Appeal. Where this discretion is invoked the number of copies made, their purpose and the charge claimed must be set out in the bill. If copies have been made out of the office the cost should be shown as a disbursement. If made in the office, a charge equivalent to the commercial cost should be claimed. A charge based on the time expended by a member of the solicitor's staff will not be allowed.

1.16 Charges as between a principal solicitor and a solicitor agent will continue to be dealt with on the established principle that such charges, where appropriate, form part of the principal solicitor's charges. Where these charges relate to the items 1, 2 and 3 they should be included in their chronological order. Where they relate to work done under item 4 they may either be included in the principal solicitor's item or be shown as a separate item properly detailed following afterwards. Solicitors are reminded that agency charges for advising the principal how to proceed are not recoverable.

1.17 No details of the work done need be provided for item 5(a) but on taxation the party entitled to the costs must justify the amount claimed. In general the drawing of a bill of costs is not fee-earner's work and, save in exceptional circumstance, no charge should be sought for such work. Charges paid to an agent will not be allowed.

1.18 Details of the work done should be provided for any charge claimed under item 5(b). When objections are lodged they should be set out under the following column headings: number of objection; page of bill; description of item; amount claimed; amount allowed; grounds for objection.
    The grounds for objection should refer to any reasons given by the taxing officer for the reduction or disallowance and state why the objector disagrees. The grounds should include authorities and references relied on.
1.19 When bills are lodged for taxation they should be supported by the relevant papers arranged as specified in r 29(7)(d). Failure to observe this requirement substantially increases the time and expense of the taxation process and may result in the bill being refused or the allowance for taxation reduced or disallowed.

1.20 *Statement of parties*. (a) Inaccurate completion of this form, from which the Supreme Court Taxing Office derives its information about the identity of the parties, causes considerable delays. The statement must include the name and address, document exchange number, reference, telephone and fax number for each solicitor or litigant in person on the record. The Supreme Court Taxing Office will communicate with the principals unless a specific written request is made for correspondence to be sent to London agents. All communications will be sent to the solicitors on the record and not to costs draftsmen. (b) If the costs are payable out of a trust fund, the names and addresses of the residuary or other beneficiaries who will ultimately bear the costs should be given (with the proportion of their interest in the fund). If appropriate, directions can then be given pursuant to RSC Ord 62, r 26 to enable them to make representations on the taxation. (c) References for taxation will not be given if the statement of parties is illegible or does not comply with the r 29(7)(b).

1.21 *Signing of bills*. RSC Ord 62, r 29(7)(c)(iii) requires that every bill be signed in his own name by a partner in the firm of solicitors whose bill it is. This signature implies that the solicitor personally vouches for the accuracy of the bill, that it is complete and that the signatory is responsible for the factual accuracy of the bill. The name of the solicitor signing the bill must also be shown in block letters. When there has been a change of solicitor in a non-legally-aided case each solicitor may sign the part of the bill relating to his firm's costs. In a legally-aided case every solicitor must sign the appropriate part of the bill.

1.22 *Papers lodged in support of the bill*. It is the responsibility of the solicitor to ensure that everything necessary to justify the bill is readily accessible. Much time has been wasted in the past because papers lodged are incomplete or in disarray. Solicitors are asked to have particular regard to the following points: (a) Only one set of papers should be supplied. All duplicate and irrelevant papers should be removed from the files before papers are lodged. (b) The various items in the bill should be readily correlated with supporting papers (eg instructions and briefs to counsel should be in bill order and clearly identified by a consecutive number or letter on the item and in the bill). (c) A note should be made on the bill if a supporting document is missing. (d) Originals of documents (especially instructions and briefs to counsel, drafts of documents settled by counsel and experts' reports) should be lodged. Any which are not available should be noted on the bill. (e) In legal aid cases a separate bundle in date order containing the certificate, amendments and authorities should be lodged together with the relevant correspondence with the Legal Aid Board seeking such amendments and authorities and copies of any consent required from the assisted person. (f) A distinction should be made between time properly recorded and time estimated. It is helpful if the relevant part of item 4 (preparation for trial) in the bill shows the date and duration of each attendance of substance. Where the time claimed on documents is substantial the receiving party should, when serving the bill, provide the paying party with a schedule of the total time claimed under item 4 (preparation), Pt A(ix) (documents) showing: (i) the date when the work was done; (ii) a description of the work; (iii) the status of the fee-earner who did the work; (iv) how long the work took. The schedule of times spent on documents should be supplied with the bill on lodging the bill and papers at the Supreme Court Taxing Office, but the schedule will not be required if either the information is already contained in the bill or the documents item is agreed.

1.23 *Calderbank offers*. A party liable to pay costs to a party other than an assisted person may make a 'Calderbank offer' (see *Calderbank v Calderbank* [1975] 3 All ER 333, [1976] Fam 93) under the provisions of Ord 62, r 27(3). Subject to r 27 if the offer is accepted the party whose bill it is may apply for the bill to be withdrawn and for the taxing fee to be abated in whole or in part. The existence of a *Calderbank* offer must not be made known personally to the taxing officer to whom the taxation has been referred.

The attention of the profession is drawn to the judgment in *Platt v GKN Kwikform Ltd* [1992] 1 WLR 465.

Direction 2: Ancillary matters
2.1 *Appointments and adjournments*. RSC Ord 62, r 30(1) requires that not less than 14 days' notice of a taxation be given. Any appointment which becomes ineffective within that time cannot therefore be allocated to another case. If an appointment given is inconvenient or a case is settled, notice should be given to the Supreme Court Taxing Office immediately, preferably by fax. The interests of other litigants awaiting an appointment must be borne in mind. Applications for adjournments made within 14 days of the appointment will therefore be granted only in the most exceptional circumstances. A very strong case will have to be made for any later application, opposed or unopposed, to succeed. This direction only applies to

adjournments, not to cases where appointments are vacated because a settlement has been reached.

2.2 *Abatement of taxing fees.* The Supreme Court Fees Order 1980, SI 1980/821, Schedule, s 5 provides for the payment of such fee as may be reasonable having regard to the work done in the court office. As a general guide, where a bill is withdrawn more than 21 days prior to the taxation the taxing fee will be not less than 50 per cent. Where the bill is withdrawn within 7 days of taxation the fee will be not less than 75 per cent. The taxing officer has a discretion to impose a different fee where the circumstances require it.

2.3 *Identification of matters in issue.* In an effort to save time the paying party is required to identify areas of disagreement and to notify the receiving party thereof well in advance of the taxation to enable those issues to be identified and clarified in advance. The paying party should outline the reason for disputing an item and where a reduction is sought should suggest the reduced figure. The taxing officer should be given this information and any response at least seven days before the taxation.

2.4 *Removal of papers.* All papers must be removed immediately after the taxation. Any papers not removed will be treated as abandoned and sent for destruction without notice. No responsibility whatsoever will be accepted for papers left after taxation, or after a proposed taxation has been settled.

2.5 *Summons to review taxations—papers for use of the court.* Applicants for reviews of taxation are required to lodge with the Chief Clerk three bundles of documents for the use of the judge and assessors.

Upon receipt of the summons to review the Chief Clerk will send notice to the applicant requesting that the bundles be lodged, which should consist of copies of the following documents: the summons to review; order/judgment or other instrument providing for the taxation; bill of costs; objections; respondent's answers (if any); master's answers and certificate; affidavits filed during the course of the taxation; the legal aid certificate, any relevant amendments thereto and authority to apply for review where applicable; any correspondence or other documents to which reference is intended to be made at the hearing of the review.

Bundles must be clearly paginated with an index at the front of the bundle listing all the documents and giving a page reference for each one. The bundles must be bound together. Loose documents will not be accepted.

The bundles must be lodged within 21 days from the receipt of notice from the Chief Clerk or such other time as the Chief Clerk may direct.

2.6 *Masters' Secretariat.* Any questions or application relating to any taxation referred to a master should be referred to the Masters' Secretariat, which is situated in room 2.14 (telephone number 071-936 6605/6505, fax number 071-936 6344), who will seek the master's directions. The sitting master whose name is printed in the Daily Cause List is available to deal with practice queries and urgent appointments.

Direction 3: Wasted costs orders and delay
3.1 *Applications under RSC Ord 62, r 28: allegations of misconduct, neglect, delay or wasted costs*
(i) Any party wishing to make an application under r 28 of Ord 62 must do so on summons in accordance with RSC Ord 32. The summons may be issued at any time after commencement of proceedings for taxation.
(ii) The summons should be so drawn as to give the other parties adequate notice of the case to be met and thus to minimise the risk of applications for adjournments.
(iii) The summons should indicate whether the party intends to rely upon (a) r 28(1) and r 10(1) (misconduct or neglect in the conduct of any proceedings), (b) r 28(2) and s 51(6) of the Supreme Court Act 1981 (personal liability of legal representative for costs) or (c) r 28(4) (failure to commence or conduct taxation proceedings in accordance with Ord 62 or delay in lodging a bill for taxation).
(iv) A summons under r 28(1) or (2) should give brief particulars of the facts complained of and the relief sought.
(v) A summons under r 28(4) should identify any failure or delay relied upon, the facts complained of and the relief sought.
(vi) The party making the application must indicate the time required for the application or, if it be preferable, request a short directions hearing. If possible a date and time of hearing will be given immediately; if that is not possible the applicant will be notified of the time and place as soon as possible. Once an order has been made Ord 42, r 4 will apply. The order must normally

be drawn up and it is the responsibility of the applicant to do so (Ord 42, r 5). In Chancery Division proceedings it will be the responsibility of the parties to draw up the order unless the master directs otherwise. Three copies of the order must be prepared, one for sealing at the Supreme Court Taxing Office and return, one for filing at the Supreme Court Taxing Office and one for filing in room 81 (Queen's Bench Division) or the Chancery Registry as the case may be.

(vii) The party having carriage of the order must serve a copy of the order upon any opposing party.

(viii) In the event of either party being dissatisfied with the taxing officer's decision under RSC Ord 62, r 28, an appeal lies to the judge in chambers in accordance with RSC Ord 58. This must not be confused with the procedure for carrying in of objections and summons for review before the judge, which continue to be governed by RSC Ord 62, Pt VI, rr 33–35.

(ix) Any enforcement proceedings will be in the Queen's Bench Division or Chancery Division as the case may be.

Direction 4: Legal aid
4.1 *Assessment of costs*
Regulation 106(1) and (2) of the Civil Legal Aid (General) Regulations 1989, SI 1989/339, provides:
'(1) Where, in proceedings to which an assisted person (or a former assisted person) has been a party and which have been brought to an end by a judgment, decree or final order, there has been an agreement as to the costs to be paid by any other party to the assisted person (or former assisted person) which that person's solicitor and counsel (if any) is willing to accept in full satisfaction of the work done, the amount of those costs shall be assessed by the Area Director. (2) Where costs are to be assessed in the circumstances specified in paragraph (1), the Area Director may, if he thinks fit, request the taxing officer of the court in which the proceedings were conducted to assess the costs on the standard basis without a taxation.'
If such request is made by the Area Director to the Supreme Court Taxing Officer or Admiralty Registrar the appropriate taxing officer will: (i) in the normal course, assess the costs without requiring the attendance of the solicitor; (ii) issue a certificate of assessment of the costs.

4.2 *Interest of the assisted person*
(i) The attention of solicitors is drawn to regs 118 and 119 of the Civil Legal Aid (General) Regulations 1989, which deal with the position applying when the assisted person (a) has no interest or has an adverse interest in a taxation (reg 118) or (b) has a financial interest in the taxation (reg 119).

(ii) Whenever an assisted person has a financial interest in the taxation (which includes any case in which he has been awarded costs), the solicitors must before lodging their bill for taxation: (a) send the assisted person a copy of the bill; (b) explain the extent of his interest in the taxation, which should cover in particular the power of the taxing officer to order payment out of the legal aid fund (hence by the assisted person personally) of any relevant part of the costs claimed inter partes, and the steps which can be taken to safeguard that interest; and (c) inform him that he has a right to appear on the taxation if he so wishes.

(iii) The bill of costs must be indorsed with a certificate in Form A in the schedule hereto. If the assisted person has expressed a wish to attend the taxation his address and telephone number must be included in the statement of parties.

(iv) Regulation 119(b) provides that an assisted person shall not be required to make any contribution to the fund in respect of the costs of taxation proceedings when he has a financial interest in a taxation. To enable these costs to be ascertained by the Legal Aid Board they will be separately certified in the taxing master's certificate. The legal aid summary to be completed by solicitors on each bill must show the costs of taxation separately and should be in the Form B in the schedule hereto.

4.3 The arithmetical accuracy of the summary on every taxed bill is the responsibility of the solicitor whose bill it is. Every bill, whether or not it includes costs payable out of the legal aid fund, lodged for the issue of a taxing master's certificate must contain a certificate that the castings are correct in Form C in the schedule which must be signed by a partner in the firm.

Direction 5: Directions withdrawn
5.1. The following Practice Directions are hereby withdrawn:
1. *Practice Direction No 1 of 1986*, 9 April 1986 (*Supreme Court Practice 1993*, Vol 1, para 62/A5/6);
2. *Practice Direction No 3 of 1986*, 10 June 1986 (*Supreme Court Practice 1993*, Vol 1, para 62/A5/7);
3. *Practice Direction No 4 of 1986*, 27 June 1986 ([1986] 3 All ER 724, [1986] 1 WLR 1054, *Supreme Court Practice 1993*, Vol 1, para 62/A5/8);

4. *Practice Direction No 5 of 1986*, 16 July 1986 ([1986] 3 All ER 725, [1986] 1 WLR 1053, *Supreme Court Practice 1993*, Vol 1, para 62/A5/9);
5. *Practice Direction No 1 of 1989*, 18 May 1989;
6. *Practice Direction No 2 of 1989*, 18 May 1989 ([1989] 2 All ER 480, [1989] 1 WLR 688, *Supreme Court Practice 1993*, Vol 1, para 62/A5/12);
7. *Practice Direction No 4 of 1989*, 1 December 1989 ([1989] 3 All ER 960, [1989] 1 WLR 1399, *Supreme Court Practice 1993*, Vol 1, para 62/A5/13);
8. *Practice Direction No 1 of 1990*, 26 June 1990 ([1990] 3 All ER 24, [1990] 1 WLR 1089, *Supreme Court Practice 1993*, Vol 1, para 62/A5/14);
9. *Practice Direction No 2 of 1990*, 20 August 1990 ([1990] 3 All ER 458, [1990] 1 WLR 1486, *Supreme Court Practice 1993*, Vol 1, para 62/A5/15);
10. *Practice Direction No 1 of 1991*, 31 January 1991 ([1991] 1 All ER 703, [1991] 1 WLR 177, *Supreme Court Practice 1993*, Vol 1, para 62/A5/17).

Schedule

Form A (para 4.2)

Certificate pursuant to regulation 119
I certify that a copy of this bill has been sent to the assisted person pursuant to regulation 119 of the Civil Legal Aid (General) Regulations 1989, with an explanation of his/her interest in the taxation and the steps which can be taken to safeguard that interest in the taxation. He/she has/has not requested that the taxing officer be informed of his/her interest and has/has not requested that notice of the taxation appointment be sent to him/her.

Signed . . .

Partner in the firm of. . .

Form B (para 4.2)
Legal aid summary to be indorsed on any bill of costs payable out of the legal aid fund

Form B (para 4.2)

Legal aid summary to be indorsed on any bill of costs payable out of the legal aid fund

*Profit costs	£	
	VAT	£
Counsel's fees		£
	VAT	£
*Other disbursements		£
	VAT	£
Costs of taxation allowed interpartes		£
	VAT	£
Costs of taxation allowed against the legal aid fund		£
	VAT	£
	£	

* Profit costs and disbursements do *not* include the costs of taxation

Form C (para 4.3)

Certificate to be indorsed on all bills
I certify that the castings of this bill are correct.

Signed . . .

Partner in the firm of . . .

Dated . . .

2024 Costs—taxation—review of taxation

Under RSC Ord 62, r 12(1) where costs are taxed on a standard basis a reasonable amount must be allowed in respect of all costs reasonably incurred and any doubts as to reasonableness are construed in favour of the paying party. Order 62, App 2, Pt I contains a list of factors to be taken into account by the taxing master when allowing costs and states that the bill of costs must consist of items specified in Pt II, together with an allowance for general care and conduct. Pt II, Item 4 consists of "Preparation" which is split into three parts; Pt A includes a list of 13 items in relation to work reasonably done arising out of or incidental to the proceedings.

Judgment was given against the applicant in a series of related cases concerning his financial position. The applicant applied for an order that the taxation of legal aid costs by the taxing master be reviewed. The four principal issues to be considered were: (1) the hourly rate, (2) the percentage uplift for general care and conduct, (3) the amount allowed for the item "Documents" under the heading "Preparation", and (4) whether dictation time in relation to attendance notes and file notes should be allowed. *Held*, (1) the hourly rates were appropriate on the principles set out in *Johnson v Reed Corrugated Cases Ltd* [1992] 1 All ER 169. (2) To justify an uplift of 100 per cent there had to be some factor indicating that the case was exceptional. One case was particularly difficult; there was a large amount at stake and litigation was of crucial importance to the applicant. The appropriate uplift would therefore be 90 per cent. The other case was not an unusual piece of litigation involving preventing a substantial claim from being struck out. Despite the problem of running two cases side by side, an uplift of 75 per cent as decided by the taxing master was correct. (3) The taxing master made an underestimate of time reasonably and properly spent in relation to the documents and the time should be increased. (4) Work properly and reasonably done in furthering the client's interests reasonably included the preparation of attendance and file notes recording work done by the solicitor. A claim for unrecorded work would not be allowed. In the present case however the work was excessive. In relation to time spent by solicitors in informal discussion with counsel and communicating with the court, the 13 factors laid down in Pt A under the heading "Preparation" were not exclusive. There was no reason why a solicitor could not recover for time reasonably spent communicating with the court or in the interests of his client, however, only a notional allowance would be made for time spent by a solicitor acting as a courier. Work done by a secretary which was appropriate for a fee-earner would be allowed, but not to the extent that it could properly be described as clerical work. An extended legal aid certificate granted at a later date could not have retrospective effect to permit recovery of fees for work done before the extension was granted. An order would be granted accordingly.

Brush v Bower Cotton & Bower (A Firm) [1993] 1 WLR 1328 (Queen's Bench Division: Brooke J).

2025 Costs—taxation—wardship proceedings—fair remuneration

A firm of solicitors who acted for a legally-aided client in a wardship matter in 1990 had their costs taxed at £45 per hour for a partner and £30 per hour for a legal executive. The firm appealed against those figures on the ground that the average expense rate of a solicitor in a comparable firm in the same part of the country was considerably higher than that amount, and they adduced evidence from a Law Society survey in support of that claim. *Held*, the survey was a useful piece of information to assist in a taxing assessment, but it was not an overwhelming factor in comparison with the experience of taxing officers in the principal registry, who had knowledge of rates charged by numerous firms. There were no grounds for interfering with the assessment, and the appeal would be dismissed.

L v L (1993) Times, 8 February (Family Division: Cazalet J and District Judge White).

2026 Costs—vouching bills of costs—certificate

The Chief Taxing Master has, with the concurrence of the Senior District Judge of the Family Division, issued the following *Practice Direction* ([1993] 4 All ER 58), which replaces *Practice Direction* [1976] 2 All ER 446 and *Practice Direction* [1984] 1 All ER 679.

1. In order to reduce the labour involved in vouching bills of costs, a certificate in the following form may be accepted as evidence of payment of any disbursement not exceeding £500 (other than a fee to counsel) provided the paying party does not require otherwise, and subject to any direction to the contrary that may be given by the taxing officer:

We AB & Co

HEREBY CERTIFY that all disbursements listed in the taxed bill in the matter of *C v D* No . . . which individually do not exceed £500 (other than those relating to counsel's fees) have been duly discharged.

Signed . . .

(Partner, AB & Co)

2. This direction is to apply from 1 October 1993 to all costs in the Supreme Court taxed under the respective jurisdictions of the Family Division and the Supreme Court Taxing Office.

2027   County courts—procedure
See COUNTY COURTS.

2028   Courts and Legal Services Act 1990—commencement
The Courts and Legal Services Act 1990 (Commencement No 9) Order 1993, SI 1993/2132, brings into force, on 23 July 1993, ss 7(1), (3), (4) (leave to appeal to the Court of Appeal), 58 (conditional fee agreements) and, on 1 October 1993, s 7(2), and certain repeals in Sch 20. For a summary of the Act, see 1990 Abr para 1861. For details of commencement, see the commencement table in the title STATUTES.

2029   Criminal proceedings
See CRIMINAL EVIDENCE AND PROCEDURE.

2030   Discovery of documents
See DISCOVERY.

2031   Dismissal of action—abuse of process—collateral attack exception
The plaintiff initiated an action against the defendant, his solicitor, alleging that in acting for him in earlier proceedings, he failed in breach of duty to advance an appeal upon a point of law which would have caused the decision against the plaintiff to be set aside. The defendant successfully applied for the action for be struck out as an abuse of the process of the court. On appeal by the plaintiff, *held*, it was clear that the judge had followed the dictum of Lord Diplock in *Hunter v Chief Constable of West Midlands Police* [1982] AC 529, HL. However, that decision had not stated that the initiation of proceedings in a court of justice for the purpose of mounting a collateral attack upon a final decision was necessarily an abuse of process, but that it might be. The issue as to whether it was an abuse of process had to be answered having regard to all the evidence, including fresh evidence, before the court on the application to strike out. Therefore, a failure by a solicitor acting for a plaintiff in breach of duty to advance an appeal upon a point of law, which would have caused the decision against the plaintiff to be set aside, might constitute an exception to the principle that the initiation of proceedings in a court of justice for the purpose of mounting a collateral attack upon a final decision of the court could be an abuse of the process of the court. Accordingly, the appeal would be allowed.

    Walpole v Partridge & Wilson (a firm) (1993) Times, 8 July (Court of Appeal: Ralph Gibson, Beldam and Peter Gibson LJJ).

2032   Dismissal of action—want of prosecution—delay—acquiescence in delay
The plaintiff brought an action for personal injuries against the defendant. Following a lengthy delay by the plaintiff's advisers the defendant made an application for the action to be struck out for want of prosecution. The plaintiff contended that the conduct by the defendant in offering facilities to the plaintiff and his advisers to watch a video which they believed to be relevant to demonstrate the extent of the plaintiff's injuries and in negotiating for settlement had amounted to acquiescence. The application was rejected and the defendant appealed. *Held*, there had been inordinate and inexcusable delay by the advisers acting for the plaintiff which had caused more than minimal prejudice to the defendants. Neither negotiations towards an offer of a settlement, nor a payment into court would in itself amount to acquiescence on the part of the defendant or estop him from applying to have the plaintiff's action struck out. Accordingly, the appeal would be allowed.

    Draper v Ferrymasters Ltd (1993) Times, 10 February (Court of Appeal: Glidewell LJ and Sir John Megaw).

2033   Dismissal of action—want of prosecution—delay—delay before and after expiry of limitation period

Out of a period of six years and five months between the issue of a writ and the application to dismiss the action for want of prosecution, three periods of delay amounting to three years in total elapsed. The first two periods of delay ocurred before the expiry of the limitation period; the third period ocurred after its expiry. On an application to dismiss the action for want of prosecution, it fell to be determined whether the court was entitled to take account of all three periods of delay and whether the delay was inordinate and inexcusable. *Held*, (1) RSC Ord 3, r 6 placed no obligation on a defendant who wished to apply to strike out an action for want of prosecution to do so within the one month period of notice under that rule. The defendants had taken no active step to induce in the plaintiffs a belief that the defendants consented to the action continuing, so that the defendants were not estopped from applying to have the action dismissed for want of prosecution because of the plaintiffs' delay. Where a defendant applied after the expiry of the limitation period to strike out an action for want of prosecution, inordinate and inexcusable delay by the plaintiff after the issue of the writ but within the limitation period could be relied upon to support the application. It followed that all three periods of delay were relevant and could be taken into account by the court in deciding whether to strike out the action. Those periods, amounting together to three years in total, out of a period of six years and five months between the issue of the writ and the application to strike out, constituted inordinate and, for the most part, inexcusable delay on the part of the plaintiffs. However, since that delay had not given rise to a substantial risk that it would not be possible to have a fair trial, nor had it caused serious prejudice to the defendants, the application to strike out would be dismissed.

Trill v Sacher [1993] 1 All ER 961 (Court of Appeal: Neill and Glidewell). *Rath v C S Lawrence & Partners (a firm) (P J Crook & Co (a firm), third party)* [1991] 3 All ER 679, CA (1991 Abr para 1954) applied. For related proceedings, see *Trill v Sacher (No 2)* (1992) Times, 14 November, CA (1992 Abr para 1983).

2034   Dismissal of action—want of prosecution—delay—delay in setting action down for hearing

Antigua and Barbuda

Under a rule of court, which has no equivalent in the English Rules of the Supreme Court, if a plaintiff failed to take the appropriate steps within specified time limits to have an action set down for hearing, the action would be automatically struck out and could not be restored. After the close of pleadings in an action, the plaintiff obtained directions for the amendment of the pleadings. The plaintiff requested that the action be set down for trial and sought further directions. The defendant successfully applied to have the plaintiff's application struck out and obtained a declaration that the action was deemed to be abandoned. On appeal, *held*, the purpose of the rule in question was to ensure that actions were set down for trial when they were ready for trial and not before. The effect of the rule was that a plaintiff's failure to comply with the strict time limits prescribed could not be regarded as a mere irregularity and the court had no discretion to grant relief. However, on the correct construction of the rule the time limits did not begin to run against the plaintiff at the close of pleadings but only when an order was made giving directions as to the trial of the cause or matter. In the present case, since no order as to the place or mode of trial was ever made, the plaintiff's action could not be deemed to have been abandoned. Accordingly, the appeal would be allowed.

Barbuda Enterprises Ltd v A-G of Antigua and Barbuda [1993] 1 WLR 1052 (Privy Council: Lords Keith of Kinkel, Bridge of Harwich, Browne-Wilkinson, Slynn of Hadley and Woolf).

2035   Dismissal of action—want of prosecution—delay—effect of delay within limitation period

It has been held that a defendant who acquiesces in a plaintiff's inexcusable, inordinate and prejudicial delay in prosecuting an action is consequently precluded from having it dismissed for want of prosecution. Any "post-acquiescence" delay by the plaintiff is not to be relied on by the defendant to entitle him to have the action dismissed unless the further delay in question is shown to cause some additional prejudice. Estoppel, waiver or acquiescence are only exercisable if prejudice in some form is shown. To attempt to justify dismissal for want of prosecution without proof of any prejudice flowing from the relevant subsequent delay is contrary to established law. The conduct of the defendants in these cases is particularly relevant whereby if they had accepted the consequences of previous delays without making their acceptance conditional on there being no further delays, they cannot later complain of those same consequences, notwithstanding that further delays, not themselves having any significant consequences, have occurred.

Harwood v Courtaulds Ltd [1993] PIQR P284 (Court of Appeal: Nourse, Steyn and Evans LJJ).

2036 Dismissal of action—want of prosecution—delay—estoppel from reliance on delay

The plaintiff suffered personal injuries in a road accident. Three years later a writ was issued and it was not until three years after that that a statement of claim was served. Two and a half years on the defendants served an "unless" order in respect of further and better particulars served by the plaintiff. Three years later the defendants made an application to strike out, which was granted by the master but reversed by the judge who conceded that although there had been inordinate and inexcusable delay on the plaintiff's part, the defendants would be estopped by their conduct from relying on the delay. On the defendants' appeal, *held*, to invoke the doctrine of estoppel successfully a plaintiff would have to establish that he had been induced to act to his detriment. Though it was accepted that the obtaining of the "unless" order, amounted to a representation of the defendants' willingness to go on with the action, that representation would not have been regarded as an intimation of willingness to accept further avoidable delay and consequential further prejudice. Further, the final period of delay had given rise to such additional prejudice as would put at risk the prospects of a fair trial and as the plaintiff had conducted the action in a way which had amounted to an abuse of process the action would not be allowed to proceed. Accordingly, the appeal would be allowed.

Culbert v Stephen G Westwell & Co Ltd and John Bryant [1993] 1 PIQR P54 (Court of Appeal: Parker, Nolan and Kennedy LJJ).

2037 Dismissal of action—want of prosecution—delay—evidence of delay

The plaintiff began proceedings against the defendant after suffering injuries in an accident at work. It was accepted on his behalf that there was inordinate and inexcusable delay in prosecuting the plaintiff's claim. His claim was struck out for want of prosecution and an appeal against that decision was unsuccessful. On the plaintiff's further appeal, *held*, to succeed in an application to strike out a plaintiff's claim for want of prosecution, a defendant had to produce some evidence either that there had been a significant addition to the substantial risk that there could not be a fair trial caused by the period after the commencement of proceedings or by periods of inordinate and inexcusable delay or that there had been a significant addition to the prejudice to the defendant. There had to be some indication of the prejudice, for example that no statement was taken at the time of the material events so that a particular witness who would have been called on a particular issue had no means of refreshing his memory, or that a particular witness who was to be called on a particular issue was of an advanced age and no longer wished, or was unable, to give evidence. In the present case, as the defendants had not identified the particular witnesses nor the particular respects in which their evidence had been impaired, the plaintiff's appeal would be allowed.

Hornagold v Fairclough Building Ltd (1993) Times, 3 June (Court of Appeal: Glidewell and Roch LJJ).

2038 Distribution of proceedings—distribution between High Court and county courts

See para 640.

2039 European Communities—Community decisions

See EUROPEAN COMMUNITIES.

2040 Family Division

See CHILDREN AND YOUNG PERSONS.

2041 Group action—striking out—benefit to plaintiffs versus injustice to defendants—consideration by court

The plaintiffs, who were legally-aided, had brought a group action against the manufacturers of certain benzodiazepine drugs, alleging negligence; in certain cases prescribers were joined as defendants. If liability had been established against the manufacturers, they would have been liable for all the damage caused, and it was clear that the amount of damages recoverable from the prescribers if liability was established only against them, would be very small. The actions were struck out pursuant to RSC Ord 18, r 19, on the grounds that they were vexatious and an abuse of the process of court, because the costs of the prescribers were out of proportion to any benefit likely to accrue to the plaintiffs from the litigation. On appeal, *held*, in the majority of cases it was inappropriate for the court to enter a cost benefit analysis, which had been carried out by the judge at first instance. Alternatively, it was for the defendant to decide whether to settle and in making this decision he had to take account of the fact that the plaintiff was legally-aided. However, in the present case, it was clear that the defendants would incur substantial costs in defending the claims whereas the benefit to the plaintiffs would be very modest, and this would involve great injustice. There were no rules of court to deal with group actions and the judge to whom they were assigned should devise particular procedures to deal with the specific problems involved in that type of litigation. Accordingly, the appeal would be dismissed.

AB v John Wyeth & Brother Ltd (No 2) (1993) Times, 1 December, Independant 15 December (Court of Appeal: Balcombe, Stuart-Smith and Peter Gibson LJJ).

2042 High Court—distribution of business—Family Division

The High Court (Distribution of Business) Order 1993, SI 1993/622 (in force on 5 April 1993), assigns to the Family Division all proceedings in the High Court under the Child Support Act 1991.

2043 House of Lords—appeal—leave to appeal—petition—supporting documents

The Principal Clerk and Fourth Clerk at the Table has made the following addition ([1993] 1 All ER 573) to the *Practice Directions and Standing Orders applicable to Civil Appeals* (the *Blue Book*, January 1992) of the House of Lords.

Practice Direction 3
  At the end of para 3.1 insert:
"Supporting documents, including extracts from *Hansard*, will only be accepted in exceptional circumstances."

The following addition to the *Practice Directions applicable to Criminal Appeals* (the *Red Book*, June 1992) of the House of Lords has been made.

Practice Direction 5
  At the end of para 5.1 insert:
"Supporting documents, including extracts from *Hansard*, will only be accepted in exceptional circumstances."

2044 Interim payment—application for interim payment of damages— consideration by court of use to which sums are put

RSC Ord 29, r 11 states that, in relation to interim payments of damages, if the court is satisfied that the plaintiff has obtained judgment against the respondent for damages to be assessed, it may order the respondent to make a payment of such amount as it thinks just, not exceeding a reasonable proportion of the damages which in the opinion of the court are likely to be recovered by the plaintiff, after taking into account any relevant contributory negligence.

The plaintiff had been left a tetraplegic after she was involved in an accident with the defendant's car whilst crossing on a pelican crossing, with the lights in her favour. She had obtained judgment with damages to be assessed and contributory negligence was agreed at 5 per cent. The plaintiff had received two interim payments totalling £87,000 and an application had been made for a further interim payment of £100,000, to adapt a house for the plaintiff. At that time she was residing in unsuitable housing, placing her family under substantial strain. The judge had been concerned that if too large an amount was spent on the house there would be too little remaining for the plaintiff's care and the application had been rejected. On appeal, *held*, the judge had made an error in having concerned himself with what was to be done with the interim payment. Once the conditions in Ord 29 were satisfied, the court had to make a payment of such amount as it thought was just, but not exceeding a reasonable proportion of the damages. Accordingly, the appeal would be allowed.

Stringman v McArdle (1993) Times, 19 November (Court of Appeal: Butler-Sloss and Stuart-Smith LJJ and Sir Tasker Watkins).

2045 Judge—allegation of bias—application for removal of judge

The defendants in an action concerning the misappropriation of funds requested the judge to discharge himself from the trial of the action on the ground that the judge had made comments in an unconnected case which suggested apparent bias. The judge, after giving full reasons, refused to withdraw from the case. On the defendants' appeal, *held*, a charge of apparent bias was not to be lightly made, even in a case such as the present where any suggestion of actual bias was disclaimed. An application to remove a judge was never justified simply by the instructions of a client. Counsel's duty to the court and to the interests of justice required that he should not make such an application unless he was conscientiously satisfied that there was material upon which he could properly do so. Although the English courts did not sanction the premature expression of factual conclusions or anything which might prematurely indicate a closed mind, an expression of scepticism was not suggestive of bias unless the judge conveyed an unwillingness to be persuaded of a factual proposition whatever the evidence might be. Although the judge would have been wiser not to have made any allusions to the present case, no reasonable and fair-minded observer could have supposed on all the relevant facts that he was expressing conclusions adverse to the defendants. Accordingly, the appeal would be dismissed.

Arab Monetary Fund v Hashim (1993) Independent, 30 April (Court of Appeal: Sir Thomas Bingham MR, Stuart-Smith and Beldam LJJ).

2046 Lands Tribunal—decision—appeal—appeal to Court of Appeal

The President of the Lands Tribunal has issued the following *Practice Note* (Estates Gazette, 25 September 1993, p 159).

1. The provisions of the Lands Tribunal Act 1949, s 3(4) restrict the right of appeal from a decision of the tribunal to "any person aggrieved by the decision as being erroneous in point of law". The tribunal's decision on matters of fact is final. The procedure in the Court of Appeal is governed by RSC Ord 61, r 1.

2. A proposed appellant who requires the tribunal to state a case for the decision of the Court of Appeal may set out the grounds of appeal in the application to the tribunal. If no grounds of appeal are specified in the application, the applicant will be invited to specify within 14 days the point or points of law which it is sought to raise in the Court of Appeal.

3. It is the obligation of the proposed appellant to define concisely and with reasonable precision the question or questions of law which it is sought to raise. Unless the point at issue is already plainly identified in the tribunal's decision, a question of law stated in general or vague terms such as "whether upon the findings of fact it came to a correct decision in law" will not be accepted.

4. Subject to the above, such grounds of appeal as are specified in the application or subsequently, and which in the view of the tribunal raise a point of law for the decision of the Court of Appeal, will normally be reproduced in the case stated. The tribunal will decline to state a case if no grounds of appeal are specified, or if the grounds of appeal when specified, in the view of the tribunal, disclose no point of law.

5. This *Practice Note* supersedes previous directions and notes relating to the case stated procedure.

2047 Legal aid

See LEGAL AID AND ADVICE.

2048 Mareva injunctions

See INJUNCTIONS.

2049 Payment into court—defendant's right—two or more plaintiffs

Under RSC Ord 22, r 1(1), in any action for a debt or damages any defendant may at any time pay into court a sum of money in satisfaction of the cause of action in respect of which the plaintiff claims or, where two or more causes of action are joined in the action, a sum or sums of money in satisfaction of any or all of those causes of action. Where a single sum of money is paid into court in respect of two or more causes of action, then, if it appears to the court that the plaintiff is embarrassed by the payment, the court may order the defendant to amend the notice of payment so as to specify the sum paid in respect of each cause of action: Ord 22, r 1(5).

The two plaintiffs claimed damages for breach of contract. The defendants made three payments into court without making any apportionment between the claims. Each plaintiff was pursuing his own separate cause of action and, although one of them would have accepted half of the total sum paid in, the defendants refused to apportion the payment. The plaintiffs contended that they should be required to do so. *Held*, although Ord 22, r 1, referred to "the plaintiff", it nevertheless enabled a payment to be made into court, where there was more than one plaintiff, in satisfaction of the cause of action in respect of which the plaintiffs claimed or, where two or more causes of action were joined in the action, a sum or sums of money in satisfaction of any or all of those causes of action. The statement to the contrary in Halsbury's Laws, Vol 37, para 285, note 6, citing *The Bosworth (No 1)* [1960] 1 All ER 146 and *The Talamba and The Troll* [1965] 2 All ER 775, was incorrect. The court's power to direct amendment only arose if it appeared to it that the plaintiff was embarrassed by the payment. The rules did not define "embarrassed" but, in that context, the underlying concept was that a plaintiff was embarrassed if he was placed in a difficulty which he ought not fairly have to face. The payment should be in a form which enabled each plaintiff to know where he stood. In requiring the defendants to apportion the sum paid in between the two plaintiffs, the court would give the defendants an opportunity to revise the sum paid in and permit them to amend the notices of payment and withdraw payments in.

Walker v Turpin [1993] 4 All ER 865 (Court of Appeal: Sir Donald Nicholls V-C, Butler-Sloss and Peter Gibson LJJ).

2050 Pleading

See PLEADING.

2051 Queen's Bench Division—commercial cases—Midland and Oxford Circuit—Birmingham Mercantile List

Lord Taylor of Gosforth CJ has issued the following *Practice Note* ([1993] 4 All ER 381) at the sitting of the court. The purpose of the note is to create a new and improved structure for the hearing of cases of a commercial or business character on the Midland and Oxford Circuit.

    1. With effect from 1 October 1993 there will be a new Queen's Bench Division list in the Birmingham district registry which will be known as "The Mercantile List (Birmingham)".

    2. It will be permissible to include in this list any action which relates to a commercial or business transaction in a broad sense, eg contractual disputes in the following categories would generally qualify for inclusion: sale of goods, hire purchase, agency, banking, guarantee, carriage of goods and insurance.

    3. At the time of commencing an action the plaintiff may issue the originating process in the said list, in which event the originating process must be marked with the name of the registry and the words "The Mercantile List (Birmingham)". Every pleading and every summons in any action in the Mercantile List (Birmingham) must contain as part of its title the words "Mercantile List".

    4. One or more circuit judges must be designated as "circuit mercantile judges" and must unless otherwise directed hear all interlocutory applications entered in the mercantile list and be the judge at the trial of such actions. Initially, only one circuit judge has to be so designated.

    5. The designated circuit mercantile judges will sit as High Court judges appointed by the Lord Chancellor under the Supreme Court Act 1981, s 9.

    6. RSC Ord 72 does not apply to actions in this list. The actions will be Queen's Bench actions and will be governed by the Rules of the Supreme Court governing such actions.

    7. Notwithstanding para 6 above, in actions in this list practitioners will be expected to ensure the expeditious and economical disposal of such cases by the exchange and lodging of chronologies, lists of dramatis personae and issues and brief skeleton arguments and by providing a page numbered core bundle. To that extent practitioners will be expected to comply with the spirit of the *Guide to Commercial Court Practice* (see *The Supreme Court Practice 1993* Vol 1, paras 72/A1–72/A31).

    8. With the approval of the Lord Chief Justice or the Senior Presiding Judge, the presiding judges of the Midland and Oxford Circuit may from time to time issue further directions as to the practice and procedure to be adopted in relation to cases in this list.

    9. (1) A designated circuit mercantile judge will have the power (a) on application by a party, to add an action to the list; (b) on application by a party, or on his own motion, to remove an action from the list, in which case it will remain a Queen's Bench action; (c) to transfer an action in the list to the lists of (i) the Chancery Division, (ii) the circuit official referees, (iii) a county court or, with the consent of the designated circuit mercantile judge of the Mercantile List (Manchester), to that list; (d) to certify that an action in this list must be heard by a High Court judge of the Queen's Bench Division, in which case it will be removed from this list.

    (2) Any application to transfer an action to the Commercial Court in London must be referred to a judge of that court.

10. A party to an action in this list has the right to apply to any High Court judge of the Queen's Bench Division or the Chancery Division, who is sitting on circuit, to hear any application in this list. The High Court judge may accede to such an application if, in the exercise of his unfettered discretion, he deems it appropriate to do so.

2052 Queen's Bench Division—commercial cases—Western Circuit—Bristol Mercantile List

Lord Taylor of Gosforth CJ has issued the following *Practice Note* ([1993] 4 All ER 1023. The purpose of the direction is the setting up of a new list or court, to be called the Bristol Mercantile Court, for the hearing of cases of a commercial or business character in the south west of England.

1. With effect from 10 January 1994 there will be a new Queen's Bench list in the Bristol district registry, which will be known as "The Bristol Mercantile Court List".

2. It will be possible to include in the Bristol Mercantile Court List any action which relates to a commercial or business matter in broad sense, other than those which ought properly to be listed in the Chancery Division or before an official referee. Thus, in particular, disputes relating to the sale of goods (national and international, and including commodities), the provision of services, carriage of goods, agency, banking (including credit arrangements and negotiable instruments), commercial fraud and professional negligence in the commercial field will generally qualify for inclusion.

3. At the commencement of an action, the plaintiff may issue the originating process in the Bristol Mercantile Court. Subject to the Rules of the Supreme Court and to the relevant paragraphs of this practice direction, an action may be transferred to the Bristol Mercantile Court. The originating process and all subsequent pleadings and other documents bearing the title of the action must be marked with the words "Bristol Mercantile Court", and in the case of transfer all such pleadings and documents coming into being after the transfer must be so marked.

4. One or more circuit judges will be designated as "circuit mercantile judges in the Bristol Mercantile Court", and will, unless otherwise directed, hear all interlocutory applications in the Bristol Mercantile Court and be the judge at the trial of actions in the court. Initially only one such judge will be designated.

5. Such designated mercantile judges will sit as judges of the High Court appointed by the Lord Chancellor under the Supreme Court Act 1981, s 9.

6. Actions in the Bristol Mercantile Court will be Queen's Bench actions governed by the relevant Rules of the Supreme Court, and RSC Ord 72 (commercial actions) will not apply. None the less the court will to a substantial extent follow Commercial Court practice as set out in the *Guide to Commercial Court Practice* (see *The Supreme Court Practice 1993*, Vol 1, paras 72/A1–72/A31). In particular, the lodging and exchange of brief skeleton arguments, of chronologies, of dramatis personae and of a page numbered core bundle will be required.

7. With the approval of the Lord Chief Justice or the Senior Presiding Judge, the presiding judges of the Western Circuit may from time to time issue further directions as to the practice and procedure to be adopted in the Bristol Mercantile Court.

8. (1) A designated mercantile judge has power: (a) on application by a party to an action proceeding in the Queen's Bench Division, to add the action to the mercantile court list; (b) to transfer an action in the list to (i) the Chancery Division, (ii) an official referee, (iii) a county court or (iv) with the consent of the judge in charge of the relevant list, to another mercantile list; (c) on the application of a party, or on his own motion, to remove an action from the list, in which case it will remain a Queen's Bench action and will be tried only by a High Court judge subject to release by the presiding judges. (2) Any application to transfer an action to the Commercial Court in London must be made to a judge of that court. (3) Prior to the hearing of any application in the Chancery Division to transfer an action proceeding in that division to the Mercantile Court, the consent of the mercantile judge to the proposed transfer must be obtained.

9. The commencement date set out in para 1 above does not prevent the earlier issuing of process in the Bristol Mercantile Court or the earlier transfer of cases to that court.

10. A party to an action in the Bristol Mercantile Court may apply to any High Court judge of the Queen's Bench Division or the Chancery Division, who is sitting on circuit, or to a judge of the Commercial Court in London, to hear any application in the Bristol Mercantile Court. Such judge may, if he sees fit, proceed to hear the application.

11. The presiding judges of the Western Circuit may designate a circuit judge, or a Queen's Counsel authorised under the Supreme Court Act 1981, s 9 to act as a judge of the High Court to hear such matters proceeding in the Bristol Mercantile Court as may be released to him by the mercantile judge.

2053   Queen's Bench Division—lists—judge in chambers list—procedure

Lord Taylor of Gosforth CJ has issued the following *Practice Direction* ([1993] 3 All ER 846), which replaces *Practice Direction (Judge in Chambers: Procedure), Pt A* [1983] 1 WLR 433 (as amended).

1. All inter partes applications and appeals to the Queen's Bench judge in chambers will initially be entered in a general list. They will be listed for hearing in Room E101.

2. Any matter which cannot be dealt with in 30 minutes will not be taken on the date given for the general list appointment. If the parties agree that it cannot be so disposed of the applicant or appellant must, as soon as practicable and not less than 24 hours before the date given, transfer the case to the chambers appeals list or, for all matters other than appeals, the special appointments list. If the parties do not agree, or agree less than 24 hours before the date given, the parties must attend on the date given.

3. Cases in the special appointments list will usually be heard on a date fixed by the judge in chambers department, Room W15 after application to fix has been made by the parties. The application must be accompanied by an agreed estimate of the length of the hearing signed by the applicant's counsel or solicitor who it is intended should appear on the application.

4. Cases in the chambers appeals list will be listed by the clerk of the lists, Room W14 and the parties will be notified by the court of the date on which such appeals will enter the warned list. Cases in the warned list may be listed for hearing at any time on or after that date. Fixtures will only be given in exceptional circumstances.

5. The original exhibits to affidavits should be retained by the parties but must be available for production at the hearing.

6. So as to ensure that a complete set of papers in proper order is available for perusal by the judge before the hearing, the parties must in advance of the hearing lodge in Room W15 a bundle, properly paged in order of date and indexed, containing copies of (1) the notice of appeal or summons; (2) the pleadings, if any; (3) copies of all affidavits, together with copy exhibits, upon which any party intends to rely; and (4) any relevant order made in the action. The bundle should be agreed if possible. In all but simple cases a skeleton argument and, where that would be helpful, a chronology should also be lodged.

7. Where a date for the hearing has been fixed, the bundle must be lodged not later than three clear days before the fixed date. For appeals where there is no date fixed for hearing, the bundle must be lodged not later than 48 hours after the parties have been notified that the case is to appear in the warned list. For cases in the general list, the bundle must be lodged at least 48 hours before the hearing. Skeleton arguments, with chronology, must be lodged not later than 24 hours before the hearing.

8. Except with leave of the judge, no document may be put in evidence or relied upon unless a copy of it has been included in the bundle. If any party seeks to rely on an affidavit which has not been included in the bundle, that party must lodge the original, with copy exhibits, in Room W15 in advance of the hearing or with the clerk or associate before the hearing begins.

2054   Queen's Bench Division—lists—jury list—summonses for directions and interlocutory applications

Drake J has, in the light of the experience of an experimental period when all summonses for directions and subsequent interlocutory applications were required to be issued for hearing before the judge in charge of the jury list, issued the following *Practice Direction* ([1993] 4 All ER 416).

1. Summonses for directions and all applications prior to setting down should be made to the master. The master will use his discretion to refer the matter to the judge if he thinks it right to do so.

2. Interlocutory applications *after* setting down should be made to the judge.

3. If a party believes that the master is very likely to refer any application to the judge (eg where there is an application for a substantial striking out) the matter should first be referred informally to the master on notice to other parties (ie without waiting for a private room appointment). The master will then decide whether the application should be referred to the judge.

4. This revised procedure should be followed as from 27 July 1993.

2055   Queen's Bench Division—lists—masters—short notice list—urgent applications

The Senior Master of the Queen's Bench Division has, with the approval of the Lord Chief Justice, issued the following *Practice Direction* ([1993] 1 WLR 221).

1. Under this practice direction, which only concerns litigation proceeding before the masters of the Queen's Bench Division, a new list is introduced on an experimental basis. The new list is called the Short Notice List and is available from 20 April 1993.

2. The Short Notice List is intended for applications which are expected to last for no more than five minutes and are fairly to be described as urgent. Applications for "unless" orders are normally to be considered as suitable for inclusion in the list.

3. The Short Notice List may only be used if either all the following conditions, ie (i) all parties concerned in the summons are represented by solicitors; (ii) all such solicitors have offices or agents who have been duly instructed in the London postal districts EC, WC, W1 and SW1; (iii) all such solicitors are equipped with fax equipment and their fax numbers appear on their printed stationery, are met or all parties to the summons consent to the summons being entered in the Short Notice List, in which case a certificate of such consent must be endorsed on the backsheet of the document lodged.

4. To enter a summons in the Short Notice List it must be typed or printed as required by RSC Ord 66 and the appropriate fee must be paid. The document on which the receipt of the fee is marked must then be lodged in Room E216 at the Royal Courts of Justice. When issued in accordance with para 6 below this document will become the original summons.

5. The backsheet of the document lodged in Room E216 must be endorsed as follows: "For entry in Short Notice List. We certify that the minimum number of clear days required by the rules of court to elapse between the service of this summons and the return day is . . . [fill in] days". The backsheet must also show the fax number, the telephone number and the reference number of each party to the summons and the name of the assigned master. If no master has been assigned, the backsheet must be endorsed with the words "No assigned master".

6. As soon as practicable after the lodging of the document, the Queen's Bench Masters' Secretary's Listing Officer must insert on it the date, time and place of the hearing and the name of the master in whose Short Notice List the summons will be heard. He must then issue the summons by applying the court seal.

7. A copy of the original summons must then be transmitted by the court by fax to all parties to the summons at the fax numbers shown on the backsheet.

8. On receipt of confirmation through the court's fax equipment that successful transmission has been effected to all parties to the summons, the listing officer must forthwith enter the summons for hearing in the Short Notice List. If confirmation of successful transmission to all parties is not received through the court's fax equipment, the listing officer must forthwith inform any party to whom a copy of the summons has been successfully transmitted that the hearing is cancelled by reason of inability to serve all parties. Such information may be communicated by telephone, fax or otherwise at the court's discretion.

9. The party who lodged the document pursuant to paragraph 4 above is responsible for retrieving the original summons before the hearing and must hand it to the master at the hearing. Any order made on the hearing of the summons will be endorsed by the master on the original summons and not on a fax copy.

10. If the assigned master is on leave or for any other reason temporarily absent from the Royal Courts of Justice, the Queen's Bench Masters' Secretary's Listing Officer may insert on the document to be issued the name of some other master. In this event, it must be assumed that a transfer has been effected pursuant to RSC Ord 4, r 8(1).

2056 Queen's Bench Division—masters—private room appointments—form of application

The Senior Master of the Queen's Bench Division has made the following *Practice Direction* ([1993] 4 All ER 768).

The application for appointment before a master form in the third cumulative supplement to *The Supreme Court Practice 1993*, Vol 2, p 165, para 20 (application by post for private room appointments before the masters) (see *Practice Direction* [1976] 2 All ER 312 at 319, [1976] 1 WLR 489 at 496, para 22) has been revised and should be deleted and the following form substituted. This form, which is available in the masters' secretary's department, may conveniently also be used for those seeking a private room appointment by personal attendance.

Application for appointment before a Queen's Bench Master

Assigned Master (if no Master has yet been assigned, write 'None') . . . .

Parties in action . . . .

Type of summons (or, if assessment of damages, nature of claim) . . . .

Value of claim (or, if unliquidated, the approximate sum the plaintiff reasonably expects to recover) . . . .

Applicant's affidavit evidence in support:
(tick box if it has been or is ready to be served)   ☐
(if none required, write 'None') . . . .
Estimated length of hearing (the court must be informed forthwith of any material change) . .

Earliest date when all parties will be ready for hearing and other convenient dates . . . . .

Dates to be avoided . . . .

Are counsel attending? . . . .

Names of counsel (if known) . . . .

Date application made . . . .

Solicitors making the application . . . .

Telephone number, fax number and reference . . . .

2057   Rules of the Supreme Court

The Rules of the Supreme Court (Amendment) 1993, SI 1993/2133 (in force on 1 October 1993), (1) provides that a probate cause or matter can only be transferred under RSC Ord 4, r 5 to Chancery Chambers or to one of the Chancery district registries; (2) extends the period within which Admiralty writs in rem remain valid for service from 4 months to 12 months; (3) specifies when leave is necessary for an appeal to the Court of Appeal; (4) enables litigants to have the grant or refusal of leave to appeal reviewed by two Lords Justices instead of a single Lord Justice; (5) amends certain provisions relating to the provision of copies of documents for other parties; (6) requires a party who ceases to act through a solicitor in the circumstances mentioned in RSC Ord 67, r 7 to provide an address for service within the jurisdiction, and outlines the consequences of failure to do so; (7) applies the rules for an application for registration of judgments under the Civil Jurisdiction and Judgments Act 1982, s 4 to authentic instruments and court settlements to which the 1982 Act applies; (8) enables the affidavit in support of an originating summons under RSC Ord 88 (mortgage action in the Chancery Division for possession or payment) to contain previously inadmissible statements of information and belief; (9) provides that applications relating to the powers exercisable by a master of the Queen's Bench Division under the County Courts Act 1984, s 56 with regard to the taking of evidence abroad in family proceedings must be made to a district judge of the Principal Registry of the Family Division; and (10) amends the form of writ of fieri facias to enforce Northern Irish or Scottish judgments to show the element of the judgment which relates to interest on the principal debt.

The Rules of the Supreme Court (Amendment No 2) 1993, SI 1993/2760 (in force on 1 December 1993), (1) provides that leave under RSC Ord 11, r 1 to serve a writ out of the jurisdiction may be given in proceedings under the Immigration (Carriers' Liability) Act 1987; and (2) amends the procedure for bringing appeals to the Court of Appeal on a question of law from a final determination of an Immigration Appeal Tribunal with leave by specifying (a) the date from which time for appealing begins to run, (b) the persons on whom notice of appeal must be served, (c) the documents that must be lodged by the appellant prior to the hearing of the appeal, and (d) that RSC Ord 59, r 13 (which provides that an appeal must not operate as a stay of execution or of the proceedings) does not apply to such appeals.

2058   Service of process—death of plaintiff prior to service—failure to amend title of action

The plaintiff had issued a writ claiming damages against the defendant for personal injuries caused by an accident while he was a guest at the defendant's hotel. However, he died before the writ was served. After the plaintiff's death, his widow became his personal representative but did not apply for an order to amend the title of the action under RSC Ord 15, r 7, until five months after the writ was served on the defendant. The defendant applied to have the action struck out on the ground that the proceedings were a nullity as service had been effected on behalf of a plaintiff who did not exist at the date of service. The action was struck out, but on appeal the action was allowed to continue. On further appeal, *held*, by virtue of Ord 15, r 7(1), the plaintiff's cause of action did not abate upon his death but vested in his widow in her capacity ·as his personal representative. Although the title of the action had not been amended to reflect this at the date of service, there had never been a stage in the proceedings when the cause of action had not been vested in a living and existing party. The failure to amend the writ before service was an irregularity that did not go to the root of the proceedings so as to render them a nullity and the court could rectify it under RSC Ord 2, r 1(2). Accordingly the appeal would be dismissed.

　Fielding v Rigby [1993] 4 All ER 294 (Court of Appeal: Sir Thomas Bingham MR, Mann and Peter Gibson LJJ).

2059　Service of process—defect in service—extension of time—extension by consent

A writ, issued by the plaintiff one month before the limitation period expired, had been amended but was not served within the period permitted. The writ was served with a statement of claim which was not accompanied by a medical report or statement of special damages as required by RSC Ord 18, r 12(1A). The defendant filed an acknowledgement of service and an oral agreement between the parties extended the time for service of the defence until 14 days after the plaintiff served a medical report and schedule of special damages. The agreement was confirmed in writing. The plaintiff served his medical evidence but not a schedule of special damages. On the defendant's application to set aside service of the writ, *held*, by virtue of Ord 3, r 5(3), the parties could do by consent that which the court could do on an application under Ord 3, r 5(2). The written consent given by the plaintiff validly extended the time for service of the defence. An extension of time for service of the defence automatically involved an extension of time for making an application under Ord 12, r 8(1) to set aside service of the writ, since the defendant was entitled to see the nature of the claim properly pleaded in the statement of claim before deciding whether to challenge the jurisdiction or deal with the case on the merits. The application to set aside the service had been made within the extended period so that the defendant was not deemed irrevocably to have submitted to the jurisdiction by failing to apply within the prescribed time. Since the statement of claim was defective because it did not comply with Ord 18, r 12(1A), the defendant was not to be taken, simply by taking a step in the action by inviting the plaintiff or the court to extend the time for service of the defence, to have waived its right to apply under Ord 12, r 8(1) to set aside the writ until the plaintiff had made good the defective service of the statement of claim. Accordingly, the defendant's application would be granted and service of the writ set aside.

　Lawson v Midland Travellers Ltd [1993] 1 All ER 989 (Court of Appeal: Sir Thomas Bingham MR, Stuart-Smith and Simon Brown LJJ).

2060　Service of process—service out of the jurisdiction—establishment of good arguable case

The plaintiffs commenced proceedings against the defendants following the defendants' refusal to make payments on the first and second presentation of a letter of credit issued by them to the plaintiffs. The plaintiffs applied for leave to serve the writ out of the jurisdiction under RSC Ord 11. Leave was granted in respect of the claim relating to the first presentation but refused with respect to the claim relating to the second presentation on the ground that that claim was insufficiently strong on its merits. The decision was upheld by the Court of Appeal, which held that the claim did not disclose a good arguable case and that therefore, leave could not be given. On appeal, *held*, the principle of forum conveniens and the assessment of the merits of the plaintiff's claim were separate and distinct elements. The standard of proof applicable when considering whether the jurisdiction of the court had been sufficiently established under Ord 11, r 1(1) was the "good arguable case" test. When considering the merits of the claim under Ord 11, rr 1(1) and 4, the standard of proof could broadly be stated to be whether, on the evidence before the court, there was a serious issue to be tried. Accordingly, the plaintiff's appeal would be allowed.

　Seaconsar Far East Ltd v Bank Markazi Jomhouri Islami Iran [1993] 4 All ER 456 (House of Lords: Lords Templeman, Griffiths, Goff of Chieveley, Browne-Wilkinson and Mustill). Decision of Court of Appeal [1993] 1 Lloyd's Rep 236 (1992 Abr para 2018) reversed.

The plaintiffs, a company formerly controlled by the first defendant, claimed that he had fraudulently misappropriated substantial sums belonging to the plaintiffs. They sought leave to serve a writ out of the jurisdiction on a foreign bank which maintained an account through which some of the sums in question had passed on the ground that, as the first defendant owed a fiduciary duty to the plaintiff and that the payments to the bank were in breach of that duty, the bank must, or ought, to have known of the fraud. *Held*, McCowan LJ dissenting, although the bank might have been curious as to the kind of business the plaintiff or the first defendant was carrying on, there were no grounds for saying that it should have suspected dishonesty. A large increase in the scale of transfers into the account was not a sufficient reason for the bank to question the transactions. Further, inconsistencies in the evidence of the governor of the bank and the lack of evidence of results from inquiries instituted by the bank and the government of the country in which the bank carried on its business did not entitle the court to conclude that the bank, at the material time, had in its possession information which ought to have put it on inquiry, which it now sought to conceal. The plaintiff had failed to make out a sufficiently strong case for service out of the jurisdiction and, accordingly, the application would be dismissed.

Polly Peck International plc v Nadir (No 3) (1993) Times, 22 March (Court of Appeal: Glidewell, McCowan and Hoffmann LJJ). Decision of Knox J (1992) Times, 28 July, Independent, 2 September (1992 Abr para 2020), reversed.

2061 Service of process—service out of the jurisdiction—irregularity in service

The plaintiff had sustained serious injuries in an accident at a hotel managed by the defendants, an American-registered corporation with a place of business in the United Kingdom. The plaintiff brought a personal injuries action and served a writ on the defendants, who applied to have the writ set aside on the ground that the Companies Act 1985, s 695 required that the writ should have been addressed to the person whose name appeared on the companies register as a person resident in the United Kingdom and authorised to accept service of process on the company's behalf. That application had been dismissed by the master, but his decision was reversed by the judge in chambers. On the plaintiff's appeal against that decision, *held*, although the matter was not entirely free from doubt, it appeared that the combined effect of RSC Ord 10, r 1(7) and RSC Ord 65, r 3(1) was to limit legitimate methods of service to those prescribed in the 1985 Act, s 695. The plaintiff's failure to address the writ to the correct person meant service had not been properly effected, but the court was satisfied that in the interests of justice it ought to exercise its discretionary power to cure that irregularity, in accordance with RSC Ord 2, r 1, in the plaintiff's favour. Accordingly, the appeal would be allowed and the writ reinstated.

Boocock v Hilton International Co [1993] 4 All ER 19 (Court of Appeal: Neill, Mann and Hoffmann LJJ).

2062 Stay of proceedings—personal injury action—stay pending vocational assessment of plaintiff

In an action for damages for personal injuries, the plaintiff claimed that his injuries rendered him unfit for employment. He sought substantial damages for past and future loss of earnings but was unwilling to submit to an interview with the defendants' employment consultant who wished to obtain an opinion as to his future employability. The defendants applied for a stay of proceedings pending a vocational assessment of the plaintiff by their employment consultant. *Held*, the vocational assessment, which would include an interview and testing of vocational skills by the defendants' employment consultant, was analogous to a medical examination. It did not appear that the permitting of such an interview would tend to make the trial longer and more expensive by burdening the court with inadmissible material under the guise of expert opinion. If there were to be any danger of inadmissible evidence resulting form such an interview and testing, that might be resolved at a later stage. A stay of proceedings unless the plaintiff submitted to the vocational assessment was an appropriate remedy and, accordingly, would be granted.

Bird v Longridge (19 February 1993, unreported) (Mayors and City of London County Court: Judge Oddie) (Kindly submitted for publication by Jacobs, Solicitors, London). *Larby v Thurgood* [1993] ICR 66 (1992 Abr para 1154) distinguished.

2063 Striking out—pleadings

See PLEADINGS.

2064 Summary judgment

See JUDGMENTS AND ORDERS.

2065   Supreme Court—fees

The Supreme Court Fees (Amendment) Order 1993, SI 1993/3191 (in force on 11 January 1994), amends the 1980 Order, SI 1980/821. The amendments include (1) the exemption of persons on income support from liability to pay prescribed fees; (2) the increase of the fees payable in respect of the commencement and progress of proceedings, the enforcement of judgments, proceedings in the Admiralty Registrar's and Marshall's Office, appeals to the Court of Appeal and insolvency proceedings; (3) the reduction of the fee payable on sealing an originating summons for the appointment of a guardian of a child's estate; (4) the increase of the fee payable in respect of a judge sitting as an arbitrator or umpire and the extension of that fee to cover the appointment of an official referee to be an arbitrator and to provide fees for the second and subsequent days upon which he hears a reference in that capacity; and (5) the extension of the fees payable on proceedings under the Companies Act 1985 and the Insolvency Act 1986 to encompass an appeal in bankruptcy and the filing of a notice of cross-appeal or a respondent's notice.

2066   Transfer of proceedings—transfer between divisions—grounds for transfer

The plaintiffs commenced proceedings in the Chancery Division and subsequently applied for a transfer to the Queen's Bench Division in the hope that a trial in the Commercial Court would be speedier. *Held*, a transfer would only be ordered if an action was begun in an inappropriate division, and applications for transfer, merely to jockey for position were to be deprecated. Accordingly, the application would be dismissed.

O'Brien v Hughes-Gibb & Co Ltd (1993) Times, 20 October (Chancery Division: Harman J). *Pantheon Ltd v Chandler Hargreaves Ltd* [1989] NLJR 329, CA (1989 Abr para 1857) applied.

2067   Transfer of proceedings—transfer from High Court to county court—striking out of proceedings by High Court

The County Courts Act 1984, s 40(1), as amended by the Courts and Legal Services Act 1990, s 2(1), provides that where the High Court is satisfied that any proceedings before it are required to be in a county court it must (a) order the transfer of the proceedings to a county court; or (b) if the court is satisfied that the person bringing the proceedings knew, or ought to have known, of that requirement, order that they be struck out.

It has been held that the court is not obliged to strike out an action where the circumstances set out in the 1984 Act, s 40(1)(b) apply. The appropriate sanction is in costs, in particular under the Supreme Court Act 1981, s 51 whereby the taxing master can order a 25 per cent reduction in costs otherwise payable. The court's discretion to strike out ought only to be applied in the most serious cases, for example where failure to start an action in the county court is a deliberate tactic rather than a bona fide mistake.

Restick v Crickmore; Nisbet v Granada Entertainment Ltd; Reed v Department of Employment; Warren v Hinchcliffe [1993] NLJR 1712 (Court of Appeal: Butler-Sloss and Stuart-Smith LJJ and Sir Tasker Watkins). Decision of Wilcox J (30 April 1993, unreported) reversed in part.

2068   Writ—issue without authority—validity of ratification

See *Presentaciones Musicales SA v Secunda*, para 64.

2069   Writ—validity—renewal

The plaintiffs, trustees of a will, claimed that the defendants had acted negligently in their advice concerning the exercise of an option to renew a lease. The writ in the action had been issued but not immediately served as the plaintiffs had been advised that they ought to make an application for a *Beddoe* order before pursuing their claim. The plaintiffs applied for and were granted ex parte an extension of the validity of the writ so that the *Beddoe* application could be heard. The defendants' application to set aside the extensions was dismissed at first instance but allowed by the Court of Appeal. On appeal by the plaintiffs, *held*, the power of the court under RSC Ord 6, r 8 to extend the validity of a writ was only to be exercised for good reason. The plaintiffs' desire to complete collateral litigation against third parties did not ordinarily constitute good reason for failure to serve a writ. There was no reason to treat a *Beddoe* application differently from other collateral litigation and accordingly, the appeal would be dismissed.

Dagnell v JL Freedman & Co [1993] 1 WLR 388 (House of Lords: Lords Templeman, Oliver of Aylmerton, Goff of Chieveley, Browne-Wilkinson and Mustill). *Re Beddoe* [1893] 1 Ch 547, CA, considered.

The plaintiff issued a writ against his employers claiming damages for an accident at work, but did not serve it within its validity period. He was granted an extension of the period of validity of the writ to seven months under RSC Ord 6, r 8(2A). On appeal by the defendant, *held*, any application for extension of the validity period must be made during the initial four month validity period or the four months after that. Only one extension could be granted on a particular application and could not be for a period of over four months. The court would consider an application to extend validity under RSC Ord 2, r 1 but only in exceptional circumstances and where the interests of justice so required. The judge at first instance had not interpreted RSC Ord 6, r 8(2A) correctly. The rule only allowed the court to extend the validity period by up to twelve months if it is satisfied that despite all reasonable efforts, it may not be possible to serve the writ within four months. There was nothing in this case to suggest any difficulty in serving the defendant within the four month period and the fact that the plaintiff's lawyer had not served the writ by mistake was not a good enough reason for the delay. Accordingly, the appeal would be allowed and the validity of the writ would not be extended.

Singh v Duport Harper Foundries Ltd (1993) Times, 15 November (Court of Appeal: Neill, Farquharson and Henry LJJ).

PRESS, PRINTING AND PUBLISHING

Halsbury's Laws of England (4th edn) Vol 37, paras 1001–1100

2070 Articles

Confidence and Privacy, Patrick Milmo: 143 NLJ 1647
Confidence in the Press, M Thompson: [1993] Conv 347
Pressing Matters, David Newell and Santha Rasaiah (on the effect of EC law on the UK media): LS Gaz, 22 September 1993, p 17
Principle in Mind, Daniel Alexander and Delia Watson (on *Secretary of State for the Home Department v Central Broadcasting Ltd* (1993) Times, 28 January, CA: 143 NLJ 156
Secrecy in Court, Andrew Nicol: LS Gaz, 1 December 1993, p 28

2071 Reports of judicial proceedings—reporting restrictions—risk of prejudice to further proceedings

A judge ordered three separate trials in the case of eleven defendants who were to be tried in connection with a number of drug offences. The effect of his decision was that seven defendants would be tried together in one trial, and two other trials involving two defendants each would be held after the first had been concluded. The judge made a very wide order under the Contempt of Court Act 1981, s 4(2) which prevented the media from reporting any details of any of the proceedings until all the trials had been concluded, and a number of news organisations, and the defendants in the later trials, applied for that order to be varied on the ground that its provisions were unnecessarily wide. *Held*, once the judge had decided that there would be a substantial risk of prejudice to the administration of justice if he did not impose reporting restrictions he should have considered whether an order was necessary to avoid such a risk, and he had erred in making his decision solely on the basis of how that risk could best be eliminated. The case was the first major trial concerning a drug commonly known as "ecstasy". It had attracted considerable and legitimate public interest and the public interest was best served by allowing the media to report it. Accordingly, the appeal would be allowed and no restrictions would be placed on publication of the judgment in the first trial.

Ex p The Telegraph plc [1993] 2 All ER 971 (Court of Appeal: Lord Taylor of Gosforth CJ, Auld and Curtis JJ).

PRISONS

Halsbury's Laws of England (4th edn) Vol 37, paras 1101–1300

2072 Articles

Prisoner—Group 4, J P Bean: 143 NLJ 648.
Suicide Attempts in Male Prisons, Alison Liebling: 143 NLJ 649.

2073 Contracting out of prisons—powers of Secretary of State—extension

The Criminal Justice Act 1991 (Contracted Out Prisons) Order 1993, SI 1993/368 (in force on 24 February 1993), amends the Criminal Justice Act 1991, s 84(1) so as to enable the Secretary of State to enter into a contract for the running of any prison. Prior to the 1993 Order the Secretary of State was, under an amendment to s 84(1) made by SI 1992/1656, only entitled to enter into such contracts in relation to prisons established after 31 October 1991. SI 1992/1656 is revoked.

2074 Prison authorities—actions of prison officers—liability of Home Office

The plaintiff, a remand prisoner, issued writs for damages against prison officers, claiming damages for negligence, assault and battery and misfeasance in public office from alleged ill-treatment by prison officers. The Home Office successfully applied to strike out part of the writ, relating to misfeasance in public office. The plaintiff's appeal was dismissed on the ground that the Home Office could not be vicariously liable for misfeasance in public office by the officers. On further appeal by the plaintiff, *held*, striking out a claim based on misfeasance in public office could only be justified if the inevitable result was that the unauthorised acts of the prison officers were so unconnected with their authorised duties as to be independent of and outside those duties. It was likely to be a question of fact and degree whether the prison officers were engaged in a misguided unauthorised method of performing their authorised duties or engaged in what amounted to an unlawful frolic of their own. It was impossible to determine the precise character of the prison officers, on which the liability or otherwise of the Home Office would depend, from a perusal of the pleadings alone. That could only be done after the facts had been established. The appeal would accordingly be allowed.

Racz v Home Office [1994] 1 All ER 97 (House of Lords: Lords Templeman, Goff of Chievely, Jauncey of Tullichettle, Browne-Wilkinson and Mustill). Decision of Court of Appeal (1992) Times, 17 December (1992 Abr para 2047) reversed.

2075 Prison rules—discipline

The Prison (Amendment) Rules 1993, SI 1993/516 (in force on 5 April 1993), further amend the 1964 Rules, SI 1964/388, so that "officer", for the purpose of the rule by virtue of which a prisoner required to be taken in custody anywhere outside a prison must be kept in the custody of an officer appointed under the Prison Act 1952, s 3 or a police officer, now includes a prisoner custody officer who is authorised to perform escort functions in accordance with the Criminal Justice Act 1991, s 89.

The Prison (Amendment) (No 2) Rules 1993, SI 1993/3075 (in force on 1 January 1994), further amend the 1964 Rules supra, by (1) extending the rule dealing with legal correspondence to all correspondence between a prisoner and his legal adviser or a court, whether or not legal proceedings have been commenced, and setting out the circumstances in which such correspondence may be opened, read or stopped; (2) increasing from three days to 14 days the maximum period for which a governor may impose a punishment of cellular confinement; and (3) limiting the punishments normally available in relation to inmates aged under 21 when the offences were committed to the punishments available in relation to young offenders under the Young Offender Institution Rules 1988, SI 1988/1422.

2076 Prisoner—determinate sentence prisoner—release and recall

The Home Secretary's directions to the Parole Board for the release and recall of determinate sentence prisoners (replacing the criteria for selection for parole operative from 1975 to 1992) are published as App A to the board's annual report for 1992 (HC 712). In the case of determinate sentence prisoners, the decision whether to recommend parole focuses primarily on the risk to the public of the commission of a further offence when the offender would otherwise be in prison. Against this factor, there should be balanced the benefit of early release into the community under supervision, which might help rehabilitation and lessen the risk of reoffending. Each case is considered on its merits, without discrimination. The board should not recommend parole unless it is satisfied that (1) the longer period of supervision provided by parole is likely to reduce the risk of the commission of further imprisonable offences (a small risk of the commission of an offence of violence being regarded as more serious than a larger risk of the commission of a non-violent offence), (2) the offender has shown by his attitude and behaviour that he is willing to address his offending and has made positive efforts and progress in that direction, and (3) the resettlement plan will help the offender's rehabilitation. The board must also have regard to the supervising officer's recommendation as to suitability for release, co-operation with a programme of supervision and adherence to the licence conditions. In considering the recall of a long-term prisoner released on licence, or in confirming an emergency recall, the board should consider whether the offender's continued liberty would present a serious risk to the safety of others or the likelihood of the commission of further imprisonable offences (the consideration as to violent and non-violent offending noted above applies); the extent to which the offender either has or has not complied with licence conditions and co-operation with the supervising officer; and, in the event of the offender remaining on licence, the unlikelihood of compliance with licence conditions and submission to supervision. In relation to the recall of offenders on licence, the board must also have regard to the supervising officer's recommendation as to the offender's remaining on licence and also to any representations made by the offender. Other factors to which the board should generally have regard both in relation to the release of determinate sentence offenders and in relation to the recall of offenders on licence ("training guidance") are also listed in App A to the report.

2077 Prisoner—escort arrangements—search of prisoner

The Prisoner Escorts Rules 1993, SI 1993/515 (in force on 5 April 1993), set out the conditions under which a prisoner custody officer authorised to perform escort functions may search a prisoner for whose delivery or custody he is responsible in pursuance of prisoner escort arrangements.

2078 Prisoner—high security risk prisoner—determination of security category— reasons for decision

The applicant was a category A prisoner serving a life sentence for murder. The Secretary of State refused to disclose to the applicant the gist of the reports which had led to a decision that he should continue to be classified as a category A prisoner or to give reasons for that decision. On an application for judicial review, *held*, although there was no general duty to give reasons for an administrative decision, the authorities showed an ever increasing variety of situations where, depending on the nature of the decision and the process by which it had been reached, fairness required that reasons be given. As long as a prisoner remained in category A his prospects for release on parole were nil. A decision to continue the classification of a prisoner as category A had a direct impact on the liberty of the subject. Fairness required that the applicant be granted the declarations sought. Accordingly, before his case was next considered by the category A section, the applicant would be entitled, subject to necessary exceptions arising from public interest immunity, to be informed of the gist of any matter of fact or opinion relevant to the determination of his security category, and would be entitled to be given reasons for any future decision which resulted in him remaining a category A prisoner.

R v Secretary of State for the Home Department, ex p Duggan (1993) Times, 9 December (Queen's Bench Division: Rose LJ and McKinnon J).

2079 Prisoner—human rights

See HUMAN RIGHTS.

2080 Prisoner—rights—prisoner's letters—examination of letters

The Prison Rules 1964, SI 1964/388, r 33(3) provides that every letter to or from a prisoner may be read or examined by the governor or an officer deputed by him and the governor may stop any letter that is objectionable or of inordinate length. The 1964 Rules, r 37A provides that a prisoner can correspond with his legal adviser in connection with any legal proceedings to which he may be a party, and that unless the governor had reason to suppose any such correspondence contained material not relating to the proceedings, it should not be read or stopped under r 33.

On the question of the validity of the 1964 Rules, r 33(3), *held*, the language of r 33 clearly covered correspondence with solicitors. A convicted prisoner, in spite of his imprisonment, retained all civil rights which were not taken away expressly or by necessary implication. The power in the Prison Act 1952, s 47(1) to make rules to regulate prisons included a power to make rules about prisoners' correspondence. By necessary implication, s 47(1) conferred a rule-making power which could limit a prisoner's general civil rights in respect of the confidentiality both of his general correspondence and of his communications with solicitors. However, every citizen had a right of unimpeded access to a court. A prisoner's unimpeded right of access to a solicitor for the purpose of receiving advice in connection with the possible institution of civil proceedings formed an inseparable part of the right to access to the court itself. Section 47(1) did not therefore authorise the making of any rule which created an impediment to the free flow of communications between a solicitor and a client about contemplated legal proceedings. Rule 37A showed that there was no objective need for a rule as wide as r 33(3). Rule 37A was unobjectionable as far as it went, but a prisoner's right of access to justice ought not to be dependent on whether or not a writ had been issued. To this extent, r 33(3) was invalid.

R v Secretary of State for the Home Department, ex p Leech (No 2) (1993) Times, Independent, 20 May (Court of Appeal: Neill, Steyn and Rose LJJ).

2081 Release on licence—life sentence—discretionary life prisoner—evaluation of risk to public

It has been held that in exercising its duty under the Criminal Justice Act 1991, s 34(4) to satisfy itself that it was no longer necessary for the protection of the public that a discretionary life prisoner should be confined, the Parole Board was not limited to the consideration of medical evidence in evaluating the risk to the public. The board, which had the final decision, was entitled to take into account the evidence of many kinds of experts.

R v Parole Board, ex p Telling (1993) Times, 10 May (Queen's Bench Division: Leggatt LJ and McCullough J).

2082 Release on licence—life sentence—relevant part of sentence—powers of Secretary of State

The Criminal Justice Act 1991, s 34, provides that the Home Secretary must refer a life prisoner to the Parole Board once the prisoner has served the relevant part of his sentence. The "relevant part" is to be specified in an order made by the sentencing court. If the prisoner was sentenced prior to the Act coming into force, the "relevant part" is certified by the Home Secretary under the 1991 Act, Sch 12 if he believes that, had the 1991 Act been in force, the court would have ordered that s 34 applied.

The applicant was convicted of murder and ordered to be detained during Her Majesty's pleasure. He was later transferred to a mental hospital by order of the respondent. He contended that, had he not been transferred, he would have been eligible for referral to the Parole Board under the 1991 Act, s 34 and Sch 12. The respondent claimed that this right did not exist for patients, who were adequately protected under the Mental Health Act 1983. On an application for judicial review, *held*, a life prisoner who later became a patient would remain a life prisoner for the purposes of the 1991 Act, and would therefore be eligible for referral to the Parole Board. Accordingly the application would be granted.

R v Secretary of State for the Home Department, ex p Hickey (1993) Times, 28 October (Queen's Bench Division: Kennedy LJ and Pill J).

The applicant was convicted of attempted murder and sentenced to life imprisonment with a recommendation that he serve at least 25 years in prison. Under the Criminal Justice Act 1991, Sch 12 the Home Secretary certified that the relevant part of the applicant's sentence was 25 years. On an application by the Home Secretary, the Lord Chief Justice recommended that a more appropriate period of time for the relevant part would be 20 years, but the Home Secretary decided not to revise his certificate. On an application for judicial review of the Home Secretary's decision, *held*, the 1991 Act did not specify that the Home Secretary had to consult a member of the judiciary before issuing a certificate. He should however consider the views of the sentencing court to determine whether that court would have invoked the 1991 Act, s 34 relating to early release. In the present case, the applicant ought to have been given the opportunity to comment on the calculation of the relevant part of his sentence prior to the certificate being issued. When, after he issued the certificate, the Home Secretary sought the views of the Lord Chief Justice, he was not bound to accept those views. Nevertheless, once those views were sought, the Home Secretary had a duty to give the applicant the opportunity to comment on them before reaching a decision. However, the Home Secretary had made clear that he would always consider written representations relating to the sentences imposed on life prisoners. Accordingly, the application would be dismissed.

R v Secretary of State for the Home Department, ex p McCartney (1993) Times, 28 October (Kennedy LJ and Pill J).

2083   Release on licence—life sentence—relevant part of sentence—specification of relevant part

Lord Taylor of Gosforth CJ has issued the following *Practice Direction* ([1993] 1 All ER 747).

1. The Criminal Justice Act 1991, s 34 empowers a judge when passing a sentence of life imprisonment, where such a sentence is not fixed by law, to specify by order the part of the sentence ("the relevant part") that must be served before the prisoner may require the Secretary of State to refer his case to the Parole Board.

2. The discretionary life sentence therefore falls into two parts (a) the relevant part, which consists of the period of detention imposed for punishment and deterrence, taking into account the seriousness of the offence and (b) the remaining part, during which the prisoner's detention is governed by considerations of risk to the public.

3. The judge is not obliged by statute to use the provisions of the 1991 Act, s 34 when passing a discretionary life sentence. However, the judge must do so save in the very exceptional case where he considers the offence is so serious that detention for life is justified by the seriousness of the offence alone, irrespective of the risk to the public. In such a case, the judge must state this in open court when passing sentence.

4. In cases where the judge is to specify the relevant part of the sentence under s 34, he must permit counsel for the defence to address the court as to the appropriate length of the relevant part. Where no relevant part is to be specified, counsel for the defence must be permitted to address the court as to the appropriateness of this course of action.

5. In specifying the relevant part of the sentence, the judge must have regard to the specific terms of s 34 and indicate the reasons for reaching his decision on the length of the relevant part.

6. Whether or not the court orders that s 34 should apply, the judge must not, following the imposition of a discretionary life sentence, make a written report to the Secretary of State through the Lord Chief Justice, as has been the recent practice.

2084   Release on licence—life sentence—tariff—prisoner's right to information

Under his scheme for fixing the penal element of mandatory life sentences, the Home Secretary would invite the judiciary to advise him as to the period that should be served for the purposes of retribution and deterrence (the "tariff" period) but would not necessarily adopt the judicial view. In fixing the penal element of a sentence, he would take into account certain other factors, such as the public interest. The four applicants, all mandatory life prisoners, sought judicial review of his refusal to give reasons for departing from the judicial view, contending that the way in which the scheme was administered fell below minimum standards of fairness. *Held*, although the Home Secretary was entitled to depart from the judicial view when fixing the penal element in a mandatory life sentence, the requirements of fairness attaching to his decision meant that the prisoner, who had the right to make representations on it, should know what factors the Home Secretary would take into account. The information to which he was entitled included the substance of the judges' advice, comprising not only the term of years which they recommended as the penal element, but also their reasons. The prisoner also had the right to be given the reasons for any departure by the Home Secretary from the judges' recommendation as to the penal element of the sentence. His refusal to give reasons was not fair and, accordingly, his decision was susceptible to judicial review.

Doody v Secretary of State for the Home Department [1993] 3 All ER 92 (House of Lords: Lords Keith of Kinkel, Lane, Templeman, Browne-Wilkinson and Mustill). Decision of Court of Appeal [1992] 3 WLR 956 (1992 Abr para 2058) affirmed.

2085   Release on licence—revocation of licence—access to reports

The applicant was convicted of murder when he was aged 15 and sentenced as a young offender to be detained during Her Majesty's pleasure, under the Children and Young Persons Act 1933, s 53(1). Following a recommendation by the Parole Board he was released on licence, under the Criminal Justice Act 1967, s 61(1). He was subsequently arrested for an alleged offence of obtaining property by deception and after a further recommendation by the board his licence was revoked and he was recalled to prison. The criminal charges against the applicant never came to trial as the indictments were tendered out of time. The applicant sought to have his case referred back to the board under the 1967 Act, s 62(4). He applied for judicial review and sought an order for certiorari to quash the decision of the board not to recommend the applicant's immediate release on licence, and a declaration that he was entitled to see, subject to any claim for public interest immunity, all the reports before the board on that date. *Held*, it was likely that the board was influenced by the prosecution evidence which the applicant did not see, and it was in the interests of fairness that the applicant ought to have had an opportunity to see the material before the board reached its decision. The applicant had made good his claim that natural justice entitled him to see all the reports, and accordingly, the application would be granted.

R v Secretary of State for the Home Department, ex p Singh (1993) Times, 27 April (Queen's Bench Division: Evans LJ and Morland J).

2086   Young offenders—young offender institutions—rules

The Young Offender Institution (Amendment) Rules 1993, SI 1993/3076 (in force on 1 January 1994), amend the 1988 Rules, SI 1988/1422, by (1) providing that the rule dealing with legal correspondence now applies to all correspondence between an inmate and his legal adviser or a court, whether or not legal proceedings have been commenced; (2) increasing the maximum period for which a governor may impose a punishment of confinement to a cell on an inmate from 3 days to 7 days; and (3) increasing the maximum period for which a governor may impose a punishment of confinement to a cell on a woman prisoner of 21 years of age or over from 3 days to 14 days.

PUBLIC HEALTH

Halsbury's Laws of England (4th edn) Vol 38, paras 1–700

2087   Air pollution

See ENVIRONMENT.

2088   Building regulation—building works—disputes between owners— jurisdiction of surveyors

See *Woodhouse v Consolidated Property Corpn Ltd,* para 1969.

2089   Building regulation—building works—notice to adjoining building owner— definition of building owner

The plaintiffs were owner-occupiers of a property. The defendant and his wife were joint tenants of an adjoining property. The defendant's agents informed the plaintiffs that works were proposed in the defendant's property. Later, notice under the London Building Acts (Amendment) Act 1939 was purportedly given to one of the plaintiffs on behalf of the defendant. The plaintiffs' solicitors informed the defendant that as the notice had only been given to one of the plaintiffs and as the defendants were joint tenants of their flat, the notice was invalid. The defendant contended that the service of a notice by one of two joint tenants was valid. *Held,* the notice was invalid as the defendant and his wife constituted the "building owner" under the 1939 Act for the purpose of serving a notice under s 47 or exercising any rights under s 46. The definition of owner in the London Building Act 1930, s 5 included "every person in possession . . . or in the occupation of any land", and "in the occupation" must be construed restrictively. Where there were joint tenants occupying the premises, it could not be said that either alone was in the occupation of the premises. Both were in occupation and must both serve a notice under s 47.

Lehmann v Hermann [1993] 16 EG 124 (Chancery Division: M R Reid QC).

2090   Building regulation—building works—notice to local authority—definition of person carrying out work

It has been held that for the purposes of the requirement to give notice to the local authority under the Building Regulations 1985, SI 1985/1065, reg 14(3), the owner of premises can be the "person carrying out the work". The term does not apply exclusively to the person who physically carries out the work.

Blaenau Gwent Borough Council v Khan (1993) Times, 4 May (Queen's Bench Division: Stuart-Smith LJ and Potts J).

2091   Clean Air Act 1993

See para 1206.

2092   Contaminated land—statutory local authority registers—withdrawal of proposals for implementation

See para 1208.

2093   Control of pollution—anglers' lead weights

The Control of Pollution (Anglers' Lead Weights) (Amendment) Regulations 1993, SI 1993/49 (in force on 10 February 1993), amend the 1986 Regulations, SI 1986/1992, by revoking the restriction on the importation of certain sizes of lead weights.

2094   Dangerous substances—classification, packaging and labelling

The Chemicals (Hazard Information and Packaging) Regulations 1993, SI 1993/1746 (in force on 1 September 1993), replace the Classification, Packaging and Labelling of Dangerous Substances Regulations 1984, SI 1984/1244. The new regulations, which regulate the classification, packaging and labelling of substances and preparations dangerous for supply or carriage, implement various Community provisions, except insofar as those directives relate to the provision of child resistant fastenings for certain packages containing dangerous substances and preparations.

2095   Fire Safety and Safety of Places of Sport Act 1987—commencement

The Fire Safety and Safety of Places of Sport Act 1987 (Commencement No 7) Order 1993, SI 1993/1411 brings into force on 1 August 1993 ss 15 (automatic means for fighting fire), 49(1), Sch 4 (repeals). For a summary of the Act, see 1987 Abr para 2118. For details of commencement, see the commencement table in the title STATUTES.

2096   Genetically modified organisms—import and acquisition

The Genetically Modified Organisms (Contained Use) Regulations 1993, SI 1993/15 (in force on 1 February 1993), make provision for the restriction of the import and acquisition of genetically modified organisms under the Environmental Protection Act 1990, s 108(1) by prescribing the period for which records of risk assessments carried out under the Act before importing or acquiring genetically modified organisms must be kept. Certain organisms are exempt from the provisions of the regulations.

2097   Notifiable disease—removal of infected person to hospital—disclosure of person's name

A local authority made an ex parte application under the Public Health (Control of Diseases) Act 1984, s 37 for a person (X) to be removed to a hospital on the grounds that he was suffering from a notifiable disease. The magistrate made an order prohibiting, until further order, publication of X's name. The next day the applicant, a local newspaper, applied to vary or discharge the prohibition order on the ground of public interest. The magistrate refused on the grounds that disclosure would cause unnecessary panic and concern and that X's family might be victimised. On appeal against the order, *held*, the court was acting as a court within the meaning of the Contempt of Court Act 1981, s 11 and had the power to allow the patient's name to be withheld from the public. However, it was a constrained power, which would only be justified to the extent that the court reasonably believed it to be necessary to serve the needs of justice. Once all reasonable opportunity to challenge such an order had passed the event of the order became historic, and therefore it would be against the public interest and the fair administration of justice for the order to continue. Accordingly, the appeal would be allowed.

Birmingham Post and Mail Ltd v Birmingham City Council (1993) Times, 25 November (Queen's Bench Division: Mann LJ and Holland J).

2098   Pollution control—controlled waste—seaweed—need for disposal licence

It has been held that within the meaning of the Control of Pollution Act 1974, s 3(2) seaweed is not "controlled waste" and a disposal licence is therefore not required under the 1974 Act, s 5. The definition of "controlled waste" under the 1974 Act, s 30 is limited to household, commercial and industrial waste, or any combination or permutation of those three classes of waste. Accordingly, seaweed is not to be included as such.

Thanet District Council v Kent County Council [1993] Crim LR 703 (Queen's Bench Division: Farquharson LJ and Wright J).

2099   Prevention and control of disease—anthrax—restrictions on importation

See para 1363.

2100   Smoke control areas—authorised fuels

The Smoke Control Areas (Authorised Fuels) (Amendment) Regulations 1993, SI 1993/2499 (in force on 15 November 1993), further amend the 1991 Regulations, SI 1991/1282, by authorising specified additional fuels, and taking account of changes in names of certain authorised fuels.

2101   Sports grounds—safety—designated grounds

The Safety of Sports Grounds (Designation) Order 1993, SI 1993/2090 (in force on 15 September 1993), amends the 1985 Order, SI 1985/1063, by designating certain grounds as sports grounds requiring safety certificates under the Safety of Sports Grounds Act 1975, as amended.

2102   Waste—controlled waste—disposal in waste site

The Control of Pollution Act 1974, s 3(1) provides that except in prescribed cases, a person may not deposit controlled waste on any land or cause or knowingly permit controlled waste to be deposited on any land or use any plant or equipment for the purpose of disposing of controlled waste or of dealing in a prescribed manner with controlled waste, unless the land is occupied by the holder of a licence.

In committal proceedings against a company, it was decided not to commit the company to stand trial in respect of alleged offences under s 3(1). In separate proceedings, a magistrates' court quashed a notice issued by a local authority requiring the defendants to remove controlled waste from their land which had been deposited there in contravention of s 3(1). In both cases, it was held that s 3(1) did not apply where the acts complained of related to waste which was not in its final resting place, but which was to be transferred to another site. On an application by a waste regulation body for judicial review of the decision not to commit the company and on an appeal by the local authority by way of case stated from the decision to quash the notice, *held*, s 3(1) was not concerned only with final deposits or disposals, it also applied to waste which was on the site temporarily. To hold otherwise would involve an unnecessary erosion of the efficacy of the Act which was as much concerned with the environmental damage that might be caused by a waste transfer station as with the effects created on or by a site where the waste reached its final resting place. Judgment would accordingly be given in favour of the waste regulatory body and the local authority.

R v Metropolitan Stipendiary Magistrate, ex p London Waste Regulation Authority; Berkshire County Council v Scott [1993] 3 All ER 113 (Queen's Bench Division: Watkins LJ, Auld and Brooke JJ).

RACE RELATIONS

See BRITISH NATIONALITY, IMMIGRATION AND RACE RELATIONS.

RAILWAYS, INLAND WATERWAYS AND PIPE-LINES

Halsbury's Laws of England (4th edn) Vol 38, paras 701–1102

2103   Articles

Transport and Works Act 1992, Michael Hackett: 137 SJ 220, 256

2104   British Coal and British Rail (Transfer Proposals) Act 1993

See para 1802.

2105　British Railways Board—employees—sickness payments

See *British Railways Board v Franklin*, para 1507.

2106　British Railways Board—level crossing—enforcement of statutory duty

See *Tayside Regional Council v British Railways Board*, para 4.

2107　British Railways Board—occupational pension fund—employer's obligations

See *London Regional Transport Pension Fund Company Ltd v Hatt*, para 1930.

2108　Channel Tunnel

See TRANSPORT.

2109　Inland waterways—transport and works—applications for orders

The Transport and Works Applications (Inland Waterways Procedure) Regulations 1993, SI 1993/1119 (in force on 1 June 1993), provide for the assimilation of the procedures for the making of applications for orders under the Transport and Works Act 1992, s 6, and proposals for orders under s 7, and the making of orders under the Transport Act 1968, s 104(3), 105(3) or 112, and the holding of inquiries in respect of them in cases when an order under the 1968 Act is required in consequence of proposals contained in an application under, or made by virtue of, the 1992 Act. The procedures are modified so that (1) a person applying for an order under the 1992 Act, s 6 must submit with the application a draft of the proposed order under the 1968 Act; (2) the procedures laid down by that Act in respect of publicity and the notification of and consultation with interested bodies are altered in such a case; and (3) the rules which apply to inquiries held under the 1992 Act into applications for, or proposals by the Secretary of State to make, orders under that Act are applied to concurrent inquiries held under the 1968 Act.

2110　Railways Act 1993

The Railways Act 1993 provides for the appointment and functions of a Rail Regulator and a Director of Passenger Rail Franchising and of new consultative committees for the railway industry. Provision is also made in respect of the provision of railway services. The Act deals with the grant and acquisition of rights over certain assets and their disposal or other transfer. The functions of the British Railways Board are amended, and provision is made with respect to the safety of railways and the protection of railway employees and members of the public from personal injury and other risks. The Act received the royal assent on 5 November 1993, and certain provisions came into force on that date, on 24 December 1993 and on 6 January 1994: SI 1993/3237. The remaining provisions come into force on a day or days to be appointed. For details of commencement, see the commencement table in the title STATUTES.

Part I (ss 1–83) The Provision of Railway Services
Section 1 together with Sch 1 empower the Secretary of State to appoint the Rail Regulator ("the Regulator") and the Director of Passenger Rail Franchising ("the Franchising Director"), who may each appoint such staff as he may need, subject to Treasury approval. Section 2 and Sch 2 provide for the establishment of rail users' consultative committees to replace the existing transport users' consultative committees. The Central Rail Users' Consultative Committee is established by s 3, Sch 3. This replaces the existing Central Transport Consultative Committee. Section 4 specifies the general duties of the Secretary of State and the Regulator under Pt I of the Act. Section 5 deals with the general duties of the Franchising Director. By virtue of s 6, it is an offence for a person to be the operator of a railway asset unless he is authorised by a licence or is exempted, by s 7, from the need for authorisation. The circumstances in which the Secretary of State and the Regulator may grant a licence authorising a person to be the operator of a railway asset are specified by s 8. Sections 9 and 10 concern licence conditions. A licence is capable of being assigned: s 11. By virtue of s 12, the Regulator may, with the consent of the licence holder and after giving the requisite notice, make modifications of licence conditions. Further provision with respect to the modification of licences is made by ss 13–16. It is provided by s 17, that a railway facility owner must, if so directed by the Regulator, enter into an access agreement conferring on another person the right to use the railway facility owner's facilities for the provision of railway services. Sections 18–22, Sch 4 make further provision in relation to access agreements, including provision concerning access agreements requiring the approval of the

Regulator (s 18), the granting of exemptions to access requirements (s 20) and the publication of model clauses for inclusion in access contracts (s 21). A duty is imposed on the Franchising Director, by s 23, to designate certain railway passenger services as eligible for provision under a franchise agreement. The Secretary of State may exempt specified passenger services from being so designated: s 24. Public sector operators are excluded from becoming franchisees by virtue of s 25. Section 26 deals with invitations to tender for franchises and s 27 concerns the transfer of franchise assets and shares. Further provision with regard to the franchising of passenger services is made by ss 28–31. Sections 32–36 relate to the Passenger Transport Authorities and Executives. The Transport Act 1968 is amended, by the 1993 Act, s 32, so as to enable Passenger Transport Executives to enter into agreements with wholly owned subsidiaries of the British Railways Board following restructuring of its businesses. Section 33 deals with the re-negotiation of 1968 Act, s 20(2) agreements (agreements for securing railway services in designated areas) as a result of the 1993 Act. Section 34 sets out provisions governing the nature and extent of the role of the Executives and the Authorities in franchising. Section 35 deals with the termination and variation of s 20(2) agreements by the Franchising Director. Related amendments to the 1968 Act are made by s 36. Sections 37–50, Sch 5 make provision in relation to closures. Sections 37–42 establish the notification and publication procedures which must be followed where an operator proposes to discontinue the operation of specified services, networks or other railway facilities. The functions of the Regulator and of the relevant rail users' consultative committee when a closure has been proposed are set out in s 43. Section 44 provides for reference to the Secretary of State of decisions taken by the Regulator concerning proposed closures. Closure conditions and the variation of closure conditions are set out in ss 45 and 46. Section 47 allows for the provision of bus substitution services to replace railway passenger services which have been discontinued or temporarily interrupted. The closure procedure for certain experimental passenger services is set out: s 48. Section 49, Sch 5 abolishes the existing statutory closure procedures for railways and enables the Secretary of State by order to exempt railway passenger services, networks and other railway facilities from the closure provisions. Section 50 deals with the exclusion of liability for breach of statutory duty. Supplementary powers of the Franchising Director are contained in ss 51–54, including the powers of the Franchising Director to form and finance companies and to acquire and dispose of assets (s 53). Sections 55–58 deal with enforcement by the Regulator and the Franchising Director, including provision regarding the validity and effect of orders (s 57) and the power to require information (s 58). Section 59, Schs 6, 7 set out the meaning and effect of railway administration orders, apply certain provisions of the Insolvency Act 1986, with adaptations, where a railway administration order is made, and provide for the transfer of relevant activities in connection with railway administration orders. Further provision is made regarding railway administration orders, winding up and insolvency by ss 60–65. In particular, s 63 provides for Government financial assistance where railway administration orders are made. Section 66 makes amendments to provisions of the Fair Trading Act 1973 in respect of monopoly and merger references in relation to the provision of railway services. Section 67 enables the Regulator to exercise concurrently with the Director General of Fair Trading some of the Director General's functions under the Fair Trading Act 1973 and the Competition Act 1980. Other functions of the Regulator are set out in ss 68–71. The Regulator's investigatory functions are set out in s 68. The Regulator is required to keep under review the provision of railway services in Great Britain and elsewhere and collect information with respect to the provision of those services, with a view to facilitating the exercise of his functions: s 69. Section 70 provides that the Regulator must prepare, publish and encourage the adoption and implementation of a code of practice for protecting the interests of rail users who are disabled. The Regulator must also publish information and advice to give to rail users or potential rail users: s 71. Section 72 requires the Regulator to maintain a register. Similar provision is made in respect of the Franchising Director by s 73. Sections 74 and 75 deal with annual reports of the Regulator and Franchising Director respectively. Sections 76–79 concern the Central Committee and the consultative committees. The General duties of the Central Committee (s 76) and the consultative committees (s 77) are set out. Section 78 amends the Transport Act 1962, s 65 in order to transfer to the consultative committees the remaining functions of the former Area Transport Users Consultative Committees. Section 79 deals with annual reports. The British Railways Board, any of its wholly owned subsidiaries and any holder of a network or station licence is required, by virtue of s 80, to provide the Franchising Director with such information as he may request. Sections 81–83 deal with interpretation.

Part II (ss 84–116) Re-organisation of the Railways
Section 84 concerns the powers of the British Railways Board to form companies for various purposes. Section 85 empowers the Board to make transfer schemes concerning the transfer of

property, rights and liabilities between itself, its subsidiaries, any publicly owned railway company, the Franchising Director, any company which is wholly owned by the Franchising Director or any franchise company. The powers of the Franchising Director to make transfer schemes for the transfer of franchise assets are set out in s 86. Provision is made by s 87 for the transfer to the Secretary of State or the Franchising Director of the British Railways Board's function of making transfer schemes. Section 88 deals with transfers of interests in certain companies. By virtue of s 89, the Secretary of State may direct the Board to make disposals and specify the manner of those disposals. Section 90 enables the Secretary of State to issue directions to the Board about the exercise of rights conferred on it by its holding of interests in companies. Supplemental provision in relation to transfer schemes is made: ss 91–97. These provisions include the power of the Secretary of State or the Franchising Director to require the provision of information in connection with transfer schemes (s 95) and the functions of the Secretary of State in relation to transfer schemes (s 96). Section 97 introduces Sch 8 which makes supplementary provision with respect to transfers under a transfer scheme. Sections 98–101 deal with the ownership of successor companies. Section 98 concerns the initial share holding in successor companies. The Treasury or the Secretary of State may acquire securities of a successor company: s 99. Section 100 provides for the appointment of nominees to act on behalf of the Treasury or the Secretary of State for these purposes. By virtue of s 101, provision is made with respect to the fixing of a target investment limit in relation to any Government shareholding in a successor company which has ceased to be wholly publicly owned. Sections 102–106 deal with the finances of successor companies. Section 102 provides that any powers which a successor company's articles of association confer on the Secretary of State to restrict the borrowings of that company must be exercised in the national interest. Government lending to certain successor companies is dealt with by s 103. Section 104 concerns Treasury guarantees for loans made to certain successor companies. The Secretary of State may, subject to Treasury approval, give grants to certain successor companies: s 105. Section 106 provides for the extinguishment of certain liabilities of successor companies. Sections 107 and 108 contain provisions with respect to the flotation of successor companies. Other financial provision is made by virtue of ss 109–111. Section 112, Sch 9 makes provision with respect to stamp duty and stamp duty reserve tax. The objectives of the Secretary of State and the corresponding duties of the British Railways Board are set out: s 113. It is provided by s 114 that the Secretary of State, the Franchising Director and the Board are not to be regarded as shadow directors of certain railway companies. Section 115 concerns parliamentary disqualification. Section 116 deals with the interpretation of terms used in Pt II.

Part III (ss 117–154) Miscellaneous, General and Supplemental Provisions
Section 117 applies the Health and Safety at Work etc Act 1974 to all types of railways. Section 118 concerns the control of railways in time of hostilities, severe international tension or great national emergency. Provision with respect to security is made by ss 119–121. Section 119 concerns the power of the Secretary of State to give instructions, s 120 deals with enforcement notices and s 121 with inspections. Section 122 deals with statutory authority as a defence to actions in nuisance. It is provided by s 123 that no person is to be regarded as a common carrier by railway. Section 124 removes the powers conferred on the Post Office by the Post Office Act 1953 to impose on railway operators obligations with respect to the carriage of mail on trains. Railway heritage (historical records and artefacts) is dealt with by s 125. Section 126 concerns the general duties and powers of the British Railways Board, providing that the Board be progressively discharged from its duties to provide certain railway services. The power of the Board to provide business support services is contained in s 127; this power is to be progressively removed as the Board ceases to provide such services. The Transport Act 1962, s 13 is amended by s 128. Section 129 makes provision with respect to bye-laws. The Secretary of State may make regulations for the charging of penalty fares by authorised passenger service operators in prescribed circumstances: s 130. Section 131 provides for the disapplication of the Restrictive Trade Practices Act 1976 from specified railway agreements. Sections 132, 133, Sch 10 make provision in connection with the transport police. Section 134, Sch 11 make provision with respect to pensions, giving the Secretary of State various powers to make orders for the purpose of reorganising the British Railways Board's existing pension schemes and establishing new schemes. Provision is made by s 135 in respect of concessionary travel for railway staff. Sections 136–142 contain financial provisions. Section 136 replaces the Railways Act 1974, s 3 with respect to the imposition of obligations and the payment of grants and subsidies under specified regulations of the European Economic Community. The Secretary of State may make payments in respect of track access charges in connection with railway goods services: s 137. Section 138 concerns grants and other payments towards facilities for public passenger transport to and from airports and harbours. Provision is made, by ss 139 and 140, in respect of grants to assist the

provision of facilities for freight haulage by railway and inland waterway. Section 141 deals with financial assistance for employees seeking to acquire franchises or parts of the British Railways Board's undertaking. Any administrative expenses incurred by the Secretary of State or the Treasury in consequence of the Railways Act 1993 are to be paid out of money provided by Parliament: s 142. Sections 143–154 deal with other miscellaneous and general matters, including general restrictions on the disclosure of information (s 145), the making of false statements (s 146), offences by bodies corporate (s 147), the service of documents (s 149) and Crown application (s 150). Section 151 sets out the general interpretation of the Act. Minor and consequential amendments, transitional provisions and repeals are contained in s 152, Schs 12–14. The power to make consequential modifications in other Acts is set out in s 153. Section 154 deals with short title, commencement and extent.

2111   Railways—rail crossings—extinguishment and diversion orders—procedural requirements

See para 1370.

2112   Railways—transport—carriage of coal and steel—international tariffs

See para 2731.

RATING AND THE COUNCIL TAX

Halsbury's Laws of England (4th edn) Vol 39, paras 1–300

2113   Articles

Appeals After the Deadline, Alan Murdie: Estates Gazette, 3 November 1993, p 116
Council Tax—A Better Solution? Garry Treagust: 143 NLJ 932
Landlords' Problems, Alan Murdie: Estates Gazette, 24 July 1993, p 82
Occupational Hazards, David Wainman (on the council tax): Tax Journal, Issue 227, p 16
Rating—Alteration of the List, Roger Sherlock: Estates Gazette, 3 July 1993, p 90

2114   Appeal—valuation tribunal

The Valuation and Community Charge Tribunals (Amendment) Regulations 1993, SI 1993/292 (as amended by SI 1993/615) (in force in part on 12 March 1993 and in part on 1 April 1993), amend the 1989 Regulations, SI 1989/439, by prescribing procedures for dealing with appeals in relation to the council tax. In particular, provision is made as to the jurisdiction of tribunals, procedure prior to a hearing and the disposal of appeals by way of written representations. Requirements as to notice of hearings are set out and certain persons are disqualified from participating in the hearing of appeals. Provision is also made as to the conduct of hearings, evidence, the making and review of decisions and orders, and appeals. The 1993 Regulations also contain amendments to existing provision consequent on the Local Government Finance Act 1992.

2115   Community charge—abolition—consequential amendments and repeals

The Local Government Finance (Repeals, Savings and Consequential Amendments) Order 1993, SI 1993/616 (in force on 1 April 1993), makes provision in consequence of the abolition of the community charge and the introduction of the council tax.

2116   Community charge—administration and enforcement

The Community Charges (Administration and Enforcement) (Amendment) Regulations 1993, SI 1993/775 (in force on 1 April 1993), amend the 1989 Regulations, SI 1989/438, as follows: (1) the definition of net earnings is amended to require that, where deductions are being made under an attachment of earnings order in respect of unpaid council tax, account be taken of the amount deducted in calculating the amount to be deducted under any subsequent attachment of earnings order in respect of unpaid community charge; (2) local authorities are permitted to require a person against whom a liability order for unpaid community charge has been made to provide information as to deductions or expected deductions from his earnings under any attachment of earnings order for unpaid council tax made in relation to him; (3) the order in which attachment of earnings orders made after 31 March 1993 under the 1989 Regulations or under those regulations and the Attachment of Earnings Act 1971 are to be dealt with is amended; (4) protection is given against the seizure of certain goods of a debtor against whom a liability order for unpaid community charge has been made; (5) the relationship between enforcement remedies is amended; (6) the prescribed form of attachment of earnings order is amended; and (7) the charges for matters connected with distress for unpaid community charge are revised.

2117 Community charge—enforcement—deductions from income support

The Local Government Finance Act 1992 (Recovery of Community Charge) Saving Order 1993, SI 1993/1780 (in force on 16 August 1993), provides that regulations which permit recovery of community charges by deduction from income support will continue to have effect in order that amendments to the Community Charge (Deductions from Income Support) (Scotland) Regulations 1989, SI 1989/507, and the Community Charge (Deductions from Income Support) (No. 2) Regulations 1990, SI 1990/545, can be made.

2118 Community charge—personal community charge—enforcement—committal to prison—rejection of offer to pay out of income support

The applicant was found guilty of wilful neglect for his failure to pay community charge. The justices rejected his offer to make repayment by fortnightly deductions from his income support, under the Community Charges (Deductions from Income Support) Regulations 1990, SI 1990/1107, and committed him to prison for 90 days. On his application for judicial review, *held*, committal was not intended to be a punishment for non-payment but merely a means of extraction, employed only in relation to those who wilfully neglected to pay. Thus the justices' failure to consider a viable offer of payment before deciding to commit a recalcitrant payer to prison was wrong. Accordingly, certiorari would be granted and the decision would be quashed.

R v Alfreton Justices, ex p Gratton (1993) Times, 7 December (Queen's Bench Division: Macpherson J).

2119 Community charge—standard community charge—company in liquidation

A company owned the freehold of certain sites that it planned to develop as flats. The company encountered financial difficulties and receivers were appointed. The flats were subsequently completed after the company went into liquidation. The company was billed for standard community charge on each of the completed flats. When no payment was forthcoming, the local authority sought liability orders against the company. The liquidators sought to stay the orders and sought directions on how the company's liability for standard community charge ranked in the winding up in view of the fact that all the relevant periods for the purposes of community charge commenced after the company had gone into liquidation, and that it was the receivers who were in possession of the flat throughout the relevant periods. *Held*, although the company was liable for the charge, the obligation was an unsecured debt, and the amount due was not provable as a debt in the winding up of the company because the company's liability did not exist at the date when it went into liquidation. The obligation only arose because the company was the freehold owner of the flats throughout the relevant periods. No direction would be given that the charges should be an expense in the liquidation as that would enable the charging authority to achieve indirectly via the liquidators what it could not achieve by a claim against the receivers. It would also act as a stepping stone enabling the local authority to reach the receivers and funds in their hands and be paid ahead of even the mortgagees. An order would be made accordingly.

Powdrill and Lyle (Joint Liquidators of Kentish Homes Ltd) v Tower Hamlets London Borough Council [1993] RA 39 (Chancery Division: Sir Donald Nicholls V-C).

2120 Community charge benefit

See SOCIAL SECURITY AND SOCIAL SERVICES.

2121 Council tax—administration and enforcement

The Council Tax (Administration and Enforcement) (Amendment) Regulations 1993, SI 1993/196 (in force on 15 February 1993), amend the 1992 Regulations, SI 1992/613, by providing that where a billing authority issued a demand notice before 1 April 1993, and received information relevant to the dwelling concerned from the valuation officer which differed from that shown in the draft valuation list, it was required to use that later information in estimating the amount of council tax payable for the financial year 1993/94. Where a billing authority had not received such information, it was required to use the draft valuation band. Where a demand notice is issued on or after 1 April 1993, the estimate is to be based on the calculation list which came into force on that day.

The Council Tax (Administration and Enforcement) (Amendment) (No 2) Regulations 1993, SI 1993/773 (in force on 1 April 1993), further amend the 1992 Regulations supra to provide that, where deductions are being made under an attachment of earnings order in respect of unpaid community charge, those deductions must be taken into account in calculating deductions under an attachment of earnings order in respect of unpaid council tax. A billing authority may now require a person subject to a liability order for unpaid council tax to provide information about deductions from his earnings under any attachment of earnings order for unpaid community charge made in relation to him. Certain goods of debtors are protected from seizure and sale following the making of a liability order for unpaid council tax. Where, following the making of a liability order, deductions from income support are being made, no other method of enforcement can be used. Certain charges for matters connected with distress for unpaid council tax are also amended.

2122 Council tax—demand notices

The Council Tax and Non-Domestic Rating (Demand Notices) (England) Regulations 1993, SI 1993/191 (in force on 15 February 1993), provide for the content of council tax demand notices. The notices must identify the dwelling to which they relate, specify the valuation band applicable to the dwelling and explain how the amount to be paid has been calculated. Further the notices must contain explanatory notes and a detailed breakdown of the planned expenditure of the billing authority. Where a council tax demand notice is invalid because it fails to contain the requisite matters, the demand for payments under it will remain effective provided that the payments were properly calculated.

The Council Tax (Demand Notices) (Wales) Regulations 1993, SI 1993/255 (in force on 19 February 1993), make provision for the content of, and the information to be supplied with, council tax demand notices issued by billing authorities in Wales. Demand notices must, in particular, identify the dwelling to which they relate, specify the valuation band applicable to the dwelling and explain how the amount required to be paid has been calculated. Unless a notice relates to a financial year which has ended and is served at the same time as a demand notice relating to the current financial year, it must also be accompanied by specified further information. Such further information must be supplied in Welsh and English where it appears to the billing authority to be requisite. Where a demand notice is invalid because it fails to contain the requisite matters, the failure to do so was due to a mistake and the amounts required to be paid were demanded in accordance with the Council Tax (Administration and Enforcement) Regulations 1992, SI 1992/613, Pt V, the requirement to pay those amounts applies as if the notice were valid. In such circumstances, the billing authority must give the council tax payer a correct statement of the relevant matters as soon as practicable after the mistake is discovered. To enable billing authorities to comply with the 1993 Regulations, major precepting authorities are required to supply them with appropriate information.

2123 Council tax—discount disregards

The Council Tax (Additional Provisions for Discount Disregards) (Amendment) Regulations 1993, SI 1993/149 (in force on 24 February 1993), further amend the 1992 Regulations, SI 1992/552, by including, for days in the period after 30 April and before 30 November in any year, persons under 20 years of age who have left further or higher education during that period as a class of persons to be disregarded for the purposes of discount.

2124 Council tax—exempt dwellings

The Council Tax (Exempt Dwellings) (Amendment) Order 1993, SI 1993/150 (in force on 24 February 1993), further amends the 1992 Order, SI 1992/558, by amending the classes of dwelling which are exempt from liability for council tax payable from 1 April 1993. Substantial amendments are made to class A, which now relates to unoccupied dwellings which require or are undergoing major repair work to render them habitable, are undergoing structural alteration which has not been substantially completed, or have been vacant for a continuous period of not less than six months, and minor amendments are made to most other classes. In addition, a new class Q is added, which exempts unoccupied dwellings in relation to which a trustee in bankruptcy would otherwise be liable for council tax.

2125 Council tax—liability for owners

The Council Tax (Liability for Owners) (Amendment) Regulations 1993, SI 1993/151 (in force on 24 February 1993), amend the 1992 Regulations, SI 1992/551, with respect to houses in multiple occupation. The definition of a tenant is extended to include leaseholders whose interest is granted for six months or more, and the definition of houses in multiple occupation is extended to dwellings occupied by one person but originally constructed or subsequently adapted for occupation by persons who do not constitute a single household. The 1993 Regulations also provide that liability to pay council tax in respect of a house in multiple occupation rests with the person who has the most inferior interest, whether freehold or leasehold, in the whole of the dwelling or, where there is no such person, the freeholder of the whole or any part of the dwelling.

2126 Council tax—reductions for disabilities

The Council Tax (Reductions for Disabilities) (Amendment) Regulations 1993, SI 1993/195 (in force on 15 February 1993), amend the Council Tax (Reductions for Disabilities) Regulations 1992, SI 1992/554, in relation to the term "relevant valuation band". Where a billing authority issues a demand notice before 1 April 1993, and has received from the listing officer information concerning the relevant dwelling which departs from the information in the draft valuation list, the authority is required to use that later information in its calculation of reductions and their application to a person to whom the 1992 Regulations apply. Where the information has not been received by the billing authority, it is required to use the valuation band shown in the draft list. Where a demand notice is issued on or after 1 April 1993, the calculation is to be based on the valuation band shown in the valuation list which comes into force on that day.

2127 Council tax—transitional reduction scheme

The Council Tax (Transitional Reduction Scheme) (England) Regulations 1993, SI 1993/175, 253 (in force on 15 February 1993), provide for the reduction in certain cases of the amount that a person is liable to pay a billing authority in England by way of council tax. The amount of reduction will generally be the amount by which the billing authority's council tax scheme exceeds the sum of its community charge scheme and an amount which varies according to the variation band applicable to the dwelling in question.

2128 Council tax—valuation lists—alteration of lists and appeals

The Council Tax (Alteration of Lists and Appeals) Regulations 1993, SI 1993/290 (in force on 1 April 1993), make provision for the alteration of council tax valuation lists. The alteration of a valuation band is subject to the restrictions specified in the regulations which also provide for the circumstances and periods in which a proposal for the alteration of a list may be made, the procedure to be followed after a proposal has been made, the day from which an alteration has effect and the notification by a listing officer of an alteration. The regulations also make provision for appeals to valuation tribunals where a disagreement arises between a listing officer and another person making a proposal for the alteration of a list in respect of an alteration.

2129 Council tax benefit

See SOCIAL SECURITY AND SOCIAL SERVICES.

2130 Distress for rates

See DISTRESS.

2131 Housing benefit

See SOCIAL SECURITY AND SOCIAL SERVICES.

2132 Lands Tribunal—decision—appeal—appeal to Court of Appeal

See *Practice Note*, para 2046.

2133 Local Government Finance Act 1992—commencement

The Local Government Finance Act 1992 (Commencement No 7 and Amendment) Order 1993, SI 1993/194 brings into force on 1 April 1993 certain minor and consequential amendments in Sch 13, paras 1, 27, 28, 94 and so much of Sch 14 as repeals the Local Government Finance and Valuation Act 1991. The order also brings into force the 1992 Act, Sch 13, para 32 on 1 February 1993 instead of on 1 April 1993 as provided by SI 1992/2454 which is, accordingly, amended. For details of commencement, see the commencement table in the title STATUTES.

2134 Non-domestic rating—central rating lists

The Central Rating Lists (Amendment) Regulations 1993, SI 1993/166 (in force on 25 February 1993), amend the 1989 Regulations, SI 1989/2263, so as to (1) amend the description of certain water supply hereditaments for the purposes of rating those hereditaments en bloc to reflect the consolidation of legislation relating to water; and (2) amend (with effect from 31 March 1992) the designation of persons in relation to water supply hereditaments in consequence of a specified water company ceasing to be a water undertaker for the purposes of the Water Industry Act 1991.

2135 Non-domestic rating—collection and enforcement

The Non-Domestic Rating (Collection and Enforcement) (Amendment and Miscellaneous Provision) Regulations 1993, SI 1993/774 (as amended by SI 1993/894) (in force on 1 April 1993), amend the 1989 Regulations, SI 1989/1058, and the Non-Domestic Rating (Collection and Enforcement) (Miscellaneous Provisions) Regulations 1990, SI 1990/145. The 1993 Regulations provide (1) that a rate demand notice cannot be served before the billing authority has set amounts of council tax for the year to which the demand notice relates; (2) for the protection from seizure of certain goods of a debtor against whom a liability order in respect of unpaid non-domestic rates has been made; (3) for the amendment of the charges that may be made for matters connected with the seizure and sale of goods for unpaid non-domestic rates; and (4) that, where a liability order has been made against joint owners or occupiers, certain of the charges for distress may be levied only once.

The Non-Domestic Rating (Collection and Enforcement) (Local Lists) (Amendment) Regulations 1993, SI 1993/1493 (in force on 6 July 1993), amend the 1989 Regulations, SI 1989/1058, in consequence of the Non-Domestic Rating Act 1993 by providing for adjustments to be made to the amount of non-domestic rates which falls to be paid and modifying collection arrangements.

The Non-Domestic Rating (Collection and Enforcement) (Central Lists) (Amendment) Regulations 1993, SI 1993/1494 (in force on 6 July 1993), amend the 1989 Regulations, SI 1989/2260, in consequence of the Non-Domestic Rating Act 1993 by providing for adjustments to be made to the amount of non-domestic rates which falls to be paid and modifying collection arrangements.

2136 Non-domestic rating—contributions

The Non-Domestic Rating Contributions (England) (Amendment) Regulations 1993, SI 1993/1496 (in force on 6 July 1993), amend the 1992 Regulations, SI 1992/3082, by amending the rules for the calculation of payments of non-domestic rating contributions by billing authorities. Provision is also made for the recalculation of the provisional amount of an authority's non-domestic rating contribution for the financial year beginning on 1 April 1993, and for the making of repayments to authorities by the Secretary of State, or of reduced payments to the Secretary of State by authorities, in consequence of a recalculation.
  Corresponding provision is made for Wales by the Non-Domestic Rating Contributions (Wales) (Amendment) Regulations 1993, SI 1993/1505 (in force on 6 July 1993), which amend the 1992 Regulations, SI 1992/3238.

The Non-Domestic Rating Contributions (England) (Amendment) (No 2) Regulations 1993, SI 1993/3082 (in force on 31 December 1993), amend SI 1992/3082 supra for the financial year beginning on 1 April 1993 by providing for an allowance to be made for certain computer costs and by making changes to the allowance for costs of collection and recovery.
  Corresponding provision is made for Wales by the Non-Domestic Rating Contributions (Wales) (Amendment) (No 2) Regulations 1993, SI 1993/3077 (in force on 31 December 1993), which amend SI 1992/3238 supra.

2137   Non-domestic rating—demand notices—Wales

The Non-Domestic Rating (Demand Notices) (Wales) Regulations 1993, SI 1993/252 (in force on 15 February 1993), make provision for the contents of rate demand notices in Wales. Notices may be in English or in Welsh or in both languages, with translations where it appears requisite. They are required to contain specified particulars and must be accompanied by explanatory notes in the appropriate language and certain further information. Where a notice is invalid because, due to a mistake, it fails to contain the prescribed matters, demands for payment remain effective provided the payments are properly calculated, although billing authorities must take steps to rectify the mistake. To enable billing authorities to supply the prescribed further information when they serve demand notices, the relevant county councils are required to supply them with appropriate information.

The Non-Domestic Rating (Demand Notices) (Wales) (Amendment) Regulations 1993, SI 1993/1506 (in force on 6 July 1993), amend the 1993 Regulations supra by requiring each Welsh billing authority to supply with its rate demand notices for the financial year beginning on 1 April 1993 issued after the coming into force of the Non-Domestic Rating Act 1993, s 1 (see the commencement table in the title STATUTES) explanatory information which takes account of the changes to transitional provisions made by the 1993 Act.

2138   Non-domestic rating—domestic property—timeshare accommodation

The Non-Domestic Rating (Definition of Domestic Property) Order 1993, SI 1993/542 (in force on 1 April 1993), amends the Local Government Finance Act 1988, s 66 in order to exclude timeshare accommodation from the definition of domestic property.

2139   Non-domestic rating—hereditaments—educational hereditaments

The Non-Domestic Rating (Miscellaneous Provisions) (No 2) (Amendment) Regulations 1993, SI 1993/544 (in force on 1 April 1993), amend the 1989 Regulations, SI 1989/2303, by amending, in consequence of the Further and Higher Education Act 1992, the definition of "educational hereditament", contained in that Act.

2140   Non-domestic rating—multiplier—special authority

Under the Local Government Finance Act 1988, different provisions for the setting of a rating multiplier apply in the case of a "special authority". The Common Council of the City of London is the only charging authority which meets the definition of "special authority".

The City of London (Non-Domestic Rating Multiplier) Order 1993, SI 1993/180 (in force on 28 February 1993), makes provision as to the calculation of the non-domestic rating multiplier by the Common Council of the City of London for the financial year beginning in 1993.

2141   Non-domestic rating—rating lists—alteration of lists—appeals

The Non-Domestic Rating (Alteration of Lists and Appeals) Regulations 1993, SI 1993/291 (in force on 1 April 1993), revoke the 1990 Regulations, SI 1990/582, and the Non-Domestic Rating (Alteration of Central Lists) (Amendment) Regulations 1991, SI 1991/723. The regulations make provisions concerning the alteration of non-domestic rating lists by valuation officers, proposals for such alterations from other persons and appeals to valuation tribunals where there is a disagreement about a proposal between the valuation officer and another person. These include (1) specifying, in relation to local non-domestic rating lists, the procedure following proposals for alterations, the time from which an alteration is to have effect and the manner in which a valuation officer notifies other persons of any alteration; (2) applying those procedures, subject to modifications, to cross-country pipe-lines; (3) making alterations to central non-domestic rating lists; and (4) allowing specified appeals and prescribing the appropriate procedure to be followed.

2142   Non-domestic rating—rating lists—alteration of lists—payment of interest

The Non-Domestic Rating (Payment of Interest) (Amendment) Regulations 1993, SI 1993/1495 (in force on 6 July 1993), amend the 1990 Regulations, SI 1990/1904, by providing that no interest is payable where a repayment or credit is made following the alteration of the central non-domestic rating list in consequence of the Non-Domestic Rating Act 1993.

2143 Non-domestic rating—valuation—public utilities

The Water Undertakers (Rateable Values) (Amendment) Order 1993, SI 1993/772 (in force on 16 March 1993), further amends the 1989 Order, SI 1989/2479. The regulations make special provision for the calculation of the rateable value of combined hereditaments in consequence of the transfer of property between water undertakers as a result of the coming into force of certain schemes under the Water Industry Act 1991, Sch 2.

2144 Non-Domestic Rating Act 1993

The Non-Domestic Rating Act 1993 amends for the period beginning with 1 April 1993 and ending with 31 March 1995 the transitional arrangements which phase in the effects of the introduction of the national non-domestic rate and the compilation of non-domestic rating lists following a revaluation of non-domestic property. The Act received the royal assent on 27 May. Certain provisions were brought into force on 4 June 1993 and the remaining provisions on 6 July 1993: see SI 1993/1418, 1512. For details of commencement, see the commencement table in the title STATUTES.

Section 1 of the Act provides that phased in rate increases in the financial year 1993–94 are to be limited to the level of inflation. Under s 2, the Secretary of State must add to the distributable amount in the non-domestic rating pool an amount in respect of the estimated shortfall arising from the implementation of the provisions of the Act, and must adjust the non-domestic rating account in consequence. Section 3 deals with the funding of the additional costs arising from the Act. Section 4 enables subordinate legislation to be made under the Local Government Finance Act 1988 and provides for such legislation to have retrospective effect. Under s 5, amendments made to the 1988 Act by the 1993 Act, s 1 are deemed to relate back to 1 April 1993, although where the right to pay rates by instalments has been forfeited because of a failure to pay in full an instalment due before the coming into force of s 1, that right cannot be revived by the provisions of the 1993 Act. Section 6 deals with short title, commencement and extent.

2145 Valuation and community charge tribunal—decision—appeal against decision—time limit

The Valuation and Community Charge Tribunals Regulations 1989, SI 1989/439, reg 32(2) provide that an appeal against a decision of a valuation and community charge tribunal might be dismissed if it is not brought within 28 days of the date of the decision.

The appellants wished to appeal against a decision of a valuation and community charge tribunal, but they failed to bring their application within the 28-day time limit laid down by the 1989 Regulations. Their application for an extension of time was refused. On their appeal, *held*, once the 28-day time limit had expired the right to appeal could only be revived or extended if the court decided to extend time under RSC Ord 3, r 5. The court would always be loath to grant an extension, particularly if the delay had been substantial or if granting an extension would cause significant prejudice to the respondent, because the requirement that persons who wished to challenge decisions of statutory tribunals should do so within a limited period of time was in the interests of good administration. A refusal to extend the time limit would be prejudicial to the appellants, but that was not a significant factor. Accordingly, the appeal would be dismissed.

Regalbourne Ltd v East Lindsey District Council (1993) Times, 16 March (Court of Appeal: Sir Thomas Bingham MR, Kennedy and Evans LJJ). *Costellow v Somerset County Council* [1993] 1 WLR 256, CA (1992 Abr para 2030) considered.

REAL PROPERTY

Halsbury's Laws of England (4th edn) Vol 39, paras 301–800

2146 Articles

Negligent Valuations, James Behrens: 137 SJ 354, 368
Quantifying Beneficial Interest in Residential Property, Josephine Hayes: 137 SJ 22
Sales by Fixed-Charge Receivers, Judith Fishman and Christopher Morris (on sales by and purchases from Law of Property Act receivers): Estates Gazette, 3 November 1993, p 122
Title Investigation—Business Acquisitions, Clive Lampard: Estates Gazette, 3 July 1993, p 94

Valuation Problems, Kerry Stephenson: 137 SJ 130
Who Owns the Power of Sale? H W Wilkinson: 143 NLJ 448

2147 Conveyancing

See CONVEYANCING.

RECEIVERS

Halsbury's Laws of England (4th edn) Vol 39, paras 801–1000

2148 Powers—collection of debts—accountability for tax

See *Sargent v Customs and Excise Comrs*, para 2622.

REGISTRATION CONCERNING THE INDIVIDUAL

Halsbury's Laws of England (4th edn) Vol 39, paras 1001–1200

2149 Births, deaths and marriages—registration—fees

The Registration of Births, Deaths and Marriages (Fees) Order 1993, SI 1993/3116 (in force on
1 April 1994) replaces SI 1992/2982 and SI 1993/589 (which replaced SI 1993/377), and in
doing so increases certain fees payable under the Marriage Act 1949, ss 27(6), 51(1) and 57(4).
Other fees relating to the registration of births, deaths and marriages remain at their current
level.

REVENUE

Halsbury's Laws of England (4th edn) Vols 5(1) (reissue), 12, 19, 23 (reissue), 24 (reissue), 44

2150 Appropriation Act 1993

The Appropriation Act 1993 applies the sum of £118,866,507,000 out of the Consolidated
Fund to the service of the year ending 31 March 1994, appropriates the sum of
£211,667,093,154·72 for supply services, and repeals the following enactments: the Consolidated
Fund (No 2) Act 1990, the Consolidated Fund Act 1991, the Consolidated Fund (No 2) Act
1991 and the Appropriation Act 1991. The Act received the royal assent on 27 July 1993 and
came into force on that date.

2151 Budget—summary

The Chancellor of the Exchequer delivered his budget speech on 30 November 1993. The
following is a brief summary of the proposals contained in it. See further *Butterworth's 1993
Budget Tax Tables*.

Income tax
The lower, basic and higher rates remain at 20 per cent, 25 per cent and 40 per cent for 1994–
95. The lower rate band is increased to £3,000. The higher rate threshold remains at £23,700.
The personal allowances and the income limit for age allowance are unchanged. For 1994–95,
the relief for the married couple's allowance, married couple's age allowance, additional personal
allowance, widow's bereavement allowance and certain maintenance payments will be restricted
to the lower rate of tax. The married couple's age allowance will be increased by £200. The
blind person's allowance is increased by £120. Relief at 20 per cent in 1994–95, and at 15 per
cent in 1995–96 applies to mortgage interest relief related to an only or main residence (other
than loans used for purchase of life annuities), and to certain maintenance payments to a divorced
or separated spouse. The qualifying maximum for mortgage interest relief remains at £30,000

for 1994–95 and 1995–96. Relief for medical insurance premiums in respect of individuals aged 60 or over is limited to 25 per cent for premiums paid after 5 April 1994. There are certain changes to the administrative arrangements concerning this scheme.

Provision is to be made for self-assessment and the "current years basis" for 1996–97 onwards. Under self-assessment, income tax will be payable on 31 January and 31 July in the tax year. Capital gains tax will be due at the same time as the tax return is submitted, on 31 January after the tax year.

Employment
Amendments have been made to the provisions concerning beneficial loans to take account of the restriction to mortgage interest relief. From 6 April 1994, a new relief applies for cheap or interest-free loans which do not exceed £5,000, excluding qualifying loans such as home loans. This will exempt from tax most season ticket loans made by employers. Loans made on a normal commercial basis to employees are also exempt. Provision will be made to enable the Treasury to set a lower official rate of interest for foreign currency loans where interest rates are significantly lower in that country than in the United Kingdom. Relief will only apply if the individual normally lives in that country and has actually lived there in the year or the previous five years.

From 1994–95 onwards, the assessable benefit of a car calculated under the new rules is based on 35 per cent of the list price of the car plus extra accessories less any capital contributions.

From 1 December 1993, the use of marketable commodities and other assets to pay employees' bonuses will attract a national insurance contribution charge. Regulations are to be introduced from 6 April 1994 requiring PAYE to be charged on assets used to pay bonuses.

Amendment will be made to the PAYE Regulations so that a United Kingdom employer who has employees of a non-resident company working for him will be required to account for PAYE even if the foreign company pays the salaries. The approved profit-sharing scheme provisions will be changed to ensure that the charge applicable to a man aged 60 or over, in respect of shares allocated to him, will not exceed that for a woman of the same age. Approved profit-sharing schemes will also be able to retain qualifying corporate bonds received on or after royal assent in exchange for shares as part of a reorganisation. The profit-related pay rules are changed for schemes registered after 30 November 1993 in order to ensure that profit-related pay is genuinely variable pay and to counter the payment of disproportionately large amounts to individuals in special schemes.

Pensions
From 6 April 1994, the earnings cap, by reference to which the maximum relief on contributions to personal pension schemes and benefits under certain occupational pension schemes are calculated is increased from £75,000 to £76,800. The rules governing the taxation of funded unapproved retirement benefit schemes are to be changed, in particular those set up offshore the income or gains of which are wholly or partly tax free and which provide a larger tax free lump sum on retirement than would be available from a similar onshore fund the income of which is taxable. The difference between the contributions into and receipts from the schemes are to be taxed at the employer's marginal rate.

Corporation tax
The rates of corporation tax are unchanged for the financial year from 1 April 1994, at 33 per cent for the standard rate and 25 per cent for the small companies' rate. The upper and lower limits for the small companies' rate are increased to £300,000 and £1,500,000. The rate at which companies pay advance corporation tax (ACT) is further reduced to 20 per cent for dividends paid after 5 April 1994. The optional foreign income dividend scheme is to be introduced in relation to dividends paid after 30 June 1994 with the intention of enabling companies to obtain repayment of surplus ACT when they pay dividends out of foreign source profits. A company which is treated as non-resident in the United Kingdom under the provisions of a double taxation treaty will be treated as non-resident for all tax purposes. This new rule applies in determining residence for any period beginning after 29 November 1993 but, under transitional provisions, a dual resident company which was regarded as not resident under a double taxation treaty before 30 November 1993 will be treated as ceasing to be resident in the United Kingdom from the start of 30 November 1993. The tax on accrued gains arising as a result of cessation of residence under this rule can be deferred until the assets are sold but not beyond six years. In relation to controlled foreign companies, the rules determining whether a non-trading company has pursued an acceptable distribution policy are changed in respect of accounting periods ending after 29 November 1993. Provision is to be made to ensure that, for contracts entered into after a date to be announced, the rules for accounting for tax on manufactured dividends are applied where securities are sold and repurchased, and the

compensation to the seller for not receiving a dividend or interest payment is reflected in a reduction in the repurchase price. Changes are to be made to the legislation, not yet in force, on companies' foreign exchange gains and losses. New rules will be introduced, from a date to be appointed, to reform the tax treatment of financial instruments used by companies for managing interest rate and currency risk. Profits or losses on financial instruments concerned will be taxed as income. The rules applying to interest paid and received by companies are to be reviewed. Legislation is to be introduced to counter schemes under which companies are sold in circumstances which result in their corporation tax liabilities, arising prior to the date of sale, being non-collectable.

Businesses

In order to prevent the back dating of claims for capital allowances, time limits for claiming allowances are to be introduced for expenditure not notified to the Revenue prior to 30 November 1993. With effect from that date, the definition of machinery and plant is restricted by excluding any item which constitutes land, buildings or structures; this rule is subject to specific prior decisions of the courts as to what constitutes plant. In relation to commercial buildings in enterprise zones and qualifying hotels, further changes have been made to transfers at tax written down value between connected persons. New rules will make it easier for a creditor to obtain relief in respect of certain trade debts given up as part of a voluntary arrangement under the Insolvency Act 1986. For the debtor, the amount given up by the creditor in such circumstances will no longer be taxable.

Investments

The business expansion scheme will not apply to shares issued after 31 December 1993. It will be replaced by an enterprise investment scheme applying to new equity shares in unquoted trading companies issued after that date. There will be income tax relief on investments of up to £100,000 per annum from 1994–95 (limited to a lower figure in 1993–94). Income tax relief for the amount invested is limited to 20 per cent, together with exemption from capital gains on first disposal of the qualifying shares, and either capital gains tax or income tax relief for any losses made on first disposal of the shares. The new scheme will not extend to private rented housing. A new scheme for venture capital trusts, a new type of investment trust investing a substantial part of their assets in unquoted trading companies, is to be introduced; it is envisaged that dividends and capital gains accruing to investors in the trust in relation to their trust holdings would be free of tax.

A number of amendments are to be made to the changes, introduced by the Finance Act 1993, in the taxation of dividends which distorted the tax position of authorised unit trusts; the amendments will take effect for distribution periods beginning after 31 March 1994.

Capital gains tax

The annual exempt amount remains at £5,800 for individuals for the year 1994–1995. For disposals occurring after 29 November 1993, indexation allowance will only be available to reduce a capital gain. In future, it will not be available to increase or create a capital loss. For disposals after 29 November 1993, any chargeable gain made by an individual or most trustees are to be deferred where the gain is reinvested in shares in a qualifying unquoted trading company or holding company of a trading group. The limits on the amounts of gains qualifying for retirement relief are increased for disposals occurring after 29 November 1993. Relief is available for the first £250,000 of gains and 50 per cent relief is available on gains between £250,000 and £1m.

Value added tax

From 1 December 1993, the registration limit is increased to £45,000; the deregistration limit is increased to £43,000. The recovery of input tax is to be permitted from 1 January 1994 on vehicles purchased by businesses leasing cars to private taxi, self-drive hire or driving schools. The repayment supplement system is to be amended so that the time between a value added tax return being received and Central Unit raising inquiries with the local value added tax office will count towards the 30-day time limit after which supplement is payable. The minimum supplement is increased from £30 to £50 or 5 per cent of the repayment. Businesses will no longer be eligible for supplement where their repayment claim is received late.

Inheritance tax

The inheritance tax threshold for 1994–95 remains at £150,000; the rate of inheritance tax remains at 40 per cent. The period within which replacement property must be acquired by the transferee following a gift to which business or agricultural property relief applied is extended from one year to three years for charges arising as a result of deaths after 29 November 1993.

Stamp duty
It is proposed to charge duty on the exchange of an interest in land or buildings for another such interest. Ad valorem duty is to be charged when the consideration payable on the sale of land or buildings is unascertainable at the time of execution of the conveyance. When transfers are executed on or after 8 December 1993, stamp duty will be payable on such transactions as if the property had been sold for its open market value. Where rent payable under a lease cannot be ascertained at the time the lease is executed, duty will be payable on the open market rent of the property. Agreements to surrender a lease will also be charged to ad valorem duty. Surrenders effected by operation of law without a formal deed will now be subject to duty. This change will apply to agreements made on or after 8 December 1993.

2152 Capital gains tax
See CAPITAL GAINS TAXATION.

2153 Capital transfer tax
See INHERITANCE TAXATION.

2154 Consolidated Fund Act 1993
The Consolidated Fund Act 1993 applies the sum of £1,893,716,000 out of the Consolidated Fund, for the year ending 31 March 1993. The Act received the royal assent on 18 February 1993 and came into force on that date.

2155 Consolidated Fund (No 2) Act 1993
The Consolidated Fund (No 2) Act 1993, applies the sum of £131,142,154·72 out of the Consolidated Fund for the year ending 31 March 1992, and the sum of £2,654,112,000 for the year ending 31 March 1993. The Act received the royal assent on 29 March 1993 and came into force on that date.

2156 Consolidated Fund (No 3) Act 1993
The Consolidated Fund (No 3) Act 1993 applies the sum of £2,159,605,000 out of the Consolidated Fund for the year ending 31 March 1994, and the sum of £92,463,143,000 for the year ending on 31 March 1995. The Act received the royal assent on 17 December 1993 and came into force on that date.

2157 Customs and excise
See CUSTOMS AND EXCISE.

2158 Finance Act 1991—commencement
The Finance Act 1991, section 58, (Commencement No 3) Regulations 1993, SI 1993/933, specify 22 April 1993 as the relevant day for bringing into effect the Income and Corporation Taxes Act 1988, s 736A, Sch 23A and s 737, as amended, in relation to manufactured overseas dividends on overseas securities as defined in Sch 23A. For a summary of the 1991 Act, see 1991 Abr para 2056. For further details of commencement, see the commencement table in the title STATUTES.

2159 Finance (No 2) Act 1992—commencement
The Finance (No 2) Act 1992, section 62, (Commencement) Order 1992, SI 1992/2642, brings into force on 6 April 1993 s 62 (qualifying maintenance payments: maintenance assessments etc) of the Act.

The Finance (No 2) Act 1992, Schedule 9, (Appointed Day) Order 1993, SI 1993/236 appoints 19 February 1993 for the coming into force of Sch 9 of the Act which concerns friendly societies and amends the Income and Corporation Taxes Act 1988, the Capital Gains Tax Act 1979 and the Taxation of Chargeable Gains Act 1992.

The Finance (No 2) Act 1992 (Commencement No 6 and Transitional Provisions and Savings) Order 1993, SI 1993/2272, appoints 13 October 1993 for the coming into operation of s 12,

Sch 18, Pt IV, which effect the repeal of statutory provisions by virtue of which certain vehicles which are used for the purposes of disabled people are exempt from excise duty. Transitional provisions and savings are made in order to preserve the exemption from duty in particular cases. For details of commencement, see the commencement table in the title STATUTES.

2160　Finance Act 1993

The Finance Act 1993 grants and alters certain duties, amends the law relating to the national debt and the public revenue and makes further provision in connection with finance. The Act received the royal assent on 27 July 1993 and certain provisions came into force on that date. For details of commencement, see the commencement table in the title STATUTES.

Part I (ss 1–50) Customs and Excise and Value Added Tax

Chapter I General

Section 1 and Sch 1 increase, as from 16 March 1993, excise duties on beer, wine, made-wine and cider, and s 2 increases, as from 1 June 1993, the rate of beer duty under the new system for charging duty on the volume and alcoholic strength of beer at the end of the production process. Beer with lower alcoholic content is brought within the excise control arrangements but no duty is chargeable on beer which is below the previous minimum strength: s 3. Provision is made by s 4 for the repeal, with effect from 1 September 1993, of the drawback arrangements for refund of duty on beer deposited in an excise warehouse; the drawback arrangements are also to be repealed in respect of beer exported to the Isle of Man when a revenue-sharing agreement with the United Kingdom comes into effect under which duty on beer would be charged at the same rates in both countries. Except as regards drinks mixed on the premises where they are to be consumed or in other specified circumstances, the blending and mixing of alcoholic liquors to produce a dutiable liquor for sale is restricted to permitted premises and excise warehouses: s 5. The quantity of spirit which may be mixed with wine in an excise warehouse is increased but the permitted maximum strength of the product is reduced: s 6. The specification of sparkling wine is extended to include any wine or made-wine kept in a container with a mushroom-shaped stopper held in place by a tie or fastening, regardless of the pressure in the container: s 7. Provision may be made by regulations to treat as methylated spirits, exempt from excise duty, imported denatured alcohol which complies with requirements of other member states: s 8. Increases in the duties on light oil and heavy oil, and in the rebates on fuel oil and gas oil, unleaded petrol and light oil for use as furnace oil took effect on 16 March 1993: s 9. Mineral oils, such as orimulsion, may by Treasury order be treated for excise duty purposes as the nearest equivalent hydrocarbon oil: s 10. Duty is to be charged on other fuel substitutes, such as lead compounds and biofuels, when set aside for use as fuel or fuel additives; this will supersede the existing provisions for petrol substitutes and power methylated spirits: s 11. Hydrocarbon oil duty is to be charged on liquids by reference to volume measured at a standard temperature instead of bulk litres at the ambient temperature on delivery: s 12. Increases in the duties on cigarettes, cigars, hand-rolling tobacco and other smoking tobacco and chewing tobacco took effect on 16 March 1993: s 13. The specification of hand-rolling tobacco is widened to include some coarser cut tobacco and any tobacco of a kind used for making into cigarettes: s 14. The rates of duty, except for the lower-rated small-prize machines where the maximum play is 5p or less, are increased with effect for licensing periods beginning after 30 April 1993: s 15. Duty on the lower-rated small-prize machines is to be abolished from 1 November 1993: s 16. For licences taken out after 16 March 1993, the rate of duty on private cars, light goods vehicles and other vehicles in the same category is increased to £125; other rates, except for heavier lorries, are also increased: s 17. The rates for special type vehicles used to transport exceptional loads are increased with provision for a further increase from a day to be appointed: s 18. The rate of duty for trade plates is tied to the rates for cars and motorcycles respectively: s 19. The duty concession for vintage motorcycles will cease to be subject to restrictions on engine capacity and weight: s 20. The Secretary of State for Transport is empowered to alter the form and presentation of the tables of rates of duty on goods vehicles by statutory instrument, but not so as to increase the rate of duty on any vehicle: s 21. The value added tax provisions for mutual recovery and disclosure of information with other member states are extended to excise duties: s 22. An excise licence may be refused for an unregistered vehicle brought into the United Kingdom if any value added tax or customs duty on the acquisition or importation of the vehicle has not been secured: s 23.

Chapter II Lottery duty

Lottery duty is introduced by s 24; the new duty will apply from a day to be appointed (s 41) but the imposition of duty will not legitimise an unlawful lottery: s 40. It is intended to be chargeable on the sale of tickets in the proposed National Lottery (s 40); specific exemptions are made for bingo and other lotteries and the exemptions may be amended by regulations: ss 24, 38. The rate of lottery duty is to be 12 per cent of the price of the ticket: s 25. Regulations may provide for payment of duty to be deferred or for payments on account: ss 26, 38. The duty will be payable by the promoter, or any other person specified by regulations as a person responsible for the lottery, including in the case of a company any of its directors; provision is made for recovery of unpaid duty with penalties: s 27. Lottery duty is under the care and management of the Commissioners of Customs and Excise (s 40) who are given a general power to make regulations for its administration and enforcement backed by statutory penalties for non-compliance: ss 28, 38. The promoter or other responsible person will be required to register with the commissioners who may make regulations concerning registration; there are statutory penalties for failure to register: ss 29, 38. The revenue trade provisions of the Customs and Excise Management Act 1979, including powers for the commissioners to estimate duty due and requirements for traders to maintain and preserve records, are applied to lottery duty: 1993 Act, s 30. There are new criminal offences relating to fraudulent evasion of lottery duty and making false statements in connection with lottery duty (s 31) and, where the offence is committed by a company, the company's officers at the time of the offence may also be charged: s 32. Goods used in the promotion and conduct of, or otherwise related to, a lottery in respect of which an offence has been committed will be liable to forfeiture: s 33. Immunity is provided for those acting on the instructions of the commissioners: s 34. A certificate by the commissioners is prima facie evidence of facts as to registration, returns and payment and photographic copies of documents, certified by the commissioners, are admissible in place of the originals: s 35. Lottery duty falling due within the previous 12 months is a preferential debt in insolvency: s 36. Provision is made for disclosure of information between the commissioners and the Gaming Board or the Secretary of State, their respective officers or persons designated by the Secretary of State: s 37. Lotteries are excluded from pool betting duty: s 39.

Chapter III Value Added Tax
From 1 April 1994, supplies of fuel and power for domestic, residential or non-business charity use cease to be zero-rated, although, as a transitional measure value added tax is chargeable on such supplies at a special 8 per cent rate until 1 April 1995: s 42. The discount for high business mileage in the scales for charging value added tax on fuel supplied for private use in business cars is abolished for return periods beginning after 5 April 1993: s 43. By virtue of s 44, a supply by a person who belongs in another member state involving the installation or assembly of goods in the United Kingdom for a trader registered in the United Kingdom may be treated as an acquisition from that person instead of a taxable supply by him; the provision allowing unregistered overseas suppliers to account for value added tax through customers in the United Kingdom is repealed. A special scheme is introduced by s 45, under which the buyer of gold is required to account for the value added tax on the sale; the scheme may be extended by Treasury order to supplies involving precious or semi-precious metal or stones. A value added tax tribunal's jurisdiction in relation to appeals concerning input tax credit for anything in the nature of a luxury, amusement or entertainment is limited to a supervisory review of the reasonableness of the commissioners' decision: s 46. The relief for the supply of samples is amended so that it is no longer necessary for the recipient to be an actual or potential customer of the business but, where two or more identical samples are supplied to the same recipient, the relief applies only to one of them: s 47. The period which must elapse from the time of the supply before relief may be claimed is reduced to six months for claims made after 31 March 1993: s 48. Substantial changes are made to the value added tax penalty system: s 49, Sch 2. The provisions as to valuation and collection of car tax on vehicles brought to the United Kingdom from other member states following the introduction of the Single Market have become obsolete on the abolition of car tax from 12 November 1992 and are omitted: s 50.

Part II (ss 51–184) Income Tax, Corporation Tax and Capital Gains Tax

Chapter I General
For 1993-94, the lower, basic and higher rates of income tax remain unchanged at 20 per cent, 25 per cent and 40 per cent respectively; the lower rate limit is increased to £2,500 but the basic rate threshold remains £23,700: s 51. There is no indexed increase in the personal and married couple's allowances for 1993-94; these allowances, and the additional personal allowance and widow's bereavement allowance, remain at the 1992-93 amounts: s 52. For the financial year 1993, which began on 1 April 1993, the rate of corporation tax is unchanged: s 53. The small companies rate is also unchanged and the accelerating fraction for marginal relief on profits between £250,000 and £1,250,000, the lower and upper profits limits, remains $\frac{1}{50}$: s 54. The mortgage interest relief limit, the qualifying maximum, is unchanged at £30,000 for 1993-94: s 55. By virtue of s 56, where the borrower buys a new home and substitutes the new

property as security for an existing loan or loans at least one of which was a qualifying loan, mortgage interest relief may be continued for the qualifying loan or loans as if they had been new qualifying loans made at the time of the substitution; the amount qualifying for relief, the relevant amount, is restricted where other qualifying loans have been, or are later, used to fund the purchase. It is no longer necessary for a borrower who has moved out of his home with the intention of disposing of it, to take out a loan to buy a new home in order to continue to qualify for mortgage interest relief on the old loan for up to 12 months after ceasing to reside at the mortgaged property; this relief is also available for life annuity purchase loans to persons aged over 65: s 57. Assessment powers, interest charges, and penalties for incorrect returns, are applied to the recovery of amounts overclaimed by MIRAS lenders: s 58. Interest may be paid gross to individuals not ordinarily resident in the United Kingdom by other deposit-takers as well as banks or building societies: s 59. In connection with the new rules for taxation of companies' foreign exchange gains and losses (see ss 125-170, infra), the deduction for interest paid on a loan repayable by reference to a currency other than that in which it was made, is restricted to a commercial return on the amount repayable expressed in terms of the original currency: s 60. New anti-avoidance provisions treating interest as arising for tax purposes as it accrues, are aimed at interest on qualifying debts; these are debts owed to United Kingdom resident companies by their associated non-resident companies, either directly or through arrangements with a third party: s 61. There are three categories of exempted debt (1) loans at a fixed rate of interest payable at intervals of 12 months or less with no premium on redemption after more than 12 months, (2) loans where the avoidance motive was not a main reason for the terms agreed and either those terms would have been agreed or accepted by the resident company if an associated company had not been involved or after the first two years the interest is payable as it accrues at intervals of 12 months or less, and (3) where the associated company is insolvent and is to be wound up or dissolved: s 62. Where the qualifying debt has the characteristics of an accrued income security, a deep discount security, or a deep gain security, the charging provisions relating to those securities are applied to determine the amounts of interest chargeable to tax on an accruals basis: ss 63-65. A double charge to tax is precluded where a single security is treated as both an accrued income security and a deep gain security, and where the same debt is deemed to be a debt on two separate securities; and income taxed on an accruals basis is not also taxable when it is actually paid to the company: s 66. The minimum amount for single donations to charity by close companies, and for single cash donations by individuals under the gift aid scheme, is reduced to £250, applicable to donations made after 15 March 1993: s 67. The maximum total amount which may be donated annually by an employee under the payroll deduction scheme is increased to £900 with effect from 1993-94: s 68. Payments made by an employer towards the expenses of an approved agent operating the employer's payroll deduction scheme are deductible for tax purposes: s 69. The flat rate cash equivalents for employee car benefits are increased for 1993-94: s 70. The corresponding amounts for car fuel benefits are also increased and there is no longer a reduction in the scale fuel benefit where business travel exceeds 18,000 miles: s 71. From 1994-95, a new method of charging car benefits to tax will apply: s 72, Sch 3. A flat rate cash equivalent is introduced for vans available for an employee's private use, with effect from 1993-94: s 73, Sch 4. There is no charge in respect of a heavier commercial vehicle unless its use by the employee is wholly or mainly for purposes other than business travel: s 74. Subject to various exceptions, the provision of sporting and recreational facilities for use by employees and their families is not taxable as an employee benefit from 1993-94 onwards; further exceptions and conditions may be imposed by regulations: s 75. The tax relief for employees in respect of removal expenses and relocation benefits provided by their employers is altered; the new rules apply to job changes and relocations after 5 April 1993: s 76, Sch 5. From 1993-94, income tax on company distributions is generally charged at the lower rate instead of the basic rate; but where an individual taxpayer is liable to higher rate tax on his total income, such distributions are liable to higher rate tax as the top part of that income; this treatment also applies to foreign dividends, stock dividends and the deemed distribution on release of a close company loan: s 77. Although the rate of advance corporation tax will reflect the lower rate of income tax in later years, for the financial year 1993 it is reduced only to 22·77 per cent; the tax credit is nevertheless limited to the lower rate unless, with some specific exceptions, the distribution forms part of a company's franked investment income: s 78. Numerous amendments, consequential on the change in the rate of tax on distributions, are made to existing legislation: s 79, Sch 6. Charities, certain heritage bodies and scientific research organisations, which are entitled to repayment of the tax credit on dividends, can claim transitional relief in the form of special additional payments on a reducing scale for the years 1993-94 to 1996-97: s 80. Advance corporation tax in respect of distributions after 15 March 1993, following a change in the ownership of the company and a major change in the nature or conduct of its trade, cannot be carried back to be set off against corporation tax liability arising before the change of ownership: s 81.

For 1993-94, the annual exempt amount of gains of individuals, and trusts for the mentally disabled etc, is unchanged; the exempt amount for other trusts is £2,900: s 82. From 1994-95, the indexed increase of the annual exempt amount will be calculated by reference to the retail prices index figures for September: s 83. By virtue of s 84, debentures issued after 15 March 1993 in exchange for shares on a company reconstruction are deemed to be securities and corporate bonds, ensuring that they are within the charge to tax as debts on a security and that any gains accrued on the shares are held over until disposal of the debentures. The capital gains tax identification rules may be modified by regulations in their application to transfers of shares into a personal equity plan: s 85. Community agricultural quotas for ewe and suckler cow premium form a new class of assets qualifying for roll-over relief; the new class applies where either the disposal of the old asset or the acquisition of the new asset takes place after 31 December 1992; further classes of assets may be added by Treasury order: s 86. For disposals after 15 March 1993, retirement relief is extended and new provision in relation to relief on the reinvestment of certain gains is made: s 87, Sch 7. Relief by set-off within a group for capital losses which accrued to a company before it joined the group is restricted by ring-fencing the pre-entry loss; these provisions apply for accounting periods ending after 15 March 1993 as regards deductions from chargeable gains accruing after that date in respect of losses where the company joined the group after 31 March 1987: s 88, Sch 8. From the introduction of the pay and file scheme (see s 120, infra) the timing of the charge on the deemed disposal of assets received from other group members by a company leaving the group is changed to the later of the beginning of the company's last accounting period in the group and its deemed reacquisition of the assets: s 89. A technical error in the consolidation of the Taxation of Chargeable Gains Act 1992, s 211, concerning transfers of long-term business between insurance companies not both resident in the United Kingdom, is corrected: 1993 Act, s 90. The annual deemed disposal of holdings in authorised unit trusts forming part of an insurance company's long-term business does not apply to accounting periods commencing before 1 January 1993; the computation of the amount of the resulting gains or losses to be spread over the current and next six accounting periods, and the transitional run-off and replacement reliefs, are amended: s 91. For the purposes of corporation tax, a company's trading profits or losses are generally required to be computed and expressed in sterling: s 92. However, in certain circumstances the company may elect to compute the profits or losses of all or part of its trade in a foreign currency, including the ECU; the conditions which must be satisfied for such an election to be effective are to be set out in regulations made by the Treasury: ss 93-95. With effect from the date appointed for commencement of new rules for the tax treatment of companies' exchange gains and losses (see ss 125-170, infra), the profits and losses of a controlled foreign company are to be computed in the currency used in the foreign company's accounts: s 96. New rules, applying to accounting periods beginning after 31 December 1992, for computing the corporation tax liability of United Kingdom branches of overseas life insurance companies are introduced: s 97, Sch 9. The categories of asset linked to particular areas of a life insurance company's business, which apply for the purpose of the deemed disposal on transfer of an asset between different categories, are modified in their application to overseas life insurance companies: s 98. An overseas life insurance company is entitled to tax credits for dividend income from United Kingdom companies referable to the life assurance business of its United Kingdom branch and may claim to treat this income as profits chargeable to corporation tax against which trading losses, charges on income, management expenses and certain capital allowances, may be set off: s 99. The exemption for non-residents from United Kingdom tax on securities of foreign states or foreign dividends does not apply to investment income attributable to the basic life assurance and general annuity business of the United Kingdom branch of an overseas life insurance company; and, where the investment income attributable to such business includes interest on Treasury securities free of tax to non-residents, any relief for management expenses is proportionately reduced: s 100. The special rules for calculating the trading receipts of a life insurance company, and the share of its profits attributable to policyholders, are modified for the United Kingdom branch of an overseas life insurance company in line with the new corporation tax rules: s 101, Sch 10. There are further modifications of the rules for calculation of companies' chargeable gains as they apply to the United Kingdom branch: s 102, Sch 11. The definition of "overseas life insurance company" is amended to apply to any non-resident insurance company carrying on life assurance business through a United Kingdom branch or agency: s 103. The market value rule does not apply to the grant of a share option after 15 March 1993 under an approved scheme; only the amount, if any, actually paid by the employee for the option is taken into account in computing the company's gain or loss: s 104. The relief on a disposal of shares acquired under an approved share option scheme for amounts charged to income tax on the grant of the option to the employee, in respect of the difference in value between the option price and the market value of the shares, is restored retrospectively: s 105. The earnings cap, the maximum earnings in respect of which contributions to approved occupational pension schemes or personal pension schemes are eligible for relief, is unchanged at £75,000 for 1993-94: s 106. From 1994-95, the indexed increases of the income tax bands, personal and married couple's allowances, and the earnings cap for approved pension provision, will be calculated by reference to the retail prices index figures for September in view of the earlier date of the Budget; a drafting omission is corrected to ensure that the earnings cap is unaltered where the change in the retail prices index is negative: s 107.

Expenditure in respect of certain counselling services for full-time employees who lose their jobs after at least two years service is exempted from tax, the provision of such services, or payment of fees or travelling expenses incurred by the employee in connection with the counselling services, is not liable to Schedule E tax on the employee and, where such expenditure is incurred by the employer, it is deductible in computing profits: s 108. Where a business commences after 31 March 1993, the deduction for pre-trading expenditure is extended to include expenditure incurred up to seven years before commencement; relief is also given for charges on income paid by a company after 31 March 1993 wholly and exclusively for the purposes of the prospective trade: s 109. The relief for expenditure in connection with waste disposal sites is amended to include expenditure to comply with authorisations for disposal of radioactive waste and pre-trading expenditure on site preparation: s 110. Relief under the scheme is denied for shares issued after 15 March 1993 where a loan is made to the investor which would not have been made, or would have been on different terms, if he had not subscribed for the shares: s 111. For periods of account ending after 5 April 1993, tax relief for employers' contributions to occupational pension schemes is explicitly limited to amounts actually paid, not mere provisions or accruals; relief is excluded for contributions paid after 5 April 1993 to the extent that deductions have previously been allowed for provisions in excess of contributions paid; relief on the same basis applies to statutory contributions required to make up a deficiency in the scheme after the employer's business has been discontinued: s 112. A 20 per cent initial allowance is provided for a limited period for expenditure under contracts made in the year ended 31 October 1993 on industrial and agricultural buildings brought into use by 31 December 1994; the temporary initial allowance for industrial buildings is introduced by adapting the enterprise zone allowance; the allowance is also available for buildings bought unused under contracts made in the year ended 31 October 1993: s 113. Corresponding provisions are made as regards the temporary initial allowance for agricultural buildings: s 114, Sch 12. On the same temporary basis, a 40 per cent first year allowance is provided, instead of the first year's writing-down allowance, for expenditure on machinery and plant incurred in the year ended 31 October 1993: s 115, Sch 13. The restriction on writing-down allowances for assets leased abroad within 10 years, the requisite period, of being brought into use is amended; the changes apply the restriction where a tax treaty relieves the lessee from liability to United Kingdom tax and ensure that the requisite period is not reduced where the assets are leased in the United Kingdom before being leased abroad: s 116. The right to elect for transfers of industrial buildings between connected persons to be treated as made at the tax written down value of the building is extended to qualifying hotels, commercial buildings in enterprise zones, and scientific research assets; the election can only be made where both parties are entitled to capital allowances: s 117. From 1993-94, a beneficiary, whose interest in the income of a United Kingdom resident trust governed by Scots law is equivalent to an interest in possession under an English trust, is treated for income tax purposes as entitled to the trust income as it arises: s 118. As regards profits arising after 15 March 1993, a foreign company is treated as being subject to a lower level of taxation if it pays less than 75 per cent of the tax which would have been payable if it had been resident in the United Kingdom: s 119. The pay and file scheme, which will apply to accounting periods ending after 30 September 1993, is further amended: s 120, Sch 14. The Treasury is empowered to make regulations to apply, with modifications, to the investment income of tax-exempt activities of friendly societies the arrangements for provisional repayments of tax on insurance companies' exempt pension business: s 121. From 1993-94, government departments become liable for failure to deduct tax and may incur interest and penalties: s 122. Criminal payments incurred after 10 June 1993 are disallowed as a deduction from income for tax purposes: s 123. The exemption from income tax for members of the House of Commons on reimbursements of travelling expenses is extended to reimbursements paid after 31 December 1991 for travel between the United Kingdom and Community institutions in Brussels, Luxembourg or Strasbourg: s 124.

Chapter II Exchange Gains and Losses
Sections 125-170, Schs 15-18 introduce new rules for the tax treatment of foreign exchange gains and losses of companies other than charities, authorised unit trusts and approved investment trusts: s 152. An exchange gain or loss accruing on a qualifying asset or liability (ss 125, 153-156), or on a contract to buy or sell currency (ss 126, 157), is recognised as an initial exchange gain or loss. Qualifying assets and liabilities comprise certain debts, currency, and certain shares: s 153. In the case of assets and liabilities, the initial exchange gain or loss (s 125) is measured by the difference in the local currency equivalent (ss 149, 164) of the basic valuation (s 159) of the asset or liability at the start and end of an accrual period: s 158. In the case of a currency contract, there is an initial exchange gain or loss (s 126) where there is a difference between the local currency equivalent of one currency at the start and end of the accrual period. A special method of calculating initial exchange gains or losses applies where the asset or liability consists of a debt the nominal amount of which varies during the accrual period; the local currency equivalent of the debt at the start of the accrual period is adjusted by adding or subtracting respectively the local currency equivalent of each increase or decrease in the period as they occur: s 127. There is an alternative method of calculating the initial exchange gain or loss, which may be applied by regulations to exclude exchange differences to the extent that they arise on assets, liabilities or contracts held or owed for certain tax-exempt activities, on debts or currency representing income which cannot be remitted to the United Kingdom, or on liabilities which the company has elected to match with prescribed assets: s 134, Sch 15. If the initial exchange gain or loss accrues in respect of an asset, liability or contract held or owed for the purposes of a trade, it is an exchange gain or loss of the trade for the accounting period in which the accrual period falls and is treated as a taxable trading receipt or allowable trading loss for that period; otherwise the initial gain or loss is a non-trading exchange gain or loss; where the asset, liability or contract is held or owed for trade purposes for only part of the period, the initial exchange gain or loss is apportioned on a just and reasonable basis. Exchange gains or losses arising otherwise than under the new rules are ignored in computing the profits or losses of the company's trade: s 128. The non-trading exchange gains or losses of an accounting period are aggregated: s 129. A net gain is charged to tax under Schedule D, Case VI: s 130. There is a limited form of relief for a net loss. The company may surrender the loss as group relief or claim loss relief against other profits of the same period; subject to that, it may carry back the relievable amount for set off against net exchange gains of periods in the last three years, taking later periods first. Any unused relievable amount is carried forward for aggregation with non-trading exchange gains and losses of the next accounting period (s 131); but net exchange losses carried forward cannot qualify for group relief or loss relief against other profits of later accounting periods: s 132. Provision is made as to the interaction of relief for non-trading exchange losses and other reliefs: s 133. Exchange losses on a foreign currency loan are ignored if the accrual of an exchange loss is a main benefit that might be expected to arise from borrowing or lending in the chosen currency: s 135. Relief for exchange losses on a loan or currency contract on special terms between parties not at arm's length may be limited to corresponding exchange gains from the same transaction: ss 136-138. The company may elect (s 139) to defer an unrealised exchange gain to the next accrual period if it accrues in respect of certain long-term capital assets or liabilities (s 140) and the lesser of the company's net unrealised exchange gains from long-term assets or liabilities accruing in the accounting period, and its total net exchange gains on qualifying debts and currency contracts accruing in that period, exceeds $\frac{1}{10}$ of its taxable profits for the period. That excess is the maximum amount which may be deferred: s 141. Where the asset or liability is used for a trade for which the local currency is foreign, the amounts to be used to calculate the deferral are first translated into their sterling equivalents: s 142. A gain attributable to a decrease in a variable debt cannot be deferred; the long-term assets or liabilities in respect of which a deferral election can be made are defined; the deferral provisions may be modified by regulations to take account of the replacement of a debt, to make provision for groups of companies, and to provide for reductions from the amount of profits used in calculating eligibility for deferral: s 143. Where all or part of a debt owed to, or by, a company is irrecoverable, the asset or liability is treated as having ceased or decreased accordingly: s 144. If an amount treated as irrecoverable becomes recoverable, the recoverable amount is treated as a new debt or an increase in the existing debt: s 145. Where a currency contract is terminated early, before any currency has been received or paid under it, and the company has a net gain or loss in respect of the contract, a balancing adjustment is made to recover or give relief, as appropriate, in the accounting period in which the termination occurs: s 146. A currency contract which is closed out by means of a reciprocal contract is treated as having been terminated early and exchange gains or losses on the second contract are ignored: s 147. Regulations may be made to provide for balancing adjustments to counter any excess charge made or relief given; where the asset shows an overall loss but exchange gains have accrued to

the company, relief may be given; conversely, where the asset shows an overall gain but exchange losses have accrued to the company, there may be a charge to tax: s 148. The local currency to be used in computing exchange gains and losses is generally sterling; however, where the asset, liability or contract is held for the purposes of a trade, the local currency or currencies of the trade (s 163) are used to establish the exchange gain or loss of the trade: s 149. There are detailed rules to determine the exchange rate to be used in calculating the local currency equivalent of the basic valuation of an asset or liability, and the local currency equivalent of amounts of debt and currency: s 150. These are modified for calculations required to ascertain the local currency equivalent of an increase or decrease in a variable debt: s 151. Qualifying companies, and qualifying assets and liabilities (s 153), are defined along with terms used in connection with assets, liabilities, and contracts: ss 152–155, 157. The construction of transactions involving the creation of assets or liabilities, and the effect of the accounting treatment of transactions, are considered: s 156. There is a translation time when the company becomes, or ceases to be, entitled to an asset or contract or subject to a liability, and whenever an accounting period ends between those times; accrual periods begin and end with a translation time: s 158. The basic valuation of an asset or liability is defined: s 159. There are rules to determine the nominal currency of assets and liabilities, the settlement currency and the nominal amount of a debt, and the local currency of a trade: ss 160–163. Shorter definitions or references are provided for several other expressions used in the rules: s 164. The new rules apply to a company as regards assets, liabilities and contracts held or acquired on or after its commencement day, the beginning of the first accounting period of the company to begin on or after the day to be appointed by Treasury order: ss 165,167. Transitional provision may be made by regulations for the treatment of gains or losses attributed to the company's existing assets, liabilities and contracts at its commencement day: s 165, Sch 16. A change of accounting date which reduces exchange gains or increases exchange losses under the new rules may be ignored if that was one of the purposes of the change: s 166. Wide-ranging powers to make further provision for the purposes of these rules by orders or regulations, including the modification or amendment of other legislation, are exercisable by the Treasury: s 167. Special rules may be made by regulations as to the treatment of exchange gains and losses arising in respect of assets of insurance companies: s 168. Gains and losses on disposals by a qualifying company of qualifying assets subject to the new rules are excluded from being chargeable gains or allowable losses: s 169, Sch 17. To take account of the new rules, and in particular the reliefs for exchange losses, there are amendments to provisions relating to interest on overdue tax, interest on overpaid tax, Schedule D, Case VI, the set-off of losses against surplus franked investment income, offshore funds, and deep gain securities: s 170, Sch 18.

Chapter III Lloyd's Underwriters etc
All the profits of an individual's underwriting business as a member of Lloyd's including, from 6 April 1993, income from assets of ancillary trust funds, are chargeable to income tax as trading profits under Schedule D, Case I; losses can be set against the individual's general income of the same year of assessment, and of the preceding year if he was also a member for that year: ss 171, 184. From 1993-94, all underwriting profits are treated as earned income: s 180. The profits or losses of a member's underwriting business for a year of assessment include his share of syndicate profits or losses arising in, and gains or losses on revaluation of assets in a premiums trust fund allocated to, the corresponding underwriting year and, from 1993-94, other profits or losses from payments made or received, after 5 April 1993, in the corresponding underwriting year: s 172. The existing administrative provisions for assessing and collecting tax on a syndicate's profits from underwriting and premiums trust funds are restated for 1992-93 and later years of assessment; these cover the method of determining syndicate profits and losses, returns and payments on account of tax by members' agents, and repayment of tax deducted and tax credits in respect of the syndicate's investment income: s 173, Sch 19. The assets of a premiums trust fund, including assets lent out under a stock lending arrangement, are revalued at the start and end of each underwriting year; where the member is not domiciled in the United Kingdom, and is either not resident or not ordinarily resident for the year, Treasury securities free of tax to non-residents are excluded from the revaluation: s 174. Provision is made for the tax treatment of a new special reserve scheme to be established by the Council of Lloyd's: s 175, Sch 20. Gains or losses on disposals of assets in other Lloyd's funds, apart from a member's premiums trust fund and special reserve fund, are not profits or losses of the underwriting business and remain subject to capital gains tax: ss 176, 184. Relief for payment of premiums for reinsurance to close a syndicate's account is disallowed as an expense of the continuing member's underwriting business in the reinsured syndicate to the extent that the amount of the premium exceeds a fair and reasonable assessment of the value of the liabilities covered; the amount disallowed is deductible from profits of his underwriting business as a member of the reinsuring syndicate: s

177. Amounts payable for stop-loss insurance, payments into Lloyd's High Level Stop Loss Fund, and payments under quota share contracts, are deductible as expenses of the underwriting business. Conversely, proceeds of stop-loss insurance, and payments out of the High Level Stop Loss Fund, are taxable as trading receipts: s 178. The final year of assessment of a member's underwriting business is the year corresponding to the underwriting year in which his Lloyd's deposit is repaid or, if he died on or before the end of that underwriting year, the year of assessment in which he died: s 179. The extended time limit for claims by authorised underwriting agents to deduct emoluments paid after the end of the period of account ceases to apply for periods ending after 29 June 1993: s 181. Regulations may make further provision for the assessment and collection of tax, make amendments to take account of changes in the rules or practice of Lloyd's, modify the rules in certain cases, and provide for foreign tax credits; provision may also be made to extend the general time limits for claims, elections and applications made by a member or a member's spouse; regulations may apply with effect from the year next but one preceding the year in which they were made; existing regulations in force at 6 April 1992 under earlier enactments are continued: s 182. Several amendments are made to existing legislation consequential on these changes in the taxation of Lloyd's underwriters: s 183. Section 184 deals with interpretation of Pt II, Chapter III.

Part III (ss 185–195) Oil Taxation
Petroleum revenue tax is abolished for oil and gas fields where no development consent was granted before 16 March 1993; expenditure for, or apportioned to, a non-taxable field is not allowable expenditure: ss 185, 195. For chargeable periods ending after 30 June 1993, the rate of petroleum revenue tax on taxable fields is reduced to 50 per cent; there is a corresponding reduction in the limit on interest payable in respect of repayments in respect of chargeable periods ending after 30 June 1993 resulting from losses carried back; and repayments of advance petroleum revenue tax are brought within the limit: ss 186, 195. The requirements as to returns and information are confined to taxable fields. New powers are given to require documents from the taxpayer and third parties in the same terms, and subject to the same restraints, as the corresponding powers in relation to corporation tax: s 187, Sch 21. Relief for exploration and appraisal expenditure is restricted to expenditure incurred before 16 March 1993: s 188. This is subject to transitional relief for expenditure incurred within two years of that date to which a company was committed under certain pre-16 March 1993 contracts (s 188) and for up to £10m of expenditure incurred between 16 March 1993 and 31 December 1994 inclusive by existing licensees and their associates: s 189. When a non-dedicated mobile asset becomes dedicated to a non-taxable field, the allowance for unrelieved expenditure on the asset is restricted: ss 190, 195. Detailed rules are introduced to determine the time at which expenditure is incurred as regards claims received after 16 March 1993; the new rules are also applied in clarification of the existing restriction on relief for costs incurred in transactions between connected persons: s 191. Field-related expenditure allowed on a claim received after 16 March 1993 cannot be brought into account for any chargeable period ending before the last day of the claim period in which it was incurred; abortive exploration expenditure, other exploration and appraisal expenditure and research expenditure incurred after 31 March 1993 cannot be brought into account for any period prior to that in which it was incurred: s 192. Tariff receipts allowance is not available for tariff receipts paid from a non-taxable field; relief is denied for payments by participators in taxable fields to connected persons as participators in non-taxable fields; the application of the tax to participators in foreign fields, and to the foreign parts of multi-national fields, is amended in line with the changes as regards United Kingdom fields: ss 193, 195. Treaty relief may be given in respect of petroleum revenue tax and the provision for exchange of information with foreign revenue authorities is extended to include that tax: s 194. Assessments, determinations and decisions may be amended to give effect to these changes: s 195.

Part IV (ss 196–200) Inheritance Tax
The nil rate band of £150,000 is not increased: s 196. From 6 April 1994, the indexed increase of the rate bands for inheritance tax will be calculated by reference to the retail prices index figures for September in view of the earlier date of the Budget: s 197. For deaths occurring after 15 March 1992, the relief for falls in value of shares forming part of the deceased person's estate is extended to investments which are cancelled within a period of 12 months: s 198. For deaths occurring after 15 March 1990, a claim to substitute sale values for the values at death of land sold within three years of the death will also apply to land sold in the fourth year if the sale value does not exceed the value at death: s 199. Questions as to the value of land may be referred to the Lands Tribunal by the Special Commissioners or the High Court: s 200.

Part V (ss 201–204) Stamp duty
The threshold for the 1 per cent duty on sales of land is increased to £60,000; no duty is chargeable in respect of the consideration on a conveyance or transfer, or on the premium for a new lease, if the amount or value of the consideration or premium does not exceed £60,000 and the document contains a certificate of value to that effect; the new threshold applies to documents executed after 15 March 1993 unless stamped before 23 March 1993: s 201. Stamp duty on a conveyance or lease made under the statutory "rent to mortgage" scheme in England and Wales, where the final consideration includes a percentage of the market value of the property on redemption, is charged on the consideration, market value less discount, which would be due under the statutory "right to buy" scheme: s 202. Corresponding provision is made concerning the "rent to loan" scheme which applies in Scotland: s 203. The way in which payment of stamp duty is recorded on documents, currently by die-impressed stamp, may be altered by Treasury regulations: s 204.

Part VI (ss 205–214) Miscellaneous and General
To facilitate the change to an earlier Budget, the period for which provisional effect is given to tax changes passed as Budget resolutions is brought forward; corporation tax and advance corporation tax are added to the taxes for which provisional effect can be given to Budget changes: s 205. Specific authority is provided for corporation tax assessments to be made in accordance with rate reductions contained in Budget resolutions subject to adjustment if the reduction is not included in a Finance Act passed within six months of the resolution: s 206. The period for which stamp duty changes can have temporary effect under Budget resolutions is also extended to allow 30 days for the Finance Bill second reading and six months for the Finance Act to be passed: s 207. From 1993-94, the fact that a person has living accommodation available in the United Kingdom will not be taken into account when deciding whether his residence in the United Kingdom is merely temporary: s 208. Exclusion from gas levy is extended to gas sold after termination of a tax-exempt contract on the ground that the continued supply had ceased to be commercially viable; but the petroleum revenue tax exemption for up to 5 per cent of cumulative production of the field outside the old tax-exempt contract does not apply after liability to gas levy lapses: s 209. The Government Trading Funds Act 1973 is amended to permit opening capital to be financed by reserves, to enable the use of public dividend capital to finance any expenditure by a trading fund, and to make consequential alterations to the borrowing limits of trading funds: 1993 Act, s 210, Sch 22. To facilitate the raising of money by issues of gilt-edged securities, the National Debt Commissioners are given power to acquire and transfer such securities: s 211. Sections 212, 213, Sch 23 deal with interpretation and repeals and s 214 with the short title of the Act.

2161 Government trading funds

The following trading funds were established, on 1 April 1993, under the Government Trading Funds Act 1973:

Trading Fund	Established by SI 1993 No
Chessington Computer Centre	948
Defence Research Agency	380
Land Registry	938
Medicines Control Agency	751

2162 Income and corporation tax
See INCOME TAXATION.

2163 Inheritance tax
See INHERITANCE TAXATION.

2164 Petroleum revenue tax
See PETROLEUM REVENUE TAXATION.

2165 Stamp duties
See STAMP DUTIES.

2166   Value added tax
See VALUE ADDED TAX.

ROAD TRAFFIC

Halsbury's Laws of England (4th edn) Vol 40, paras 1–993

2167   Articles
Interim Disqualifications and Interim Arrangements: Procedural or Penalty, J N Spencer: 157 JP Jo 115
Road Traffic Act 1991, Laurence Cramp and John Spencer: 155 JP Jo 827, 156 JP 8, 22, 38, 54
Sentence for Disqualified Driving, Alec Samuels: 157 JP Jo 488
The Penalty for not having a Vehicle Excise Licence and the Unit Fine System, JN Spencer: 157 JP 419
Transport and Works Act 1992, Michael Hackett: 137 SJ 220, 256
Without Reasonable Excuse, Christine Clayson (on the failure to provide a specimen): 137 SJ 1260

2168   Accident—duty to report accident as soon as reasonably practicable—onus of establishing failure to report
Scotland
The appellant was in a road accident which involved no other vehicles. He immediately contacted his company by car telephone to arrange for the local breakdown service to attend and also called his wife who came to collect him. The police arrived at the scene after the appellant had left and went on to call at the appellant's house one hour later. The appellant was subsequently charged with failure to provide his name and address, and failure to report the accident as soon as reasonably practicable pursuant to the Road Traffic Act 1988, s 170(3), (4). There was evidence that the police stations closest to the appellant's home were closed at the time of the accident although the station near the scene of the accident was open. The appellant maintained that he had intended to contact the police the following day. On appeal against conviction, *held*, the time period concerned was relatively short. There was no evidence to suggest that if the appellant had asked his wife to take him to the police station at the time of the accident, or if he had telephoned the open station and waited for a police officer to come to his home, he would have been in a position to report the accident any sooner than he did. The onus was on the Crown to establish that there was a failure on the part of the appellant to report the accident as soon as reasonably practicable. That must mean that it would have been reasonably practicable for the appellant to report the accident sooner than he did, and the Crown had not established that on the evidence. Accordingly, the appeal would be allowed.
    Hornall v Scott 1993 SLT 1140 (High Court of Justiciary).

2169   Accident—hospital charges
The Road Traffic Accidents (Payments for Treatment) Order 1993, SI 1993/2474 (in force on 8 November 1993), increases the maximum amount payable under the Road Traffic Act 1988, s 157(2) for hospital treatment of traffic casualties from £2,780 to £2,856 for in-patients and from £278 to £286 for out-patients. The amount payable under s 158(2) in respect of the emergency treatment fee is increased from £20·10 to £20·65 and in respect of a medical practitioner's travelling expenses in providing such treatment from 39p to 40p per mile.

2170   Careless driving—sentencing guidelines—aggravating and mitigating factors
See *R v Shepherd (Attorney-General's Reference (No 14 of 1993)); R v Wernet (Attorney-General's Reference (No 24 of 1993))*, para 2250.

2171   Careless driving—standard of proof
The Road Traffic Act 1988, s 3 provides that if a person drives a motor vehicle on a road without due care and attention, or without reasonable consideration for other persons using the road, he is guilty of an offence.

The defendant was the driver of a van which crashed into the back of a stationary car, shunting it into the back of another car. He gave a number of reasons for the accident but was charged under the 1988 Act, s 3. The court acquitted him on the grounds that the prosecution had failed to establish the cause of the accident and therefore failed to prove beyond reasonable doubt that the defendant had breached the 1988 Act, s 3. On appeal against the court's decision, *held*, the prosecution had to prove beyond reasonable doubt that the defendant was not exercising the degree of care and attention that a reasonable and prudent driver would exercise in the circumstances. The standard was an objective one, impersonal and universal, fixed in relation to the safety of other users of the highway. In the absence of an explanation put forward by the defendant, or if that explanation was objectively inadequate, and the only possible conclusion was that the defendant was careless, he should be convicted. On the facts of this case, the only possible conclusion was that the defendant was driving without due care and attention. Accordingly, the appeal would be allowed.

DPP v Cox (1993) 157 JP 1044 (Queen's Bench Division: Kennedy LJ and Clarke J).

2172 Carriage by road

See CARRIERS.

2173 Common transport policy

See EUROPEAN COMMUNITIES.

2174 Disqualification—disqualification for life—effect on rehabilitation

The defendant was charged with damaging property with intent to endanger life, contrary to the Criminal Damage Act 1971, s 1(2). The defendant was alleged to have deliberately driven his motor car in the wrong direction along a one-way street towards another car, approaching in the correct direction, at some 20 to 30 mph causing an accident. The defendant then reversed his car, drove off and was not arrested until some 9 months later. Following his conviction the defendant was sentenced to 6 years' imprisonment and disqualified from driving for life. On appeal against sentence, *held*, in the absence of psychiatric evidence or evidence of previous convictions indicating that he would be a danger to the public, it was inappropriate to impose a disqualification from driving for the rest of the defendant's life. When considering the imposition of an order of disqualification and its length, a court ought to have regard to the effect upon the defendant's prospects of effective rehabilitation. The defendant did not have any previous convictions involving either dangerous or careless driving or the use of a vehicle as a weapon, therefore the order was wrong in principle and excessive. Further, the length of sentence of imprisonment was excessive in the light of the defendant's antecedents and the circumstances of the case. Accordingly, the appeal would be allowed, the disqualification would be reduced to five years and the sentence of imprisonment reduced to three years.

R v King [1993] RTR 245 (Court of Appeal: Steyn LJ, Henry and Morland JJ).

2175 Disqualification—disqualification for life—requirement to take further driving test before disqualification removed

The appellant pleaded guilty to reckless driving, driving whilst disqualified and to two other offences of driving with excess alcohol and with no insurance. On his appeal against a sentence of disqualification for life, with a requirement that he take a test of competence to drive before being allowed to drive, *held*, such a requirement was included because it would be open to the appellant to apply in five years' time for the restoration of his licence. However, it offended against the principle that, where a period of disqualification was imposed, no reference should be made to the statutory provision enabling the offender, having been disqualified, to seek a reduction in the disqualification after the appropriate period. The appeal would be allowed to the extent of substituting a period of disqualification of ten years.

R v Lark (1992) 14 Cr App Rep (S) 196 (Court of Appeal: Lord Taylor of Gosforth CJ, Simon Brown and Roch JJ).

2176 Disqualification—driving whilst disqualified—special reasons for not ordering disqualification

Scotland

The Road Traffic Offenders Act 1988, s 28 provides that where a person is convicted of two or more traffic offences committed on the same occasion and involving obligatory endorsement, the total number of penalty points to be attributed is the number or highest number that would be attributed on a conviction of one of them. Section 44 of the 1988 Act provides that the court need not endorse a licence if for special reasons it thinks fit not to do so.

The defendant had been disqualified from driving but appealed, and an order was made suspending his disqualification pending the appeal. Due to his solicitor's failure to lodge certain documents in time, the defendant's appeal was deemed to have been abandoned although the defendant himself was not aware of this fact. He was subsequently seen driving and charged with two offences of driving whilst disqualified, to which he pleaded guilty. At first instance, it was decided that the mere fact that the two offences occurred within an hour of each other in streets very close to each other did not mean that they occurred on the same occasion for the purposes of the 1988 Act, s 28 and consequently the defendant's licence was endorsed with six penalty points on each of the two charges to which he had pleaded guilty. It was also decided that the fact that the defendant was unaware that his appeal had been abandoned was not a special reason for not ordering endorsement under the 1988 Act, s 44 as he could not avoid liability by delegating his obligations to his solicitor. On appeal, *held*, if the defendant had been engaged on a single, uninterrupted course of driving while disqualified, the proper view to take would have been that he was committing a single offence even though it was being committed in different streets as he travelled from one place to another in the course of his journey. In this case, however, the offences were committed on different occasions and were not all part of a single incident and had to be dealt with separately. The fact that the defendant was genuinely unaware of his disqualification due to a failure of his solicitor was capable of amounting to a special reason for ordering that there should be no endorsement of his licence under the 1988 Act, s 44. Accordingly, the appeal would be allowed and the order for endorsement of the defendant's licence would be quashed.

Robertson v McNaughtan 1993 35 SLT 1143 (High Court of Justiciary).

2177   Drink-driving—blood specimen—failure to provide specimen—right to have sample taken by defendant's own medical practitioner

The defendant was convicted on a charge of failing to provide a blood specimen contrary to the Road Traffic Act 1988, s 7(6). He had insisted that his own medical practitioner take a specimen of blood. On appeal by way of case stated, *held*, there was no general right to insist that a specimen be taken by a driver's own medical practitioner. *Bayliss v Chief Constable of Thames Valley Police* [1978] RTR 328, DC (1978 Abr para 2334) was a special case on its own facts, as in that case, the driver's own medical practitioner had been at the police station at the relevant time.

DPP v Smith (1993) Times, 1 June (Queen's Bench Division: Watkins LJ and Tuckey J).

2178   Drink-driving—breath test—failure to provide specimen—disqualification

An information laid against the defendant alleged that, having been driving or attempting to drive a motor vehicle on a road, being a person who was required under the Road Traffic Act 1988, s 7 to provide a specimen, he failed without reasonable excuse to provide such a specimen. Following his conviction, the justices stated that while the evidence supported the submission that he was in charge of his vehicle it did not go so far as to establish that he was not driving or attempting to drive at the time the specimen was required. If the defendant had been driving or attempting to drive at the material time, the sentence was a mandatory period of disqualification but if he was only in charge of the vehicle the magistrates had a discretion as to whether to disqualify and for what period. The defendant was fined and given the mandatory disqualification of three years. On his appeal against sentence, *held*, the justices had failed to make it clear on what basis the defendant was being sentenced. The case would be remitted to the justices to consider whether or not to disqualify.

Crampsie v DPP [1993] RTR 383 (Queen's Bench Division: Evans LJ and Otton J).

2179   Drink-driving—breath test—failure to provide specimen—evidence irregularly obtained

The defendant was observed by policemen driving in a dangerous manner. They followed him home, signalling for him to pull over although he ignored their signals. He was approached by one policeman as he walked up the drive of his house and was dragged to the roadside where he was asked to undertake a breath test which he refused to do. The policemen arrested him and took him to the police station where a breath test showed he was severely over the alcohol limit. He was then charged with driving with excess alcohol in his body. At first instance, the defendant claimed that the policemen had trespassed and acted in an oppressive manner and requested the court to issue two witness summonses so that his neighbours could give evidence of the policemen's oppressive conduct thereby enabling the court to consider exercising their discretion to exclude the evidence under the Police and Criminal Evidence Act 1984, s 78. The court refused on the ground that the evidence disclosed by the witnesses would add nothing material to the case, and that whatever they said the court would not exclude the breath test as evidence. On appeal by the defendant, *held*, the conduct of the policemen in stopping and arresting the defendant was relevant to the court's exercise of its discretion under the 1984 Act, s 78. By stating that it would not exclude the breath test as evidence whatever the witnesses may say, the court had not exercised its discretion under the 1984 Act, s 78. The court had therefore erred in excluding the evidence of the two witnesses by not issuing the witness summonses and accordingly, the appeal would be allowed and the conviction would be quashed.

Sharpe v DPP [1993] RTR 392 (Queen's Bench Division: Staughton LJ and Buckley J).

2180 Drink-driving—breath test—failure to provide specimen—reasonable excuse

The Road Traffic Act 1988, s 7(6) provides that it is an offence for a person, without reasonable excuse, to fail to provide a specimen when required to do so by a police constable investigating a drink-driving offence.

The respondent was acquitted of contravening the 1988 Act, s 7(6) by failing to comply with a requirement to provide two breath specimens at a police station. She provided one specimen, which exceeded the limit, but failed to provide a second. The inspector in charge observed that she was anxious and that her speech was nasal, but there was nothing to indicate that she was suffering from any medical condition that would have prevented her providing a second specimen. Medical evidence was given that she had a history of nervous asthma and a low anxiety threshold. On appeal, *held*, justices were not entitled to act upon material beyond the evidence put before them. When considering whether the defence of reasonable excuse was made out, they had to confine themselves to the actual evidence before them and not apply experiences or knowledge of their own, as they had done in the present case, which was not supported by the evidence. Accordingly, the appeal would be allowed but, in the particular circumstances, the case would not be remitted to the justices with an order for conviction.

DPP v Curtis (1993) 157 JP 899 (Queen's Bench Division: Watkins LJ, Tucker JJ).

2181 Drink-driving—breath test—power to require breath test—correct procedure

The defendant was charged with driving with excess alcohol. When arrested, he was required to provide two specimens of breath. He was then offered the option of providing a specimen of blood or urine under the Road Traffic Act 1988, s 7(4). He declined the offer. The police officer who made the offer said, in evidence, that she completed the standard procedure form but was unable to recall the exact words used. She was not cross-examined on this point. The defendant submitted that there was no evidence to show that he had been warned, in accordance with the 1988 Act, s 7(7), that failure to provide the blood or urine specimen might make him liable to prosecution. This was accepted by the justices but they decided that as no prejudice had been caused to the defendant the specimens of breath provided would not be rendered inadmissible. The defendant was convicted and appealed on the basis that the breath tests should not have been admitted. *Held*, failure to follow the correct procedure would result in the specimen not being admissible in evidence. However, as there was no cross-examination of the officer, the justices ought to have asked her to explain or remind them of the procedure and, if necessary, to produce the standard procedure form. The standard procedure form ought to be produced by prosecutors in breathalyser cases and justices ought to ensure that where a submission of the kind made in the instant case was made it did not succeed where it was permissible for them to allow further evidence to be called. Accordingly, the appeal would be allowed.

Murray v DPP [1993] RTR 209 (Queen's Bench Division: Watkins LJ and Laws J).

Scotland

A driver was arrested after failing a roadside breath test. The court found that there was no case for him to answer because it had not been established in evidence that the police officers who administered the roadside test or the subsequent tests at the police station had been in uniform when the tests were carried out, as required under the Road Traffic Act 1988, s 6. The Crown appealed, contending it could rely on the results of the breath samples carried out at the police station because those samples had been obtained in the course of an investigation into an offence under the 1988 Act, ss 4, 5, and that consequently it was unnecessary to establish that the officers had been in uniform when the roadside breath test was given. *Held*, it was not necessary for the procedure in the 1988 Act, s 6 to have been followed at all so long as the procedure governing the taking of samples at a police station, as laid down in the 1988 Act, s 7, had been observed.

Accordingly, even though there was no evidence that the officers had been in uniform, the evidence regarding the specimens of breath provided at the station was clearly sufficient to constitute a case to answer. The appeal would be allowed, and the case remitted to the sheriff's court for the proceedings to continue.

Orr v Urquhart 1993 SLT 406 (High Court of Justiciary).

2182 Drink-driving—breath test—specimen—unreliable readings

A driver was convicted of driving with excess alcohol in his breath, contrary to the Road Traffic Act 1988, s 5(1)(a). He provided a positive sample of breath at the roadside and was then arrested. At the police station he was required to provide two samples of breath on an intoximeter. On analysis both gave positive, but significantly different, readings. The police officer therefore made a request for a blood or urine sample under the 1988 Act, s 7(3)(b) and a sample of blood was subsequently provided which gave a reading consistent with the higher of the two breath specimens. At the prosecution's request, the magistrate only considered the offence in relation to breath and dismissed the charge in relation to blood. On appeal, the accuracy of the intoximeter came into issue and in order to resolve that matter the court had regard to the blood analysis. The court accepted evidence that although the intoximeter was capable of giving inconsistent readings if the person providing the samples did not use the same force of breath on each occasion, it was accurate at the time the defendant provided the samples and dismissed the appeal. On further appeal, *held*, where a police officer decided that a breath analysis device was unreliable and required the provision and analysis of a specimen of blood, a subsequent prosecution should be based solely on the analysis of blood and not on that of breath. Accordingly, the appeal would be allowed and the conviction would be quashed.

McLellan v DPP [1993] RTR 401 (Court of Appeal: Rose LJ and Pill J). *Badkin v DPP* [1988] RTR 401, CA applied.

2183 Drink-driving—disqualification—disqualification for life—appropriateness

The defendant had been disqualified from driving on 24 previous occasions and had nine previous convictions for driving with excess alcohol. He was subject to a ten-year disqualification when he was seen driving a car on two occasions. On the second occasion, he was found to have a blood alcohol level over the legal limit. He was sentenced to 13 months' imprisonment and disqualified from driving for life. On appeal, *held*, the defendant was a menace to other people, but there were no exceptional circumstances requiring disqualification for life, and it could not be said that the defendant would be a danger to the public indefinitely. Accordingly, the period of disqualification would be reduced to ten years.

R v Rivano (1993) 14 Cr App Rep (S) 578 (Court of Appeal: Stuart-Smith LJ, May and Ward JJ).

2184 Drink-driving—moped—meaning of driving

The defendant set a moped in motion by sitting astride it and propelling it with his feet in a paddling motion. His hands were on the handlebars and he was controlling the movement and direction of the machine, although the lights were not on and the engine did not start. He was arrested and subsequently convicted of driving a moped with excess alcohol, on the grounds that it was irrelevant that the vehicle was not moving under its own power and that the manner and use of the moped would unequivocally be seen and interpreted by a passer-by as driving. He appealed by way of case stated, contending that he was not driving the moped. *Held*, the justices had correctly directed themselves as to the law, and there was ample material to justify their conclusion that a passer-by would regard the use of the vehicle as driving. The appeal would accordingly be dismissed.

Gunnell v DPP [1993] Crim LR 619 (Queen's Bench Division: Rose LJ and Waller J).

2185 Drink-driving—option of providing blood or urine specimen—inability to provide specimen

The respondent had been arrested after failing a roadside breath test. He opted to provide a specimen of blood or urine to replace the breath test and was informed by the officer that the replacement specimen would be one of blood. However, on arrival at the police station, it was found that no doctor was available to take the specimen and the police officer asked the respondent to provide a urine specimen instead. The respondent was unable to do so. At the respondent's trial on a charge of driving with excess alcohol, the Crown sought to rely on the evidence provided by the breath specimen, but the justices decided it was not entitled to rely on that evidence and dismissed the information. The Crown appealed by way of case stated. *Held*, the Road Traffic Act 1988, s 8(2) stated that a driver had to provide a specimen of blood or urine if the breath specimen was not to be used. The fact that the respondent's inability to provide either specimen had been due to circumstances beyond his control did not justify the decision to prevent the Crown from relying on the breath specimen at trial. Accordingly, the appeal would be allowed and the case remitted to the justices with a direction to continue the hearing.

DPP v Winstanley [1993] RTR 222 (Queen's Bench Division: Kennedy LJ and Clarke J).

2186 Drink-driving—option of providing blood or urine specimen—preference

Scotland

The Road Traffic Act 1988, s 7 provides that in the course of investigating whether a person has committed an offence under the 1988 Act, s 5(1), a constable can: (1) require that person to provide a specimen of blood or urine at a police station for laboratory tests, and (2) decide whether the specimen should be of blood or urine.

The defendant was arrested, charged with driving while unfit through drink contrary to the 1988 Act, s 5(1)(a) and taken to a police station where a blood sample was requested under the 1988 Act, s 7. Before the sample was taken a standard form was read out which stated that the type of sample would be decided by the constable, but that any reason that the defendant offered in response to that decision would be taken into account. A submission of no case to answer was made on the grounds that the defendant was denied his implied right under the standard form to influence the decision as to the type of sample taken and therefore the specimen of blood was improperly obtained and inadmissible. The sheriff upheld that submission and acquitted the defendant. The prosecution appealed by way of case stated. *Held*, the 1988 Act, s 7 unequivocally stated that the choice between the types of specimen was to be decided by the constable who required the sample to be taken, and there was no requirement for him to invite the driver to express a preference. Although the wording of the standard form was misleading it did not affect the statutory position. Accordingly, the appeal would be allowed and the case remitted to the sheriff.

McLeod v MacFarlane 1993 SLT 782 (High Court of Justiciary).

Scotland

The Road Traffic Act 1988, s 7 provides that in the course of investigating whether a person has committed an offence under the 1988 Act, s 5, a constable can: (1) require that person to provide a specimen of blood or urine at a police station for laboratory tests, and (2) decide whether the specimen should be of blood or urine.

The appellant was convicted of driving whilst unfit through alcohol, contrary to the 1988 Act, s 5. He had been found slumped over his steering wheel unconscious and apparently injured. He was taken to hospital where the police required him to provide a blood specimen for a laboratory test. At the close of the Crown case, a submission of no case to answer was made on the grounds that the failure to inform the appellant that he was required to supply a specimen of blood or urine was contrary to authority and thus unfair. The sheriff dismissed the submission. On appeal, *held*, the choice between the two types of specimen was to be decided by the constable making the requirement. The appellant had no right to express any preference and thus a constable was not obliged to inform him that he was required to give blood or urine. It was sufficient for the constable simply to require the appellant to provide a specimen of blood. Accordingly, the appeal would be dismissed.

Simpson v McClory 1993 SLT 861 (High Court of Justiciary). *McLeod v MacFarlane* 1993 SLT 782 supra and *DPP v Warren* [1992] 3 WLR 884, HL (1992 Abr para 2189) followed.

2187 Driving at excessive speed—speed measuring devices

The defendant was served by the prosecution with a speeding report and witness statement that his speed had been checked by a police officer using a radar gun. His solicitor, doubting the accuracy of the measurements, sought unsuccessfully to obtain from the prosecution relevant information on the radar gun. The defendant submitted there was no case to answer as no evidence had been given by the police officer that the radar gun was an approved device as certified by the Home Secretary and therefore the evidence of speed measurement was inadmissible on the basis of the Road Traffic Offenders Act 1988, s 20. On appeal against conviction, *held*, the prosecution was required to prove that the Home Secretary had approved the use of the radar gun before the measurement of speed could be admitted in evidence. The approval was to be established by the production of the necessary schedule or by the police officer giving evidence that the device used was an approved one and without that material the conviction could not be sustained. Accordingly, the appeal would be allowed. *Roberts v DPP* [1994] RTR 31 (Queen's Bench Division: Stuart-Smith LJ and Judge J).

The Road Traffic Offenders (Prescribed Devices) Order 1993, SI 1993/1698 (in force on 9 August 1993), prescribes (1) a device designed or adapted for recording a measurement of the speed of motor vehicles activated by means of sensors or cables on or near the surface of the highway, and (2) a device designed or adapted for recording a measurement of the speed of motor vehicles activated by means of a light beam or beams, as speed detection devices for the purposes of the Road Traffic Offenders Act 1988, s 20.

2188 Driving instructors—registration—fees

See para 2561.

2189 Driving licence—disability—erroneous interpretation of the law

When vocational and ordinary driving licences were replaced by a unified driving licence (in implementation of Council Directive (EC) 80/1263), a drafting error in the regulations resulted in more lenient criteria being applied for visual acuity for holders of driving licences permitted to drive heavy goods vehicles and public service vehicles than was intended. The regulations provided a standard below which a driver was prevented from holding a licence by reference to three criteria (visual acuity in the better eye (with corrective lenses if necessary), and that in the worse eye (again with corrective lenses if necessary) and the uncorrected acuity in each eye). In fact, the three criteria had been intended to be alternatives, the intended standard being more stringent. Drivers who had previously held a vocational driving licence were permitted to continue to hold such by reference to the standards previously applicable, provided that their eyesight had not subsequently deteriorated to the extent of becoming a prescribed disability.

In practice, the officers within the Driver and Vehicle Licensing Agency ("the DVLA") handling applications for vocational driving entitlement applied the standards which it had been intended to enact in the regulations. In the course of so doing and in response to an inquiry regarding a driver who had held a licence to drive heavy goods vehicles for a number of years, the DVLA advised the driver's employer that the driver did not meet the required eyesight standards and recommended that he was unfit to hold a licence permitting him to drive heavy goods vehicles. The employer expressed surprise and pointed out that the driver's career was at stake. On 12 July 1991, the DVLA stated that it had no alternative but to revoke the driver's licence so far as it related to heavy goods vehicles. The driver was subsequently dismissed after some 20 years' employment.

Earlier in July 1991, however, doubt had been cast on the DVLA's interpretation of the regulations. It had been suggested that the effect of the eyesight test as enacted was cumulative and that a driver could only be said to suffer from a prescribed disability if he failed all three criteria. On 30 July 1991, the DVLA deferred processing applications which they would hitherto have refused on eyesight grounds, and on 5 August the processing of the deferred applications was resumed in the light of the actual legal requirements. As a result of the DVLA's heavy workload, there was considerable delay in reviewing the cases of persons who had been adversely affected by the erroneous interpretation of the regulations.

The driver's case was referred to the Parliamentary Commissioner for Administration. He criticised both the basic drafting errors in the regulations and the DVLA for failing to ensure that their instructions to staff corresponded to the regulations as enacted. The DVLA's letter to the driver's employer referring to the revocation of his licence would not have been sent had the DVLA acted more promptly when a serious doubt was cast on their interpretation of the regulations. The commissioner expressed the strongest criticism of the DVLA's failure to take prompt action to correct their earlier error in revoking the driver's licence and in failing to act more promptly in respect of other persons who had been similarly adversely affected. The DVLA has undertaken to pay suitable compensation to the driver and to contact all other persons adversely affected to ascertain whether they also have suffered ascertainable losses.

Decision on Loss of Employment caused by Mistaken Revocation of a Licence to Drive a Heavy Goods Vehicle, Parliamentary Commissioner for Administration (HC 13).

2190 Driving licence—fees

The Motor Vehicles (Driving Licences) (Amendment) Regulations 1993, SI 1993/1602 (in force on 16 July 1993), further amend the 1987 Regulations, SI 1987/1378, by (1) increasing from one year to five years the period of normal residence in Great Britain or the United Kingdom during which the holder of an exchangeable licence is eligible for the grant of a licence under the Road Traffic Act 1988, Pt III (ss 87–109); (2) increasing the fee for an ordinary test taken before 4.30 pm on a weekday in the case of a test of competence to drive a motor vehicle other than a motorcycle or a moped from £23·50 to £26; (3) increasing the fee for an ordinary test taken at or after 4.30 pm on a weekday from £44 to £45 in the case of a test of competence to drive a motorcycle or a moped, and from £35 to £36 in the case of any other test; (4) increasing the fee for an ordinary test taken on a Saturday from £44 to £45 in the case of a test of competence to drive a motorcycle or a moped, and from £35 to £36 in the case of any other test; (5) increasing the fee for an extended driving test taken on a weekday in the case of a test of competence to drive a motor vehicle other than a motorcycle or a moped from £47 to £48·50; (6) increasing the fee for an extended driving test taken on a Saturday from £90 to £92 in the case of a test of competence to drive a motorcycle or a moped, and from £75 to £77·50 in the case of any other test; and (7) increasing the fee for a test to drive a London cab from £23·50 to £26.

2191   Driving whilst unfit through drink or drugs—driving on road or other public place—meaning of "public place"—club car park

The appellant had been convicted of being in charge of a motor vehicle on a road or other public place whilst unfit through drink or drugs contrary to the Road Traffic Act 1988, s 4. The car was parked in the car park of a community centre, and the car park was accessible to the public. To use the facilities of the centre one had to become a member, which involved being nominated by an existing member. The magistrates concluded that the appellant's membership of the club did not distinguish him in any way from members of the public in the area. The question arose as to whether the magistrates had failed to consider if the car park had in fact been used by members of the public at any time. It was argued that the magistrates had been wrong in their conclusion that members of the club and the general public were in the same position. On appeal, *held*, the appellant had used the car park as a member of a club and the club was not so large that it could not be distinguished from the general public in the area. A member of a bona-fide club used a club car park as part of his membership and not in his capacity as a member of the public. Accordingly the appeal would be allowed.

    Havell v DPP [1993] Crim LR 621 (Queen's Bench Division: Rose LJ and Waller J). *DPP V Vivier* [1991] RTR 205 DC, (1991 Abr para 2082) considered.

2192   Goods vehicles—drivers' hours—calculation of driving and rest periods

See *Criminal proceedings against Charlton*, para 2732.

2193   Goods vehicles—operator's licence—fees

The Goods Vehicles (Operators' Licences, Qualifications and Fees) (Amendment) Regulations 1993, SI 1993/301 (in force on 1 April 1993), further amend the 1984 Regulations, SI 1984/176, by increasing the fee for the grant or variation of a goods vehicle operator's licence from £70 to £170.

2194   Goods vehicles—operator's licence—temporary use in Great Britain

The Goods Vehicles (Operators' Licences) (Temporary Use in Great Britain) (Amendment) Regulations 1993, SI 1993/1416 (in force on 1 July 1993), further amend the 1980 Regulations, SI 1980/637, so as to extend the definition of "combined transport", in the provision relating to exemptions for Northern Ireland or foreign goods between member states, to include journeys made partly by road and partly by sea.

The Goods Vehicles (Operators' Licences) (Temporary Use in Great Britain) (Amendment) (No 2) Regulations 1993, SI 1993/2120 (in force on 28 September 1993), further amend the 1980 Regulations supra by modifying the Transport Act 1968, Pt V (ss 59–94), so as to exempt the operator of any Albanian goods vehicle from the need to obtain an operator's licence in order to carry goods in Great Britain on an international journey.

2195   Goods vehicles—operator's licence—unlicenced use—tractor used for towing

The Transport Act 1968, s 60(1) provides that no person may use a goods vehicle on a road for the carriage of goods for hire or reward or for or in connection with trade or business carried on by him, unless he has an operator's license. "Goods" are defined in the Act as goods or burden of any description. The Vehicles (Excise) Act 1971, s 8(1) provides that excise duty is payable on any mechanically propelled vehicle which is not exempt. A vehicle used for the conveyance of goods or burden but not for hire or reward or in connection with a trade or business is one of the exemptions under the Act.

The defendant repaired and tested trailers which he towed with a tractor unit for which he did not have an operator's or excise license. He was prosecuted under the 1968 and 1971 Acts but contended that the trailers did not constitute goods under the 1968 Act and that the tractor unit was not being used for the conveyance of goods or burden for hire or reward or for or in connection with a trade or business under the 1971 Act. He was found guilty at first instance and appealed. *Held*, whether the trailers were goods or not under the 1968 Act was a question of fact to be determined by the justices at first instance. Their finding could not be challenged unless it was perverse. In this case, their finding had clearly not been perverse and would therefore stand. The same principle applied to their finding in relation to the 1971 Act. Accordingly, the appeal would be dismissed.

Booth v DPP [1993] RTR 379 (Queen's Bench Division: Watkins LJ and Laws J).

2196 Goods vehicles—plating and testing

The Goods Vehicles (Plating and Testing) (Amendment) Regulations 1993, SI 1993/2048 (in force on 1 October 1993), further amend the 1988 Regulations, SI 1988/1478. The regulations provide, in particular, that (1) an examiner is not required to accept a vehicle for examination if it or any motor vehicle accompanying it emits substantial quantities of avoidable smoke; (2) the fee for a retest is less than the fee for a first examination or periodical test in some circumstances and free in certain other circumstances regardless of whether the vehicle is submitted to the testing station which carried out the first examination or periodical test; (3) provisions relating to the maintenance of speedometers, requiring certain goods vehicles to be fitted with speed limiters and to have a plate in the cab giving certain particulars relating to the limiter fitted to the vehicle are now prescribed statutory requirements; (4) provisions relating to front retro-reflectors on trailers, hazard warning signal devices, front position lamps on trailers and rear registration plate lamps are now prescribed construction and use requirements; and (5) there is no longer a right of appeal to the area mechanical engineer, appeals now lying direct to the Secretary of State.

The Goods Vehicles (Plating and Testing) (Amendment) (No 2) Regulations 1993, SI 1993/3013 (in force on 2 January 1994), further amend the 1988 Regulations supra by (1) reducing the fee payable on an application for a first examination or periodical test in the case of a motor vehicle with two axles, from £34·70 to £32·70, and in the case of a motor vehicle with three axles, from £34·70 to £33·70. The fee on an application for such an examination or test in the case of a motor vehicle with four or more axles remains at £34·70; (2) reducing the fee payable on an application for a first examination or periodical test in the case of a trailer with one axle, from £17·90 to £16·70, and in the case of a trailer with two axles, from £17·90 to £17·10. The fee on an application for such an examination or test in the case of a trailer with three or more axles remains at £17·90; (3) reducing the fee payable for a re-test or further re-test within 14 days after the examination or earlier re-test from £17·60 to £16·60 in the case of a motor vehicle and from £9·70 to £8·30 in the case of a trailer; (4) reducing the fee payable for re-tests in circumstances other than those referred to in (3) supra, as in (1) supra; (5) reducing the fee payable on a request for an amendment to a plating certificate following a notifiable alteration or for a re-examination where a particular in the certificate is or may be no longer applicable from £13·90 to £13·50. The regulations also amend the provision for counting the number of axles of a vehicle.

2197 Goods vehicles—training of drivers—carriage of dangerous goods by road

The Road Traffic (Training of Drivers of Vehicles Carrying Dangerous Goods) (Amendment) Regulations 1993, SI 1993/1122 (in force on 30 July 1993), amend the 1992 Regulations, SI 1992/744, by requiring drivers of certain road tankers carrying radioactive material to possess the certificate of driving training which is required on vocational training for certain drivers of vehicles carrying dangerous goods by road.

See also para 1360.

2198 Goods vehicles—type approval

The International Transport of Goods under Cover of TIR Carnets (Fees) (Amendment) Regulations 1993, SI 1993/3068 (in force on 2 January 1993), further amend the 1988

Regulations, SI 1988/371, by reducing (1) from £68·40 to £64·60 the fee for an inspection of a vehicle design-type in connection with the grant of TIR design-type approval where the inspection is of a design-type which is a variation of a design-type for which a TIR design-type approval has been granted and from £419·30 to £396·20 the fee for such an inspection in any other case; (2) from £6 to £5·70 the fee for the issue of a TIR vehicle approval certificate for a vehicle which is of a design-type for which TIR design-type approval has been granted and from £6 to £5·70 the fee for the issue of a duplicate of such certificate; and (3) from £46·30 to £43·70 the fee for an inspection of a TIR vehicle approval certificate where the inspection is carried out following refusal of such a certificate for the vehicle and from £66·20 to £62·60 the fee for such inspection in any other case.

2199 Goods vehicles—vehicle excise duty—simplification of goods vehicles rates
See para 868.

2200 Motor insurance
See INSURANCE.

2201 Motor vehicles—approval marks
The Motor Vehicles (Designation of Approval Marks) (Amendment) Regulations 1993, SI 1993/1710 (in force on 10 August 1993), further amend the 1979 Regulations, SI 1979/1088, by prescribing new markings relating to motor vehicles approved in respect of safety-belt anchorages.

2202 Motor vehicles—competitions and trials
The Motor Vehicles (Competitions and Trials) (Amendment) Regulations 1993, SI 1993/2233 (in force on 11 October 1993), further amend the 1969 Regulations, SI 1969/414, by making provision for the authorisation of competitions or trials involving the use of motor vehicles on highways whose route mileage does not exceed ten miles. The fees payable for such events are prescribed and are less than those for events the route mileage of which exceeds ten miles, which are increased. The regulations also amend the standard conditions for events and the Schedule of specified events.

2203 Motor vehicles—removal and disposal
The Removal and Disposal of Vehicles (Amendment) Regulations 1993, SI 1993/278 (in force on 1 June 1993), amend the 1986 Regulations, SI 1986/183, so as to empower a traffic warden to remove or arrange for the removal of a vehicle parked or broken down in a road if it is causing an obstruction, is likely to cause danger to road users, or an offence is being committed under certain enactments by or under which prohibitions or restrictions on the waiting of vehicles on roads are imposed.

The Removal and Disposal of Vehicles (Amendment) (No 2) Regulations 1993, SI 1993/1475 (in force on 5 July 1993), further amend the 1986 Regulations supra, so as to empower a parking attendant to remove or arrange for the removal of a vehicle parked in a designated parking place in Greater London in contravention of a prohibition or restriction.

The Removal and Disposal of Vehicles (Amendment) (No 3) Regulations 1993, SI 1993/1708 (in force on 12 July 1993), is made as a consequence of a defect in SI 1993/1475 supra which it re-enacts with modifications.

2204 Motor vehicles—removal, storage and disposal—sums and charges
The Removal, Storage and Disposal of Vehicles (Prescribed Sums and Charges etc) (Amendment) Regulations 1993, SI 1993/550 (in force on 12 April 1993), further amend the 1989 Regulations, SI 1989/744, by increasing from £95 to £105 the sum or charge payable in respect of the removal by the police or a local authority of vehicles found outside Greater London. SI 1992/385 is revoked.

The Removal, Storage and Disposal of Vehicles (Prescribed Sums and Charges etc) (Amendment) (No 2) Regulations 1993, SI 1993/1415 (in force on 5 July 1993), further amend the 1989

Regulations supra, so as to extend the sum or charge payable in respect of the removal of a vehicle by the police or a local authority to vehicles found inside Greater London.

2205 Motor vehicles—seat belts—definition of seat belt

The Road Vehicles (Construction and Use) Regulations 1986, SI 1986/1078, reg 47 defines a seat belt as "a belt intended to be worn by a person in a vehicle and designed to prevent or lessen injury to its wearer in the event of an accident to the vehicle.

The defendant was stopped by a policeman for not wearing a seat belt in contravention of the Motor Vehicles (Wearing of Seat Belts) Regulations 1982, SI 1982/1203, reg 4. He had been using a clip which was designed and manufactured specifically to allow the belt to be worn loosely. The prosecution contended that, unless the belt was worn in such a way that would "prevent or lessen injury to its wearer in the event of an accident", it was not a seat belt for the purposes of the regulations and therefore the defendant could not be said to have been wearing a seat belt. The court at first instance declared that there was insufficient evidence to show that the clip would prevent the seat belt from preventing or lessening injury and therefore found for the defendant. On appeal by way of case stated, *held*, no point of law arose from the case. It was essentially a matter of fact whether, in an individual instance, a seat belt as adapted would not prevent or lessen injury to its wearer. It was for the justices to decide, which they had done in favour of the defendant. Accordingly, the appeal would be dismissed.

DPP v Shaw (1993) 157 JP 1035 (Queen's Bench Division: McCowan LJ and Popplewell J).

1982 Regulations replaced by Motor Vehicles (Wearing of Seat Belts) Regulations 1993, SI 1993/176, para 2206.

2206 Motor vehicles—seat belts—wearing of seat belts

The Motor Vehicles (Wearing of Seat Belts) Regulations 1993, SI 1993/176 (in force on 2 February 1993), which replace the 1982 Regulations, SI 1982/1203, the 1989 Regulations, SI 1989/1219 and the 1991 Regulations, SI 1991/1255, provide for the wearing of seat belts in the front or rear of motor vehicles by adults and for the wearing of seat belts and other restraints by children in the rear of motor vehicles. The requirement that a person driving, or riding in a front seat of, a motor vehicle, or that a person riding in a rear seat of a motor car or a passenger car which is not a motor car, wear an adult belt does not apply if the driver's seat is not provided with an adult belt or if an adult belt is not available in the front or rear of the vehicle as the case may be. The description of seat belt that must be worn if available now includes belts approved by other member states. A medical certificate, which includes a certificate issued under the law of another member state, issued on or after 1 January 1995 stating that it is inadvisable on medical grounds for a person to wear a seat belt will have to state its period of validity and bear a specified symbol. The exemptions in respect of emergency vehicles and persons in lawful custody have been extended. A small child (ie a child aged under 12 years and under 150 centimetres in height) in the rear of a vehicle is now required to wear a suitable child restraint if one is available or, if one is not available, a small child over three years of age must wear an adult belt if one is available. Provision is also made in respect of restraints approved by, and medical certificates issued under the law of, other member states.

The Motor Vehicles (Wearing of Seat Belts by Children in Front Seats) Regulations 1993, SI 1993/31 (in force on 2 February 1993), replace the 1982 Regulations, SI 1982/1342, so that it is now unlawful to drive a vehicle with a small child (see supra) in the front unless he is wearing a suitable restraint. It is an offence to drive a vehicle with a large child (ie a person under 14 years of age who is not a small child) in the front without a seat belt if a child restraint or an adult belt is available in the front of the vehicle. A medical certificate, which now includes a certificate issued under the law of another member state, issued on or after 1 January 1995 stating that it is inadvisable on medical grounds for a person to wear a seat belt will have to state its period of validity and bear a specified symbol.

2207 Motor vehicles—tests

The Motor Vehicles (Tests) (Amendment) Regulations 1993, SI 1993/3011 (in force on 2 January 1994), further amend the 1981 Regulations, SI 1981/1694, by (1) increasing from £10·35 to £10·80 the fee payable for the test examination of a motor bicycle without a side car; (2) increasing from £17·30 to £18·20 the fee payable for the test examination of a motor bicycle with a side car; (3) increasing from £20·30 to £21·30 the fee payable for the test examination of a vehicle in Class III; (4) increasing from £24 to £25·30 the fee payable for the test examination of a vehicle in Class IV; (5) increasing from £30·35 to £32 the fee payable for the test examination of a vehicle in Class V; (6) increasing from £26·50 to £27·94 the fee payable for the test examination of a vehicle in Class VII; (7) increasing the fees payable, in the case of vehicles other than those in Class VI, on an appeal, where a notice of the refusal of a test certificate has been issued and the fees payable for a duplicate test certificate; (8) reducing the fee payable for an examination of a vehicle constructed or adapted to carry more than 12 passengers from £42·70 to £40·30 but the supplement for such an examination, at the applicant's request, on a Saturday, remains at £27·50; (9) reducing the fee payable for a re-examination of such a vehicle within 14 days of the date of the issue of the notice of refusal of a test certificate from £21 to £19·80 but the supplement for such an examination, at the applicant's request, on a Saturday, remains at £13·75; (10) reducing the fee payable for the re-examination of such a vehicle within 14 days from the issue of the notice of refusal from £42·70 to £40·30 but the supplement for such an examination, at the applicant's request, on a Saturday, remains at £27·50; (11) reducing the fee payable for an examination of a vehicle in any other case from £29·80 to £28·20 but the supplement for such an examination, at the applicant's request, on a Saturday, remains at £20; (12) reducing the fee payable for a re-examination of such a vehicle within 14 days of the date of the issue of the notice of refusal of a test certificate from £14·90 to £14·10 but the supplement for such a re-examination, at the applicant's request, on a Saturday, remains at £10; (13) reducing the fee payable for a re-examination of such a vehicle later than 14 days from the date of the issue of the notice of refusal from £29·80 to £28·20 but the supplement for such a re-examination, at the applicant's request, on a Saturday, remains at £20; (14) reducing the fee payable for the supply of 100 forms of test certificate from £36 to £27; and (15) increasing the fees payable, in the case of Class VI vehicles, on an appeal, where a notice of the refusal of a test certificate has been issued and the fees payable for a duplicate test certificate.

2208   Motor vehicles—type approval—alternative requirements

The Motor Vehicles (Type Approval) (Great Britain) (Amendment) Regulations 1993, SI 1993/2201 (in force on 1 October 1993), further amend the 1984 Regulations, SI 1984/981, by applying the type approval requirements concerning exhaust emissions to any vehicle, whenever manufactured, except one with fewer than four wheels or one fuelled solely by liquid petroleum gas; and revising the type approval requirements concerning exhaust emissions, rear view mirrors, brakes, noise, seats and anchorages.

The Motor Vehicles (EC Type Approval) (Amendment) Regulations 1993, SI 1993/1221 (in force on 1 June 1993), amend the 1992 Regulations, SI 1992/3107, so as to implement changes made by certain Community provisions in respect of the permissible sound level and exhaust systems of motor vehicles and the external projections forward of the cab's rear position panel of motor vehicles of category N.

The Motor Vehicles (EC Type Approval) (Amendment) (No 2) Regulations 1993, SI 1993/2198 (in force on 1 October 1993), further amend the 1992 Regulations supra so as to implement changes made by Community provisions in respect of the measures to be taken against air pollution by emissions from motor vehicles.

The Motor Vehicles (Type Approval for Goods Vehicles) (Great Britain) (Amendment) Regulations 1993, SI 1993/2200 (in force on 1 October 1993), further amend the 1982 Regulations, SI 1982/1271, by making it clear that type approval requirements apply to vehicles until they are registered under the Vehicles (Excise) Act 1971; applying the type approval requirements concerning exhaust emissions to any vehicle, whenever manufactured, except one with fewer than four wheels or one fuelled solely by liquid petroleum gas; and revising the type approval requirements concerning exhaust emissions, brakes and noise.

2209   Motor vehicles—type approval—fees

The Motor Vehicles (Type Approval and Approval Marks) (Fees) Regulations 1993, SI 1993/630 (in force on 6 April 1993), replace the 1992 Regulations, SI 1992/489. The principal changes relate to (1) the fee amounts and the inclusion of fees in connection with activities related to the examination, and issue of certificates, for European whole vehicle type approval and low volume type approval; (2) the introduction of fees for the consideration of certain changes in detail to vehicles issued with national type approval certificates; (3) the introduction of an hourly fee for examination of premises with a view to them being approved for the purposes of carrying out examinations in accordance with a type approval scheme, or a Community instrument or Regulation; (4) the introduction of an hourly fee for advising a manufacturer whether his arrangements for securing conformity of production are likely to be accepted by the Secretary of State; and (5) the introduction of fees in respect of motorcycle and moped exhaust emissions, motorcycle brakes, steering of goods vehicles, identification of motorcycle controls, measurement of maximum speed limiters, and vehicle masses.

The Motor Vehicles (Type Approval and Approval Marks) (Fees) (Amendment) Regulations 1993, SI 1993/2903 (in force on 20 December 1993), amends a drafting error in SI 1993/630 supra.

2210   Motor vehicles—tyres—safety

The Motor Vehicles Tyres (Safety) (Amendment) Regulations 1993, SI 1993/2877 (in force on 31 December 1993), further amend the 1984 Regulations, SI 1984/1233, by (1) specifying which retreaded tyres may be supplied; (2) making provision for retreaded tyres which satisfy the requirements of, or are recognised by, other member states of the European Community; and (3) providing that the exemption for used retreaded tyres no longer depends on a tyre being marked.

2211   Parking penalties—enforcement

See para 636.

2212   Parking places—London—parking adjudicators

The Road Traffic (Parking Adjudicators) (London) Regulations 1993, SI 1993/1202 (in force on 1 July 1993), prescribe the procedure to be followed in relation to proceedings before parking adjudicators appointed under the Road Traffic Act 1991, s 73.

2213   Parking places—London—parking attendants—wearing of uniforms

The Parking Attendants (Wearing of Uniforms) (London) Regulations 1993, SI 1993/1450 (in force on 5 July 1993), prescribe functions under the Road Traffic Regulation Act 1984, s 99 (removal of vehicles illegally, obstructively or dangerously parked, or abandoned or broken down), and the Road Traffic Act 1991, ss 66(1) (fixing of penalty charge notice to a stationary vehicle in a designated parking place in London, or giving such a notice to a person appearing to be in charge of a vehicle), 69 (immobilisation of vehicles in parking places in London), and 77(4) (fixing of immobilisation device to a stationary vehicle in a special parking place in London) for the purposes of the 1984 Act, s 63A(4), which provides that parking attendants in Greater London must wear such uniform as the Secretary of State may determine when exercising prescribed functions, and must not exercise any of those functions when not in uniform.

2214   Parking places—London—road traffic debts—enforcement

The Enforcement of Road Traffic Debts Order 1993, SI 1993/2073 (in force on 1 September 1993), specifies (1) parking charges payable under the Road Traffic Act 1991, Sch 6, and (2) certain sums awarded as costs by a parking adjudicator on adjudications under that Act, as debts the payment of which may be enforced by bailiffs certificated in accordance with the Enforcement of Road Traffic Debts (Certificated Bailiffs) Regulations 1993 infra. The regulations also specify the requirements which must be satisfied before payment may be enforced by execution against goods and by other means. A number of provisions of the County Courts Act 1984 are modified in relation to the enforcement of specified debts by certificated bailiffs.

The Enforcement of Road Traffic Debts (Certificated Bailiffs) Regulations 1993, SI 1993/2072 (in force on 1 September 1993), apply the Distress for Rent Rules 1988, SI 1988/2050, with modifications, for the purposes of the certification of bailiffs under the Road Traffic Act 1991, s 78, by virtue of which certain road traffic debts may be enforced by certificated bailiffs. The regulations also provide for the fees to be charged by them.

2215   Parking places—power to provide parking places

See *Vickers v Dover District Council*, para 521.

2216   Passenger and goods vehicles

See TRANSPORT.

2217 Public service vehicles

See TRANSPORT.

2218 Reckless driving—causing death by reckless driving—alternative verdict

See *R v Hammett*, para 786.

2219 Registration marks—retention

The Retention of Registration Marks Regulations 1992 (Amendment) Regulations 1993, SI 1993/988 (in force on 1 May 1993), amend the 1992 Regulations, SI 1992/510, for the purpose of applying them in respect of applications, made before 1 May 1993, for the grant of a right of retention of a registration mark.

The Retention of Registration Marks Regulations 1993, SI 1993/987 (in force on 1 May 1993), replace the provisions contained in the 1992 Regulations supra for applications, made on or after 1 May 1993, for the grant of a right of retention of a registration mark and provide (1) for a person in whose name a vehicle is registered to be granted a right to have the registration mark for the time being assigned to the vehicle assigned to another vehicle, being a vehicle registered either in that person's name or in the name of some other person nominated by him; (2) for a fee, payable on application, for the grant of a right of retention of £25 and a sum equal to the amount of the charge which could have been made under the Finance Act 1976, s 12(1) on the assignment of a mark; (3) for a refund of the fee to be made where a right of retention is revoked or the period in which the right could have been exercised has expired; and (4) for the extension, on one or more occasions and on payment of the prescribed fee of £25, of the period of one year from the date on which the retention document is issued in which the right of retention may be exercised.

2220 Registration marks—sale

The Sale of Registration Marks (Amendment) Regulations 1993, SI 1993/986 (in force on 1 May 1993), amend the 1989 Regulations, SI 1989/1938, by setting out a new scheme, which replaces the existing scheme in respect of applications made after 1 May 1993, for the sale of registration marks. Under the new scheme, (1) a sum will be payable, in addition to the purchase price of a relevant right, when the agreement to purchase such right is made instead of at the time when the registration mark is assigned to the vehicle; (2) if a relevant right is revoked by the Secretary of State, or if the time in which it could have been exercised has expired, a refund may be made; (3) the period of one year from the date on which the certificate of entitlement of the right is issued in which a relevant right may be exercised may be extended on one or more occasions; and (4) on an application for an extension, the prescribed fee of £25 may be retained whether or not the application is granted.

2221 Road Traffic Act 1991—commencement

The Road Traffic Act 1991 (Commencement No 6 and Transitional Provisions) Order 1993, SI 1993/1461, as amended by SI 1993/1686, 2229, brings into force on 5 July 1993 ss 41, 42 (variation of charges at off-street parking places and at designated parking places), 66(7) (parking penalties), 70–72 (exemptions from immobilisation of vehicles in parking places, representations in relation to removal or immobilisation of vehicles, appeals to parking adjudicator), 79 (application to Crown and visiting forces), 83, Schs 6 (parking penalties), 8 (certain repeals). It also brings into force on that date in respect of the London borough of Wandsworth only ss 64, so far as it is not already in force (charges at designated parking places), 65 (contravention of certain orders relating to parking places), 66, so far as it is not already in force (parking penalties in London), 69 (immobilisation of vehicles in parking places), 81 (minor and consequential amendments), Sch 7, para 5, so far as it is not already in force (amendment to Road Traffic Regulation Act 1984, s 55). Sections 67, 68 (recovery of vehicles or of proceeds of disposal, charges for removal, storage and disposal of vehicles) are also brought into force on the same date to a limited extent. Transitional provision is also made.

The Road Traffic Act 1991 (Commencement No 7 and Transitional Provisions) Order 1993, SI 1993/2229, amends the 1993 Order, SI 1993/1461, and brings into force on 4 October 1993 in respect of the London boroughs of Bromley, Hammersmith and Fulham and Lewisham, ss 64, so far as not already in force (charges at designated parking places), 65 (contravention of certain orders relating to parking places), 66, so far as not already in force (parking penalties in

London), 69 (immobilisation of vehicles in parking places), 81, Sch 7, para 5, so far as not already in force (amendment to Road Traffic Regulation Act 1984, s 55). On the same date, ss 67(4), (6), for the purpose of their application to vehicles found in those boroughs, 68(2)(b), for the purpose of its application in relation to the councils of those boroughs (recovery of vehicles or of proceeds of disposal, charges for removal, storage and disposal of vehicles) are also brought into force. Transitional provision is also made.

The Road Traffic Act 1991 (Commencement No 8 and Transitional Provisions) Order 1993, SI 1993/2803, brings into force on 6 December 1993 in respect of the London boroughs of Camden, Hackney and Hounslow, ss 64, so far as not already in force, 65, 66, so far as not already in force, 69, 81, Sch 7, para 5, so far as not already in force. On the same date, s 67(4), (6), for the purpose of their application to vehicles found in those boroughs, and s 68(2)(b), for the purpose of its application in relation to the councils of those boroughs (recovery of vehicles or of proceeds of disposal, charges for removal, storage and disposal of vehicles) are also brought into force. Transitional provision is also made.

The Road Traffic Act 1991 (Commencement No 9 and Transitional Provisions) Order 1993, SI 1993/3238, brings into force on 31 January 1994 in respect of the London boroughs of Richmond upon Thames and Southwark, ss 64, so far as not already in force, 65, 66, so far as not already in force, 69, 81, Sch 7, para 5, so far as not already in force. On the same date, s 67(4), (6), for the purpose of their application to vehicles found in those boroughs, and s 68(2)(b), for the purpose of its application in relation to the councils of those boroughs are also brought into force. Transitional provision is also made.

For a summary of the Act, see 1991 Abr para 2113. For details of commencement, see the commencement table in the title STATUTES.

2222 Road Traffic (Driving Instruction by Disabled Persons) Act 1993

The Road Traffic (Driving Instruction by Disabled Persons) Act 1993 makes provision for enabling persons with certain physical disabilities to be authorised, in certain circumstances, to give paid instruction in the driving of motor cars. The Act received the royal assent on 20 July 1993 and comes into force on a day to be appointed.

Section 1 amends the Road Traffic Act 1988 by adding new sections 125A, 125B which provide for the registration of disabled persons as driving instructors. Section 2 amends the 1988 Act, s 129 to provide for the grant of licences allowing disabled persons to give instruction so as to obtain practical experience. New sections 133A–133D are added to the 1988 Act by the 1993 Act, s 3–5, to provide for the assessment of a disabled person's ability to control a motor car in an emergency and to provide for the creation of offences; there is a duty to disclose further disability. Section 6 and the Schedule make consequential amendments and s 7 deals with short title, commencement and extent.

2223 Road traffic offences—sentencing

See SENTENCING.

2224 Road vehicles—construction and use—regulations

The Road Vehicles (Construction and Use) (Amendment) (No 1) Regulations 1993, SI 1993/1946 (in force on 1 September 1993), further amend the 1986 Regulations, SI 1986/1078, by making provision for the fitment of speed limiters to coaches, buses and goods vehicles and for the fitment of a plate which gives information about the speed limiter fitted to any such vehicle.

The Road Vehicles (Construction and Use) (Amendment) (No 2) Regulations 1993, SI 1993/2199 (in force on 1 October 1993), further amend the 1986 Regulations supra by introducing compulsory compliance with the limits on emissions from light-duty vehicles first used before 1 October 1994 specified by Council Directive (EC) 93/59; providing for such vehicles used before that date and other vehicles whenever first used to comply with those limits as an alternative to existing requirements; and providing for vehicles required to comply with various Council Directives to comply with equivalent Community Regulations as an alternative to the Directives.

The Road Vehicles (Construction and Use) (Amendment) (No 3) Regulations 1993, SI 1993/3048 (in force on 1 January 1994), further amend the 1986 Regulations by re-enacting in similar terms the regulations introduced by SI 1993/1946 in order to make it clear that a speed limiter meets the prescribed requirements if it is calibrated to a set speed below 70 mph instead of at a set speed of 70 mph.

2225 Road vehicles—registration and licensing

The Road Vehicles (Registration and Licensing) (Amendment) Regulations 1993, SI 1993/1760 (in force on 9 August 1993), further amend the 1971 Regulations, SI 1971/450, by increasing the fee for the issue of a duplicate licence from £3·50 to £5·50.

2226 Speed limits—principal roads

The Road Traffic Regulation Act 1984 (Amendment) Order 1993, SI 1993/35 (in force on 23 January 1993), amends the 1984 Act, Sch 9, by removing from the orders for which the consent of the Secretary of State would otherwise be required under Sch 9, para 13 or 14 any order which contains no provision falling within Sch 9, para 13(1)(a)–(f) other than a provision (1) directing that a principal road is to be, or cease to be, a restricted road, or (2) being, in the case of an order for the purposes of s 84(1) (orders for speed limits on roads other than restricted roads), a provision applying to a principal road. Accordingly, orders imposing, varying or cancelling a speed limit on a principal road may now be made without the Secretary of State's consent.

2227 Taxi cabs

See TRANSPORT.

2228 Traffic orders—local authorities—procedure

The Local Authorities' Traffic Orders (Procedure) (England and Wales) (Amendment) Regulations 1993, SI 1993/1500 (in force on 5 July 1993), amend the 1989 Regulations, SI 1989/1120. Various changes are made, including the following: (1) the procedure whereby local authorities may vary parking charges by giving notice is prescribed; (2) following the introduction of the concept of the "traffic authority" by the New Roads and Street Works Act 1991, consequential amendments are made to the regulations; (3) amendments are made to the provisions relating to the requirement for local authorities to consult certain bodies before making an order; and (4) further exceptions are added to the consultation requirements.

2229 Traffic wardens—functions

The Functions of Traffic Wardens (Amendment) Order 1993, SI 1993/1334 (in force on 1 June 1993), amends the 1970 Order, SI 1970/1958, in order to extend the powers and functions of traffic wardens. Traffic wardens may now carry out the functions of a constable under the Road Traffic Regulation Act 1984, s 100(3) (interim disposal of removed vehicles) and may, in carrying out their functions, exercise the powers conferred on constables by the 1984 Act, ss 104, 105 (power to immobilise vehicles). They may also exercise the powers conferred on constables by the Road Traffic Act 1988, s 164(1), (2) and (6) (power to require production of driving licence and statement of date of birth) where they have reasonable cause to believe that an offence of stopping a vehicle on a pedestrian crossing in breach of pedestrian crossing regulations or of leaving a vehicle in a dangerous position has been committed. Such powers may also be exercised where a traffic warden is employed to perform custodial functions in respect of vehicles removed from a road or land in the open air in pursuance of regulations made under the 1984 Act, s 99 or from a parking place in pursuance of a street parking place order, and where he has reasonable cause to believe that an offence of obstructing a road, or certain other offences, have been committed in respect of the vehicle. The functions of wardens are further extended to include the enforcement of the law with respect to offences of stopping vehicles on pedestrian crossings in breach of pedestrian crossing regulations and the exercise of the functions of constables under the fixed penalty scheme in respect of the offences of obstructing a highway (where the offence is committed in respect of a vehicle) and leaving a vehicle in a dangerous position.

2230 Transport

See TRANSPORT.

ROYAL FORCES

Halsbury's Laws of England (4th edn) Vol 41, paras 1–600

2231 Articles
War and Order, Captain Keith Raynor (on the jurisdiction of Army courts martial): LS Gaz, 22 September 1993, p 30

2232 Army—imprisonment and detention
An officer was charged with an offence under the Official Secrets Act 1989, and held under close arrest which nearly amounted to solitary confinement. She applied for a writ of habeas corpus on the ground that there had been excessive and oppressive delay in the investigation of her case. *Held*, though there was a duty on army authorities to proceed with expedition in these matters, the investigation was long and complex, containing potentially very serious accusations. Excessive delay had not yet been demonstrated and the detention of the officer for 75 days had been lawful due to the proper investigation of the allegations made. If the matter came before the court again it would have to be satisfied that the investigations were proceeding as rapidly as could reasonably be expected. Accordingly, the application would be dismissed.
    Re Maychell (1993) Independent, 26 February (Queen's Bench Division: Kennedy LJ and Clarke J).

2233 Army, Air Force and Naval Discipline Acts—continuation
The Army, Air Force and Naval Discipline Acts (Continuation) Order 1993, SI 1993/1804 (in force on 20 July 1992), continues in force the Army Act 1955, the Air Force Act 1955 and the Naval Discipline Act 1957 until 31 August 1994.

2234 Discipline—service courts—evidence—evidence through live television link
The Criminal Justice Act 1988 (Application to Service Courts) (Evidence through Television Links) Order 1993, SI 1993/244 (in force on 8 March 1993), applies to proceedings before service courts the provisions of the Criminal Justice Act 1988, s 32(1)–(3) relating to the giving of evidence by witnesses other than the accused through live television links in certain circumstances and with appropriate modifications. Service courts are (1) courts-martial constituted under the Army Act 1955 or the Air Force Act 1955; (2) courts-martial constituted under the Naval Discipline Act 1957 and disciplinary courts constituted under the 1957 Act, s 50; (3) the Courts-Martial Appeal Court; and (4) standing civilian courts.

2235 Member of royal forces—child support maintenance—recovery
See para 374.

2236 Member of royal forces—voting at elections
See para 1121.

2237 Navy—duty of care—naval airman—drunkenness
See *Barrett v Ministry of Defence*, para 1882.

2238 Pensions
See PENSIONS AND SUPERANNUATION.

2239 Visiting forces—claim for personal injury—right of action
The Agreement regarding the Status of Forces of Parties to the North Atlantic Treaty 1951, art VIII, para 5 provides that claims arising out of acts or omissions of "members of a force or civilian component" done in performance of an official duty, for which a member of that force or a civilian attached thereto was responsible, and causing damage in the "receiving state" to "third parties other than any of the contracting parties" are to be dealt with under the laws of the receiving state and any resulting damages are to be payable by the governments of the receiving state and the visiting force.

The plaintiff, a member of the United States Air Force stationed in England, brought proceedings against the United States government and the Ministry of Defence, claiming damages for personal injuries arising out of medical treatment received at a United States military hospital. The Ministry of Defence successfully applied to have its name struck out of the writ on the ground that the 1951 Agreement did not confer a right of action on the plaintiff against the United Kingdom government. On the hearing of the plaintiff's action, it was held that the US Government was immune from suit under the 1951 Agreement. On the plaintiff's appeal, *held*, the 1951 Agreement had not been incorporated into English municipal law, and accordingly, the agreement was irrelevant to the plaintiff's claims. As a matter of first impression, it would be astonishing if the plaintiff were able, in a foreign court, to recover from the state in whose forces he served, in respect of treatment provided by that state as an adjunct to that service, compensation on a basis not sustainable in the court of that state. The nature of the treatment, the identity of those involved and the place where it was given were factors which together pointed irresistibly to the conclusion that the treatment was the exercise of sovereign, immune authority on the part of the United States government. The appeal would therefore be dismissed.

Littrell v Government of the United States of America (1993) Times, 24 November, Independent, 2 December (Court of Appeal: Nourse, Rose and Hoffmann LJJ). For earlier related proceedings, see [1992] 3 All ER 218 (1992 Abr para 2248).

SALE OF GOODS

Halsbury's Laws of England (4th edn) Vol 41, paras 601–692

2240 Articles

Feudal Hangover, Michael Nash (on market overt): 143 NLJ 592

2241 Consumer protection

See CONSUMER PROTECTION.

2242 Price marking

See CONSUMER PROTECTION.

2243 Rights of suppliers—retention of title provision—charge—registration

See *Compaq Computer Ltd v Abercorn Group Ltd*, para 467.

2244 Rights of suppliers—retention of title provision—effect of receivership

It has been held that where a supplier supplies goods on credit, which are sold subject to a retention of title provision, to a company which then goes into receivership, the suppliers will be adequately protected by an undertaking given by the administrative receivers that, should the suppliers vindicate their claim to title, the receivers should pay them the value of any goods used or sold during the receivership.

Lipe Ltd v Leyland Daf Ltd (1993) Times, 2 April (Court of Appeal: Lloyd, Kennedy and Hoffmann LJJ).

2245 Rights of suppliers—retention of title provision—product from processing

See *Modelboard Ltd v Outer Box Ltd (in liquidation)*, para 466.

2246 Unascertained goods—transfer of title—Law Commission recommendations

The Law Commission and the Scottish Law Commission have jointly published a report *Sale of Goods forming part of a Bulk* (HC 807; Law Com No 215; Scot Law Com 145). The report focuses on the rule in the Sale of Goods Act 1979, s 16 that no property in unascertained goods passes to a buyer until the goods are ascertained. Difficulties have been experienced with the present rule when, after a buyer has paid for unascertained goods and received a document of title, the seller becomes insolvent and the goods are retained for the benefit of the seller's secured creditors. The commissions recommend that property in an undivided share in bulk should pass before the goods are ascertained. The proposed rule would only apply where the contract was for the sale of a specified quantity of unascertained goods, where the goods formed part of an identified bulk and where the buyer had paid for some, at least, of the goods. If those requirements were met, the property in the goods would pass, under the proposed rule, at such time as the parties agreed; in the absence of agreement on that point, the property would pass as soon as the bulk had been identified and the price for some, at least, of the goods paid. Parties would be free to choose that the existing rule under s 16 should apply. A buyer's undivided share in the bulk, under the proposed rule, would be that proportion that the goods due bore to the total quantity in bulk, subject to a rule on ascertainment by exhaustion and a rule that the aggregate of two shares could not exceed the whole. Specific rules would be enacted in relation to consents by co-owners and liabilities inter se. A draft Bill which would implement the proposals is appended to the report.

SALE OF LAND

Halsbury's Laws of England (4th edn) Vol 42, paras 1–400

See CONVEYANCING.

SENTENCING

Halsbury's Laws of England (4th edn) Vol 11(2) (reissue), paras 1187–1351

2247 Articles

A Method of Achieving Fair Unit Fines, Bryan Gibson and Geoffrey Levy: 157 JP Jo 147
Breach, Revocation and Amendment, Alan Armbrister (on community orders): 157 JP Jo 499
Changes in Sentencing—Back to the Drawing-Board, Robert Stevens: 157 JP Jo 724
Community Service—Who Works, P Lloyd and N Perry: 157 JP Jo 794
Diversion from Custody, Phil Fennell (on alternatives to sending mentally disordered offenders into custody): LS Gaz, 30 June 1993, p 18
Health and Safety at Work—Sentencing, Alec Samuels: 157 JP Jo 763
Life Sentences: Law, Practice and Release Decisions, 1989–93, Lord Windlesham: [1993] Crim LR 644
Meaning of Life, Gregory Treverton Jones (on the mandatory life sentence): LS Gaz, 1 December 1993, p 23
Penalties for the Possession of Class B and C Drugs, JN Spencer: 157 JP Jo 451
Post Criminal Justice Act 1991—A Probation Based Initiative, Kevin Downing: 157 JP Jo 426
Problem Child, Hugh Howard (on the subtext in pre-sentence reports for juvenile crime): 138 SJ 47
'Seriousness' of the Offence, Ian McLean: 137 SJ 177
The Consequences of Re-Offending During The Currency of A Suspended Sentence: 157 JP Jo 791
The New Probation Order and Probation Help by the Back Door: 157 JP Jo 826
Unnecessary Legislative Changes, Anthea Hucklesby (on the Bail (Amendment) Bill): 137 NLJ 233
Will Johnny Be Good?—New Powers of Remand for Persistent Young Offenders, Katharine Marshall: 157 JP Jo 166

2248 Attempted unlawful sexual intercourse—unduly lenient sentence

The defendant was convicted of attempted unlawful sexual intercourse with a girl under 13 and sentenced to two years' probation. The Attorney General contended that the sentence was unduly lenient and applied for a review. *Held*, the imposition of a custodial sentence was appropriate for actual or attempted unlawful sexual intercourse with a young girl and where there was a need for deterrence. The victim, in the present case, was a nine-year-old and a probationary sentence failed to reflect the gravity of the offence. Accordingly, a four-month custodial sentence would be imposed.

A-G's Reference No 13 of 1993 (1993) Independent, 30 July (Court of Appeal: Lord Taylor of Gosforth, CJ, Alliott and Buckley JJ).

2249   Burglary—custodial sentence—previous convictions—mitigating factors

The appellant and a co-defendant had been caught by the police whilst committing a burglary. The sentencing court declared that the offence in this particular case was so serious that only a custodial sentence was justified. The appellant was therefore sentenced to twelve months' detention in a young offender institution but his co-defendant was only made subject to a community service order. On appeal against the sentence, *held*, the finding that only a custodial sentence was justified for the offence did not mean that the court could not take into account mitigating factors. The co-defendant had never been involved in any offence of burglary previously and had agreed to undertake community service if the court considered that to be appropriate. In contrast, the appellant had previous convictions for burglary and had declined to say he would be willing to do community service, expressing a preference for probation instead. The sentence in his case was therefore no longer than was appropriate for the offence. Accordingly, the appeal would be dismissed.

R v Reynolds (1993) 14 Cr App Rep (S) 694 (Court of Appeal: Beldam LJ and Schiemann J).

2250   Causing death by careless driving—sentencing guidelines—aggravating and mitigating factors

It has been held that the sentencing guidelines set out in *R v Boswell* [1984] 3 All ER 353 (1984 Abr para 2365) apply to the offence of careless driving introduced by the Road Traffic Act 1988, s 3A, as amended by the Road Traffic Act 1991, s 3. This means that the consumption of alcohol or drugs is an aggravating feature which will usually necessitate a custodial sentence, unless the alcohol level at the time of the offence is just over the borderline, the carelessness is momentary and there is strong mitigation. Normally, the severity of the sentence will depend on the number of people killed, to reflect public opinion in this regard. The Criminal Justice Act 1992, s 67 increased the maximum sentence for dangerous driving from five years to ten. In light of this, the guidelines in *R v Boswell* need to be reconsidered to the extent that drivers who drive with reckless disregard for the safety of others after taking alcohol should now expect, in bad cases, to be sentenced for upwards of five years and, in the worst cases, for a term of years in the upper range of those permitted by Parliament.

R v Shepherd (A-G's Reference (No 14 of 1993)); R v Wernet (A-G's Reference (No 24 of 1993)) (1993) Times, 27 December (Court of Appeal: Lord Taylor of Gosforth CJ, Popplewell and Scott-Baker JJ).

2251   Causing death by reckless driving and driving with excess alcohol— sentencing practice—aggravating factors

The Criminal Justice Act 1991, s 29(2) provides that where any aggravating factors of an offence are disclosed by the circumstances of other offences committed by the offender, nothing prevents the court from taking those factors into account for the purposes of forming an opinion as to the seriousness of the offence.

The offender was driving his motor cycle whilst under the influence of excess alcohol and fatally injured a police officer who was directing traffic into a lay-by. He pleaded guilty to the offence of causing death by reckless driving and was sentenced to three months' imprisonment and disqualified from driving for four years. The Attorney General applied for a review of the sentence as being unduly lenient under the Criminal Justice Act 1988, s 36. He contended that the offender's consumption of alcohol to a level which impaired his ability to drive properly and his history of previous convictions for drink-driving were aggravating features which should have been considered when determining the appropriate sentence. *Held*, the circumstances of the previous offences of driving with excess alcohol showed a determination to continue driving with excess alcohol despite past experience. That indicated a mental element of deliberation which was an aggravating factor in the present case and ought to have been considered when sentence was passed. The sentence was unduly lenient and would be varied by substituting a sentence of 18 months' imprisonment and eight years' disqualification. Accordingly, the Attorney General's application for review would be allowed.

R v Hayton [1993] RTR 310 (Court of Appeal: Lord Taylor of Gosforth CJ, Mantell and Smith JJ).

The offence of causing death by reckless driving has been replaced by the offence of causing death by dangerous driving in the Road Traffic Act 1988, s 1 as substituted by Road Traffic Act 1991, s 1.

2252 Causing death by reckless driving and driving with excess alcohol— sentencing practice—response to public concern

The appellant was convicted of causing death by dangerous driving and driving with excess alcohol. He was sentenced to three years' imprisonment and disqualified from driving for five years. On his appeal against sentence, *held*, in the light of the justified public concern in respect of the grossly anti-social conduct of persons who, having drunk to excess, drove and by reckless driving caused death, courts could be expected to respond by passing more severe sentences on such drivers. The appeal would be dismissed.

R v Craig (1993) Times, 25 May (Court of Appeal: Rose LJ and Turner J).

2253 Community service order—revocation of order—imposition of custodial sentence

The defendant pleaded guilty to burglary and was ordered to perform community service. A year later he made an application under the Powers of Criminal Courts Act 1973, s 17(2)(b) for revocation of the order on the ground that he was unable to carry out the work under the order because he was suffering from a back injury. The Crown Court revoked the order and in its place imposed a sentence of four months' imprisonment, suspended for one year. The defendant appealed against the imposition of the revised sentence. *Held*, under the 1973 Act, s 17(2)(b) the court had the power to revoke a community service order and deal with the offender in any manner in which he could have been dealt with for the offence if the order had not been made. Although the court had the power to impose a custodial sentence, it was inappropriate to do so where the defendant had been unable to carry out the sentence through no fault of his own. Accordingly, the appeal would be allowed, the suspended sentence would be revoked and in view of the lapse of time since the original order was made no further sentence would be imposed.

R v Fielding (1993) 14 Cr App Rep (S) 494 (Court of Appeal: Steyn LJ, Pill and Wright JJ).

2254 Compensation order—compensation for injury—causal connection between offence and injury

The defendant was involved in an incident in a public house in which a woman suffered injuries from being struck in the face with a glass held by the defendant. He admitted that, as he made to throw beer over the woman, her face made contact with the glass. He pleaded guilty to common assault but was acquitted of unlawful wounding. He was ordered to pay compensation of £250 to the woman. On his appeal against the compensation order, he contended that, in view of his acquittal of unlawful wounding, the court had no power to make the order. *Held*, under the Powers of Criminal Courts Act 1973, s 35, which enabled a court to order a convicted person to pay compensation for any personal injury, loss or damage resulting from the offence of which he had been convicted, there had to be some causal connection between the offence and the injury, loss or damage before the payment of compensation could be ordered. The offence need not be the sole cause of the injury etc; it would suffice if it could be fairly said that the injury resulted from the offence. The defendant's acquittal of the charge of unlawful wounding simply meant that the jury was not satisfied that the defendant had intended to harm the woman or was reckless as to whether he harmed her or not. It did not answer the question of causation which was simply whether the defendant's involuntary act of making to throw beer over the woman had resulted in the injury to her. His intention was irrelevant for this purpose. The question of causation was one for the judge who had decided that the assault had resulted in the injury in the sense that the woman would not have been struck in the face if the defendant had not made as if to throw beer over her. The compensation order was properly made and the appeal would be dismissed.

R v Corbett (1993) 14 Cr App Rep (S) 101 (Court of Appeal: Mann LJ, Phillips and Tuckey JJ).

A man unknown to the defendant bumped into her in a public house and poured beer over her. The defendant responded by throwing empty beer bottles at him. A beer bottle hit an innocent bystander, who suffered a wound to the head. The defendant was sentenced to 200 hours' community service and ordered to pay compensation to the man hit by the bottle. On appeal, *held*, the basis of the defendant's plea was that there was no causal link between her conduct in the affray and the injury actually suffered by the victim. By virtue of the Powers of Criminal Courts Act 1973, s 35, compensation could only be made the subject of an order of the court where there was a proven causal link between the offence of which the defendant was charged and the injury in respect of which the compensation order was made. There was no such proven causal link and the judge accordingly had no jurisdiction to make the order. The order would be quashed.

R v Deary (1993) 14 Cr App Rep (S) 648 (Court of Appeal: Farquharson LJ and Ognall J).

2255 Compensation order—false accounting—offence by third party

The defendant was the manager of a public house, part of whose duties included filling in the weekly takings sheet. He went to visit an ill relative without permission and on his return discovered that a large amount of the weekly takings were missing. Instead of reporting the loss to his superiors, the defendant tried to cover up the deficiency by falsifying the records. He pleaded guilty to false accounting and was sentenced to a community service order together with a compensation order for the loss suffered by his employers, the costs of his prosecution and his own legal aid contribution for his own defence. On appeal against the sentence, *held*, the loss of the employer's funds was not caused by the defendant's deception but by an unknown third party. Therefore, the compensation order for the employer's loss would be quashed. The defendant having already made some contribution to his legal aid, it was not within the power of the court to order him to make any further contribution. Accordingly, the compensation order in relation to the legal aid would also be quashed and the only order to be left standing would be that in relation to payment towards the prosecution costs.

R v Graves (1993) 14 Cr App Rep (S) 791 (Court of Appeal: Glidewell LJ and Garland J).

2256 Compensation order—means of offender—inquiries

It has been held that before a compensation order is countenanced, the court has a duty to enquire scrupulously into the existing financial position of the defendant. Such an order should not be made on the basis of pure speculation as to the defendant's future prospects.

R v Ellis (1993) Times, 26 October (Court of Appeal: McCowan LJ, Ognall and Gage JJ).

2257 Compensation order—order in addition to custodial sentence—appropriateness of order

The appellant was convicted of handling stolen goods and was sentenced to six months in a young offender institution. In addition, the court made a compensation order in favour of the victim. On appeal against the sentence, *held*, the trial judge had failed to assess the loss which actually resulted from the offence and, since a large proportion of the stolen property was recovered, a compensation order was inappropriate. Further, it was wrong in principle to have made the order because the six-month sentence was itself sufficient to mark the seriousness of the offence. Accordingly, the compensation order would be quashed and the appeal allowed to that extent.

R v Tyce (1993) Times, 15 October (Court of Appeal: Lord Taylor of Gosforth CJ, Turner and Dyson JJ).

2258 Conditional discharge—breach of conditional discharge—aggravating feature of subsequent sentence

The Criminal Justice Act 1991, s 31(2) provides that for the purposes of the Act, an offence is associated with another if the offender is convicted of it in the same proceedings in which he is convicted of the other offence, or, although convicted of it in earlier proceedings, is sentenced for it at the same time as he is sentenced for that offence.

The defendant altered names and forged signatures on her employer's cheques so as to make them payable to her. She pleaded guilty to nine counts of theft and was sentenced to 18 months' imprisonment on each count to run concurrently. Two years earlier, the defendant had been convicted of obtaining property by deception and given a conditional discharge, which was now activated. The judge decided to take the breach of the conditional discharge into account as an aggravating feature when assessing the length of the sentence that he imposed rather than imposing a separate penalty. On appeal against sentence, *held*, the Criminal Justice Act 1991, s 29 did not allow the breach of the conditional discharge to be taken into account as an aggravating feature as it limited aggravating factors to those disclosed by the circumstances of other offences committed by the offender and there was not sufficient indication of the circumstances of the previous offence before the court to enable advantage to be taken of that provision. Neither could the earlier offence be taken into account as an associated offence as the defendant had not been sentenced for it except by way of conditional discharge and it did not therefore come within the ambit of the 1991 Act, s 31(2). There were mitigating factors such as the fact that the defendant had pleaded guilty and had lost a child born to her during the time between the two trials. She was also well-educated and industrious. Accordingly, a sentence of 12 months' imprisonment would be substituted.

R v Godfrey (1993) 14 Cr App Rep (S) 804 (Court of Appeal: Lord Taylor of Gosforth CJ, Pill and Sedley JJ).

2259 Confiscation order—enforcement—designated countries and territories

The Criminal Justice Act 1988 (Designated Countries and Territories) (Amendment) Order 1993, SI 1993/1790 (in force on 30 July 1993), amends the 1991 Order, SI 1991/2873. The 1991 Order provides that the Criminal Justice Act 1988, Pt VI (confiscation of the proceeds of offences) applies to orders made by the courts of designated countries or territories for the purposes of recovering property obtained by conduct corresponding to an offence to which the 1988 Act, Pt VI applies, recovering the value of property so obtained or depriving a person of a pecuniary advantage so obtained. The 1993 Order adds Canada and India to the list of designated countries to which the 1991 Order applies.

The Criminal Justice Act 1988 (Designated Countries and Territories) (Amendment) (No 2) Order 1993, SI 1993/3147 (in force on 1 February 1994), further amends the 1991 Order supra by adding Bulgaria, Isle of Man, Netherlands and Switzerland to the list of designated countries to which the 1991 Order applies.

2260 Confiscation order—proceeds of drug trafficking—assessment of value of proceeds

The defendant, who had been convicted of a number of drug offences, sought leave to appeal against the extent of a confiscation order made against him on the ground that it was of an amount considerably greater than that claimed by the prosecution. *Held*, by virtue of the Drug Trafficking Offences Act 1986, s 1(4), once the court had determined that a defendant had benefited from drug trafficking, it had to determine in accordance with s 4 the amount to be recovered from him. Section 4(1) provided that the amount to be recovered under the order was to be the amount the court assessed to be the value of the defendant's proceeds of drug trafficking. Accordingly, the court was not merely entitled, but was bound, to reject the prosecution's suggestion that the scope of the inquiry should be restricted. The application would be refused.

R v Atkinson (1993) 14 Cr App Rep (S) 182 (Court of Appeal: Lord Taylor of Gosforth CJ, Simon Brown and Roch JJ).

The Drug Trafficking Offences Act 1986, s 2(2), (3)(a), provides that the court may, for the purposes of determining whether the defendant has benefited from drug trafficking and, if he has, of assessing the value of the proceeds make the following assumptions: that any property appearing to the court (i) to have been held by him at any time since his conviction, or (ii) to have been transferred to him at any time since the beginning of the period of six years ending when the proceedings were instituted against him, was received by him as a payment or reward in connection with his drug trafficking.

The defendant, who had been convicted of a drug trafficking offence, appealed against a confiscation order imposed under the 1986 Act and against his sentence of 12 years' imprisonment. *Held*, on a correct construction of the 1986 Act, s 2(3)(a) "appearing to the court" meant there must be prima facie evidence which entitled the judge to make the prescribed assumptions which could be rebutted by evidence called by the defendant. It was not enough that the court had some reason to suspect that the defendant had benefited from drug trafficking. On this basis the original confiscation order was quashed and a confiscation order for a lower sum substituted. The defendant was sentenced on the assumption that he was the ringleader of the conspiracy, but in fact there was someone beyond the jurisdiction who was more senior. The defendant's original sentence was therefore quashed and a sentence of ten years' imprisonment substituted. Accordingly, the appeal would be allowed.

R v Rose [1993] 2 All ER 761 (Court of Appeal: Watkins LJ, Leonard and Alliott JJ). *R v Dickens* [1990] 2 All ER 626, CA (1990 Abr para 2117) applied. Dicta of Staughton LJ in *R v Redbourne* [1993] 2 All ER 753 at 758, 759 CA (1992 Abr para 2267) doubted.

2261   Confiscation order—proceeds of drug trafficking—designated countries and territories

The Drug Trafficking Offences Act 1986 (Designated Countries and Territories) (Amendment) Order 1993, SI 1993/1792 (in force on 30 July 1993), amends the 1990 Order, SI 1990/1199, which provides that the Drug Trafficking Offences Act 1986 applies to orders made by courts in designated countries or territories for the purpose of recovering payments received in connection with drug trafficking and to proceedings which have been or are to be instituted in a designated country or territory and may result in such orders being made there. The 1993 Order adds Antigua and Barbuda, Belarus, Bulgaria, Burkina Faso, Burundi, Denmark, Fiji, Iran, Japan, Kenya, Luxembourg, Morocco, Niger, Panamá, Romania, the Russian Federation, Slovenia, South Africa, Suriname and Ukraine to the list of designated countries, and removes Hungary and the Union of Soviet Socialist Republics (including the Byelorussian Soviet Socialist Republic) from that list.

The Drug Trafficking Offences Act 1986 (Designated Countries and Territories) (Amendment) (No 2) Order 1993, SI 1993/3158 (in force on 1 February 1994), further amends the 1990 Order supra. The list of designated countries is extended to include Armenia, Azerbaijan, Bosnia and Herzegovina, Brunei, Colombia, Croatia, Dominica, Dominican Republic, El Salvador, Macedonia, Mauritania, Netherlands, Slovakia, Zambia and Zimbabwe.

2262   Confiscation order—proceeds of drug trafficking—evidence of earlier dealing

The defendant pleaded guilty to possessing a class B drug with intent to supply, and to possessing a sawn-off shotgun without a certificate. He was sentenced to two years' imprisonment for possessing a controlled drug, with two and a half years' consecutive for possessing a firearm, and a confiscation order was made under the Drug Trafficking Offences Act 1986. The defendant appealed against the sentence on the grounds that the drugs which were the subject of the charge did not come within the 1986 Act, ss 1(3), 2(3) as being a payment or reward in connection with drug trafficking carried on by the offender or another and that the sentence passed for the firearms offence was excessive. *Held*, in the instant case the judge had taken the view that it was the defendant's first drug trafficking offence and that the drugs had been purchased on a single occasion. It was therefore impossible to say that the drugs constituted a payment or reward in connection with drug trafficking and it followed that the confiscation order was contrary to the provisions of the 1986 Act and would therefore be set aside. It was correct to impose a consecutive sentence for the firearm offence, but two and a half years was too long and a term of 18 months would be substituted.

R v Butler (1993) 14 Cr App Rep (S) (Court of Appeal: Lord Taylor of Gosforth CJ, Popplewell and Laws JJ).

2263   Confiscation order—proceeds of drug trafficking—payment to intermediary

It has been held that a confiscation order under the Drug Trafficking Offences Act 1986 may be made against an intermediary in a drug trafficking chain in respect of payments received by the intermediary from the buyer of the drugs and passed on by the intermediary to the manufacturer of the drugs.

R v Simons (1993) Times, 4 June (Court of Appeal: Watkins LJ, Henry and Pill JJ).

2264   Confiscation order—proceeds of drug trafficking—power to revise order

The defendant was convicted of offences contrary to the Drug Trafficking Offences Act 1986 and sentenced to 20 years' imprisonment. A confiscation order was also imposed pursuant to the 1986 Act. In applying the procedure under the 1986 Act, the court found that the defendant had benefited from drug trafficking but that only half of the amount by which he had benefited was realisable at the time of making the confiscation order. An order in the sum realisable was therefore made. The judge imposed a three year term of imprisonment in default of payment. The confiscation order was made prior to the commencement of the Criminal Justice (International Co-Operation) Act 1990. Two years later a receiver was appointed to recover an outstanding sum under the confiscation order and applied under the 1990 Act, s 16 for a certificate that the amount which ought to have been realised from the defendant was greater than the amount taken into account in making the confiscation order against him after his conviction. The application was refused and the receiver appealed on the ground that the 1990 Act ought to have had retrospective effect. *Held*, the 1986 Act was expressed to operate where payment had been received from drug trafficking whether before or after the commencement of the 1986 Act, s 1. However, there was no provision under the 1986 Act to increase the sum previously ordered and any provision which increased a money judgment retrospectively, particularly if coupled with an additional liability to imprisonment, would adversely effect a defendant's property rights. A defendant was not to be prejudiced by laws being construed as having retroactive effect unless it was clear that it was Parliament's intention to do so. No such intention appeared in the 1990 Act. Accordingly, the appeal would be dismissed.

Re Barretto [1994] 2 WLR 149 (Court of Appeal: Sir Thomas Bingham MR, Staughton and Roch LJJ).

2265 Conspiracy to pervert the course of justice—avoidance of conviction of serious offence

An elderly man had been found in the appellants' flat with severe injuries which rendered him unable to speak, write or walk. The appellants claimed that the man had been mugged by people in the street and had been brought back to their flat. The police, however, discovered evidence that he had been mugged in the flat. The appellants were charged with causing grievous bodily harm with intent and robbery, to which they pleaded not guilty. They were not convicted on these counts because the police were unable to ascertain exactly who had carried out the mugging. They pleaded guilty to conspiring to pervert the course of justice and were each sentenced to five years' imprisonment. On appeal against sentence, *held*, the sentence was excessive and left the appellants with the perception that they were dealt with on the basis that they were guilty of the offences for which they had not been convicted. Justice to the victim could not be achieved by loading the sentence for conspiracy. Accordingly, the appeal would be allowed and the sentence of five years' imprisonment would be reduced to three years' imprisonment.

R v Walsh (1993) 14 Cr App Rep (S) 671 (Court of Appeal: McCowan LJ and Otton J).

2266 Crown Court—information as to antecedents

Lord Taylor of Gosforth CJ has issued the following *Practice Direction* ([1993] 4 All ER 863).

1. Procedures setting interim minimum standards as to the level of antecedent information to be provided in the Crown Court have been agreed to facilitate the implementation of recommendations and assist counsel in presenting antecedents to the Crown Court. Where current local arrangements exceed these standards, they must be maintained. Details of the circumstances of previous convictions for offences of a similar nature, or having similar victims, will in many cases be of considerable assistance to sentencing courts. Officers should ensure that any such available information is included in the antecedents as set out in 2(b) below (see also *Manual of Guidance*, para 7.11.4(viii)(b)). The interim standards set out below have not been designed to meet all the requirements for information that judges might have, and therefore have to be regarded as the minimum information to be provided. In a case where additional information concerning, for example, the circumstances of the current or previous offences is available, it should be included. Judges might also require additional information in any individual case.

2. The following standard forms are to be used:

(a) Form NIB74C for personal and other details. Information contained in paras 1–11 of the form must be completed from information provided by the defendant while in police custody following arrest. No action is to be taken to verify any personal information. Where information is refused or is not available, that must be stated on the form. Paragraphs 9–11 of the form should contain brief details only.

(b) Form MG16 for previous convictions. Brief details of the circumstances of the last three similar offences must be shown on the form alongside the relevant conviction. Spent convictions must be marked in accordance with the *Manual of Guidance*, para 7.15.3.

(c) Form MG 17 for recorded cautions.

These forms must be completed by the police and each document must be typed.

3. The Crown Court antecedents must be prepared by the police immediately following committal proceedings or upon receipt of a notice of appeal. Ten copies of the set of antecedent documents must be prepared in each case. Two copies must be provided to the Crown Prosecution Service direct, the remainder to the court. The court must send two copies to the defence and one to the probation service. The remaining copies are for the court's use, including one for the note taker. The antecedent documents must be served within 21 days of committal in each case. Any points arising from the antecedent information must be raised with the police, by the defence solicitor, at least seven days before the listing so that the matter can be resolved

prior to the hearing. Seven days before the hearing date, the police must check the conviction details and any additional convictions shown must be listed on an additional MG16A and served as above to be attached to the documents already supplied. Details of any additional outstanding cases must also be provided at this stage.

4. Form NIB74C, para 12 must identify any current orders breached, outstanding offences known and liability for driving disqualification, if known. Details of outstanding fines must not be shown. Where more than four previous convictions are recorded, para 13 of the form must contain a summary of total convictions recorded under the following heads: offences against the person; offences against property; fraud and kindred offences; theft and kindred offences; public order offences; and others. Paragraph 13 must also show details of the time spent in custody on the impending case.

5. The preparation of forms for the acceptance of last-minute offences to be taken into consideration is the responsibility of the Crown Court police liaison officer at the court centre, who must also activate any police circulations resulting therefrom. Any exhibits required in guilty plea cases must be brought to court by the police and thereafter be the responsibility of the court police liaison officer. Executed bench warrants must be returned via the police liaison officer, who must deliver them direct to the clerk present in court.

6. *Practice Direction (Crime Antecedents)* [1966] 2 All ER 929 is revoked.

2267 Disqualification from driving—road traffic offences

See ROAD TRAFFIC.

2268 Drug offence—aggravation—offence committed while offender on bail for earlier offence

The three defendants pleaded guilty to conspiring to evade the prohibition on the importation of a Class A controlled drug. The drugs involved had a street value of between £60,000 and £100,000. The offence was committed while two of the defendants were on bail for other offences. All three defendants were sentenced to two and a half years' imprisonment. On a reference by the Attorney General on the ground that the sentences were too lenient, *held*, a sentence of between seven and ten years was appropriate for offences involving Class A drugs worth up to £10,000 on a plea of not guilty. The sentences imposed were very much below the guidelines in *R v Aramah* (1982) 76 Cr App Rep 190, CA (1982 Abr para 2666) and revised in *R v Bilinski* (1987) 86 Cr App Rep 146, CA (1987 Abr para 2431) and were unduly lenient. The fact that two of the defendants were on bail when the offence was committed constituted an aggravating factor of the conspiracy so as to be relevant to the appropriate sentence. Their sentences would be increased to five years. The sentence of the third offender, allowing for certain mitigating factors peculiar to him, would be increased to four years.

A-G's References (Nos 3, 4 and 5 of 1992) (1993) 14 Cr App Rep (S) 191 (Court of Appeal: Lord Taylor of Gosforth CJ, Simon Brown and Roch JJ).

2269 Drug offence—possession of cannabis with intent to supply—suspended sentence combined with community service order

The defendant pleaded guilty to possession of 3·5 grammes of cannabis with intent to supply. He was subject to a conditional discharge in respect of an offence of possessing cannabis. For the offence of possessing cannabis with intent he was sentenced to 12 months' imprisonment, suspended for two years and for the offence for which he had been conditionally discharged a community service order was imposed. On appeal against sentence, *held*, in following *R v Starie* (1979) 1 Cr App Rep (S) 179 it was not good sentencing practice to combine a suspended sentence with a community service order on the same occasion. Accordingly, the suspended sentence would be varied to a community service order to run concurrently with the existing community service order.

R v Campbell (1993) 14 Cr App Rep (S) 401 (Court of Appeal: Leggatt LJ, Rougier and Sedley JJ).

2270 Forfeiture order—overseas order—enforcement

The Criminal Justice (International Co-operation) Act 1990 (Enforcement of Overseas Forfeiture Orders) (Amendment) Order 1993, SI 1993/1791 (in force on 30 July 1993), amends the 1991 Orders, SI 1991/1463 (England and Wales) and SI 1991/1464 (Northern Ireland), which make provision for the enforcement in England, Wales and Northern Ireland of orders made by courts in designated countries or territories for the forfeiture and destruction of property used in the commission of drug trafficking offences. The 1993 Order adds Antigua and Barbuda, Belarus, Bulgaria, Burkina Faso, Burundi, Denmark, Fiji, Iran, Japan, Kenya, Luxembourg, Morocco, Niger, Panama, Romania, the Russian Federation, Slovenia, South Africa, Suriname and Ukraine to the list of designated countries for the purposes of drug trafficking offences, and removes Hungary and the Union of Soviet Socialist Republics (including the Byelorussian Soviet Socialist Republic) from that list. The 1993 Order also extends the provisions of the 1991 Orders to offences corresponding to indictable offences to which the Criminal Justice Act 1988, Pt VI applies (all other indictable offences except offences under the Prevention of Terrorism (Temporary Provisions) Act 1989, Pt III) and designates Canada, India, Italy, Nigeria and Sweden for this purpose.

The Criminal Justice (International Co-operation) Act 1990 (Enforcement of Overseas Forfeiture Orders) (Amendment) (No 2) Order 1993, SI 1993/3148 (in force on 1 February 1994), further amends the 1991 Orders supra. The 1993 Order adds Armenia, Azerbaijan, Bosnia and Herzegovina, Brunei, Colombia, Croatia, Dominica, Dominican Republic, El Salvador, Macedonia, Mauritania, Netherlands, Slovakia, Zambia and Zimbabwe to the list of designated countries for the purposes of drug trafficking offences, and Bulgaria, Isle of Man, Netherlands and Switzerland to the list of designated countries for the purposes of offences corresponding to indictable offences to which the Criminal Justice Act 1988, Pt VI applies.

2271   Indecent assault—assault analogous to rape

The defendant pleaded guilty to two counts of exposing his person and two of indecent assault. The defendant approached women, who were strangers to him, while they were walking alone and indecently exposed himself to them and indecently assaulted them. On the first occasion he pushed a woman off her bicycle, told her that he had a knife, forced her to masturbate him and attempted oral sex. On the second occasion he again caused a woman aged 69 to fall off her bicycle and attempted oral sex. The defendant had no previous convictions and was described as having a personality disorder. He was sentenced to nine years' imprisonment and appealed. *Held*, although the label indecent assault had to be attached to the offences, the invasion of a woman's body by her mouth could be regarded as every bit as serious as rape. Had the instant case been a case of rape, there would have been little doubt that the judge would have considered an indeterminate sentence. The total sentence was clearly justified by the conduct which had actually occurred and accordingly, the appeal would be dismissed.

   R v Wilson (1993) 14 Cr App Rep (S) 627 (Court of Appeal: Lord Taylor of Gosforth CJ, Auld and Curtis JJ).

2272   Insider dealing—disqualification from acting as director of a company—power to make disqualification order

See *R v Goodman*, para 474.

2273   Magistrates' court—decision on sentence—challenge—appropriate mode of challenge

See *R v Ealing Justices, ex p Scrafield*, para 1736.

2274   Manslaughter—death caused by motor vehicle—victim attempting to prevent theft of vehicle

The defendant was observed by the victim stealing a van. The victim climbed onto the van in an attempt to force the defendant to stop but, by swerving, the defendant threw the victim off the roof causing him fatal head injuries. The defendant was sentenced to nine years' detention in a young offender institution and was disqualified from driving for ten years. On appeal against the sentence, *held*, the offence of manslaughter by a motor vehicle was not the same as death by reckless driving. Whether manslaughter was an appropriate charge or not was a matter for the prosecuting authority to consider anxiously, bearing in mind that the more grave offences should only be charged where there was a very high risk of death. This was such a case and accordingly, the appeal would be dismissed.

   R v Pimm (1993) 14 Cr App Rep (S) 730 (Court of Appeal: Lord Taylor of Gosforth CJ, Henry and Blofeld JJ).

2275   Manslaughter—involuntary manslaughter—aggravating circumstances

The defendant struck the deceased in the face, causing him to fracture his skull when he fell. The deceased suffered a haemorrhage and died. The defendant was convicted of manslaughter and sentenced to three years' imprisonment. On appeal against sentence, *held*, in *R v Coleman* (1991) 12 Cr App Rep (S) 508, CA (1991 Abr para 2162), it was suggested that the starting point for sentence in a case of involuntary manslaughter was 12 months' imprisonment on a plea of guilty. However, in this case, the defendant had not admitted his guilt; he had behaved aggressively throughout and there was no reason for him to strike the blow. The sentence of three years was excessive; the proper sentence would have been two years. To that extent, the appeal would be allowed.

R v Bryant (1993) 14 Cr App Rep (S) 621 (Court of Appeal: Lord Taylor of Gosforth CJ, Auld and Curtis JJ).

2276 Manslaughter—involuntary manslaughter—asphyxiation during sexual intercourse

The appellant was convicted of the manslaughter of his partner, who died as a result of asphyxiation during sexual intercourse. He was sentenced to four years' imprisonment. On appeal, *held*, those who indulged in such practices were likely to receive substantial sentences of imprisonment, but in the circumstances of the present case the appellant's sentence would be reduced to three years' imprisonment. Accordingly, the appeal would be allowed to that extent.

R v Williamson (1993) Times, 19 October (Court of Appeal: Lord Taylor of Gosforth CJ, Otton and Kay JJ).

2277 Mitigation—defendant victim of crime—offences committed against alleged perpetrator of crime

The first defendant lost a number of items of property in a theft. The police advised him that they were not hopeful of recovering the items or apprehending those responsible for the theft. He obtained information about the crime and reported it to the police. Although arrests followed as a result of the information, those arrested were later released without charge. Having been given the name of a 16-year-old boy who had allegedly committed the theft, the first and second defendants went to the boy's home, forced him into a van, and questioned and threatened him for 20 minutes. The boy suffered superficial injuries. The defendants pleaded guilty to kidnapping the boy and were each sentenced to five years' imprisonment. On appeal against sentence, *held*, the kidnapping and interrogation with threats of a 16-year-old boy was a serious offence, even if there was proven wrongdoing by the victim. Although the physical injury suffered by the boy was trivial, the true gravity of the case lay in its threat to public order. Civilised society could not tolerate individuals taking the law into their own hands. The frustration felt when a crime was committed and the offender was not brought to justice was understandable, but such frustration could never justify the defendants' conduct. Under the Criminal Justice Act 1991, s 5 a suspended sentence could be justified only by exceptional circumstances. To regard the fact that the defendants had a grievance and took the law into their own hands because they were dissatisfied with the progress made by the police as an exceptional circumstance would be to validate the conduct that it was the court's business to deter. Immediate custodial sentences were therefore justified. However, the sentences passed were grossly disproportionate and the appropriate sentence for each defendant would be six months' imprisonment.

R v Chapman; R v Bond (1993) Times, 29 June (Court of Appeal: Lord Taylor of Gosforth CJ, Ognall and Sedley JJ).

2278 Plea of guilty—discount in sentence—failure to give discount

The appellant was part of a group involved in a fight outside a pub in which two youths were severely injured. There was no evidence to show the appellant had been directly responsible for the injuries. He was charged with causing grievous bodily harm with intent. During the trial a count of violent disorder was added to the indictment, to which the appellant pleaded guilty. He was given the maximum sentence for violent disorder of five years' imprisonment. On appeal against sentence, *held*, the sentence was excessive. Although it was a serious offence, the appellant had indicated before trial that he was willing to plead guilty if the count of violent disorder were added to the indictment. The sentencing judge had subsequently failed to give the appellant any credit for his plea of guilty and it was therefore wholly inappropriate to impose the maximum term of five years' imprisonment. Accordingly, the appeal would be allowed and the sentence would be reduced to three years' imprisonment.

R v Greene (1993) 14 Cr App Rep (S) 682 (Court of Appeal: McCowan LJ and Otton J).

2279   Plea of guilty—divergence between prosecution and defence as to facts—duty of accused's legal representatives

See *R v Mohun*, para 783.

2280   Probation order—breach of probation order—custody prior to probation order being made

The defendant was sentenced to twelve months' detention in a young offender institution for burglary and handling stolen goods, together with nine months for breach of a probation order. He had been in custody for four months prior to being placed on probation. He appealed against his sentence for breach of the probation order on the ground that the four-month custody period prior to the order being made ought to have been taken into account. *Held*, when deciding on a sentence for breach of a probation order, a sentencing court ought to take into account any period spent in custody prior to the order being made, as this period of custody cannot be deducted from the original sentence as a "relevant period" under the Criminal Justice Act 1967, s 67. In this case, more credit ought to have been given to the defendant for the period spent in custody and for the fact that he had satisfactorily completed three-quarters of the probation order. Accordingly, the appeal would be allowed and the sentence for breach of the probation order reduced to three months.

R v Neville (1993) 14 Cr App Rep (S) 768 (Court of Appeal: Glidewell LJ and Garland J). *R v McDonald* (1988) 10 Cr App Rep (S) 458 applied.

2281   Rape—aggravating factors—death of victim

The defendant had broken into an elderly woman's house and burgled it. He then raped the woman, whom he had first blindfolded and gagged, and left her tied to her bed. Two days later, the woman had a fatal stroke. The defendant pleaded guilty to counts of rape and burglary but not guilty to a count of manslaughter. He was given concurrent custodial sentences of three and a half years for the burglary, five years for the rape and seven years for manslaughter. On a reference by the Attorney General on the ground that the sentence was unduly lenient, *held*, it had been established in *R v Billam* [1986] 1 All ER 985, CA (1986 Abr para 2368) that where a rape was committed by a man who had broken into or otherwise gained access to a place where a victim was living, the starting point should be eight years' imprisonment. There were a number of aggravating factors listed in *Billam* of which three were relevant in this case: (1) violence was used over and above the force necessary to commit the rape (2) the victim was very old and (3) the effect upon the victim, whether physical or mental, was of special seriousness. Taking into account the fact that the defendant had pleaded guilty and had had to undergo the ordeal of awaiting the outcome of the reference, the sentence of seven years' imprisonment for manslaughter would be replaced by one of eleven years' imprisonment.

A-G's Reference (No 33 of 1992) (1993) 14 Cr App Rep (S) 712 (Court of Appeal: Lord Taylor of Gosforth CJ, Henry and Blofeld JJ).

2282   Rape—life sentence—risk of future offending

The defendant was convicted of rape, aggravated burglary, false imprisonment, causing grievous bodily harm with intent, assault occasioning actual bodily harm, abducting a woman by force, robbery and malicious wounding. The defendant committed six rapes, some on women who were attacked in their homes, threatened with a knife and treated with violence. He was sentenced to life imprisonment. A psychiatric report indicated that the defendant was not suffering from a mental disorder. The defendant appealed against sentence on the ground that it was unlikely that he would commit such offences in the future. *Held*, the three criteria for the imposition of a sentence of life imprisonment were that the offence or offences were in themselves grave enough to warrant a very long sentence, that it appeared from the nature of the offences or the offender's history that he was a person of unstable character likely to commit further such offences in the future, and that if such offences were committed the consequences to others would be specially injurious. It was clear that the first and third criteria were clearly satisfied. Since there was no evidence that the defendant's character would change and that he would not be a danger if released, the sentence was correct and the appeal would be dismissed.

R v Chandler (1993) 14 Cr App Rep (S) 586 (Court of Appeal: Watkins LJ, Auld and Curtis JJ).

The defendant, who had been employed on a number of occasions as a nanny to small children with whom he had committed indecent acts and of which acts he taken photographs, was convicted of two offences of rape, five of indecent assault and one of taking an indecent photograph. On appeal against a sentence of life imprisonment, *held*, there was no medical evidence that the defendant was suffering from mental illness. However, it was open to a court sometimes to infer from the circumstances that there was something radically wrong with a defendant, in the sense that he had a disturbed mind which, even though a psychiatrist could not put a label on it, amounted to a condition which satisfied one of the three main criteria for the imposition of a life sentence. The court was satisfied that, if released in the near future, the defendant would be a menace to small children. He had to be kept in prison or in some other place of safety for a very long time and released only when the appropriate authorities were sure that it was safe both for him and the public. The appeal would be dismissed.

R v Stevenson (1993) 14 Cr App Rep (S) 22 (Court of Appeal: Watkins LJ, Macpherson and Judge JJ).

2283   Rape—young offender—review of non-custodial sentence

The respondent, aged 15, had been convicted of rape and indecent assault. He had been made the subject of a three-year supervision order, with a condition that he attend a specified activities programme, and his parents had been ordered to pay £500 compensation to the complainant. The Attorney General applied for a review of the sentence under the Criminal Justice Act 1988, s 33 on the ground that it was unduly lenient. *Held*, although the Magistrates' Court Act 1980, s 24 provided that a person aged under 18 who was charged with an indictable offence other than homicide should be tried summarily except in specified circumstances, the Court of Appeal had jurisdiction to entertain the Attorney General's application because an offence of rape was triable only on indictment under the 1988 Act, s 35(3)(a). Their Lordships understood the reluctance of the trial judge to impose a custodial sentence, bearing in mind that the probation service had strongly recommended a community sentence, but a non-custodial sentence was simply not tenable in the circumstances. Accordingly, the appeal would be allowed and the sentence replaced with one of two years' detention, pursuant to the Children and Young Persons Act 1933, s 53(2).

R v W (1993) Times, 16 March (Court of Appeal: Lord Taylor of Gosforth CJ, Henry and Blofeld JJ).

2284   Reckless driving—guilty plea—discretion to impose maximum sentence

The appellant was convicted of reckless driving, and the maximum sentence of two years' imprisonment was imposed. For additional charges of taking without consent and driving while disqualified, the appellant received concurrent sentences. For breach of probation offences, he received sentences of six months' imprisonment on each count, consecutive to the two year term, but concurrent with each other. On appeal against the sentence, the appellant claimed that the imposition of the maximum sentence of imprisonment for reckless driving had made no allowance for his guilty plea. *Held*, the court had given credit for the guilty plea when imposing the overall sentence. It did not necessarily follow that because the maximum sentence was passed on the individual count, no credit was given for the appellant's guilty plea. Furthermore the judge could have dealt with the appellant more severely in respect of the other offences. Accordingly, the appeal would be dismissed.

R v Yapp (1993) 157 JP 312 (Court of Appeal: Steyn LJ and Wright J).

2285   Recommendation for deportation—refugee

The appellants, who had both been granted refugee status at some time before their trial, were convicted of obtaining money by deception. On their appeals against sentence, which included a recommendation for their deportation, the question arose whether the recommendation was appropriate in the case of persons having refugee status. *Held*, the granting of refugee status was in no sense an order made by the Secretary of State exempting an individual from the provisions of the Immigration Act 1971, s 8(2). The principles upon which a court should act in considering whether to make a recommendation for deportation were set out by the Court of Appeal in *R v Nazari* (1980) 71 Cr App Rep 87 (1980 Abr para 1506). The court had to consider whether the accused's continued presence in the United Kingdom was to the country's detriment. It had power to make the recommendation but the final decision was to be made by the Secretary of State who had power to make the order for deportation.

R v Villa (1993) 14 Cr App Rep (S) 34 (Court of Appeal: Farquharson LJ, Turner and Cazalet JJ).

2286   Remission—effect of sentence on rights of remission

The appellant received sentences totalling twelve months' imprisonment for assault and a number of road traffic offences, and a consecutive sentence of 14 days' imprisonment for two offences of failing to surrender to bail. He appealed against sentence on the ground that the additional 14 days' imprisonment would reduce his entitlement to remission from one half to one third. *Held*, the court would express no view on the question of whether it would ever be proper for the sentencing court to have regard to the effect that the sentence would have upon rights of remission. However, where a court was imposing a total sentence of imprisonment as long as 12 months it would seldom be appropriate or desirable to add a very short consecutive sentence for offences such as failing to surrender to bail, and the appeal would be allowed to the extent that the sentence of 14 days' imprisonment would be served concurrently with the other sentences.

R v Gorman (1992) 157 JP 74 (Court of Appeal: Watkins LJ, Phillips and Tuckey JJ). *R v Burnley Magistrates' Court, ex p Halstead* (1991) 155 JP 288 (1990 Abr para 2154) considered.

2287   Restrictions on sentencing—breach of probation order

It has been held that, unless invited by an offender or an offender's probation officer, justices have no power to deal with an offender for breach of a probation order made before the Criminal Justice Act 1991, Sch 13 came into force. The powers of justices and the Crown Court are considerably different in this area. The Crown Court is able to proceed of its own volition to deal with such an offender while the justices may only deal with him if he or his probation officer has made an application under Sch 2, para 7.

R v Ipswich Justices, ex p Best (1993) 14 Cr App Rep (S) 685 (Queen's Bench Division: Watkins LJ and Owen J).

2288   Restrictions on sentencing—custodial sentence—guidelines

It has been held that when sentencing a defendant for two or more offences and those offences are combined to require an immediate custodial sentence under the Criminal Justice Act 1991 the sentencing judge is required to indicate which two he has in mind and make it clear, using the language of the sections of the 1991 Act, how he was arriving at his sentence. It is important that judges comply with the framework of sentencing as prescribed in the 1991 Act.

R v Husbands (1993) 14 Cr App Rep (S) 709 (Court of Appeal: Lord Taylor of Gosforth CJ, Henry and Blofeld JJ).

2289   Restrictions on sentencing—suspended sentence—activation—whether activation amounts to passing a sentence

The Criminal Justice Act 1991, s 1(2)(a) provides that the court must not pass a custodial sentence unless it is of the opinion that the offence, or the combination of the offence and one other offence associated with it, was so serious that only a custodial sentence can be justified. Section 31(2) provides that an offence is associated with another if the offender is convicted of it in the proceedings in which he is convicted of the other offence or (although convicted of it in earlier proceedings) is sentenced for it at the same time as he is sentenced for that offence. The defendant was sentenced in the Crown Court to three months' imprisonment for shoplifting and 6 months' imprisonment to run consecutively for activation of an earlier sentence for shoplifting suspended for two years. Also committed to the Crown Court was a breach of an earlier three month sentence for shoplifting suspended for two years. On the defendant's appeal against sentence, *held*, the earlier offence was not associated with the later one within the meaning of the 1991 Act, s 31(2) as it was distinct from it and had been the subject of a separate sentence. As a matter of law, activating a suspended sentence was not passing a sentence. Therefore the circumstances of the earlier offences, or either of them, could be taken into account only if they disclosed any aggravating factors in relation to the later offence. As the earlier offences did not disclose any such aggravating factors, the earlier offences ought not to have been taken into account and the defendant's appeal would be allowed.

R v Crawford (1993) 157 JP 667 (Court of Appeal: Lord Taylor of Gosforth CJ, Pill and Sedley JJ).

2290   Robbery—"obituary burglary"—custodial sentence

It has been held that a robbery which takes place at the home of a person whose death has been recently announced in the newspapers (known as an "obituary burglary") is of such a serious nature that only a custodial sentence can be justified.

R v Lewis (1993) 14 Cr App Rep (S) 744 (Court of Appeal: Lord Taylor of Gosforth CJ, Pill and Sedley JJ).

2291 Robbery—tariff—court's discretion

The defendant was convicted of robbing a building society with a handgun, two counts of criminal damage and common assault. He admitted the offences but the trial was contested on the grounds that he was in an abnormal state of mind and suffering from depression at the time of their commission. He was sentenced to 18 months' imprisonment concurrent for robbery, to run concurrently with lesser sentences for the other offences. The Attorney General appealed, contending that the sentence was unduly lenient. *Held*, tariffs and guideline cases were not immutable and special treatment was appropriate in extraordinary cases. Ordinarily, a sentence of 18 months' imprisonment for armed robbery would be wholly inadequate. However, this was not a mainstream example of a building society robbery: the defendant was of low intelligence and suffered from depression, he committed the offence on the spur of the moment and immediately afterwards confessed to the robbery. The sentence was lenient but, given the exceptional circumstances of the case, it was not unduly lenient and, accordingly, the appeal would be dismissed.

R v Bigby (1993) Times, 14 October (Court of Appeal: Lord Taylor of Gosforth CJ, Turner and Dyson JJ).

2292 Suspended sentence—activation—subsequent minor offences

The defendant had been given two suspended sentences of imprisonment, one for attempted burglary and obtaining property by deception and the other for theft. He was subsequently convicted of obtaining unemployment benefit by deception and being in breach of bail requirements. The court decided that the latter two crimes were not serious enough to justify custodial sentences. It therefore imposed no penalty for the bail offence and a nominal sentence of one day for the deception offence but passed a sentence of imprisonment for breach of the suspended sentences. On appeal against the sentence, *held*, if a subsequent offence committed by an offender who is subject to a suspended sentence was not itself one which the court regarded as serious enough to justify a custodial sentence, then, except in exceptional circumstances, the court ought not to activate the suspended sentence. There were no exceptional circumstances in this case so the appeal would be allowed and the custodial sentence would be replaced by a probation order.

R v Bee (1993) 14 Cr App Rep (S) 703 (Court of Appeal: Beldam LJ and Schiemann J).

2293 Suspended sentence—offence involving breach of trust—theft and false accounting

The defendant, a police officer, pleaded guilty to 11 counts of false accounting. As a result of his wife becoming seriously disabled the defendant was obliged to carry out some building works on his house. He initially understood that he would receive a grant for the total cost of the work, however once he was committed to the work it materialised that a grant would not be available for the full cost and he would have to make up the shortfall. The defendant, in the course of his duties, collected fines paid at police stations for the discharge of warrants issued at magistrates' courts. He issued receipts for the moneys received, but failed to pay over the money to the court office. He was sentenced to three months' imprisonment. As a consequence of the offences, the defendant lost his job, his house, had made two suicide attempts and was now receiving psychiatric care for reactive depression. He appealed on the ground that there were exceptional circumstances under the Powers of Criminal Courts Act 1973, s 22(2) to justify the imposition of a suspended sentence. *Held*, the offences were a serious breach of trust and there was no doubt that a custodial sentence was justified for the purposes of the Criminal Justice Act 1991, s 1(2)(a). Where a person in a position of trust broke that trust he would frequently find that the consequences went far beyond the immediate impact of any sentence that might be imposed on him. In the instant case, although there were substantial mitigating factors, the defendant's circumstances did not amount to exceptional circumstances and as such would not justify the imposition of a suspended sentence. However, the court recognised that there was a case for mercy and reduced the sentence to 42 days' imprisonment to effect the defendant's immediate release.

R v Lowery (1993) 14 Cr App Rep (S) 485 (Court of Appeal: Steyn LJ, Pill and Wright JJ).

The defendant, a sub-postmistress, pleaded guilty to theft and false accounting. She and her husband had taken on substantial loans to obtain the post office and were now bankrupt with the husband unemployed and presently in hospital. The defendant was sentenced to four months' imprisonment on each count, the sentences to run concurrently. She appealed against the sentence on the ground that there were exceptional circumstances which justified a suspended sentence. *Held*, in considering *R v Barrick* (1985) 7 Cr App Rep (S) 142, CA it was accepted that a custodial sentence would be required and that four months would be regarded as the shortest sentence for a breach of trust case. The circumstances could not be described as exceptional and therefore the sentence passed was correct. However, as it was not a case in which there was deliberate dishonesty from the start, and in the light of the husband's situation and the defendant's financial plight the sentence would be reduced to two months to allow the immediate release of the defendant.

R v Robinson (1993) 14 Cr App Rep (S) 559 (Court of Appeal: Lord Taylor of Gosforth CJ, Owen and Curtis JJ).

2294 Theft—theft from telephone box—policy

The defendant was convicted of the theft of money from a telephone box and was sentenced to two months' imprisonment, with suspended sentences totalling ten months being activated consecutively. He appealed against the sentence. *Held*, it was a matter of policy to deter thefts from telephone boxes. There was evidence that the defendant provided himself with the necessary tools and went on a deliberate expedition to rob telephone boxes of their contents. It was an offence capable of being so serious as to justify a custodial sentence. However, the defendant's appeal would be allowed to the extent of making the sentence of imprisonment concurrent with the activated suspended sentences.

R v Decino (1993) Times, 10 May (Court of Appeal: Beldam LJ, Connell and Ebsworth JJ).

2295 Time spent on bail—extent to which allowance should be made

It has been held that simply because a defendant has been on bail for a considerable time pending an appeal, no substantial reduction in his sentence is justified. In the current state of the lists, a sentence might well have been served by the time an appeal was heard, and judges should not be discouraged from granting bail in cases where it was appropriate to do so.

R v Callan (1993) Times, 1 July (Court of Appeal: Staughton LJ, Laws and Smith JJ).

2296 Unlawful wounding—mitigation—provocation and aggravation

The defendant was a woman sentenced to 18 months' imprisonment after pleading guilty to unlawful wounding. In the past, her victim had claimed that she had slept with the defendant's partner and was pregnant by him, sent the defendant threatening correspondence and attacked the defendant causing her injury. The incident leading to the conviction occurred outside a club where the victim again taunted the defendant, causing the defendant to lose her temper and strike the victim over the head with a beer bottle. On appeal against the sentence, *held*, there was considerable mitigation in this case as there was much provocation and aggravation revealed by the circumstances, although this did not justify the defendant in losing her temper. Because of the very considerable mitigation, a sentence as long as 18 months was not necessary and, accordingly, a suspended sentence of 12 months would be substituted.

R v Huntley (1993) 14 Cr App Rep (S) 795 (Court of Appeal: Glidewell LJ and Garland J).

2297 Wounding with intent—evidence of previous convictions for violence

The Criminal Justice Act, s 2(2)(b), states that in relation to a custodial sentence imposed, other than one that is fixed by law, where the offence is violent the sentence must be for such longer term as in the opinion of the court is necessary to protect the public from serious harm from the offender. Section 29(2) states that where any aggravating factors of an offence are disclosed by the circumstances of other offences committed by the offender, nothing in that part of the Act shall prevent the court from taking those factors into account for the purpose of forming an opinion as to the seriousness of the offence.

The appellant had been involved in a knife fight in which a man had been seriously scarred. The appellant was convicted of unlawful wounding with intent to cause grievous bodily harm, contrary to the Offences Against the Person Act 1861, s 18, and had been sentenced to six years' imprisonment. The appellant had a record of convictions for violence. On appeal against the length of the sentence, *held*, the court could not disregard the evidence of the appellant's previous offences, which showed a ready resort to violence and to weapons, with or without provocation. These offences made his commission of the present offence more serious. Circumstances which showed some added gravity of criminal purpose were a legitimate consideration under s 29(2).

In the present case the appellant provoked the fight and such an individual was a danger to the public, and the public was entitled to such protection as could properly be given. The 1991 Act, s 2(2)(b) therefore applied, and the sentence of six years was justified. Accordingly, the appeal would be dismissed.

R v Utip (1993) 14 Cr App R (S) 746 (Court of Appeal: Lord Taylor of Gosforth CJ, Pill and Sedley JJ). *R v Bexley* (1992) 14 Cr App R (S) 462 (1992 Abr para 2273), applied.

2298 Wounding with intent—unduly lenient sentence—deferred sentence

The defendant pleaded guilty to wounding with intent to cause grievous bodily harm. He accosted a young woman in a night club and when stopped by her boyfriend hit him in the face with a beer glass causing six lacerations requiring 18 stitches. The defendant's sentence was deferred for six months. The Attorney-General asked the Court of Appeal to review the sentence on the ground that it was unduly lenient. The defendant submitted that a case in which sentence had been deferred was not a final order, and therefore not capable of being referred to the Court of Appeal by the Attorney-General as it was not a sentence. *Held*, if a deferment was not a sentence for the purposes of the Criminal Appeal Act 1968, s 50(1) there would be no right of appeal against a deferment, and an Attorney-General's reference could not be made until the final disposal had been ordered by the trial court. Thus the offender would fall to be dealt with three times, rather than twice. The Criminal Justice Act 1988, s 35(6) provided that sentence for the purposes of that Act had the same meaning as in the 1968 Act which provided that sentence included any order made by a court when dealing with an offender. The court was satisfied that the sentence was strikingly and unduly lenient, and a sentence of 30 months' imprisonment would be substituted as the lowest sentence which could be passed.

A-G's Reference (No 22 of 1992) [1994] 1 All ER 105 (Court of Appeal: Lord Taylor of Gosforth CJ, Potts and Judge JJ).

2299 Wounding with intent—unduly lenient sentence—duty to give reasons

The defendant pleaded guilty to wounding with intent to cause grievous bodily harm contrary to the Offences Against the Person Act 1861, s 18 and was sentenced to three months imprisonment for stabbing the victim twice. The sentence was referred to the Court of Appeal by the Attorney General under the Criminal Justice Act 1988, s 36. *Held*, the recorder did not specify any reasons or explain the process by which she arrived at the sentence. Since the date of the trial the offender had served the sentence and had been at liberty for eight months. There was a report before the Court of Appeal from a consultant forensic psychiatrist who was of opinion that the offender had been suffering from a severe schizophrenic illness and had responded well to medical treatment. The court was in favour of the medical treatment continuing. Although it was an unduly lenient sentence, the court was of the view that the special medical circumstances which had emerged subsequent to the trial and the Attorney General's reference were such that the case was quite exceptional, and therefore the court would not interfere with the sentence. It was stated that if those who had to pass sentence specified reasons or explained the process by which they arrived at that sentence, then that would bring them to consider the likely effect and public reception of that sentence.

R v Skinner (1993) Times, 23 March (Court of Appeal: Lord Taylor of Gosforth CJ, Pill and Sedley JJ).

2300 Young offender—detention in a young offender institution—plea of guilty—discount for plea

The defendant, aged 16, pleaded guilty to criminal damage. He was sentenced to 12 months' detention in a young offender institution, the maximum sentence available. On appeal against sentence, he contended that, in view of his plea of guilty, the maximum sentence should not have been imposed. *Held*, where a juvenile pleaded guilty to an offence, he should normally receive a sentence of less than the maximum. In the case of offences punishable with 14 years' imprisonment or more where a juvenile could be ordered to be detained under the Children and Young Persons Act 1933, s 53(2), a sentence of 12 months' detention in a young offender institution following a plea of guilty was not objectionable if the offence in question would have justified a sentence of detention under s 53(2) and a discount in respect of the plea was made by detention in a young offender institution being chosen instead of detention under s 53(2). An appropriate discount should have been made for the defendant's plea. The appeal would be allowed and the sentence reduced to ten months.

R v George (1993) 14 Cr App Rep (S) 12 (Court of Appeal: Watkins LJ, Boreham and Cresswell JJ).

SET-OFF AND COUNTERCLAIM

Halsbury's Laws of England (4th edn) Vol 42, paras 401–600

2301   Mortgage—action for possession—set-off and counterclaim by mortgagor
See *National Westminster Bank plc v Skelton; Ashley Guarantee plc v Zacaria*, para 1828.

2302   Set-off—equitable right of set-off—contracting out of right to deduct— whether right of set-off excluded
See *Connaught Restaurants Ltd v Indoor Leisure Ltd*, para 1629.

SETTLEMENTS

Halsbury's Laws of England (4th edn) Vol 42, paras 601–1100

2303   Misdrafting of settlement—solicitor's duty to beneficiary
See *Hemmens v Wilson Browne*, para 2424.

2304   Settlement of shares—shares allotted as part of company demerger— treatment as income or capital
A testator left shares in a company to her husband for life and then to her son absolutely. The company carried out a reorganisation under which a new company was created. The new company was to belong to the shareholders of the original company in the same proportions as their original shareholding. The shares were issued by the new company as fully paid up in consideration for the transfer by the original company of shares in a wholly owned subsidiary, and shares in the new company were allotted and issued direct to the shareholders in satisfaction of a dividend declared by the original company. In a test case, the trustee of the settlement sought a determination as to whether in the hands of trustee shareholders the shares in the new company were to be treated as income belonging to the life tenant or capital belonging to the remainderman. *Held*, to regard the transaction as a distribution of profits, akin to the payment of a dividend and hence income, would be to exalt company form over commercial substance to an unacceptable extent. The general principles of law governing such cases were designed to give effect to the assumed intention of the testator. When the inflexible application of those principles would produce a result manifestly inconsistent with the presumed intention of the testator, the court ought not to apply them slavishly. Accordingly, the shares in the new company were to be treated as capital.
Re Lee; Sinclair v Lee [1993] 3 All ER 926 (Chancery Division: Sir Donald Nicholls V-C).

2305   Trustee—overseas trust—capital gains tax
See *De Rothschild v Lawrenson*, para 283.

SEX DISCRIMINATION

Halsbury's Laws of England (4th edn) Vol 16, Supp paras 767–771:38

2306   Articles
A Pause Over Pregnancy, Brian Napier: LS Gaz, 3 February 1993, p 21
Community Law and Awards for Discrimination, Brian Napier: 143 NLJ 1184
Recession Hits Women, Sean Webster (on redundancies in solicitors' firms): 137 SJ 242
The EEC Code of Conduct on Sexual Harassment, Toni Lester: 143 NLJ 1473, 1540
Women's rights, Kate Harrison: 143 NLJ 621

2307   Discrimination—employment—redundancy—additional payment
See *EC Commission v Kingdom of Belgium*, para 2753.

2308   Discrimination—employment—selection—doctor—refusal of application for employment by family health services authority
The Sex Discrimination Act 1975, s 6(1)(a) provides that it is unlawful for an employer to discriminate against a man or woman in the arrangements he makes for the purpose of determining who should be offered employment.

A general practitioner complained that he was the victim of sex discrimination under the 1975 Act, s 6(1)(a) by a family health services authority which had not appointed him to a vacancy for which he had applied. On a preliminary assessment of the complaint, an industrial tribunal decided that it had jurisdiction to hear the doctor's case. The authority appealed against this preliminary finding. *Held*, the sources of the obligations between a doctor and the family health services authority were statutory, not contractual. The appointment of a general practitioner did not constitute employment under the 1975 Act, s 82(1). The remedy in cases such as this one was by way of appeal to the Secretary of State during which allegations of discrimination could be made. Section 6(1)(a) was not satisfied in this case as the arrangements for determining who should be offered employment were not made by the family health services authority but were instead governed by a statutory procedure. Such a statutory arrangement, which was fixed, was not therefore one made by an employer. Accordingly, the industrial tribunal had no jurisdiction to hear the doctor's complaint and the appeal would be allowed.

Ealing Hammersmith and Hounslow Family Health Services Authority v Shukla [1993] ICR 710 (Employment Appeal Tribunal: Wood J presiding). *Wadi v Cornwall and Isles of Scilly Family Practitioner Committee* [1985] ICR 492 (1985 Abr para 2103) followed. *Roy v Kensington and Chelsea and Westminster Family Practitioner Committee* [1990] 1 Med LR 328, CA (1990 Abr para 1648) not followed. *Roy v Kensington and Chelsea and Westminster Family Practitioner Committee* [1992] 1 AC 624, HL (1992 Abr para 1807) considered.

2309   Discrimination—employment—unfair dismissal—compensation—limit
See *Marshall v Southampton and South West Hampshire Area Health Authority (No 2)*, para 2754.

2310   Discrimination—occupational pension scheme—retirement age—bridging pension
See *Birds Eye Walls Ltd v Roberts*, para 2755.

2311   Discrimination—occupational pension scheme—retirement age—definition of "pay"
A nurse's pension entitlement was derived from a scheme established by statute for providing pensions for local government employees. It was a compulsory scheme to which the employer and employee were required to contribute. The applicant's pension was reduced the day before her sixtieth birthday, the effect of the the National Insurance (Modification of Local Government Superannuation Schemes) Regulations 1969, SI 1969/793. On appeal by the applicant from an industrial tribunal hearing that the pension payments were not "pay" within the scope of the Treaty of Rome, art 119 regarding equal pay and that therefore a claim of sex discrimination under the treaty was precluded, *held*, a retirement pension established within the framework of a social security scheme laid down by legislation did not come within the definition of "pay" in art 119. The applicant's scheme was a statutory one governed by exhaustive rules which left the employer no discretion at all and which applied to a general category of local government workers throughout the country. Therefore the applicant whose pension benefits were reduced from the age of sixty was precluded under the treaty from making a claim of sex discrimination. Furthermore as the applicant had retired before the European Communities Act 1972 came into force, to apply art 119 would have given retrospective force to the 1972 Act. There was no statutory justification for that conclusion and the appeal tribunal would not construe the legislation to give it that retrospective effect. Accordingly, the appeal would be dismissed.

Griffin v London Pension Authority [1993] ICR 564 (Employment Appeal Tribunal: May J presiding)

2312 Discrimination—occupational pension scheme—survivor's pension for widows only

See *Ten Oever v Stichting Bedrijfspensioenfonds voor het Glazenwassers en Schoonmaakbedrijf*, para 2755.

2313 Discrimination—public house admissions policy—male wearing earrings

Northern Ireland

The defendant owned a bar which had an admissions policy stipulating that the minimum standard of dress was "smart, clean casual wear". The plaintiff was asked to leave the bar as he was wearing two relatively small stud earrings in the lobe of his left ear. The plaintiff claimed that he had been unlawfully discriminated against on grounds of sex by the defendant contrary to the Sex Discrimination (Northern Ireland) Order 1976, art 30(1) in respect of the provision of facilities or services. At first instance the claim was dismissed, the judge stating that the fact that the defendant did not treat female and male customers in an identical way did not necessarily mean that they were not dealt with on a basis of equality and concluded that there was nothing in the evidence to suggest that the discrimination alleged by the plaintiff "was against him by reason of his gender". On appeal, *held*, the judge had erred in finding that the defendant had not discriminated against the plaintiff on grounds of sex by refusing to provide him with refreshment facilities because he was wearing earrings. The defendant had refused to serve the plaintiff with refreshment facilities "in the like manner and on the like terms" within the meaning of the 1976 Order, art 30(1). It was clear that in today's conditions it would not be possible to say that there was a difference between men and women as regards the wearing of personal jewellery. The reason for the defendant refusing to serve the plaintiff was because he was a man, and therefore the defendant had unlawfully discriminated against the plaintiff on the grounds of sex. Accordingly, the appeal would be allowed.

McConomy v Croft Inns Ltd [1992] IRLR 561 (Queen's Bench Division: Murray LJ).

The Sex Discrimination (Northern Ireland) Order 1976, art 30(1) is analogous to the Sex Discrimination Act 1976, s 29(1).

2314 Discrimination—sexual harassment—European guidelines

Commission Recommendation (EC) 92/131 on the protection of the dignity of women and men at work, adopted by the EC Commission, recommends that the member states take action to promote awareness that conduct of a sexual nature or other conduct based on sex affecting the dignity of women and men at work, including conduct of superiors and colleagues, is unacceptable if (1) such conduct is unwanted, unreasonable and offensive to the recipient; (2) a person's rejection of or submission to such conduct on the part of the employers or workers (including superiors or colleagues) is used explicitly or implicitly as a basis for a decision which affects that person's access to vocational training, access to employment, continued employment, promotion, salary or other employment decisions; (3) such conduct creates an intimidating, hostile or humiliating work environment for the recipient; and that such conduct may, in certain circumstances, be contrary to the principle of equal treatment within Directive (EC) 76/207. The accompanying Code of Practice defines "sexual harassment" as unwanted conduct of a sexual nature, or other conduct based on sex affecting the dignity of women and men at work, and provides that this definition can include unwelcome physical, verbal or non-verbal conduct.

The plaintiff made a complaint of sexual discrimination against her employers, alleging that the employers' conduct included personal insults, rude comments and sexist remarks ridiculing women. The complaint was dismissed by an industrial tribunal. On appeal, *held*, "sexual harassment" was not a definitive phrase in law and it was helpful to note European trends. Guidance could be received from the recommendations made by the Commission and the definition contained in the Code of Practice might also be helpful when considering such matters. Harassment indicated a degree of repetition rather than a single act, although this would depend on the circumstances of an individual case. In this case, the tribunal failed to make findings of primary fact. There was insufficient direction in law from which it could be established what the industrial tribunal had in mind as the principles to be applied. The appeal would be allowed and the case remitted to an industrial tribunal.

Wadman v Carpenter Farrer Partnership (1993) Times, 31 May (Employment Appeal Tribunal: Wood J presiding).

2315   Discrimination—social security—invalidity pension—assumption about mother

See *Schuler-Zraggen v Switzerland*, para 1417.

2316   Discrimination—social security—severe disablement allowance and invalid care allowance—entitlement according to pensionable age

See *Thomas v Chief Adjudication Officer*, para 2757.

2317   Equal pay—remedies

The Sex Discrimination and Equal Pay (Remedies) Regulations 1993, SI 1993/2798 (in force on 22 November 1993), repeal the Sex Discrimination Act 1975, s 62(2) which provided that an award of compensation by an industrial tribunal under Pt II could not exceed a specified sum. An industrial tribunal which makes an award under the sex discrimination legislation may now include a sum by way of interest on the amount awarded. Such interest is to be calculated at a rate which accrues from day to day, and the rates of interest to be used are specified. Provision is made for an industrial tribunal to depart from these rules where applicable. Written details must be given if no interest is awarded.

2318   Equal pay—work of equal value—material difference other than sex

The employees worked on an evening shift composed entirely of women. They brought equal pay claims, comparing their work in a packing department with a man similarly employed in a different packing department. It was conceded that the work was of equal value but the employer's defence was that the difference in pay was due to the fact that the comparator received a shift premium because he worked rotating shifts. An industrial tribunal and the Employment Appeal Tribunal both upheld the defence. On the employees' further appeal, *held*, there was no error of law in the tribunal's identification of the material factor to which the variation in pay was due. The fact that some indeterminate part of the shift premium represented compensation for working unsociable hours did not necessarily preclude a finding that the payment of the shift premium was genuinely due to working rotating shifts. The tribunal was entitled to conclude that the inconvenience caused by a rotating shift was the sole cause of the variation in pay. Accordingly, the appeal would be dismissed.

   Calder v Rowntree Mackintosh Confectionery Ltd [1993] IRLR 212 (Court of Appeal: Balcombe, Kennedy and Evans LJJ).

The Equal Pay Act 1970, s 1(3) provides that an equality clause will not operate in relation to a variation between a woman's contract and a man's contract if an employer proves that the variation is genuinely due to a material factor which is not the difference of sex.

   A male colleague, who was engaged in the same work as the female plaintiff, was mistakenly paid more than the plaintiff. As a result the plaintiff applied to an industrial tribunal on the ground that she was entitled to equal pay. It was held that she was entitled to equal pay and the employer appealed on the ground that the industrial tribunal had erred in law in requiring an objective justification of the difference in pay, and had failed to apply the correct test namely whether there was a material factor other than sex which was a material difference between her and the comparator causing the variation in pay within the meaning of the Equal Pay Act 1970, s 1(3). *Held*, the correct test was laid down in *Calder v Rowntree Mackintosh Confectionery Ltd* [1992] ICR 372 (1992 Abr para 2333) (affirmed on appeal supra) where it was held that in a case of direct discrimination it was not necessary for the employer to justify objectively the difference in pay. There was no evidence of intention to discriminate or of actual discrimination and the difference occurred because of a mistake and not because of anything which was tainted with gender-based discrimination. Therefore, the employer was able to rely on his own mistake in paying one of his employees a salary greater than another employee engaged in the same work. Accordingly, the appeal would be allowed.

   Yorkshire Blood Transfusion Service v Plaskitt (1993) Times, 17 August (Employment Appeal Tribunal: Tuckey J presiding).

Scotland

The plaintiffs were female employees at the defendant's factory, engaged in work indirectly related to shopfloor production. They sought equal pay with male clerical workers, whose work was directly related to production. Direct and indirect workers had previously been employed on the same hourly rates, although the direct workers worked longer hours, and it was conceded by the defendant that the indirect workers were engaged in equal work to that of the direct workers. A negotiated settlement between the defendant and the union representing the clerical workers resulted in a reduction in the direct employees' hours of work, giving rise to an anomaly in hourly rates between the groups. The plaintiffs' claim for equal pay was dismissed at first instance, on the ground that the defendant had established a defence under the Equal Pay Act 1970, s 1(3) by showing that the difference in pay between the plaintiffs and their comparators resulted from a collective bargaining agreement untainted by sex discrimination. On appeal, *held*, the correct approach was to consider whether the employers had shown that the difference between the plaintiffs and their comparators was genuinely due to a material factor other than sex. It could not be accepted that an employer could discharge that burden by proving that the variation was free from sex discrimination, as there could be a cause for a variation which was not a material factor other than the difference of sex. The difference in hourly rates arose from a collective agreement, which did not show any objective factor justifying or supporting the result produced. The difference in pay was incidental, resulting in a pay difference not due to any material factor other than a difference of sex. The appeal would accordingly be allowed.

Barber v NCR (Manufacturing) Ltd [1993] IRLR 95 (Employment Appeal Tribunal: Lord Coulsfield presiding).

See also *Enderby v Frenchay Health Authority*, para 2752.

2319　Equal treatment—Sunday trading—indirect discrimination

A local authority sought to restrain a retailer from opening a store in its area on a Sunday. The applicants, female shop assistants employed at the retail outlet, contended that as women substantially outnumbered men among those who were able to be, and were in fact, working on a Sunday, the closure of a retail outlet on that day would mean more women than men were deprived of a job. In addition, they contended that the enforcement of the Shops Act 1950, s 47, which provided that shops had to remain closed on a Sunday except for the purpose of specified transactions, was in contravention of Council Directive (EC) 76/207 as it was liable to have the effect of introducing a condition or selection criterion for jobs that was indirectly discriminatory. They sought a declaration that the Sunday trading provisions of the Shops Act 1950 were unlawful and unreasonable as a part of EC law and an injunction to restrain the defendant local authority from seeking to enforce the Sunday trading provision in relation to their store. The local authority and the Attorney General sought to strike out the employees' claim, as disclosing no cause of action, and the authority sought an interlocutory injunction, restraining the retailer from opening its shop. *Held*, the effect of s 47 in prohibiting the staff from working on a Sunday was not a requirement that staff be dismissed or subjected to some other detriment. Section 47 was not a new provision which made unlawful that which had previously been lawful. Its practical effect had not been to require dismissals or to subject employees to detriment, but to prohibit the retailer from lawfully offering job opportunities on Sundays. The retailer was in clear breach of a valid law. The injunction sought by the local authority, and the application to strike out the applicants' claim, would be granted.

Chisholm v Kirklees Metropolitan Borough Council; Kirklees Metropolitan Borough Council v B & Q plc [1993] ICR 826 (Chancery Division: Ferris J).

SHIPPING AND NAVIGATION

Halsbury's Laws of England (4th edn) Vol 43, paras 1–1247

2320　Articles

Assignments of Earnings—Who Ferryman Pays? Andrew Murray (on *Pan Ocean Shipping Co Ltd v Creditcorp Ltd* [1993] 1 Lloyd's Rep 345, CA (para 2326)): (1993) 8 JIBFL 496
Bills of Lading, Fidelma White and Robert Bradgate: LS Gaz, 16 June 1993, p 23
Freedom of Contract in Maritime Law, Jan Ramberg: [1993] 2 LMCLQ 178
Shipping Lawyers—Land Rats or Water Rats? Stewart Boyd: [1993] 3 LMCLQ 317
The Revised Maritime Section of the Korean Commercial Code, Rok Sang Yu and Jongkwan Peck: [1993] 3 LMCLQ 403

2321　Admiralty jurisdiction

See ADMIRALTY.

2322   Carriage of goods by sea—force majeure clause—scope

The sellers contracted to deliver a cargo of oil on a cif sale to the buyers. The contract provided that ship's nomination was to be given to the buyers at the latest at the time the vessel passed Gibraltar. There was also a force majeure clause in the contract which provided that neither party was to be liable for any breach, delay or non-performance which indirectly resulted from or was caused, in whole or in part, by impairment or interference with the sellers' means of supply or which directly or indirectly resulted from any cause beyond the sellers' control. The sellers nominated, by telex, a specified vessel. The buyers then confirmed acceptance of the vessel. On the same day, the sellers withdrew the nomination, but no substitute was nominated. The sellers later informed the buyers that due to unforeseen difficulties, oil of the contracted specification could not be delivered until after the agreed arrival date. Despite the offer of a different specification cargo, the parties were unable to agree on a price adjustment for it. The buyers sought damages for breach of contract. It was held at first instance that the most that the buyers accepted was that the sellers were entitled to substitute another vessel for the original and since no substitution had been made, the sellers were still obliged to make delivery of the original vessel, and that the sellers could not rely on a force majeure clause. On appeal by the sellers, *held*, the nomination telex effectively locked the original vessel into the contract subject only to the right to substitute another contractual vessel with another contractual cargo in immediate replacement of the original vessel. The sellers' option to substitute was not an obligation but a right and fell outside the scope of a force majeure clause. Although there was a principle that where a seller had enough goods to fulfil some contracts, but was prevented by force majeure from fulfilling all of them, it was no answer to a plea of force majeure for a buyer who did not receive his contractual quantity to say that the failure to deliver to him was not caused by force majeure but by the seller preferring other buyers, as long as the seller allocated the available goods in a reasonable manner. This principle did not apply in the present case, as there was no allocation and no shortage. The sellers were not allowed to invoke this principle ex post facto in relation to a shortage which only later came to light. The appeal would accordingly be dismissed.

Coastal (Bermuda) Petroleum Ltd v VTT Vulcan Petroleum SA, The Marine Star [1993] 1 Lloyd's Rep 329 (Court of Appeal: Nourse, McCowan and Hirst LJJ).

2323   Carriage of goods by sea—general average—accidental damage—temporary repairs

A vessel was accidentally damaged at sea and put into a port of refuge where it underwent temporary repairs to enable it to complete its voyage. Having completed the voyage, it underwent permanent repairs. General average, which was to be settled according to the York-Antwerp Rules 1974, was declared. It fell to be determined whether the shipowner was entitled to recover the appropriate proportion of the cost of the temporary repairs as a substituted expense under the York-Antwerp Rules. *Held*, Hoffmann LJ dissenting, a shipowner's obligation under his contract was to carry the cargo to its destination. If the ship was damaged but still capable of repair, he had to repair it. At common law, the expenses of repair were particular average expenses incurred by the shipowner and, in the absence of some contractual provision, there was no right to claim substituted expenditure as general average. Under the York-Antwerp Rules, the expense which fell to be compared with the cost of the temporary repairs was the expense which would have been incurred but had been saved and which would have been allowed in general average if the temporary repairs had not been effected. The rules could not be construed so as to require an assumption that the temporary repairs could not have been effected. Unless such an assumption was made, the owners were faced with an insuperable difficulty: they could not show that repairs in dry dock were necessary for the safe prosecution of the voyage because all that was necessary for this purpose were the temporary repairs which could be carried out afloat and were effected at the port of refuge. Unless the repairs were necessary for the safe prosecution of the voyage, the handling and other specified charges could not be admitted as general average. Accordingly, the temporary expenditure was not allowable in substitution and the vessel owners' claim would fail.

Marida Ltd v Oswal Steel, The Bijela [1993] 1 Lloyd's Rep 411 (Court of Appeal: Neill, Mann and Hoffmann LJJ). Decision of Hobhouse J [1992] 1 Lloyd's Rep 636 (1992 Abr para 2342) affirmed.

2324   Carriage of goods by sea—loss or damage—time limits

The United States Carriage of Goods by Sea Act 1936, s 3(6) provides that in any event a carrier and a ship will be discharged from all liability in respect of loss or damage unless the suit is brought within one year after delivery of the goods or the date when the goods ought to have been delivered.

The plaintiff charterers entered into a charterparty with the defendant shipowners. The charterparty provided that any disputes would be referred to arbitration in London and that they would be governed by English Law. The plaintiffs claimed that in breach of the charter, the vessel was presented for loading with tanks that were dirty and unsuitable for the carriage of cargo, which necessitated the cleaning of the tanks, which in turn delayed the start of the loading, and allegedly caused consequential financial loss and expense to the plaintiffs. No suit was brought within the year immediately following the allegations and when an appointment with an arbitrator finally took place the defendants successfully contended that the action was time-barred. The plaintiffs then sought a declaration that the action was not time-barred. This was rejected and on appeal, *held*, the issue was the construction of the 1936 Act, s 3(6) which was an exact counterpart of the Hague Rules, art 3, r 6. In following *Gouladris v Goldman* [1951] 1 QB 74 loss or damage within the meaning of the 1936 Act, s 3(6) was to be given a wide construction and extended to loss or damage relating to the goods and not just physical loss of or damage to them. Accordingly, the appeal would be dismissed.

Cargill International v CPN Tankers (Bermuda) Ltd (1993) Times, 10 June (Court of Appeal: Hirst and Roch LJJ and Sir David Croom-Johnson).

2325 Charterparty—arbitration clause—validity of arbitration clause
Australia
The parties entered into a voyage charterparty for the carriage of goods, the appellant as owner and the respondent as charterer. The charter contained a clause referring any dispute to arbitration in London under English law. When the particular dispute arose, the parties agreed to an Australian arbitrator and arbitration under Australian law and that decision was to be final. The arbitrator found for the respondent who subsequently issued a claim for the disputed sum. The appellant refused to pay, contending that the arbitrator's decision was void: the agreement to submit to Australian arbitration was invalid because legislation prohibited the purported ouster of the jurisdiction of the English court. The respondent then obtained a winding-up order against the appellant. On appeal, *held*, correctly construed, the relevant legislation did not render the agreement to submit to an Australian arbitration void. It followed that the arbitrator's award was valid and, accordingly, the appeal would be dismissed.

Bulk Chartering & Consultants Australia Pty Ltd v T & T Metal Trading Pty Ltd, The Krasnogorsk (1993) 114 ALR 189 (Supreme Court of New South Wales).

2326 Charterparty—assignment of shipowners' rights—recovery of advance payment of hire
An assignee received an advance payment of hire under a charterparty but the hire was subsequently not earned. The charterers applied to recover the charter hire paid to the assignees of the shipowners' rights on the ground that subsequent to the payment of hire there had been a failure of consideration under the charterparty. The application was granted and the assignees appealed. *Held*, the charterers contended that the payments of advance hire under the charterparty were similar to other advance payments of hire made in respect of a period which at the time of payment lay in the future and where the payments would only be conditional or provisional. It was accepted that an advance payment of hire under a charterparty was provisional in that if the hire was not earned for the whole period covered by the payment, the charterer would be entitled to recover a proportion of that amount. However those rights were between an owner and a charterer. The fact that the payment might have been "provisional" as between the charterers and the owners did not mean that the moneys retained some special characteristic when they reached the hands of a third party. In the circumstances there was no basis on which a claim for money had and received or for money paid for a consideration which had wholly failed would be brought against the assignees. The assignees were in a position analogous to that of a *bona fide* purchaser for value and accordingly, the appeal would be allowed.

Pan Ocean Shipping Co Ltd v Creditcorp Ltd (1993) Times, 28 January (Court of Appeal: Neill, Beldam and Kennedy LJJ).

This decision has been affirmed on appeal: [1994] 1 All ER 470.

2327 Charterparty—time-charter—legitimacy of last voyage order
It has been held that the legitimacy of an order by a charterer for a last voyage under a time-charter ought to be judged at the date the order was given rather than at the date when it became effective and the vessel was required to comply with it, namely, at or immediately prior to the

outset of the final voyage.
Torvald Klaveness A/S v Arni Maritime Corporation, The Gregos (1993) 2 Lloyd's Rep 335
(Court of Appeal: Russell, Hirst and Simon Brown LJJ).

2328 Fishing vessels

See FISHERIES.

2329 Limitation of liability—limitation action—costs of obtaining limitation decree

Liability for a collision between the plaintiffs and the defendants had been settled. The defendants
brought a limitation action against the plaintiffs and obtained a declaration that they were
entitled to limit their liability. The question then arose as to the costs of the limitation action.
The former practice under the Merchant Shipping Act 1894 was that the plaintiff in a limitation
action (ie the defendant in the present case), should pay the costs unless the defendant
unreasonably raised any issue. The defendants contended that the practice followed under the
1894 Act was not appropriate where limitation was sought under the Convention on Limitation
of Liability for Maritime Claims 1976, as incorporated by the Merchant Shipping Act 1979,
s17, Sch4, and submitted that costs should follow the event. *Held*, the application of the
Convention was very different from that of the 1894 Act. Under the latter the shipowner had
to establish absence of fault and privity and where he alone had access to the facts needed to
establish these, the shipowner should pay the costs of investigating the facts. Under the
Convention he merely had to establish that the claim was within the Convention, art 2, to
obtain a decree, unless the claimant proved the facts in art 4. If the claimant could prove facts
which defeated the right of limitation he would be entitled to costs. However if he could not do
this, costs should follow the event. This approach struck a fair balance between the parties.
The Celebration (1993) Times, 5 October (Queen's Bench Division: Clarke J).

2330 Merchant shipping—fees

The Merchant Shipping (Fees) (Amendment) Regulations 1993, SI 1993/1340 (in force on 1
June 1993), amend the 1991 Regulations, SI 1991/784, by prescribing fees for and in connecton
with boatmasters' licences issued under the Merchant Shipping (Local Passenger Vessels)
(Master's Licences and Hours, Manning and Training) Regulations 1993, SI 1993/1213.

2331 Merchant shipping—light dues

The Merchant Shipping (Light Dues) (Amendment) Regulations 1993, SI 1993/475 (in force
on 1 April 1993), provide for an increase of approximately 3,5 per cent in the scale of light dues
payable under the 1990 Regulations, SI 1990/364.

2332 Merchant shipping—load lines—unregistered ships

The Merchant Shipping (Load Lines) Act 1967 (Unregistered Ships) Order 1993, SI 1993/1994
(in force on 3 September 1993), replaces the 1991 Order, SI 1991/2543 (as amended), which
contained an error. The order applies the Merchant Shipping (Load Lines) Act 1967 to certain
classes of unregistered British ships as if they were ships registered in the United Kingdom. As a
result, the Secretary of State for Transport may exempt such ships from the provisions of the
Merchant Shipping (Load Lines) Act 1967, the Merchant Shipping (Load Lines) Rules 1968, SI
1968/1053, and from certain other provisions which may be specified in a Load Line Exemption
Certificate.

2333 Merchant shipping—local passenger vessels—masters' licences and hours—manning and training

The Merchant Shipping (Local Passenger Vessels) (Masters' Licences and Hours, Manning and
Training) Regulations 1993, SI 1993/1213 (in force in part on 1 June 1993 and in part on 1
October 1993) impose requirements in relation to local passenger vessels, in particular the
licensing of masters of such vessels, the hours of work of such masters, the manning of such
vessels and the training of the crew in emergency procedures.

2334 Merchant shipping—merchant seamen—child support maintenance—recovery

See para 374.

2335 Merchant shipping—navigational equipment

The Merchant Shipping (Navigational Equipment) Regulations 1993, SI 1993/69 (in force on 15 February 1993), revoke and re-enact the Merchant Shipping (Navigational Equipment) Regulations 1984, SI 1984/1203, as amended. The regulations align the radar equipment requirements and radar maintenance arrangements on United Kingdom vessels as well as the United Kingdom's magnetic compass and direction finder requirements with reg V/12 of the International Convention for the Safety of Life at Sea. The regulations refer to a merchant shipping notice which specifies the navigational equipment performance standards adopted by the International Maritime Organisation and the relevant standards which apply to United Kingdom vessels.

2336 Merchant shipping—overseas territories—prevention of collisions

The Merchant Shipping Act 1979 (Overseas Territories) (Amendment) Order 1993, SI 1993/1786 (in force on 21 August 1993), amends the 1989 Order, SI 1989/2400, by updating the reference to the Merchant Shipping (Distress Signals and Prevention of Collisions) Regulations 1989, SI 1989/638, to include a reference to the amendments to those regulations which came into force on 19 April 1991.

2337 Merchant Shipping (Registration, etc) Act 1993

The Merchant Shipping (Registration, etc) Act 1993, amends and restates the law relating to the registration of ships. The Act received the royal assent on 1 July 1993. Certain provisions came into force on 21 March 1994 and 1 May 1994: SI 1993/3137. For details of commencement, see the commencement table in the title STATUTES.

Section 1 establishes a central register for ships in the United Kingdom under the control of the Registrar General of Shipping and Seamen. The new register will contain those ships which are registered under the Merchant Shipping Act 1894, Pt I, small boats registered under the Merchant Shipping Act 1983, s 5 and fishing vessels registered under the Merchant Shipping Act 1988, s 13. Section 2 sets out the basic criteria for entitlement to register a ship and identifies the circumstances in which registration may be refused or terminated. The Secretary of State is empowered by s 3 to make regulations in connection with the registration of ships as British ships which will provide for all matters of administration and detail in respect of such registration.

Section 4 identifies those offences which relate to a ship's British connection, including furnishing false information to the Registrar General of Shipping and Seamen and intentionally altering suppressing, concealing or destroying a document containing information relevant to the British connection. It is an offence for an unregistered fishing vessel to fish for profit or to appear to be a registered British fishing vessel when unregistered: s 5. Section 6 sets out the private law provisions for registered ships, including provision as to the title to, and the registration of mortgages over, such ships.

The scope of registration is expanded by s 7 to enable ships registered elsewhere to be bareboat chartered-in and to be registered temporarily by charterers who are qualified to register British ships, subject to limitation. Section 8 deals with consequential amendments, the re-enactment of certain provisions of the Merchant Shipping Acts relating to British ships and the British flag. Sections 9, 10 deal with interpretation, short title and commencement.

2338 Merchant shipping—registration of ships

The Merchant Shipping (Registration of Ships) Regulations 1993, SI 1993/3138 (in force on 21 March 1994), provides for the registration of merchant ships, fishing vessels and small ships in accordance with the Merchant Shipping (Registration, etc) Act 1993. The regulations govern who is qualified to register such ships and the methods of application and renewal for registration.

2339 Merchant shipping—safety—equipment and installations

The Merchant Shipping (Pilot Ladders and Hoists) (Amendment) Regulations 1993, SI 1993/3232 (in force on 31 January 1994), amend the 1987 Regulations, SI 1987/1961, to implement the amendments made to the International Convention for the Safety of Life at Sea 1974, Chap V, reg 17, adopted by the Maritime Safety Committee of the International Maritime Organisation on 23 May 1991. More stringent requirements will apply to equipment or arrangements supplied or modified after the date on which the regulations come into force. The 1987 Regulations will continue to apply unamended to arrangements made, or equipment and installations fitted, before that date.

2340 Merchant shipping—safety—fire appliances

The Merchant Shipping (Fire Appliances) (Amendment) Regulations 1993, SI 1993/3162 (in force on 31 January 1994), further amend the 1980 Regulations, SI 1980/544, to implement the amendments made to the Annex of the International Convention for the Safety of Life at Sea 1974, Chap II-2, adopted by the International Maritime Organisation on 11 April 1989. Provision is made for alternative requirements for inert gas systems on chemical tankers and gas carriers, and the regulations require paint lockers to be protected by fire-extinguishing systems and new fire hoses to be of non-perishable material.

2341 Merchant shipping—safety—fire drills and extinguishing appliances

The Merchant Shipping (Musters and Training) (Amendment) Regulations 1993, SI 1993/3231 (in force on 31 January 1994), amend the 1986 Regulations, SI 1986/1071, to implement the amendments made to the Safety of Life at Sea Convention 1974, Chap III, reg 18, adopted by the Maritime Safety Committee of the International Maritime Organisation on 23 May 1991, both for ships to which the Convention applies and certain other ships. The regulations set down requirements as to drills and instructions in the use of fire extinguishing appliances.

2342 Merchant shipping—safety—fire protection

The Merchant Shipping (Fire Protection) (Amendment) Regulations 1993, SI 1993/3163 (in force on 31 January 1994), amend SI 1984/1218 and SI 1992/2360 so as to give effect to amendments to the Annex to the International Convention for the Safety of Life at Sea 1974. Provision alternative to the existing requirements for inert gas systems on chemical tankers and gas carriers is made. Provision is also made for fire-extinguishing systems for paint lockers and flammable liquid lockers. Various provision is made in respect of ships constructed on or after 1 February 1992, including the following: requirements are set out in relation to helicopter decks; amendments are made in relation to the restrictions as to the use of combustible materials in the structure of a ship; provision is made for fire hoses to be of non-perishable material; and requirements for ships carrying dangerous goods are extended to United Kingdom cargo ships of less than 500 gross tons. In addition, further requirements are set out for passenger ships constructed on or after 1 January 1994 with public spaces spanning three or more decks.

The Merchant Shipping (Fire Protection) (Non-United Kingdom) (Non-SOLAS Ships) (Amendment) Rules 1993, SI 1993/3161 (in force on 31 January 1994), amend the 1986 Rules, SI 1986/1248, so as to give effect to certain amendments to the International Convention for the Safety of Life at Sea 1974. The amendments include provision relating to (1) alternative requirements for inert gas systems on chemical tankers and gas carriers; (2) requirements for fire-extinguishing systems for paint lockers and flammable liquid lockers; (3) requirements in respect of helicopter decks on ships constructed on or after 1 February 1992; and (4) the extension of the requirements for ships carrying dangerous goods to ships of less than 500 gross tons constructed on or after 1 February 1992.

The Merchant Shipping (Fire Protection) (Ships Built Before 25th May 1980) (Amendment) Regulations 1993, SI 1993/3164 (in force on 31 January 1994), further amend the Merchant Shipping (Fire Protection) (Ships Built Before 25th May 1980) Regulations 1985, SI 1985/1218, to implement the amendments made to the Annex of the International Convention for the Safety of Life at Sea 1974, Chap II-2, adopted by the International Maritime Organisation on 11 April 1989. Provision is made for alternative requirements for inert gas systems on chemical tankers and gas carriers, and the regulations require paint lockers to be protected by fire extinguishing systems and new fire hoses to be of non-perishable material.

2343 Merchant shipping—safety—reasonable steps—owner's vicarious liability

A limited company was convicted of failing to take all reasonable steps to secure that a ship was operated in a safe manner contrary to the Merchant Shipping Act 1988, s 31 on the ground that the chief engineer of the company's ship was only allowed 2 hours 50 minutes to familiarise himself with the ship before sailing. The company appealed, by way of case stated, on the grounds that the justices had made no finding as to who had decided that the ship would go to sea, that they had concluded that failure by anybody in the company to take all reasonable steps gave rise to an offence under the 1988 Act, s 31 and that the company, as owner of the ship, was not vicariously liable for the omissions of all its employees. *Held*, Parliament had not intended to create a criminal liability on the part of the owner for an omission by any or all of its employees and as such the owner was not to assume vicarious liability for everything done in operating the ship. Where the owner was a limited company the duty to take all reasonable steps had to be performed by those who managed the ship for the company. The justices had failed to make a finding as to how the company was managed, their reasoning being that somebody must have failed to take all reasonable steps and that that somebody must have been an employee. Accordingly, the appeal would be allowed.

Seaboard Offshore Ltd v Secretary of State for Transport [1993] 3 All ER 25 (Queen's Bench Division: Staughton LJ and Buckley J).

2344 Merchant shipping—vessels in commercial use for sport or pleasure

The Merchant Shipping (Vessels in Commercial Use for Sport or Pleasure) Regulations 1993, SI 1993/1072 (in force in part on 13 May 1993 and in part on 1 April 1994), amend various regulations and rules which have a definition of either "pleasure yacht" or "pleasure craft" so as to substitute a new definition, "pleasure vessel". This has the effect of excluding vessels in commercial use. In addition, the Merchant Shipping (Load Line) Rules 1968, SI 1968/1053, as amended, are applied to vessels used for sport or recreation when in commercial use.

2345 Pilotage—negligence of pilot—liability of harbour authority

The plaintiffs' ship was damaged in a collision while in the charge of a compulsory pilot employed by the harbour authority. The plaintiffs brought proceedings against the harbour authority, claiming that it was vicariously liable for the alleged negligence of the pilot because it owed a positive duty to provide pilotage services under the Pilotage Act 1987. The plaintiffs further claimed that the harbour authority was liable in contract, having contracted to supply pilotage services subject to a statutory or common law implied term that they would be performed with reasonable skill and care. On the trial of a preliminary issue, *held*, the 1987 Act, s 2 did not create new duties for harbour authorities, but gave statutory definition to duties assumed under earlier legislation. Under s 2 the harbour authority was required to supply properly authorised pilots for ships, but was not under a duty to pilot ships. In the light of the fact that the plaintiffs had not alleged that the pilot was incompetent or that the harbour authority was in breach of duty in providing a pilot who was not properly qualified, the authority was not vicariously liable in tort for the negligence of the pilot on board the plaintiffs' ship. As the arrangement between the parties was merely one to discharge the plaintiffs' statutory obligation by taking a compulsory pilot and paying for his services, there was no contract between the parties. Accordingly, the plaintiffs' claim would be dismissed.

Oceangas (Gibraltar) Ltd v Port of London Authority, The Cavendish (1993) Times, 24 May (Queen's Bench Division: Clarke J).

2346 Pollution—prevention

The Merchant Shipping (Prevention of Oil Pollution) (Amendment) Order 1993, SI 1993/1580 (in force on 7 July 1993), further amends the 1983 Order, SI 1983/1106, by enabling regulations to be made to give effect to certain amendments to the Annex of the Protocol of 1978 relating to the International Convention for the Prevention of Pollution from Ships 1973 adopted by the Marine Environment Protection Committee of the International Maritime Organisation.

The Merchant Shipping (Prevention of Oil Pollution) (Amendment) Regulations 1993, SI 1993/1680 (in force on 20 July 1993), further amend the 1983 Regulations, SI 1983/1398, by giving effect to amendments to the International Convention for the Prevention of Pollution from Ships 1973, Annex I adopted by the Marine Environment Protection Committee (MEPC) of the International Maritime Organisation. The main purpose of the amendments adopted by the MEPC are the designation of the Antarctic as a special area, the introduction of a requirement for ships to carry oil pollution emergency plans, an increase in the stringency of discharge criteria, enhancement of the design criteria for new oil tankers, and modification of the survey and construction requirements for existing tankers.

The Merchant Shipping (Prevention of Pollution by Garbage) (Amendment) Order 1993, SI 1993/1581 (in force on 7 July 1993), amends the 1988 Order, SI 1988/2252, by enabling regulations to be made to give effect to certain amendments to the 1978 Protocol relating to the International Convention for the Prevention of Pollution from Ships 1973, Annex 5 adopted by the Marine Environment Protection Committee of the International Maritime Organisation.

The Merchant Shipping (Prevention of Pollution by Garbage) (Amendment) Regulations 1993, SI 1993/1681 (in force on 20 July 1993), further amend the 1988 Regulations, SI 1988/2292. The regulations implement the amendments to the International Convention for the Prevention of Pollution from Ships 1973, Annex V which have been adopted by the Marine Environment Protection Committee (MEPC) of the International Maritime Organisation. The Antarctic has been added to the list of special areas to which stricter discharge requirements apply and ships entering the area are required to have capacity for the retention of garbage while in the area.

2347 Protection of wrecks—restricted areas

The Protection of Wrecks (Designation No 1) Order 1993, SI 1993/976 (in force on 22 April 1993), designates as a restricted area for the purposes of the Protection of Wrecks Act 1973 an area off Lacada Point in County Antrim, Northern Ireland, round the site of what is believed to be the wreck of the vessel "Girona" which is of historical and archaeological importance.

SOCIAL SECURITY AND SOCIAL SERVICES

Halsbury's Laws of England (4th edn) Vol 33, paras 301–1077

2348 Articles

Access Denied, David Thomas (on social security law): LS Gaz, 1 December 1993, p 19
Challenging the Vires of Social Security Regulations—*Chief Adjudication Officer v Foster*, Neville
    Harris (on *Chief Adjudication Officer v Foster* [1993] 1 All ER 705, HL (1992 Abr para 2455)):
    56 MLR 710

2349 Accommodation—provision by local authority—assessment of resources

The National Assistance (Assessment of Resources) (Amendment No 2) Regulations 1993, SI 1993/2230 (in force on 4 October 1993), make further amendments to the 1992 Regulations, SI 1992/2977, which relate to the assessment by local authorities of the resources of residents in accommodation arranged under the National Assistance Act 1948, Pt III. Provision is made that income derived from certain premises occupied by a third party is no longer to be treated as capital.

2350 Accommodation—provision by local authority—persons in residential care

The Residential Accommodation (Relevant Premises, Ordinary Residence and Exemptions) Regulations 1993, SI 1993/477 (in force on 1 April 1993), enable local authorities to make residential accommodation arrangements for certain categories of people who are in or temporarily absent from independent sector residential care and nursing homes on 31 March 1993. The regulations extend the definitions of relevant premises contained in the National Assistance Act 1948, s 26A(2), to cover other premises in which residents may qualify for preserved rights. Residents are to be treated as ordinarily resident in relevant premises if they are in fact resident in such premises or if they are temporarily absent from such premises. The regulations set out the categories of people for whom local authorities will be entitled to make arrangements.

2351 Accommodation—provision by local authority—sums for personal requirements

The National Assistance (Sums for Personal Requirements) Regulations 1993, SI 1993/462 (in force on 1 April 1993), set out the weekly sums which local authorities are, in the absence of special circumstances, to assume that residents in accommodation arranged under the National Assistance Act 1948, Pt III will need for their personal requirements. From 12 April 1993 all residents will be assumed to need £12·65 per week, in addition to any attendance allowance, constant attendance allowance or the care component of any disability living allowance payable, unless that allowance is otherwise disregarded.

2352 Attendance allowance—blind person—no other relevant disability— entitlement

The applicant was blind and walked about his own flat without danger to himself although he did require assistance when taking a bath and cutting up food. In 1989 a medical practitioner determined that the applicant did not satisfy any of the conditions of the Social Security Act 1975, s 35(1) for an attendance allowance. The determination was reconsidered by another practitioner and was again rejected and later a third delegated medical practitioner refused to revise the decision. On appeal against the refusal, *held*, Nolan LJ dissenting, a blind person who suffered from no other significant physical or mental disability, was entitled to an attendance allowance if he required attention throughout the day in connection with frequently performed bodily functions. If a blind person required attention in connection with the bodily function of walking, on the basis that he needed the help of a guide when in unfamiliar surroundings, then his right to attendance allowance would depend upon factors which included how often in each day he claimed to need to go to unfamiliar surroundings and the extent to which his asserted need was accepted as a requirement. Walking in unfamiliar surroundings, in connection with which the applicant needed assistance, was not a bodily function within the concept set out in the 1975 Act. Accordingly, the appeal would be dismissed.

Mallinson v Secretary of State for Social Security (1993) Times, 2 April (Court of Appeal: Ralph Gibson, Mann and Nolan LJJ).

1975 Act, s 35(1) now Social Security Contributions and Benefits Act 1992, s 64.

2353 Benefits—claims and payments

The Social Security (Claims and Payments) Amendment Regulations 1993, SI 1993/478 (in force on 1 April 1993), amend the 1987 Regulations, SI 1987/1968. The regulations provide that a person in receipt of income support, either alone or with certain other benefits, who is liable to make payments in place of child support maintenance under the Child Support Act 1991, s 43(1) may, subject to certain restrictions, have deductions made from those benefits to satisfy that liability.

The Social Security (Claims and Payments) Amendment (No 2) Regulations 1993, SI 1993/1113 (in force on 12 May 1993), amend the 1987 Regulations supra by adding unemployment benefit, income support, sickness benefit, invalidity benefit and severe disablement allowance to the list of benefits which may be paid by automated credit transfer.

The Social Security (Claims and Payments) Amendment (No 3) Regulations 1993, SI 1993/2113 (in force in part on 27 September 1993, in part on 25 October 1993), amend the 1979 Regulations, SI 1979/628, by permitting the record of industrial accidents which employers are required to keep to be kept by electronic means. The 1987 Regulations supra are amended in order to deal with the case where it is impossible to determine the date on which a request for a claim form for disability living allowance was received. Other amendments include a provision to permit amounts of family credit or disability working allowance of not more than £4 a week to be paid in a lump sum. An extension of the time allowed for applying for someone to be appointed to make a claim for benefit to which a deceased person was entitled and for making the claim is also provided for. Other amendments relate to the suspension of benefit pending an appeal, to the extinguishment of the right to payment of benefit and permitting benefit to be paid direct to the proprietor of a residential home. The Community Charges (Deductions from Income Support) (No 2) Regulations 1990, SI 1990/545, and the Council Tax (Deductions from Income Support) Regulations 1993, SI 1993/494, are amended to deal with the priority to be given when more than one application for deductions from income support in respect of council tax or community charge is received.

The Social Security (Miscellaneous Provisions) Amendment Regulations 1993, SI 1993/846 (in force in part on 4 April 1993 and in part on 19 April 1993), amend the Income Support (General) Regulations 1987, SI 1987/1967. The regulations provide that for the purposes of calculating a claimant's entitlement to income support, maintenance payments made under the Child Support Act 1991 are to be treated as income. The regulations specify how that income is to be calculated. It is further provided that provisions in the Social Security (Payments on Account, Overpayments and Recovery) Amendment Regulations 1993, SI 1993/650 (see para 2358), which refer to the present regulations, will come into force on 19 April 1993.

2354 Benefits—community care

The Social Security Benefits (Miscellaneous Amendments) Regulations 1993, SI 1993/518 (in force on 1 April 1993) amend a number of other social security benefit regulations in order to take account of the changes to care in the community which were introduced on 1 April 1993. SI 1991/2740 and SI 1991/2890 are amended so that persons residing in residential care or nursing homes before 1 April 1993 retain the right to receive attendance and disability living allowance. These allowances are not available to persons in residential care homes owned and managed by local authorities. SI 1992/3147 is amended to provide the circumstances in which persons living in small residential care homes on 31 March 1993 which were not registered under the Registered Homes Act 1984 have preserved rights to attendance allowance or the care component of disability living allowance. SI 1987/1967 is amended to make specific provisions in the income support scheme for persons living in or temporarily absent from residential accommodation on 31 March 1993 as well as providing that some or all of voluntary or charitable payments made to a person to enable him to live in a home of his choice must be disregarded when assessing the income of a resident of a residential care or nursing home. SI 1987/1971 is amended to make specific provision, in relation to housing benefit, for persons who occupied or were temporarily absent from residential accommodation on 31 March 1993.

2355 Benefits—deductions—child support maintenance

See para 2383.

2356 Benefits—general

The Social Security (Miscellaneous Amendments) (No 2) Regulations 1993, SI 1993/963 (in force on 22 April 1993), amend the Income Support (General) Regulations 1987, SI 1987/1967, the Family Credit (General) Regulations 1987, SI 1987/1973, the Housing Benefit (General) Regulations 1987, SI 1987/1971, the Council Tax Benefit (General) Regulations 1992, SI 1992/1814, and the Disability Working Allowance Regulations 1991, SI 1991/2887. The 1993 Regulations establish two new funds, payments from which are to be disregarded in determining the entitlement of a person to income support, housing benefit, council tax benefit, family credit or disability working allowance.

2357 Benefits—income-related benefits—general

The Income-related Benefits Schemes (Miscellaneous Amendments) Regulations 1993, SI 1993/315 (in force on dates between 29 March and 13 April 1993), further amend the Income Support (General) Regulations, SI 1987/1967, by reducing, from two years to one year, the period of time a person must have been unemployed before his applicable amount can be reduced in cases of his failure to attend courses. Such courses may be provided by or on behalf of the Secretary of State. The deduction to be made in the case of non-dependants and their partners is specified. In relation to the calculation of income, the regulations further amend the notional income provisions in respect of occupational pensions, and they provide a disregard in respect of the earnings of a claimant or partner who is entitled to the carer premium. The Family Credit (General) Regulations 1987, SI 1987/1973, and the Disability Working Allowance (General) Regulations 1991, SI 1991/2887, are further amended to provide that where a child or young person has capital in excess of £3,000, any maintenance income of that child or young person is to be treated as the income of the claimant. In addition, the method of calculation of weekly maintenance is amended. Statutory maternity pay may no longer be treated as earnings, and the regulations provide that a guardian's allowance may be disregarded.

Amendments are also made to 1987 Regulations, SI 1987/1967, 1973, and the 1991 Regulations, SI 1991/2887, consequential on the introduction of the council tax.

The Income-related Benefits Schemes (Miscellaneous Amendments) (No 2) Regulations 1993, SI 1993/1150 (in force on 25 May 1993), amend the Housing Benefit (General) Regulations 1987, SI 1987/1971, the Income Support (General) Regulations 1987, SI 1987/1967, the Community Charge Benefits (General) Regulations 1989, SI 1989/1321, and the Council Tax Benefit (General) Regulations 1992, SI 1992/1814. Now, in reviewing claims for specified benefits, the question of whether the Secretary of State exceeded his powers in making a provision in a regulation or order is not a question arising in connection with an authority's or a review board's power to review on the ground of a mistake of law. In addition, the regulations provide that in calculating a claimant's applicable amount for housing benefit, income support or council tax benefit, where he has a partner who is blind or treated as blind, that person's presence will not prevent the claimant from satisfying the qualifying condition for a severe disability premium.

The Income-related Benefits Schemes (Miscellaneous Amendments) (No 3) Regulations 1993, SI 1993/1540 (in force on dates between 1 August and 7 September 1993), further amend the Council Tax Benefit (General) Regulations 1992, SI 1992/1814, the Disability Working Allowance (General) Regulations 1991, SI 1991/2887, the Family Credit (General) Regulations 1987, SI 1987/1973, the Housing Benefit (General) Regulations 1987, SI 1987/1971 and the Income Support (General) Regulations 1987, SI 1987/1967, so as to increase the amount to be allowed in respect of the cost of books and equipment in calculating a student's grant income and increasing the amount of the deduction to be made in calculating a student's eligible rent in respect of housing benefit.

The Income-related Benefits Schemes (Miscellaneous Amendments) (No 4) Regulations 1993, SI 1993/2119 (in force in part on 4 October 1993, in part on 5 October 1993), amend the Income Support (General) Regulations 1987, SI 1987/1967, the Family Credit (General) Regulations, SI 1987/1973, and the Disability Working Allowance (General) Regulations 1991, SI 1991/2887. The amendments include the introduction and amendment of certain definitions and an alteration in the circumstances in which a person is to be treated as being a member of the household. Provision is made that the disregard of a specified amount of certain war pensions and payments is not to apply where the pension or payment falls to be disregarded under other specified provisions, with respect to the calculation income other than earnings. £200 of certain payments made as a training bonus is to be disregarded with respect to the calculation of capital. The amendments made to the 1987 Regulations, SI 1987/1967, include a provision that a person is not to be treated as if he is in remunerative work if he is absent from work due to illness or maternity. The 1993 Regulations also alter the element of personal expenses contained in the applicable amount of people in specified types of accommodation and amend the provision relating to the disregard of certain earnings where the employment has been terminated or the claimant has ceased to be engaged in work with respect to the calculation of earnings of employed earners. The amendments made to SI 1987/1973 and SI 1991/2887 include a provision that a person who is absent from work owing to illness or maternity is not to be regarded as on holiday.

The Income-related Benefits Schemes and Social Security (Recoupment) Amendment Regulations 1993, SI 1993/1249 (in force in part on 14 May 1993, in part on 3 June 1993), further amend the Family Credit (General) Regulations 1987, SI 1987/1973, the Housing Benefit (General) Regulations 1987, SI 1987/1971, the Income Support (General) Regulations 1987, SI 1987/1967, the Disability Working Allowance (General) Regulations 1991, SI 1991/2887, and the Council Tax Benefit (General) Regulations 1992, SI 1992/1814. The regulations provide that payments from a specified charitable trust are to be disregarded in determining the entitlement of a person to specified benefits. The Social Security Recoupment Regulations 1990, SI 1990/322, are also amended in order to exempt payments made into the specified trust from the effects of the Social Security Act 1992, s 82. The 1987 Regulations, SI 1987/1971, are further amended in order to extend the circumstances in which a claim for benefit is required to be referred to a rent officer to make a determination with respect to a person's rent.

2358 Benefits—overpayment—method of recovery

The Social Security (Payments on account, Overpayments and Recovery) Amendment Regulations 1993, SI 1993/650 (in force on 5 April 1993), amend the 1988 Regulations, SI 1988/664, in order to provide that where an interim payment of income support is made to a person entitled to child support maintenance under the Child Support Act 1991, or under a court order or a maintenance agreement, there is no longer a requirement that he must be given notice of his liability to have the payment brought into account and to repay it. The regulations also provide for child support maintenance in respect of the period between the effective date of a maintenance assessment and the making of that assessment to be prescribed income for the purposes of the Social Security Administration Act 1992, s 74(1).

2359 Benefits—overpayment—misrepresentation

The Social Security Act 1986, s 53 provides that where it has been determined that, whether fraudulently or otherwise, a person has misrepresented, or failed to disclose, any material fact and in consequence of the misrepresentation or failure a payment has been made in respect of a benefit to which s 53 applies, the Secretary of State will be entitled to recover the amount of any payment which he would not have made but for the misrepresentation or failure to disclose.

The plaintiff, who was in receipt of income support, later went to an unemployment benefit office and made a further claim for unemployment benefit. He was given form B1 on which he stated that he had claimed unemployment benefit but had not received any. He then received both income support and unemployment benefit. On receiving his weekly payments of benefit from the Post Office he made the standard declaration that he had correctly reported any fact which would affect the amount of his payment and that he was entitled to the amount calculated. It was later discovered that the amount of income support had been wrongly calculated and that he had been overpaid. The Department of Health and Social Security successfully sought to recover the amount he was overpaid. The plaintiff's appeal to a social security commissioner was dismissed. On further appeal, *held*, Evans LJ dissenting, it was common ground that the receipt of unemployment benefit affected the amount of income support payable and also that the plaintiff had not reported the fact that he had received unemployment benefit, as opposed to the fact that he had claimed it. The plaintiff was aware that he was in receipt of unemployment benefit and was also aware that that affected the amount of income support to which he was entitled and as such, that constituted a failure to disclose a material fact. The signing of the declaration by the plaintiff constituted non-disclosure of a material fact and as such was a misrepresentation. Therefore, the failure to declare receipt of income support when claiming unemployment benefit was a misrepresentation within the meaning of the 1986 Act, s 53 and any overpayment would be recoverable. Accordingly, the appeal would be dismissed.

Jones v Chief Adjudication Officer; Sharples v Chief Adjudication Officer [1994] 1 All ER 225 (Court of Appeal: Dillon, Stuart-Smith and Evans LJJ).

2360   Benefits—up-rating

The Social Security Benefits Up-rating Order 1993, SI 1993/349 (in force on 22 February 1993), increases the rates and amounts of certain benefits. The order increases (1) the rates of certain workmen's compensation and industrial disease benefits; (2) the lower rate of statutory maternity pay; (3) the rate of graduated retirement benefit; (4) the weekly rates of (a) disability living allowance; and (b) child benefit and one parent benefit. The weekly rates of statutory sick pay are also specified, and the earnings limits for child dependency increases are set out. The applicable amounts for family credit, disability working allowance are also specified. The order states the amount of sums relevant to the applicable amount for the purposes of income support, housing benefit and council tax benefit. The Social Security Benefits Up-rating Order 1991, SI 1991/503, and the Social Security Benefits Up-rating (No 2) Order 1991, SI 1991/2910, are both revoked.

The Social Security Benefits Up-rating Regulations 1993, SI 1993/723 (in force on 12 April 1993), provide that where a question has arisen about the 1993 Order supra on a benefit already in payment, the altered rates will not apply until the question is determined by an adjudicating authority. The regulations also increase the earnings limits applying to (1) unemployability supplement; (2) those undertaking work in certain circumstances while receiving sickness or invalidity benefit; and (3) child dependency increases payable with invalid care allowance. The 1992 Regulations, SI 1992/469, are revoked.

2361   Child benefit—adjustment of rates—single parents

The Child Benefit and Social Security (Miscellaneous Amendments) Regulations 1993, SI 1993/965 (in force on 12 April 1993), further amend the Child Benefit and Social Security (Fixing and Adjustment of Rates) Regulations 1976, SI 1976/1267, so that a single parent is disentitled to the increase in the weekly rate of child benefit if one of the benefits specified is paid to him. Guardian's allowance is removed from the list of specified benefits. In addition, an amendment is made to the Social Security (Overlapping Benefits) Regulations 1979, SI 1979/597, so as to provide that there will be no adjustment of guardian's allowance in respect of any increase in the weekly rate of child benefit for single parents.

2362   Community charge benefit—general

The Local Government Finance Act 1992 (Community Charge Benefits) Saving Order 1993, SI 1993/502 (in force on 31 March 1993), provides that the power conferred by the Social Security Administration Act 1992, s 63(3) to make regulations for reviews of determinations relating to community charge benefits in relation to any year which ends before 1 April 1993, may be exercised as if the amendment made to s 63(3) by the Local Government Finance Act 1992, Sch 9, para 14 (which replaces the reference to community charge benefit by a reference to council tax benefit) had not been made.

2363   Community charge benefit—savings and transitional provision

The Local Government Finance Act 1992 (Community Charge Benefit) Savings and Transitional Order 1993, SI 1993/232 (in force on 9 March 1993), provides that, notwithstanding the amendments made to the Social Security Administration Act 1992, ss 140, 163(2)(d) by the replacement of references to community charge benefit subsidy by references to council tax benefit subsidy, those provisions are to have effect as originally enacted in respect of community charge benefit subsidy in relation to any year ending before 1 April 1993. Accordingly, the Secretary of State may make provision, in relation to any such year, in respect of community charge benefit subsidy as if the amendments had not been made. Transitional provision is also made to enable the Secretary of State to withold, adjust or deduct sums from payments of council tax benefit subsidy due to a billing or levying authority in order to settle claims by an authority for community charge benefit subsidy.

2364   Community charge benefit—subsidy—calculation

See para 2378.

2365   Community provisions

See EUROPEAN COMMUNITIES.

2366   Contributions—regulations

The Social Security (Contributions) Amendment Regulations 1993, SI 1993/260 (in force on 11 April 1993), further amend the 1979 Regulations, SI 1979/591, by (1) providing that where a person starts or ends self-employment, or wishes to pay or cease paying voluntary contributions, he must notify the Secretary of State in writing. A person paying such contributions must also notify any change of address. Amendments are made to the method of, and time for, payment of Class 2 and Class 3 contributions. Provision is made for the Secretary of State to issue bank giro credit forms to facilitate payment, and an amendment is made in respect of the date by which Class 3 contributions are to be paid. Other minor amendments are made.

The Social Security (Contributions) Amendment (No 2) Regulations 1993, SI 1993/281 (in force on 6 April 1993), further amend the 1979 Regulations supra by increasing the weekly lower and upper tax earnings, to £56 and £420 respectively, for the tax year beginning 6 April 1993. The abatement of percentage rates of Class 1 contributions payable by and in respect of serving members of the forces is increased to 0·5 per cent.

The Social Security (Contributions) Amendment (No 3) Regulations 1993, SI 1993/282 (in force on 6 April 1993), further amend the 1979 Regulations supra by increasing the special rate of Class 2 contributions payable by share fishermen from £7·00 to £7·75.

The Social Security (Contributions) Amendment (No 4) Regulations 1993, SI 1993/583 (in force on 6 April 1993), further amend the 1979 Regulations, SI 1979/591, in respect of payments to be disregarded. The regulations provide that certain payments made to employees in respect of travel or accommodation arising out of a disruption to public transport caused by a strike or other industrial action, are not to be treated as earnings. Subject to certain conditions, certain payments in respect of foreign travel expenses are to be disregarded as earnings.

The Social Security (Contributions) Amendment (No 5) Regulations 1993, SI 1993/821 (in force on 19 April 1993), further amend the 1979 Regulations supra. The new regulations provide for interest to be payable on Class 1 contributions unpaid after the fourteenth day after the end of the tax year in respect of which they were due and on Class 1A contributions unpaid after the fourteenth day after the end of the tax year in which they were due to be paid. Interest is also now payable in certain circumstances to employers who have overpaid either Class 1 or Class 1A contributions. Provision is also made for the repayment and remission of interest in certain circumstances.

The Social Security (Contributions) Amendment (No 6) Regulations 1993, SI 1993/2094 (in force on 21 September 1993), further amend the 1979 Regulations supra. The regulations provide that for the purpose of satisfying the contribution conditions for contributory benefit, where payment of a Class 2 or Class 3 contribution is made by the due date, after the date when a person could otherwise have received a contributory benefit, the payment is to be treated as having been made by the earlier date, except in certain circumstances.

The Social Security (Contributions) Amendment (No 7) Regulations 1993, SI 1993/2925 (in force on 1 December 1993), further amend the 1979 Regulations supra by providing that where a payment of earnings is made by way of a beneficial interest in any asset which is capable of being traded on a recognised investment exchange and which has a published selling price, the value of the payment is to be determined by reference to the selling price. The regulations also add to the list of assets not to be disregarded as payments in kind for the purpose of calculating earnings.

The Social Security (Contributions) (Miscellaneous Amendments) Regulations 1993, SI 1993/2736 (in force on 30 November 1993), further amend the 1979 Regulations supra so as to provide that where an employer pays, or makes a contribution towards, an employee's liability for council tax, that payment is to be disregarded as earnings where the employer provides the accommodation. Such provision does not give rise to a liability to income tax under Schedule E. In addition, the regulations amend the Social Security Contributions and Benefits Act 1992, s 10 by providing that the Class 1A contribution due in respect of fuel provided by the employer for the employee's private motoring is no longer reduced by 50 per cent where an employee's business travel exceeds 18,000 miles a year.

2367 Contributions—re-rating

The Social Security (Contributions) (Re-rating) Order 1993, SI 1993/280 (in force on 6 April 1993), increases the amounts of weekly earnings specified in the secondary earnings brackets of the Social Security Contributions and Benefits Act 1993, s 9(3). The specified rates of Class 2 and Class 3 contributions in the Act are increased, as is the amount of earnings below which an earner may be excepted from liability for Class 2 contributions. The lower and upper limits of specified profits or gains between which Class 4 contributions are payable are also increased.

2368 Council tax benefit—entitlement

The Council Tax Benefit (General) Amendment Regulations 1993, SI 1993/688 (in force on 1 April 1993), amend the 1992 Regulations, SI 1992/1814. The changes include (1) providing for the calculation of the amount to be deducted in respect of income tax in relation to a claimant's earnings to take account of the lower rate of income tax; (2) excepting certain payments from the meaning of earnings with regard to self-employed earners; (3) amending the way in which the income of a child or young person is calculated; (4) amending the provisions specifying how notional capital attributed to a claimant is to be reduced; (5) increasing the payment towards the cost of books to be excluded from a student's grant in calculating his income; (6) amending the calculation of a person's maximum council tax benefit; (7) providing for the disregard of certain payments in calculating the income of non-dependents; (8) amending the provision prescribing the residents of a dwelling in respect of whom entitlement to an alternative maximum council tax benefit does not arise; (9) amending the provision governing the day when a change of circumstance is to have effect where two or more changes take place in the same benefit week; (10) further specifying the evidence and information which may be required in respect of a claim; (11) enabling community charge benefit review boards to undertake further reviews of council tax benefit determinations in certain cases; and (12) amending the income and capital of a claimant which are to be disregarded.

2369 Council tax benefit—general

See para 2376.

2370 Council tax benefit—permitted total

The Council Tax Benefit (Permitted Total) Order 1993, SI 1993/689 (in force on 1 April 1993), outlines the basis for calculating the permitted total of council tax benefit for any year for authorities granting such benefit under the Social Security Contributions and Benefits Act 1992 and limits the amount by which council tax benefit payments may be increased.

2371 Disability (Grants) Act 1993

The Disability (Grants) Act 1993 empowers the Secretary of State to make grants to certain organisations concerned with disabled persons. The Act received the royal assent on 27 May 1993 and came into force on that date.

2372   Disability living allowance—conditions of entitlement

The Social Security (Disability Living Allowance) (Amendment) Regulations 1993, SI 1993/1939 (in force on 26 August 1993), amend the 1991 Regulations, SI 1991/2890. In relation to assisted dialysis, the circumstances in which a person who is undergoing renal dialysis in a National Health Service hospital is to be taken to satisfy the conditions of entitlement to the care component of a disability living allowance are modified, and references to certain provisions are substituted consequential on the consolidation of the law relating to social security.

2373   Disability living allowance—introduction

The Social Security (Introduction of Disability Living Allowance) (Amendment) Regulations 1993, SI 1993/408 (in force on 1 April 1993), further amend the 1991 Regulations, SI 1991/2891. The regulations extend the period during which a transition from mobility allowance and attendance allowance to the two components of disability living allowance must be made.

The Social Security (Introduction of Disability Allowance) (Amendment) (No 2) Regulations 1993, SI 1993/1739 (in force on 6 August 1993) as amended by SI 1993/2704 (in force on 25 November 1993), amend the 1991 Regulations supra by providing for the termination of awards of disability living allowance for persons who have two awards of disability living allowance for fixed periods ending on different days. Excepted persons are to be treated as having been awarded one award of disability living allowance, and the 1993 Regulations also provide for the rate of payment of awards of disability living allowance. Further provision for the manner in which awards of disability living allowance are to be paid is also made.

2374   Earnings factors—revaluation

The Social Security Revaluation of Earnings Factors Order 1993, SI 1993/1159 (in force on 25 May 1993), increases the earnings factors relevant to the calculation of the additional pension in the rate of any long-term benefit, or of any guaranteed minimum pension, or to any other calculation required under the Social Security Pensions Act 1975, Pt III, for the tax years 1978–79 to 1992–93, by specified percentages varying from 310·4 per cent (1978–79) to 5 per cent (1992–93).

2375   Housing benefit—amount—reduction—suitable alternative accommodation

The applicants originally owned their own property but due to unemployment were forced to sell. The applicants moved to another house which was let to them on an assured shorthold tenancy where they applied for housing benefit. The rent officer determined that the correct market rent was less than what the applicants were paying in rent. The local authority then reduced the housing benefit payable. The applicants unsuccessfully appealed to the Housing Benefit Review Board, on the grounds that the contractual rent did not exceed the market rent and that there was no accommodation at lower prices available in the private sector for letting. A further application for judicial review was also refused. On appeal, held, there was no satisfactory answer to the issue as to how the Review Board had formulated its opinion that alternative accommodation suitable for the reasonable needs of the applicants was available on the market at the level of rent allowed and upon which basis they felt able to reject the contrary case which the applicant advanced. The decision letter provided to the applicants was defective in that the evidence appeared to have been entirely general and unspecific. The evidence upon which the Review Board purported to rely did not justify its conclusion as a matter of law, and accordingly, the appeal would be allowed.

R v Housing Benefit Review Board, ex p Gibson (1993) 25 HLR 487 (Court of Appeal: Bingham MR, Kennedy and Evans LJJ).

2376   Housing benefit—general

The Housing Benefit (General) Amendment Regulations 1993, SI 1993/317 (in force on dates between 29 March and 5 April 1993), further amend the 1987 Regulations, SI 1987/1971. The major changes made by the regulations include (1) further specifying, in certain cases, the circumstances in which a person is to be treated as occupying a dwelling as his home; (2) enabling authorities to substitute a higher figure for unreasonably low ineligible service charges; (3) providing that certain payments in respect of children accommodated with a claimant are not to be treated as the earnings of a self-employed earner, and providing that when certain payments are used to pay the claimant's rent, the rent to be taken into account is the claimant's eligible rent less certain deductions in respect of non-dependants; (4) providing that where a child or young person has capital in excess of £3,000, any of his income consisting of maintenance is to be treated as income of the claimant; (5) specifying, in relation to the calculation of a person's maximum housing benefit, the deduction to be made in the case of non-dependants and their partners; (6) providing, with respect to the calculation of income, a disregard of guardian's allowance and a disregard in respect of the earnings of a claimant or a partner entitled to the carer premium and remove the disregard of maintenance payments made by a claimant. The amount to be disregarded in relation to certain claimants entitled to higher pensioner premium is specified and the disregards in respect of charitable and voluntary payments and income arising from disregarded capital is amended.

The Housing Benefit and Council Tax Benefit (Miscellaneous Amendments) Regulations 1993, SI 1993/2118 (in force on 4 October 1993), amend the Housing Benefit (General) Regulations 1987, SI 1987/1971 and the Council Tax Benefit (General) Regulations 1992, SI 1992/1814. Various changes are made by the regulations with respect to each benefit, including the following: (1) two definitions, namely "date of claim" and "maternity leave", are added; (2) a person absent from work due to illness or maternity leave is not to be treated as engaged in remunerative work; (3) provision is made to treat certain capital of a child or young person as income; (4) the period by reference to which the earnings of self-employed earners are to be estimated is altered from 52 weeks to one year; (5) provision is made with respect to the calculation of earnings of employed earners, including further specification of the amounts which are to be included as earnings, and the amendment of provisions relating to the disregard of certain earnings where the employment has been terminated or the claimant has ceased to be engaged in work; (6) amendments are made to provisions specifying the amount to be deducted in relation to social security contributions, with respect to the calculation of earnings of self-employed earners; (7) with respect to the calculation of a person's applicable amount, amendments are made to the conditions relating to severe disability premium; (8) in relation to the calculation of income other than earnings, the disregard of a specified amount of certain war pensions and payments is not to apply where the pension or payment falls to be disregarded under other specified provisions; and (9) in relation to housing benefit only, amendments are made to the provisions specifying the circumstances in which a person is to be treated as being or not being a member of the household.

2377   Housing benefit—non-dependant—meaning of adult child

The Housing Benefit (General) Regulations 1987, SI 1987/1971, reg 3(1) provides that "non-dependant" means any person who normally resides with the claimant, with certain exceptions. Regulation 3(2) provides that an exception to reg 3(1) exists for a person who jointly occupies the claimant's dwelling.

The claimant sought judicial review of a decision to make deductions from their benefit in respect of his adult sons, who normally resided with him, on the ground that they were "non-dependants" within reg 3(1). The claimant contended that his sons' residence with him fell within one of the exceptions in reg 3(2) as persons who jointly occupied the claimant's dwellings. It was held that the deductions had been properly made and the claimant's application was dismissed. On appeal, held, "jointly occupies" had to mean something narrower than "normally residing with" or there would be no non-dependants. The word "jointly" was a technical expression connoting a legal relationship. In this case the claimant was liable to a non-dependant deduction from his housing benefit and his appeal would be dismissed.

R v Chesterfield Borough Council, ex p Fullwood (1993) Times, 15 June (Court of Appeal: Balcombe, Leggatt and Hoffmann LJJ). Decision of Henry J (1992) 24 HLR 706 (1992 Abr para 2419) affirmed.

2378   Housing benefit—subsidy—calculation

The Housing Benefit and Community Charge Benefit (Subsidy) (No 2) Order 1993, SI 1993/935 (in force on 31 March 1993), replaces SI 1993/484, which contained a defect. The order sets out the way in which the housing benefit and community charge benefit subsidy payable to the local authorities who administer those benefits is calculated for the year ending 31 March 1993. The manner of calculating the additional sum payable to the relevant authority in respect of the cost of administering both benefits is also specified. Provision is also made in respect of additions or deductions from the subsidy in respect of rent rebates or allowances and in respect of community charge benefit.

2379 Housing benefit—subsidy—claims

The Housing Benefit and Community Charge Benefit (Subsidy) Amendment (No 2) Regulations 1993, SI 1993/945 (in force on 1 April 1993), replace SI 1993/485, which contained a defect. The regulations provide that the particulars which must be given to the Secretary of State by a local authority where a claim for housing benefit subsidy or community charge subsidy is being made, must include certain details of the total number of benefit overrun weeks during the relevant year. Information relating to the average rents of local authority properties rented out on specified days must also be included.

2380 Housing benefit—subsidy—rent officers' functions

The Rent Officers (Additional Functions) (Amendment) Order 1993, SI 1993/652 (in force 1 April 1993), amends the 1990 Order, SI 1990/428, which conferred functions on rent officers in connection with housing benefit and rent allowance subsidy. Provision is made for the case where an application is made by a local authority to a rent officer for a determination of rent and such application is required during a transitional period under social security legislation.

2381 Income support—deductions—child support maintenance

See para 2383.

2382 Income support—deductions—council tax

The Council Tax (Deductions from Income Support) Regulations 1993, SI 1993/494 (in force on 1 April 1993), provide for deductions to be made from income support to meet sums due in respect of council tax owed by a person where a liability order, summary warrant or decree has been obtained against that person. An adjudication officer, to whom applications to make such deductions must be referred, will decide whether there is sufficient income support to allow such deductions to be made. Provision is also made with respect to the circumstances, time of making and termination of deductions and provisions allowing a right of appeal are set out.

2383 Income support—deductions—debts

The Deductions from Income Support (Miscellaneous Amendment) Regulations 1993, SI 1993/495 (in force on 1 April 1993), further amend the Social Security (Claims and Payments) Regulations 1987, SI 1987/1968, to include, with respect to provisions relating to deductions from income support in respect of certain debts, references to council tax, fines and child support.

2384 Income support—entitlement—claimant receiving free in-patient hospital treatment

The National Health Service Act 1977, s 128 defines a hospital as any institution for the reception and treatment of persons suffering from illness or requiring medical rehabilitation. The Income Support (General) Regulations 1987, SI 1987/1967, reg 21(3) defines a patient as a person receiving free in-patient treatment within the meaning of the Social Security (Hospital In-Patients) Regulations 1975, SI 1975/555, reg 2(2), which provides for the reduction of personal benefits after the beneficiary has received free in-patient treatment in a hospital or similar institution maintained or administered under the National Health Service.

The plaintiff was one of several psychological patients transferred from hospital to a private nursing home by the local authority. It was agreed that the former patients were entitled to income support, payable to the nursing home. The plaintiff's claim for income support (as an invalidity benefit) was rejected on the grounds that the plaintiff was a hospital in-patient and his income exceeded the applicable amount. On appeal, the social security appeal tribunal found that community care rather than hospitalisation was appropriate for the plaintiff, that the nursing home was not a hospital for the purposes of the 1977 Act, s 128, and he was thus entitled to income support. That decision was upheld by the social security commissioner. On the defendant's further appeal, held, the nursing home was a hospital for the purposes of the 1977 Act, s 128. It was under a contractual obligation to the local authority to make a bed available for the plaintiff and to provide appropriate levels of nursing staff. The arrangement thus fell within the scope of the 1975 Regulations, reg 2. Accordingly, the appeal would be allowed.

White v Chief Adjudication Officer (1993) Times, 2 August (Court of Appeal: Ralph Gibson, Russell and Stuart-Smith LJJ). *Minister of Health v Royal Midland Counties Home for Incurables* [1954] 1 CH 530, CA applied.

2385   Income support—general

The Income Support (General) Amendment Regulations 1993, SI 1993/30 (in force on 2 February 1993), further amend the 1987 Regulations, SI 1987/1967, by providing that the interest on loans acquired to meet a service charge in respect of repairs or improvements to a dwelling house is to be included amongst the eligible housing costs for the purpose of income support. Certain provisions relating to eligible housing costs in the 1987 Regulations have been omitted.

The Income Support (General) Amendment (No 2) Regulations 1993, SI 1993/1219 (in force on 31 May 1993), further amend the 1987 Regulations supra. The regulations provide that, for the purposes of the residential allowance, a person living in a residential care home or nursing home may be treated as continuing to live in that home while he is temporarily absent from it for up to three weeks. Where he is absent because he is in hospital, he is regarded as continuing to reside in that home for the first six weeks of any absence.

The Income Support (General) Amendment No 3 Regulations 1993, SI 1993/1679 (in force on 2 August 1993), further amend the 1987 Regulations supra. The main changes made include the exclusion of payments on so much of any loan or loans exceeding £150,000 (or £125,000 from 11 April 1994) from the mortgage interest payments taken into account in determining a person's applicable amount. Provision is also made for the disregard of certain payments made under a mortgage protection policy in the calculation of income other than earnings.

The Income Support (General) Amendment (No 4) Regulations 1993, SI 1993/3121 (in force on 10 January 1994), further amend the 1987 Regulations supra by providing that amounts for service charges for repair and improvements to either the dwelling occupied as the home or where the dwelling is part of a building, to any part of that building containing that dwelling, are not to be taken into account in determining housing costs.

2386   Income support—periodical payments—relevant period

B's former husband paid her £40 per month on a voluntary basis until he was made redundant. B then claimed and received supplementary benefit. She subsequently received a lump sum from her husband's redundancy pay, thereby becoming ineligible for supplementary benefit. She later applied for income support which replaced supplementary benefit. It was found that she was not entitled to this benefit as her weekly income exceeded her weekly applicable amount for the purposes of income support; the sum being a payment other than a periodical payment, and the period over which it was to be taken into account was to be determined in accordance with the Income Support Regulations 1987, SI 1987/1967, reg 57. This decision was upheld by a social security tribunal on appeal. On further appeal, the adjudication officer held that the redundancy money was a periodical payment, and it was decided to remit the case to a tribunal to decide when the relevant period started. B appealed against this decision. *Held*, the agreement to pay the redundancy money was reached 13 months after the last payment was made. By that time there could not be said to be either any agreement for maintenance or that there was any pattern of regular payments. The sum was a payment other than a periodical payment, and accordingly, the period over which the payment was to be taken into account was to be obtained in accordance with reg 57(1)–(3) from a date decided in accordance with regs 57(4), 59(2), instead of in accordance with reg 51(4) and for a period calculated under reg 56(1), beginning on a date specified in accordance with reg 59(1). The appeal would be allowed.

Bolstridge v Chief Adjudication Officer [1993] 2 FLR 657 (Court of Appeal: Neill, Steyn and Rose LJJ).

2387   Industrial injury—adjudication

The Social Security (Industrial Injuries and Adjudication) Regulations 1993, SI 1993/861 (in force on 19 April 1993), amend the Social Security (Adjudication) Regulations 1986, SI 1986/2218, so as to (1) permit adjudicating medical pratitioners and specially qualified adjudicating medical practitioners to deal with matters in relation to industrial injuries and prescribed diseases; (2) allow a medical practitioner to adjudicate upon a claim where he has prepared a report on the case of a claimant, if he proposes to determine the question in favour of the claimant; and (3) make changes consequential upon the Social Security (Industrial Injuries) (Prescribed Diseases) Amendment Regulations 1993, SI 1993/862 (see para 2389). In addition, various consequential changes are made to the Social Security (Industrial Injuries) (Prescribed Diseases) Regulations 1985, SI 1985/967.

2388 Industrial injury—disablement pension and unemployability supplement— permitted earnings

The Social Security (Industrial Injuries) (Dependency) (Permitted Earnings Limits) Order 1993 (in force on 12 April 1993), revokes the 1992 Order, SI 1992/524, and increases the earnings limits in respect of dependent children set out in the Social Security Contributions and Benefits Act 1992, Sch 7, para 4(a) and (b) from £115 to £120 and from £15 to £16 respectively.

2389 Industrial injury—prescribed diseases

The Social Security (Industrial Injuries) (Prescribed Diseases) Amendment Regulations 1993, SI 1993/862 (in force on 19 April 1993), further amend the 1985 Regulations, SI 1985/967, so as to (1) provide for the prescription of two further industrial diseases, namely carpal tunnel syndrome, where the disease is contracted as a result of the use of hand-held vibrating tools, and primary carcinoma of the lung accompanied by silicosis, which is prescribed in relation to occupations associated with the use of free silica; (2) extend the existing prescription of primary neoplasm of the bladder; (3) amend the description of the disease "lung cancer" to "primary carcinoma of the lung"; (4) disapply, in the case of carpal tunnel syndrome, the presumption that a prescribed disease is due to the nature of a person's employment; and (5) revoke the Social Security (Industrial Injuries) (Prescribed Diseases) Amendment Regulations 1991, SI 1991/1938, reg 3.

The Social Security (Industrial Injuries) (Prescribed Diseases) Amendment (No 2) Regulations 1993, SI 1993/1985 (in force on 13 September 1993), further amend the 1985 Regulations supra by prescribing chronic bronchitis and emphysema as industrial diseases, where either condition has, or both conditions have, been contracted after working for twenty years underground in a coal mine.

2390 Invalid care allowance—earnings

The Social Security (Invalid Care Allowance) Amendment Regulations 1993, SI 1993/316 (in force on 12 April 1993), further amend the 1976 Regulations, SI 1976/409, by increasing the earnings permitted under ibid, reg 8(1) to £50. The 1992 Regulations, SI 1992/470, are amended in consequence.

2391 Invalid care allowance—pensionable age—sex discrimination

See *Thomas v Chief Adjudication Officer*, para 2757.

2392 Invalid care allowance—time spent caring for severely disabled persons

The Social Security (Invalid Care Allowance) Amendment (No 2) Regulations 1993, SI 1993/1851 (in force on 17 August 1993), amend the 1976 Regulations, SI 1976/409, by providing that a person who cares for at least two severely disabled persons is to be treated as regularly and substantially engaged in caring for a severely disabled person only where at least 35 hours a week are spent in caring for any one of the severely disabled persons.

2393 Invalidity pension—assumption about mother—sex discrimination

See *Schuler-Zraggen v Switzerland*, para 1417.

2394 Medical appeal tribunal—decisions—guidelines

The Social Security (Adjudication) Regulations 1986, SI 1986/2218, reg 31(4) provides that when considering an applicant's eligibility for certain benefits under the Social Security Act 1975, a medical appeal tribunal must make a written record of their decision, signed by all members of the tribunal, including a statement of the reasons for their decision and their findings on all facts material to the decision.

The Court of Appeal has laid down guidelines for appellate courts to follow when considering whether the decision of a medical appeal tribunal complied with the 1986 Regulations, reg 31(4) so as to be a lawful decision. The court emphasised that the guidelines were given in broad terms and that much would depend on the facts of the individual case: (1) the tribunal's decision should record the medical question it was required to answer and the answer should be so directed to the question that the parties are able to identify the issues to which the tribunal has addressed itself, (2) where the tribunal makes a medical examination of the patient, its findings should be recorded and these might give sufficient reason why a particular decision was reached, (3) the tribunal might need to explain why it made one diagnosis rather than another if the clinical findings did not lead to an obvious diagnosis, particularly if the tribunal's diagnosis differed from that of another qualified practitioner, and (4) the tribunal might need to ensure it gives adequate reasons, rather than just the conclusion, for a decision as to causation, especially where an applicant has previously been in receipt of benefit and there was no question of malingering or bad faith on his part. Since the underlying principle was fairness, the applicant should be given sufficient explanation to enable him to know why his claim has failed or where the chain of causation has broken in case he wished to reapply.

Evans v Secretary of State for Social Services (1993) Times, 14 September, Independent, 17 September (Court of Appeal: Neill, Nolan and Evans LJJ).

1975 Act consolidated in Social Security Contributions and Benefits Act 1992 and Social Security Administration Act 1992.

2395 National assistance—assessment of resources

The National Assistance (Assessment of Resources) (Amendment) Regulations 1993, SI 1993/964 (in force on 22 April 1993), amend the 1992 Regulations, SI 1992/2977, so as to take account of the implementation of the Child Support Act 1991. Other changes of substance lay down the circumstances in which payments by a third party towards the cost of a resident's accommodation are to be treated as income, and require local authorities to disregard the value of any premises occupied in whole or in part by a child whom the resident is liable to maintain by virtue of the National Assistance Act 1948, s 42(1). The regulations establish two new trust funds, and certain drafting errors in the 1992 Regulations are corrected.

2396 Occupational pensions

See PENSIONS AND SUPERANNUATION.

2397 Pension Schemes Act 1993

See para 1944.

2398 Personal pensions

See PENSIONS AND SUPERANNUATION.

2399 Residential care home—community care—contracts—negotiation of contracts

Under the National Health Service and Community Care Act 1990 and the Community Care (Residential Accommodation) Act 1992, local authorities were required to make arrangements for the accommodation of persons in need of care, and could make arrangements with voluntary organisations, including registered homes. A local council decided to require residential care home owners to submit to certain contractual conditions for the provision of residential care. The conditions included the provision of lifts and minimum room sizes and services for residents. A local care home applied for judicial review of the decision on the grounds that some of the terms of the contract were impossible to comply with without considerable expense, were inappropriate and impracticable, and that the council's refusal to negotiate the terms of the proposed contract was an abuse of power or unreasonable. *Held*, the legislation made changes to the existing law regarding the provision of accommodation to those in need. The principal change was that the responsibility for funding for new residents in need passed from central government to local authorities with the purpose of involving the private sector in the provision of residential care. The council's decision not to negotiate the terms of the draft contract was susceptible to judicial review because the consequences of the decision sufficiently related to the purpose of the legislation so as to provide statutory underpinning. The council's action was likely to defeat the purpose of the National Health Service and Community Care Act 1990 with the result that homes in the private sector faced closure and potential residents' choice would be curtailed. Given the consequences, the council had acted unreasonably in requiring the home owners to submit to the terms of the proposed contract. Accordingly, the application would be granted and the council's decision quashed.

R v Cleveland County Council, ex p Cleveland Care Homes Association (1993) Independent, 30 December (Queen's Bench Division: Potts J).

2400   Residential care home—registration—contractual terms

A council was required to make arrangements to provide accommodation for persons in need of care and attention under the National Assistance Act 1948, as amended by the Community Care (Residential Accommodation) Act 1992. The council provided residential care by entering into contracts with the operators of residential care homes registered under the Registered Homes Act 1984. The council's standard form of agreement for the provision of social care and nursing home care imposed obligations on the operator additional to those under the 1984 Act. An association of owners of residential care and nursing homes, registered under the 1984 Act, applied for a declaration that the council's standard form was ultra vires and/or unreasonable. They submitted that the mixing of statutory standards and contractual requirements conflicted with the 1984 Act and created uncertainty as to the respective operation of the two. *Held*, there was no reason in law why a local authority should not impose a stricter contractual regime on the operators to enable the council to fulfil its duties under the 1948 Act, as amended. The contractual requirements did not conflict with, or affect, the rights and duties imposed by the 1984 Act, nor were they unreasonable. Where a local authority had a statutory duty to provide services, funded wholly or in part from taxpayers' money, it had to balance its statutory duty to provide services with its fiduciary duty not to waste the money of those paying for them. An insistence on contractual standards coupled with firm and economical enforcement was an essential means of achieving such a balance. Neither the 1948 Act, as amended, nor the 1984 Act imposed a public law duty of restraint on local authorities in respect of the contractual terms they sought to rely on when making arrangements with operators of registered residential care homes. Accordingly, the application would be dismissed.

R v Newcastle upon Tyne City Council, ex p Dixon (1993) Times, 26 October (Queen's Bench Division: Auld J).

2401   Residential care home—registration—temporary residents

The appellant was convicted under the Registered Homes Act 1984 of exceeding the condition in her certificate of registration as to the number of persons for whom residential accommodation could be provided. On appeal against her conviction, *held*, the issue was whether residential accommodation could be provided in a residential care home when accommodation was made available to persons intending to stay only for a short time. The word "resident" had been considered in connection with other statutes in which some degree of permanence or continuity had gone to the meaning of the definition. The court did not see that continuity was a relevant concept under the 1984 Act, as the Act was primarily concerned with the safety, health and care of those who were in residential homes. It was the accommodation that had to be residential and if residential accommodation was provided it did not matter if the occupier intended to stay a short or a long time. Accordingly, the justices had been correct in finding that temporary or short stays were not excluded under the 1984 Act, and accordingly the appeal would be dismissed.

Swindells v Cheshire County Council (1993) Times, 18 February (Queen's Bench Division: Staughton LJ and Buckley J).

2402   Retirement benefit—graduated retirement pension—age addition

The Social Security (Widow's Benefit and Retirement Pensions) Amendment Regulations 1993, SI 1993/1242 (in force on 7 June 1993), further amend the 1979 Regulations, SI 1979/642, by prescribing graduated retirement benefit as a payment, the receipt of which by persons aged over 80 years may entitle them to age addition. The conditions otherwise prescribed for persons to receive an age addition under the 1979 Regulations, reg 17(2) are also amended.

2403   Severe disablement allowance—equal treatment

The Social Security (Severe Disability Allowance) Amendment Regulations 1993, SI 1993/3194 (in force on 13 January 1994), implement Council Directive (EEC) 79/7 on the progressive implementation of the principle of equal treatment for men and women in social security matters. The regulations extend the qualification entitlement for a non-contributory invalidity pension to certain women who had previously failed to qualify because of a condition which applied to married women.

2404   Severe disablement allowance—pensionable age—sex discrimination

See *Thomas v Chief Adjudication Officer*, para 2757.

2405   Social fund—cold weather payments

The Social Fund (Cold Weather Payments (General) Amendment Regulations 1993, SI 1993/2450 (in force on 1 November 1993), further amend the 1988 Regulations, SI 1988/1724, by providing that persons whose income support applicable amount includes a residential allowance, are no longer entitled to cold weather payments out of the social fund. Changes to residential areas linked to the national climatological stations by way of post office postcodes are also made.

2406   Social fund—maternity and funeral expenses

The Social Fund Maternity and Funeral Expenses (General) Amendment Regulations 1993, SI 1993/479 (in force on 1 April 1993), further amend the 1987 Regulations, SI 1987/481, so that a claimant may be entitled to funeral expenses where he or his partner has been awarded the appropriate maximum council tax benefit but not the alternative maximum council tax benefit, or is a person in respect of whom the alternative maximum council tax benefit may be awarded. In addition, in relation to cremations, the regulations add the cost of an ordinary urn to the expense for which a funeral payment may be made.

2407   Social Security Act 1993

The Social Security Act 1993 amends the Social Security Act 1986, ss 3 and 85, to provide for the making of certain payments into the National Insurance Fund. The Act received the royal assent on 28 January 1993 and comes into force for certain purposes on that date. For details of commencement, see the commencement table in the title STATUTES.

Section 1 of the Act amends the Social Security Act 1986, s 3 in relation to minimum contributions to personal pension schemes and the calculation of contributions. It also amends the 1986 Act, s 85 by providing for the payment out of the National Insurance Fund into the Consolidated Fund, sums which the Secretary of State may estimate to be administrative expenses incurred by him in the exercise of his functions. Section 2 provides that during the tax year 1993-94 there must be paid into the National Insurance Fund out of money provided by Parliament, sums to be determined by the Secretary of State not exceeding in aggregate 20 per cent of estimated benefit expenditure for the financial year ending with 31 March 1994 and amends the Social Security Contributions and Benefits Act 1992, s 1(1) accordingly. Section 3 makes corresponding provision for Northern Ireland. Section 4 provides for the interpretation of the term "tax year" and provides that enactments specified in the Schedule to the Act are repealed to the extent there specified. Section 5 deals with the short title, commencement and extent.

2408   Social Security (Consequential Provisions) Act 1992—appointed day

The Social Security (Consequential Provisions) Act 1992 Appointed Day Order 1993, SI 1993/1025, appoints 19 April 1993 in respect of Sch 4, paras 8, 9 (which amend the Social Security Contributions and Benefits Act 1992, Sch 2, para 6) so that, from that date, interest may be charged on Class 4 contributions which are overdue.

2409   Statutory sick pay—rate of payment

The Statutory Sick Pay (Rate of Payment) Order 1993, SI 1993/350 (in force on 6 April 1993), increases the lower rate of statutory sick pay to £46·95. The earnings band is also increased and the higher rate now becomes payable when the employee's earnings are £195 or more per week. Certain transitional provisions are included. The 1990 Regulations, SI 1990/257, are revoked.

2410   Training for work—Learning for Work programme—miscellaneous provisions

The Learning for Work (Miscellaneous Provisions) Order 1993, SI 1993/1949 (in force on 6 September 1993), provides that for the purpose of specified subordinate legislation, a person using facilities provided under the Learning for Work programme is to be treated as not being employed but as participating in arrangements for training under the Employment and Training Act 1973, s 2, and any payment made to a person in connection with his use of those facilities is to be treated in the same manner as a payment made in respect of such training. A payment made in connection with his use of such facilities must not be treated as earnings for the purpose of the Social Security Contributions and Benefits Act 1992, Pt I.

2411 Training for work—payments

The Training for Work (Miscellaneous Provisions) Order 1993, SI 1993/348 provides that for the purposes of certain specified subordinate legislation, a person using facilities provided under the Training for Work programme is to be treated as participating in arrangements for training under the Employment and Training Act 1973, s 2. Any payment made to such a person in connection with his use of those facilities is to be treated in the same manner as a payment made in respect of such training. Payment to a person in connection with his use of such facilities must not be treated as earnings for the purposes of the Social Security Contributions and Benefits Act 1992, Pt I.

2412 Unemployment benefit—entitlement—student—power to make regulations

The applicant, a mature student at a polytechnic, sought judicial review by way of certiorari to quash the Social Security Benefits (Student Loans and Miscellaneous Amendments) Regulations 1990, SI 1990/1549, reg 6(2) and a declaration that the Social Security (Unemployment, Sickness and Invalidity Benefit) Amendment (No 2) Regulations 1986, SI 1986/1011, and the 1990 Regulations, reg 6(2) were invalid on the ground that both were ultra vires the Secretary of State's powers conferred by the Social Security Act 1975. *Held*, the Secretary of State had power under the Social Security Act 1975, ss 17(2)(a), 166(2)(a) to make regulations for the purpose of determining entitlement to unemployment benefit which excluded from entitlement those days of unemployment which fell within a period beginning with the commencement of a course of full-time study and ended with its termination. Accordingly, the application would be dismissed.

 R v Secretary of State for Social Security, ex p Moore (1993) Times, 9 March (Court of Appeal: Sir Thomas Bingham MR, Kennedy and Evans LJJ). Decision of Popplewell J (1993) Times, 1 February affirmed.

2413 Unemployment benefit—entitlement—voluntary work

The Social Security (Unemployment, Sickness and Invalidity Benefit) Amendment Regulations 1993, SI 1993/1754 (in force on 11 August 1993), further amend the 1983 Regulations, SI 1983/1598. The regulations provide that a person engaged in voluntary work is deemed to be available for employment on that day if he would be ready for employment on 48 hours' notice, except where the voluntary work is for a member of his family.

2414 Welfare foods—free milk and vitamins

The Welfare Food Amendment Regulations 1993, SI 1993/1105 (in force on 17 May 1993), further amend the 1988 Regulations, SI 1988/536, by (1) making new provisions concerning applications for vitamins and the purchase of welfare food; (2) enabling the Secretary of State to request documentary evidence in support of a claim for reimbursement for the supply of milk or dried milk to children in day care; (3) increasing the price of dried milk to those entitled to purchase it at a reduced price; (4) altering the provisions concerning the issue and use of milk tokens; and (5) providing an alternative entitlement to vitamins for nursing mothers.

2415 Workmen's compensation—pneumoconiosis—amount of payments

The Pneumoconiosis etc (Workers' Compensation) (Payment of Claims) (Amendment) Regulations 1993, SI 1993/1158 (in force on 1 May 1993), further amend the 1988 Regulations, SI 1988/668, by increasing, by approximately 2·5 per cent, the amount of payments made under the Pneumoconiosis etc (Workers' Compensation) Act 1979 in any case in which a person first becomes entitled to payment on or after the date when these regulations came into force.

2416 Workmen's compensation—supplementation

The Workmen's Compensation (Supplementation) Amendment Scheme 1993, SI 1993/422 (in force on 14 April 1993), further amends the 1982 Scheme, SI 1982/1489, by substituting a new schedule of lower rates of lesser incapacity allowance for beneficiaries.

SOLICITORS

Halsbury's Laws of England (4th edn) Vol 44, paras 1–400

2417 Articles

Can Negligent Solicitors Hide Behind the Limitation Act? Hugh Brayne: 137 SJ 10
Place your Bets, Ferrier Charlton (on contingency fees): LS Gaz, 7 July 1993, p 19
Recession Hits Women, Sean Webster (on redundancies in solicitors' firms): 137 SJ 242
The Crisis in Solicitors' Training, Robert Abbey: 143 NLJ 1780
The Narrow Pool, Russell Hill (on the recruitment of trainee solicitors): 143 NLJ 1310

2418 Costs—liability for costs—express or implied agreement with client—contingency fees

The Environmental Protection Act 1990, s 82(12) provides that the court must order a defendant to pay to the person bringing proceedings under the Act, such amount as the court considers reasonably sufficient to compensate him for any expenses properly incurred in the proceedings.

The respondent had taken action against the applicants under the 1990 Act, and was awarded a sum for costs of the proceedings pursuant to s 82(12). The applicants appealed against the decision and submitted that because the respondent was on income support and had no legal aid for her action, there must have been an express or implied agreement between the respondent and her solicitors that they would not expect their costs from her. In that case s 82(12) would not apply as the respondent would not have incurred any liability for costs. Held, in the circumstances there must have been an understanding between the solicitors and the respondent that they would look to her for costs only if she was successful in her action, and this amounted in law to a contract. This agreement was therefore unlawful under the Solicitors Act 1974, s 59(2) and the Solicitors' Practice Rules 1990, r 8(1). However, provided the professional standards of solicitors were followed, so that it was made clear that the client was liable for costs, a solicitor could wait until after the case had been determined and then make a decision not to reclaim his costs from the client. Accordingly the appeal would be allowed.

British Waterways Board v Norman (1993) Times, 11 November (Queen's Bench Division: McCowan LJ and Tuckey J).

2419 Costs—security for costs—equality of treatment under Community law

See *Hubbard v Hamburger*, para 2725.

2420 Disciplinary proceedings—purpose of disciplinary orders—requirement for severe sanctions

A solicitor acted in a transaction for the sale of a flat by his wife to her brother and had received moneys from the mortgagees to hold until the property was conveyed to the purchaser and security documents had been executed in favour of the mortgagees. Instead he disbursed all the moneys almost immediately, the sale was never completed and the security documents were never executed. The solicitor made good the moneys when the matter came to light. The Solicitors Disciplinary Tribunal suspended him from practising as a solicitor for two years. On appeal, a Queen's Bench Divisional Court quashed the penalty and substituted a fine of £3,000. The Law Society appealed. Held, the Divisional Court ought to be very slow to interfere with a penalty imposed by a professional tribunal in a case of professional misconduct. In the present case the Divisional Court had given no good reason for interfering with the tribunal's decision and had acted contrary to settled principles in doing so. Practising lawyers were required to discharge their professional duties with integrity, probity and complete trustworthiness. If a solicitor did not discharge his duties in such a way he had to expect that severe sanctions would be imposed on him by the tribunal. Although some disciplinary orders would have a punitive and deterrent element, in most cases the fundamental purpose of the tribunal's order would be to maintain the reputation of the profession and to sustain public confidence in the integrity of the profession. In the present case, although the Divisional Court had erred in principle, as the matters complained of had occurred two years previously, the appeal would be dismissed.

Bolton v The Law Society (1993) Times, 8 December (Court of Appeal: Sir Thomas Bingham MR, Rose and Waite LJJ).

2421 Disciplinary proceedings—striking off—application—applicant in person

A former client of a firm of solicitors complained to the Law Society that various solicitors in the firm had practised without valid practising certificates. The Law Society issued a warning to the solicitors, but did not consider it appropriate for the complaint to be prosecuted before the disciplinary tribunal. Some time later the client applied under the Solicitors Act 1974, ss 50, 51 to strike off the solicitors, making allegations of serious misconduct in support of the application. On the solicitors' application to dismiss the client's claim, *held*, the court, in order to avoid lurid claims by disgruntled litigants, could not entertain an application under the 1974 Act, ss 50, 51 unless it was made by counsel. It did not have jurisdiction to entertain an application made by an applicant in person. Even if it did have such jurisdiction, it could only be exercised in exceptional cases. Accordingly, as the client had not shown sufficient grounds to justify striking off the solicitors, her claim would be dismissed.

Re Solicitors, ex p Peasegood [1994] 1 All ER 298 (Queen's Bench Division: Stuart-Smith LJ and Judge J).

2422 Disciplinary proceedings—unbefitting conduct—conduct less culpable

Two solicitors were charged with drawing money from a client account other than as permitted by the Solicitors' Accounts Rules 1986, r 7 contrary to r 8, failing to maintain properly written account books contrary to r 11 and permitting a cheque to be drawn on their client account to be dishonoured upon presentation. Each charge was prefaced by the allegation of conduct unbefitting a solicitor. The solicitors admitted the charges and the Solicitors' Disciplinary Tribunal reprimanded both of them and struck one off the Roll. They appealed on the ground that although they both admitted the charges their conduct in relation to all three charges had wrongly been given added gravity by being treated as conduct unbefitting a solicitor. *Held*, it would only be appropriate in exceptional circumstances to go behind the decisions of the tribunal. However the tribunal pitched its findings at a much less culpable level than could be characterised as conduct unbefitting a solicitor and drew no distinction between breaches of the 1986 Rules and conduct unbefitting a solicitor. In the circumstances the solicitors ought not to be tied to their admissions of such conduct and on the basis of the tribunal's findings, their liability ought to be limited to breaches of the 1986 Rules, rr 7, 8 and 11. Accordingly, the appeal would be allowed, and the appropriate lesser findings would be substituted under the Solicitors Act 1974, s 49(4).

Re Solicitors (1993) Independent, 20 July (Court of Appeal: Lord Taylor of Gosforth CJ, Alliott and Buckley JJ).

2423 Duty of care—failure to prepare will—duty to beneficiary

After a family argument, the testator made a will which disinherited his two daughters. Following a reconciliation, the testator instructed the defendant solicitor to draw up a new will. Owing to the defendant's negligence, this was never done. The daughters claimed in negligence against the defendant. At first instance, it was held that although there had been a breach of professional duty by the solicitor, the damage alleged was too speculative and uncertain in extent to be recoverable, and the daughters' claim was dismissed. On appeal, *held*, although in general a solicitor owed a duty of care to his client and no-one else, instructions to prepare a will were different to other instructions to a solicitor. The failure to carry them out resulted in the client's purpose being thwarted, but left the client's estate with no effective remedy. There was a special relationship between the solicitor and the intended beneficiary which should attract a liability if the solicitor was negligent, and it could not be accepted that the damage was too speculative and uncertain to be recoverable. The appeal would accordingly be allowed.

White v Jones [1993] 3 All ER 481 (Court of Appeal: Sir Donald Nicholls V-C, Farquharson and Steyn LJJ).

2424 Duty of care—misdrafting of settlement document—duty to beneficiary

A client instructed his solicitors to draft a document giving the plaintiff a present right to call at an unspecified time in the future for a sum of money to enable her to purchase a house. The document as executed gave the plaintiff no enforceable rights. The plaintiff subsequently called on the client to perform the promise, but he refused to do so. The plaintiff claimed that the solicitors were in breach of their duty of care and sought to recover from them the sum to which she would have been entitled under the document. *Held*, there could be circumstances in which a solicitor might owe a duty of care in carrying out an inter vivos transaction, for example where a settlor, acting on the advice of his solicitor, executed an irrevocable deed of settlement conferring benefits on the wrong beneficiary, the solicitor might be liable to the intended beneficiary. However, such a duty did not arise in all inter vivos transactions. Applying *Caparo v Dickman*, the plaintiff's claim was defeated by the principle that the situation had to be one where it was fair, just and reasonable for the law to impose the duty of care on one party for the benefit of the other. In the present case, the client was still alive and the matter was not irremediable. The only reason why the situation had not been rectified was that the client had changed his mind. In these circumstances, it would offend against common sense to grant the plaintiff a remedy against the solicitor. Further, the client had an adequate remedy against the solicitor because, as there had been a breach of contract, he was entitled to repudiate the contract and refuse to pay the solicitors' bill. If he had already paid, he could instruct another solicitor to draft an appropriate document and could recover the additional charges as damages for breach of contract. In neither event was it necessary to give the plaintiff a remedy. Accordingly, the plaintiff's claim would be dismissed.

Hemmens v Wilson Browne (a firm) [1993] 4 All ER 826 (Chancery Division: Judge Moseley). *Caparo Industries plc v Dickman* [1990] 1 All ER 568, HL (1990 Abr para 294) applied.

2425   Duty to client—breach of trust—payment of money prior to completion of sale of land

See *Target Holdings Ltd v Redferns*, para 2577.

2426   Duty to client—conflict of interest—confidential information

Canada

The respondent law firm was retained to represent a number of plaintiffs in asbestos-related litigation against the appellants. The respondent was one of three domestic firms affiliated to an international partnership, another member of which had previously been retained by the appellants. Although the affiliated firms expressly agreed to continue as separate, independent and competing practices in Canada, the appellants contended that where firms represented themselves as affiliated they must be treated as one firm for the purposes of the confidentiality rule. Accordingly, the appellants unsuccessfully sought an order that the respondent was ineligible to act against them because of a conflict of interest. On appeal, *held*, the court had to consider whether a reasonably informed person would be satisfied that no confidential information concerning the appellant had been, or would be, passed to the respondent. The stringent arrangements to maintain the independence of the domestic firms ensured that interaction between the partners of the affiliated firms was minimal. A reasonably informed person would thus conclude that any appearance of conflict was not well founded and that there was no appearance of impropriety. Accordingly, the appeal would be dismissed.

Re Manville Canada Inc and Ladner Downs (1993) 100 DLR (4th) 321 (British Columbia Court of Appeal).

2427   Duty to client—conflict of interest—limits of duty

New Zealand

The plaintiff executed a mortgage over her property in order to secure a loan made to her son. The son's own solicitor, who was a family friend, had refused to act and so the plaintiff was taken to the defendant solicitor, who acted for both parties. The son went bankrupt leaving the plaintiff liable to repay the principal sum and arrears of interest. The plaintiff brought an action for breach of contract, breach of fiduciary duty and negligence, claiming the solicitor had failed to ensure that she received independent advice, should not have acted for her, had failed to reveal that the son's original solicitor had refused to act, that he should have advised her not to sign the mortgage and that he should have told the plaintiff he knew nothing concerning the son's ability to pay the mortgage. Her claim was dismissed at first instance and upheld on appeal. On appeal by the defendant solicitor to the Privy Council, *held*, there was no general rule of law that a solicitor could never act for both parties in a transaction where there was a potential conflict of interest. A solicitor could act for both parties to a transaction if he obtained their informed consent. Consent was informed if both parties were aware of the conflict and that the solicitor might be prevented from revealing information to one party which might be to the detriment of the other party. It was also necessary to establish exactly what services the solicitor was requested to provide. In this case the solicitor was instructed to carry out the conveyance and to explain the implications of the transaction. The solicitor had advised the plaintiff on several occasions to seek independent advice and that she would lose her house if the son defaulted. She had declined to seek independent advice and therefore there was no duty on the solicitor to refuse to act. Where the client had not asked for advice, the solicitor had no duty to go beyond the scope of the instructions by giving such advice on the wisdom of a particular transaction. On the question of whether there was a fiduciary duty to disclose material facts, such a duty could not be relied upon to widen the scope of the contractual duties. As the solicitor owed no contractual duty to advise against entering into the mortgage, the plaintiff could not argue that there was a fiduciary obligation to offer that advice. In addition, any duty to disclose facts would relate to actual knowledge and not to lack of knowledge. Accordingly the appeal would be allowed.

Clark Boyce v Mouat [1993] 4 All ER 268 (Privy Council: Lords Goff of Chieveley, Jauncey of Tullichettle, Slynn of Hadley, Lowry and Mustill).

2428   Duty to client—divorce proceedings—duty to protect wife's financial position

See *Griffiths v Dawson*, para 1017.

2429   Law Society—delegation of powers—delegation to a named individual

The applicant sought judicial review of a resolution of the Council of the Law Society that delegated the power to authorise the renewal of conditional practising certificates to the director and any assistant director of the Solicitors Complaints Bureau. He claimed that the resolution was a breach of the Solicitors Act 1974, s 79 in that power had not been delegated to a named individual. The application for judicial review was dismissed. *Held*, nothing in the 1974 Act, s 79 provided that there was a duty on the Council to ascertain the name of the person performing the particular function, provided he was objectively identifiable. The presumption of deliberate selection must give way to a consideration of the practical realities of the exercise of the power to delegate, and therefore the concept of 'individual' in the 1974 Act, s 79 also covered the holder of a particular office from time to time. It was important to bear in mind that the power to authorise renewal of certificates was regulatory, not disciplinary and Parliament had to be credited with intending a system of delegation which best served the regulatory system under the 1974 Act, as well as the public interest. Accordingly, the appeal would be dismissed

R v Law Society, ex p Curtin (1993) Times, 3 December (Court of Appeal: Russell, McCowan and Steyn LJJ).

2430   Legal Services Ombudsman—annual report

The annual report for 1992 of the Legal Services Ombudsman has been published (see HC 696). Only a small percentage of the complaints made to the Solicitors Complaints Bureau are brought to the attention of the ombudsman and most complainants are presumed to be satisfied with the outcome of their complaints. The ombudsman refers to some specific matters which are matters for concern or interest; in relation to written estimates of costs required to be given by solicitors to clients he states that, in the absence of evidence that such written information has been given, he is inclined to prefer a client's view that such information has not been given to any contrary view advanced by a solicitor (paras 4.6, 5.8). He suggests that beneficiaries under wills should have the same rights as clients to have complaints investigated by the bureau, and should not be made to wait until the administration of the estate has been completed (para 4.9). He also calls for an improvement in the arrangements for referring cases to the Solicitors' Indemnity Fund instead of expecting complainants to instruct independent solicitors to pursue claims of negligence (para 4.13). The practice of sending a standard letter with space for a handwritten message is criticised when the handwritten message is barely legible (para 4.15), as is the practice of returning to complainants their letters of complaint (para 4.17). As a result of advice from counsel, the ombudsman no longer regards the fact that a complaint concerns conduct in court as answering the question whether he can investigate either the complaint or the way in which it was handled by the Bar Council (cf the Courts and Legal Services Act 1990, s 22(7)(b)); his chief concern is to decide whether the complaint can be investigated without undermining the finality of any judicial decision in the case giving rise to the complaint. Where a complaint relates to counsel's breach of contract or negligence, the allegations about the handling of the complaint frequently relate to the Bar Council's methods and procedures which fall within the ombudsman's jurisdiction, as do complaints about conduct in court (other than breach of contract or negligence) (para 4.22).

2431   Undertaking—solicitor's innocent misrepresentation as to client's bona fides—enforcement

Company A sought to instruct the plaintiff solicitors to draw up a loan contract under which company A agreed to lend company B certain sums provided that company B gave company A a letter of credit in advance. The plaintiffs only accepted instructions after the defendant solicitors gave an unconditional professional undertaking to pay the plaintiffs' costs and disbursements. After exchange of contracts, but before company A took possession of the letter of credit, it became evident that company A had no funds and had intended to defraud company B. When presented with a bill for the plaintiffs' costs the defendants refused to pay, contending that the plaintiffs had made an innocent misrepresentation as to their client's bona fides which released the defendants from their undertaking, given in relation to an honest client. The plaintiffs then issued an originating summons seeking to enforce the undertaking. *Held,* the fact that a solicitor acted for a client did not constitute a representation that the client was bona fide. The plaintiffs were entitled to rely on the defendants' undertaking despite their client's bad faith. Accordingly, the summons would be granted.

Rooks Rider (a firm) v J R Steel [1993] 4 All ER 716 (Chancery Division: Knox J).

STAMP DUTIES

Halsbury's Laws of England (4th edn) Vol 44, paras 601–800

2432 Conveyance—new buildings—consideration—computation

The Inland Revenue has issued a Statement of Practice SP 8/93, which replaces previous statements published in 1957 and 1987, explaining how the law on stamp duty applies to contracts for the sale or lease of a building plot where, at the date of the contract, building work on the plot has not commenced or is incomplete but, at the time of the conveyance, building work has commenced or has been completed. Where there is a contract for a conveyance or lease of land and, as a separate transaction, a further contract for building works, stamp duty on the conveyance or lease will be calculated without regard to the further contract. Where there is one transaction implemented by two contracts, one for the sale or lease of the building plot and one for the building works themselves, the amount of ad valorem stamp duty charged depends on the amount of the consideration, which in turn depends on whether the contracts can be shown to be genuinely independent of each other. The statement does not apply where the transaction concerned, or any part of it, involves a sham or artificial transaction. Where unconditional contracts have been entered into before or within 28 days of 12 July 1993, ie the date of the statement, stamp duty can be paid on the basis which applied before the statement if that is more beneficial. See further *STI,* 15 July 1993.

2433 Stamp duty reserve tax

The Stamp Duty Reserve Tax (Amendment) Regulations 1993, SI 1993/3110 (in force on 1 January 1994), amend the 1986 Regulations, SI 1986/1711, by making further modifications to the Taxes Management Act 1970 as it applies to stamp duty reserve tax. New provisions are added relating to regulations about jurisdiction and practice and procedure, the power of Special Commissioners to order costs and publish reports of decisions, the issue of demand notes and receipts, appeals against penalty determinations, and penalty proceedings before commissioners and before the court.

STATUTES

Halsbury's Laws of England (4th edn) Vol 44, paras 801–1006

2434 Commencement of Statutes

The following table contains detailed commencement provisions of all statutes passed in 1993. Repealed provisions are omitted. Schedules are included but not those sections which simply introduce schedules. The table also contains details of all commencement orders made in 1993, which in certain cases relate to statutes passed before 1993. Revoked orders are omitted.

An asterisk (*) indicates that a section, subsection or schedule is in force only in part or only for certain purposes.

The table refers to statutes only in so far as they relate to England and Wales.

STATUTE	COMMENCEMENT	AUTHORITY
Agriculture Act 1993		
• s 26(1)	no date	s 26(2)
• ss 55, 59	4 August 1993	s 65(3); SI 1993/2038
• ss 50–53	27 September 1993	s 65(2)
• s 1(1)(a), 21	1 October 1994	ss 1(2)(b) (but appropriate authority may by order provide that s 1(2)(b) is to have effect with substitution for 1 October 1994 of such later date before 1 January 1996 as may be specified in the order: s 1(3)), 21(2), (3)
• remaining provisions	27 July 1993	
Appropriation Act 1993	27 July 1993	
Asylum and Immigration Appeals Act 1993		
• 1*, 2, 3, 12–16	1 July 1993	
• ss 1*, 4–11, Schs 1, 2	26 July 1993	s 14; SI 1993/1655
Bail (Amendment) Act 1993		
• s 1	no date	s 2(2)
• s 2	20 July 1993	
British Coal and British Rail (Transfer Proposals) Act 1993	19 January 1993	
Charities Act 1993		
• ss 41–49, 69, Sch 6 (para 21(3))	no date	s 99(2)
• remaining provisions	1 August 1993	s 99(1)
Clean Air Act 1993	27 August 1993	s 68(2)
Coal Industry Act 1992		
• ss 2, Schedule (Pt II)	20 November 1993	s 3(4); SI 1993/2514
Consolidated Fund Act 1993	18 February 1993	
Consolidated Fund (No 2) Act 1993	29 March 1993	
Consolidated Fund (No 3) Act 1993	17 December 1993	
Courts and Legal Services Act 1990		
• ss 7(1)*, (3), (4), 58	23 July 1993	SI 1993/2132
• s 7(1)*, (2), Sch 20*	1 October 1993	SI 1993/2132
Criminal Justice Act 1993		
• ss 1–16, 18, 24(1)–(11), 25, 26(1), 27–32, 36–43, 47–64, 72, 74, 78, Schs 1, 2, 4, 5 (paras 1, 3–22), 6*	no date	s 78(3)
• s 79(1)–(12), Sch 5 (para 2)	27 July 1993	s 78(2)
• ss 66, 67	16 August 1993	SI 1993/1968
• s 65, Schs 3, 6*	20 September 1993	SI 1993/1968
• ss 70, 71	27 September 1993	s 78(1)
• ss 20(1), 21(1), (2), (3)(a), (b), (d)–(h), 22(1), 23, 34(1), 35, 44–46, 73	1 December 1993	SI 1993/2734
Disability (Grants) Act 1993	27 May 1993	

STATUTE	COMMENCEMENT	AUTHORITY
Education Act 1993		
• ss 3, 4, 6–21, 22(2)(b)★, (c), (4), 36(3)–(5), 47(1)–(4), 48–54, 68–70, 78, 81–91, 93–135, 136(2), 138–151, 153(3), (5), 154, 159, 160, 161(1)–(4), 162–176, 177(1), 180(3)–(6), 182–191, 196, 197(5), 217(2), 224–226, 228(4), 229(1)★, (2), (3), 230(1)★, (2), (6), 231–237, 241, 252–258, 261, 262, 272, 273, 277–279, 289, 295–298, 304, Schs 1, 2, 3 (Pt II), 8–10, 11 (paras 1–13), 15, 18, 19 (paras 2, 6, 9, 10, 12, 13, 16–19, 20(b), 21, 23(b), 24(a)(i), 26, 27, 31, 33, 34★, 36–38, 44–54, 55(a), 57–63, 65–67, 70, 71, 73, 74, 76, 77(b), 79, 81, 82★, 85–89, 90★, 91–108, 109(b)(ii), (c), (d), 110, 111, 113–117, 120, 121, 125, 126★, 127–129, 130★, 136, 137★, 138(b)(i)★, 139(a)(i), 140, 142, 145–148, 151, 154★, 156–161, 163(b), 167(a), 168, 169, 171, 172, 173(1)(a)), 20 (paras 2, 4), 21★	no date	s 308(3)
• ss 240, 301–303, 305, 306, 308	27 July 1993	
• Sch 19 (para 173(2), (3), (5), (6), (8)(a), 9(a))★	1 August 1993	SI 1993/1975
• ss 5, 204–212, Sch 19 (para 173(1)(c), (2)★, (3)★, (4), (5)★, (6)★, (7))	1 September 1993	SI 1993/1975
• ss 1, 2, 192(1)–(5), (6)★, (7)★, (8), 193–195, 197(1)–(4), (6), 198–203, 229(1)★, 230(1)★, (3)–(5), 242–245, 247–251, 259, 260, 263–265, 269, 270, 280, 282–286, 293, 294, Schs 14, 19 (paras 1, 3–5, 7, 8, 11, 14, 15, 20(a), 23(a)(i)★, 24(a)(ii), (iii), 25, 28, 30, 32, 34★, 35, 40–43, 56, 64, 68, 69, 72, 75, 77(a), 78, 80, 84, 112, 118(b)–(d), 119, 122, 124, 131, 132, 141, 149, 152, 154★, 155, 170, 173(1)(b), (8)(a)★, (b), 9(a)★, (b), 175), 21★	1 October 1993	SI 1993/1975
• s 24	9 December 1993	SI 1993/3106
• ss 22(1), (2)(a), (b)★, (3), 23, 25–35, 36(1), (2), 37–46, 47(5)–(9), 55–67, 71–77, 79, 80, 92, 136(1), (3), 137, 152, 153(1), (2), (4), 155–158, 161(5), 177(2)–(6), 178, 179, 180(1), (2), 181, 213–216, 217(1), 218–223, 227, 228(1)–(3), 238, 239, 246, 266–268, 271, 274–276, 281, 287, 288, 290–292, 299, 300, Schs 3 (Pt I), 4–7, 11 (para 14), 12, 13, 16, 17, 19 (paras 7, 22, 23(a)★, 24(a)(iv), (b), 29, 39, 55(b), 82★, 83, 90★, 109(a), (b)(i), (e), 118(a), (e), 123, 126★, 130★, 133–135, 137★, 138(a), (b)(i)★, (ii), 138(b)(i)★, 139(a)(ii), (b), (c), 143, 144, 150, 153, 162, 163(a), (c), 164–166, 167(b), 174), 20 (paras 1, 3, 5–7), 21★	1 January 1994	SI 1993/3106
Education (Schools) Act 1992		
• ss 9(7)★, 14★, Schs 2 (paras 1–3), 4 (para 4★)	1 May 1993	SI 1993/1190
• ss 9(1)–(6), (7)★, 13, 14★, Schs 2 (paras 6–15), 5★	12 June 1993	SI 1993/1491

STATUTE	COMMENCEMENT	AUTHORITY
• s 15*, Sch 5*	1 September 1993	SI 1993/1491
• s 15*, Sch 5*	1 September 1994	SI 1993/1491
Environmental Protection Act 1990		
• ss 35(6), 36(1), 37(3)*, 38(7)*, 39(3), 40(3), 41(2), (4), (5), 42(8)*, 43(8), 54(14), 63(1), 64(1), (4), (8), 65(2), 66(7), 74(6), Schs 15 (para 21), 16*	18 February 1993	SI 1993/274
• Sch 16*	1 May 1993	SI 1993/274
European Communities (Amendment) Act 1993	23 July 1993	s 7
European Economic Area Act 1993	5 November 1993	
European Parliamentary Elections Act 1993		
• s 1	no date	s 3(3)
• ss 2, 3	5 November 1993	
Finance Act 1989		
• s 178(1) (appointed day for the purposes of Social Security Contributions and Benefits Act 1992, Sch 1, para 6)	6 April 1993	SI 1993/754
• s 158(2)	6 April 1993	SI 1993/753
• s 158(1)	19 April 1993	SI 1993/753
Finance Act 1991		
• s 58*	22 April 1993	SI 1993/933
• s 7(2), (3), (5), Sch 2 (paras 3(1), (2), 5(1), (3), (4), 13, 14)	1 May 1993	SI 1993/1152
• s 7(1), (4), (6), (7), Schs 2 (paras 1, 2, 3(3), 4, 5(2), 6–12, 15–20, 22), 19 (Pt II)	1 June 1993	SI 1993/1152
Finance Act 1993		
• ss 4(2)(b), (d), (3), 11, Sch 23*	no date	ss 4(8), 11(5), 12(8), 41, 211(9)
• s 105(3)	1 January 1992	s 105(4)
• ss 1, 9, 13, Sch 1	16 March 1993	s 1(4)
• s 201	23 March 1993	s 201(4)
• s 48	1 April 1993	s 48(2)
• s 2	1 June 1993	s 2(2)
• s 4(2)(a), (c), (4)–(6)	1 September 1993	s 4(7)
• s 12(2), (4)–(6), (8)	13 September 1993	s 12(8); SI 1993/2215
• Sch 2, para 4	1 October 1993	Sch 2, para 4(3); SI 1993/2214
• s 12(1), (3), (7)	15 October 1993	s 12(8); SI 1993/2215
• appointed day for the purposes of s 18(2)	30 November 1993	SI 1993/2446
• appointed day for the purposes of ss 24(1)(b), (2)–(5), 25–28, 29(2)–(8), 30–38, 40, 41, Sch 2, paras 1, 2	1 December 1993	SI 1993/2782, 2842
• appointed day for the purposes of s 211	9 December 1993	SI 1993/2831
• ss 24(1)(a), 29(1), 39, Sch 23, Pt I*	1 February 1994	SI 1993/2842
• remaining provisions (subject to the exception that certain provisions are expressed to take effect on various dates)	27 July 1993	see various provisions of the Act
Finance (No 2) Act 1992		
• Sch 9	19 February 1993	Sch 9, para 22; SI 1993/236
• ss 1(5)*, 3(1)*, Schs 1*, 2*	1 June 1993	ss 1(8), 3(2); SI 1993/1341
• s 12, Sch 18, Pt IV	13 October 1993	s 12(2); SI 1993/2272

STATUTE	COMMENCEMENT	AUTHORITY
Fire Safety and Places of Sport Act 1987 • s 15, Sch 4*	1 August 1993	SI 1993/1411
Football Spectators Act 1989 • s 9	1 August 1993	SI 1993/1690
Foreign Compensation (Amendment) Act 1993	27 July 1993	s 3(1)
Friendly Societies Act 1992 • ss 27–57*, 58–61, 62–79*, 80, 81, 82(1)–(4), 83, 114, Schs 11–13*, 14 (paras 1–6, 8–17)*, 16 (paras 2(1)(a), (3), 25, 26, 28), 19 (para 9), 22*	13 January 1993	SI 1993/16
• ss 5–26, 93(1)–(4), 94, 98*, 99, 101–113, 115, 125, Schs 2, 3 (paras 1–8, 9(1), (3)–(7), 10–15), 4–10, 16 (paras 4(a), (c), 5–7, 10, 16, 19, 24*, 32(1)–(7), 37, 38(a), 42(a), 45, 47, 48(b), (e), 52), 18*, 19 (paras 2(1), (2)*, 3*, 4*, 5(1)(a)*, (b)*, (d)*, (e)*, (2)(a)*, 6, 11*, 12, 13–16*), 20, 21 (paras 1, 5–11), 22*	1 February 1993	SI 1993/16
• Sch 22*	5 February 1993	SI 1993/197
• ss 51–54*, 56*, 57*, 62–64*, 65–67*, 98*, Schs 16 (paras 3, 34–36, 38(b), (c)*, 39–41), 18 (para 3*), 19 (paras 2(2), 3, 4, 5(1)(a)*, (b)*, (d)*, (e)*, (2)(a)*, 11*, 13*, 15*, 16*), 22*	28 April 1993	SI 1993/1186
• ss 27(5)*, 32(1)–(6)*, (8)*, (9)*, 33–43*, 44(8)*, 45*, 46(1)*, (3)*, (8)*, 48(1), (2), (6), (7), 49(1)*, 50*, 70(5)*, (6)*, (7)*, 71(1), (2), 72(2), 85–92, Schs 11 (para 16*), 12 (para 7*), 13*, 14 (paras 7(4), 17*), 15, 16 (paras 29, 31, 32*, 33), 19 (para 14*), 22*	13 September 1993	SI 1993/2213
• ss 27–31*, 32(7)*, 44*, 46–48*, 49*, 55*, 68–79*, 82(5), 93(5)–(15), 96, 98*, 124, Schs 11*, 12*, 14 (paras 1–6*, 7(1)–(3)*, (4), (5)–(7)*), 16 (paras 1*, 2(1)(b), (2), 4(b), 8, 9, 11–15, 17, 18, 20–23, 27, 30, 32*, 38(c)*, 42(b), (c), 43, 44, 46, 48(a), (c), (d), 49–51), 18*, 19 (paras 5(1)(c), (2)(b), 7), 21 (paras 18, 19), 22*	1 January 1994	SI 1993/2213, 3226
• s 31*	1 July 1994	SI 1993/2213
• s 31*	1 January 1995	SI 1993/3226
Gas (Exempt Supplies) Act 1993	no date	s 4(2)
Health Service Commissioners Act 1993	5 February 1994	s 22(4)
Incumbents (Vacation of Benefices) (Amendment) Measure 1993	no date	s 16(2)
Judicial Pensions and Retirement Act 1993	no date	s 31(2)
Leasehold Reform, Housing and Urban Development Act 1993 • ss 132*, 184, Schs 21 (para 2), 22*	no date	s 188(2)
• ss 126, 127, 135–140, 181(1), (2), (4), 186, 188, Sch 22*	20 July 1993	s 188(2)
• ss 26(9), 75*, 88*, 91*, 98, 99*, 100, 108*, Schs 21 (paras 4, 7, 27), 22*	2 September 1993	SI 1993/2134

STATUTE	COMMENCEMENT	AUTHORITY
• ss 104–107, 108*, 109–120, 123–125, 128–131, 133, 134, 174, 176, 178, 179, 180*, 182, Schs 16, 21 (paras 10–25), 22*	11 October 1993	SI 1993/2134
• ss 1–25, 26(1)–(8), 27–74, 75*, 76–87, 88*, 89, 90, 91*, 92–97, 99*, 101–103, Schs 1–15, 21 (paras 1, 5, 9, 26, 30), 22*	1 November 1993	SI 1993/2134
• ss 132*, 158–173, 175, 177, 180*, 181(3), 183, 185, Schs 17–20, 21 (3, 6, 8, 28, 29, 31, 32), 22*	10 November 1993	SI 1993/2762
• s 121	1 December 1993	SI 1993/2762
• s 122	1 February 1994	SI 1993/2762
Local Government Act 1992		
• Sch 1 (para 12)	6 January 1994	s 30(3); SI 1993/3169
Local Government (Amendment) Act 1993	20 September 1993	s 3(2)
Local Government and Housing Act 1989		
• Sch 11 (para 14)	25 January 1993	SI 1993/105
• ss 67–70*, 72*, 73	7 October 1993	SI 1993/2410
Local Government Finance Act 1992		
• Sch 13 (para 32)	1 February 1993	SI 1993/194
• Schs 13 (paras 1, 27, 28, 94), 14*	1 April 1993	SI 1993/194
Local Government (Overseas Assistance) Act 1993	20 September 1993	s 2(2)
Maintenance Orders (Reciprocal Enforcement) Act 1992	5 April 1993	s 3; SI 1993/618
Merchant Shipping (Registration, etc) Act 1993		
• Schs 4*, 5 (Pt II*)	no date	s 10(2)
• ss 1–7, 9, 10, Schs 1–3, 5 (Pt I)	21 March 1994	s 10(2), (3); SI 1993/3137
• Schs 4*, 5 (Pt II*)	1 May 1994	s 10(2), (3); SI 1993/3137
National Lottery etc Act 1993		
• ss 48–59, Schs 7–9, 10*	no date	s 65
• ss 1–15, 17, 19, 20, 26(1), (3)–(5), 40–44, 60–63, 65, 66, Schs 1–3, 6	25 October 1993	s 60(5); SI 1993/2632
• ss 16, 18, 21–25, 26(2), 27–39, 45–47, Schs 4, 5, 10*	21 December 1993	s 60(5); SI 1993/2632
Noise and Statutory Nuisance Act 1993		
• s 9, Sch 3	no date	s 12(2)
• remaining provisions	5 January 1994	s 12(1)
Non-Domestic Rating Act 1993		
• ss 1(2), 4	4 June 1993	SI 1993/1418
• remaining provisions	6 July 1993	SI 1993/1512
Nurses, Midwives and Health Visitors Act 1992		
• s 1, 3, 4*, 5–14, 16, 17, Schs 1, 2, 3*	1 April 1993	SI 1993/588
Offshore Safety Act 1992		
• ss 3(1)(a), (e), (2), Sch 2*	30 November 1993	s 7(3); SI 1993/2406
Ordination of Women (Financial Provisions) Measure 1993	5 November 1993	
Osteopaths Act 1993	no date	s 42(2)

STATUTE	COMMENCEMENT	AUTHORITY
Pension Schemes Act 1993	no date	s 193(2)
Priests (Ordination of Women) Measure 1993	no date	s 12(2)
Probation Service Act 1993	5 February 1994	s 33(2)
Radioactive Substances Act 1993	27 August 1993	s 51(2)
Railways Act 1993		
• ss 2, 3, 4(1)*, (2), (3)*, (4)–(6), (7)*, (8), (9)*, 5, 6(1), (3), (4), 7–22, 23(1), (2), 24, 25(1)*, (2)*, (3)–(9), 26–28, 29(1)–(7), 30, 31, 34–80, 83(1)*, (2), 86, 87(1)*, (3), (4), 93(3)(b), 117–125, 129, 132, 133, 135–140, 141(1)(a), 145(5)(a), (b)(i), (7), 150(4), Schs 2–7, 10, 11 (paras 9(3)*, 11), 12 (paras 1–3, 6(6), 9, 14(4)–(6), 15–22, 25, 27, 29, 32), 13, 14*	no date	s 154(2)
• s 1, Sch 1	5 November 1993	s 154(2)
• ss 4(1)*, (3)*, (7)*, (9)*, 32, 33, 81, 82, 83(1)*, (2), 142–144, 145(1)–(4), (5)(b)(ii), (6), 146, 147, 149, 150(1)–(3), 151(1)*, (5), 154	24 December 1993	s 154(2); SI 1993/3237
• ss 6(2), 23(3), (4), 25(1)*, (2)*, 29(8), 83(1)*, 84, 85, 87(1)*, (2), (5), 88–92, 93(1), (2), (3)(a), (4)–(13), 94–116, 126–128, 130, 131, 134(2), (3), 141(1)(b), (2)–(5), 151(1)*, (2)–(4), (6)–(9), 153, Schs 8, 9, 11 (paras 1–8, 9(1), (2), (3)*, (4), 10, 12–14), 12 (paras 4, 5, 6(1)–(5), (7), 7, 8, 10–13, 14(1)–(3), 23, 24, 26, 28, 30, 31), 14*	6 January 1994	s 154(2); SI 1993/3237
Reinsurance (Acts of Terrorism) Act 1993	27 May 1993	
Representation of the People Act 1993	20 July 1993	
Road Traffic Act 1991		
• ss 64(1)*, 65*, 66(1)–(6)*, 67(4)*, (6)*, 68(2)(b)*, 69*, Sch 7 (para 5*)	4 October 1993	SI 1993/2229
• ss 64(1)*, 65*, 66(1)–(6)*, 67(4)*, (6)*, 68(2)(b)*, 69*, Sch 7 (para 5*)	6 December 1993	SI 1993/2803
• ss 64(1)*, 65*, 66(1)–(6)*, 67(4)*, (6)*, 68(2)(b)*, 69*, Sch 7 (para 5*)	31 January 1994	SI 1993/3238
Road Traffic (Driving Instruction by Disabled Persons) Act 1993	no date	s 7(2)
Sexual Offences Act 1993	20 September 1993	s 2(2)
Social Security Act 1993		
• s 1(3)	25 July 1986	s 5(3)
• ss 2, 3, 4(1), 5	29 January 1993	
• ss 1(1), (2), 4(2), Schedule	6 April 1993	s 5(2)
Social Security (Consequential Provisions) Act 1992	1 July 1992	s 7(2)
• appointed day for the purposes of Sch 4, paras 8, 9	19 April 1993	SI 1993/1025
Statute Law (Repeals) Act 1993		
• Sch 1, Pt IX*	no date	s 4(2), (3)
• remaining provisions	5 November 1993	

STATUTE	COMMENCEMENT	AUTHORITY
Trade Union Reform and Employment Rights Act 1993		
• ss 23, 24*, 25, 31, 32, Schs 2, 3, 7 (paras 3(b)*, 5*, 6(b)*), 8 (paras 12, 13, 15, 16*, 17–19, 20(b), 25(a), 26(a)(ii), (iii), (b)–(e), 27, 28(a), 31, 32(a), 35, 76*, 77*), 9, 10*	no date	s 52
• ss 52–55	1 July 1993	
• ss 1–6, 10–13, 15–22, 24(2)*, (3)*, 28–30, 33–35, 36(3)*, 38–41, 43, 44, 47, 48, Schs 1, 5, 6, 7 (paras 1, 2, 13–27), 8 (paras 2, 6, 7, 11, 14, 16*, 20(a), 21, 24, 26(a)(i), 29, 32(b), 36–41, 43(b), 46, 47, 49, 52–61, 62(b), 63, 64(b), (c), 65, 66(b), 67–75, 76*, 77*, 78–84, 86–89), 9 (paras 1, 2, 4, 5), 10*	30 August 1993	s 52; SI 1993/1908
• Schs 7 (para 7), 8 (paras 28(b), (c), 30), 10*	15 October 1993	s 52; SI 1993/2503
• ss 14, 26, 27, 32, 36*, 37, 42, 45*, Schs 4, 7 (paras 3(a), (b)*, 5*, 6(a), (b)*, 8–12), 8 (paras 10, 22, 23, 25(b), 48, 50, 51, 85), 9 (para 3), 10*	30 November 1993	SI 1993/1908, 2503
• ss 8, 9, Schs 8 (paras 42, 43(a), 44, 45, 62(a), 64(a), 66(a)), 10*	1 January 1994	SI 1993/1908
• ss 45*, 46*, Schs 8 (paras 1, 3–5, 8, 9, 33, 34)*, 10*	1 April 1994	SI 1993/2503
• ss 45*, 46*, Schs 8 (paras 1, 3–5, 8, 9, 33, 34)*, 10*	1 April 1995	SI 1993/2503
• s 7, Sch 10*	1 April 1996	s 7(4); SI 1993/1908
Video Recordings Act 1993	20 September 1993	s 6(2)
Welsh Language Act 1993		
• ss 30, 31, 35(2), Sch 2*	no date	s 36(2)
• remaining provisions	21 December 1993	s 36(1)

2435 Legislation—validity after repeal

See *R v Folkestone Justices, ex p Kibble*, para 27.

2436 Statute Law (Repeals) Act 1993

The Statute Law (Repeals) Act 1993 promotes the reform of the statute law by the repeal, in accordance with recommendations of the Law Commission, of certain enactments which are no longer of practical utility. The Act received the royal assent on 5 November 1993 and came into force, with certain exceptions, on that date. For details of commencement, see the commencement table in the title STATUTES.

2437 Welsh Language Act 1993

The Welsh Language Act 1993 establishes the Welsh Language Board (Bwrdd yr Iaith Gymraeg) to promote and facilitate the use of the Welsh language, and to provide for the preparation by public bodies of schemes giving effect to the principle that in the conduct of public business and the administration of justice in Wales the English and Welsh languages should be treated on a basis of equality. The Act received the royal assent on 21 October 1993 and, with certain exceptions, came into force on that date. For details of commencement, see the commencement table in the title STATUTES.

Sections 1–4, Sch 1 establish the board, provides for its constitution and membership, set out its functions of promoting and facilitating the use of the Welsh language, and require the board to comply with directions given by the Secretary of State. Section 5 requires public bodies notified by the board to establish Welsh language schemes for the purpose of giving effect to the principle that Welsh and English should be treated on an equal basis. Sections 6, 7 define public bodies and empower the board to issue notices to such bodies. Section 8 provides for objections to be made against time limits specified in a s 7 notice. Under ss 9–11 the board must issue guidelines as to the form and content of schemes, must prepare and consult on draft guidelines and must from time to time revise its guidelines. Sections 12, 13 require notified public bodies to submit schemes to the board within specified time limits and to carry out consultations on the preparation of schemes. Section 14 provides for the approval of schemes or for their referral to the Secretary of State. Under s 15, the board may require a public body to review an approved scheme in the light of revised guidelines issued by the board under ss 9–11. Section 16 provides for amendments to be made to schemes. Sections 17–20 provide for investigations by the board into non-compliance with schemes. Section 21 deals with application to the Crown.

Sections 22–24 re-enact with modifications provisions of the Welsh Courts Act 1942 and the Welsh Language Act 1967, concerning the use of Welsh in legal proceedings, the power to make rules prescribing translations of oaths and affirmations in Welsh for use in court and rules to provide for interpreters in courts in Wales. There are powers to give Welsh names to statutory bodies, offices or places and to prescribe Welsh forms: ss 25–27. Sections 28, 29 enable industrial and provident societies and credit unions to adopt fully Welsh titles. Sections 30, 31 make provision for documents relating to Welsh companies and publicity for limited liability status of Welsh companies. Sections 32, 33 enable the statutory declaration required on certain documents as to the status of a registered charity or a charity which is a company to appear in Welsh. Section 34 provides for the service of any notice required under ss 5–21. Repeals, consequential amendments, commencement and short title are dealt with in ss 35–37, Sch 2.

STOCK EXCHANGE

Halsbury's Laws of England (4th edn) Vol 45, paras 1–300

2438 Articles
City Comment, Nicholas Sayers (on the changes to the Yellow Book): LS Gaz, 8 September 1993, p 26
Statutory Regulation of Insider Dealing in Malaysia, Singapore and Hong Kong—A Comparative Analysis, Shahril Ridzuan: [1993] 2 MLJ XXV

2439 Stock Exchange Rules—amendment
The London Stock Exchange Rules Amendment No 16 incorporates the changes made by several Stock Exchange notices to the London Stock Exchange Rules.

The changes made to the Rules include amendments made to the procedure of the Disciplinary Committee. An existing provision in the Rules that a member firm must state on its business letters, notices and other official publications that it is a member of the London Stock Exchange is added to. Now the firm may state instead that it is a member of the International Stock Exchange of the United Kingdom and the Republic of Ireland.

The dealing and reporting rules are amended so as to add a new rule relating to market maker conduct. International Equity Market Practice Notes (IEMPNs) may be issued from time to time prescribing standards of conduct expected from market makers when transacting business in SEAQ (Stock Exchange Automated Quotations System) International securities. Any market maker failing to comply with the requirements of an IEMPN may be required to justify its actions to the Exchange. Provision is made whereby a market maker possessing a system capable of automatically changing its quotations in any SEAQ International security must register the system with the stock exchange and obtain the Stock Exchange's permission before using the system. The member firm must also register with the Stock Exchange any change to the capabilities or proposed uses of the system. Minor amendments are made to the dealing and reporting rules for a member firm market maker with a non-member principal.

New provisions relating to the developing markets sector on SEAQ International are included in the Rules. The Regulation and structure of the sector are set out, as are the requirements for market maker registration. The Rules require that amendments to the list of securities quoted on the developing markets sector will be published from time to time by the Stock Exchange.

The Rules remove the existing provisions relating to the registration of accredited dealers in the Equity Market and their obligations, and amend the rules regarding fast markets and indicative markets. The rules concerning reporting are also amended.

The Rules make provision for the use of SEATS (Stock Exchange Alternative Trading System), in particular for the obligations of corporate brokers and market makers, access to SEATS, satisfaction of firm orders placed, company announcements and order exposure for SEATS securities.

In the gilt-edged market, new restrictions are imposed on member firms dealing with one another, and amendments are made to traditional options.

TELECOMMUNICATIONS AND BROADCASTING

Halsbury's Laws of England (4th edn) Vol 45, paras 301–900

2440 Articles

Broadcast Coverage of International Sports Events, Ian Blackshaw: 143 NLJ 1290
The Myth of the Moratorium, (ITC powers to prevent take-overs of Channel 3 licensees), Adrian C Laing: 137 SJ 449.

2441 Broadcasting—Broadcasting Complaints Commission—jurisdiction

The Broadcasting Complaints Commission upheld complaints against a television production company for a broadcast concerning allergies. The findings were challenged on the basis that the Commission had no jurisdiction under the Broadcasting Act 1990, s 143(1) and that the findings were unreasonable in that there had been no infringement of privacy as claimed. In an application for judicial review by the producers, *held*, the Broadcasting Complaints Commission was entitled to decide that though the matter had previously been reported, there had been an infringement of privacy. The fact that some private matter had been published many years ago and was now forgotten by the public did not in any way diminish the hurt or upset of it being repeated. As to the complaint that the programme makers unfairly edited the interviews they gave so as to present the opposite views to those which were actually expressed in the interviews, the Broadcasting Complaints Commission was correct in deciding that the contributions had been unfairly edited. The Broadcasting Complaints Commission was within its jurisdiction and was not unreasonable in taking the view that there was an infringement of privacy despite the fact that the matter had previously been reported and was already in the public domain. Accordingly, the application would be dismissed.

R v Broadcasting Complaints Commission, ex p Granada Television Ltd (1993) Times, 31 May (Queen's Bench Division: Popplewell J).

2442 Broadcasting—Channel 3—licensing

The Broadcasting (Restrictions on the Holding of Licences) (Amendment) (Order) 1993, SI 1993/3199 (in force on 1 January 1994), amends the Broadcasting (Restrictions on the Holding of Licences) Order 1991, SI 1991/1176, removing certain restrictions on the holding of two licences to provide regional Channel 3 services except where the services are provided for London.

2443 Broadcasting—foreign satellite programmes—specified countries

The Broadcasting (Foreign Satellite Programmes) (Specified Countries) (Amendment) Order 1993, SI 1993/3047 (in force on 14 December 1993) amends the 1991 Order, SI 1991/2124, by substituting a new schedule to the 1991 Order specifying additional countries which are added as one of the steps necessary to implement the European Convention on Transfrontier Television.

2444 Broadcasting—foreign satellite service—proscription order

The Foreign Satellite Service Proscription Order 1993, SI 1993/1024 (in force on 1 May 1993), in accordance with the Broadcasting Act 1990, s 177, proscribes the foreign satellite service known as Red Hot Television.

See also *R v Secretary of State for the National Heritage, ex p Continental Television BV*, para 1524.

2445 Broadcasting—non-domestic satellite service—prescribed countries

The Broadcasting (Prescribed Countries) (Amendment) Order 1993, SI 1993/3046 (in force on 14 December 1993) amends the 1991 Order, SI 1991/1820, by substituting a new schedule to the 1991 Order specifying additional countries which are added as one of the steps necessary to implement the European Convention on Transfrontier Television.

2446 Interception of communications—quotas for warrants

In his 1992 annual report under the Interception of Communications Act 1985 (Cm 2173), the commissioner refers to the ceiling on the number of active warrants for interceptions which the Home Secretary has imposed on himself. These quotas have been gradually increased over the years and are regarded as a valuable discipline. The quotas, however, lack any statutory authority and the commissioner questions whether the Secretary of State should circumscribe his discretion to authorise the issue of warrants by reference to an arithmetical norm. The report also refers to a misunderstanding whereby the Post Office delayed implementing a cancellation of a postal warrant and unauthorised interceptions occurred as a result; it adds that arrangements have now been made to ensure that telephone messages cancelling such warrants are promptly confirmed in writing, that cancellation instruments are passed to the Post Office at once, and that the Post Office ceases interceptions on the date a warrant expires unless notified in writing of its renewal. The report refers to some instances where the Act has been contravened; deficiencies in procedure have been remedied and no use has been made of unauthorised materials; moreover, the commissioner is satisfied that the lapses were not symptomatic of laxity or casualness in approach.

2447 Telecommunications—leased lines

The Telecommunications (Leased Lines) Regulations 1993, SI 1993/2330 (in force on 20 October 1993), modify various licences granted under the Telecommunications Act 1984, s 7 so as to implement Council Directive (EC) 92/44 (application of open network provision to leased lines, harmonising the technical characteristics for leased lines on the public telecommunication network and providing for certain requirements relating to access to leased lines and to availability of information about conditions of supply of such lines).

2448 Telecommunications—public telecommunications systems

By virtue of his powers under the Telecommunications Act 1984, s 9, the Secretary of State has designated the telecommunications systems specified in the licences granted to the bodies named below as public telecommunications systems; accordingly, those bodies become telecommunications operators.

Body	Designated by SI 1993 No
Bradford Cable Communications Ltd	2172
City of London Telecommunications Ltd	1879
Energis Communications Ltd	1935
Ionica L3 Ltd	1880
MFS Communications Ltd	2899
Torch Communications Ltd	2898

2449 Television licences—fees

The Wireless Telegraphy (Television Licence Fees) (Amendment) Regulations 1993, SI 1993/476 (in force on 1 April 1993), amend the 1991 Regulations, SI 1991/436 by increasing the fees payable for the issue of television licences. In particular, the basic fee for a television in the case of monochrome is increased to £27·50 and in the case of colour to £83. In the case of instalment licences the issue fee for the Standard Instalment Licence is increased from £40 to £41·50 with instalment fees raised from £20 to £20·75. For the Premium Instalment Licence the issue and instalment fees of £21·25 are both increased to £22.

The Wireless Telegraphy (Television Licence Fees) (Amendment) (No 2) Regulations 1993, SI 1993/2205 (in force on 1 October 1993), make provision for an additional type of colour television licence for which the fees are payable by instalments. They provide for the payment of one of seven specified issue fees and five equal instalments thereafter. In each case the total amount payable is £83·00.

2450 Video Recordings Act 1993

The Video Recordings Act 1993 amends the Video Recordings Act 1984. The Act received the royal assent on 20 July 1993 and came into force on 20 September 1993.

Section 1 amends the 1984 Act, s 4 to make provision for titles to be assigned to video works for identification purposes. Section 2 introduces a new s 14A into the 1984 Act which provides a general defence to offences under the 1984 Act. A time limit for prosecutions under the 1984 Act is introduced by the 1993 Act, s 3. Section 4 extends the procedure for the admissibility in evidence of certificates stating relevant facts and s 5 makes similar provision in relation to Scotland. Section 6 deals with short title, commencement and extent.

2451 Videos—supply to persons under age

A company was charged with supplying a video to a person under the age specified in the classification. On appeal against conviction, *held*, the question was whether the defence contained in the Video Recordings Act 1984, s 11(2) that the accused neither knew nor had reasonable grounds to believe that the person had not attained that age was concerned with the knowledge and information of the company by those who managed its affairs, or the knowledge and information of the employee who made the sale. It was absurd to suppose that those who managed a vast company had any knowledge or information as to the age of casual purchasers of video films. It was the employee who sold the video at the check-out who had the knowledge or reasonable belief and it was his knowledge or reasonable belief that was relevant. If it were otherwise, the statute would be wholly ineffective against companies. Therefore the knowledge and information of the employee who made the sale was relevant and could be imputed to the company. Accordingly, the appeal would be dismissed.

Tesco Stores Ltd v Brent London Borough Council [1993] 2 All ER 718 (Queens Bench Division: Staughton LJ and Buckley J).

2452 Wireless telegraphy—land mobile-satellite service—exemptions

The Wireless Telegraphy Apparatus (Land Mobile-Satellite Service) (Low Bit Rate Data) (Exemption) Regulations 1993, SI 1993/21 (in force on 15 February 1993), provide for exemptions from the licensing requirements of the Wireless Telegraphy Act 1949, s 1(1). Exemption is provided for mobile earth stations which send low bit rate data communications by wireless telegraphy via a land mobile-satellite service provided by or through the European Telecommunications Satellite Organisation or the International Maritime Satellite Organisation or a signatory to those organisations or TRAK-SAT Communications Limited with land earth stations in that service. Accordingly, it will not be necessary to hold a licence to establish and use the stations to which these regulations apply.

2453 Wireless telegraphy—short range devices—exemptions

The Wireless Telegraphy (Short Range Devices) (Exemption) Regulations 1993, SI 1993/1591 (in force on 26 July 1993), provide for the exemption from the licensing requirements of the Wireless Telegraphy Act 1949, s 1(1) of various short range devices, formerly known as low power devices. For the exemption to apply, the short range device must be approved under the Telecommunications Act 1984, s 84. Short range devices will from 1 January 1996 have to comply with the type approval requirements set out in the Electromagnetic Compatibility Regulations 1992, SI 1992/2372, Pt VI before being supplied or taken into service.

THEATRES AND OTHER PLACES OF ENTERTAINMENT

Halsbury's Laws of England (4th edn) Vol 45, paras 901–1100

2454 Films—co-production agreements

The Films Co-Production Agreements (Amendment) Order 1993, SI 1993/1805 (in force on 10 August 1993), amends the 1985 Order, SI 1985/960, by extending the list of agreements made between the government of the United Kingdom and the governments of certain other countries to include an agreement with New Zealand.

2455 Public entertainment—licence—condition

Public entertainments licences may be granted and renewed by a local authority on such terms and conditions and subject to such restrictions as may be specified: London Government Act 1963, Sch 12, para 1(2).

The applicant's entertainments and exhibition licences were renewed on condition that it would require organisers of events to ensure that all advertisements would encourage visitors to events to use public transport. On an application for judicial review of that condition, *held*, in order to be reasonable, a condition imposed under Sch 12, para 1(2) had to be sufficiently precise to enable an applicant for a licence to know what its obligations were. Although conditions could be imposed which were for a public purpose in connection with the licensed use of premises, they could not be such that no reasonable licensing authority could have imposed them. A condition was unreasonable in the *Wednesbury* sense if its meaning was so obscure that an originating summons as to its construction had to be issued under RSC Ord 7. The relief sought would not be granted because the applicant had a statutory right of appeal under the 1963 Act, Sch 12, para 19.

R v Hammersmith and Fulham London Borough Council, ex p Earls Court Ltd (1993) Times, 15 July (Queen's Bench Division: Kennedy LJ and Buckley J).

TORT

Halsbury's Laws of England (4th edn) Vol 45, paras 1201–1536

2456 Articles

Ethical Triumph, or Surgical Rape? Barbara Hewson (on court orders for Caesareans): 137 SJ 1182

Harassment—A Recognised Tort? Margaret Noble: 143 NLJ 1685

Lessons From New Zealand, Michael Whincup (on the developments in the law of tort in New Zealand): LS Gaz, 29 September 1993, p 22

Protection of Privacy the Common Law gets a Grip, Philip Turl: [1993] Fam Law 640

References—How Far Can You Go? Sylvia Elwes (on *Spring v Guardian Assurance* [1993] 2 All ER 273 (1992 Abr para 1846)): 137 SJ 1196

The Emergence of Harassment as a Recognised Tort, John Murphy: 143 NLJ 926

The New Law of Privacy, Patrick Milmo QC: 143 NLJ 1182

Toxic Torts and Group Actions, Charles Pugh and Valerie Easty: 143 NLJ 1293

Trespass to the Person—A Tort Too Far, Irvine Marr and Paul Coppin (on *Stubbings v Webb* [1993] 1 All ER 322 (1992 Abr para 1629)): 137 SJ 654

Unlawful Strip Searching, Heather Williams and Jane Deighton (on a new tort of trespass to the person): 137 SJ 377

2457 Breach of statutory duty—child in local authority care—failure of authority to further child's best interests

The plaintiff, who had been in local authority care from the age of three until she was 18, had been assessed and educated as if mentally handicapped and severely subnormal. She was placed, when aged 18, in a residential establishment on the ground that she was educationally subnormal and unable to look after herself. She was, in fact, of normal intelligence and claimed damages against the local authority, in its capacity both as parent, by virtue of a care order, and as local education authority, and against the school which she had attended for most of the period, for breach of their statutory duties and/or negligence for failing to further her best interests and to afford her the opportunity for proper development of her character and abilities and aptitudes and her special educational needs, contrary to the Education Act 1944, ss 33(2), 36 and/or the Education (Miscellaneous Provisions) Act 1953, s 6(2)(b). The authority and the school sought to strike out the claims against them. *Held*, where a statute imposed a duty but provided no remedy, either civil or criminal, for its breach, there was an assumption that a private law remedy was available to the plaintiff; this depended on the construction of the statute in question. A defined and specific duty, not one owed to the public at large, had to be established.

There were duties under both Acts owed by authorities in loco parentis to a particular person. The plaintiff was such a person and, therefore, was in a particular class to which duties were owed under the care order. The authority could not be sued as education authority but could be sued for breach of its obligations while in loco parentis to the plaintiff. The authority's application would be refused. However, as it was not just and reasonable for the school to owe the duty of care pleaded, the claim against it would be struck out.

   Holtom v Barnet London Borough Council (1993) Times, 30 September (Queen's Bench Division: Judge Oddie).

2458   Breach of statutory duty—liability of employer

See HEALTH AND SAFETY AT WORK.

2459   Deceit—company officers' fraudulent misrepresentations—liability of company

See *Dixon v Deacon Morgan McEwan Easson*, para 469.

2460   Deceit—defence of contributory negligence—availability

See *Alliance & Leicester Building Society v Edgestop Ltd; Same v Dhanoa; Same v Samra; Mercantile Credit Co Ltd v Lancaster*, para 1813.

2461   False imprisonment—arrest for likely breach of the peace—hunt saboteur

See *Kelly v Chief Constable of Hampshire*, para 673.

2462   False imprisonment—store detective—store detective acting as informant to police

A store detective mistakenly considered that the plaintiff had been involved in the theft of a cassette from a shop and informed the police. As a result, a police officer, in exercise of his discretion under the Police and Criminal Evidence Act 1984, s 24(6), arrested the plaintiff. No charge was brought against the plaintiff and the plaintiff brought an action for damages for false imprisonment against the store detective. The claim was withdrawn from the jury, and the plaintiff appealed against the decision. *Held*, the store detective had merely given information to the officer who had decided, in the exercise of his discretion, to make an arrest. She had neither encouraged, promoted nor requested the plaintiff's arrest. Accordingly, the appeal would be dismissed.

   Davidson v Chief Constable of North Wales Police (1993) Times, 26 April (Court of Appeal: Sir Thomas Bingham MR, Staughton and Waite LJJ).

2463   Interference with performance of contract—act causing breach of contract—intention

The plaintiffs, a record producer and a number of musicians, claimed that, because the first defendant, a singer, had refused to perform her contract with the second defendant, a company which had engaged the services of the plaintiffs to work on an album of songs to be performed by the first defendant, the second defendant had broken its contract with the plaintiffs thereby causing them to suffer loss and damage. The claim was struck out on the ground that it disclosed no reasonable cause of action because, even if the allegations were made out, the plaintiffs had failed to allege or establish that the first defendant had acted with an intention to cause loss or damage to them, or that her actions were directed at them. On appeal by the plaintiffs, *held*, Peter Gibson LJ dissenting, a person intentionally interfered with a contract between two other parties either by persuading one to break his contract with the other or, by some unlawful act, directly or indirectly preventing one party from performing his contracts. The first defendant voluntarily broke her agreement with the second defendant knowing of the plaintiffs' contract the performance of which would be impossible if she refused to perform her obligations under her agreement with the second defendants. As she must have realised that her performance of her obligations under her contract was essential and irreplaceable, she must have intended that the second defendant would be unable to perform its obligations to the plaintiffs. Accordingly, it seemed unnecessary to assert a specific intention to interfere with the performance of the plaintiffs' contracts which must necessarily follow from the first defendant's refusal to perform her obligation to the second defendant. In the absence of any explanation from the first defendant, the only reasonable inference was that in refusing to perform she must have had a purpose of her own to serve which she pursued at the expense of the plaintiffs' right to contractual performance by the second defendant of its obligations. The appeal would be allowed.

Peter Gibson LJ dissenting said that the ambit of the tort of procuring a breach of contract should be restricted by requiring the plaintiff to show that the defendant by his conduct intended to, and with that intention did break, or otherwise interfere with, a contract to which the plaintiff was a party.

Millar v Bassey (1993) Independent, 26 August (Court of Appeal: Ralph Gibson, Beldam and Peter Gibson LJJ).

2464 Joint tortfeasors—settlement agreement by one tortfeasor—effect

The defendant's action for libel against the two plaintiffs was successful and judgment for £1,500,000 was entered against them. A settlement between the defendant and the first plaintiff was agreed in which the defendant accepted the payment of £10,000 in full and final settlement of the judgment provided that certain other conditions were met. The second plaintiff, with the first plaintiff's consent, was sent a copy of the agreement. His trustee in bankruptcy claimed contribution against the first plaintiff. The plaintiffs claimed that the agreement was a release by the defendant of all his rights against either plaintiff arising out of the libel action. *Held*, the parties to the agreement did not intend that the second plaintiff be immediately discharged from all further liability. The settlement was concerned with the defendant's rights against the first plaintiff. While a term as to the reservation of rights against the second defendant might be implied into such an agreement, there could be no implication as to rights of contribution. The agreement was clearly subject to an implied term that the defendant's rights against the second plaintiff would be reserved. The plaintiffs' claim would be dismissed.

Watts v Aldington; Tolstoy v Aldington (1993) Times, 16 December (Court of Appeal: Neill, Steyn and Simon Brown LJJ).

2465 Libel and slander

See LIBEL AND SLANDER.

2466 Misfeasance by prison officer—abuse of power—liability of Home Office

See *Racz v Home Office*, para 2074.

2467 Negligence

See NEGLIGENCE.

2468 Nuisance

See NUISANCE.

2469 Personal injury—explosion—illegality of activity—entitlement to damages

Canada

The plaintiff, aged 14, was injured by an accidental explosion of a pipe bomb made by his friends which had been left briefly, against the plaintiff's wishes, in his possession. The plaintiff was convicted of possessing a pipe bomb and subsequently started an action against his friends who made the bomb and the supplier of gunpowder used in it. At first instance the action was dismissed on the grounds of the ex turpi causa doctrine. On appeal by the plaintiff, *held*, owing to the comparatively trivial nature of the illegality it was not appropriate to dismiss the action summarily. Accordingly, the appeal would be allowed.

Zickefoose v Barotto Sports Ltd (1993) 99 DLR (4th) 57 (Alberta Court of Appeal). Decision of Alberta Court of Queen's Bench (1991) 91 DLR (4th) 116 (1992 Abr para 2534) reversed.

2470 Trespass—trespass to land—damages—measure of damages—property let at concessionary rent

See *Ministry of Defence v Ashman; Ministry of Defence v Thompson*, para 971.

2471 Trespass—trespass to land—remedy—right of self-redress—availability

See *Burton v Winters*, para 1897.

2472   Trespass—tresspass to the person—search by prison officer—strip search

The plaintiffs, one a female aged 18 and the other a male aged 17, visited the prison where the female's brother was a category A inmate. They were both asked to submit to a search and told that the visit would not go ahead if they refused. They agreed and were taken in turn into a small anteroom by two officers of the same sex as themselves where they were told to remove all their clothes, which they did. There was a glass window in the door of the room which was only partially covered. Prison officers and members of the public were passing by outside the door, although there was no evidence of anyone actually looking in. The plaintiffs were given a small, flimsy piece of curtain to put in front of their bodies. The search left both plaintiffs feeling very upset and humiliated and as a result the female experienced symptoms of post-traumatic stress disorder for several months after the incident. The plaintiffs sought damages from the Secretary of State with responsibility for the prison service, relying on various forms of the tort of trespass to the person. *Held*, the Prison Rules 1964, r 86 provides prison officers with the power to search any person entering or leaving a prison. That power would be exercised unlawfully, firstly, if more than reasonable force was employed, secondly, if the decision to search was perverse and, thirdly, if the search was not conducted in a reasonably seemly and decent manner. Following a finding that the searches were not conducted in a reasonably seemly and decent manner the judge declared the existence of the tort of trespass to the person by unlawfully inducing a person to remove his or her clothes. The judge accordingly awarded compensatory and exemplary damages to each plaintiff.

Bayliss v Home Secretary (1993) Legal Action Bulletin, February, p 17 (Liverpool County Court: Judge Marshall Evans).

TOWN AND COUNTRY PLANNING

Halsbury's Laws of England (4th edn) Vol 46 (reissue), paras 1–768

2473   Articles

Breach of Condition Notices—Theory and Practice, David Hainsworth (on the Town and Country Planning Act 1990, s 187A): [1993] JPL 903
Certificates of lawful Use or Development—The New System, Richard Max: Estates Gazette, 20 November 1993, p 172
Councils, Councillors and Costs, J Cameron Blackhall (on costs at planning enquiries): [1993] JPL 112
High Street Finance, Alec Samuels (on the balance between retail and financial services in shopping centres): 137 SJ 793
Multiple Implementation of Planning Permissions, Neil Collar: [1993] JPL 627
Planning and Compensation Act 1991, Alec Samuels: 157 LG Rev 862
Planning and Pollution Control, Gill Castorina: Estates Gazette, 2 October 1993, p 113
Planning and Transportation, Transportation and Planning, Alec Samuels: 157 LG Rev 401
Planning Conditions—Enforcement and Variation, Simon Payne: [1993] Conv 119
Planning for Development, Felix Bourne (on the policies of local planning authorities): LS Gaz, 29 September 1993, p 27
Planning Gain in Ten Dimensions, Richard Fordham: [1993] JPL 719
Planning Law (Update), Charles Mynors: 137 SJ 375
Public Rights of Way—By-Ways over Private Land, Mary Welstead: [1993] Conv 129
Some Aspects of Deregulation, Jon Vivian and Mark Heighton (on how the Sunday trading rules will apply under the Planning Acts): Estates Gazette, 9 October 1993, p 130
Sustainability" A Long-Established Concern of Planning, Denzil Millichap [1993] JPL 1111
The Government's Consultation Paper "Reform of the Caravan Sites Act 1968"—A Solution to Gipsy Site Provision? Geoffrey Holgate: [1993] Conv 39, 111
The Need to Check Planning Conditions, John Martin: Estates Gazette, 7 August 1993, p 62
The Subdivision of Single Dwelling-houses into Flats and the Applicability of the Four Year Enforcement Rule, John Trimbos: [1993] JPL 311

2474   Advertisements—control of display—knowledge or consent of offender

The Town and Country Planning Act 1990, s 224(3) provides that if any person displays an advertisement in contravention of certain regulations made under the Act, he is guilty of an offence. Section 224(5) provides that a person is not guilty of an offence under s 224(3) by reason only of his being the owner or occupier of the land on which the advertisement is displayed or of his goods, trade, business or other concerns being given publicity by the advertisement, if he proves that it was displayed without his knowledge or consent.

Advertisements for an extreme political party were displayed without the consent of the defendants, the chairman and the regional officer of the party. They only discovered the existence of the advertisements when they received a letter from the local authority requesting the removal of the advertisements. Following the failure of the defendants to remove the advertisements, an action was brought against them, and the defendants were convicted of displaying an advertisement contrary to the Town and Country Planning (Control of Advertisements) Regulations 1989, SI 1989/670, regs 5, 26 and the 1990 Act, s 224(3). The justices held that once the defendants had received the letters, they had a responsibility to remove the advertisements or be guilty of an offence. The defendants appealed by way of case stated. *Held*, the proper construction of s 224(5) provided a defence where it was proved that the display was made without the knowledge or consent of the offender. It was contrary to the fundamental principles of law for someone to become guilty of a criminal offence simply on acquiring knowledge on a state of affairs for which he was not responsible. Accordingly, the appeal would be allowed and the convictions quashed.

Edmonds v Merton London Borough Council; Tyndall v Same (1993) Times, 6 July (Queen's Bench Division: Kennedy LJ and Buckley J).

2475 Advertisements—control of display—separate advertisements

It has been held that the display of different posters on different dates without the consent of a local authority constitute separate advertisements under the Town and Country Planning (Control of Advertisements) Regulations 1992, SI 1992/666, regs 5, 27. Separate advertisements are therefore to be regarded as separate offences, not one continuing offence.

Kingston upon Thames Royal Borough Council v National Solus Sites Ltd (1993) Times, 24 June (Queen's Bench Division: Glidewell J).

2476 Appropriation of land—appropriation for planning purposes—power to override easements—sale of land for redevelopment

The plaintiff local authority was the freehold owner of a piece of land, on which it operated a children's home for a number of years. The land was expressed to be subject to restrictive covenants limiting the number of properties which could be built on the land. The plaintiff later wished to sell the land and gained outline planning permission for redevelopment by the erection of several detached houses. The defendants claimed the benefit of the restrictive covenants. In order to obtain the benefit of the Town and Country Planning Act 1971, s 127, which provided for the overriding of easements and other rights on land which had been appropriated by a local authority for planning purposes, the plaintiff passed a resolution that "pursuant to the Local Government Act 1972, s 122, the site be appropriated from social services to planning purposes". The plaintiff applied by way of originating summons to determine whether the site had been validly appropriated for planning purposes. The defendants contended that the plaintiff had to show that it had acquired or appropriated the land for some purpose connected with its planning functions. *Held*, the land had not been appropriated for planning purposes. Section 122 provided that a local authority could appropriate for any purpose for which it had power to acquire land by agreement. The plaintiff could not acquire land by agreement to sell for redevelopment. By the 1971 Act, s 112, it was necessary to show that the land was required to secure the carrying out of one or more of the following activities, namely "development, redevelopment and improvement" or "for a purpose which it is necessary to achieve in the interests of proper planning of an area in which the land is situated". The proposed sale of the land for development pursuant to the planning permission granted was not an acquisition of land for planning purposes, and the originating summons would be dismissed.

Sutton London Borough Council v Bolton [1993] 33 EG 91 (Chancery Division: Judge Baker).

1971 Act, ss 112, 127 now consolidated in the Town and Country Planning Act 1990, ss 226, 237.

2477 Blight notice—plans affecting part of claimant's land—counter-notice—request for purchase of whole of claimant's land

A council planned to build a road which would pass through part of the claimant's land. As a result, the claimant was unable to sell the whole of the land and served a notice under the Town and Country Planning Act 1990, s 150, requesting the council to purchase all of the land. The council served a counter notice on the ground that they would only purchase that part of the land affected by the building of the new road. Subsequently, the council adopted a new scheme whereby the road would be realigned so as not to encroach on any part of the claimant's land. On an application to determine whether the council's objection to the blight notice was well founded, *held*, the jurisdiction of the tribunal was limited to deciding whether or not the ground stated in the counter notice was well founded and the council could not rely on a ground not stated in the counter notice. The potential loss of the part of the land affected would cause material detriment to the remainder of the property. The council would therefore be required to buy the whole property even though no part of it was required for the purpose of the realigned road. Accordingly, it was declared that the objection made by the council was not well founded and the blight notice served by the claimant was valid and effective.

Entwistle Pearson (Manchester) Ltd v Chorley Borough Council (1993) 66 P & C R 277 (Lands Tribunal: Mr J C Hill, TD, FRICS).

2478   Caravan site—licensing—exemption—site providing accommodation for annual workers

The Caravan Sites and Control of Development Act 1960, Sch 1, para 7 provides that a site licence is not required for the use of agricultural land as a caravan site on which persons employed in farming operations are accommodated during a particular season.

The respondents kept poultry and traded in free-range eggs on a large area of land owned by them. They used part of the land as an unlicensed caravan site on which they provided accommodation for persons employed in their poultry business. The local authority laid an information alleging that the respondents' failure to obtain a licence for the site contravened the 1960 Act, Sch 1, para 7. The justices dismissed the information on the ground that poultry farming was seasonal work for which a licence was not required. On appeal by the local authority, *held*, the legislation was intended to apply to work which was genuinely seasonal, such as hop-picking, not work which went on throughout the year. If "a particular season" was construed to mean "a whole year" and was applied to work which was not genuinely seasonal, the legislation would be rendered meaningless. The respondents' poultry business was not genuinely seasonal, and, accordingly, the local authority's appeal would be allowed.

Vale of White Horse District Council v Mirmalek–Sani & Mirmalek–Sani (1993) 25 HLR 387 (Queen's Bench Division: Kennedy LJ and Clarke J).

2479   Caravan site—site for gipsies—injunction—contempt of court

See *Guildford Borough Council v Valler*, para 581.

2480   Caravan site—site for gipsies—injunction—judicial review

See *R v West Sussex County Council, ex p Wenman*, para 6.

2481   Caravan site—site for gipsies—meaning of "gipsies"

The Caravan Sites Act 1968 defines "gipsies" as persons of nomadic habit of life, whatever their race or origin.

The applicants were travellers who sought various reliefs from a local authority under the 1968 Act, claiming that they fell within the definition of "gipsies" in the Act. *Held*, the definition of "gipsies" in the 1968 Act included any people leading a nomadic habit of life, even if they were not traditional gipsies. However, the words imported something more than just wandering and travelling but suggested people moving from place to place with a purpose in mind which was a necessary and characteristic part of their lives. It would take a while to acquire this purpose as well as establish the nomadic habit of life, neither of which were sufficiently present in this case to entitle the applicants to come within the definition of "gipsies" under the 1968 Act. Accordingly the applications would be dismissed.

R v South Hams District Council, ex p Gibb; R v Gloucestershire County Council, ex p Davies; R v Warwickshire County Council, ex p Walker (1993) Times, 15 November (Queen's Bench Division: Harrison J).

2482   Development Board for Rural Wales—transfer of housing stock

The Development Board for Rural Wales (Transfer of Housing Stock) Regulations 1993, SI 1993/1808 (in force on 12 August 1993), make provision for the transfer of the housing stock of the Development Board for Rural Wales. The regulations provide that the board may be

required by the Secretary of State to make proposals for the disposal of its housing stock. Further
provision is made regarding the price at which property is to be transfered, land registration
requirements and the transfer of housing stock.

2483   Development plan—development of residential area—provision of open spaces

A construction company was refused planning permission for the construction of residential
flats because the local authority felt the company's proposals in relation to open spaces with
public access did not comply with the area's development plan. The company's appeal was
allowed because the inspector was satisfied with the company's assurances that open spaces would
be available, although the company had refused to enter into a legal agreement with the local
authority to ensure that would be the case. The local authority appealed under the Town and
Country Planning Act 1990, s 228, contending the inspector should not have taken the
company's verbal assurances into account because there was nothing in those assurances which
would prevent the company from denying access to the public at a later date. *Held*, there had
not been inconsistencies in the inspector's decision. He had accepted that the public would not
have a legal right to use the land, but in the light of the company's assurances he had felt the
public were likely to be given access. It had not been unreasonable for him to rely on those
assurances, and there was no need to consider whether those assurances could be enforced if they
were breached. Accordingly, the appeal would be dismissed.

   Crawley Borough Council v Secretary of State for the Environment and Fairbriar Homes Ltd [1993]
JPL 148 (Queen's Bench Division: David Widdicombe QC).

2484   Development plan—material considerations—draft local plan

A district council refused consent for a change of use from residential/bed and breakfast to office
accommodation. Subsequently, a planning inspector decided not to grant planning permission
and the Secretary of State dismissed an appeal against his decision. On an application to quash
the dismissal of the appeal, *held*, a draft local plan, which contained emerging policies, had been
approved for consultation. Although it was still at the earliest stage, it was capable in law of
being a material consideration. The inspector should have recognised its existence and indicated
the extent to which his decision had been influenced by it. The application would be granted.

   Kissel v Secretary of State for the Environment (1993) Times, 22 July (Queen's Bench Division:
Sir Graham Eyre QC).

2485   Development plan—material considerations—interpretation of legislation

The Town and Country Planning Act 1990, s 70(1),(2) provides that when dealing with an
application for planning permission a local planning authority should have regard to the
development plan, so far as material to the application, and to any other material considerations.
Section 54A, as added by the Planning and Compensation Act 1991, provides that where, in
making any determination under the planning Acts, regard is to be had to the development
plan, the determination must be made in accordance with that plan unless material considerations
indicate otherwise.
   A district council refused an application for planning permission for the redevelopment of a
public house into offices on the grounds that the proposals did not comply with the area's
development plan. The defendant developers appealed, a local inquiry was held and the inspector
allowed the appeal. The council applied to the High Court for an order to quash the decision.
The council contended that the procedure by which the inspector had reached his decision was
incorrect: he relied exclusively on the 1990 Act, s 70(2) and failed to apply, or even consider s
54A. Moreover, the inspector had failed to distinguish between the development plan policies
and other policies and had not recognised the presumption in favour of the development plan.
Held, the inspector had clearly failed to refer expressly to s 54A, but provided that the
requirements of that section were met this would not prove fatal to the decision. However, the
fact that he appeared to have followed s 70(2) and not to have applied the approach prescribed
by s 54A would entitle the court to quash the decision. Nevertheless, since a reconsideration by
the Secretary of State on the basis of s 54A, would not produce a different decision, the court
would exercise its discretion not to quash the inspector's decision. Accordingly, the application
would be dismissed.

   St Albans District Council v Secretary of State for the Environment (1992) 66 P & CR 432
(Queen's Bench Division: David Widdicombe QC).

2486 Enforcement notice—appeal—application for leave to appeal out of time

The Town and Country Planning Act 1990, s 289(6), as amended by the Planning and Compensation Act 1991, s 6(5), provides that leave is required before an appeal may be made to the High Court on a point of law arising from the making of an enforcement notice.

Due to oversights by its advisers, a local authority failed to lodge an appeal against an inspector's decision on an enforcement notice in time. The local authority applied for an extension of time, and it fell to be determined whether leave should be granted in accordance with the 1990 Act, s 289(6). *Held*, there was no indication in the 1990 Act, s 289(6), as amended, as to the standard which had to be applied by the court in deciding whether to grant leave, nor was there any authority to which the court could turn for guidance. The intention of the amendment was to weed out frivolous appeals which were doomed to failure, so the court ought to apply the same standards as those which would be applied when deciding whether to grant leave for judicial review, namely whether the application disclosed arguable grounds of appeal. The material facts of the application did not reveal arguable grounds, and, accordingly, the application would be dismissed.

R v Secretary of State for the Environment and Gojkovic, ex p Kensington and Chelsea Royal London Borough Council [1993] JPL 139 (Queen's Bench Division: Hutchison J).

2487 Enforcement notice—appeal—costs

See *Rozhon v Secretary of State for Wales*, para 2011.

2488 Enforcement notice—appeal—variation—potentially unjust consequences of variation

The appellant converted a workshop into an extension to his house, but sold the extension as separate accommodation contrary to the Town and Country Planning Act 1971, s 22(3)(a). The appellant subsequently sought planning permission for the extension to be used as a separate house, but this was refused. His appeal against refusal was dismissed, and the local authority issued an enforcement notice requiring (1) the cessation of the use of the premises as two separate dwellings, and (2) its restoration to use as a single dwelling. On appeal against the enforcement notice the inspector upheld the first step because access to the extension was inadequate for a single dwelling, but he struck out the second step on the ground that it was excessive and unreasonable. The appellant appealed against that decision, contending it was hopelessly ambiguous because neither he nor the other homeowner knew what they had to do to comply with it. *Held*, the amended notice could be satisfied by either homeowner moving out so that one of the properties was no longer used as a dwelling, or by both homeowners moving out so that neither property was used as a dwelling. The fact that there were alternative ways of complying with the notice had not rendered it ambiguous even though the homeowners did not know who was obliged to move. However, the amended enforcement notice could result in the extension remaining in use as a dwelling and the original house falling empty, and as neither the local authority nor the inspector had intended that result the matter ought to be remitted to the Secretary of State for his determination. To that extent, the appeal would be allowed.

Bennett v Secretary of State for the Environment and East Devon District Council [1993] JPL 134 (Queen's Bench Division: Lionel Read QC).

1971 Act, s 22(3)(a) superseded by Town and Country Planning Act 1990, s 55(3)(a).

2489 Enforcement notice—application for adjournment of hearing—planning permission sought prior to hearing for breach

It has been held that where a defendant is prosecuted for breach of the terms of a planning enforcement notice and then applies for planning permission prior to the hearing, the magistrates ought still to hear and determine the guilt or innocence of the defendant notwithstanding that the planning application has been made. The discretion to adjourn must only be used in exceptional cases and depends on individual circumstances with the predominant concern being the just and convenient management of the case before the court rather than sympathy for the defendant.

R v Beaconsfield Magistrates, ex p South Buckinghamshire District Council (1993) 157 JP 1073 (Queen's Bench Division: Staughton LJ and Buckley J).

2490   Enforcement notice—division of one site into separate enforcement notice sites—separate consideration of notices

The appellant was served with ten enforcement notices alleging material changes of use of certain buildings on his agricultural holding from agricultural use to uses such as vehicle repairs and storage. Nine of the notices related to individual buildings and land on which separate businesses were being conducted; the tenth notice related to the entire site comprising the previous agricultural holding. The inspector concluded that the uses and traffic thereby generated detracted from the character and appearance of the area, that the objections could not be overcome by conditions or partial approval, and that it would be unjust to single out some businesses for approval when all contributed to the overall problem. On appeal against his dismissal of appeals against the notices, *held*, the inspector had to consider whether planning permission should be granted in respect of the land to which a notice related. He had, therefore, to consider the circumstances obtaining in the case of each particular enforcement notice site. It was neither proper nor lawful to refuse permission for a use on a particular site because of uses on other sites unless there was some convincing or legitimate reason for so doing. In concluding that it would be unjust to single out some businesses for approval and some for refusal when all contributed to the overall problem, the inspector was wrong. Such potential injustice was not a planning consideration. The local planning authority had divided up the overall site into separate enforcement notice sites; the inspector should, therefore, have considered whether permission should have been granted in relation to each part comprised within each enforcement notice. The appeal would be allowed and the case remitted for rehearing and determination.

Reed v Secretary of State for the Environment and Tandridge District Council (1992) 65 P & CR 50 (Queen's Bench Division: Malcolm Spence QC).

2491   Enforcement notice—non-compliance—lack of knowledge of enforcement notice

The Town and Country Planning Act 1971, s 89(5) sets out the penalties for non-compliance with enforcement notices. Section 243(2) deals with the validity of enforcement notices.

The appellants appealed against their respective convictions in relation to the contravention of certain enforcement notices and argued that s 89(5) of the 1971 Act did not create an absolute offence and therefore the local authority had to establish that the appellants were aware of the enforcement notices before being convicted. *Held*, an offence under s 89(5) was not truly criminal. The presumption that mens rea was required could be displaced if the statute made it clear that Parliament did not intend that mens rea was necessary. This was especially the case if this construction was in accordance with the purpose of the statute. It was clear when reading s 89(5) together with s 243(2) that knowledge of a notice was not a fundamental part of the offence. Section 243 made it clear that the statute intended those who had an interest in the land to make efforts to inform themselves of the planning position in relation to that land. The intention of Parliament was that the person intending to use the land should have the burden of establishing whether the use of the land was prohibited. Enforcement notices had to be registered as land charges and each district planning authority had a duty to keep a public register of notices under the Local Government and Planning (Amendment) Act 1981. It was therefore the policy of the 1971 Act to impose absolute liability to encourage owners and users of land to be vigilant. Accordingly the appeals would be dismissed.

R v Collett; R v Furminger; R v Nazari; R v Pope; R v Bandar (1993) Times, 28 October (Court of Appeal: Nolan and Tuckey LJJ and Latham J).

The Town and Country Planning Act 1971, ss 89(5), 243(2) now the Town and Country Planning Act 1990, ss 179(2) and 285(2).

2492   Enforcement notice—time limit

The Town and Country Planning Act 1990, s 172(4)(b) provides that an enforcement notice in respect of a failure to comply with any condition which relates to the carrying out of building operations on land and subject to which planning permission was granted for the development of that land must be issued within a period of four years from the date of the breach.

A council granted planning permission for the construction of a farmhouse on condition that its occupation should be limited to a person employed, or last employed locally in agriculture or in forestry or a dependant of such a person. An enforcement notice was served on the occupants of the farmhouse who had resided in it for more than four years on the ground that neither of them fulfilled that condition. On their appeal against the notice, it was held to have been out of time. On appeal by the council, *held*, Rose LJ dissenting, the condition imposed upon the grant of planning permission related exclusively to occupancy and was in no way concerned with the building as such. It did not "relate to the carrying out of building . . . operations" within the meaning of s 172(4)(b). Only conditions relating to the physical and visible characteristics of the building were protected by the time limit imposed for enforcement. The appeal would be allowed.

Rose LJ, dissenting, held that the operational development for which permission was granted was the construction of a new dwelling and that a condition as to agricultural use or occupancy was imposed in relation to the permitted development.

Newbury District Council v Secretary of State for the Environment (1993) 67 P & CR 68 (Court of Appeal: Russell, Hirst and Rose LJJ). *Harvey v Secretary of State for Wales* (1989) 88 LGR 253, CA (1989 Abr para 2347) distinguished.

1990 Act, s 172 now as substituted by Planning and Compensation Act 1991, s 5.

2493 Lands Tribunal—decision—appeal—appeal to Court of Appeal

See *Practice Note*, para 2046.

2494 Leasehold Reform, Housing and Urban Development Act 1993

See para 1612.

2495 Listed building—enforcement notice—non-compliance with notice— reasonable steps taken to comply with notice

See *Mid-Devon District Council v Avery*, para 1900.

2496 Planning permission—appeal—amendment of plan for site to which appeal relates—duty to inform persons affected

On an appeal against a local planning authority's refusal of an application for planning permission for a gipsy caravan site, the inspector accepted an amended plan which increased the site area by 50 per cent, thereby enabling the site to accommodate more caravans and bringing it significantly closer to three nearby residences. He considered that the amendment did not substantially alter the proposed site and that the persons affected did not need to be informed. He stated that, as agricultural work was available in the area, there would be no working areas on the site itself and, therefore, no serious harm to the occupiers of nearby dwellings. On an application to quash his order granting planning permission, *held*, a main, although not the only, criterion as to whether an amendment was substantial was whether the development was so changed that to allow the amendment would deprive those who should have been consulted on the changed development of the opportunity of such consultation. The amendment to the plan was substantial; the decision that it was not was perverse under the *Wednesbury* principle. The Town and Country Planning (Appeals) (Written Representations Procedure) Regulations 1987, SI 1987/701, by expressly providing for third parties to be heard on an appeal by written representations, impliedly gave them the right to be informed of any amendment to the application which materially affected them. The availability of agricultural work in the area was a principal issue in the case; the inspector had failed to give adequate reasons for his determination in respect of that matter. The owners and occupiers of the three residences near the application site, the parish council and other local residents were all entitled to be consulted on the changed development. The application would be allowed.

Breckland District Council v Secretary of State for the Environment (1992) 65 P & CR 34 (Queen's Bench Division: David Widdicombe QC).

2497 Planning permission—appeal—application out of time—constructive registration

The plaintiff issued a notice of motion against the Secretary of State's decision to dismiss his appeal against the refusal by the district council to grant him planning permission under the Town and Country Planning Act 1990, s 288. The notice of motion was sent to the Queen's Bench Division to be registered in the Crown Office in accordance with RSC Ord 94, r 2(1). However, on receipt of the application it was sent to the Chancery Division and by the time the application was returned to the Queen's Bench Division it was outside the six-week time limit for appeals set out under the 1990 Act, s 288(3). The plaintiff's application was dismissed for being out of time. On appeal, *held*, it was assumed that due to an administrative error and through no fault of the plaintiff's, the document did not arrive at the Crown Office until after the time limit had expired. The plaintiff had done everything required of him by posting his completed notice of motion, and as such that was a constructive entry for registration in the

Crown Office. Accordingly, the appeal would be allowed.

Low v Secretary of State for Wales (1993) Times, 18 March (Court of Appeal: Nourse, Stuart-Smith and Waite LJJ).

2498   Planning permission—condition—enforceability

A district council granted the plaintiff outline planning permission, subject to an agricultural occupancy condition, for the erection of a bungalow on a specified ordnance survey location. The bungalow was subsequently built on land some distance away from that in respect of which the planning permission was granted. In a preliminary application, the plaintiff contended that the bungalow was built in the wrong place, in breach of planning permission, and thus was not bound by the occupancy restriction because the restriction was a term of the planning permission that had no relevance to the bungalow. *Held,* where planning permission was granted for the erection of a building, the fact that the building failed to comply with it did not mean that the permission was to be treated as a nullity. The plaintiff had relied on the permission to erect the bungalow and it would be strange if, as a result of the plaintiff's own default in failing to comply with the plan, the plaintiff was not bound by the occupancy restriction. Accordingly, the application would be rejected.

Handoll v Warner, Goodman and Street (a firm) (1992) 66 P & CR 78 (Chancery Division: Mervyn Davies J). *Kerrier District Council v Secretary of State for the Environment* (1980) 41 P & CR 284, DC (1981 Abr para 2955) applied.

2499   Planning permission—condition—reasonable prospect test

The applicant had applied for planning permission to develop some of its land. An inspector recommended that planning permission be granted subject to the condition that an access road be built over land owned by the local authority. The local authority declined to allow the road to be built on environmental grounds and refused to grant planning permission. On appeal by the applicant, the Secretary of State claimed that he was prevented by law from granting permission which was subject to conditions that appeared to have no reasonable prospect of fulfilment within the statutory five-year period. On further appeal by the applicant, *held,* the mere fact that a planning permission condition had no reasonable prospects of being fulfilled did not, by itself, mean that planning permission must be refused. The appropriate decision to be taken depended on the particular facts of the application and the discretion of the planning authority. Accordingly, the appeal would be allowed.

British Railways Board v Secretary of State for the Environment (1993) Times, 29 October (House of Lords: Lords Keith of Kinkel, Templeman, Jauncey of Tullichettle, Browne-Wilkinson and Mustill). Decision of Court of Appeal [1993] JPL 342 reversed. *Jones v Secretary of State for Wales* [1990] JPL 907 (1990 Abr para 2428) overruled.

2500   Planning permission—condition—validity

The Town and Country Planning Act 1971, s 52 provides that a planning authority can enter into an agreement with a landowner for the purposes of restricting or regulating the development or use of land.

A district council granted a farmer planning permission to build a house on his land, which was in the metropolitan green belt, subject to conditions that occupation of the house be limited to persons wholly or mainly employed in agriculture and that he enter into a covenant under the Town and Country Planning Act 1971, s 52, binding the farm in the hands of successive owners. He subsequently sold the farm to the appellants. They wished to sell the house free from the occupational restriction and unsuccessfully applied for a declaration that the covenant was null and void. On appeal, *held,* the extent of a planning authority's powers under the 1971 Act, s 52 was determinable by reference to that section. Thus, where an authority, with the consent of the landowner, made an agreement for the purposes of restricting or regulating the development or use of the land, it would be valid. The fact that the purpose for which the agreement was made could not have been attained under the 1971 Act, s 29 was irrelevant because the two statutory provisions were distinct. Accordingly, the appeal would be dismissed.

Good v Epping Forest District Council (1993) Times, 11 November (Court of Appeal: Ralph Gibson, Hirst and Peter Gibson LJJ).

1971 Act, s 52 now Town and Country Planning Act 1990, s 106.

2501   Planning permission—refusal—application to quash refusal—time limit

On an application under the Town and Country Planning Act 1990, s 288 to quash a decision of the Secretary of State refusing planning permission for a change of use and new building works, it has been held that the six-week time limit for making the application, which begins on the date of the decision not the date on which it is received, includes in its calculation days such as Christmas Day and bank holidays.

Stainer v Secretary of State for the Environment and Shepway District Council (1992) 65 P & CR 310 (Queen's Bench Division: David Widdicombe QC). *Griffiths v Secretary of State for the Environment* [1983] 2 AC 51, HL (1983 Abr para 3287) followed.

2502 Planning permission—refusal—replacement of old buildings on ground of appearance

An inspector refused planning permission for the replacement of a number of old and dilapidated buildings in a national park with new buildings on the ground that if he granted permission he might be setting a precedent for allowing visually harmful buildings to be replaced by more attractive buildings. The Secretary of State upheld his decision. On appeal against the Secretary of State's decision, *held*, if permission were allowed on the ground that new was better than old, existing buildings might be neglected and allowed to decay. It was a matter of fact and degree as to whether the existing buildings would cause a problem in the future. Accordingly, the court could not impugn the inspector's decision and the appeal would be refused.

Bride Brick Co Ltd v Secretary of State for the Environment (1993) Times, 19 July (Queen's Bench Division: Sir Graham Eyre QC).

2503 Planning permission—warehouse club—definition of "retail shop"

Company A was intending to open a warehouse club which would sell certain goods in bulk to members of the club. Membership could be obtained by persons who had paid an annual subscription and who were either in business or within a specified employment group. Company A was granted planning permission in an area which was classed as a "primary industrial and commercial area" and conditions were set down in an agreement pursuant to the Town and Country Planning Act 1990 s 106, restricting use to non-retail use. The agreement also acknowledged that using the club for retail sale of goods to visiting members of the public within class A1 of the Town and Country Planning (Use Classes) Order 1987 (SI 1987/7647), would constitute a change of use requiring planning permission. The applicants applied for judicial review of the local authority's decision to grant planning permission and argued that (1) Company A's proposals included an element of retail use and the borough council had not given planning permission for this; (2) the agreement was too vague and not sufficient to restrict Company A as required; and (3) that the courts would not impose an injunction on company A if the use of the premises breached the planning permission. *Held*, if there was a restriction on those who could buy from the warehouse, the premises were not prima facie for the sale of goods to "visiting members of the public" within class A1. The applicants' other arguments were also rejected. Accordingly, the application would be dismissed.

R v Thurrock Borough Council, ex p Tesco Stores Ltd (1993) Independent, 28 October, Times, 5 November (Queen's Bench Division: Schiemann J). *Lewis v Rogers* (1984) 82 LGR 670 (1984 Abr para 2746) distinguished.

2504 Stop notice—ambiguous notice—construction

The defendant was granted planning permission for a single storey extension to his property. In contravention of the grant he built a two-storey extension. An enforcement notice was issued requiring him to remedy the breach by reducing those parts of the development which exceeded the permission. The defendant continued the work and a stop notice was then issued under the Town and Country Planning Act 1971, s 90 which stated that all the activities specified in the notice ought to cease. Following his failure to stop the building the defendant was prosecuted for contravention of the stop notice. The defendant appealed on the ground that the stop notice was invalid. *Held*, the stop notice purported to prohibit all operational development on the site. It was not confined, as it ought to have been, to that part of the work, the continuation of which would be in breach of the planning permission. Since the contravention of the stop notice was the subject matter of the prosecution and because of the penal consequences that flowed from such a contravention the terms of the stop notice ought to have been strictly construed. Further, if the meaning was unambiguous, assistance was not to be derived from other documents. Accordingly, the appeal would be allowed.

R v Dhar [1993] Crim LR 615 (Court of Appeal: Russell LJ, Morland and Mantell JJ).

1971 Act, s 90 now Town and Country Planning Act 1990, s 183, as amended by Planning and Compensation Act 1991, s 9.

2505   Tree preservation order—appeal—time for consultation
It has been held that when considering an appeal against tree preservation orders and replanting orders, an inspector of the Department of the Environment is not obliged to allow time for consultation so that a notice of appeal might be treated as an amended application. There is no obligation for consultation as there is in the case of applications for planning permission.

Batchelor v Secretary of State for the Environment (1993) Times, 15 February (Queen's Bench Division: Popplewell J).

TRADE AND INDUSTRY

Halsbury's Laws of England (4th edn) Vol 47, paras 1–651

2506   Anti-competitive practice—operation of bus service—undertaking in respect of service
An established bus company (Southdown) found a newcomer (Easy Rider) competing on one of its routes. Southdown saturated its services over the route by increasing the frequency of its services although there had been no increase in demand and the increase resulted in heavy losses, the services failing to cover their variable costs. Although the fares charged were comparable to those on other Southdown services and similar to those charged by Easy Rider, they were clearly uneconomic. Eventually, Easy Rider withdrew from the market. The Monopolies and Mergers Commission found (see Cm 2248: a report on the conduct of Southdown Motor Services Ltd in respect of its operation of local bus services in routes 262 and 242 in Bognor Regis) that the competition from Easy Rider had been of advantage to passengers, resulting in lower fares than elsewhere in the area and in higher levels of service. It found that the loss of competition might be expected to result in higher fares and in reduced levels and quality of service on the route and those in adjacent corridors and hence to operate against the public interest. The commission recommended that Southdown should be required to limit fare increases on the affected routes to increases in inflation over the next two years and that it should be required to undertake during that time not to reduce the level of service on the affected routes.

2507   Assisted areas
The Assisted Areas Order 1993, SI 1993/1877 (in force on 1 August 1993), revokes the 1984 Order, SI 1984/1844 as amended. The order designates development areas and intermediate areas. The description of the new areas is by reference to travel to work areas or wards within such areas.

2508   Competition policy—EC
See EUROPEAN COMMUNITIES.

2509   Consumer protection
See CONSUMER PROTECTION.

2510   Export controls
See CUSTOMS AND EXCISE.

2511   Monopolies and mergers—merger situation—bus services
The Monopolies and Mergers Commission was asked to investigate whether enterprises carried on by Lancaster City Transport Ltd (LCT) had ceased to be distinct from enterprises carried on by Stagecoach Holdings plc. When it was decided to privatise LCT's bus operations and its coach subsidiary, Stagecoach decided not to bid for the business because of a possibility of a reference to the commission. It realised, however, that LCT's depot would be a commercially attractive acquisition and made a successful bid for that, for a number of vehicles and for certain plant and equipment. Although Stagecoach had not taken over LCT's bus business it registered all LCT's services and operated them from the time when LCT ceased to do so. Stagecoach argued that the transaction had concerned a transfer of assets but not the creation of a merger situation within the meaning of the Fair Trading Act 1973, s 65(1)(a). The commission stated

(*Stagecoach Holdings plc and Lancaster City Transport Ltd*, a report on a merger situation: Cm 2423) that the phrase in the 1973 Act, s 65(1)(a) "brought under common ownership or common control" had to be construed with regard to its context and the purpose of the Act; further, that the intention of the Act was to enable the commission to consider commercial realities and results and it did not have to confine its attention to the results of legally enforceable agreements and arrangements. In looking at the commercial realities, it regarded the continuity of the bus services previously provided by LCT as significant; but the decisive point was what had made that continuity possible, ie the acquisition of the depot. By acquiring the depot, Stagecoach had ensured that it could operate the services previously provided by LCT economically and the connection between the depot and the commercial operation of those services was fundamental (a fact which was emphasised by the fact that Stagecoach was prepared to pay a high price to secure it). The commission considered that the requirements of s 65(1)(a) were satisfied and that the enterprises carried on by LCT and by Stagecoach had ceased to be distinct. It believed also that a merger situation qualifying for investigation had been created and that, by reason of the loss of competition in the area concerned, it might be expected to operate against the public interest. The commission considered that divestment would be disproportionate and that any form of regulation of fares or service levels would be inconsistent with the deregulation of the bus industry and might inhibit adjustments of services to changes in demand. It recommended that Stagecoach should undertake that if it should respond to competition with its services in the district of Lancaster by reducing fares or by increasing frequencies, it would not raise fares or reduce frequencies if the competitor should withdraw the competing services for three years after such withdrawal. It also recommended that Stagecoach should undertake not to operate additional services in competition with a competitor's services within a shorter interval before the competing service than the competitor operated against itself. In the absence of such undertakings, the commission recommended divestment of the newly-acquired depot. The commission also suggested that Stagecoach should be required to publish information (to be agreed with the Office of Fair Trading) on the financial performance of its operations in the district of Lancaster and to supply to the office similar information on certain other profit centres for comparison.

2512   Monopolies and mergers—merger situation—newspaper merger—transfer of newspapers to new owner

The Monopolies and Mergers Commission investigated, under the Fair Trading Act 1973, s 59, the proposed transfer of Argus Newspapers Ltd from Argus Press Ltd to Trinity International Holdings plc (*Argus Press Ltd and Trinity International Holdings plc* (Cm 2373), a report on the proposed transfer) to ascertain whether the proposed transfer would operate against the public interest. Its investigation concerned three areas in particular: the accurate presentation of news and the free expression of opinion; the concentration of ownership and competition for readers and advertising; and matters relating to employment. The commission noted that it had on two recent occasions looked into the editorial and advertising policies of Trinity (Cm 1772 and Cm 2374: see infra) and stated that there was no reason to believe that Trinity would change its existing policy in respect of editorial independence. It found therefore that the proposed transfer would not endanger the accurate presentation of news and the free expression of opinion. The accretion of Argus newspapers to Trinity would make the latter the sixth largest publisher of regional and local newspapers, with an approximate market share of 4·9 per cent. The increase in concentration was not a matter of concern, even taking into account a further accretion of titles under the investigation reported at Cm 2374. There was no geographic overlap between the areas in which the Trinity and Argus newspapers were distributed and hence no increased concentration at regional or local level, nor any loss of competition for readers or distributors. The commission found that there would be no adverse effect on competition for readers or advertisers. It noted that Argus was one of the few significant newspaper publishers which had not introduced direct input technology; when that technology was introduced, job losses at Argus were inevitable, regardless of the proposed transfer. The commission investigated the position regarding the Argus pension scheme; the scheme was in slightly greater surplus than at the time of the last valuation in 1990 and Trinity had informed the commission that former Argus employees would have the alternative of remaining with an Argus pension scheme or joining the Trinity scheme. The commission concluded that, so far as employment matters were concerned, there was no justification for interfering with the proposed transfer and that overall the proposed transfer was not expected to operate against the public interest.

The Monopolies and Mergers Commission investigated, under the Fair Trading Act 1973, s 59, an offer to purchase the share capital of Joseph Woodhead & Sons Ltd by Trinity International

Holdings plc (*Trinity International Holdings plc and Joseph Woodhead & Sons Ltd* (Cm 2374), a report on the proposed transfers of controlling interests). Woodhead was a privately-owned company involved with newspaper printing and publishing. The commission concentrated on the three issues affecting the public interest which it had considered in its report at Cm 2373 (see supra). It concluded that there was no danger to the accurate presentation of news and the free expression of opinion in the proposed acquisition; there being no geographic overlap between the areas in which the Woodhead and Trinity newspapers were distributed, the proposed acquisition would have no adverse effects on competition either for readers or for advertising. The effects on employment would be minimal, the Woodhead pension fund was well funded and Trinity had no plans to change that scheme, of which existing employees would be able to retain membership if they chose. The commission accordingly concluded that the proposed acquisition was not expected to operate against the public interest.

2513 Monopolies and mergers—monopoly situation—monopoly of bus services—public interest

The Monopolies & Mergers Commission found (see *The supply of bus services in Mid and West Kent* (Cm 2309)) that Maidstone and District Motor Services Ltd ("M & D") effectively operated a monopoly of bus services in mid and west Kent. In order to protect its network and revenues, M & D ran extra journeys, usually shortly ahead of its competitors' services, and sometimes reduced the fares on such services. M & D maintained that the additional costs of such activities were lower than the revenue thereby created or protected. The commission stated that it did not accept the short-term incremental cost identified by M & D as adequate to assess the acceptability of its response to competition; any such response should be fair and not designed to eliminate the competitor. It ruled that the running of additional journeys that did not cover their variable and semi-variable costs operated (or might be expected to operate) against the public interest; as also did M & D's introduction of additional journeys timed immediately before a competitor's; the operation of unregistered buses with a view to interfering with a competitor's services; the registration by M & D of commercial services over certain tendered routes operated by competitors as a response to competitive action by the competitors on these or related routes; and the use of selective fare reductions targeted against a competitor's attempt to enter a market. The commission noted that the Transport Act 1985 was intended to ensure that existing bus operators would not be able to prevent other operators from using important bus stations. It found that the terms and conditions under which M & D offered access to one bus station provided competitors neither with reasonable facilities nor the security of enjoying them; this failure to offer access on reasonable terms also operated against the public interest (or might be expected so to operate). The commission suggested that undertakings should be sought from M & D not to register journeys on the same routes as its competitors within a shorter interval before its competitor's services than the competitor itself had registered; to maintain its frequency of service on any route from which a competitor had withdrawn for at least one year after the withdrawal; not to register commercial services against competitors' tendered services; not to make selective fare reductions on services running immediately before a competitor's; and to offer competitors equal access to the bus station on reasonable terms.

2514 Monopolies and mergers—monopoly situation—monopoly of fragrance supply—public interest

Following complaints that suppliers were exercising unfair discrimination in refusing to supply two retailers, the Monopolies and Mergers Commission investigated the supply of fine fragrances in the United Kingdom (see *Fine Fragrances* (Cm 2380), a report on the supply in the United Kingdom for retail sale of fine fragrances). It found that a complex monopoly situation existed, in which the leading fragrance houses refused to supply retailers other than those authorised by them; all but one recommended resale prices which most leading retailers observed for most of the time. The commission was aware, in making its investigation, of the EC Commission decisions, *Yves St Laurent Parfums* (Case IV/33.342) OJ L 12, 18 January 1992, pp 24–35, and *Parfums Givenchy* (Case IV/33.542) OJ L 236, 19 August 1992, pp 11–22, which had allowed the companies concerned to take account of a number of factors in deciding whether to supply a retail outlet with goods, including fine fragrances. The Monopolies and Mergers Commission concluded that the operation of selective distribution by the fragrance houses in the United Kingdom did not operate against the public interest; there was increasing competition in a market where the emphasis was on non-price competition; the grey market was increasing, and prominent retailers were entering the market through grey-market sources of supplies; and the EC Commission had insisted that fragrance houses should be free to sell to their authorised retailers throughout the Community. Similarly, the recommending of resale prices was not against the public interest, in that the recommendations did not in practice prevent price competition and unauthorised retailers were taking full advantage of the recommendations to draw attention to their price-cutting; further, there was merit in the argument that recommended resale prices were a convenience to retailers, especially the small ones. By using qualitative criteria to determine whether to supply a retail outlet, the fragrance houses were indulging in uncompetitive practices; but these were appropriate for the product concerned and were compatible with the criteria approved by the EC Commission; hence, although the procedures were susceptible to improvement, they did not operate against the public interest. On the evidence, the Monopolies and Mergers Commission also concluded that the provisions, included in the agreements between the fragrance houses and the authorised retailers, concerning range-stocking and minimum purchases might encourage new retailers to apply for authorised status and were not against the public interest.

2515 Monopolies and Mergers Commission—reference to commission—content of reference

The applicants sought judicial review of a decision of the Director General of Fair Trading to make a reference to the Monopolies and Mergers Commission concerning the operation of bus services following the completion of a report by the director which had been concerned only with the conduct of two specific bus routes. *Held*, the purpose of an investigation by the Director General was to establish whether there was, or had been conduct amounting to anti-competitive practice. The director's report of his investigation had to contain his reasoned opinion whether the course of conduct described in the report in connection with the services specified was anti-competitive. The reference to the commission could not specify as subjects for investigation any services not specified or any course of conduct not described in the original report. The director's report and the investigation giving rise to it were concerned essentially with the conduct of two specific bus services. A course of conduct could only be referred to the commission if it had been described in the report in such a way as to indicate that it related to specified goods or services, that it had been the subject of an investigation and that it was worthy of a reference. The mere mention in a report of a course of conduct as part of the trading background or by way of comparison did not qualify. The director's reference to the commission specified a course of conduct in connection with bus services generally whereas his report specified the conduct of only two bus routes. This was unlawful and accordingly the application would be granted.

R v Director General of Fair Trading, ex p Southdown Motor Services Ltd (1993) Times, 18 January (Queen's Bench Division: Auld J).

2516 Motor manufacturer—insolvency—debt owed to supplier—supplier's refusal to continue to supply—whether abuse of dominant position

Receivers had been appointed in respect of a manufacturer of motor vehicles which had become insolvent and which owed one of its suppliers over £750,000. The supplier said it would stop supplying vital parts to the manufacturer until it received the money it was owed, and the manufacturer contended that the supplier's ultimatum amounted to an abuse of a dominant position within the EC Treaty, art 86. The court refused to grant the manufacturer's application for an order in those terms and, on the manufacturer's appeal, *held*, the supplier could not be said to have been in a dominant position within the terms of art 86 because it had supplied parts according to the manufacturer's specifications, and those parts could have been made by a number of alternative suppliers. In any event, the supplier had been exercising its normal common law rights in not providing any more supplies until it was paid the amount owed, and the court had acted correctly in refusing the application. Accordingly, the appeal would be dismissed.

Leyland Daf Ltd v Automotive Products plc (1993) Times, 9 April (Court of Appeal: Dillon, Steyn and Rose LJJ). Decision of Sir Donald Nicholls V-C (1993) Times, 6 April affirmed.

2517 Public procurement—award of contracts—competitive tendering—exclusion of contractor

See *General Building and Maintenance plc v Greenwich London Borough Council*, para 1712.

2518 Public procurement—award of contracts—competitive tendering—information

The Utilities Supply and Works Contracts (Amendment) Regulations 1993, SI 1993/3227 (in force on 13 January 1994), amend the 1992 Regulations, SI 1992/3279. The regulations implement Council Directive (EC) 90/531, art 3(2)(b) in accordance with Commission Decision

(EC) 93/327 which provides that a member state must ensure that a utility communicates information relating to contracts awarded by it to the Commission under conditions defined by the Commission. The regulations also make certain other amendments to the 1992 Regulations.

2519 Public procuremnent—Community provision
See paras 2707, 2708, 2709.

2520 Public procurement—public services contracts
The Public Services Contracts Regulations 1993, SI 1993/3228 (in force on 13 January 1994), implement Council Directive (EC) 92/50 relating to the co-ordination of procedures for the award of public services contracts. The regulations, which apply to certain public bodies referred to as "contracting authorities", deal in particular with the treatment to be accorded to services providers or potential services providers who are nationals of, and established in, member states. The regulations make detailed provision with respect to public services contracts, including the following: (1) the categories of services are specified; (2) provision is made in relation to technical specifications in contract documents; (3) the procedures leading to the award of a public services contract are set out; (4) provision is made with regard to the selection of services providers; (5) the criteria for the award of a public services contract are set out; (6) various miscellaneous matters are dealt with, including the holding of designs contests, obligations relating to employment protection and working conditions, the publication of notices and confidentiality of information; (7) provision for the enforcement of obligations; and (8) the Public Supply Contracts Regulations 1991, SI 1991/2679, are amended so as to ensure that not more than one set of regulations applies to any contract.

2521 Restraint of trade—customer lists—recovery
See *Roberts v Northwest Fixings*, para 1995.

2522 Restraint of trade—restrictive covenant—notice period
See *GFI Group Inc v Eaglestone*, para 1140.

2523 Restraint of trade—restrictive covenant—validity
Under a restrictive covenant in a severance agreement between the plaintiff, the defendant's former employer and the defendant, the latter was paid the equivalent of a year's emoluments on condition that he worked for no trade competitor within one year of leaving his former employ. He took up employment with a competitor and the plaintiff sought to enforce the covenant. The trial judge granted an interlocutory injunction. On appeal by the defendant, it fell to be determined whether the court should construe the covenant in such a way as to make it reasonable in its scope and, therefore, enforceable. *Held*, as a matter of policy, the court should not attempt to find within restrictive covenants which were apparently too wide implicit limitations which would justify imposing such limitations. The court would neither whittle down the scope of the present covenant in order to grant a more limited form of injunctive relief, nor ignore it as unenforceable but nevertheless enjoin the defendant by way of ancillary order so as to ensure that he would not breach his continuing duty of confidentiality. Such a residual duty of confidentiality in respect of the plaintiff's trade secrets was enforceable by a covenant preventing the defendant working for a trade rival. However, such a covenant in the instant case was too wide and, therefore, unenforceable. Accordingly, the appeal would be allowed.

J A Mont (UK) Ltd v Mills [1993] IRLR 172 (Court of Appeal: Glidewell, Beldam and Simon Brown LJJ).

Two companies, one of which was controlled by the defendant, were merged to form a new company. The defendant covenanted to refrain from doing business with "any person, firm or company who had done business with the group (ie the new company) at any time in the year before he left the group". The company subsequently sold its business to the plaintiffs without the defendant's consent, and on the same day the plaintiffs dismissed the defendant. The plaintiffs sought an interlocutory injunction to enforce the covenant, but their application was refused on the ground that, in accordance with the Transfer of Undertakings (Protection of Employment) Regulations 1981, SI 1981/1794, reg 5, the plaintiffs had been substituted for the word "group" in the covenant, so that the covenant restrained the defendant in relation to persons with whom the plaintiffs, not the group, had done business in the previous year. On appeal by the plaintiffs, *held*, the 1981 Regulations, reg 5 gave the plaintiffs the power to restrain the defendant from doing things which he had covenanted not to do, notwithstanding that the plaintiffs had not employed the defendant at the time the covenant was made. The terms of the covenant were unlimited in area and unrestricted as to the type of business concerned, but it was not so wide as to render it unenforceable, and the fact that the new company had sold its business without the defendant's consent had not operated to discharge his obligations. Accordingly, the appeal would be allowed and an interlocutory injunction granted.

Morris Angel & Son Ltd v Hollande [1993] 3 All ER 569 (Court of Appeal: Dillon and Bingham LJJ). *Home Counties Dairies Ltd v Skilton* [1970] 1 All ER 1227, CA applied.

2524 Restraint of trade—solicitation and competition—ex-employee

See *Hanover Insurance Brokers Ltd v Schapiro*, para 1141.

2525 Restrictive trade practices—agreements, decisions and concerted practices in the insurance sector—exemption from Community rules prohibiting concerted behaviour

See para 2738.

2526 Restrictive trade practices—registered agreements—inspection and copy fees

The Registered Restrictive Trading Agreements (Inspection, Copy and Certification) (Fees) Regulations 1993, SI 1993/1376 (in force on 1 July 1993), increase the fees payable by members of the public for inspecting agreements placed by the Director General of Fair Trading on the register kept by him under the Restrictive Trade Practices Act 1976. The 1977 Regulations, SI 1977/612, are revoked.

2527 Restrictive trade practices—standards and arrangements

The Restrictive Trade Practices (Standards and Arrangements) (Services) Order 1993, SI 1993/2453 (in force on 1 November 1993), approves standards of performance in the provision of services, and standards of dimension, design, quality or performance in respect of goods used in providing them, adopted by Electricity Association Services Limited, and an arrangement as to the provision information or advice, also adopted by that body. For the purpose of determining whether an agreement is one to which the Restrictive Trade Practices Act 1976, applies, no account is, therefore, to be taken of any term in the agreement by which the parties or any of them agree to comply with, or to apply, such approved standards and arrangement.

The Restrictive Trade Practices (Standards and Arrangements) (Goods) Order 1993, SI 1993/2473 (in force on 1 November 1993), approves certain standards adopted by Electricity Association Services Limited in relation to goods and services. In determining whether the Restrictive Trade Practices Act 1976 applies to an agreement, the effect of the order is that no account is taken of any term in which the parties agree to comply with or apply the approved standards.

2528 Statistics of trade—Census of Production

The Census of Production Order 1993, SI 1993/3037 (in force on 31 December 1993), deals with the Census of Production which will be taken in 1994 as well as subsequent years. It prescribes the undertakings to which the census is confined, the matters to which returns relate and exempted persons. The 1981 Order, SI 1981/1487, and 1984 Order, SI 1984/1762, are revoked.

2529 Sugar beet—research and education

The Sugar Beet (Research and Education) Order 1993, SI 1993/397 (in force on 1 April 1993), provides for the carrying into effect for the year 1993–94 of the programme of research and education in matters affecting the growing of home grown beet. It also provides for the assessment of contributions towards the expenditure on the programme and for the collection of the contributions from the processors and growers of sugar beet.

2530   Sunday trading—government proposals for reform

The Home Secretary has published *Reforming the Law on Sunday Trading: A guide to the options for reform* (Cm 2300) in which four approaches to reforming the law on Sunday trading are described. All four are incorporated into a draft Bill which is appended to the white paper. Parliament is to be given the opportunity to vote on the main options for reform and the government will allow its supporters a free vote. The first option is total deregulation which would bring the law in England and Wales into line with that in Scotland. The second option is partial deregulation; all small shops (ie those with up to 280 sq m of floor space) would be allowed complete freedom to open on Sundays, but larger shops, subject to exceptions including pubs, restaurants and petrol filling stations, would be restricted to opening for six consecutive hours between 10 am and 6 pm and would need to give written notice of their intention to the appropriate local authority. The third option would permit only a limited range of shops to open on Sundays; some shops would be entirely exempt from any restrictions (eg pubs, restaurants, chemists selling medicines, vehicle hire shops, shops at airports, banks, bureaux de change, post offices providing postal services, and funeral undertakers); other small shops (defined as above) would also be exempt if restricting their trade (eg general convenience stores, newsagents, video hire shops, florists, garden centres, motor supplies shops, "do-it-yourself" shops, chemists, farm shops, kiosks and stalls not exceeding 10 sq m) or on account of their location (eg tourist shops selling items with a local association, hospital shops and shops at sporting events); certain types of larger shops (garden centres, motor supplies shops and "do-it-yourself" shops) would be permitted to open between 9 am and 8 pm for the sale of a restricted range of products. The fourth option is similar in outline to the third option, but would allow a wider range of shops to open on Sundays (unlike the third option, antique shops, craft shops, wine warehouses, banks (without restriction), travel agents, estate agents and building societies would be allowed to open, all markets would be allowed to trade, and all shops would be allowed to open on the four Sundays before Christmas). Enforcement under all options, other than deregulation, would remain the responsibility of local authorities. Express provision is made for Jewish shops. Provision is also made for employment rights; "protected shop workers", as defined, would be given the right not to be dismissed and the right not to suffer detriment for refusing to work on Sundays. The definition does not cover persons not employed in shops at the relevant commencement date. Any contract of employment of a protected shop worker, to the extent that it required shop work on a Sunday, would be unenforceable by the employer.

2531   Sunday trading—restrictions on trade—validity

Two local authorities sought injunctions to restrain a trader from opening its shops on a Sunday, contrary to the Shops Act 1950, s 47. Following an indication by the judge that he would grant the injunctions the trader gave an undertaking not to open its shops on Sundays notwithstanding its contention that the 1947 Act, s 50 had a restrictive effect on Community trade and as such was inconsistent with the provisions of EC Treaty, art 30. The trader appealed to the House of Lords, and following a reference for a preliminary ruling under EC Treaty, art 117 to the European Court of Justice, *held*, the European Court of Justice had stated that the prohibition laid down in art 30 did not apply to national rules which prohibited retailers from opening on Sundays if the restrictive effects which that prohibition had on Community trade did not exceed the intrinsic effects of rules of that kind. The House of Lords was obliged to follow the European Court of Justice's ruling, and, accordingly, the trader's appeals would be dismissed.

   Stoke-on-Trent City Council and Norwich City Council v B & Q plc [1993] 2 All ER 297n (House of Lords: Lords Goff of Chieveley, Bridge of Harwich, Brandon of Oakbrook and Ackner). Decision of Hoffmann J [1991] 2 WLR 42 (1990 Abr para 2461) affirmed.

A local authority brought charges against the applicant in respect of 43 separate offences of Sunday trading contrary to the Shops Act 1950, s 47. The applicant sought judicial review of the decision of justices to prosecute it in respect of the offences on the ground that, as it was uncertain whether s 47 was in conformity with Community law, the bringing of the charges was an abuse of process because it would be unfair to try the applicant. *Held*, the local authority had a duty to institute proceedings under s 71 and a wider power, under the Local Government Act 1972, s 222, to institute legal proceedings if it were in the interests of the inhabitants of its area and that the purpose of bringing the charges with the threat of possible future convictions was to act as a deterrent. Pending the determination by the European Court of Justice of the question of whether the 1950 Act, s 47 was in conformity with Community law, the domestic legislation remained in force. Neither a local authority nor a trader might assume otherwise unless that legislation had been disapplied pending the decision of the European Court. The laying of the multiplicity of charges was not an abuse of process and the application would be dismissed.

R v Lincoln Magistrates' Court, ex p Wickes Building Supplies Ltd (1993) Times, 6 August (Queen's Bench Division: Mann LJ and Sedley J).

A council prosecuted the applicant company in respect of Sunday trading contrary to the Shops Act 1950, s 47. The company applied for judicial review of the council's decision on the grounds that the council's policy for enforcing Sunday trading legislation breached the 1950 Act, s 71. The company contended that the council lacked an adequate system for detecting contraventions of the 1950 Act, s 47, was unaware of the extent of Sunday trading in its area, and selectively prosecuted nationally recognised stores which had advertised an intention so to trade. *Held*, the duty under the 1950 Act, s 47 was a general one and was not discharged by a discriminatory enforcement policy. In practice, due to its scarce resources and many other duties, the council was restricted to warning smaller stores which traded on Sundays and was unable rigorously to enforce its policy. The council had prosecuted the applicant fairly and rationally, in compliance with the 1950 Act, s 71 and, accordingly, the application would be dismissed.

R v Kirklees Metropolitan Borough Council, ex p Tesco Stores Ltd (1993) Times, 26 October (Queen's Bench Division: McCowan LJ and Leonard J).

See also *Chisholm v Kirklees Metropolitan Borough Council; Kirklees Metropolitan Borough Council v B & Q plc*, para 2319.

TRADE DESCRIPTIONS

Halsbury's Laws of England (4th edn) Vol 48, paras 281–324

2532   Articles

A Licence to Sell Counterfeit Goods? Victor Smith: 137 SJ 822.
Disclaiming False Trade Descriptions, RG Lawson: 157 JP Jo 595.
Why Are We Waiting? Geoff Holgate (on *R v Avro plc* (1993) 157 JP 759 (para 2533): 137 SJ 914.

2533   False trade description—airline ticket

The plaintiff was issued with a flight ticket from Gatwick to Alicante by the defendant company. The return flight was stated to be with another carrier and was to take off at a specified time on the return date. On the outward flight the plaintiff was given a replacement ticket for the return flight. This ticket was issued by a different carrier and was due to take off one hour before the previous stated time on the relevant day. On arrival at Alicante airport, he was informed that the destination airport on the return flight was Southend and that the original return flight did not exist. The defendant company pleaded guilty on two counts under the Trade Descriptions Act 1968, s 14. On appeal, *held*, the statement that the return flight from Alicante was at a certain time was a statement of existing fact despite the fact that the time was stated in the ticket as subject to alteration. At the time when the statements were read by the plaintiff the statements were false to the knowledge of the defendant. This was in no way affected by the contractual right to cancel the flight or vary the time or destination. Accordingly, the appeal would be dismissed.

R v Avro plc (1993) 157 JP 759 (Court of Appeal: Lloyd LJ, Potter and Buckley JJ).

2534   False trade description—football shirt—indication of approval by football club

The defendant was a street trader who sold t-shirts and badges near a football ground. The shirts and badges displayed an emblem similar to the registered trademark of the football club. There was nothing on the goods which identified them as officially approved by the club. The defendant was charged and convicted of two offences of supplying goods to which a false trade description was applied. On appeal, *held*, it could not be stated that the t-shirts contained any indication as to who had authorised them to be produced or whether they conformed with any authorised type or who they were produced by. It was clear from the writing on the rear of the t-shirts that it was not possible for them to have been authorised by the football club. In the circumstances there was insufficient evidence to convict the defendant, and further there was also a doubt in relation to the badges. Accordingly, the appeal would be allowed and the convictions quashed.

R v Veys (1992) 157 JP 567 (Court of Appeal: Staughton LJ, Waterhouse and McCullough JJ).

2535 False trade description—stove top grill—description in advertisement—misleading instructions

The plaintiff manufactured a stove top grill that was advertised in a national newspaper as being able to fit "every burner-gas, electric or propane". A woman purchased one of the grills, only to find that when she followed the instructions for installation, it would not work. Tests showed that the grill would have worked if she had not removed the grate but the instructions had recommended removing the grate for a better fit. The plaintiff was prosecuted under the Trade Descriptions Act 1968 for applying a false description to goods it advertised and supplied, and convicted at first instance. On appeal, *held*, it was implicit in the advertisement that the words "fits any burner" would be taken to mean that the grill would physically fit any burner in accordance with any instructions provided, as those instructions would be understood by the reasonable purchaser. The instructions were misleading in this respect as one would expect the reasonable consumer to do what the instructions said, namely to remove the grate for a better fit in order to use the grill. The words used in the advertisement were therefore capable of being a false trade description within the meaning of the 1968 Act and accordingly, the appeal would be dismissed.

Janbo Trading Ltd v Dudley Metropolitan Borough Council (1993) 157 JP 1056 (Queen's Bench Division: Kennedy LJ and Clarke J).

2536 Price marking—price label—position of label on goods

See *Allen v Redbridge London Borough Council*, para 576.

TRADE MARKS, TRADE NAMES AND DESIGNS

Halsbury's Laws of England (4th edn) Vol 48, paras 1–500

2537 Articles

Champagne and Elderflowers, Bernadette Lynch (on *Taittinger v Allbev* [1993] 2 CMLR 741, CA (para 2540)): 143 NLJ 1304

Shopping Habits and Passing Off, Joanna Rasamalar Jeremiah: [1993] 2 MLJ cxxxi

True or False? Geoff Holgate (on counterfeiting): 137 SJ 784

2538 Design right—semiconductor topographies

The Design Right (Semiconductor Topographies) (Amendment) Regulations 1993, SI 1993/2497 (in force on 10 November 1993) amend the 1989 Regulations, SI 1989/1100, by adding two new parts that list the additional classes of qualifying persons enjoying legal protection of topographies of semiconductor products. In particular, Liechtenstein, the United States, Iceland and Norway are added to the list of specified persons.

2539 Passing off—misrepresentation—advertising—restraint of advertising—interlocutory injunction

The plaintiffs had developed and marketed a range of pain-killers and the defendants wished to market what they regarded as an equivalent but cheaper slow-release pain-killer. The defendants published advertisements which included a two-page spread with a green apple out of which a large bite had been taken and promised savings of about 25 per cent compared to the plaintiffs' product. The advertisement was similar to the plaintiffs' own publicity in which a large green apple was always featured. In an action by the defendants to discharge an interlocutory injunction restraining them from issuing advertisements similar to those already published or promoting their products. *Held*, the evidence had established that the two products enjoyed, for practical purposes, equivalent therapeutic characteristics and the defendants' product had been granted the requisite product licence by the relevant authorities. It was therefore not arguable that a misrepresentation had been made. Advertisements made by the defendants for the therapeutic equivalent of a rival's established pain-killing drug, as being in effect just as good but cheaper, did not justify the grant to the rival, pending the trial of its action for passing off, an interlocutory injunction restraining such advertisements. Accordingly, the application would be allowed.

Ciba Geigy plc v Parke Davis & Co Ltd (1993) Times, 6 April (Chancery Division: Aldous J).

2540 Passing off—misrepresentation—damage to reputation and goodwill—champagne

The defendant produced and sold a carbonated non-alcoholic fruit drink under the name "elderflower champagne" in bottles similar to champagne bottles. The word "elderflower" appeared on the front label in prominent letters with the word "champagne" below in smaller but readable letters. The product was sold in health food stores and supermarkets. The plaintiffs, a producer of champagne and bodies involved in regulating the production of French wines, sought an injunction on the ground that the use of the word "champagne" in the name was a passing off and was also prohibited by Council Regulation (EC) 823/87. On appeal from the refusal of an injunction, *held*, there had been a misrepresentation in that the defendant's product was called champagne and the impression the name conveyed was strongly reinforced by the shape of the bottle. If the defendant was permitted to use the name "champagne", the goodwill in the distinctive name "champagne" would be eroded with serious consequences for the champagne houses. Although the Council Regulation could not be enforced through the British implementing enforcement provisions because the plaintiff did not have standing to sue under them, the regulation had direct effect. Although the grant of an injunction under domestic law was discretionary, where the plaintiff's Community law right was infringed and the defendant offered no undertaking, an injunction would be granted in any ordinary circumstances. Accordingly, an injunction would be granted both under English and Community law to restrain the defendants from referring to the word champagne. That did not prevent sale of the defendant's product, provided it was not called champagne. The appeal would be allowed.

Taittinger v Allbev Ltd [1993] 2 CMLR 741 (Court of Appeal: Sir Thomas Bingham MR, Mann and Peter Gibson LJJ). Decision of Sir Mervyn Davies [1993] 1 CMLR 597 reversed.

2541 Registered designs—protection of industrial property—convention countries

The Designs (Convention Countries) Order 1993, SI 1993/1257 (in force on 14 June 1993), declares Belarus, Croatia, the Czech Republic, Kazakhstan, the Slovak Republic, Slovenia, the Russian Federation and the Ukraine to be convention countries for the purposes of the Registered Designs Act 1949 following the accession of those countries to the International Convention for the Protection of Industrial Property.

2542 Trade mark—infringement—disclosure of information—use of information against third parties

In an action for the infringement of a trade mark, the defendants, pursuant to undertakings given in a consent order, swore affidavits naming third parties to whom they had supplied counterfeit goods. The defendants sought an order restraining the plaintiffs from using the information disclosed in the affidavits save for the purpose of the present proceedings, arguing that the plaintiffs had given an implied undertaking to this effect. *Held*, the plaintiffs had the twin objectives of stopping the activities of the defendants and of obtaining information to enable them to pursue a cause of action against the third parties. There was no implied obligation in such cases restricting the use of documents and information disclosed on discovery for the purposes of the action only. To create such an obligation would be to impose a considerable and unjustified limitation on the principle in *Norwich Pharmacal Co v Customs and Excise Comrs* (compelling discovery of the names of infringers by the defendant and others on the application of the plaintiff). Accordingly, the defendants' application would be dismissed.

Levi Strauss & Co v Barclays Trading Corpn Inc [1993] FSR 179 (Chancery Division: Judge Bromley). *Norwich Pharmacal Co v Customs and Excise Corms* [1974] AC 133, HL applied.

2543 Trade mark—infringement—mark not used on goods—mark used on invoices

The defendant purchased herbicide from the plaintiffs in Belgium and resold it in the United Kingdom. The herbicide purchased in Belgium was the same as the herbicide sold by the plaintiffs in the United Kingdom. The defendant sold the herbicide with the same unaltered packaging and used the plaintiffs' registered trade mark on delivery notes and subsequent invoices. The plaintiffs applied for summary judgment alleging infringement of their registered trade mark. The defendant argued that there was no infringement because the registered trade mark was not used on the container and that its use on subsequent invoices was not in the course of trade. The defendant applied for a reference to the European Court of Justice, arguing that the plaintiffs' rights in the registered trade mark had been exhausted by the sale of the same product in different member states of the European Community. *Held*, use of a registered trade mark on invoices and delivery notes was just as much an infringement as stamping the mark on a container for the goods. Use of a registered trade mark on an invoice, even if rendered long after the sale and delivery, was still a use in the course of trade. The use of different marks in different countries, in the absence of other evidence, did not demonstrate a disguised restriction on trade. Accordingly, the application would be dismissed.

Cheetah Trade Mark [1993] FSR 263 (Chancery Division: Morritt J).

2544   Trade mark—infringement—product with similar name

Australia

The applicants were the registered proprietor of a trade mark, "Polo", in respect of various products including sheets and bath towels. The respondents began to sell bed linen products under the brand name "Polo Club" prompting the applicants to seek an injunction and damages for infringement of their trade mark. The respondents contended that: (1) their use of the word "Club" provided a sufficient differentiation, (2) the goods were sold in rival stores which differed in standard, and (3) their use of the mark was not likely to deceive or confuse consumers and thus they could rely on a statutory defence. *Held,* (1) the respondents' trade mark was deceptively similar to the applicants' and the word "Club" was not a sufficient distinction since many consumers would assume "Polo Club" was associated with the longer-standing "Polo" mark. Therefore, the respondents had infringed the applicants' trade mark, the essential feature of which was the word "Polo". (2) The fact that the goods were sold in rival and supposedly differing standard stores was no defence. (3) Since consumers were likely to find the trade marks confusing, the respondents could not rely on the statutory defence. Accordingly, the application would be granted.

Polo Textile Industries Pty Ltd v Domestic Textile Corpn Pty Ltd (1993) 114 ALR 157 (Federal Court).

2545   Trade mark—registration—product with similar name

An application was made to register a trademark in respect of wound dressings called "Inadine". The opponents owned the marks "Anadin" and "Anadin Extra" for "analgesic preparations". It was conceded that the opponents had established a substantial reputation in respect of analgesics in tablet and capsule form sold over the counter. The application was allowed and the opponents appealed. *Held,* the applicants' mark could reasonably be pronounced as "IN-A-DIN" by a substantial number of people allowing for imperfect recollection and careless pronunciation and as such the marks were so close as to be likely to cause confusion when used on similar goods. Customers purchasing "Anadin" for themselves were unlikely to take away a wound dressing if the shop assistant misheard the request but customers often made purchases for third parties and in cases where they had an imperfect recollection of what they had been asked to buy the nature of the product was likely to cause confusion. Both analgesic tablets and wound dressings were often purchased when the patient had no symptoms and someone asked to obtain a branded product would not necessarily be informed of the type of product required. Registration would offend the Trade Marks Act 1938, s 11 as the applicants had not established the use of their mark in a manner which would not cause deception and confusion. Accordingly, the appeal would be allowed.

Inadine Trade Mark [1992] RPC 421 (Chancery Division: Aldous J).

2546   Trade marks and service marks—fees

The Trade Marks and Service Marks (Fees) (Amendment) Rules 1993, SI 1993/3029 (in force on 29 December 1993), abolish the payment of a fee in relation to an application for conversion of a specification from the old classification in the Trade Marks and Service Marks Rules 1986, SI 1986/1319, Sch 3, to the new classification in Sch 4.

2547 Trade marks and service marks—priority application—relevant countries
The Patents and Marks (Convention and Relevant Countries) Order 1993, SI 1993/1258 (in force in part on 14 June 1993 and in part on 1 July 1993), amends the Trade Marks and Service Marks (Relevant Countries) Order 1986, SI 1986/1303, to take account of the accession of Belarus, Croatia, the Czech Republic, Kazakhstan, the Slovak Republic, Slovenia, the Russian Federation and the Ukraine to the International Convention for the Protection of Industrial Property, and declares those countries to be convention countries for the purposes of the Patents Act 1977, s 5. The 1993 Order also amends the 1986 Order supra to take account of the reunification of Germany.

TRADE UNIONS

Halsbury's Laws of England (4th edn) Vol 47, paras 491–584

2548 Ballots—refund of expenditure—abolition
The Funds for Trade Union Ballots Regulations (Revocation) Regulations 1993, SI 1993/233 (in force on 1 April 1993), revoke (with effect from 1 April 1996) the 1984 Regulations, SI 1984/1654, which provide for the refund by the Certification Officer of certain expenditure incurred by trade unions in the conduct of certain ballots. The 1993 Regulations also progressively reduce the proportion of expenditure which is to be refunded in respect of ballots conducted during the period prior to 1 April 1996 and provide that no refund is to be made if the Certification Officer considers that a statutory requirement applying to the conduct of a ballot has not been complied with.

2549 Ballots—supervision of ballots—scrutineer—qualifications
The Trade Union Ballots and Elections (Independent Scrutineer Qualifications) Order 1993, SI 1993/1909 (in force on 30 August 1993), specifies the qualifications required by a person in order to be eligible for appointment as an independent scrutineer of certain trade union ballots and elections. The 1993 Order also provides that certain named bodies are eligible for appointment as scrutineers and revokes the 1988 Order, SI 1988/2117.

2550 Certification Officer—fees
The Certification Officer (Amendment of Fees) Regulations 1993, SI 1993/936 (in force on 1 May 1993), revoke SI 1992/461 and amend the following fees payable to the Certification Officer: (1) on an application for approval of a proposed instrument of amalgamation or transfer, from £1,241 to £1,347; (2) on an application for approval of a change of name, from £71 to £90; (3) for an inspection of documents kept by the Certification Officer in respect of trade union or employers' association amalgamations, from £38 to £55; (4) for the entry of the name of an amalgamated organisation in the lists maintained by the Certification Officer where the name of each of the amalgamating organisations is already entered, from £110 to £127; (5) on application by an organisation of workers to have its name entered in the list of trade unions maintained by the Certification Officer, from £288 to £291; and (6) on an application by a trade union for a certificate of independence, from £448 to £436.

2551 Collective agreements—incorporation of terms in contracts of employment
See *Lee v GEC Plessey Telecommunications*, para 1136.

2552 Industrial action—restraint—action aimed at non-contracting party
The trade union represented a number of persons who had been dismissed by the employer, and in protest the union proposed to distribute leaflets outside supermarkets urging members of the public not to buy goods which the employer had produced. The employer obtained an interlocutory injunction restraining the union from embarking on the leaflet campaign until trial or further order on the ground that the proposed action amounted to direct interference by the union with the employer's contracts with the supermarkets concerned. On appeal by the union, *held*, the leaflets were not directed at the supermarkets but at their customers. They did not exhort the supermarkets' managers to stop selling the employer's product, and the employer's

contention that the distribution of leaflets outside the supermarkets might dissuade those managers from selling its product was not a sufficient reason for finding that the leaflet campaign would be tortious. The campaign would bring direct pressure on persons who were strangers to the contract, but because any effect on the contracting party would be indirect it would be necessary to show that the union proposed to employ unlawful means in the leaflet campaign if its conduct was to be actionable. There was no evidence that the campaign would involve the use of unlawful means, and accordingly the appeal would be allowed and the injunction lifted.

Middlebrook Mushrooms Ltd v Transport and General Workers Union [1993] ICR 612 (Court of Appeal: Neill, Mann and Hoffmann LJJ).

2553   Industrial action—teachers—refusal to carry out assessments—whether "trade dispute"

A trade union representing teachers proposed to ask its members to refuse to carry out certain tests and assessments under the National Curriculum in order to persuade the Secretary of State to reduce the excessive workload that the tests would place on teachers. A local education authority sought an injunction restraining the union's action. The authority's application was dismissed on the ground that the action was a "trade dispute" within the meaning of the Trade Union and Labour Relations (Consolidation) Act 1992, s 244(2)(b) and thereby protected from liability in tort. The authority appealed, arguing that the action was not a trade dispute as it did not wholly or mainly relate to terms and conditions of employment but was primarily concerned with the objections of union members to the procedures to be used for the tests. *Held*, the history of the dispute showed that the union had been increasingly concerned about working time, and that that concern had come to a head as the date for the tests approached. Although union members had criticisms to make about the National Curriculum on educational grounds, the union's prime concern was the excessive workload that it imposed on teachers. It was also of considerable importance that the wording of the ballot paper stated that the protest was to be against the excessive workload that the testing and assessment would cause. Accordingly, the dispute related mainly to the terms and conditions of employment of the union's members within the meaning of the 1992 Act, s 244 and the appeal would be dismissed.

Wandsworth London Borough Council v National Association of Schoolmasters and Union of Women Teachers [1993] IRLR 344 (Court of Appeal: Neill, Steyn and Rose LJJ). Decision of Mantell J (1993) Times, 7 April affirmed.

2554   Industrial relations—derecognition of union—effect on individual member

The Employment Protection (Consolidation) Act 1978, s 23(1)(a) provides that every employee has the right not to have action short of dismissal taken against him as an individual by his employer for the purpose of preventing or deterring him from becoming or seeking to become a member of an independent trade union or penalising him from doing so.

The plaintiffs were members of an independent trade union. The employers made a significant pay offer to employees in lieu of the former process of collective bargaining with the union. Accepting the pay offer meant relinquishing the right to union membership. The plaintiffs refused the offer and as a result were not offered the pay rise. An industrial tribunal held that the employers had acted in contravention of s 23(1). The employers successfully appealed, the Employment Appeal Tribunal holding that s 23(1) only applied if dissuading employees from being union members was the purpose of the employer's action. On the plaintiffs' appeal, *held*, there was no doubt that the employer's purpose in offering extra pay to those who signed the new contracts was to persuade the plaintiffs to abandon union representation. The industrial tribunal had rightly decided that the purpose of the employers' actions contravened the 1978 Act, s 23(1), and the Employment Appeal Tribunal had erred in overturning its decision. Accordingly, the plaintiffs' appeal would be allowed.

Associated British Ports v Palmer [1994] ICR 97 (Court of Appeal: Dillon, Butler-Sloss and Farquharson LJJ). Decision of Employment Appeal Tribunal [1993] ICR 101, EAT (1992 Abr para 2618) reversed.

The plaintiff's union was derecognised by the defendant employer. Collective bargaining was terminated and each employee was required to sign individual contracts. A substantial pay increase was offered to those who signed the new contracts, but not to those, like the plaintiff, who did not sign. An industrial tribunal upheld the plaintiff's claim that the employer had acted in breach of the Employment Protection (Consolidation) Act 1978, s 23(1). On the employer's appeal, however, it was held that the union derecognition did not fall within s 23(1) as it was done collectively for all employees, and the change in salary did not sufficiently affect the plaintiff's union membership or cause loss of benefit. On appeal by the plaintiff, *held*, the purpose of the employer's action was to reduce the power of the union so that it was totally negated. This action had the wholly foreseeable consequence of deterring employees, within the meaning of s 23(1), from being union members. The appeal would accordingly be allowed.

Associated Newspapers Ltd v Wilson [1994] ICR 97 (Court of Appeal: Dillon, Butler-Sloss and Farquharson LJJ). Decision of Employment Appeal Tribunal [1992] ICR 681, EAT (1992 Abr para 2618) reversed.

2555 Industrial relations—independent trade union—certification—staff associations

A staff federation of a company which had been formed as a trade union for employees applied to the Certification Officer for a certificate that it was an independent trade union. The application was rejected on the ground that it was a condition of service that employees could not be members of trade unions other than a departmental staff association approved by the director of the company, which had the consequence that the staff federation was liable to interference by the employer within the meaning of the Trade Union and Labour Relations (Consolidation) Act 1992, s 5(b) and therefore could not be said to be independent. On appeal by the staff federation, *held*, the staff federation was liable to interference by the employer within the meaning of the 1992 Act, s 5(b). As it was a condition of service that employees were not permitted to be members of any other trade union the statutory employment rights had been withdrawn from employees at the company and it was to be expected that those conditions would continue. Accordingly, the appeal would be dismissed.

Government Communications Staff Federation v Certification Officer [1993] ICR 163 (Employment Appeal Tribunal: Wood J presiding).

2556 Member—discrimination against member—promotion

The applicant held a full-time union post as group assistant secretary. Following an unsuccessful application for promotion he took action against his employer on the ground that by refusing to promote him to a higher grade his employer's promotion board had taken action against him for the purpose of deterring him from taking part in trade union activities within the meaning of the Employment Protection (Consolidation) Act 1978, s 23. An industrial tribunal held that the applicant had suffered discrimination under the 1978 Act, s 23. The employer appealed on the ground that the decision of the promotion board and their suggestion that the employee should obtain further experience of work other than his union job was not action taken against him for the purpose of deterring him from taking part in the activities of a trade union within the meaning of the 1978 Act, s 23. *Held*, it was important that the provisions of the 1978 Act, s 23 were carefully analysed and the issues separated. The industrial tribunal had failed to ask itself (i) what was the action short of dismissal of which complaint was made, and (ii) what was its purpose? Accordingly, the appeal would be allowed and remitted for a fresh hearing.

Department of Transport v Gallacher [1993] ICR 654 (Employment Appeal Tribunal: Wood J presiding).

This decision has been affirmed on appeal: (1994) Times, 25 March, CA.

2557 Right to join trade union—requirement to join union—whether violation of human rights

See *Sibson v United Kingdom*, para 1410.

2558 Trade Union Reform and Employment Rights Act 1993

The Trade Union Reform and Employment Rights Act 1993 makes further reforms of the law relating to trade unions and industrial relations and amends the law relating to employment rights, including the abolition of the right to statutory minimum remuneration. The Act received the royal assent on 1 July 1993. Certain provisions came into force on that date and certain other provisions were brought into force on various dates in 1993–1996: see SI 1993/1908, 2503. The remaining provisions come into force on a day or days to be appointed. For details of commencement, see the commencement table in the title STATUTES.

Part I (ss 1–22) Trade Unions etc
Sections 1–7 deal with union elections and ballots. Section 1 provides that when a union appoints an independent scrutineer for an executive election, the appointment must require him to inspect the register of names and addresses of the members of the union whenever it appears to

him appropriate to do so and, in particular, at the request of a union member or election candidate who suspects that the register is not up-to-date and accurate. A union is required to supply the scrutineer with a copy of the register of names and addresses of its members by reference to which the election is being held, and the scrutineer's appointment must require him to examine that copy in the same circumstances as he is required to inspect the register. The scrutineer's report on the election must state whether he has inspected the register of names and addresses or examined the copy of the register supplied to him, and whether such inspection or examination has revealed any matter which should be drawn to the attention of the trade union in order to secure that the register is accurate and up-to-date. Section 2 requires a union to ensure that the voting papers in an executive election are stored and distributed, and the votes counted, by one or more independent persons appointed by the union. The scrutineer's report on the election must state the name of the person appointed or, if no such person was appointed, that fact, and must indicate whether the scrutineer is satisfied with the performance of the independent person. Section 3 and Sch 1 make similar provision in relation to the conduct of political fund ballots. Section 4 provides that ballots on union mergers are to be fully-postal and subject to independent scrutiny. Section 5 provides that the notice to be sent out with voting papers for union merger ballots must not make a recommendation or express an opinion about the proposed merger. Section 6 requires a trade union to impose a duty of confidentiality, in relation to the register of members' names and addresses, on any scrutineer or independent person appointed by the union for the purposes of an election, political resolution and union merger ballots covered by the Trade Union and Labour Relations (Consolidation) Act 1992, Pt I, Chapters IV (ss 46–61), VI (ss 71–96) and VII (ss 97–108). Section 7 repeals the 1992 Act, s 115 which empowers the Secretary of State to establish a scheme to fund union ballots, and s 116, which requires an employer to allow a recognised trade union to use his premises for a secret ballot in certain circumstances. Both repeals are to take effect on 1 April 1996.

Sections 8–12 relate to the financial affairs of unions. Section 8 provides that a union's annual return to the Certification Officer must contain details of the salary and other benefits paid to each member of the executive, the president and the general secretary by the trade union, and a statement of the number of names on the union's register of members and the number of those names which are not accompanied by an address. Section 9 requires a trade union to take all reasonable steps to secure that, not later than eight weeks after the submission of its annual return to the Certification Officer, all its members are provided with a written statement containing certain information about the conduct of its financial affairs (and other related matters) during the period to which that return relates. The statement must also include an indication of what a member may do if he suspects an irregularity in the conduct of the union's affairs. The union is required to supply a copy of the statement to the Certification Officer as soon as reasonably practicable after it is provided to its members; the union is also required to supply a copy of the statement to an individual member if he requests such a copy not later than two years after the submission of the annual return to the Certification Officer. Section 10 enables the Certification Officer to direct a trade union to produce documents relating to its financial affairs, if he thinks there is good reason to do so. The Certification Officer may appoint one or more inspectors to investigate the financial affairs of a union and to report on them, if it appears to the Certification Officer that the financial affairs of a union are being conducted fraudulently or unlawfully, or that persons concerned with the management of those affairs have been guilty of fraud, misfeasance or other misconduct, or that the union has failed to comply with any duty imposed by the 1992 Act or by a rule of the union relating to its financial affairs. Provision is made for reports of investigations to be produced and published, and for the recoupment of the expenses of investigations in certain circumstances. Section 11 creates offences and sets out penalties. There are specified time limits for bringing proceedings for such offences. Section 12 provides that persons convicted of certain offences in connection with the financial affairs of a trade union are disqualified from being a member of a union's executive or from being the president or general secretary of a union for five or ten years, depending on the gravity of the offence.

Sections 13–16 deal with rights in relation to union membership. Section 13 amends the 1992 Act, s 148 and is intended to clarify the law relating to action short of dismissal on grounds related to union membership or activities, following the decision of the Court of Appeal in *Associated British Ports v Palmer* (1993) Times, 5 May, and *Associated Newspapers Ltd v Wilson* [1994] ICR 97 (para 2554). As a result of the amendment, an employer who takes reasonable action to change his relationship with his employees will not be acting in contravention of s 146. The 1993 Act, s 14 provides that an individual may not be excluded or expelled from a trade union unless it is for a permitted reason. An individual who claims to have been excluded or expelled in contravention of this provision may present a complaint to an industrial tribunal within specified time limits. Section 15 provides that an employer must ensure that no unauthorised subscription deductions are made from a worker's wages pursuant to "check-off" arrangements. Section 16 extends the conduct for which an individual may not be disciplined by a trade union, so as to include conduct which consists in failing to agree, or withdrawing agreement, to the deduction of union subscriptions from wages as part of "check-off" arrangements; resigning or proposing to resign from the union or from another union, becoming or proposing to become a member of another union, refusing to become a member of another union, or being a member of another union; working with or proposing to work with individuals who are not members of the union or who are or are not members of another union; working for or proposing to work for an employer who employs or has employed individuals who are not members of the union or who are or are not members of another union; or requiring the union to do an act which it is required to do under the 1992 Act on the application or request of a member.

Sections 17–22 relate to industrial action. Sections 17–19 provide that if the organisation of industrial action by a union is to be protected against certain civil law proceedings, it must be preceded by a fully-postal ballot, subject to a limited exception for certain merchant seamen, written notice of the union's intent to ballot its members on industrial action must be given to the employer not later than seven days before the opening day of the ballot, and the union must take steps as soon as reasonably practicable after the ballot to provide the employer of the members balloted with the result of the ballot. Where the number of members entitled to vote in the ballot exceeds 50, s 20 requires that the ballot in respect of the industrial action must be subject to independent scrutiny, each ballot voting paper must comply with certain requirements, and the scrutineer must make a report to the union on the ballot stating whether he is satisfied as to certain matters. Section 21 provides that the union must, not later than seven days before the industrial action is intended to start or first take place, give written notice to an employer of those of his employees whom the union intends to induce to take part in the action, indicate whether the industrial action concerned is intended to be continuous or discontinuous, and state when the action is intended to start (if it is to be continuous) or the days on which it is intended to take place (if it is to be discontinuous). Section 22 enables an individual who claims that the supply of goods or services to him has been or will be prevented, delayed or reduced by unlawfully organised industrial action to bring proceedings to restrain that unlawful action. The new Commissioner for Protection Against Unlawful Industrial Action may grant an individual assistance for proceedings against a trade union.

Part II (ss 23–34) Employment Rights
Sections 23–25 and Schs 2, 3 implement Council Directive (EC) 92/85 on the rights of pregnant workers. Section 23 and Sch 2 give a new right to all employees, irrespective of their length of service, to fourteen weeks' maternity leave. Section 24 provides for all employees, irrespective of their length of service, the right not to be dismissed on grounds of pregnancy or childbirth. Section 25 and Sch 3 provide that an employee who would otherwise have to be suspended from work on maternity grounds for health and safety reasons has a right to be offered suitable alternative work (if available), and a right to be paid during her suspension.

Section 26 and Sch 4 give every employee who works at least eight hours a week the right to be given a written statement of his terms and conditions of employment within two months of beginning that employment (thereby implementing Council Directive (EC) 91/533 on an employer's obligation to inform employees of the conditions applicable to the contract or employment relationship). Section 27 provides that an employee who works for at least eight hours a week is entitled to an itemised pay statement from his employer, unless the number of persons employed by the employer is less than twenty. Section 28 and Sch 5 provide additional protection against dismissal and action short of dismissal for health and safety representatives and other employees in certain circumstances where health and safety is in issue. Section 29 provides that an employee is unfairly dismissed if the reason for dismissal was that he brought proceedings against his employer to enforce a relevant statutory right, or that he alleged that his employer had infringed the right in question. Section 30 provides that the statutory limit on compensation for unfair dismissal may be exceeded in certain cases where reinstatement or re-engagement orders have not been fully complied with, and the final compensation would otherwise be less than the cost of fully complying with the reinstatement or re-engagement order. Section 31 applies individual employment rights under certain provisions of the Employment Protection (Consolidation) Act 1978 to service as a member of the naval, military or air forces of the Crown.

Section 32 enables an individual to present a complaint to an industrial tribunal challenging the validity of the terms of a collective agreement or the rules of an employer which may be applied to him where the terms or rules may contravene the principle of equal treatment. If the tribunal finds the complaint to be well-founded, it must make an order declaring the term or rule to be void. Section 33 amends provisions of the Transfer of Undertakings (Protection of

Employment) Regulations 1981, SI 1981/1794, relating to employees' rights on the transfer of undertakings, and an employer's duty to inform and consult trade union representatives, so as to bring those provisions fully into line with Council Directive (EC) 77/187 (the EC Acquired Rights Directive). It also clarifies the position following the decision of the European Court of Justice in *Katsikas v Konstantinidis, Skreb v PCO Stauereibetrieb Paetz & Co Nachfolger GmbH, Schroll v PCO Stauereibetrieb Paetz & Co Nachfolger GmbH* [1993] IRLR 179 (para 1177); an employee may inform the transferor or the transferee that he objects to becoming employed by the transferee, in which case his contract of employment terminates, but he is not treated as having been dismissed. Section 33 also removes the possibility of "technical" redundancy payments being claimed by civil servants who continue to do the same work after privatisation. Section 34 amends provisions of the 1992 Act, relating to consultation on collective redundancies, so as to bring those provisions fully into line with Council Directive (EC) 92/56 (the EC Directive on Collective Redundancies).

Part III (ss 35–47) Other Employment Matters
Section 35 repeals the Wages Act 1986, Pt II (ss 12–26), thereby abolishing wages councils and the requirement for employers to pay statutory minimum remuneration in line with wages orders made by them.

Section 36 amends the constitution of industrial tribunals, so as to permit industrial tribunal chairmen to sit alone, without lay members, in the case of certain proceedings. Section 37 amends the constitution of the Employment Appeal Tribunal, so as to permit it to be fully constituted by a judge sitting alone, without lay members, in the case of appeals from an industrial tribunal where the tribunal consisted of the chairman sitting alone. Section 38 makes technical amendments so as to extend the power to confer jurisdiction on industrial tribunals in respect of claims for damages for breach of contract of employment and similar claims. Section 39 and Sch 6 provide that an agreement to refrain from instituting or continuing specified proceedings before an industrial tribunal is not void providing the conditions regulating compromise agreements are satisfied in relation to the agreement. Section 40 enables regulations to be made restricting publicity in proceedings before an industrial tribunal involving sexual misconduct. Section 41 makes similar provision in relation to the Employment Appeal Tribunal. Section 42 gives the Employment Appeal Tribunal power to make a restriction of proceedings order where it is satisfied that a person has habitually and persistently and without any reasonable ground instituted vexatious proceedings. Such an order may only be made on an application by the Attorney General.

Section 43 removes the particular requirement to encourage the extension, development and reform of collective bargaining from the statutory terms of reference of the Advisory, Conciliation and Arbitration Service (ACAS), simplifies the power enabling ACAS to give advice on industrial relations matters, and enables the chairman of ACAS to be appointed on a part-time basis. Section 44 enables ACAS to charge a fee for its services when it considers it appropriate, and provides a reserve power for the Secretary of State to direct ACAS to charge fees for its services.

Section 45 imposes on the Secretary of State (instead of on local education authorities) a duty to secure the provision of careers services for those at or leaving school or further education, and a power to secure the provision of such services for others. Section 46 enables local education authorities to supply goods and services for a period of two years to any person who provides, or arranges for the provision of, careers services. Section 47 applies to Scotland only.

Part IV (ss 48–55) Supplementary
Section 48 contains interpretation provisions. Section 49 and Schs 7, 8 contain miscellaneous and consequential amendments. Section 50 and Sch 9 concern transitional provisions and savings; s 51 introduces Sch 10 (repeals); and ss 52–55 concern commencement, financial provision, Northern Ireland, and the short title, respectively.

TRANSPORT

2559 Channel tunnel—international arrangements—criminal jurisdiction

The Channel Tunnel (International Arrangements) Order 1993, SI 1993/1813 (in force 2 August 1993), gives qualified effect to the Protocol between the United Kingdom and French Governments Concerning Frontier Controls and Policing, Co-operation in Criminal Justice, Public Safety and Mutual Assistance Relating to the Channel Fixed Link. The order includes a provision for the extension of English criminal jurisdiction to conduct in the United Kingdom control zone which, if taking place in England, would constitute an offence under a frontier control enactment. A presumption is created as to jurisdiction over offences committed in the tunnel system where it is uncertain on which side of the frontier they were committed. Further provision is made enabling constables and customs officers to assist French officers by taking into temporary custody persons arrested by the latter in the French control zone.

2560 Common transport policy
See EUROPEAN COMMUNITIES.

2561 Licensing and testing—fees—matters to be taken into account
The Department of Transport (Fees) (Amendment) Order 1993, SI 1993/1601 (in force on 22 June 1993), amends the 1988 Order, SI 1988/643, by providing that when the fees for entering and retaining a person's name in the register of approved driving instructors, and the test fees and charges for forms evidencing successful completion of approved training courses by learner motorcyclists are fixed, account can be taken of past deficits incurred by the Secretary of State and/or the registrar in discharging their functions in relation to the register, the tests and the training courses.

2562 Passenger and goods vehicles—drivers' hours—community drivers—temporary exception
The Community Drivers' Hours (Passenger and Goods Vehicles) (Temporary Exception) Regulations 1993, SI 1993/67 (in force on 19 January 1993), provide that, until 31 January 1993, any time spent driving in the exceptional circumstances occasioned by severe weather conditions in Scotland or the effects or consequences of such exceptional circumstances must not be taken into account for the purposes of the application of EC Council Regulation 3820/85, arts 6, 8, and 9.

2563 Passenger and goods vehicles—drivers' hours—exemption—revocation
The Drivers' Hours (Passenger and Goods Vehicles) (Exemption) (Revocation) Regulations 1993, SI 1993/158 (in force on 2 February 1993), revoke the Drivers' Hours (Passenger and Goods Vehicles) (Exemption) Regulations 1993, SI 1993/66.

2564 Passenger and goods vehicles—drivers' hours—recording equipment—approval of fitters and workshops
The Passenger and Goods Vehicles (Recording Equipment) (Approval of Fitters and Workshops) (Fees) (Amendment) Regulations 1993, SI 1993/3066 (in force on 2 January 1994), further amend the 1986 Regulations, SI 1986/2128, by reducing the fees for the approval of fitters or workshops for the installation or repair of recording equipment from £254 to £240 and for the renewal of an approval from £103 to £97·30.

The Motor Vehicles (Driving Licences) (Large Goods and Passenger-Carrying Vehicles) (Amendment) Regulations 1993, SI 1993/1603 (in force on 16 July 1993), further amend the 1990 Regulations, SI 1990/2612, by increasing the fee payable for a test of competence to drive a large goods or passenger-carrying vehicle from £55·50 to £60 for a test taken on a weekday and from £75 to £77·50 for a test taken on a Saturday.

2565 Private hire vehicle—licensing—licences issued by different local authorities
The appellants, operators of private hire vehicles, had operators' licences issued by one controlling authority but their vehicles and drivers were licensed by a neighbouring controlling authority. The appellants were convicted of operating a private hire vehicle without a licence, contrary to the Local Government (Miscellaneous Provisions) Act 1976, s 46, on the ground that an operator who held an operators' licence issued in one controlled district could only operate with vehicles and drivers licensed in the same district. On their appeal against conviction by way of case stated, held, the 1976 Act required licensed private hire operators to make use only of vehicles and drivers licensed by the council of the district in which the operators were licensed. That interpretation of the legislation required one licensing authority to take responsibility for issuing all three types of licence, so that the conditions on the granting of licences could be inter-related and effective steps could be taken to ensure that they were observed. The appeals would

be dismissed.

Dittah v Birmingham City Council; Choudhry v Birmingham City Council [1993] RTR 356 (Queen's Bench Division: Kennedy LJ and Clarke J).

2566 Private hire vehicle—licensing—unlicensed operation within controlled area—advertising outside controlled area

The Local Government (Miscellaneous Provisions) Act 1976, s 80(1) provides that, in relation to the licensing of private hire vehicles, "operate" means in the course of business to make provision for the invitation or acceptance of bookings for such a vehicle.

The offices of a mini-cab operator were situated in a town outside a controlled district within which a private hire vehicle operator's licence was required pursuant to the 1976 Act, s 55. The operator placed advertisements for his business in local telephone directories circulating in towns both within and outside the controlled district. However, he made provision for the acceptance of bookings only in the town where the office was situated. In proceedings brought by the local authority, he was acquitted of operating a private hire vehicle within a controlled area without a licence contrary to s 46(1)(d) of the Act. On appeal by the local authority, *held*, the 1976 Act, s 80(1) was concerned with the areas where provision was made to deal with an invitation of bookings and not with the areas the invitation might reach. As the advertisements informed the public that the operator had made provision in the area where his office was based, and as he had made no such provision in the other areas where the directories were circulated, he did not "operate" within the meaning of s 80(1). Accordingly, the appeal would be dismissed.

Windsor and Maidenhead Royal Borough Council v Khan (t/a Top Cabs) (1993) Times, 7 May (Queen's Bench Division: Leggatt LJ and McCullough J).

2567 Public service vehicles—conditions of fitness, equipment, use and certification

The Public Service Vehicles (Conditions of Fitness, Equipment, Use and Certification) (Amendment) Regulations 1993, SI 1993/3012 (in force on 2 January 1994), amend the 1981 Regulations, SI 1981/257, by reducing the fee payable for (1) a certificate of initial fitness on a first application and on a subsequent application when the test required is a test of stability, from £136·50 to £129 and, on any other subsequent application, from £16·30 to £15·40; (2) type approvals, from £788 to £744·70, £74 to £69·90, £390 to £368·60 and £1685 to £1592·30, as the case may be; and (3) a duplicate certificate, from £9·30 to £8·80.

2568 Public service vehicles—operators' licences

The Public Service Vehicles (Operators' Licences) (Amendment) Regulations 1993, SI 1993/2753 (in force on 1 December 1993), amend the 1986 Regulations, SI 1986/1668, by increasing the fee for the grant of a licence (other than a special licence) from £3·50 to £4·50 for each month, or part of the month, during which the licence is expressed to be in force. The fee for the second and every subsequent disc issued to the holder of a licence is increased from £3·50 to £4·50 for each month, or part of the month, during which the disc may be used.

2569 Public service vehicles—registration of local services—fees

The Public Service Vehicles (Registration of Local Services) (Amendment) Regulations 1993, SI 1993/2752 (in force on 1 December 1993), amend the 1986 Regulations, SI 1986/1671. Although the fee for an application to register or vary particulars of a community bus service with the traffic commissioner remains unchanged at £10, the fee to register any other type of service has been increased from £30 to £38 and the fee to vary particulars of such a service has increased from £27 to £38.

2570 Public service vehicles—traffic commissioners—publication and inquiries

The Public Service Vehicles (Traffic Commissioners: Publication and Inquiries) (Amendment) Regulations 1993, SI 1993/2754 (in force on 1 December 1993), amend the 1986 Regulations, SI 1986/1629, by increasing the fee for a copy of "Notices and Proceedings" supplied by a traffic commissioner pursuant to the Public Passenger Vehicles Act 1981, s 5(2)(b) from £2·50 to £3·50.

2571 Railways

See RAILWAYS, INLAND WATERWAYS AND PIPE-LINES.

2572 Road traffic

See ROAD TRAFFIC.

2573 Taxi cabs—fares—London

The London Cab Order 1993, SI 1993/1093 (in force on 24 April 1993), further amends the 1934 Order, SR & O 1934/1346, by increasing the fares payable for the hiring of a motor cab in the Metropolitan Police District and the City of London in respect of all journeys beginning and ending there.

2574 Transfer schemes—modifications

The Transport Act 1985 (Modifications in Schedule 4 to the Transport Act 1968) (Further Modification) Order 1993, SI 1993/2797 (in force on 6 December 1993), makes further amendments to the Transport Act 1968, Sch 4, by adapting its provisions to transfer schemes under the Transport Act 1985, s 61.

The Transport Act 1985 (Modifications in Schedule 4 to the Transport Act 1968) (Further Modification) (Amendment) Order 1993, SI 1993/2909 (in force on 5 December 1993), amends the 1993 Order supra by changing the date on which that Order comes into force.

TRUSTS

Halsbury's Laws of England (4th edn) Vol 48, paras 501–975

2575 Articles

Alternatives on Scrip Issues, Christopher McCall QC: LS Gaz, 28 July 1993, p 17
A Safe Harbour, Syren Johnstone (on fiduciary law): 143 NLJ 1162
Asset Protection Trusts and Gibraltar's Legislation, BJS Marrache and GV Davis: 143 NLJ 721
Bringing Trustees up to Date, Beatrice Toll (on the Trustee Investment Act 1961): 137 SJ 435
Carers and Wills, Another Application of Estoppel and Constructive Trusts, Elizabeth Hailstone: [1993] Fam Law 415
Clayton's Case—When to Apply it, Richard SJ Marshall (on *Clayton's Case* (1816) 1 Mer 572): 137 SJ 770
Constructive Trusts of Homes—A Bold Approach, DJ Hayton: (1993) 109 LQR 485
Constructive Trusts, Proprietary Estoppel and Wavering Equity, Josephine Hayes: 137 SJ 606
In the Mire With Miras, Peter Trevett QC: Tax Journal, Issue 223, p 14
The Real Costs of Scrip Dividends, Howard Nowlan: Tax Journal, Issue 223, p 10
The Remedial Constructive Trust in Commercial Transactions, SR Scott: [1993] 3 LMCLQ 330
Trust Law and Occupational Pension Schemes, David Hayton: [1993] Conv 283
Trusts of the Family Home—The Irish Experience, John Mee: [1993] Conv 359
Wills Containing Provision for a Mentally Handicapped Child, District Judge Gordon Ashton: 143 NLJ 1190

2576 Constructive trust—breach of fiduciary duty—acceptance of bribe

New Zealand

The respondent was employed as the Director of Public Prosecutions for Hong Kong. During his career, he accepted bribes in breach of the fiduciary duty he owed to the Crown. He pleaded guilty to offences under the Prevention of Bribery Ordinance and was sentenced to imprisonment. With the moneys received as bribes the respondent acquired three freehold properties in New Zealand which had been conveyed to himself and his co-respondents. The Attorney General of Hong Kong registered caveats against the title of the three properties, and he then sought to renew the caveats to prevent any dealing with the property pending the hearing of proceedings which had been initiated for the purposes of claiming the properties on a constructive trust. All the respondents opposed the renewal of the caveats on the ground that the Crown had no equitable interest in the properties. At first instance the court ordered that the caveats lodged by the Attorney General against the respondents should lapse. Following an unsuccessful appeal, the Attorney General appealed to the Privy Council. *Held*, the decision in *Lister & Co v Stubbs* (1890) 45 ChD 1, was not consistent with the principles that a fiduciary must not be allowed to benefit from his own breach of duty, that the fiduciary ought to account for the bribe as soon as he received it, and that equity regarded as done that which ought to be done. As soon as the respondent received a bribe in breach of the duties he owed to the government of Hong Kong, he became a debtor in equity to the Crown for the amount of that bribe. A fiduciary who accepts a bribe in breach of his duty holds the bribe in trust for the person to whom the duty is owed, and the fiduciary is accountable not only for the original amount of the bribe but also for the increased value of the property representing the bribe. Accordingly, the appeal would be allowed.

A-G for Hong Kong v Reid [1994] I All ER I (Privy Council: Lords Templeman, Goff of Chieveley, Lowry, Lloyd and Sir Thomas Eichelbaum).

2577　Constructive trust—knowing assistance in fraudulent breach of trust—receipt of trust money—payment prior to completion of sale of land

The defendant solicitors had acted for a mortgagee who was lending money to a prospective purchaser and mortgagor of land. The solicitors had received the mortgage money from the mortgagee and held it on a bare trust. They had implied authority to pass the money to the purchaser when the property had been transferred. The money was subsequently paid over before completion of the transfer. The mortgagee brought a claim for breach of trust and an order was made on a motion for summary judgment, giving the solicitors leave to defend provided an interim payment of £1m was made to the mortgagee against a guarantee of repayment and also allowing a cross-appeal by the mortgagee for summary judgment in the full amount claimed. The solicitors appealed against that order. *Held*, the breach of trust had been conscious and deliberate. A trustee or other fiduciary who disposed of trust property to a stranger was under an immediate duty to make restitution of the money which had been lost, which in this case was the money paid over by the solicitors. The solicitors should however receive a credit for any money recovered by the mortgagee on realisation of the property. Accordingly, the appeal would be dismissed.

Target Holdings Ltd v Redferns (1993) Times, 24 November, Independent, 3 December (Court of Appeal: Ralph Gibson, Hirst, and Peter Gibson LJJ).

2578　Declaration of trust—certainty of intention—issued share capital

Following the trial of an action the court held that the defendant had declared himself to be a trustee for the plaintiff as to a five per cent holding in the issued share capital of a company to which the plaintiff had thereupon become absolutely beneficially entitled. By a notice of motion the defendant applied to have the judgment in the action recalled and set aside on the ground that the purported trust had failed for want of certainty of the subject matter. *Held*, a purported declaration of trust was sufficiently certain as to subject matter if, immediately after the purported declaration, the court could have made an order for the execution of the trust. In the case of a trust of intangible assets the requirement of certainty did not necessarily entail segregation or appropriation of the specific property which was to form the subject matter of the trust. Since the shares were of such a nature as to be indistinguishable one from another and were therefore all equally capable of satisfying the trust, it was unnecessary to identify any particular shares and as such, the trust was not void for uncertainty of subject matter. Accordingly, the motion would be dismissed.

Hunter v Moss [1993] I WLR 934 (Chancery Division: Colin Rimer QC).

2579　Pension fund trustees—action for breach of trust—action by employees—pre-emptive costs order

The plaintiffs were employees of a company and were entitled to certain benefits under a pension scheme, the terms of which prohibited the trustees from making any payments to the employer or making any amendment which might prejudice the members' interests. The company was taken over and the employees were invited to transfer to one of two new funds on the same terms as before but with the guarantee that the trust deeds would prevent any alteration to the prejudice of members' rights. The funds were then sold and the trustees were replaced. A series of complicated financial transactions were then made by the various companies involved, resulting in the alteration of the trust deeds and the company which had purchased the funds allegedly being reimbursed for their purchase. The employees, in a consolidated action, brought a claim for breach of trust and applied for a pre-emptive costs order that costs of the action be paid out of the fund. *Held*, the order should be made on the basis of the factors set out in the case of *National Anti-Vivisection Society v Duddington* (1989) Times, 16 November (1989 Abr para 1789). The order would not restrict the judge from awarding costs at trial but would establish that the trustees had a lien on the trust fund for any costs, including those awarded against them, to the extent that they had carried out their duties correctly. The claims were not insubstantial and if independent trustees were appointed they would no doubt apply for authority to pursue them. The beneficiaries, who were employees, could not reasonably be expected to have the financial resources to proceed with litigation and in view of the fact that they had contributed money to the fund, they had the right to ensure that the fund was correctly administered by trustees in a way which reflected their legitimate expectations. Because the actions would not be heard for some time it would be unfair to leave the administration of the funds to trustees whose honesty was in doubt. A judicial trustee would therefore be appointed. The application would be granted accordingly.

McDonald v Horn (1993) Times, 12 October (Chancery Division: Vinelott J).

2580 Public Trustee—fees

The Public Trustee (Fees) (Amendment) Order 1993, SI 1993/619 (in force on 1 April 1993), further amends the withdrawal fee rate fixed by the Public Trustee (Fees) Order 1985, SI 1985/373.

2581 Resulting trust—failure of purpose of trust—determination of interest in property

The plaintiff was a secure tenant of a council house. He had substantial savings which he intended to bequeath to the defendants under his will. The parties came to an arrangement whereby the plaintiff would anticipate his testamentary benefaction to the defendants by providing in his lifetime a sum to enable them to buy a house instead of having to rent accommodation. Under the arrangement the plaintiff would be entitled to live at the house rent free for the rest of his life. Following a dispute, the arrangement came to an end and the plaintiff was forced to move into alternative accommodation provided by the council. He sought a beneficial interest in the house by way of resulting trust. At first instance the judge held that by way of proprietary estoppel the defendants would be ordered to repay the plaintiff for his expenditure. On their appeal, *held*, the plaintiff had not lost the whole of the sum contributed by him to purchase the house but merely the right to rent-free occupation for the rest of his life. He was entitled to a sum commensurate with the extent of his equity. It would be unconscionable for the defendants not to satisfy the interest they had promised to the plaintiff and there was no reason in conscience why that interest should in part be satisfied at the public expense from housing benefit. The appeal would be allowed and the case remitted for an assessment to be made of the compensation payable.

Baker v Baker (1993) 25 HLR 408 (Court of Appeal: Dillon, Beldam and Roch LJJ).

2582 Resulting trust—money paid under ultra vires contract

See *Westdeutsche Landesbank Girozentrale v Islington London Borough Council*, para 607.

2583 Resulting trust—purchase of land—illegality—effect on claim under trust

The plaintiff and the defendant purchased a house using funds from a joint business venture. The property was vested in the sole name of the plaintiff to assist the parties in making false claims for social security benefit, but it was understood between them that they were to be joint beneficial owners. The parties quarrelled and the plaintiff vacated the property, leaving the defendant in occupation. The plaintiff brought proceedings claiming possession and asserting sole ownership of the property. The defendant counterclaimed for an order for sale and for a declaration that the property was held by the plaintiff on trust for the parties in equal shares. The plaintiff's appeal against the dismissal of her claim and judgment for the defendant on the counterclaim was unsuccessful. On her further appeal, *held* (Lords Keith and Goff dissenting), it was clearly established that at law, as opposed to equity, property in goods or land could pass under or pursuant to an illegal contract. English law had a single law of property made up of legal and equitable interests and a distinction could not be drawn between property rights enforceable at law and those requiring the intervention of equity. If the law was that a party was entitled to enforce a property right acquired under an illegal transaction, the same rule ought to apply to any property right so acquired, whether such right was legal or equitable. The plaintiff claimed under a resulting trust, the creation of which depended not on a contractual obligation but on a common intention, acted upon by the parties to their detriment. Where two parties provided the purchase money to buy a property which was conveyed into the name of only one of them, that party was presumed to hold the property on a resulting trust for both parties, in shares proportionate to their contributions. Where the presumption of resulting trust applied, a party claiming under it did not have to rely on illegality. If he proved that the property was vested in the name of the other party alone but that he provided part of the purchase money, or voluntarily transferred the property to the other party, he could establish a claim under a resulting trust unless the contrary was shown. In the present case, the defendant simply pleaded the common intention that the property should belong to both herself and the plaintiff and that she contributed to the purchase price. She was not forced to rely on the illegality to prove her equitable interest, and the illegality only emerged because the plaintiff sought to raise it. The defendant had raised the presumption of a resulting trust and there was no evidence to rebut that presumption. Accordingly, the appeal would be dismissed.

Tinsley v Milligan [1993] 3 All ER 65 (House of Lords: Lords Keith of Kinkel, Goff of Chieveley, Jauncey of Tullichettle, Lowry and Browne-Wilkinson).

2584 Trust property—shares—shares allotted as part of company demerger—treatment as income or capital

See *Sinclair v Lee*, para 2304.

2585 Trustee—overseas trust—capital gains tax

See *De Rothschild v Lawrenson*, para 283.

2586 Variation of trust—use of memorandum—failure to sign embodying deed

A testator, in his will, bequeathed a sum of money to his housekeeper who had worked for him for 52 years; the residue of his estate was to be divided equally between the defendants, his 16 cousins. After the testator's death concern was expressed about the lack of provision in the will for the housekeeper and it was suggested by the first plaintiff, one of the executors, that the defendants might agree to vary the terms of the will so as to give her a larger pecuniary legacy and the freehold of a bungalow where she had lived. In agreement with the suggestion each of the defendants thereupon signed an identical memorandum stating "that the terms of the will be varied" by giving the housekeeper a larger pecuniary legacy and the freehold of the bungalow, and reciting that he or she was "prepared to enter into a deed to formalise" the gift. When the deed embodying the arrangements set out in the memoranda had been prepared, the first four defendants refused to sign it. The executors issued a summons to determine whether the devolution of the testator's estate had been effectively varied by the memoranda. *Held*, the memorandum signed by each of the residuary legatees showed on its face an intention to create a document having immediate legal effect. Since there were no grounds for inferring that the residuary legatees did not intend the documents signed by them to have legal effect, or that some material fact had not been disclosed to them, the memoranda took effect to vary the distribution of the deceased's estate as soon as they were communicated to the executors.

Crowden v Aldridge [1993] 1 WLR 433 (Chancery Division: Jonathon Sumption QC).

VALUE ADDED TAX

Halsbury's Laws of England (4th edn) Vol 12, paras 864–990

2587 Articles

Compensating Measures, David Hanman (on avoiding VAT liability): LS Gaz, 15 September 1993, p 17

Land and Property Consultation, Anthony Davis (on VAT legislation in the land and property sphere): Tax Journal, Issue 226, p 8

Let Property—Transfer of Going Concern Relief, Richard Pincher: Tax Journal, Issue 235, p 11

Reverse Payments and Rent-Free Periods, Peter Hewitt: Tax Journal, Issue 239, p 11

Taking Stock of the Transitional VAT System, Peter Jenkins: Tax Journal, Issue 223, p 12 and Issue 224, p 9

The New (Very) Expanded Reverse Charge, Martin Lynchehan (on the Value Added Tax Act 1983, s 7): Tax Journal, Issue 234, p 4

To Pay or Not to Pay That is the Question, Neil Warriner and Michael Sedlaczek (on VAT payments before an appeal can be heard): Tax Journal, Issue 238, p 10
VAT and Local Authorities, Michael Jacobs: Tax Journal, 25 February 1993, p 8
VAT Avoidance and Mitigation, Ian Saunders: 137 SJ 100
VAT Avoidance and the National Audit Office, Gavin McFarlane: 1993 SLT 232
What is a Tour Operator? Marzenna Cummings: Tax Journal, Issue 237, p 5
Zero Rating of Domestic Building Works, Richard Pincher: Tax Journal, Issue 230, p 11

2588 Accounting and records

The Value Added Tax (Accounting and Records) (Amendment) Regulations 1993, SI 1993/761 (in force on 17 March 1993), amend the 1989 Regulations, SI 1989/2248, by increasing from £1,000 to £2,000 the maximum amount of the difference between underdeclarations and overdeclarations of liability for the purpose of the correction of a person's value added tax account.

2589 Accounting for tax—cash accounting

The Value Added Tax (Cash Accounting) (Amendment) Regulations 1993, SI 1993/762 (in force on 1 April 1993), further amend the 1987 Regulations, SI 1987/1427, by increasing the value of taxable supplies in a year for the purposes of admission to, and remaining in, the cash accounting scheme, from £300,000 to £350,000, and by dispensing with the requirement for formal authorisation by the Commissioners of Customs and Excise for admission to the scheme.

The Value Added Tax (Cash Accounting) (Amendment) (No 2) Regulations 1993, SI 1993/3028 (in force on 3 January 1994), further amend the 1987 Regulations, SI 1987/1427, by relaxing conditions for admission to, and remaining in, the cash accounting scheme; and by reducing to six months the period in respect of which outstanding tax has to be accounted for when a person who has been operating the scheme ceases to trade.

2590 Accounting for tax—practice—misdirection by customs officers

The owner of a hairdressing business was registered for value added tax. He engaged the services of stylists who, on professional advice, were self-employed and responsible for accounting for their takings from customers. On two occasions, the accounting practice of the business was checked by visiting customs officers but on neither occasion was it suggested that the accounting practice with regard to the stylists was unacceptable. On a third visit, however, an officer decided that the practice was incorrect and an assessment was issued for value added tax owing since the previous visit by an officer. The view of the third officer was upheld by the local value added tax office. The owner could not afford to appeal to a value added tax tribunal because of the assessment to back tax. The question whether the change in accounting practice should take effect only in the future was raised with the Parliamentary Commissioner for Administration. The chairman of the Commissioners of Customs and Excise accepted that there was some substance to the point raised and agreed that the failure of the two officers to correct the owner's accounting practice amounted to a misdirection; the full amount of the tax assessed and paid as a result of the third officer's visit, together with interest, was remitted. The chairman also asked the local value added tax office to agree reasonable compensation with the owner for costs and inconvenience caused.

Case C.729/92, Selected Cases 1993, Vol 3, p 24, Parliamentary Commissioner for Administration.

2591 Appeal—appeal to tribunal—costs—conduct of appellant

The taxpayer ran an independent school on a non-profit-making basis. It was advised by the Commissioners of Customs and Excise that education and training otherwise than for profit was exempt from value added tax. The taxpayer supplied a Customs officer, at his request, with a set of draft accounts. They showed that the taxpayer had made a profit. It was informed that it was, accordingly, obliged to register for value added tax. On its appeal against that requirement, the taxpayer eventually provided final audited accounts which showed that it had actually made a loss. On its application for costs "of and incidental to and consequential upon the appeal", *held*, costs generally followed the event. The taxpayer had not acted in such a way as to make an award of costs inappropriate. As it was not registered, or obliged to register, for value added tax, it was not required to keep records and was not in breach of any duty to the commissioners in providing draft accounts which proved to be both inaccurate and unfavourable to itself. Further, it had not attempted to mislead the commissioners. Accordingly, its application would be granted.

Surrey College Ltd v Customs and Excise Comrs [1992] VATTR 181 (Value added tax tribunal).

2592 Appeal—appeal to tribunal—costs—litigant in person

It fell to be determined whether the taxpayer, who had prepared and conducted a successful appeal to a value added tax tribunal himself and who had been obliged to close his business pending the appeal, was entitled to costs in respect of the loss of income from the business, the loss of profit for the time spent on the case by the taxpayer, his partners and staff, and interest on any sums awarded as costs. *Held,* as the value added tax tribunal was not identified in the Litigant in Persons (Costs and Expenses) Act 1975, s 1(1) nor specified in an order made under that provision by the Lord Chancellor, the Act did not apply so as to entitle litigants in person to recover their profit losses before a tribunal. RSC Ord 62, r 18, by virtue of which a litigant in person was entitled to remuneration for the time spent by him in the conduct of an appeal, was introduced to provide the machinery necessary to implement the 1975 Act and dealt only with proceedings identified by that Act. The Value Added Tax Tribunal Rules 1986, SI 1986/590, r 29, which applied RSC Ord 62 "with the necessary modifications" in cases where a value added tax tribunal directed that the costs of, incidental to and consequent on, the appeal of the successful party might be taxed by a taxing master of the Supreme Court, referred to such modifications as were required to reflect the true position in law. In the present case, those words disapplied Ord 62, r 18. Accordingly, an award of costs to a successful litigant in person following an appeal to a value added tax tribunal could not exceed those costs recoverable at common law. The losses sustained as a consequence of the closure of the taxpayer's business were not recoverable under the rubric "costs" in the 1986 Rules, r 29. The words "consequent upon the appeal" connoted costs incurred following, or resulting from, the appeal so that, even if the losses could be recovered as costs, they could not be properly described as costs "consequent upon" the appeal as the loss was sustained before the appeal was embarked upon. The tribunal's order for costs was not a judgment within the Judgments Act 1838. Under the 1986 Rules, r 29(5), costs awarded under r 29 were recoverable as a civil debt so that the taxpayer was not entitled to recover interest on the costs recovered from the date of the tribunal's order.

Nader (trading as Try Us) v Customs and Excise Comrs [1993] STC 806 (Court of Appeal: Farquharson, Beldam and Henry LJJ). *Customs and Excise Comrs v Ross* [1990] 2 All ER 65 approved.

2593 Appeal—appeal to tribunal—right of appeal against amended assessment

The taxpayer appealed against an assessment to value added tax. He also applied to a value added tax tribunal to waive the requirement that the tax assessed should be paid before the hearing of the appeal on grounds of hardship. The tribunal directed that the disputed tax should be paid to, or deposited with, the Commissioners of Customs and Excise within 3 months or the appeal would be dismissed without further hearing. Meanwhile the commissioners issued an amended assessment in a reduced sum. The taxpayer appealed against the amended assessment and made a new application on hardship grounds. The commissioners applied for the consolidation of the two appeals and subsequently when the tax was not deposited within the time limit as directed by the tribunal, they applied for the dismissal of the original appeal. The taxpayer opposed the commissioners' application to consolidate the two appeals and applied for the original appeal to be allowed. The tribunal allowed the application for consolidation of the two appeals and directed that they both be dismissed without the need for further hearing. The taxpayer appealed, contending that the tribunal had erred (1) in holding that the two appeals were the same and that there was no right of appeal against the amended assessment; and (2) in dismissing the appeal against the amended assessment for non-compliance with the direction of the tribunal made in respect of the original appeal. *Held,* where the amount of an assessment had been reduced by an amendment subsequent to the lodging of an appeal by the taxpayer, the taxpayer could not appeal separately against the amended assessment and treat the first appeal as allowed because (1) there was power to reduce the assessment under the Value Added Tax Act 1983, Sch 7, para 4(9) and (2) there was no provision for a further appeal against the amended assessment if the original assessment had already been appealed against. Accordingly, there was in truth only one appeal, namely the appeal against the original assessment, and after the amendment, the assessment in its reduced form and that appeal continued to exist until it was withdrawn, decided or compromised, and the tribunal's order relating to that appeal had to be complied with. The taxpayer's appeal would accordingly be dismissed.

Sitar Tandoori Restaurant v Customs and Excise Comrs [1993] STC 582 (Queen's Bench Division: Henry J).

2594   Appeal—appeal to tribunal—taxpayer discharged bankrupt—locus standi

An assessment to value added tax was made on a partnership in 1983. The partnership had been dissolved in 1981 and all of the partners had subsequently been declared bankrupt. It fell to be determined whether the taxpayer, one of the partners and now a discharged bankrupt, who had been given leave in 1991 to appeal against the assessment out of time, had the right to appeal to a value added tax tribunal against the assessment. *Held*, the right of appeal vested in the trustee in bankruptcy by virtue of the Bankruptcy Act 1914, s 48(5), as a "thing in action". Discharge from bankruptcy under the Insolvency Act 1986, s 11 did not by virtue of s 281 re-vest the right of appeal in the discharged bankrupt. The trustee in bankruptcy had delayed winding up the bankruptcy in order to enable the taxpayer to produce evidence relating to the assessment. In spite of the lapse of time, it was still open to the Commissioners of Customs and Excise to prove for the debt arising from the assessment. If they did so, the trustee in bankruptcy might assign the right of appeal under the Value Added Tax Tribunal Rules 1986, SI 1986/590, r 13. If no such assignment were made, the taxpayer would have no locus standi.

Hunt v Customs and Excise Comrs [1992] VATTR 255 (Value added tax tribunal).

1914 Act, s 48(5) now Insolvency Act 1986, s 311(4).

2595   Assessment—invalidity—amendment

The taxpayer contended that a second assessment to value added tax, which included periods covered by a first assessment, was invalid. *Held*, as evidence relied on in making the second assessment had been available when the first assessment was made and evidence of facts relied on in making the first assessment were sufficient to justify the making of the first assessment, the second assessment could not be said to have been made to the best of the judgment of the Commissioners of Customs and Excise. An assessment not so made was invalid. It could not be saved by the deletion of those parts of it which were incorrect by reducing it in accordance with the Value Added Tax Act 1983, Sch 7, para 4(9). As an assessment had to be considered as a whole, an invalid assessment had to be withdrawn. If still within the time limit, another correct assessment might then be raised.

Barber v Customs and Excise Comrs [1992] VATTR 144 (Value added tax tribunal).

2596   Assessment—multi-period assessments

It fell to be determined whether a value added tax assessment in respect of 24 accounting periods constituted a single assessment and was, therefore, null and void because it was made more than six years after the end of the first prescribed accounting period included in the assessment. *Held*, a global assessment was invalid if any single part of it was invalid. The crucial question was whether there were 24 individual assessments. It had previously been held that it was wholly unreal to treat a series of running assessments as constituting separate assessments rather than one assessment in a total sum. There was in effect one global assessment covering all of the periods.

Customs and Excise Comrs v Le Rififi Ltd [1993] STC 725 (Queen's Bench Division: Leonard J). Dicta of Dillon LJ in *Don Pasquale (a firm) v Customs and Excise Comrs* [1990] STC 556 at 560, CA (1990 Abr para 2538) followed.

2597   Budget—summary

See para 2151.

2598   Common system of value added tax—uniform basis of assessment—local tax—tax other than turnover tax

See *NV Giant v Commune of Overijse*, para 2742.

2599   Default surcharge—liability to surcharge—reasonable excuse for failure to pay tax on time

Scotland

A substantial reclaim in respect of value added tax was due to an associated property company of the taxpayer. The property company issued a mandate authorising the Commissioners of Customs and Excise to make the repayment to the taxpayer instead of to it against the taxpayer's value added tax liability. The commissioners applied the repayment against the total debt owed by the taxpayer, including value added tax, default surcharges and interest. The taxpayer had general cash flow problems and the repayment was insufficient to extinguish its value added tax liability. On its appeal against 13 default surcharge assessments, the taxpayer contended that the commissioners' delay in making the repayment was the reason why it had failed to meet its value added tax liability. *Held*, the only excuse being put forward was an insufficiency of funds accompanied by an explanation as to why the funds or part of them were not available. Further, the taxpayer, having failed to avail itself of the statutory provisions allowing companies to be registered as a group, was merely asserting that some repayment had not been made to an entirely separate legal persona, the property company. The appeal would be dismissed.

Artful Dodger (Kilmarnock) Ltd v Lord Advocate [1993] STC 330 (Inner House).

2600 Exempt supply—education—training and retraining

The Value Added Tax (Education) (No 2) Order 1993, SI 1993/1124 (in force on 22 April 1993), varies the Value Added Tax Act 1983, Sch 6, Group 6 so as to extend the scope of the exemption thereunder to supplies of training and retraining for any trade, profession or employment, including work experience, and the supply of goods and services essential thereto, provided as part of a government funded training programme under the Employment and Training Act 1973, s 2; and so as to take account of the revised arrangements for the provision and funding of further education under the Further and Higher Education Act 1992. The 1993 Order revokes SI 1993/763 which inadvertently omitted from the definition of "school" a reference to voluntary schools within the meaning of the Education Act 1944.

2601 Exempt supply—insurance—pension fund trustees—investment of contributions in insurance policies

The taxpayer operated a pensions and employee benefits consultancy and acted as trustee and administrator of pension schemes. It invested the contributions received from employers and employees in insurance policies. It fell to be determined whether the services supplied by the taxpayer were exempt from value added tax as being either or both of the making of arrangements for the provision of any insurance and the handling of insurance claims by insurance agents under the Value Added Tax Act 1983, Sch 6, Group 2, items 3, 4. *Held*, as trustee and administrator of the schemes, the taxpayer was vested with the appropriate rights and obligations. The standard charges made by the taxpayer in relation to the schemes were made by it by virtue of its right to charge as trustee conferred on it by the scheme rules. Most of the services supplied by it under the schemes were services that it was required to provide under the trust deeds and the rules. The only rights that members and their dependants had were those given by the trust deeds and rules against the taxpayer as trustee. Accordingly, the taxpayer did not supply any services of arranging for the provisions of insurance within Sch 6, Group 2, item 3. When it made claims under insurance policies, it did so as principal, not as agent and, therefore, it could not properly be described as handling insurance claims as agent within Sch 6, Group 2, item 4. The taxpayer made a single composite supply of trusteeship and administrative services which were standard-rated. Its appeal would be dismissed.

Federated Pensions Services Ltd v Customs and Excise Comrs [1992] VATTR 358 (Value added tax tribunal).

2602 Exempt supply—land—yacht used for habitation—mooring fees

The taxpayers lived aboard a yacht which they owned and on which they had carried out certain works of improvement to make it habitable and seaworthy. Such work included the replacement of its engine, although the new engine was not properly installed, the yacht had no propeller or electrical system and was not capable of self-propulsion. Work to render the yacht capable of self-propulsion could have been carried out within a few weeks. The taxpayers contended that the mooring fees paid by them to the local authority were exempt from value added tax because they used the yacht as their home. *Held*, the yacht was properly described as "a ship, boat or vessel" within the Value Added Tax Act 1983, Sch 6, Group 1, item 1(f) because that provision did not require that the vessel in question be capable of use for navigation at the relevant time. The yacht had not been designed solely as a place of permanent habitation nor had it been adapted for that purpose. Accordingly, the mooring fees were standard-rated.

Roberts v Customs and Excise Comrs [1992] VATTR 30 (Value added tax tribunal).

2603 Finance Act 1985—interest on tax—prescribed rate

The Finance Act 1985 (Interest on Tax) (Prescribed Rate) Order 1993, SI 1993/421 (in force on 6 March 1993), provides that, for the purposes of the 1985 Act, s 18, the prescribed rate of interest on tax recovered or recoverable by assessment is 6·25 per cent.

The Finance Act 1985 (Interest on Tax) (Prescribed Rate) (No 2) Order 1993, SI 1993/3168 (in force on 6 January 1994), provides that, for the purposes of the 1985 Act, s 18, the prescribed rate of interest on tax recovered or recoverable by assessment is 5·50 per cent.

2604 Finance Act 1993

See para 2160.

2605 General regulations

The Value Added Tax (General) (Amendment) Regulations 1993, SI 1993/119 (in force on 26 January 1993), further amend the 1985 Regulations, SI 1985/886, by restoring reg 29(2)–(6) (determination of longer period applicable to a taxable person where exempt input tax is treated as being attributable to taxable supplies), which were inadvertently removed by SI 1992/3102.

The Value Added Tax (General) (Amendment) (No 3) Regulations 1993, SI 1993/856 (in force in part on 31 March 1993 and in part on 1 April 1993), made as a consequence of a defect in SI 1993/764, which is revoked, further amend the 1985 Regulations supra by requiring that for any supply in respect of which the buyer must account for the output tax on behalf of the seller, both that fact and the amount of tax to be accounted for must be shown on the tax invoice.

The Value Added Tax (General) (Amendment) (No 4) Regulations 1993, SI 1993/1224 (in force on 31 May 1993), made as a consequence of a defect in SI 1992/3102, further amend the 1985 Regulations supra by substituting reg 9A which sets out the notification requirements placed upon persons who exercise the place of supply option in relation to distance sales.

The Value Added Tax (General) (Amendment) (No 5) Regulations 1993, SI 1993/1639 (in force on 1 August 1993), further amend the 1985 Regulations supra by amending the provisions relating to input tax and partial exemption so as to (1) make clear that nothing in those provisions is to be construed as allowing a taxable person to deduct the whole or any part of tax on the importation or acquisition by him of goods or the supply to him of goods or services where those goods or services are not used or to be used by him in making supplies in the course or furtherance of a business carried on by him; (2) widen the definition of exempt input tax to include input tax on goods and services used in the making of supplies outside the United Kingdom which would be exempt if made in the United Kingdom, where that input tax is not deductible; (3) extend the scope of the provision as to the adjustment of attribution of input tax to include the input tax now contained in the definition of exempt input tax in (2) supra; and (4) add a new provision by virtue of which supplies outside the United Kingdom which do not give rise to the right to deduct input tax are distinguished from those which do give rise to that right regardless of where the supplies take place.

The Value Added Tax (General) (Amendment) (No 6) Regulations 1993, SI 1993/1941 (in force on 2 August 1993), further amend the 1985 Regulations supra by (1) requiring traders from other member states who make supplies of goods to customers in the United Kingdom and who intend to treat those supplies as falling within the Value Added Tax Act 1983, s 8D(1) to notify the Commissioners of Customs and Excise and the customers in writing of their intention to do so, (2) requiring traders from other member states who install or assemble goods in the United Kingdom and who intend to treat those supplies as falling within s 8D(2) similarly to notify the commissioners and the customers of that intention, (3) requiring the issue of invoices in a prescribed form by United Kingdom traders who make supplies which are to be treated as if they were subject to the law corresponding, in the other member states where the customers are, to s 8D(1), (4) prescribing the time and form in which a trader from another member state who has elected to treat supplies in the United Kingdom as falling within s 8D(1) is required to issue invoices to his customers, and (5) prescribing the time and form in which a trader from another member state who has elected to treat supplies of goods installed or assembled in the United Kingdom as falling within s 8D(2) is required to issue invoices to his customers.

The Value Added Tax (General) (Amendment) (No 7) Regulations 1993, SI 1993/3027 (in force on 1 January 1994), further amend the 1985 Regulations supra by providing that distress for failure to pay value added tax or any amount recoverable as if it were tax may now be levied by an officer of rank not below that of Higher Executive Officer who may also direct an unauthorised person to levy; and by providing for the debtor to be liable for all costs and charges in connection with the distress. There is no longer a requirement that the goods distrained be independently appraised or that they be sold only by public auction.

2606   Imported goods—counterfeit currency

See *Witzemann v Hauptzollamt München-Mitte*, para 2710.

2607   Imported goods—goods from other member states—principle of non-discrimination

See *EC Commission v Italian Republic; EC Commission v Kingdom of Spain; EC Commission v Italian Republic*, para 2745.

2608   Input tax—deduction—dividends paid to holding company

See *Satam SA v Minister responsible for the Budget*, para 2743.

2609   Input tax—deduction—supply for purposes of business—supply for work different from normal business of taxpayer

The taxpayer company specialised in electron beam welding. Its managing director obtained estimates from a number of building firms, including the taxpayer, for alterations to his house. The work was undertaken by the taxpayer which, although it had wide objects covering general construction works, did not normally do such work and, therefore, sub-contracted some of the work. The taxpayer's claim to deduct input tax on the costs of the work was refused by the Commissioners of Customs and Excise on the ground that it was not part of the taxpayer's business under the Value Added Tax Act 1983, s 14(3). On appeal by the taxpayer, *held*, although the work was not work usually done by the taxpayer, it was no less an "economic activity" within the meaning of Council Directive (EC) 77/388, art 4(4) than the taxpayer's usual work. Its past and present construction activities were more than enough to enable construction work to qualify as one of its economic activities. The work in question qualified for the deduction of input tax and, accordingly, the appeal would be allowed.

Fusetron Ltd v Customs and Excise Comrs [1993] 2 CMLR 613 (Value added tax tribunal).

2610   Input tax—exceptions to right to deduct—furniture

The taxpayer company installed wardrobes of standard design into newly built houses. The wardrobes were formed on two sides by the walls of the house and on the third side by a portion of wall whose only purpose was to separate the wardrobe from the room it served. The skirting boards, architraves and frames on which the wardrobe doors were hung were fitted to the walls. The taxpayer claimed credit for input tax paid on the materials used in constructing the wardrobes, including mirror doors, tracks and hanging shelves. The Commissioners of Customs and Excise raised assessments to recover the deductions made in respect of all the materials. Under the Value Added Tax Act 1983, s 14, the rule that a taxable person might deduct his input tax was restricted by the Value Added Tax (Special Provisions) Order 1981, SI 1981/1741, art 8 the effect of which was that credit for input tax on disputed materials might only be claimed if they were neither finished or prefabricated furniture nor materials for the construction of such furniture. A value added tax tribunal held that neither the wardrobes nor the materials came within art 8. On the commissioners appeal, *held*, art 8 was applied to speculative builders to establish equality between those who purchased a house already fitted out on which no value added tax was payable and those who fitted out a house themselves paying value added tax on fixtures. In looking at the finished product the tribunal had used the correct approach as it was clear that the wardrobes were not furniture. Accordingly, the appeal would be dismissed.

Customs and Excise Comrs v McLean Homes Midland Ltd [1993] STC 335 (Queen's Bench Division: Brooke J).

2611   Input tax—motor cars

The Value Added Tax (Cars) (Amendment) Order 1993, SI 1993/2951 (in force on 1 January 1994), amends provisions of the 1992 Order, SI 1992/3122, concerning the self-supply of a motor car where an input tax deduction has been taken and the output tax relief for secondhand motor cars. Accordingly, where businesses which lease cars to private taxi firms, self-drive hire firms and driving schools and which have reclaimed the value added tax on purchases of such motor cars (see infra) sell those cars, value added tax is charged on their full selling price. Where an input tax deduction has been taken but the car has been put to a non-qualifying use, there is now a self-supply.

The Value Added Tax (Input Tax) (Amendment) Order 1993, SI 1993/2954 (in force on 1 January 1994), amends the 1992 Order, SI 1992/3222, by enabling businesses which lease cars to private taxi firms, self-drive hire firms and driving schools to reclaim the value added tax on purchases of motor cars for that purpose.

2612 Input tax—registration as intending trader—sale of business before taxable supplies made—repayment of input tax

The taxpayer purchased land which he intended to plant up as a woodland. He registered for value added tax and reclaimed input tax on the costs of preparing the land and planting out but he sold the woodland before making any taxable supplies. The Commissioners of Customs and Excise sought to recover input tax paid to him on the ground that he had made no taxable supplies. *Held*, the sale of the woodland was an exempt supply of both land and trees. The whole of the input tax on supplies to the taxpayer was used in making that exempt supply even though, when he claimed and received the input tax, he had not contemplated that an exempt supply would take place. The taxpayer's activities in relation to the land and the trees were predominantly concerned with making taxable supplies. Accordingly, there was a business within the Value Added Tax Act 1983, s 2(1) or an economic activity carried on by the taxpayer within Council Directive (EC) 77/388, art 4(2). In so far as it was a business of a continuing nature and capable of being transferred, it was a going concern within the Value Added Tax (Special Provisions) Order 1981, SI 1981/1741, art 12. The commissioners' claim would fail.

Hordern v Customs and Excise Comrs [1992] VATTR 382 (Value added tax tribunal).

2613 Input tax—taxable and exempt supplies—apportionment

The taxpayer company converted a large house into ten self-contained flats to be let as holiday accommodation. It so advertised the flats but only some were let as holiday accommodation. It granted a one-year lease of the whole building to a company for the purpose of accommodating its employees. The Commissioners of Customs and Excise sought to recover part of the input tax credited to the taxpayer in respect of the supplies of goods and services used in the conversion of the house on the ground that an exempt supply (ie the lease) had been made before the intended supply (ie the holiday accommodation). *Held*, there was no supply of holiday accommodation unless the flats were provided to tenants to whom they had been advertised as holiday accommodation. The provision of accommodation, not the publication of the advertisement, made such a supply taxable under the Value Added Tax Act 1983, Sch 6, Group 1, item 1(aa). As there was no causative nexus between the publication of the advertisement of the holiday flats and the letting of the whole building for a different purpose, there was no provision of holiday accommodation within the meaning of Sch 6, Group 1, item 1(aa). No entitlement to deduct value added tax, under Council Directive (EC) 77/388, art 17(2)(a), arose until the goods and services had been used in a taxable supply. Article 17(5)(c), which permitted member states to authorise a deduction of value added tax on the basis of the use of all or part of the goods and services, applied to both a conventional once-and-for-all deduction where no time elapsed between intended use and actual use and to a scheme of provisional deduction and subsequent adjustment to such deduction. Accordingly, the input tax for which credit had been claimed had to be apportioned between the charge on supplies used in the making of taxable supplies of holiday accommodation and those used in the making of the exempt supply of the one-year lease.

Cooper and Chapman (Builders) Ltd v Customs and Excise Comrs [1993] STC 1 (Queen's Bench Division: Brooke J).

2614 Misdeclaration—serious misdeclaration—reasonable excuse

The taxpayer company's value added tax return overstated its entitlement to a repayment of tax and understated its tax liability. As the amount of the repayment of input tax claimed was not unusually high, the company secretary was not alerted to the possibility of an error when she signed the return. On its appeal against a serious misdeclaration penalty, the taxpayer contended that an inexperienced accounts clerk had failed to notice an error made by an unidentified employee and that pressure of work of the company secretary made it effectively impossible for the error to be detected so that the taxpayer had a reasonable excuse for the error. *Held*, the Finance Act 1985, s 33(2)(b), which provided that when reliance was placed on any other person to perform any task, neither the fact of such reliance, nor any dilatoriness or innacuracy by that other person was a reasonable excuse, did not impose more stringent requirements for the establishment of a reasonable excuse in cases where the taxpayer had relied on other persons than where no such reliance had been placed. The taxpayer had failed to establish a reasonable excuse for its misdeclaration and its appeal would be dismissed.

Frank Galliers Ltd v Customs and Excise Comrs [1993] STC 284 (Queen's Bench Division: Hutchison J).

2615 Overpayments—interest—prescribed rate

The Value Added Tax Act 1983 (Interest on Overpayments etc) (Prescribed Rate) Order 1993, SI 1993/192 (in force 6 February 1993), reduces the prescribed rate of interest payable under the Value Added Tax Act 1983, s 38A in cases of official error from 10·25 per cent to 8 per cent.

2616 Payments on account

The Value Added Tax (Payments on Account) Order 1993, SI 1993/2001 (in force on 2 September 1993), replaces the Value Added Tax (Payments on Account) (No 2) Order 1992, SI 1992/1668. The new order continues to require a taxable person whose value added tax liability in respect of a specified period exceeded £2m to make payments on account of tax that he may become liable to pay in respect of his tax periods but now applies also to taxable persons whose value added tax liability did not exceed that amount in the specified period but exceeds that amount in a subsequent period of a year. If the total amount of tax which a taxable person, who is under a duty to make payments on account, is less than £1,600,000, the duty ceases. The time for payment remains unchanged but now, where a taxable person has agreed with the Commissioners of Customs and Excise to pay tax by credit transfer, his time for making any payment on account is extended by seven days. Provision is made for reduction and increase of payments in specified circumstances.

2617 Refund of tax—repayment to Community traders

The Value Added Tax (Repayment to Community Traders) (Amendment) Regulations 1993, SI 1993/1223 (in force on 31 May 1993), made in consequence of a defect in SI 1992/3098, which is revoked, further amends the 1980 Regulations, SI 1980/1537, so as to enable Community traders whose taxable supplies fall to be taxed in accordance with the Value Added Tax Act 1983, s 32B (overseas suppliers accounting through their customers) to be entitled to repayment of tax under the regulations.

2618 Refund of tax—repayment to third country traders

The Value Added Tax (Repayments to Third Country Traders) (Amendment) Regulations 1993, SI 1993/1222 (in force on 31 May 1993), made in consequence of a defect in SI 1992/3153, which is revoked, amends the 1987 Regulations, SI 1987/2015, so as to enable third country traders whose taxable supplies fall to be taxed in accordance with the Value Added Tax Act 1983, s 32B (overseas suppliers accounting through their customers) to be entitled to repayment of tax under the regulations.

2619 Registration—duty to furnish return—period to which return relates—period exceeding 12 months—compatability of statute with Community law

B had traded as an unregistered trader for value added tax purposes for several years. B then registered for value added tax and the business was taken over by the appellant firm, with B as one of the partners. During a visit by a Customs and Excise officer it was discovered that the business should have been registered at an earlier date. The appellant firm was requested by Customs and Excise to produce a return and details of turnover for the 12-year period before registration. No return was submitted and the Customs and Excise Commissioners then raised an assessment and imposed penalties for failure to register during the 12-year period. A value added tax tribunal dismissed an appeal by the appellant firm against the assessment. The appellant firm appealed against the decision of the tribunal and argued that: (1) the commissioners could not lawfully require the production of a return for a period exceeding one year as this was contrary to Council Directive (EC) 77/388, art 22(4), which provides that a tax period must not exceed one year. If the Value Added Tax (General) Regulations 1985, SI 1985/886, reg 58(1)(c), permitted the commissioners to extend the length of a return period then it was ultra vires the enabling statute in that the extension was retrospective and this was not authorised. (2)

As a penalty was imposed for failure to notify liability to register for value added tax, the appellant firm should not also have to account for tax which had not been received from its customers. (3) Since it was B and not the appellant firm who was required to be registered during the 12-year period, the wrong person had been assessed. *Held*, (1) the commissioners were entitled to ask for a return covering the 12-year period as it was merely an accumulation of the quarterly returns which should have been made by the appellant firm and which the commissioners were permitted to ask for. Accordingly, reg 58(1)(c), under which the commissioners purported to vary the first period for returns, was not ultra vires the enabling statute, or in conflict with art 22(4) of the directive. The 12-year period concerned was made up of a number of periods which individually did not exceed a year. (2) The imposition of a penalty and the assessment of tax due were not alternative processes. (3) The original obligation to account for the tax was on B. However the appellant firm had taken over B's registration and had undertaken to pay any value added tax due by B, therefore the assessment was valid. Accordingly, the appeal would be dismissed.

Bjellica v Customs and Excise Comrs [1993] STC 730 (Queen's Bench Division: Leonard J).

2620 Registration—liability to be registered—increase of limits

The Value Added Tax (Increase of Registration Limits) Order 1993, SI 1993/766 (in force in part on 17 March 1993 and in part on 1 May 1993), amends the Value Added Tax Act 1983 by increasing from £36,600 to £37,600 the value added tax registration limits for taxable supplies and acquisitions from other member states and increasing the limit for cancellation of registration in the case of taxable supplies from £35,100 to £36,000, with effect from 1 May 1993, and in the case of acquisitions from £36,600 to £37,600, with effect from 17 March 1993.

The Value Added Tax (Increase of Registration Limits) (No 2) Order 1993, SI 1993/2953 (in force in part on 1 December 1993 and in part on 1 January 1994), amends the Value Added Tax Act 1983 by increasing the value added tax registration limits for taxable supplies and acquisitions from other member states from £37,600 to £45,000, with effect from 1 December 1993 in the case of taxable supplies and from 1 January 1994 in the case of acquisitions; and by increasing the limit for cancellation of registration in the case of taxable supplies from £36,000 to £43,000, with effect from 1 December 1993, and in the case of acquisitions from £37,600 to £45,000, with effect from 1 January 1994.

2621 Registration—liability to be registered—reasonable excuse for failure to register

The taxpayer, a tunnel miner, worked for a building contractor who registered him as self-employed for income tax purposes. The taxpayer engaged the services of an unqualified accountant to look after his tax affairs. The building contractor advised the taxpayer to obtain a value added tax number. The taxpayer completed and signed a value added tax form sent to him by his accountant and believed that he would then be registered. He discovered subsequently that the accountant had submitted no income tax return on his behalf and that he was not registered for value added tax. The accountant could not be traced. On the taxpayer's appeal against a penalty for failure to notify his liability to be registered, *held*, the taxpayer knew of the basic requirement to be registered for value added tax and had taken immediate steps to register. He had not relied on a third party who was inaccurate or dilatory; he had employed an accountant who did nothing at all but had misrepresented the true position to the taxpayer who was a working man with only a basic education. There was a reasonable excuse for the taxpayer's failure to register and his appeal would be allowed.

Chapman v Customs and Excise Comrs [1992] VATTR 402 (Value added tax tribunal).

2622 Registration—taxable person becoming incapacitated—person carrying on business of taxable person

A company to which a bank had granted a loan facility to acquire three properties failed to pay interest due on the loan. The bank, therefore, appointed a receiver to collect the rents from the tenants of the properties. The company, having elected to waive its exemption from value added tax, was registered for value added tax. It fell to be determined whether the receiver was liable to account to the Commissioners of Customs and Excise for the value added tax element in the rents collected by him or whether he might apply it in discharge of the principal and interest due to the bank. The receiver contended that he was not an administrative receiver and had not been involved in carrying on the business of the company or dealing with its assets generally. *Held*, by virtue of the Value Added Tax Act 1983, s 31, which empowered the commissioners to make provision for persons carrying on the business of a taxable person who had become "incapacitated" (which included a company in receivership), the commissioners might treat as a taxable person any person carrying on the business in question. The receiver was carrying on the business of the company in relation to the three properties. The commissioners had to be able to collect the revenues collected by others in the name of the primary taxable person. The receiver was the company's agent. The company remained the primary taxable person. The receiver, therefore, was liable to account to the commissioners for the value added tax in question.

Sargent v Customs and Excise Comrs [1994] STC 1 (Chancery Division: Judge Paul Baker QC). *Re John Willment (Ashford) Ltd* [1979] 2 All ER 615 (1979 Abr para 357) followed.

2623 Registration—voluntary registration—intention to trade

The taxpayer company applied for registration as an intending trader. It provided evidence of its formation and objects, the opening of a bank account and the purchase of a fax machine. It operated from the home of a director but, at the time of application, had incurred no other expenditure and carried on no business activity although it claimed that it was negotiating with potential customers and suppliers. The Commissioners of Customs and Excise sought more precise evidence that its intention to trade was genuine. On the taxpayer's appeal against the refusal of registration, *held*, the onus was on the taxpayer to show that it intended to make taxable supplies. The requirement of United Kingdom law to satisfy the commissioners of the intention to make taxable supplies under the Value Added Tax Act 1983, Sch 1, para 5(b) did not conflict with the general right to deduct input tax under Council Directive (EC) 77/388, arts 17, 22(8). In view of the commissioners' duty to protect the Revenue, they were justified in requiring further evidence from the taxpayer whose appeal would be dismissed.

Golden Pyramid Ltd v Customs and Excise Comrs [1993] 2 CMLR 321 (Value added tax tribunal).

2624 Supply of goods and services—credit service—group of companies—representative member of group—self-finance credit

The taxpayer was the holding company of a group of companies consisting of retail outlets and a consumer credit service which provided a credit card for use by customers of the retail outlets. It was assessed for value added tax, under the Value Added Tax Act 1983, s 29, as the representative member of the group. It fell to be determined whether value added tax became payable on the supply of goods to the customer or when the taxpayer received payment from the credit service. *Held*, the taxpayer was entitled to be treated as carrying on both the credit and retail businesses of the group. Accordingly, the supply of credit was a supply of self-finance credit. Value added tax was payable, therefore, when the taxpayer received payment from the credit service.

Customs and Excise Comrs v Kingfisher plc [1994] STC 63 (Queen's Bench Division: Popplewell J).

2625 Supply of goods and services—fuel for private use—consideration for fuel—increase

The Value Added Tax (Increase of Consideration for Fuel) Order 1993, SI 1993/765 (in force for prescribed accounting periods beginning after 5 April 1993), substitutes the Finance Act 1986, Sch 6, Table A so as to increase by 20 per cent the fixed scale used as the basis for charging value added tax on road fuel provided by businesses for private motoring.

The Value Added Tax (Increase of Consideration for Fuel) (No 2) Order 1993, SI 1993/2952 (in force for prescribed accounting periods beginning after 5 April 1994), substitutes the Finance Act 1986, Sch 6, Table A so as to increase by 6 per cent the fixed scale used as the basis for charging value added tax on road fuel provided by businesses for private motoring. The order also amends SI 1993/765 supra.

2626 Supply of goods and services—modification of retail scheme—deductions for agents' own purchases

The taxpayer was the representative member of a group of companies which sold goods by mail order through agents. Agents received a ten per cent rebate for agent's own purchases (AOPs). As some of the goods supplied were standard-rated for the purposes of value added tax, and some were zero-rated, the taxpayer had agreed with the Commissioners of Customs and Excise to operate a modified version of Retail Scheme H whereby the split between standard-rated and zero-rated goods was assessed and applied to gross takings. When assessing output tax, it was also necessary to make reductions on the gross takings to take account of the AOP rebate. An arrangement was therefore made whereby the percentage of AOPs would be estimated from a test sample and the tax liability worked out accordingly. This arrangement was applied for a few years until the taxpayer discovered that the AOP percentages had been incorrectly estimated in the past and began to use a revised percentage for subsequent payments. The commissioners accepted in correspondence that the revised percentage could be used for subsequent accounting periods but rejected the taxpayer's claims to apply it retrospectively. The commissioners issued two assessments, the smaller one in respect of tax undeclared by the taxpayer in the then current accounting period and the larger one to recover the deductions claimed by the taxpayer retrospectively. A value added tax tribunal upheld the larger assessment but ruled in favour of the taxpayer in relation to the smaller assessment. The taxpayer appealed against the decision in relation to the larger assessment and the commissioners appealed against the decision in relation to the smaller assessment. *Held*, it was plain that the taxpayer had adopted a modified version of Retail Scheme H for the purpose of calculating the proportion of receipts derived from AOPs. Letters exchanged between the parties constituted offers to cover the ensuing three-year period which, when taken up by the submission of the first return on the offered basis, were binding on the taxpayer for the next three years. Moreover, even if the arrangements were not a modification of Retail Scheme H, the correspondence taken as a whole evidenced an agreement between the parties which stood on its own. Having entered into such an agreement, the taxpayer could not now resile from it without securing the agreement of the commissioners. Accordingly, the taxpayer's appeal would be dismissed and the commissioners' appeal would be allowed.

GUS Merchandise Corp Ltd v Customs and Excise Comrs (No 2) [1993] STC 738 (Queen's Bench Division: Hutchison J).

2627 Supply of goods and services—retailers' scheme—change in rate of tax

The taxpayer, a retailer of, and mail order trader in, both standard-rated and zero-rated goods, used one of a number of retail schemes under which it did not account for value added tax until a customer paid for goods instead of when the goods were supplied to the customer. The standard rate of value added tax was increased and an Appendix to the schemes provided that tax was due at the higher rate in respect of supplies made before the date of the increase. The taxpayer appealed against an assessment based on the new rate of tax in respect of supplies made before the date of the increase but for which it had not received payment until after that date. *Held*, by virtue of Council Directive (EC) 77/388, art 10, value added tax became chargeable when goods were delivered. Member states were entitled, under art 10(2), to institute retail schemes and were neither required to notify the EC Commission nor to obtain its consent to such measures. In instituting such schemes, they were entitled to derogate from art 10. Where a member state did institute a scheme, the rate of tax became, by virtue of art 12(1)(a), that in force at the time of receipt of payment for a supply, not the time of delivery. The retail schemes in question did derogate from art 10. By virtue of art 27(1), derogations from Community legislation intended to simplify the procedure for charging tax could not affect the amount of tax due at the final consumption stage except to a negligible extent. For the purpose of notifiable derogations under art 27(1), the final consumption stage was the time of delivery. The Appendix affected the amount of tax due at the final consumption stage to a material extent. The provisions relating to changes in the rate of tax were, therefore, invalid. The appeal would be allowed.

Next plc v Customs and Excise Comrs [1993] 2 CMLR 993 (Value added tax tribunal).

2628 Supply of goods and services—supply for a consideration—economic activity—grant of building rights over immovable property

See *van Tiem v Staatssecretaris van Financiën*, para 2749.

2629 Supply of goods and services—supply for a consideration—purchase by credit card—commission deducted by credit card issuer

See *SA Chaussures Bally v Ministry of Finance, Belgium*, para 2747.

2630 Supply of goods and services—supply for a consideration—right to occupy premises rent-free while carrying out repairs

The taxpayer company agreed to lease a sawmill from an associated company for 25 years of which the first three years were to be rent-free while the taxpayer carried out repairs and modifications to the sawmill, and thereafter at an annual rent which was to be subject to rent reviews every five years. The taxpayer claimed and received input tax on the value added tax charged on the goods and services supplied in connection with the building works. The Commissioners of Customs and Excise assessed the taxpayer to value added tax on the basis that the work carried out to the sawmill was a supply to the lessor. On the taxpayer's appeal against the assessment, *held*, under the agreement, the taxpayer was to receive the right to occupy the sawmill for three years rent-free in return for undertaking the repairs and modifications. The three-year rent-free period was directly linked to the taxpayer's undertaking and was properly to be regarded as consideration for the supply of services which consisted of the building work. That agreement was incorporated into the lease. The taxpayer was liable to account for value added tax on those services supplied to the landlord.

Ridgeons Bulk Ltd v Customs and Excise Comrs [1992] VATTR 169 (Value added tax tribunal).

2631 Supply of goods and services—supply of hairdressing services—self-employed stylists supplying services on taxpayer's premises

The taxpayer company carried on business as hairdressers. It entered into agreements with senior hair stylists, previously employed by it, under which they agreed to operate on the taxpayer's premises as self-employed hairdressers. The Inland Revenue accepted that they were self-employed for income tax purposes. It fell to be determined for value added tax purposes whether the stylists supplied their services to the customers on their own behalf as self-employed persons or on behalf of, or as agents of, the taxpayer. *Held*, the question as to whom the services were supplied depended on the relationship between the stylists and the taxpayer. In determining that issue, it was not crucial how the customers perceived the matter. The stylists' hairdressing activities were more consistent with contracts for services than contracts of service. Accordingly, they supplied their services as self-employed hairdressers to the customers, not to the taxpayer.

Customs and Excise Comrs v MacHenrys (Hairdressers) Ltd [1993] STC 170 (Queen's Bench Division: Potts J).

2632 Supply of goods and services—supply of services

The Value Added Tax (Supply of Services) Order 1993, SI 1993/1507 (in force on 1 August 1993), provides that a person carrying on a business who puts services which have been supplied to him to any private use or uses them, or makes them available to any person for use, for a purpose other than a purpose of the business is to be treated as supplying those services in the course or furtherance of the business. In such circumstances, where the taxable person has treated as his input tax the whole of the value added tax charged to him on the supply of the services, the total tax charge cannot exceed the amount of the input tax deducted.

2633 Supply of goods and services—supply of single service or separate services—services supplied by company for unrecognised government

The international community had not recognised Bophuthatswana as an independent sovereign state and it was therefore unable to maintain an accredited diplomatic mission in the United Kingdom. The taxpayer company was established and funded by the Bophuthatswanan government to own and maintain houses and rent offices in the United Kingdom for the purposes of the Bophuthatswanan government, to develop trading opportunities and encourage investment in Bophuthatswana. A value added tax tribunal declared that the taxpayer was liable to tax on the basis that it was providing a single supply of services of the kind that would be supplied by an accredited diplomatic mission. On appeal, it was held that the supply made by the taxpayer was not a single supply of services but the supply of a number of separate services, some or all of which were zero-rated. On appeal by the Commissioners of Customs and Excise, *held*, it was acceptable to approach a supply of goods or services as if it involved a single transaction where the supply was a single simple transaction or type of transaction involving two or more elements, and it was necessary to decide what was the true and substantial nature of the consideration given for the payment. However, although there was only a single commercial relationship between the taxpayer and the government of Bophuthatswana, in the present case the individual supplies of goods and services in the course of that relationship appeared to vary widely both in nature and in taxability or potential taxability. It was not right to cast over them a blanket label of "services of the sort ordinarily provided by a diplomatic mission" and conclude that, since these words did not appear in the relieving provisions of the Value Added Tax Act 1983, the whole of the services must be charged at the standard rate. It was essential to analyse the individual supplies of goods and services by reference to the specific taxing and relieving provisions of the 1983 Act, as a preliminary to deciding whether any of them were no more than ancillary or incidental to another or others and if so, how the money paid by the Bophuthatswana government should appropriately and fairly be apportioned between them. Accordingly, the appeal would be dismissed.

Bophuthatswana National Commercial Corp Ltd v Customs and Excise Comrs [1993] STC 702 (Court of Appeal: Neill, Nolan and Evans LJJ). Decision of Rose J [1992] STC 741 (1992 Abr para 2717) affirmed.

2634 Supply of goods and services—supply received from abroad—reverse charge

The Value Added Tax (Reverse Charge) Order 1993, SI 1993/2328 (in force on 1 November 1993), revokes the 1992 Order, SI 1992/3128, and varies the Value Addded Tax Act 1983, Sch 3, so as to extend the application of the reverse charge provisions of s 7 to all supplies of services not already covered where the customer is registered in the United Kingdom, thereby making the customer liable for value added tax instead of the overseas supplier.

2635 Supply of goods and services—taxi cab hire—whether proprietor acting as principal

The taxpayer traded as a mini-cab driver and private-hire proprietor. He had arrangements with drivers (journeymen) under which he provided them with vehicles and bore expenses. In return, the drivers paid him a percentage of the takings. The taxpayer also had arrangements with owner drivers who paid him for the use of radio and booking services. Although most customers paid by cash, some paid by credit. A Customs and Excise Commissioner determined that in such cases the taxpayer was acting, not as he contended, as the principal, with the journeymen and the owners acting as his employees, but as agent for the drivers concerned, and as such had made supplies liable to Value Added Tax. On appeal, a value added tax tribunal determined that the question it had to decide was who supplied the services when providing transport for credit customers. The tribunal found that there was no special arrangement between the taxpayer and the journeymen or owners as regards credit customers, that there was only one form of contractual relationship between the taxpayer and both the journeymen and owners and that the taxpayer had incorrectly dealt with the income and expenditure relating to the credit customers so far as such affected his liability to value added tax. On appeal, *held*, the tribunal did not err in law either by posing the wrong question or by failing to take material considerations into account. Its decision was one which was plainly open to it on the material before it and it could not be said that it was a decision inconsistent with the only proper construction of the facts proved. The taxpayer's appeal would accordingly be dismissed.

Carless v Customs and Excise Comrs [1993] STC 632 (Queen's Bench Division: Hutchison J).

2636 Supply of goods and services—value of supply—determination of value

By virtue of the Value Added Tax Act 1983, Sch 4, para 3, where the whole or part of a business carried on by a taxable person consists in supplying to a number of non-taxable persons goods to be sold, whether by them or others, by retail, the Commissioners of Customs and Excise may direct that the value of any such supply is to be taken to be its open market value.

The taxpayer company was the parent company of a group of trading companies. One of its subsidiaries carried on a mail order business, selling its goods through agents. The agents, who were not registered for value added tax, bought the goods for less than the full price advertised in the subsidiary's catalogues. Goods ordered by the agents were either retained by them for themselves or resold to customers. The Commissioners of Customs and Excise gave a direction, under the 1983 Act, Sch 4, para 3, that the value of the supply of goods to the agents should be taken to be its open market value on a sale by retail. On appeal against the notice, the taxpayer contended that the direction was invalid because, when it supplied goods to the agents, it neither knew nor cared whether the agents would resell the goods, and it was inconsistent with Council Directive (EC) 77/388. *Held*, the taxpayer was capable of finding out what proportion of an agent's orders were for resale and it could not escape the incidence of tax by failing so to find out. The commissioners' direction simply mirrored the language of the statutory provision empowering them to act as they had done. That language had not been held invalid by the European Court of Justice. The direction required the taxpayer to estimate the open market value of the goods supplied by it. As it was impossible or excessively difficult to ascertain the actual prices at which the goods were sold to all the customers, the commissioners were entitled to use the open market value as the basis of their assessments. The direction did not conflict with any principle of Community law. The appeal would be dismissed.

Fine Art Developments plc v Customs and Excise Comrs [1993] STC 29 (Queen's Bench Division: Brooke J).

2637   Taxable person—activity engaged in as public authority—activity entrusted to third party—exemption

See *Ayuntamiento de Sevilla v Recaudodores de las Zonas Primera y Segunda*, para 2748.

2638   Tribunal—direction—failure to comply with direction

Scotland

The taxpayer appealed against the refusal of his claim for a refund of value added tax. He withdrew his objection to the application of the Commissioners of Customs and Excise for an extension of time to serve their statement of case and list of documents on the understanding that they would be required to file the documents by a particular date. The tribunal made a direction to that effect but the commissioners failed to lodge the documents by that date. At the hearing of the appeal, the taxpayer contended that the tribunal should, accordingly, in the exercise of its discretion, allow his appeal. The tribunal allowed the appeal. On appeal by the commissioners, *held*, the question was whether the tribunal had exercised its discretion reasonably and in a judicial manner. The test of unreasonableness or injustice had to be applied to the facts and circumstances before the tribunal at the time it exercised its discretion. No reason or excuse had been presented to the tribunal to justify it excusing the commissioners' failure to comply with the direction which had been given to avoid further delay. The tribunal was entitled to expect them to comply strictly with the direction. In the absence of any mitigating circumstances, the tribunal was entitled to exercise its discretion to allow the appeal. The appeal would be refused.

Customs and Excise Comrs v Young [1993] STC 394 (Inner House).

2639   Zero rating—building work—construction of building

Scotland

The taxpayer school was granted planning permission to build a new accommodation block on condition that the sewage treatment plant serving the existing buildings was replaced. It fell to be determined whether the installation of the replacement sewage treatment plant, which included civil engineering work, was standard-rated or zero-rated for value added tax purposes. *Held*, in the Value Added Tax Act 1983, Sch 5, Group 8, item 2, by virtue of which the supply of any services in the course of the construction of a building was zero-rated, the expression "any services" was unqualified. Services of a civil engineering nature might qualify for zero-rating provided that they were supplied in the course of the construction of a relevant building. The critical question was whether the installation of the replacement sewage treatment plant was supplied in the course of construction of the new accommodation block. "In the course of" referred to services done contemporaneously or consecutively in relation to a new building and had a substantial connection with the new building. That was a question of degree. The new sewage treatment plant was constructed only because the new accommodation block was built at the school and approximately two-thirds of the cost of the new sewage treatment plant could reasonably be treated as attributable to the needs of the new accommodation block. The installation of the new sewage treatment plant was contemporaneous or consecutive to the building of the new accommodation block with the construction of which it had a substantial connection. It fell to be regarded as services of a civil engineering nature supplied in the course of the construction of the new accommodation block and was, accordingly, zero-rated.

Customs and Excise Comrs v Rannoch School Ltd [1993] STC 389 (Inner House).

2640   Zero rating—building work—conversion, reconstruction, alteration or enlargement of existing building

In the first case, planning permission was granted for the replacement of an old church by a new church provided that the old church tower was retained. The tower was blocked off and repaired. Only ten per cent of the old church, excluding the tower, remained. In the second case, a new building, adjoining an existing nursing home, was constructed. The existing building housed the dining room, the kitchen and the administrative offices of the home and was connected to the new building, which contained 12 bedrooms, bathrooms and staff accommodation, by a passageway. In the third case, a derelict cottage with no roof and only 65 per cent of its original walls remaining was partially demolished and a new house was constructed. About 35 per cent of the original walls were used in the new house. It fell to be determined whether the supplies made in the course of each of the building works were zero-rated, under the Value Added Tax Act 1983, Sch 5, Group 8, item 2, on the ground that they were made "in the course of the construction of a building" or whether the works constituted "the conversion, reconstruction, alteration or enlargement of an existing building", under Sch 5, Group 8, note (9)(a), and, as such, were not to be regarded as "construction" so that the supplies were standard-rated. *Held*, the word "alteration" would not be applied to any work to the fabric of a building short of complete erection or complete destruction. Where it was beyond argument that a building was in existence before the work began, all Sch 5, Group 8, note 9(a) required was to consider the building as it was, to consider the end result and to ask whether the work done amounted to the conversion, reconstruction, alteration or enlargement of an original building, in the sense in which those words were commonly used, or whether the end result was a new building. Whether the work amounted to the conversion, reconstruction, alteration or enlargement of an original building was a question of fact and degree. In the first case, there had been virtually total demolition and a new building which absorbed no more than cosmetic details from the old building. The work on the tower was a separate project with separate supplies; that work, even if regarded as incorporated in the main project did not make the rest of the work an alteration or enlargement of an existing building. The supplies in respect of that work were zero-rated. In the second case, the planning permission had required there to be a connecting door between the existing building and the new structure; and the new accommodation could only be used in conjunction with the facilities provided in the existing building. The new structure was an extension to an existing building which provided internal access to it. The supplies in respect of that work were also zero-rated. In the third case, the cottage had been an existing building at the outset but, after demolition, what remained was not an existing building so that the work concerned did not amount to the reconstruction of an existing building. The supplies in respect of that work were standard-rated.

Customs and Excise Comrs v London Diocesan Fund; Customs and Excise Comrs v Elliott; Customs and Excise Comrs v Penwith Property Co Ltd [1993] STC 369 (Queen's Bench Division: McCullough J). Dictum of Lord Diplock in *Customs and Excise Comrs v Viva Gas Appliances Ltd* [1983] STC 819 at 823, HL (1983 Abr para 3530), not followed.

2641 Zero rating—clothing and footwear—protective boots and helmets

The Value Added Tax (Protective Boots and Helmets) Order 1993, SI 1993/767 (in force on 6 April 1993), amends the Value Added Tax Act 1983, Sch 5, Group 17 so that protective boots and helmets for industrial use and motor cycle crash helmets which satisfy the provisions of Council Directive (EC) 89/686 and bear the appropriate EC mark of conformity are treated for tax purposes as articles which satisfy standards approved by the British Standards Institution and bear a marking indicating compliance with the appropriate specification.

2642 Zero rating—food—beverages

The Value Added Tax (Beverages) Order 1993, SI 1993/2498 (in force on 1 December 1993), amends the Value Added Tax Act 1983, Sch 5, Group 1, by extending the standard rate of value added tax from manufactured beverages to all beverages, except for milk and other beverages included in the items overriding the exceptions.

2643 Zero rating—services for overseas purposes—supplies of training to overseas governments for sovereign activities

An extra-statutory concession allows zero rating for training services, other than exempt training, supplied in the United Kingdom to overseas governments for the purpose of their sovereign activities. The concession replaces a similar relief previously in the Value Added Tax Act 1983, Sch 5, Group 9. The relief is intended for the training in the United Kingdom of overseas government officials, public servants and members of organisations such as the armed forces, the police, the emergency services and similar bodies answerable to the government in question. In order for the relief to apply, the supplier of the services must retain a statement in writing from the relevant government or its accredited representative certifying that the trainees are employed in furtherance of its sovereign activities. The relief does not apply to the training of personnel from government-owned businesses or sponsored commercial organisations such as state airlines or nationalised industries but value added tax charged on supplies to such businesses may be reclaimed under specified arrangements. The concession has effect from 1 October 1993. See further *STI*, 21 October 1993.

2644 Zero rating—transport—repair or maintenance of ship

The taxpayer carried on business as marine engineers and ship repairers. It was engaged to carry out work on a 50-year-old harbour tug which had been purchased by a company for use as a support vessel for racing yachts owned by it. The work included repairs and refurbishment as well as the installation of specialised navigational computer equipment. A repair workshop and an area for entertaining yacht crews and journalists were also installed. On the taxpayer's appeal against an assessment to value added tax made on the basis that the services and goods supplied by it to the tug's owners were standard-rated, *held*, the work carried out by the taxpayer did not constitute "a treatment or process" to the tug in her original condition within the Value Added Tax Act 1983, Sch 2, para 2, nor was such work either repair or maintenance of the tug within Sch 5, Group 10, item 1. Accordingly, the goods and services supplied by the taxpayer were not zero-rated but were standard-rated. The work carried out to the tug could be described as "modifications" of the vessel within Council Directive (EC) 77/388, art 5(4), (5). As the terms of art 15 were unconditional and sufficiently precise, the taxpayer could rely on them to exempt the work from tax if the tug was used for commercial activities. However, the tug was not so used because its owners, who used the equipment on the tug for evaluating the performance of yachts with which they competed in races, used the tug for recreation or pleasure not for reward or as part of a business carried on by them. The work was standard-rated and, therefore, the appeal would be dismissed.

A & P Appledore (Falmouth) Ltd v Customs and Excise Comrs [1992] VATTR 22 (Value added tax tribunal).

VALUERS AND APPRAISERS

Halsbury's Laws of England (4th edn) Vol 49, paras 1–100

2645   Articles

The Environmental Factor, Philip Freedman and Halina Ward (on the effect of environmental factors on valuations): Estates Gazette, 27 November 1993, p 132
Valuation for Local Taxation—The Appeals System, Christopher Lewsley: [1993] 33 RVR 113
Valuation Tribunals—The New Procedures, Brian Hill: Estates Gazette, 7 August 1993, p 67

2646   Duty of care—exclusion of liability—unfair contract term

See *Melrose v Davidson*, para 599.

WAR, ARMED CONFLICT AND EMERGENCY

Halsbury's Laws of England (4th edn) Vol 49, paras 101–200

2647   Chemical weapons—prohibition—international Convention

A Convention on the prohibition of the development, production, stockpiling and use of chemical weapons and on their destruction (Cm 2331) was signed in Paris on 13 January 1993. It will come into force 180 days after the deposit of the 65th ratification (provided that this is not made within two years). The Convention requires parties to make certain declarations, eg as to whether they own or possess chemical weapons (as defined), and reports, eg as to the existence on their territories of such weapons belonging to other countries, within 30 days of the entry of the Convention into force in respect of each country (art III). Provision is made for the destruction of chemical weapons in accordance with the Verification Annex; before their destruction, they are subject to inspection and may not be moved for any purpose other than their destruction (art IV). Parties to the Convention will immediately cease all production of chemical weapons; their production facilities will be subject to inspection and will have to be closed and eventually destroyed in accordance with the Verification Annex (art V). Certain activities are expressly excluded from the application of the Convention (art VI). National laws will have to prohibit natural and legal persons within their jurisdiction from undertaking any activity which is prohibited by the Convention; this prohibition will extend beyond national boundaries. Such laws will also have to prevent any such activity from occurring within any place under their control (art VII). An Organisation for the prohibition of Chemical Weapons will be established under art VIII to implement the Convention. It will be based in The Hague and will comprise a conference of states parties, an executive council and a technical secretariat. The organisation will enjoy legal capacity within the territories of the states parties and also the appropriate privileges and immunities. Any dispute between states, or between a state and the organisation, regarding the interpretation or application of the Convention may, after negotiation, be referred to the International Court of Justice, provided that both parties to the dispute so agree (art XIV). The Convention is of unlimited duration (art XVI) and states may not accede to it subject to reservations, although reservations may be made in respect of the Verification Annex (art XXII). The Convention has not been ratified by the United Kingdom.

2648 Civil defence—local authority—functions

The Civil Defence (General Local Authority Functions) Regulations 1993, SI 1993/1812 (in force on 1 August 1993), replace the 1983 Regulations, SI 1983/1634. The 1993 Regulations set out the civil defence functions of county councils and district councils in non-metropolitan counties. In relation to metropolitan counties and Greater London, the principal civil defence functions of the metropolitan county fire and civil defence authorities and the London Fire and Civil Defence Authority are transferred to the councils of districts and London boroughs and the City of London. The regulations also provide for it to be the function of fire and civil defence authorities to carry out civil defence functions on behalf of any councils in their areas and, at the request of the designated minister or a council, to assist councils in the carrying out of those functions.

2649 Northern Ireland

See NORTHERN IRELAND.

2650 Pensions

See PENSIONS AND SUPERANNUATION.

WATER

Halsbury's Laws of England (4th edn) Vol 49, paras 201–939

2651 Control of pollution—anglers' lead weights

The Control of Pollution (Anglers' Lead Weights) (Amendment) Regulations 1993, SI 1993/49 (in force on 10 February 1993), amend the 1986 Regulations by revoking the restriction on the importation of certain sizes of lead weights.

2652 Control of pollution—bathing water—failure to comply with Community law

See *EC Commission v United Kingdom of Great Britain and Northern Ireland*, para 2703.

2653 Drainage—drainage charges—calculation

The General Drainage Charges (Relevant Quotient) Regulations 1993, SI 1993/165 (in force on 2 February 1993), make provision for the method of ascertaining the quotient to be used to calculate drainage charges for local flood defence districts. They provide for the quotient to be determined by the application of a formula which varies the quotient calculated in respect of the financial year 1989/90.

2654 Internal drainage boards—finance—drainage rates

The Drainage Rates (Forms) Regulations 1993, SI 1993/223 (in force on 3 March 1993), revoke the 1990 Regulations, SI 1990/173, and re-act their provisions with modifications to take account of the abolition of an owner's rate by the Internal Drainage Boards (Finance) Regulations 1990, SI 1990/72.

2655 National Rivers Authority—finance—power to issue levies

The National Rivers Authority (Levies) Regulations 1993, SI 1993/61 (in force on 16 January 1993), replace the 1990 Regulations, SI 1990/118 and confer on the National Rivers Authority a power to raise revenue in order to meet its expenses in respect of local flood defence districts, by the issue of levies to certain local authorities in respect of financial years beginning in or after 1993.

2656 Nitrate sensitive areas—designation

The Nitrate Sensitive Areas (Designation) (Amendment) Order 1993, SI 1993/3198 (in force on 11 January 1994), amends the 1990 Order, SI 1990/1013. Under the Water Resources Act 1991, s 95 the Minister of Agriculture, Fisheries and Food may, in areas designated as nitrate sensitive areas, enter into agreements with farmers imposing obligations on them with respect to land-management in return for payments. The principal order differentiated between basic and premium scheme agreements and provided for a review of payments. The 1993 Order increases the rates of payment for agreements made under the premium scheme in respect of claims for payment made after the period beginning on 1 August 1993.

2657 Pollution—discharge into controlled waters by third party—liability of company

See *National Rivers Authority v Wright Engineering Co Ltd*; *National Rivers Authority v Yorkshire Water Services Ltd*, para 1214.

2658 Towpath—right to use—River Thames

The plaintiff company, the registered proprietor of freehold land, appealed against the dismissal of its claim for possession against the owners of two houseboats moored to the bank of a river by the plaintiff's land. The moorings were by ropes secured to poles and trees on the sloping bank between the towpath and the water's edge. There were also gangplanks from the houseboats which rested on, and were embedded some six inches deep into, the towpath. *Held*, it was not disputed that along the towpath ran a public footpath. However, a public right of foot over a path and a public right of towage were separate and distinct rights. A right of way on foot did not include any right over the river bank. The right of towage, if it still existed, clearly included the right to pass a towrope from the horse on the towpath to the vessel being towed to the land. Neither right extended to the rights claimed by the houseboat owners to maintain their moorings and gangplanks on the bank. Accordingly, the appeal would be allowed.

Sussex Investments Ltd v Jackson (1993) Times, 29, July (Court of Appeal: Balcombe and Farquharson LJJ and Sir Robert Parker).

2659 Water supply and sewerage services—customer service standards

The Water Supply and Sewerage Services (Customer Service Standards) (Amendment) Regulations 1993, SI 1993/500 (in force on 1 April 1993), further amend the 1989 Regulations, SI 1989/1159, so that the right to a payment or credit is no longer restricted to domestic users or to customers who are liable to pay the undertaker's charges. New provisions are introduced which give customers rights of compensation if undertakers fail to comply with certain requirements relating to the interruption of water supplies, the installation of water meters and the escape of effluent into a customer's building. References in the 1989 Regulations to the Water Act 1989 are replaced by references to the corresponding provisions of the Water Industry Act 1991.

WEIGHTS AND MEASURES

Halsbury's Laws of England (4th edn) Vol 50, paras 1–200

2660 Articles

Froth-Blowers Lament, Christine Clayson (on DTI policy towards beer measures): 137 SJ 1192.

2661 Capacity serving measures—intoxicating liquor

The Capacity Serving Measures (Intoxicating Liquor) (Amendment) (Regulations) 1993, SI 1993/2060 (in force on 20 September 1993), amend the 1988 Regulations, SI 1988/120. The regulations remove the obligation to mark a line of a particular thickness and or a minimum length and at a minimum distance from the brim of line measures; remove the obligation to mark the nominal capacity of brim and line measures in characters of a minimum height; and allow inspectors testing the fitness of such measures for use for trade to accept test reports and results from approved bodies in other member states of the European Community for the purpose of avoiding duplicate testing of capacity serving measures imported from those states.

2662 Measuring instruments—non-automatic weighing machines—EC requirements—fees

The Measuring Instruments (EC Requirements) (Fees) Regulations 1993, SI 1993/798 (in force on 9 April 1993), consolidate the Measuring Instruments (EC Requirements) (Fees) Regulations 1988, SI 1988/1184, as amended, and the Non-automatic Weighing Instruments (EC Requirements) (Fees) Regulations 1992, SI 1992/3093. The regulations stipulate the new fees payable in connection with services provided by the Department of Trade and Industry with regard to measuring instruments and non-automatic weighing instruments. All fees in the regulations are payable monthly in arrears except for fixed fees which are payable on completion of the work.

2663 Weights and Measures Act 1985—commencement—revocation

The Weights and Measures Act 1985 (Commencement) (Revocation) Order 1993, SI 1993/2698, revokes the 1992 Order, SI 1992/770, which appointed 1 April 1994 for the coming into force of s 43 (ascertainment of quantity of beer and cider for specified purposes), the only provision of the Act which is not in force. For a summary of the Act, see 1985 Abr para 2880. For details of commencement, see the commencement table in the title STATUTES.

WILLS

Halsbury's Laws of England (4th edn) Vol 50, paras 201–655

2664 Articles

Inheritance (Provision for Family and Dependants) Act 1975, Giles Harrap and Miranda Allardice: 137 SJ 41
The Conduct of Probate Sales, Leslie Dubow: 143 NLJ 1438
Why Make a Will? David A Chatterton: 137 SJ 397

2665 Construction of will—description of property—transfer of money from one account to another—bequest of sums in account

The deceased left certain sums to be added to an existing trust fund, under the terms of her will. The residue after payment of other bequests was left to charities, who were the first and second defendants. In her lifetime the deceased had received an income from the trust fund which had been administered by the third defendant. The third defendant had an enduring power of attorney to deal with her affairs and in order to obtain higher rates of interest he had opened a new account and transferred the funds from the original account. This had been done without the knowledge of the deceased and the third defendant had been unaware of the terms of the will. The executrix made an application for the will to be construed and the question arose as to whether the money in the deceased's account at the time of her death passed as a specific legacy to the trust, or whether it passed as residue to the charities. *Held*, the money in the original account was in the nature of a fund because nearly all the sums in the account had been received from the trust. It could therefore be inferred that the deceased had intended sums from that account which were not spent, to be returned to the trust. If the deceased had intended to bequeath sums held elsewhere to the trust, this would have involved tracing which was a complex matter. In addition, the arrangements for the first and second accounts were on very similar terms. Thus the interest of the deceased in the second account was substantially the same as that in the first account and the change from one account to another was effectively only a change of name. Accordingly, the money would pass to the trust under the terms of the will.

Re Dorman (Deceased) [1994] 1 All ER 804 (Chancery Division: David Neuberger QC).

2666   Construction of will—intention of testator—effect of subsequent legislation

Scotland

The granddaughter of a testator died, leaving three children. The father of those children had been married to another woman at the time of their birth, so he and the granddaughter had not married until some years after their last child had been born. The court had determined that the granddaughter's children could inherit under the terms of the testator's will on the ground that references in the trust disposition to "issue" and "great-grandchildren" meant issue and great-grandchildren who had been legitimate by the time of vesting upon the granddaughter's death. On appeal by another great-grandchild against that decision, *held*, a provision in Scots law that children whose parents subsequently married were legitimate only if the parents of the child had been free to marry each other at the date of conception had been removed by the Legitimation (Scotland) Act 1968, so there was no doubt that at the date of vesting in 1989 the great-grandchildren had been recognised as legitimate. However, the case turned on whether the maker of the disposition had intended that possession of the status of legitimacy at the period of vesting should be determinative of the qualification to take as a beneficiary, and there was no reason to suppose that the testatrix had contemplated the possibility that the law would be changed before the period of vesting so as to result in the legitimation of persons previously incapable of it. The more natural intention to attribute to the testator was that the succession should be regulated by the law as it had stood at the time of the testator's death, rather than by the law as it stood at the time of his granddaughter's death, and, accordingly, the appeal would be allowed.

Miller v Callender (1993) Times, 4 February (House of Lords: Lords Keith of Kinkel, Jauncey of Tullichettle, Lowry, Mustill and Slynn of Hadley).

2667   Deed of variation—validity—omission

See *Schnieder v Mills*, para 978 and *Crowden v Aldridge*, para 2586.

2668   Dissolution or annulment of marriage—effect on will

The Law Commission has published a report, *Family Law: The Effect of Divorce on Wills* (Cm 2322; Law Com No 217), in which it considers the present law that, in the absence of a contrary intention, a former spouse should not benefit from a will made before the marriage was dissolved or anulled. The Commission proposes further amendments to the Wills Act 1837, s 18A (effect of dissolution or annulment of marriage on will) so that property devised or bequeathed to a former spouse should, in the absence of any contrary intention, pass as if the former spouse had died on the date on which the marriage was dissolved or annulled; and any provision appointing the former spouse executor or trustee or conferring a power of appointment on such spouse should take effect as if the spouse had died on such date. The Commission also proposes that the Children Act 1989, s 6 (revocation of appointment of guardian) should be amended so that, in the absence of any contrary intention in the instrument of appointment, any appointment of the former spouse as guardian is revoked as from the date of the dissolution or annulment of the marriage. A draft Bill which would give effect to these recommendations is appended. The Commission expressly states that it does not recommend any change to the present law in relation to secret trusts, contracts to dispose of property by will, testamentary clauses to pay debts owed to or relieve liabilities owed by the former spouse, or to the right of a former spouse to apply under the Inheritance (Provision for Family and Dependants) Act 1975.

2669   Mutual wills—application of doctrine—property left to beneficiaries rather than testators

A married couple each made a will the terms of which were the same. The wills bequeathed all real and personal property in favour of the plaintiff daughter and the defendant son in equal shares and appointed them as executors. The father died without having altered or revoked his will. Probate of his will was granted to the plaintiff and the defendant. Several months later the mother made a new will, revoked all former wills and testamentary dispositions and appointed the defendant to be her executor. She bequeathed to the plaintiff a small sum of money and bequeathed the remainder of her property to the defendant. The mother died several months later. The plaintiff issued a writ alleging that her mother and father had entered an agreement as to the disposition of their respective estates and on the death of her father, her mother had become bound in equity to give effect to the agreement and to dispose of her estate pursuant to the terms of the will but that wrongfully and in breach of that agreement she had revoked that will and left all her estate, excluding a small sum of money, to her defendant brother. She alleged that the consequence was that her brother now held the real and personal estate of the mother as a trustee for herself and himself in equal shares. On a question of law, tried as a preliminary issue, *held*, the basic doctrine of mutual wills was well established and not in dispute. However the doctrine was not to be limited only to cases where the second testator to die gained a benefit under the will of the first testator to die, as the aim of the doctrine was to prevent the first deceased testator from being defrauded by the refusal of the second testator to perform his part of the agreement. It was a logical extension of the rule therefore that the doctrine was also applicable in cases where the two testators had left their property to particular beneficiaries rather than each other. Accordingly, the decision on the preliminary issue would be decided in favour of the plaintiff.

Re Dale [1993] 4 All ER 129 (Chancery Division: Morritt J).

2670 Preparation of will—failure to prepare will—liability of solicitor
See *White v Jones*, para 2423.

2671 Probate
See EXECUTORS AND ADMINISTRATORS.

EUROPEAN COMMUNITIES

Halsbury's Laws of England (4th edn) Vols 51 and 52

The material below comprises cases heard before the European Court of Justice and important legislative developments from the EC Council and Commission. The arrangement of the material conforms with Vols 51 and 52.

2672 Articles
A Trading Nation, Gavin McFarlane: LS Gaz, 24 March 1993, p 17
Acquisition Financing in Europe, Julian Harris: 143 NLJ 1653
Beyond *Frankovic*, Malcolm Ross (on *Frankovic v Italy* [1992] IRLR 84): 56 MLR 55
Criminal Common Law Remedies Against Citizens for Breach of Community Law, David
    Pedley: 157 JP Jo 435, 158 JP Jo 3
EC Practice Briefing, Peter Duffy: 137 SJ 299
EC Services Directive, John Bennett and Stephen Cirell: 137 SJ 18
Enforcement of EC Directives by Individuals, Oliver Hyams: 137 SJ 448
Financial Self-regulation and EC directives, Michel Tison: [1993] LMCLQ 60
Free Selections, Paul Egerton-Vernon (on EC Trade): LS Gaz, 31 March to 23 April 1993
Letting in the Competition, Susan Singleton (on EC competition law): 137 SJ 812
Maternity Rights: The New European Directive, Tess Gill: 137 SJ 8
Multimodal Transport and EC Competition Law, Nick Maltby: [1993] LMCLQ 79
New Era of Trust Within the European Community? Joseph Daly and Robert MacLean: 137
    SJ 325
Proving Equal Value—The European Court Lends a Hand, Brian Napier: 143 NLJ 1648
Services in the Single Market, Peter Hewitt: Tax Journal, Issue 204, p 13
State Aid Challenge, Isabelle Zornoza (on the implications of *CIRFS v Commission* (C-313/90):
    LS Gaz, 7 July 1993, p 31
Sunday Trading Revisited, Paul Diamond: 137 SJ 604
The Effectiveness of European Community Law, Francis Synder: 56 MLR 19
The European Convention on Human Rights—Time to Incorporate, Sir Thomas Bingham
    MR: (1993) 109 LQR 390
The Undeniable Supremacy of EC Law, Emma Chown: 143 NLJ 377
The World Cup and Competition Law, Susan Singleton: 143 NLJ 748

THE COMMUNITIES

**2673 Administration—education—higher education—European co-operation
scheme—Tempus II**
Council Decision (EC) 93/246 adopts the second phase of the trans-European co-operation scheme for higher education (Tempus II) for the years 1994–1998. The objectives of the Tempus

scheme are to promote the development of the higher education systems in the eligible countries, with regard to issues of curriculum development, the reform of higher education structures and institutions and their management, and the development of skill-related training to address specific higher and advanced level skill shortages during economic reform, in particular through improved and extended links with industry. The decision is effective as from 29 April 1993. (OJ L112 6.5.93 p 34.)

2674   Community treaty—agreement between member states and San Marino

The European Communities (Definition of Treaties) (Agreement on Customs Union and Co-operation between the European Economic Community and the Republic of San Marino) Order 1993, SI 1993/1783 (in force on a date to be notified in the London Gazette) declares the Agreement on Customs Union and Co-operation between the European Economic Community and the Republic of San Marino to be a Community Treaty as defined in the European Communities Act 1972, s 1(2). The aim of the Agreement is to contribute to the social and economic development of the Republic and to strengthen relations between the parties. The principal effect of declaring the Agreement to be a Community Treaty is to invoke the provisions of the 1972 Act, s 2, which provides for the implementation of treaties so specified.

2675   Community treaty—European Investment Bank—creation of European Investment Fund

The European Communities (Definition of Treaties) (European Investment Fund) Order 1993, SI 1993/3157 (in force on a date to be notified in the London Gazette), declares the Act amending the Protocol on the Statute of the European Investment Bank (signed by the member states at Brussels on 25 March 1993) to be a Community Treaty as defined in the European Communities Act 1972, s 1(2). The Act amends the Protocol by adding a new article enabling the Board of Governors of the Bank to create the European Investment Fund. The declaration of the Act as a Community Treaty, brings into effect in relation to it the provisions of the 1972 Act, s 2 which provides for the implementation of specified treaties.

2676   EC Commission—Rules of Procedure

The EC Commission has adopted new Rules of Procedure to replace the provisional Rules of Procedure of 1967. The new rules deal with such things as meetings of the Commission, decision-making procedures, departmental and interdepartmental structures and deputising. The rules came into force on 11 September 1993. (OJ L230 11.9.93 p 15.)

2677   European Communities (Amendment) Act 1993

See para 544.

2678   European Parliament—right to vote and stand as a candidate

Council Directive (EC) 93/109 has been adopted laying down detailed arrangements for the exercise of the right to vote and stand as a candidate in elections to the European Parliament for citizens of the Union who are residing in a member state of which they are not nationals. According to art 3, any person who is a citizen of the Union, within the meaning of the EC Treaty, art 8(1) who is not a national of the member state of residence but satisfies the same conditions in respect of the right to vote and stand as a candidate as that state imposes by law on its own nationals, has the right to vote and to stand as a candidate in elections to the European Parliament in the member state of residence unless deprived of those rights by arts 6, 7 of the directive. No person may stand as a candidate in more than one member state at the same election. The right to vote is exercisable either in the member state of residence or in the home member state. No person may vote more than once at the same election. The directive is to be implemented in the member states no later than 1 February 1994. (OJ L329 30.12.93 p 34.)

2679   General provisions—EC Council documents—public access

Council Decision (EC) 93/731 on public access to EC Council documents has been adopted. Article 1 of the decision states that the public is to have access to Council documents (defined as "any written text, whatever its medium, containing existing data and held by the Council"), subject to the conditions laid down in the decision. However, access to a Council document will not be granted where its disclosure could undermine the protection of the public interest, the protection of the individual and of privacy, the protection of commercial and industrial secrecy, the protection of the Community's financial interests, and the protection of confidentiality as requested by the natural or legal person who supplied any of the information contained in the document or as required by the legislation of the member state which supplied any of the information. The decision is in force as of 1 January 1994. (OJ L340 31.12.93 p 43.)

2680 Principles, objectives and tasks—EC Treaty—establishment of internal market—area without internal frontiers—free movement of persons

See *R v Secretary of State for the Home Department, ex p Mehmet Colak*, para 220.

THE COURT OF JUSTICE

2681 Actions—annulment—locus standi—decision of direct and individual concern

Council Directive (EC) 83/416 on the authorisation of scheduled inter-regional air services for the transport of passengers, mail and cargo between member states was amended by Council Directive (EC) 89/463 which laid down new rules giving airlines greater scope to develop markets and to promote the development of direct services between the various regions in the Community rather than indirect services. Pending the coming into operation of the co-operation arrangements agreed between the governments of Spain and the United Kingdom, Gibraltar airport was excluded from the territorial scope of the new rules. Gibraltar sought the annulment of this exclusionary measure. *Held*, the measure affected equally all air carriers who wished to operate a direct inter-regional air service between another Community airport and Gibraltar airport and, more generally, all those using the latter airport. Accordingly, it applied to objectively defined situations. There were other airports also temporarily excluded from the scope of the directive. In view of the differences between Spain and the United Kingdom concerning sovereignty over the territory on which Gibraltar airport was situated and the operational problems resulting from those differences, the development between that airport and the other airports within the Community was conditional on the implementation of the co-operation arrangements agreed between those two states. The measure in question could not be regarded as constituting a decision within the meaning of the EC Treaty, art 173(2), which had the technical meaning employed in art 189 (by virtue of which a decision was binding in its entirety upon those to whom it was addressed) and which enabled a person to institute proceedings against a decision which, although in the form of a regulation or decision addressed to another person, was of direct or individual concern to the former person. The measure in question was of the same general nature as Directive 89/463. The application by Gibraltar was inadmissible and would be dismissed.

Case C-298/89: Government of Gibraltar v EC Council (supported by Kingdom of Spain, United Kingdom and Commission, interveners) (1993) Times, 9 July (ECJ: Full Court).

2682 Ancillary and other proceedings—court or tribunal—definition

It has been held that the words "court or tribunal" in the EC Treaty, art 177 only relate to an authority which is a third party in relation to the body or person adopting the decision which forms the subject matter of the proceedings.

Case C-24/92: Corbiau v Administration des Contributions (1993) Times, 20 May (ECJ: Full Court).

2683 Court of First Instance—extension of jurisdiction

Council Decision (ECSC, EC, Euratom) 93/350 amends Decision 88/591, on the creation of the Court of First Instance, so as to include actions brought by natural or legal persons pursuant to the EC Treaty, arts 178, 181. This effectively means that, with effect from the date of applicability of the decision, the court will be able to hear any case which an individual or a company refers to it, other than anti-dumping matters. The decision is in force on the first day of the second month following that of its publication in the Official Journal. (OJ L144 16.6.93 p 21.)

2684 Preliminary ruling—interpretation of Community law—insufficient information provided by national court

In a dispute relating to competition within the broadcasting industry, an Italian court referred a number of questions concerning the interpretation of certain Community provisions to the

European Court of Justice for a preliminary ruling under the EC Treaty, Art 177. *Held*, the references for a preliminary ruling had lacked detail with regard to the elements of fact and law which would make it possible to establish the purpose of the questions submitted and thereby to understand their meaning and scope. An interpretation of Community law which would be useful for a national court could only be given if the court which made the application had defined the factual and legislative background to the questions which it submitted or had explained the premise on which those questions were based, and in the instant case the information given by the national court had been too fragmentary to enable the European Court of Justice to interpret the Community competition rules in the light of the situation which had arisen in the national court. Accordingly, the European Court of Justice would refuse to answer the questions submitted to it.

Joined Cases C-320–322/90: Telemarsicabruzzo SpA v Circostel (1993) Times, 10 February (ECJ: Full Court).

In a reference to the European Court of Justice on a matter concerning the importation of manufactured tobacco and the interpretation of various EC Treaties and directives, *held*, the interpretation of Community law required the national court to define the factual and legislative background to the reference. The national court had confined itself to referring to the Italian monopoly for manufactured tobacco, without specifying the discrimination complained of in regard to the procurement and sale of goods. The excessively vague reference did not allow the court to give a useful interpretation of Community law and therefore pursuant to the Rules of Procedure, art 92, the questions submitted to the Court for a preliminary ruling were inadmissible. Accordingly, the application would be dismissed.

Case C-157/92: Pretore di Genova v Banchero (1993) Times, 20 May (ECJ: Full Court).

2685 Reference from national court—Convention—jurisdiction—compensation claim—civil actions

The respondents were the relations of a German pupil who during a school trip to Italy was the victim of a fatal accident. The accompanying teacher was prosecuted for manslaughter before an Italian criminal court. The respondents joined those proceedings as civil parties in order to obtain an award for damages. The teacher subsequently lodged an appeal, against the enforcement of that decision in his own country, and made a claim that the relevant public authority should bear the cost of compensating the damage caused, in the event that the proceedings went against him. The appeal was dismissed and on further appeal the proceedings were stayed and a reference was made to the European Court of Justice on the interpretation of the 1968 Convention on Jurisdiction and the Enforcement of Judgments in Civil and Commercial Matters, *held*, (1) "civil matters" within the meaning of the first indent of the Convention art 1, covered an action for damages brought before a criminal court even in cases where social insurance provided liability under public law. In the legal systems of the contracting states the right to obtain compensation for damage suffered, following behaviour deemed to be contrary to criminal law, was generally recognised as being civil in nature. An action could only fall outside the scope of the Convention where the person against whom it had been brought was to be regarded as a public authority having acted in the exercise of its public authority powers. Therefore a claim for damages brought in the context of criminal proceedings against a teacher in a state school who in the course of his duties caused injury to a pupil by reason of a breach of his official duties fell within the definition of "civil matters" under the Convention, art 1. (2) The Convention had established an enforcement procedure which constituted an autonomous and complete system, including the matter of appeals and it followed that art 36, excluded procedures whereby interested parties might challenge an enforcement order under domestic law. Article 37 excluded any action by interested third parties against a decision given in the context of proceedings brought under art 36, even where the domestic law of the state enabled such parties to appeal. (3) The non recognition of a decision for the reasons indicated in the Convention, art 27(2) was only possible where the defendant was in default in the original proceedings. The provision could not be relied upon where the defendant entered an appearance. A defendant was deemed to have entered an appearance where in the context of a claim for compensation connected to criminal proceedings, the defendant stated his position to the criminal proceedings during the hearing of the main issue but not on the civil proceedings which were also subject to argument. Judgment would be given accordingly.

C-172/91: Sonntag v Waidmann (1993) Times, 18 May (ECJ: Full Court).

2686 Specific principles of Community law—force majeure

See *An Bord Bainne Co-operative Ltd v Intervention Board for Agricultural Produce*, para 73.

EXTERNAL RELATIONS

2687   United Nations—sanctions—Serbia and Montenegro—application of EC Treaty where member state imposes restrictive sanctions

See *R v HM Treasury, ex p Centro-Com Sarl*, para 1323.

ECONOMIC AND MONETARY POLICY

2688   European Communities (Amendment) Act 1993

See para 544.

ENVIRONMENT AND CONSUMERS

2689   Consumers—Community Eco-label—standard contract

Commission Decision (EC) 93/517 on a standard contract covering the terms of use of the Community eco-label has been adopted. The Annex to the decision contains a copy of the standard contract and includes articles concerning rights and obligations; advertising; compliance monitoring; confidentiality; suspension and withdrawal; limitation of liability and indemnity; fees; complaints; and contract duration and applicable law. The decision has been adopted in accordance with Council Regulation (EC) 880/92, art 12 on the Community eco-label award scheme (see 1992 Abr para 2787) and is in force as of 15 September 1993. (OJ L243 29.9.93 p 13.)

2690   Consumers—consumer information—tobacco products—labelling

Council Directive (EC) 89/622 on the approximation of the laws, regulations and administrative procedures concerning the labelling of tobacco products required, by arts 3, 4, indications on cigarette packets of tar and nicotine yields, and warnings that tobacco was a serious damage to health to cover at least 4 per cent of the surfaces on which they were printed. The Tobacco Products Labelling (Safety) Regulations 1991, SI 1991/1530, required such indications and warnings to cover at least 6 per cent of those surfaces. It fell to be determined whether the requirements of those regulations were permitted by the directive. *Held*, the directive was designed to eliminate barriers to trade which might arise as a result of differences in national provisions on the labelling of tobacco products and thereby impede the establishment and operation of the internal market. For that purpose, it contained common rules concerning the health warnings and the indications of tar and nicotine yields which were to appear on cigarette packets. The directive was addressed to the member states and not to the manufacturers, who had no interest in using a greater surface area for the indications and warnings in question. In view of the public awareness of the health risks associated with tobacco consumption, the expression "at least" in arts 3, 4 of the directive was to be interpreted as meaning that member states were free, if they considered it necessary, to decide that indications and warnings were to cover a greater surface area than that specified. Accordingly, member states were free to require, so far as domestic production was concerned, that the warnings on cigarette packets might cover a greater surface area of the packet than that required by the directive.

Case C-11/92: R v Secretary of State for Health, ex p Gallagher (1993) Times, 28 June (ECJ: Fifth Chamber).

2691   Consumers—contracts—unfair terms

Council Directive (EC) 93/13 on unfair terms in consumer contracts has been adopted. According to the directive, a contractual term which has not been individually negotiated is to be regarded as unfair if, contrary to the requirement of good faith, it causes a significant imbalance in the parties' rights and obligations arising under the contract, to the detriment of the consumer. A term is to be regarded as not individually negotiated where it has been drafted in advance and the consumer has therefore not been able to influence the substance of the term, particularly in the context of a pre-formulated standard contract. The Annex to the directive contains an indicative and non-exhaustive list of the terms which may be regarded as unfair. These terms include those which have the object or effect of excluding or limiting the legal liability of the seller or supplier in the event of death or personal injury resulting from an act or omission of the seller or supplier; those terms automatically extending a contract of fixed duration where the consumer does not indicate otherwise, when the deadline fixed for the consumer to express his desire not to extend the contract is unreasonably early; those terms which enable the seller or supplier to alter the terms of the contract unilaterally without a valid reason which is specified in the contract; those terms which enable the seller or supplier to alter unilaterally without a valid reason any characteristics of the product or service to be provided; and those terms which exclude or hinder the consumers' right to take legal action or exercise any other legal remedy particularly by requiring the consumer to take disputes exclusively to arbitration not covered by legal provisions. The directive is to be implemented in the member states not later than 31 December 1994. (OJ L95 21.4.93 p 29.)

2692 Consumers—foodstuffs—contaminants in food—Community procedure

Council Regulation (EC) 315/93 lays down a procedure for the adoption of harmonised Community rules in respect of contaminants which may enter into food at any stage from production to consumption. A "contaminant" is any substance not intentionally added to food which is present in such food as a result of the production, manufacture, processing, preparation, treatment, packing, packaging, transport or holding of such foods, or as a result of environmental contamination. The regulation is not to apply to contaminants which are the subject of more specific Community rules. Under art 2, food containing a contaminant in an amount which is unacceptable from the public health viewpoint, and in particular at a toxicological level, is not to be placed on the market. When a member state, as a result of new information or of a reassessment of existing information, has reason to suspect that a contaminant in food, although complying with Regulation 315/93, constitutes a health risk, it may temporarily suspend or restrict application of the provision in question in its territory (OJ L37 13.2.93 p 1.)

2693 Consumers—foodstuffs—hygiene

Council Directive (EC) 93/43 on the hygiene of foodstuffs has been adopted. Food hygiene is defined as being applicable to all measures necessary to ensure the safety and wholesomeness of foodstuffs. The measures are to cover all stages after primary production, during preparation, processing, manufacturing, packaging, storing, transportation, distribution, handling and offering for sale or supply to the consumer. Detailed guidelines of food hygiene are set out which include general requirements for food premises; specific requirements where foodstuffs are prepared, treated or processed; requirements for movable and/or temporary premises, premises used primarily as a private dwelling house, premises used occasionally for catering purposes, and vending machines; transport; equipment requirements; food waste; water supply; personal hygiene; and training. Member states are to bring into force the laws, regulations and administrative provisions necessary to comply with the directive not later than 30 months after adoption. The directive was adopted on 14 June 1993. (OJ L175 19.7.93 p1).

2694 Consumers—health and safety—products which may jeopardise health or safety—exchange of information

Council Decision (EC) 93/580 concerning the institution of a Community system for the exchange of information in respect of certain products which may jeopardise consumers' health or safety has been adopted. Under art 1, any member state which decides to adopt measures to prevent, restrict or attach particular conditions to the marketing or use of a product because it does not comply with Community rules and may jeopardise the health and safety of consumers, must notify the EC Commission. Further, wherever possible the producer, distributor or importer of the product should be consulted first. The decision applies to all products intended for use by consumers except products intended exclusively for professional use. The decision is in force as from 25 October 1993, but only applies until 29 June 1994. (OJ L278 11.11.93 p 64.)

2695 Consumers—health and safety at work—mineral-extracting industry

Council Directive (EC) 92/104 on the minimum requirements for improving the safety and health protection of workers in surface and underground mineral-extracting industries has been adopted. The directive contains a list of general health and safety obligations. These include protection from fire, explosions and health endangering atmospheres; escape and rescue facilities; communications, warning and alarm systems; and an obligation to ensure that the workers receive health surveillance appropriate to the health and safety risks incurred by them. The directive was adopted on 3 December 1992 and is to be implemented in the member states within 24 months of that date. (OJ L404 31.12.92 p 10.)

2696   Environment—air pollution—nitrogen oxides—control of national annual emissions

Council Decision (EC) 93/361 concerns the accession of the Community to the Protocol to the 1979 Geneva Convention on long-range transboundary air pollution in respect of the control of emissions of nitrogen oxides or their transboundary fluxes. Under the Protocol, a copy of which is attached to the decision, the parties are under an obligation to take effective measures to control and/or reduce their national annual emissions of nitrogen oxides, or their transboundary fluxes, so that, by 31 December 1994, they do not exceed the national annual emissions of nitrogen oxides or their transboundary fluxes of such emissions for the year 1987 (or any previous year to be specified). The parties are also under an obligation to make unleaded fuel sufficiently available along main international transit routes to facilitate the circulation of vehicles equipped with catalytic converters. The Protocol is to enter into force on the ninetieth day following the date on which the sixteenth instrument of ratification, acceptance, approval or accession has been deposited. The decision of the Community as to accession to the Protocol is effective as of 17 May 1993. (OJ L149 21.6.93 p 14.)

2697   Environment—carbon dioxide emissions—energy efficiency

Council Directive (EC) 93/76 on the limitation of carbon dioxide emissions has been adopted. The objective of the directive is the attainment of a reduction in carbon dioxide emissions by improving energy efficiency. According to the directive, this can be done by implementing programmes in the areas of energy certification of buildings; the billing of heating, air-conditioning and hot water costs on the basis of actual consumption; third-party financing for energy efficiency investments in the public sector; thermal insulation of new buildings; regular inspection of boilers; and energy audits of undertakings with high energy consumption. The directive, applying the principle of subsidiarity, allows the measures taken to be determined by the individual member states, on the basis of potential improvements in energy efficiency, cost effectiveness, technical feasibility, and environmental impact. Such programmes can take the form of laws, regulations, economic and administrative instruments, information, education and voluntary agreements whose impact can be objectively assessed. The member states are to implement the directive as soon as possible, but no later than 31 December 1994. (OJ L237 22.9.93 p 28.)

2698   Environment—industrial activities—eco-management and audit scheme

Council Regulation (EC) 1836/93 has been adopted allowing voluntary participation by companies in the industrial sector in a Community eco-management and audit scheme. The purpose of the scheme is to evaluate and improve the environmental performance of industrial activities and the provision of the relevant information to the public. The objective of the scheme is to promote continuous improvements in environmental performance by (1) the establishment and implementation of environmental policies, programmes and management systems by companies, in relation to their sites; (2) the systematic, objective and periodic evaluation of the performance of such elements; and (3) the provision of information as to environmental performance to the public.

The scheme is open to companies operating a site or sites where an industrial activity is performed. In order for a site to be registered, a company must carry out certain obligations, such as the adoption of a company environmental policy and the carrying out of environmental audits, ensuring that they meet the requirements of the regulation. The regulation came into force on 13 July 1993. (OJ L168 10.7.93 p 1.)

2699   Environment—ionising radiations—outside workers

See para 1357.

2700   Environment—land pollution—hazardous waste—control of transboundary movements—Basel Convention

Council Decision (EC) 93/98 has been adopted concerning the conclusion, on behalf of the Community, of the Convention on the Control of Transboundary Movements of Hazardous Wastes and their Disposal (the Basel Convention). The Convention, the text of which is attached to the decision, places an obligation on the parties to the Convention to inform the other parties of any prohibition of imports of hazardous wastes. Each party must avoid the export of hazardous wastes to the parties that have expressly prohibited the import of such wastes. Further, the parties to the Convention are to take appropriate measures to ensure that the generation of hazardous wastes is reduced to a minimum, ensure the availability of adequate disposal facilities, and prevent the import of hazardous wastes and other wastes if there is reason to believe that the wastes in question will not be managed in an environmentally sound manner. The Convention is to enter into force on the 90th day after the date of deposit of the 20th instrument of ratification, acceptance, formal confirmation, approval or accession. (OJ L39 16.2.93 p 1.)

2701 Environment—protection against pollution—north-east Atlantic

Council Decision (EC) 93/550 has been adopted concerning the conclusion of the Co-operation Agreement for the protection of the coasts and waters of the north-east Atlantic against pollution. The decision approves the agreement, as adopted in Lisbon in 1990. A copy of the text of the agreement is attached to the decision which is in force as of 20 October 1993. (OJ L267 28.10.93 p 20.)

2702 Environment—radiation pollution—radioactive substances—shipments between member states

Council Regulation (Euratom) 1493/93 on the shipment of radioactive substances applies to shipments between member states of sealed sources, other relevant sources and radioactive waste. Under the regulation, a holder of radioactive substances who intends to carry out a shipment of such sources or waste must obtain a prior written declaration by the consignee of the radioactive substance to the effect that the consignee has complied, in the member state of destination, with all applicable provisions implementing Council Directive (EC) 80/836 (on the basic safety standards for health protection of the general public and workers against the dangers of ionising radiation), art 3 and with national requirements for safe storage, use or disposal of that waste. The regulation is in force as from 9 July 1993. It ceases to apply to radioactive waste on 1 January 1994. (OJ L148 19.6.93 p 1.)

2703 Environment—water pollution—sea water—bathing water

The EC Commission sought a declaration that, by failing to take all the necessary measures to ensure that the quality of bathing water in the bathing areas of certain seaside resorts in England conformed with Council Directive (EC) 76/160, the United Kingdom was in breach of its Community obligations. The United Kingdom contended that it had taken all practicable steps to conform with the directive and that the definition of "bathing water" in art 1(2)(a) was too imprecise to enable member states to identify the waters falling within its scope. *Held*, according to that provision, "bathing water" meant all running or still fresh waters, or parts thereof, and sea water in which bathing was not prohibited and was traditionally practised by a large number of bathers. That expression was to be interpreted in the light of the underlying objectives of the directive which included the protection of the environment and public health and the improvement of living conditions. Those objectives would not be attained if the waters of bathing resorts equipped with facilities such as changing huts, toilets, markers indicating bathing areas, and supervised by lifeguards could be excluded from the scope of the directive solely because the number of bathers was below a certain threshold. Such facilities and the presence of lifeguards constituted evidence that the bathing area was frequented by a large number of bathers whose health had to be protected. The bathing areas in question had for long been bathing resorts meeting those criteria and, accordingly, as from the notification of the directive, they should have been considered bathing areas within the meaning of the directive. The time limits laid down in the directive began to run from the date of notification of the directive. It required the member states to take steps to ensure that certain results were attained and, apart from specified derogations, they could not rely on particular circumstances to justify a failure to fulfil that obligation. The contention that all practicable steps had been taken to comply with the directive was not a further ground, in addition to the derogations expressly permitted, justifying the failure to fulfil the obligations in question. The declaration sought would be granted.

Case C-56/90: EC Commission v United Kingdom of Great Britain and Northern Ireland (1993) Times, 15 July (ECJ: Full Court).

ENERGY OTHER THAN FROM COAL

2704 Nuclear energy—supply—safeguards

The applicant company exported two containers which it believed to be empty but which in fact contained nuclear material. It informed the EC Commission's safety inspectorate and the

Euratom supply agency of the error. The Commission placed the applicant under administration for a period of four months for breach of the Euratom Treaty, art 79 concerning accounting and operating records relating to nuclear material. The applicant sought the annulment of the Commission's decision on the ground that the penalty imposed was too severe. *Held,* any failure to fulfil one of the obligations laid down in Commission Regulation (EC) 3227/76, which defined the nature and scope of the Euratom Treaty, art 79, entitled the Commission to adopt one of the sanctions laid down in art 83 in respect of any persons or undertakings responsible for the infringement in question. It was not relevant that the export had been carried out inadvertently. In adopting any particular sanction, the Commission was not required to take into account whether or not the particular infringement of art 79 had been brought to an end. Any failure by an undertaking to observe those provisions of the Euratom Treaty which sought to prevent the diversion of nuclear materials from their intended uses constituted a serious infringement. The reasons for the applicant's error did not justify the imposition of a less severe penalty. The application would be dismissed.

Case C-308/90: Advanced Nuclear Fuels GmbH v EC Commission [1993] 3 CMLR 241 (ECJ: Sixth Chamber).

2705   Renewable energy sources—Altener programme

Council Decision (EC) 93/500 has been adopted, setting up a programme to promote renewable energy sources within the context of the Altener programme (specific actions for greater penetration of renewable energy sources). The programme is to last for five years and the amount of Community funds estimated as necessary for implementation of the programme is 40m Ecu for the period 1993–1997. The four categories of actions that are to be financed under the programme include (1) studies and technical evaluations for defining technical standards or specifications; (2) measures to support member states' initiatives for extending or creating infrastructures; (3) measures to foster the creation of an information network; and (4) studies, evaluations and other appropriate measures aimed at assessing the technical feasibility and the advantages for the economy and for the environment of the industrial exploitation of biomass for energy purposes. Annex I contains a list of Community objectives for reducing carbon dioxide emissions by developing renewable energy sources. The decision is to apply from 1 January 1993 to 31 December 1997. (OJ L235 18.9.93 p 41.)

UNDERTAKINGS

2706   Companies—capital—increase in capital

A public sector organisation which took the form of a public company and acted in the common interest under the control of the state took over the management of a private sector company whose share capital it decided to increase by virtue of certain statutory powers under Greek law but without the assent of the existing shareholders. The latter were given a right of pre-emption to acquire the new shares. It fell to be determined whether the law in question was contrary to Community law. *Held,* Council Directive (EC) 77/91, art 25, required an increase in a company's capital to be decided in the company's general meeting. Accordingly, the unilateral increase in the company's capital was prohibited. Although a decision of the EC Commission had approved the law in respect of state aid under the EC Treaty, art 93, that decision could not alter the state's obligations under other provisions of Community law. Although, by virtue of that decision, Greece had been given a time limit to bring its law into accordance with Directive 77/91, art 25, that decision could not alter the illegality before the time limit had expired. The law in question, therefore, was in breach of art 25 and contrary to Community law.

Cases C-134–135/91: Kerafina v The Republic (Greece) [1993] 2 CMLR 246 (ECJ: Sixth Chamber).

2707   Public contracts—utilities—co-ordination of procedures

Council Directive (EC) 93/38 has been adopted co-ordinating the procedures of entities operating in the water, energy, transport and telecommunications sectors. The directive replaces the 1990 utilities directive, Council Directive (EC) 90/531, with effect from 1 July 1994, except with regard to Spain, which has until 1 July 1997, and Portugal and Greece, which have until 1 January 1998, to implement the directive. By virtue of the 1993 Directive, art 45(1), all references to the 1990 Directive are to be construed as references to Directive 93/38. (OJ L199 9.8.93 p 84.)

2708 Public supply contracts—procedures for award—consolidation of original texts

Council Directive (EC) 93/36 has been adopted co-ordinating procedures for the award of public supply contracts. The directive repeals and replaces the earlier public supply contracts directive, Council Directive (EC) 77/62, and makes minor editorial changes, in order to align it with the provisions of the directives on public works (Council Directive (EC) 93/37), services (Council Directive (EC) 92/50) and utilities (Council Directive (EC) 93/38). By virtue of Directive 93/36, art 33, references to the 1977 Directive are to be construed as references to Directive 93/36 and are to be read in accordance with the correlation table set out in Directive 93/36, Annex IV. The directive is to be implemented in the member states by 14 June 1994. (OJ L199 9.8.93 p 1.)

2709 Public works contracts—procedures for award—consolidation of original texts

Council Directive (EC) 93/37 has been adopted co-ordinating procedures for the award of public works contracts. The directive repeals and replaces the earlier public works contracts directive, Council Directive (EC) 71/305, and makes some technical changes. By virtue of the 1993 Directive, art 36, references to the 1971 Directive are to be construed as references to the 1993 Directive and are to be read in accordance with the correlation table set out in the 1993 Directive, Annex VIII. The directive is to be implemented in the member states in accordance with the deadlines laid out in Annex VII but is without prejudice to the obligations of the member states concerning their deadlines for transposition into national law. (OJ L199 9.8.93 p 54.)

CUSTOMS UNION AND FREE MOVEMENT OF GOODS

2710 Free movement of goods—combined nomenclature—bank notes—counterfeit bank notes

The taxpayer acquired counterfeit money in Italy. He took it by car to Germany where he intended to sell it. He was arrested in Germany and the money was seized. He was convicted of the offence of counterfeiting currency and sentenced to a term of imprisonment. It fell to be determined whether customs duty and value added tax were due on the importation of the money into Germany. *Held*, it was already established that, since imports of narcotic drugs into the Community otherwise than through strictly controlled economic channels were prohibited in all the member states by virtue of international commitments, no customs debt could arise on the importation of such drugs because they could not be marketed and integrated into the economy of the Community. That principle applied a fortiori to counterfeit currency, which was subject to absolute prohibition on importation and marketing in all member states, so that no customs debt could arise on the importation of such currency into the customs territory of the Community. It was also already established that import value added tax and customs duty displayed comparable essential features and that illegal imports of drugs were wholly alien to the provisions of Council Directive (EC) 77/388 and could not give rise to a value added tax debt. That principle applied a fortiori to imports of counterfeit currency so that value added tax could not be charged on the importation of counterfeit currency into the Community.

Case *C-343/89: Witzemann v Hauptzollamt München-Mitte* [1993] STC 108 (ECJ: Sixth Chamber). Cases *221/81: Wolf v Hauptzollamt Düsseldorf* [1982] ECR 3681, ECJ, *240/81: Einberger v Hauptzollamt Freiburg* [1982] ECR 3699, ECJ (1983 Abr para 1342), and *294/82: Einberger v Hauptzollamt Freiburg* [1984] ECR 1177, ECJ (1985 Abr para 3116) followed.

2711 Free movement of goods—quantitative restrictions and equivalent measures—exports—cultural objects—unlawful removal

The EC Treaty, art 36 permits member states to retain the right to restrict the import and export of their national treasures. Under Council Regulation (EC) 3911/92 the export of cultural goods outside the customs territory of the Community is subject to the presentation of an export licence. Under article 2 of the regulation, an export licence may be refused where the cultural goods come within the ambit of Council Directive (EC) 93/73. This directive concerns the return of cultural objects unlawfully removed from the territory of a member state and defines "cultural objects" as those objects classified, before or after the removal, as among the "national treasures possessing artistic, historic or archaeological value" under national legislation or administrative procedures within the meaning of article 36 of the Treaty. The cultural objects must also belong to one of the categories listed in the Annex to the directive. The directive only applies to cultural objects unlawfully removed from the territory of a member state on or after 1 January 1993. "Unlawful removal" is defined by the directive as being the removal from the territory of a member state in breach of its own rules on the protection of national treasures or in breach of Regulation 3911/92, or the retention of an object at the end of a period of lawful removal, or any breach of another condition governing such temporary removal. The directive was adopted on 15 March 1993 and stipulates that implementation in the member states is to take place within nine months of its adoption, except in respect of Belgium, Germany and the Netherlands. These countries are to implement the provisions of the directive within twelve months of its adoption. (OJ L74 27.3.93 p 74.) Regulation 3911/92 (OJ L395 31.12.92 p 1.) on the export of cultural goods entered into force on 30 March 1993 and was implemented with effect from 1 April 1993 by Commission Regulation (EC) 752/93 (OJ L77 31.3.93 p 24.), the Annex to which contains sample licence forms.

2712 Free movement of goods—quantitative restrictions and equivalent measures—national provisions restricting or prohibiting particular selling arrangements

The defendant was prosecuted for reselling products in an unaltered state at prices lower than their actual purchase prices contrary to a French law which prohibited resale at a loss. It fell to be determined whether such a law was compatible with Community law on the free movement of goods. *Held*, a national law imposing a general prohibition on resale at a loss was not intended to regulate trade in goods between member states. While it might restrict the volume of sales and, therefore, the volume of sales of products from other member states by depriving traders of a method of sales promotion, that was not sufficient to characterise the law as a measure having equivalent effect to a quantitative restriction on imports. The application to products from other member states of national provisions restricting or prohibiting particular selling arrangements was not such as to hinder directly or indirectly, actually or potentially, trade between member states within the meaning of the decision of the European Court of Justice in *Case 8/74: Procureur du Roi v Dassonville* [1974] ECR 837 provided that those provisions applied to all affected traders operating within the national territory and provided that they affected in the same manner, in law and in fact, the marketing of domestic products and those from other member states. Such provisions fell outside the scope of the Community law on the free movement of goods.

Joined Cases C-267 and 268/91: Criminal proceedings against Keck (1993) Times, 25 November (ECJ: Full Court).

2713 Free movement of goods—quantitative restrictions and equivalent measures—pre-contractual relations—duty to provide information to consumers

The defendant purchased a brand Y motor cycle from the plaintiff, a German dealer who was not an authorised dealer for any particular brand. The French dealer from whom the German importer had purchased the motor cycle assured the importer that purchasers could rely upon the guarantee at any brand Y dealer. Under the contract, the defendant was entitled to rely on her rights to the guarantee as against either the vendor or other undertakings approved by the manufacturer or by the importer. The plaintiff failed to inform the defendant that, in spite of those conditions, German authorised dealers would usually refuse to carry out repairs on motor cycles imported by parallel importers because they believed that, as net prices in France were lower than in Germany, such imports gave rise to an unjustified competitive advantage. The defendant refused to take delivery of the motor cycle. It fell to be determined whether a vendor's obligation, under German contract law, to provide information to a consumer in pre-contractual relations constituted a measure having equivalent effect to quantitative restrictions on imports within the meaning of the EC Treaty, art 30. *Held*, the obligation to provide information applied, at least in so far as products of Community origin were concerned, indistinctly to all contractual relations governed by German contract law. It did not seek to control trade with other member states. The obligation to provide information did not give rise to the risk of hindering the free movement of goods. The fact that certain distributors of the particular brand concerned refused to provide services under guarantee on motor cycles which had been purchased through a parallel import gave rise to that risk. The restrictive effects which the obligation to provide information might have on the free movement of goods were too uncertain and indirect for such an obligation to be considered as liable to hinder trade between member states.

Case C-93/92: CMC Motorradcenter GmbH v Baskiciogullari (1993) Times, 27 October (European Court of Justice: Sixth Chamber).

2714   Free movement of goods—quantitative restrictions and equivalent measures—prohibition of eye-catching comparative price advertising

A German law, intended to protect consumers from misleading advertisements including price comparisons, prohibited advertising which used eye-catching price comparisons. A subsidiary of a French company, which sold products supplied by the parent company and manufactured mainly in France, distributed a brochure in Germany which showed beside the price at which goods had been formerly sold the new lower price of the products in bold red characters. In proceedings against the subsidiary, a question arose as to the compatibility of the German law with Community law. *Held*, it was established that all trading rules of member states which were capable of hindering, directly or indirectly, actually or potentially, intra-Community trade were to be considered as measures having an effect equivalent to quantitative restrictions on imports contrary to the EC Treaty, art 30 and that national legislation which limited or prohibited certain forms of publicity or certain means for promotion of sales, although it did not directly affect imports, might be such as to limit the volume of such imports because it restricted the possibilities of distribution of imported products. For a trader to be required to adopt another system of publicity or promotion of sales according to the member states concerned, or to give up the use of a system which he thought would be particularly effective, might constitute an obstruction to imports even if such legislation was indistinctly applicable to national and imported products. The prohibition in question, which applied to eye-catching advertising using price comparisons whether true or false, went beyond the requirements of the aim pursued by the legislation. Correct price comparisons which were prohibited by German law could in no way distort conditions of competition; the prohibition of such comparisons, on the contrary, was likely to restrict competition. The prohibition in question was likely to restrict imports from one member state to another and thereby constituted a measure having an equivalent effect within art 30.

Case C-126/91: Schutzverband gegen Unwesen in der Wirtschaft v Yves Rocher GmbH (1993) Times, 10 July (ECJ: Full Court).

2715   Free movement of goods—quantitative restrictions and equivalent measures—restrictions on Sunday trading

See *Stoke-on-Trent City Council and Norwich City Council v B & Q plc*, para 2531.

AGRICULTURE

See AGRICULTURE.

FREEDOM OF MOVEMENT FOR WORKERS

2716   Derogations—protection of public against misuse of university diplomas—principle of proportionality

Under German law, the holder of a university diploma issued by a German higher education establishment was entitled to use his diploma in Germany without special authorisation. However, German nationals and foreigners, including Community nationals, who had obtained a university diploma from a foreign higher education establishment were required to apply for authorisation in order to use the diploma in Germany. It fell to be determined whether that requirement constituted an impediment to the free movement of persons and discrimination contrary to the EC Treaty. *Held*, art 52 on the right of establishment could not be interpreted so as to exclude from the benefit of Community law a member state's own nationals who, because they had lawfully resided in another member state and there acquired a professional qualification recognised by Community law, were, with regard to their member state of origin, in a situation similar to that of any other persons who enjoyed the rights and freedoms guaranteed by the Treaty. The same reasoning applied to art 48 on the free movement of workers. However, the German law in question sought to protect the public against the misleading use of university diplomas acquired outside German territory. That was a legitimate interest justifying a restriction of the fundamental freedoms of movement and establishment under the Treaty. The procedure for authorisation of a diploma was, nevertheless, subject to the principle of proportionality. *Case C-19/92: Kraus v Land Baden-Würtemberg* (1993) Times, 6 April (ECJ: Full Court).

2717 Employment—European Employment Service—Eures

Commission Decision (EC) 93/569 has been adopted implementing Council Regulation (EC) 1612/68 on the freedom of movement for workers within the Community. Whereas the current system for the exchange of job vacancies (SEDOC) no longer corresponds to the requirements of the labour market in Europe, it has been decided that the EC Commission and the employment services of the member states should create a European network of services, known as Eures. The Eures network is a network made up of national employment services, their eventual partners and the Commission, and is responsible for exchanging information specified by Regulation 1612/68, and providing that information to potential users. The information concerned relates to "vacancies which could be filled by nationals of other member states", also known as 'Euro-vacancies", and they are defined as those vacancies which are "more likely to be filled if advertised at Community level, as more quality applications shall be received". Annex II contains a list of the types of vacancies with a Community dimension that come within the ambit of the scheme. The decision is in force as of 22 October 1993. (OJ L274 6.11.93 p 32.)

2718 Material scope—students—right of residence

Council Directive (EC) 93/96 on the right of residence for students has been adopted. In order to guarantee access to vocational training, it has been decided to grant the right of residence to students for the duration of the course of studies in question. The right of residence is to be evidenced by the issue of a document known as a "residence permit for a national of a member state of the Community". The permit is to be renewed on an annual basis unless the duration of the course of studies is less than one year, in which case the permit is only valid for that period of time. The spouse and the dependent children of a national of a member state entitled to the right of residence within the territory of a member state are to be entitled to take up any employment anywhere within the territory of that member state. The directive does not establish any entitlement to the payment of maintenance grants by the host member state on the part of students benefiting from the right of residence. The directive was to be implemented in the member states by 31 December 1993. (OJ L317 18.12.93 p 59.)

2719 Specific sectors—medical services—advertising of specialist qualifications

See *R v Secretary of State for Health, ex p Goldstein*, paras 1771, 2729.

RIGHT OF ESTABLISHMENT AND FREEDOM TO PROVIDE SERVICES

2720 Copyright—protection—non-nationals

It has been held that copyright and related rights, because of their effect on intra-community trade and services, fall within the scope of the application of the EC Treaty and are therefore subject to the general principle of non-discrimination laid down in art 7.
Case C-92/92: Phil Collins v Imtrat Handelsgesellschaft mbH; Case C-326/92: Patricia Im-und Export Verwaltungsgesellschaft mbH v EMI Electrola GmbH [1993] 3 CMLR 773 (ECJ: Full Court).

2721 General—beneficiaries—companies—location of registered office

The taxpayer, a company incorporated under German law whose registered office was in Germany, had a branch in the United Kingdom through which a number of loans had been granted to United States companies. It received a refund of corporation tax paid in the United Kingdom on the interest received from the companies as, under a double taxation convention between the United Kingdom and the United States, interest paid by a United States company was taxable in the United Kingdom only when it was paid to a United Kingdom company or a company resident for tax purposes in the United Kingdom. The taxpayer's claim for a repayment supplement equal to interest on the amount overpaid was refused on the ground that the supplement was payable only to United Kingdom residents. It fell to be determined whether the residence requirement constituted a restriction on the right of freedom of establishment and indirect discrimination on the ground of nationality. *Held*, the freedom of establishment granted to nationals of a member state by the EC Treaty, art 52 included, pursuant to art 58, the right of companies or firms formed under the law of a member state and having their registered office, central administration or principal place of business within the Community to pursue their activities in the member state concerned through a branch or agency. The use of the criterion of fiscal residence within national territory for the purpose of granting a repayment supplement on overpaid tax was liable to work more particularly to the disadvantage of a company having its seat in another member state. The fact that the exemption from tax which gave rise to the refund was available only to non-resident companies could not justify a rule of a general nature withholding the benefit. The rule was, therefore, discriminatory and contrary to arts 52, 58.

Case C-330/91: R v IRC, ex p Commerzbank AG [1993] 4 All ER 37 (ECJ: Full Court). For earlier English proceedings, see [1991] STC 271 (1991 Abr para 1367).

2722 General—implementation—alien—entry rights as representative of Community company

See *Pasha v Secretary of State for the Home Department*, para 245.

2723 General—recognition of qualifications—measures intended to avoid possible abuse—legitimate interest of state

See *Kraus v Land Baden-Würtemberg*, para 2716.

2724 General—rights of entry and stay—student—spouse and dependent children—employment rights

See para 2718.

2725 General—scope of principle of non-discrimination—person exercising a profession—lodging of security for costs

The plaintiff, an English solicitor, acting in his capacity as executor of a will under English law, applied to a German court for the transfer to his name of assets situated in Germany which were part of the estate. At the request of the defendant, the court required the plaintiff to lodge security for costs under a law by virtue of which foreign nationals who brought proceedings before German courts were required, on application by the defendant, to provide a guarantee for lawyers' expenses and fees. It fell to be determined whether the requirement that the plaintiff lodge security for costs infringed Community law. *Held*, a member state was prohibited from requiring the lodging of security for costs by a person exercising a profession who was established in another member state and who had brought proceedings before one of the courts of the first member state on the sole ground that such person was a national of another member state and in circumstances where nationals of that member state were not required to do so; the requirement constituted discrimination on the ground of nationality contrary to the EC Treaty, arts 59, 60. The right of equality of treatment under Community law could not depend upon the existence of reciprocal agreements concluded between member states. The fact that the main proceedings were based upon the law of succession could not set aside the application of the right of freedom to provide services under Community law in respect of a member of a profession responsible for the transaction in question.

Case C-20/90: Hubbard v Hamburger (1993) Times, 16 July (ECJ: Sixth Chamber).

2726 General—scope of principle of non-discrimination—translation of name— risk of confusion to potential clients

The applicant, a Greek national, resided in Germany where he practised as a self-employed masseur and hydrotherapy assistant. He wished to have the spelling of his name in the register of marriages amended in order to correspond with the spelling which gave the best indication to German speakers of the correct pronunciation of his name and as it had been transcribed in Latin characters in his Greek passport. As the name appearing in the register of marriages had to correspond to the name in his birth certificate, a translation of his birth certificate was ordered. The transcription was carried out in accordance with rules which provided for transliteration and resulted in a further version of his name. He disputed the transcription on the ground that it distorted the pronunciation of his name. *Held*, the EC Treaty, art 52, one of the fundamental provisions of the Community, required nationals of other member states to be assimilated to nationals of the country of establishment by prohibiting any discrimination resulting from national laws, regulations or practices. The question was whether the German rules on transcription were capable of putting the applicant in a less favourable legal or factual position than that of a national of Germany in similar circumstances. Nothing in the EC Treaty prevented the transcription of a Greek name into Latin characters in the registers of civil status of a member state which used the Latin alphabet; it was for the member state concerned to lay down the appropriate rules of transcription. Those rules were only incompatible with art 52 to the extent to which their application might cause difficulties to the person concerned such that in practice they restricted his right of freedom of establishment. Article 52, therefore, prohibited the applicant from being required to use a spelling of his name which distorted its pronunciation as a consequence of which he was exposed to a risk of being confused with other persons by his potential clients.

Case C-168/91: *Konstantinidis v Stadt Altensteig-Standesamt* [1993] 3 CMLR 401 (ECJ: Sixth Chamber).

2727   Investment firms and credit institutions—capital adequacy

Council Directive (EC) 93/6 on the capital adequacy of investment firms and credit institutions has been adopted. Under art 3 of the directive, investment firms which hold clients' money and/or securities and which offer one or more of the following services must have an initial capital of 125,000 ECU: the reception and transmission of investors' orders for financial instruments; the execution of investors' orders for financial instruments; or the management of individual portfolios of investments in financial instruments, provided that they do not deal in any financial instruments for their own account or underwrite issues of financial instruments on a firm commitment basis. Member states may, however, reduce the amount to 50,000 ECU where a firm is not authorised to hold clients' money or securities, to deal for its own account, or to underwrite issues on a firm commitment basis. All other investment firms are to have an initial capital of 730,000 ECU. Member states are to implement the provisions of the directive by 31 December 1995. (OJ L141 11.6.93 p 1.)

2728   Investment services—securities

Council Directive (EC) 93/22 on investment services in the securities field has been adopted. Under the directive, each member state is to make access to the business of investment firms subject to authorisation for investment firms of which it is the home member state. The authorisation is to specify which particular investment service the undertaking is authorised to provide. Further, each member state is to ensure that any investment firm which is a legal person and which, under its national law, has a registered office, has its head office in the same member state as its registered office; and any other investment firm has its head office in the member state which issued its authorisation and in which it actually carries on its business. The competent authorities are not to grant authorisation unless an investment firm has sufficient initial capital in accordance with the rules laid down in the capital adequacy directive (Directive 93/6), and the persons who effectively direct the business of an investment firm are of sufficiently good repute and are sufficiently experienced. Member states are to adopt the necessary laws, regulations and administrative provisions necessary for them to comply with this directive by 1 July 1995 and the provisions of the directive are to be implemented by 31 December 1995 at the latest. (OJ L141 11.6.93 p 27.)

2729   Specific sectors—medical, dental and veterinary services—doctors—mutual recognition of diplomas, etc

Council Directive (EC) 93/16 has been adopted to facilitate the free movement of doctors and the mutual recognition of their diplomas, certificates and other evidence of formal qualifications. The directive repeals Directives 75/362, 363 on the mutual recognition of diplomas, etc and Directive 86/457 on specific training in general medical practice. Directive 93/16 lists the diplomas, certificates and other evidence of formal qualifications that are to be recognised by the member states. It applies to the activities of doctors working in a self-employed or employed capacity who are nationals of the member states. It came into force on 27 July 1993. (OJ L165 7.7.93 p 1.)

See also *R v Secretary of State for Health, ex p Goldstein*, para 1771.

TRANSPORT

2730 Air transport—competition—concerted practices—exemption from rules of competition

Commission Regulation (EC) 1617/93 has been adopted concerning the application of the EC Treaty, art 85(3) to certain categories of agreements and concerted practices. The regulation exempts from the application of art 85(1) agreements between undertakings in the air transport sector, decisions by associations of such undertakings and concerted practices between such undertakings which have as their purpose one or more of the following: joint planning and co-ordination of the schedule of an air service between Community airports; the joint operation of a scheduled air service on a new or on a low-density route between Community airports; the holding of consultations on tariffs for the carriage of passengers, with their baggage, and of freight on scheduled air services between Community airports; slot allocation and airport scheduling in so far as they concern air services between airports in the Community. The regulation entered into force on 1 July 1993. (OJ L155 26.6.93 p 18.)

2731 Inland transport—railway transport—carriage of coal and steel—international tariffs

The European Communities (Definition of Treaties) (International Railway Tariffs Agreements) Order 1993, SI 1993/944 (in force on 10 April 1993), declares the 1986 Protocols to the European Coal and Steel Community Agreements with Switzerland and Austria of 1956 and 1957 on the introduction of through international railway tariffs for the carriage of coal and steel to be Community Treaties. The Protocols enable Spain and Portugal to accede to the Agreements in accordance with the 1972 Act, art 4(2) concerning the Conditions of Accession of Spain and Portugal to the EC.

2732 Inland transport—road transport—carriage of goods by road—driving periods

Under Council Regulation (EC) 3820/85, art 7(1), a driver to whom the regulation applied was required, after four-and-a-half hours' driving, to observe a 45-minute break unless he began a rest period; and, under art 7(2), that break might be replaced by breaks of at least 15 minutes each distributed over the driving period or immediately after that period. In criminal proceedings for various infringements of the regulation, questions arose concerning the interpretation of art 7. *Held*, art 7 prohibited drivers to whom the regulation applied from driving continuously for more than four and a half hours. However, where a driver had taken a 45-minute break either as a single break or as several breaks of at least 15 minutes during or at the end of a four-and-a-half hour period, the calculation provided for by art 7(1) was to begin afresh, without taking account of the driving time and breaks previously completed by the driver. The calculation provided for by art 7(1) began at the moment when the driver set in motion the recording equipment provided for by Council Regulation (EC) 3821/85 on recording equipment in road transport and began driving.

Case C-116/92: Criminal proceedings against Charlton (1993) Times, 27 December (ECJ: Sixth Chamber).

COMPETITION

2733 Application of rules of competition—EC Commission enforcement—discretionary powers

In the first case, an Italian car dealer complained to the EC Commission that a car manufacturer had contravened the EC Treaty, art 85 by ceasing to supply the dealer with vehicles under an agreement between them. The Commission rejected the dealer's application for an injunction compelling the manufacturer to resume supplies and for termination of the infringement. In the second case, a number of importers of Japanese vehicles complained to the Commission under art 85 that other importers had agreed, under the auspices of the French authorities, a total quota on imports of national sales to be shared between them and that, as a consequence, obstacles to parallel imports had been introduced. Their request to the Commission to deal with their complaint under art 175 was rejected. Questions arose as to the nature and extent of the Commission's obligation to act on a complaint by a private party under Regulation 17, art 3. *Held*, in the first case, the Commission had no power under art 85(1) to adopt an injunction ordering the manufacturer to supply the dealer; it had a discretionary power as to whether to conduct an investigation. In order to determine the degree of priority to be accorded to a matter before it, the Commission was entitled to consider Community interest. Having examined the complaint adequately before deciding not to proceed with an investigation, the Commission was entitled to refer the dealer to the national courts for the protection of its rights under art 85(1). In the second case, the Commission, by informing the importers that it did not intend to proceed with their complaint, had taken the required action before the court had delivered its judgment. Accordingly, the court was no longer required to give a decision. A provisional letter of the Commission informing the importers that it was not proceeding with their complaint could not be the subject of proceedings for annulment under art 173 and an action under art 175 could not be converted for that purpose.

Case T-24/90: Automec Srl v EC Commission; Case T-28/90: Asia Motor France SA v EC Commission [1992] 5 CMLR 431 (CFI: Full Court).

2734   Application of rules of competition—terms and conditions of employment— discriminatory rules—rules not constituting state aid

The provisions of certain German shipping rules allowed German shipping companies to employ crew members from non-member states on terms and conditions of employment and remuneration which were less favourable than those applicable to crew members who were German nationals. It fell to be determined on a preliminary ruling whether the German rules amounted to state aid which distorted competition within the meaning of EC Treaty, art 92, and if so whether they were amenable to judicial review under art 117. *Held,* art 92 provided that aid granted through the state or through the resources of the state and which had the effect of distorting competition was contrary to Community law. However, the German scheme had not been created by the state but by the shipping companies themselves, and the European Court of Justice had no power to interfere with such a scheme even though it gave German shipping companies an advantage over companies based in other member states. In any event, neither the social objectives which art 117 sought to achieve nor the measures taken by each state to achieve those means were amenable to judicial review.

Joined Cases C-72/91 and C-73/91 Firma Sloman Neptun Schiffahrts AG v Seebetriebsrat Bodo Ziesemer (1993) Times, 26 March (ECJ: Full Court).

2735   Rules of competition—abuse of dominant position—threat to stop supplying product

See *Leyland Daf Ltd v Automotive Products plc,* para 2516.

2736   Rules of competition—agreements, decisions and concerted practices—air transport—exemption from rules

See para 2730.

2737   Rules of competition—exercise of intellectual property rights—copyright— satellite broadcasting and cable retransmission

Council Directive (EC) 93/83 on the co-ordination of certain rules concerning copyright and rights related to copyright applicable to satellite broadcasting and cable retransmission has been adopted. Article 2 of the directive states that member states are to provide an exclusive right for the author to authorise the communication to the public by satellite of copyright works, subject to certain provisions, eg that the authorisation may be acquired only by agreement. Under article 4, for the purposes of communication to the public by satellite, the rights of performers, phonogram producers and broadcasting organisations are protected in accordance with certain provisions of Council Directive (EC) 92/100 (1992 Abr para 2830), which concerns the rental and lending rights related to copyright in the field of intellectual property. Article 8 of Directive 93/83 states that member states are to ensure that when programmes from other member states are transmitted by cable in their territory the applicable copyright and related rights are observed, and that such retransmission takes place on the basis of individual or collective contractual agreements between copyright owners, holders of related rights and cable operators. Member states are to bring into force the laws, regulations and administrative provisions necessary to comply with the directive before 1 January 1995. (OJ L248 6.10.93 p 15.)

2738   Rules of competition—insurance sector—application of EC Treaty, art 85(3)

Commission Regulation (EC) 3932/93 has been adopted concerning the application of the EC Treaty, art 85(3) to certain categories of agreements, decisions and concerted practices in the insurance sector. Pursuant to art 85(3), art 85(1) is not to apply to agreements, decisions by associations of undertakings and concerted practices in the insurance sector which seek co-operation with respect to (1) the establishment of common risk-premium tariffs based on collectively ascertained statistics or on the number of claims; (2) the establishment of standard policy conditions; (3) the common coverage of certain types of risks; or (4) the establishment of common rules on the testing and acceptance of security devices. The regulation is in force as at 1 April 1993 and applies until 31 March 2003. (OJ L398 31.12.92 p 7.)

2739   Rules of competition—public undertaking—service of general economic interest—exclusive rights—obstruction

A Belgian trader provided within his city and neighbouring areas a service which consisted of the collection of mail from the sender's address and the distribution of that mail before noon the next day, provided that the addresses were within that geographic area. Mail to be sent to addresses outside that area was collected by the trader and posted by him. In criminal proceedings against him for infringement of the exclusive right of the Postal Administration ("PA"), a public sector undertaking, to collect, transport and distribute throughout Belgium all correspondence of any kind, questions arose concerning the compatibility of such criminal law with Community law. *Held,* the PA was an undertaking to which the state had granted special or exclusive rights within the meaning of the EC Treaty, art 90(1), which prohibited member states from enacting or maintaining in force any measure contrary to the Treaty and in particular the rules on competition. By virtue of art 90(2), undertakings entrusted with the operation of services of general economic interest were to be subject to the rules of competition in so far as the application of those rules did not obstruct the performance, in law or in fact, of the particular tasks assigned to them. The PA was responsible for a service of general economic interest consisting in the obligation to ensure the collection, transport and distribution of mail, for all users throughout the territory of Belgium, at uniform tariffs and under similar conditions relating to quality, without regard to specific situations or to the level of profitability of each individual transaction. The exclusion of competition in the provision of postal services could not be justified where specific services were concerned which were dissociable from the service of general interest and satisfying specific needs of traders by providing certain additional services which the traditional postal service did not offer while not calling in question the economic equilibrium of the service of general economic interest provided by the holder of an exclusive right. It was for the national court to examine whether the services in question fell within those criteria.

Case C-320/91: Criminal proceedings against Paul Corbeau (civil party: Régie des posts) (1993) Times, 21 July (ECJ: Full Court).

TAXATION

2740   Value added tax—chargeable event—change in rate of tax—simplification procedures

See *Next plc v Customs and Excise Comrs,* para 2627.

2741   Value added tax—compliance with directive—return period exceeding 12 months

See *Bjellica v Customs and Excise Comrs,* para 2619.

2742   Value added tax—effect on other taxes—local tax

A local tax was charged annually on persons who habitually or occasionally organised public performances or entertainments within the locality and charged an entrance fee to persons attending or participating. The tax, which was charged on the gross amount of all receipts, was payable on the total amount of entrance fees, rental and cloakroom charges, the sale of programmes or dance cards and the proceeds from all refreshments and any contributions or consideration which might replace or supplement such amounts, as well as any other charges. On the taxpayer's appeal against an assessment to tax on the performances and entertainments, the question arose whether the local tax was a turnover tax affecting all the commercial transactions on which value added tax had already been charged and, therefore, prohibited by Council Directive (EC) 77/388, art 33. *Held,* the tax in question did not possess the characteristics of a turnover tax because it did not have the effect of compromising the functioning of the common system of value added tax by levying a charge on the movement of goods and services and on commercial transactions in a way comparable to value added tax. It applied only to a limited category of goods and services and was not a general tax: it was charged annually, not at each stage of the production and distribution process, and it was levied on the gross amount of all receipts, not on the value added at each transaction. The imposition of such a tax was not prohibited by art 33.

Case C-109/90: NV Giant v Commune of Overijse [1993] STC 651 (ECJ: Fourth Chamber). Cases 295/84: Rousseau Wilmot SA v Caisse de Compensation de l'Organisation Autonome Nationale de l'Industrie et du Commerce (Organic) [1985] ECR 3759, ECJ (1985 Abr para 3033) and 252/86: Bergandi v Directeur Général des Impôts [1991] STC 529, ECJ (1991 Abr para 2699) considered.

2743   Value added tax—holding company—dividends

The taxpayer was the holding company of a group of companies. Its income was derived from payment for goods and services supplied by it which were subject to value added tax and from dividends paid by companies in the group which were not so subject. It fell to be determined whether it was entitled to deduct from its value added tax liability the whole of the amount of value added tax paid on its purchases of goods and services. Held, the right of deduction was to be applied in such a way that its application corresponded, so far as possible, to the field of activity of the taxpayer. A holding company whose sole purpose was the acquisition of holdings in other companies, where there was no involvement in the management of the other companies, was not a taxable person for the purposes of value added tax and, therefore, had no right to deduct under Council Directive (EC) 77/388, art 17. As the receipt of dividends was not within the scope of value added tax, dividends arising from the holding of shares fell outside the scheme of deductions. Accordingly, dividends were to be excluded from the deductible proportion of input tax under arts 17, 19.

Case C-333/91: Satam SA v Minister responsible for the Budget (1993) Times, 22 July (ECJ: Full Court).

2744   Value added tax—illegal imports—counterfeit currency

See Witzemann v Hauptzollamt München-Mitte, para 2710.

2745   Value added tax—imports—imports from other member states— discrimination between domestic goods and goods from other member states

Italy charged value added tax on goods imported from other member states by non-taxable persons even though value added tax had already been charged in the other member state and the supply of similar goods in Italy was not subject to value added tax. The EC Commission sought a declaration that, by failing to adopt the measures necessary to permit such persons to obtain a refund of tax, Italy had failed to fulfil its obligations under the EC Treaty, art 95, which prohibited discriminatory taxation. Italy contended that no member state could be held responsible for the fact that Community provisions, despite being well-developed in the area of value added tax, still left citizens of member states in uncertainty as to the extent of their rights. Held, art 95 prohibited discriminatory taxation of imported goods. That provision had direct effect and created personal rights for individuals which national courts were bound to protect. On the importation of goods by a non-taxable person, where value added tax was not charged on the supply of similar goods by non-taxable persons within the member state of importation, art 95 required account to be taken of the amount of value added tax paid in the member state of exportation which was still contained in the value of the goods at the time of importation, so that the value added tax already paid was not included in the taxable amount and was also deducted from the value added tax payable on importation. Although the provisions of art 95 were directly effective making it possible for a non-taxable importer to rely on art 95 before the national courts, that was only a minimum guarantee which was not sufficient to ensure the full and complete implementation of the EC Treaty. The legal rules of member states should be worded unequivocally so as to give the persons to whom they applied a clear and precise understanding of their rights and obligations and to enable national courts to ensure that those rights and obligations were observed. By failing to adopt the measures necessary to permit non-taxable importers to deduct from the value added tax due on importation the amount of value added tax paid in the member state of exportation which was still contained in the value of the

goods at the time of their importation, Italy had failed to fulfil its obligations under art 95.
  Case C-120/88: EC Commission v Italian Republic [1993] STC 136 (ECJ: Full Court). *Cases
15/81: Gaston Schul Douane Expediteur BV v Inspecteur der Invoerrechten en Accijnzen, Roosendaal*
[1982] ECR 1409, ECJ (1982 Abr para 1340); *47/84: Staatssecretaris van Financiën v Gaston
Schul Douane-Expediteur BV* [1985] ECR 1491, ECJ (1985 Abr para 3119); *299/86: Drexl v
Italy* [1988] ECR 1213, ECJ (1989 Abr para 2589); *168/85: EC Commission v Italy* [1986] ECR
2945, ECJ (1988 Abr para 2681); and *257/86: EC Commission v Italy* [1988] ECR 3249, ECJ
(1991 Abr para 2702), applied.

In similar proceedings against it, Spain contended that a right to a deduction in the member
state of importation was at odds with the inherent nature of value added tax as a tax on
consumption and with a fair and equitable apportionment of tax revenue between the member
state of exportation and that of importation. *Held*, Spain had similarly failed to fulfil its
obligations under the EC Treaty, art 95.
  Case C-119/89: EC Commission v Kingdom of Spain [1993] STC 136n (ECJ: Full Court).

In similar proceedings against it, Greece contended that although it was not opposed in principle
to the elimination of double taxation of imported goods, that was a matter which required clear
and precise rules in the form of a Community directive and that was the only way to apply the
relevant principles uniformly. *Held*, Greece had similarly failed to fulfil its obligations under the
EC Treaty, art 95.
  Case C-159/89: EC Commission v Hellenic Republic [1993] STC 160n (ECJ: Full Court).

2746 Value added tax—right to deduct

See *Golden Pyramid Ltd v Customs and Excise Comrs*, para 2623.

2747 Value added tax—taxable amount—goods purchased by credit card—commission deducted by credit card issuer

In cases where a purchase of shoes sold by the taxpayer was made by credit card, the credit card
issuer paid the taxpayer the sum paid by the purchaser less a commission of about five per cent.
It fell to be determined whether the taxpayer was liable to pay value added tax on an amount
which included the commission. *Held*, by virtue of Council Directive (EC) 77/388, art
11(A)(1)(a), the taxable amount within the territory of the country for the supply of goods was
everything which constituted the consideration which had been, or was to be, obtained by the
supplier from the purchaser, the customer or a third party. Where the supplier of goods
calculated the value added tax to be paid by the purchaser on the basis of the total price, with a
view to levying it on behalf of the tax authorities, that was the taxable amount which was to be
taken into consideration in order to determine the corresponding amount of value added tax
which the supplier was to hand over to the tax authorities. The fact that the purchaser did not
pay the price agreed directly to the supplier but paid by the intermediary of the card issuer, who
retained a percentage based on the price, could not change the taxable amount. The deduction
carried out by the card issuer constituted the consideration for the service which it offered to
the supplier. That service was a separate transaction with regard to which the purchaser of the
goods was a third party. The means of payment used in a transaction between purchaser and
supplier could not change the taxable amount for value added tax purposes. Accordingly, the
amount of the commission deducted by the card issuer was to be included in the taxable amount
for the calculation of the value added tax which the taxpayer was liable to pay.
  Case C-18/92: SA Chaussures Bally v Ministry of Finance, Belgium (1993) Times, 22 July
(ECJ: Sixth Chamber).

2748 Value added tax—taxable person—activity undertaken as public authority—activity entrusted to third party

Under Spanish law, tax collectors were appointed by local authorities under the control of
whose treasuries they carried out their activities. The tax collectors were required to provide
the security fixed by the authority which had appointed them. They received no salary from
the authority nor was there any contract of employment between the authority and a tax
collector. They set up their own offices and recruited their own staff. They were remunerated
by way of a collection premium which was a percentage of the tax collected by them and a
proportion of the supplements added on in the event of enforced recovery. It fell to be
determined whether, in the calculation of the collection premium, value added tax was to be
added on. *Held*, under Council Directive (EC) 77/388, art 4(1), persons who independently

carried out certain economic activities were taxable persons. The word "independently" in art 4(4) excluded from the charge to value added tax persons bound by legal ties creating the relationship of employer and employee as regards working conditions, remuneration and the employer's liability. No such ties bound the tax collectors to the authorities so that their activities were to be regarded as being carried out independently within art 4(1), (4). By virtue of art 4(5), an activity might be considered non-taxable if it was carried out by a body governed by public law and was carried out by that body acting as a public authority. An activity carried out by a private individual was not excluded from the scope of value added tax merely because it consisted of acts falling within the prerogatives of the public authority. Article 4(5) was inapplicable where a public authority had entrusted the collection of taxes to an independent third party.

Case C-202/90: Ayuntamiento de Sevilla v Recaudodores de las Zonas Primera y Segunda [1993] STC 659 (ECJ: Fifth Chamber).

2749   Value added tax—taxable person—economic activity—grant of building rights over immovable property for a consideration

The taxpayer bought privately a building plot on which he paid value added tax. He granted building rights over the plot for a period of 18 years subject to an annual payment that included value added tax. A "building right" under Dutch law was a right in rem to erect or install buildings, works or plant on land belonging to another person. The taxpayer's exemption from value added tax in respect of the grant of the building rights was waived on the ground that the waiver concerned the letting of immovable property. He deducted the value added tax charged to him on the purchase of the land. The tax authorities disputed his right to do so on the ground that, in granting the building rights, the taxpayer had not acted as a trader for the purposes of Dutch law. Questions on certain provisions of Council Directive (EC) 77/388 were referred to the European Court of Justice. Held, under art 4(2), the exploitation of tangible or intangible property for the purpose of obtaining income from it on a continuing basis was to be considered an economic activity. The term "exploitation" referred to all transactions, whatever their legal form, by which it was sought to obtain income from goods on a continuing basis. The grant, therefore, by an owner of immovable property to another person of building rights in respect of that property, by authorising that person to use the immovable property for a specified period in return for a consideration, was to be regarded as an economic activity involving the exploitation of tangible property for the purpose of obtaining income from it on a continuing basis for the purposes of art 4(2). Where a member state had exercised the option provided by art 5(3) to treat rights in rem giving the holder of them a right of user over immovable property as tangible property, "transfer" in art 5(1), by virtue of which a supply of goods meant the transfer of the right to dispose of tangible property as owner, had to be treated as including the creation of such a right in rem. The scope of art 4 was unaffected by whether a member state had exercised the option of treating the creation of building rights as a supply of goods, as provided for in art 5(3).

Case C-186/89: van Tiem v Staatssecretaris van Financïen [1993] STC 91 (ECJ: Third Chamber).

SOCIAL POLICY

2750   Drugs—European Monitoring Centre for Drugs and Drug Addiction

Council Regulation (EC) 302/93 setting up a European Monitoring Centre for Drugs and Drug Addiction, has been adopted. The Centre's objective is to provide the member states with objective, reliable and comparable information at European level concerning drugs and drug addiction and their consequences. The priority areas of activity are the demand and reduction of the demand for drugs; national and Community strategies and policies; international co-operation and geopolitics of supply; control of trade in narcotic drugs, psychotrophic substances and precursors, as provided for in the relevant present or future international Conventions and Community Acts; and the implication of the producer, consumer and transit countries, within areas covered by the treaty, including money laundering. The regulation is to enter into force on the day following the decision of the competent authorities on the seat of the Centre. (OJ L36 12.2.93 p 1.)

2751   Employment and working conditions—transfer of undertakings—employment relationship

See Katsikas v Konstantinidis, para 1177.

2752   Equal pay and treatment—justification for difference in pay—objective justification

A female speech therapist employed by a health authority complained of sex discrimination on the ground that, at her level of seniority within the National Health Service members of her profession, which was predominantly a female profession, were considerably less well paid than members of comparable professions in which, at an equivalent professional level, there were more men than women. It fell to be determined (1) whether the principle of equal pay for men and women required the employer to prove, by providing objective justification, that a difference in pay between two jobs assumed to be of equal value, of which one was carried out almost exclusively by women and the other predominantly by men, did not constitute sex discrimination; (2) whether the employer could rely as sufficient justification for the difference in pay upon the fact that the rates of pay of the jobs in question were decided by collective bargaining processes which, although carried out by the same parties, were distinct and which, considered separately, had no discriminatory effect; and (3) to what extent the fact that part of the difference in pay was attributable to a shortage of candidates for one job and to the need to attract them by higher salaries could objectively justify that pay differential. *Held*, (1) where significant statistics disclosed an appreciable difference in pay between two jobs of equal value, one of which was carried out almost exclusively by women and the other predominantly by men, the EC Treaty, art 119 required the employer to show that difference was based on objectively justified factors unrelated to any discrimination on the ground of sex. (2) The fact that the respective rates of pay of two jobs of equal value, one carried out almost exclusively by women and the other predominantly by men, were arrived at by collective bargaining processes which, although carried out by the same parties, were distinct and, taken separately, had in themselves no discriminatory effect, was not sufficient objective justification for the difference in pay between those two jobs. (3) It was for the national court to determine, if necessary by applying the principle of proportionality, whether and to what extent the shortage of candidates for a job and the need to attract them by higher pay constituted an objectively justified economic ground for the difference in pay between the jobs in question.

Case C-127/92: Enderby v Frenchay Health Authority [1994] 1 All ER 495 (ECJ: Full Court). For proceedings in the Court of Appeal, see [1992] IRLR 15 (1992 Abr para 2334).

2753   Equal pay and treatment—redundancy—additional payment

Under Belgian law, employees aged 60 or over who were made redundant were entitled to an additional monthly payment from their last employer provided that they were entitled to unemployment benefit. Women ceased to be eligible for unemployment benefit when they reached the age of 60; men continued to be eligible until the age of 65. It fell to be determined whether the legislation discriminated against women contrary to the EC Treaty, art 119. The Belgian government contended that the additional monthly payment was a social security benefit which did not fall within the scope of pay for the purposes of art 119. *Held*, the payment constituted "pay" within art 119 rather than a social security benefit because it was the responsibility of the last employer of the employee dismissed; it was due by reason of the employment relationship which existed. It had its origins in a national collective agreement which had subsequently been given the force of law. It was contrary to art 119 for female employees who were made redundant to be ineligible for the payment in circumstances where male employees in the same position were entitled to it.

Case C-173/91: EC Commission v Kingdom of Belgium [1993] IRLR 404 (ECJ: Full Court).

2754   Equal pay and treatment—unfair dismissal—compensation—limit

The termination of a female employee's employment by an area health authority constituted unlawful discrimination on grounds of sex. Compensation recoverable by her under the Sex Discrimination Act 1975, s 65, was limited to an amount which, in view of the assessment of her financial loss, was inadequate. It fell to be determined whether, by virtue of Council Directive (EC) 76/207, art 6, on the implementation of the principle of equal treatment for men and women as regards working conditions, a victim of sex discrimination on the part of an authority which was an emanation of the state was entitled to full reparation for the loss or damage sustained by him or her and whether art 6 enabled that person to contest the applicability of national legislation which was intended to give effect to the directive but set limits to the compensation recoverable. *Held*, where financial compensation was the measure adopted for the purpose of achieving the objective of real equality of opportunity, it had to be adequate in that it had to enable the loss and damage actually sustained as a result of discriminatory dismissal to be made good in full. It might not be limited to a fixed upper limit or by excluding an award of interest to compensate for the loss sustained by the recipient of the compensation as a result of the effluxion of time until the capital sum awarded was actually paid. A person injured in such circumstances might rely on the provisions of art 6 as against an authority of the state acting in its capacity as employer in order to set aside a national provision which imposed limits on the amount of compensation recoverable by way of reparation.

Case C-271/91: Marshall v Southampton and South West Hampshire Area Health Authority (No 2) [1993] 4 All ER 586 (ECJ: Full Court). For earlier proceedings, see 1990 Abr para 1000.

2755 Social security—occupational pension—sex discrimination

Under an occupational pension scheme, an employer paid a bridging pension, financed entirely by it, to employees who were obliged to take early retirement because of ill health before reaching the statutory retirement age. It fell to be determined whether the method by which the pension was calculated, which resulted in a woman between the ages of 60 and 65 receiving less than a man of the same age whose position was comparable in all other respects, was contrary to the principle of equal treatment for men and women under the EC Treaty, art 119. *Held*, the bridging pension constituted "pay" within art 119. The principle of equal treatment presupposed that the men and women to whom it applied were in identical situations. Where the deferred payment which an employer made to those of his employees who were obliged to take early retirement because of ill health was regarded as a supplement to the financial resources of the man or woman in question, they were not in identical situations. The assessment of the amount of a bridging pension was not frozen at a particular moment; it varied according to changes occurring in the financial position of the man or woman in question with the passage of time. Until the age of 60, the financial position of a woman taking early retirement on the ground of ill health was comparable to a man in a similar situation because neither of them was yet entitled to payment of the state pension. Between the ages of 60 and 65, men and women were no longer in a comparable position because women started drawing the pension at 60. The difference in the amount of the bridging pension paid to men and women between the ages of 60 and 65 was based on an objective difference between their respective financial situations so that it could not be regarded as discriminatory. Further, in calculating the bridging pension, it was not contrary to art 119 to take account of the full state pension which a married woman would have received had she not opted to pay pension contributions at a reduced rate, entitling her to a reduced pension only or not entitling her to a pension, or of the widow's pension which might be drawn by the woman concerned and which was equivalent to a full state pension.

Case C-132/92: Birds Eye Walls Ltd v Roberts [1993] 3 CMLR 822 (ECJ: Second Chamber).

Prior to her death, the claimant's wife had been a member of an occupational pension scheme, funded by employers and employees, the rules of which provided for a survivor's pension for widows only. That entitlement was extended to widowers two months after the death of the claimant's wife. It fell to be determined whether the claimant was entitled to a widower's pension on the ground that the pension was to be treated as pay within the meaning of the EC Treaty, art 119 and that no discrimination between men and women was permissible. *Held*, it was established that the concept of pay within the meaning of art 119(2) comprised any consideration, whether in cash or in kind, whether immediate or future, provided that the worker received it, albeit indirectly, in respect of his employment from his employer. Even though certain benefits were paid after the end of the employment relationship, they nevertheless constituted pay within the meaning of art 119. The concept of pay so defined did not apply to social security schemes or benefits such as retirement pensions which were directly governed by legislation without any element of agreement within the undertaking or the occupational branch concerned and which were obligatorily applicable to general categories of workers. The rules of the pension scheme in question were not laid down directly by law but were the result of an agreement between both sides of the industry concerned. The scheme was funded wholly by the employers and employees with no public financial contribution. From all those factors, it would be inferred that the survivor's pension fell within the scope of art 119. By virtue of the European Court of Justice judgment of 17 May 1990 in *Case C-262/88: Barber v Guardian Royal Exchange Assurance Group* [1990] 2 All ER 660 (1990 Abr para 2706), the direct effect of the EC Treaty, art 119 might be relied upon, for the purpose of claiming equal treatment in the matter of occupational pensions, only in relation to benefits payable in respect of periods of employment subsequent to the date of that judgment, subject to the exception in favour of workers or those claiming under them who had, before that date, initiated legal proceedings or raised an equivalent claim under the applicable national law.

Case C-109/91: Ten Oever v Stichting Bedrijfspensioenfonds voor het Glazenwassers en Schoonmaakbedrijf (1993) Times, 12 October (ECJ: Full Court).

2756 Social security—retirement pension—sex discrimination

See *Griffin v London Pension Authority*, para 2311.

2757 Social security—severe disablement allowance—sex discrimination

United Kingdom law denied severe disablement allowance or invalid care allowance to women who had attained the age of 60 who had not been entitled to the benefit immediately before reaching that age; men might continue to receive such benefits until the age of 65. Questions arose concerning the compatibility of such discrimination with Council Directive (EC) 79/7, art 7(1)(a), which enabled member states to exclude from the scope of the directive the determination of pensionable age for the purposes of granting old-age and retirement pensions and its possible consequences for other benefits. *Held*, where, by virtue of art 7(1)(a), a member state prescribed different retirement ages for men and women for the purposes of granting old-age and retirement pensions, the scope of the permitted derogation, defined by the words "possible consequences thereof for other benefits" in that provision, was limited to forms of discrimination existing under the other benefit schemes which were necessarily and objectively linked to the difference in retirement age. Forms of discrimination provided for in benefit schemes other than old-age and retirement schemes could be justified, as being the consequence of determining a different retirement age according to sex, only if such discrimination was objectively necessary in order to avoid disrupting the complex financial equilibrium of the social security system or to ensure consistency between retirement pension schemes and other benefit schemes.

Case C-328/91: Thomas v Chief Adjudication Officer [1993] 3 WLR 581 (ECJ: Sixth Chamber). For earlier proceedings, see *Thomas v Adjudication Officer and Secretary of State for Social Security; Morley v Chief Adjudication Officer and Secretary of State for Social Security* [1990] IRLR 436, CA (1990 Abr para 2183).

2758 Transfer of undertakings—EC Directive—application

A company contracted out the running of a staff canteen to the defendants, on the understanding that the defendants would be paid a monthly fee to cover costs relating to management, wages, clothing and insurance. The company agreed to supply the premises and electricity free of charge, and the defendants in return agreed to employ the existing canteen staff on the same pay as they were earning before the agreement came into force. One of the plaintiffs complained that the date on which her salary was paid had been unilaterally varied, and she was dismissed when she announced that she would not continue working for the defendants if her salary was not paid in the previous way. Both plaintiffs complained that they no longer received allowances for clothes and shoes, although the total amount of their payment was unchanged. The defendants argued that the agreement with the company did not constitute a transfer of undertaking within the meaning of Council Directive (EC) 77/187 on the approximation of the laws of the member states relating to the safeguarding of employees' rights in the event of transfer of undertakings, businesses or parts of businesses. On a referral from the national court on the interpretation of the Directive, art 1(1), and on the question of whether it was a breach of art 3(2) to vary the date on which salaries were to be paid to the employees concerned and/or to vary the composition of the salary paid even though the total remained unchanged, *held*, the crucial criterion for deciding whether there was a transfer of undertaking within the meaning of art 1(1) was whether the relevant business retained its identity. The directive could apply where the owner of an undertaking entrusted, by contract, to the owner of another the responsibility of providing a service for employees for a fee and other benefits on agreed terms. It was for the national judge to assess whether all the factual circumstances were characteristic of a transfer of undertaking within the meaning of the directive. The directive did not prevent a variation of the employment relationship with the new employer insofar as national law allowed such an alteration independently of the transfer of the undertaking. The directive was intended to add to the protection given to employees where an undertaking was transferred, and it could only be relied on to ensure that the employee was protected in his relations with the transferee to the same extent as he was protected in his relations with the transferor under national law. A ruling would be given accordingly.

Case C-209/91: Rask v ISS Kantineservice A/S [1993] IRLR 133 (ECJ: Third Chamber).

INDEX

The titles under which the *Abridgment* is arranged are listed on pp 9–11. The references in the list and in this index are to paragraphs, not pages.

administrative law
administrative powers, invalid legislation, severance, 556
judicial control, Prime Minister's authority, conclusion of contract, 3
judicial review. *See* judicial review
natural justice, breach of, 50
statutory appeals, Law Commission consultation, 49
tribunals and inquiries, friendly societies, 51

Admiralty
action in rem, arrest of ship, jurisdiction, 52, 53
jurisdiction, 54
practice, harmonisation of practice with Commercial Court, 56

adoption
See under children and young persons

agency
commercial agents, rights and obligations, 59
contract of insurance, undisclosed principal, 65
estate agents, commission, 61, 62, 63
Lloyd's, members agents, duty of care, 1552
ratification, time for, limitation, 64

agriculture
agricultural business, grants, 67
agricultural holdings—
arbitration, 69
model clauses, breach of, 69
notice to quit, service of, 70
succession to tenancy, 72
agricultural marketing—
grants, 77
guaranteed prices—
potatoes, 77, 78
wool, 77
milk and milk products—
export sales, 73
milk marketing, 77
scheme of reorganisation, 74
Common Agricultural Policy, wine, 79
crop burning, restrictions, 81
dairy produce, quotas—
procedure before tribunal, 75
transfer of quotas, 76
feeding stuffs, 82
fishing, decommissioning, 1276
hill livestock, allowances, 83
Home-Grown Cereals Authority, rates of levy, 84
integrated administration and control system, 85
livestock—
artificial breeding, sheep and goats, 86
beef special premium, 87
bovine embryo, 88
bovine semen, importation, 89
hill livestock, allowances, 83

agriculture—*continued*
livestock—*continued*
sheep and suckler cow premium quotas, 105, 106
Meat and Livestock Commission levy scheme, 90
plant breeders' rights—
fees, 91
reproductive material, 92, 93
schemes, 94
plant health—
forestry, 1325
import and export, 96
plant passports, fees, 95
potatoes, seed potatoes, 97
seeds—
beet seeds, 98
cereal seeds, 99
fees, 100
fodder plants, 101
oil and fibre plants, 102
registration, licensing and enforcement, 103
vegetable seeds, 104
set aside scheme, claim, 68
sheep, premiums, 105
suckler cows, premiums, 106
wool, guaranteed prices, arrangements, 108

animals
abandonment, 110
animal pathogens, import, 111
diseases—
approved disinfectant, 113
foot-and-mouth disease, 114
therapeutic substances, 115
dogs, dangerous dogs—
public place—
car, 118
garden path, 119
strict liability, 120
tattooing of, 116
types of dangerous dogs, 117
export, veterinary and zootechnical checks, 121
identification, marking and breeding, records, 112
importation—
bees, 122
post-import controls, 123
veterinary and zootechnical checks, 121
movement, markets, 125
offences, cruelty, 110
poultry—
breeding flocks and hatcheries, 127
fees, 126
testing and registration, 128
scientific procedures—
establishments, fees, 129
protected animals, 130
spring taps, 131
veterinary surgeons and veterinary practitioners, registration, 134

791